WINFIELD AND JOLOWICZ
ON TORT

EIGHTEENTH EDITION, 2010

BY

W. V. H. ROGERS, M.A.

of Gray's Inn, Barrister;
Senior Fellow in the University of Nottingham

SWEET & MAXWELL

THOMSON REUTERS

First Edition	(1937) The Author
Second Edition	(1943) The Author
Third Edition	(1946) The Author
Fourth Edition	(1948) The Author
Fifth Edition	(1950) The Author
Sixth Edition	(1954) T. Ellis Lewis
Seventh Edition	(1963) J. A. Jolowicz and T. Ellis Lewis
Eighth Edition	(1967) J. A. Jolowicz with T. Ellis Lewis
Ninth Edition	(1971) J. A. Jolowicz with T. Ellis Lewis and D. M. Harris
Tenth Edition	(1975) W. V. H. Rogers
Eleventh Edition	(1979) W. V. H. Rogers
Twelfth Edition	(1984) W. V. H. Rogers
Reprinted	(1986)
Thirteenth Edition	(1989) W. V. H. Rogers
Fourteenth Edition	(1994) W. V. H. Rogers
Fifteenth Edition	(1998) W. V. H. Rogers
Reprinted	(1999)
Reprinted	(2000)
Sixteenth Edition	(2002) W. V. H. Rogers
Reprinted	(2004)
Seventeenth Edition	(2006) W. V. H. Rogers
Eighteenth Edition	(2010) W. V. H. Rogers

Published in 2010 by Thomson Reuters (Legal) Limited
(Registered in England & Wales Company No 1679046,
Registered Office and address for service:
100 Avenue Road, London, NW3 3PF) trading as
Sweet & Maxwell.
For further information on our products and services visit:
www.sweetandmaxwell.co.uk
Typeset by Interactive Sciences Ltd, Gloucester
Printed in the UK by
CPI William Clowes Beccles NR34 7TL

*A CIP catalogue record
for this book is available
from the British Library*

*No natural forests were destroyed to make this product,
only farmed timber was used and re-planted.*

ISBN 978–1847–03793–0

PREFACE TO THE EIGHTEENTH EDITION

In the last few years I have become accustomed to the House of Lords making some radical changes to tort law at the end of the legal year when this book had already been set up. Last time, for example, six-and-a-half pages of a seven-and-a-half-page Preface had to be devoted to this phenomenon. Those late developments, like *Barker v Corus* and *Customs and Excise v Barclays Bank*, have been woven into this edition. This time, the schedule requires submission of the Preface rather earlier. Whether or not the Supreme Court has something up its sleeve this Term, there are upcoming appeals in *Sienkiewicz v Greif (UK) Ltd* (proof of causation, Ch.6), *Morrison Sports v Scottish Power* (breach of statutory duty, Ch.7) and *Bocardo v Star Energy* (damages for subterranean trespass, Ch.13). On the legislative front there is not a great deal of lawyer's law in the last four years. It is now nine years since the Law Commission proposed a cleansing of the Augean stables of limitation of actions but that did not appear even in the *draft* Civil Law Reform Bill of 2009, though it had been promised. For that nine years of inaction, the legislation on crime, criminal justice, policing and terrorism covers at least 3,347 pages of the statute book.

This is a book about tort doctrine, the substantive law; but tort law in operation is the focus of the current crisis (not too strong a word) over costs and the financing of litigation, It may be that the most significant event since the last edition is the appearance of Jackson L.J.'s *Review of Civil Litigation Costs*. This monumental report (produced with astonishing speed) appeared not long before the text had to be submitted, but some of its principal recommendations are outlined in the context of personal injuries in Ch.1. It is proposed that the success fees and after the event insurance (ATE) premiums associated with Conditional Fee Agreements should cease to be recoverable by the successful claimant, since these are the main factors which have driven up costs over the last few years. Nor is it just a matter of defendants' liability insurers having to pay more, for there has been litigation on a pretty heroic scale between ATE insurers and claimants' solicitors who, the insurers allege, failed properly to vet the strength of claims brought with ATE policies (*Axa Insurance v Akther & Derby*, Ch.26).

As far as the basic structure of the law is concerned, the restatement of the economic torts in *OBG v Allan* (Ch.18) is easily the most important development (though it is ironic that hardly anyone studying Torts nowadays will ever be exposed to this). *Revenue & Customs v Total* on conspiracy ensures that we have not got a wholly "symmetrical" system but there is no doubt that we have made progress in simplifying this area. In the last few years, litigation on trade disputes has tended to be about the details of ballots; now we shall have to see how the statutory structure of immunities written in the *"Thomson v Deakin/Rookes v Barnard"* era will operate after *OBG v Allan*.

The Duty of Care War (now 40 years old if we treat *Home Office v Dorset Yacht Co* as the first engagement) seems to have been a little quieter than in the period covered by the last edition, but the relationship between tort law and public law continues to give trouble. If the defendants' application for permission to appeal in *Connor v Surrey C.C.* (Ch.5) is successful, the Supreme Court will have another opportunity to look at the issue. The Law Commission has produced provisional proposals in this area, which are outlined in Ch.5, but they do not seem to have been generally very well received.

Defamation continues to give trouble, despite the clarification of the *Reynolds* principle in *Jameel v Wall Street Journal* (Ch.12). After submission of the text, the CA in *British Chiropractic Association v Singh* (briefly mentioned in Ch.12 at proof stage) held that a statement that the defendants "happily promoted bogus treatments" was capable of being read as meaning, "promoted treatments for which the defendant believed there was no scientific support" and hence fell within the scope of fair comment. In that sense the case turns on its particular facts, for one cannot lay down "rules" about the difference between facts and opinions (or "value judgments" as the European Court of Human Rights likes to call them). But that conceals a deeper problem. The claimants had not taken on the newspaper in which the statement appeared but only the author and, as Lord Judge C.J. put it at [12], the, "unhappy impression [had] been created that this [was] an attempt by the BCA to silence one of its critics", the issue of the efficacy of chiropractic being a matter of very legitimate interest to patients. The claim has now been abandoned and the BCA will be liable for large costs; but the defendant will have suffered the stress of nearly two years of litigation and will no doubt be out of pocket. There is to be another review of defamation law and readers may care to look at Lord Lester's Defamation Bill (May 26, 2010), the purpose of which is probably to inform the review. No doubt defamation law is imperfect, but like much else in the law the real problem is less the substantive rules than the way in which quite small issues can quickly rack up alarming costs expenditure for both sides. A particular area of controversy has been "libel tourism". Americans are not diffident about promoting the merits of their own institutions and rarely pay much regard to what happens outside their shores in this respect, seeming to believe, as Lord Hoffmann said in his 2010 Ebsworth Memorial Lecture, "the whole world should share their view about how to strike the balance between freedom of expression and the defence of reputation". It is not surprising that he got a good deal of abuse for his views but what is disheartening (though not surprising) is that nowhere in the "serious newspaper" comment on this issue would you have discovered that the supposedly antiquated law here on the reporting of matters of public concern is of quite recent growth and is more or less the same everywhere *except* the United States: Australia, New Zealand, Canada (at the end of 2009) and Ireland (by statute in 2009). But slogans are easier than facts.

No doubt there will be further important decisions before this book is published but I would draw attention to the following cases, which occurred or came to my attention after submission but could not be incorporated.

(1) The current complexity of limitation law has been referred to above. An illustration is *Williams v Lishman, Sidwell, Campbell & Price Ltd* [2010] EWCA Civ 1418. D causes a loss to C which he deliberately conceals for the purposes of s.32 of the Limitation Act 1980; there then occurs a second loss (arising from the same breach of duty) which D does not conceal. Is the first loss a "fact relevant to the plaintiff's right of action" so as to prevent time running? On the facts it was held that both losses occurred simultaneously so the issue did not arise but Rix L.J. inclined to the view that on the other hypothesis s.32 would operate in favour of the claimant. There are:

"[O]dd consequences whichever solution is adopted. It may be said that there is no logic or justice in allowing a potentially small concealed loss to extend the time for bringing a claim when the claimant subsequently incurs a much larger loss but still has not acted sufficiently promptly with respect to that loss. As against that, why should the existence of a small second loss, which a claimant may well consider is not worth suing for, set time running against a claimant who only discovers too late that he has suffered a far greater earlier loss that has been concealed from him?"

(Elias L.J.).

(2) In Ch.22, *Muuse v Secretary of State for the Home Department* is cited as illustrating that exemplary damages may be awarded for misfeasance in a public office. The CA ([2010] EWCA Civ 453)

reversed the judge's decision that a case of misfeasance had been made out on the facts because it had not been established that the officials knew of or were reckless as to the legality of their actions (as opposed to the effect on the claimant). However, the court upheld the award of exemplary damages on the basis of the alternative claim for false imprisonment, the behaviour of the officials (protected by a Home Office policy of anonymity) being plainly outrageous. There is no suggestion that the exemplary damages would not have been available on the misfeasance claim if it had been made out.

(3) Credit hire and mitigation issues continue to arise after property damage in road accident cases: see *Beechwood Birmingham Ltd v Hoyer Group UK Ltd* [2010] EWCA Civ 647.

(4) The tort of abuse of process had a rare outing in *Land Securities Plc v Fladgate Fielder* [2009] EWCA Civ 1402; [2010] 2 W.L.R. 1265. The allegation was that D started judicial review proceedings against Westminster CC over a grant of planning permission to C in order to put pressure on C to help D relocate its offices. The CA upheld a summary judgment in favour of D. Etherton L.J. said that:

> "[E]ven if the tort can be committed outside circumstances of compulsion by arrest, imprisonment or other forms of duress, there is no reasonably arguable basis for extending the tort beyond the other particular heads of damage which must exist for invocation of the tort of malicious prosecution. A different conclusion would not only go beyond the factual context of [the earlier cases], but would be inconsistent with the refusal of the House of Lords in *Gregory* to extend the tort of malicious prosecution to all civil proceedings. It makes no sense severely to limit the cause of action for malicious prosecution, an essential ingredient of which is that the proceedings had been brought without reasonable or probable cause, to three particular heads of damage, but to extend to all cases of economic loss a tort of abuse of process which can apply even where the alleged 'abuser' had a good cause of action."

Mummery L.J. was of the view that the:

> "[C]ourts have a range of wide discretionary powers to control the conduct of the parties, to safeguard the public interest and to protect the courts themselves from misuse of legal process e.g. powers to stay or strike out proceedings, to impose a range of conditions on the conduct of the litigation, and to order payment of legal costs and expenses. There is no pressing need to supplement procedural law by expansive substantive tortious liability in

order to protect litigants in civil proceedings from malicious or abusive claims."

So this is not a likely growth area.

(5) The HCA upheld the refusal of the NSWCA in *Gett v Tabet* (Ch.6) to reformulate the law of causation in terms of loss of a chance: see [2010] HCA 12. It is interesting that Keifel J. (at [145] and notes) refers to the differences in the formal standard of proof in common law and some civil law countries as being relevant to apparent differences on this issue.

The University of Nottingham, which was kind enough to take me back after a long absence, has provided as congenial an environment as could be wished for over the last few years and, in Stephen Bailey and Stephen Todd, has provided me with access to the wisdom of two amiable colleagues of real stature in Torts. Once again, I must express my thanks to the editorial staff of the publishers for their assistance and efficiency. This is not just a ritual incantation—we go back a long way and I cannot really recall a cross word.

HORSFORTH   W.V.H.R.
June, 2010.

CONTENTS

TABLE OF CASES

Hinks v Fleet [1986] 2 E.G.L.R. 243 9–24
Hinz v Berry [1970] 2 Q.B. 40 5–62
Hiort v Bott (1874) L.R. 9 Ex. 86 .... 17–9, 17–13
Hiort v London & North Western Ry Co (1879) 4 Ex. D. 188 17–5
Hiscox Syndicates Ltd v The Pinnacle Ltd [2008] EWHC 145 14–6
HL v UK [2004] E.H.R.R. 32 .... 4–16, 4–30, 25–35
Hoadly v Dartford DC [1979] R.T.R. 359 6–48
Hoare & Co v McAlpine [1923] 1 Ch. 167 .... 15–6, 15–18
Hobbs (Farms) Ltd v Baxenden Chemical Co Ltd [1992] 1 Lloyd's Rep. 54 .... 10–3, 15–11
Hobbs v Marlowe [1978] A.C. 16 1–19
Hocking v Matthews (1670) 1 Vent. 86 19–13
Hodge v Anglo-American Oil Co (1922) 12 Ll.L.Rep. 183 10–2
Hodgkinson & Corby Ltd v Wards Mobility Services Ltd [1994] 1 W.L.R. 1564 18–46
Hodgson v Trapp [1989] A.C. 807 .... 22–26, 22–32, 22–34, 22–35
Hodkinson v H Wallwork & Co Ltd [1955] 1 W.L.R. 1195 6–52
Hoffman v Sofaer [1982] 1 W.L.R. 1350 22–40
Hoffmann v Monanto Canada Inc [2005] SKQB 225 14–9
Hogg v Historic Buildings and Monuments Commission [1988] 3 C.L. 285 (Cty.Ct) 9–8
Hogg v Ward (1858) 27 L.J.Ex. 443 4–28
Holbeck Hall Hotel Ltd v Scarborough BC [2000] Q.B. 836 .... 6–31, 14–21
Holden v CC Lancashire [1987] Q.B. 380 22–10
Holden v White [1982] 2 Q.B. 679 9–5
Holderness v Goslin [1975] 2 N.Z.L.R. 46 20–18
Hole & Son (Sayers Common) v Harrison [1973] 1 W.L.R. 345 22–44
Hole v Ross-Skinner [2003] EWCA Civ 774 16–7
Hole v Sittingbourne Ry (1861) 6 H. & N. 488 .... 14–19, 20–24
Holland v Lampen-Wolfe [2000] 1 W.L.R. 1573 24–6
Holland v Saskatchewan [2008] SCC 42; 294 D.L.R. (4th) 193 5–46
Holleran v Bagnell (1879) 4 L.R.Ir. 740 23–10
Holley v Smith [1998] Q.B. 726 22–50
Holliday v National Telephone Co [1899] 2 Q.B. 392 .... 20–24, 20–28
Holling v Yorkshire Traction Co Ltd [1948] 2 All E.R. 662 14–16
Hollingsworth v Southern Ferries [1977] 2 Lloyd's Rep. 70 9–3
Hollington v F Hewthorn & Co Ltd [1943] K.B. 587 5–88
Hollins v Fowler (1875) L.R. 7 H.L. 757 .... 17–8, 17–11, 17–22, 17–23, 17–24
Hollins v J Davy Ltd [1963] 1 Q.B. 844 17–11
Hollis v Dow Corning (1996) 129 D.L.R. (4th) 609 .... 10–3, 10–8
Hollis v Vabu Pty Ltd [2001] HCA 44, 181 A.L.R. 263 20–3
Hollywood Silver Fox Farm Ltd v Emmett [1936] 2 K.B. 468 14–12
Holman Construction Ltd v Delta Timber Co Ltd [1972] 1 N.Z.L.R. 1081 11–21
Holmes v Ashford [1950] 2 All E.R. 76 10–5
Holmes v Bagge (1853) 1 E. & B. 782 25–31
Holmes v Mather (1875) L.R. 10 Ex. 261 4–34
Holmes v Wilson (1839) 10 A. & E. 50 13–8
Holt v Payne Skillington (1995) 49 Con L.R. 99 .... 11–21, 11–23
Holtby v Brigham & Cowan (Hull) Ltd [2000] 3 All E.R. 421 21–1
Holy Apostolic Church v Att-Gen (NSW) ex rel. Elisha (1989) 18 N.S.W.L.R. 291 18–51
Holy Monasteries v Greece (1994) 20 E.H.R.R. 1 25–36
Homburg Houtimport BV v Agrosin Pte Ltd [2003] UKHL 12; [2004] 1 A.C. 715 ... 5–41,
                                                                                                     5–42
Home Brewery Co Ltd v William Davis & Co (Leicester) Ltd [1987] Q.B. 339 ... 13–4, 25–30
Home Office v Dorset Yacht Co Ltd [1970] A.C. 1004, HL 5–4, 5–5, 5–6, 5–11, 5–18,
                                                                                 5–26, 5–31, 5–46, 5–50 6–38, 14–34
Hone v Benson (1978) 248 E.G. 1013 9–36
Hone v Going Places Leisure Travel Ltd [2001] EWCA Civ 947 20–1
Honeywell and Stein Ltd v Larkin Bros [1934] 1 K.B. 191 .... 14–19, 20–25
Hong Kong Polytechnic University v Next Magazine Publishing Ltd [1997]
     H.K.L.R.D. 514 12–18
Hooper v Rogers [1975] Ch. 43 .... 22–52, 22–53
Hope v Leng Ltd (1907) 23 T.L.R. 243 12–44
Hopper v Reeve (1817) 7 Taunt. 698 4–5

Robinson v Kilvert (1889) 41 Ch. D. 88 14–9
Robinson v Post Office [1974] 1 W.L.R. 1176 6–32
Robinson v St Helens MBC [2002] EWCA Civ 1099; [2003] P.I.Q.R. P128 .... 26–18, 26–210
Robot Arenas Ltd v Waterfield [2010] EWHC 115 (QB) 17–9
Robson v Hallett [1967] 2 Q.B. 939 .... 9–6, 13–9, 13–10
Robson v Liverpool CC [1993] P.I.Q.R. Q78 22–29
Robson-Paul v Farrugia (1969) 20 CCR 820 13–10
Roe v Minister of Health [1954] 2 Q.B. 66 .... 5–1, 5–77, 5–89, 20–6
Roe v Sheffield CC [2003] EWCA Civ 1; [2004] Q.B. 653 .... 7–5, 7–9, 14–42, 21–1
Roebuck v Norwegian Titanic Co (1884) 1 T.L.R. 117 25–14
Rogers v Kennay (1846) 9 Q.B. 594 17–16
Rogers v Nationwide News Pty Ltd (2003) 201 A.L.R. 184 12–41
Rogers v Night Riders [1983] R.T.R. 324 .... 20–1, 20–22
Roles v Nathan [1963] 1 W.L.R. 1117 .... 9–12, 9–14
Rolls-Royce New Zealand Ltd v Carter Holt Harvey Ltd [2005]] 1 NZLR 324 5–24
Romantiek v BVBA Simms [2008] EWHC 2099 (QB) 25–21
Romegialli v Marceau (1963) 42 D.L.R. (2d) 481 19–5
Romeo v Conservation Commission of the Northern Territory (1998) 152 A.L.R.
    263 9–8
Romney Marsh v Trinity House (1870) L.R. 8 Ex. 204 25–33
Roncarelli v Duplessis (1959) 16 D.L.R. (2d) 698 .... 7–20, 7–21
Rondel v Worsley [1969] 1 A.C. 191 5–60
Ronex Properties Ltd v John Laing Construction Ltd [1983] Q.B. 398 .... 21–6, 23–4
Rookes v Barnard [1964] A.C. 1129 ..... 12–79, 18–9, 18–10, 18–11, 18–17, 18–34, 18–41,
                                                22–8, 22–9, 22–10, 22–11, 22–12
Rootes v Shelton [1968] A.L.R. 33 25–13
Ropaigealach v Barclays Bank Plc [2000] 1 Q.B. 263 13–14
Rose v Ford [1937] A.C. 826 22–19
Rose v Groves (1843) 5 Man. & G. 613 14–3
Rose v Miles (1815) 4 M. & S. 101 14–3
Rose v Plenty [1976] 1 W.L.R. 141 20–12
Rosenbery v Percival [2001] HCA 18, (2001) 178 A.L.R. 577 25–4
Ross v Associated Portland Cement Manufacturers Ltd [1964] 1 W.L.R. 768 .... 6–46, 7–16,
                                                                        7–19, 8–12
Ross v Caunters [1980] Ch. 297 .... 5–37, 5–38, 5–59
Rost v Edwards [1990] 2 Q.B. 460 12–39
Roswell v Prior (1701) 12 Mod. 635 .... 14–17, 14–23
Rothwell v Chemical & Insulating Co Ltd [2006] EWCA Civ 27 22–19
Rothwell v Chemical & Insulating Co Ltd [2007] UKHL 39 .... 5–64, 5–65, 6–10
Rouse v Gravelworks Ltd [1940] 1 K.B. 489 15–11
Rouse v Squires [1973] Q.B. 889 .... 6–36, 21–1
Rowe v Herman [1997] 1 W.L.R. 1390 20–24
Rowe v Kingston-upon-Hull CC [2003] EWCA Civ 1281; [2003] E.L.R. 771 26–18
Rowland v Christian, 443 P.2d 561 (1968) 9–3
Rowlands v CC Merseyside [2006] EWCA Civ 1773 .... 22–8, 22–11
Rowley v Secretary of State for Work and Pensions [2007] EWCA Civ 598 5–16
Rowling v Takaro Properties Ltd [1988] A.C. 473 5–10
Roy v Prior [1971] A.C. 470 .... 4–32, 19–12, 24–10
Royal Aquarium Society Ltd v Parkinson [1892] 1 Q.B. 431 12–41
Royal Baking Powder Co v Wright & Co (1900) 18 R.P.C. 95 12–75
Royal Bank of Scotland v Bannerman Johnstone Mclay [2005] CSIH 39; [2005]
    P.N.L.R. 43 11–25
Royal Bank Trust Co (Trinidad) Ltd v Pamplona [1987] 1 Lloyd's Rep. 218 ..... 11–16, 11–24
Royal Brompton Hospital NHS Trust v Watkins Gray International (UK) [2002]
    UKHL 14; [2002] 1 W.L.R. 1397 21–5
Royscot Trust Ltd v Rogerson [1991] 2 Q.B. 297 .... 6–39, 11–2, 11–21
Royster v Cavey [1947] K.B. 204 24–2
Rozario v Post Office [1997] P.I.Q.R. P15 8–16
Rundle v State Rail Authority (NSW) [2002] NSWCA 354 5–23
Rushmer v Smith [2009] EWHC 94 (QB) 11–31, 24–21
Rushton v National Coal Board [1953] 1 Q.B. 495 22–16

TABLE OF STATUTES

TABLE OF STATUTORY INSTRUMENTS

TABLE OF EUROPEAN LEGISLATION:
TREATIES & CONVENTIONS

TABLE OF ABBREVIATIONS

Neutral citations to English and other cases are given in standard form (e.g. [2009] UKHL 33 or [2005] HCA 12) as are references to the Law Reports (e.g. [2009] 1 A.C. 1339).

All E.R.	All England Reports
All E.R. (Comm)	All England Reports (Commercial Cases)
A.L.R.	Australian Law Reports
art.	article
Arts	articles
Att-Gen	Attorney-General
BC	Borough Council
c.	chapter (when referring to the chapter number of an Act or SI)
CA	Court of Appeal
CC	(preceded by a location) County Council or City Council
CC	(followed by a location) Chief Constable
Ch.	Chapter (when referring to chapters of a book) or Chancery
Ch.D	Chancery Division
Chs	Chapters (when referring to chapters of a book)
cl.	Clause
Cll	Clauses
C.L.R.	Commonwealth Law Reports (Australia)

Co	Company
Corp	Corporation
County Ct.	County Court
CPR	Civil Procedure Rules
DC	District Council (also means Divisional Court)
Dir.	Direction
D.L.R.	Dominion Law Reports (Canada)
DPP	Director of Public Prosecutions
edn	edition
E.G.	Estates Gazette
E.H.R.R.	European Human Rights Reports
I.C.R.	Industrial Cases Reports
Inc	Incorporated
I.R.L.R.	Industrial Relations Law Reports
Ir. R.	Irish Reports
J.P.I.L.	Journal of Personal Injury Law
K.B.	King's Bench
LBC	London Borough Council
L.R.Ir.	Law Reports Ireland
Ltd	Limited
MBC	Metropolitan Borough Council
MC	Magistrates Court
Med.L.R.	Medical Law Reports
no.	Number
Nos	numbers
N.S.W.L.R.	New South Wales Law Reports
N.Z.L.R.	New Zealand Law Reports
p.	page
pp.	pages
para.	Paragraph
paras	Paragraphs

PD	Practice Direction
P.I.Q.R.	Personal Injury and Quantum Reports
Plc	Public limited company
P.N.L.R.	Professional Negligence Law Reports
Pt	Part
Pts	Parts
P.T.S.R.	Public and Third Sector Reports
Q.B.	Queen's Bench
Q.B.D.	Queen's Bench Division
r.	Rule
rr.	Rules
RDC	Rural District Council
reg.	Regulation
regs	Regulations
Ry	Railway
s.	Section
ss.	Sections
S.C.	Session Cases
Sch.	Schedule
Schs	Schedules
S.C.R.	Supreme Court Reports (Canada)
SI	Statutory Instrument
S.J.	Solicitor's Journal
S.L.T.	Scots Law Times
subs.	subsection
subss.	subsections
Vol.	Volume
Vols	Volumes
V.R.	Victoria Reports
W.L.R.	Weekly Law Reports

CHAPTER 1

NATURE AND FUNCTIONS OF THE LAW OF TORT

1. NATURE OF THE LAW OF TORT

NUMEROUS attempts have been made to define a "tort" or "tortious **1–1** liability", with varying degrees of lack of success. Winfield's definition is discussed below, but that was primarily a formal one designed to distinguish tortious liability from other traditional legal categories such as contract or trust. The primary need of the reader, however, must be a statement of what a book of this kind is about. We should begin, therefore, with description rather than with definition and must be content for the moment to sacrifice accuracy and completeness for the sake of simplicity. Having given a very broad description of the role of the law of tort we can then return to the problem of formal definition, and finally look at the relationship of parts of the tort system with certain other legal and social institutions pursuing similar ends.

1

A. Aims of the Law of Tort

1–2   It is not possible to assign any one aim to the law of tort, which is not surprising when one considers that the subject comprehends situations as disparate as A carelessly running B down in the street; C calling D a thief; E giving bad investment advice to F; G failing to diagnose H's dyslexia at school; or I selling J's car when he has no authority to do so. At a very general level, however, we may say that tort is concerned with the allocation of responsibility for losses,[1] which are bound to occur in our society. It is obvious that in any society of people living together numerous conflicts of interest will arise and that the actions of one person or group of persons will from time to time cause or threaten damage to others. This damage may take many forms—injury to the person, damage to physical property, damage to financial interests, injury to reputation and so on—and whenever a person suffers damage he is inclined to look to the law for redress. However, the granting of redress by the law means that some person or group of persons will be required by the law to do or refrain from doing something. This redress may take various forms. In the great majority of tort actions coming before the courts the claimant is seeking monetary compensation (damages) for the injury he has suffered, and this fact strongly emphasises the function of tort in allocating or redistributing loss. In many cases, however, the claimant is seeking an injunction to prevent the occurrence of harm in the future and in this area the direct "preventive" function of tort predominates.[2] An injunction is the primary remedy sought, for example, in cases of nuisance (wrongful interference with the enjoyment of land) and the so-called "economic torts" such as inducing breach of contract. This is not because damages are unavailable (they clearly are) but because the defendant is engaged in a continuing act and the damage suffered by the claimant may not yet have occurred or may be suffered over a long period of time. Even when the claim is for damages in respect of a completed wrong, the role of tort can only be squared in some cases with the idea of compensation by giving that word an artificially extended meaning. Thus there are some situations in which the law imposes upon the defendant an obligation to disgorge the profits he has made from his wrongdoing, whether or not the claimant has suffered any loss. In a few situations, where exemplary damages are awarded, the idea of compensation is dropped altogether in favour of overt

---

[1] This is not the same thing as "compensating for misfortune". See para.1–28 et seq., below.

[2] An award of damages against A may also have a "preventive" function in deterring B from behaving in the same way, but how far this works is controversial: para.1–29, below.

punishment; but much more frequently there are substantial awards of damages (nominally compensatory) for matters like injury to reputation and interference with liberty, which one cannot even begin to quantify in mathematical terms. A couple of nights in the police station may attract more damages than a broken arm, a libel in a national newspaper more than the loss of that arm. In these cases the law is performing a complex function incorporating vindication, deterrence and appeasement.[3] Some tort actions (for example, some claims for trespass to land) may be brought mainly as a method of obtaining a declaration of rights, notwithstanding the availability under modern procedure of a specific remedy of that nature. Associated with this is what a Canadian judge, Linden J., has called the "Ombudsman" function of tort, under which those responsible for losses (typically corporations whose activities cause major disasters) may be called upon to answer in public for their activities. Now it is clear that it is not a function of tort law to provide an alternative route to a public inquiry but there are certainly cases which come close to that. In *Ashley v Chief Constable of Sussex*[4] A had been shot dead by a police officer in a drugs raid. The officer was acquitted on a charge of murder and the Chief Constable conceded liability for negligence in a civil claim by the family. The majority of the House of Lords rejected an application to strike out as an abuse of process the family's[5] alternative cause of action based upon trespass to the person even though it was accepted that in the circumstances no greater damages could be obtained under this head than under that on which the defendants were prepared to concede liability. It was a fair inference that the family's purpose was to obtain a finding that the deceased had not merely been the victim of organisational negligence in the planning of the raid but that he had been unlawfully killed, but they had pleaded a valid cause of action and the fact that they would recover no more damages for it did not mean that they had no legitimate interest in pressing it:

"[T]he very fact that the Chief Constable remains understandably concerned to defend the claim of [trespass] tends to confirm that

---

[3] Vindication of rights may play a role even in cases of negligence. See, e.g. the award of damages in *Rees v Darlington Memorial Hospital NHS Trust* [2003] UKHL 52; [2004] 1 A.C. 309 (para.24–15, below) or the modification of causation principles in *Chester v Afshar* [2004] UKHL 41; [2005] 1 A.C. 345 (para.6–12, below).

[4] [2008] UKHL 25; [2008] 1 A.C. 962.

[5] Strictly speaking there were claims (a) by family members under the Fatal Accidents Act 1976 and (b) by A's estate: see Ch.23. Acquittal on the criminal charge and liability in the civil action are not necessarily inconsistent: both the burden of proof and the content of self-defence differ in the criminal and civil law (see para.25–30, below).

the claimants may remain, equally understandably, concerned to pursue that claim."[6]

There have also been cases in which a civil claim has been brought in order to provoke the prosecuting authorities into acting.[7]

It is perhaps unkind to call tort the dustbin of the law of obligations, but it is certainly the great residuary category. No one theory explains the whole of the law.

1–3   Even where we are concerned with material or financial loss the law clearly cannot decree that whenever one suffers loss he should automatically be entitled to redress from the author of that loss. If, for example, A begins to trade in a commodity in a district in which B has previously had a monopoly, A can clearly foresee that if he adopts superior methods of business he will cause loss to B—indeed it might be said in one sense that his purpose was to cause loss to B—but he is clearly not liable to compensate B for this loss. Indeed, the law takes quite the opposite stance by providing that many agreements between traders to restrict competition are unlawful.[8] There must be some reason in any given case for calling on the law to provide the redress sought, to shift the loss as otherwise it lies where it falls. With comparatively few exceptions this reason is fault of some kind on the part of the defendant. However, the law cannot even go so far as to order every person whose action may be regarded as "faulty" to make redress to those who suffer by it: paradoxical as it may seem, the law of tort is as much about non-liability as it is about liability.[9]

> "Acts or omissions which any moral code would censure cannot in a practical world be treated so as to give a right to every person injured by them to demand relief. In this way rules of law arise which limit the range of complainants and the extent of their remedy."[10]

Corrective justice (the principle that wrongs should be righted) points towards liability where a loss has been inflicted but the demands of distributive justice (the principle that there should be a

---

[6] At [69] per Lord Rodger. See also *Grant v Roche Products (Ireland) Ltd* [2008] IESC 35. Contrast *Birkenfeld v Kendall* [2008] NZCA 531; [2009] 1 N.Z.L.R. 499, where wilful misconduct was not alleged and the defendant had made an offer of the maximum damages payable under a statutory limitation. See also para.4–3 below.

[7] See *Halford v Brookes* [1991] 1 W.L.R. 428 (successful civil action arising from murder; defendant subsequently prosecuted and convicted: *The Times*, August 1, 1996).

[8] Competition Act 1998; and see art.81 (ex art.85) of the Treaty of Rome.

[9] Jolowicz, "The Law of Tort and Non-Physical Loss" (1972) 12 J.S.P.T.L. 91.

[10] *Donoghue v Stevenson* [1932] A.C. 562 at 580, per Lord Atkin.

fair allocation of assets and losses) also have to be taken into account.

> "The truth is that tort law is a mosaic in which the principles of corrective justice and distributive justice are interwoven. And in situations of uncertainty and difficulty a choice sometimes has to be made between the two approaches."[11]

It is the business then of the law of tort to determine when the law will and when it will not grant redress for damage suffered or threatened, and the rules for liability whereby it does this are the subject of this book. We may say, therefore, that if a claimant has suffered damage (which is by no means always confined to injury to his body or damage to his property) in circumstances covered by the rules for liability stated in a book on the law of tort, then, assuming the rules to be correctly stated, the claimant has been the victim of a tort; by this we mean no more than that a tort is a wrong, the victim of which is entitled to redress.[12] Of course, if the claimant is unable to establish a tort, it does not follow that he is without some other form of redress. The act or omission of the other party may be some other sort of wrong for which a remedy may lie in contract or restitution or according to the rules of equity governing breach of trust, matters which are briefly considered in the next section. However, all these categories of private law are, like tort, concerned with questions of liability. An action founded upon tort or other wrong is an action between persons, either natural or artificial (i.e. corporations), and the outcome can only be that one of them, the defendant, is or is not liable to do or refrain from doing something at the suit of the other. If there is no defendant whose liability can be established according to the principles of the law, then the claimant is left without redress so far as private law is concerned. He may, of course, look to the Welfare State or to a private loss insurance contract he may have made.[13] The relationship, present and future, between the law of tort and such sources of compensation must be considered in the concluding part of this chapter.

---

[11] *McFarlane v Tayside Health Board* [2000] 2 A.C. 59 at 83, per Lord Steyn. See para.24–15, below.

[12] See *S.C.M. (UK) Ltd v Whittall & Son Ltd* [1971] 1 Q.B. 337 at 347–348, per Winn L.J.

[13] Insurance of course depends on the private law of contract, but one can hardly describe the insurer's payment on the occurrence of the insured event as "redress". When a person has to pay damages for failing to deliver the goods he has promised under a contract of sale one can fairly say that he is redressing the breach of an obligation to deliver. The insurer does not promise that the insured event will not happen, he simply promises to pay a sum of money if it does.

B. Definition of Tortious Liability: Tort and Other Sources of Liability

1-4   Winfield's definition of tort was as follows:

> "Tortious liability arises from the breach of a duty primarily fixed by law; this duty is towards persons generally and its breach is redressible by an action for unliquidated damages."

At the risk of repetition, we must again stress that in framing this definition Winfield was not seeking to indicate what conduct is and what is not sufficient to involve a person in tortious liability, but merely to distinguish tort from certain other branches of law. As we shall see, it cannot be accepted as entirely accurate but it has the merit of comparative brevity and contains elements which deserve continuing emphasis. It is true that a cause of action in modern law is merely a factual situation the existence of which enables the claimant to obtain a remedy from the court[14] so he is certainly not in the position he was in 200 years ago of having to choose the right "form of action" to fit his claim. Nonetheless, even the comparatively lax modern style of pleading requires the claimant to set out the elements of the claim which he must establish, and in practice this will nearly always involve identifying the tort or other cause of action on which he relies. Furthermore, statutes and rules of procedure sometimes distinguish between, say, contract and tort with reference to matters such as limitation of actions,[15] contributory negligence,[16] service of process and jurisdiction[17] and costs[18] and the court cannot then avoid the task of classification. When a new liability develops it may be unclear exactly where it should be placed for purposes of classification. Although there is no tort of invasion of privacy as such, there is a wrong of "misuse of private information" which covers much of the same ground. This has developed out of breach of confidence, which has equitable origins, and equity—apart from providing the remedy of the injunction

---

[14] *Letang v Cooper* [1965] Q.B. 232 at 244, per Diplock L.J.

[15] Time limits for the bringing of claims. Usually called "prescription" in European legal systems (in English law prescription usually describes the *acquisition* of rights by passage of time). In contract time runs from the date of the breach, in most torts the basic rule, though heavily qualified, is that it runs from the date when the damage is suffered: see para.26–8, below.

[16] See the Law Reform (Contributory Negligence) Act 1945, in para.6–43, below.

[17] The unification of the law on cross-border litigation in Europe effected by the Brussels Convention and the Civil Jurisdiction and Judgments Act 1982 means that the concepts of "contract" and "tort" must be given an autonomous meaning which does not necessarily accord with that of the local law: *Arcado S.P.R.L. v Haviland S.A.* [1988] E.C.R. 1539; *Kalfelis v Bankhaus Schröder etc.* [1988] E.C.R. 5565.

[18] At one time the County Courts Act contained different financial limits of contract and tort for the purposes of recovery of costs and this led to a very large number of cases in which the sole issue was whether the claim sounded in contract or tort. The present legislation draws no distinction.

—had historically little to do with tort liability. However, such a wrong "violates the claimant's personality" as a continental lawyer might say, and therefore has some similarity to defamation, which is undoubtedly a tort.[19] Various opinions have been expressed by judges about its proper modern classification but it is now commonly stated to be a tort.[20]

C. Contract and Tort[21]

The first point that must be made is that from a practical lawyer's point of view there may be a considerable overlap in any factual situation between the law of contract and the law of tort. For example, a claim for damages arising from a defective product may involve a complex web of issues under the Sale of Goods Act 1979, the law of misrepresentation and collateral warranty, the tort of negligence, the Consumer Protection Act 1987 and a chain of contractual indemnities among retailer, middleman and manufacturer.[22] It is unlikely that any legal system can ever cut loose from general conceptual classifications such as "contract" and "tort" (at any rate they seem to be found everywhere) but the student will quickly come to recognise that the boundary must sometimes be crossed in the solution of a problem. It has long been trite law that a defendant may be liable on the same facts in contract to A and in tort to B (notwithstanding privity of contract[23]); it is now, after a period of uncertainty, also clearly established that there may be concurrent contractual and tortious liability to the same claimant, though he may not, of course, recover damages twice over. However, before we examine these propositions further we must make some attempt at formally distinguishing the two heads of liability.

1–5

It was Winfield's view that tortious duties exist by virtue of the law itself and are not dependent upon the agreement or consent of the persons subjected to them. I am under a duty not to assault you, not to slander you, not to trespass on your land, because the law says I am under such a duty and not because I have agreed with you to undertake such a duty. Winfield therefore considered that tortious liability could for this reason be distinguished from contractual

---

[19] In human rights law, the current view is that art.8 of the European Convention on Human Rights, which guarantees respect for private and family life, embraces both privacy and reputation (defamation): *Radio France v France* (2005) 40 E.H.R.R. 29 at [31].

[20] See para.12–82, below.

[21] "Never did a Name so obstruct a true understanding of the Thing. To such a plight has it brought us that a favourite mode of defining a Tort is to declare merely that it is not a Contract. As if a man were to define Chemistry by pointing out that it is not Physics or Mathematics": Wigmore, *Select Cases on the Law of Torts*, vii. But see *R. v Secretary of State, Ex p. Factortame Ltd (No.7)* [2001] 1 W.L.R. 942 at 965.

[22] See, e.g. *Lambert v Lewis* [1982] A.C. 225.

[23] Modified by the Contracts (Rights of Third Parties) Act 1999, but it is still the *basic* rule that only a party to a contract may sue or be sued on it.

liability and from liability on bailment, neither of which can exist independently of the parties', or at least of the defendant's, agreement or consent. There are, however, several instances of what is undoubtedly tortious liability for the existence of which some prior consent, undertaking or assumption of responsibility on the part of the defendant is essential. The liability of the occupier of premises to his visitor, for example, which is now governed by the Occupiers' Liability Act 1957, is based upon breach of a duty of care owed by the occupier to persons whom he has permitted to enter upon his premises. The duty owed to trespassers, i.e. persons who enter without his consent, is not the same.[24] Again, the duty of care owed by a person who gives gratuitous advice upon a serious occasion is, doubtless, a tortious one,[25] but its existence is dependent upon the adviser's agreement to give the advice, if not necessarily upon his agreement to accept legal responsibility for it. Still more difficult is the fact that in some situations an undertaking (whether or not by contract) by A to B to perform a service, the object of which is to confer a benefit upon C, may give rise to liability in tort to C.[26]

If it is not true that all tortious duties arise independently of the will of the defendant, it is equally not true that contractual duties are always dependent upon that will. Not only is there the obvious point that the duty not to break one's contracts is itself a duty imposed by the law, but it is also the case that contractual liability may exist even in the absence of any true consent between the parties. Whether or not there is a contract normally depends upon the outward manifestations of agreement by the parties, not on their subjective states of mind.[27]

1–6   Another mode of differentiation between tortious and contractual liability, it is suggested, is to be found in the proposition that in tort the content of the duties is fixed by the law whereas the content of contractual duties is fixed by the contract itself. If I consent to your entry upon my premises then the duty which I owe to you is the duty fixed by the Occupiers' Liability Act, i.e. by the law itself, but whether, for example, my duty is to deliver to you 10 or 20 tons of coal can only be discovered from the contract between us. Even this distinction, however, is by no means always valid, for today in many cases the content of contractual duties is also fixed by the law. Statute provides, for example, that certain quite specific obligations shall be contained in contracts for the sale or hire-purchase of goods

---

[24] But since Winfield wrote, the duty owed to trespassers has risen: see para.9–25, below.
[25] But a close relationship between adviser and advisee is required and for this purpose the relationship has been described as "equivalent to contract": *Hedley, Byrne & Co Ltd v Heller & Partners Ltd* [1964] A.C. 465 at 530, per Lord Devlin.
[26] See para.5–34, below.
[27] See, e.g. *Smith v Hughes* (1871) L.R. 6 Q.B. 597 at 607, per Blackburn J.; Treitel, *The Law of Contract* (12th edn). Winfield would have no doubt replied that the objective approach was taken merely for reasons of evidential and commercial convenience.

and cannot be excluded[28]; and it is now no longer true, as once perhaps it was, that implied terms in a contract, in the absence of a statutory rule, are always to be based upon the presumed intention of the parties.[29] Conversely, there are tortious duties which are subject to variation by agreement, whether or not that agreement amounts in law to a contract between the parties.[30]

At the risk of abandoning the limits of formal definition, a more satisfactory basis for distinguishing between contract and tort may be sought in considering the aims of the two heads of liability. The "core" of contract is the idea of enforcing promises, whereas tort aims principally at the prevention or compensation of harms, and this difference of function has two principal consequences. First, that a mere failure to act will not usually be actionable in tort, for that would be to set at naught the rule that even a positive promise will not give rise to legal liability unless it is intended as legally binding and supported by consideration or the formality of a deed; secondly, that damages cannot be claimed in tort for a "loss of expectation", or, as it is sometimes expressed, damages in contract put the claimant in the position he would have been in had the contract been performed, whereas damages in tort put him in the position he would have been in had the tort not been committed. However, major qualifications still have to be made. Failure to receive the benefits promised under a contract might be regarded as a "harm"[31] but nevertheless the harm suffered because the defendant has not delivered the goods he promised under the contract is a harm of a different type from that suffered by a person whose body or property is injured by the defendant's negligence.[32]

There are undoubtedly examples where a liability in tort arises for failure to confer a benefit on others in the sense of failing to protect their safety. Some of these are of very long standing, for example, the duty of an occupier to take steps to ensure that his visitors are not harmed by dangers on his land, even if those are not of his making. More recently, it has become common to impose tort liability upon

---

[28] Sale of Goods Act 1979; Unfair Contract Terms Act 1977.

[29] *Lister v Romford Ice & Cold Storage Co Ltd* [1957] A.C. 535 at 594, per Lord Tucker; *Liverpool CC v Irwin* [1977] A.C. 239 at 257, 258, per Lord Cross.

[30] Occupiers' Liability Act 1957 s.2(1); *Ashdown v Samuel Williams Ltd* [1957] 1 Q.B. 409. This case would be decided differently since the Unfair Contract Terms Act 1977 but is still illustrative of the general principle of law.

[31] See Burrows, *Understanding the Law of Obligations* (1998) Ch.1, who adopts "wrongful interference" as the hallmark of tort in order to avoid this overlap.

[32] If the defendant delivers non-conforming goods which cause physical damage to existing property of the claimant then that loss, too, is recoverable in contract even though it is also the type of damage dealt with by tort. *Godley v Perry* [1960] 1 W.L.R. 9 is a good example from personal injury law. The claimant's complaint was not "my catapult doesn't work" but "it broke and put my eye out".

persons for failure to perform public functions connected with safety,[33] though here there is no overlap with contract law. The major difficulty in relation to private transactions is the principle, which has gained great prominence in the modern law, that liability in tort may arise from an "assumption of responsibility" by the defendant.[34] When this is followed by reliance by the claimant in failing to take alternative measures for his own protection it may not be too difficult to say that the defendant has "harmed" the claimant, rather than merely failed to carry out a promise, as where D undertakes to check C's brakes, fails to warn C that he has not done so and lets him drive off and crash. Since, however, every contracting party presumably "relies" on the other to perform his contractual promise, we still, if we take reliance-based liability beyond physical damage, face the prospect of tort taking over much of the territory of contract. Thus if D undertakes to manage the business affairs of a syndicate of persons the members of the syndicate may sue D for negligence in the management, whether or not they have a contractual relationship with him.[35] On this basis it is not entirely easy to say why (as, it is thought, most lawyers would say is now the law), if S contracts to sell and deliver goods to B by a certain date and fails to do so, B's claim lies only in contract. Certainly the tort liability of the syndicate manager requires fault (negligence) and the duties of sellers of goods are strict, but it is hard to believe that the result would be different if it could be shown that by taking due care the seller could have delivered on time.

1–7 Liability based upon assumption of responsibility has often[36] required a very close relationship between the parties. This is also relevant to the validity of the second element of Winfield's definition, that the duty in tort is owed to persons generally. The reference now is, of course, to the primary duty, i.e. the duty not to trespass, not to slander and so on, for breach of which tortious liability is imposed. The breach of such a duty gives rise to a remedial duty, i.e. a duty to make redress, and this is always owed to a specific person or persons whatever the source of the liability. Winfield would now be forced to retreat from the claim that if the primary duty is towards a specific person or specific persons it cannot arise from tort,[37] but there is probably still some substance in his contention that the element of generality was an important factor in the definition and,

---

[33] See para.5–33, below.
[34] See para.5–34, below.
[35] *Henderson v Merrett Syndicates Ltd* [1995] 2 A.C. 145.
[36] But not always: see para.5–36, below.
[37] The claim would not accord with the law governing negligent misstatements or "assumption of responsibility" in general.

while not capable of precise definition, was sufficiently workable in the majority of cases. However, even leaving aside recent developments, it appears that everything depends upon the level of abstraction at which the duty is expressed. It can, no doubt, be truly stated that by virtue of the law of tort I am under a duty not to convert to my own use the goods of anybody else, while my contractual duty to deliver goods which I have sold is owed only to the person to whom I have sold them but this is to compare two statements at different levels. Just as I have a general duty not to commit the tort of conversion, so I have a general duty not to commit breaches of contract. If, on the other hand, we descend to the particular, then just as my duty to deliver certain goods is owed only to their buyer, so also my duty not to convert certain goods to my own use is owed only to the person in possession, or having the immediate right to possession, of them.

As to damages, the law of contract puts the claimant in the position he would have been entitled to occupy (subject to the law of remoteness) as a result of the transaction agreed between the parties. While it is clear that (assuming the claim in tort to arise from some transaction between the parties) tort does not do that, the distinction is less fundamental than might appear. If a surgeon operates negligently on a curable condition and leaves the condition incurable, the patient recovers damages on the basis that with careful surgery he would have been cured; if a solicitor negligently fails to carry out X's instructions to make a will in favour of C, C can recover as damages the value of the lost legacy[38]; and if the seller of property fraudulently[39] induces the claimant to buy it, while the claimant cannot recover as damages the profits he would have made if the representation had been true, he may be able to recover the profits he would have earned by laying out his money elsewhere.[40]

D. Concurrence of Contract and Tort

We now return to the point that contractual and tortious duties **1–8** may co-exist on the same facts. The proposition that D may incur liability in tort (in particular the tort of negligence) to C from a matter or transaction in respect of which D had a contract with B

---

[38] *White v Jones* [1995] 2 A.C. 207, para.5–37, below. See Stapleton, "The Normal Expectancies Measure in Tort Damages" (1997) 113 L.Q.R. 257, who therefore argues that from the damages point of view there is nothing revolutionary in *White v Jones*.

[39] Fraud (deceit) is a tort and subject to the tort measure of damages: para.11–14, below.

[40] *East v Maurer* [1991] 1 W.L.R. 461. But see *Clef Aquitaine S.A.R.L. v Laporte Materials (Barrow) Ltd* [2001] Q.B. 488, para.11–14, below, which appears to go further.

was clearly established in the great case of *Donoghue v Stevenson*,[41] which is the basis of the manufacturer's common law liability in tort to the ultimate consumer.[42] However, negligence rests upon the existence of a duty of care owed by the defendant to the claimant and in the last resort this is determined by the court's perception of what is fair, just and reasonable, and on that issue the contractual context in which the events take place cannot necessarily be regarded as irrelevant. Thus, for example, it has been held that a building sub-contractor was not liable in negligence for damage to the works when the main contract provided that they were to be at the risk of and insurable by the building owner,[43] and an agent answering inquiries on behalf of his principal is not personally liable in negligence in respect of their accuracy unless he has assumed some direct responsibility.[44] Similarly, too great a readiness to hold that a director owes a personal duty of care to persons with whom his company has dealings risks setting at naught the protection of limited liability.[45]

As to the other case, where it is alleged that the defendant owes concurrent duties in contract and tort to the *same* person, some legal systems have a doctrine (known in French law as *non cumul des obligations*) that this is not possible.[46] Though there were signs of this here in earlier days,[47] the weight of the modern case law was the other way and the "concurrence" approach was decisively affirmed by the House of Lords in *Henderson v Merrett Syndicates Ltd*,[48] where it was held that Names at Lloyd's might sue members' agents (with whom they had a contract) for negligence as well as for breach of contract in the management of underwriting business so as to gain the advantage of the longer time limit under the Latent Damage Act 1986.[49] As Lord Goff put it[50]:

> "[T]he result may be untidy but, given that the tortious duty is imposed by the general law, and the contractual duty is attributable to the will of the parties, I do not find it objectionable that the

[41] [1932] A.C. 502.
[42] See Ch.10.
[43] *Norwich CC v Harvey* [1989] 1 W.L.R. 828.
[44] *Gran Gelato Ltd v Richcliff (Group) Ltd* [1992] Ch. 560 (the principal will be responsible to the claimant for the acts of the agent and may recover an indemnity under his contract with the agent. The point is significant for the claimant where the principal is insolvent). See para.11–22, below.
[45] See para.24–23, below.
[46] See generally Weir in XI *International Encyclopedia of Comparative Law*, Ch.12.
[47] See, e.g. *Groom v Crocker* [1939] 1 K.B. 194; *Bagot v Stevens Scanlan & Co Ltd* [1966] 1 Q.B. 197.
[48] [1995] 2 A.C. 145.
[49] See para.26–11, below.
[50] [1995] 2 A.C. at 194.

claimant may be entitled to take advantage of the remedy which is more advantageous to him."[51]

Thus, for example, concurrent liability arises between carrier and passenger, doctor and (private) patient, solicitor and client, and employer and employee.[52] With respect to jurisdiction in Europe, the relevant treaty provisions[53] provide, as qualifications to the general rule that jurisdiction lies in the court of the defendant's domicile, that a person domiciled in a contracting state may be sued: "in matters relating to a contract, in the courts for the place of performance of the obligation in question" and, "in matters relating to tort, delict or quasi-delict, in the courts for the place where the harmful event occurred." In this context a ready acceptance of the concurrence of contract and tort could give rise to "split" jurisdiction and therefore a more restrictive approach will be taken than under English law. For example, in a case where the obligation under the contract was to inspect goods abroad, the Court of Appeal rejected an attempt to base jurisdiction here on the alleged negligence of the defendants in preparing the report which was submitted to the claimants in England, for the claim was still a "matter relating to a contract".[54] In any event, the expressions used in these provisions must, in order to ensure consistency, be given a "European" meaning which avoids the differences in classification among the laws of contracting states.[55]

The above cases have concerned "adjectival" matters and had the **1–9** issue in any of them been one of the substance of the defendant's duty it might have been a matter of indifference whether the claim was regarded as lying in contract or tort, because the duty would have been the same. For example, a doctor's duty in tort is to exercise proper professional care and skill and the implied terms in his contract are the same[56]: he does not impliedly warrant that he

---

[51] This seems to be a general trend: *BC Hydro & Power v BG Checo International* (1993) 99 D.L.R. (4th) 577; *Bryan v Maloney* (1995) 128 A.L.R. 163 at 167; *Dairy Containers Ltd v N.Z.I. Bank Ltd* [1995] 2 N.Z.L.R. 30.

[52] In the case of employer and employee no one ever seems to have doubted that with regard to safety matters a claim lay in tort, indeed lawyers would regard the claim as primarily tortious, perhaps because claims for breach of statutory duty are commonly brought in tandem. Cf. *Scally v Southern Health & Social Services Board* [1992] 1 A.C. 294.

[53] Originally the Brussels and Lugano Conventions, implemented here by Civil Jurisdiction and Judgments Acts 1982 and 1991. From March 2002 the Brussels Convention was replaced by Council Regulation 44/2001, but this did not affect the substance of the law.

[54] *Source Ltd v T.U.V. Rheinland Holdings* [1998] Q.B. 54. However, in *Raiffeisen Zentralbank Österreich A.G. v National Bank of Greece S.A.* [1999] 1 Lloyd's Rep. 408, Tuckey J., though able to distinguish *Source*, thought it could not stand with *Kleinwort Benson Ltd v Glasgow CC* [1999] 1 A.C. 153.

[55] See para.1–4, above.

[56] The implied term in a contract for the supply of a service where the supplier acts in the course of a business (which includes a profession) is found in the Supply of Goods and Services Act 1982 s.13, restating the common law.

will effect a cure, though theoretically he may do so by an express promise to that effect.[57] However, there have been a number of cases in which attempts have been made to use the general duty of care in tort to override the allocation of responsibility between the parties by contract. If the contract were to provide expressly that the defendant was not liable for "risk X" then (subject to the effect of the Unfair Contract Terms Act 1977 upon that term) it would be absurd to allow a tort duty to intrude and contradict that.[58] The same must be true where there is an implied term in the contract that the defendant is not to be liable for "X" (or, as it would be more likely to be expressed, there is no implied term that he should be liable for that risk). Hence in *Tai Hing Cotton Mill Ltd v Liu Chong Hing Bank Ltd*[59] the claimants' employees had forged some 300 cheques totalling HK$5.5 million. A forgery is a nullity and the claimants claimed a declaration that the defendant bank was not entitled to debit those cheques to their account and was therefore required to reimburse the claimants. It was established law that a customer's duty to a bank was (a) not to draw cheques in such a manner as to facilitate forgery; and (b) to notify the bank immediately of any forgery of which he becomes aware, but on the facts neither of these duties had been broken. The Privy Council rejected the defendants' contention that the claimants had been in breach of a duty of care in negligence to the bank. Similarly, the Court of Appeal has rejected claims in tort where no implied term could be established that a mortgagee owed any duty to ensure that the managing agent of a ship kept her insured for a stipulated sum[60] or that an insurer should inform the mortgagee of a ship when the owners were dishonestly jeopardising the cover.[61] However, in *Tai Hing Cotton Mill*, Lord Scarman went so far as to say that there was no, "advantage . . . in searching for a liability in tort where the parties are in a contractual relationship", a proposition which plainly no longer represents the law after *Henderson v Merrett Syndicates Ltd*.

---

[57] *Thake v Maurice* [1986] Q.B. 644 shows that a court will require very clear evidence to establish such a warranty against a doctor. Compare *Platform Funding Ltd v Bank of Scotland Plc* [2008] EWCA Civ 930; [2009] Q.B. 426, where it was held that although a valuer undertook only to use skill in the valuation he did undertake without qualification that he had valued the correct property. Similarly if a surgeon mixes up two patients and performs the wrong operation he commits trespass even if the confusion was someone else's fault.

[58] *Norwich CC v Harvey*, above, fn.43, in the three-party situation.

[59] [1986] A.C. 80. Applied in *Yorkshire Bank Plc v Lloyds Bank Plc* [1999] 1 All E.R. (Comm.) 154 so as to prevent a claim by paying bank against drawee bank when cheque fraudulently altered by person unknown.

[60] *National Bank of Greece S.A. v Pinios Shipping Co (No.1)* [1989] 3 W.L.R. 185 (on appeal, but not on this point) [1990] 1 A.C. 637.

[61] *Bank of Nova Scotia v Hellenic Mutual War Risks Association* [1990] 1 Q.B. 818 reversed on the construction of the contract, [1992] 1 A.C. 233. See also *Banque Keyser Ullmann S.A. v Skandia (UK) Insurance Co Ltd* [1991] 2 A.C. 249.

Even where the parties are not in a contractual relationship restraint may have to be exercised because sound policy may suggest that the matter should be left entirely to contract law. Thus building contracts are commonly made by a tendering process and contract law has reasonably clear rules about this. The basic principle is that the person who invites tenders has complete discretion as to which bidder shall get the contract. This may be modified in some cases by a finding that there was a promise (a collateral contract) to accept the "best" bid; or at least a promise to give honest consideration to all conforming bids; and where public works are involved there may be statutory requirements which displace the general law. There would be a serious risk of disruption of these principles if we allowed contentions that the invitor owed a "duty of care" to bidders, still more if we allowed such arguments to be advanced by sub-contractors associated with unsuccessful bidders.[62]

E. Tort and the Law of Restitution

The law of restitution[63] is concerned with the liability of a person **1–10** to pay money to another on the ground of unjust enrichment. One simple example of restitutionary liability is that to repay money which has been paid under a mistake of fact. I owe you £100. I pay the £100 to your twin brother whom I mistake for you, and he honestly believes that he is entitled to the money. Another is the liability of a seller to repay the price of goods when he fails to deliver. In both cases there is a duty to repay the money and so the defendant is under a remedial duty. Still, in the first case it cannot be said that this remedial duty is the result of the breach of some primary duty: it would be meaningless to say that your twin brother was under a duty not to accept the money from me, or that he was under a duty of any kind save the remedial duty to return the money to me because otherwise he would be unjustly enriched at my expense. In the second case there is certainly a primary duty—to deliver the goods—from which the remedial duty arises, but it is contractual, not tortious.

This is not to say that there is no connection between tort and restitution. Historically, the claimant may "waive" some torts and, instead of claiming damages for the loss he has suffered, claim in restitution what the defendant has received by the wrong.[64] Secondly, for some things which are undoubtedly wrongs, though they

---

[62] See *Design Services Ltd v Canada* [2008] SCC 22; [2008] 1 S.C.R. 737, where there appears to have been a collateral contract between the invitor and the main contractor bidders.

[63] In the past the greater part of this area of law was known as quasi-contract because recovery was granted on the basis of fictional contracts.

[64] See paras 22–13 and 26–2, below.

may lie on or beyond the fringe of what is commonly classified as the common law of torts (for example breach of confidence, breach of copyright) the claimant may directly claim, without reference to any procedural fictions, an account of the defendant's profits. However, except in those cases where the remedy of an account is granted by statute, it is more closely associated with equitable wrongdoing, in particular with breach of fiduciary duty. Thirdly, there are cases where the defendant has taken or misused the claimant's property where awards of damages are made on the basis of a "fair rental" payment, which may be compensatory in form but are arguably based in practical terms on reversal of the defendant's gain.[65]

The third element of Winfield's definition is that the breach of duty is redressable by an action for unliquidated damages. A claim is said to be "liquidated" when it is for a fixed, inelastic sum[66] or one which is calculable by the mere process of arithmetic.[67] This serves to distinguish tort from at least some of the quasi-contractual heads of restitution (for example, the claim for the return of money paid under a mistake) and from statutory actions for penalties.[68] It is not, of course, a sufficient test of tort liability that the remedy is unliquidated damages—for these are also the primary remedy for breach of contract—but it seems to be a necessary one: if, assuming the claimant can make out the elements of the case, he cannot recover unliquidated damages[69] then whatever claim he may have, it is not for tort. We should hasten to add that unliquidated damages are not the only remedy for tort and in the case of some torts they are not even, in practice, the primary remedy.[70]

F. Tort and Equitable Liability Distinguished

1–11   If a trustee misappropriates property which he holds upon trust for a beneficiary, the beneficiary can claim compensation. That compensation is not damages at all, though as a practical matter in some cases it may come close to the damages which would be awarded for

---

[65] See further para.22–13, below. A claim for the return of money paid under a void contract is neither a "matter relating to a contract" nor a "matter relating to tort, delict or quasi-delict" for jurisdiction purposes under the Brussels Convention: *Kleinwort Benson Ltd v Glasgow CC* [1999] 1 A.C. 153. Presumably, however, a case where the plaintiff had suffered a tort and claimed damages on a restitutionary basis would fall within the latter category.

[66] But the fact that the claimant claims a specific sum in his pleadings (e.g. £5,000 as the value of a wrecked car) does not make it liquidated.

[67] e.g. the price of goods sold and delivered at so much a unit or wages at so much a week.

[68] See, e.g. *Att Gen v Cantor* [1938] 2 K.B. 826 (affirmed [1939] 1 K.B. 326).

[69] But the claimant may be able to obtain a *quia timet* injunction before his cause of action is complete by suffering damage: para.22–52, below.

[70] e.g. the economic torts and nuisance.

misappropriation of property by a tort. The relationship of trustee and beneficiary is simply the best known example of a wider equitable concept of a fiduciary relationship, the distinguishing feature of which is an obligation of loyalty, and which has several consequences, for example that the fiduciary must not profit from his position or put himself in a position where there is a conflict between his own interests and those of the person to whom he owes the duty,[71] but which will also lead, where necessary, to the award of equitable compensation. Hence a claim for breach of fiduciary duty may lie in parallel with a tort claim against, for example, a solicitor on behalf of his client, and the concept has even been called in aid in Canada[72] and New Zealand[73] in cases of sexual abuse. However, equity recognises duties which do not turn on "disloyalty" and which are in substance duties of care.[74] In *Henderson v Merrett Syndicates Ltd (No.1)*[75] Lord Browne-Wilkinson said:

"The liability of a fiduciary for the negligent transaction of duties is not a separate head of liability but the paradigm of the general duty to act with care imposed by law on those who take it upon themselves to act for or advise others. Although the historical developments of the rules of law and equity have, in the past, caused different labels to be stuck on different manifestations of the duty, in truth the duty of care imposed on bailees, carriers, trustees, directors, agents and others is the same duty: it arises from the circumstances in which the defendants were acting, not from their status or description. It is the fact that they have all assumed responsibility for the property or affairs of others which renders them liable for the careless performance of what they have undertaken to do, not the description of the trade or position which they hold."

Perhaps the time is approaching to assimilate equitable wrong-doing with the law of tort[76] but the force of history is powerful in English law and for the moment it is probably safer to say that the

---

[71] See Millett L.J. in *Bristol and West Building Society v Mothew* [1998] Ch.1 at 17–18.
[72] *Norberg v Wynrib* (1992) 92 D.L.R. (4th) 449.
[73] See *S. v G.* [1995] 3 N.Z.L.R. 681. But see the warning against the assumption that this is always an alternative to a tort claim in *H. v R.* [1996] 1 N.Z.L.R. 299 at 307: "An otherwise admirable end cannot be met by utilising an important concept, and one which has a distinct moral and functional presence in the law, by watering down the basic concept of a fiduciary." For an optimistic attempt to establish a fiduciary duty see *Calvert v William Hill Credit Ltd* [2008] EWCA Civ 1427; [2009] Ch 330.
[74] A tactical reliance on the equitable duty in order to avoid principles of causation and damage applicable at common law will meet with a hostile response: *Target Holdings Ltd v Redferns* [1996] A.C. 421; *Bristol and West Building Society v Mothew*, above, fn.71. *Cia de Seguros Imperio v Heath (REBX) Ltd* [2001] 1 W.L.R. 112 (limitation) goes further.
[75] [1995] 2 A.C. 145 at 205.
[76] See Birks, "Definition And Division" in *The Classification of Obligations* (1997).

streams run in different channels even though the patterns they produce may have similarities. Even now, although law and equity have long been fused and questions relating to trusts may incidentally arise in tort cases, actions related to matters of trust are allocated to the Chancery Division of the High Court. The distinctiveness of equity (at least at a theoretical level) has been affirmed in situations which might have been absorbed into the tort of negligence. Thus a mortgagee of property exercising a power of sale may have to take care to obtain a proper price and a receiver who carries on a debtor's business for the creditor may have to run it properly, but these duties are owed in equity and not in negligence on the basis of "neighbourhood".[77]

G. Tort and Liability on Bailment

1-12   A bailment[78] involves the custody of one person's goods by another. The person who delivers the goods is called a "bailor", the person to whom they are delivered is the "bailee". Common examples of bailment are hire of goods, such as hire of a car from a garage; gratuitous loan of goods, such as lending this book to a friend; and pawn or pledge. In very many cases the delivery is on a condition, express or implied, that the goods shall be restored to the bailor, or according to his directions, as soon as the purpose for which they are bailed is completed but it seems that this is not a necessary condition. For example, a standard hire-purchase agreement involves a bailment followed by an option to purchase and if the hire charges and option fee are paid the purpose of the exercise is that the bailee should become the owner.[79] If the bailee misuses or damages the goods he is, of course, liable in a civil action to the bailor. Is this liability to be distinguished from liability in tort? Many bailments arise out of contract, but it is undoubtedly possible

---

[77] *Downsview Nominees Ltd v First City Corp Ltd* [1993] A.C. 295; *Medforth v Blake* [2000] Ch. 86. But see the remark of Scott V.C. at [2000] Ch. 102: "I do not accept that there is any difference between the answer that would be given by the common law to the question what duties are owed by a receiver managing a mortgaged property to those interested in the equity of redemption and the answer that would be given by equity to that question. I do not, for my part, think it matters one jot whether the duty is expressed as a common law duty or as a duty in equity. The result is the same. The origin of the receiver's duty, like the mortgagee's duty, lies, however, in equity and we might as well continue to refer to it as a duty in equity." A liquidator or administrator owes no duty to individual creditors: *Nam Tai Electronics v Hague* [2008] UKPC 13; [2008] P.N.L.R. 27; *Kyrris v Oldham* [2003] EWCA Civ 1506.

[78] Palmer, *Bailment*, 3rd edn (2009).

[79] It seems inaccurate to say that the bailor gives up any right to the return of the goods upon the exercise of the option since that right would only arise if the hire charges were not paid. In *Yearworth v North Bristol NHS Trust* [2009] EWCA Civ 37; [2009] 3 W.L.R. 118 a transaction under which A put goods in B's custody on terms that the goods were to be used according to A's wishes in certain circumstances but under which they could not be restored to A was a bailment.

for bailment to exist without contract and where this is the case, as
in the gratuitous loan of something for the use of the borrower, what
is the nature of the liability? Winfield's opinion was that the bailee's
liability is not tortious because, he said, the duty arises from a
relation, that of bailor and bailee, which is created by the parties. No
one need be a bailee if he does not wish to be one and no one can
have liability for the safe custody of goods thrust upon him against
his will.[80] It is certainly true that a person cannot be subjected to the
duties of a bailee without his consent but as we have already seen,
there are duties which are undoubtedly tortious and which can only
exist if there has been some prior agreement between the parties, so
it may be argued that there is no good reason for distinguishing the
common law duties of a bailee from duties of this kind. Assumption
of responsibility has been an important idea in the expansion of the
modern law of negligence[81] but a little before this occurred it was
said on high authority that the obligation of the bailee, "arises
because the taking of possession in the circumstances involves an
assumption of responsibility for the safe keeping of the goods".[82]
Furthermore, while it is a requirement of a bailment that the bailee
voluntarily takes custody of the goods, it seems that it is not
necessary that the bailor should consent to their custody.[83] If the
bailor's claim is necessarily founded upon some specific provision
in a contract, then, no doubt, the bailee's liability is not tortious but
contractual; but if the bailor's claim rests upon a breach by the
bailee of one of the bailee's common law duties, then might one not
contend that his liability as much attributable to the law of tort as is
the claim of a visitor against the occupier of premises under the
Occupier's Liability Act?[84] However, the Court of Appeal has held
that a gratuitous bailment may create a legal obligation independent
of that in tort, though on the facts there was also a parallel liability
under that head.[85] Sometimes the legislature lays down rules by
reference to the contract/tort distinction and no other. For example,
the legislation on limitation of actions contains elaborate provisions
on contract and tort but says nothing about bailment. The courts

---

[80] See para.17–9, below. Winfield's view is set out in full in *Province of the Law of Tort*,
Ch.5, where he makes the point that bailment is more fittingly regarded as a distinct branch
of the law of property under the title "Possession" than as appropriate to either the law of
contract or the law of tort.

[81] See para.5–34, below.

[82] *Gilchrist Watt and Sanderson Pty. Ltd v York Products Pty. Ltd* [1970] 1 W.L.R. 1262 at
1268, PC.

[83] *The Pioneer Container* [1994] 2 A.C. 324.

[84] *Turner v Stallibrass* [1898] 1 Q.B. 56 at 59, per Collins L.J.; *Morris v C. W. Martin & Sons
Ltd* [1966] 1 Q.B. 716; *Chesworth v Farrar* [1967] 1 Q.B. 716; *Gilchrist, Watt and
Sanderson Pty Ltd v York Products Pty Ltd* [1970] 1 W.L.R. 1262.

[85] *Yearworth v North Bristol NHS Trust* [2009] EWCA Civ 37; [2009] 3 W.L.R. 118. Where
the bailment involves specific undertakings by the bailee the measure of damages may be
more akin to that in contract than tort: at [50].

have nevertheless managed to accommodate bailment cases within this structure.[86] All this is typical of the common law's willingness to be pragmatic about "classification" and to admit parallel causes of action.

H. Tort and Crime Distinguished

1–13   Crime and tort overlap. Many torts are also crimes, sometimes with the same names and with similar elements (for example, assault and battery) and sometimes a civil action in tort is deduced from the existence of a statute creating a criminal offence.[87] The more serious, "traditional" criminal offences are likely to amount to torts[88] provided there is a victim who has suffered damage[89] but the scope of tort is wider: it is broadly true to say that causing physical damage by negligence is always tortious, but it is criminal only in certain circumstances or conditions.[90] A driver who causes injury in a road accident may well be guilty of a crime, such as careless driving, but his civil liability arises entirely from the tort of negligence (although the detailed rules of the criminal law governing road traffic may be called in aid to demonstrate what is or is not due care in driving).

There is no real difficulty in distinguishing criminal prosecutions from tort claims, if only because they are tried in different courts by different procedures. Generally, criminal proceedings are brought by the Crown Prosecution Service or some authorised body and although a private prosecution is still possible, the object of the proceedings in any case is the imposition of some sanction in the nature of punishment, for example imprisonment or a pecuniary fine, even though the sanction imposed may have a reformative rather than a strictly punitive purpose. Nevertheless, there are functional overlaps between the two categories. At least some of tort law, like crime, has the purpose of deterrence and in a very limited class of cases tort imposes overt punishment upon defendants in the shape of exemplary damages.[91] On the other side, criminal proceedings may lead to a compensation order in favour of the victim (a matter which is outlined later).[92] In this respect the distinction between crime and tort has become more blurred, though since tort originated in trespass, which to our eyes was in medieval times quasi-criminal,

---

[86] See, e.g. *Chesworth v Farrar* [1967] 1 Q.B. 716. See also *American Express Co v British Airways Board* [1983] 1 W.L.R. 701 (protection from action in tort under Post Office Act 1969 extended to bailment or the legislation would be ineffective).
[87] See Ch.7.
[88] But not always, e.g. perjury: para.24–10, below.
[89] There is no law of "attempted tort".
[90] But with the rather anomalous exceptions of manslaughter and causing death by careless or reckless driving, the occurrence of damage is generally irrelevant to criminality.
[91] See para.22–8, below.
[92] See para.4–2, below.

the law may only be returning to its roots. Furthermore, the compensatory sums awarded under these provisions are, until the court specifies their exact amount, quite uncertain and are therefore just as "unliquidated" as are damages in tort. There is, however, one peculiarity which marks them off from damages in tort. In every case they are obtainable only as a result of a process the primary purpose of which, when it is initiated, is the imposition of punishment, or something in the nature of punishment. In crime, the award of compensation is ancillary to the criminal process: in tort it is normally its very object.

It should also be borne in mind that criminal proceedings may act in an auxiliary role to a civil case. For example, a prosecution in respect of a traffic accident is likely to take place before the trial or settlement of a civil action arising from it and a conviction may be used as evidence of negligence in the civil action.[93]

I. Law of Obligations?

At this stage we may, perhaps, claim to have given some reason **1–14** why a book on the law of tort need not concern itself with restitution, crime or breach of trust, and to have gone a little way towards distinguishing tortious from contractual liability. As to the last, we have seen that the boundaries between the two types of liability are by no means easy to state (nor are they immutable)[94] and that there are plentiful opportunities for both forms of liability to coexist on one and the same set of facts. The claimant in such a case cannot recover damages twice over under different heads of legal liability. Would it not, therefore, be advantageous to bring tortious and contractual liability together in one book under some such titles as "The Law of Obligations"? There is a great deal to be said for this and it will be essential where one aims at a study of a particular factual area of legal liability, such as product liability or "professional negligence". However, the practicality of the exercise depends on the level of detail required. A general book on the law of obligations ought to include the whole of the law of contract and torts, the law of restitution and, even if it did not include the whole law of trusts, should certainly contain a good deal of equity, and thus risks becoming unmanageably large. Furthermore, while there are undoubtedly points at which our legal categories interconnect and

---

[93] See para.5–88, below.
[94] With changes in the law a topic may "move" from contract into tort, an important example being the imposition of a tortious duty to take care in making statements in *Hedley, Byrne & Co Ltd v Heller & Partners Ltd* [1964] A.C. 465, Ch.11, below.

cross, and it is vital that the lawyer should grasp the implications of this, there are also large areas where they travel alone. The law of tort is concerned with the incidence of liability.[95] Books on contract or on trusts are, no doubt, concerned with the incidence of liability for loss or damage suffered, as are those on tort, but there, liability only forms a part, and sometimes a small part, of their subject matter. Equally, if not more important, are such questions as the ways in which a contract may be concluded or a trust set up, the various modes of discharge or dissolution and the nature of the property rights these institutions may create. But the central question for the law of tort is always that of liability, and it is this which really forms the link between the various topics covered in this book. We are not here concerned with the creation of legal relationships or rights of property, though it may be necessary to mention them incidentally from time to time.

2. FOUNDATION OF TORTIOUS LIABILITY

1–15 Winfield's definition of tortious liability has been criticised on the ground that it is formal, not material, and does nothing to indicate the lawfulness or otherwise of a given act. This, it seems, Winfield admitted, for he agreed that the layman must be told that no one but a professional lawyer can say whether or not the loss inflicted on him by the action or inaction of a neighbour will entitle him to a remedy by civil action against the neighbour, and added:

> "[A] layman is not remarkable for wisdom if he imagines that he can safely say that he is entitled to sue his neighbour for tort or for breach of contract, or for any conceivable claim without consulting a professional lawyer first."

Winfield did devote several pages of early editions of this work to discussion of a familiar controversy concerning the foundation of tortious liability which has some bearing on the problem of a material definition. Salmond had asked[96]:

> "Does the law of torts consist of a fundamental general principle that it is wrongful to cause harm to other persons in the absence

---

[95] In this sense tort most closely resembles crime.
[96] *Torts*, 2nd edn (1910), pp.8–9.

of some specific ground of justification or excuse, or does it consist of a number of specific rules prohibiting certain kinds of harmful activity, and leaving all the residue outside the sphere of legal responsibility?"

He chose the second alternative.[97] From the point of view of the practical lawyer concerned with the law at a particular moment there can be no doubt that the second view is the correct one: for example, a recording company was held to have no civil action in respect of "bootlegging" of its artists' performances where it was unable to prove any of the economic torts or the distinct tort of breach of statutory duty,[98] even though the defendants' conduct was criminal and no justification for it could be offered. Despite occasional judicial canvassing of the idea,[99] English law has not adopted what in the United States is known as the "prima facie tort theory" whereby:

"The intentional infliction of temporal damages is a cause of action, which, as a matter of substantive law, whatever may be the form of the pleading, requires a justification if the defendant is to escape".[100]

Nevertheless, it should be noted that we have for a good many years had something very close to a generalised principle of liability in situations where the defendant's purpose is the infliction of physical harm[101] on the claimant,[102] and despite the caution which

---

[97] To take two modern examples, in *Furniss v Fitchett* [1958] N.Z.L.R. 396 at 401, Barrow-clough C.J. said: "The well known torts do not have their origin in any all-embracing general principle of tortious liability." In *Bollinger v Costa Brava Wine Co Ltd* [1960] Ch. 262 at 283, Danckwerts J. said: "The substance of [the argument for the defendants] was that, before a person can recover for loss which he suffered from another person's act, it must be shown that his case falls within the class of actionable wrongs. But the law may be thought to have failed if it can offer no remedy for the deliberate act of one person which causes damage to the property of another."

[98] *R.C.A. Corp v Pollard* [1983] Ch. 135. See *Dunlop v Woolahra MC* [1982] A.C. 158; *Lonrho Ltd v Shell Petroleum Co Ltd (No.2)* [1982] A.C. 173.

[99] e.g. *Mogul SS Co Ltd v McGregor Gow & Co* (1889) 23 Q.B.D. 598 at 663, per Bowen L.J. The High Court of Australia's flirtation in *Beaudesert SC v Smith* (1966) 120 C.L.R. 145 with the principle that independently of the "nominate" torts, "a person who suffers harm or loss as the inevitable consequence of the unlawful, intentional and positive acts of another is entitled to recover damages from the other" no longer represents the law there: *Northern Territory v Mengel* (1995) 185 C.L.R. 307.

[100] *Aikens v Wisconsin* 195 U.S. 194 (1904), per Holmes J. But see Dobbs, "Tortious Interference with Contractual Relationships" (1980) 34 Ark. L.Rev. 335.

[101] The American doctrine was primarily focused on interference with economic interests. We have had similar problems in attempting to generalise the economic torts.

[102] *Wilkinson v Downton* [1897] 2 Q.B. 57, para.4–36, below.

characterises the courts' attitude to the duty of care in negligence[103] it will be an unusual case in which the defendant is not liable where his act has caused foreseeable physical damage to the claimant or his property.

1–16   Winfield conceded the correctness of the "narrow" view as a practical, day-to-day matter,[104] but he contended that from a broader outlook there was validity in the theory of a fundamental general principle of liability, for if we take the view, as we must, that the law of tort has grown for centuries, and is still growing, then some such principle seems to be at the back of it. It is the difference between treating a tree as inanimate for the practical purposes of the moment (for example, for the purpose of avoiding collision with it, it is as lifeless as a block of marble) and realising that it is animate because we know that it has grown and is still growing. The caution and slowness which usually mark the creation of new rules by the judges tend to mask the fact that they have been created, for they have often come into existence only by a series of analogical extensions spread over a long period of time. To vary the metaphor, the process has resembled the sluggish movement of the glacier rather than the catastrophic charge of the avalanche but when once a new tort has come into being, it might fairly seem to have done so, if the whole history of its development is taken into account, in virtue of the principle that unjustifiable harm is tortious.[105]

1–17   Where the courts hold that the harm is justifiable, there is, of course, no tort, and they may hold that it is justifiable for any one or more of several reasons. The claimant may be asking them to do what they think Parliament is more fitted to do; he may be alleging a particular tort, without giving proof of some essential requisite of it; he may be taking an exaggerated view of what is necessary to his own comfort or prosperity; or he may be demanding the creation of a remedy which would throw out of gear other parts of the law. Nonetheless, subject to these restrictions and looking at the law of torts in the whole of its development, Winfield still inclined to the first theory.

However, since the supporters of the second view do not deny that the law of tort is capable of development, or even that new heads of liability can come into existence, and since the supporters of the first view admit that no action will lie if the conduct which caused the

---

[103] See para.5–3, below.

[104] For an entertaining perspective on the fissiparous nature of the common law of torts, see Rudden, "Torticles" (1991–92) 617 Tulane Civil Law Forum 105.

[105] Damage for which compensation is not recoverable is known as *damnum sine injuria*; where a tort is actionable per se (without proof of loss, e.g. trespass) there is said to be *injuria sine damno*.

harm was justifiable,[106] the difference between them is perhaps less than is sometimes supposed. Summing up his investigation into the controversy, Professor Glanville Williams said this[107]:

"The first school has shown that the rules of liability are very wide. The second school has shown that some rules of absence of liability are also very wide. Neither school has shown that there is any general rule, whether of liability or of non-liability, to cover novel cases that have not yet received the attention of the courts. In a case of first impression—that is, a case that falls under no established rule or that falls equally under two conflicting rules —there is no ultimate principle directing the court to find for one party or the other... Why should we not settle the argument by saying simply that there are some general rules creating liability... and some equally general rules exempting from liability... Between the two is a stretch of disputed territory, with the courts as an unbiased boundary commission. If, in an unprovided case, the decision passes for the claimant, it will be not because of a general theory of liability but because the court feels that here is a case in which existing principles of liability may properly be extended."

3. TORT AND OTHER SOURCES OF COMPENSATION

As will be seen, much of the law of tort in practice is concerned with the problem of accidental injury to the person or damage to property, and the general approach of the law to these problems rests on two broad principles. Both are subject to a very large number of exceptions and qualifications but by and large it is the case first that the victim of accidental injury or damage is entitled to redress through the law of tort if, and only if, his loss was caused by the fault of the defendant or those for whose fault the defendant must answer, and secondly that the redress due from the defendant whose liability is established should be "full" or should, in other words, be as nearly equivalent as money can be to the claimant's loss. Nevertheless, even in those accidents which can be attributed to another's fault, the role played by the law of tort should not be exaggerated. A **1–18**

---

[106] "What is justifiable conduct? This, of course, is the whole question of tortious liability. If it means justifiable in law, the statement merely means that you must compensate for harms (and it will be noticed that what kind of harms is not specified) unless the law says you are not obliged to. In other words we still have to decide what losses the law deems worthy of compensation, and what are the circumstances producing such harm which will be considered sufficient to entail liability": Wright, "Introduction to the Law of Torts" (1944) 8 C.L.J. 240.
[107] "The Foundation of Tortious Liability" (1939) 7 C.L.J. 131.

century or so ago the law of tort was probably the primary vehicle of compensation, but poverty, ignorance or economic pressure deprived many injured persons of access to the law and threw them back on the Poor Law, charity or the assistance of a trade union or friendly society. In more recent times the development of insurance and social security has tended to relegate tort law to a more secondary role.[108] We must, therefore, turn to look at some of these other sources of compensation and their relationship with the law of tort and in doing so consider further some of the assumptions which underpin the tort system.

A. Damage to Property: Tort and Insurance

1–19   There is little in the way of state provision for loss or damage to property,[109] which obviously occupies a much lower position of priority than personal injury.[110] Private insurance is, however, of very great significance in relation to property damage. Insurance takes two basic forms, "loss" or "first party" insurance and "liability" or "third party" insurance. Under the first, the owner of property has cover against loss or damage to that property from the risks described in the policy, such as fire, flood and theft, whether or not the loss occurs through the fault of any other person.[111] Under the second, the assured himself is covered against legal liability which he may incur to a third party, and the establishment of such liability by the third party, not merely loss suffered by the third party, is an essential prerequisite to a claim on the policy. A good example of a policy combining both types of cover is a motor "comprehensive"

---

[108] This type of phenomenon is not, of course, unique to the law of tort but lawyers may tend to exaggerate the overall practical effect of legal liability. It is likely, for example, that the practice of administrative challenge to unfair exemption clauses is a much more potent protector of "consumers" than the possibility that a court may strike such clauses down: Unfair Terms in Consumer Contracts Regulations 1999, SI 1999/2083.

[109] However, the Riot (Damages) Act 1886 makes the police authority liable for property damage caused by a riot within its area, presumably on the basis that it has failed to uphold order (cf. the Criminal Injuries Compensation Scheme, para.4–2, below). The Act can be relied on by a company carrying out public functions on a "contracted out" basis: *Yarl's Wood Immigration Ltd v Bedfordshire Police Authority* [2009] EWCA Civ 1110.

[110] In an emergency such as flood or fire the social security authorities would assist with clothing, bedding and other immediate needs. Provision may sometimes be made on an ad hoc basis for widespread disasters. For various mechanisms (including, in France, a compulsory "disaster extension" to property insurance (underwritten by the state)) see Faure and Hartlief, *Financial Compensation for Victims of Disasters: a comparative legal approach* (2005).

[111] Indeed, the insured could normally claim on the policy even if the property was damaged through his own negligence (but not his own deliberate act) though the policy may restrict cover in certain circumstances, for example where the key is left in the car and it is then stolen.

policy,[112] which will (a) cover the insured against legal liability to other road users and passengers and (b) entitle the insured to claim from his insurer the cost of repairs should his vehicle be damaged or the value of the vehicle if it becomes a "write-off".[113]

Loss insurance is of very great significance in relation to damage to property, and it is safe to assume that very much more is paid out every year on property loss policies than is recovered in tort actions in such cases. The fundamental stance of the law on loss insurance is that it is irrelevant to tort liability.[114] If D damages C's property and this is fully covered by an insurance policy, that in no way precludes C suing D for the cost of repairing the property.[115] Indeed, even if C has collected on his insurance that would not provide D with a defence.[116] In fact, it is inconceivable that C would sue in the latter case because, property loss policies generally being contracts of indemnity, he would then have to reimburse the insurer with the damages recovered. A more likely outcome is that the insurer will exercise his right to be subrogated to C's rights against D, and sue D (in reality probably D's liability insurers) in C's name.[117] The principle of subrogation therefore means that the wrongdoer ends up having to save harmless someone who has already taken a premium for doing the same for the claimant. Nevertheless, the attitude of the courts is not entirely consistent. No one has yet gone so far as to hold that the fact that the claimant is insured is in itself enough to defeat his claim but the presence (or likely presence) of loss insurance has sometimes been used in combination with other factors to reach that conclusion.[118] We may note, on the other side of the

[112] The majority of motor policies are comprehensive, though all that is required by law is cover against liability for personal injuries and, from 1989, property damage to third parties. A standard householder's policy will also combine both loss and liability insurance.

[113] The fact that the accident is the assured's own fault will not prevent a claim under (b), though there will normally be conditions as to the use of the vehicle and its maintenance in a roadworthy condition, breach of which will entitle the insurer to repudiate liability. In no circumstances can the insured claim under (a) in respect of his own injuries, though many policies contain a limited element of "no-fault" loss insurance for injury to driver and passengers.

[114] See para.22–42, below. And in relation to "collateral benefits" in personal injury cases (a similar issue), para.22–32, below.

[115] Informal settlements of minor motor claims without calling on the insurance are probably quite common because of the concern of both parties to maintain their no claims bonuses.

[116] *Bee v Jenson* [2007] EWCA Civ 923; [2007] 4 All E.R. 791 (hire charges). But it might have an impact on costs: *Hobbs v Marlowe* [1978] A.C. 16.

[117] See *Castellain v Preston* (1883) 11 Q.B.D. 380; *Caledonia North Sea Ltd v British Telecommunications Plc* [2002] UKHL 4; [2002] S.C. (HL) 117 (a case of subrogation of a liability insurer).

[118] See, e.g. Lord Denning M.R. in *Lamb v Camden LBC* [1981] Q.B. 625 at 637–638, though his Lordship was probably wrong on the facts to assume that there was cover. In *Norwich CC v Harvey* [1989] 1 W.L.R. 828 the fact that D was in a chain of building contracts, one of which, between C and X, required C to maintain insurance on the works, was held to be a good reason for holding D not liable to C.

equation, that the fact that D has (or is likely to have) liability cover is equally not a good reason for making him liable but that, too, has sometimes been a strong influence in favour of liability.[119]

1–20   The opportunities for an effective exercise of the insurer's rights of subrogation may vary considerably from one type of case to another. In marine cases the right is probably commonly exercised because the size of the individual claim makes it worthwhile to do so; in home and contents insurance subrogation is probably almost nonexistent since if the loss is anyone's fault it is likely to be the householder's (against whom it cannot be exercised) or that of persons, like burglars, who will not be worth pursuing. In the case of road accidents, repairing or replacing vehicles probably represents their largest single cost. For many years nearly all motor insurers operated a "knock for knock" agreement, so that if there was a collision between car A, comprehensively insured by Company X, and car B, insured by Company Y, and the accident was caused by the fault of car A and led to damage to both vehicles, each insurer would bear its own loss in respect of the vehicle it insured and would not pursue subrogation rights against the other in that other's capacity as liability insurer. There has been no such general agreement since 1994, though that does not mean that subrogation rights will be regularly pursued. However, one should not underestimate the incidence of property-related claims, as witness the litigation about "credit hire" for fault-free drivers involved in accidents.[120]

It can be argued that to allow a tort claim in respect of property damage when loss insurance is widely held or easily available is wasteful and that this is compounded by subrogation litigation, which only shifts money around the system from one insurer to another. On the other hand, it would require a pretty major change in our intuitive ideas of corrective justice to take away C's right to claim against D when D's fault has damaged C's property, and there would still remain the problem of uninsured losses, whether by total absence of cover,[121] inadequate cover or "excess" thresholds.[122] If, as is likely, the subrogation system is of limited application in

---

[119] Again, most notably, Lord Denning M.R. in *Nettleship v Weston* [1971] 2 Q.B. 691, para.5–76, below. In German law a person who is immune from liability because of mental disorder may nevertheless be ordered to pay compensation if he has sufficient assets: BGB §829. This includes having compulsory liability insurance.

[120] See para.22–43, below. Individually these involve small amounts. However, damage to property sometimes leads to litigation on an heroic scale. It was estimated that the cost of the hearing arising from the Buncefield oil depot explosion in 2005 were £250 a minute and claimants' costs were £16 million: *Colour Quest Ltd v Total Downstream UK Plc* [2009] EWHC 823 (Comm); [2009] 2 Lloyd's Rep. 1 at [3].

[121] Compulsion to insure one's property could hardly be justified.

[122] In motor cases the loss of no claims bonus is also a significant factor.

smaller cases, it may be thought that the continued operation of tort law in large claims is not a serious social problem.

Litigation over pure financial loss caused by negligence is certainly less frequent than over damage to property, if only because the law puts serious obstacles in the claimant's way.[123] However, when it does occur it generally involves very large sums of money, sometimes far beyond the capacity of the liability insurance market to bear.

B. Personal Injuries and Death

The Royal Commission under Lord Pearson[124] reported in 1978, that tort law accounted for no more than one-quarter of the £827 million[125] per annum which was then paid in respect of compensation for personal injury. The monetary figures are now much larger, social security is rather more restricted, tort defendants now have to some extent to reimburse the social security system and it is now probably more worthwhile to make a low value tort claim; but there is no reason to believe that tort has advanced from the second rank in the intervening years. Private insurance plays a role here, too, but the major player is social security. However, what is true of the whole system is not necessarily true of part of it. For example, tort damages play a very small role with regard to accidents in the home (one of the largest categories) simply because there is rarely anyone on whom to pin liability; on the other hand, quite a high proportion of road accident victims[126] recover under the tort system (such accidents are rarely no one's fault[127] and insurance is compulsory).

1–21

C. Private Insurance, Occupational Pensions, etc.

Three main types of insurance give protection against accidental death or injury: life assurance, personal accident insurance and permanent health insurance. The first is without doubt the most important: personal accident and permanent health insurance are a good deal less common, the Pearson Commission's personal injury survey finding that such cover contributed only about 6 per cent to accident compensation. More significant are employers' occupational sick pay schemes. In fact, in 1983, sick pay from employers replaced social security payments as the method of short-term income replacement. Individual schemes vary in detail but replace

1–22

---

[123] See para.5–39, below.
[124] Cmnd. 7054.
[125] Which would be about £3.8 billion today if adjusted according to the retail price index.
[126] About 25 per cent at the time of Pearson.
[127] It may of course be entirely the victim's fault, which bars any claim.

all or part of lost income for a maximum period which may be related to length of service but which rarely exceeds six months. In cases of death or long-term injury leading to premature retirement a payment may be made under an occupational pension scheme, though the traditional "final salary" scheme is now far less common. The chance of receipt of any one or more of the above benefits is heavily influenced by the social class of the victim and the nature of his employment, but it will readily be appreciated that some accident victims or their dependants stand to get very large sums from such sources and it may be asked to what extent such receipts are taken into account in assessing tort damages for loss of earnings.[128] The question is complex and will be considered in more detail later,[129] but the broad answer is that the courts will ignore all charitable and comparable payments, all proceeds of private insurance and all occupational pension scheme payments but will make a deduction in respect of sick pay. Quite apart, therefore, from social security benefits, there is a strong possibility that some accident victims who are successful in a tort claim will receive more than they have lost in income.

D. Social Security

1–23   The social security system is hugely complex and it would be impossible to summarise it here. It is not even easy to define what "the system" is. The Criminal Injuries Compensation Scheme, for example, is a major provider of state assistance to a group of victims of misfortune, but it has not, since its inception, been within the legal framework of benefits nor has it been administered by the Department of Work and Pensions. It is outlined below in connection with intentional torts to the person, since those are generally also criminal.[130] With regard to benefits usually regarded as being in this category we still have to draw a distinction between industrial and non-industrial injuries.

1–24   **i. Non-industrial injuries.** Some benefits (for example, income support and housing benefit) are simply based on the fact that the recipient's means are below bare subsistence level and they have no connection with injury—though an accident victim may receive them if the conditions are satisfied. Otherwise, cases of injury falling

---

[128] The question usually arises in this way because the payment of such benefits nearly always precedes the recovery of tort damages. If the issue arose of whether tort damages were to be taken into account in assessing payments under the insurance policy or the pension scheme, everything would depend upon the construction of the contract. Tort damages, however, would almost invariably have no effect on payments of life or personal accident policies.

[129] See para.22–32, below.

[130] See para.4–2, below.

outside the Industrial Injuries Scheme are dealt with in the same way as sickness and the primary short-term benefit is in fact now paid by employers in the form of "statutory sick pay" for up to 28 weeks. Employers could formerly recoup the greater part of statutory sick pay payments by deducting them from national insurance contributions due to the Inland Revenue, but this is no longer so.[131] When the statutory sick pay entitlement has been exhausted it is replaced by employment and support allowance (formerly incapacity benefit) supplemented for adult and minor dependants.[132] In addition, a claimant who needs constant care or assistance or is unable to walk may receive disability living allowance or attendance alowance.[133]

ii. Industrial injuries.[134] The Workmen's Compensation Act 1897 introduced into English law the first important type of accident compensation not based on the law of tort. Under that Act, workers injured in various types of employment could recover compensation for personal injury "arising out of and in the course of employment". Unlike the modern system of industrial injury benefits, however, this compensation was payable by the employer and was recoverable by action in the courts. With the implementation of the Beveridge Report[135] the Workmen's Compensation Scheme was abolished and replaced by a system of benefits payable by the state for such accidents and diseases.[136] The Industrial Injuries Scheme[137] now covers industrial injuries (including certain prescribed diseases) and provides for payment of "disablement benefit" to the injured worker. The basic condition of award is that the injury was caused by an accident, "arising out of and in the course of employment". Injuries with short-term effects are excluded by the rule that disablement benefit is not payable for the first 15 weeks after the accident. It is most important to note that disablement benefit is not necessarily looked upon as a method of replacement of lost earnings but is based upon an objective assessment of disablement, fixed on a percentage basis either by regulations or by a medical board. For example, the regulations provide that loss of sight of one eye amounts to a 30 per cent disablement so that the victim receives

1–25

---

[131] Statutory Sick Pay Act 1994. The redundancy payments system began in this way, but the cost now falls on employers.
[132] In 2009 the rate for an adult with no dependants was up to £95.15 per week. Benefits are, of course, updated, usually annually.
[133] In a very serious case the sums involved can be very large. In *Freeman v Lockett* [2006] EWHC 102 (QB) the claimant was receiving over £50,000 a year in respect of domiciliary care.
[134] Lewis, *Compensation for Industrial Injury* (1987).
[135] Cmd. 6404 (1942).
[136] National Insurance (Industrial Injuries) Act 1946. There may of course be further provision in particular employments, e.g. the Police (Injury Benefit) Regulations, SI 2006/932.
[137] Strictly, this is a misnomer since there is no separate fund nor even, now, a separate Act.

proportionate benefit even though his earnings may not be affected at all. Formerly, disablement of less than 20 per cent attracted a lump sum gratuity but many of these cases were taken out of the system in 1986,[138] thereby making tort claims more important in "minor" cases. Disablement benefit takes the form of a pension. The maximum payment in 2009 was £145.80 per week but additional sums are payable where there is a need for constant attendance.

Payments in respect of industrial injuries are higher than in the case of other accidents, there is no contribution requirement (though the injury must be work-related) and in some cases payments may be made even though there is no interruption of employment and earnings are unaffected. The "industrial preference" therefore still exists, though now only in respect of longer-term cases and at a lower rate than formerly.[139]

E. Recovery of Social Security Payments

1–26   The question of offsetting social security payments against damages where a tort claim succeeds is governed by statute and is dealt with later.[140] Briefly, in the case of personal injuries social security payments paid in the initial five-year period after the accident are deducted by the defendant, who must reimburse the Secretary of State.[141] In this context the reader should also remember that in dealing with personal injuries the cost of provision of medical services, though not "compensation", cannot be left out of account. The cost attributable for the National Health Service and the personal social services to accidental death, injury and industrial disease is probably considerably more than the social security payments made in respect of such losses.[142] Subrogation or reimbursement of healthcare providers has long been found in a number of other legal systems and there was, for a long while, a limited right of recourse by the health service in road accident cases—this has now been extended more widely.[143]

---

[138] The threshold disability is now 14 per cent but disabilities between 14 and 19 per cent are paid at the 20 per cent rate.

[139] The preference was probably retained in the implementation of the Beveridge reforms in the 1940s because work-related accidents had for 50 years received a "preference" under the Workmen's Compensation Acts. At the inception of the national insurance scheme the preference was 73 per cent in cases of short-term injury.

[140] See para.22–34, below.

[141] See Lewis, "England and Wales" in Magnus (ed.), *The Impact of Social Security Law on Tort Law* (2003).

[142] Well over half of those who do make a tort claim make a full recovery within two years of the accident: Law Com. No.257, §3.37.

[143] See para.22–36, below. Note that the number of NHS "bed days" attributable to house accidents in 1994/1995 was nearly six times that attributable to road accidents: Hansard, H.L., January 27, 1998, col.WA26.

4. PAYING FOR THE OPERATION OF THE TORT SYSTEM

As we have seen, we have a mixed system of compensation in which   **1–27**
tort plays a significant but secondary role. How is the operation of
the tort system financed? In the case of personal injuries the great
majority of claims are brought against defendants who are insured
against liability, a point which is discussed below in relation to
deterrence. Very few claims, even if successful, progress right
through the system to a judgment against the defendant; the great
majority being settled at some stage, often before the issue of
proceedings. The method of financing the handling of claims underwent a major change at the end of the 20th century. Some people
have legal expenses insurance to assist in asserting claims, but it has
probably never been very widespread in England except as a limited
"add-on" to some other policy.[144] Legal aid for personal injury
cases never formed a very large part of net civil legal aid expenditure because most claims which were supported succeeded and the
bill was passed to liability insurers. However, legal aid[145] has now
been virtually abolished in this context except for medical negligence cases and largely replaced by the conditional fee system,
under which the claimant's lawyers waive all or part of their fees
and disbursements if the claim fails but receive these (normally with
a success fee or "uplift") if it succeeds.[146] In that event the defendant will pay on the usual basis that "costs follow the event".[147] An
unsuccessful claimant remains liable to pay the legal expenses of the
successful defendant, but will normally take out a single premium
ATE[148] insurance policy to cover this risk; if the claimant is successful this cost, too, will normally be recoverable from the defendant.[149] Putting aside medical negligence, the cost of the system is
therefore very largely borne by liability or legal expenses insurers,

---

[144] Thus a motor policy may provide for legal services to pursue claims arising out of an
accident which is the other driver's fault.

[145] More accurately, litigation funding provided by the Community Legal Service: *Access to
Justice Act* 1999.

[146] This is not the same as the American contingency fee, where the fee is an agreed-upon-
in-advance proportion of the damages.

[147] C.P.R. 44.12A introduced "costs-only" proceedings where the parties have settled but the
amount of recoverable costs remains in dispute.

[148] "After the event" (insurance). Where the claimant has some form of legal expenses cover
(BTE or "before the event" insurance), it may be reasonable, for costs purposes, for him
to look to that cover first: *Sarwar v Alam* [2001] EWCA Civ 1401; [2002] 1 W.L.R. 125.
Yet another permutation is that BTE cover may be available to a claimant under the
defendant's policy. Since this will give the defendant's insurer control of the proceedings,
this is less likely to be a reasonable course to require the claimant to take.

[149] *Callery v Gray* [2002] UKHL 28, [2002] 1 W.L.R. 2000. The ATE may cover the claimant
against expenses for which he is liable to his lawyers under the terms of the conditional
fee agreement (e.g. disbursements) but the whole premium, if reasonable, is recoverable
from the defendant: *Callery v Gray (No.2)* [2001] EWCA Civ 1246; [2001] 1 W.L.R.
2142.

though that does not answer the criticism that the system is inefficient in expending large amounts of money in the transfer process (see below). The amount of the recoverable success fee quickly became a matter of great controversy, since the legislation simply set a maximum figure of 100 per cent but the House of Lords held that in "modest and straightforward damages claims" following road traffic accidents the normal maximum would be 20 per cent.[150] This did not entirely settle the matter and since October 2003 there has been an agreement for motor cases between the insurance industry and solicitors' representatives providing for a fixed solicitors' success fee of 12.5 per cent in cases which settle and one of 100 per cent in cases which go to trial.[151] A further strand in the story was that new players entered the game in the form of "claims farmers", claims management companies which advertised widely, collected potential cases and, after an initial vetting, "sold" them in bulk to firms of solicitors. Some of these went into liquidation[152] and there was concern about the marketing practices of some. The Compensation Act 2006 introduced a scheme for the regulation of these businesses.

This system has led to a very large increase in the costs faced by liability insurers. The *Review of Civil Litigation Costs* commented[153]:

"It is, of course, congenial for claimant lawyers to see their clients provided with comprehensive funding and insulated from all risk of adverse costs. It is congenial for both claimant and defendant lawyers to have a constant stream of work passing across their desks. Indeed, it is congenial for judges to know that the claimants who appear before them are not putting their personal assets at risk, whatever the outcome of the individual case. But these undoubted benefits have been achieved at massive cost, especially in cases which are fully contested. That cost is borne by taxpayers, council taxpayers, insurance premium payers and

---

[150] *Callery v Gray*, above fn.149.

[151] Subsequently a similar agreement was made in respect of employers' liability cases, but with a success fee of 25 per cent for settled cases. For the implementation of both agreements (including counsel's costs) see CPR Pt 45 (and for the background see *http://www.civiljusticecouncil.gov.uk*). The rules also provide for "predictable costs" (excluding disbursements, success fee and insurance premium) for low value motor cases based on the formula of £800 plus 20 per cent of agreed damages up to £5,000 plus 15 per cent of agreed damages between £5,000 and £10,000.

[152] In *Claims Direct Test Cases, Re* [2003] EWCA Civ 136; [2003] P.I.Q.R. P31 the court held that a large part of the charges made by the company were not an ATE premium within the meaning of the legislation and hence were not recoverable from the defendant.

[153] 2010 (ISBN 9780117064041), Ch.10, 1.10.

by those defendants who have the misfortune to be neither insured nor a large and well resourced organisation."

Although the conditional fee system with its associated ATEs and success fees largely replaced legal aid, the latter was based upon an assessment of financial need (though over the years it covered less and less people), whereas a conditional fee arrangement is available to:

"[A]ny person, whether rich or poor and whether human or corporate . . . . All that such a person needs to do is to find willing solicitors and willing insurers." [154]

The Review makes recommendations which may be broadly summarised as follows:

1. Neither the success fee nor the ATE premium should be recoverable from unsuccessful defendants. It would still be open to claimants to make conditional fee agreements with their lawyers but success fees (capped in personal injuries cases at 25 per cent of the damages recovered, excluding damages for future care and future losses) and ATE premiums would be their responsibility alone.[155] It would also be possible to make a contingency fee agreement (subject to independent advice and regulatory safeguards) whereby the fee would be a proportion of the damages. Costs would be recoverable by the claimant on the normal basis and in so far as the fee exceeded the normal charge for the work it would come out of the damages.[156]
2. To counter the impact of this on claimants two further changes should be made. First, "general damages" (i.e. for pain and suffering and loss of amenities[157]) should be raised by 10 per cent. Secondly, the traditional principle that the loser pays the costs of both sides should be radically modified so that the amount an unsuccessful claimant could be made to pay would reflect the means of the parties and their conduct of the proceedings.[158]

---

[154] Ch.10, 4.8 of the Review, above, fn.153.
[155] This would be similar to the position when CFAs were first introduced. Success fees and ATE premiums became recoverable from defendants in 2000 under the Access to Justice Act 1999.
[156] Ch.12 of the Review, see fn.153.
[157] See Chap.22, below, see fn.153.
[158] See Ch.10, Section 4 of the Review, see fn.153.

3. "Referral fees" paid by solicitors to claims management companies[159] would be banned.[160] Despite the view of the Office of Fair Trading that these promoted competition and remedied the "information asymmetry" between claimants and defendant insurers, the Review concluded that these fees did not add:

> "[A]ny commensurate value to the litigation process. On the contrary, referral fees have now escalated to such a level that some solicitors cut corners in order to (a) cover the referral fee and (b) make a profit on the case. In straightforward road traffic accident cases often more than half the fees paid to the solicitors are paid out in referral fees. This is to the detriment of the client, the solicitors and the public interest."[161]

It is thought that the effect of these changes would be to leave the majority of personal injury claimants no worse off and some whose cases settle early better off. The above proposals are essentially concerned with controlling the application of the traditional approach to costs whereby the starting point is that the successful party recovers what he has reasonably spent. An alternative approach is one of fixed costs for particular types of proceedings. We already come close to this with the regime of "predictable costs" for road traffic claims up to £10,000 but the review recommends the introduction of a fixed costs regime for all personal injury claims in the Fast Track (i.e. not exceeding £25,000 in value and capable of being tried in one day).

5. Criticisms of the Tort System in the Context of Personal Injuries

A. The "Fault Principle"

1–28   Though overall the law of tort is by no means the most important vehicle for accident compensation, an accident victim who can make out a tort claim stands to recover very substantially more than one who cannot, partly because of the rules about deductibility of

---

[159] BTE insurers (see fn.148, above) may also receive referral fees under the system commonly known as BTE 2 because rather than instructing and paying solicitors they will "sell" the claim to solicitors, who will then conduct it under a CFA.

[160] It seems that there is widespread non-compliance by solicitors with the rules governing referral to them by claims management companies: *Claims Management Regulation, Impact of Regulation, One Year Assessment,* Ministry of Justice (2008), Ch.8, appendix.

[161] Ch.20, 4.7, see fn.153.

other compensation payments from tort damages and partly because tort damages, unlike social security payments, are subject to no financial limits and take into account matters like pain and suffering, loss of amenity,[162] loss of promotion prospects and extra expenses incurred as a result of the injury. The claimant in a tort action must generally show that his injuries were caused by the defendant's fault and until comparatively recently it was taken as almost axiomatic that payment of higher compensation to the victims of fault was justified, but the development of insurance, particularly in the form of the social security system, has led many commentators[163] to take a different view.

Since the law of tort is a system of establishing liability it is obvious that it could never have compensated all victims of misfortune. At the very least there must be some causal link between an activity of the defendant and the injury to the claimant. There is, however, no logically compelling reason why the law should have chosen fault as the determinant of this liability.[164] What justification, then, can be advanced for the adoption of the fault principle?

B. Tort and Deterrence

The principle that a person should be called upon to pay for **1–29** damage caused by his fault may be thought to have an affinity with the criminal law (which the law of tort as a whole certainly did have much earlier in its history) in the sense that one of its purposes is deterrence, the prevention of harmful conduct. It is certainly true that at least some parts of the law dealing with premeditated conduct do help serve this purpose as well as that of deciding whether or not redress for damage already suffered should be ordered: newspaper editors, for example, take steps to avoid publication of defamatory matter, and trade union officials have recognised the efficiency of the "economic" torts as an instrument for controlling conduct by demanding, and receiving, statutory exemption from some of them so as to secure for themselves greater freedom of industrial action.[165] It is a recurring complaint that the partial withdrawal of the traditional exemption since 1980 has unduly altered the balance

---

[162] Industrial disablement benefit, above, is however based upon loss of faculty.
[163] Lord Parker C.J. in (1965) 18 *Current Legal Problems* 1 was one of the earliest critics of the present system. The leading academic monograph is Cane, *Atiyah's Accidents, Compensation and the Law*, 6th edn. Sugarman, *Doing Away With Personal Injury Law* (1989) gives a United States perspective.
[164] Earlier law was perhaps more inclined to admit specific defences than to postulate a general requirement of fault.
[165] See para.18–36, below.

between employers and unions. It is, however, more controversial
how far there is any effective deterrent force in those parts of the law
relating to accidental injury, where liability is based upon negligence. There are a number of reasons for this. First, a generalised
instruction to people to take care, which is all that the law gives, is
of little practical use in guiding their behaviour in a given situation.
Certain driving practices, for example driving at 60 mph down a
crowded shopping street, could be recognised as negligent by ordinary people without any judicial assistance, but the majority of cases
do not present such clear-cut issues and the number of variable
factors is so great that one case is hardly even of persuasive value in
another.[166] The force of this criticism probably varies from one type
of accident to another. It is particularly strong in the case of road
accidents, where the activity is, in the case of an experienced driver,
largely instinctive and where a momentary lapse of attention can
lead to catastrophic results with few realistic possibilities of taking
other precautions to minimise or avoid the risk.[167] Where, however,
the accident arises from an alleged defect in a system of work or the
organisation of a business, it is possible that a tort judgment may
play a part in exposing the risk and leading others to take measures
to prevent recurrence, whether voluntarily or at the insistence of
their insurers.[168]

1–30 The second reason why the deterrence argument is of limited
validity relates to the sources from which damages are in fact paid.
If it were the case that tort damages were paid out of the tortfeasor's
own resources it could hardly be denied that the threat of legal
liability would deter,[169] but in practice damages are, far more often

[166] Statutory duties are often (but not always) more precise in this respect. Breach of such
duties often gives rise to civil liability (see Ch.7, below) but does not generally do so in
the field of road traffic. Statements that merely exceeding the statutory speed limit does not
automatically amount to civil negligence are commonplace.

[167] But car users can wear safety belts and it is interesting that the courts held that failure to
take this preliminary precaution amounted to contributory negligence even before their use
became compulsory: para.6–53, below. A number of surveys have found a correlation
between the introduction of "no fault" motor schemes and increased accident rates:
Laudes (1982) 25 J.L. & Econ. 49; McEwin (1989) 9 International Rev. L. & Econ. 13;
Sloan (1994) 14 International Rev. L. & Econ. 53. However, the figures may be affected
by factors unrelated to tort liability, e.g. guarantees of compensation to drivers (thereby
reducing the self-preservation deterrent), changes in traffic laws or in reporting or car use
patterns.

[168] This argument would be particularly applicable to work accidents, defective products and
some medical misadventures. However, some argue that liability may have the opposite
effect in tending to encourage a lack of openness among those responsible for
accidents.

[169] "If it were not for insurance, the common law would operate with intolerable harshness in
its application to driving": *Imbree v McNeilly* [2008] HCA 40 at [23] per Gleeson C.J.
Damages may be much larger than any fine likely to be imposed by a criminal court for
comparable conduct.

than not, paid by an insurer[170] rather than by the tortfeasor himself,[171] which undoubtedly blunts the deterrent edge. Liability insurance is now actually compulsory so far as concerns road accidents affecting third parties[172] and most work accidents[173] and to meet the problem of the uninsured driver[174] there is an agreement under which the Motor Insurers' Bureau (i.e. the road traffic insurers acting collectively) satisfies claims.[175] Of course, the presence of insurance does not necessarily altogether take away the deterrent effect, for the premium may be related not only to the general risk presented by the activity or the actor (the nature of the employer's trade or the age of the driver) but the record of the particular insured. However, the setting of insurance premiums may depend on many factors and while, say, motor premiums are quite strongly "experience-related",[176] this appears to be less so in relation to employers' liability.[177] Where the defendant is in the business of supplying goods or services to the public, the cost of obtaining insurance cover (or of paying damages if he carries his own risk) will be reflected in the price charged to the public or in a reduced profit margin so that those who actually pay it are either the consumers or the shareholders or both.[178] Nevertheless, the overall cost of the harmful

[170] The general position is that the claim is against the insured tortfeasor in person, though of course in practice his insurer will handle the claim. However, in the case of motor claims there is, without prejudice to the claim against the tortfeasor, a direct right of action against the insurer: European Communities (Rights Against Insurers) Regulations SI 2002/3061, implementing Directive 2000/26/EC.

[171] See Lewis, "Insurers and Personal Injury Litigation: Acknowledging the Elephant in the Living Room" [2005] J.P.I.L. 1. However, some large organisations, public and private, act as self-insurers. The National Health Service Litigation Authority administers a risk-pooling scheme for NHS Trusts established in 1995.

[172] Road Traffic Act 1988 s.143, replacing earlier legislation and, from the end of 1988, extended to cover property damage as well as personal injury. Cover must be unlimited in respect of personal injury but is generally only up to £20 million in respect of property damage.

[173] Employers' Liability (Compulsory Insurance) Act 1969 s.1.

[174] i.e. where there is no policy at all. Where there is a policy and the car is driven by a person not entitled to drive it (even if he has unlawfully taken the car) the insurer must pay: see e.g. *Miller v Hales* [2006] EWHC 1529 (QB).

[175] There is a supplementary agreement covering claims by untraced drivers. The agreements are not strictly enforceable by the claimant, but the Bureau will never take the point. The Bureau may require the claimant to pursue any claims at law that he may have or to assign claims to it, but the existence of the Bureau means that we are far less likely than some countries to have tort claims against third parties who are in some way involved in the events leading up to an accident with an uninsured driver (see, e.g. *Childs v Desormeaux* [2006] SCC 18; [2006] 1 S.C.R. 643). By virtue of Directive 84/5/EC the agreements must provide protection equivalent to that which would be available against an insured and identified driver: *Byrne v M.I.B.* [2008] EWCA Civ 574; [2009] Q.B. 66 (shorter time limit under untraced drivers' agreement).

[176] But the greater part of motor insurance premiums go to pay for property damage, which, in the case of damage to the insured's own car, has nothing to do with tort.

[177] See Cane, *Atiyah's Accidents, Compensation and the Law*, 6th edn, p.372.

[178] See Lord Griffiths in *Smith v Eric S. Bush* [1990] 1 A.C. 831: "There was once a time when it was considered improper even to mention the possible existence of insurance cover in a lawsuit. But those days are long past."

conduct is still (in theory) reduced because if others can provide similar goods and services without this additional cost they will gain an increased share of the market.

Deterrence is not only produced of course by the threat of direct imposition of a financial penalty. It is perfectly possible that a person may be induced to take greater care by the harm to his reputation which may be caused by a successful tort suit against him.[179] Again, this effect would probably only be produced in certain fields of liability such as professional negligence, injuries caused by defective products and work injuries. While experience shows that a powerful force of public opinion can be mobilised against a drug company which was alleged to have produced a drug which had injured children, it is very unlikely that people would take much interest in a road accident caused by one of its delivery vans. In any event, a large corporate defendant which has the wherewithal is capable of avoiding much adverse publicity by an out-of-court settlement, and the speed with which substantial compensation has been offered in the wake of some mass disasters suggests that in practice the victim's chances of recovery are in direct proportion to the scale of the accident and, hence, the amount of public attention it receives.

1–31   We may conclude, therefore, that the prospect of tort liability will have some influence on conduct but that this influence is variable and limited. Even if it had a greater deterrent effect it would not necessarily justify a fault-based system, for strict liability would, presumably, have just as great an effect. Professor Gary Schwartz, after a survey of the empirical evidence in the United States, concluded that:

> "[T]he information suggests that the strong form of the deterrence argument is in error. Yet it provides support for that argument in its moderate form: sector-by-sector tort law provides something significant by way of deterrence."[180]

Our ambivalence on this surfaces in judicial decisions here. Thus Staughton L.J. said in 1994 that:

> "[O]ne advantage that is claimed for imposing a duty of care is that it encourages people not to be negligent. I very much doubt if that is the case. The great expansion of tortious liability over the last hundred and fifty years has had the remarkable feature that

---

[179] See Linden (1973) 51 Can. Bar Rev. 155.
[180] G. Schwartz, "Reality in the Economic Analysis of Tort Law: Does Tort Law Really Deter?" (1994) 42 U.C.L.A. Law Rev. 377. He is speaking in a context in which the predominant requirement is "fault" but with a major enclave of strict product liability.

the direct financial consequences almost invariably fall on someone whose purse is assumed to be bottomless, such as an insurance company or a large commercial concern or an organ of
central or local government"[181]

However, in the same case Sir Thomas Bingham M.R. said that he
could not:

"[A]ccept, as a general proposition, that the imposition of a duty
of care makes no contribution to the maintenance of high standards. The common belief that the imposition of such a duty may
lead to overkill[182] is not easily reconciled with the suggestion that
it has no effect."[183]

C. Tort and Responsibility

The other argument in favour of a tort system based on fault (or
at least of a tort system, as opposed to other mechanisms of compensation) is still more difficult to assess but cannot be dismissed
out of hand on that basis. It is that the notion of responsibility is a
powerful, intuitive factor in people's attitudes to accidents and that
there is a deep-seated idea that those who have caused damage to
others should pay: "corrective justice" requires that those who have
caused harm to others should correct what they have done and in
practice, in most cases, the payment of money is the only practical
correction available. This argument is not necessarily rebutted by
the fact that the money may come from an insurer; indeed, since few
awards of damages would otherwise be paid, it might be regarded as
buttressing it. Of course there is no logical reason why such a duty
to correct harm should arise only where the defendant is at fault
(though it seems inevitable that there should be a minimum requirement that he has caused the harm): one might, for example, say that
it arose where the defendant, in pursuit of his own purposes,
imposed an exceptional or "non-reciprocal" risk upon the claimant.
However, even if it is only the product of a long-standing system
dominated by fault, one may confidently say that the call for the
duty to correct harm is stronger where there is fault. It is now an
economic commonplace that an activity should bear its own costs,
rather than "externalise" them so that they fall on others. Not many
years ago the watchword was "loss distribution", but now there is
a good deal more interest in allocating ultimate responsibility to
those who generate the resulting costs, as witness the schemes for

1–32

---

[181] *M. v Newham LBC* [1994] 4 All E.R. 602 at 631 (on appeal *sub nom. X v Bedfordshire CC*
[1995] 2 A.C. 633, para.5–52, below).
[182] e.g. "defensive medicine". See para.1–43, below.
[183] [1994] 4 All E.R. at 619.

the recoupment from tortfeasors of social security benefits and accident treatment costs.[184] This sort of reallocation inevitably involves costs, but these particular arrangements seem to be comparatively cheap.

1–33   Linked to this (and here fault clearly has a necessary role to play) is the idea that people should answer for their damaging actions. For example, a persistent refrain in discussions of compensation for medical misadventure is that if we move away from a liability system some means will have to be found of ensuring that medical staff are accountable for blameworthy mistakes. There may, however, be more effective and efficient means of achieving such aims. The most obvious is the criminal law. The criminal law's response to negligently caused harm is more partial than that of the civil law: there are fairly comprehensive sanctions on careless conduct on the road and (as far as employers are concerned) at work, but there are other areas of activity (medical treatment, for example) where the criminal law only operates if the fault is very bad and death ensues. A surgeon who kills his patient by gross negligence commits manslaughter; one who by the same means renders him quadriplegic commits no offence at all. That, of course, is not the whole story, for the surgeon is exposed to disciplinary proceedings, and since the outcome of these may be exclusion from the profession (whereas any tort damages will be paid by the hospital trust or insurer) they are a far more effective sanction. Again, however, the system operates in a random way: there is no equivalent of the General Medical Council for plumbers or electricians. In other cases, where there is a major disaster, there will commonly be a public inquiry and that may "point the finger" more effectively than a civil suit. Certainly it will avoid the underlying flaw in the argument that the "day in court" in a civil suit ensures accountability—the simple fact that an out-of-court settlement will avoid that. The NHS Redress Act 2006 created an extra-judicial mechanism for the settlement of smaller claims. This would not so much replace tort law as provide an alternative mechanism for its administration, because compensation (probably up to £20,000) would be only be available if there is tort liability, but the Act provides for "redress" to include the giving of an explanation and apology as well as compensation. However, because of a reorganisation of the general complaints system within the NHS the Act has not yet been brought into force.

On the other hand, tort is a crude mechanism for apportioning blame, for it ignores massive disproportions between the defendant's negligence and the consequences for which he is obliged to pay. Suppose two drivers career off the motorway on to a railway track below and cause a train wreck in which there are dozens of

---

[184] See paras 22–34 and 22–36, below.

casualties. The first has had no sleep the night before and knows full well that he is unfit to drive; the second merely commits a momentary piece of inattention. As far as tort law is concerned the outcome of both cases is the same: the driver (in reality his insurer) pays all the resulting damages in full.

At a less theoretical level, there are other criticisms of the tort system.

D. Expense and Inefficiency

The tort system based upon fault is undoubtedly expensive to **1–34** administer when compared with, say, social security. The Pearson Commission estimated that in personal injury claims the cost of operation was about 85 per cent of the value of compensation paid through the system, whereas the corresponding figure for social security was about 11 per cent.[185] Up-to-date, across the board figures are hard to come by and there is of course likely to be a substantial difference between a claim which settles early and one which goes to trial. The relative cost of operation of the system as a whole has probably increased substantially in the last ten or fifteen years, probably because of the new methods of funding claims which have been outlined above.[186] Most claims are for comparatively small amounts of money and then even fairly minimal legal input will loom quite large in the equation; the amount of costs incurred in a settled motor claim for £2,000 is likely to be proportionately a good deal more than in one for £200,000.[187] Claimant's costs tend to be higher than defendants', which is hardly surprising since the claimant has to make the running, but where the claim is successful (and most claims which get to the stage of proceedings being issued are) these have to be borne by the defendant. This disparity is particularly marked in medical negligence cases: in 2008–09 the National Health Service Litigation Authority paid

---

[185] The figures, however, favour social security because they conceal the fact that the cost of collection of contributions falls outside the account, i.e. on the employer. However, the estimate by the Civil Justice Review (Cm. 394, 1986) was that the cost of the tort system was between 50 and 70 per cent of personal injury damages awarded. According to the Association of British Insurers (*Delivering a Fair and Efficient Compensation System*, 2005) claimant's costs (which are usually higher than defendant's) average 38 per cent of sums recovered in motor claims.

[186] See para.1–27, above. One sample (*Review of Civil Litigation Costs: Preliminary Report* (2009), Vol 1, Appendix 1a) of 280 successful personal injury claims provided to the Review showed a costs/damages ratio of 1:8:1 (and this seems not to include insurers' in-house costs). Compare the figures in Appendix 10, base costs without ATE premium and success fee.

[187] Graph A11 in Appendix 21 to Vol 1, above, is instructive in the medical negligence context. Only one case where the damages exceeded £500,000 incurred greater total legal costs; most of those between £25,000 and £50,000 did so.

about £730 million in damages, total claimant costs were nearly £140 million and total defence costs about £65 million.[188]

In considering these points, however, one must bear in mind that in a very large number of cases liability will not be contested at all and the cost will be generated by, for example, the issue of the quantum of damages, which would also arise if the law imposed liability without fault. So to some extent the criticism on efficiency grounds is directed not so much at the fault system as at the *tort* system.

1–35   Secondly, there is the problem of delay. The Pearson Commission concluded that delay was:

> " . . . [T]he most important reason for dissatisfaction with the legal system . . . delay is sometimes justifiable but it can often aggravate pressure on the claimant to settle prematurely, and can be a source of worry and distress. Nor is it necessarily in the interests of the defendant. The problem of delay is also linked with the medical condition sometimes known as 'compensation neurosis'."

Since then there has been a major shift of personal injury cases to the county court (where all claims for less than £50,000 must now be started) and the Civil Procedure Rules of 1999 have led to a fundamental change in responsibility for the handling of civil litigation from the parties to the courts, based on an interventionist judicial role in case management. There is some evidence that this can actually increase costs by leading to steps being taken earlier, and therefore sometimes unnecessarily ("front-loading"), than would have been the case in the past, though it has been concluded that in a personal injury context the benefits of the changes in promoting settlement outweigh this factor.[189] In any event , there is not a great deal that procedural reform can do about delay prior to the issue of proceedings, which need not be done for (normally) three years after the injury.

1–36   Thirdly, the unpredictability of the result of cases based upon fault liability may put claimants under pressure to settle their claims for amounts less than they would receive if their claim went successfully to trial. The vast majority of personal injury claims are settled without trial, most of them without even the issue of proceedings. It is true that of claimants who make a claim most will receive some payment but, though there is no clear statistical evidence on the point, many of those payments will be for substantially less than would be awarded if the matter went to trial. Since there is always

---

[188] Graph A3.
[189] *Review of Civil Litigation Costs* (2010), Ch.35, Section 7, 7.2.

some risk that the claimant's claim will founder in whole or in part at the trial, the defendant's insurers are in a position to exploit this factor by making a discount in the amount they offer in settlement.[190] This element of risk, leading to pressure to settle, is of course present in virtually all litigation but it is peculiarly powerful in the case of personal injuries because a very large part of the claimant's future wealth may be at stake. The problem is exacerbated—though the matter may be of more direct concern to his lawyers than to him—by the fact that even if he wins at the trial on liability there may be a large element of irrecoverable costs if the defendant's insurers have made an accurately-calculated Part 36 offer of settlement.[191] On the other hand, a claimant may now also make a Part 36 settlement offer, with penal consequences to the defendant on interest and costs if a higher award is made at trial. The Review of Civil Litigation Costs[192] proposes that the effects of refusal of a claimant's Part 36 offer be given teeth comparable to those of the claimant's refusal in the reverse situation by entitling him to an uplift of 10 per cent in his damages as well as the costs sanctions.[193] Not surprisingly perhaps, small claims may be over-compensated: their "nuisance value" may make insurers willing to buy-off claimants with fairly generous offers. Under-compensation in serious cases may also have been contributed to by the practice of assessing damages on a lump-sum basis; until very recently payment by instalments was only available via an out-of-court settlement.[194]

We have already noted that the victim of a mass disaster may have a valuable ally in the form of public opinion. Such a claimant is also now likely to find his claim handled by a specialist firm of solicitors (or by a co-ordinated group of them) who are adept at using publicity and who can match the experience and expertise in claims handling of a major insurer.[195] Such cases are also likely to be handled so that selected "lead claims" will be used to determine the main issues.[196]

---

[190] See Genn, *Hard Bargaining* (1987); Phillips and Hawkins, "Some Economic Aspects of the Settlement Process: A Study of Personal Injury Claims" (1976) 39 M.L.R. 497.

[191] Under CPR Pt 36 the defendant may offer a sum in satisfaction of the claim. If the claimant does not accept it and the action goes to trial, the judge is not informed of the offer and, if his award is not more advantageous than the offer, the claimant bears the costs of the action from the date of the offer.

[192] See para.1–27, above.

[193] See Ch.41 of the Review.

[194] See para.22–23, below.

[195] Apart from experience, specialism may produce a difference in attitude to initiating litigation.

[196] But we are still a long way from the American "class action" where one claim is made on behalf of the group. For American experience with "mass torts" see Fleming, *The American Torts Process*, Ch.7.

6. Alternatives

1–37 These criticisms do not complete the tally of objections to the present law of tort so far as it concerns personal injury accidents,[197] but similar problems have been encountered in other jurisdictions and there has been a widespread debate about alternative solutions. Any reform of the law governing compensation for personal injuries might adopt one of two basic solutions—an extension of strict liability (i.e. liability imposed without proof of fault), which would retain the law of tort though in a different form; and the "insurance" technique (whether private or public), which would mean the abolition or bypassing of the law of tort in whole or in part.

A. Strict Liability

1–38 Despite the continuing dominance of fault liability, the English law of tort does contain certain limited principles of strict liability[198] with regard to personal injuries. Some of these are of common law origin and of respectable antiquity, others have been the creation of modern statutes and have either been limited in their practical importance[199] or of rather haphazard application.[200] It is unlikely that any consistent policy has been followed in the creation of these areas of strict liability, though it is perhaps possible to discern behind some of them a very hazy idea of unusual or increased risk. However, the strictness of the liability varies considerably along a spectrum from near absolute liability to little more than a reversed burden of proof, and in nearly every case the defendant may plead the contributory fault of the claimant as a defence or in diminution of damages. While there may be some merit in a system of strict liability for unusual risks it can hardly make much contribution to the accident compensation problem as a whole when common risks

---

[197] Other criticisms voiced to the Pearson Commission were that the system was difficult for the injured person to understand and operate (Vol.1, para.250); that the adversarial nature of the system had a damaging effect on family relations, friendships and employment relations (para.260); and that the system could be unfair to the tortfeasor, particularly where his reputation was affected by allegations made in litigation (para.256).

[198] Some would argue that a strict liability is not a liability in tort at all. But the CA in *Bedfordshire Police Authority v Constable* [2009] EWCA Civ 64 was clear that there could be strict liability torts and that they were based on responsibility. However, the issue in the case was not whether the statutory liability to pay compensation was a liability in tort but whether it was a liability to pay "damages" for the purposes of an insurance policy and it was held that it was.

[199] The liability under the Nuclear Installations Act 1965 (para.15–24, below) is probably the strictest known to English law.

[200] See, e.g. the many statutory duties arising under industrial safety legislation, some of which are considered in Ch.8, below.

are left to the law of negligence.[201] As a result of an EEC initiative one such risk has been brought into the strict liability fold, namely losses caused by defective products, though the liability is by no means absolute.[202] French law has always had an element of strict liability for motor accidents[203] because of the provision in art.1384 of the *Code civil* governing damage caused by a "thing" in one's custody, but the law of July 5, 1985[204] goes further by allowing victims (other than drivers) to recover damages even though they themselves are at fault. Only if the victim's fault is "inexcusable" and is the sole cause of the accident is he barred. Ordinary contributory negligence remains relevant, however, to claims by drivers or to claims for property damage.[205] The exclusion of contributory negligence is very important because its retention would require the same kind of investigation into the facts of the accident as does the present law, and hence lose much of the advantage of strict liability. By contrast, our legislation on product liability retains contributory negligence. Those who believe that tort law has a deterrent role will object to the exclusion of contributory negligence, for logically it is necessary to give claimants as well as defendants the incentive to avoid accidents. In any event, as has been pointed out above, there will always remain the problem of disputes about damages rather than liability. Another problem is that if we make the (realistic) assumption that strict liability would apply to identified activities rather than across the board, we end up attributing the cost of an accident to the strict liability activity when many accidents are the product of the interaction of more than one activity.

Of course a statutory strict liability is confined to cases where its specified conditions are fulfilled and may be narrower in scope than an equivalent general fault liability. Thus the Warsaw Convention makes an air carrier liable without fault for bodily injury suffered by a passenger caused by accident.[206] "Bodily injury" does not, in this context, include psychiatric trauma[207] and an "accident" requires some unexpected event external to the passenger (deep vein thrombosis caused by cramped but normal seating is not an accident in this

---

[201] See Spencer, "Motor Cars and the Rule in *Rylands v Fletcher*" [1983] C.L.J. 65, who, while conceding that social security may be a better method of handling road accidents than liability in tort, concludes that this is a case where the best is the enemy of the good.

[202] See Ch.10, below.

[203] A majority of European countries have some form of strict liability for motor accidents.

[204] Loi no.85–677.

[205] Art.12 puts the onus upon the liability insurer to make an offer of amends to the victim within eight months and there are stiff financial penalties for failure to do so or for making an inadequate offer.

[206] For some unusual situations see *Disley v Levine* [2001] EWCA Civ 1087; [2002] 1 W.L.R. 785 and *Laroche v Spirit of Adventure (UK) Ltd* [2009] EWCA Civ 12; [2009] 3 W.L.R. 351.

[207] *Morris v KLM Royal Dutch Airlines* [2002] UKHL 7; [2002] 2 A.C. 628.

sense, nor is a fall by a passenger when the aircraft is in its normal state).[208] Nor, in this context (though not necessarily in others), can the claimant fall back on a common law duty based on failure to warn or instruct, because the Convention is an exclusive basis for the carrier's liability.[209]

B. Non-tort Compensation

1–39 An alternative approach is to abandon tort liability and create direct compensation rights. This can be done either by ad hoc compensation schemes for particular types of accidents or by a broader extension of social security rights.

The Workmen's Compensation Scheme, abolished in England in 1948 (but still existing in various forms in the United States and Australia) was an early form of ad hoc no-fault compensation, but although it was not tort, it involved adversarial litigation between the claimant and his employer, who was liable to pay the compensation. No-fault, insurance-based schemes have, however, proliferated and about half the states in the United States operate them in the field of road accidents, as do some Australian states. However, while they generally take the form of cover bought by the motorist which allows any person injured as a result of the operation of the vehicle to claim against the insurer, they vary greatly in the amount and range of benefits and in the extent to which they limit the right to claim tort damages. Generally they do not cover non-pecuniary loss such as pain and suffering, but in order to reduce the number of tort claims for this, some jurisdictions impose a minimum threshold on this loss.

Though nearly all ad hoc, selective no-fault schemes have been created in the context of transport accidents or criminal injuries,[210] there are instances of their application to other types of case, for example, the medical accident schemes which operate in Sweden and Finland.[211]

1–40 Much more far reaching than anything we have mentioned so far is the scheme now operating in New Zealand. The origin of the scheme is the Report of the Woodhouse Commission, which had been appointed to deal only with compensation for work injuries but

---

[208] *Deep Vein Thrombosis and Air Travel Group Litigation, Re* [2005] UKHL 72; [2006] 1 A.C. 495; *Povey v Qantas Airways Ltd* [2005] HCA 33; *Barclay v British Airways Plc* [2008] EWCA Civ 1419; [2009] 3 W.L.R. 369.

[209] *Sidhu v British Airways* [1997] A.C. 430.

[210] For the English scheme on this see para.4–2, below.

[211] See Brahams (1988) 138 N.L.J. 14. But the schemes by no means guarantee compensation. For example, in Sweden a causative link with the treatment must be shown and it does not apply if the injury constitutes an unavoidable complication of a measure which was justified from a medical viewpoint.

which felt unable to limit itself to its terms of reference and proposed an all-embracing no-fault system of compensation financed by the State and based on the five guiding principles of community responsibility, comprehensive entitlement, "real" compensation (including non-pecuniary loss), the promotion of rehabilitation, and administrative efficiency. Most of the proposals were implemented by the Accident Compensation Act 1972.[212] The scheme was somewhat restricted in its coverage by changes in 1992 and has been further modified several times; the law is now to be found in the Injury Prevention, Rehabilitation and Compensation Act 2001 as amended. Claims are handled administratively with reviews and ultimate appeals on a question of law to the High Court and Court of Appeal.

The statutory definition is complex but, broadly speaking, the scheme gives cover for personal injury by accident, for occupational disease and for personal injury by medical "treatment injury" . The last concept[213] replaced the former "medical misadventure", which took two forms: medical error, such as failure to diagnose (which was effectively the same as common law negligence) or medical mishap (a severe adverse reaction to proper treatment likely to occur in less than 1 per cent of cases and of the risk of which the patient was unaware). Now treatment injury is defined negatively as an injury which is not a necessary part or ordinary consequence of the treatment and which is not (a) wholly or substantially caused by the person's underlying health nor (b) solely attributable to a resource allocation decision nor (c) the result of unreasonably withholding consent to treatment. In practice this may not be very different from what went before.[214] Cover for mental injury (other than that related to physical injury) is now confined to cases involving certain sexual offences and to a single work-related event which the person experiences directly. As injury arising from an intentional act is "accidental" as far as the victim is concerned, there is no need for a separate criminal injuries compensation scheme in New Zealand. The original plan envisaged the extension of the scheme to disease in general and to disability; there now seems no prospect of this happening.

Where the compensation scheme applies the right of action in tort is abolished (though it remains for cases outside the scheme[215]). In

---

[212] For a full account of the current scheme see Todd, *Law of Torts in New Zealand*, 5th edn (2009). In Australia, a National Committee of Inquiry in 1974 proposed a scheme that would cover all incapacity, whether caused by accident or illness, but the proposal was lost with a change of government in 1975.

[213] Introduced by the Injury Prevention, Rehabilitation and Compensation Amendment Act (No.2) 2005.

[214] See Todd, above, fn.212, 2.4.04.

[215] Hence there is still common law litigation in New Zealand in "nervous shock" cases. See e.g. *Queenstown Lakes DC v Palmer* [1999] 1 N.Z.L.R. 549.

the case of total incapacity for work, compensation is at the rate of 80 per cent of earnings, subject to a statutory maximum. This is considerably more than would be payable under the general social security scheme but such a sum will, of course, be payable to very few claimants. The original scheme provided for fairly modest lump sum payments for non-pecuniary loss which could not exceed NZ$27,000 (£10,000) in the worst case but these were entirely abolished by the 1992 Act,[216] being replaced with periodical "independence allowance" in cases of disability above 10 per cent. Lump sum payments were, however, restored (with a maximum of NZ$100,000) by the 2001 Act. The according of a low priority to non-pecuniary loss is a feature of most of the radical proposals for reform put forward in recent years. It is no doubt true that "loss" of this description is very different from the loss of something having an obvious monetary value and that damages are awarded at common law more by way of "solace for unpleasantness and misfortune" than by way of replacement of something of which a person has been deprived. It is also true that it is difficult to find a basis for the assessment of some types of non-pecuniary damage.[217] On the other hand, there is no a priori reason for saying that those who suffer pain or loss of amenity are undeserving of such solace as the payment of money can bring them. The reply of the radical reformers is that compensation of this kind should be given to none until such time as the basic income losses of all can be restored through the chosen compensation system.

Even in cases to which the scheme applies it does not exclude the recovery of exemplary damages, which may be awarded in New Zealand in a very bad case of negligence.[218]

1–41   The merits and demerits of the various approaches to the problem of personal injury compensation received detailed consideration in the Report of the Royal Commission on Civil Liability and Compensation for Personal Injury, the Pearson Report.[219] The Commission was appointed in 1973 as a result of widespread public concern with accident compensation generated by the thalidomide affair, in which some 400 children in the UK were born with deformities caused by the taking by their mothers of the drug thalidomide between 1958 and 1961. For the purposes of this chapter the crucial and principal point of the Report is that it did not recommend the creation of a comprehensive scheme of state compensation on the lines of the New Zealand Accident Compensation Act. The Report states that consideration of a comprehensive scheme was precluded

---

[216] The cost of the scheme had been growing at an average of 16.5 per cent per annum before the 1992 changes.

[217] See para.22–22, below.

[218] *A v Bottrill* [2002] UKPC 44; [2003] 1 A.C. 449.

[219] Cmnd. 7054 (1978).

by the terms of reference. There is, however, some internal evidence in the Report that this attitude to the terms of reference concealed some disagreement among the members of the Commission as to the desirability of a comprehensive state scheme. The final chapter of the Report[220] speaks of three schools of thought on the ultimate objectives of compensation. One school would welcome the extension of no-fault compensation (and, by implication, of state-financed no-fault compensation) to all accidents and, in the long run, to sickness. Others hoped that there would always be a role for tort damages because they were able to deal more discriminatingly than social security payments with individual losses and embodied a recognition of the principle of responsibility. A third group thought that it would be better to assess the consequences of the Commission's limited proposals before trying to judge in which direction it would be appropriate to move next.

It is not, therefore, surprising that what the Report proposed was adjustments of the compromise arrived at with the birth of the Welfare State rather than any radical change. Perhaps the most important proposal was for a scheme for road accidents whereby there would be payment by way of social security benefits (financed by a levy on petrol) at the same rates as under the Industrial Injuries Scheme in respect of injury and death suffered as the result of the use of a motor vehicle on land to which the public has access. The right to sue in tort would have remained. Nothing has happened on this front, though the prevalence of strict tort liability in that area in Europe may produce pressure for a move in that direction, though that would, of course, be tort-based.[221]

Radical reformers have concentrated upon the relative equity **1–42** between "fault" and "non-fault" victims and have advocated moderate automatic benefits to which the abolition of the costs (including transfer costs) of the tort system could make a major contribution. The price of this might be a reduction in compensation for non-pecuniary loss to those who can at present prove fault and for pecuniary loss in the case of high-income earners, but the reformers would respond that as to the first, income support should occupy a higher place in the scale of priorities and as to the second, this group can protect themselves by insurance. A decent meal for all is preferable to a banquet for some. However, public debate over medical negligence and some mass-disaster cases suggests that

---

[220] Ch.33.
[221] For many years, Germany had a two-track system for road accidents, a strict liability regime with a cap on total liability and no damages for non-pecuniary loss, and full recovery under the general fault provisions of the BGB. The latter restriction on strict liability was removed in 2002. See Fedtke, "Germany" in Koziol and Steininger (eds) *European Tort Law 2001* (2002).

expectations of the "proper" level of compensation are at a level well beyond that which could be financed without additional taxation. This may be irrational and retributive, but it cannot be ignored if any reform is to be effected. Even if this difficulty can be surmounted, however, there remains the problem of the scope of no-fault compensation. The Pearson Commission's reasons for singling out the victims of road accidents for preferential treatment would by no means command universal assent and the savings stemming from the abolition of tort liability will not go very far if spread across the whole spectrum of accident compensation. A comparatively high proportion of road accident victims recover tort damages so there would be a substantial sum available to finance a road scheme. However, road accidents comprise less than 20 per cent of all accidents and the only other areas in which tort damages play a major role are those of accidents at work and medical injuries, in which the proportion of tort recoveries is lower. The scale of the problem even in one area of compensation may be illustrated by an estimate made by the Chief Medical Officer in 2003.[222] In 2000/2001 the NHS spent about £400 million handling clinical negligence claims. At current levels of damages a true no-fault scheme based on the harm being caused by the treatment and with 28 per cent[223] of eligible persons making claims, the annual cost would be nearly £4 billion. Even if payments were reduced to 50 per cent of their present levels and only 19 per cent of people claimed, under a more rigorous test of "preventability", the cost would still be nearly £1–2 billion. On any view, a comprehensive accident scheme would have to fund compensation for a very large proportion of its claimants on a scale which the savings made from the abolition of tort liability would come nowhere near meeting. Indeed, it is widely felt among reformers that a rational compensation system cannot even confine its coverage to accident victims, since the needs of a person under disability are not mitigated by the fact that it has arisen from illness or congenital cause rather than by accident.[224] On this view, even the comprehensive New Zealand scheme suffers from the vice of cause-related compensation.[225] However, if we bring in illness, we enter a wholly different statistical dimension, since it is generally thought that the contribution of accidents to all forms of disability is not more than about 10 per

---

[222] Department of Health, *Making Amends*, 2003. This is the basis of the NHS Redress Act 2006 (para.1–33, above, which will make alternative provision for handling smaller claims, though still on the basis of tort).

[223] The estimates of likely claimants were based partly on Swedish experience and partly on a survey of patients.

[224] See Stapleton, *Disease and the Compensation Debate*.

[225] More so since the 1992 changes.

cent.[226] Reform in this area is as much about politics as principle, and the present system contains a whole range of firmly entrenched misconceptions about the nature and quantum of compensation, not to mention vested interests (of particular classes of victims as well as of personal injury lawyers). If there were no social security system and all persons suffering disability for non-fault reasons were condemned to utter destitution, it might be possible to raise a sufficient head of steam for a new and comprehensive approach but the basic social security system does exist and reform may well be perceived by the public as "fine tuning" brought about at the price of taking away existing rights—and there are no votes in that. Even the present social security system is proving difficult to sustain and the prospect of the additional funding necessary to support general disability compensation at more than subsistence level appears remote. There is perhaps more chance of the introduction of limited, ad hoc no-fault schemes, but these are likely to make comprehensive change even more difficult by creating further enclaves of preferential treatment. Professor Atiyah, the foremost critic of the tort system for personal injury, has suggested that the best way forward might be simply to abolish tort liability across the board and leave it up to people to buy loss insurance cover for themselves and their families, though he would have a compulsory no-fault cover for road accidents (based on policies paid for by car owners) because the existing structure of mixed liability/property damage loss insurance in that area could be adapted without undue difficulty.[227]

7. Tort and the Compensation Culture

So tort law is not a very efficient means of compensating misfortune, but one might reply that it never set out to do that, but to right wrongs. The question nevertheless arises whether, even in that more modest frame, it has not become rather out of control. We have all been brought up to believe that the United States has long been the home of rampant tort law, of multi-million dollar recoveries arising out of cars which did not prove crash-proof or cups of coffee which scalded the buyer. In 1991 an American writer asserted that, "the American links adversity with recompense whereas the Englishman or woman accepts adversity as a routine part of life"[228] but recent events cast some doubt on the second proposition.

1–43

---

[226] Pearson Report, Vol.2, p.12. Of course, tort liability applies to the wrongful causing of disease and is of importance in the employment context but, despite sporadic litigation about matters like smoking diseases, hepatitis and CJD, the overall impact of tort must be small outside the employment context.

[227] See Atiyah, *The Damages Lottery* (1997).

[228] Kritzer, "Propensity to Sue in England and the United States of America: Blaming and Claiming in Tort Cases" [1991] *Journal of Law and Society* 400.

1–44   "Tort reform" has long been a matter of debate in the United
States and has led to various forms of legislative action, most
commonly in the form of putting caps on damages, especially for
non-pecuniary loss, and abolishing or modifying the traditional
common law rule that each of a number of tortfeasors causing
indivisible harm is liable for the whole loss.[229] More recently there
has been very large scale legislative action in most Australian states,
driven by a perceived insurance crisis. The New South Wales Civil
Liability Act 2002 is typical and contains provisions of three main
types. First, some basic principles of the common law are "restated"
in a way presumably intended to render them immune from judicial
tampering.[230] So, for example, under s.5I(2) a person is not liable for
a risk which cannot be avoided by the exercise of reasonable care
and skill (except in so far as it is appropriate to require him to warn
of such a risk). In this way, at least part of the common law in this
area has been "codified". Secondly, certain recent developments
extending liability under the local common law are reversed. Thus
it is provided that a person may not recover damages in respect of
the cost of upbringing of a normal but unwanted child[231] and a
person whose conduct amounting to a criminal offence punishable
by six months or more materially contributed to his injury cannot
recover damages.[232] Thirdly, radical restrictions are introduced on
the quantum of damages for personal injury. Pecuniary loss damages
are capped at three times average earnings.[233] Furthermore, the fund
of damages is assumed to earn 5 per cent per annum net,[234] twice the
figure in England, something which has a dramatic effect on the
amount. An index-linked cap (about £220,000 at the end of 2008)
was put on non-pecuniary loss. Perhaps the impact is even greater
on smaller claims. There is now no payment at all for non-pecuniary
loss unless there is long-term impairment of at least 15 per cent,
which cuts out many, many cases of the "trip and fall" or "whiplash
injury" variety. If the impairment is more than 15 per cent but less
than 33 per cent damages are not based on a percentage of the
maximum, but on a reduced sliding scale, so someone with a 25 per
cent impairment gets 6.5 per cent of the maximum, i.e. a little over
£14,000.[235] To give a simple comparison, the victim of a broken leg

---

[229] See Dobbs, *Law of Torts*, Chs 25 and 26.
[230] The High Court of Australia may fairly be said to have shown a pro-claimant inclination
until the mid-90s, but that was rather reversed before the legislation.
[231] Civil Liability Act 2002 (NSW) s.71. On this issue see para.24–15, below.
[232] Section 54 of the NSW Act.
[233] Section 12 of the NSW Act.
[234] Section 14 of the NSW Act.
[235] Direct comparison is difficult because in England such damages are not directly assessed
on impairment percentages. However, we may assume the maximum figure of about
£250,000 here to represent 100 per cent impairment.

which heals without complications gets about £5,500 in England; in New South Wales he gets nothing because of the lack of long-term impairment.

In the last few years, there has been much discussion in England **1–45** of a supposed compensation culture and an insurance crisis.[236] The Government referred the issue to the Better Regulation Task Force, a body set up in the 1990s to keep an overview on all forms of State regulation which might impinge upon business activities. Its report[237] contended that the number of personal injury claims was actually falling,[238] and that the compensation culture was something of an urban myth (though it cannot be denied that the size of damages awards in more serious cases has increased substantially in real terms).[239] Much of the debate has been conducted at a rather superficial level and exploited for political ends.[240] Furthermore, there must be at least some doubt about the reliability of much of the statistical information used in the debate, if only because the various estimates are based on different sets of data.[241] It is, for example, difficult to state with certainty how many personal injury claims there are. The published Judicial Statistics only show proceedings commenced and most claims are abandoned or settled before that. For 2006 the insurance industry *Fourth UK Bodily Injury Awards Study* reported 258,000-odd claims on insurers for personal injury in road accidents but for the overlapping accounting year 2006–2007 the Compensation Recovery Unit (to which all claims for personal injury must be notified before any payment can be made) reported 518,000-odd such claims.[242] What does seem clear is that overall expenditure on the tort system has been driven up in the last two

[236] See, e.g. a report by the Faculty and Institute of Actuaries, *The Cost of the Compensation Culture* (2002), contending that the current overall cost of compensation, at about £10 billion, was 1 per cent of GDP, increasing at a rate of up to 15 per cent per year.

[237] "Better Routes to Redress" (2004).

[238] Of course the number of claims lodged is not the whole story since many claims are settled without the issue of proceedings but, wherever social security benefits have been paid, the Compensation Recovery Unit, which handles recoupment from tortfeasors (see para.22–34, below) must be informed of any settlement and the figures from that source apparently confirm this picture.

[239] See para.22–28, below.

[240] See, e.g. David Davis, Shadow Home Secretary, in *The Spectator*, August 20, 2004, inextricably confusing the personal injury problem with the Human Rights Act 1998. Some estimates of the annual cost of clinical negligence to the NHS simply take the total value of all unsettled claims in the pipeline and assume that they will all succeed at 100 per cent.

[241] The actuaries' estimate above includes the cost of the Criminal Injuries Compensation Scheme, which is certainly not tort. Some estimates include the cost to employers of unfair dismissal and discrimination claims, which are entirely the creation of modern statute law. The well-known American Tillinghast Towers-Perrin figures for 2000 put the cost of the UK "tort system" at 0.6 per cent of GDP, compared with 1.9 per cent for the USA, 0.8 per cent for Japan and 1.3 per cent for Germany. The first overseas figure fits our intuitive assumptions, the last two seem surprisingly high.

[242] See *Review of Civil Litigation Costs: Preliminary Report*, Vol 1, Ch.6, Section 4, 4.1 (2009).

decades by changes in the legal costs and funding system and as we
have seen there are now proposals to reverse this.[243] Substantial
increases in liability insurance premiums are an undeniable fact but
it does not follow that they are wholly caused by the increased cost
of liability. Thus political interference with the market in motor
premiums may have played a role in the Australian crisis; and in
England it is a commonplace that for a long time employers'
liability insurance was sold as a loss leader and that its unprofit-
ability (to some extent now reversed) dates from a time before the
compensation culture came on the scene. Whatever the truth about
the figures there is also no doubt that there is a social cost in the
perception of a litigation-conscious society in the form of restrictions on activities which would formerly have been perceived as
harmless[244]—safety overkill—something which the House of Lords
strove to counter in 2003.[245] The Compensation Act 2006 also
contains a rather pale imitation of the New South Wales legislation
in the form of section 1:

> "1. Deterrent effect of potential liability
> A court considering a claim in negligence or breach of statutory
> duty may, in determining whether the defendant should have
> taken particular steps to meet a standard of care (whether by
> taking precautions against a risk or otherwise), have regard to
> whether a requirement to take those steps might—
>
> (a) prevent a desirable activity from being undertaken at all, to
>   a particular extent or in a particular way, or
> (b) discourage persons from undertaking functions in connec-
>   tion with a desirable activity."

Some may consider that a rather futile exercise in the sense that
not only is it implicit or explicit in the current approach taken by the
courts[246] but it is hardly of such strength as to deter a court determined to go in the opposite direction (unlikely as that may be).[247]

---

[243] See para.1–27, above.
[244] For an example, see *Hampstead Heath Winter Swimming Club v London Corp* [2005] EWHC 713 (Admin); [2005] 1 W.L.R. 2930, para.9–17, below.
[245] *Tomlinson v Congleton BC* [2003] UKHL 47; [2004] 1 A.C. 46, para.9–17, below.
[246] See, e.g. *Tomlinson v Congleton BC*, above, fn.245; and *Bolton v Stone* [1951] A.C. 850. In *Hopps v Mott Macdonald Ltd* [2009] EWHC 1881 (QB) it is said at [92] that its purpose, "is to draw attention to, and to some extent, to expound the principle of the common law expounded by the House of Lords in *Tomlinson.*"
[247] Fulbrook, *Outdoor Activities, Negligence and the Law* (2005) is an interesting and detailed examination of the "law in action" in the context of outdoor activities, one of the contexts in which the charge of restriction of worthwhile activities by tort law has been most prominent.

The compensation culture controversy will be with us for some time yet. It revolves around the problem of personal injury compensation, to which a large part of this chapter has been devoted. But there is far more to tort law than that and it is now time to look at the principles.

CHAPTER 2

THE STRUCTURE OF TORT LAW: HISTORY AND INFLUENCES

A PRACTICAL legal system could hardly avoid the practice of, to **2–1** some degree, attaching labels to different types of tortious wrongdoing: in most systems, for example, "tort" embraces both defamation and accidents causing bodily injury[1] but it would be surprising if the rules of liability were identical for both types of case. So a French or German lawyer will in practice make use of the limited categories such as those we call "nuisance" or "defamation". Yet the codified, civil law systems typically have a rather broad, unified theory of tort liability, even if it is not usually wholly comprehensive. France is the best known example, for the framers of the *Code civil* at the beginning of the 19th century managed to get all of tort law into five short articles (two of which were about tumbledown buildings, and animals, both of which seem to attract a special rule in most legal systems). Certainly the laconic words of the *Code* have been interpreted (in some areas one might even say perverted[2]) by a mass of subsequent case law and supplemented by much special legislation (for example on road accidents) but the core remains—in France the basic source of the law is a legislative statement of a very broad nature. Here, on the other hand, the substance of tort law is a mass of case law stretching back hundreds of years. Of course the French core is 200 years old and life was in some respects simpler then, but a modern product in the European

---

[1] But not all: in New Zealand personal injury accidents are largely outside the tort system (see para.1–40, above) and some systems regard defamation as criminal only.
[2] As in the case of liability for damage caused by things in one's care under art.1384, which was probably intended simply as an introduction for the articles on buildings and animals.

style may not be very different. The newest European Code is that of the Netherlands,[3] the relevant part of which came into force in 1992, and it is instructive to look at art.6.3.1.1[4]:

> "1. A person who commits an unlawful act towards another which can be imputed to him, must repair the damage which the other person suffers as a consequence thereof.
> 2. Except where there is a ground of justification, the following acts are deemed to be unlawful: the violation of a right, an act or omission violating a statutory duty or a rule of unwritten law pertaining to proper social conduct.
> 3. An unlawful act can be imputed to its author if it results from his fault or from a cause for which he is answerable according to law or common opinion".

There are some other substantive articles (again buildings and animals feature, as well as the now obligatory products liability[5]) and provisions on ancillary matters like vicarious liability, but art.6.3.1.1 is the source, for Dutch purposes, of at least 50 per cent of the matter dealt with in this book.

1. The Forms of Action: Trespass and Case

2–2   Perhaps it might be possible to draw up a broad principle encapsulating most of the common law[6] of tort in this way (though whether it would be worthwhile is another matter) but that is not the way we have operated, and what we did in the past colours our thinking now. The law of tort grew up, like other branches of our law, behind a screen of legal procedure. Until the mid-19th century, the question which arose when a claimant sued a defendant for some alleged injury was not "Have the claimant's rights been infringed by the defendant?" or even "Has the defendant broken some duty which he owed to the claimant?" but "Has the claimant any form of action against the defendant, and, if so, what form?" If he could not fit his claim into one of the recognised forms of action, he had no legal

---

[3] The Nederlands Burgerlijk Wetboek (NBW).
[4] Transl. P.P.C. Haannapel and E. Mackaay (1990).
[5] European harmonisation has compelled us all to regard "product liability" as something special, with the result that in France the new provisions in the *Code civil* on this take up far more space than all the rest of tort law.
[6] The expression is used advisedly, for many other legal systems are based on English law. The American *Restatement of Torts* (now well into its third "edition") is nothing like a civil law code: it has affinities with a highly authoritative text, with over 800 articles and a massive commentary. There are English examples of "codification" dating from the late 19th century, such as the Bills of Exchange Act 1882 and the Sale of Goods Act 1893 (now 1979). If one codified English tort law in that style it would look more like the *Restatement* than part of a continental code.

grievance. An action was usually commenced by a royal writ issued from the Chancery, which in this sense signified not a court of law but a Government department, one of whose functions was the creation and issue of these writs. It was known also as the *officina brevium* which has been conveniently translated as "the writ-shop", for a claimant could not get a writ without paying for it. For a very considerable period of our legal history the shape of the law was no more than a classification of writs. The writs that remedied the injuries which in modern times are called torts were principally the writ of trespass and the writ of trespass on the case or "case". Trespass in common parlance now signifies unauthorised entry on another person's land, but in law it has a wider signification, as it has in the King James Bible. The writ of trespass lay for injuries to land or to goods, or to the person, though "injuries" must be read in an extended sense[7] because the tort was actionable per se, that is to say, the claimant could sue even if there had been no damage as that word would normally be understood. However, it was limited to injuries which were direct and immediate and it did not extend to indirect or consequential injuries: so it was trespass for me to throw a brick at you and hit you but not if I left an unlighted pile of bricks in the alley at the side of my house and you stumbled over them. However, these indirect injuries came to be remediable through the action on the case, though this, unlike trespass, required proof of damage. These two classes of action, "trespass" and "case", existed side by side for centuries and to them we owe most of our law of tort. There were, however, definite distinctions between these two forms of action and until the 19th century it was vital for a claimant to choose correctly between them.[8] Only after the reforms of that century had broken up the cast-iron moulds of procedure did it cease to be necessary:

"[T]o canvass the niceties of the old forms of action. Remedies now depend upon the substance of the right, not on whether they can be fitted into a particular framework".[9]

Nevertheless at least a basic knowledge of the forms of action is still necessary not only for the understanding of the old authorities but for the classification of much of the modern law[10]—in Maitland's famous phrase, "The forms of action we have buried, but they

---

[7] The sense is the Latin *iniuria*, "wrong".
[8] See Pritchard, "Trespass, Case and the Rule in Williams v Holland" [1964] C.L.J. 234.
[9] *Nelson v Larholt* [1948] 1 K.B. 339 at 343 per Denning J.
[10] For an example see *Watkins v Home Office* [2006] UKHL 17; [2006] 2 A.C. 395 (misfeasance in a public office), para.7–23, below.

still rule us from their graves".[11] In the course of time certain types
of claim acquired more specific names, such as assault, battery, libel,
slander, nuisance, negligence and so on. The fact that they acquired
such names was due to mere accidents of terminology traceable
probably to their frequent occurrence, but they still have their roots
in the ancient categories, so that even now (although trespass and
case are long gone) a lawyer might explain that the reason why a
claim for negligence requires proof of damage, whereas a claim for
battery does not, is that the former is (or was) an action on the case,
the latter one is trespass. Of course the fact that the explanation is
historical does not mean that there might not then have been, and
may still continue to be, a good policy reason for the distinction:
those torts which are actionable per se might be regarded as concerned with the vindication of rights[12] or with situations where
damage is likely but very hard to prove.[13]

2–3   So we cannot point, at least without some distortion, to any
single, comprehensive concept of wrongdoing which leads to tortious liability. One might get the impression from a reading of
modern case law that there was such a concept in the idea of
"negligence", which dominated tort law through most of the 20th
century (and which dominates tort courses even more than text-
books) but common sense and simple morality tell us that wherever
there is liability for negligence there must also be liability for
intentional harm; indeed, liability for intentional wrongdoing is, and
probably should be, wider than that for negligence.[14] In the European systems both types of conduct are easily accommodated under
the name of "fault", or at least they are both placed under the same
heading.[15] As a practical matter one may say that fault is as much a
dominant feature of tort liability here as in those systems,[16] but to
say that we had a general concept of fault would be to over-simplify

---

[11] Maitland, *Equity*, p.296. Thus the distinction between trespass to land and private nuisance
still turns upon the old distinction between trespass and case. See, e.g. *Esso Petroleum Co
Ltd v Southport Corp* [1956] A.C. 218.

[12] See *Ashley v CC Sussex* [2008] UKHL 25; [2008] 1 A.C. 962, para.1–2, above.

[13] Libel is in some respects an example of this. However, in libel and other torts actionable
per se the courts are nowadays quite ready to strike out a claim as an abuse of process
where it is clear that the damage is trivial or nonexistent and the claim is "not worth the
candle". "The claim for a shilling in damages in order to prove a point and obtain an award
of costs is history": *White v Withers LLP* [2009] EWCA Civ 1122 at [72]. So in these cases
it might now be better to say, not that damage is unnecessary, but that it is presumed.

[14] Compare para.4–36, below and Ch.18 (economic torts).

[15] As in the German Civil Code, BGB §823(1): "A person who, *wilfully or negligently*,
unlawfully injures the life, body, health, freedom, property or other right of another is
bound to compensate him for any damage arising therefrom."

[16] Indeed more so. In France strict liability under art.1384 of the CC (*Code Civil*) is now
probably more important in practice than the liability for fault under arts 1382 and 1383.
Furthermore, some systems which do not have a wide-ranging strict liability under the
general Code, have strict liability for traffic injuries, which are a very major source of tort
claims.

the law, for our intentional torts such as battery and deceit came into existence long before any general conception of negligence, and they continue to carry some of their history with them. For example, battery, as a form of trespass to the person, requires a "direct" injury to the victim. There is no doubt that if wilful physical harm is done indirectly that leads to liability in tort, but we cannot call it either battery or negligence, so we were reduced to describing it by the name of the case at the end of the 19th century—which was thought to establish that there was liability in such circumstances.[17] The current view is that the case is not in fact a good example of this idea so we are denied even that convenience.[18]

There is, therefore, no doubt that we have a collection of torts rather than a single principle but this does not prevent the courts creating new heads of liability to meet changing circumstances or changing perceptions of the need for protection from harm. Sometimes this may occur very suddenly, as happened in the middle of the 19th century, when the tort of inducing breach of contract was established[19]; on other occasions the process may involve more of a synthesis of existing principles, the culmination of an evolution rather than a revolution, as happened when the foundation of the general law of negligence was laid in 1932.[20] In the case of the latest addition to the family there is some doubt about the parentage of the offspring. The modern law has seen a marked development of the law of confidence and, propelled by the Human Rights Act 1998, this has now cut loose from any strict requirement that the information should have been *imparted* in confidence by the person to whom it relates. There is a growing tendency to refer to it as "misuse of private information", though it seems not quite to have become a general basis for the protection of privacy against wrongful intrusion.[21] The predominant view has been that the law of confidence rests upon equitable principles rather than upon tort[22] but in practical terms this is perhaps a distinction without a difference, as witness the occasional judicial reference to the "tort of breach of confidence" or the "tort of misuse of private information".[23] The traffic is, of course, not all one way: a head of tortious liability may

---

[17] *Wilkinson v Downton* [1897] 2 Q.B. 57.
[18] See below, para.4–37.
[19] *Lumley v Gye* (1853) 2 El. & Bl. 116. See para.18–2, below.
[20] *Donoghue v Stevenson* [1932] A.C. 653. See para.5–5, below. Of course, the common law judge is always reluctant to admit that a completely new departure has been made. In *Lumley v Gye* there were old cases about "enticing" servants away from their duty but the court was really making new law.
[21] See para.12–82, below.
[22] Though some years ago the Law Commission proposed that it should be codified as a statutory tort.
[23] See para.12–82, below.

be born, acquire a name and be cut off by other developments before it reaches its prime.[24]

2–4   The forms of action have long gone: for a century and a half there has been a more or less uniform process for starting all civil claims for damages, now a claim form under the Civil Procedure Rules, but it has not been in accordance with the tradition of the common law to analyse rights as something separate from the remedy given to the claimant, so that, although we have abolished the procedural restrictions of the forms of action, it is still necessary for the claimant to establish a cause of action. It is not therefore correct to say that a person has a basic right not to have untruths told about himself, for he is only able to restrain the publication of such untruths if the circumstances in which they are disseminated fall within a specific tort such as passing off, malicious falsehood or defamation.[25] To some extent this basic approach has changed under the Human Rights Act 1998, under which the English court must give effect to the rights and freedoms guaranteed by the European Convention on Human Rights.[26] This guarantees for example the rights to life, to liberty and to the enjoyment of property but it seems that, in the medium term at least, we are more likely to rely on these to modify existing rules of tort law where necessary than to rewrite the whole rule book in terms of rights[27] rather than liabilities.[28]

2–5   It is important to realise that the various torts are not exclusive of one another and that there is no reason why a given set of facts should not contain the elements of several of them. The claim form which initiates a civil case must contain a concise statement of the nature of the claim[29] and this is supplemented (later, except in the simplest cases) by particulars of claim which contain, "a concise statement of the facts on which the claimant relies."[30] The purpose of the exercise is to enable the opposing party to know what case is being made in sufficient detail to enable him properly to answer it.[31] Today the claimant does not necessarily have to specify the particular tort on which he wishes to rely, for the issue is whether what he alleges (in traditional terminology) "discloses a cause of action",

---

[24] This seems to be the effect of the Protection from Harassment Act 1997 (para.4–38, below) upon the common law tort rather tentatively advanced in *Khorasandjian v Bush* [1993] Q.B. 272.

[25] *Kingdom of Spain v Christie, Manson & Woods Ltd* [1986] 1 W.L.R. 1120 at 1129.

[26] See para.2–8, below.

[27] In *Watkins v Home Office* [2006] UKHL 17; [2006] 2 A.C. 395 the court rejected an attempt to fashion an extension of tort liability based on "constitutional rights".

[28] In most European countries the Convention has been incorporated in domestic law for a good many years but its influence on the basic structure of private law has been limited.

[29] CPR 16.2(1)(a).

[30] CPR 16.4(1)(a).

[31] *British Airways Pension Trustees Ltd v Sir Robert McAlpine & Sons Ltd* (1994) 45 Con. L.R. 1 at 4.

i.e. a set of facts for which there is a legal remedy.[32] It is, therefore, open to the claimant to assert that the factual situation gives rise to a basis of liability which has never before been expressly recognised. In practice, however, it is normally prudent,[33] and may in practical terms be essential for the claimant, to identify by name the cause of action on which he relies: judges are presumed to know the law, but they are entitled to and should receive the assistance of counsel. Furthermore, subject to the court's power to allow amendment of pleadings (probably now to be exercised less generously than in the past) no one is allowed to lead evidence of facts which he has not pleaded. If the facts alleged in the claim do not show a sustainable legal basis for the claim even if they are all proved, the defendant may apply to have the claim struck out[34] or apply for summary judgment on the ground that the claim has no reasonable prospect of success.[35] So, what is necessary to get to trial is that the facts alleged should include those essential to liability under at least one tort, without at the same time including any which are fatal to that liability. For this purpose the court is not concerned with evidence, i.e. with whether the facts alleged can be proved, but with whether the facts if proved can realistically be regarded[36] as being the possible basis of a claim.[37] However, the whole sequence of events leading up to the claimant's damage may include the essentials of more than one tort, and where this is so the position is simply that there is more than one reason why the claimant should succeed.

Put shortly, therefore, it is necessary for counsel for the claimant, in settling the particulars of claim,[38] to plead all the facts which are

---

[32] *Letang v Cooper* [1965] 1 Q.B. 232 at 242–244, where Diplock L.J. states that a "cause of action" is simply a factual situation the existence of which entitles one person to obtain from the court a remedy against another person. An alternative definition is, "every fact, though not every piece of evidence, which it would be necessary for the plaintiff to prove, if traversed, to support his right to judgment of the court": *Read v Brown* (1888) 22 Q.B.D. 128 at 131. *Black v Yates* [1992] Q.B. 526.

[33] If only because lack of clarity in the presentation of the case risks running foul of the overriding objective of the Civil Procedure Rules (CPR), to enable the court to deal with the case justly, which includes the saving of expense and allocation of resources proportionate to the complexity of the issues: CPR 1.1(2).

[34] CPR 3.4.2(a). This is the successor of what in former times was known as the demurrer procedure.

[35] CPR 24.2(a)(i). Under the old Rules of the Supreme Court summary judgment was available only to the person asserting the claim (now 24.2(a)(ii)).

[36] It is not necessary for the court to be satisfied that the claim *will* succeed as a matter of law and it is undesirable to decide complex issues of law on hypothetical facts: *Farah v British Airways, The Times*, January 26, 2001.

[37] However, under CPR 24, where the issue is simply whether the claimant has a real prospect of success, the defendant may seek summary judgment on the ground that the evidence available to the claimant is too weak. See *Three Rivers DC v Bank of England (No.3)* [2001] UKHL 16; [2003] 2 A.C. 1, especially the speech of Lord Hutton at [120], where the distinction is drawn between the "attack on the pleadings" point and the "no real prospects of success" point.

[38] Cases decided under the old RSC will refer to the "statement of claim".

essential to the particular tort or torts on which he intends to rely. One cannot, however, simply plead all the facts which led up to the claimant's injury, for this would be to go back to the creation of the world. One is bound to select from the whole complex of facts those which are relevant to the client's claim in point of law and this, of course, one cannot do save by reference to particular torts which are recognised (or at least which one hopes to convince the court should be recognised). Suppose that the defendant has orally stated of the claimant, a shopkeeper, that the claimant habitually sells goods which he knows to have been stolen. Here the defendant's words prima facie fall under the tort known as "slander of title" or "malicious falsehood"[39] and also within that form of the tort of defamation known as "slander actionable per se".[40] Now it is not normally an essential of the tort of defamation that the defendant should have used the words maliciously, but this is an essential of malicious falsehood. If, therefore, the claimant wishes to make use in argument of that tort he must allege in his pleading that the defendant acted with malice. Otherwise, even though the defendant was in fact malicious, he will be precluded from proving this at the trial and so will fail to bring his case within malicious falsehood. He will thus lose the advantage of an alternative line of argument which, on the facts as they actually occurred, should have been open to him.[41] The claimant may, of course, have practical reasons for not pursuing all the causes of action available. In *Joyce v Sengupta*[42] a statement published about the claimant was clearly defamatory on its face but the claimant sued only for the tort of malicious falsehood because legal aid was then[43] available for the tort but not available for defamation.[44] An argument that this was an abuse of the process of the court was rejected, for:

"[W]hen more than one cause of action is available to him, a plaintiff may choose which he will pursue. Usually, he pursues all available causes of action, but he is not obliged to do so. He may pursue one to the exclusion of another . . . I have never heard it

---

[39] See para.12–72, below.

[40] See para.12–6, below.

[41] But compare *Cornwall Gardens Pte Ltd v R.O.Garrard & Co Ltd* [2001] EWCA Civ 699, where the court refused to allow the claimant to dress up what was in substance a claim for malicious falsehood as one for interference with rights by unlawful means, in order to escape the limitation period.

[42] [1993] 1 W.L.R. 337.

[43] Such claims are no longer funded under the Community Legal service: Access to Justice Act 1999 Sch.2.

[44] See also *Spring v Guardian Assurance* [1995] 2 A.C. 296 (claim for negligence as a way of sidestepping privilege blocking defamation claim): para.11–33, below.

suggested before that a plaintiff is not entitled to proceed in this way... [or] that he must pursue the most appropriate remedy."[45]

We may say, therefore, that the law of tort is divided over the various torts which we are now to consider, but life itself is not similarly divided. The law of tort may say, "If A, B and C, then liability in negligence" and also "If A, B and D, then liability in nuisance". Life may produce A, B, C, D, E, F, G, H. If it does, and assuming E, F, G, and H to be legally irrelevant, the claimant should plead and prove A, B, C, D. If he does he is entitled to succeed under the rules both of negligence and of nuisance but this conclusion cannot, of course, be reached by one who is not familiar with the essentials of each particular tort.

The grouping of particular torts which have acquired names in 2–6
any sort of classification is of no value except for purposes of exposition. And even for that it cannot possibly be scientifically complete. Following his definition of tortious liability, Winfield made the liability of the defendant, and not the interest of the claimant which is infringed, the root of his classification, while there is nowadays a tendency to adopt the other course. The order followed in the succeeding chapters adheres strictly to neither course but has as its principal aim no more than the avoidance, so far as reasonably possible, of repetition and of references forward to later chapters. The object is comprehensibility and the convenience of the reader who wants to begin at the beginning and go on to the end. The result is neither "historical" nor "scientific". If it is convenient, that is enough.

2. New Influences on English Tort Law

Reference has already been made to the contrast in "style" between 2–7
the common law and the codified European systems. Our courts have tended to look not to Europe but to the development of the common law in the Commonwealth and the United States; but we are also now part of a complex of European institutions which have a political as well as an economic agenda and this has implications for the development of tort law. Of most immediate concern for any student is the impact of the European Convention on Human Rights.

---

[45] [1993] 1 W.L.R. 337 at 342 per Nicholls V.C.

A. Tort Law and Human Rights

2–8   The UK was the first state to ratify the European Convention on Human Rights and Fundamental Freedoms,[46] signed at Rome in 1950. The Convention binds its signatories on an international plane to secure to citizens the rights and freedoms defined in the Convention but does not require that a State should incorporate the Convention in domestic law so as to require local courts to apply it. Hence, until the coming into force of the Human Rights Act 1998 in October 2000, the Convention was not directly part of English law. A person who claimed to be a victim of a violation of the Convention might, however, petition the European Commission of Human Rights in Strasbourg and if that body found the complaint admissible (one condition of which was the exhaustion of local remedies) the case would go before the European Court of Human Rights.[47] If the Court found that there had been a violation of the Convention it could award the applicant monetary compensation as "just satisfaction".[48] It had no power to undo what had been done on the domestic plane (e.g. a criminal conviction or dismissal from employment) but if the state of domestic law had led to the violation or prevented any local remedy for it, the Government would feel obliged to correct that. The Convention did not give rise to rights in the English courts but it was by no means without effect. First, where a statutory provision was uncertain in its meaning, it was presumed that Parliament intended to legislate in such a way as to comply with its international obligations under the Convention[49]; secondly, the Convention was regarded as, "an articulation of some of the principles underlying the common law"[50] so that it was taken into account in formulating the common law.[51] With the approach of the implementation of the Human Rights Act 1998 the latter tendency gathered force, so that in *Reynolds v Times Newspapers Ltd*,[52]

---

[46] "ECHR" All references to decisions are to final decisions of the Court unless otherwise indicated (e.g. "Commission"). Since 1998 the Commission (which was primarily concerned with admissibility) has been merged with the Court.

[47] This must not be confused with the Court of Justice of the European Communities, commonly known as the European Court of Justice.

[48] art.41 of the Convention. Thus in *Halford v UK* (1997) 24 E.H.R.R. 523, the sum of £10,000 was awarded for intrusion into privacy by telephone tapping.

[49] *R v Home Secretary Ex p. Brind* [1991] 1 A.C. 696.

[50] *Rantzen v Mirror Group Newspapers* [1994] Q.B. 670 at 691.

[51] Among the clearest examples are *Rantzen v Mirror Group Newspapers (1986) Ltd* [1994] Q.B. 670 and the speech of Lord Goff in *Att Gen v Guardian Newspapers Ltd (No.2)* [1990] 1 A.C. 109 at 283. In *Derbyshire CC v Times Newspapers Ltd* [1992] Q.B. 770 the CA relied on the Convention to come to the conclusion that a local authority could not sue for defamation. The HL ([1993] A.C. 534) thought it unnecessary to rely on the Convention. In *John v Mirror Group Newspapers* [1997] Q.B. 586 (para.12–71, below) the CA thought it unnecessary to rely on the Convention but said that its conclusion was "buttressed" by it.

[52] [2001] 2 A.C. 127, below, para.12–53.

a case concerning libel and "political speech", Lord Steyn could say that it was:

> "[C]ommon ground that in considering the issues before the House, and the development of English law, the House can and should act on the reality that the 1998 Act will soon be in force".[53]

B. The Human Rights Act 1998

It remains the case that a complaint may ultimately be taken to the 2–9 Court in Strasbourg, but the 1998 Act gives the Convention "further effect" (a carefully chosen phrase) in English law. The core of the Act from a constitutional point of view is perhaps the provisions dealing with legislation. Under s.3 the court is to read primary and subordinate legislation in a way compatible with Convention rights, *so far as it is possible to do so.* This clearly goes well beyond the former use of the Convention to resolve ambiguities in statutes and to avoid the effect of s.3 there must be a clear indication of an intention incompatible with the Convention.[54] In that event, the court has no power to strike down primary legislation but may (at the level of the High Court or above) make a declaration of incompatibility under s.4.[55] This has no effect on the outcome of the suit in which the issue is raised, nor does it require the Government to take remedial action, though a fast-track legislative procedure is available if it chooses to do so.[56]

Perhaps more likely to be directly relevant to tort law are the provisions of the Act concerned with the acts of "public authorities". The basic principle is that it is unlawful for a public authority to act in a way which is incompatible with a Convention right[57] and the victim of such an unlawful act may bring proceedings in which a court, "may grant such relief or remedy, or make such order, within its powers as it considers just and appropriate."[58] The relief may include an award of damages but only if, taking account of all the circumstances of the case (including any other relief granted), such an award, "is necessary to afford just satisfaction to the person

---

[53] [2001] 2 A.C. at 207. The HL somewhat varied the decision of the CA in this case but the transcript of the proceedings in the latter court shows that it intended its decision to be "Convention proof".

[54] See *R v A (No.2)* [2001] UKHL 25; [2002] 1 A.C. 45 at [44].

[55] As to subordinate legislation, see Human Rights Act 1998 s.4(4).

[56] Human Rights Act 1998 s.10 and Sch.2.

[57] Convention rights are those set out in arts 2 to 12 and 14 of the Convention and certain rights governed by the First and Sixth Protocols. See, inter alia, Clayton and Tomlinson, *The Law of Human Rights*, 2nd edn (2009); Lester, Pannick and Herberg, *Human Rights Law And Practice*, 3rd edn (2009); Beatson, Grosz, Hickman, Palmer and Singh, *Human Rights: Judicial Protection in the United Kingdom*, 2nd edn (revised, 2008).

[58] Human Rights Act 1998 s.8(1).

to whom it is made".[59] The court is directed, on the issue of damages, to take into account the principles applied by the European Court of Human Rights and that body has quite frequently regarded the vindication of the right as sufficient satisfaction.[60] In this context there is a considerable overlap between the Convention and the common law. For example, art.5.2 provides that:

"[E]veryone who is arrested shall be informed promptly, in a language which he understands, of the reasons for his arrest and of any charge against him."

At common law (and now under the Police and Criminal Evidence Act 1984) a person arrested has a similar right to be informed of the reason for his arrest[61] and if he is not, he has a claim for the tort of false imprisonment, which may lead to the award of substantial damages. However, some infringements of the Convention rights by a public body would not be a tort under the common law. For example, under art.8.1 everyone has the, "right to respect for his private and family life, his home and his correspondence".[62] Now although the English common law of torts has always protected privacy in various indirect ways[63] and the law of confidence has been developed into a wrong of misuse of private information, which covers much of the ground, there is no general tort of infringement of privacy under that name. However, where the defendant is a public authority there is now a statutory wrong under the Act. This is not an action in tort for breach of statutory duty,[64] because the remedy in damages is discretionary and even where they are awarded they will be in line with the Strasbourg practice, not that of English courts in tort cases, but otherwise there is some similarity with such an action.[65] It would be impracticable in this book to provide a full account of the various Convention rights but it will be necessary to refer to them when they overlap with or qualify the common law. There is no comprehensive definition of a public authority in the Act but it includes a court or tribunal or, "any person certain of whose functions are of a public nature".[66] Organs of central or local government and the police are obviously public

---

[59] Human Rights Act 1998 s.8(3).

[60] *R. (Greenfield) v Secretary of State for the Home Dept* [2005] UKHL 14; [2005] 1 W.L.R. 673; *Gillan v UK*, January 12, 2010, Application No.4158/05. See generally Law Com. No.266, *Damages under the Human Rights Act 1998* (2000).

[61] See below, para.4–29.

[62] Subject to art.8.2, which allows lawful interference which is necessary in a democratic society for national security, the prevention of crime, etc.

[63] See below, para.12–78.

[64] See Ch.7.

[65] See Law Com. No.266, §4.20 ("in effect a form of action for breach of statutory duty").

[66] Human Rights Act 1998 s.6(3). But not Parliament.

authorities in the ordinary sense of that expression and the same may
be true of many regulatory bodies and the BBC. In some cases, it
may be difficult to decide whether a body is a public authority in this
ordinary sense or only in the extended sense quoted above, a point
which is of significance because in the latter case the Act does not
apply to acts of the body which are of a private nature.[67]

Although a court is a public authority for the purposes of the Act, **2–10**
a claim in respect of a judicial act is only to be brought by way of
appeal (or in some cases judicial review) and damages may not be
awarded in respect of judicial acts done in good faith except with
regard to wrongful detention under art.5(5) of the Convention.[68]
However, that takes us to the central area of difficulty in mapping
the relationship of the Act, the Convention and the common law of
tort. Despite the fact that the act of a court may not be subject to an
award of damages, it is still a public authority which must not act in
a way incompatible with the Convention. Does that mean that a
court, in declaring and applying the common law, is required to do
so in a way which is compatible with the Convention rights? Or, is
it enough that they simply give effect to the Convention rights by
means of the mechanisms created by the Human Rights Act? The
first approach would have very significant implications: it would
make the common law a subsidiary regime shaped by the Convention, which is expressed in terms of very broad, general rights quite
different from the common law's method of building up principle
from case to case; and, since it is plain that the international
obligations under the Convention may extend to creating and implementing a legal regime which protects the right in question against
acts in the private sphere,[69] it would have the potential to create new
causes of action against private persons, even though the Human
Rights Act applies only to public authorities. It was not the intention
of the promoters of the Act to create this "full horizontal"
effect—the Lord Chancellor said that the Act would not allow:

"[T]he courts to act as legislators and grant new remedies for
infringement of rights unless the common law itself enables them
to develop new rights or remedies."[70]

Furthermore, the broad approach would arguably be inconsistent
with the doctrine of precedent, since it would give a trial judge a

---

[67] Human Rights Act 1998 s.6(5). *Aston Cantlow etc. Parochial Church Council v Wallbank*
[2003] UKHL 37; [2004] 1 A.C. 546, e.g. a security firm which (a) operates a prison under
contract with the state and (b) guards private premises: *Quaquah v Group 4 Securities Ltd
(No.2), The Times*, June 27, 2001.
[68] Human Rights Act 1998 s.9.
[69] *Airey v Ireland* (1979) 2 E.H.R.R. 305; *X and Y v Netherlands* (1985) 8 E.H.R.R. 235;
Johnston v Ireland (1986) 9 E.H.R.R. 203.
[70] Hansard, HL, November 24, 1997, col.785.

"trump card" (at least where the matter in question had not been considered by a higher court in the context of the Convention) which would enable him to escape otherwise binding decisions. The Human Rights Act does not "incorporate" the Convention into English law and it is potentially misleading to say, metaphorically, that it does.[71]

2–11   As one would expect there is no single, simple answer to the question, though in tort law it is certainly not quite a case of *Argentoratum locutum, judicium finitum*.[72]

In one type of case a Convention right does not so much create a cause of action as militate against an existing liability at common law—for example, the right of freedom of expression under art.6 has at least the potential to restrict the ability of the law to impose liability for defamation. In such a case the court really has no choice but to alter the common law to make it compatible with the Convention, as has happened in relation to qualified privilege and reporting of matters of public concern.[73] In one case a judge declined to apply the common law rule of strict liability in "mistaken identity" libel cases even though that rule was supported by decisions of the Court of Appeal and the House of Lords before the Act (and indeed before the Convention).[74] Nonetheless, where the Convention protects a right which is not recognised or protected by the common law of tort the general tendency since the Human Rights Act 1998 has been to take the line that there may be two parallel regimes governing the situation and the court's duty not to act inconsistently with the Convention is fulfilled by its giving a remedy, via the Act, for the infringement of the Convention right itself, even if one is denied under the common law. In *Wainwright v Home Office*[75] where the events took place before the Act, the House of Lords declined to create a "high level" general tort of invasion of privacy so as to allow the United Kingdom to comply with its international obligations under art.8 and it is clear that the result is the same after the Act. A:

"[F]inding that there was a breach of art. 8 will only demonstrate that there was a gap in the English remedies for invasion of privacy which has since been filled by ss. 6 and 7 of the 1998

---

[71] *McKerr, Re* [2004] UKHL 12; [2004] 1 W.L.R. 708 at [65] per Lord Hoffmann.

[72] *Secretary of State for the Home Department v AF* [2009] UKHL 28; [2009] 3 W.L.R. 74 at [98] per Lord Rodger ("Strasbourg has spoken so the matter is closed").

[73] See para.12–54, below. In the context of defamation we are now encountering the reverse problem, i.e. that the common law gives too much protection to freedom of expression, because defences like truth and privilege give absolute protection to the defendant and unless they can be tempered with an element of proportionality, they risk art.8, which is now regarded as protecting reputation as well as privacy: para.12–2, below.

[74] *O'Shea v MGN Ltd* [2001] E.M.L.R. 40, see para.12–20, below.

[75] [2003] UKHL 53; [2004] 2 A.C. 406.

Act.[76] It does not require that the courts should provide an alternative remedy which distorts the principles of the common law."[77]

In *Smith v Chief Constable of Sussex*[78] the House of Lords held that the general rule of the common law that the police owed no actionable duty to protect individuals from crime remained, notwithstanding the positive duty in art.2 of the Convention to protect life.

There was no claim in *Smith* under the Human Rights Act but, although a violation of art.2 by the police is plainly now actionable under that Act, it should not be assumed that it is simply a mirror image of the common law tort of negligence. The primary focus of art.2 is upon the need for public authorities to have suitable systems in place to protect citizens—the provision of a criminal law and police services, the assessment of detained persons for suicide risk and so on.[79] Even if these requirements are fulfilled there may be an "operational" duty to take further steps to protect an individual but then the Strasbourg jurisprudence on art.2 requires the public authority to have reason to know of a "real and immediate risk" to life and while this cannot be equated with "gross negligence" it is nonetheless a stringent test and it should not be assumed that it is satisfied in every case where, a duty of care being established, there would be negligence at common law.[80] A public hospital is a "public authority" for the purposes of the Human Rights Act and it must take steps to secure competent staff and adequate equipment and safety systems, but there is no liability under art.2 for a negligent treatment error which would lead to liability at common law.

> "[Where] a Contracting State has made adequate provision for securing high professional standards among health professionals and the protection of the lives of patients, [the Court] cannot accept that matters such as error of judgment on the part of a health professional or negligent co-ordination among health professionals in the treatment of a particular patient are sufficient of themselves to call a Contracting State to account from the standpoint of its positive obligations under Article 2 of the Convention to protect life."[81]

---

[76] i.e. as far as public authorities are concerned.
[77] Lord Hoffmann at [52]. In fact he doubted whether there had been an infringement of art.8 but the ECHR disagreed: *Wainwright v UK*, Application No.12350/04 (Sect.4), ECHR 2006-X.
[78] [2008] UKHL 50; [2009] 1 A.C. 225.
[79] *Mitchell v Glasgow CC* [2009] UKHL 11; [2009] 1 A.C. 874 at [66].
[80] *Van Colle v CC Hertfordshire* [2008] UKHL 50; [2009] 1 A.C. 225; *Savage v South Essex Partnership NHS Trust* [2008] UKHL 74; [2009] 1 A.C. 681.
[81] *Powell v UK* , Application No.45305/99, ECHR 2000-V; *Savage*, above fn.80.

Furthermore, the mere fact that the defendant is a public authority which could have prevented the harm does not necessarily mean that it is in breach of art.2, because the matter in question may fall within the scope of the activities of another authority.[82]

An alternative possibility, of course, is that the court simply takes the view that the existing common law fulfils the Convention requirements without more—the Convention, after all, is primarily an international instrument designed to ensure compliance by States with basic standards of protection and it would be surprising if none of them had achieved that in any area before the Convention. For example, art.8 of the Convention is now seen as protecting reputation as well as privacy[83] but it might be argued that the common law of defamation (which has already had to be "reined in" to some extent to comply with art.6) already does that adequately, or more than adequately. In fact the question may turn out to be more complicated because an argument can be made that the common law, to some extent, gives too much protection to freedom of expression, because defences like truth and privilege give absolute protection to the defendant and need to be tempered with an element of proportionality.[84]

2–12   On the other hand, there are cases in which there has been something closer to "horizontality". We have already mentioned the development of misuse of private information out of the law of confidence, a process undoubtedly given impetus, even if not entirely caused by, the need to comply with art.8. A newspaper or a writer is not a public authority so there is no question of application of art.8 via the Human Rights Act, but it has been said that:

"[I]n order to find the rules of the English law [on this matter] we now have to look in the jurisprudence of articles 8 and 10. Those articles are now not merely of persuasive or parallel effect but . . . are the very content of the domestic tort that the English court has to enforce."[85]

There is no doubt that if there is a conflict between a decision of the European Court of Human Rights and one of the House of Lords or Supreme Court a judge is bound to apply the latter,[86] but in a later

---

[82] *Mitchell v Glasgow CC*, above, fn.79, at [68].
[83] See para.12–2, below.
[84] A better example comes from housing law rather than tort law. Article 8 guarantees respect for one's home, but in all but the most exceptional cases the court is entitled to assume that the various statutory mechanisms for gaining possession are art.8-compliant and there is no need for a full judicial art.8 hearing in every eviction case: *Kay v Lambeth LBC* [2006] UKHL 10; [2006] 2 A.C. 465.
[85] *McKennitt v Ash* [2006] EWCA Civ 1714; [2008] Q.B. 73 at [11].
[86] *Kay v Lambeth LBC* [2006] UKHL 10; [2006] 2 A.C. 465.

case concerning photography in a public place,[87] where there was no "conflict" because the case, unlike the relevant House of Lords authority, involved a child, the Court of Appeal was clearly influenced by the rather more claimant-friendly approach to "celebrity photography" taken by the European Court of Human Rights[88] than that which had been implied in an earlier House of Lords decision.[89]

Procedure and substance are closely intertwined in the law. In response to *Osman v UK*, which is discussed below, the English courts became much less ready to strike out claims for negligence at the initial stage on the ground that there could be no duty of care, particularly in cases of claims alleging failure by public bodies in child protection functions. Formally this was not a change in the substantive law on when there was a duty of care but a statement that whether such a duty exists may require examination of the facts of the particular case. However, sooner or later in this way we move across the map from "no duty of care" via "there may sometimes be a duty of care" to "there is generally a duty of care, though the standard imposed may require us to take account of the competing public interests"; and in that way the substantive law has in effect been altered. In *J.D. v East Berkshire Community Health NHS Trust*[90] the Court of Appeal held that in the light of subsequent developments the House of Lords case of *X v Bedfordshire CC*[91] could no longer be taken as authority that there could be no duty of care owed to children in these cases. Appeals from the *J.D.* litigation involved claims by the parents of children taken into care,[92] to which different considerations apply and the striking out of the claims was upheld by the majority of the House of Lords. If the Human Rights Act had been applicable to the case and if there had been an infringement of art.8 in relation to the parents, Lord Rodger preferred to reserve his opinion on whether it would have been appropriate to modify the law of negligence in the parent's favour.[93] Perhaps the practical answer is that all this is less a matter of what the courts *must* do, as of what they *will* do. At the highest level there

---

[87] *Murray v Express Newspapers Ltd* [2008] EWCA Civ 446; [2009] Ch 481.

[88] *Von Hannover v Germany* (2005) 40 E.H.R.R. 1.

[89] *Campbell v MGN Ltd* [2004] UKHL 22; [2004] 2 A.C. 457.

[90] [2003] EWCA Civ 1151; [2004] Q.B. 558.

[91] [1995] 2 A.C. 633.

[92] *J.D. v East Berkshire Community Health NHS Trust* [2005] UKHL 23; [2005] 2 A.C. 373.

[93] At [118]. Cf. Lord Bingham dissenting at [50]: "[The question arises] whether the law of tort should evolve, analogically and incrementally, so as to fashion appropriate remedies to contemporary problems or whether it should remain essentially static, making only such changes as are forced upon it, leaving difficult and, in human terms, very important problems to be swept up by the Convention. I prefer evolution." See also Lord Bingham's dissent in *Smith v CC Sussex* [2008] UKHL 50; [2009] 1 A.C. 225 at [58].

are few doctrines of the common law which are immune to modification by the Supreme Court.[94]

2–13   Article 6 of the Convention requires special treatment. It provides, in the context of civil litigation, that:

> "[I]n the determination of his civil rights and obligations . . .
> everyone is entitled to a fair and public hearing . . . by an inde-
> pendent and impartial tribunal established by law."

This right of access to courts administering law is of course a
fundamental element of English law, in which it can be traced back
to Magna Carta. On its face it is primarily procedural so that if the
domestic law accords a remedy in a particular situation the process
of adjudicating on a claim for the remedy must meet the Convention
requirements. However, one decision of the European Court of
Human Rights used art.6 in such a way as (arguably) to modify the
substantive law of England. In *Osman v Ferguson* the claimants
alleged that the police were negligent in failing to restrain one
Paget-Lewis, who, they said, was a threat to their safety and who
attacked them, killing one and injuring the other. The Court of
Appeal held[95] that the claim should be struck out because the
decision of the House of Lords in *Hill v CC West Yorkshire*[96] meant
that it was against public policy to hold the police liable in damages
for negligence in the investigation of crime.[97] Thus, even on the
assumption that the claimants' allegations were proved in full, the
claim was bound to fail as a matter of law because the police owed
no duty to members of the public. The claimants then proceeded to
invoke the European Convention on Human Rights, first before the
Commission and then before the European Court of Human
Rights.[98] As the law then stood, of course, the Court might order the
Government to pay compensation to the claimants for an infringement of the Convention but the decision on the human rights issue
could not directly affect the outcome of the litigation between the
claimants and the police. The Court found no violation of the
substantive right to life under art.2 of the Convention because the
claimants had not shown that there was any point before the attack
when the police knew or ought to have known that their lives were
at real or immediate risk. However, the Court went on to hold that

---

[94] Could the HL, for example, introduce into English law the doctrine of French law that the
keeper is strictly liable for damage caused by things in his charge or totally abolish the
doctrine of consideration? Probably not, though even in the case of these examples one
could equally well say that the restriction was the product of a self-denying ordinance
rather than a theoretical restriction.

[95] *Osman v Ferguson* [1993] 4 All E.R. 344.

[96] [1989] A.C. 53.

[97] See para.5–11, below.

[98] *Osman v UK* (1998) 29 E.H.R.R. 245.

the striking out of the claim without any investigation of the facts constituted a violation of art.6. Each claimant was awarded £10,000 compensation for the violation.[99]

The reasoning of the European Court of Human Rights was as follows[100]: the basis of the exclusionary rule in *Hill* was a conclusion that to allow actions against the police in respect of the investigation of crime would jeopardise the efficiency of the force and the effectiveness of the battle against crime; but a blanket rule of "immunity" would be disproportionate because it would not balance the harm suffered by the victim and the gravity of the negligence in the individual case against the harm to the public interest in imposing liability; therefore to dismiss the claim under a procedure which did not allow for determination of the facts was a contravention of art.6. This gave rise to some very serious difficulties. Although art.6 is concerned with procedural fairness in the adjudication of rights granted by the domestic law, the effect of the decision was to pass upon the validity of the substantive rules of the domestic law in granting or withholding the right in the first place: the decision proceeds upon the basis of the claimants being deprived of a civil right which *Hill* plainly stated that they did not possess. Logically there seemed to be no limits to this power to pass upon the validity of the domestic law. Suppose, for example, that A is convicted of a crime because of the evidence of B and it now turns out that this evidence was incorrect because B was stupid and credulous. If A sues B for negligence it has hitherto been plain beyond argument that the claim would be struck out. Since there is a clear rule of law that even perjured evidence does not give rise to civil liability,[101] then a fortiori the same must apply to evidence given without due care: the law decided centuries ago that a witness must not be under even the remotest threat of *any* civil consequences[102] arising from his evidence and that the only sanction is to be the comparatively narrow one of the criminal law of perjury. Was it now to be said that because in some individual cases this rule may act disproportionately its universality was now liable to attack via art.6?[103] However, in *Z v UK*[104] the majority of the European Court of Human Rights reconsidered the scope of art.6 in the context of a

[99] In practical terms, the claimants were awarded compensation for not being allowed to make a full presentation of a claim which would probably have failed, but the Convention is about the vindication of rights.

[100] Lord Browne-Wilkinson in *Barrett v Enfield LBC* [2001] 2 A.C. 550 at 558 confessed that he found it "extremely difficult to understand".

[101] See para.24–10, below.

[102] See also the defamation rule: para.12–41, below.

[103] This is in fact much more of a "blanket exclusionary rule" than that in *Hill*, which did not say that the police could *never* be sued for failing to prevent crime: the decision might well have been different if they had allowed Paget-Lewis to escape from custody and make the attack.

[104] (2002) 34 E.H.R.R. 3. See also *Fogarty v UK* (2002) 34 E.H.R.R. 12.

failure by a local authority to protect the applicants from child abuse, the claim in domestic law having been struck out by the House of Lords on the ground that there was no duty of care under the tort of negligence.[105] This time there was held to be no breach of art.6:

> "101. The applicants may not . . . claim that they were deprived of any right to a determination on the merits of their negligence claims. Their claims were properly and fairly examined in light of the applicable domestic legal principles concerning the tort of negligence. Once the House of Lords had ruled on the arguable legal issues that brought into play the applicability of Article 6 . . . of the Convention . . . , the applicants could no longer claim any entitlement under Article 6 . . . to obtain any hearing concerning the facts . . . [S]uch a hearing would have served no purpose, unless a duty of care in negligence had been held to exist in their case. It is not for this Court to find that this should have been the outcome of the striking out proceedings since this would effectively involve substituting its own views as to the proper interpretation and content of domestic law."[106]

Ironically, the fundamental proposition that there was no duty of care in such a case no longer seems to represent English law (as we have seen above) but on a more general plane one might say that this approach returned art.6 to its proper place.[107] However, in *Z v UK* there was held to be a breach of the substantive right not to be subjected to inhuman or degrading treatment under art.3 of the Convention and, in turn, a breach of art.13 in the failure of the domestic law to afford a remedy for that. Since the Human Rights Act, of course, a claim under art.3 will be directly justiciable in an English court.

2–14   The net effect of all this is that to some extent we have two parallel and overlapping legal systems, one based on tort law, the other based on vindication of Convention rights. Although the focus of the two systems is different and by and large damages are likely to be lower in Convention claims than at common law,[108] there are still remedial problems. In *Van Colle v Chief Constable of Hertfordshire*[109] the deceased was murdered by X, against whom he was to

---

[105] *X v Bedfordshire CC* [1995] 2 A.C. 633.

[106] See also *Matthews v MoD* [2003] UKHL 4; [2003] 1 A.C. 1163.

[107] The striking out procedure is considered further in the context of negligence: see para.5–3 below. There is an echo of *Osman* in *Almeda v Att Gen for Gibraltar* [2003] UKPC 81. Under the common law of Gibraltar (as originally under the common law of England) there was no liability for non-repair of the highway. The argument that there was a contravention of the guarantee in the Gibraltar Constitution of "protection of the law" was rejected: that afforded procedural guarantees but did not confer any substantive rights.

[108] *Watkins v Home Office* [2006] UKHL 17; [2006] 2 A.C. 395 at [26] ("ungenerous").

[109] [2008] UKHL 50; [2009] 1 A.C. 225.

be a witness in a criminal case, in circumstances which Cox J. held constituted a culpable failure by the police to afford the deceased protection for the purposes of art.2. The claim (by the estate of the deceased and by his parents) was brought solely under art.2. The House of Lords held that there had been no violation of art.2 because the police did not have reason to know of the "real and immediate risk" of violence and therefore did not have to address the issue of damages. However, the trial judge had awarded £15,000 to the deceased's estate and £17,500 each to his parents. Had there been a liability at common law it is not at all clear that the estate could have recovered substantial damages for his death, which was instantaneous, though it might have recovered something for his distress in the period before the fatal attack during which threats were made by X; but it is clear that his parents would have had no claim at all. They were not dependent on him for the purposes of the Fatal Accidents Act 1976 and, since he was an adult, they had no claim for statutory bereavement damages (then £10,000 between them). The Court of Appeal[110] reduced the awards to £10,000 to the estate and £7,500 each to the parents, but the total is still far more than would have been recovered by the estate at common law, indeed far more than could have been recovered against X, had he been worth suing. The Court of Appeal did accept that it was questionable whether the parents should be regarded as victims for the purposes of the Convention but the point had not been raised in the respondent's notice so the matter was not pursued. Lord Scott returned to the point of locus standi in *Savage v South Essex Partnership NHS Foundation Trust*, a case of a suicide by a mental patient. The claim failed at all stages for lack of a violation of art.2 so no assessment of damages was ever made but the husband of the deceased, who could have brought a claim for negligence on behalf of the estate and under the Fatal Accidents Act in respect of any dependency of his, had declined to do so, the art.2 proceedings being brought by the deceased's daughter. Lord Scott said:

"One problem, and it seems to me a major problem, with the respondent's claim is that a claim under section 7 of the 1998 Act may only be brought by a 'victim' of the unlawful act or omission relied on . . . I am quite unable to understand how a close family member can claim to be a 'victim' in relation to an act, in breach of the article 2(1) negative obligation, or in relation to an omission, in breach of the article 2(1) positive obligation, that had led to the death. The domestic law of a country may, as the domestic law of this country does, provide a remedy to the estate of the deceased and to the dependants of the deceased in any case where

---

[110] [2007] EWCA Civ 325; [2007] 1 W.L.R. 1821.

an act or omission unlawful under civil law has caused death. But
I do not see it as any part of the function of article 2(1) to add to
the class of persons who under ordinary domestic law can seek
financial compensation for a death an undefined, and perhaps
undefinable, class composed of persons close to the deceased who
have suffered distress and anguish on account of the death."[111]

No doubt the claimant's concern was to obtain a judicial determination about the death but that had already been made by the inquest
verdict, which found that the defendants' precautions were inadequate. Vindication certainly has a role to play in tort damages[112] and
a fortiori under the Convention, but when they are awarded on a
substantial scale they are hard to distinguish from exemplary damages, which are not allowed under the Convention. Although the
problems thrown up by parallel legal remedies are not insuperable,
perhaps one day we shall need a new Judicature Act, as we once
had, to "fuse" law and equity.

C. A European Tort Law?

2–15   This chapter began by referring to certain aspects of tort law in
other European legal systems. Private law is outside the competence
of the European Union, though certain of its functions, most notably
that of consumer protection, have produced pockets of "European
tort law" if we may use that phrase, on matters like product liability[113] and unfair contract terms. However, in the last 20 years there
has been a remarkable amount of academic activity directed towards
framing Europe-wide principles of private law.[114] A "European
Group on Tort Law" produced a series of surveys of particular
aspects of tort law which culminated in a volume of Principles.[115] A
study group on a European Civil Code was active on a broader front
in preparing principles of private law and combined with a number
of other groups to produce in 2008 Principles, Definitions and
Model Rules of European Private Law, the "Draft Common Frame

[111] [2008] UKHL 74; [2009] 1 A.C. 681 at [5].
[112] See para.22–5, below.
[113] See Ch.10, below.
[114] i.e. very broadly speaking, the law governing relations between persons but not the law
governing the special powers of the State. Contract, tort and property are therefore private
law. However, in the common law the distinction, while it undoubtedly exists, is hard to
draw. Many of the modern cases on negligence involve actions against public authorities
for carrying out their functions badly or failing to carry out those functions and such cases
are undoubtedly part of the law of torts (see, e.g. Watkins v Home Office [2006] UKHL 17;
[2006] 1 A.C. 395). In France, on the other hand, the liability of a public authority for
damage depends upon principles which are to a considerable extent separate and distinct
from those of private law in the Code civil and such cases are even heard in separate courts.
See Bell, Boyron and Whitaker, Principles of French Law, 2nd edn (2008).
[115] Principles of European Tort Law, Text and Commentary (2005).

of Reference" (DCFR). The Contract material is based on the work of the earlier Lando Commission[116] but to this is added material from the existing body of EU law, the so-called *acquis communautaire*. The DCFR[117] is an "enigmatic concept".[118] It declares itself to be, "an academic, not a politically authorised text"[119] but in the past the European Parliament has declared itself in favour of a European Civil Code[120] and the Commission has spoken in terms of a common frame of reference being used as a "legislator's toolbox", at least in the area of consumer law (though in that case it is difficult to see why it contains material on general tort law, commercial agency and unjust enrichment). People have also spoken of an "optional civil code" but while that idea has real content in relation to contracts, the option idea would seem rather unsuitable to tort.

It is a truism of comparative law that the results in different **2–16** systems are often rather similar, though the routes by which they are reached may be different. Let us take the provisions from the DCFR and the Principles of European Tort Law which deal with a broadly similar issue.

DCFR:
"VI. –2:101 Meaning of legally relevant damage
(1) Loss, whether economic or non-economic, or injury is legally relevant damage if

(a) one of the following rules of this Chapter so provides;
(b) the loss or injury results from a violation of a right otherwise conferred by the law; or
(c) the loss or injury results from a violation of an interest worthy of legal protection.

(2) In any case covered only by sub-paragraph (b) or (c) of paragraph (1) loss or injury constitutes legally relevant damage only if it would be fair and reasonable for there to be a right to reparation[121] . . .
(3) In considering whether it would be fair and reasonable for there to be a right to reparation . . . regard is to be had to the ground of accountability, to the nature and proximity of the

---

[116] Lando and Beale (eds), *Principles of European Contract Law, Parts I and II* (2000); Lando and others (eds), *Principles of European Contract Law, Part III* (2003).
[117] The Interim Outline Edition of 2008 contains the text and an introduction. The full version (2009) with comments and notes runs to six volumes.
[118] Eidenmüller, Faust, Grigoleit, Jansen, Wagner, Zimmermann, "The Common Frame of Reference for European Private Law—Policy Choices and Codification Problems" (2008) 28 O.J.L.S. 659 at 661.
[119] Introduction, para.4.
[120] Resolution of May 1989.
[121] Equivalent provisions relating to prevention of damage are here omitted.

damage . . . , to the reasonable expectations of the person who
suffers . . . the damage, and to considerations of public policy."

Principles of European Tort Law:

"Art. 2:102. Protected interests
(1) The scope of protection of an interest depends on its nature;
the higher its value, the precision of its definition and its obvious-
ness, the more extensive is its protection.
(2) Life, bodily or mental integrity, human dignity and liberty
enjoy the most extensive protection.
(3) Extensive protection is granted to property rights, including
those in intangible property.
(4) Protection of pure economic interests or contractual relationships may be more limited in scope. In such cases, due regard
must be had especially to the proximity between the actor and the
endangered person, or to the fact that the actor is aware of the fact
that he will cause damage even though his interests are necessarily valued lower than those of the victim.
(5) The scope of protection may also be affected by the nature
of liability, so that an interest may receive more extensive protection against intentional harm than in other cases.
(6) In determining the scope of protection, the interests of the
actor, especially in liberty of action and in exercising his rights, as
well   as   public   interests   also   have   to   be   taken   into
consideration."

Those who progress through this book will be able to recognise,
even if "through a glass darkly", a good deal of this in current
English tort law, in particular the approach to the duty of care and
the differing extent of protection of certain interests according to
whether we are dealing with negligent or intentional conduct,
though there are of course provisions in both drafts which are simply
incompatible with current English law. However, some of those
incompatibilities (most obviously the absence in England of strict
liability for motor accidents) are really political rather than issues of
legal doctrine. Nor are the incompatibilities a case of "English law
v the Rest". The idea that "the Civil Law" is some monolithic unity
is far from the truth: thus acceptance of either set of proposals
would, for example, require German law to take a fundamentally
different approach to liability for employees and neither draft contains anything resembling the French liability for damage done by
things, a most distinctive feature of French tort law to which they
are probably rather attached. A more important question is whether,

even if such substantive problems could be overcome, any "unification" of tort law in Europe (which is always there in the background, even if everyone involved in these projects seems to want to
distance himself from such an idea) is at all feasible. The legal
cultures are very different even if they all embrace much the same
principles at the highest level of abstraction. Thus the extracts above
seem to assume open exposition and discussion at the highest level
which are quite familiar in English judgments (and indeed in German ones) but which are quite alien to the tradition of the Cour de
Cassation in France, where the tradition is that one must give
reasons but not *explain* the reasons. Although English appellate
procedures have become markedly more "paper-based" in recent
years the fundamental idea of the oral trial which settles all issues
between the parties is still the underlying foundation of the procedural system, even though most cases are of course settled; and
matters which on the face of it have nothing to do with substantive
law may have major implications for the substantive principles. For
example, in English civil cases the standard of proof is on a balance
of probabilities: if something is shown to be just more likely than
not it is treated as having been conclusively established for most
purposes. In some European systems on the other hand the damage
must be proved with "certainty".[122] It would be wrong to equate this
with the English "beyond a reasonable doubt" of the criminal
standard and it is hard to pin down. However, it does seem more
onerous than the balance of probability standard. That has obvious
implications for the approach the particular system will take to the
substantive law issue of claims based on "loss of a chance". One
must also not forget the considerable uncertainty which would result
from unification, and the massive burden of re-education,[123] not to
mention the natural human fondness for the familiar. Perhaps most
important of all is the fact that even if everyone adopted the same
text, how would one prevent the system simply breaking up very
quickly by divergences in local interpretation? In a few very narrow
areas of private law (principally matters of jurisdiction) the European Court of Justice acts as the ultimate appellate court for an
"autonomous" European law but it is inconceivable that we could
have a Supreme Court of Private Law for the whole of Europe or
that we could expect local courts to keep up with legal developments
in all the other countries.

It seems unlikely that there will be wholesale unification or **2–17**
harmonisation in the foreseeable future (even of the law of contract,

---

[122] Thus in the *Principles of European Tort Law* art.2:105 damage, "must be proved according
to normal [national] procedural standards".
[123] Something German lawyers were wont to emphasize in the period after the enactment of
the BGB. When the current Dutch Civil Code was introduced in the 1990s, law faculties
had apparently been teaching it for a decade.

which might appear more desirable and which would probably be a good deal easier than in the case of tort). If EU legislators in their activities impinging on private law do make substantial use of the DCFR as a legislative toolbox then that will have an impact on English law and make life more complicated.[124] However, even if nothing like this happens and these documents and proposals remain academic texts, it must also be borne in mind that for a century the English courts have been "comparatists" in the sense that they have been willing to look at developments in other common law countries and in the last 20 years at the highest level they have shown an increasing inclination to look at civil law systems.[125] So it is not inconceivable that at the highest level English courts might make "voluntary" use of things like the DCFR.

3. TORTS NOT TREATED IN THIS BOOK

2–18   There are some wrongs which are certainly torts but which are rather outside the scope of an elementary book. First, there are those matters which are commonly treated as specialised legal subjects in their own right. Technically speaking, actions for infringement of the intellectual property rights of copyright, patents, and trade marks are actions in tort (albeit statutory) but these matters are far too specialised and complex for inclusion in a book of this kind[126] and the statutory causes of action for wrongful discrimination are best looked at in the context of employment law, where they most commonly arise.[127] Then there is a range of minor tort causes of action based on the common law.[128] For example, there is a group of wrongs concerned with interference with a franchise—a royal privilege, or branch of the Queen's prerogative, subsisting in the hands of a subject.[129] The forms of it are various, but examples are the franchise of a number of persons to be incorporated and subsist as

---

[124] Consider the example of product liability. The current Directive (EC 85/374) applies to personal injury and a very limited range of property damage but it leaves it to English law to determine what types of damages are obtainable. A replacement Directive which legislated by reference to the DCFR might bring in rules about damages which are either not reconcilable with English law or which are expressed in such imprecise terms that a question would arise whether there was a "margin of appreciation" for more specific local rules: e.g. VI-2:202, 6:101(2), 6:103, 6:202, 6:203.

[125] Three well-known examples are *Henderson v Merrett Syndicates* [1995] 2 A.C. 145, *White v Jones* [1995] 2 A.C. 207 and *Fairchild v Glenhaven Funeral Services* [2002] UKHL 22; [2003] 1 A.C. 32. Such overt external references, even to another civil law system, would be very unusual in Europe.

[126] Even the comprehensive Clerk & Lindsell, *Torts*, 19th edn, deals with them all in an abbreviated form in one chapter (q.v. for references to specialised works).

[127] But note that these may overlap on the facts with common law claims: see *Farah v MPC* [1998] Q.B. 65 at 69.

[128] See Rudden, "Torticles" (1991–92) 6–7 Tulane Civ L.F. 105.

[129] Blackstone, *Comm*, ii, 37.

a body politic; and franchises to have waifs, wrecks, strays, royal fish; and to hold markets or fairs, to take tolls for bridges and ferries.[130] In another sense, "franchise" signifies the right to vote at a parliamentary or municipal election. In the famous case of *Ashby v White*,[131] a returning officer was held liable in damages for wrongfully refusing to take the claimant's vote at a parliamentary election. From this point of view the case is now wholly obsolete since by statute the remedy is criminal not civil,[132] but it remains a relevant authority on the tort of breach of statutory duty. Sometimes Parliament may sweep away whole areas of tort law, as happened with the group of torts which related to interference with family relationships.[133] Others may be preserved like legal fossils, the social circumstances which underlay them having passed away, for the time being at least. An example is usurpation of a public office.[134]

---

[130] See Clerk & Lindsell, *Torts*, 14th edn, Ch.26 (not in the current edition). Some of this is by no means obsolete, see, e.g. *Iveagh v Martin* [1961] 1 Q.B. 232; *Wyld v Silver* [1963] 1 Q.B. 169; *Sevenoaks DC v Patullo* [1984] Ch. 211.
[131] (1703) 2 Ld. Raym. 938.
[132] Representation of the People Act 1985.
[133] See para.18–2, below.
[134] See the 13th edn of this work, p.554.

CHAPTER 3

GENERAL CHARACTERISTICS OF TORTIOUS LIABILITY

THERE are different ways in which liability in tort may arise: **3–1**

1. Liability may be imposed as a legal consequence of a person's act, or of his omission if he is under a legal duty to act. Liability may also be imposed upon one person as the legal consequence of the act or omission of another person with whom he stands in some special relationship such as that of employer and servant. That is known as vicarious liability and is the subject of a separate chapter.[1]
2. In most cases liability is based upon fault: sometimes an intention to injure is required but more often negligence is sufficient. In other cases, which are called cases of strict liability, liability is in varying degrees independent of fault.
3. Whereas most torts require damage resulting to the claimant which is not too remote a consequence of the defendant's conduct, a few, such as trespass in some, or perhaps all, of its various forms and libel, do not require proof of actual damage.

1. INTENTION OR NEGLIGENCE OR THE BREACH OF STRICT DUTY

A. Intention

Some torts require intention on the part of the wrongdoer. It is, of **3–2**
course, impossible for the law to do more than to infer a person's

---

[1] See Ch.20, below.

intention, or indeed any other mental state, from his conduct.[2] The law may frequently attribute to him an intention which a metaphysician would at most consider very doubtful. Centuries ago, Brian C.J. said: "It is common knowledge that the thought of man shall not be tried, for the Devil himself knoweth not the thought of man."[3] On the other hand, Bowen L.J. in 1885 had no doubt that, "the state of a man's mind is as much a fact as the state of his digestion".[4] There is no contradiction in these dicta. All that Brian C.J. meant was that no one can be perfectly certain of what passes in the mind of another person but Brian would certainly not have dissented from the proposition that in law what a person thinks must be deduced from what he says and does and that is all that Bowen L.J. meant.

Given this basic premise that intention can only be inferred from conduct we are still left with the problem of defining intention. Everyone agrees that a person intends a consequence if it is his desire or motive to bring it about, but beyond that it is probably not possible to lay down any universal definition for the purposes of tort. In crime, the law now is that the jury is entitled (but not, it seems, required) to infer intention where the defendant was aware that the harm was "virtually certain" to result from his act.[5] There has been much less discussion of intention in tort and there are probably at least two reasons for this (apart from the relative infrequency of cases on intentional torts). First, since the abolition of the forms of action the claimant may sometimes be able to fall back upon a wider principle of liability for negligence: if I strike you, then provided I cause you hurt and that hurt could have been foreseeable to a reasonable man then my conduct amounts to the tort of negligence even if the court is in doubt whether I acted intentionally.[6] Secondly, while the criminal law may insist that the defendant's intention must extend to all the elements and consequences of his act making up the definition of the crime, the law of tort may separate the initial interference with the victim from the consequences of that interference (remoteness of damage[7]) and while intention or foresight may be necessary as to the former it may not be as to the latter. Thus if A strikes B intending some slight harm but B suffers greater harm (because, for example, he falls as a result of the blow) A is responsible for the greater harm if it is a direct consequence of the blow: he need not even foresee the possibility of

---

[2] Including his conduct in the witness box.
[3] Year Book Pasch. 17 Edw. 4, fol. 2, pl. 2.
[4] *Edgington v Fitzmaurice* (1885) 29 Ch. D. 459 at 483.
[5] *R. v Nedrick* [1986] 1 W.L.R. 1025 (intent in murder).
[6] However, the limits of this freedom are not entirely clear: see the next section.
[7] See Ch.6, below.

the greater harm, let alone intend it.[8] Indeed, the defendant is liable for the greater harm even if it is the result of some unusual susceptibility of the claimant, a principle developed primarily in the context of negligence[9] but applying with even more force to intentional wrongdoers.[10]

In one tort, conspiracy to injure, intention has the very narrow   **3–3** meaning of single-minded purpose to do harm, so that the defendant does not "intend" even what he foresees as inevitable if his purpose is to advance his own interests.[11] Other torts in the area of unlawful interference with economic interests now require either that very narrow "purpose" intention *or* that the defendant acts so as to cause harm to the claimant as the means to some other end which it is his purpose to achieve: the claimant must therefore be the "target" of the defendant's actions.[12] In the context of trespass to land it has been said that indifference to a risk that trespass will occur by animals in the defendant's charge amounts to intention[13] and it is thought that the same approach should be taken in all the trespass torts: if D throws his coffee dregs out of the window of his office, knowing that others may be passing, that should be trespass if anyone is hit, whether the street is so crowded that it is a virtual certainty or is comparatively unfrequented.[14] Or to take a more realistic example, consider the case of someone who places a bomb for political reasons; he may give a warning on the basis of which the emergency services may be expected to act and he may not "intend" personal injury in the sense of desiring it but he can hardly deny that he appreciates the real risk of something going wrong.[15] This is the state of mind referred to in the criminal law as "subjective recklessness", that is to say, the wrongdoer is conscious of the risk he is taking.[16] Where recklessness as to consequences will do in tort, so will recklessness as to circumstances. Thus the tort of misfeasance in a public office is committed when a public officer acts knowingly outside the scope of his powers with the intent that the claimant will thereby be injured or if he is recklessly indifferent

---

[8] *Wainwright v Home Office* [2001] EWCA Civ 2081; [2002] Q.B. 1334 at [69] (on appeal [2003] UKHL 53; [2004] 2 A.C. 406); *Williams v Humphrey, The Times*, February 20, 1975.

[9] See para.6–32, below.

[10] *Allan v New Mount Sinai Hospital* (1980) 109 D.L.R. (3d) 634.

[11] para.18–23, below.

[12] para.18–13, below.

[13] See *League Against Cruel Sports v Scott* [1986] Q.B. 240 at 252.

[14] This is the view taken in *Bici v MoD* [2004] EWHC 786 (QB), *The Times*, June 11, 2004, but cf. *Restatement of Torts*, 3d, Tentative Draft No.1, §1 ("substantial certainty").

[15] See *Breslin v McKenna* [2009] NIQB 50.

[16] Though using "intention" to embrace this state of mind is a convenient shorthand it is open to criticism as being wider than the proper usage. As Finnis points out, "Intention in Tort Law" in Owen (ed.) *Philosophical Foundations of Tort Law* (1995), lecturers know that what they say will inevitably confuse some of their audience but it would be difficult to say that they intend to do so.

to the legality of his acts and the damage he may inflict on the claimant.[17]

B. Negligence

3–4   "Negligence" is an independent tort with a number of elements. What we are concerned with at this point[18] is negligence as the state of mind which is one element of the tort (and of course of some other torts). In this sense it usually signifies inadvertence by the defendant to the consequences of his behaviour, simple examples being the motorist who daydreams, the solicitor who forgets about the approach of the limitation period or the doctor who forgets that the patient is allergic to a treatment. It may be that the word should only be used in this sense[19] but for the purposes of the tort of negligence a defendant clearly cannot always escape liability because he adverted to the risk if the case is one where even inadvertence would saddle him with liability. An illustration of advertence is *Vaughan v Menlove*,[20] where the defendant had been warned that his haystack was likely to overheat and catch fire, which might spread to the land of his neighbour. He said that he would "chance it" and he was held liable for the damage which occurred when the stack actually took fire. There is, therefore, a certain degree of overlap between negligence and recklessness in the sense described under the previous heading, though recklessness is not an independent tort, merely an alternative element to intention in certain torts where mere negligence will not do. Liability for intentional or reckless behaviour in those torts is generally more rather than less extensive than liability for negligence[21] but in the past there was , paradoxically, at least one case in which the reverse was true. Thus the general limitation period (the period within which the claim must be brought) for tort is six years. For the tort of negligence (where it causes personal injury) it is three years but with the two important qualifications that (1) time does not begin to run until the claimant knows or ought to know that he has a claim and (2) even when the period has expired the court may "disapply" the limitation period.[22] At one time it was held that the fixed, six-year period

---

[17] *Three Rivers DC v Bank of England (No.3)* [2001] UKHL 16; [2003] 2 A.C. 1. See also *White v White* [2001] 2 All E.R. 43 (a requirement that a person "knows" something will generally be satisfied if he suspects that it is so but takes the attitude that he will not ask further because he would rather not know).

[18] As to the other elements of the tort, see Chs 5 and 6, below.

[19] See the remarks of Lord Reid in *I.C.I. v Shatwell* [1965] A.C. 656 at 672.

[20] (1837) 3 Bing N.C. 468.

[21] e.g. (i) liability for certain sorts of loss (in particular economic loss) may be recoverable if the conduct is intentional, but not if it is negligent (ii) the remoteness of damage rules may be more severe on the defendant (see para.6–19, below) and (iii) exemplary or aggravated damages may be available (see para.22–8, below).

[22] See Ch.26.

applied to battery (involving intention/recklessness) which meant that the claimant might be worse off under the law of battery than under the law of negligence. That particular problem has now gone away because the more flexible provision in the limitation statute has been interpreted as covering battery. The freedom of the claimant to frame his claim as the lesser wrong if it suits him to do so is not entirely clear. The case which formerly held that the fixed limitation period applied to battery suggests that it is not unlimited. However, if we imagine a case in which the claimant, a trespasser, is shot at night by the defendant firing a gun into his garden, it is hard to believe that even if the claimant has some evidence that the defendant shot him intentionally or recklessly he is required to frame his claim as one for battery if instead he prefers simply to allege negligence.[23] Perhaps the answer is that the defendant is not to be allowed to set up his own worse wrongdoing in objection to that alleged by the claimant.[24] The problem is probably more theoretical than real but it arises from the different historical origins of trespass and negligence.[25]

C. Breach of Strict Duty

In some torts, the defendant is liable even though the harm to the **3–5** claimant occurred without intention or negligence on the defendant's part. Thus it was laid down in the celebrated case of *Rylands v Fletcher*[26] that:

> "[I]f a person brings or accumulates on his land anything which, if it should escape, may cause damage to his neighbours, he does so at his peril. If it does escape and cause damage, he is responsible, however careful he may have been, and whatever precautions he may have taken to prevent damage."

This is sometimes styled "absolute" liability, but the epithet is misplaced, as there are possible defences even to torts of this kind, for example, the act of a third party excludes liability under the rule in *Rylands v Fletcher.* Liability in nuisance may be strict where the defendant himself or someone for whom he is responsible has created the nuisance.[27] Liability for breach of a statutory duty is often not dependent on proof of negligence,[28] and where an Act

---

[23] Cf. *Revill v Newberry* [1996] Q.B. 567. In that case the defendant had been acquitted of a crime requiring intention or recklessness, though that would not have been conclusive on those issues in a civil action.

[24] Even if he could, the claimant could amend his claim.

[25] See para.2–2, above.

[26] (1868) L.R. 3 H.L. 330 at 340, Ch.15, below.

[27] See para.14–13, below.

[28] See para.7–15, below.

requires something to be done without qualification, contravention of the statute automatically establishes liability.[29]

D. "Reasonable" and "Reasonable Man"

3–6   It is convenient to insert here an explanation of the terms "reasonable" and "reasonable man". They recur so frequently in the law of tort, and indeed in every branch of the law, that their meaning must be grasped at the outset of this exposition. As to the law of tort, reasonableness is an essential ingredient in the law of negligence, whether that word be used to indicate an independent tort or a mental element in the commission of certain other torts and more will be said of this in the chapter on negligence. However, there are many other torts in which, in one way or another, the idea appears. If any broad sense can be extracted from the various significations of "reasonable conduct" it might be described as the behaviour of the ordinary person in any particular event or transaction, including in such behaviour obedience to the special directions (if any) which the law gives him for his guidance in that connection. This is, of course, an abstraction. Lord Bowen visualised the reasonable man as "the man on the Clapham omnibus"[30] an American writer as "the man who takes the magazines at home, and in the evening pushes the lawn-mower in his shirt sleeves".[31] Despite the inveterate use of the masculine gender, there is no doubt that the personification includes the reasonable woman in the sense that the abstraction is not intended to embody peculiarly masculine values or patterns of behaviour[32] and no doubt "reasonable person" is gradually becoming the preferred expression. The reasonable person has not the courage of Achilles, the wisdom of Ulysses nor the strength of Hercules, nor has he "the prophetic vision of a clairvoyant".[33] He will not anticipate folly in all its forms, but he never puts out of consideration the teachings of experience and so will guard against

---

[29] *John Summers & Sons Ltd v Frost* [1955] A.C. 740. On terminology in this context see Smith L.J. in *Allison v London Underground Ltd* [2008] EWCA Civ 71; [2008] I.C.R. 719 at [31]. Liability under the Nuclear Installations Act 1965 will exist even if the damage is attributable to an act of God, but not if it is attributable to hostile action in the course of armed conflict: s.13(4).

[30] A similar character is sometimes called up as the personification of public opinion on a legal issue. Here the current tendency is to call him the "passenger on the Underground": *McFarlane v Tayside Health Board* [2000] 2 A.C. 59; *Frost v CC South Yorkshire* [1999] 2 A.C. 455.

[31] Cited by Greer L.J. in *Hall v Brooklands Auto Racing Club* [1933] 1 K.B. 205 at 224. Eldredge, *Modern Tort Problems*, p.3: "The reasonable man is a fiction—he is the personification of the court and jury's social judgment".

[32] But cf. Bender, "A Lawyer's Primer on Feminist Theory and Tort" (1988) 38 J. Legal Educ. 3.

[33] *Hawkins v Coulsdon & Purley UDC* [1954] 1 Q.B. 319 at 341 per Romer L.J. Pace Lord Bramwell, who occasionally attributed to the reasonable man the agility of an acrobat and the foresight of a Hebrew prophet.

the negligence of others when experience shows such negligence to be common.[34] He is reasonable but he is neither a perfect citizen nor a "paragon of circumspection".[35] While one does not expect the reasonable person to be all-seeing and all-knowing, and he can therefore make "reasonable mistakes", he is not the "average person". In reality no individual is infallible and even the most careful person will probably on a few occasions fail to foresee a risk when he has no excuse for doing so. In the limited sense that the legal personification of due care will never fall below the standard set by the law he does not resemble any living human being. This is good so far as it goes, but it must be added that where a person exercises any calling, the law requires him, in dealing with other people in the course of that calling, to exhibit the degree of skill or competence which is usually associated with its efficient discharge.[36] Nobody expects the passenger on the Clapham omnibus to have any skill as a surgeon, a lawyer, a pilot, or a plumber, unless he is one; but if he professes to be one, then the law requires him to show such skill as any ordinary member of the profession or calling to which he belongs, or claims to belong, would display.

The description of "reasonable" just given is, and can only be, a rough approximation to exactness. As was indicated in it, if the law gives special directions for the guidance of the ordinary person, he must regulate his conduct by them if his conduct is to be regarded as reasonable. Now these directions are often so precise and technical that a person, if he is to ascertain and act upon them, strikes one as anything but a commonplace person, and seems to need the Clapham lawyer at his elbow on many occasions. Here the judicial method, being what it is, shows two rather conflicting tendencies. One is to get as near exactness as may be in the rules relating to what is regarded as reasonable. The other is to recognise that complete exactness is neither attainable nor desirable.[37] Nor is this all. The judge has to decide what "reasonable" means, and it is inevitable that different judges may take variant views on the same question

---

[34] *L.P.T.B. v Upson* [1949] A.C. 155 at 173 per Lord Uthwatt, and at 176 per Lord de Parcq; *Lang v London Transport Executive* [1959] 1 W.L.R. 1168 at 1175 per Havers J. See the *Restatement of Torts*, 2d, §289, 290: "What is customarily regarded as requisite for the protection of others, rather than that of the average man in the community".

[35] *A. C. Billings & Sons Ltd v Riden* [1958] A.C. 240 at 255 per Lord Reid. For a brilliant caricature of "this excellent but odious creature" see Sir Alan Herbert, *Uncommon Law*, pp.1–5.

[36] General and approved practice may, however, fall below the standard of the reasonable man, and if so, it is not a good defence.

[37] The latter tendency is dominant at the present day, but with the disappearance of juries in civil cases and the expansion of law reporting, there is a danger that judges' decisions of fact may come to be treated as laying down detailed rules of law: *Qualcast (Wolverhampton) Ltd v Haynes* [1959] A.C. 743, especially per Lord Somervell at 757–758 per Lord Denning at 759–761.

with respect to such an elastic term.[38] An extreme example of this was a case in which "reasonable cause" was an element and the very same act was held by an appellate criminal court to be a felony punishable with penal servitude for life, and by an appellate civil court to be not even a tort.[39] Conflicts of this sort are very unusual, and although we shall find the reasonable person doing some things which a moralist would regard as quixotic and a good many other things which he would condemn as slovenly or even cowardly, the law on the whole strikes a fair average between these extremes.

3–7   Several other phrases will be encountered in the law reports which have sometimes, but not always, a meaning equivalent to "reasonable". Such are "fair", "just", "natural justice". Like certain other phrases (for example "judicial discretion"), they show that although law and ethics are distinct topics, it is impossible to make or to administer a civilised system of law without taking account of current ethical ideas,[40] which include not only corrective justice (the notion that harm should be redressed) but also distributive justice (the fair distribution of losses and burdens in society).[41] The notion of what is "fair, just and reasonable" now plays a major, overt role in determining the existence and scope of the duty of care which is the foundation of negligence.[42]

2. MOTIVE AND MALICE

3–8   Motive may be conveniently treated here. It signifies the reason for conduct. Unfortunately it has become entangled with the word "malice" which is used quite differently in the law of tort. It may mean what the layman usually takes it to be—"evil motive" or spite—or the purpose of causing harm to someone, or it may simply signify doing an act wilfully without just cause or excuse. The last two senses have really nothing to do with motive but refer to intention, a term which ought to be confined to advertence to

---

[38] *Glasgow Corp v Muir* [1943] A.C. 448 at 457 per Lord Macmillan, who deals with some of the attributes of a reasonable man. Though invested with power to decide what is reasonable, it does not follow that the judge will always behave like a reasonable man himself: *O'Connor v State of South Australia* (1976) 14 S.A.S.R. 187.

[39] *R. v Denyer* [1926] 2 K.B. 258; *Hardie & Lane Ltd v Chilton* [1928] 2 K.B. 306. This conflict was resolved in *Thorne v Motor Trade Association* [1937] A.C. 797, cf. the differing views expressed in the Court of Appeal and in the House of Lords in *Woods v Duncan* [1946] A.C. 401.

[40] Winfield, "Ethics in English Case Law" (1931) 45 Harv. L. Rev. 112–135, reprinted in *Select Legal Essays* (1952), pp.266–282.

[41] See the speeches of Lord Hoffman in *Frost v CC South Yorks* [1999] 2 A.C. 455 (para.5–69, below) and Lord Steyn in *McFarlane v Tayside Health Board* [2000] 2 A.C. 59 (para.24–15, below).

[42] See para.5–17, below.

conduct and its consequences, and which is quite colourless as to the motive which influences the actor. The meaning of malice has to be considered in the context of each tort where it is said to be relevant—for example, defamation, malicious prosecution and misfeasance in a public office.

A. Motive Generally Irrelevant

As to motive in its proper meaning, the general rule is that, if **3–9** conduct is presumptively unlawful, a good motive will not exonerate the defendant, and that, if conduct is lawful apart from motive, a bad motive will not make him liable. We shall see that there are several exceptions to the second part of this rule. To the first part of it, defences like necessity and private defence are exceptions, for they depend to a certain extent on a good motive on the part of the defendant.

The general irrelevancy of evil motive was affirmed by the House of Lords in *Bradford Corp v Pickles*.[43] Pickles was annoyed at the refusal of the Corporation of Bradford to purchase his land in connection with the scheme of water supply for the inhabitants of the town. In revenge, he sank a shaft on his land. The water which percolated through his land in unknown and undefined channels from the land of the corporation on a higher level was consequently discoloured and diminished when it passed again to the lower land of the corporation. For this injury Pickles was held not liable. "It is the act", said Lord Macnaghten:

"[N]ot the motive for the act that must be regarded. If the act, apart from motive, gives rise merely to damage without legal injury, the motive, however, reprehensible it may be, will not supply that element."[44]

Three years later this was again emphasised by the House of Lords in *Allen v Flood*[45] and, for better or worse,[46] it remains the

---

[43] [1895] A.C. 587.
[44] [1895] A.C. 587 at 601. See further as to this case, para.14–12, below.
[45] [1898] A.C. 1.
[46] Many Civil Law systems recognise the concept of abuse of rights. See, e.g. the Dutch Civil Code, art.3–13(2): "Instances of abuse of right are the exercise of a right with the sole intention of harming another or for a purpose other than that for which it was granted or the exercise of a right where its holder could not reasonably have decided to exercise it, given the disproportion between the interest to exercise the right and the harm caused thereby". See also van Gerven, Lever and Larouche, *Tort Law (Common Law of Europe Casebooks)* (2000), p.231.

general rule today. As we shall see, however, there are certain
exceptional cases in which the evil motive of the defendant, if
proved, will tip the scales of liability against him.[47]

---

[47] One exception, misfeasance in a public office (see *Three Rivers DC v Bank of England*
[2003] 2 A.C. 1 at 191 and Ch.7 below) had been almost forgotten when *Bradford v
Pickles* was decided but is now a rather fashionable cause of action, though success in it
seems rare.

CHAPTER 4

TRESPASS TO THE PERSON AND RELATED MATTERS

TRESPASS to the person involves direct interference with a person's **4–1** body or liberty. In its original legal meaning "trespass" signified no more than "wrong"[1] and in early times the great bulk of trespasses were dealt with in the local courts. A trespass which was also a breach of the king's peace, however, fell within the jurisdiction of the king's courts, and in course of time the allegation that the trespass was committed *vi et armis*[2] came to be used as common form in order to preserve the jurisdictional propriety of an action brought in those courts, whether or not there was any truth in it.[3] In its developed form the writ of trespass covered injuries to land, to

---

[1] Milsom, *Historical Foundations of the Common Law*, 2nd edn, p.285; Milsom, "Trespass from Henry III to Edward III" (1958) 74 L.Q.R. 195, 407, 561.

[2] By force and arms.

[3] See, e.g. the case of 1317, cited by Milsom, *Historical Foundations of the Common Law*, 2nd edn, p.289.

goods and to the person, but the first two are today more conveniently considered in separate chapters.

There is no doubt that as a matter of history trespass to the person might be committed negligently, i.e. inadvertently as well as by intention,[4] though this is probably not the law in England today. We return to this point later,[5] but for the moment we shall treat trespass to the person as requiring intention. There are three main forms, namely, assault, battery and false imprisonment[6] and their common element is that the wrong must be committed by "direct means". What precisely this means is difficult to say. The classical illustration was of throwing a log into the highway and hitting a passer-by. In contrast if someone were to stumble on the log that would be indirect, or "case". The broad idea of the notion is easy enough to understand in the case of battery, where it seems to mean something in the nature of a blow (though even that may be hard to define with precision).[7] It is more difficult to give directness a clear meaning in the related torts of assault and false imprisonment: the former requires no physical contact and may now, it seems, be committed by making threats over the telephone,[8] and while the obvious form of the latter is physical seizure of the claimant by an officer, it is clear that the tort is equally committed if the claimant submits to a legal authority asserted by the officer.[9] In neither case is there much meaning in "directness", save that both situations involve a threat, express or implied, of the infliction of force, though in the latter it is qualified. The point is really of very limited importance because where some physical harm is intentionally inflicted by indirect means liability in tort still arises,[10] and where harm has been caused negligently that, in the modern law, is the tort of negligence.[11] However, these forms of liability do not cover all the ground covered by trespass. For example, where there is a trespass to the person the claimant may recover substantial damages for distress or humiliation even though he suffers no physical injury whatever —trespass is actionable per se—but, if the defendant uses indirect means to inflict humiliation or distress on the claimant it seems that

---

[4] *Weaver v Ward* (1616) Hob. 134; *Dickensen v Watson* (1681) T. Jones 205; *Dodwell v Burford* (1670) 1 Mod. 24; *Gibbon v Pepper* (1695) 2 Salk. 637; *Scott v Shepherd* (1773) 2 W.Bl. 892.

[5] See para.4–33, below.

[6] Trespass to the person was also the parent of some torts, now abolished, which protected family and service relationships: see para.18–1, below.

[7] See para.4–6, below.

[8] See para.4–13, below.

[9] See para.4–15, below.

[10] See para.4–36, below.

[11] In earlier times both intentional and negligent indirect infliction of injury would have fallen under the "action on the case".

in English common law[12] there may be no action[13] in the absence of some physical harm (which for this purpose includes a recognised mental illness).[14]

A distinction between what is "direct" and "indirect" is found in other contexts of tort law. For example, at one time the leading test of remoteness of damage in negligence[15] was based on the theory that the defendant was liable for directly inflicted harm even though it was unforeseeable. It seems unlikely that "direct" had precisely the same meaning there as it does here.[16] More recently, a majority of the House of Lords drew a distinction between the direct and indirect infliction of physical harm by negligence, a duty of care with regard to the former being easier to establish than with regard to the latter,[17] but there is no overt suggestion that the distinction is meant to reflect the concept of directness in the trespass torts.[18]

No doubt it is necessary to draw distinctions between the different types of intentional torts to the person: one might, for example, wish to restrict the category of cases actionable per se to situations where there was some very immediate and intrusive interference with the claimant.[19] However, it is questionable whether the way in which the distinction is now drawn, on the basis of the historical distinction between trespass and case, is defensible for all purposes. For example, it is difficult to see why the two cases of D stabbing C and D surreptitiously poisoning C[20] should be regarded in the civil law as two different torts (as they must be if it is correct to say that the second injury is not a battery) even if that is now unlikely to give rise to any practical difficulty.

Acts of trespass to the person are generally crimes as well as torts.[21] It is therefore necessary to outline briefly the mechanisms for   **4–2**

---

[12] But in some cases there may be liability for the statutory wrong under the Protection from Harassment Act 1997: para.4–38, below.

[13] Unless of course the conduct amounts to some other tort actionable per se, such as libel.

[14] Cf. *Nickerson v Hodges* 84 So. 37 (La. 1920) (the "pot of gold" case).

[15] See Ch.6, below.

[16] Thus in the classical example, when the wayfarer stumbled over the log on the highway his damage was surely not too remote for the purposes of an action on the case.

[17] *Marc Rich v Bishop Rock Marine* [1996] A.C. 211, para.5–13, below.

[18] The conduct complained of (failing to prevent a vessel sailing with a defective hull) could plainly have never amounted to trespass to goods. However, the example given of direct harm (causing a fire by dropping a cigarette) presumably could be, if done with the requisite mental state.

[19] See below, para.4–6.

[20] It may be that the criminal law has a rather broader notion of battery (see para.4–6, below) and it is in any case not required in the more serious offences involving grievous bodily harm. Poisoning is a specific offence.

[21] One cannot, however, assume that the mens rea of the crimes always equates exactly with the mental element of the torts. There is perhaps a certain ambivalence in *R. v Barnes* [2004] EWCA Crim 3246; [2005] 1 W.L.R. 910 on whether the court is simply giving advice on prosecutorial policy or stating substantive differences between tort and crime.

awarding compensation for crimes which arise outside the context of tort law.

First, criminal proceedings may lead to compensation of the victim by the offender without a separate civil action,[22] for, since 1972 the criminal courts have had power to order an offender to pay compensation to his victim. Indeed, "power" is a slightly misleading expression, for the court is now required to give reasons, on passing sentence, if it does not make a compensation order.[23] A magistrates' court is not to order compensation in excess of £5,000[24] and losses resulting from road accidents are generally excluded but the compensation which may be awarded may include a sum for bereavement or anxiety and distress.[25] A compensation order should only be made where the convicted person's responsibility is clear[26] but civil liability is not a precondition,[27] so that an order might be made where, for example, there was no civil liability for breach of statutory duty.[28] This summary procedure is obviously unsuitable for cases where there are complex questions of quantification of the loss[29] and a civil action may offer the claimant other advantages,[30] but in minor matters a compensation order is obviously a much more sensible course than requiring the victim to take separate civil proceedings.

The main source of compensation for victims of violent crime is the Criminal Injuries Compensation Scheme. The original Scheme was introduced on a non-statutory basis in 1964, paying compensation from public funds for personal injury caused by a crime of violence[31] broadly in line with common law damages for tort,

---

[22] Some civil law systems allow the victim to join in criminal proceedings as a *partie civile*. See art.2 of the French *Code pénal*.

[23] Powers of Criminal Courts (Sentencing) Act 2000, s.130 (this Act consolidates the Powers of the Criminal Courts Act 1973 and its amendments, in particular those in the Criminal Justice Act 1988).

[24] The majority of awards are for much less.

[25] *Bond v CC Kent* [1983] 1 W.L.R. 40.

[26] *R. v Chappell* (1984) 128 S.J. 629; *R. v Horsham JJ., Ex p. Richards* [1985] 1 W.L.R. 986.

[27] *R. v Chappell*, above, fn.26. Where civil liability is established in subsequent proceedings sums recovered as compensation are to be brought into account.

[28] See Ch.7.

[29] "It seems to me obvious, and this court has often reiterated, that the magistrates' court is not a suitable court in which to entertain any but simple, straightforward claims for compensation": *R. v Liverpool Crown Court, Ex p. Cooke* [1997] 1 W.L.R. 700 at 706 per Leggatt L.J.

[30] e.g. a lower burden of proof than that necessary to establish the criminal guilt which is a precondition to a compensation order, a higher likelihood of recovery because the defendant may be able to call on a policy of insurance and, in suitable cases, exemplary damages. Furthermore, civil damages are a matter of right, not of discretion: it would be inappropriate to make a compensation order where the offender's only asset was a home but that would not prevent the victim obtaining a civil judgment and enforcing it by selling the home.

[31] The Scheme does not cover property damage. However, under the Riot (Damages) Act 1886 the police authority must compensate owners for damage to buildings and contents

subject to restrictions on quantum for loss of earnings and deduction in respect of benefits coming to the victim from other sources (for example, social security payments and pensions). Although the Scheme was put on a statutory basis in 1988 this was never implemented because the Government came to the view that the Scheme was too expensive[32] and in 1993 it was proposed to replace it with a "tariff" scheme giving fixed amounts for specified injuries but making no additional payments in respect of loss of earnings and expenses.[33] The implementation of the new Scheme was declared unlawful in judicial review proceedings[34] and the Scheme we now have is a political compromise introduced by the Criminal Injuries Compensation Act 1995.[35]

The Scheme is administered by the Criminal Injuries Compensation Authority. Applications are considered by claims officers and appeals are decided by adjudicators. Very broadly, a person is eligible for compensation if he has sustained personal injury directly attributable to a crime of violence or the apprehension of an offender or the prevention of an offence.[36] Mental trauma constitutes personal injury, but if the victim is not physically injured he must generally show the elements necessary for a claim by a "primary" or "secondary" victim for "nervous shock" at common law.[37] Compensation for pain and suffering and loss of amenity is on the basis of a tariff ranging from £250,000 for quadriplegia or serious brain damage to £1,000 for minor injuries like a fractured rib with significant pain lasting more than six weeks. Some of these figures are broadly comparable to those which would be awarded by a court assessing damages for personal injuries at common law but some are a good deal lower.[38] Unlike the abortive tariff scheme which was

---

caused by a riot. This was held to fall within a standard public liability policy in *Bedfordshire Police v Constable* [2009] EWCA Civ 64 (as to the scope of the Act see *Yarl's Wood Immigration Ltd v Bedfordshire Police* [2009] EWCA Civ 1110).

[32] In its first year of operation the Scheme made 1,164 awards. By 1992–1993 there were 37,000 awards and the cost had increased 38-fold to £152 million.

[33] See Cm. 2434 (1993). The combination of a sharp reduction in awards in more serious cases and simpler administration was expected to cut the cost of the Scheme by about a half.

[34] *R. v Home Secretary, Ex p. Fire Brigades Union* [1995] 2 A.C. 513.

[35] The Act is the barest of frameworks. The substance is found in the Scheme itself (currently 2008). Since 2006 there has been a Europe-wide requirement for Member States to have schemes, "on compensation to victims of violent intentional crimes committed in their respective territories, which guarantee fair and appropriate compensation to victims": Directive 2004/80/EC, art.12.

[36] In the last two cases the applicant must have been taking an exceptional and justifiable risk: para.12 of the Scheme.

[37] para.9. See para.5–61, below.

[38] Thus the loss of one arm attracted a civil award of not less than £87,500 in 2009 but under the Scheme the awards are £33,000 and £55,000 for non-dominant and dominant arm respectively. In the period after 1995 some awards under the Scheme were higher than awards of civil damages because the tariff figures under the abortive planned scheme were based on average awards under the original scheme, which included loss of earnings.

declared unlawful, the current Scheme does provide for compensation for loss of earnings and expenses, subject to a number of restrictions: (1) no compensation is payable under this head in respect of the first 28 weeks' loss of earnings; (2) the net rate of earnings compensated for cannot exceed one and a half times the gross median national wage; and (3) almost all collateral benefits are deductible.[39] Furthermore, there is a maximum payment of £500,000 under all heads. The cost of private medical treatment is compensable only when both the treatment and its cost are reasonable.[40] Where the financial loss is an ongoing one, the process of assessment is comparable to that for the assessment of lump sum damages for loss of earnings at common law, that is to say the application of a multiplier to the net annual loss.[41] In 2007–2008 the Scheme paid £225 million.[42]

The Criminal Injuries Compensation Scheme has been subject to severe criticism on the ground that it lacks theoretical foundation and is merely an attempt to single out yet another group of unfortunates for special treatment, though it can no doubt be said that the State has a more direct interest here than in the case of accidental injuries because of its responsibility for maintaining law and order. From a theoretical point of view the Scheme is of course supplementary to the law of torts, since it is virtually inevitable that the actual offender has committed a tort but the number of cases of serious injury in which the victim recovers substantial compensation from the offender must be very small, so there is no analogy with, say, the Motor Insurers' Bureau arrangements, where the responsibility of the minority of uninsured motorists is passed to the insured majority. What really underpins the Scheme (apart from the political difficulty of withdrawing a benefit once conferred) seems to be sympathy, coupled perhaps with a fear that without it penal policies designed to reform offenders may give the impression that there is no concern for the victim.

4–3   In comparison with the volume of offences against the person handled by the criminal courts or the number of civil actions for

These tariff figures were carried forward into the 1995 scheme even though that did allow payments for loss of earnings. Since then civil awards have increased substantially. Awards for "bereavement" and loss of dependency may be made in fatal cases but there are considerable differences of detail compared with the provisions of the Fatal Accidents Act 1976: para.38.

[39] However, charitable payments or certain payments made under privately effected insurance are not deductible. Sums received from a civil action against the offender or under a compensation order made by the criminal court are deductible.

[40] para.35(c).

[41] para.32. See para.22–26, below. There is no provision for periodical payments as such under the Scheme but with the applicant's consent an annuity may be purchased with the lump sum.

[42] Power to seek recovery from the offender was given by s.57 of the Domestic Violence, Crime and Victims Act 2004.

negligence, civil actions for trespass to the person are not common. No doubt this has always been so, for in trivial cases the claimant is likely to hesitate at the risks of civil litigation once tempers have cooled, and in serious cases the defendant may well not be worth pursuing. Furthermore, even in serious cases the existence of the Criminal Injuries Compensation Scheme and the power of the criminal court to make direct compensation orders against defendants nowadays do much to remove the incentive to bring a civil action. Though there may be cases in which an award of damages against a private defendant will exceed the sum awarded under the Criminal Injuries Compensation Scheme, the number of cases in which the necessary conditions are fulfilled and in which the defendant is worth suing is likely to be small.[43] In less serious cases the modest sums the criminal court may award by way of direct compensation from the offender are likely to be as much as the claimant would receive in practice by enforcing a civil judgment, whatever the size of that judgment might be. However, as we have seen, civil suits are sometimes brought for rather indirect motives, for example to make a "point of principle" or to get an individual investigation or to provoke the prosecution authorities into acting.[44] In other cases there may be the prospect of recovery of large damages because from a civil point of view someone is vicariously liable for the act of the wrongdoer, even though it amounts to a crime. The best example is the large number of actions brought in respect of abuse in children's homes, sometimes many years after the event.[45] What appears to be (and what has probably been for 200 years) the most important context of these trespass torts is suits against the police and other public bodies. Here the law of tort may be serving more as a vindicator of personal liberty than as a vehicle for compensating harm, a point emphasised by the court's power to award exemplary damages in such cases.[46] Even in this context, however, the use of tort law is often said to be primarily motivated by perceived deficiencies in the procedures for complaints and discipline in respect of police conduct.[47]

From a practical point of view the law has now become more **4–4** complicated in the area of conduct covered by the trespass torts. An adviser may, for example, have to consider civil liability under the

---

[43] Cf. *Raja v van Hoogstraten* [2005] EWHC 2890 (Ch) (arranging murder); *Lawson v Glaves-Smith* [2006] EWHC 2865 (QB) (rape and false imprisonment; £239,000 under various heads).
[44] See para.1–2, above.
[45] The limitation difficulties in these cases were ameliorated by *A v Hoare* [2008] UKHL 6; [2008] 1 A.C. 844, para.26–18, below.
[46] See para.22–9, below.
[47] See *Ashley v CC Sussex* [2008] UKHL 25; [2008] 1 A.C. 962, para.1–2, above; but vindication is not confined to police action: *Breslin v McKenna* [2009] NIQB 50.

Protection from Harassment Act 1997 (outlined later in this chapter[48]) which, although it requires some element of repetition, is in other respects much wider than trespass. Furthermore, a "public authority" may incur civil liability under the Human Rights Act 1998 for acting in a way incompatible with rights under the European Convention on Human Rights, though the overlap here is likely to arise in the context of false imprisonment rather than assault and battery.

1. ASSAULT AND BATTERY

4–5 *Battery is the intentional and direct application of force to another person.*

Assault is an act of the defendant which causes the claimant reasonable apprehension of the infliction of a battery on him by the defendant.

In popular language,[49] the word "assault" is used to describe either or both of these torts, but in this chapter it will be used in its strict sense. So, to throw water at a person is an assault but if any drops fall upon him it is battery[50]; riding a horse at a person is an assault but riding it against him is a battery. Pulling away a chair, as a practical joke, from one who is about to sit on it is probably an assault until he reaches the floor, for while he is falling he reasonably expects that the withdrawal of the chair will result in harm to him. When he comes in contact with the floor, it is a battery. Throwing over a chair on which another person is actually sitting is either a battery or one of the forms of residuary trespass to the person; either way the defendant is liable.[51]

A. Meaning of Force

4–6   If there is a forcible contact no damage is necessary, for trespass is actionable per se. Any physical contact with the body of the claimant (or his clothing) is sufficient to amount to "force": there is a battery when the defendant shoots the claimant from a distance

---

[48] See para.4–38, below.

[49] Sometimes in law. Thus "common assault" in the Criminal Justice Act 1988, s.40, embraces battery as well as assault in the strict sense: *R. v Lynsey* [1995] 3 All E.R. 654. See also under the Offences Against the Person Act 1861, s.47: *R. v Ireland* [1998] A.C. 147. Williams, *Criminal Law*, 2nd edn, p.172, points out that while "assault" is a verb in common use, there is no such verb to describe the action of battery.

[50] *Pursell v Horne* (1838) 3 N. & P. 564 and, as Pollock noted (*Torts*, 15th edn, p.159), there is much older authority in Reg. Brev (ed. 1687), 108b (*de liquore calido super aliquo projecto*). So also, to spit at a person is an assault, and if the spittle hits him that is a battery.

[51] Per Gibbs C.J. in *Hopper v Reeve* (1817) 7 Taunt. 698 at 700.

just as much as when he strikes him with his fist and the same is probably true when the defendant deliberately runs into the car in which the claimant is sitting, shaking him up.[52] Whether the infliction of such things as heat or light[53] or blowing smoke[54] on a person would be battery is uncertain, though the answer is probably no. Smoke is, from a scientific point of view, particulate matter but for the purposes of trespass to land it has been treated as an intangible and therefore falling into the realm of nuisance. If exposing a person to smoke were to be treated as trespass to the person we would have to decide whether the defendant was liable for exposure which he merely foresaw: it can hardly be the law that a smoker commits battery on all the non-smokers near him, even if they show they object.[55] Of course, if injury were intended and caused by exposure to such things it would be actionable even though it was not battery.[56] Mere passive obstruction has been said not to be battery,[57] though in a criminal case there was held to be a battery where the defendant innocently drove his car on to the victim's foot and declined to move it.[58]

Some situations raise the problem of "directness", which we have already touched on. Depending on the view one takes of this in the modern law it may not be battery if I daub with filth a towel which I hope that you will use and you unwittingly do so and befoul your face[59]—a case in which one cannot fall back on liability for intentional harm because there seems to be no "damage"; but again in a modern criminal case putting acid in a hand dryer so that it injured the next person to use it was held to amount to battery.[60] However, a rather similar uncertainty about "directness" is to be found in the criminal cases. In *R. v Martin*,[61] where the defendant barred the doors of a theatre and then caused a panic in which patrons were injured trying to get out, two of the judges thought that this, or

---

[52] *Clark v State* 746 So. 2d 1237 (Fla. 1999).
[53] It has been held in Northern Ireland that photographing a person is not an assault: *Murray v Ministry of Defence* [1985] 12 N.I.J.B. 12.
[54] "Secondary smoking" claims in this country have tended to be against employers for negligence in allowing smoking so as to injure the claimant's health.
[55] There are some entertaining American cases collected in 46 A.L.R. 5th 813.
[56] In *Kaye v Robertson* [1991] F.S.R. 62 Glidewell L.J. thought it might well be that if a bright light was shone into a person's eye and injured his sight or damaged him in some other way that would be a battery but this seems to ignore the fact that damage is irrelevant to liability in trespass. If the harm to sight was intended it is actionable as intentionally inflicted harm, if it ought to have been foreseen it is negligence.
[57] *Innes v Wylie* (1844) 1 C. & K. 257 at 263 per Lord Denman.
[58] *Fagan v MPC* [1969] 1 Q.B. 439.
[59] This is battery according to the *Restatement of Torts*, 2d, s.18, comment, but US law has clearly abandoned the "direct" requirement: see Dobbs, *Torts* (2000) §28.
[60] *DPP v K* (1990) 1 W.L.R. 1067 (offence of "assault" under s.47 of the Offences Against the Person Act 1861). In *Breslin v McKenna* [2009] NIQB 50 (a civil action) planting a bomb set to go off later was held to be trespass.
[61] (1881) 8 Q.B.D. 54.

digging a hole for a person to fall into,[62] would be a battery. However, the conviction was for the offence of unlawfully and maliciously inflicting grievous bodily harm under the Offences Against the Person Act 1861, which does not require a battery, and the modern view seems to be that "inflict" is, for practical purposes, virtually synonymous with "cause".[63] Even where battery is directly in issue, rather than facing the issue head-on, the tendency seems to be to give a broad meaning to "directly". Thus in *Haystead v CC Derbyshire*[64] the defendant struck W in the face, with the result that the baby she was holding fell to the floor. He was charged with an offence of assault (which in this context includes battery) on the baby and his conviction was upheld by the Divisional Court on the basis that:

> "[T]he movement of W whereby she lost hold of the child was entirely and immediately the result of the [defendant's] action in punching her. There is no difference in logic or good sense between the facts of this case and one where the defendant might have used a weapon to fell the child to the floor, save only that this is a case of reckless and not intentional battery."[65]

Of course in the civil law, if the baby had been injured, there would have been the plainest possible case of negligence even if the defendant never gave any thought to the likely effect on the baby.

For battery there must be a voluntary act by the defendant intended to bring about the contact with the claimant. I do not commit battery against you if X seizes my arm and uses it like a club—here X and X alone is liable but the act need be intentional only as to the contact, and intention to bring about the harmful consequence is not required: if D pushes C into a swimming pool and injury occurs, then, assuming D's act to be "hostile", there is liability for the injury even though it was neither desired nor even foreseen by D.[66] However, it seems clear that for the purposes of this tort intention includes conscious and unjustifiable risk taking—recklessness.[67]

---

[62] This is regarded as indirect for civil purposes in *Wong v Parkside Health NHS Trust* [2001] EWCA Civ 1721; [2003] 3 All E.R. 932 at [9].

[63] *R. v Burstow* [1998] A.C. 147 at 160, 164.

[64] [2000] 2 Cr. App. R. 339.

[65] The court did not consider an alternative approach based on "transferred malice" but was dubious about its success: see para.4–35, below.

[66] *Wilson v Pringle* [1987] Q.B. 237 at 249; *Williams v Humphrey, The Times*, February 20, 1975.

[67] See para.3–3, above.

B. Hostility

Life would be difficult if all bodily contact were actionable unless   **4–7**
it could be brought within a specific justification or defence and the
courts have struggled to find some further ingredient to distinguish
battery from legally unobjectionable contact. In *Cole v Turner*[68]
Lord Holt C.J. said that, "the least touching of another in anger is a
battery" but this would be too narrow, for an unwanted kiss is as
much actionable as a blow and "anger" might well be an inapt
description of the defendant's motive. In *Collins v Wilcock*[69] Robert
Goff L.J. said that, quite apart from specific defences such as lawful
authority in effecting an arrest or the prevention of crime, bodily
contact was not actionable if it was generally acceptable in the
ordinary conduct of everyday life. This is more satisfactory than the
somewhat artificial approach whereby a person is deemed to consent
to the multitude of minor contacts, including physical contacts,
which take place in, for example, a crowded Underground station in
the rush hour. Of course, absence of consent is often relevant in the
sense that it is open to a person to make it plain that he objects to
contacts that most people find trivial and thereby render actionable
what would not be so if done to others, but there must be limits on
this: the passenger on the crowded Underground train can hardly be
allowed to appropriate to himself a disproportionate share of the
space because he objects to being touched by others.[70] In *Wilson v
Pringle*,[71] however, the Court of Appeal, while not rejecting what
was said in *Collins*, laid down that a battery involves a "hostile"
touching. The actual decision was that the trial judge had been
wrong to grant summary judgment to the claimant under Order 14 of
the Rules of the Supreme Court (which was based upon there being
no triable defence to the claim[72]) where the defendant, a schoolboy,
had on his own admission pulled the claimant's bag from his
shoulder and thereby caused him to fall to the ground and injure
himself: such horseplay, it seems, may or may not be battery,
according to whether the tribunal of fact can discern the ingredient
of "hostility".[73] However, since the court expressly said that hostility did not require ill will or malevolence, the requirement seems
hardly to mean any more than that the defendant has interfered in a
way to which the claimant might object. Perhaps the closest we can
get to the central idea is to say that the interference must be

[68] (1704) 6 Mod. 149.
[69] [1984] 1 W.L.R. 1172. See also the same judge in *F, Re; F v West Berkshire HA* [1990] 2
A.C. 1. *Collins* applied in *McMillan v CPS* [2008] EWHC 1457 (Admin).
[70] And consider the example above of smoking in a place where that is permitted.
[71] [1987] Q.B. 237.
[72] See now CPR Pt 24 ("defendant has no real prospect of successfully defending the claim
or issue").
[73] The point gains significance now that it is clear that for the purposes of negligence the
standard is that of a reasonable child of that age: see para.5–78, below.

"offensive" in the sense that it infringes the claimant's right to be physically inviolate, to be "let alone". To say, however, that there must be something offensive to dignity seems to be going too far,[74] at least if *Nash v Sheen*[75] is correctly decided: it was held to be battery where the claimant went for a permanent wave and the defendant, without her consent, applied a tone rinse which produced a skin reaction. Even this rather vague formulation may not cover every case: for example, indecent touching of a small child is clearly a battery even though the child may have insufficient understanding to "take offence".

Whatever the theoretical basis of liability, we can say that touching another in the course of conversation or to gain his attention[76] is not a battery. Even some persistence may be justifiable, for:

> "[T]he lost or distressed may surely be permitted a second touch, or possibly even more on a reluctant or impervious sleeve or shoulder, as may a person who is acting reasonably in the exercise of a duty. In each case, the test must be whether the physical contact so persisted in has in the circumstances gone beyond generally accepted standards of conduct."[77]

Into the assessment of this must enter not only any limitations laid down by the claimant but also the relationship (or lack of it) between the parties. An embrace of a complete stranger may be a battery[78]; an embrace in an attempt to settle a lovers' tiff may not be, even if the other has forbidden it.

C. Consent and Battery

4–8   Where there is consent to the contact there is no battery[79] and the same is true where the claimant, though not in fact consenting, so conducts himself as to lead the defendant reasonably to believe that consent exists.[80] Subject to lawful authority, such as a power of

---

[74] The *Restatement*, 2d, §18 says "harmful or offensive to personal dignity" but there is some difficulty in saying that there is a battery where the act is neither offensive nor *intended* to cause harm: see Dobbs, *Torts*, §30.

[75] *The Times*, March 13, 1953.

[76] *Wiffin v Kincard* (1807) 2 Bos. & Pul. 471; *Coward v Baddeley* (1859) 4 H. & N. 478.

[77] *Collins v Wilcock* [1984] 1 W.L.R. 1172 at 1178.

[78] But even here *de minimis non agit sapiens*.

[79] It seems that the claimant has to prove absence of consent: see para.25–3, below. For a discussion of the relationship between consent and "offensiveness" see *Non-Marine Underwriters at Lloyd's v Scalera* [2000] SCC 24; [2000] 1 S.C.R. 551.

[80] See, e.g. *O'Brien v Cunard SS Co* 28 N.E. 266 (Mass. 1891) (holding up arm in vaccination line).

arrest, an adult of full understanding has at common law an absolute right to the inviolability of his body and therefore has an absolute right to choose whether or not to consent to medical treatment, even if the treatment is necessary to save his life,[81] or, in the case of a pregnant woman, the life of her unborn child.[82] Similarly, an adult of full capacity has the right to choose whether to eat or not:

"Even if the refusal is tantamount to suicide, as in the case of a hunger strike, he cannot be compelled to eat or forcibly fed".[83]

The same seems to be true even if the would-be suicide is a prisoner in lawful custody and the practice of forcible feeding, which was followed when suicide and attempted suicide were crimes,[84] has ceased: imprisonment limits a person's autonomy but does not deprive him of the power to choose to end his life.[85] Nor can the defendant contend that his well-meaning life-saving acts should attract only nominal damages, for that would be to make the principle of autonomy no more than symbolic. In Canada damages of CAN\$20,000 were awarded where the defendants ignored the claimant's known religious objections to a blood transfusion.[86]

---

[81] *St George's Healthcare NHS Trust v S* [1999] Fam. 26; *Airedale NHS trust v Bland* [1993] A.C. 789 at 891; *T (Adult, Refusal of Treatment), Re* [1993] Fam. 95; *A (Children) (Conjoined Twins: Surgical Separation), Re* [2001] Fam. 147; *R. (Burke) v General Medical Council* [2005] EWCA Civ 1003; [2005] 3 W.L.R. 1132.

[82] *St George's Healthcare NHS Trust v S* [1999] Fam. 26; and see *Winnipeg Child and Family Services v G* [1997] 3 S.C.R. 925 (mentally competent woman addicted to glue sniffing). It is not possible to sidestep the problem via the wardship procedure for that does not arise until the child is born: *F (in utero), Re* [1988] Fam 122.

[83] *B v Croydon HA* [1995] Fam. 133 at 137.

[84] See *Leigh v Gladstone* (1909) 26 T.L.R. 139.

[85] This seems clearly to be accepted in *Reeves v MPC* [2001] 1 A.C. 360, though that case involved the question of whether the gaoler could be liable to the prisoner for failing to take steps to ensure that the suicide was not facilitated: see para.5–33, below. In *Secretary of State for the Home Dept v Robb* [1995] Fam 127, a declaration was granted that the prison authorities might lawfully abide by the prisoner's refusal to take food. However, despite the negative form of the declaration the tenor of the judgment is plainly that the prison authorities would have been behaving unlawfully if they had chosen *not* to abide by the prisoner's decision. Yet in *R. v Collins, Ex p. Brady*, Unreported, March 10, 2000, Maurice Kay J. inclined to the view, without deciding the issue, that a custodian might be entitled to prevent the suicide of a person with full mental capacity. He remarked that it, "would be somewhat odd if there is a duty to prevent suicide by an act (for example, the use of a knife left in a cell) but not even a power to intervene to prevent self-destruction by starvation". However, the applicant was mentally disordered and the case turned on s.63 of the Mental Health Act 1983. Note also that the European Commission on Human Rights has held that forcible feeding of a person in custody can be justified under the Human Rights Convention on the basis of art.2 (right to life): *X v Federal Republic of Germany* (1984) (10565/83).

[86] *Malette v Shulman* (1990) 67 D.L.R. (4th) 321. Compare *B v An NHS Hospital Trust* [2002] EWHC 429 (Fam.); [2002] 2 All E.R. 449, where the claimant sought only nominal damages and £100 was awarded.

4–9   These principles apply if the person has full capacity[87] to make decisions but although it is clear at common law that the court must not infer incapacity from the fact that the decision is "irrational" in the sense that it is not one that would be made by the vast majority of sane adults,[88] where this is the case it is obviously likely that in any litigation the capacity will be called into question. This issue most frequently arises in the context of medical care and treatment and the law is now to be found in the Mental Capacity Act 2005,[89] though this is generally similar to the common law.

The first point is that the Act does not confer any right to impose treatment unless the person lacks capacity (or, in certain cases, is reasonably believed to lack it) and it is presumed that a person has capacity unless the contrary is shown; nor is he to be treated as lacking capacity merely because the decision he makes is an unwise one.[90] A person lacks capacity in relation to any matter[91]:

"[I]f at the material time he is unable to make a decision for himself in relation to the matter because of an impairment of, or a disturbance in the functioning of, the mind or brain".[92]

If this requirement is fulfilled then any act done for or decision made for or on behalf of the incapable person must be in his best interests,[93] though provided the person doing the act or making the decision complies with the requirements of s.4 it is sufficient if he reasonably believes that it is in the best interests of the person concerned.[94] The Act is not confined to acts of medical care or

---

[87] Even where the claimant has the mental capacity to give a valid consent, any consent must be given freely and not under threats or improper pressure or undue influence. See *T (Adult, Refusal of Treatment), Re* [1993] Fam. 95 (mother's religious influence). It seems possible that nowadays a case like *Latter v Braddell* (1881) 50 L.J.Q.B. 448 (housemaid compelled to submit to medical examination on suspicion of pregnancy) would go the other way and that threats of violence would not be required. In *Wainwright v Home Office* [2003] UKHL 53; [2004] 2 A.C. 406 this issue was not pursued because the limits on the strip-search procedure to which the claimant was said to have consented were exceeded by the defendants.

[88] So in *C, Re* [1994] 1 W.L.R. 291 an injunction was granted restraining amputation of the claimant's leg even though he was a paranoid schizophrenic committed to Broadmoor. In *Matter of Gordy* 658 A. 2d 613 (Del. 1994) an American court found a 96-year-old with Alzheimer's disease sufficiently competent to refuse treatment.

[89] In force October 1, 2007.

[90] Mental Capacity Act 2005 s.1. So *Re C*, above, would be decided in the same way. The mere fact that a person is mentally ill does not necessarily mean that he lacks capacity.

[91] Clearly there will be many cases in which a person has full capacity to decide matters relating to issue A but not issue B.

[92] Mental Capacity Act 2005 s.2(1). This may be permanent or temporary. The definition is amplified by s.3 by reference to understanding, retaining and using information and communication decisions.

[93] Mental Capacity Act 2005 s.1(5).

[94] Mental Capacity Act 2005 s.4(9).

treatment but this is specifically dealt with by s.5. If the person doing the act has reasonably concluded, after proper inquiries, that the person concerned lacks capacity and reasonably believes that it will be in his best interests, then he does not incur any liability in relation to the act that he would not have incurred if the person treated had had capacity and had consented.[95] So if C is brought into hospital in a coma and life-saving treatment, which cannot be postponed until he recovers consciousness,[96] is administered to him by D, D has a defence to any action for battery (as indeed he would have had at common law, though on the vaguer basis of "necessity").

If a person is not unconscious but, say, suffering from mental disorder, it may be necessary to "restrain" him, that is to say, to use or threaten force or restrict his liberty of movement.[97] If that is the case then the person doing the act must also comply with two further conditions set out in s.6: (i) that he reasonably believes it is necessary to do the act to prevent harm to the person subjected to it; and (ii) the act is a proportionate response to the likelihood of harm and its potential seriousness.

The Act contains, in ss.24 to 26 provisions on "advance decisions **4–10** to refuse treatment", that is to say, decisions made by a person with capacity that if at some future time he becomes incapable treatments specified by him may not be carried out or continued. Such a decision is only applicable to life-sustaining treatment if (a) it is in writing, signed by the person and witnessed and (b) contains an express statement that it is to apply even if there is a risk to life.[98] This would seem to have changed the law, at least if *Malette v Shulman*[99] represents the common law position in England, since the card carried by the claimant and prohibiting blood transfusion would not have complied with the requirements of this part of the Act. That of course is not the end of the story. Under the factors specified in s.4, going to the requirement that treatment must be in the patient's best interests, the person administering it must:

"[C]onsider, so far as is reasonably ascertainable ... [the patient's] past and present wishes and feelings (and, in particular,

---

[95] Mental Capacity Act 2005 s.5(2).

[96] If it can be, the person administering the treatment is likely to fall foul of s.4(3).

[97] Mental Capacity Act 2005 s.6(4). This section does not cover "deprivation of liberty" under art.5 of the European Convention on Human Rights. Restraint amounting to this is governed by amendments to the Act (ss.4A, 4B, 16A and Sch.A1) inserted by the Mental Health Act 2007.

[98] Mental Capacity Act 2005 s.25(5),(6).

[99] (1990) 67 D.L.R. (4th) 321, para.4–8, above.

any relevant written[100] statement made by him when he had capacity)."

However, while going against an advance declaration complying with s.25 automatically makes the treatment wrongful,[101] the wishes of the patient are merely a factor to be considered in the other situation and the ultimate question is whether the doctor reasonably believes that he is acting in the patient's best interests.[102]

4–11   A minor who has reached the age of 16 years may give a valid consent to medical treatment himself under s.8 of the Family Law Reform Act 1969 and he may do so at common law even below that age if he is capable of a full understanding of the consequences.[103] In these cases the child's power to consent to treatment is concurrent with that of the parents[104] and a parental consent may render lawful treatment to which the child objects,[105] though no doctor can be compelled to administer treatment and in deciding whether or not to do so he will be influenced by the child's wishes. When the child has the capacity to give a valid consent and does so, the parents' objection to the treatment will not invalidate the child's consent.[106] In all cases involving a minor the court has an inherent jurisdiction to override the child's objection to treatment or the child's consent to treatment.[107] In the case of young children the consent of the parents or guardian to medical treatment which is reasonably necessary or to procedures which, though not therapeutic, are generally acceptable,[108] constitutes a valid consent on behalf of the child.

---

[100] It seems odd that an oral statement should be irrelevant.

[101] This is the effect of s.26(1).

[102] This is the approach taken to s.4 in the context of making a will for an incapable person in *Re P (Statutory Will)* [2009] EWHC 163 (Ch); [2010] 2 W.L.R. 253 at [42]: "Although the fact that P makes an unwise decision does not on its own give rise to any inference of incapacity . . . , once the decision-making power shifts to a third party (whether a carer, deputy or the court) I cannot see that it would be a proper exercise for the third party decision-maker consciously to make an unwise decision merely because P would have done so."

[103] *Gillick v West Norfolk AHA* [1986] A.C. 112.

[104] *R, Re* [1992] Fam. 11.

[105] This is the effect of s.8(3) of the 1969 Act: *W, Re* [1993] Fam. 64.

[106] *W, Re* [1993] Fam. 64.

[107] Where the child has no capacity to consent the doctor should respect the parents' refusal to consent, but may apply to the court, which may override the parents' decision: *A (Children) (Conjoined Twins: Surgical Separation), Re* [2001] Fam. 147. The Mental Capacity Act has no relevance in such cases because although the child lacks capacity it is not because of, "an impairment of, or a disturbance in the functioning of, the mind or brain".

[108] e.g. testing of blood to determine paternity (*S v McC* [1972] A.C. 240); ritual circumcision or ear-piercing (*R. v Brown* [1994] 1 A.C. 212 at 231) but not tattooing: Tattooing of Minors Act 1969. A parent clearly could not give a valid consent to the sterilisation of a minor (as opposed to a necessary therapeutic procedure of which sterility was a byproduct). Where it is thought that sterilisation would be in the best interests of a minor because of mental incapacity the leave of the court should be sought as in the case of a mentally incompetent adult.

D. Assault

Assault of course requires no contact because its essence is **4–12** conduct which leads the claimant to apprehend the application of force. In the majority of cases an assault precedes a battery, perhaps by only a very brief interval, but there are examples of battery in which the claimant has no opportunity of experiencing any apprehension before the force is applied, for example a blow from behind inflicted by an unseen assailant.[109] Just as there can be a battery without an assault, so also there can be an assault without a battery, as where the defendant does not carry his threat through or even has no intention of doing so but knows that the claimant is unaware of this.[110] Similarly if the blow is intercepted or prevented by some third person. In *Stephens v Myers*[111] the defendant, advancing with clenched fist upon the claimant at a parish meeting, was stopped by the churchwarden, who sat next but one to the claimant. The defendant was held to be liable for assault. It is irrelevant that the claimant is courageous and is not frightened by the threat or that he could easily defeat the defendant's attack: "apprehend" is used in the sense of "expect". The claimant must, however, have reason to apprehend that the defendant has the capacity to carry out the threat immediately.[112] It would not be an assault for the defendant to wave his fist (as opposed to pointing a gun) at the claimant on a passing train, nor where the claimant was under the effective protection of the police.[113] Pointing a loaded pistol at someone is of course an assault, but despite a curious statement to the contrary,[114] the law is exactly the same if the pistol is unloaded, unless the person at whom it is pointed knows this (or unless his distance from the weapon is so great that any reasonable person would have realised he was out of range, in which case there would be no assault even if it was loaded).[115] Assault involves reasonable apprehension of impact of something on one's body and, unless some such factor as is mentioned above is present, that is exactly what occurs when a firearm is pointed at one by an aggressor.

[109] A Biblical instance in point is the slaying of Sisera by Jael, the wife of Heber the Kenite. She drove a tent-peg through his head while he was asleep. The shooting of F.B. in *Bici v MoD* [2004] EWHC 786 (QB), *The Times*, June 11, 2004 seems to be a modern example.
[110] e.g. *Herbert v Misuga* (1994) 111 D.L.R. (4th) 193.
[111] (1840) 4 C. & P. 349.
[112] See, e.g. *Mbasogo v Logo Ltd* [2006] EWCA Civ 1370; [2007] Q.B. 846 (presence of coup plotters in city insufficient); *Darwish v Egyptair Ltd* [2006] EWHC 1399 (QB). Holding out a baton in such a way as to show an intent to prevent the claimant's exit was an assault in *Hepburn v CC Thames Valley* [2002] EWCA Civ 1841.
[113] What is sufficiently "immediate" is a question of fact. Perhaps *Thomas v NUM (South Wales Area)* [1986] Ch. 20 is a rather "tough-minded" decision in this respect (violent threats and gestures by pickets at persons going into work in vehicles by a police cordon).
[114] *Blake v Barnard* (1840) 9 C. & P. 626 at 628.
[115] See the *Restatement*, 2d s.29.

4–13	For many years it was said that some bodily movement was required for an assault and that threatening words alone were not actionable. This was rejected by the House of Lords in *R. v Ireland*,[116] a criminal case, but there seems no reason to doubt that the reasoning also applies to tort. Hence threats on the telephone may be an assault provided the claimant has reason to believe that they may be carried out in the sufficiently near future to qualify as "immediate".[117] In fact the court in *Ireland* went further and held that an assault could be committed by malicious silent telephone calls. The defendant's purpose was to convey a message to the victim just as surely as if he had spoken to her.[118]

> "The victim is assailed by uncertainty about his intentions. Fear may dominate her emotions, and it may be fear that the caller's arrival at her door may be imminent. She may fear the possibility of immediate personal violence".[119]

While words alone may constitute an assault, they may negative the threatening nature of a gesture which would otherwise be an assault, as where the defendant laid his hand upon his sword and said, "If it were not assize time, I would not take such language from you": as it was assize time, he was held not to have committed an assault.[120] Similarly it would be no assault if a landowner were to insist that a trespasser leave his land and show that he would use reasonable force in the event of a refusal; but the highwayman could not defend an action for assault by showing that he offered the claimant the opportunity to escape violence by handing over his money.

Where the threat lacks the quality of immediacy necessary for an assault, it does not follow that there is no remedy. First, if the claimant suffers actual damage (for example psychiatric illness) as a result of a threat of unlawful action, he may have a claim on the basis exemplified in *Wilkinson v Downton*[121] or perhaps intimidation.[122] More important in practice is likely to be the Protection from Harassment Act 1997.[123]

---

[116] [1998] A.C. 147.
[117] [1998] A.C. 147 at 162, Lord Steyn refers to a threat which is to be carried out "in a minute or two". No doubt that should not be taken as the outer limit of "immediate" but it is submitted that a threat in a call which the claimant knows is coming from Australia is not an assault.
[118] Per Lord Hope at 166.
[119] Per Lord Steyn at 162.
[120] *Turbervell v Savadge* (1669) 1 Mod. 3.; cf. *R. v Light* (1857) Deers & B. 332, where the physical act was perhaps rather more immediate.
[121] See para.4–36, below.
[122] See para.18–15, below.
[123] See para.4–38, below.

E. Relationship to Criminal Proceedings

Assault and battery are crimes as well as torts, and the Offences **4–14** Against the Person Act 1861 makes criminal proceedings in certain circumstances a bar to any subsequent civil proceedings. By ss.42 to 45, where a person is prosecuted before a court of *summary jurisdiction* and, after a hearing on the merits,[124] either the summons is dismissed, and a certificate of dismissal is granted by the magistrates, or he is convicted and has served his imprisonment or paid the whole amount awarded against him, no further proceedings, civil or criminal, for the same cause,[125] shall lie at the instance of anyone against that person. The Act is only a defence: (1) if the proceedings are instituted by or on behalf of the party aggrieved, and not by someone else; (2) if the summons is dismissed on the merits of the case and not for some technical defect; or (3) if the proceedings are summary and not by way of indictment. The Act does not prevent proceedings against anyone other than the defendant, so that the conviction of an employee for an assault committed in the course of his employment is no bar to an action against his employer.[126] Quite apart from the statutory provision there is a common law principle, founded upon public policy, whereby a person will not be allowed, in a civil action, to mount a collateral attack upon the final decision of a criminal court of competent jurisdiction. Thus where at his trial X contended that his confession was involuntary because he had been beaten up by Y, but the trial judge found that it was voluntary, X's subsequent attempt to bring an action for battery against Y was dismissed as an abuse of the process of the court.[127] However, this principle would not prevent the commencement of a civil action because the defendant had been acquitted in the criminal court[128]: apart altogether from any substantive differences between the statutory crime and the tort, the standards of proof are different and a verdict of acquittal in the criminal case is quite consistent with a finding of liability in the civil action. Nor does a conviction prevent the defendant from contesting liability in a case where a civil action can be brought against him. That would be inconsistent with s.11 of the Civil Evidence Act 1968, which provides that a criminal conviction is, in civil proceedings, prima facie but not conclusive evidence that the defendant committed the offence.[129]

---

[124] *Reed v Nutt* (1890) 24 Q.B.D.; *Ellis v Burton* [1975] 1 All E.R. 395 (guilty plea).
[125] Where D has been prosecuted and convicted this precludes not only a civil action for assault, but also an action using the assault as the basis for some other cause of action: *Wong v Parkside Health NHS Trust* [2001] EWCA Civ 1721; [2003] 3 All E.R. 932.
[126] *Dyer v Munday* [1895] 1 Q.B. 742.
[127] *Hunter v CC West Midlands* [1982] A.C. 529.
[128] This is not inconsistent with art.6(2) of the European Convention on Human Rights, provided the civil proceedings do not question the acquittal: *Ringvold v Norway* (2003) Application No.34964/97.
[129] *J v Oyston, The Times*, December 11, 1998. *Brinks-Mat Ltd v Abu-Saleh* [1995] 1 W.L.R.

2. FALSE IMPRISONMENT[130]

4–15 *This is the infliction of bodily restraint which is not expressly or impliedly authorised by the law.*

Both "false" and "imprisonment" are somewhat misleading terms. "False" does not here necessarily signify "mendacious" or "fallacious", but is used in the less common sense of "erroneous" or "wrong" and it is quite possible to commit the tort without "imprisonment" of a person in the common acceptance of that term. In fact, neither physical contact nor anything resembling a prison is necessary. If a lecturer locks his class in the lecture room after the usual time for dismissal has arrived, that is false imprisonment; so, too, if a person be restrained from leaving his own house or any part of it,[131] or be forcibly detained in the public streets.[132] "Imprisonment", says the old *Termes de la Ley*[133]:

> "[I]s the restraint of a man's liberty whether it be in the open field, or in the stocks or cage in the street, or in a man's own house, as well as in the common gaol. And in all these places the party so restrained is said to be a prisoner, so long as he hath not his liberty freely to go at all times to all places whither he will, without bail or mainprize".[134]

This definition (with due elimination of the archaisms in it) was accepted by the Court of Appeal in *Meering v Grahame-White Aviation Co Ltd*.[135] There is no false imprisonment where the claimant consents to the defendant's order, but he is not to be taken as consenting simply because he does not resist by force.[136] A difficult line must be drawn between consent on the one hand and peaceful

---

1478 cannot be supported if it lays down any other rule: *McCauley v Hope* (1999) 149 N.L.J. 228.

[130] It is a crime as well as a tort.

[131] *Warner v Riddiford* 4 C.B.(N.S.) 180 (1858).

[132] Blackstone, Comm., iii, 127. Cf. the wedding guest detained by Coleridge's Ancient Mariner:

> "He holds him with glittering eye—
> The wedding-guest stood still,
> And listens like a three years' child,
> The Mariner hath his will."

Would restraint by post-hypnotic suggestion suffice? There seems to be no reason why it should not be false imprisonment if the victim would not have assented to it. On false imprisonment by brainwashing, see Dobbs, *Torts* (2000) §37.

[133] Its first edition was about 1520.

[134] A person bailed is theoretically in the custody of his sureties; a person mainprized (now wholly obsolete) is at large.

[135] (1920) 122 L.T. 44 at 51, 53.

[136] He is entitled to resist by force (*Hepburn v CC Thames Valley* [2002] EWCA Civ 1841) but resistance to arrest is generally unwise, because the arrest may turn out to be lawful.

but unwilling submission to express or implied threats of force or asserted legal authority (whether valid or not) on the other.[137]

A. Knowledge of Claimant[138]

It had been held in *Grainger v Hill*[139] that imprisonment is **4–16** possible even if the claimant is too ill to move in the absence of any restraint. In *Meering*'s case the court went much further by holding that the tort is committed even if the claimant did not know that he was being detained.[140] The facts were that the claimant, being suspected of stealing a keg of varnish from the defendants, his employers, was asked by two of their police to go with them to the company's office. He assented and at his suggestion they took a short cut there. On arrival he was taken or invited to go to the waiting room, the two policemen remaining in the neighbourhood. In an action for false imprisonment the defence was that the claimant was perfectly free to go where he liked, that he knew it and that he did not desire to go away but it was held by a majority of the Court of Appeal that the defendants were liable because the claimant from the moment that he came under the influence of the police was no longer a free man. Atkin L.J. said:

"It appears to me that a person could be imprisoned without his knowing it. I think a person can be imprisoned while he is asleep, while he is in a state of drunkenness, while he is unconscious, and while he is a lunatic.[141] . . . Of course the damages might be

[137] See Prosser and Keeton, *Torts*, 5th edn, pp.50–51. Thus there is no false imprisonment when the claimant complies with a police request to accompany them to the police station, but the tort is committed if the "request" is made in such a manner as to lead the claimant to believe he has no choice in the matter. See *Myer Stores Ltd v Soo* [1991] 2 V.R. 597.

[138] Authority is not very clear on the state of mind of the defendant. Historically, there is something to be said for the view that negligence should suffice (e.g. locking a room without checking whether there is anyone inside) but false imprisonment is a species of trespass to the person and intention is probably now required for all forms of this wrong. That was the view of Smith L.J. in *Iqbal v Prison Officers Association* [2009] EWCA Civ 1310. In *R. v Governor of Brockhill Prison Ex p. Evans (No.2)* [2001] 2 A.C. 19 at 28 it is said to be a tort of strict liability; but the point at issue there was different: the defendant knew he was detaining the claimant, he simply mistakenly thought he had lawful authority to do so. It is one thing to say that a person exercising a power to deprive another of liberty must get it right at his peril, another to impose liability for a restraint of which the defendant is wholly unconscious. However, if damage is suffered, an action on the case for negligence will lie and being deprived of one's liberty for a substantial period is damage: *Karagozlou v MPC* [2006] EWCA Civ 1691; [2007] 1 W.L.R. 1881 (misfeasance in a public office).

[139] (1838) 4 Bing. N.C. 212.

[140] Contra the *Restatement of Torts*, 2d, ss.35, 42, but the *Restatement* imposes liability if the claimant is harmed by the confinement and gives a wide meaning to harm.

[141] Even if it be accepted that the tort is committed in these cases, did not Meering consent to remaining in the room?

diminished and would be affected by the question whether he was conscious of it or not."

The learned Lord Justice's ground for this opinion was that, although a person might not know he was imprisoned, his captors might be boasting elsewhere that he was.[142] This point might be regarded as more relevant to defamation than to false imprisonment, but Atkin L.J.'s view has been approved, obiter,[143] by the House of Lords in an appeal from Northern Ireland, *Murray v Ministry of Defence*[144] though with the rider that a person who is unaware that he has been falsely imprisoned and has suffered no harm can normally[145] expect to recover no more than nominal damages. The basis of the law as stated in *Meering* and *Murray* is no doubt that personal liberty is supremely important so that interference with it must be deterred even where there is no consciousness nor harm. There must, however, be a detention. A patient who is in a coma after an accident is not "detained" by the hospital. A more difficult case is *R. v Bournewood etc. NHS Trust*,[146] where a patient, who because of mental disorder lacked the capacity to consent or to object, was admitted as a "voluntary" patient. In fact the court held that the hospital's actions were justified at common law by necessity but the majority were of the view that he was not "detained" by being kept in an unlocked ward, even though he was sedated and closely supervised and, if he had attempted to leave, the hospital would have considered his compulsory detention under the Mental Health Act.[147]

B. Restraint must be Complete

4–17   The tort is not committed unless motion be restrained in every direction. In *Bird v Jones*[148] the defendants wrongfully enclosed part

---

[142] (1920) 122 L.T. 44 at 53–54.

[143] On the facts the claimant was aware she was under restraint.

[144] [1988] 1 W.L.R. 692; *Herring v Boyle* (1834) 1 Cr.M. & R. 377 must be regarded as wrongly decided.

[145] Perhaps this is intended as a reference to the possibility of exemplary damages where there is arbitrary, oppressive or unconstitutional action: para.22–9, below. However, a person who is aware that he is detained is imprisoned during periods thereafter when he is asleep: *Roberts v CC Cheshire* [1999] 1 W.L.R. 662.

[146] [1999] 1 A.C. 458.

[147] Compare Lord Steyn, dissenting on this issue: "The suggestion that L was free to go is a fairy tale" (at 495). Even the majority, however, were of the view that he was detained while being taken to the hospital by ambulance. The European Court of Human Rights held that he had been deprived of his liberty for the purposes of art.5 of the Convention: *H.L. v UK* [2004] E.H.R.R. 32. While it did not—indeed could not—question the correctness of the decision on false imprisonment, the difference seems odd.

[148] (1845) 7 Q.B. 742.

of the public footway on Hammersmith Bridge, put seats in it for the use of spectators of a regatta on the river, and charged for admission to the enclosure. The claimant insisted on passing along this part of the footpath, and climbed over the fence of the enclosure without paying the charge. The defendants refused to let him go forward, but he was told that he might go back into the carriageway and cross to the other side of the bridge if he wished. He declined to do so and remained in the enclosure for half an hour. The defendants were held not to have committed false imprisonment.[149] What will amount to a complete restraint must be a question of degree. A person would plainly be imprisoned if locked inside a large building,[150] even though he had full freedom to roam around inside it, and it has been suggested that unlawful conscription is theoretically capable of being false imprisonment[151] but it seems unlikely that an action for false imprisonment would lie if, for example, the claimant was wrongfully prevented from leaving this country.[152] If, however, there is a total restraint upon the claimant's liberty, that is false imprisonment even though it lasts for only a brief period of time. This means that many acts which are "primarily" battery may also involve false imprisonment, as where C is raped by D.

C. Means of Escape

If a person has the reasonable[153] means of escape, but does not **4–18** know it, it is submitted that his detention is nevertheless false imprisonment unless any reasonable person would have realised that he had an available outlet. Thus, if I pretend to turn the key of the door of a room in which you are and take away the key, it would seem unreasonable if you made no attempt to see whether the door was in fact locked. A more difficult case is that in which you have

---

[149] But if the claimant suffers damage by being prevented from going in a certain direction (e.g. misses an important appointment), an action on the case might lie. Obstruction of the highway may be a public nuisance even though the claimant is not totally detained.

[150] Or marooned on an island: Napoleon was certainly imprisoned on St Helena. Cf. *Guzzardi v Italy* (1980) 3 E.H.R.R. 333. By these standards there could be no argument but that detaining people in Oxford Circus was imprisonment: *Austin v MPC* [2007] EWCA Civ 989; [2008] Q.B. 660 (on appeal on other issues [2009] UKHL 5; [2009] 1 A.C. 564).

[151] *Pritchard v MoD* [1995] C.L.Y. 4726.

[152] See *Louis v Commonwealth* (1986) 87 F.L.R. 277. Protocol 4, art.2 of the European Convention on Human Rights guarantees the rights to liberty of movement and to leave a country, but these have not been enacted by the Human Rights Act 1998. There is no common law tort of imposing exile upon a person, even though it is forbidden by Magna Carta. It is necessary to show trespass to the person or some other tort: *Chagos Islanders v Att Gen* [2004] EWCA Civ 997.

[153] See *McFadzean v Construction Forestry Mining and Energy Union* [2007] VSCA 289 for a full discussion.

a duplicate key in your pocket but have forgotten its existence. A reasonable person may suffer from a lapse of memory.

D. Defences

4–19　　Most of the defences depend upon conditions which in general negate liability in tort.[154] Some particular cases may be mentioned here. It must be emphasised that these matters are defences in the true sense, that is to say, it is for the defendant to raise and to establish them[155]: it is for an officer who effects an arrest to show that he had lawful authority to do so, not for the claimant to show that he did not, and the claimant certainly does not have to prove negligence or malice, the question is whether the detention was justified or not. In *R. v Governor of Brockhill Prison, Ex p. Evans (No.2)*[156] the claimant was released from prison by habeas corpus when a decision of the Divisional Court disapproved earlier cases dealing with the method of calculation of the release date for prisoners with concurrent sentences, and he recovered £5,000 damages for the 59 days he had spent in prison after his proper release date. This was despite the fact that before the new ruling was given the prison governor would plainly have had no authority to release him. The governor was acting in accordance with the law as it was then perceived to be, but the general rule of the law[157] is that decisions which are overruled are regarded as never having had legal force, subject to any issue being res judicata between parties who have previously litigated the issue.[158] However, in some situations a person may be justified in acting on facts as he reasonably believes them to be: a power of arrest which depended upon the arrested person being guilty of the offence would be a very risky thing to exercise and the law therefore generally provides that there

---

[154] See Ch.25.

[155] *R. v Deputy Governor of Parkhurst Prison, Ex p. Hague* [1992] 1 A.C. 58 at 162.

[156] [2001] 2 A.C. 19.

[157] It is not a universal rule, for example it does not apply in procedural matters. The HL in *Evans* declined to embark on a full review of the declaratory theory, while accepting that it might need further modification. See also *Kleinwort Benson v Lincoln CC* [1999] 2 A.C. 349 and *National Westminster Bank Plc v Spectrum Plus Ltd* [2005] UKHL 41; [2005] 2 A.C. 680.

[158] A governor is not guilty of false imprisonment for detaining a prisoner under a sentence which the court, it is subsequently held, had no power to impose, for he must obey an order of the court unless at that time it is invalid on its face, but that was not the position in *Evans*: the governor misinterpreted the effect of the sentence. The sentence of the court was X years and the issue was the impact on the actual time served of the legislation governing the period on remand. *Olotu v Home Office* [1997] 1 W.L.R. 328 is also different from *Evans*. Although the claimant was detained beyond the proper period of her detention she was to be released on the order of the court and until the court did so her detention was lawful as far as the governor was concerned. See also *Quinland v Governor of Swaleside Prison* [2002] EWCA Civ 174; [2003] Q.B. 306.

may be an arrest on reasonable suspicion.[159] What is rather curious about the *Evans* decision is that an arresting officer may also treated more favourably if he acts on what turns out with hindsight to be an erroneous view of the law. In *Percy v Hall*[160] an action for false imprisonment failed where the claimant was arrested under a bye-law which was subsequently held to be invalid. So, on facts like *Evans*, if the claimant had escaped after the expiry of his proper sentence and had been arrested before the decision of the Divisional Court and had then, after that decision, sued the arresters, they might have had a defence whereas the prison governor would not.[161]

i. Reasonable condition. It is not a tort to prevent a person from leaving your premises because he will not fulfil a reasonable condition subject to which he entered them. In *Robinson v Balmain Ferry Co Ltd*[162] the claimant paid a penny for entry to the defendants' wharf from which he proposed to cross the river by one of the defendants' ferry boats. A boat had just gone and, as there was not another one for 20 minutes, the claimant wished to leave the wharf and was directed to the turnstile which was its exit. There he refused to pay another penny which was chargeable for exit, as was stated on a noticeboard, and the defendant declined to let him leave the wharf unless he did pay. The Judicial Committee held that this was not false imprisonment:

4–20

"There is no law requiring the defendants to make the exit from their premises gratuitous to people who come there upon a definite contract which involves their leaving the wharf by another way ... The question whether the notice which was affixed to these premises was brought home to the knowledge of the plaintiff is immaterial, because the notice itself is immaterial".[163]

The court regarded the charge of a penny for exit as reasonable. It must be stressed that it was crucial to the decision in this case that the claimant had contracted to leave the wharf by a different route. Nonetheless, the decision is a strong one because it amounts, in

---

[159] See below.
[160] [1997] Q.B. 24.
[161] See Judge L.J. in *Evans* in the CA at [1999] Q.B. at 1077. In *Percy v Hall* it is suggested that while the Crown would not be liable for the consequences of issuing the invalid bye-law it should be. The effect of *Evans* was that the Crown paid, via the Prison Service, for the errors of the courts. In *Quinland*, above, no one paid even though the claimant served an extra six weeks. The governor was entitled and bound to take the court's order at its face value and the failure of the Criminal Appeal office to expedite the correction of the judge's error was held to fall within exemption for judicial functions in s.2(5) of the Crown Proceedings Act 1947 (as to which, see para.24–3, below).
[162] [1910] A.C. 295.
[163] [1910] A.C. at 299. Cf. Viscount Haldane L.C. in *Herd v Weardale Steel Co Ltd* [1915] A.C. 67 at 72.

effect, to recognising extra-judicial imprisonment as a method of enforcing contractual rights.[164]

4–21   **ii. Imprisonment, arrest and detention.** By s.12(1) of the Prison Act 1952, "a prisoner, whether sentenced to imprisonment or committed to prison on remand pending trial", is lawfully confined in the prison, so that there is no action for false imprisonment against the prison governor or any prison officer acting under his authority.[165] However, it would not be quite right to say that the law of false imprisonment is inoperative within a prison: the prisoner could, for example, bring such a claim against a fellow prisoner who locked him in a shed (or even an individual prison officer who locked him in his cell without authority[166]). Nor is there false imprisonment where a prisoner is kept in intolerable conditions. The proper remedy at common law is by way of judicial review or, if harm is suffered, by an action for negligence.[167] It may also amount to inhuman or degrading treatment contrary to art.3 of the European Convention on Human Rights, for which damages will be available under the Human Rights Act 1998.

---

[164] A right denied in *Bahner v Marwest Hotel* (1970) 12 D.L.R. (3d) 646. The claimant in *Robinson*'s case was, after a short time, allowed to leave by squeezing past the turnstile. Could the defendants have kept him there indefinitely?

Winfield also put the cases of a person getting on the wrong bus and not being allowed to leave without paying the minimum fare and of a student who mistakenly enters the wrong lecture room and is not allowed by the lecturer to leave until the end of the hour on the ground that he will interrupt the discourse (though one would have thought that the effort of keeping him there would cause a good deal more interruption). He suggested that in each case the decision must turn upon whether, (1) the mistake was a reasonable one, and (2) the condition as to exit was a reasonable one.

Tan Keng Fen in "A Misconceived Issue in the Tort of False Imprisonment" (1981) 44 M.L.R. 166 argues that neither *Robinson*'s case nor *Herd v Weardale Steel Co*, below, supports the view stated in the text, and that a person may always withdraw his consent to restraints upon his liberty, though he may not demand instant release if that would be unduly inconvenient. However, he admits that the result of neither case is easily reconcilable with this view.

[165] *R. v Deputy Governor of Parkhurst Prison, Ex p. Hague* [1992] 1 A.C. 58. Similarly, art.5 (as opposed to arts 3 and 8) of the European Convention on Human Rights is concerned with the lawfulness of detention, not its conditions: *Ashingdane v UK* (1985) 7 E.H.R.R. 528 at [44]; *R. (Munjaz) v Mersey Care NHS Trust* [2005] UKHL 58; [2006] 2 A.C. 148 (cf. the dissent of Lord Steyn); *Davies v Secretary of State for Justice* [2008] EWHC 397 (Admin). The fact that the Parole Board has acted unlawfully in administrative law terms in relation to considering the prisoner's release does not render his detention unlawful for the purpose of false imprisonment: *Dunn v Parole Board* [2008] EWCA Civ 374; [2009] 1 W.L.R. 728.

[166] Where action is taken in bad faith there may be liability for misfeasance in a public office: *Hague* at 123: *Karagozlou v MPC* [2006] EWCA Civ 1691; [2007] 1 W.L.R. 1881 (move to closed prison; however, the claim was based on false information said to have been supplied by the police).

[167] On ordinary principles this would require a physical injury or injury to health, but Lord Bridge in *Hague*'s case contemplates intolerable pain or discomfort as sufficient. Nor do the Prison Rules give rise to an action for breach of statutory duty.

False imprisonment is a form of trespass and "not doing is no **4–22** trespass". Nevertheless it is clear that the failure of a prison governor to release a prisoner at the end of his sentence is false imprisonment—or at least no one thought to argue the contrary in *R. v Governor of Brockhill Prison, Ex p. Evans (No.2)*.[168] However, in *Iqbal v Prison Officers Association*[169] the claimant was not allowed to leave his cell during one day because of unlawful strike action by prison officers. The direct cause of the confinement was the order of the governor. No action lay against him[170] but the claim for false imprisonment was brought against the prison officers association. A majority of the Court of Appeal held that the claim failed: false imprisonment was not generally committed by omission, the *Brockhill* case being explicable by the fact that the prisoner had a positive right, as against the governor, to be released at the end of his sentence, whereas the prison officers, although they knew that the consequences of their actions would be confinement of prisoners for longer than normal, had merely failed to carry out their contractual duties to the prison service. As Lord Neuberger M.R. pointed out:

"[T]he court should be reluctant to reach a conclusion whose implications could lead to many small private law damages claims arising from what may often be little more than poor timekeeping by prison officers, and whose outcome may often turn on issues such as whether an officer in an undermanned prison could better have organised his working day to ensure that a prisoner was let out of his cell at precisely the time stipulated by the governor."[171]

The issue might arise outside a prison context. In *Herd v Weardale, etc. Co Ltd*[172] a miner, in breach of his contract of employment with the defendants, refused to do certain work allotted to him in the mine, and demanded to be taken to the surface by the lift five hours before his shift expired. He was not allowed to leave for 20 minutes. The claim for false imprisonment failed because the claimant had no right to be brought up until the end of the shift[173] and the House of Lords did not discuss what the position would have been if he had been kept down the mine after that time, though in the Court of Appeal Buckley and Hamilton L.JJ. were of the view that the only claim would have been for breach of contract.[174]

---

[168] para.4–19, above.
[169] [2009] EWCA Civ 1310.
[170] para.4–21, above.
[171] At [40]. But Sullivan L.J., dissenting, thought that it was a case of deliberate disobedience to orders which could not be equated with an omission.
[172] [1915] A.C. 67. Cf. *Whittaker v Sandford* 85 A. 399 (1912).
[173] See para.4–20, above.
[174] [1913] 3 K.B. 771.

4–23   A lawful arrest is, of course, no false imprisonment and it follows that a person who arrests another in pursuance of a valid warrant cannot be sued.[175] If an arrest is authorised, it does not become unauthorised because excessive force is used in effecting it (though an action for battery would lie).[176] Only an outline of powers of arrest is given here and more detail must be sought in books on constitutional law or civil liberties. Traditionally the common law has been concerned to restrain intrusions into personal liberty even if not accompanied by circumstances of aggravation or high-handedness and substantial damages may be awarded for even quite brief unlawful detentions.[177] The vindication of liberty has symbolic and admonitory values and, while most of us would probably prefer a night in the cells to a broken leg it does not follow that the damages for the latter should exceed those for the former.[178] Awards of damages for false imprisonment by the police can be very substantial even without the addition of aggravated or exemplary damages.[179] Where the unlawful detention is continuing the claimant may seek a writ of habeas corpus: this is not often used but it has certainly not fallen into disuse. A person who is unlawfully detained may use self-help to escape, including reasonable force[180] though this is a risky course since the power of arrest is likely to depend not only upon the commission of an offence but, in the alternative, upon a reasonable suspicion thereof. Hence, even an innocent person who forcibly resists arrest may be liable in tort for battery if the arrester had reasonable grounds for his suspicion.[181]

4–24   First, the common law gives the police no power to detain for questioning[182] but Part I of the Police and Criminal Evidence Act 1984 gives a police officer power to stop and search any person or vehicle for stolen or prohibited[183] goods if he has reasonable grounds to believe that such goods will be found. Originally, the law

---

[175] See para.24–11, below.

[176] *Simpson v CC South Yorkshire*, *The Times*, March 7, 1991.

[177] See *Thompson v MPC* [1998] Q.B. 498. But one must bear in mind that minor acts of physical interference by a constable (e.g. with a drunken person) may fall within what is acceptable in ordinary life (see para.4–7, above): *McMillan v CPS* [2008] EWHC 1457 (Admin).

[178] The rather dismissive approach in *Fayed v MPC* [2004] EWCA Civ 1579 may have been produced by the claimants' behaviour which led up to the arrest.

[179] See para.22–8, below.

[180] Though it is a question of fact, one might ask what force is reasonable to avoid a few hours in police custody?

[181] In the criminal law the defendant's mistaken belief in circumstances which, if they existed, would make his resistance lawful may provide him with a defence even if the mistake is unreasonable (*Beckford v R.* [1988] A.C. 130) but the civil law seems to be less generous: para.25–30, below.

[182] A person who voluntarily attends at a police station for questioning cannot be detained there unless he is lawfully arrested: Police and Criminal Evidence Act 1984 s.29.

[183] i.e. offensive weapons or things used for offences of dishonesty. There are also powers to stop and search vehicles and their passengers under the prevention of terrorism and public order legislation.

of arrest without warrant turned on the distinction between felonies and misdemeanours. The Criminal Law Act 1967, which abolished these categories, introduced the concept of the "arrestable offence" and the law was re-enacted with modifications in the Police and Criminal Evidence Act 1984.[184] These powers of arrest were replaced by new provisions of that Act substituted by the Serious Organised Crime and Police Act 2005.

A distinction is drawn between the powers of police officers[185] and others. By s.24 of the Act, as amended:

"(1) A constable may arrest without a warrant—

(a) anyone who is about to commit an offence;
(b) anyone who is in the act of committing an offence;
(c) anyone whom he[186] has reasonable grounds for suspecting to be about to commit an offence;
(d) anyone whom he has reasonable grounds for suspecting to be committing an offence.

(2) If a constable has reasonable grounds for suspecting that an offence has been committed, he may arrest without a warrant anyone whom he has reasonable grounds to suspect of being guilty of it.

(3) If an offence has been committed, a constable may arrest without a warrant—

(a) anyone who is guilty of the offence;
(b) anyone whom he has reasonable grounds for suspecting to be guilty of it."

If, therefore, Constable D[187] arrests C on reasonable suspicion that he is committing an offence then (provided the other requirements of the section are fulfilled) there is a defence to any action for false imprisonment even though it turns out that C was not, in fact, guilty. Under the old law it was held that the plain meaning of the statute required that the arresting officer should be in possession of information which gives him reasonable cause to suspect the claimant and it was not enough that such information was in the possession of another officer who gave an order to arrest which the

---

[184] An arrestable offence was one in respect of which the penalty was fixed by law or which was punishable with five years' imprisonment or which was specified by legislation.

[185] The Police Reform Act 2002 gives a chief constable power to designate civilians such as police authority employees and contracted-out staff to perform certain police functions. Their powers depend upon the designation.

[186] The "he" is important. If the officer knows that the arrested person is not about to commit an offence but a reasonable observer would think he was, there is no power of arrest.

[187] In practice, of course, a claim will be brought against the chief constable on the basis of vicarious liability for the acts of D.

defendant officer obeyed.[188] Whether or not this is necessarily realistic in modern conditions,[189] the statute was founded, "on the longstanding constitutional theory of the independence and accountability of the individual officer".[190] There seems no reason to believe that the new legislation effects any change.[191]

There is no longer any distinction between arrestable offences and others: the power applies to *any* offence. However, by s.24(4) the power to arrest is only applicable if the constable has reasonable grounds for believing that for any of the reasons mentioned in subs.(5) it is necessary to arrest the person in question. The reasons are:

"(a) to enable the name or address of the person in question to be ascertained[192];

(b) to prevent the person in question[193]—

    (i) causing physical injury to himself or any other person;

    (ii) suffering physical injury;

    (iii) causing loss of or damage to property;

    (iv) committing an offence against public decency[194]; or

    (v) causing an unlawful obstruction of the highway;

(c) to protect a child or other vulnerable person from the person in question;

(d) to allow the prompt and effective investigation of the offence or of the conduct of the person in question;

(e) to prevent any prosecution for the offence from being hindered by the disappearance of the person in question."

To a large extent these reasons replicate the "general arrest conditions" which had to be fulfilled under the original 1984 Act to

---

[188] *O'Hara v Chief Constable, Royal Ulster Constabulary* [1997] A.C. 286; cf. *Keegan v CC Merseyside* [2003] EWCA Civ 936; [2003] 1 W.L.R. 2187.

[189] *Raissi v MPC* [2008] EWCA Civ 1237; [2009] Q.B. 564 at [33]. The European Convention on Human Rights, art.5, may be less restrictive: *O'Hara*'s case at 292.

[190] [1997] A.C. 286 at 293 per Lord Steyn.

[191] The statute in question in *O'Brien* was the Prevention of Terrorism (Temporary Provisions) Act 1984, but for this purpose it was identical with the Police and Criminal Evidence Act 1984 s.24, and there seems to be no material difference in the new version of s.24. The arresting officer does not, of course, have to investigate the matter himself: he may rely on apparently reliable information given to him by another officer: *Clarke v CC North Wales*, April 5, 2000, CA. Any deficiencies in his briefing do not invalidate the arrest, though they may render the briefing officer liable for some other tort, e.g. misfeasance in a public office: *Alford v CC Cambridgeshire* [2009] EWCA Civ 100.

[192] s.24(5)(a),(b).

[193] s.24(5)(c).

[194] This applies only where members of the public going about their normal business cannot reasonably be expected to avoid the person in question: s.24(6).

justify an arrest without warrant for a non-arrestable offence.[195]
These did not apply to an arrestable offence but it was held that
since the arresting officer had a discretion he must exercise it in
good faith and without taking into account irrelevant matters: reasonable suspicion was a condition precedent of the rightfulness of an
arrest, but it was not conclusive. It would seem that the reasons in
s.24(5) (which are now applicable to all offences) *replace* the issue
of discretion, but the two may well overlap in some cases. Thus in
Mohammed-Holgate v Duke[196] it was held that the constable's belief
that the claimant would be more likely to confess by being questioned at the police station was a legitimate reason for exercising the
discretion to arrest and did not render the arrest unlawful.[197] No
doubt it would now be argued that such a reason would fall within
the "prompt and effective investigation" reason in s.24(4). In fact a
"formal" arrest preparatory to questioning is nowadays almost common form, even if the person arrested has voluntarily attended the
police station and has expressed willingness to co-operate. Whether
the exercise of a power of arrest is "necessary" in such cases
remains to be seen.[198] At any rate one thing seems clear: the burden
of showing the unreasonableness of an arrest in administrative law
terms is on the claimant, but it is for the police to show that one of
the reasons in s.24(5) was present.

The powers of arrest of a private citizen are governed by **4–25**
s.24A:

"(1) A person other than a constable may arrest without a
warrant—

(a) anyone who is in the act of committing an indictable
offence;
(b) anyone whom he has reasonable grounds for suspecting
to be committing an indictable offence.

(2) Where an indictable offence has been committed, a person
other than a constable may arrest without a warrant—

(a) anyone who is guilty of the offence;
(b) anyone whom he has reasonable grounds for suspecting
to be guilty of it."

There are three clear differences between the powers of a constable and a private citizen. First, the citizen's power of arrest is

---

[195] Police and Criminal Evidence Act 1984 s.25.
[196] [1984] A.C. 437.
[197] Using detention to question the suspect was described by the Royal Commission on
Criminal Procedure as "one of the primary purposes of detention upon arrest". Cmnd.
8092 (1981), para.3.66.
[198] See *Fayed v MPC* [2004] EWCA Civ 1579, which displays a fairly indulgent attitude
towards the practice.

confined to indictable offences, that is to say, offences triable on indictment rather than on information only in the magistrates' court. Secondly, the citizen has no power to make a "preventive" arrest: an offence must be in progress or he must reasonably believe that it is. Thirdly, in the case of the citizen there is no equivalent of s.24(2). Where an indictable offence *has been committed*, any person may arrest without warrant anyone who is guilty of the offence or anyone whom he has reasonable grounds for suspecting to be guilty of it. In other words, where the offence has been committed there may be a defence even if the arrester "gets the wrong man"; but if in fact no offence has been committed by anyone the arrest is unlawful.[199]

As in the case of the police officer, the private citizen effecting an arrest has to satisfy further alternative conditions. Three of these are similar to those applicable to constables—that he has reasonable grounds to believe that the arrest is necessary to prevent the arrestee causing physical injury to himself or another, suffering injury or causing loss of or damage to property.[200] The fourth is that he has reasonable grounds to believe that it is necessary to prevent the arrestee, "making off before a constable can assume responsibility for him."[201] Finally, in all cases it must appear to the person making the arrest, "that it is not reasonably practicable for a constable to make it instead".[202]

4–26   In addition to these statutory powers of arrest, any person may use such force (which may include detention)[203] as is reasonable in the circumstances[204] in the prevention of crime, or in effecting or assisting in the lawful arrest of offenders, suspected offenders or persons unlawfully at large.[205] There also still exists a common law

---

[199] There is therefore preserved the somewhat anomalous rule in *Walters v WH Smith & Son Ltd* [1914] 1 K.B. 595, whereby the liability of a private person for false imprisonment may depend upon the outcome of a criminal trial (not necessarily of the person arrested) which takes place after the arrest was made. A private person arresting on suspicion of an arrestable offence must prove not only reasonable grounds for his suspicion but also that the arrestable offence in question has been committed by someone. See *R. v Self* [1992] 1 W.L.R. 657. In *Davidson v CC North Wales* [1994] 2 All E.R. 597 the police officer was protected but if the store detective had made the arrest herself she would have been liable for false imprisonment.

[200] Police and Criminal Evidence Act 1984 s.24A(4)(a)–(c).

[201] PACE 1984 s.24A(4)(d).

[202] PACE 1984 s.24A(3)(b).

[203] *Albert v Lavin* [1982] A.C. 546.

[204] Clearly there must be some proportionality between the force and the crime prevented, but the issue is treated as one of fact: *Att Gen for Northern Ireland's Reference (No.1 of 1975)* [1977] A.C. 105. This is open to criticism, inter alia, on the ground that it gives insufficient guidance to persons using force. See generally Doran (1987) 7 L.S. 291. Compare the European Convention on Human Rights, art.2, which allows fatal force where "absolutely necessary" to prevent unlawful violence, to effect a lawful arrest or quell riot or insurrection. However, art.2 allows the law enforcement authority to act on the basis of the situation as it reasonably believes it to be: *McCann, Farrell and Savage v UK* (1995) 21 E.H.R.R. 97.

[205] Criminal Law Act 1967 s.3.

power to arrest to prevent an imminent breach of the peace by the person arrested[206] and this complies with art.5 of the European Convention on Human Rights.[207] In order to prevent an imminent breach of the peace there may also be detention short of arrest[208] but there is no doctrine that such action may be justified on lesser grounds than those applicable to an arrest: in either case the apprehended breach of the peace must be about to happen, not merely reasonably anticipated at some time in the future.[209] In the past most cases about arrest and detention arose from the apprehension of individual persons for crime or from restraint of mentally disordered persons and the principles forged in that context are not easy to apply to action which may be taken to restrain or restrict the movement of large numbers of persons in the course of demonstrations and assemblies. For example, where there is disorder at point A large numbers of people may be temporarily detained, perhaps for long periods of time, at point B in order to prevent the aggravation of the disorder but it may be impossible reasonably to regard all, or even most, of them as bent on disorder or breaches of the peace; nevertheless, such action may be justified "in extreme and exceptional circumstances" on the principle of necessity.[210]

The position in all these matters is rather different where the **4–27** arrested person has been convicted of an imprisonable offence. Under s.329 of the Criminal Justice Act 2003 a defendant sued by a claimant who has been convicted of an imprisonable offence has a defence to any claim for trespass to the person on the same occasion as the offence if he proves that he acted only because he believed that the claimant was about to commit an offence (or was in the course of committing it or had committed it immediately beforehand; or that he acted to defend himself or another; or to protect or recover property; or to prevent the commission of an

---

[206] *R (Laporte) v CC Gloucestershire* [2006] UKHL 55; [2007] 2 A.C. 105 (a claim for judicial review seeking a declaration that the action of the defendant was unlawful).

[207] *Steel v UK* (1998) 28 E.H.R.R. 603.

[208] An arrest, but not a detention of this type, requires that the arrested person be brought before a magistrate and the provisions of the Police and Criminal Evidence Act 1984 apply: *Williamson v CC West Midlands* [2003] EWCA Civ 337; [2004] 1 W.L.R. 14.

[209] *R (Laporte) v CC Gloucestershire*, above, fn.206. In *Murray v Ministry of Defence* [1998] 1 W.L.R. 692 it is suggested that there is a power to restrain the movement of A for a short time if necessary to effect the lawful arrest of B; and there is power to restrict the movement of occupants while premises are searched: *DPP v Meaden* [2003] EWHC 3005 (Admin); 2004 1 W.L.R. 945; *Connor v CC Merseyside* [2006] EWCA Civ 1549; [2007] H.R.L.R. 6.

[210] *Austin v MPC* [2007] EWCA Civ 989; [2008] Q.B. 660. There as no appeal to the HL on the false imprisonment/necessity issue: [2009] UKHL 5; [2009] 2 A.C. 564, though the HL held that there had been no infringement of art.5 of the Convention. Compare the situation where the police may restrict movement on a motorway for some time after an accident so as to prevent further accidents. In *Austin* the point is made that in the case of demonstrations it may be preferable to rely on police powers to give directions under ss.11–14 of the Public Order Act 1986 because the gravamen of offences thereunder is failure to obey directions rather than any ulterior criminal intent.

offence; or to apprehend the offender) *and* that his act was not grossly disproportionate in the circumstances.[211] "Belief" here is actual belief even if unreasonable.[212] So if the defendant (whether a police officer or a private person) arrests the claimant for, say, burglary on totally inadequate evidence but matters which later come to light lead to his conviction (for that or any other imprisonable offence) no action can be brought unless what the defendant did was "grossly disproportionate". The claimant requires the court's permission to bring proceedings and this can only be given if there is evidence that the condition as to the defendant's belief was not satisfied or that his act was grossly disproportionate.[213]

4–28   (a) *The burden and standard of proof.* In an action for false imprisonment the burden of proof of justifying an arrest is upon the person effecting it[214] and if he fails to do so he is liable for false imprisonment and, where there has been a threatened or actual use of force (no matter how minor) for assault or battery as well. Unless it can be shown that the claimant was guilty of the offence or was about to commit it, the power of arrest depends on reasonable grounds for suspicion and in this connection it is obviously necessary first to establish that the arrester actually did suspect the claimant[215]; but there must also be an objective basis for that state of mind. It also seems clear as a matter of statutory language that the burden of proof lies on the arrester in respect of the presence of one of the "reasons" which justify arrest.[216] Reasonable suspicion is less than prima facie proof,[217] if only because the latter must be based on admissible evidence, whereas suspicion can take into account other matters as well[218] and Lord Devlin said that:

---

[211] This is a paraphrase: for the precise wording see the section.

[212] Criminal Justice Act 2003 s.329(8)(b).

[213] Criminal Justice Act 2003 s.329(3). Failure to seek permission does not render the proceedings a nullity: *Adorian v MPC* [2009] EWCA Civ 18; [2009] 1 W.L.R. 1859.

[214] Where action short of arrest such as detaining a crowd is taken on the basis of necessity (see above) it is for the police to show that the general course they took was necessary but for the individual claimant to show that the refusal to release him was *Wednesbury* unreasonable: *Austin v MPC* [2007] EWCA Civ 989; [2008] Q.B. 660 at [70].

[215] *Siddique v Swain* [1979] R.T.R. 474.

[216] s.24(5) and 24A(4). See paras 4–24 and 4–25, above. Note, however, that the arrester must have reasonable grounds for *believing* in the existence of the reason, not *suspecting* it. It is suggested above (para.4–24) that these reasons replace the "unreasonable exercise of discretion" issue which was present under the previous law. On that, the burden of proof was on the claimant: see *Fayed v MPC* [2004] EWCA Civ 1579 at [83].

[217] Where a small number of people could be identified as the only ones capable of having committed the offence, that may afford reasonable grounds for suspecting each of them, in the absence of any information that could or should enable the police to reduce the number further: *Cumming v CC Northumbria* [2003] EWCA Civ 1844; *The Times*, January 2, 2004.

[218] *Hussien v Chong Fook Kam* [1970] A.C. 943 at 949.

"[S]uspicion in its ordinary meaning is a state of conjecture or surmise where proof is lacking: 'I suspect but I cannot prove.' Suspicion arises at or near the starting point of an investigation of which the obtaining of prima facie proof is at the end".[219]

In *Dallison v Caffery*[220] where a theft had undoubtedly been committed, the defendant police officer had received trustworthy information that the claimant had been identified as the man responsible and it was held that therefore the arrest was justified. In *Hogg v Ward*,[221] on the other hand, a police constable was held liable for arresting the claimant on a mistaken charge of theft made by the owner of some harness because the constable ought to have known, from the claimant's open use of the property and his immediate statement of facts which raised a reasonable inference that he had acquired it honestly, that arrest was not justifiable in the circumstances.

(b) *Information of charge.* It was established at common law in **4-29** *Christie v Leachinsky*[222] that in ordinary circumstances a person arrested must be informed of the ground on which he is arrested, otherwise the arrest is unlawful[223]: the officer is not entitled to remain silent or to fabricate[224] a "holding charge". The law is now to be found in s.28 of the Police and Criminal Evidence Act 1984 and the position with regard to arrest by a police officer is as follows: where a person is arrested otherwise than by being informed that he is under arrest (for example, where he is physically

---

[219] *Hussien v Chong Fook Kam* [1970] A.C. 943 at 948. See also *Raissi v MPC* [2008] EWCA Civ 1237; [2009] Q.B. 564 at [20]. Code A under the Police and Criminal Evidence Act 1984 dealing with police powers of "stop and search" provides that reasonable suspicion, "can never be supported on the basis of personal factors alone without reliable supporting intelligence or information or some specific behaviour by the person concerned. For example, a person's race, age, appearance, or the fact that the person is known to have a previous conviction, cannot be used alone or in combination with each other" as a basis for reasonable suspicion. Code G, dealing with arrest simply says that, "there must be some reasonable, objective grounds for the suspicion, based on known facts or information which are relevant to the likelihood the offence has been committed and the person to be questioned committed it" but it would be curious if there were a difference.

[220] [1965] 1 Q.B. 348, decided under the common law where the test was whether there was reasonable and probable cause for the arrest.

[221] (1858) 27 L.J.Ex. 443.

[222] [1947] A.C. 573.

[223] However, if the arrested person is convicted of an imprisonable offence committed on that occasion s.329 of the Criminal Justice Act 2003 (above) would appear to block any claim unless failure to inform of the grounds is automatically "grossly disproportionate" (which seems unlikely).

[224] But if there is a charge in respect of which the officer has reasonable grounds for suspecting guilt, an arrest in respect of that is lawful even if the officer's real purpose is to investigate a more serious offence. In this sense a "holding charge" is a "well known and respectable aid to justice": *R. v Chalkely* [1998] Q.B. 848.

seized) he must as soon as practicable[225] be informed[226] that he is under arrest even if the fact is obvious and also of the ground for the arrest, again even if it is obvious. The only qualification to these duties is that they do not apply if it was not reasonably practicable for the information to be given because the claimant escaped from custody before it could be given. It has been held that an arrest is a continuing state of affairs so that if the information is not given promptly but is given at a later stage the arrest becomes lawful from that point, which may affect the quantum of damages.[227] Where the arrest is by a private individual he does not have to inform the claimant of the fact of the arrest or of the ground where it is obvious. It has been said that *Christie v Leachinsky*, s.28 and art.5(2) of the European Convention on Human Rights ("everyone who is arrested shall be informed promptly, in a language which he understands, of the reasons for his arrest and of any charge against him") all express the same principle[228] and that the essential idea is that, having regard to the information available to the arresting officer, the arrested person must be told the "essential legal and factual grounds for his arrest".[229] As to what is required by way of information, technical or precise language need not be used[230] but sufficient detail should be given to enable him to understand the factual as well as the legal nature of what he is accused of, so that, for example, "you are under the arrest for burglary" is insufficient without information of when and where.[231]

4–30   (c) *The European Convention on Human Rights*. Article 5(1) of the Convention provides that everyone has "the right to liberty and security of person". It then goes on to provide an exhaustive list of circumstances in which deprivation of liberty is justified and these include:

---

[225] Quaere whether this is more onerous than "reasonably practicable". In *Murray v Ministry of Defence* [1988] 1 W.L.R. 692, where the arrest was under emergency legislation, it was held lawful to postpone the words of arrest until the premises had been searched, for fear of violent resistance from other persons.

[226] Not necessarily by the arresting officer: *Dhesi v CC W Midlands, The Times*, May 9, 2000.

[227] *Lewis v CC South Wales* [1991] 1 All E.R. 206.

[228] *Taylor v CC Thames Valley* [2004] EWCA Civ 858; [2004] 1 W.L.R. 3155.

[229] *Fox, Campbell and Hartley v UK* (1990) 13 E.H.R.R. 157 at [40]. However, the Convention requires that the information be given "promptly" whereas the 1984 Act requires it at the time of arrest or as soon as practicable thereafter, which may be more stringent. Thus it seems that in *Taylor* information given in the custody suite would have been too late but cf. *Fox, Campbell and Hartley* at [42].

[230] Hence "you are under arrest for killing X" would be sufficient and if the ground given was "the murder of X" the arrest is valid even if the charge is eventually manslaughter.

[231] *R. v Telfer* [1976] Crim.L.R. 562; *Newman v Modern Bookbinders Ltd* [2000] 1 W.L.R. 2559.

"The lawful arrest or detention of a person effected for the purpose of bringing him before the competent legal authority on reasonable suspicion of having committed an offence or when it is reasonably considered necessary to prevent his committing an offence or fleeing after having done so".[232]

Where the detention is by the police or some other public authority it is now common form to add a claim under the Human Rights Act 1998.[233] There is an enormous degree of overlap between the two bases of liability but they are not identical: there may be cases where a claim for false imprisonment would succeed and a claim under the Convention would fail, or vice versa.[234] Thus a very brief restraint without formal arrest may not be a "deprivation of liberty" under the Convention[235] but would be "imprisonment" at common law.[236] On the other hand the Strasbourg court held that art.5 was engaged in *R. v Bournewood etc. NHS Trust*,[237] even though the majority of the House of Lords held that there was no imprisonment.[238] Detention is allowed by the Convention on certain grounds which are unknown as such to English law, e.g. of alcoholics and vagrants[239] but it has been held that the Convention requires compliance with domestic law, so that wherever the arrest is unjustified in English law and there is a sufficient deprivation of liberty there is a breach of the Convention.[240] Since the list of permissible circumstances in art.5(1) is exhaustive, there is some difficulty in entirely reconciling the common law with the Convention. For example, necessity may clearly provide a justification for a detention which

---

[232] art.5(1)(c).

[233] See para.2–8, above. A right to compensation is specifically granted by art.5(5).

[234] So also there may be an overlap between the torts of assault and battery and inhuman or degrading treatment under the Convention. The Constitution of the Bahamas contains guarantees against deprivation of liberty and inhuman or degrading treatment in terms similar to those in the Convention. In *Merson v Cartwright* [2005] UKPC 38 the JCPC said at [9] that, "in some cases the overlap may be complete—two concentric circles of equal radius, so to speak. In other cases, the circles may simply intersect, with each having a segment common to both".

[235] See *Guenat v Switzerland,* Application No.24722/94 (admissibility decision). However, the conduct might have been justifiable in English law on the basis of necessity.

[236] False imprisonment was not in issue in *R. (Gillan) v MPC* [2006] UKHL 12; [2006] 2 A.C. 307 where the court considered the stop and search provisions of the Terrorism Act 2000. The European Court of Human Rights found a violation of art.8 but found it unnecessary to decide on art.5: *Gillan v UK*, January 12, 2010, Application No.4158/05.

[237] See para.4–16, above.

[238] *H.L. v UK* (2005) 40 E.H.R.R. 32. If D keeps C under house arrest for large portions of the day but allows him to go out alone for a few hours C would not be "imprisoned" during the latter periods; but in some circumstances there might be a deprivation of liberty throughout such a regime: see *Secretary of State for the Home Dept v JJ* [2007] UKHL 45; [2008] 1 A.C. 385.

[239] art.5(1)(e).

[240] *Steel v UK* (1999) 28 E.H.R.R. 603.

would amount to imprisonment[241] but it is nowhere mentioned in art.5. The answer can only be found by applying the principle that apparently absolute protections conferred by the Convention may have to be interpreted in the light of proportionality to other legitimate public interests. Hence in *Austin v Metropolitan Police Commissioner*[242] the claimants were imprisoned when they were confined in Oxford Circus for some hours while the police struggled to control a nearby demonstration but that detention was justified by necessity[243]; but although their freedom of movement was seriously restricted[244] they were not, in view of the legitimacy of the police action, deprived of their liberty.

4–31   (d) *Detention after arrest.* Where the arrest is by a private individual the arrested person must be taken before a magistrate or a police officer, not necessarily forthwith, but as soon as is reasonably possible. For example, a person arrested in the street by a store detective on suspicion of shoplifting may be taken back to the store while the matter is reported to the store manager, and may be detained there while the police are sent for.[245] It is unlikely that he would be allowed to take the suspect to the suspect's house to see whether any of the stolen property is there, though it was held that a police officer could do so.[246]

The position after a police arrest was radically modified by the Police and Criminal Evidence Act 1984. By s.30 a person arrested otherwise than at a police station must be taken to a police station as soon as practicable after his arrest, unless his presence elsewhere is necessary in order to carry out such investigations as it is reasonable to carry out immediately.[247] The time for which and the conditions in which he may be held are then governed by Part IV of the Act and since s.34(1) provides that a person, "shall not be kept in police detention" except in accordance with Part IV, a contravention of this creates a case of false imprisonment.[248] These provisions are much too detailed to examine here but very broadly the position is that there must be periodic reviews of the detention by the police and,

---

[241] See para.4–26, above. Thus while art.5(1) allows "detention" as well as arrest, this is only for the purpose of bringing him before the court or to prevent his committing an offence and not, on the face of it, for the general public order and safety purpose in *Austin v MPC* [2007] EWCA Civ 989; [2008] Q.B. 660. However, both the CA and HL declined to give a concluded view on the scope of the justifications in art.5(1): [2009] UKHL 5; [2009] 1 A.C. 564.

[242] [2009] UKHL 5; [2009] 1 A.C. 564.

[243] [2007] EWCA Civ 989; [2008] Q.B. 660. This issue was not on appeal to the HL.

[244] It is significant that art.2 of the Fourth Protocol gives the right to liberty of movement but that has not been ratified by the UK.

[245] *John Lewis & Co Ltd v Tims* [1952] A.C. 676.

[246] *Dallison v Caffery* [1965] 1 Q.B. 348.

[247] Thus preserving *Dallison v Caffery* [1965] 1 Q.B. 348.

[248] *Roberts v CC Cheshire* [1999] 1 W.L.R. 662.

with the authority of a senior officer the detainee may be held for up to 36 hours without charge. Thereafter, the authority of a magistrates' court is required for further detention without charge up to 96 hours. After that period the suspect must either be released or charged and brought before a magistrates' court as soon as practicable.[249] In any event, even if these time limits have not been exceeded, an arrested person must be released as soon as the need for detention has ceased to apply and if he is not, there is false imprisonment from that time, notwithstanding that the initial arrest was lawful.[250]

Various matters ancillary to detention are dealt with in Part V. Contravention of the provisions on searches and fingerprinting will presumably lead to liability for battery but will not render the detention unlawful. There is no damages sanction attached to the provisions dealing with the suspect's right to have someone informed of his arrest or access to legal advice. Contravention does not render the detention unlawful, and there is no claim for breach of statutory duty; nor is any right under the European Convention on Human Rights infringed unless the effect is to deprive the claimant of a fair trial.[251]

E. Distinction from Abuse of Procedure

A defendant may be liable for false imprisonment even though he **4–32** did not personally detain the claimant, so long as he acted through an intermediary who exercised no independent discretion of his own. In *Austin v Dowling*[252] a police inspector refused to take the responsibility of arresting B on a charge made by A, but finally did arrest B when A signed the charge sheet. It was held that A could be liable for false imprisonment. There can, however, be no false imprisonment if a discretion is interposed between the defendant's act and the claimant's detention. If, for example, A makes a charge against B before a magistrate and the magistrate then decides to order the arrest of B, A has set in motion not a ministerial but a judicial officer exercising a discretion of his own and A cannot be liable for false imprisonment.[253] In modern conditions it is very

---

[249] When the suspect has been charged the Prosecution of Offences Act 1985 and regulations made thereunder prescribe time limits within which the prosecution must proceed.
[250] *Taylor v CC Thames Valley* [2004] EWCA Civ 858; [2004] 1 W.L.R. 3155.
[251] *Cullen v CC Royal Ulster Constabulary* [2003] UKHL 39; [2003] 1 W.L.R. 1763. However, if access is refused in bad faith there might be liability for misfeasance in a public office: at [71]. The case concerned s.15 of the Northern Ireland (Emergency Provisions) Act 1987 but this is modelled on the equivalent provision of the Police and Criminal Evidence Act 1984 and the reasoning would seem to apply.
[252] (1870) L.R. 5 C.P. 534.
[253] *Austin v Dowling* (1870) L.R. 5 C.P. 534 at 540 per Willes J.; *Sewell v National Telephone Co Ltd* [1907] 1 K.B. 557.

likely that where the police arrest on the basis of information or complaint they will be held to be exercising an independent discretion[254] but that is not inevitably so, as for example where there is a request or encouragement to arrest on information provided solely by the defendant.[255] The liability of an informant for abuse of legal procedure[256] is an entirely different matter which is considered in detail in a later chapter. For the present it is sufficient to note that whereas in false imprisonment the claimant need prove no more than his detention, leaving it to the defendant to prove its lawfulness if he can, in malicious prosecution, the best known form of abuse of procedure, the claimant must prove that the defendant (1) instituted a prosecution of him which (2) ended in his favour and (3) was instituted without reasonable and probable cause and (4) was malicious. It is true the claimant may still succeed in the absence of both (1) and (2) if he was actually arrested[257] but he must still prove as distinct matters both absence of reasonable and probable cause and also malice.

3. TRESPASS TO THE PERSON AND NEGLIGENCE

4–33   In terms of cases coming before the courts, negligence is the dominant tort of the modern law. Having outlined the elements of the various forms of trespass to the person, it is now necessary to consider in some detail the structural relationship of trespass and negligence and then to deal with the residual category of intentional wrongdoing which is neither trespass nor negligence.

It is unlikely that it was ever the law that a person could be held liable in trespass if he was wholly without fault.[258] However, it certainly was once the law that if the defendant inflicted a "direct" injury on the claimant he was liable unless he established some defence. This is still the case in many situations: for example, if the claimant sues a police officer for false imprisonment there is no doubt that it is up to the officer to prove the exercise of a lawful power of arrest. The claimant must prove that he was arrested; the officer must prove that he was lawfully arrested if this is the case. At one time this approach was also taken to the basic, mental element

---

[254] See, e.g. *Davidson v CC North Wales* [1994] 2 All E.R. 597 (so held even though the informant was a store detective).

[255] *Ahmed v Shafique* [2009] EWHC 618 (QB). Cf. *Coles Myer Ltd v Webster* [2009] NSWCA 299 (invention of allegation led to liability).

[256] A claim for defamation will fail because it is now held that even a malicious informant is protected by absolute privilege: see para.12–41, below.

[257] *Melia v Neate* [1863] 3 F. & F. 757; *Roy v Prior* [1971] A.C. 470. See Ch.19.

[258] Winfield, "The Myth of Absolute Liability" (1926) 42 L.Q.R. 37 cf. Milsom (1958) 74 L.Q.R. at 582–583. See also Winfield and Goodhart, "Trespass and Negligence" (1933) 49 L.Q.R. 359; *Fowler v Lanning* [1959] 1 Q.B. 426 at 433 per Diplock J.

of the tort. Since a party is generally only required to plead and to prove those matters in respect of which the burden of proof lies on him, a declaration (or particulars of claim, in modern terminology) which alleged that "the defendant struck the claimant" was perfectly good. If the claimant proved that, by evidence, he did not necessarily win the case, for the defendant might show that it was a blameless accident; but failure by the defendant to plead and to prove that meant (assuming there was no other defence like lawful arrest in issue) that the claimant won—it was not incumbent on him to show that the defendant struck the blow intentionally or was negligent.[259] In contrast, where the injury was caused by indirect means the proper[260] cause of action was "case" and the claimant bore the burden of showing that the defendant's act failed to come up to the standard required by law.[261]

To the rule about the burden of proof in trespass, collisions on the highway were an exception.[262] The origin of this rule is obscure and Winfield, in common with most other writers, regarded it as both exceptional and historically unjustifiable.[263] Nevertheless, in *National Coal Board v Evans*[264] Cohen L.J. said that he could see no logical justification for restricting it to highway accidents, and in *Fowler v Lanning*[265] Diplock J. held generally that the burden of proving negligence in actions for unintentional trespass to the person lay upon the claimant.[266] Accordingly, the statement of claim, which recorded laconically that "the defendant shot the plaintiff", was struck out as disclosing no cause of action since it lacked an allegation of intention or negligence.

Fowler v Lanning was concerned only with the burden of proof as reflected in the principles of pleading: it did not hold that there could not be a negligent trespass. Some years later the relationship between trespass and negligence came before the Court of Appeal in

4–34

---

[259] In *Weaver v Ward* (1616) Hob. 134, there was an accident during militia exercises rather similar to that in *Fowler v Lanning*. On demurrer it was held that the defendant's plea did not amount to "inevitable accident" but the court said: "no man shall be excused of a trespass ... except it may be judged utterly without his fault as if a man by force take my hand and strike you or if here the defendant had said that the plaintiff ran across his [musket] when it was discharging, or had set forth the case with the circumstances so as it had appeared to the court that it had been inevitable and that the defendant had committed no negligence to give occasion to the hurt."

[260] But after *Williams v Holland* (1833) 10 Bing. 112, it was held that the claimant might sue in case if the injury, though direct, was not intentional.

[261] Of course then as now the happening of the accident might raise an inference of negligence for the purposes of proof.

[262] *Holmes v Mather* (1875) L.R. 10 Ex. 261; *Southport Corp v Esso Petroleum Co Ltd* [1956] A.C. 218 at 225–227 per Devlin J. affirmed by the House of Lords.

[263] The question could still be the subject of dispute in South Australia in 1980: *Lord v The Nominal Defendant* (1980) 24 S.A.S.R. 458.

[264] [1951] 2 K.B. 861 at 875.

[265] [1959] 1 Q.B. 426.

[266] The same result had been reached in Massachusetts as long ago as 1850: *Brown v Kendall* 6 Cush. 292.

the context of limitation of actions. In *Letang v Cooper*[267] the defendant drove his car over the legs of the claimant, who was sunbathing on a piece of grass outside a hotel where cars were parked. She did not issue a writ until more than three years had passed, which meant that a claim for negligence was statute-barred,[268] but she argued that she had an alternative claim in trespass, which was not statute-barred, the general tort limitation period being six years. This argument was rejected by the Court of Appeal for two reasons. One was that the three-year period prescribed by statute applied to all claims for personal injuries no matter what the cause of action.[269] However, the other reason is not a mere matter of statutory interpretation and concerns the structure of the law in this area. Lord Denning M.R. (with whom Danckwerts L.J. agreed) expressed his agreement with *Fowler v Lanning* but added:

> "I would go this one step further: when the injury is not inflicted intentionally but negligently, I would say the only cause of action is negligence and not trespass."[270]

On this view, trespass to the person is a tort only of intention (including within that term "subjective recklessness").[271] Diplock L.J. would not have gone quite so far. For him, a cause of action was simply a factual situation the existence of which entitles a person to obtain a remedy from the court and an action founded upon a failure to take reasonable care is an action for negligence notwithstanding that it can also be called an action for trespass to the person.[272] In particular, the claimant in such a case of "unintentional trespass" must show damage (whereas trespass proper is actionable per se) and has the burden of proof of negligence. In other words, the claimant gains no advantage from framing his claim in this way and the trespass liability becomes merely an alternative label for some cases of negligence.[273] Though it is true that the matter has not been fully explored in England since *Letang v Cooper*,[274] the net result appears to be that the action for unintentional trespass to the person

---

[267] [1965] 1 Q.B. 232.
[268] Nowadays the court might simply "disapply" the limitation period: see para.26–20, below.
[269] This view was subsequently declared to be wrong but has now been restored to favour. See para.26–18, below.
[270] [1965] 1 Q.B. at 240.
[271] As to this, see para.3–3, above.
[272] [1965] 1 Q.B. at 242–244.
[273] His Lordship would also presumably have accepted that claims for unintentional trespass to the person fall within the Law Reform (Contributory Negligence) Act 1945. As to intentional conduct, see para.6–44, below.
[274] In *Wilson v Pringle* [1987] Q.B. 237, the CA referred to the necessity for the touching in trespass to be "deliberate" and that is really the only view reconcilable with the requirement of hostility emphasised in that case.

has disappeared in practice (for Diplock L.J.) or even in name (for Lord Denning).[275]

To classify liability in this way according to the mental state of the defendant rather than solely according to the directness of the injury is, it is submitted, a welcome rationalisation of the law,[276] at least as far as concerns assault and battery. If claimants have lost a theoretical right to sue in respect of a negligently caused contact which causes no damage, that is something about which we need not lose any sleep. The reason why battery is actionable per se is because it protects and vindicates the claimant's autonomy and dignity and while those are seriously infringed by wilful conduct (in which we include conscious risk-taking) they are not (or at least not to the same degree) by negligent conduct.[277] A claimant who can establish a trespass may not need to show that the injury suffered thereby was foreseeable to the defendant, but it is thought that this advantage can be justified by reference to the wilful nature of the defendant's conduct.[278] In any event, even the law of negligence goes a good way down this road, since (1) it is not necessary that the precise nature or amount of the injury be foreseeable and (2) if any injury was foreseeable the defendant is liable even if, because of the claimant's pre-existing susceptibility, it is different to what would have been suffered by a normal person.[279] It is also true that in a case of negligence the claimant has to show that he was owed a duty of care by the defendant, a concept which serves the functions of eliminating or restricting certain types of claim for reasons of "policy" and of limiting the range of the defendant's liability in

4–35

---

[275] See *Bici v MoD* [2004] EWHC 786 (QB), *The Times*, June 11, 2004, where Elias J. held that intention or subjective recklessness was required.

[276] However, this view has not found favour in some other parts of the common law world. There is some support in Australia for the view that unintentional trespass to the person survives as an alternative to negligence, even to the extent of giving the claimant an advantage on the burden of proof. However, the High Court in *Hackshaw v Shaw* (1984) 155 C.L.R. 614 did not find it necessary to decide the issue. In Canada among cases supporting the survival of trespass, see *Larin v Goshen* (1975) 56 D.L.R. (3d) 719 and *Bell Canada v Cope (Sarnia) Ltd* (1980) 119 D.L.R. (3d) 254.

[277] See *Ashley v CC Sussex* [2008] UKHL 25; [2008] 1 A.C. 962, para.1–2, above.

[278] For a similar reason aggravated damages may be obtained for trespass but not for negligence: see para.22–8, below.

[279] D unlawfully shoots at X, misses and hits C. If D ought to have been aware of the risk to C, no doubt it is a case of negligence. However, C's presence may have been unforeseeable or C may wish to pursue a claim for aggravated or exemplary damages, obtainable only if there is a trespass. The criminal law has a well-developed doctrine of "transferred intent", which would make D guilty of assault of C in such circumstances. In the USA this is firmly embedded in tort law (see Prosser, "Transferred Intent" (1967) 45 Texas L.Rev. 650) and was applied by the Northern Ireland CA in a civil action in *Livingstone v MoD* [1984] N.I. 356 (D fired baton round and hit C, liable for battery even if he intended to hit another person unless he could show justification. Of course, if D was justified with regard to the other person, that would not necessarily preclude a claim for negligence by C). Followed in *Bici v MoD* [2004] EWHC 786 (QB), *The Times*, June 11, 2004, but with doubt whether the principle could be applied to assault as opposed to battery.

respect of such claims as are admitted.[280] In fact the first function is rarely relevant in cases of personal injury, where a duty of care exists almost without qualification and in so far as it may be relevant it is hard to believe that any court would have ignored the issue of policy merely because the claimant's claim was framed as "unintentional trespass".[281] With regard to the second function, we apply the test of whether the claimant was a reasonably foreseeable victim of the defendant's act. As to this, it is hardly surprising that the trespass cases were not concerned with it because trespass already has its own built-in and usually more restrictive control device in the form of the requirement of directness. It is the law, as we have seen,[282] that where A aims a blow at B, misses and hits C, then A commits battery against C even if no contact with him was foreseeable. That, it is suggested, is sound policy where A is a wilful wrongdoer but (once again) it is difficult to see why it should apply to the case where A is not wilful just because the contact he makes with C happens to be "direct".

4. Acts Intended to Cause Physical Harm, Other than Trespass to the Person

4–36   If the argument in the previous section be accepted one situation remains to be dealt with. All claims for unintentional harm would fall under the head of negligence but history confines trespass to the infliction of harm by direct means.[283] So what is the position in the situation where the harm is intentionally but indirectly inflicted —the surreptitious poisoning, for example? It is not battery but one can hardly describe attempted murder as "negligence". The problem is really one of terminology, arising from the fact that we have chosen the term negligence to describe what our ancestors would have called "the action on the case". Plainly it cannot be the law that if D is liable for doing a thing negligently he escapes liability if he does it intentionally. For many years it has been customary to say

---

[280] See para.5–3, below.

[281] The major type of personal injury case where the duty of care has been restricted is the case arising out of nervous shock suffered from witnessing injury to others (see para.5–66, below). But it is hard to see how a trespass-based claim could be relevant in such a case since the claimant is *ex hypothesi* not within the area of danger and not fearful for his own safety. Nevertheless in *Breslin v McKenna* [2009] NIQB 50 some claimants appear to have recovered damages for psychiatric injury on the basis of trespass even though they were not in the vicinity of the explosion.

[282] See fn.279, above.

[283] Of course it might be better if history were different. Compare the simple provision of §823(1) of the German BGB: "A person who *wilfully or negligently* unlawfully injures the life, body, health, freedom, property or other right of another is bound to compensate him for any damage arising therefrom."

that such liability rests upon the case of *Wilkinson v Downton*.[284] D, by way of a practical joke, falsely told C, a married woman, that her husband had met with an accident in which both his legs had been broken, was lying at The Elms at Leytonstone and that she was to go in a cab to fetch him home. The effect of this upon the claimant, who was found to be a person of normal fortitude, was that she suffered a violent shock:

"[P]roducing vomiting and other more serious and permanent physical consequences at one time threatening her reason, and entailing weeks of suffering and incapacity."[285]

In holding D liable to C, Wright J. said that:

"[T]he defendant has ... wilfully done an act calculated to cause physical harm to the plaintiff-that is to say, to infringe her legal right to safety, and has in fact thereby caused physical harm to her. That proposition without more appears to state a good cause of action, there being no justification alleged for the act."[286]

The principle was approved and applied by the Court of Appeal on somewhat similar facts in *Janvier v Sweeney*[287] where a private detective, in order to get papers from the claimant, falsely represented that he was a police officer and that she was in danger of arrest for association with a German spy, thereby causing her psychiatric trauma.

The difficulty with regarding *Wilkinson v Downton* as resting on a liability for intentionally caused harm is that it is most unlikely that Downton intended to produce the result which he did or even foresaw it, indeed Wright J.'s judgment implies that he did not.[288] "Calculated to cause harm" is ambiguous, for the phrase could refer to harm actually contemplated by the defendant—subjective recklessness—or to harm which a reasonable person would foresee as a

4–37

---

[284] [1897] 2 Q.B. 57.
[285] In comparison with other nervous shock victims the claimant was perhaps treated generously, no doubt because of the outrageous behaviour of the defendant. Note that if D had in fact injured C's husband in the way stated and she had suffered this shock on being told by X, she could not have recovered damages from D: see para.5–68, below.
[286] [1897] 2 Q.B. 57 at 58–59. Described by Stuart-Smith L.J. in *W v Essex CC* [1999] Fam. 90 at 114 as "the peculiar tort".
[287] [1919] 2 K.B. 316.
[288] See [1897] 2 Q.B. 57 at 59; *Wong v Parkside Health NHS Trust* [2001] EWCA Civ 1721; [2003] 3 All E.R. 932 at [8]. But in *Janvier v Sweeney* the jury specifically found that the defendant knew that injury might be caused.

probable result[289] and it is the latter which fits the facts.[290] It has since been pointed out[291] that the real problem in *Wilkinson v Downton* was a different one, namely that a few years before, the Privy Council in *Victorian Ry Commrs v Coultas*[292] had held that "nervous shock" was not a recoverable head of damage in a claim arising from a negligent act and that Wright J. seems really to have been concerned to escape the shackles of that case by declining to apply it to an imputed or "deemed" intention. Although the liability for nervous shock is still very different from that for other forms of injury arising from negligence,[293] the *Coultas* restriction disappeared from the law within a few years of *Wilkinson v Downton* and it has been said in *Wainwright v Home Office* that, "there is no point in arguing about whether the injury was in some sense intentional if negligence will do just as well" and that *Wilkinson v Downton*, "has no leading role in the modern law".[294] This, however, seems to go too far, if we are talking about principle rather than the mechanism by which that case would be decided today. If harm is inflicted intentionally (that is to say, with the purpose of causing it or knowingly reckless as to its occurring) it is surely a misuse of language to describe it as falling within a claim for negligence, even if the historical origin of our law of negligence is an action on the case which also comprehended intentional harm. Many other cases could be imagined where the source of the harm is something other than a statement or where the harm is something other than psychiatric injury. For example, I might scare a person into nervous shock by dressing up as a ghost[295] or subject the claimant to some terrifying spectacle.[296] Nor need the principle be confined to shock. If I

---

[289] Thus "calculated to" in the Defamation Act 1952, s.3, plainly means "likely to" whether or not the defendant actually foresaw the consequence.

[290] Cf. *Hall v Gwent Healthcare NHS Trust* [2005] EWCA Civ 919, an even more terrible warning against practical joking, where the lies were told to a third person who inflicted the damage and which would not even have passed the latter threshold.

[291] *Wainwright v Home Office* [2003] UKHL 53; [2004] 2 A.C. 406 at [37] per Lord Hoffmann.

[292] (1888) 13 App. Cas. 222.

[293] See paras 5–61 to 5–74, below.

[294] *Wainwright*, above, fn.29, at [41]. However, it was applied in *C v D* [2006] EWHC 166 (QB) where the defendant was found to be reckless as to the causing of psychiatric injury.

[295] Although a claim for shock based on negligence by a person who is abnormally susceptible may not be sustainable (see para.5–66, below) there is no reason to apply such a rule to wilful conduct, even, perhaps, if D is not aware of C's susceptibility.

[296] See *Blakely v Shortal's Estate* 20 N.W. 2d 28 (1945) (D cut his throat in C's kitchen). Cf. *Bunyan v Jordan* (1937) 57 C.L.R. 1 and *Bradley v Wingnut Films Ltd* [1994] E.M.L.R. 195 (where it was found that the defendants had no reason to anticipate causing shock). Liability for negligence is well established where, in C's presence, D negligently kills or injures (or even puts in danger) C's loved one (see para.5–66, below). A fortiori, there must be liability where D wilfully harms the loved one. See, e.g. *Johnson v Commonwealth* (1927) 27 S.R. (N.S.W.) 133. One might question whether, in view of D's wilful behaviour one should insist in such cases on a tie of love and affection between C and the person attacked.

suddenly shout at a child who is descending a difficult staircase, intending the child to fall, I am surely liable if it does so and breaks its neck. The administration of a noxious drug to an unwitting victim might be another illustration, assuming it not to be battery because there is no element of "force" (if accompanied by false representations it might also be the tort of deceit[297]).[298] It is perfectly true that at the end of the day the defendant will be liable whether he desired to kill, or foresaw death as a possibility but was indifferent to it, or thought there was no risk of death but making the claimant ill would be a good joke, or merely left the poison out by complete inadvertence in circumstances where it might be consumed—but it looks very odd to treat all these scenarios as if they were exactly the same: wicked people are worse than careless people and we should not forget it.[299] We recognise the vindicatory role of the trespass torts[300] and the same should be true of wilful wrongdoing which, for technical, historical reasons, does not fall within them. Nor are the objections purely linguistic, for it cannot be assumed that there are no substantive consequences. Thus the law of damages differs: it is far from clear that aggravated damages are available for negligence and exemplary damages certainly are not, but sometimes they are where the defendant acts intentionally.[301] However, one problem which was formerly a frequent source of "classification" issues has largely gone away: the expression "negligence, nuisance or breach of duty" in the Limitation Act 1980 is capable of including claims for personal injury caused by trespass.[302]

Whether we subsume these cases within negligence or continue to classify them differently, a more serious practical problem is the nature of the damage which they cover. Mrs Wilkinson suffered shock, which is now well-recognised in law as a variety of personal injury. However, in the United States liability under a theory for extreme and outrageous conduct has been extended to cover distress or humiliation without psychiatric trauma amounting to illness. Such "harm" is plainly recoverable as part of the damages for

---

[297] In *Wilkinson v Downton* the claimant recovered a total of £100 1s. 10½d., the 1s. 10½d being recovered in deceit as representing the cost of the railway fares of persons she sent to Leytonstone.

[298] Similarly the principle might in some cases extend to the intentional infection of another person with disease. See *R v Dica* [2004] EWCA Crim 1103; [2004] Q.B. 1257, para.25–5, below.

[299] In *Breslin v McKenna* [2009] NIQB 50 the explosion of a bomb with a timing device was held to be battery but if it had not been the judge would have applied *Wilkinson v Downton*. He took the view, on the basis of *Wong v Parkside Health NHS Trust*, above, fn.288, that there was a middle ground between intention/recklessness and negligence whereby the, "degree of harm is sufficiently likely to result that the defendant cannot be heard to say that he did not 'mean' it to do so" and that where personal injury (as opposed to mere distress) had been caused, this view had been neither approved nor disapproved in *Wainwright*.

[300] *Ashley v CC Sussex* [2008] UKHL 25; [2008] 1 A.C. 962, para.1–2, above.

[301] On aggravated and exemplary damages see para.22–8, below.

[302] See para.26–18, below.

trespass to the person or other torts, such as libel, which are action-able per se; equally plainly, it does not amount to sufficient damage to found an action for negligence[303] or any other action stemming from "case". On the existing authorities English common law does not go so far as American law in this respect.[304] Lord Hoffmann has reserved his opinion on whether the law should be extended, but only on the basis that a real intention is present and with the caveat that:

> "[I]n institutions and workplaces all over the country, people constantly do and say things with the intention of causing distress and humiliation to others. This shows lack of consideration and appalling manners but I am not sure that the right way to deal with it is always by litigation".[305]

One reason for caution in extending the common law is that the statutory tort of harassment[306] allows recovery of damages for "among other things ... anxiety".

5. The Protection from Harassment Act 1997

4–38 Section 1 of this Act makes it an offence to pursue a course of conduct[307] which the defendant knows or ought to know[308] amounts to harassment of another[309] and by s.3 this is civilly actionable, leading to, "damages ... for (among other things) any anxiety caused by the harassment and any financial loss resulting from the

---

[303] For an extreme illustration, see *Hicks v CC South Yorkshire* [1992] 2 All E.R. 65 (fear of approaching death). However, where physical injury has been suffered, matters like worry and anxiety may increase those damages in their non-pecuniary aspect: see para.22–19, below.

[304] *Wong v Parkside Health NHS Trust* [2001] EWCA Civ 1721; [2003] 3 All E.R. 932 at [11]. See also *Giller v Procopets* [2008] VSCA 236.

[305] *Wainwright v Home Office* [2003] UKHL 53; [2004] 2 A.C. 406 at [46]. Cf. Lord Scott at [62]: it does not and it should not extend to such "harm". However, there are now extensive statutory provisions rendering unlawful harassment at work on the basis of matters on which the law forbids discrimination. The definition of harassment is not identical with that in the Protection from Harassment Act 1997 and there is no express requirement of repetition. See, e.g. s.3B of the Disability Discrimination Act 1995, added by the Disability Discrimination Act 1995 (Amendment) Regulations 2003, SI 2003/1673.

[306] Below.

[307] Conduct includes speech: s.7(3).

[308] But this is to be decided without reference to any mental illness or characteristic of the accused: *R. v C* [2001] EWCA Crim 1251; *The Times*, June 14, 2001; and see *Banks v Ablex Ltd* [2005] EWCA Civ 173; [2005] I.C.R. 819.

[309] A corporate body is incapable of being harassed within the meaning of the Act: *Daiichi UK Ltd v Stop Huntington Animal Cruelty* [2003] EWHC 2337 (QB); [2004] 1 W.L.R. 1503 (but see *SmithKlineBeecham Plc v Avery* [2009] EWHC 1488 (QB)).

harassment".[310] Damages may, therefore, be awarded for the sort of psychiatric damage that was suffered by the victim in *R. v Ireland*,[311] but also for lesser degrees of psychic disturbance.[312] An injunction may also be granted in respect of future conduct.[313] A "course of conduct" must involve conduct on at least two occasions.[314] Putting a person in fear of violence on at least two occasions by a course of conduct is a more serious offence under the Act but is not made civilly actionable as such. Plainly, however, the greater includes the lesser and such conduct will fall under the general crime of harassment and will therefore be civilly actionable by that route. Beyond this the Act makes no attempt to define harassment. It has been said that one has to draw a distinction between conduct which is, "unattractive, even unreasonable, and conduct which is oppressive and unacceptable"[315] and in doing this one must take account of the context in which the conduct takes place.[316] It has been held at first instance that chanting intended to disrupt a graduation ceremony was not harassment because there was insufficient evidence that anyone was "alarmed, distressed, threatened or frightened" even though they were annoyed, though the line between distress and annoyance may be hard to draw.[317] At

[310] In accordance with general principle an employer is vicariously liable for conduct by an employee which contravenes the Act, including conduct directed at fellow employees, provided there is a sufficiently close connection between the conduct and the employment: *Majrowski v Guy's and St. Thomas's NHS Trusts* [2006] UKHL 34; [2007] 1 A.C. 224. The standard of proof in civil cases is the ordinary civil one of a balance of probabilities: *Jones v Hipgrave* [2004] EWHC 2901 (QB). The, "only real difference between the crime of s.2 and the tort of s.3 is standard of proof": *Ferguson v British Gas Trading Ltd* [2009] EWCA Civ 46; [2010] 1 W.L.R. 785 at [17].

[311] See para.4–13, above. See also *Singh v Bhakar*, Cty Ct, July 24, 2006.

[312] *S & D Property Investments Ltd v Nisbet* [2009] EWHC 1726 (Ch). However, such damages are likely to be modest: at [76].

[313] The exercise of this power in a proper case does not infringe art.10 of the European Convention on Human Rights: *Howlett v Holding* [2006] EWHC 41 (QB).

[314] Thus the conduct in *Janvier v Sweeney* [1919] 2 K.B. 316 would presumably be harassment in the ordinary sense of that word but might not be actionable under the Act because it was committed on only one occasion. See *Dowson v CC Northumbria* [2009] EWHC 907 (QB). D engages in covert surveillance of C on a number of occasions. On, say, the sixth occasion C finds out and becomes concerned. If C has reason to believe it may be repeated that falls within the Act: *Howlett v Holding*, above, fn.313. By s.1(1A) inserted by the Serious Organized Crime and Police Act 2005, where the harassment is of two or more persons there need only be conduct on one occasion in relation to each person, but s.1(1A) does not give rise to a civil claim for damages. Section 1(3) provides that the Act does not apply to a course of conduct pursued for the purpose of preventing or detecting crime but it has been suggested that in the light of the Human Rights Act 1998, s.1(3) contains a requirement of necessity or proportionality: *KD v CC Hampshire* [2005] EWHC 2550 (QB). In any event it does not give carte blanche to any citizen to set up as a vigilante: *Howlett v Holding*.

[315] *Majrowski v Guy's and St Thomas's NHS Trusts* [2006] UKHL 34; [2007] 1 A.C. 224 at [30].

[316] *Conn v Sunderland CC* [2007] EWCA Civ 1492; [2008] I.R.L.R. 324.

[317] *University of Oxford v Broughton* [2008] EWHC 75 (QB) (an application for an interim injunction); but an injunction had earlier been granted against disruption of examinations: at [25].

any rate harassment goes well beyond causing fear of violence. It is capable of embracing, for example, persistent following, questioning or "doorstepping" by journalists; methods of debt collection which are humiliating, threatening or distressing[318] or persistent unjustified demands for payment[319]; newspaper articles[320] or other publications[321]; or conduct in the course of a neighbour dispute which is designed to distress, for example, playing loud music or banging on walls. There is, therefore, a good deal of overlap with liability at common law[322] and legislation prompted by the phenomenon of "stalking" has become a formidable engine of control of offensive behaviour.

Harassment in its ordinary sense seems to imply something sustained and intended to distress.[323] So if D quarrels with C in 2000 and makes an abusive telephone call to him on that occasion and this is repeated in 2001, but as a result of a wholly independent quarrel, that would not, it is submitted, fall within the Act.[324] Nor would one describe the constant playing of loud music, caused not by spite but by selfish indifference to neighbours, as harassment,[325] though it may amount to a common law nuisance and an offence under other legislation governing noise. If there are criminal proceedings for harassment, the court dealing with the offender may make a restrain-

---

[318] *S & D Property Investments Ltd v Nisbet* [2009] EWHC 1726 (Ch). This may enable the claimant to set off the damages against the debt sought to be enforced.

[319] *Allen v Southwark LBC* [2008] EWCA Civ 1478; *Ferguson v British Gas Trading Ltd* [2009] EWCA Civ 46; [2010] 1 W.L.R. 785. A corporate defendant cannot necessarily escape by saying, "Oh well, everyone knows computerised systems produce silly errors and you cannot prove that anyone particular person here knew about it": *Ferguson*. Cf. *Bowden v Spiegel Inc.* 216 P.2d 571 (Cal. 1950) where a claim under the Act would fail, because the conduct was only on one occasion.

[320] *Thomas v News Group Newspapers Ltd* [2001] EWCA Civ 1233; [2002] E.M.L.R. 4. But press criticism which is robust and likely to cause distress is not harassment unless it is an abuse of press freedom.

[321] *Howlett v Holding,* above, fn.313.

[322] Thus the journalists' doorstepping would be trespass and the conduct by the neighbour would be nuisance. The rather protean nature of the Act makes it difficult to decide where to place it in a book like this. There is also some overlap with the power to make anti-social behaviour orders under the Crime and Disorder Act 1998.

[323] The conduct must be targeted at an individual: *Thomas v News Group Newspapers Ltd* [2001] EWCA Civ 1233; [2002] E.M.L.R. 4 at [30] but presumably in an employment context this condition might be satisfied if the claimant made it known that he objected to persistent conduct not particularly directed at him.

[324] Even where the incidents arise out of the same matter, it has been said that the fewer the incidents and the wider apart they are, the less likely they are to constitute harassment: *Lau v DPP, The Times*, March 29, 2000.

[325] s.1(2) provides that, "the person whose course of conduct is in question ought to know that it amounts to harassment of another if a reasonable person in possession of the same information would think the course of conduct amounted to harassment of the other." This would cover, e.g. conduct directed at the victim which the defendant regards as a joke but which a reasonable person would regard as going beyond that.

ing order prohibiting the defendant from doing anything described in the order[326] and in practice this seems likely to be more important than civil claims under the Act for an injunction.

[326] See s.5.

CHAPTER 5

NEGLIGENCE: DUTY AND BREACH

5–1 As was stated earlier, negligence may mean a "mental" element in
tortious liability (or, indeed, any other form of liability) or it may
mean an independent tort. In this chapter we are concerned with
negligence in the latter sense.[1]

*Negligence as a tort is a breach of a legal duty to take care which
results in damage to the claimant.* Thus its ingredients are, (1) a
legal duty on the part of D towards C to exercise care in such
conduct of D as falls within the scope of the duty; (2) breach of that
duty, i.e. a failure to come up to the standard required by law; and
(3) consequential damage to C which can be attributed to D's
conduct.[2] This chapter deals with the first two elements; consequential damage is discussed in Ch.6, as is the contributory fault of the
claimant. As the concept of foreseeability plays a part in all of these
elements they cannot always be kept apart, and it has been said that,
"they are simply three different ways of looking at the same problem".[3] Suppose, for example, that D jostles X, causing X to drop
something and this sets off a very unexpected train of events which
causes injury to C, standing many feet away.[4] If one wished to hold
that D was not liable to C one might say that D owed him no duty
of care because he could not foresee injury to him; or that he owed
him a duty of care but had not broken it because he could not foresee
that his conduct would cause C harm; or that he owed him a duty of
care and had broken it but the damage was not legally attributable to
him because no one could have foreseen it. The orthodox answer is
the first (which has the advantage of solving the case at the first step)
but they are all plausible and some may think that the second is the
most convincing. Nevertheless, while it must always be borne in
mind that the three elements overlap and their separation is artificial
in some cases,[5] this structure does accord with the way in which
most cases are approached by the English courts. However, because
we use words in a rather loose way, we must be alert that we do not,
merely because the word "duty" is used, put the legal issue in the
wrong box. For example, there is no doubt that the user of a vehicle
is liable to other road users if an accident occurs because it is not
kept in roadworthy condition. Suppose that in a particular case (the
example is entirely imaginary) a road accident is caused by a burst
tyre, that the defect in the tyre would have been observed if the user
had checked his car before setting off on Tuesday but that the court

---

[1] For history, see Winfield, "The History of Negligence in the Law of Torts" (1926) 42
L.Q.R. 184; Fifoot, *History of the Common Law*, Ch.8.
[2] This approach has been said to be "technically wrong" but since in the same case it is said
to be "commonplace" and "convenient" we shall stick to it: *Sam v Atkins* [2005] EWCA
Civ 1452; [2006] R.T.R. 171 at [14].
[3] *Roe v Minister of Health* [1954] 2 Q.B. 66 at 86, CA per Denning L.J.
[4] See *Palsgraf v Long Island R.R.* 162 N.E. 99 (N.Y. 1928), para.5–21, below.
[5] See further, para.5–23, below.

rejects the claim because the defendant had checked the tyres on Monday, as he always did. One might very well say that the defendant "owed no duty to check the tyres before each trip" but the issue is clearly one of breach ((2) above) not of duty of care. It is self-evident that he owes other road users a duty to take care for their safety and that this includes the maintenance of the vehicle; what we are concerned with is how he must behave in order to fulfil it.

It is also important to be aware of the relationship between elements (1) and (3) above. It has been said to be meaningless to ask whether D owes C a duty of care without also considering the type of damage in question: while the defendant may be under a duty to safeguard the claimant against one type of damage (for example, physical damage to his property) he may not be under such a duty in respect of another type of damage (for example, pure financial loss).[6]

Although the tort of negligence is of very general application it frequently occurs in a number of standard situations: accidents on the road or at work, medical misadventure, defective premises, professional advice and so on. In some of these cases, although liability is essentially based upon negligence it is put into statutory form[7] or there are important additional statutory provisions which rest on some other basis[8]; in others, although there has been little statutory intervention, there are enough special features in the way the law is applied to justify a separate treatment.[9] The first part of this chapter is concerned with the theoretical basis of the duty of care concept and examines certain areas in which this problem has been particularly prominent in the modern law. Some of the other areas form the basis of subsequent chapters.

1. DUTY OF CARE: GENERAL

It is not for every careless act that a person may be held responsible **5–2** in tort law, nor even for every careless act that causes damage. He will only be liable in negligence if he is under a legal duty to take care. It may be objected that "duty" is not confined to the law of negligence and that it is an element in every tort, because there is a legal duty not to commit assault or battery, not to commit defamation, not to commit nuisance and so on. In a sense that is true, but all that "duty" signifies in those torts is the comparatively simple proposition that you must not commit them: they have their own,

[6] *Caparo Industries Plc v Dickman* [1990] 2 A.C. 605 at 627; *S v Gloucestershire CC* [2001] 2 W.L.R. 909 at 932. See para.6–27, below.
[7] See occupiers' liability: Ch.9.
[8] See employer's liability for work accidents, Ch.8, and liability for defective products, Ch.10.
[9] See Ch.11, liability for statements.

detailed, internal rules which define the circumstances in which they are committed and duty adds nothing to those.[10] But in the tort of negligence, "duty" is the core ingredient of the tort. A general liability for carelessly causing harm to others would, at least as things are perceived by the courts, be too onerous for a practical system of law and we shall see that there are areas of activity and types of loss where the law of negligence does not intervene or intervenes only in a limited way.[11] Thus there can be no liability in respect of loss caused by incorrect evidence given in court; there is no general liability for failing to assist or protect others; and while one cannot say that there is *no* duty of care in respect of economic loss caused by negligence, the liability which exists in that context is considerably more restricted than that in respect of physical damage. What was said by du Parcq L.J. in 1946 is as true now as it was then (even though the range of recognised duties has increased substantially in the intervening years), namely, that:

> "[I]t is not true to say that whenever a person finds himself in such a position that unless he does a certain act another person may suffer, or that if he does something another person will suffer, it is his duty in the one case to be careful to do the act and in the other case to be careful not to do the act."[12]

On the facts the defendant, an employer of a pantomime artiste, was not liable for failing to take steps to provide secure locks on the theatre dressing rooms because there was no duty to guard employees' property against theft. Duty is the primary control device which allows the courts to keep liability for negligence within what they regard as acceptable limits and the controversies which have centred around the criteria for the existence of a duty reflect differences of opinion as to the proper ambit of liability for negligence.

A. The Place of the Duty Issue in the Law

5–3   The concept of the duty of care has in modern times shown signs of becoming an arcane mystery. An Australian judge in 1998,

---

[10] In rejecting the argument that battery was a "breach of duty" in the context of the Limitation Act 1980 s.11, Lord Griffiths said: "If I invite a lady to my house one would naturally think of a duty to take care that the house is safe but would one really be thinking of a duty not to rape her?". *Stubbings v Webb* [1993] A.C. 498 at 508, HL. However, the Act is now given a broader interpretation: para.26–18, below.

[11] Contrast French law, where the concept of "duty" is entirely absent from the *Code civil* and the case law. Of course this is not the whole story—a claim for economic loss which in England would be thrown out at the duty level might be rejected in France for an inadequate causal link. But that is less a "question of law" and more a matter for the impression of the trial judge. German tort law has no concept of duty but the way the Civil Code (the BGB) is structured around protected interests sometimes produces much the same result as the English cases.

[12] *Deyong v Shenburn* [1946] K.B. 227 at 233, CA.

having referred to the "foundation" judgment of Lord Atkin in *Donoghue v Stevenson*,[13] remarked that, "the modern abundance of authority [on the duty of care] ... would not make Lord Atkin much wiser."[14] Nevertheless, much difficulty will be avoided if it is grasped at the outset that duty is fulfilling two functions. It is true that the question in every case is "did *this* defendant owe a duty of care to *this* claimant?" for the courts do not decide academic issues but disputes between parties. Nevertheless, in most of the cases in this section the courts have been concerned with broader questions which transcend the particular dispute and which are essentially concerned with whether, and if so how far, the law of negligence should operate in a situation of a particular type. Discussion is therefore couched in terms of general categories, such as "Is there a duty of care not to cause economic loss by statements?" or "Is there a duty to prevent a third party inflicting harm on another?" and the court is essentially concerned with mapping the limits of the law of negligence and identifying those areas in which there are factors (fairness, practicability, risk of untoward consequences) which suggest that the law should not give a remedy for negligent conduct or at least should do so only to a limited extent. It was, therefore, perfectly possible for the House of Lords in *Hedley Byrne & Co Ltd v Heller & Partners Ltd*[15] to decide[16] (1) that there was a duty of care recognised by English law in respect of statements; but (2) no duty was owed on the facts by the defendant to the claimant.[17] In the sense now being considered the issue of duty is a question of law. The question duty or no duty ultimately depends in most (and perhaps all) cases on the court's assessment of what is fair, just and reasonable,[18] but that question is asked not in the context of justice as between the particular parties to the case but in the context of all cases of that type.

> "Once the decision is taken that, say, company auditors though liable to shareholders for negligent auditing are not liable to those proposing to invest in the company[19] ... that decision will apply to all future cases of the same kind."[20]

Accordingly, to traditional thinking the issue was often suitable to be dealt with on a striking out application or as a preliminary issue,

[13] See para.5–5, below.
[14] Priestley J.A. in *Avenhouse v Hornsby SC* (1998) 44 N.S.W.L.R. 1, NSWCA.
[15] [1964] A.C. 465, para.11–16, below.
[16] It is unrealistic to say that because of proposition (2) proposition (1) was obiter.
[17] On the facts this was because of a disclaimer and disclaimers are no longer automatically valid (see para.11–30, below).
[18] See para.5–13, below.
[19] See para.5–14, below.
[20] *Barrett v Enfield LBC* [2001] 2 A.C. 550 at 560 per Lord Browne-Wilkinson. *Cooper v Hobart* [2001] SCC 79; [2001] 3 S.C.R. 537 at [37].

where the case would be decided on the assumption that the facts alleged by the claimant could be proved at the trial. For a while it looked as if this expedited procedure would be blocked altogether by the fair trial guarantee in art.6 of the European Convention on Human Rights. It now seems clear that this is not so and that it is legitimate, in the context of art.6,[21] for the substantive law to lay down that liability may be excluded in all situations of a particular type so long as that is a proper and proportionate response to what it conceives to be the needs of public policy.[22] However, the question of what is fair, just and reasonable may not lend itself to "bright line" rules established without close examination of the facts[23] and this is particularly so:

"[I]n an area of the law which [is] uncertain and developing . . . [where] it is not normally appropriate to strike out . . . [I]t is of great importance that such development should be on the basis of actual facts found at trial not on hypothetical facts assumed (possibly wrongly) to be true for the purpose of the strike out".[24]

This is particularly likely to be so where the case turns on the exercise of a discretionary power by a public authority.[25] On the other hand, where the matter can be dealt with at a preliminary stage as an issue of law the court should not hesitate to do so.[26] The Civil Procedure Rules enable these matters to be dealt with in a rather more flexible way than was once the case. There is no longer any complete embargo on adducing evidence on a striking out application and in the alternative the defendant may apply for summary judgment on the ground that the case has no real prospect of success, which extends further than objections to the pleaded case.[27] By proper use of these procedures it may be possible to dispose of weak claims without a full trial in a manner which satisfies the requirements of art.6.[28]

---

[21] But that does not preclude a challenge under one of the guarantees of substantive rights. So in *Z v UK* (2002) 34 E.H.R.R. 3 (see para.2–13, above) the ECHR disclaimed any power to consider the rule of tort law under art.6 but held that the state of the domestic law amounted to a breach of art.3 of the Convention.

[22] See para.2–13, above.

[23] Even "quite feeble" particulars of negligence may prevent a striking out nowadays: *Strickland v Hertfordshire CC* [2003] EWHC 287 (QB). In a criminal case of gross negligence manslaughter the existence of a duty of care is a matter for the judge, not the jury: *R v Evans* [2009] EWCA Crim 650; [2009] 1 W.L.R. 1999.

[24] *Barrett v Enfield LBC*, above, fn.20, at 557 per Lord Browne-Wilkinson.

[25] As to which see para.5–45, below.

[26] *Kent v Griffiths* [2001] Q.B. 36 at 51.

[27] *Sutradhar v National Environment Research Council* [2006] UKHL 33; [2006] 4 All E.R. 490. So it is no longer always necessary for the defendant to show that the claim must plainly and obviously fail as a matter of law.

[28] *S v Gloucestershire CC* [2001] 2 W.L.R. 909, especially at 935–937.

In the sense now being considered, the issue of duty arises **5-4** comparatively rarely in the day-to-day business of the courts and tends to be the preserve of the Court of Appeal and the House of Lords.[29] Most cases of negligence arise from acts directly causing physical damage to persons or property and there the law is much more straightforward. No one would think of opening a running-down case by citing authorities to show that a duty of care was owed by a driver to a pedestrian.[30] Speaking of damage to property (and if anything the proposition must be even more true with regard to personal injury) the Privy Council[31] has said that:

"[T]he question of the existence of a duty of care does not give rise to any problem because it is self-evident that such a duty exists and the contrary view is unarguable"[32]

and in *Caparo Industries Plc v Dickman*[33] Lord Oliver said that in the case of physical damage, "the existence of the nexus [of duty] between the careless defendant and the injured plaintiff can rarely give rise to any difficulty".

"Personal or physical injury directly inflicted is the first building block of the law of negligence. Unless such injury is excused, it will almost always be a component of a breach of a duty of care owed by the person inflicting the injury to the person or the owner of the material object injured."[34]

Of course, it would be going too far to say that there is a universal duty in respect of foreseeable physical damage. For example, one might pause before holding one safe-blower liable to another for

---

[29] The issue of the duty of care has come before the House of Lords or Privy Council remarkably frequently since 1970.

[30] Compare *Langley v Dray* [1998] P.I.Q.R. P314, an unsuccessful attempt to complicate a simple road traffic case with a duty issue.

[31] Speaking through Lord Brandon, whose dissent in *Junior Books v Veitchi* [1983] 1 A.C. 520 marks a turning point in the reaction against liability for other types of loss in the 1980s.

[32] *Mobil Oil Hong Kong Ltd v Hong Kong United Dockyards Ltd* [1991] 2 Lloyd's Rep. 309 at 328.

[33] [1990] 2 A.C. 605 at 633.

[34] *Sandhar v Dept of Transport* [2004] EWCA Civ 1440; [2005] P.I.Q.R. P13 at [38] per May L.J. Note the "directly"—the position is by no means necessarily the same where the injury is directly inflicted by a third party and the complaint is that the defendant failed to prevent that: see para.5–26 below. In *K v Secretary of State for the Home Dept* [2002] EWCA Civ 775; *The Times*, July 22, 2002, Laws L.J. attempted a synthesis whereby the role of a "third agency" (which might include market forces as well as the actions of human beings) in the infliction of the harm explained most of the cases, whether of economic loss or of physical damage, in which the law drew back from imposing a duty of care. However, Arden L.J. had reservations and Simon Brown L.J. preferred to express no opinion.

mismanaging the gelignite,[35] and there are cases where the imposition of liability even for physical damage might be undesirable because it would cut across some other legal regime governing damage of that type.[36] Nevertheless, it remains true that in physical damage cases there are few "duty" problems of this type. It would, therefore, be wrong to envisage negligence as a sea of non-liability surrounding areas of liability. If anything, the true picture is the reverse, for as Lord Goff said[37]:

> "[T]he broad general principle of liability for foreseeable damage is so widely applicable that the function of the duty of care is not so much to identify cases where liability is imposed as to identify those where it is not",

a proposition which it is thought, as a practical matter in terms of cases coming before the courts, has survived the subsequent attacks on the decision in which it has its origin.[38]

If, however, a duty does exist in this general sense then there may be an issue whether it is applicable to the particular facts before the court or, as it is sometimes said, whether it was owed to the particular claimant. For example, the House of Lords in *Donoghue v Stevenson*[39] was concerned with the general question whether a manufacturer owed a duty of care to the ultimate user of his products and the conclusion was that he did. If, however, the product had been stolen from his factory and taken to Australia where, many years later, it caused injury to C, then it might be a difficult question to determine whether a duty was owed to C, that is to say, whether C was a foreseeable victim of the initial negligence in manufacture. This is the second sense of duty[40] but if there is no duty in the first, general, sense we never get to the second question. As is explained below, we might arguably dispense with duty in the second sense[41] but without duty in the first sense we have no means of explaining at least some of those situations in which foreseeable damage goes without legal redress.

Many duties of care are long established (for example, the duties owed by drivers to other road users and of employers in respect of the safety of their workers). Others are of more recent vintage

---

[35] See para.25–20, below.
[36] See *Marc Rich & Co A.G. v Bishop Rock Marine Co Ltd* [1996] A.C. 211, para.5–13, below.
[37] *Smith v Littlewoods Organisation Ltd* [1987] A.C. 241 at 280, HL.
[38] Lord Goff was referring to the speech of Lord Wilberforce in *Anns v Merton London Borough* [1978] A.C. 758: see below.
[39] [1932] A.C. 562, para.5–5, below.
[40] Earlier editions of this book referred to the first question as the "notional duty" and to this as "duty in fact".
[41] See para.5–23, below.

but nonetheless firmly fixed in the law, though they may still be in the course of development (for example, the duty of a person who has "assumed responsibility" for a task[42]). Is there any universal principle which explains the duties of care which exist and those cases where a duty has been rejected? Alternatively, since in a novel case the court must take a decision as to whether a new duty should be recognised,[43] is there any principle to guide it in this task? Three periods in the history of the law must be distinguished.

B. Law Before Anns v Merton

The first attempt to formulate a general principle was made by 5–5 Brett M.R. in *Heaven v Pender*[44] but by far the most important generalisation is that of Lord Atkin in *Donoghue v Stevenson*.[45] A manufacturer of ginger beer sold ginger beer in an opaque bottle to a retailer. The retailer resold it to A, who treated a young woman of her acquaintance with its contents. It was alleged that these included the decomposed remains of a snail which had found its way into the bottle at the factory. The young woman alleged that she became seriously ill in consequence and sued the manufacturer for negligence. The doctrine of privity of contract prevented her bringing a claim founded upon breach of a warranty in a contract of sale, but a majority of the House of Lords held that the manufacturer owed her a duty to take care that the bottle did not contain noxious matter and that he would be liable in tort if that duty was broken. Lord Atkin said[46]:

> "In English law there must be, and is, some general conception of relations giving rise to a duty of care, of which the particular cases found in the books are instances. The liability for negligence, whether you style it such or treat it as in other systems as a species of 'culpa,' is no doubt based upon a general public sentiment of moral wrongdoing for which the offender must pay. But acts or omissions which any moral code would censure

---

[42] See para.5–34, below.

[43] An extreme view was sometimes advanced that liability for negligence could only exist where there was a duty recognised by previous judicial decision. See Landon (1941) 57 L.Q.R. 183: "Negligence is not actionable unless the duty to be careful exists. And the duty to be careful exists where the wisdom of our ancestors has deemed that it shall exist." There are echoes of this in the dissent of Viscount Dilhorne in *Home Office v Dorset Yacht Co Ltd* [1970] A.C. 1004, HL, but it is quite inconsistent with the law since 1932. To emphasise the need for respect for precedent, as the courts now do (para.5–8, below) is not at all the same thing as saying that new duties cannot be created: *Mills v Winchester Diocesan Board* [1989] 1 All E.R. 317 at 332.

[44] (1883) 11 Q.B.D. 503 at 509.

[45] [1932] A.C. 562. For the history of litigation and of Mrs Donoghue, see A. Rodger, QC, "Mrs. Donoghue and Alfenus Varus" [1988] C.L.P. 1.

[46] [1932] A.C. at 580.

cannot in a practical world be treated so as to give a right to every person injured by them to demand relief. In this way rules of law arise which limit the range of complainants and the extent of their remedy. The rule that you are to love your neighbour becomes, in law, you must not injure your neighbour and the lawyer's question, Who is my neighbour? receives a restricted reply. *You must take reasonable care to avoid acts or omissions which you can reasonably foresee would be likely to injure your neighbour. Who, then, in law is my neighbour? The answer seems to be—persons who are so closely and directly affected by my act that I ought reasonably to have them in contemplation as being so affected when I am directing my mind to the acts or omissions which are called in question."*[47]

There could be no denying that *Donoghue v Stevenson* established that manufacturers owed a duty not to cause physical damage to ultimate consumers of their wares[48] (what is sometimes called the "narrow rule" in *Donoghue v Stevenson*) but it seems plain from the structure of Lord Atkin's speech that what we may call the "neighbour principle" was a vital step on the road to this general conclusion of law, not merely a test for determining whether the claimant was a foreseeable victim of the defendant's negligence, an issue which was anyway not before the House of Lords in any meaningful sense.[49] Nevertheless for a long time there was a marked judicial reluctance to accept that the "neighbour principle" had much relevance to determining whether a duty of care might exist in other areas of activity, though it might determine the spatial and temporal limits of such duties as were held to exist.[50] Still less did it have any impact where, before 1932, duties had been specifically rejected. There continued to be no duty of care in making statements or in disposing of tumbledown houses—words were not like deeds and a dwelling was inherently different from a ginger beer bottle. Certainly new "duty situations" continued to be recognised, for as Lord Macmillan had said in *Donoghue v Stevenson*, "the categories of negligence are never closed"[51] but little reliance was placed upon this generalised concept.[52]

---

[47] Emphasis added.
[48] A duty which was stated with greater precision in a subsequent passage: see para.10–2, below.
[49] The case came before the House of Lords from Scotland as what in modern English procedural terms would be called a preliminary issue of law (see CPR 3.1(2)) and no trial of the truth of the averments seems to have taken place: see Rodger, [1988] C.L.P. 1 and Heuston (1957) 20 M.L.R. 2.
[50] i.e. duty in the second sense above.
[51] [1932] A.C. at 619.
[52] Thus in the Court of Appeal in *Home Office v Dorset Yacht Co Ltd* [1969] 2 Q.B. 412 no reference was made to *Donoghue v Stevenson*.

C. Law as Stated in Anns v Merton

In *Home Office v Dorset Yacht Co Ltd*,[53] Lord Reid had suggested **5–6**
that the time had come to regard the "neighbour principle" of
Donoghue v Stevenson as applicable in all cases where there was no
justification or valid explanation for its exclusion. The suggestion
was taken up by the House of Lords in *Anns v Merton London
Borough*,[54] in particular in the speech of Lord Wilberforce, who
said[55] that the matter should be approached in two stages. First, one
must ask whether there was a sufficient relationship of "proximity
or neighbourhood" between claimant and defendant such that in the
defendant's reasonable contemplation carelessness on his part might
cause damage to the claimant. If so, a prima facie duty of care arose.
Then, at the second stage, it was necessary to consider whether there
were any considerations which ought to "negative, or to reduce or
limit" that duty.[56] The enthusiasm with which some judges took up
this elegant rationalisation of the law and used it to attack previously
well-entrenched principles of non-liability produced a remarkably
swift reaction so that within a decade it could be said that it no
longer represented the correct general approach to the establishment
of a duty of care.[57] One of the most radical manifestations of this
expansive reliance on *Anns* was *Junior Books Ltd v Veitchi Co Ltd*[58]
where a majority of the House of Lords in dealing with a loss which,
at least on one view, was economic in nature, imposed a liability
which appeared to conflict with hitherto well-established
principles.[59]

D. Present Law

After three decisions at the highest level in the mid-1980s which **5–7**
had cast doubts on the *Anns* approach,[60] the decisive case in the
"counter-revolution" was probably the decision of the Privy Council in *Yuen Kun Yeu v Attorney-General of Hong Kong*,[61] in which
Anns was subjected to reinterpretation. A statutory officer, the Commissioner of Deposit-taking Companies, registered as a deposit-

---

[53] [1970] A.C. 1004 at 1027.
[54] [1978] A.C. 728.
[55] [1978] A.C. 728 at 751–752.
[56] Whether as to its scope or the class of persons to whom it was owed or the damages to
which a breach of it might give rise.
[57] The actual decision concerned liability for defective premises. Even in this respect it is
virtually dead: para.9–33, below.
[58] [1983] 1 A.C. 520.
[59] See the dissenting speech of Lord Brandon at 551. The case is dealt with more fully,
para.5–44, below.
[60] *Governors of the Peabody Donation Fund v Sir Lindsay Parkinson Ltd* [1985] A.C. 210,
HL; *Candlewood Navigation Corp v Mitsui O.S.K. Lines* [1986] A.C. 1, PC; *Leigh and
Sillavan Ltd v Aliakmon Shipping Co Ltd* [1986] A.C. 786 (para.5–40, below).
[61] [1988] A.C. 175.

taker a company which subsequently went into liquidation with the
result that the claimants lost the money they had deposited with it.
They alleged that the Commissioner knew or ought to have known
that the affairs of the company were being conducted fraudulently
and speculatively, that he failed to exercise his statutory powers of
supervision so as to secure that the company complied with its
obligations and that he should either never have registered the
company or have revoked its registration. On a preliminary issue of
law and assuming these allegations to be well founded, the Privy
Council upheld the judgment of the Hong Kong Court of Appeal in
favour of the Commissioner. It is hard to take exception to the
decision itself, even though the Commissioner's function was of
course the protection of depositors, for the facts were replete with
characteristics which have been relied upon in many other cases as
justifying denial of a duty. The loss was economic in nature; the
claimants were unascertained members of a huge class of persons
depositing money with Hong Kong financial institutions and had no
"special relationship" with the Commissioner; the loss had been
directly inflicted by the wrongful act of a third party and there is no
general duty to confer protection against such loss; the Commissioner had neither the legal power nor the resources to control the
day-to-day running of the many companies subject to this jurisdiction so that no duty which could fairly and practicably be imposed
on him would be likely to forestall fraud by those determined to
practise it; and the failure of the legislature to impose a civil
sanction in the legislation[62] was at least a pointer towards rejecting
a common law duty of care.[63] No doubt a court faithfully applying
Anns v Merton might have rejected a duty at the second stage on all
or any of these grounds[64] but the Privy Council held that it was not
necessary to pass beyond the first stage because these were matters
which on a proper view of the law were part of the notion of
"proximity". There were, said the court, two possible interpretations of the first stage of the *Anns* formula: the first was that

---

[62] The legislation was subsequently amended to give the Commission immunity from civil
suit. For comparable English provisions giving immunity see the Financial Services and
Markets Act 2000 Sch.1 Pt IV, para.19 (replacing legislation in 1986) and the Banking Act
1987 s.1(4). The position here is not altered by EC Directive 77/780: *Three Rivers DC v
Bank of England (No.3)* [2003] 2 A.C. 1. However, the impact of the Human Rights Act
1998 and the Convention is uncertain. The 2000 Act ducks the problem by providing that
it does not apply, "so as to prevent an award of damages made in respect of an act or
omission on the ground that the act or omission was unlawful as a result of section 6(1)
of the Human Rights Act 1998".

[63] However, this factor had not inhibited the court in *Anns v Merton* from finding a common
law duty superimposed upon a statutory power.

[64] As, indeed, Huggins V.P. and Fuad J.A. in the Hong Kong Court of Appeal had done:
[1986] L.R.C. (Comm.) 300. See also *Mills v Winchester Diocesan Board* [1989] 2 All
E.R. 317.

proximity meant merely reasonable foreseeability of injury, all matters of "policy" then being relegated to the second stage; the other, which was favoured by the Privy Council, was that proximity included other factors which should enter into the decision whether a duty of care should be imposed.

Three "tests". Since *Yuen Kun Yeu* the stream of authority has   **5-8** flowed unabated and at present it is possible to identify three approaches to the question of the determination of the duty of care: (i) the so-called "tripartite (or threefold) test" in *Caparo Industries Plc v Dickman*,[65] which asks whether the harm was foreseeable, whether there was sufficient proximity between the parties and whether the imposition of a duty of care would be fair, just and reasonable; (ii) the test which asks whether the defendant has "assumed responsibility" to the claimant with regard to the matter from which the harm arises; and (iii) the "incremental test", whereby the law should develop novel categories of negligence incrementally and by analogy with established categories. It would be as well to repeat at the outset that the issue arises comparatively rarely on the ground[66] and to say that, while "test" is the common shorthand, one will look in vain for anything sufficiently precise to serve as a litmus paper in this area, and it has been said that:

"[T]he unhappy experience with the rule so elegantly formulated by Lord Wilberforce in *Anns v Merton London Borough Council* ... suggests that appellate judges should follow the philosopher's advice to 'Seek simplicity, and distrust it'."[67]

All three were considered at length by the House of Lords in *Customs and Excise Commissioners v Barclays Bank Plc*.[68] The claimants had obtained a freezing order against the assets of two companies in respect of outstanding VAT. This was served on the Bank, which wrote in acknowledgment of its obligation to obey but before that letter was received (indeed, probably before it was sent)

---

[65] [1990] 2 A.C. 605.

[66] See para.5–4, above. One suspects that in terms of cases tried, only a small minority ever involve a "duty of care" inquiry, just as probably only a minute number of contract disputes involve such a conceptual fundamental as consideration

[67] Lord Rodger in *Customs and Excise Commissioners v Barclays Bank Plc* [2006] UKHL 28; [2007] 1 A.C. 181 at [51]. What was said in Australia a few years ago is true here: "What the ... shifts in authority over fairly short periods demonstrate is the unlikelihood that any [judge] who tackles the subject, even in a final court of appeal, can claim thereafter a personal revelation of an ultimate and permanent value against which later responses must suffer in comparison": *Vairy v Wyong SC* [2005] HCA 62, 223 C.L.R. 422 at [67]. For an even bleaker view see Hayne J. in *Brodie v Singleton SC* [2001] HCA 29, 206 C.L.R. 512 at [318]

[68] Above.

the companies managed to withdraw large sums, which were irrecoverable. The House of Lords held that the Bank did not owe a
duty of care to the claimants. None of the judgments purports to
state any universal test, though one can probably say that the
incremental approach cannot be regarded as a solvent in its own
right because it gives no indication of where the increments should
stop—one might simply reach a radically different result in three
steps rather than one leap. However, it is not without value as a
reminder that, "caution and analogical reasoning are generally valuable accompaniments to judicial activity" and as a cross-check
against the other approaches.[69] Assumption of responsibility came
to prominence in the context of liability for statements and it was
subsequently extended to cases in which the defendant undertook to
perform a task for the claimant (it is hardly suitable for the general
run of cases in which there has been no contact between the parties
before the harm is suffered[70]); and because the loss in such cases
tends to be economic rather than physical, it remains prominent
where that type of loss is in issue. However, it is not confined to
such cases,[71] nor is it a universal solvent of them. Thus *Caparo
Industries Plc v Dickman*, the leading case on the tripartite test, was
itself a statement case involving economic loss; and in *Spring v
Guardian Assurance*,[72] a case of a statement made to a third party,
one member of the majority relied on assumption of responsibility
but the others upon the tripartite test. Voluntary assumption of
responsibility does not require that the defendant should actually
intend to be legally liable for what he says or does, it is assessed
objectively,[73] but on the facts of *Customs and Excise Commissioners*, an economic loss case, it clearly could not be satisfied—the
Bank had no choice, it was bound by law to comply with the order
and was potentially liable for contempt if it did not (though on the
facts its error did not attract that penalty). That, however, was not
the end of the matter, for the decision in favour of the Bank was
ultimately based on the tripartite test. The dissipation of the account

---

[69] At [84], [93]. Further, "the closer the facts of the case in issue to those of a case in which
a duty of care has been held to exist, the readier a court will be . . . to find that there has
been an assumption of responsibility or that the proximity and policy conditions of the
threefold test are satisfied. The converse is also true": at [7].

[70] So it surprising that Lord Hoffmann says at [37] that *Henderson v Merrett Syndicates*
[1995] 2 A.C. 145 (a "task" case) was "a re-run of *Donoghue v Stevenson* in a claim for
economic loss. . . . To say that the managing agents assumed a responsibility to the
Names to take care not to accept unreasonable risks is little different from saying that a
manufacturer of ginger beer assumes a responsibility to consumers to take care to keep
snails out of his bottles."

[71] See para.5–36, below.

[72] [1995] 2 A.C. 296, para.11–33, below.

[73] *Customs and Excise Commissioners* at [5], [73], [86].

was certainly foreseeable, but whether or not the "notoriously elusive"[74] proximity requirement was satisfied, it would not be fair, just and reasonable to impose liability. This was a case where the liability was modest in relation to the defendants' resources and, unlike in many other economic loss cases, the amount of potential liability was known, but one might conceive of others where noncompliance with an order in a manner which would constitute civil law negligence but not attract the penalties for contempt would involve a ruinous liability. It was to the contempt jurisdiction and not to the law of negligence that one should look for the sanctions attached to freezing orders.

> "The common law has ... developed a system offering very significant protection for claimants, together with very considerable incentives, backed by ample sanctions, for banks and other third parties to do their best to comply. Having imposed such an obligation on a third party, I do not consider that it should go further by imposing a duty on the third party towards a claimant to take care to prevent abstractions committed by the defendant in breach of a freezing order. This would not be analogous with or incremental to any previous development of the law. The position as it is without any such duty of care seems to me to represent a fair and normally effective balance between the respective interests involved."[75]

Lord Hoffmann thought there was a close analogy with a statutory duty which did not give rise to civil liability and which could not automatically be made the foundation of a common law duty of care:

> "[Y]ou cannot derive a common law duty of care directly from a statutory duty. Likewise, as it seems to me, you cannot derive one from an order of court. The order carries its own remedies and its reach does not extend any further."[76]

So the overall picture seems to be that assumption of responsibility, the *Caparo* tripartite test and incrementalism all have a role to play in suitable cases, perhaps in a mutually supportive way, for there are some signs of running the concepts together.[77] Indeed, this

---

[74] Lord Bingham at [15].
[75] Lord Mance at [113].
[76] At [39].
[77] Lord Hoffmann at [35], Lord Rodger at [65]–[66] and Lord Walker at [73]. This has occurred before. In *Merrett v Babb* [2001] EWCA Civ 214; [2001] Q.B. 1174 at [41] May L.J. thought that the *Caparo* "strand" and the assumption of responsibility "strand" in reality merged.

is probably inevitable. Although it has been said that if the case falls within the principle of assumption of responsibility there should be no need to embark on any further enquiry whether it is fair, just and reasonable to impose liability,[78] it may be impossible to avoid issues which figure in the tripartite test in order to determine whether there is an assumption of responsibility in the relevant sense. For example, a seller of goods clearly "assumes responsibility" in the ordinary sense of those words to deliver them but the current law is that he is not liable in tort (as opposed to contract) for failing to do so. One cannot escape the ultimate question of whether it is fair, just and reasonable (the context of those issues in this example being the general structure of the law[79]).

All this said, it is the tripartite test which has figured most frequently in the greatest variety of cases so we need to look more closely at that. The *Caparo* case, "though it is no rule-book, represents the modern backdrop against which to judge any putative negligence claim."[80]

5–9   *Caparo v Dickman. Caparo Industries Plc v Dickman*[81] concerned the liability of an auditor for financial loss suffered by investors and is considered from this point of view in more detail below[82] but for the moment we are concerned with what it said about the general approach to the duty of care. There are now three separate steps or issues in the "duty of care" inquiry. First, it must of course be reasonably foreseeable that the conduct of the defendant will cause damage to the claimant. This requirement is essential even in a situation of a type (road or industrial accidents, for example) where the existence of a duty of care has long been well established. In such cases it will be the only inquiry unless, indeed, even this element is regarded as self-evident. Secondly, there must be sufficient "proximity" between the parties, and thirdly:

> "[T]he situation [must] be one in which the court considers it fair, just and reasonable that the law should impose a duty of care of a given scope on the one party for the benefit of the other".[83]

We must examine the second and third of these in more detail but at the outset two warnings must be given.

5–10   The first warning is that the content of these steps and the relationship between them is imprecise rather than "scientific" and

---

[78] *Henderson v Merrett Syndicates Ltd* [1995] 2 A.C. 145 at 181.
[79] See para.5–16, below.
[80] *Connor v Surrey CC* [2010] EWCA Civ 286 at [102] per Laws L.J.
[81] [1990] 2 A.C. 605.
[82] See para.11–25, below.
[83] Lord Bridge in *Caparo* at [1990] 2 A.C. 617.

one cannot reconcile all the judgments in form even if they all point the same way in substance. It is, "reaching for the moon ... to expect to accommodate every circumstance which may arise within a single short abstract formulation"[84] and one must beware of using the ideas we do have as slogans.[85] As Lord Roskill put it in *Caparo*[86]:

> "There is no simple formula or touchstone to which recourse can be had in order to provide in every case a ready answer to the questions whether, given certain facts, the law will or will not impose liability for negligence or, in cases where such liability can be shown to exist, determine the extent of that liability. Phrases such as 'foreseeability', 'proximity', 'neighbourhood', 'just and reasonable', 'fairness' ... will be found used from time to time in different cases. But ... such phrases are not precise definitions. At best they are but labels or phrases descriptive of the very different factual situations which can exist in particular cases and which must be carefully examined in each case before it can be pragmatically determined[87] whether a duty of care exists and, if so, what is the scope and extent of that duty".

The second warning is that these imprecise concepts are likely to be called in aid less frequently than might appear. Though orthodoxy may sometimes be overturned in the Supreme Court, when a duty is well established in a situation of the type before the court, it will not generally return *de novo* to issues like proximity and fairness,[88] for that would be a recipe for inconsistency and uncertainty.[89]

> "It is a truism to say that any case must be decided taking into account the circumstances of the case, but where those circumstances comply with established categories of liability, a defendant should not be allowed to seek to escape from liability by

[84] *Merrett v Babb* [2001] EWCA Civ 214. [2001] Q.B. 1174 at [41] per May L.J.

[85] *Customs and Excise Commissioners* at [35].

[86] [1990] 2 A.C. at 628.

[87] The exercise of discovering a duty of care has been described as "intensely pragmatic": *Rowling v Takaro Properties Ltd* [1988] A.C. 473 at 501.

[88] It has been pointed out that "incrementalism" can apply "the other way round" so that it will be "particularly difficult to establish a duty of care in a situation closely analogous to one where the law has already denied the existence of such a duty": *M v MPC* [2007] EWCA Civ 1361 at [41].

[89] Of course general ideas like fairness will play a part in deciding what should be the *content* of an established duty of care. A judge will not ask himself whether it is fair that an employer should owe a duty of care to protect the safety of workers. But his notions of fairness and practicability are likely to determine whether the employer's behaviour in, e.g. failing to supply a safety device, falls below the standard required by law. On the typical analysis this is a matter of breach rather than duty.

appealing to some vaguer concept of justice or fairness; the law cannot be re-made for every case."[90]

Even in those situations where a duty of care is denied or admitted only to a very restricted degree there is a tendency, via one or more appellate decisions, to develop rather more precise criteria of liability for the area in question. Thus in the case of a person who suffers psychiatric trauma from shock at injury to another it is now established that the claimant must have a sufficient relationship of love and affection with the direct victim and that he must witness the event or its immediate aftermath.[91] These are in effect the law's standard assessments of proximity and of what is fair and reasonable in shock cases. The more general concepts are likely to be called in aid where the court is deciding whether to venture into an entirely novel area of liability or where a "new" duty has been established and it is in the course of development.

The court's assessment of what is fair, just and reasonable is not much of a "test" in comparison with the laws of science and logic, but it can be argued that it does provide an ultimate statement of principle.[92]

5–11   **i. Proximity.** As a matter of ordinary language, the word "proximity" is capable of meaning the equivalent of foreseeability, for its primary meaning is "nearness",[93] especially in a spatial sense. "The pedestrian was in proximity to the car and therefore it was foreseeable that he should be injured".[94] Of course even in this sense it cannot be confined to nearness in space, as Lord Atkin recognised in *Donoghue v Stevenson*:

> "I think that this[95] sufficiently states the truth if proximity be not confined to mere physical proximity, but be used, as I think it was

[90] Hobhouse L.J. in *Perrett v Collins* [1998] 2 Lloyd's Rep. 255 at 263.
[91] See para.5–66, below.
[92] In two modern cases, *Frost v CC South Yorkshire* [1999] 2 A.C. 455 (para.5–69, below) and *McFarlane v Tayside Health Board* [2000] A.C. 59 (para.24–15, below) some members of the HL have used the principle of distributive (as opposed to corrective) justice to deny a duty of care. But distributive justice is what the court regards as setting a fair limit on the responsibility for loss and seems to be part and parcel of the "fair, just and reasonable" element in *Caparo*: see *Parkinson v St James etc. University Hospital NHS Trust* [2001] EWCA Civ 530; [2002] Q.B. 266 at [37]–[39]. At any rate it is, "not a principle of English law recently adopted so as to allow free rein to ignore basic principles long established": *Thompstone v Tameside and Glossop etc NHS Trust* [2008] EWCA Civ 5; [2008] 1 W.L.R. 2207 at [47].
[93] Lord Oliver in *Caparo* at [1990] 2 A.C. 633 refers to its literal meaning as "closeness". Much the same point can be made about "neighbour".
[94] Cf. in US law, "proximate cause" which means what we commonly call "remoteness of damage". Although the English phrase also has spatial overtones, the real sense of both is "operative" or "legally adequate" (an expression often used by European lawyers).
[95] i.e. what A. L. Smith L.J. said in *Le Lievre v Gould* [1893] 1 Q.B. 491 at 504, where he had referred to proximity.

intended, to extend to such close and direct relations that the act complained of directly affects a person whom the person alleged to be bound to take care would know would be directly affected by his careless act."[96]

This seems to be the sense in which the word was often used in the post *Anns v Merton* period. But while there would still undoubtedly be legal proximity between the driver and the pedestrian in our example, the legal sense is now different. According to the Privy Council in *Yuen Kun Yeu*, proximity means, "the whole concept of necessary [i.e. necessary to produce a duty of care] relationship between the plaintiff and defendant". Now while this plainly introduces elements other than foreseeability, it is not, it is submitted, the formulation of a test or criterion at all, for it gives no indication of what, in any case, are the other ingredients of the necessary relationship. It is rather as if a tax Act said that a special tax should be levied on, "vehicles more than four metres long and having certain other characteristics". What is clear, however, is that proximity differs from one situation to another because a closer or more direct nexus will be required with reference to some types of damage or some types of conduct.[97] Where the defendant has directly caused physical harm to the claimant or his property by an act, a duty may readily be established by showing foreseeability and nothing else.[98] In such a case:

"[I]t is enough that the plaintiff happens to be (out of the whole world) the person with whom the defendant collided or who purchased the offending ginger beer".[99]

Where, however, there is a failure to act or the loss is economic in nature or is a mental trauma or for some other reason the imposition of liability based upon foreseeability is perceived to be problematic, the law will, if it does not deny liability completely, insist on a substantially closer relationship between the parties. Thus (although the terminology was not in vogue at the time of the decision) while there is clearly under the common law[100] no general duty in D to protect C against damage which B (for whom D is not

---

[96] [1932] A.C. 562 at 581.
[97] See generally Kidner, "Resiling from the Anns principle: the Variable Nature of Proximity in Negligence" (1987) 7 L.S. 319.
[98] *Mobil Oil Hong Kong Ltd v Hong Kong United Dockyards Ltd* [1991] 1 Lloyd's Rep. 309 at 368, PC; *Caparo Industries v Dickman* [1990] 2 A.C. 605 at 632; *Customs and Excise Commissioners v Barclays Bank Plc* [2006] UKHL 28; [2007] 1 A.C. 181 at [31]. There are many other statements to the same effect and they are in no way affected by *Marc Rich & Co A.G. v Bishop Rock Marine Co Ltd* [1996] 1 A.C. 211, para.5–13, below.
[99] *Caparo* in the CA per Bingham L.J. [1989] 1 Q.B. 653 at 686.
[100] As to the European Convention on Human Rights, see para.2–13, above.

vicariously liable) wilfully chooses to do to C, there would be proximity between officers in charge of young offenders who allow them to escape and owners of property in the immediate vicinity which is damaged by the offenders during the escape.[101] The foundation of the duty is the custody of the offenders, even if the case involves a step beyond that where the defendant has custody of both the wrongdoer and the victim (for example where one prisoner is attacked by others). However, there will not be proximity between the police and victims of crime in general. In *Hill v CC West Yorkshire*[102] a 20-year-old student was murdered by one Sutcliffe, known as the "Yorkshire Ripper", who had committed a number of similar offences in Yorkshire. After his apprehension her estate brought an action against the police,[103] who, it was alleged, had been guilty of negligence in failing to catch Sutcliffe and thereby prevent her murder. The House of Lords held that there was nothing to take the case out of the general rule denying a duty of care in respect of wilful wrongdoing by others: the police did not have the wrongdoer in their custody and there was no special relationship between the police and the claimant, who was a member of the public at large. The risk which the alleged negligence presented to her was no different from that presented to many thousands of young women in Yorkshire, any of whom might be Sutcliffe's victim.[104] This was one of two alternative bases of the decision: the other was that it was undesirable to impose a duty of care in respect of the investigation of crime because it would have deleterious effects on police efficiency. Despite some earlier doubts about this in view of the Human Rights Act 1998 it has subsequently been confirmed so that there may be no liability even though the victim is identifiable to the police.[105] The insistence on a close relationship between the parties is most consistently apparent in cases where the claimant complains that he has suffered loss by acting on incorrect information or advice given by the defendant and one of the judges in the leading case spoke of the necessity of a relationship "equivalent to contract".[106]

5–12   Sometimes proximity is used in a rather different sense, as indicating not the relationship between the parties but the relationship

---

[101] *Home Office v Dorset Yacht Co* [1970] A.C. 1004. See further para.5–31, below.

[102] [1989] A.C. 53.

[103] Rather unusually (see para.4–3, above) civil actions had already been successfully brought against Sutcliffe by some of his victims.

[104] But if the defendant had been a canning company whose negligence had poisoned the claimant she could have been anyone in England (or, subject to the rules governing the jurisdiction of the courts, anyone in the world) and there would have been a duty.

[105] See para.5–20, below.

[106] Lord Devlin in *Hedley, Byrne v Heller & Partners* [1964] A.C. 465 at 529. For a somewhat unusual example of a claim which failed for lack of proximity see *Goodwill v British Pregnancy Advisory Service* [1996] 1 W.L.R. 1397.

between the defendant and the source of harm. In *Sutradhar v National Environment Research Council*[107] the defendant Council, funded by the Overseas Development Agency, undertook a survey of the quality of water sources in Bangladesh. This tested for 31 chemical elements but not arsenic and the report said nothing about arsenic. The conventional wisdom at the time was that the presence of arsenic would be highly unlikely. Nor did it purport to be a report on potability, the purpose of the exercise being to use spare funds which might contribute to knowledge about fish farming. The claimant (one of some 699 identified) contended that he had suffered injury to his health as a result of drinking water contaminated with arsenic and that the defendant was in breach of a duty of care to him. The claim went through various formulations but ended up as one based on a duty not to release a report which might give the impression that the water was free of arsenic and fit to drink. The House of Lords affirmed the decision to strike out the claim. There were cases in which persons had undertaken inspections or laid down safety requirements in respect of matters like airworthiness or medical facilities at boxing matches and liability had been imposed when these were found wanting[108] but in those cases there had been, "proximity in the sense of a measure of control over . . . the potentially dangerous situation",[109] there was a "direct and immediate connexion" between the defendants' role and the claimants' injuries. Here the defendants had no control whatever over the supply of water in Bangladesh. That was enough to strike out, but under modern procedure the court may also take a broader approach to whether the claim has some prospect of success and the claimant would clearly face formidable problems in establishing that even if there had been an implied representation of the unlikelihood of arsenic in the water that would have caused the authorities in Bangladesh to question then current orthodoxy and do something about the situation.

It will be necessary to return to the issue of proximity later, for there is a tenable view that it is really no more than a statement of the conclusion that there is or is not a duty. However, first we must examine the third element in the *Caparo* trilogy.

ii. Fair, just and reasonable. Even if there is the requisite degree **5–13** of proximity,[110] a duty may still be denied if in the court's view the

---

[107] [2006] UKHL 33; [2006] 4 All E.R. 490.
[108] See para.5–36,below.
[109] At [38] per Lord Hoffmann.
[110] Or so it is said, see para.5–17, below.

imposition of liability would not be fair, just and reasonable.[111] In
Marc Rich & Co A.G. v Bishop Rock Marine Co Ltd[112] the vessel
The Nicholas H developed a crack while carrying a cargo from
South America to Italy. Off Puerto Rico a surveyor employed by
N.K.K., a marine classification society,[113] was called in by the
master. The surveyor eventually[114] pronounced that the vessel was
fit to complete the voyage with temporary welding work. A few
days later she sank with the total loss of the cargo. The claimants,
owners of the cargo, obtained US$500,000 by settlement against the
shipowners (this being the limit of their liability under the conventions governing carriage by sea) and claimed the balance of US$5.7
million against N.K.K. On a preliminary issue of law, for the
purposes of which it was assumed that the surveyor was negligent
and that the loss of the cargo was a foreseeable consequence of that,
a majority of the House of Lords held that N.K.K. owed no duty of
care to the cargo owners. Like one of the judges in the Court of
Appeal[115] the majority proceeded upon the assumption (without so
deciding) that the requirement of proximity was satisfied but the
cumulative effect of a number of policy factors pointed against a
decision in favour of the owners. Of these the most important related
to the structure of the network of transactions involved in carriage
by sea. The liability of the shipowner was limited by statute[116] to so
much per ton of the ship's tonnage[117] and if the cargo owner were
allowed to bypass this by the device of a claim against the classification society (which is beyond the protection of the tonnage limitation) such bodies would be likely to seek to pass on the cost of their
liability insurance to shipowners or to seek indemnities against
them, thereby disturbing the balance between cargo owners and
carriers set by international convention.[118] Even if this did not

---

[111] Although three words are used it should not be thought that there will be a minute
disjunctive analysis. All three words convey the same idea of "judicial policy" in slightly
different ways.

[112] [1996] A.C. 211.

[113] These bodies inspect ships and give them certificates of seaworthiness for insurance
purposes.

[114] His initial advice had been for an immediate major repair in dry dock, a recommendation
at which the shipowners naturally balked.

[115] Mann L.J.: [1994] 1 W.L.R. 1071 at 1085.

[116] See now the Merchant Shipping Act 1995 s.185 and Sch.7. The right to limit is lost where
the carrier causes the damage intentionally or recklessly: Sch.7, art.4.

[117] There was some confusion over this aspect of the case, for in the CA the limitation was
treated as based on the provisions of the Hague Rules governing bill of lading contracts but
in the view of the majority of the HL the point was unimportant. "Tonnage limitation is
a part of the international code which governs the claims under consideration. It is as
relevant as any limitation under the Hague Rules": [1996] 2 A.C. 211 at 238.

[118] Much the same point has arisen in different ways in two other areas. First, the issue in
Leigh & Sillavan v Aliakmon Shipping [1986] A.C. 785 (para.5–40, below); secondly, in
actions against stevedores and other sub-contractors to the carriage contract: see cases such
as *New Zealand Shipping Co v Satterthwaite* [1975] A.C. 154 and *The Mahkutai* [1996]
A.C. 650.

happen, another layer of insurance cover (the liability cover of the classification society) would be wastefully introduced into the structure.[119] Furthermore, there was a risk that classification societies would decline to survey high risk vessels, thereby causing potential damage to their function of acting for the public welfare in respect of safety at sea.[120]

These issues are complex and the weight of the arguments and the conclusions difficult to assess[121] and this is not the place to pursue in detail the position of classification societies. What is clear, however, is that the House of Lords was basing its decision upon an array of factors which are based neither upon foreseeability nor upon any technical legal doctrine. Quite small differences may, therefore, produce a contrary result. There is an obvious similarity between the function of the classification society in *Marc Rich* and that of a person carrying out an airworthiness inspection under the Air Navigation legislation. Yet in *Perrett v Collins*,[122] the Court of Appeal held that the inspector acting for a non-profit making organisation which carried out the statutory function was liable for negligence in granting a certificate to a private light aircraft which led to the injury of the claimant, who was a passenger. The legislation in question had as at least one of its major purposes the safeguarding of human life[123] and, while it was true that the law had generally

---

[119] This also seems to be the idea behind *Norwich CC v Harvey* [1989] 1 W.L.R. 828 where, the building owner having contracted with the main contractor to insure the works, a subcontractor (who was not a party to the main contract) carelessly set fire to them. The court held that the sub-contractor owed the owner no duty of care and made no reference to the various cases on the liability of stevedores to cargo owners, which had approached the matter via the law of privity of contract and had gone to some trouble to evade that. In some cases now, of course, a non-party may be able to rely on someone else's exclusion clause via the Contracts (Rights of Third Parties) Act 1999. Compare *British Telecommunications v James Thomson & Sons (Engineers) Ltd* [1999] 1 W.L.R. 9, HLSc., where the fact that the main contract exempted "nominated" sub-contractors reinforced rather than negatived the duty of care owed to the owner by "domestic" sub-contractors.

[120] The cargo owners in such a case would acquire no rights against the classification society under the Contracts (Rights of Third Parties) Act 1999 because (a) the contract would not "purport to confer a benefit" on them and (b) in practice they would not be identified in it. See s.1.

[121] For the other view see the strong dissent of Lord Lloyd. He points out that as a general rule: (1) liability may be imposed upon A to B notwithstanding the existence of a contract between A and C; (2) the existence, absence or feasibility of loss or liability insurance is not overtly taken into account by the courts; and (3) many defendants such as doctors and hospitals are undoubtedly public benefactors but this has not hitherto been regarded as a reason for granting them immunity from liability. The decision of the CA in *Capital and Counties Plc v Hampshire CC* [1997] Q.B. 1004 rejecting immunity for the fire service is very much in line with Lord Lloyd's reasoning in *Marc Rich*: see [1997] Q.B. at 1038–1044. See also Stapleton, "Tort, Insurance and Ideology" (1995) 58 M.L.R. 820.

[122] [1998] 2 Lloyd's Rep. 255.

[123] Compare *Philcox v Civil Aviation Authority, The Times*, June 8, 1995, where the CA held that an inspector was not liable to the owner of the aircraft when it was destroyed in a crash. The function of the inspection was to protect the public against owners rather than provide a service for the benefit of owners. Claims against marine surveyors by purchasers

extended a similar protection to property damage (which was what was at issue in *Marc Rich*) as to personal injury, there was no doubt that there was a tendency to regard the latter type of loss as having a higher value in the scale of things and it did not therefore follow that a restriction on liability which could be justified in the context of one type of loss should automatically be applied to the other.[124] The role of the inspector was more fundamental than that of the classification society since he had been closely involved in the supervision of the aircraft's construction and it was for him to say whether it should fly or not. Furthermore, on the facts of the case the element of wastefully adding another defendant to the loop (as Hobhouse L.J. put it[125]) did not apply, since there could be cases in which the only remedy would be against the inspector.[126] One factor that influenced the decision in *Marc Rich* was that the damage was done "indirectly": the result would probably have been different if, say, the inspector had dropped a cigarette and set fire to the cargo,[127] though the impact on the structure of arrangements for carriage by sea would have been the same—it is difficult to manipulate things in the defendant's favour when the act amounts to what, in former times, would have been regarded as trespass. However, while there is an obvious difference between advice by D to B which causes damage to C's property and D breaking that property himself, there is no real discussion of what "direct" meant. It could hardly have been used in the old trespass sense, for what the defendant in *Donoghue v Stevenson* did was not a trespass and that case contains reference to persons "closely and directly affected by my act".[128] In *Perrett* one of the judges[129] thought that the damage was "direct" in

---

of the vessel relying on a certificate of seaworthiness have failed: *Reeman v DoT* [1997] 2 Lloyd's Rep. 648; *The Morning Watch* [1990] 1 Lloyd's Rep. 547; *Att Gen v Carter* [2003] NZCA 48; [2003] 2 N.Z.L.R. 160. The losses were truly economic. The boats did not sink, they were worth less than the buyers paid for them.

[124] On this reasoning if a sailor had been drowned in *Marc Rich* his dependants might have had a claim against N.K.K. What if the boat owner in *Reeman v DOT* (above, fn.123) had been drowned when the defective vessel sank?

[125] [1998] 2 Lloyd's Rep. at 259.

[126] This aspect of the case is not very fully dealt with. As a gratuitous passenger in a private aircraft the international conventions and domestic legislation on the liability of air carriers would not have been applicable to the claimant. Yet, as the defendants argued, the application of the case to other circumstances might offer the opportunity to bypass the legislation by taking aim at those responsible for inspection rather than the commercial carrier. For Buxton L.J. such a case would have to be dealt with as it arose (at 276). However, the liability of commercial carriers, while not absolute, is not generally dependent on proof of fault and is therefore more onerous than that of an inspection agency. Furthermore, the scope of financial limitation of liability by European carriers has been reduced by Council Regulation (EC) No. 2027/97 and a similar process will occur in other countries as the Montreal Convention of 1999 is ratified.

[127] [1996] 1 A.C. at 237.

[128] [1932] A.C. at 580.

[129] Buxton L.J. at [1998] 2 Lloyd's Rep. 274.

the sense required because of the major role of the inspector[130] but that even if it was not, the justice of the case in the particular context dispensed with it; another thought that "directly inflicted loss" was no part of the requirements for liability in case of personal injury.[131]

While *Marc Rich* (and some other duty of care cases)[132] may be   **5–14** regarded as involving attempts to pass liability around from a subrogated loss insurer to a defendant's liability insurer, in many cases a decision against a duty of care really does mean that the loss lies where it falls. Thus in *Caparo Industries Plc v Dickman*[133] the House of Lords held that defendants carrying out the statutory audit of a public company owe a duty of care (by contract) only to the company and therefore to the general body of shareholders as a collectivity, but not to individual buyers of the company's shares (even if they are existing shareholders) nor to creditors of the company. Reliance on the accounts for such purposes is certainly foreseeable (Lord Bridge described it as highly probable)[134] and it may even be that statements of accounting standards[135] or auditors' manuals[136] draw attention to the likelihood of such reliance; but that is not enough. A number of reasons underlie this restrictive approach. The most obvious is a fear of a multiplicity of claims and a belief that the liability insurance market cannot in practice bear the risk of exposure to the full range of foreseeable loss arising from an inadequate audit of a major company, with the consequent risk, if a duty is imposed, of ruinous[137] liability out of all proportion to the

---

[130] See also *Clay v A.J. Crump & Sons Ltd* [1964] 1 Q.B. 533.
[131] Hobhouse L.J. at 264.
[132] e.g. *Leigh & Sillavan v Aliakmon Shipping Co* [1986] A.C. 785 (para.5–41, below). The insurer, having paid the claim, takes over the rights of the insured against the tortfeasor. It is rarely clear from the report that a case is an insurer's subrogation action, since the claim is made in the name of the insured, but this must frequently be so.
[133] [1990] 2 A.C. 605. For further discussion see para.11–25, below
[134] [1990] 2 A.C. 605 at 625.
[135] As did the Australian Accounting Standards at issue in *Esanda Finance v Peat Marwick Hungerfords* (1997) 188 C.L.R. 241.
[136] See, e.g. *Columbia Coffee & Tea Pty v Churchill* (1992) 29 N.S.W.L.R. 141, rejected in *Esanda*, above, fn.135.
[137] At the time of these cases auditors generally practised as partnerships with unlimited personal liability of the members. It is true that the Limited Liability Partnerships Act 2000 now offers some safeguard against personal liability since it puts partners in such firms in much the same position as shareholders in a company. However, it is not thought that this justifies a change in the law on auditors' liability. Even before the Act some firms had hived off the auditing activity to corporate entities. English law of course allows the defendant, subject to the Unfair Contract Terms Act 1977, to limit his liability by agreement or even by notice (there is special provision for auditors in the Companies Act 2006, see para.11–25, below) and sometimes, as in the case of merchant shipping or carriage by air, there is a statutory regime of limitation of liability. However, professional bodies sometimes restrict the power to limit liability. Where the defendant operates as a company or a limited liability partnership his personal "liability" is de facto limited to the value of his investment in the company or firm.

fault of the defendant,[138] that is to say, the "floodgates" argument often deployed in cases of economic loss and psychiatric trauma. Furthermore, though, there are also reasons which might be brought under the general heading of fairness. For Lord Bridge in *Caparo*, to hold the auditor liable to anyone in the world who happens to deal with the company on the basis of the audit report is:

> "[T]o confer on the world at large a quite unwarranted entitlement to appropriate for their own purposes the benefit of the expert knowledge or professional experience attributed to the maker of the statement,"[139]

for which, it may be added, they have not paid.[140] For McHugh J. in the similar case of *Esanda Finance v Peat Marwick Hungerford*[141] an important factor is that investors and creditors as a group are commonly not "dependent" upon the audit. They may possess considerable financial sophistication and they:

> "[A]re likely to be in a better position to know the likely extent of their losses. The investor or creditor knows the maximum extent of any likely loss. Unlike most plaintiffs in negligence cases, these investors and creditors can take steps to protect themselves against loss. Some creditors and investors will have the staff or means to investigate and verify that part of the audited person's financial affairs that is relevant to the loan or investment. They can seek verification of the report and accounts from the auditors and rely on any representations or assurances (whether for reward or otherwise) that the auditors give. Creditors can assign debts to factoring organisations and in some cases may even be able to insure their debts. They can spread the loss against successive years of revenue by making provision against bad and doubtful debts. Investors can spread their risk by diversifying their investments."[142]

---

[138] See Lord Oliver in *Caparo* at [1990] 2 A.C. 643 and McHugh J. in *Esanda* (1997) 188 C.L.R. 241.

[139] [1990] 2 A.C. 605 at 621. Compare Lord Hoffman's "economic reason" for not imposing liability for omissions in *Stovin v Wise* [1996] A.C. 923 at 944 (para.5–26, below). Another troublesome factor about audit cases, to which McHugh J. in the *Esanda* case below refers, is that the cause of the financial problems which the audit fails to reveal will commonly be the fraud or mismanagement of those running the company but the personal remedy against them will rarely be of as much value as a claim against the auditor. Since under our system each person causing the same damage to the claimant is liable to the claimant for the full loss (see Ch.21, below) the auditor is likely to end up bearing that, for if the claimant's rights against the primary wrongdoer are worthless so also will be the auditor's right of contribution or indemnity. For a full discussion, see *Feasibility Investigation of Joint and Several Liability*, Ch.10.2, DTI, HMSO, 1996.

[140] Cf. *Smith v Eric S. Bush* [1990] 1 A.C. 831 (para.11–26, below).

[141] (1997) 188 C.L.R. 241. See also Stapleton (1995) 111 L.Q.R. 301.

[142] See also *Bily v Arthur Young & Co* 834 P. 2d 745 (Cal. 1992).

Looked at in terms of who can most efficiently absorb the losses involved, there is no evidence that it is the auditors rather than investors and on balance it seems likely to be the reverse since the investors are many and the auditors few.[143] Of course these arguments will not be applicable to some individual cases: there may be individual investors who have no sophisticated financial knowledge, no ability to spread risks and who may be ruined by reliance on the audit report but the law has to frame a rule for the generality of cases.[144]

No doubt there is a good deal to be said on both sides in the above examples but in some cases the rejection of a duty of care has the air of inevitability. Such would be the case where a claim was made for injuries suffered as the result of the negligence of the armed forces during active operations against an enemy. As it was put by Dixon J. in the High Court of Australia in *Shaw Savill and Albion Co Ltd v The Commonwealth*[145]: **5–15**

"It could hardly be maintained that during an actual engagement with the enemy or a pursuit of any of his ships the navigating officer of a King's ship of war was under a common law duty of care to avoid harm to such non-combatant ships as might appear in the theatre of operations. It cannot be enough to say that a conflict or pursuit is a circumstance affecting the reasonableness of the officer's conduct as a discharge of the duty of care, though the duty itself persists. To adopt such a view would mean that whether the combat be by sea, land or air our men go into action accompanied by the civil law of negligence, warning them to be mindful of the person and property of civilians. It would mean that the courts could be called upon to say whether the soldier on the field of battle or the sailor fighting on his ship might reasonably have been more careful to avoid causing civil loss or damage. No one can imagine a court undertaking the trial of such an issue, either during or after a war. To concede that any civil liability can rest upon a member of the armed forces for supposedly negligent acts in the course of an actual engagement with the enemy is opposed alike to reason and to policy."

---

[143] In *Spartan Steel & Alloys v Martin* [1973] 2 Q.B. 27 (para.5–36, below) Lord Denning M.R. used a similar argument to deny a duty of care to C where C suffers economic loss as a result of D's interference with a public utility supply.

[144] Book 6, art.109 of the Dutch Civil Code has an interesting provision (of quite general application) which might allow the imposition of liability but protect the auditor against ruin: "The judge may reduce a legal obligation to repair damage if awarding full reparation would lead to clearly unacceptable results in the given circumstances, including the nature of the liability, the juridical relationship between the parties and their financial incapacity." However, many would find such a vague provision unacceptable.

[145] (1940) 66 C.L.R. 344 at 361.

For such reasons, the Court of Appeal in *Mulcahy v Ministry of Defence*[146] struck out a claim by a soldier for deafness suffered by alleged negligence during an artillery bombardment during the Gulf War. It is true that it has been held that for the purposes of art.2 of the European Convention on Human Rights (duty to protect life) a soldier abroad is protected but this was in the context of the duty to hold an inquest into a death from heatstroke which raised issues about medical assessment of his suitability.[147] Whatever the Convention might one day say about combat injuries it is inconceivable that the common law on this point can have been affected.[148]

E. Relationship with Other Legal Principles

5–16   What is "fair, just and reasonable" is not merely a matter of the proper balance of rights and duties between persons placed in the position of the claimant and defendant or of the impact on society of the imposition of liability. A factor which frequently appears in the case law is the effect of the imposition of a duty of care upon the relationship between negligence and other parts of the legal system, a point we have already encountered in considering the relationship of contract and tort.[149] The courts have shown some concern lest an ever-expanding liability for negligence should eat up other rules developed by the courts and Parliament. Where there is a statutory regime a:

> "[C]ommon law duty must not be inconsistent with the performance by the authority of its statutory duties and powers in the manner intended by Parliament, or contrary in any other way to the presumed legislative intention."[150]

In *C.B.S. Songs Ltd v Amstrad Consumer Electrics Plc*[151] the defendants manufactured tape-to-tape domestic audio systems

---

[146] [1996] Q.B. 732; *Post Traumatic Stress Disorder Litigation, Re*; *Multiple Claimants v MoD* [2003] EWHC 1134 (QB). See further para.5–18, below. Cf. *Bici v MoD* [2004] EWHC 786 (QB), *The Times*, June 11, 2004 (policing function rather than combat). The immunity does not preclude liability for deficiencies in medical treatment for psychiatric illness caused by military service: *Post Traumatic Stress Disorder Litigation, Re*, above. In the *Shaw Savill* case the action was allowed to proceed because the collision did not occur in combat conditions.

[147] *R (Smith) v Oxfordshire Assistant Deputy Coroner* [2009] EWCA Civ 1441; [2009] 3 W.L.R. 1099.

[148] For the striking out of a bizarre claim for negligence in giving spiritual advice on inter-denominational communion see *Clark v Roman Catholic Archdiocese of Brisbane* [1998] Qd. R. 26. Even California law would seem to accord: *Nally v Grace Community Church* 763 P. 2d 948 (1988). Sexual or financial exploitation by abuse of the role of spiritual adviser is, of course, another matter.

[149] See para.1–5, above.

[150] *Stovin v Wise* [1996] AC 923 at 935 per Lord Nicholls.

[151] [1988] A.C. 1013.

which facilitated illegal copying of copyright material. In rejecting any duty of care by the manufacturers to the owners of the copyright, the House of Lords pointed out that in the copyright legislation Parliament had produced what could reasonably be regarded as a code governing the rights of copyright owners and that imposed liability only where copying had been authorised, a requirement plainly not satisfied on the facts since purchasers were warned against illegal copying by notices on the equipment. To impose liability for negligence would subvert the statutory regime. In *Murphy v Brentwood DC*[152] this "structure of the law" argument was relied on in two ways. The House of Lords held that a builder was not liable in negligence to the owner of a house built by him in respect of defects of construction which did not cause personal injury or damage to other property (for example, the contents). Where neither of these elements was present the owner's complaint was essentially that he had acquired something which was less valuable than the price he had paid for it and the remedying of such loss was the function of the law of contract rather than negligence.[153] In addition, however, the Defective Premises Act 1972 had imposed liability upon the builder of a dwelling, transmissible from one owner to another, for just such defects of quality as were being complained of.[154] The limitation period under the statute is a fixed one of six years from completion, whereas for the common law duty it could be a good deal longer.[155]

"It would be remarkable to find that similar obligations . . . applicable to buildings of every kind and subject to no such limitations or exclusions as are imposed by the 1972 Act, could be derived from the builder's common law duty of care."[156]

In *Rowley v Secretary of State for Work and Pensions* the claim was based on alleged incompetence in processing an application for a child maintenance assessment and it was struck out on the basis that it would be inconsistent with the statutory scheme, which contained a substantial degree of protection against the consequences of incompetence. The fact that the scheme might not cater for all losses (such as the psychiatric harm alleged by one claimant

---

[152] [1991] 1 A.C. 398: para.9–33, below.
[153] As is also the case with a product which is shoddily made and does not work: para.10–9, below.
[154] See para.9–37, below.
[155] Both under general principles and under the Latent Damage Act 1986: para.26–9, below.
[156] [1991] 1 A.C. 398 at 480 per Lord Bridge. Lord Oliver at 491 points out that it is curious that the legislation receives little or no discussion in the earlier cases. The absence of similar legislation in New Zealand is one reason justifying a different approach in that country: *Invercargill CC v Hamlin* [1996] A.C. 624.

or the need to leave the matrimonial home) did not mean that the common law was available to fill the gaps. It was not for the courts to evaluate the merits of the structure created by Parliament.[157]

However, if this approach were taken to its logical conclusion there would never be any expansion of tort law, indeed it would be a good deal narrower in its scope than it now is, for there is almost always some legal regime governing the situation and if it gives no civil remedy in damages to the claimant it might be argued that that reflects a proper view of public policy.[158] That this is not the law is shown dramatically by *Spring v Guardian Assurance Plc*[159] in which the House of Lords held that the writer of a reference might be under a duty of care to the subject of the reference notwithstanding that until then it had been assumed that the only liability arose in the torts of libel and malicious falsehood, both of which in such a case required proof of malice.[160] Indeed, the case illustrates a point which is perhaps rather obvious but which tends to be forgotten in discussions dominated by the need to keep liability under control. This is that what the court conceives to be fair, just and reasonable may be just as much a reason for imposing a duty of care as for denying one.[161] The need for free and frank disclosure in references points towards a narrow rule of liability requiring malice but the interests of the subject of the reference are to be given more weight than may formerly have been the case. Against the demands of free speech:

"[L]ooms the probability, often amounting to a certainty, of damage to the individual, which in some cases will be serious and may indeed be irreparable. The entire prosperity and happiness of someone who is the subject of a damning reference which is given carelessly but in perfectly good faith may be irretrievably blighted."[162]

Donoghue v Stevenson itself was a decision that, notwithstanding the restrictions imposed by privity of contract, an injured consumer required a remedy against the negligent manufacturer of a defective product[163] and Lord Atkin considered that the absence of such a

---

[157] [2007] EWCA Civ 598; [2007] 1 W.L.R. 2861. See also *Jones v Dept of Employment* [1989] Q.B. 1.
[158] See generally Sir Robin Cooke, "An Impossible Distinction" (1991) 107 L.Q.R. 46.
[159] [1995] 2 A.C. 296, para.11–33, below.
[160] Although libel does not generally require proof of malice, it does when the occasion is one of qualified privilege and the giving of a reference is such an occasion.
[161] See also *Perrett v Collins* [1998] 2 Lloyd's Rep. 255.
[162] [1995] 2 A.C. 296 at 326 per Lord Lowry.
[163] The public good is now conceived to demand a strict liability in such cases: para.10–12, below.

remedy would be a "grave defect in the law".[164] Perhaps the most remarkable decision of all is that in *White v Jones*[165] holding that a solicitor in preparing a will owed a duty of care to intended beneficiaries under the will. Liability was based upon an "assumption of responsibility" by the solicitor but was carried further than in any previous case because there was no reliance by the claimants, which had been assumed to be a necessary element under that concept. What Lord Goff described as "the impulse to do practical justice"[166] was, however, an overriding consideration, for the estate in such a case has no claim against the solicitor since it has suffered no loss. Underlying the majority judgments in this case seems to be a perception that it is necessary to impose a duty of care to fulfil a quasi-disciplinary function.[167]

F. Relationship between Proximity and what is Fair, Just and Reasonable

Although in *Caparo* "proximity" is separated from what is "fair, just and reasonable", the point has been made above that the former does not provide any measure or test which can be applied to a set of facts because it is something which varies from one type of case to another: sometimes nothing more than foreseeability of injury is required, sometimes there must be a very close relationship between the claimant and the person causing the loss, and it appears to be the court's perception of what is fair, just and reasonable which determines the point chosen on this scale of necessary proximity. In most cases of personal injury or property damage proximity seems to be an unnecessary wheel on the coach, since its application does not appear to achieve anything that has not already been accomplished by reasonable foreseeability. Take, for example, *Mulcahy v Ministry of Defence*,[168] where both foreseeability and proximity were conceded by the defendants.[169] The claimant was standing at a point forward of the firing line to which he had been sent by his officer so that damage to his hearing was a foreseeable, indeed an obvious, risk. What is usefully added by the proposition that there was proximity between them? Indeed, given the ordinary meaning of the word (from which its legal meaning should not perhaps become entirely detached) it would be very odd to say that they were not in proximity and the decisive stage, if a duty of care is to be rejected, must be what is fair, just and reasonable. Where the court adopts

5–17

---

[164] [1932] A.C. at 582.
[165] [1995] 2 A.C. 207, para.5–37, below.
[166] [1995] 2 A.C. 207 at 259.
[167] See para.5–37, below.
[168] [1996] Q.B. 732. See para.5–15, above.
[169] [1996] Q.B. at 749.

restricted proximity then of course there is an apparent difference between foreseeability and proximity: to take facts like those of *Caparo*, it is readily foreseeable that open market investors relying on an audit report may suffer loss even if most people would agree that they are a good deal more remote in spatial or temporal or causal terms than the company being audited. However, even in this case it remains true that the decision to adopt restricted proximity is the result of the court's view of what is fair.[170] The *Caparo* test *looks* as if it runs:

"(1) Auditors do not owe a duty to investors who rely upon audit reports because there is no proximity and (2) A further reason for denying a duty is that it would impose an unreasonable burden upon them to hold them liable to investors who rely upon audit reports in view of the uninsurability of the risk and the complexity of audit decisions etc."

but the true proposition appears to be:

"(1) It would impose an unreasonable burden upon auditors etc. and (2) therefore we will say that the duty of care is owed only to the audited company and not to more remote persons."

The necessary degree of proximity is the product of the court's conclusion on what is fair, just and reasonable.[171] The point is indeed recognised in *Caparo* itself by Lord Oliver:

"It is difficult to resist a conclusion that what have been treated as three separate requirements are, at least in most cases, in fact merely facets of the same thing, for in some cases the degree of foreseeability is such that it is from that alone that the requisite proximity can be deduced, whilst in others the absence of that essential relationship can most rationally be attributed simply to

---

[170] It is therefore difficult to agree with Longmore L.J. in *Customs and Excise Commissioners v Barclays Bank Plc* [2004] EWCA Civ 1555; [2005] 1 W.L.R. 2082 at [31] that "fairness . . . is something of a 'label' attached by the court if it decides that public policy requires a duty of care to be imposed". Rather fairness is the *reason* why the duty is imposed.

[171] "The result of a process of reasoning rather than the process itself, but it remains a useful term because it signifies that the process of reasoning must be undertaken. But to hope that proximity can describe a common element underlying all those categories of case in which a duty of care is recognised is to expect more of the term than it can provide": Dawson J. in *Hill v Van Erp* (1997) 188 C.L.R. 159. See also La Forest J. in *Canadian National Ry Co v Norsk Pacific SS Co* (1992) 91 D.L.R. (4th) 289 and *Hercules Managements Ltd v Ernst & Young* (1997) 146 D.L.R. (4th) 577.

the court's view that it would not be fair and reasonable to hold the defendant responsible".[172]

There are a number of other judicial statements to the same effect, for example by Lord Nicholls in *Stovin v Wise*:

"The *Caparo* tripartite test elevates proximity to the dignity of a separate heading. This formulation tends to suggest that proximity is a separate ingredient, distinct from fairness and reasonableness, and capable of being identified by some other criteria. This is not so. Proximity is a slippery word. Proximity is not legal shorthand for a concept with its own, objectively identifiable characteristics. Proximity is convenient shorthand for a relationship between two parties which makes it fair and reasonable one should owe the other a duty of care. This is only another way of saying that when assessing the requirements of fairness and reasonableness regard must be had to the relationship of the parties."[173]

G. Judicial Approaches to "Policy"

Despite the plethora of case law on the subject it seems likely that **5–18** the precise formulation of the general approach to the duty of care is of limited practical importance. What is more significant is the clear recognition in modern judgments that the duty issue depends heavily upon what is fair, just and reasonable, matters which take in a much broader range of questions than technical issues of law. Common law courts are rather more open than their civil law brethren about expounding "policy" issues (and since appellate courts are not infrequently divided a case can look rather like a debate) but there is still a certain, one might almost say, "coyness" about policy. Twenty years ago in *McLoughlin v O'Brian*, where the issue was the limits of liability for psychiatric trauma, Lord Scarman said that:

"[T]he policy issue where to draw the line is not justiciable.[174] The problem is one of moral, economic and financial policy. The

---

[172] [1990] 2 A.C. 605 at 633. In *Osman v UK* (para.2–13, above) the ECHR, while rejecting any "immunity" based on policy, regarded *Hill v CC West Yorkshire* (para.5–11, above) as correct on the basis of proximity. This presents an obvious difficulty if the concepts are related: see Pill L.J. in *Palmer v Tees HA* [2000] P.I.Q.R. P1.

[173] [1996] A.C. 923 at 932. Lord Nicholls dissented as to the result (see para.5–43, below) but not on the general approach to duty. See also *Islington LBC v University College London Hospital NHS Trust* [2005] EWCA Civ 596; [2006] P.I.Q.R. P3 at [21].

[174] This has now changed: see para.5–66, below.

considerations relevant to a decision are not such as to be capable of being handled within the limits of the forensic process"[175]

Yet in the same case Lord Edmund Davies described this as a proposition which was "as novel as it is startling".[176] More recently, in *McFarlane v Tayside Health Board*[177] the House of Lords was concerned with the question whether the parents of a healthy child could claim damages for the cost of its upbringing when there was negligence in treatment designed to render the father sterile. The answer, overturning 20 years of English case law, was no—it was not fair, just and reasonable to impose such liability. However, the speeches show a strong reluctance to accept that the issue turns on "public policy,"[178] that "unruly horse".[179] Certainly a court does not act like a committee of ministers, civil servants and advisers, which may propose any result it feels can pass the test of political practicality: the court is constrained by precedent, by its constitutional position and by the need for stability and coherence in the structure of the law. However, if, as Lord Steyn thought, the result was dictated by the need for distributive justice to temper corrective justice in this context[180] what is that but "public policy"? After all, it is the competition between those two concepts of justice which underlies the general debate about whether compensation for personal injuries should be handled through the law of negligence or through some other mechanism which would bring basic compensation to a larger number of people[181] and no one would protest about that being described as a matter of public or social policy. Of course no court could overturn the present personal injury system but that is not because of the inherent nature of the issue, it is because the court is more constrained than is the legislature. The courts can, however, very substantially modify its impact, as they have recently done in the contexts of mental injury[182] and the assessment of damages.[183] Perhaps we can say with Lord Millett that the issue in *McFarlane* is one of "legal policy"—"our more or less inadequately expressed idea of what justice demands"[184]—a narrower canvas, but one which still involves ethical and practical, rather than strictly legal, considerations. "Policy", whether concealed in the language of proximity or out in the open, means simply that the

[175] [1983] 1 A.C. 410 at 431.
[176] [1983] 1 A.C. 410 at 427.
[177] [2000] 2 A.C. 59.
[178] See [2000] 2 A.C. 59 at 73, 83, 95 ("social policy"), 100 104, 108.
[179] *Richardson v Mellish* (1824) 2 Bing. 229 at 252.
[180] [2000] 2 A.C. at 82.
[181] See para.1–28, above.
[182] See para.5–61, below.
[183] See para.22–22, below.
[184] [2000] 2 A.C. at 108, quoting Prosser and Keeton, *Torts*, 5th edn, p.264.

court must decide (subject to the doctrine of precedent) whether there should be a duty, taking into account the established framework of the law and also the implications that a decision one way or the other may have for the operation of the law in our society. This (what Lord Goff described as "an educated reflex to facts"[185]) is an inescapable part of the judicial process (unless all foreseeable harm is to be compensated or no harm at all) and it is better to recognise it as such rather than to cloud the issue by saying that, "policy need not be involved where reason and good sense ... will point the way",[186] for in the last analysis these apparently contrasted concepts are surely one and the same thing.

Given all that, however, the problem remains that the policy question may be a very difficult one and the court is usually necessarily dependent upon the arguments presented by counsel for the parties, who have a closer interest in the outcome of the particular case than in the broader public interest.[187] Perhaps this does not matter too much where the policy issue is "the shape of the law" —for example the relationship between contract and tort[188]—but in other cases the court may be faced with considerable uncertainty about the practical background or about the practical effects of a decision one way or the other.[189] The *Marc Rich* case,[190] which has been outlined above, is a good example and Lord Lloyd's dissent emphasises the limited nature of the evidence on insurance practice which was before the court.[191] So, too, in *Hill v CC West Yorkshire*[192] one of the reasons for the decision was the risk of damage to the public interest by promoting "defensive policing". This may be correct, but judging by the report the conclusion seems to be

5–19

---

[185] *Smith v Littlewoods Organisation Ltd* [1987] A.C. 241 at 271.

[186] Lord Morris in *Home Office v Dorset Yacht Co Ltd* [1970] A.C. 1004 at 1039.

[187] Counsel is rarely instructed to appear as amicus curiae in negligence cases.

[188] Though even on technical legal issues one may compare the elaborate consultations undertaken by the Law Commission before proposing changes in the law.

[189] See, e.g. Hoffmann J. at first instance in *Morgan Crucible v Hill Samuel Bank* [1991] Ch. 295 at 305, remarking that the courts, "do not have the information on which to form anything other than a very broad view of the economic consequences of their decisions". In *Islington LBC v University College London Hospital NHS Trust* [2005] EWCA Civ 596; [2006] P.I.Q.R. P3 at [37] Buxton L.J. said: "it is quite impossible for a court to know, within the confines of a particular case and with the benefit only of a sparse amount of evidence and its own common sense, what are the wider implications of the move that it is being asked to make."

[190] [1996] A.C. 211.

[191] See also *Perrett v Collins* [1998] 2 Lloyd's Rep. 255 at 277; *Vowles v Evans* [2003] EWCA Civ 318; [2003] 1 W.L.R. 1607 at [12]. In *McLoughlin v Grovers* [2001] EWCA Civ 1743; [2002] Q.B. 1312 at [30] (a case of mental breakdown arising from alleged negligence by solicitors) Brooke L.J. said, "I have no very clear insight into what the ordinary person on the London Underground, or in a Glasgow public house, or in any other place where he or she may be found, would regard as fair in this case".

[192] [1989] A.C. 53.

based upon a judicial hunch rather than evidence[193] and similar arguments about "defensive fire-fighting" or "defensive medicine" have not impressed the courts.[194] In *Spring v Guardian Assurance Plc*[195] Lord Lowry remarked that:

> "It has been said that public policy should be invoked only in clear cases in which the potential harm to the public is incontestable, that whether the anticipated harm to the public will be likely to occur must be determined on tangible grounds instead of on mere generalities and that the burden of proof lies on those who assert that the court should not enforce a liability which prima facie exists."

However, many cases do not satisfy this stringent test. The danger of proceeding upon incorrect assumptions has underlain greater reluctance to strike out claims against public authorities without trial or further investigation of the facts,[196] but it is not clear how far the courts can go in practice in modifying the approach to the process whereby judges assess the weight of policy factors.

5–20   Hunch or not, the line taken in *Hill* has since been decisively reaffirmed by a majority of the House of Lords in *Smith v Chief Constable of Sussex*.[197] This was again a case of a criminal attack but unlike in *Hill* the claimant had complained about threats and was therefore known to be the specific target. The "core principle" of *Hill* was upheld and even though Lord Phillips was uncertain how far liability would impact upon the police's performance of their duties,[198] Lord Brown was in no doubt[199]:

> "[As to the] concern that the imposition of the liability principle[200] upon the police would induce in them a detrimentally defensive frame of mind. So far from doubting whether this would in fact be so, it seems to me inevitable. If liability could arise in this context (but not, of course, with regard to the police's many other tasks in investigating and combating crime) the police would be likely to treat these particular reported threats with especial caution at the expense of the many other threats to life,

---

[193] The same point can be made about the rejection in *Spring v Guardian Assurance* [1995] 2 A.C. 295, para.11–33, below, of the argument that a decision in favour of the subject of the reference would lead to referees being less frank.

[194] *Capital & Counties Plc v Hampshire CC* [1997] Q.B. 1004.

[195] [1995] 2 A.C. at 326.

[196] See para.5–3, above.

[197] [2008] UKHL 50; [2009] 1 A.C. 225.

[198] At [102].

[199] At [132].

[200] This is in fact his response to the "liability principle" proposed by Lord Bingham, dissenting, which would have been confined to cases of specific and imminent threats from the third party, whose whereabouts were known.

limb and property of which they come to learn through their own and others' endeavours. They would be likely to devote more time and resources to their investigation and to take more active steps to combat them. They would be likely to arrest and charge more of those reportedly making the threats and would be more likely in these cases to refuse or oppose bail, leaving it to the courts to take the responsibility of deciding whether those accused of making such threats should remain at liberty. The police are inevitably faced in these cases with a conflict of interest between the person threatened and the maker of the threat. If the police would be liable in damages to the former for not taking sufficiently strong action but not to the latter for acting too strongly, the police, subconsciously or not, would be inclined to err on the side of over-reaction. I would regard this precisely as inducing in them a detrimentally defensive frame of mind. Similarly with regard to their likely increased focus on these reported threats at the expense of other police work."

There may be liability in such cases under the Human Rights Act 1998 where there is a real and immediate threat to life but there was no claim on this basis in *Smith* and the majority declined to remodel the common law in line with the Convention, despite the fact that he possibility of such a claim to some extent weakens the impact of the arguments used to deny liability at common law.

In *Brooks v Metropolitan Police Commissioner*[201] the police were sued by a witness to a murder who claimed that his shock reaction to the event had been exacerbated by the police failure to offer him the support and protection to which he was entitled (though there was no allegation that he was subjected to specific threats). Again the claim was struck out on the *Hill* principle and here it is difficult to contest the likely deleterious effects of a duty. As Lord Steyn said:

"[W]hilst focusing on investigating crime, and the arrest of suspects, police officers would in practice be required to ensure that in every contact with a potential witness or a potential victim time and resources were deployed to avoid the risk of causing harm or offence. Such legal duties would tend to inhibit a robust approach in assessing a person as a possible suspect, witness or victim."[202]

In stark contrast to these decisions stands that of the majority of the Supreme Court of Canada in *Hill v Hamilton-Wentworth*

---

[201] [2005] UKHL 24; [2005] 1 W.L.R. 1495.
[202] At [30]. See also *M v MPC* [2007] EWCA Civ 1361 (claim based on negligent failure to prosecute).

Regional Police Services Board[203] to the effect that there may be liability to a *suspect* for negligent investigation even though previously the field was thought to be occupied only by malicious prosecution and misfeasance in a public office, both of which are singularly difficult to establish.[204] The "defensive policing" arguments (now reversed) were dismissed as speculative.

All this is not to say, of course, that the police enjoy any general immunity from liability for negligence. A police officer is liable for negligence causing a road accident or for failing to protect someone in custody from attack or (where there is reason to suspect the risk) self-harm[205]; and he may assume responsibility to someone at risk of attack.[206] *Hill v CC West Yorkshire* is a case of failing to prevent crime; but while every allowance may have to be made for operational exigencies, there is no reason why a duty should be denied in respect of positive acts in preventing crime or danger.[207] Other persons having duties to control or supervise those with criminal proclivities may also face claims from their victims and such cases are considered below.[208]

H. Duty to this Claimant

5–21   Though the order is not perhaps logical, it is desirable—before turning to examine some of the categories where a duty of care is denied or restricted—to say some more about the other role played by the duty of care. Let us assume a case of physical injury caused by an act of the defendant, a situation in which the duty of care is at its most expansive. It is still necessary, however, that on the particular facts the defendant owed a duty to the claimant.

In such a case the test is whether injury to the claimant would have been in the contemplation of a reasonable man. Despite the reference in *Donoghue v Stevenson* to "neighbours" the test is not one of physical closeness[209] but of foresight, for my neighbours are, "persons who are so closely and directly affected by my act that I

---

[203] [2007] SCC 41; [2007] 3 S.C.R. 129.
[204] See Chs. 19 and 7, below.
[205] See para.6–41, below
[206] *Costello v CC Northumbria* [1999] I.C.R. 752.
[207] As is accepted in *Hill* at [1983] A.C. 59. Hence it is surprising that *Hill* is relied on in *New South Wales v Klein* [2006] NSWCA 95, where the issue was whether there was a duty of care to relatives in respect of a shooting by the police. In *Desmond v CC Nottinghamshire* [2009] EWHC 2362 (QB) it was held arguable that there was a duty of care in relation to processing an application for an enhanced criminal record certificate.
[208] See para.5–31, below.
[209] One is tempted to say "proximity" but now that the word has been elevated to the status of a legal "code word" it is best avoided.

ought reasonably to have them in contemplation".[210] Sometimes claimant and defendant may be physically close but there is no duty because, for example, the latter has no reason to expect the former's presence; conversely, there may be a duty even though goods are negligently manufactured in Newcastle and cause damage in Southampton. In other cases, the physical propinquity of the parties or lack of it will be a factor to be taken into account in determining what a reasonable man would have had in contemplation.[211]

Negligence "in the air" or towards some other person is not enough: the claimant cannot build on a wrong to someone else.[212] The point is graphically illustrated by the famous United States case of *Palsgraf v Long Island Railroad.*[213] The facts as presented to the New York Court of Appeals[214] were that the defendants' servants negligently pushed X, who was attempting to board a moving train, and caused him to drop a package containing "fireworks". The resulting explosion knocked over some scales, many feet away, which struck the claimant, injuring her. By a majority the court reversed a decision for the claimant. It might well have been that the defendants' servants were negligent with regard to the man carrying the package, at least as far as his property was concerned, but there was nothing in the appearance of the package to suggest even to the most cautious mind that it would cause a violent explosion. In the words of Cardozo C.J.:

"If no hazard was apparent to the eye of ordinary vigilance, an act innocent and harmless, at least to outward seeming, with reference to her, did not take to itself the quality of a tort because it happened to be a wrong, though apparently not one involving the risk of bodily insecurity, with reference to someone else . . . The orbit of the danger as disclosed to the eye of reasonable vigilance would be the orbit of the duty."

On this side of the water, *Bourhill v Young*[215] the case of the pregnant fishwife who sustained nervous shock at witnessing the aftermath of a road accident, is to the same effect. As Lord Russell of Killowen put it, a duty of care:

---

[210] Hence an employer may owe a duty of care to a member of a worker's family in respect of a foreseeable risk from the worker's employment: *Hewett v Alf Brown's Transport* [1992] I.C.R. 530; *Maguire v Harland & Wolff Plc* [2005] EWCA Civ 1; [2005] P.I.Q.R. P21 (though the claim failed on the facts in the light of the knowledge available to the defendants at the relevant time). Cf. *Caltex Refineries (Qd) Pty Ltd v Stavar* [2009] NSWCA 258, where an Australian court made more of a meal of such an issue.

[211] Or, if one prefers, what the court thinks a fair limit on the defendant's responsibility.

[212] *Bourhill v Young* [1983] A.C. 92 at 108 per Lord Wright. This may sometimes be qualified for procedural purposes: *Wall v Radford* [1991] 2 All E.R. 741.

[213] 162 N.E. 99 (N.Y. 1928). See also *Schlink v Blackburn* (1993) 109 D.L.R. (4th) 331.

[214] There is much doubt as to what actually happened.

[215] [1943] A.C. 92.

"[O]nly arises towards those individuals of whom it may reasonably be anticipated that they will be affected by the act which constitutes the alleged breach."[216]

5–22 When we say that the claimant must be a foreseeable victim we do not mean that he need be identifiable by the defendant. It is enough that he should be one of a class within the area of foreseeable injury.[217] In *Haley v London Electricity Board*[218] the defendants, with statutory authority, excavated a trench in the street. They took precautions for the protection of passers-by which were sufficient for a normal-sighted person, but the claimant, who was blind, suffered injury because the precautions were inadequate for him. It was held that the number of blind persons who go about the streets alone was sufficient to require the defendants to have them in contemplation and to take precautions appropriate to their condition. It is not even necessary that the claimant should be in existence at the time when the negligent act is done. If, for example, D carelessly repairs the brakes on a car and this leads to injury to the owner's child born thereafter, there is no doubt that the child would have a cause of action.[219] Indeed, a duty is owed to one who has not been born when the injury to his mother (causing disability to him) is suffered, even though a foetus does not have an independent legal personality.[220]

I. Overlap of Duty and Breach

5–23 For convenience we often categorise duties by reference to relationships. For example, we say that manufacturers owe duties to ultimate consumers, drivers to other road users and so on. This does no harm (indeed, it is necessary in so far as we must identify those areas in which a duty of care is rejected or limited) provided it is

---

[216] [1943] A.C. 92 at 102. For the problem of nervous shock, see para.5–61, below. The claimant heard the accident but did not see it and was in no physical danger from it. A solicitor may be liable to disappointed beneficiaries for mismanaging the making of a will (para.5–37, below) but if a motorist knocked down the testator while the latter was on the way to make the will, he would owe a duty to the testator but not to the beneficiaries since the loss to them would be unforeseeable, quite apart from the absence of any relationship between the motorist and the beneficiaries which would be likely to attract a duty of care in respect of such financial loss.

If A damages property in B's custody he is in breach of a duty of care to any persons unknown who have sufficient interest in the goods to bring a claim (see Ch.17) even if B has represented that he is the only such person: *Awad v Pillai* [1982] R.T.R. 266. However, cf. *The Pioneer Container* [1994] 2 A.C. 324.

[217] He may join the class after the negligent act but before the damage is suffered: *Aiken v Stewart Wrightson Members Agency Ltd* [1995] 1 W.L.R. 1281.

[218] [1965] A.C. 778.

[219] *Burton v Islington HA* [1993] Q.B. 204; *X & Y v Pal* (1991) 23 N.S.W.L.R. 26 at 30.

[220] *Burton v Islington HA* above, fn.219. Post-1976 births are governed by legislation: para.24–13, below.

remembered that it is normally not the existence of the relationship alone which makes the claimant the defendant's neighbour, but the fact that the defendant ought in the court's view to have had the claimant in contemplation[221] when directing his mind to the acts or omissions which are called in question, i.e. the alleged acts of negligence themselves. It follows that the test can only be applied ex post facto.[222] It also follows that it is impossible always to keep separate from each other questions of the existence of a duty, of the breach of that duty and of remoteness of damage. The foresight of the reasonable man is of critical importance in the first two questions and plays a not insignificant role in the third, and it has been said that:

> "[I]t is, on final analysis, the need for care lest someone be injured that both creates the duty and determines what amounts to a breach of it."[223]

Indeed, it can be argued that the only necessary function performed by the duty of care concept in the present law is to deal with those cases where liability is denied not because of lack of foreseeability but for reasons of legal policy and that in all other cases (the great majority, where there is physical damage caused by an act) everything can be handled by asking whether the defendant behaved with the prudence of a reasonable man[224] or whether the damage was too remote a consequence of the negligence. In *Page v Smith*[225] the issue was whether the defendant, who caused a collision of moderate severity with the claimant's car, was liable for the loss caused by the fact that a rare but dormant mental condition of the claimant's was triggered by the accident. Distinguishing the case of a very minor parking "bump" Lord Lloyd said:

> "[I]f . . . the defendant bumped into his neighbour's car while parking on the street, in circumstances in which he could not

---

[221] Of course, the existence of the relationship may be a necessary precondition to liability under a particular heading, e.g. the relationship of occupier and visitor under the Occupiers' Liability Act 1957: see Ch.9.

[222] "It is here, as elsewhere, a question of what the hypothetical reasonable man, viewing the position, I suppose ex post facto, would say it was proper to foresee": *Bourhill v Young* [1943] A.C. 92 at 110 per Lord Wright. There are some difficult passages in *Page v Smith* [1996] A.C. 155, suggesting that this is a special rule for nervous shock (Lord Keith) or at least for the situation where D causes shock to C by endangering B (Lord Lloyd). But the use of "as elsewhere" seems to indicate that Lord Wright was simply making the point that it is inevitable that the court (the hypothetical reasonable man) sees the matter from the point of view of hindsight.

[223] *Voli v Inglewood SC* [1963] Qd.R. 256 at 257 per Windeyer J.

[224] For the former "controversy" on this subject see Winfield, "Duty in Tortious Negligence" in *Select Legal Essays* and Lawson, "Duty of Care in Negligence: a Comparative Study" (1947) 22 Tulane L.Rev. 111–130.

[225] [1996] A.C. 155.

reasonably foresee that the occupant would suffer any physical injury at all, or suffer injury so trivial as not to found an action in tort, there would be no question of his being held liable for the onset of hysteria. Since he could not reasonably foresee any injury, physical or psychiatric, he would owe the plaintiff no duty of care."

While the conclusion on liability is certainly correct, one might just as well say—indeed it seems more natural to do so—that the defendant did owe the claimant a duty of care but the damage suffered was not a reasonably foreseeable consequence of his negligence.[226] There is no doubt that the defendant in the example did owe the claimant a duty of care in respect of the claimant's property. To that it may be properly replied that a duty of care does not exist in the abstract: it must relate to the kind of loss suffered by the claimant[227] and property damage is a different kind of loss from personal injury. However, it is hard to see why there is no duty of care in respect of personal injury even in a parking manoeuvre: sudden pressure on the wrong pedal could cause a substantial impact sufficiently great to damage the occupant of the car.

The point that in a case which is really about *breach* one may find the court speaking in terms of the defendant's *duty* to do such-and-such is illustrated by an Australian case, *Rundle v State Rail Authority (NSW)*.[228] The 15-year-old claimant's "hobby" was vandalizing trains by spray-painting graffiti. Windows of coaches were designed so that the horizontal opening would be very small, though if the rubber grommets were worn this could double in size. In the latter event it was possible for a person of slim build, with considerable effort and agility, to project the top half of his body through the window. This the claimant did in order to spray the roof of the coach and he was struck by some lineside object and seriously injured. Not surprisingly, the appeal court upheld the dismissal of his claim. Although many of the windows were not "perfect" they were still

---

[226] "It does not . . . matter whether one speaks of a duty to take care, the existence of which depends upon physical injury being foreseeable to the particular claimant, or of a general duty to take care not to cause physical injury to anyone which is only broken in relation to the claimant if some kind of physical injury to him or her was foreseeable": *Maguire v Harland & Wolff Plc* [2005] EWCA Civ 1; [2005] P.I.Q.R. P21 at [62] per Mance L.J. (a dissenting judgment, but on the facts rather than the law).

[227] *Banque Bruxelles Lambert SA v Eagle Star Insurance Co Ltd* [1997] A.C. 191 at 211 per Lord Hoffmann; and see Lord Bridge in *Caparo v Dickman* [1990] 2 A.C. 605 at 627: "It is never sufficient to ask simply whether A owes B a duty of care. It is always necessary to determine the scope of the duty by reference to the kind of damage from which A must take care to save B harmless." See para.6–27, below.

[228] [2002] NSWCA 354, [2002] Aust Torts Reports 81–678. *Tomlinson v Congleton BC* [2003] UKHL 47; [2004] 1 A.C. 46, para.9–17, below, has similar elements. The case mainly concerned the Occupiers' Liability Act 1984 s.1(3) of which well illustrates the running together of the duty and breach issues.

completely adequate as a safeguard against what a passenger making an ordinary use of the train might be expected to do, for example leaning out of the window to get a better view or to relieve sickness, and a system of frequent inspection of the window fittings to maintain the smaller opening would have been expensive and would have interfered with the operation of the railway, since 94 per cent of the coaches were in use at any one time. The trial judge put his decision in terms of there being no duty to take effective steps to prevent the claimant behaving like this and it is therefore not surprising that most of the appeal judgment is couched in similar terms, but as the court accepted there was no doubt that the railway owed the claimant a duty, namely to take reasonable care to provide a coach which was fit to carry him. That duty was not breached because he was only able to put himself in the way of an obvious risk of harm by making extraordinary efforts in order to achieve his aim of spraying the roof. Indeed, the court accepted that the factors which had led the trial judge to reject a duty were, "convincing reasons for concluding that if there was a duty it was not breached".

It has to be accepted that the analysis of the elements of the tort of negligence is not a scientific exercise—they overlap to some extent and opinions will differ as to where each case should be "located",[229] but the fact remains that the existence of a duty of care, breach of that duty and remoteness of damage are regularly treated as separate ingredients of the tort of negligence and this continues to have advantages from the point of view of exposition. In some cases there is no doubt whatever that the defendant's conduct was negligent towards someone, what is seriously in issue is whether the defendant was negligent towards the claimant and this is most conveniently considered in terms of duty; in other cases there is no doubt that if the defendant was negligent at all then he was negligent towards the claimant, and these cases are most conveniently discussed in terms of breach. If there is a duty and a breach then the extent of the liability to that claimant will be considered as a matter of remoteness.

J. Other Jurisdictions

The search for "ultimate principle" has not been confined to **5–24** England and there are now some disparities in the various

---

[229] In *Sydney Water Corp v Turano* [2009] HCA 42 the defendants were not liable for a road accident caused by the collapse of a tree in 2001 which had been brought about by non-obvious effect of their installation of a water main in 1981. Perhaps it is more intuitive to say that they did not owe a duty to road users at that location 20 years later than that they had not broken a duty. Again it makes no practical difference.

approaches to the duty of care question in the various Commonwealth countries, though how much difference that makes to the
outcome of cases is difficult to judge. Canada applies a somewhat
recast *Anns* model, though as can be seen from a fairly recent
statement of it,[230] it shades into something like the *Caparo*
formula:

> "In *Odhavji Estate v. Woodhouse*[231] . . . the Court affirmed the
> *Anns* test and spoke . . . of three requirements: reasonable fore-
> seeability; sufficient proximity; and the absence of overriding
> policy considerations which negate a *prima facie* duty established
> by foreseeability and proximity . . . . Some cases speak of foresee-
> ability being an element of proximity where 'proximity' is used in
> the sense of establishing a relationship sufficient to give rise to a
> duty of care . . . . *Odhavji*, by contrast, sees foreseeability and
> proximity as separate elements at the first stage; 'proximity' is
> here used in the narrower sense of features of the relationship
> other than foreseeability. There is no suggestion that *Odhavji* was
> intended to change the *Anns* test; rather, it merely clarified that
> proximity will not always be satisfied by reasonable foresee-
> ability. What is clear is that at stage one, foreseeability and factors
> going to the relationship between the parties must be considered
> with a view to determining whether a *prima facie* duty of care
> arises. At stage two, the issue is whether this duty is negated by
> other, broader policy considerations.
>
> The plaintiff bears the ultimate legal burden of establishing a
> valid cause of action, and hence a duty of care: *Odhavji*. How-
> ever, once the plaintiff establishes a *prima facie* duty of care, the
> evidentiary burden of showing countervailing policy considera-
> tions shifts to the defendant, following the general rule that the
> party asserting a point should be required to establish it."

The New Zealand position is not radically different. It was
described as follows in *Te Mata Properties Ltd v Hastings District
Council*[232]:

> "The Court in [*South Pacific Manufacturing Co Ltd v New Zea-
> land Security etc Ltd*[233]] emphasised the importance of consider-
> ing all the relevant circumstances in deciding whether a duty of

---

[230] *Childs v Desormeaux* [2006] SCC 18; [2006] 1 S.C.R. 643 at [12]. The Singapore CA
considered it was stating an approach substantially similar in *Spandeck Engineering Pte
Ltd v Defence Science and Technology Agency* [2007] SGCA 37; [2007] 4 S.L.R. 100.
[231] [2003] SCC 69; [2003] 3 S.C.R. 263.
[232] [2008] NZCA 446; [2009] 1 N.Z.L.R. 460 at [33]. See also *Rolls-Royce New Zealand Ltd
v Carter Holt Harvey Ltd* [2005] 1 NZLR 324.
[233] [1992] 2 N.Z.L.R. 282.

care should be imposed, and that the question was of an intensely pragmatic character, well suited for gradual development but requiring most careful analysis. It took the view that the two broad fields of inquiry are the degree of proximity or relationship between the alleged wrongdoer and the person who has suffered damage—which is not of course a simple question of foreseeability of harm as between the parties and involves the degree of analogy with cases in which duties are already established—and whether there are other policy considerations tending to negative or restrict the duty in that class of case. They warned against laying down hard and fast rules as to when a duty of care arises, and stressed the importance of a step by step application to the facts of particular cases."

It has been observed in the Supreme Court there that the changes of emphasis since *Anns* have produced no substantial difference in result.[234]

The formal position in Australia is rather different. The High Court in *Sullivan v Moody*[235] rejected the *Caparo* approach on the ground that neither proximity nor fairness had the necessary precision to serve as practical tests and that the latter was capable of being misunderstood as an invitation to formulate policy rather than to search for principle. The current Australian approach is summarised in *Caltex Refineries (Queensland) Pty Limited v Stavar*[236] as involving a:

"[C]lose analysis of the facts bearing on the relationship between the plaintiff and the putative tortfeasor by references to the 'salient features' or factors affecting the appropriateness of imputing a legal duty to take reasonable care"

and there follows a non-exhaustive list of 17 commonly recurring factors. The process has been described[237] as not a matter of policy but as, "an evaluative judgment which includes normative considerations as to the appropriateness of the imputation of legal responsibility and the extent of thereof." Yet the High Court in *Sullivan* based its conclusion on the view that there would be a clash between the contended for duty and (a) the law of defamation and (b) the defendants' statutory functions. These are just such matters as have been considered by English courts under the third element in *Caparo*. There are certainly some radical differences between English and Australian tort law (even leaving aside the changes

[234] *Couch v Att Gen* [2008] NZSC 45; [2008] 3 N.Z.L.R. 725 at [52]
[235] [2001] HCA 59; 207 C.L.R. 562.
[236] [2009] NSWCA 258 at [102]–[105].
[237] *Makawa Pty Ltd v Randwick CC* [2009] NSWCA 412 at [17].

which were made there by legislation at the beginning of the century to curb tort liability)—in the approach to economic loss or the liability of advocates, for example. But it would be difficult to contend that these have been brought about by differences in the formal approach to the duty of care.

2. Duty of Care: Specific Problems

5–25 Although so far we have concentrated upon the general approach to determining whether a duty of care exists, the cases are of course concerned with producing a result on a particular set of facts. The range of situations in which the "duty issue" may arise is almost infinite but there are a number of standard situations in which it has arisen very frequently and it is necessary to say more about these. Unfortunately the categories are not watertight and there is a good deal of overlap between them so that, for example, a case about the activities of a public authority, the fourth category in what follows, may also involve discussion[238] in terms of omissions and assumption of responsibility, or even economic loss.[239] With the warning, therefore, that the reader must be prepared to move between different sections (and, indeed, to refer back to the section on the general approach to duty) we turn to five of these common situations.

A. Failure to Act

5–26 The basic rule has always been—and seems still to be—that one must take care not to cause injury to others, but there is no general duty to act for the benefit of others. The rule is that I must not harm my neighbour (misfeasance) not that I am required to save him (nonfeasance).

> "The very parable of the good Samaritan . . . which was invoked by Lord Atkin in *Donoghue v Stevenson* . . . illustrates, in the conduct of the priest and the Levite who passes by on the other side, an omission which was likely to have as its reasonable and probable consequence damage to the health of the victim of the thieves, but for which the priest and the Levite would have incurred no civil liability in English law."[240]

---

[238] The emphasis in a particular judgment may be affected by the way in which the case has been argued. In *Calvert v William Hill Credit Ltd* [2008] EWCA Civ 1427; [2009] Ch. 330 the judge found that a bookmaker owed no general duty to protect clients against gambling but that the defendants had to a limited extent assumed responsibility to the claimant. The main battleground of the appeal was on causation.

[239] In comparison, the liability of lawyers and psychiatric injury are comparatively self-contained categories.

[240] *Home Office v Dorset Yacht Co Ltd* [1970] A.C. 1004 at 1060 per Lord Diplock.

There is dissatisfaction in some quarters with the suitability of the rule in modern conditions[241] and in 1987 one member of the House of Lords, while accepting the existence of the rule, said that it might one day have to be reconsidered.[242] However, in *Stovin v Wise* the rule was regarded as justifiable by both the majority and the minority in the House of Lords. Lord Hoffmann for the majority said:[243]

"There are sound reasons why omissions require different treatment from positive conduct. It is one thing for the law to say that a person who undertakes some activity shall take reasonable care not to cause damage to others. It is another thing for the law to require that a person who is doing nothing in particular shall take steps to prevent another from suffering harm from the acts of third parties ... or natural causes. One can put the matter in political, moral or economic terms. In political terms it is less of an invasion of freedom for the law to require him to consider the safety of others in his actions than to impose upon him a duty to rescue or protect. A moral version of this point may be called the 'Why pick on me?' argument. A duty to prevent harm to others or to render assistance to a person in danger or distress may apply to a large and indeterminate class of people who happen to be able to do something. Why should one be held liable rather than another? In economic terms, the efficient allocation of resources usually requires an activity should bear its own costs. If it benefits from being able to impose some of its costs on other people (what economists call 'externalities') the market is distorted because the activity appears cheaper than it really is. So liability to pay compensation for loss caused by negligent conduct acts as a deterrent against increasing the cost of the activity to the community and reduces externalities. But there is no similar justification for requiring a person who is not doing anything to spend money on behalf of someone else. Except in special cases (such as marine salvage) English law does not reward someone who voluntarily confers a benefit on another. So there must be some special reason why he should have to put his hand in his pocket."

---

[241] See, e.g. Linden, "Rescuers and Good Samaritans" (1971) 34 M.L.R. 241; Weinrib, "The Case for a Duty to Rescue" (1981) 90 Yale L.J. 247; Markesinis, "Negligence, Nuisance and Affirmative Duties of Action" (1989) 105 L.Q.R. 104 cf. Honoré "Are Omissions Less Culpable?" in Cane and Stapleton (eds.) *Essays for Atiyah*. For European systems see van Gerven, Lever and Larouche, *Tort Law (Common Law of Europe Casebooks)* (2000), Ch.3.1.

[242] Lord Goff in *Smith v Littlewoods Organisation Ltd* [1987] A.C. 241 at 271.

[243] [1996] A.C. 923 at 943.

The rule applies to public bodies as well as private persons. The defendants in *Stovin v Wise* were a highway authority; and where a horse fair had been held in a small town for hundreds of years the local authority was under no obligation to take steps to ensure adequate arrangements for the control of horses or that horse traders had liability insurance against the risk of visitors to the fair being injured by horses for:

> "[T]he general policy of the law does not extend to holding D legally to blame for injury to C caused by the negligence of T on the ground that D could have prevented it . . . . As a matter of generality, to hold a person liable to a victim for injury for which the defendant was not directly to blame, but was caused by the negligence of a third person which the defendant could have foreseen and prevented, would shift the basis of tort liability towards a system for the transfer of losses resulting from injuries not merely caused by the default of the defendant but which a defendant might have been able to prevent."[244]

The rule is probably in practice less frequently determinative than might be thought for two reasons: what may from one point of view seem to be nonfeasance may be treated in law as misfeasance and in many cases the relationship between the parties or some other factor may lead to the imposition of a duty to act.

5–27   **i. Cases where there is not a true omission.** The first point is that an apparent omission may be treated as simply an item in a chain of active negligent conduct. A driver must take active steps to meet emergencies which arise and no one would seriously contend that his failure to brake at a junction was an omission in the sense here discussed[245] and maintaining one's speed in a deliberate attempt to balk an overtaking driver who had "run out of road" would be actionable negligence.[246] So also, a doctor's prescription of a drug without warning the patient that it was dangerous if taken with alcohol would be as much negligence as giving him the wrong information on dosage. Nonetheless, in some cases it is impossible to regard the omission as part of a course of conduct in this way. Thus in England the common understanding is (though there appears to be no case precisely in point) that refusal by a doctor in

---

[244] *Glaister v Appleby in Westmorland Town Council* [2009] EWCA Civ 1325; [2010] P.I.Q.R. P6 at [46].

[245] Rigby L.J. in *Kelly v Metropolitan Ry Co* [1895] 1 Q.B. 944 at 947 said of a driver's failure to shut off steam so that his train ran into the dead end, "the proper description of what was done was that it was a negligent act in so managing the train as to allow it to come into contact with the dead-end".

[246] This seems to be accepted in *Smith v Cribbens* [1994] P.I.Q.R. P 218, where, however, maintaining speed was a sensible thing to do in the circumstances.

an emergency to go to the aid of a person who is not his patient would not be actionable.[247] Equally, of course, what contains elements of positive conduct may still, for the purposes of tort law be an omission. Starting something does not of itself impose a legal duty to finish it.[248] In *Stovin v Wise* the defendant road authority had resolved to improve a junction and then let the matter go to sleep. Had the work been done, the claimant would probably not have been involved in the accident which took place but the accident was nevertheless caused by what the authority failed to do (improve the junction) not by anything it did. In contrast, a person who is hit by a driver who fails to brake may plausibly say that he was injured by the car being driven too fast.[249] In *East Suffolk Rivers Catchment Board v Kent*[250] the defendants, acting under statutory powers, began to repair a breached sea wall on the claimant's property. A competent work force could have done the job and stopped the flooding in about 14 days but in fact it took them 178 days. The House of Lords dismissed the claimant's claim because, as Lord Porter put it[251]:

"[T]heir duty was to avoid causing damage, not either to prevent future damage due to causes for which they were not responsible or to shorten its incidence. The loss which the respondents suffered was due to the original breach, and the appellants' failure to close it merely allowed the damage to continue during the time which they took in mending the broken bank."

It goes without saying, of course, that if a person engaged in a rescue which he was not obliged to undertake negligently inflicts

---

[247] In *Capital & Counties Plc v Hampshire CC* [1997] Q.B. 1004 at 1060, a case about a fire brigade, Stuart-Smith L.J., giving the judgment of the court, said that, "a doctor who happened to witness a road accident . . . is not under any legal obligation to [assist], save in certain limited circumstances which are not here relevant, and the relationship of doctor and patient does not arise." What the "limited circumstances" are is not specified. However, a majority of the NSWCA has held that a doctor may be under a duty to respond to a call for help for a non-patient: *Woods v Lowns* (1996) Aust. Torts Rep. 81–376, though local legislation on professional conduct had some influence on the decision.

[248] In *Capital & Counties*, above, fn.247, at 1035 Stuart-Smith L.J. thought that if the doctor volunteers his assistance his only duty was not to make the patient worse, but presumably that may include making him worse by dissuading others from seeking other assistance. At any rate it is plainly the law that a hospital which admits a patient must treat him, not ignore him: *R. (Burke) v GMC* [2005] EWCA Civ 1003; [2006] Q.B. 273 at [32]. Where a patient of sound mind refuses treatment it is unlawful to administer it but where he consents to it, the source of the duty to administer it is not his wishes but the duty to care for him which the hospital has undertaken.

[249] See Lord Hoffmann [1996] A.C. at 945.

[250] [1941] A.C. 74.

[251] [1941] A.C. 74 at 104.

some positive harm upon the claimant he may be liable for that[252] for he has then left the claimant worse off than he was before.[253] "You made me worse" sounds properly in tort; "you failed to save me" sounds, if at all, in contract.[254] The fire brigade are not liable to a property owner for being tardy in responding to a call, but if, once they get there, they negligently turn off the sprinkler system which would have saved the property or reduced the damage, they are.[255]

"Sometimes the additional feature [necessary to found a duty of positive action] may be found in the manner in which the victim came to be at risk of harm or injury. If a defendant has played some causative part in the train of events that have led to the risk of injury, a duty to take reasonable steps to avert or lessen the risk may arise."[256]

A defendant who without wrongdoing creates a source of danger is liable if he does not take proper steps to safeguard others against it: so if I dig a hole in the pavement I must take proper steps to fence

---

[252] A rare example is *Davis v Stena Line Ltd* [2005] EWHC 420 (QB); [2005] 2 Lloyd's Rep. 13 (where, however, there was clearly a duty to attempt rescue). "Both priest and levite ensured performance of any common law duty of care to the stricken traveller when, by crossing to the other side of the road they avoided any risk of throwing up dust in his wounds": Deane J. in *Jaensch v Coffey* (1984) 54 A.L.R. 417 at 440. Thus the result in *Stovin v Wise* might have been different if, as a result of "improving" the junction the authority had made it more dangerous but in a true rescue situation allowance will have to be made for the exigency of the emergency. *O.L.L. Ltd v Secretary of State for Transport* [1997] 3 All E.R. 897 is a difficult case. The issue was whether the coastguard could be liable, not for tardy response to an emergency, but for misdirecting (as was alleged) a lifeboat and helicopter attending an emergency at sea. While accepting that a defendant might be liable for a positive act at the scene which caused direct physical injury, May J. struck out the claim on the basis that since the coastguard would plainly, in accordance with the *Capital & Counties* case (below), not be liable if it misdirected its own boat or helicopter, nor should it be if it misdirected someone else. Nonetheless the defendant has deprived the claimant of the assistance of others: see Lord Bingham in *Smith v CC Sussex* [2008] UKHL 50; [2009] 1 A.C. 225 at [57]. Suppose a passing motorist said that he would take an unconscious casualty to hospital and other people at the scene forbore to call an ambulance. Would he not be liable if he stopped for refreshments, whereby the patient died? Why should it matter that he intervenes "at the scene"? Note, however (1) in the *OLL* case proving cause and effect might have been very difficult, though this could not have been dealt with on the striking out application (2) the claim was not a very attractive one since it was a claim for contribution by defendants one of whose officers was convicted of manslaughter in respect of the event.

[253] *Stovin v Wise* [1996] A.C. at 949.

[254] Thus if in the *East Suffolk* case there had been a contract no doubt the defendants would have been in breach of an implied term to do the work with reasonable efficiency, but see below as to "assumption of responsibility".

[255] *Capital & Counties Plc v Hampshire CC* [1997] Q.B. 1004; cf in Scots law *Burnett v Grampian Fire and Rescue Service* [2007] CSOH 3; 2007 S.L.T. 61. See also *Alexandrou v Oxford* [1993] 4 All E.R. 328 (police and 999 call).

[256] *Mitchell v Glasgow CC* [2009] UKHL 11; [2009] 1 A.C. 874 at [40] per Lord Scott. For the crime of gross negligence manslaughter see *R. v Evans* [2009] EWCA Crim 650; [2009] 1 W.L.R. 1999.

it and if my car breaks down on the highway I must take steps to prevent it causing danger to other traffic.[257] Whether one regards that as an element in a positive course of conduct or as depending upon a separate principle would seem not to matter.[258]

ii. Relationships. Even where there is a "true" omission the law　**5–28** may impose a duty to act; and it not infrequently does so. It is impossible to catalogue the situations but a number of factors which seem typically to point towards a duty of affirmative action are considered below. The situation where liability is imposed because the defendant has "assumed responsibility" for a task is considered in the following section but there is a good deal of overlap between the two categories and in most cases where a duty is imposed because there is a "special relationship" between the parties it might be said that in entering that relationship the defendant had assumed responsibility for the claimant's safety or well-being but some such assumption or relationship distinguishes the defendant from a mere stranger.

(a) *Relationships of dependence.* A duty to act may be imposed　**5–29** where the claimant is under the care or control of the defendant and is incapable of protecting himself. Thus claims have succeeded against schools for failing to safeguard pupils[259] against injury,[260] the police are liable for failure to protect a mentally disturbed person in their custody from self-inflicted harm[261] and the same is of course true of a mental hospital with regard to a patient who is a suicide risk.[262] In many of these cases the defendant will be a public

---

[257] *Wright v Lodge* [1993] 4 All E.R. 299. See also *Johnson v Rea* [1962] 1 Q.B. 373; *McKinnon v Burtatowski* [1969] V.R. 899. But it is not enough that some act of the defendant has created the opportunity for someone else to do damage. In *C.B.S. Songs Ltd v Amstrad Consumer Electronics Plc* [1988] A.C. 1013 the defendants produced tape recorders which made it easy to copy copyright material. The House of Lords emphatically denied that they were under any duty of care to the owners of the copyright material, whose rights were to be found in the copyright legislation alone and that had not been infringed.

[258] It may not take much to convince the court that the defendant has created the danger as opposed to failing to remedy it: *Kane v New Forest DC* [2001] EWCA Civ 878; [2002] 1 W.L.R. 312 (requiring construction of footpath on development without ensuring safe egress to road).

[259] But a university incurs no liability for failing to control the private lives of its students, allowing them to be seduced, become associated with criminals or become drug addicts: *Hegel v Langsam* 273 N.E. 2d 351 (1971).

[260] On the extent to which a school may have a duty to take action to prevent bullying out of school see *Bradford-Smart v West Sussex CC* [2002] EWCA Civ 7; [2002] ELR 139. While a school is under a duty to protect a pupil from physical harm in, e.g. playing sports, it is not obliged to take out accident insurance for the child, nor to advise the parents to do so: *Van Oppen v Bedford School* [1990] 1 W.L.R. 235.

[261] *Kirkham v CC Greater Manchester* [1990] 2 Q.B. 283 (as to suicide by sane persons in custody, see para.5–33, below).

[262] See *Savage v S. Essex Partnership NHS Foundation Trust* [2008] UKHL 74; [2009] 1 A.C. 681 at [47].

authority so there is the prospect of an alternative claim, via the Human Rights Act 1998, based on art.2 of the Convention, though the primary focus of that is on the requirement that the state should ensure adequate "systems" to guard against the risk. It might seem obvious as a matter of principle that a tort duty is owed by a parent to his child and this seems to be the law in England.[263] The point has been little litigated, perhaps because of the likely absence of liability insurance, but it should be noted that the imposition of a duty would allow an insured defendant to claim contribution from an uninsured parent (for example in a case arising out of a road accident where the parent had failed to supervise the child).[264]

5–30   (b) *Other relationships with the victim.* The previous cases may be said to involve relationships of dependence but duties of affirmative action are imposed across a much wider range of relationships, in at least some of them probably because the defendant gains some benefit from his relationship with the claimant. Thus an employer must not only take proper steps to secure safety in the workplace[265] but must look after a worker who is injured or falls ill at work even if the employer is not responsible for the emergency[266]; and the same is true of a carrier with regard to his passenger.[267] Indeed, the Supreme Court of Canada has extended this so as to hold that a private boat owner was obliged to take steps to rescue a guest who fell overboard.[268] An occupier is under a duty to take reasonable care to ensure that his premises are reasonably safe for the purposes for which his visitor enters and owes a duty (although a rather more

[263] *Surtees v Kingston on Thames BC* [1992] P.I.Q.R. P101 (foster parent) but the duty is not a high one and the case emphasises that it must take account of the distractions of everyday life. See also Saville L.J. in *Marc Rich & Co A.G. v Bishop Rock Marine* [1994] 1 W.L.R. 1071 at 1077 (no duty in stranger to save blind man from road accident, but duty in parent to prevent child running into the road). The criminal offence of allowing the death of a child or vulnerable adult under s.5 of the Domestic Violence, Crime and Victims Act 2004 may extend beyond persons who have "assumed responsibility" at common law, though the primary purpose of the provision seems to have been to sidestep the common tactic of "cross incrimination" where one of two persons could have been responsible.
[264] Hence the caution of the High Court of Australia about imposing liability in *Hahn v Conley* (1971) 126 C.L.R. 378 unless the parent has embarked on some activity. See further para.6–51, below.
[265] See Ch.8. This does not extend to a duty to arrange accident insurance for workers abroad in a country with no developed system of motor insurance: *Reid v Rush and Tompkins Group Plc* [1989] 3 All E.R. 228. Cf. *Van Oppen v Bedford School*, above, fn.260.
[266] *Kasapis v Laimos* [1959] 2 Lloyd's Rep. 378. He is under no duty to safeguard the employee's property against theft: *Deyong v Shenburn* [1946] 1 K.B. 236.
[267] A duty to try to rescue a man overboard was conceded in *Davis v Stena Line Ltd* [2005] EWHC 420 (QB); [2005] 2 Lloyd's Rep. 13. A duty to take action was imposed in *Silva Fishing Corp (Pty) Ltd v Maweza* [1957 (2)] SA 256 where the defendants hired a vessel to the claimants on a profit sharing basis.
[268] *Horsley v Maclaren, The Ogopogo* [1971] 2 Lloyd's Rep. 410. It would be impracticable to impose a duty of care on a taxi driver to assess the sobriety of his passenger and to set him down only where a drunken person would be safe: *Griffiths v Brown, The Times*, October 23, 1998.

restricted one) to trespassers and both of these may clearly require positive steps, for example to do repairs or put up warnings,[269] though the occupier is not required to prevent people from encountering obvious risks like climbing trees or swimming in lakes.[270] However, one cannot slip from the mere existence of a relationship to the assumption that there is a protective duty: a social landlord who took action against an abusive tenant was not liable when the tenant responded by killing the person who had initiated the complaint.[271]

"The [landlord's] . . . obligation to [the deceased] was to act as a responsible landlord and to take steps to terminate [the abuser's] tenancy in order to remove him from the locality where he was causing such trouble. That obligation cannot . . . suffice to justify treating the [landlord] as having assumed responsibility for [the deceased's] safety."[272]

How far is a defendant providing an ordinary service, such as the sale of alcohol, under a duty to protect a claimant of full age and understanding against his own weakness? In *Barrett v Ministry of Defence*[273] the defendants operated a military base at an isolated site in Northern Norway at which alcohol was available cheaply and drinking was a principal recreation. The claimant's husband died after consuming a large quantity of alcohol. The Court of Appeal rejected the contention that the defendants were under a duty to monitor and control the consumption of alcohol at the base, despite the fact that the disciplinary code contained provisions designed to curb excessive consumption. Beldam L.J., delivering the judgment of the Court of Appeal, pointed out that the level of consumption which might put a person in danger varied considerably from person to person and that it was:

"[F]air, just and reasonable for the law to leave a responsible adult to assume responsibility for his own actions in consuming alcoholic drink. No one is better placed to judge the amount that he can safely consume or to exercise control in his own interest as well as in the interest of others. To dilute self-responsibility and to blame one adult for another's lack of self-control is neither just

[269] See generally Ch.9.
[270] See para.9–17, below. See also *Fowles v Bedfordshire CC* [1995] P.I.Q.R. P380 (merely providing facilities for gymnastics; no duty to take active steps to prevent an adult using them in a foolish manner dangerous to himself; liability was based on having encouraged the manoeuvre by giving inadequate instruction in it).
[271] *Mitchell v Glasgow CC* [2009] UKHL 11; [2009] 1 A.C. 874.
[272] At [44] per Lord Scott. See also *X v Hounslow LBC* [2009] EWCA Civ 286; [2009] P.T.S.R 1158.
[273] [1995] 1 W.L.R. 1217. Cf. *Jacobson v Nike Canada* (1996) 133 D.L.R. (4th) 377.

nor reasonable and in the development of the law of negligence is an increment too far."[274]

The defendants were, however, liable for the death, subject to a two-thirds reduction on account of contributory negligence, because of the way in which they had dealt with the deceased[275] after he was found in a collapsed state.[276] In *Jebson v Ministry of Defence*,[277] on the other hand, the defendants were held liable for an injury caused by their failure to supervise the claimant soldier during his return journey from an evening's drinking organised by the company commander.[278] Perhaps that case is to be explained by the context that the soldiers were under military discipline. The High Court of Australia has firmly rejected the view that a commercial seller of alcohol is under any tort duty to monitor the consumption of his customers or restrain them from leaving if he considers, for example, that they are unfit to drive. Such a duty would require surveillance and inquiries which would be seriously invasive of customers' autonomy and potentially destructive to peaceful social relations.

"To encourage interference by publicans, nervous about liability, with the individual freedom of drinkers to choose how much to drink and at what pace is to take a very large step. It is a step for legislatures, not courts, and it is a step which legislatures have taken only after mature consideration. It would be paradoxical if members of the public who may deliberately wish to become intoxicated and to lose the inhibitions and self-awareness of sobriety, and for that reason are attracted to attend hotels and restaurants, were to have that desire thwarted because the tort of negligence encouraged an interfering paternalism on the part of those who run the hotels and restaurants."[279]

There may be exceptional cases where the drinker is beyond any rational action or mentally ill but the case was not made exceptional because the drinker had asked the bar owner to store his motorcycle and then demanded it back.

---

[274] [1995] 1 W.L.R. at 1224. Nor is a bookmaker under any general duty to safeguard punters against the risks of gambling: *Calvert v William Hill Credit Ltd* [2008] EWCA Civ 1427; [2009] Ch 330.

[275] The defendants had "assumed responsibility" for him but it is submitted that as his quasi-employers on those premises they were bound to do so.

[276] *Crocker v Sundance Northwest Resorts* (1988) 51 D.L.R. (4th) 321 and *Jordan House v Menow* (1973) 38 D.L.R. (3d) 105 were distinguished: in the first D had permitted C to take part in a ski race as well as supplying drink and in the second he had put the obviously intoxicated C out of the bar on a highway.

[277] [2000] 1 W.L.R. 2055.

[278] There was 75 per cent contributory negligence.

[279] *CAL No 14 Pty Ltd v Scott* [2009] HCA 47 at [54]. See also *Cole v South Tweed Heads Rugby League Football Club Ltd* [2004] HCA 29; 217 C.L.R. 469.

(c) *Relationship with person causing the harm.* A relationship **5–31**
between the defendant and the person who is the cause of the harm
to the claimant may lead to liability to the claimant.[280] For this
reason a school authority was liable for letting a small child out of
school in circumstances where it was foreseeable that he would
cause an accident in which a driver was killed trying to avoid him[281]
and in a suitable case this may extend even to wilful wrongdoing.
Thus in *Home Office v Dorset Yacht Co Ltd* borstal authorities who
failed in their duty of supervision were responsible for damage done
by escaping inmates in the immediate vicinity and in the course of
the escape.[282] Where the defendant has control of both the claimant
and the wrongdoer (for example, in a case where there is an assault
on a prisoner by fellow inmates[283]) the case for the imposition of a
duty is particularly strong.

In the *Dorset Yacht* case the wrongdoers were subject to a form of
custody by the defendants. We have seen that the police incur no
liability for failing to get wrongdoers into custody, but there may be
intermediate cases where there is a duty of supervision. In *Couch v
Att Gen*[284] the nominal defendant was sued as representing the New
Zealand probation service on the basis that they had allowed X
during his parole from a sentence for aggravated robbery to take up
employment at premises where there were large quantities of alcohol and cash and at which he had injured the claimant and murdered
three other people during the course of theft. The Supreme Court of
New Zealand held that this disclosed an arguable claim of negligence, though three members of the court were of the view that the
claimant would have to establish that she was a member of a class
especially vulnerable in view of X's record[285] and her position as a
fellow employee or the premises being an attractive target for theft
would not do that.

We have seen that a person who supplies alcohol to another is
entitled to assume that the other is the best judge of what he can
safely consume,[286] but does the same apply if the other gets drunk

---

[280] In some cases of course the relationship (generally only that of employer and employee)
between D and the wrongdoer may make D vicariously liable for the wrongdoer's act: see
Ch.20, below. Here it is assumed that there is no vicarious liability, hence there must be
a duty in D and breach of it by him: *Smith v Leurs* (1945) 70 C.L.R. 256.

[281] *Carmarthenshire CC v Lewis* [1955] A.C. 549. As to the duty to the child, see above.

[282] [1970] A.C. 1004. Cf. *Fleming v Securities Commission* [1995] 2 N.Z.L.R. 514, where it
was held that a newspaper carrying advertisements contravening securities legislation
owed no duty of care to the public.

[283] *Ellis v Home Office* [1953] 2 Q.B. 135.

[284] [2008] NZSC 45, [2008] 3 N.Z.L.R. 725. Since there is no general liability for negligence
for personal injuries in NZ the claim was one for exemplary damages which are available
there (but not here) for that tort in certain circumstances. Cf. *X v South Australia* [2007]
SASC 125.

[285] Cf. the "proximity" reason in *Hill v CC W Yorks*.

[286] *Barrett v MoD*, para.5–30, above.

and causes a road accident which injures a pedestrian? The reasoning which might deny liability to the driver does not necessarily apply to the pedestrian, who has done nothing to contribute to the accident. The matter has not been litigated here, though it has been said in the Supreme Court of Canada that:

> "[T]here is no doubt that commercial vendors[287] of alcohol owe a general duty of care to persons who can be expected to use the highways."[288]

If this is to be the law then there may of course be serious evidentiary difficulties and in practical terms the duty cannot be a very high one, since the barman cannot be expected to keep a detailed tally of the consumption of all his customers. In an English case it has been said, obiter, that a person who entrusted a car to a drunk might bear liability for an accident but that a dealer who sold a car to a known alcoholic would not be liable for an accident caused by intoxication a few weeks later.[289] The policy considerations in relation to those who serve alcohol of course overlap with those in cases where it is the drinker who comes to grief and the High Court of Australia has observed that the view in Canada that there is a duty to the third party is:

> "[R]egarded . . . as a logical step from the conclusion that there is a duty to the customer. In [Australia], since there is generally no duty to the customer, the step cannot be taken on that ground. Whether it is open on some other ground must be left to a case raising the issue."[290]

A duty to control the behaviour of patrons on the premises is another matter[291]: that falls naturally within the scope of the defendant's duty as occupier. It should be noted, however, that in the road traffic context litigation against providers of alcohol is less likely in England than in some other jurisdictions because of the existence of compulsory motor liability insurance in an unlimited amount and of

---

[287] However, the Supreme Court of Canada has rejected any general duty on a private host to monitor guests' drinking at a party: *Childs v Desormeaux* [2006] SCC 18; [2006] 1 S.C.R. 643.

[288] *Stewart v Pettie* (1994) 121 D.L.R. (4th) 222 at 231. The claimant was a passenger in the car who had visited the establishment with the driver but the reasoning plainly applies to any road user. The duty was found not to have been broken.

[289] Lord Goff in *Paterson Zochonis & Co Ltd v Merfarken Packaging Ltd* [1986] 3 All E.R. 522 at 540.

[290] *CAL No 14 Pty Ltd v Scott* [2009] HCA 47 at [57].

[291] *Adeels Palace Pty Ltd v Moubarak* [2009] HCA 48.

the MIB as a back-up in cases where the driver is uninsured[292]: in other jurisdictions the claimant may take action against the third party where there is no cover or its limits have been exceeded.

iii. Property owners. An occupier is under a duty not only to his **5–32** visitors but to take steps to remove a hazard on his land which threatens neighbouring property even though it has arisen from the act of nature or of a third party—property is a source of obligation as well as of rights.[293] In principle this can extend to taking steps to prevent a third party gaining access to the property and using it to inflict damage on the claimant but wilful human conduct is not normally sufficiently likely to require the defendant to contemplate it as a reasonable probability rather than a remote possibility. So in *Smith v Littlewoods Organisation Ltd*[294] the defendants were not liable when vandals entered an empty cinema scheduled for redevelopment and caused a fire which spread to property next door.[295]

"So far as Littlewoods knew, there was nothing significantly different about these empty premises from tens of thousands of others up and down the country. People do not mount 24-hour guards on empty properties and the law would impose an intolerable burden if it required them to do so save in the most exceptional[296] circumstances."[297]

This is to approach the matter as one of a general duty to take steps to ensure property does not become a source of danger to others and then to handle individual cases as matters of breach of duty. Lord Goff on the other hand adopted the position that in the

---

[292] Though at least in theory the MIB could require the claimant to sue the third party; Uninsured Driver Agreement (1999) para.14.1. This could not of course apply where the inebriated person injures himself. In *Cal No 14 Pty Ltd*, above, fn.290, the Motor Insurance Board was a co-claimant, seemingly on the basis of the limited "no fault" payments it made to accident victims.

[293] See para.14–21, below.

[294] [1987] A.C. 241.

[295] What if the claim arises from criminal injury inflicted on the premises by some third party? Such a case probably does not fall within the Occupiers' Liability Act 1957 (Ch.12). It may be going too far to say that an occupier can never be under a duty to protect visitors against attack (consider, for example a hotel or nursery without any security). But it is quite unrealistic to expect the occupier to do much in relation to, say, a car park. See *Modbury Triangle Shopping Centre v Anzil* [2000] HCA 61; 175 A.L.R. 164 and *Proprietors of Strata Plan 17226 v Drakulic* [2002] NSWCA 381; 55 N.S.W.L.R. 659.

[296] The old film stock on the property did not present any special fire hazard.

[297] [1987] A.C. 241 at 251 per Lord Griffiths. "Unless the needle that measures the probability of a particular result flowing from the conduct of a human agent is near the top of the scale it may be hard to conclude that it has risen sufficiently from the bottom to create the duty reasonably to foresee it": at 261 per Lord Mackay.

absence of special circumstances there was no duty to guard against such risks: such a duty would be an unreasonable burden[298] and, at least in the case of theft, the primary obligation to protect his property should rest on the owner of it.[299] In practice on such facts there may be no great difference between the two approaches.[300] It has since been said in the House of Lords that Lord Goff's approach is to be preferred but that was in a case which did not involve the defendant's property being a source of danger.[301]

5–33   **iv. Safety services.** The traditional approach has been that a public body or service is in the same position with regard to omissions as a private person. The successful defendants in some of the leading cases were, after all, public authorities.[302] If a public authority gave an undertaking to assist and the claimant relied on that so as to change his position there might be liability, but that argument would frequently not be open because no alternative steps were available: a person whose house is on fire is not likely to be able to assert that when the fire service said it was on its way he desisted from organising a chain of neighbours with buckets. However, the political, moral and economic arguments which are said to underpin the general rule of non-liability[303] hardly apply to a service the function of which is to guard the public against danger and that service will also be under some form of pre-existing public law duty (albeit not enforceable by a private law claim for damages) in respect of the performance of its functions. It may be significant that when, in *Hill v CC West Yorkshire*[304] the House of Lords rejected a duty of care on the police in respect of the investigation of crime, the reasoning was based on lack of proximity between the police and the

---

[298] See Lord Goff's example at 277 in the *Littlewoods* case of the family going on holiday who forget to lock their door (*P. Perl (Exporters) Ltd v Camden London Borough* [1984] Q.B. 342) whereby a burglar gains access to neighbouring premises.

[299] In many cases the contest would effectively be between the defendant's liability insurer and the neighbour's subrogated loss insurer.

[300] Lord Keith in *Littlewoods* felt able to agree with both Lord Goff and Lord Mackay. Lords Brandon and Griffiths agreed with Lord Mackay.

[301] *Mitchell v Glasgow CC* [2009] UKHL 11; [2009] 1 A.C. 874 at [20], [56]. In *Topp v London Country Bus* [1993] 1 W.L.R. 976 the Court of Appeal held that the defendants were not liable for a hit and run death caused by persons who took their unsecured minibus. See also *Bohdal v Streets* [1984] Tas. R. 83 (private car in drive). The oddity about *Topp*'s case is that the court closely followed the view of Lord Goff in *Littlewoods*, even though that is plainly not the majority view. See Howarth (1994) 14 L.S. 88. Victims of untraced drivers may sue the MIB and it appears from the report of the case at first instance that the MIB had required the proceedings to be brought against the bus company: [1993] 3 All E.R. 448.

[302] *East Suffolk v Kent*; *Stovin v Wise*; *Capital & Counties v Hampshire CC*; *Mitchell v Glasgow CC*, above.

[303] See para.5–26, above.

[304] [1989] A.C. 53, para.5–11, above.

victim and the perceived deleterious effects of liability on police
efficiency, not on the simple fact that they *failed* to catch the
criminal. In *Kent v Griffiths*[305] the claimant suffered an asthma
attack at home, her doctor called for an ambulance and was assured
that it was on its way. In fact the ambulance did not arrive until well
after the "target" time (something for which there was no explanation) and the claimant suffered a respiratory arrest, which would
probably have been avoided by timely arrival of the ambulance. The
doctor gave evidence that if she had been informed of the likely
delay she would have had the claimant driven to hospital by other
means, so a decision in favour of the claimant could easily have
been reached on the basis of "undertaking and reliance", yet this
figures hardly at all in the Court of Appeal's judgment.[306] Rather the
duty seems to have arisen simply from the acceptance of the call and
it seems that the result would have been the same even if the
claimant had been in a remote place with no alternative means of
transport. That may be "illogical" in the light of traditional assumptions about the nature of contract and tort but most people would
probably find it shocking if the law drew a distinction between the
two situations. The Court emphasised that it was not concerned with
a situation where a decision had been taken by the public body about
the allocation of limited resources, nor with a case where, with the
benefit of hindsight, a "wrong" decision had been taken in an
emergency on the basis of limited information: it is for the ambulance service, not the courts, to take decisions on the first matter and
as to the second, to be wrong is not necessarily to be negligent. The
cases of the fire service[307] and the police were distinguished on the
basis that their duty was owed to the public at large.[308] No doubt that
explains why the police are not liable to some unidentifiable member of the public injured by a criminal whom they fail to catch but
it is less easy to see why the fact that the fire service may have to
take into account the risks to other property when fighting a fire
necessarily means that they have no duty of care to fight it efficiently
as far as the owner of the burning house is concerned. If there is to
be a difference between the cases it seems better to recognise that it
lies in the fact that the fire service is primarily concerned with
saving property and that imposing liability would tend to enure for
the benefit of subrogated fire insurers who have taken a premium to

[305] [2001] Q.B. 36.
[306] The doctor's evidence is mentioned in the statement of facts at [2001] Q.B. 42 and at the
    end of the judgment (at 54) it is said that, "if wrong information had not been given about
    the arrival of the ambulance, other means of transport could have been used."
[307] On the non-liability of the fire service see para.5–27, above.
[308] [2001] Q.B. at 52.

cover the risk,[309] though that would hardly justify a different result where life was at risk from the fire.[310]

While such cases may not be easy to reconcile it does now seem to be the case that a public service may incur liability for failing to save an identifiable person whose protection from personal injury it can be said to have assumed. Another straw in the wind is *Reeves v Metropolitan Police Commissioner*[311] where the police were held liable for negligence in failing to prevent the suicide of a sane[312] person in custody in their cells. In fact the existence of a duty of care was never challenged in either appeal and the matter was fought in the House of Lords on the issue of whether the deliberate act of the deceased broke the chain of causation[313] but the clear implication is that the defendants' concession on the issue of duty in the appeals was rightly made.[314] However, a duty to prevent others of full age and capacity harming themselves will be rare, for, "on the whole people are entitled to act as they please, even if this will inevitably lead to their own death or injury."[315] So the existence of the duty turned on the fact that the deceased was in the police cells and the police had reason to know that he was a suicide risk[316]: the police are not required to take special precautions for every person in custody.[317] Nor will they owe a duty of care to prevent a person who has just been arrested escaping and injuring himself in the process.[318] In Australia it was held that there was no duty to intervene when police officers came upon a man who appeared to be preparing

[309] See Lord Hoffmann in *Stovin v Wise* [1996] A.C. at 955. So also, in relation to the facts of that case, drivers can generally take care against obvious road hazards. It should be noted that respect for the home and the peaceful enjoyment of possessions are guaranteed by, respectively, art.8 and art.1 of the First Protocol to the Convention and the European Court of Human Rights has said that, "although the object of Article 8 is essentially that of protecting the individual against arbitrary interference by the public authorities, it does not merely compel the State to abstain from such interference: in addition to this primarily negative undertaking, there may be positive obligations inherent in effective respect for [the guaranteed right]": *Guerra v Italy* (1998) 26 E.H.R.R. 357 at 383. But while the state must clearly establish a fire service, it would be surprising if a Convention claim could extend to acts of operational negligence.

[310] And is not the coastguard service nowadays rather like the ambulance despatch service, despite *O.L.L. Ltd v Secretary of State for Transport*, para.5–27, above?

[311] [2000] 1 A.C. 360.

[312] The evidence as to his mental condition was not very satisfactory, but this is the basis on which the case was fought.

[313] See para.6–41, below.

[314] See particularly Lord Hope at [2000] 1 A.C. 379. On this case and the principle of autonomy see para.4–8, above.

[315] Lord Hope at [2000] 1 A.C. 379. "Under the domestic law of the United Kingdom there is no general legal duty on the state to prevent everyone within its jurisdiction from committing suicide": *Savage v S. Essex Partnership NHS Foundation Trust* [2008] UKHL 74; [2009] 1 A.C. 681 at [25]. See also para.9–17, below.

[316] Such a person is in that category of vulnerable groups, which also includes mental patients and conscripts, which attracts a duty of protection under art.2 of the European Convention on Human Rights: *Savage*, above, fn.315.

[317] *Orange v CC W. Yorkshire* [2001] EWCA Civ 611; [2002] Q.B. 347.

[318] *Vellino v CC Greater Manchester* [2001] EWCA Civ 1249; [2002] 1 W.L.R. 218.

to commit suicide by gassing himself in his car but who, upon being questioned, appeared rational and said that he had changed his mind. Later that day he did commit suicide by that method. The officers had statutory power to detain a person who appeared to be mentally ill and about to commit suicide but their testimony that they believed neither condition to be satisfied was not challenged and the statutory power was not therefore triggered. Whatever might have been the position had this not been so (and Australian law may be rather more generous than English law in finding a common law duty of care in the context of a statutory power[319]) the result was that the police officers no more owed a duty of care than would any other visitor to the car park.[320] The result would surely be the same at common law in England[321] and, even assuming that art.2 of the Convention could be extended to a case where there was no element of control it might be difficult to establish the requisite "real and immediate risk" to life.

B. Assumption of Responsibility

In *Hedley, Byrne & Co Ltd v Heller & Partners Ltd*[322] the House of Lords held that in English law there might be liability in tort for merely financial loss[323] caused by negligent misstatement and the court spoke in terms of the maker of the statement having assumed or undertaken a responsibility towards the other and that other having relied upon it. This is considered at a later point in the particular context of statements.[324] However, while it cannot serve as a general "test" for all duty of care questions, it is now clear that the broad principle of the case goes beyond liability for statements and extends to the situation where the defendant undertakes to perform a task or service for the claimant. That, it will immediately be observed, brings us very close to the realm of contract and that was essentially the point of *Henderson v Merrett Syndicates Ltd.*[325] The claims were brought by "Names" at Lloyd's who had incurred

5–34

---

[319] See *Graham Barclay Oysters Pty Ltd v Ryan* [2002] HCA 54; 211 C.L.R. 540. For English law see para.5–46, below. In any event the position of public bodies exercising statutory powers in Australia must now be considered in the light of uniform legislation illustrated by ss.42–46 Civil Liability Act 2002 (NSW).

[320] *Stuart v Kirkland-Veenstra* [2009] HCA 15.

[321] In Australia at one time an attempt was made to explain the position of safety regulators in terms of "general reliance". However, while the concept was referred to by Lord Hoffmann in *Stovin v Wise* [1996] A.C. at 954 it has also been said that there is "little if any support for it in English law" (*Capital & Counties Plc v Hampshire CC* [1997] Q.B. at 1027). Indeed, it was never very clear exactly what it was and it seems to have disappeared in the land of its birth: *Vairy v Wyong SC* [2005] HCA 62; 223 C.L.R. 422.

[322] [1964] A.C. 465.

[323] There was probably liability before this at least in certain cases of physical damage, e.g. misleading instructions accompanying a medicine.

[324] See Ch.11.

[325] [1995] 2 A.C. 145. For the concurrence of contract and tort, see para.1–8, above.

heavy personal liabilities arising out of alleged negligent underwriting by the managing agents of syndicates of which they were
members. In some cases a "members' agent" was interposed
between the Names and the managing agents so that prima facie
there was no privity of contract and the claim was tort or nothing[326];
in other cases there was a direct contractual link but the Names were
asserting a tort claim in order to gain the advantage of the Latent
Damage Act 1986 on limitation of actions.[327] In holding that a duty
of care arose in tort in both situations, Lord Goff said:

> "There is in my opinion plainly an assumption of responsibility[328]
> in the relevant sense by the managing agents towards the names
> in their syndicates. The managing agents have accepted the names
> as members of a syndicate under their management. They obvi-
> ously hold themselves out as possessing a special expertise to
> advise the names on the suitability of risks to be underwritten, and
> of the circumstances in which, and the extent to which, reinsur-
> ance should be taken out and claims should be settled. The names,
> as the managing agents well knew, placed implicit reliance on that
> expertise, in that they gave authority to the managing agents to
> bind them to contracts of insurance and reinsurance and to the
> settlement of claims. I can see no escape from the conclusion that,
> in these circumstances, prima facie a duty of care is owed in tort
> by the managing agents to such names ... Furthermore, since
> the duty rests on the principle in *Hedley, Byrne*, no problem arises
> from the fact that the loss suffered by the names is pure economic
> loss."[329]

The House of Lords was concerned with pure, preliminary issues
of law in this case and not with the details of the alleged negligent
conduct. In fact the complaint was of negligent underwriting by
taking on greatly excessive aggregate risks and far too little reinsurance cover but the reasoning in the case would plainly apply to the
situation in which A undertook the management of B's business
affairs and then, while giving the contrary impression, did nothing at
all. Nor can it necessarily be objected that the real nature of the case
is that the claimant has been prevented from making a gain: loss, by
reliance, of the opportunity to employ one's money profitably is as

---

[326] In fact it was held that the terms of the members' agents' contracts made them responsible
to the Names for the default of underwriting agents.

[327] See para.26–9, below.

[328] The phrase had been criticised by Lord Griffiths in *Smith v Eric S. Bush* [1990] 1 A.C. 831
at 862 (para.11–26, below) but the point he had been concerned to make was that the
assumption of responsibility was more often deemed from the circumstances than
expressly undertaken.

[329] [1995] 2 A.C. 145 at 182.

much a loss actionable in tort as loss of the money itself.[330] The loss is, of course, purely economic and in certain cases that is a bar to recovery,[331] but that is clearly not so under *Hedley Byrne*. Statements rarely give rise to any type of loss other than economic loss and if, in *Hedley Byrne*, the House of Lords had held that there was a duty of care in respect of statements, but that it did not extend to economic loss, that would have strangled the new duty at birth. So the economic loss argument is no more valid in an "undertaking" case than in a "statement" case.

This approach does not go so far as to impose a liability exactly   **5–35** equivalent to that in contract because of the requirement of reliance[332] (unnecessary where there is a contract supported by consideration) but nevertheless it goes a very long way down the road of creating a parallel liability in respect of services and one which is more than merely academic because it may lead to different results. For example, one of the underlying problems of *Henderson* was the fact that the claims of some claimants had become statute-barred before they knew about them and the imposition of a duty in tort enabled them to outflank the problem via the Latent Damage Act. Now it may well be the case that the non-applicability of the Act to contractual negligence is not a very sensible rule anyway, but it might be argued that in the case of recent legislation the correct approach is direct amendment of the legislation rather than unsettling the boundary between contract and tort claims.[333] On the other hand, some would take the view that in this type of case we have really moved into a different sort of obligation altogether, neither contract nor tort.[334]

Since *Henderson,* assumption of responsibility has been the basis   **5–36** of recovery in a very wide range of situations and as we have seen it is to some extent a rival to the *Caparo* test as the general approach to the duty of care question. It has been used to justify (in some cases in tandem with the *Caparo* approach) the imposition of a duty of care on an educational psychologist called in by a local authority to advise on a child,[335] on the British Boxing Board of Control in respect of the adequacy of medical arrangements at fights taking

---

[330] See *East v Maurer* [1991] 1 W.L.R. 461. See the nature of the loss in *White v Jones,* para.5–37, below.

[331] See the next section.

[332] It is also the case that there must be negligence—but that is anyway generally a requirement of contracts to provide services.

[333] See more generally Whittaker, "The Application of the 'Broad Principle of Hedley Byrne' Between Parties to a Contract" (1997) 17 L.S. 169.

[334] See McBride and Hughes, "Hedley Byrne in the House of Lords: an Interpretation" (1995) 15 L.S. 376. See also McBride, "A Fifth Common Law Obligation" (1994) 14 L.S. 35. McBride and Hughes argue that the liability equates most closely to a fiduciary one ("letting others down"): see Lord Browne-Wilkinsons's view in *White v Jones,* para.5–37, below.

[335] *Phelps v Hillingdon LBC* [2001] 2 A.C. 619.

place under its aegis,[336] on a referee of an amateur rugby match[337] and on a solicitor acting for a borrower to take care to ensure, for the benefit of an unrepresented lender, that the security was effective.[338] It has also been called in aid to impose a duty limited to a particular type of loss, by asking, in a case where the defendant was obviously under a potential liability for some type of harm, for what consequences of his action he could fairly be regarded as assuming responsibility.[339]

In few, if any, of these cases has the defendant expressly assumed responsibility in the sense that he has recognised that he will incur a legal liability if he fails in it, but this is not necessary—the assumption of responsibility in question is one which is based on the law's objective assessment of the situation[340]; but one must be able to say that the defendant has undertaken to "see to it" and that this is based on something more than a recognition that he is under a legal compulsion to perform the task. As we have seen, in *Customs and Excise Commissioners v Barclays Bank Plc*[341] it was held that a bank does not assume responsibility to the holder of an injunction freezing a customer's account by writing to acknowledge that he has received it: he has no choice but to obey the court's order. Of course a person may go beyond his legal duty, as in *Neil Martin Ltd v Revenue and Customs Commissioners*[342] where, although there was no actionable statutory duty on the part of the Revenue to process an application promptly and therefore no common law duty to do so could have arisen in its place, the defendants could be vicariously liable for an employee's decision to make (without authority) a declaration on the claimants' behalf. Even if there is no element of legal compulsion, care must be taken to focus on what the defendant has undertaken (or is to be deemed to have undertaken) responsibility for, otherwise we are on a slippery slope towards outflanking the basic principle that one is not required to take positive action to assist others: an employer no doubt assumes responsibility for his

---

[336] *Watson v British Boxing Board of Control Ltd* [2001] Q.B. 1134. See also *Wattleworth v Goodwood Racing Co Ltd* [2004] EWHC 140; [2004] P.I.Q.R. P25 (motor sport association advising on safety at tracks).

[337] *Vowles v Evans* [2003] EWCA Civ 318; [2003] 1 W.L.R. 1607. "Rarely if ever does the law absolve from any obligation of care a person whose acts or omissions are manifestly capable of causing physical harm to others in a structured relationship into which they have entered": at [25].

[338] *Dean v Allin & Watts* [2001] EWCA Civ 758; [2001] 2 Lloyd's Rep. 249. See also *Killick v Pricewaterhouse Coopers* [2001] Lloyd's Rep. P.N.18 (valuation of shares).

[339] *Parkinson v St. James etc. NHS Trust* [2001] EWCA Civ 530; [2002] Q.B. 266.

[340] *Smith v Eric S. Bush* [1990] 1 A.C. 831 at 862; *Henderson v Merrett Syndicates Ltd* [1995] 2 A.C. 145 at 181; *Phelps v Hillingdon LBC* [2001] 2 A.C. 619 at 654.

[341] [2006] UKHL 28; [2007] 1 A.C. 181, para.5–8, above.

[342] [2007] EWCA Civ 1041; [2007] S.T.C. 1802.

workers' safety[343] but he is not to be taken as volunteering to act as a pensions adviser[344]; and an insurer that paid benefits under a health insurance scheme arranged with an employer did not assume responsibility to a worker in respect of the assessment of his condition—the worker's entitlement under the scheme was by contract with his employer and if he contended that the payments had been wrongfully withheld, the proper course was an action against the employer.[345] Nor do fire officers "assume responsibility" to the owners of property when they arrive at the scene of a fire.[346]

i. Responsibility without reliance. Assumption and reliance are **5–37** flexible concepts[347] but while the first may be found by implication in almost any circumstances in which a person takes on a task, reliance by the claimant is sometimes plainly absent. Such was the case in *White v Jones*.[348] A testator, having made a will disinheriting his daughters after a family quarrel, became reconciled with them and instructed the defendant solicitors to prepare a new will. There was a delay by the defendants which amounted to negligence and the testator died before the will could be made, with the result that the "old" will governed the devolution of his estate. The delay was a breach of contract to the testator but since the estate was in no way diminished in size that would have given rise only to nominal damages. Hence as far as the law of contract was concerned:

> "[T]he only persons who might have a valid claim (the testator and his estate) have suffered no loss, and the only person who has suffered a loss (the disappointed beneficiary) has no claim."[349]

---

[343] Though despite *Costello v CC Northumbria* [1999] I.C.R. 752 and *Mullaney v CC W. Midlands* [2001] EWCA Civ 700 it hardly seems necessary to rely on that concept in such a case.

[344] *Outram v Academy Plastics* [2000] I.R.L.R. 499. Cf. *Lennon v MPC* [2004] EWCA Civ 130; [2004] 1 W.L.R. 2694, where there was an assumption of responsibility in response to an inquiry.

[345] *Briscoe v Lubrizol* [2000] I.C.R. 694. The contract between the employer and the insurer would probably have barred a claim by the worker under the Contracts (Rights of Third Parties) Act 1999 had it been in force. In such a case the insurer is concerned to avoid litigation by individuals who may be impecunious.

[346] *Capital & Counties Plc v Hampshire CC* [1997] Q.B. 1004 at 1036. However, perhaps the ambulance service does when it books an emergency call: para.5–33, above.

[347] *Hedley Byrne* was also the basis of Lord Goff's reasoning in *Spring v Guardian Assurance Plc* [1995] 2 A.C. 256 (para.11–33, below) where the House of Lords held that the provider of a reference might owe a duty of care to the subject of the reference but the other judges spoke in more general negligence terms. The case is more like *Hedley Byrne* in that it concerned a statement but the statement was made not to the claimant but to a third party and in such a case undertaking to and reliance by the subject may be tenuous.

[348] [1995] 2 AC. 207.

[349] [1995] 2 A.C. 207 at 259 per Lord Goff; *Ross v Caunters* [1980] Ch. 297 at 303 per Megarry V.C. The result of the rather similar case of *Ross v Caunters* is approved, but not its reasoning, for its reliance on the broad *Donoghue v Stevenson* principle failed to meet the conceptual problems of the situation: [1995] 2 A.C. at 267.

A majority of the House of Lords upheld a decision in favour of the beneficiaries based on the tort of negligence.[350] On such facts, where the beneficiaries are aware of the testator's intention it might be possible to contend that they had relied on the solicitors by forbearing to put pressure on them or on the testator to finalise the matter, but the case was argued and decided on the basis that no such reliance was necessary, despite the additional objections that the solicitor's primary duty arises by contract with his client, that his negligence lay in simply failing to carry out the client's instructions,[351] that the beneficiaries had not been deprived of anything which they possessed or to which they had any right, since the testator could have cut them out again for no reason at all[352] and that the practical result was to increase the size of the testator's bounty at the expense of the solicitors, since the legatee under the unrevoked will could plainly keep what the testator did not intend to give him.[353] Persons who foreseeably rely on an auditor's report cannot sue,[354] whereas those who find that they were the object of the intended bounty of a long-lost relative can.

For Lord Goff, in the majority, the dominant factor seems to have been a strong "impulse for practical justice"[355] bolstered by a need for the law to recognise the role of solicitors in relation to testators and legatees[356] and the fact that other jurisdictions seemed all to have come down in favour of liability.

"In my opinion, therefore, your Lordships' House should in cases such as these extend to the intended beneficiary a remedy under the *Hedley Byrne* principle by holding that the assumption of responsibility by the solicitor towards his client should be held in law to extend to the intended beneficiary who (as the solicitor can reasonably foresee) may, as a result of the solicitor's negligence, be deprived of his intended legacy in circumstances in which

---

[350] In *Hill v Van Erp* (1997) 188 C.L.R. 159 the majority of the High Court of Australia also came to the conclusion that a solicitor owed a duty to a disappointed beneficiary.

[351] At least in *Ross v Caunters*, above, fn.349, it was a case of "active" negligence in that the will had been improperly executed.

[352] The case was not one which would have attracted the Inheritance (Provision for Family and Dependants) Act 1975.

[353] "What is plain is that the family as a whole are better off because of the appellants' negligence": Lord Nolan [1995] 2 A.C. at 293. Hence the view of some that the answer lies in a modification of the law of succession: see (1995) 111 L.Q.R. 357. Cf. (1996) 112 L.Q.R. 54.

[354] See para.5–11, above.

[355] [1995] 2 A.C. at 259.

[356] There is a good deal of emphasis in the majority judgments on the role of the "family solicitor" and references to "individual citizens" and "persons of modest means" but it seems impossible to contend that the decision is inapplicable to, e.g. a beneficiary which is a major charity.

neither the testator nor his estate will have a remedy against the solicitor."[357]

It must also be pointed out that such a situation does not normally involve any possibility of wide-ranging or indeterminate liability. In such a case the defendant's contemplation of the claimant is: "actual, nominate and direct. It is contemplation by contract, though of course the contract is with the testator."[358]

The reasoning of Lord Browne-Wilkinson, who delivered the other main majority judgment, is rather different.[359] "Assumption of responsibility", far from being invented in *Hedley Byrne*, was traceable to the decision in *Nocton v Lord Ashburton*[360] where, despite the general rule then prevailing that there was no duty of care in respect of information or advice, the House of Lords had accepted liability arising out of a fiduciary relationship. *Hedley Byrne* was simply the recognition of another category of special relationship which would give rise to a duty of care on the basis of assumption of responsibility. It was true that a necessary element in the liability arising from statements to the claimant was reliance by the claimant[361] for that was the only way in which the claimant could show damage, but reliance was not necessary in the case of a special relationship of the fiduciary variety: in the paradigm fiduciary relationship, that of trustee and beneficiary, a:

> "[T]rustee is under a duty of care to his beneficiary whether or not he has had any dealing with him: indeed he may be as yet unborn or unascertained and therefore any direct dealing would be impossible".[362]

White v Jones fell neither within the category of fiduciary relationships nor was it a case of damage caused by a statement, but there was no reason why the law should not create new categories of

---

[357] [1995] 2 A.C. at 268. Whether "all the conceptual problems ... can be seen to fade innocuously away" (at 269) must, however, be debatable.

[358] *Ross v Caunters* [1980] Ch. 297 at 308. However, it is not wholly true to say that the quantum of the liability is certain. Suppose A intends to make a will leaving all his estate to B and A wins the National Lottery or discovers a Rembrandt in the attic. It is also possible in theory that there could be claims by persons who were unidentifiable at the time of the transaction (e.g. unborn members of a class). Lord Goff in *White v Jones* was content to leave such cases to be decided when they arose: [1995] 2 A.C. at 269.

[359] However, like Lord Goff his Lordship emphasises public reliance and dependence on solicitors in relation to wills.

[360] [1914] A.C. 932.

[361] Cf. statements by the defendant about the claimant to other persons who act on them to the claimant's detriment: *Spring v Guardian Assurance* [1995] 2 A.C. 256, para.11–33, below.

[362] [1995] 2 A.C. at 271. Whether the analogy is a good one is debatable: the trustee is dealing with the beneficiary's property.

"special relationships" and no reason why it should always require reliance.

> "What is important is not that A knows that B is consciously relying on A, but A knows that B's economic well being is dependent upon A's careful conduct of B's affairs."[363]

While the liability recognised in *White v Jones* is one in tort, the assumption of responsibility has its origin in the contract with the testator[364] and in failing to carry out the instructions the solicitor breaks that contract. One view is that a better way to deal with this type of situation is via the law of contract, which is the solution of German law (which is more restrictive than English law in relation to recovery of economic loss in tort).[365] However, such a radical step was beyond the powers of the House of Lords, nor has it been brought about by the Contracts (Rights of Third Parties) Act 1999. That allows a third party to enforce a term in a contract between others if the term purports to confer a benefit on him and there is no intention against such enforcement by the contracting parties. However, the contract between the solicitor and the testator is not one which confers a benefit on the beneficiary: the contract is a means whereby the testator may confer such a benefit by the will.[366] In some cases a party to the contract may be able to recover damages on behalf of the third party even though he (the contract promisee) has not suffered any loss, as where A commissions work on a building by B and then, before the breach by B, transfers the building to C,[367] but that is no help in a situation like *White v Jones* for in the building case the loss is "transferred" to C, that is to say it is one which A would have suffered if he had retained the building, whereas the loss suffered by the beneficiary (loss of the gift) is one which never could have been suffered by the testator. For the same reason one cannot get round the problem by assignment.

5–38   Some developments since *White v Jones* in the factual context of that case are outlined in a later section.[368] It was, however, at first difficult to know how far *White v Jones* was to be taken—a rather

---

[363] [1995] 2 A.C. at 272. Cf. *Longstaff v Birtles* [2001] EWCA Civ 1219; [2002] 1 W.L.R. 470 (clear route to recovery on basis of fiduciary relationship; wrong to try to construct alternative case of assumption of responsibility).

[364] Lord Mustill's point that the contract was not merely part of the history as it was in *Donoghue v Stevenson* (see [1995] 2 A.C. at 280) seems unanswerable.

[365] The *Vertrag mit Schutzwirkung fur Dritte* (contract with protective effect for third parties): see [1995] 2 A.C. at 263.

[366] At any rate, that was the Law Commission's intention: Law Com. No.242 (1997) §7.20. It was held in *Gartside v Sheffield, Young & Ellis* [1983] 1 N.Z.L.R. 37 that the rather similar wording of the Contracts (Privity) Act 1982 s.4, did not give the beneficiary a claim.

[367] *Linden Gardens Trust Ltd v Lenesta Sludge Disposals Ltd* [1994] 1 A.C. 85.

[368] See para.5–58, below.

narrow rule about solicitors and wills, or a "super-principle", merging law and equity and transcending the boundaries of contract and tort?[369] Even if it does not go as far as the second, it is now clear that, as Lord Mustill predicted in his dissent, it does not exist, "simply to create a specialist pocket of tort law, with a special type of proximity, distinct from the main body of doctrine".[370] He said:

"[T]he present case does not as it seems to me concern a unique and limited situation, where a remedy might be granted on an ad hoc basis without causing serious harm to the general structure of the law for I cannot see anything sufficiently special about the calling of a solicitor to distinguish him from others in a much broader category. If the claim in the present case is sound, for any reasons other than those given by my noble and learned friends,[371] it must be sound in every instance of the general situation which I have already identified, namely: where A promises B for reward to perform a service for B, in circumstances where it is foreseeable that performance of that service with care will cause C to receive a benefit, and that failure to perform it may cause C not to receive that benefit. To hold that a duty exists, even prima facie, in such a situation would be to go far beyond anything so far contemplated by the law of negligence."[372]

In *Gorham v British Telecommunications Plc*[373] the deceased had opted out of his employer's occupational pension scheme and had taken out a personal money purchase pension plan with SLA. SLA

---

[369] Lord Nolan in a comparatively short speech agreed with both Lord Goff and Lord Browne-Wilkinson. He thought that the case fell within the general *Caparo* principles and, like the CA, was impressed by the fact that *Ross v Caunters* had stood for 15 years with no apparent ill-effects. It could be said ([1995] 2 A.C. at 293) that if, "the defendant drives his car on the highway, he implicitly assumes a responsibility towards other road users, and they in turn implicitly rely on him to discharge that responsibility. By taking his car on to the road, he holds himself out as a reasonably careful driver. In the same way ... a professional man or an artisan who undertakes to exercise his skill in a manner which, to his knowledge, may cause loss to others if carelessly performed, may thereby implicitly assume a legal responsibility towards them." It may be argued that there are very substantial differences between the cases: (1) while the driver no doubt chooses to go on the road, if we are to say that the liability depends on assumption of responsibility then every negligence case does; (2) the driver does not undertake to do anything for anybody; (3) the driver acts rather than fails to act; (4) the damage is physical.
[370] [1995] 2 A.C. at 291.
[371] Lord Mustill disagreed with those reasons.
[372] McHugh J. dissenting in *Hill v Van Erp* (1997) 188 C.L.R. 159 asked whether an accountant commissioned to assess a business which the client was considering buying as a gift for a relative owed a duty to the relative or whether an insurance broker commissioned to effect a life insurance policy owed a duty to persons who were beneficiaries of the estate of the proposed insured. See *Hughes v Richards* [2004] EWCA Civ 266; [2004] P.N.L.R. 35.
[373] [2000] 1 W.L.R. 2129.

had been negligent towards the deceased in failing to advise him that the employer's scheme was better.[374] The Court of Appeal held that the defendants owed a duty not only to the deceased (with whom they had a contract) but, by analogy with *White v Jones*, also a duty in tort to his dependants, who were therefore able to sue in their own right for the loss of certain death in service benefits which would have been available under the employer's scheme.[375] However, such a situation is more complex than *White v Jones* in one respect, for the wishes of the person taking out the pension plan might conflict with the best interests of his family, for example, he might wish to enhance his pension during his own lifetime at the expense of his widow after his death. The duty was not, therefore, one to see that the dependants were "properly provided for" but one not to advise so as to cause unnecessary loss to the dependants within the scope of the provision the pension taker wished to make.[376]

C. Economic Loss[377]

5–39   As we have seen, much of the controversy about the role of the duty of care in negligence has arisen in cases which have involved the problem of "economic loss" but so far we have not examined that concept closely. The expression is liable to mislead: if a car is destroyed, that is "economic" in the sense that the owner's assets are thereby diminished, but in legal terms it is classified as damage to property and the owner is entitled to its value as damages. Even if the loss is unquestionably only financial in nature, no difficulty is felt about allowing its recovery if it is a *consequence* of physical injury or damage to the claimant's property: for example, the claimant in *Donoghue v Stevenson* could have recovered lost earnings and medical expenses and a company whose machinery was damaged by negligence would recover lost profits while the machinery was out

---

[374] A seller is not of course generally required to inform the buyer of the superiority of others' products but the regulations governing the selling of pensions required the defendants to give the claimant a degree of impartial advice.

[375] Would the Contracts (Rights of Third Parties) Act 1999 affect this case? Even if one regards the duty to the deceased as contractual, it seems difficult to say that *that term* "purports to confer a benefit upon" the dependants. It is the policy which does that.

[376] The major difficulty in this case arose from the fact that the defendants had "come clean" at a stage where it would have been possible to remedy the matter in part, but the claimant had managed to delude himself that he had somehow rejoined the employer's scheme and did nothing: para.6–51, below.

[377] There is a huge amount of literature on this topic. See inter alia, Cane, *Tort Law and Economic Interests*, 2nd edn; Feldthusen, *Economic Negligence*, 5th edn; Atiyah, "Negligence and Economic Loss" (1967) 83 L.Q.R. 248; Dwyer, "Negligence and Economic Loss" in Cane and Stapleton (eds) *Essays for Atiyah*; McGrath, "The Recovery of Economic Loss in Negligence" (1985) 3 O.J.L.S. 350; Stapleton, "Duty of Care and Economic Loss: A Wider Agenda" (1991) 107 L.Q.R. 249.

of action.[378] We are concerned with cases which fall into neither of these categories.

The cases concern a number of distinct situations and the same considerations of policy are not necessarily applicable to each: there is certainly no blanket rule forbidding recovery of economic loss caused by negligence, as we have seen in connection with liability based on assumption of responsibility. There are considerable difficulties in expounding the law in this area because the issue of economic loss frequently coincides with other factors which inhibit the imposition of liability for negligence. For example, if a local authority acting under statutory powers fails to carry out an adequate inspection of a house in the course of construction and is subsequently sued by the owner in respect of defects (a frequent source of litigation in the 1970s and 1980s) at least three potential "problems" arise: (1) the loss suffered by the claimant is economic in nature despite the fact that it manifests itself in physical defects in the building; (2) the authority's conduct is essentially an omission—failure to prevent the builder erecting a shoddy structure; (3) since the local authority cannot devote infinite resources to such matters, the question arises of how far the courts will interfere with the authority's decision on allocation. As the law has developed the judicial emphasis on these various factors has varied from time to time. Thus it is the first which is now the principal reason why there is no liability,[379] but earlier the tendency was to deny that the loss was economic in its nature. The third element was clearly recognised in the leading case (now overruled) in which such liability was imposed[380] and this led to serious difficulties over the relationship between the principles of tort law and of public law. As to the second element, it is probably fair to say that it was hardly acknowledged until 1996, when the duty in such a case had already been rejected.[381] Some degree of overlap is therefore inevitable in any exposition. In this section we consider two situations where the loss is caused by the negligent act of the defendant and where the emphasis is on the nature of the loss: (a) where damage to the person or property of a third person causes financial loss to the claimant; and (b) where the claimant suffers financial loss because of defects in the quality of goods or property supplied to him.[382] The situation

---

[378] It is assumed in both cases that the loss is not too "remote" in the sense considered in the next chapter and that the claimant has acted reasonably to mitigate his loss—e.g. in the second example by hiring a replacement machine if one is available. Where A damaged B's ship and this led to oil spillage which damaged C, a voluntary payment by B to C was not recoverable by B in his action against A in the absence of an assignment of C's claim against A: *Esso Petroleum Co Ltd v Hall Russell & Co Ltd* [1989] A.C. 643.

[379] *Murphy v Brentwood DC* [1991] 1 A.C. 398, para.9–33, below.

[380] *Anns v Merton London Borough* [1978] A.C. 728.

[381] See *Stovin v Wise* [1996] A.C. 923, para.5–26, above.

[382] This is taken up in more detail in Chs 9 and 10, below.

where financial loss is caused by the defendant's failure to fulfil an undertaking to perform a service has already been considered[383] and the liability for financial loss arising from statements is dealt with in Ch.11.

It would help to note two points at the outset. First, the restrictive approach to economic loss is most marked in the law of negligence; there is less difficulty about its recovery in the case of intentional torts such as deceit or intentional interference with contract. Secondly, there is similarly no difficulty if the claimant can frame his claim in contract: most claims for breach of contract involve economic loss and nothing else.[384]

While in most cases it is obvious into which category the injury falls, there may be difficult borderline cases on what amounts to physical damage. It has been said that fabric would be damaged if it were subjected to large deposits of dust which require professional cleaning[385]; so is a gas appliance which is rendered unusable by the ingress of water[386]; and a ship is "damaged" if it is doused in hydrochloric acid and requires decontamination even if there is no appreciable permanent effect on the plating.[387] Contamination of land by radioactive material requiring removal of the topsoil has been held to be physical damage.[388] It has even been held to be arguable that livestock are damaged when, as a result of a movement restriction imposed in a foot and mouth outbreak caused by the defendants, they cannot be sold at their intended price because they have become oversized.[389] However, the fact that the alteration of the physical state of something may be damage does not necessarily mean that the owner can recover damages.

> "If a skilful painter overpaints X's daubs unasked, he inflicts property damage ... even if the world will pay more for the canvas now than it would have done before he came on the scene. If a lump of concrete is dropped on X's car, property damage has

---

[383] See para.5–34, above.

[384] Thus the paradigm case of breach of contract is where S contracts to deliver goods by a certain day and fails to do so and B claims as damages the difference between the contract price and the higher market price on the delivery date, i.e. the extra cost of obtaining a substitute.

[385] *Hunter v Canary Wharf Ltd* [1996] 2 W.L.R. 348 (reversed, but not on this point, [1997] A.C. 655).

[386] *Anglian Water Services Ltd v Crawshaw Robbins Ltd* [2001] B.L.R. 173.

[387] *The Orjula* [1995] 2 Lloyd's Rep. 395. See also *Att Gen for Ontario v Fatehi* (1984) 15 D.L.R. (4th) 1323 (spilling petrol on highway requiring it to be cleaned).

[388] *Blue Circle Industries Plc v MoD* [1999] Ch. 289. Cf. *Merlin v B.N.F.L.* [1990] 2 Q.B. 557.

[389] *D. Pride & Partners v Institute for Animal Health* [2009] EWHC 685 (QB) (but the claim was struck out because the movement order rather than the outbreak was the direct cause of the loss).

been inflicted even if someone can persuade an avant garde gallery curator that the resultant object is a work of art worth more than X paid for the car. What if anything X can recover is a separate question which does not fall to be answered at this stage of the enquiry."[390]

i. Economic loss resulting from damage to property belonging to a third party or from injury to a third party.[391] If D negligently damages the property of X, X can sue D for that damage and consequential loss resulting from it (for example unavoidable loss of revenue while the property is being repaired[392])[393] but if C suffers loss because he is prevented from using that property as a result of the damage, C generally cannot sue D. Similarly, if D negligently kills X, who employs C and C thereby loses his job, or D injures X and C incurs care responsibilities to X,[394] C cannot, at common law, sue D,[395] though in the related context of loss of support from a family member there is a very major statutory modification of this.[396]

5–40

The point about property damage is neatly illustrated by *Spartan Steel & Alloys Ltd v Martin & Co (Contractors) Ltd.*[397] A power cut caused by the defendants' negligence caused material to solidify in the claimants' furnace. The claimants recovered the reduction in value of the solidified "melt" (which had undergone a chemical change from partial processing) and the profit they would have made from its sale as an ingot, but they recovered nothing for the loss of profit on four further melts which would normally have been processed during the time the electricity was interrupted, for this was not a consequence of any damage to their property but simply of the

---

[390] *Jan de Nul (UK) Ltd v Axa Royal Belge SA* [2002] EWCA Civ 209; [2002] 1 Lloyd's Rep. 583 at [92].
[391] These cases are commonly labelled "relational economic loss".
[392] D collides with C's tram. All other tram traffic is delayed and C incurs financial penalties under its franchise agreement. Is this economic loss consequential on damage to the tram? See *Metrolink Victoria Pty Ltd v Inglis* [2009] VSCA 227 where, however, the case was not argued this way.
[393] If D negligently loses the property or allows it to be stolen then, too, an action lies in tort—at least if D is a bailee—but where D allowed X's aircraft (leased to D's company) to be seized by the authorities for non-payment of navigation charges, a Scots court classified that as economic loss: *Nordic Oil Services v Bearman* 1993 S.L.T. 1164.
[394] *Islington LBC v University College London Hospital NHS Trust* [2005] EWCA Civ 596; [2006] P.I.Q.R. P3. See para.22–37, below.
[395] Scots law is the same: *Robertson v Turnbull* 1982 S.C., HL 1.
[396] The Fatal Accidents Act 1976, allowing the dependants of the deceased to sue the tortfeasor who caused the death: see Ch.23, below. There was once a common law action *per quod* in favour of a husband for injury to his wife and an employer for injury to his servant but this has been abolished: para.18–2, below.
[397] [1973] 2 Q.B. 27.

interruption of the electricity supply. In duty language the defendants owed the claimants a duty in respect of damage to their property but did not owe them any duty with respect to mere loss of profits unconnected therewith.[398] Of course property damage was the source of the whole of the claimants' loss but with regard to the lost profits on the four melts it was a consequence of damage to the property of the electricity undertaking, which had suffered no loss other than the cost of repairing the damaged cable[399] and, perhaps, loss of revenue while the supply was interrupted. In other words, the claimant may only sue for damage to property or loss consequent on that if it is his property which is damaged[400]—though ownership is not necessary,[401] possession (or even an immediate right to possession[402]) will do.[403] For this purpose an equitable owner of the property may recover, certainly if the legal owner is joined in the action and perhaps even without that formality.[404] It is not, however, enough that the claimant has merely contractual rights with respect to the property which are rendered less valuable as a result of the damage or that he has contractual obligation in respect of it which becomes more onerous.[405] If, therefore, the electricity supply in

---

[398] Lord Denning M.R. hesitated about classifying such cases as belonging to duty or remoteness but it is submitted that this doubt disappears when it is recognised that D may owe C a duty with respect to loss "A" but not loss "B": *Banque Bruxelles Lambert SA v Eagle Star Insurance Co Ltd* [1997] A.C. 191.

[399] One might be inclined to dismiss this as relatively trivial but damage to utility cables is a huge problem. In 1998/99 BT raised over 10,000 claims for telephone line damage totalling more than £15 million: *British Telecommunications Plc v Geraghty & Miller International Inc*, July 29, 2004, Leeds Mercantile Court. In *Transco Plc v United Utilities Water Plc* [2005] EWHC 2784 (QB) a simple mistake in turning off a valve cost the gas company £174,000 (the trespass claim looks stronger than the negligence one).

[400] This is the reason why if an insurer insures A's property and B negligently destroys it the insurer cannot sue the wrongdoer in its own name, though it may be subrogated to A's rights: *Simpson & Co v Thompson* (1877) 3 App. Cas. 279 (where the right of subrogation was no use since the owner of the damaged ship and the owner of the negligent ship were the same person, who could not sue himself).

[401] It is sufficient, even though an owner out of possession and with no immediate right to it may not be able to sue for other wrongs such as trespass and conversion: *East West Corp v DKBS AF 1912 A/S* [2003] EWCA Civ 83; [2003] Q.B. 1509.

[402] *Colour Quest Ltd v Total Downstream UK Plc* [2009] EWHC 640 (Comm); [2009] 2 Lloyds Rep 1 and cases cited therein (upheld on this point, *Shell UK Ltd v Total UK Ltd* [2010] EWCA Civ 180).

[403] The common law always equated possession and ownership for this purpose: hence a bailee could sue for the full value of the goods bailed to him (even though his interest was limited) whether or not he would be responsible to the owner for the loss. The amount which a bailee can recover may now be restricted by statute: para.17–19, below.

[404] *Shell UK Ltd v Total UK Ltd* [2010] EWCA Civ 180.

[405] *Cattle v Stockton Waterworks* (1875) L.R. 10 Q.B. 453. Thus it would seem that fishermen who lost their livelihood as a result of oil pollution could not sue at common law: *Landcatch Ltd v International Oil Pollution Compensation Fund* [1999] 2 Lloyd's Rep. 316; *R.J.Tilbury & Sons (Devon) Ltd v Alegrete Shipping Co Inc.* [2003] EWCA Civ 65; [2003] 1 Lloyd's Rep. 327; contra, *Union Oil Co v Oppen* 501 F. 2d 558 (1974) described as a "special rule" in *State of Louisiana v M/V Testbank* 752 F. 2d 1019 (1985). They probably have a statutory right of action under the Merchant Shipping Act 1995, para.15–25, below.

Spartan Steel had been speedily restored but the cooling had caused damage to the furnace, loss of production during the time taken to effect repairs to it would, it seems,[406] have been recoverable.[407] Equally the claimants would have succeeded if the cable, at the point at which it was severed, had been vested in them.

After a period of doubt[408] this approach was reaffirmed by the Privy Council in *Candlewood Navigation Corp Ltd v Mitsui O.S.K. Lines Ltd*[409] where time charterers of a damaged vessel (who did not have possession of it) failed to recover the hire which they had to pay even when the vessel was out of action and the revenue which they lost through being unable to make use of the vessel. It will be observed that there was nothing unforeseeable about the loss to the charterers (such loss being a highly likely consequence of damage to a cargo ship[410]) and that D escaped part of the liability which they would otherwise have incurred had the charterer been in possession of the vessel, for then the lost revenue would have been a consequence of damage to "their" property. The person from whom the charterer had hired the use of the vessel could not sue for this loss since he had not suffered it, nor did he suffer loss of hire, since the charterer had to go on paying it. Of course if the charterer had been relieved under the charter of their obligation to pay hire while the vessel was laid up, that would have been recoverable by the person from whom it had been hired. The extent of the tortfeasor's liability in such a case therefore turns on the contractual arrangements[411]

---

[406] The contrary view seems to be taken at first instance in Scotland in *Coleridge v Millar Construction Co Ltd*, 1997 S.L.T. 211, relying on the emphasis in *Marc Rich & Co A.G. v Bishop Rock Marine Co Ltd* [1996] A.C. 211, para.5–13, above, on "direct" physical damage. Although the damage to the first melt in *Spartan Steel* was in a sense "indirect" (since it was a consequence of the damage to the electricity undertaking's cable) there is no overt suggestion in *Marc Rich* that the decision in the claimant's favour on that item was wrong. In any event, the physical damage in *Coleridge* was found to be unforeseeable.

[407] It is assumed that damage to the furnace was reasonably foreseeable by D (Cf. the *Coleridge* case above). Cf. *Londonwaste Ltd v Amec Civil Engineering Ltd* (1997) 53 Con.L.R. 66, where there was some damage to the claimant's turbines but the cause of the loss of revenue was held to be the severing of the cable, which was vested in a third party. For a complex case on the relationship between physical damage and economic loss, see *The Orjula* [1995] 2 Lloyd's Rep. 395.

[408] Caused by *Junior Books v Veitchi* [1983] 1 A.C. 520, para.5–44, below.

[409] [1986] A.C. 1.

[410] A charterer with possession would be the exception rather than the rule.

[411] Legal changes wholly unconnected with tort law may affect the application of the rule. British Rail owned all its track and rolling stock so damage to a BR bridge automatically attracted liability for loss of BR revenue but now the track owner and train operators are completely separate entities. Persons carrying out works likely to affect the line sometimes give the train operator a contractual indemnity: *Tesco Stores v Constable* [2008] EWCA Civ 362. In *Bow Valley Husky (Bermuda) Ltd v St John Shipbuilding Co Ltd* (1997) 153 D.L.R. (4th) 385, C1 had been incorporated as an offshore company by C2 and C3 for fiscal reasons. As to the "common adventure" theory, see below.

between the owner[412] of the damaged property and the person making use of it.[413]

5–41   The apparently arbitrary nature of liability in these cases is demonstrated even more clearly by the subsequent decision of the House of Lords in *Leigh and Sillavan Ltd v Aliakmon Shipping Co Ltd*[414] X sold a cargo of steel coils c&f to C, the property remaining with X during transit but the risk being imposed on C.[415] The coils were damaged by bad stowage by D, the carrier, and C's action against D failed, since although C later acquired ownership of the goods by performance of the sale contract he had neither ownership nor possession while they were at sea. At first sight this result looks extraordinary but closer examination reveals a more complicated picture in the context of carriage by sea. The factual situation in the case was atypical because in most cases at that time the buyer would acquire property in the goods by endorsement to him of the bill of lading and when that happened he would take over, by virtue of the Bills of Lading Act 1855, the rights of the seller against the carrier under the contract of carriage, which would give the right to sue for damage during transit—in other words, there was a statutory exception to the rule of privity of contract and there was no need for tort law to operate.[416] Indeed, there were generally positive reasons why tort should not operate, because contracts involving carriage by sea are made on standard forms based on international agreement and contain detailed exemptions and limitations for the purpose of allocating risks between the carrier and the consignor/consignee, and allowing a right of action in negligence would create the risk that this allocation could in effect be disturbed.[417] In *Leigh and*

---

[412] Confusingly, the claimant in *Candlewood* was the owner of the vessel! It had chartered it by demise to X (which gives possession to X) and then time chartered it back again. The claimant's losses were not suffered in its capacity as owner. In non-marine terms, a charter by demise is like hiring a self-drive van; a time (or voyage) charter is like engaging a removal firm.

[413] Cf. *White v Jones* [1995] 2 A.C. 207, para.5–37, above, where a desire to ensure that a negligent defendant does not escape "scot free" seems to play some part in the decision to impose liability.

[414] [1986] A.C. 786.

[415] i.e. C had to pay X in full even if the cargo was lost or damaged. This is the normal position in international sales.

[416] Alternatively, in some cases there might be an implied contract between the buyer and the carrier if he took delivery from the carrier and paid the freight: *Brandt v Liverpool etc. Steam Navigation Co* [1924] 1 K.B. 575.

[417] Cf. the interesting judgment of Robert Goff L.J. in the Court of Appeal ([1985] Q.B. 350 at 399) where he proposed a theory of recovery of "transferred loss", i.e. when D owes a duty of care not to damage X's property and commits a breach of that duty in circumstances in which the loss foreseeably falls on C by reason of the contract between X and C, then D would be liable in tort to C, but the duty would be modified by the terms of the contract between X and D. Cf. the German law theory of *Drittschadensliquidation* discussed by Markesinis, "An Expanding Tort Law—the Price of a Rigid Contract Law" (1987) 103 L.Q.R. 354. The House of Lords in *Leigh and Sillavan* did not think that a duty of care could be modified in this way but if a duty of care can be rejected because of the contractual arrangements lying behind the event (as it was in the *Marc Rich* case,

Sillavan the normal mechanism failed to operate because a last minute variation took the contract between buyer and seller outside the scope of the 1855 Act.[418] That Act has now been replaced by the Carriage of Goods by Sea Act 1992 and the law amended so that it is much less likely that the buyer with risk in the goods will not be able to sue the carrier[419] under the contract of carriage.[420]

It must also be pointed out in the context of *Leigh and Sillavan* that the fact that C may have no claim because the property belonged to X when the damage was done does not mean that X has no claim in respect of the damage, even though the risk is on C and C has to pay X. In *Leigh and Sillavan* the sellers could have sued the carriers for breach of contract, though any damages they recovered would then have been held for the buyers[421] and, as the House of Lords pointed out, even though the sellers might have had little incentive to sue, it would have been open to the buyers, on variation of the contract, to have protected themselves by requiring the sellers to exercise this right on their account or by taking an assignment from them.

In *Leigh and Sillavan* both the act of negligence and all the damage to the cargo took place before the claimants acquired title, but what if some or all of the damage occurs after the claimant acquires title, as where it passes during the voyage? As a matter of general principle there must be cases in which a defendant owes a duty in respect of property damage to persons who have no title to the property when he is negligent, as where D in 2008 manufactures a component which is installed in a factory acquired by C in 2009 and which causes the factory to be burned down in 2010. To say that "English law does not recognise and never has recognised a duty of care upon a shipowner to anyone who was not the owner of the

---

para.5–13, above) why should a duty not be modified? Note, however, that while it may be possible to speak of the loss being "transferred" on the facts of *Leigh and Sillavan*, the consequential losses of a property owner and a "relational" victim may be very different: *Bow Valley Husky (Bermuda) Ltd v St John Shipbuilding Co Ltd* (1997) 153 D.L.R. (4th) 385.

[418] What started as an ordinary c&f contract was varied to a sale ex warehouse performed when the buyers eventually paid.

[419] Note, however, that it seems extremely unlikely that a buyer in international trade will not have insured the goods. The "real" claimant is therefore likely to be an insurer exercising subrogation rights (see, e.g. *Mitsui & Co Ltd v Flota Mercanta Grancolombiana SA* [1988] 1 W.L.R. 1145). At the moment that is generally legally irrelevant (though cf. the *Marc Rich* case, para.5–13, above) but may have significance in a court's perception of what is argued to be a "hard case".

[420] The Act is short but complex and details must be sought in specialist works. Very broadly, the Act (1) removes the necessity that the claimant should have acquired property, "upon or by reason of the transfer of the bill of lading"—it is enough that he becomes the lawful holder of the bill; (2) extends the transfer of the contractual rights of the seller against the carrier to persons who take delivery under certain other shipping documents now commonly in use, e.g. sea waybills. The Act is not affected by the Contracts (Rights of Third Parties) Act 1999.

[421] See *The Albazero* [1977] A.C. 774.

goods at the time when the tort was committed"[422] is not inconsistent with this for the tort is not complete until there is damage and
in the example the claimant is owner or possessor at that time.
However, in *Homburg Houtimport BV v Agrosin Pte Ltd*[423] timber
shipped for two cargo owners deteriorated on voyage because of bad
stowage at the outset. It was held that their claim in tort failed. More
than insignificant damage had been done before they acquired property in the timber and what happened after that was merely a
worsening of damage which was complete in law: it was not possible to apportion the damage by time or among the owners at
different stages.[424]

5–42   While there may be a good deal to be said against tort liability on
facts like *Leigh and Sillavan*, the rule in the case is one of general
application and is applicable to other cases where there is no special
legislation.[425] The distinction it draws between economic and physical harm has been described as "Jesuitical"[426] and it has been
rejected by high authority in other common law jurisdictions.[427] The
rule certainly rests in part upon the "floodgates" (or "where is it to
end?") argument, the spectre of a liability, in Cardozo J.'s famous
words, "in an indeterminate amount for an indeterminate time to an
indeterminate class."[428] This risk is certainly present in the case of
interruption of public utility supplies, though it has been contended
that it is exaggerated because individual losses may be small and
unlikely to lead to much litigation.[429] However, the physical conse-

---

[422] Roskill L.J. in *Margarine Union GmbH v Cambay Prince Steamship Co Ltd* [1969] 1 Q.B.
219 at 254.
[423] [2003] UKHL 12; [2004] 1 A.C. 715.
[424] The HL dealt with the matter very briefly and adopted the reasoning of Rix L.J. below:
[2001] EWCA Civ 55; [2001] 1 Lloyd's Rep. 437.
[425] Some cases may be affected by the Latent Damage Act 1986 s.3 (see para.26–13, below).
This provides, in effect, that where D causes damage to X's property and X disposes of it
to C, then C has a cause of action against D (running, for limitation purposes, from the date
on which X's accrued), provided that X had not become aware of the damage when he was
owner. The legislative history of s.3 revolves around latent damage to buildings and the
law of limitation against successive owners. It is unlikely to have occurred to anyone that
it would be relevant to the context with which we are now dealing and it would be
inapplicable where, as in *Leigh and Sillavan* itself, the damage is discovered before the
acquisition by C. Nevertheless its relevance to non-building cases seems to be assumed in
the CA in *Homburg Houtimport*, above, fn.423, where permission to amend so as to rely
on it was refused.
[426] *Coleridge v Miller Construction* 1997 S.L.T. 485 at 491.
[427] It is still the predominant US view, though there are cases the other way, such as *People
Express Airlines v Consolidated Rail* 495 A. 2d 107 (1985).
[428] *Ultramares Corp v Touche* 174 N.E. 441 at 444 (1931). In fact, a negligent misstatement
case, where there is no such hard and fast rule against recovery of economic loss.
[429] *New Zealand Forest Products v Att Gen* [1986] 1 N.Z.L.R. 14. In *Spartan Steel* itself it
seems that there was no widespread interruption of supplies. However, for a case where
more than a million households and businesses were affected (and where the economic
loss claims failed) see *Johnson Tiles Pty Ltd v Esso Australia Pty Ltd* [2003] VSC 27.

quences of an accident may be very wide ranging[430] and in that context the courts do not (at least overtly) deny a remedy because it will be available to many and may bankrupt defendants.[431] Furthermore, the rule is applicable even in a case (like *Leigh and Sillavan*) where there is no real risk of wide-ranging liability and a loss which in other circumstances might have been expected to fall upon A falls upon B. The virtue the present rule does have is that it provides a mechanical and fairly easily applied test for the resolution of disputes (and hence for the avoidance of prolonged litigation[432]) and in many cases where it would produce an unjust result it may be open to a potential claimant, if he chooses to do so, to restructure his arrangements to avoid its impact. This was the reasoning of the members of the Supreme Court of Canada who broadly accepted the "English rule" in *Canadian National Ry Co v Norsk Pacific SS Co Ltd*,[433] where D's barge rammed and damaged a railway bridge owned by X but almost exclusively used by C.[434] One judge imposed liability on the basis of foreseeability of loss to an identifiable claimant.[435] The three other judges found for liability on the basis of "proximity", McLachlin J. saying that a:

"[C]omprehensive ... consideration of proximity requires that the court review all of the factors connecting the negligent act with the loss; this includes not only the relationship between the parties but all forms of proximity—physical, circumstantial, causal or assumed indicators of closeness. While it is impossible to define comprehensively what will satisfy the requirements of proximity or directness, precision may be found as types of

---

[430] See Fleming James in (1972–1973) 12 J.S.P.T.L. 105, who instances damage from nuclear installations (for which, however, there are special statutory provisions) and the London and Chicago fires. See also *The Grandcamp* [1961] 1 Lloyd's Rep. 504, where an explosion caused 500 deaths and 3,000 personal injuries. The damages were US$70 million, though on appeal it was held that the explosion was not foreseeable to the defendants.

[431] Parliament sometimes limits liability (see, e.g. the merchant shipping legislation limiting liability in accordance with the defendant ship's tonnage).

[432] "When ... courts formulate legal criteria by reference to indeterminate terms such as 'fair', 'just', 'just and equitable' and 'unconscionable', they inevitably extend the range of admissible evidentiary materials. Cases then take longer, are more expensive to try, and, because of the indeterminacy of such terms, settlement of cases is more difficult, practitioners often having widely differing views as to the result of cases if they are litigated. Bright line rules may be less than perfect because they are under-inclusive, but my impression is that most people who have been or are engaged in day-to-day practice of the law at the trial or advising stage prefer rules to indeterminate standards": *Perre v Apand Pty Ltd* [1999] HCA 36; 198 C.L.R. 180 at [81] per McHugh J.

[433] (1992) 91 D.L.R. (4th) 289.

[434] La Forest J. speaking for the judges who followed the English rule emphasised that the risk was obvious to X and to C (such incidents had happened before) and they could have altered the incidence of liability by restructuring their contract, e.g. by leasing the bridge to C, but such arrangements would be unlikely to be possible in cases of interruption of public utility supplies.

[435] The use of the bridge by CNR was obvious to everyone using the river.

relationships or situations are defined in which the necessary closeness between negligence and loss exists."

All, it would seem, were agreed that the line must be drawn well short of recovery on the basis of foreseeability and it seems unlikely that those who based themselves on proximity would have found a duty to, say, a sub-buyer in *Leigh and Sillavan*; and in a subsequent case the Supreme Court of Canada rejected liability where a company suffered loss as a result of injury to a "key employee".[436] Nevertheless it must be questionable whether the proximity approach provides a predictable test of liability,[437] and this seems to be borne out by another decision of the Supreme Court of Canada, *Bow Valley Husky (Bermuda) Bermuda Ltd v St John Shipbuilding Ltd*,[438] in which it returned to the issue.

C2 and C3 were involved in oil exploration and for fiscal reasons incorporated C1 to own and operate a rig, contracting to pay C1 hire. The rig was disabled as a result of the negligence of D. C1 recovered damages but the claims of C2 and C3 were dismissed. The leading judgment[439] attempts a reconciliation of the opposing views in *Norsk Pacific* but on balance it seems that it is the minority view in that case which now prevails, i.e. there is a general exclusionary rule subject to more or less defined exceptions[440] and the facts of *Bow Valley* fell into none of these. While it was possible for the court to recognise new exceptions, it should not assiduously seek to do so, "for what is required is a clear rule predicting when recovery is available". From a policy point of view, the denial of liability was justified because (1) it was not possible to draw a rational line between C2 and C3 and other investors in the project on the basis that the claimants were "identifiable" or "users" of the rig or had "relied" on the defendants,[441] (2) there was ample deterrent content in the law in C1's property damage claim[442] and (3) the three claimants had had ample opportunity to allocate their various risks by contract and had in fact done so. A great diversity of views is

---

[436] *D'Amato v Badger* (1996) 137 D.L.R. (4th) 129.
[437] Non-common law systems provide a variety of answers. Thus German law, while it knows no duty of care, gives much the same answer as English law because it restricts liability by reference to the loss suffered: see Markesinis, *A Comparative Introduction to the German Law of Torts*, 2nd edn. French law draws no formal distinction between physical and economic loss but seems generally to adopt a restrictive approach to proof of causation where there is economic loss caused *par ricochet*. See van Gerven, Lever and Larouche, *Tort Law (Common Law of Europe Casebooks)* (2000), Ch.2.3.
[438] (1997) 153 D.L.R. (4th) 385.
[439] McLachlin J.
[440] Or so thought Iacobucci J.
[441] The case arose from a failure to warn of a fire hazard but the reliance of C2 and C3 was no different from that of any person upon the manufacturer of a product.
[442] Which amounted to CAN$5 million.

found in the High Court of Australia's decision[443] in *Perre v Apand Pty Ltd*,[444] where the defendants supplied potato seed (which they should have known was diseased) to S in South Australia, who as a result produced a crop with bacterial wilt. This did not infect the crops of neighbouring growers but they lost their valuable markets in Western Australia, which prohibited the import of crops grown within 20 kilometres of an outbreak. All the members of the High Court held that the defendants were liable, though there was disagreement about those losses suffered in the claimants' capacity as processors. Although the Court spoke with seven different voices there is some emphasis on what McHugh J. called "vulnerability",[445] that is to say the total control exercised by the defendants on the supply and the inability of the claimants to protect themselves by contract or otherwise, though the 20 kilometre limit was also significant as preventing indeterminacy and producing an identifiable class of claimants.

Before leaving this area we should note a principle of English law **5–43** of uncertain ambit which qualifies the general rule above. If, as a result of the negligence of D, damage is caused to X's vessel, the owners of cargo in the vessel have to contribute rateably to expenditure necessary to meet the emergency (a "general average contribution") and a cargo owner may sue D for this even though there is no physical damage to his portion of the cargo. In the leading case Lord Roche said:

" . . . [I]f two lorries A and B are meeting one another on the road, I cannot bring myself to doubt that the driver of lorry A owes a duty to both the owner of lorry B and to the owner of goods then carried on lorry B. Those owners are engaged in a common adventure with or by means of lorry B and if lorry A is negligently driven and damages lorry B so severely, while no damage is done to the goods in it, the goods have to be unloaded for the repair of the lorry and then reloaded or carried forward in some other way and the consequent expense is (by reason of his contract or otherwise) the expense of the owner of the goods, then, in my judgment, the owner of the goods has a direct cause of action to recover such expense. No authority to the contrary was cited, and I know of none relating to land transport."[446]

While the decision of the proponents of "proximity" in the *Norsk Pacific* case does not perhaps rest on this, it certainly seems to have

---

[443] Not for the first time in this context: see *The Willemstad* (1976) 136 C.L.R. 529.
[444] [1999] HCA 36; 198 C.L.R. 180.
[445] At [50]. See Gaudron J. at [42] and Gummow J. (with whom Gleeson C.J. agreed) at [216].
[446] *Morrison SS Co Ltd v Greystoke Castle* [1947] A.C. 265 at 280.

been influenced by it.[447] However, in England it has been said that
Lord Roche's "common adventure" principle is confined to the
maritime context or at least to precisely analogous situations involving carriage by land and it was therefore held inapplicable to the
relationship between a power generator and an electricity supplier.[448] The judges in *Norsk Pacific* who denied liability distinguished Lord Roche's principle because in their view the
relationship between the owner of a bridge and a person who is
allowed to use it is not "a common adventure".[449]

5–44   **ii. Defects of quality in goods or property supplied.** In *Muirhead v Industrial Tank Specialities Ltd*,[450] the claimant, an enter-
prising fishmonger, conceived a scheme to supply the market in
lobsters at times of high demand by keeping them in tanks. He
purchased the tanks from ITS but the pumps in the tanks failed to
function properly, a large number of lobsters died and the claimant
suffered loss in being unable to proceed with his project. There was
a good claim for breach of contract against ITS but they were
insolvent. Accordingly, the claimant sued the French manufacturers
of the pumps (with whom he had no contract) alleging that they
were negligent in supplying equipment which was not properly
adapted for use under English voltages. Damages were recovered
for the dead lobsters and for certain consequential losses but the
claimant failed in his claim for the cost of the pumps and the profits
that would have been made in the business had the pumps func-
tioned properly. It is certainly the law that the manufacturer of goods
owes a duty of care to ultimate consumers who are not in a contractual relationship with him[451] but this duty is not to cause damage
to persons or to property[452] and the major part of the claimant's
claim in this case was that he had suffered a loss of business because

---

[447] See (1992) 91 D.L.R. (4th) 289 at 376 (McLachlin J.).
[448] *Londonwaste Ltd v Amec Civil Engineering Ltd* (1997) 53 Con.L.R. 66; *Colour Quest Ltd
v Total Downstream UK Plc* [2009] EWHC 640 (Comm); [2009] 2 Lloyds Rep 1.
[449] It was rejected by the whole court in *Bow Valley*.
[450] [1986] Q.B. 507.
[451] *Donoghue v Stevenson* [1932] 562, para.10–2, below.
[452] A agrees to sell a quantity of water to C. D bottles it in unhygienic conditions, it develops
mould and has to be destroyed. C has no claim against D, D "damaged" A's water. C of
course has a claim for breach of contract against A. *M. Hasegawa & Co v Pepsi Bottling
Group (Canada) Co* (2002) 213 D.L.R. (4th) 663. No doubt A had a claim in tort against
D but he also had a contract. Cf. *Bacardi-Martini Beverages Ltd v Thomas Hardy
Packaging Ltd* [2002] EWCA Civ 549; [2002] 2 Lloyd's Rep. 379 (B supplies CO_2, which
is applied to concentrate and water supplied by A1 and A2 and the whole consignment of
the resulting drink has to be destroyed because of contamination in the CO_2; for the
purpose of interpretation of a contractual provision relating to "direct physical damage to
property" this was not a case of damage to the concentrate and water (which were never
intended to continue to exist in their original form) but of the creation of a defective new
product.

the pumps were unsuitable for their purpose,[453] a claim which lay in contract against ITS but not in tort against the manufacturers. Similarly in *Murphy v Brentwood DC*[454] the House of Lords ended a long period of controversy by reaffirming that defects in a building which cause it to be less valuable or even potentially dangerous constitute economic loss and do not at common law[455] give rise to any claim except via a contract with the defendant.[456]

A decade or so earlier the claim in *Muirhead* would probably never have been presented. What prompted it was the difficult case of *Junior Books Ltd v Veitchi Co Ltd*.[457] The defenders were engaged as sub-contractors to lay a floor in the pursuer's factory. There was no contractual relationship between the parties and the main contractors were not involved in the proceedings. The pursuers alleged that the floor was defective (though not dangerous), that this was caused by the negligence of the defenders and that they had suffered damage totalling some £207,000, being the cost of replacing the floor and various other items of consequential loss. On a preliminary issue of law, the majority of the House of Lords held that the pursuers' allegations disclosed a cause of action for negligence. Quite why this was so is less clear: certainly the pursuers were owners of the floor, but to say that this meant that there was damage to their property is tantamount to saying that supply of an article which is shoddy and breaks is actionable in negligence and that is not the law. Some saw in the case the beginnings of a major extension of liability for economic loss, but by subsequent interpretation it has largely been relegated to a rather narrow decision on specialised facts.[458] Lord Keith in *Murphy v Brentwood* suggested that the case fell within the *Hedley Byrne* principle and that may well be the case provided this is understood in the broad sense of "assumption of responsibility" rather than in the narrower sense governing statements of information or advice.[459] The defenders, as nominated sub-contractors,[460] would have been chosen by the pursuers (no doubt after direct negotiations between them) and were

---

[453] The business was not lost because the lobsters died, but because the pumps were unusable.
[454] [1991] 1 A.C. 398. See para.9–33, below.
[455] See the Defective Premises Act 1972, para.9–37, below.
[456] The Contracts (Rights of Third Parties) Act 1999 will not generally affect either of these situations because (a) the contract will not generally purport to confer a benefit on the third party claimant and (b) will not identify him.
[457] [1983] 1 A.C. 520.
[458] In *The Orjula* [1995] 2 Lloyd's Rep. 395 Mance J. described *Junior Books* as a case that appeared to have, "joined the slumber of the uniquely distinguished from which it would be unwise to awaken it without very solid reason".
[459] In so far as the defendants "said" anything expressly or by implication in *Junior Books* it was much more akin to a promise than information or advice.
[460] Doubt has been cast on whether they were in fact nominated sub-contractors: *Lancashire etc. Baptist Churches Inc v Howard & Seddon Partnership* [1993] 3 All E.R. 467 at 479, but this is the basis upon which the case was decided by the HL: [1983] 1 A.C. at 542.

therefore in a "uniquely proximate"[461] relationship with them, more so than is normally the case between a building owner and a sub-contractor. The relationship was not contractual but it was all but a contract. In contrast, although the ultimate user of goods no doubt "relies" on the manufacturer's producing a good and suitable product the relationship is far less proximate.[462] However, even this explanation is not free from difficulty, though the difficulty is one that applies to almost any "assumption of responsibility" case. It is that we are imposing a contract-type liability between parties who have structured their relationship in such a way as not to create a contract.[463]

D. Negligence and Public Law[464]

5–45   While the principles of administrative law impinge upon the law of negligence, English law has no separate system of administrative liability: the starting point is that on the one hand a public body is subject to the general law of tort in the same way as a trading company or a private individual,[465] and on the other hand an act or decision which is invalid in public law terms and subject to judicial review does not for that reason become civilly actionable in damages. The same is generally true of an individual servant of a public body.[466] However, the functions of public bodies are carried out under statutes[467] (or, in the case of central government, the Prerog-

---

[461] Lord Bridge in *D.&F. Estates Ltd v Church Commissioners* [1989] A.C. 177 at 202. However, Lord Goff in *Henderson v Merrett Syndicates Ltd* [1995] 2 A.C. 145 at 196, was of the view that the case does not represent a general rule even for nominated sub-contractors.

[462] Unless, say, there were an assurance by the manufacturer, but in that case there would very likely be a collateral contract anyway: *Shanklin Pier v Detel Products Ltd* [1951] 2 K.B. 854. The standard of quality that may legitimately be expected of goods may be set by the terms of the contract between the manufacturer and the intermediary to whom the goods are first sold or to whose order they are made (thus the Sale of Goods Act recognises that the price of goods is a factor in determining whether they are of satisfactory quality) and there might be difficulty in importing the contractual standard into the duty of care owed to the ultimate user. Cf. *Leigh and Sillavan Ltd v Aliakmon Shipping Co Ltd* [1986] A.C. 786 at 818, para.5–41, above. However, this is not regarded as a fatal obstacle where goods cause physical damage.

[463] As Robert Goff L.J. admits in *Muirhead* at [1986] Q.B. 528 there is no legal reason, though it is not the practice, why a building contract should not involve direct contracts between the building owner and specialists who are normally sub-contractors.

[464] Booth and Squires, *The Negligence Liability of Public Authorities*; Markesinis et al, *Tortious Liability of Statutory Bodies*; Fairgrieve, Andenas and Bell, *Tort Liability of Public Authorities in Comparative Perspective*; Law Com. Consultation Paper No.187, *Administrative Redress: Public Bodies and the Citizen* (2008).

[465] *Barrett v Enfield LBC* [2001] 2 A.C. 550; *Capital & Counties Plc v Hampshire CC* [1997] Q.B. 1004.

[466] See *Northern Territory v Mengel* (1995) 185 C.L.R. 307 but one tort is unique to public bodies and servants: misfeasance in a public office, as to which see para.7–20, below.

[467] A governmental body is not liable in negligence for the consequences of a legislative act: *Kimpton v Canada* [2004] BCCA 72; 236 D.L.R. (4th) 324. However, in some cases there can be a liability under European Union law: para.7–12, below.

ative) and these typically give an element of discretion as to how the functions shall be performed and what resources shall be devoted to them, a discretion which is obviously necessary and which must be reflected in the law if the body is sued: perhaps it goes too far to say that "a government must be entitled to govern free of the restraints of tort law"[468] but tort law must certainly not hamper good government. There is no real disagreement as to the aim, the difficulty lies in finding a formula to achieve it.

i. Statutory duties and powers and the common law. The first **5–46** question is whether there is a statutory duty, breach of which is actionable in tort. This issue is considered in more detail later[469] but for the moment it is sufficient to note that the answer depends on the proper construction of the statute and that there is no general rule of liability; indeed non-liability rather than liability is the rule. If, on the proper construction of the statute, no civil action arises, one cannot fall back on a liability for negligence in performance of the duty. There is no tort of "negligent performance of a statutory duty". If the situation will support a common law duty of care under ordinary principles there may be liability[470] but the statutory duty itself does not give rise to a duty of care.[471] A common law duty of care cannot, "grow parasitically out of a statutory duty not intended to be owed to individuals"[472] (and the same is a fortiori true where there is a statutory power rather than a duty). Thus there is a non-actionable duty in the National Health Service Act 1977 under which that service provides health care, but in so far as a hospital is liable for clinical negligence its duty arises from what it has done in accepting a patient for treatment.[473] However, one cannot assume that there is such a common law assumption of responsibility merely because the defendant is exercising a statutory function which may be regarded as for the protection of persons such as the claimant.[474]

---

[468] *Samson v Canada* (1991) 80 D.L.R. (4th) 741 at 749 per Linden J.A.

[469] See Ch.7, below.

[470] See e.g. *Rice v Secretary of State for Trade and Industry* [2007] EWCA Civ 289; [2007] I.C.R. 1469 where the statutory framework itself gave rise to no liability but created a relationship between the claimant and the National Dock Labour Board which was in some respects similar to that of employee and employer.

[471] *X v Bedfordshire CC* [1995] 2 A.C. 633 at 734, explaining *Geddis v Proprietors of the Bann Reservoir* (1878) 3 App. Cas. 430 at 455–456 and *Home Office v Dorset Yacht Co Ltd* [1970] A.C. 1004 at 1030. *Holland v Saskatchewan* [2008] SCC 42; 294 D.L.R. (4th) 193.

[472] *Gorringe v Calderdale MBC* [2004] UKHL 15; [2004] 1 W.L.R. 1057 at [71] per Lord Scott. *Sandhar v Dept of Transport* [2005] EWCA Civ 1440; [2005] P.I.Q.R. P183 at [37]; *Neil Martin Ltd v Revenue and Customs Comrs* [2007] EWCA Civ 1041; [2007] S.T.C. 1802.

[473] *Gorringe v Calderdale MBC*, above (fn.472) at [38]; *Sandford v Waltham Forest LBC* [2008] EWHC 1106 (QB).

[474] *X v Hounslow LBC* [2009] EWCA Civ 286 (fn.472); [2009] P.T.S.R. 1158.

5–47   We have already touched on the position of public services when dealing with the general approach to omissions. Most of the "public law" cases in fact involved an omission if that is taken in the broad sense of including incompetent exercise of a power so as to fail to protect the claimant from harm directly inflicted by another agency. However, the point was rather glossed over in the modern case law until it came to the fore in *Stovin v Wise*.[475] S was injured in an accident at a dangerous junction caused by the negligence of W and recovered damages against W. W then sought a contribution[476] from Norfolk CC, the highway authority, and a precondition of this was that the authority, if sued, would have been liable to S.[477] There is a civilly actionable statutory duty to maintain the highway[478] but this was inapplicable because it concerns the state of repair of the roadway and the danger at the junction arose from poor visibility. There was a statutory power[479] to require the removal of an obstruction but after negotiations with the frontager the authority decided to remove it itself. However, the matter then "went to sleep" for nearly a year before the accident. There was plainly no basis upon which the case could have been brought within any of the recognised exceptions to the general rule of "no duty to act",[480] though the reasons underpinning that rule are not so obviously applicable to a public body, and the majority of the House of Lords declined to find a common law duty of care. The statute itself gave rise to no liability and its breach could not be the basis of a liability at common law: there was no way, as Lord Hoffmann put it, in which the statutory "may" could be turned into a common law "ought".[481] The position of "uncompromising orthodoxy"[482] is that:

> "[A]lthough a public authority may be under a public duty, enforceable by mandamus, to give proper consideration to the question whether it should exercise a power, this duty cannot be

---

[475] [1996] A.C. 923. See also para.5–26, above.

[476] Civil Liability (Contribution) Act 1978. See Ch.21, below.

[477] This was of course a matter of indifference on the facts to S, since whatever W's rights of contribution against the authority, she was liable in full to S.

[478] Highways Act 1980, see para.14–42, below.

[479] Highways Act 1980 s.79. The distinction between a power and a duty may not always be clear and in any event a duty may contain wide elements of discretion: *R. v CC Sussex, Ex p. International Trader's Ferry Ltd* [1999] 2 A.C. 418; *Larner v Solihull MBC* [2001] P.I.Q.R. P17. In *T v Surrey CC* [1994] 4 All E.R. 577 a statute required a local authority to maintain a register of child minders but then gave the authority various discretionary powers about registration and deregistration. A child placed with a registered child minder was injured by her when the authority had information which should have led it at least to suspend her. A judgment in favour of the claimant was based upon—and only upon—an express assurance to the mother that the child minder was a suitable person.

[480] See para.5–26, above.

[481] [1996] A.C. at 948.

[482] [1996] A.C. at 951.

equated with, or regarded as a foundation for imposing, a duty of care on the public authority in relation to the exercise of the power. Mandamus will compel proper consideration of the authority of its discretion, but that is all."[483]

The majority in *Stovin v Wise* left open[484] the possibility that a common law duty of care might arise in the context of a statutory power if two conditions were satisfied: (1) that on the facts it would have been irrational not to exercise the power (in other words that a decision not to do so would have been outside the scope of a proper exercise of discretion); and (2) that there are exceptional grounds for holding that the policy of the statute requires compensation to be paid to persons who suffer loss because the power was not exercised.[485] However, this was later rejected in *Gorringe v Calderdale Metropolitan Borough Council*,[486] another case of failure to improve the highway (by erecting warning signs). The first matter might be relevant in administrative law proceedings aimed at requiring the highway authority to consider exercising its statutory powers but not to the common law of negligence.

"[The] mere fact that, in a given case, a reasonable council would have exercised its powers by providing an additional sign does not alter the fact that they would have been under no common law duty to do so. Conversely, even if it would have been wholly unreasonable for the council not to provide an additional sign, this does not mean that they were in breach of a common law duty to do so."[487]

---

[483] *Sutherland SC v Heyman* (1985) 60 A.L.R. 1 at 13 per Mason J. Cf. Lord Nicholls in *Stovin v Wise* at [1996] A.C. 936.

[484] The majority approach may be a compromise.

[485] [1996] A.C. at 953. These conditions were not satisfied in *Stovin v Wise*. It would have been extremely difficult to contend that not improving the junction was irrational in public law terms (the first condition) for it was one of many in the area (and by no means the worst) to which the authority's limited resources might have been devoted. As to the second element, the legislative scheme pointed away from liability rather than towards it, since the improvement power dated from an era in which there was no civil liability even for non-repair of the roadway itself.

[486] [2004] UKHL 15; [2004] 1 W.L.R. 1057, disapproving *Larner v Solihull MBC* [2001] P.I.Q.R. P17, a curious case which had purported to follow both the majority and the minority in *Stovin v Wise* (see also *Thames Trains v H.S.E.* [2003] EWCA Civ 720). The practical implications of the contrary view are apparent from both *Larner* and *Gorringe*, viz. the need for a massive investigation of the history of the authority's road safety activities in order to establish "unreasonableness".

[487] At [92] per Lord Rodger. An attack on a failure to act at common law via assumption of responsibility will be much easier to establish if there is direct contact between the claimant and the public body. However, perhaps it should not be altogether ruled out even in a road traffic case.

Of course if the highway authority installed misleading road markings or signs there would be no difficulty about finding it liable because it would then have created a source of danger.[488]

5–48   **ii. Direct and vicarious liability.** In this context, one needs to be aware that a claim may be presented in one or more of three alternative ways. First, as a claim for breach of statutory duty. If there is such an actionable duty it is likely that will be imposed directly upon the public body, though whether it has fulfilled it will, of course, demand examination of the acts of its human agents. Secondly, on the basis that the public body is itself under a duty of care under the general law of negligence, as it would be, for example, in relation to the maintenance of its vehicles or the selection of its staff ("direct liability"). Such a duty may exist in parallel with a statutory duty or alone even if no actionable statutory duty exists. Thirdly, an individual human agent of the public body may owe a personal duty to the claimant for the breach of which the body may be vicariously liable in the normal way. Again, this may exist in parallel with one or both of the other duties or alone. If we take as an example the area of failure to provide suitable educational services, the modern cases generally take the line that the statutory provisions do not give rise to a duty of the first type because they are not intended to give rise to civil actions for damages but only to public law remedies and whatever modes of redress (such as appeal) they themselves provide. Duties of the second type have also, as we shall see below, generally been rejected because they have involved issues of policy in which the courts should not interfere but a more welcoming attitude has sometimes[489] been shown to duties of the third type, given the:

> "[L]ong and well-established, now elementary [rule], that persons exercising a particular skill or profession may owe a duty of care in the performance to people who it can be foreseen will be injured if due skill and care are not exercised".[490]

Even in this situation, however, one should guard against the process of reasoning which runs:

---

[488] This is clearly accepted in *Gorringe* but the application of it in *Bird v Pearce* [1979] RTR 369 is doubted. Could this apply to the *design* of a new highway? For an Australian view see *Roads and Traffic Authority of NSW v Refrigerated Roadways Pty Ltd* [2009] NSWCA 263.

[489] However, not always, because the court may take the view that a duty of care on the individual may discourage the proper performance of his professional duty: see para.5–20, above.

[490] *Phelps v Hillingdon LBC* [2001] 2 A.C. 619 at 653 per Lord Slynn.

"The public body has this statutory function; it employs X to carry that out; therefore (and without more) X owes a duty to the claimant for the breach of which the public body is vicariously liable".

Any duty of care owed by X to the claimant must be grounded on the recognised principles of private law, in particular those concerning the giving of advice and assumption of responsibility,[491] taking account of whatever policy factors may be relevant in the particular context.[492]

iii. Administrative law invalidity. If the relationship between 5–49 claimant and defendant is one which might prima facie attract a duty of care absent the statute, consideration must be given to the question whether the statutory framework modifies or excludes the common law duty. The difficulties which arise at the interface between public and private law have increased since the law of negligence has expanded its scope beyond the direct infliction of physical damage by act. If we take the example of a local authority, its powers and duties derive from statutory authority conferred by Parliament, which will have intended to confer on the authority a measure of discretion as to the extent to which and the means by which those functions are fulfilled. That discretion is conferred on the authority, not on the courts, as our system of administrative law recognises. If a challenge to the exercise of the functions is mounted by way of judicial review, that will, according to traditional thinking, succeed only if the exercise is ultra vires, that is to say if it was illegal (for example, purporting to run a tram service under authority to run a bus service) or the exercise of the discretion was affected by impropriety (taking into account irrelevant matters when reaching the decision) or was irrational (*"Wednesbury* unreasonable"[493]). It is the last which has figured most prominently in the tort cases: the test is not whether the court agrees that the decision was the best one that could be taken, but whether a sensible authority could have come to that conclusion. It may well be that this threshold is not so high as

[491] See Mummery L.J. in *Carty v Croydon LBC* [2005] EWCA Civ 19; [2005] 1 W.L.R. 2312 at [83]–[84]. Where the statutory function carried out by the employer does not give rise to a duty of care one cannot say that the employee assumes responsibility to the claimant in carrying out that function. Compare *Neil Martin Ltd v Revenue and Customs Commissioners* [2007] EWCA Civ 1041; [2007] STC 1802 where the employee went beyond carrying out the function.
[492] Domestic tort law says that social workers owe no duty of care to the parents of children taken into care (see para.5–53, below). In *B v Reading BC* [2007] EWCA Civ 1313; [2008] 1 F.L.R. 797 this was held also to bar an alternative claim based on a "direct" duty of the authority to have in place a proper system for training and supervision of social workers. In the final analysis this would still require the claimants to establish that a social worker had acted incompetently because of the absence of such a system.
[493] *Associated Provincial Picture Houses Ltd v Wednesbury Corp* [1948] 1 K.B. 223.

it once was and that now there may be an element of "proportionality" in the matter, something which is clearly the test when human rights are in issue,[494] but even under that test the court is not to substitute its judgment for that of the administrator: the latter has a "margin of appreciation" with which the court should not interfere.

5–50   How these principles should be reconciled with the application of the law of negligence has been the subject of varying approaches since the issue came to the fore in the 1970s.[495] It is clear enough that some decisions are simply non-justiciable in a private law action.[496] These may be high political decisions ("shall we go to war?",[497] "shall we join the EMU?") but they may also extend to decisions on the allocation of resources or the infliction of risks. To take an example based loosely on *Home Office v Dorset Yacht Co*,[498] suppose that the Home Office resolves to institute a policy of open, non-secure young offender institutions with a view to promoting their reformation. Claims in tort by neighbours of the institution whose homes are burgled by absconding offenders will plainly fail even if there is a sharp increase in burglaries in the area, just as a direct challenge to the policy by judicial review would fail (assuming the correct procedures had been followed to arrive at the policy). The threshold is impassable because if:

> "[T]he factors relevant to the exercise of the discretion include matters of policy, the court cannot adjudicate on such policy and therefore cannot reach the conclusion that the decision was outside the ambit of the statutory discretion."[499]

This includes:

> "[S]ocial policy, the allocation of finite financial resources between the different calls made upon them or ... the balance between pursuing desirable social aims as against the risk to the public inherent in doing so."[500]

---

[494] See *R. (Daly) v Home Secretary* [2001] UKHL 26; [2001] 2 A.C. 522. For housing possession cases the test has been said to be, "a decision which no reasonable person would consider justifiable": *Doherty v Birmingham CC* [2008] UKHL 57; [2009] A.C. 367 at [110].

[495] *Home Office v Dorset Yacht Co Ltd* [1970] A.C. 1004 is probably the first case.

[496] *Carty v Croydon LBC*, above (fn.491) at [21].

[497] The legality of a war is irrelevant even under art.2 of the European Convention on Human Rights in a claim based on failure to protect the lives of troops: *R (Gentle) v Prime Minister* [2008] UKHL 20; [2008] 1 A.C. 1356.

[498] [1970] A.C. 1004.

[499] *X v Bedfordshire CC* [1995] 2 A.C. 633 at 738 per Lord Browne-Wilkinson.

[500] *X v Bedfordshire CC* [1995] 2 A.C. 633.

One approach attempted to distinguish between "policy" and "operational" decisions, the first being normally non-justiciable, the second more likely to lead to liability, though still containing elements of discretion in some cases.[501] The line between the two categories cannot be sharply drawn, for the decision to do an operational act may easily involve and flow from a policy decision.[502] The very fine lines which have to be drawn may be illustrated by two immigration cases. In *W v Home Office*[503] the claimant was detained on arrival as an asylum seeker because of a low score on a test designed to assess his knowledge of his asserted country of origin. Subsequently he easily passed the test and it was discovered that he had not taken the test on the earlier occasion but someone else's results had been placed on his file by mistake. Although this was the purest "operational" error it was the process of gathering information about the claimant's status that was outside the scope of any private law remedy and he was owed no duty of care by the immigration service. In *R. (A) v Secretary of State for the Home Dept*[504] the claimants, having been allowed to remain for asylum reasons were, by administrative error, given a classification which prevented them claiming benefits. This was eventually corrected but there was no mechanism for making retrospective payments. It was held that the Secretary of State owed a duty to them[505] and *W* was distinguished on the basis that there the mishandling of information took place at the stage of making the judgment whether the claimant should be allowed entry, whereas here the decision on the claimants' status had already been taken and it was merely a matter of the administrative implementation of that decision.[506] In truth:

"[T]his kind of classification does not appear to provide any absolute test for determining whether the case is one which allows or excludes a duty of care ... [though it] may provide some

---

[501] See *Anns v Merton LBC* [1978] A.C. 728.

[502] *Barrett v Enfield LBC* [2001] 2 A.C. 550 at 571 per Lord Slynn. See Bailey and Bowman "The Policy/Operational Dichotomy—A Cuckoo in the Nest" [1986] C.L.J. 430.

[503] [1997] Imm. A.R. 302.

[504] [2004] EWHC 1585 (Admin).

[505] However, the case is difficult to reconcile with *Rowley v Secretary of State for Work and Pensions* [2007] EWCA Civ 598; [2007] 1 W.L.R. 2861, para.5–16, above (inconsistency with statutory scheme of remedies).

[506] However, Keith J. thought that *W* might anyway be inconsistent with later decisions. Furthermore, there was no claim for false imprisonment in *W*. Although the immigration legislation gives the executive wide powers of detention, "it seems entirely wrong that someone who has been wrongly detained by the executive because of a filing error or some other incompetence in their offices should not be entitled to compensation as of right": *I.D. v Home Office* [2005] EWCA Civ 38; [2005] I.N.L.R. 278 at [121]. An arresting police officer must have reasonable cause to believe that the person has committed an offence.

guide towards identifying some kinds of case where a duty of care may be thought to be inappropriate."[507]

Another view was that if there is any element of discretion involved, a decision by a public body must fail the administrative law test of unreasonableness before it may be made the subject of an action for damages.[508] In *X v Bedfordshire CC* Lord Browne-Wilkinson said:

> "It is clear both in principle and from the decided cases that the local authority cannot be liable in damages for doing that which Parliament has authorised. Therefore if the decisions complained of fall within the ambit of such statutory discretion they cannot be actionable at common law. However, if the decision complained of is so unreasonable that it falls outside the ambit of the discretion conferred upon the local authority, there is no a priori reason for excluding all common law liability."[509]

On this basis there might be a threefold classification of acts by public bodies: (1) matters of "high policy" which were always beyond the scope of legal challenge; (2) justiciable discretionary decisions (which would have to pass through the administrative law filter discussed above); and (3) justiciable matters of implementation. However, any absolute distinction between the second and third categories is open to the same objection as that between policy and operational decisions.[510] The example given in *X v Bedfordshire* of category (3) is running a school in respect of matters of safety but many matters of safety involve the allocation of resources and hence the exercise of "discretion": Does the roster allow us to have a

---

[507] *Phelps v Hillingdon LBC* [2001] 2 A.C. 619 at 673 per Lord Clyde; *Stovin v Wise* [1996] A.C. 923 at 951.

[508] This was sometimes taken as supporting a quite different proposition, namely that if the decision failed the administrative law test that of itself gave rise to a duty of care: *Larner v Solihull MBC* [2001] P.I.Q.R. P17. That would contradict the principle that any duty must arise from the common law of torts (see para.5–47, above).

[509] [1995] 2 A.C. at 736; and see *A v Essex CC* [2003] EWCA Civ 1848; [2004] 1 W.L.R. 1881 at [33]. If the claimant passes this threshold and the court imposes a duty, it is difficult to see what more the claimant would have to do to establish a breach. Provided some harm is foreseeable, a decision flawed for irrationality (as opposed to illegality or impropriety) could be hardly be other than "negligent".

[510] That is not to say that there may not in most cases be a recognisable difference in practice between making policy and implementing it. Thus the courts will not interfere with the decision of an adoption agency as to what information should be provided to adopters unless it is wholly unreasonable; but if there is a policy to provide information X and the agency forgets to do so it can be liable: *A v Essex CC*, above, fn.509. Similarly, the court will not tell a Minister what vessel tonnage requirement he should impose on applicants for a fishing licence; but there is no reason why he should not be liable (even if the issue is at his "absolute discretion") if an official miscalculates the tonnage of the vessel in question: *Keeping v Canada* [2003] NLCA 21; 226 D.L.R. (4th) 285.

teacher in the yard?[511] Should we fix that leaking gutter before the icy weather? Does the person supervising rugby need special training? Are these conceptually different from the decision by the education authority to cut back on school maintenance spending or not to replace teachers (presumably decisions in category (1) or at least (2))?[512] Rather than three separate categories the reality seems to be that there is a continuum. Perhaps one cannot take the matter further than Lord Hutton did in *Barrett v Enfield London Borough*[513] when he said:

"In *Rowling v Takaro Properties Ltd*[514] the judgment of the Privy Council delivered by Lord Keith of Kinkel emphasised that the non-justiciability of an allegation of negligence in the exercise of a statutory discretion is based on the need to exclude those cases which are unsuitable for judicial resolution, that the fact that the decision under attack is capable of being described as having been of a policy character does not in itself render the case unsuitable for judicial decision, but that it is necessary to weigh and analyse all the relevant considerations in considering whether it is appropriate that a court should adjudicate on the negligence alleged."

Hence, said his Lordship:

"[P]rovided that the decisions [in question] do not involve issues of policy which the courts are ill-equipped to adjudicate upon, it is preferable for the courts to decide the validity of the plaintiff's claim by applying directly the common law concept of negligence than by applying as a preliminary test the public law concept of *Wednesbury* unreasonableness . . . to determine if the decision fell outside the ambit of the statutory discretion."[515]

In *Carty v London Borough of Croydon* (a claim for failure to provide proper education) Dyson L.J. reviewed the authorities and concluded that there was:

---

[511] Cf. *Carmarthenshire CC v Lewis* [1955] A.C. 549, para.5–31, above.
[512] In *Carty v Croydon LBC* [2005] EWCA Civ 19; [2005] 1 W.L.R. 2312 at [25] Dyson L.J. said that, "a claim based on an allegation that it was negligent to build a school on site A rather than site B would almost certainly be struck out as non-justiciable." Presumably he had in mind complaints that, e.g. site B would have been more convenient or accessible but one would have thought that if the source of the complaint were that site A was contaminated land which posed a danger to pupils' health the issue would be eminently justiciable.
[513] [2001] 2 A.C. 550 at 581.
[514] [1988] A.C. 473.
[515] [2001] 2 A.C. at 586.

"[M]uch to be said for the view that there should only be two areas of potential enquiry where the issue arises whether a public authority is liable for negligence in the performance of its statutory functions. The first is whether the decision is justiciable at all. And the second is to apply the classic three stages enunciated in [*Caparo v Dickman*]: foreseeability of damage, proximity and that the situation is one in which it is fair, just and reasonable that the law should impose a duty of care."[516]

5–51   There may in fact be less difference between this apparently simple approach and that of Lord Browne-Wilkinson in *X v Bedfordshire* than at first appears, for there is a certain ambiguity in the idea of "non-justiciability" in this context. At one end of the spectrum it means—and everyone agrees on this—that no court should inquire into the wisdom of the Government's foreign or taxation policy. At the opposite extreme, in cases like *Carty*, where it is being alleged that an education officer has fallen down in carrying out an educational responsibility which he has assumed to a child, the case is no different in principle from that of, say, a doctor who culpably fails to diagnose his patient's illness. Both activities require the making of difficult judgments but that does not mean that they are outside the scope of the law of negligence; nor, of course does it mean that a defendant who, with the benefit of hindsight, has made the wrong decision incurs liability, provided he has followed recognised professional practices. But in the intermediate case, where it is claimed that the "system" adopted by the public body is deficient, we are not really saying that the court cannot adjudicate upon the validity of the system but that in doing so it should adopt a cautious approach which recognises the primacy of the discretion in matters of policy granted by Parliament to the public body. That is the basis of judicial control under the administrative law concept of unreasonableness. In that sense the issue is justiciable.[517] It may well be that the flexibility in the legal concept of negligence (though perhaps more naturally in relation to *breach* rather than *duty*) enables us to reach the same result without attempting to draw sharp preliminary lines based on administrative law concepts. After all, there may be cases in which it is undeniable that the public authority does owe the claimant a duty of care in respect of the damage complained of and this has to be accommodated within the public law framework. In *Connor v Surrey CC*[518] the claimant, a head teacher, was complaining of the failure of the local authority to fulfil

---

[516] [2005] EWCA Civ 19; [2005] 1 W.L.R. 2312 at [28]. Supported by Bailey, "Public Authority Liability in Negligence: the continued search for coherence" (2006) 26 L.S. 155 but with criticism of the continuing use of the concept of justiciability.

[517] See Hale L.J. in *A v Essex CC* [2003] EWCA Civ 1848; [2004] 1 W.L.R. 1881 at [33].

[518] [2010] EWCA Civ 286.

the well-established duty of an employer to safeguard an employee against the damaging effects of stress at work. On the facts this would have involved a decision to replace the school's governing body with an Interim Executive Board, a matter which was clearly within the scope of the authority's statutory discretion but since there had been a serious breakdown in the way the school was governed, which was prejudicing the operation of the school, the necessary constraints on interference with that discretion were met: the council's duty to correct the problems at the school and their duty of care to the claimant "plainly marched together".[519]

"What might have been the proper outcome had the two things pulled in opposite directions [would be] a question for another day and another claim."[520]

iv. Whether duty fair, just and reasonable. Even if the imposition of a duty of care would not restrict the legitimate scope for the exercise of discretion by the public body, the statutory context in which the function is carried out[521] may be of decisive importance in determining whether a duty of care exists. In effect this is an aspect of the "fair, just and reasonable" element in *Caparo v Dickman*. In the eponymous appeal in *X v Bedfordshire CC*[522] the complaint was by children who alleged that they were subject to neglect and ill-treatment and that the authority had failed to take steps to take them into care. Lord Browne-Wilkinson was inclined to the view that this was a case of a justiciable decision but it was held that even so it was not just and reasonable to impose a duty of care for a number of reasons: it would cut across the statutory system for the protection of children at risk, which involves "inter-disciplinary" procedures for the authority, the police, doctors and others[523]; the task of the authority was a delicate one and the imposition of liability might make it adopt defensive tactics which would be harmful to the broad body of children at risk; there was a high risk of vexatious complaints in this area; the statutory scheme provided

5–52

---

[519] At [111] per Laws L.J.
[520] At [124] per Sedley L.J.
[521] Just as the existence of a contractual framework may bar or modify a tort duty: see para.1–9, above. Incompatibility with a statutory scheme may also be a reason for rejecting an implied contractual term: *Johnson v Unisys Ltd* [2001] UKHL 13; [2003] 1 A.C. 518 (where claims both in contract and negligence were rejected).
[522] [1995] 2 A.C. 633. Five appeals were heard and reported together.
[523] "To introduce into such a system a common law duty of care enforceable against only one of the participant bodies would be manifestly unfair. To impose such liability on all the participant bodies would lead to almost impossible problems of disentangling as between the respective bodies the liability, both primary and by way of contribution, of each for reaching a decision found to be negligent": [1995] 2 A.C. at 750.

remedies by way of complaint and investigation[524]; and such analogous authority as existed[525] pointed away from liability. In another of the appeals, *M v Newham London Borough*, the situation was reversed and the claimants, mother and child, complained of a decision to take the child into care on suspicion of child abuse by the mother's boyfriend, a suspicion arrived at, it was alleged, after inadequate inquiries by a psychiatrist and social worker. Though there were other reasons for the decision, the policy arguments in *X v Bedfordshire* were thought equally applicable.

5–53   The later cases show more reluctance in practice to deny a duty because of a background statutory context. In *Barrett v Enfield London Borough*[526] the claim was in respect of alleged failure to take due care over the upbringing of a child in care and this was allowed to go to trial, in line with the current tendency not to be so free with the striking out procedure.[527] The policy considerations in *X v Bedfordshire* restricting the duty of care on a local authority when deciding whether or not to take action in respect of a case of suspected child abuse did not have the same force in respect of decisions taken once the child was already in local authority care.[528] *Phelps v Hillingdon London Borough*[529] was a conjoined appeal concerning allegations of failure to provide for special educational needs. The claims were in fact based on the vicarious liability of the defendants for the acts and omissions of individual employees and these were not thought, for the purposes of striking out, to present any fatal conflict with the statutory framework; but "direct" claims against the defendant authorities were also regarded as arguable. Indeed, it may be that the law has changed even in the context of *X v Bedfordshire* itself, child abuse (though this involves some difficulties from the point of view of precedent). In *D v East Berkshire Community Health NHS Trust*[530] the Court of Appeal held that in the light of subsequent developments the House of Lords case of *X v Bedfordshire* could no longer be taken as authority that there could be no duty of care owed to children in these cases. The principal

---

[524] But as Sir Thomas Bingham M.R. pointed out in the CA, claimants want compensation for their loss, not just investigation of their grievances: [1994] 4 All E.R. 602 at 619.

[525] *Yuen Kun Yeu v Att Gen of Hong Kong* [1988] A.C. 175; *Hill v CC West Yorkshire* [1989] A.C. 53.

[526] [2001] 2 A.C. 550.

[527] See para.5–3, above. See also *W v Essex CC* [2001] 2 A.C. 592.

[528] "[I do not] accept that because the court should be slow to hold that a child can sue its parents for negligent decisions in its upbringing that the same should apply necessarily to all acts of a local authority. The latter has to take decisions which parents never or rarely have to take (e.g. as to adoption or as to an appropriate foster parent or institution)": [2001] 2 A.C. at 573 per Lord Slynn.

[529] [2001] 2 A.C. 619; *Carty v Croydon LBC* [2005] EWCA Civ 19; [2005] 1 W.L.R. 2312.

[530] [2003] EWCA Civ 1151; [2004] Q.B. 558. See also *B v Att Gen of New Zealand* [2003] UKPC 61; [2003] 4 All E.R. 833.

reason was that now (though not at the time of the events in *D*) arts 3 (protection against inhuman or degrading treatment) and 8 (respect for family life) are given direct effect in English law by the Human Rights Act 1998[531] and, while these were not identical with a duty of care at common law, the policy arguments wholly excluding such a duty no longer had the same force since the court would be involved in examining the authority's conduct in the statutory context. However, the appeals to the House of Lords from the *D* litigation involved claims by the parents of children taken into care,[532] to which different considerations apply: it will always be in the parents' interests that the child is not taken into care, there is a conflict of interest between the parents and the child and the striking out of those claims was therefore upheld by the majority of the House of Lords.[533]

There is a view which decries the approach of denying a duty of care on the basis that the imposition of a duty might lead some people to adopt a defensive approach to the performance of their professional duties and argues that the problem can be dealt with adequately by reference to the undoubted principle that a person who fearlessly carries out his professional role will not be held to be negligent. So in *Barrett*'s case Lord Slynn did not appear to embrace some of the alleged policy considerations with enthusiasm even in the *X v Bedfordshire* context.[534] However, some take a more sceptical view of the effectiveness of the "breach approach" to block bad claims and in *D v East Berkshire Community Health NHS Trust*[535] Lord Brown sounded the following warning note:

"There is always a temptation to say in all these cases that no one, whether a doctor concerned with possible child abuse, a witness or a prosecutor will ever in fact be held liable unless he has conducted himself manifestly unreasonably; it is unnecessary, therefore, to deny a duty of care, better rather to focus on the appropriate standard by which to judge whether it is breached.

---

[531] The child abuse claims in *X v Bedfordshire* both resulted in successful applications to the European Court of Human Rights: *Z v UK* (2002) 34 E.H.R.R. 3; *T.P. v UK* (2002) 34 E.H.R.R. 2, respectively. There were held to be breaches of arts 3 and 8, though not of art.6, the Court disclaiming any power to pass upon domestic tort law.

[532] *D v East Berkshire Community Health NHS Trust* [2005] UKHL 23; [2005] 2 A.C. 373. See also *AD v Bury MBC* [2006] EWCA Civ 1 and *Sullivan v Moody* [2001] HCA 59; 183 A.L.R. 404.

[533] The fact that the Human Rights Act is now in force is no ground for the CA revisiting this issue: *Lawrence v Pembrokeshire CC* [2007] EWCA Civ 446; [2007] 1 W.L.R. 291 but the case is not necessarily the same if the parent is not suspected of being the abuser: *C v Merthyr BC* [2010] EWHC 62 (QB); and see, in a somewhat different context, *W v Essex CC* [2001] 2 A.C. 592 and *A v Essex CC* [2003] EWCA Civ 1848; [2004] 1 W.L.R. 1881

[534] See [2001] 2 A.C. at 568.

[535] [2005] UKHL 23; [2005] 2 All E.R. 443 at [137].

That, however, is to overlook two fundamental considerations: first, the insidious effect that his awareness of the proposed duty would have upon the mind and conduct of the doctor (subtly tending to the suppression of doubts and instincts which in the child's interests ought rather to be encouraged), and second, a consideration inevitably bound up with the first, the need to protect him against the risk of costly and vexing litigation, by no means invariably soundly based."[536]

That was said in the context of supporting a denial of a duty of care to parents suspected of abuse. The trouble is that very similar arguments can be deployed to deny a duty to the child: overreaction is just as likely as the line of least resistance.

5–54   **v. Procedure.** Before leaving the present law in this area mention must be made of a jurisdictional matter. The procedure for judicial review of administrative action is not by ordinary suit but by application under Pt 54 of the Civil Procedure Rules.[537] A claim for damages may be made in judicial review proceedings if there is a private law wrong, but there are various restrictions upon the procedure, in particular a requirement of permission to lodge a claim and a short time limit. Judicial review is not an exclusive regime for actions against public authorities: a person injured on local authority land, for example, proceeds (and must proceed[538]) by claim in the ordinary way; a person wrongfully detained may have some basis to seek judicial review but he is also entitled to proceed simply by a common law claim for false imprisonment.[539] Nor is Pt 54 applicable where some collateral public law issue arises in what is essentially a private law claim. However, in *Cocks v Thanet DC*[540] the House of Lords held that where, as a precondition to establishing a private right of action under a statute, the claimant was obliged to impugn, on public law grounds, a decision of a local authority, judicial review was the correct procedure. This does not, it has been held, prevent the bringing of an ordinary action for negligence where a common law duty arises in the context of the exercise of a

---

[536] See also *Lawrence v Pembrokeshire CC* [2007] EWCA Civ 446; [2007] 1 W.L.R. 291; the dissenting opinion of Charron, Bastarache and Rothstein JJ. in *Hill v Hamilton-Wentworth Regional Police Services Board* [2007] SCC 41; [2007] 3 S.C.R. 129 at [152], denying a duty of care by police to suspects; and the judgment of Hodgson J.A. in *Stewart v Ronalds* [2009] NSWCA 277 (report on conduct of Minister leading to his dismissal).
[537] Formerly RSC Ord.53.
[538] CPR 54.3(2).
[539] *I.D. v Home Office* [2005] EWCA Civ 38; [2005] I.N.L.R. 278.
[540] [1983] 2 A.C. 286.

statutory power, even though that may require public law impropriety to be established against the defendant.[541]

vi. The Law Commission's provisional proposals. In 2008 the **5–55** Law Commission issued a Consultation Paper, *Administrative Redress: Public Bodies and the Citizen*.[542] This began from the premise that:

"[I]n private law . . . the current situation is unsustainable. The uncertain and unprincipled nature of negligence in relation to public bodies, coupled with the unpredictable expansion of liability over recent years, has led to a situation that serves neither claimants nor public bodies."[543]

It is proposed that the present liability of a public body under the tort of negligence would remain for cases where the damage occurred in the course of an activity which has no public law elements because it is one which could be carried out by a private person, for example negligence in the maintenance of local authority premises or the driving of a local authority vehicle. However, where the activity was "truly public" the present law would be replaced by a new regime under which there would be liability in damages[544] for "serious fault".[545] An activity would be "truly public" if the defendant body:

"(a) exercised, or failed to exercise, a special statutory power; or (b) . . . breached a special statutory duty; or (c) . . . exercised, or failed to exercise, a prerogative power."[546]

The last is very obviously truly public because it is unique to the Crown; the first is intended to cover situations where a private person could not undertake the activity because it is authorised by the statute; the second is more difficult to pin down because it covers activities which could be performed by private persons but it is aimed at the cases where the public body is marked out by the statute as having a duty, the example given being the statutory duty

---

[541] *Lonhro Plc v Tebbit* [1992] 4 All E.R. 280. Thus in *X v Bedfordshire CC* [1995] 2 A.C. 633 (above) some of the claims potentially involved impugning discretionary decisions but they were all brought by ordinary action. See also *Phonographic Performance Ltd v D.T.I.* [2004] EWHC 1795 (Ch); [2004] 1 W.L.R. 2893 (action against Crown for failure to implement Directive in the nature of breach of statutory duty and suitable for private law claim).

[542] LCP No 187.

[543] Para.2.7.

[544] This claim could be brought either in judicial review proceedings where appropriate or in a free-standing action.

[545] See para.4.110.

[546] Para.4.131.

to provide housing for the homeless. The second requirement would be that the power or duty was intended to "confer a benefit" on the claimant as an individual. This is said to be based on the principle in European law governing claims against the State for failure to implement EU law.[547] Even if there was the requisite intention, the liability in damages would be confined to the interest intended to be protected so that for example a statutory system of inspection of the safety of vehicles might give rise to a claim for damages for personal injury but not to one where the claimant had simply bought a sub-standard vehicle. Finally, liability in damages would arise only if there was serious fault, this being seen as "the key" to the proposals.[548] The fault, it is said, must be "seriously aggravated".[549] Again this is said to be inspired by the approach to liability for failure to implement EU legislation, though the context there is very different. Some of the factors listed on the issue whether there is fault at all are familiar from the general "calculus of negligence" —matters such as the likelihood and seriousness of the harm and the cost of avoiding it[550]—but others are perhaps not (e.g. the "extent and duration of departures from well-established good practice" or the extent to which senior administrators are involved). It is also proposed to abandon the general rule of joint and several liability where there are a number of concurrent tortfeasors and give the court a discretion to impose only proportionate liability, a matter which might have considerable significance for claims based on failure by public bodies to exercise regulatory powers. The torts of misfeasance in a public office and breach of statutory duty (in so far as it concerned public bodies) would be abolished.

5–56   These are only provisional conclusions.[551] As to the core proposal of a standard of serious fault it is difficult to escape the conclusion that it is likely to be unpredictable and to involve very detailed factual investigations. Of course the new regime would lead to liability in some cases where at present there is no duty of care in tort; but it might also lead to the failure of some claims which now succeed where a duty of care is found. It has been suggested above that a claim based on failure by a local authority to maintain its premises would still fall under the normal negligence regime as found in the Occupiers' Liability Acts 1957 and 1984. However, a failure by a highway authority to carry out its statutory duty to

---

[547] *Francovich v Italy* (C–6/90) [1995] I.C.R. 722. See para.7–12, below. See *Three Rivers District Council v Governor of the Bank of England* [2001] UKHL 16; [2003] 2 AC 1, where a banking directive was held not to confer such rights.
[548] Para.4.152.
[549] Para.4.146.
[550] See para.5–83, below.
[551] For criticism see Cornford [2009] P.L.70.

maintain the highway would be public in terms of the proposals because it is clearly a "special statutory duty".[552] At present such cases are governed by a statutory regime which imposes a standard similar to that of the general law of negligence but imposes upon the authority the burden of showing that it had taken such steps as were reasonable and makes the authority liable, contrary to the general rule of the law, for the work of independent contractors.[553] Since this regime already recognises that one cannot expect the highway to be in perfect condition at all points because there are limits on resources, it is difficult to say how much difference the standard of serious fault would make, but a change in the burden of proof and on independent contractors presumably would weaken the claimant's position. Of course the proposals would, in the event of serious fault, open the way to claims which are not now possible, namely those in respect of failure to exercise the statutory power to *improve* the highway.[554] The proposals also indicate that, while the ordinary driving of a police car would fall under the general negligence regime, emergency, "blue light" driving would be a truly public activity, attracting the serious fault standard. Again it is difficult to say whether this would make any difference because the present law seems to allow to some extent for the "necessity of the moment" in determining what is reasonable care.[555] In other words, the existing law already goes some way to providing that modification of corrective justice[556] which the Law Commission believes should underpin the whole of public authority liability. It might be thought odd that the law should have different regimes for accidents caused by police cars according to whether or not there is an emergency justifying infringement of the criminal law speed limit (contrast French law, which puts all liability of a public body into a separate category of administrative liability) but the definitions in the Consultation Paper cannot be read as if they were statutory formulae. It indicates, for example, that police investigation of crime would be a public function under the proposals,[557] even though it would not be carried out under any special statutory power or duty or the prerogative. At the moment the common law seems to have a virtually blanket denial of a duty of care so this might be regarded as an improvement of the claimant's position but where there is a real and immediate danger of violence there is already a liability in domestic law under art.2 of

---

[552] Para.6.5.
[553] See para.14–42, below.
[554] In *Stovin v Wise* [1996] A.C. 923 the defendants decided to do the improvement work and then forgot about it. Was that "serious fault"?
[555] See para.5–85, below.
[556] See Appendix A of the Consultation Paper.
[557] See para.6.6.

the European Convention on Human Rights,[558] so it is not clear what would be added by the new liability.

5–57 It may be objected that the above situations do not lie at the heart of the proposals, which are less concerned with "accidents" than with the consequences of maladministration, and these are more likely to take the form of damage to livelihood or refusal of benefits like housing. It is perhaps significant that all of the cases analysed by the Commission in its attempt to assess the impact of the serious fault standard were applications for judicial review, and in its view only a very small proportion of these would have passed the proposed threshold.[559] However, it should not be assumed that even in this context the proposals would provide a remedy. If ever there was a case where justice calls for damages but the present common law does not provide it, it is *Jain v Trent Strategic Health Authority*,[560] where the trial judge had found that the defendants' actions leading to the closure of the claimants' care home on the grounds of wholly unfounded fears for the safety of the residents had been *Wednesbury* unreasonable and had "bordered on the reckless". Yet the House of Lords rejected any duty of care, essentially for the reason given for the rejection of a duty to parents in a child abuse case, namely that a duty to act for the protection of residents was incompatible with a duty not to damage the claimants' business. The actions were undoubtedly truly public and presumably there was serious fault in the sense of the proposals but it is difficult to see how there could be any liability under them. The purpose of the legislation may have been to confer a benefit on residents of care homes as individuals, but it certainly not intended to confer one on those running the homes. This situation, where loss is inflicted on C for the protection of B or the public as a whole, cannot be uncommon.[561] Again, however, since the coming into force of the Human Rights Act 1998, the Convention may come to the rescue, since Lord Scott thought that the facts of *Jain*, if occurring now, would attract art.6(1) and art.1 of the First Protocol.[562]

The provisional proposals originate in work which began before 2004[563] and they are concerned not only to provide remedies where they are needed but to protect public bodies from unmanageable demands. The Commission's conclusion was that:

---

[558] See para.5–19, above.
[559] Appendix C.
[560] [2009] UKHL 4; [2009] 1 A.C. 853.
[561] Childcare powers in so far as they affect suspected parents are another example. The Consultation Paper seems inconsistent on this point, since in para.4.28 cases of erroneously restricting cattle movement to prevent the spread of disease or putting the claimant on a child abuse register are given as instances of the potential injustice that the current law can cause.
[562] [2009] UKHL 4; [2009] 1 A.C. 853 at [12].
[563] See *Monetary Remedies in Public Law* (2004).

"[R]ecent history has seen an increase in governmental liability and there seems little to suggest that this increase will halt or that the extent of liability will decrease."[564]

No doubt that is true of the Human Rights Act 1998 but the introduction of that was a deliberate act of policy; with regard to the common law of negligence the proposition would be very difficult to justify in the context of the last decade.

E. Lawyers and Negligence: Third Parties and Litigation

Solicitors will generally have a contract with their clients which **5-58** will require them to exercise proper professional care and skill within the scope of the retainer. There may be no contract where the client is legally aided with a nil contribution and generally there is no contract between a barrister and a lay client[565] but there is no doubt that in these cases there is an assumption of responsibility which gives rise to the same duty in practical terms, though in tort not in contract.[566] Two matters have, however, proved controversial: the duty of the lawyer to third parties and the duty, even to his client, in the context of litigation.

i. Third parties. The paradigm case is that where the lawyer is **5-59** instructed to draw a will for X which will benefit C and fails to carry out that task properly.[567] We have seen how in *White v Jones*[568] liability was imposed in such a case on the basis of assumption of responsibility, but something more needs to be said by way of explanation of the scope of this duty. It applies as much to a financial institution offering will-making services as to a solicitor.[569] Although the duty sounds in tort the underlying basis of it is the acceptance of the client's instructions and the scope of those instructions are obviously determinative of the duty to the beneficiary. While as matter of principle there should be a duty in respect of gifts inter vivos, it has been held that there is no liability if the donor is

---

[564] Para.4.56.
[565] Any rule of law (as opposed to professional conduct) forbidding a barrister entering into a contract was abolished by the Courts and Legal Services Act 1990 s.61.
[566] However, even where there is a contract there may be a parallel duty in tort: *Midland Bank Trust Co Ltd v Hett, Stubbs & Kemp* [1979] Ch. 384, approved in *Henderson v Merrett Syndicates Ltd* [1995] 2 A.C. 145.
[567] Where the will is in order and the deceased appoints A as his executor, leaving property to C, and the defendants culpably fail to carry out A's instructions to administer the estate promptly C may suffer loss because the property is not transferred to him promptly. However, in such a case A can sue for that loss (holding the damages in trust for C) since until the estate is administered the property is vested in A: *Chappell v Somers & Blake* [2003] EWHC 1644; [2004] Ch. 19.
[568] [1995] 2 A.C. 207, para.5–37, above.
[569] *Esterhuizen v Allied Dunbar Assurance Plc* [1998] 2 F.L.R. 668.

able to rectify the error made[570]: if he chooses not to do so, the effective cause of the failure of the transaction is not the negligence of the solicitor but the decision of his client.[571] The duty extends to the drafting of the instrument[572] and its execution[573] as well as simple failure to implement the instructions.[574] There will generally be no liability to the estate[575] because it will have suffered no loss by the bequest going to the wrong destination, but the duty to the beneficiary is an independent one so that, while there must be no double liability,[576] there may be liability to the beneficiary and liability to the estate in respect of any further loss which it suffers.[577] However, the solicitor in such a situation is not the guardian of the interests of the object of the client's bounty[578] except to the limited extent of carrying out the client's instructions. So he does not owe a duty to the beneficiary to advise the testator on arranging his affairs so as to minimise the tax impact of the transaction on the

---

[570] *Hemmens v Wilson Browne* [1995] Ch. 223. Contrast *Hughes v Richards* [2004] EWCA Civ 266; [2004] P.N.L.R. 35 (A engages B to set up a trust to benefit C—the job is mishandled, the fund lost and C receives no benefit, C's claim is arguable, even though it was possible that A might recover substantial damages in alternative).

[571] As to the effect of pre-death change of mind by the testator in the case of an ineffective will see *Humbleston v Martin Tolhurst Partnership* [2004] EWHC 151 (Ch); [2004] P.N.L.R. 26.

[572] *Horsefall v Haywards* [1999] Lloyd's Rep. P.N. 332; *Martin v Triggs Turner Bartons* [2009] EWHC 1920 (Ch); [2010] P.N.L.R. 3; cf. *Fraser v McArthur Stewart* [2008] CSOH 159; 2009 S.L.T. 31. Note that under s.20 of the Administration of Justice Act 1982 the court has jurisdiction, on application within six months of representation being taken out, to rectify a will so as to carry out the intentions of the testator, if it is satisfied that the will is so expressed that it fails to carry out the testator's intentions in consequence of a clerical error or of a failure to understand his instructions. Failure to take this course may amount to failure to mitigate loss and provide a defence to the claim against the solicitor: *Walker v Geo. H. Medlicott & Son* [1999] 1 W.L.R. 727.

[573] *Ross v Caunters* [1980] 1 Ch. 297; *Esterhuizen v Allied Dunbar Assurance Plc*, above, fn.569 (normally insufficient to leave accurate written instructions on attestation, but cf. *Gray v Richards Butler* [2000] W.T.L.R. 143, decided in 1997).

[574] *White v Jones*, above, fn.568.

[575] Cf. *Worby v Rosser* [1999] Lloyd's Rep. P.N. 972 (probate of will prepared by defendant successfully opposed by beneficiaries of earlier will on grounds related to testator's capacity; costs of proceedings not recoverable by beneficiaries since those costs directly recoverable by estate if breach of duty established).

[576] *Corbett v Bond Pearce* [2001] EWCA Civ 531; [2001] 3 All E.R. 769.

[577] *Carr-Glyn v Frearsons* [1999] Ch. 326 (where the negligence lay in failing to ensure the severance of a joint tenancy with the result that it did not fall into the estate). The question whether the client and/or "the estate" has a claim may not be so easy. The deceased receives erroneous tax planning advice from D and leaves his estate to X. This has the effect that his estate incurs substantially more inheritance tax liability than need have been the case. The deceased, it seems, suffers no loss (beyond the disappointment of his hopes for X and that is not a legal loss) because inheritance tax is only payable on death and there is no tort claim to survive his death. Nor does the executor suffer any loss since he is only liable for the tax up to the amount of the estate: *Daniels v Thomson* [2004] EWCA Civ 307; [2004] P.N.L.R. 33 (where the question whether X had a claim was not in issue; if he does not, there is another "black hole"; compare *Rind v Theodore Goddard* [2008] EWHC 459 (Ch) where the issue of liability to X was not regarded as suitable for summary judgment).

[578] It is assumed that there is no direct assumption of responsibility to the third party, e.g. by answering questions from him.

beneficiary.[579] In *Clarke v Bruce Lance & Co*[580] the defendants in 1973 had drawn up a will for the testator which left a filling station to the claimant and some five years later they acted for the testator again in granting an option (at a fixed price) over the filling station to a tenant, who was virtually certain to exercise it.[581] The claimant's claim for negligence was struck out: if the defendants had owed him any duty of care they could find themselves in the intolerable position of having to seek to dissuade their client (the testator) from having to carry through a transaction upon which he had decided.

The duty to third parties is not confined to carrying out instructions for wills; for example, it has been held that a solicitor acting for a borrower may be under a duty to take care to ensure, for the benefit of an unrepresented lender, that the security given is effective.[582] However, in conducting litigation or negotiating in an adversarial situation neither client nor lawyer normally[583] owes a duty of care to their opponent.[584]

ii. Litigation: the demise of the former immunity. For many 5–60
years the law took the stance that a lawyer conducting litigation did not owe a duty of care even to his own client in the conduct of the case in court and matters closely connected therewith.[585] Various reasons were put forward for this immunity: that an advocate has a duty to the court as well as to his client and in order to fulfil the duty to the court he had to be relieved of even the possibility that actions for negligence would be brought against him by a disgruntled client; the difficulty or undesirability of retrying, in the action against the advocate, the issue which arose in the original litigation out of which the action arose; the general immunity granted to those

---

[579] *Cancer Research Campaign v Ernest Brown* [1998] P.N.L.R. 583; and see *Woodward v Wolferstans, The Times,* April 8, 1997.

[580] [1988] 1 W.L.R. 881.

[581] The option was not exercisable until the death of the testator's widow, which had not occurred at the time of the proceedings.

[582] *Dean v Allin & Watts* [2001] EWCA Civ 758; [2001] 2 Lloyd's Rep. 249; and see *Al Kandari v J.R. Brown & Co* [1988] Q.B. 665. A lawyer and an attesting witness participate in drawing up a mortgage of X's property when it is obvious to both of them that there is a serious risk that X is defrauding his co-owner. The witness is aware that his attestation is untrue. Both are liable to the co-owner for the cost of vacating the mortgage: *Graham v Hall* [2006] NSWCA 208.

[583] A New Zealand court has held that a lawyer inaccurately certifying that he has explained a divorce settlement to his client owes a duty of care to the other party in respect of loss suffered when the settlement is subsequently set aside: *Connell v Odlum* [1993] 2 N.Z.L.R. 257. In normal circumstances the other party must rely on his own lawyer but here he has no choice but to accept the certificate.

[584] *Business Corporations International v Registrar of Companies* [1988] Ch. 229; *Connolly-Martin v D* [1999] Lloyd's Rep. P.N. 790. But see the power to make a wasted costs order, para.5–60, below. As to liability for abuse of process, see Ch.19.

[585] The leading decisions of the HL were *Rondel v Worsley* [1969] 1 A.C. 191 and *Saif Ali v Sydney Mitchell & Co* [1980] A.C. 198.

involved in court proceedings; the "cab-rank" rule whereby counsel must take any case within his field of competence[586]; and the existence of professional disciplinary procedures. Now, however, the immunity has been swept away, at least in relation to claims arising out of civil proceedings, by the House of Lords in *Arthur J.S. Hall & Co v Simons*.[587] There is something in the first two of the above reasons; the third one is an incorrect analogy since the advocate is the only person in the court who can fairly be said to have assumed responsibility to his client[588]; but even taken together the first two reasons were not regarded as having sufficient force to justify the maintenance of a rule which must inevitably have been seen as special treatment of lawyers by lawyers and which must have been open to potential attack under the European Convention on Human Rights.[589] Furthermore, other jurisdictions with very similar legal systems[590] had rejected the rule without undue effects and considerable difficulty had been encountered in defining the limits of the immunity.[591] None of the cases involved in the appeal had originated from criminal proceedings[592] but four members of the House[593] were of the view that the traditional rule was equally inapplicable to claims arising from criminal proceedings.[594]

---

[586] In modern times the immunity extended to solicitors acting as advocates, but the cab-rank rule has never applied to them.

[587] [2002] 1 A.C. 615.

[588] See Lord Hoffmann at 698. The witness's duty is to tell the truth; the judge is a public officer of justice.

[589] Twenty years before, Lord Diplock in *Saif Ali v Sydney Mitchell & Co*, above, fn.585, had expressed some regret that the House had not received a more radical submission that the immunity ought no longer to be upheld.

[590] Most notably Canada. However, the High Court of Australia has rejected *Hall v Simons* and affirmed the immunity: *D'Orta Ekenaike v Victoria Legal Aid* [2005] HCA 12; 223 C.L.R. 1. Among those judges in the majority who delivered a joint judgment, the key issue is finality and procedural differences between England and Australia are emphasised. New Zealand rejected immunity in *Chamberlains v Lai* [2006] NZSC 70; [2007] 2 N.Z.L.R. 1.

[591] These were probably exacerbated by the Civil Procedure Rules: [2002] 1 A.C. at 745 per Lord Hobhouse.

[592] One was a building dispute, the others were matrimonial ancillary relief proceedings and all concerned advice on settlement.

[593] Lords Steyn, Browne-Wilkinson, Hoffmann and Millett; Lords Hope, Hutton and Hobhouse dissenting.

[594] The issue of the immunity of solicitors conducting a criminal defence has been considered by the Inner House in *Wright v Paton Farrell* [2006] CSIH 7. However, the court was somewhat divided in its views on the whole issue of immunity. The Lord President thought that solicitors in Scotland had "acquired" an immunity via *Rondel v Worsley* and that this should remain after *Hall*. Lord Johnston thought that *Hall* did not determine any part of the immunity issue for Scotland but that both solicitors and counsel should enjoy immunity in respect of criminal proceedings. Lord Osborne thought that solicitors did not enjoy immunity under Scots law but dismissed the claim on the ground that there was no relevant averment of loss caused by the defendant. In *Chamberlains v Lai*, above, fn.590, it is accepted that there may have to be differences in the scope of counsel's liability between civil and criminal proceedings.

It is not, of course, the law that an advocate is negligent because he is wrong.[595] The court:

"[M]ust make full allowance for the fact that an advocate in court, like a commander in battle, often has to make decisions quickly and under pressure, in the fog of war and ignorant of developments on the other side of the hill".[596]

Of course he faces the risk of unfounded or even vexatious claims, but that is true of any professional person who does not achieve the result that his client wants and the House of Lords thought that the power to dismiss a claim without trial on the ground that it had no reasonable prospect of success[597] was an adequate protection.[598] Furthermore, we must take account of another, procedural rule whereby an action will be struck out as an abuse of the process of the court if it involves an attack on the final decision of another court of competent jurisdiction.[599] If, for example, the claimant has been convicted of a crime and sues his counsel for negligence in the conduct of the case (assuming that *Hall* will be treated as extending to criminal cases) he must, in order to establish that he has suffered damage, impugn his conviction.[600] This is so whether the conviction was obtained after a trial or upon a plea of guilty[601] and whether or not the sentence has been served in full.[602] The rule rests upon public policy against the re-litigation of issues which have been determined and against which there has been no

[595] See *Moy v Pettmann Smith* [2005] UKHL 7; [2005] 1 W.L.R. 581.
[596] *Ridehalgh v Horsefield* [1994] Ch. 205 at 236. This statement is made in the context of the power to make a wasted costs order against an advocate because of any improper, unreasonable or negligent act or omission by him, but it is equally relevant to tort liability. On wasted costs orders see the Supreme Court Act 1981 s.51, as substituted by the Courts and Legal Services Act 1990 s.4. The existence of wasted costs orders really destroyed the foundations of the "divided loyalties" argument in support of the immunity.
[597] CPR 24.2.
[598] Indeed, Lord Hoffmann thought that lawyers were in an advantageous position in this respect since the court would have an understanding of the background without expert assistance: [2002] 1 A.C. 691. See also, in the same case, on the impact of changes in the funding of litigation.
[599] The relevance of this to a tort action where there had been prior proceedings between the claimant and some third person was made clear in *Hunter v CC West Midlands* [1982] A.C. 529. Of course where there has been a final decision on an issue between the claimant and the third person that cannot be reopened between *them* because of the separate principle of res judicata.
[600] Strictly of course the issue in the negligence case is not the same as in the criminal case, but the soundness of the conviction is nevertheless at the heart of the negligence case: *Smith v Linskills* [1996] 1 W.L.R. 763 at 769.
[601] *Somasundaram v M. Julius Melchior & Co* [1989] 1 All E.R. 129; *Hall* [2002] 1 A.C. at 706.
[602] As it had been in *Smith v Linskills*, above, fn.600. In such a case the claimant will say that his purpose is to recover damages but the attack on the previous decision is still inherent in his case.

appeal or in respect of which the appeal process has been exhausted: a final decision should, save in exceptional circumstances, be final.[603] If one allows the criminal conviction to be impugned in civil proceedings there is a risk that one may end up with:

> "[T]wo conflicting decisions of the court, one (reached by judge and jury on the criminal burden of proof) saying that [the claimant] is guilty, the other (reached by a judge alone on balance of probability) that he is not guilty."[604]

No one doubts of course that miscarriages of justice occur but it is thought that the proper method of dealing with them is by the appeal process and mechanisms for review of convictions, not by civil litigation against lawyers.[605] However, the underlying principle that conflicting decisions are unacceptable obviously does not apply where the conviction has been set aside. The "final decision" procedural rule was in the past supported on the *additional* ground of the difficulty of determining what would have been the outcome of the previous proceedings if due care had been used but that was also a foundation of the rejected substantive immunity rule. If the first decision has been set aside the action against the advocate must therefore proceed unless it can be said at the preliminary stage that on the facts it has no reasonable prospect of success. The reason for the final decision rule, that the administration of justice will be brought into disrepute, is far less powerful where the first decision is a civil one:

> "[W]hether the original decision was right or wrong is usually a matter of concern only to the parties and has no wider implications. There is no public interest objection to a subsequent finding that, but for the negligence of his lawyers, the losing party would have won."[606]

Where the claimant has been represented by solicitor and counsel and he sues the former the relationship between the two lawyers must be considered. A solicitor who has consulted counsel will

---

[603] Is this principle, too, vulnerable to attack under art.6 of the European Convention on Human Rights? See Lord Hope at [2002] 1 A.C. 723.

[604] [2002] 1 A.C. at 684 per Lord Browne-Wilkinson.

[605] Cf. Lord Hobhouse at [2002] 1 A.C. 751.

[606] [2002] 1 A.C. at 706 per Lord Hoffmann, who gives as a possible exception a case where the claimant in the first proceedings for libel brought against him by X, had failed on a plea of justification.

prima facie be entitled to rely on his advice[607] but he cannot, "rely blindly and with no mind of his own on counsel's view".[608]

A witness enjoys immunity from civil liability,[609] which is not confined to defamation, and this extends to preliminary investigations carried out by him with a view to litigation, otherwise the immunity could easily be outflanked.[610] Unlike the case of the advocate, this is still one where it is believed that immunity is necessary lest the witness be deterred from performing his duty to the court. However, in relation to civil proceedings this does not create a blanket immunity for an expert who is engaged to advise the claimant on the merits of his claim.[611] The court must, difficult as it is, determine what is the principal purpose for which the work was done: if the purpose was primarily for use in court or for disclosure to the other side[612] it will be immune, but if its principal purpose was to inform the claimant it will not. There will generally be less difficulty in a criminal case, where experts are unlikely to be engaged until the proceedings are on foot or at least imminent.[613]

The prosecutor in a criminal case is at once client, lawyer and also a minister of justice but the accused as a general rule has no cause of action for negligence[614] against those engaged in prosecuting him on behalf of the community.[615] This rests on general grounds of public policy and not on the former advocate's immunity.[616] How-

---

[607] *Somasundaram v M. Julius Melchior & Co*, above, fn.601; *Matrix Securities Ltd v Theodore Goddard* (1997) 147 N.L.J. 1847; *McFaddens v Platford* [2009] EWHC 126 (TCC) at [56].

[608] *Davy-Chieseman v Davy-Chieseman* [1984] Fam. 48; *Locke v Camberwell HA* [1991] 2 Med.L.R. 249; *Bond v Royal Sun Alliance* [2001] P.N.L.R. 30. Where the solicitor is liable it is likely that counsel will bear the greater share of the damages for the purposes of contribution: *Pritchard Joyce & Hinds v Batcup* [2008] EWHC 20 (QB); [2008] P.N.L.R. 18.

[609] In relation to evidence in court this extends even to perjured evidence. However, the immunity has not been extended so as to prevent professional disciplinary proceedings: *Meadow v GMC* [2006] EWCA Civ 1390; [2007] Q.B. 462. See also *Phillips v Symes* [2004] EWHC 2330 (Ch); [2005] 4 All E.R. 519 (costs).

[610] *Evans v London Hospital Medical College* [1981] 1 W.L.R. 184. However, dishonest fabrication of evidence out of court is another matter: see para.12–40, below.

[611] *Palmer v Durnford Ford* [1992] Q.B. 483.

[612] *Stanton v Callaghan* [2000] Q.B. 75 (joint expert report). The issue of the status of *Stanton* was thought suitable for a direct appeal to the Supreme Court in *Jones v Kaney* [2010] EWHC 61 (QB). In *N v Agrawal* [1999] P.N.L.R. 939 a prosecution witness was held not to be liable to the victim for failing to turn up but if the claimant's expert in a civil case failed to turn up, that would be a breach of contract.

[613] *Karling v Purdue* [2005] P.N.L.R. 13. OH (where there is an exhaustive view of the authorities).

[614] There may be liability for malicious prosecution or misfeasance in a public office (see Ch.19, and para.7–20, below respectively) but these require "malice".

[615] *Elguzouli-Daf v MPC* [1995] Q.B. 335. So in *Cran v NSW* [2004] NSWCA 92 the claimant had no action where, as he alleged, his confinement was unnecessarily prolonged because the authorities were unnecessarily slow in getting material analysed for drugs.

[616] *Arthur J.S. Hall & Co v Simons*, above, at [2002] 1 A.C. 679, 697. The alleged negligence in the two appeals reported as *Elguzouli-Daf* could hardly have fallen within the immunity.

ever, in *Welsh v CC Merseyside*[617] a claim that the Crown Prosecution Service had failed to inform the court that certain offences had been taken into consideration in other proceedings was held to disclose a cause of action based upon assumption of responsibility via an undertaking given to the claimant.

F. Psychiatric Injury[618]

5–61   The first point is one of terminology. For many years it has been customary to refer to this form of damage as "nervous shock". That has the advantage of serving as a reminder that this head of liability has in most cases required something in the nature of a traumatic response to an *event*.[619] That is not necessarily so in some cases where the claimant is directly affected by the defendant's conduct[620] but it is still the law that the spouse of a brain-damaged accident victim who foreseeably succumbs to psychiatric illness from the strain of caring for the victim has no cause of action against the tortfeasor.[621] However, the expression seems to be falling into disuse[622] and "psychiatric injury" or "mental injury"[623] is becoming a more frequent terminology.

Psychiatric injury is a form of "personal injury"[624] but it is more problematical for the law than most physical injury for two reasons. First, despite advances in scientific knowledge of the working of the mind there is still a belief, right or wrong, that it presents a greater risk of inaccurate diagnosis[625] or incorrect attribution of cause and

---

[617] [1993] 1 All E.R. 692. However, that part of the reasoning which considers s.2(5) of the Crown Proceedings Act 1947 is doubted in *Quinland v Governor of Swaleside Prison* [2002] EWCA Civ 174; [2003] Q.B. 306.

[618] Mullany and Handford, *Tort Liability for Psychiatric Damage*, 2nd edn. For the Law Commission's proposals, see the end of this section.

[619] Cf. *Tame v New South Wales* [2002] HCA 35; 211 C.L.R. 37 (the *Annetts v Australian Stations* appeal).

[620] See para.5–71, below.

[621] *Alcock v CC South Yorkshire* [1992] 1 A.C. 310 at 396, 401, 416; *Jaensch v Coffey* (1984) 155 C.L.R. 549. See the criticism in *Campbelltown CC v Mackay* (1989) 15 N.S.W.L.R. 501.

[622] See *Alcock*'s case, above, fn.621, and the criticism by Bingham L.J. in *Attia v British Gas Plc* [1988] Q.B. 304 at 317.

[623] Evans L.J.'s preference in *Vernon v Bosley (No.1)* [1997] 1 All E.R. 577 at 597, though he admitted that "nervous shock" remained the lawyer's favourite.

[624] For historical reasons it is not "bodily injury" under the Warsaw Convention, governing liability of air carriers: *Morris v K.L.M. Royal Dutch Airlines* [2002] UKHL 7; [2002] 2 A.C. 628, para.1–38, above.

[625] In *Vernon v Bosley (No.2)* [1999] Q.B. 18 C at the trial recovered some £643,000 damages for the traumatic consequences of witnessing the aftermath of the death of his children. In matrimonial proceedings decided three weeks before judgment, the court had proceeded upon much more optimistic evidence of the prognosis of P's condition than had been before the Queen's Bench judge. However, in *Frost v CC South Yorkshire* [1997] 3 W.L.R. 1194 at 1217, Henry L.J. put the risk of fraudulent shock claims as no greater than in, "cases involving back injuries where there is often a wide gap between observable symptoms and complaints."

effect,[626] and the incidence or the basis or even the very existence of some conditions is controversial.[627] A further difficulty is that the line between "mental" and "physical" is still not fully scientifically understood: nowadays, for example, there is support for the view that certain forms of depression are the product of physical changes in the brain[628] and if these can be produced by a sudden shock the only basis for treating such a case differently from physical lesion by impact must rest on legal policy. The current practice is to regard some injuries which are undoubtedly physical (such as a stroke or a miscarriage) but which are produced by shock as falling within the special rules in this section but in other contexts they may be equated with more direct physical harm. Secondly, while the physical effects of an accident are limited by the laws of inertia, physical injury to one person, or even the threat of it, may produce mental trauma in others, witnesses, relatives, friends and so on.[629] "The contours of tort law are profoundly affected by distinctions between different types of damage"[630] and mental injury is as "special" as economic loss.

i. A recognised psychiatric illness. The early view was that   **5–62** mental injury unaccompanied by physical injury was not compensable at all[631] but this was discarded around the end of the 19th century, both for intentional wrongdoing[632] and for negligence,[633] though it took rather longer to reach the position where the claimant might recover damages for shock caused by endangerment of another. However, it is still the law that the sensations of fear or mental distress or grief[634] suffered as a result of negligence[635] do not

---

[626] See, e.g. *Page v Smith (No.2)* [1996] 1 W.L.R. 855.
[627] See No.137 Law Com., Cm. (1995), Part III. This has been particularly so of the condition variously known as ME, CFS or PVFS, which was the basis of the claim in *Page v Smith* [1996] A.C. 155.
[628] See *Weaver v Delta Airlines Inc* (1999) 56 F Supp 2d 1190, discussed in *Morris v K.L.M.*, above, fn.624.
[629] In this respect the problem has affinities with relational economic loss: para.5–40, above.
[630] *Frost v CC South Yorkshire* [1999] 2 A.C. 455 at 492 per Lord Steyn.
[631] *Victorian Ry Commissioners v Coultas* (1888) 13 App. Cas. 222.
[632] *Wilkinson v Downton* [1897] 2 Q.B. 57, (but see current criticism of this view of the case: para.4–36, above).
[633] *Dulieu v White* [1901] 2 K.B. 669.
[634] There is a limited statutory right of action for bereavement: para.23–12, below.
[635] The position is different in the case of the intentional torts actionable per se because damages are then said to be at large: see para.22–8, below. E.g. in a case of libel the award of damages will reflect (though obviously not in any precise mathematical way) the distress suffered by the claimant at the publication and in a case of false arrest the damages may be aggravated by the distress suffered by the claimant because of the high-handed treatment of him. Some statutory wrongs such as race or sex discrimination and harassment also allow damages for distress.

in themselves give rise to a cause of action.[636] There must be some recognisable and acknowledged psychiatric illness[637] (though of course a physical injury resulting from a shock—heart failure, a fall, a miscarriage—is also compensable[638]). Thus where a claim alleged negligence in the conduct of a police disciplinary investigation the submission that actionable damage had occurred in the form of anxiety and vexation was described by the House of Lords as unsustainable[639] and claimants failed in their claim when they suffered claustrophobia and fear at being trapped in a lift.[640] A claim was also rejected where the victims of a disaster were trapped, fully conscious, for some time before they suffered a swift death from asphyxia.[641]

Assuming the mental injury suffered qualifies as damage in the above rather imprecise sense, the cases have been said to:

> "[B]roadly divide into two categories, that is to say, those cases in which the injured plaintiff was involved, either mediately or immediately, as a participant, and those in which the plaintiff was no more than a passive and unwilling witness of injury caused to others."[642]

5–63   **ii. Claimant physically threatened by the negligence—a primary victim.** The simplest case is that where the claimant suffers shock from a reasonable fear for his own safety caused by the

---

[636] A claimant who has suffered a physical injury may in principle recover damages for the distress caused to him by the injury even though it does not amount to a recognisable psychiatric illness. In practice in the majority of cases this will be "lost" in the conventional figures for loss of amenity (para.22–22, below) but, e.g. damages for facial scarring will take account of the psychological effect on the victim. Even a breach of contract wholly unconnected with personal injury may give rise to damages for non-pecuniary loss if the contract concerns the claimant's "peace of mind": *Farley v Skinner* [2001] UKHL 49; [2002] A.C. 732.

[637] Among many statements of this requirement, see *Hinz v Berry* [1970] 2 Q.B. 40 at 42; *Alcock v CC South Yorkshire* [1992] 1 A.C. 310 at 401, 416; *Jaensch v Coffey* (1984) 155 C.L.R. 549 at 559, 587; *Wainwright v Home Office* [2003] UKHL 53; [2004] 2 A.C. 406 (which considers the effect of intentional wrongdoing).

[638] Another possibility is that shock causes a personality change which renders the claimant more susceptible to some physical harm. Such a case will raise problems of causation. For an extreme example, see *Commonwealth v MacLean* (1997) 41 N.S.W.L.R. 389 (shock causing increased consumption of alcohol and tobacco; throat cancer developing after many years).

[639] *Calveley v CC Merseyside* [1989] A.C. 1228.

[640] *Reilly v Merseyside RHA* [1995] 6 Med. L.R. 246.

[641] *Hicks v CC South Yorkshire* [1992] 2 All E.R. 65. Where a person's life expectancy is shortened by an injury, distress at that is a compensable item of damage. No doubt in *Hicks* there was a momentary interval between the onset of physical injury by crushing and death but it was too short sensibly to attract this principle.

[642] *Alcock v CC South Yorkshire* [1992] 1 A.C. 310 at 407 per Lord Oliver.

defendant's negligence (the "near miss"): then he may recover damages. In *Dulieu v White*[643] the claimant succeeded in a claim for shock, resulting in a miscarriage, when a horse-drawn van was negligently driven into the bar of the public house where she was serving. It is not necessary that the claimant should actually be in danger, provided he reasonably believes he is.[644] However, if the fear is not reasonably entertained (for example if the claimant is a hysterical personality who suffers shock from the noise of a collision on the other side of the street) there is no action.[645] The scope of this category of liability is nonetheless enlarged by the majority decision of the House of Lords in *Page v Smith*.[646] The claimant was involved in a collision caused by the defendant's negligence which caused property damage but no physical injury.[647] However, as a result of the experience the claimant suffered a recurrence of myalgic encephalomyelitis (ME) or chronic fatigue syndrome (CFS) which had affected him on and off for 25 years but which now became chronic and permanent.[648] The case was decided in the House of Lords on the basis that the circumstances of the accident were not such as to cause foreseeable psychiatric injury to a person of normal fortitude[649] but some physical injury was plainly foreseeable from it. In the view of the majority, psychiatric injury was but a variety of the broader genus of "personal injury"[650] and therefore the claimant was entitled to recover on the basis of the "thin skull" principle. This says that once the defendant owes a duty to the claimant and is in breach of it, his liability is not limited to the

---

[643] [1901] 2 K.B. 669.

[644] *McFarlane v E.E. Caledonia Ltd* [1994] 2 All E.R. 1 at 10.

[645] [1994] 2 All E.R. 1 at 11, though on the facts the CA took the view that C was not in fact in fear for his own safety at the time. See also *Hegarty v E.E. Caledonia Ltd* [1997] 2 Lloyd's Rep. 259; *Monk v P.C. Harrington Ltd* [2008] EWHC 1879 (QB); [2009] P.I.Q.R. P3.

[646] [1996] A.C. 155; *Giblett v Murray, The Times*, May 25, 1999.

[647] Lord Rodger's reference in *British Steel Plc v Simmons* [2004] UKHL 20; [2004] I.C.R. 585 at [56] to physical *and* psychiatric injury should be read as a reference to the facts of that case.

[648] The findings of the trial judge that (1) this controversial condition existed and (2) that the claimant suffered from it were not challenged on appeal. In a further appeal on causation (*Page v Smith (No.2)* [1996] 1 W.L.R. 855) the CA held that the judge had been entitled to come to the conclusion that the accident had made a material contribution to the recurrence of the condition: para.6–7, below. Note that the damages were reduced to about 60 per cent of the loss to reflect the fact that the claimant was vulnerable to the recurrence of the condition from other causes.

[649] Lord Ackner and Lord Lloyd in the majority thought this conclusion was probably wrong. "When cars collide at 30 miles an hour, the possibility that those involved will suffer nervous shock, resulting from some form of psychiatric illness, is not lightly to be brushed aside": Lord Lloyd at 197.

[650] As Lord Lloyd pointed out at 190, a standard English statutory formula in the Limitation Acts and elsewhere is, " 'personal injury' includes any disease and any impairment of a person's physical or mental condition".

injuries which were reasonably foreseeable at the time of the accident but extends to more serious injuries brought about by the claimant's pre-existing weakness.[651] The limits of *Page v Smith* are not easy to state. How stringently is the "zone of danger" to be defined? If the defendant drives furiously down a crowded street there may be hundreds of people momentarily in the zone of physical danger created by his negligence: can any of them who happens to have an "eggshell personality" sue if he suffers shock?[652] However, the case is not confined to the simple situation where D's negligence puts C in danger of injury by *accident*: thus where the negligence of the police force in failing to provide a functioning surveillance device required an officer to make repeated surreptitious visits to a car belonging to gangsters in order to make it work, the defendants were held liable when the stress of this, combined with his existing hypertension (of which they were unaware) precipitated a psychiatric condition and a stroke.[653]

Nor is the category of primary victim confined to those who suffer mental injury from fear for their own safety. The House of Lords applied *Page v Smith* to a case where the pursuer's anger at the happening of the accident in which he was injured was the trigger which made a material contribution to his depressive illness.[654] It is enough, it seems, that the claimant is within the zone of physical danger even if what triggers the mental injury is the sight of what happens to others. In *Chadwick v British Transport Commission*[655] the claimant was a volunteer helper at the scene of a rail disaster and suffered mental trauma as a result. For many years this case was regarded as resting on the basis that a duty was owed to him as a rescuer but the existence of any separate category of rescuers for this

---

[651] See para.6–32, below. The previous authorities regarded injury by shock as of a different "kind" from physical harm. "The test of liability for shock is foreseeability of injury by shock": *King v Phillips* [1953] 1 Q.B. 429 at 441; *The Wagon Mound (No.1)* [1961] A.C. 388 at 426; *Alcock v CC South Yorkshire* [1992] 1 A.C. 310 and 400. However, according to Lord Lloyd at 196 the courts in these cases did not have in mind the position of a primary victim threatened by physical injury. In *Frost v CC South Yorkshire* [1999] 2 A.C. 455 at 475 Lord Goff, dissenting, disagreed with this approach, taking the view that the thin skull rule only applied once there was some physical damage.

[652] *Glen v Korean Airlines Co Ltd* [2003] EWHC 643 (QB); [2003] Q.B. 1386 would provide an example but the point was not in issue in the proceedings. *Fagan v Goodman*, November 30, 2001 (QB) indicates a restrictive approach

[653] *Donachie v CC Greater Manchester* [2004] EWCA Civ 405; *The Times*, May 6, 2004. See also *A v Essex CC* [2003] EWCA Civ 1848; [2004] 1 W.L.R. 1881. An adoption agency failed to carry out a decision to make information available to adopters which would have revealed the child's very disturbed state. The adopters suffered psychiatric disorder because of his behaviour. Was this damage foreseeable? No, but, "it was foreseeable that [W] might assault them and damage their property. In those circumstances, the principle in *Page v Smith* . . . indicates that there is liability for whatever harm ensues" (at [71]).

[654] *British Steel Plc v Simmons* [2004] UKHL 20; [2004] I.C.R. 585.

[655] [1967] 1 W.L.R. 912.

purpose was rejected in *Frost v CC South Yorkshire*[656] and *Chadwick*'s case was regarded as correctly decided on the basis that the claimant had been in physical danger from the collapse of the wreckage, even though the judge[657] found that it was the horrific nature of the experience rather than fear for himself which had affected him.[658] This approach may be supported on the grounds that in some cases it may be extremely difficult to determine whether or how far the claimant suffered shock from fear for himself or from the sight of what happened to others, and there may be cases in which there is a damaging impact on his psyche without his consciously suffering anything that could be called fear. Nevertheless, it is a mechanical approach and one can conceive of cases where it might operate in the claimant's favour even though he was at the time entirely unaware of any danger to himself.[659]

In all these cases there is a close degree of temporal proximity between the defendant's negligence and the infliction of mental trauma on the claimant. We are now familiar with the situation where the defendant exposes the claimant to some harmful risk (a pollutant or some harmful chemical, for example) which has not caused any direct harm but the claimant's knowledge of this affects his mental state. Although he might be said to be in the "zone of danger", *Page v Smith* does not stretch this far. In *Rothwell v Chemical & Insulating Co Ltd*[660] one of the appellants, G, had been exposed to asbestos and developed asymptomatic pleural plaques. These did not in any way interfere with his physical health and would not themselves lead to any illness but they were a signal that asbestos had penetrated the body and that there was some more than normal risk of the development of an asbestos-related condition, something which G discovered when he was told about it by a doctor over 30 years after the exposure, though he had been concerned about the risk of developing an asbestos-related disease for years before that. That would not amount to damage which created

5–64

---

[656] [1999] 2 A.C. 455. See also *Young v Charles Church (Southern) Ltd* (1997) 39 B.M.L.R. 146.

[657] The father of the trial judge in *Frost*.

[658] Cf. *Hunter v British Coal* [1998] Q.B. 140, decided before *Frost*, where the claimant had been in some danger (though he was not aware of it) when he was near a defective hydrant but when the hydrant exploded and killed a workmate he was out of sight and some distance away.

[659] Cf. the example given by Toulson J. in *Coleman v British Gas Services Ltd*, April 12, 2002 (QB) at [62] of the passenger in a car who is asleep and unaware of an emergency which causes a neck injury to another passenger and who, on learning of this afterwards, wrongly convinces himself that he, too, has such an injury: no liability.

[660] [2007] UKHL 39; [2008] A.C. 281. See also *The Creutzfeldt-Jakob Disease litigation*; *Group B Plaintiffs v Medical Research Council* [2000] Lloyd's Rep. Med. 161 (decided in 1997); *Fletcher v Commissioners of Public Works* [2003] 1 I.R. 465; *Coleman v British Gas Services Ltd*, April 12, 2002 (QB).

a cause of action. However, G worried so much about the risk that he developed a clinical depressive condition. While it is obvious that this knowledge would cause anxiety to anyone, the case was conducted on the basis that there was no evidence that a person of reasonable fortitude would react so strongly as to become mentally ill. On that basis the House of Lords held that *Page v Smith* could not be extended to such a situation. The case is obviously very far removed on its facts from *Page*, not least because of the very long gap between the "exposure to danger" and the mental consequences of it, though the reasons for distinguishing that decision are variously expressed. Unlike *Rothwell*, *Page* was a case of psychiatric injury, "arising as an immediate consequence of an obvious accident"[661]; the chain of causation in *Rothwell* was, "stretched far beyond that which was envisaged in *Page*"[662]; and:

> "[I]t would be an unwarranted extension of [*Page*] to apply it to psychiatric illness caused by apprehension of the possibility of an unfavourable event which had not actually happened."[663]

The result in *Rothwell* might have been different if the pleural plaques had constituted "damage" for it is well-established that even anxiety falling short of mental illness at the consequences of a physical injury is a proper item of damages.[664] There would still, however, have been a difficulty, for the plaques themselves were not dangerous, they were simply an indication of penetration of the body by asbestos and one would be saying that:

> "[A] claimant with plaques would have a claim for damages for the risk that he would develop asbestosis or mesothelioma, when a claimant without plaques, but with exactly the same risk of developing those diseases, would have no claim".[665]

It may well be impossible in such a case to disentangle the mental processes which lead to the claimant's anxiety but one may say that a wholly rational person would be worried by the exposure, not the plaques. On the other hand, given the basic premise of *Page v Smith* that physical injury and mental injury are but different forms of "personal injury" the fact that on this hypothesis some physical

---

[661] Lord Mance at [104]; "an immediate response to a past event": Lord Rodger at [95].
[662] Lord Hope at [55].
[663] Lord Hoffmann at [33].
[664] See para.22–19, below.
[665] [2007] UKHL 39; [2008] A.C. 281 at [91] per Lord Rodger.

injury has occurred would make it impossible to avoid the application of the thin skull rule.[666]

Rothwell's case proceeds on the basic premise that claims do not **5–65** lie for exposure to risk.[667] "Risk of damage" is not "damage" and the case aims to prevent sidestepping this by blocking claims based on genuine but exaggerated reactions to exposure to risk. In that sense it might be justified on the basis of having to draw the line somewhere, "thus far and no further" as has been said in another mental injury context.[668] However, the case reveals some doubt in the House of Lords about the very desirability of the *Page* rule.[669]

iii. Claimant a witness of danger to others—a secondary **5–66** **victim.** The situation here is that D's negligence causes injury to B (or puts B in danger of injury[670]) and C (who is neither injured nor in danger[671]) suffers shock as a result of the incident. The leading case is *Alcock v CC South Yorkshire*.[672] The 10 appellants had suffered psychiatric injury[673] as a result of the disaster in 1989 at

---

[666] In Scotland s.1 of the Damages (Asbestos-Related Conditions) (Scotalnd) Act 2009 (asp) provides:

"(1) Asbestos-related pleural plaques are a personal injury which is not negligible.

(2) Accordingly, they constitute actionable harm for the purposes of an action of damages for personal injuries.

(3) Any rule of law the effect of which is that asbestos-related pleural plaques do not constitute actionable harm ceases to apply to the extent it has that effect.

(4) But nothing in this section otherwise affects any enactment or rule of law which determines whether and in what circumstances a person may be liable in damages in respect of personal injuries."

This has retroactive effect (other than in respect of claims settled or determined) and would clearly allow recovery for mere anxiety about plaques but damages will presumably be modest. In England, the Ministry of Justice on February 25, 2010, announced that it was to make payments of £5,000 to persons who had begun but not resolved claims for pleural plaques before *Rothwell* but that it was not minded to reverse that decision. A private member's Bill similar to the Scottish Act was lost with the 2010 election.

[667] Cf. *Pratt v Scottish Ministers* [2009] CSOH 31; [2009] S.L.T. 429 (failure to provide counselling about risk arising from an incident at work).

[668] *Frost v CC South Yorkshire* [1999] 2 A.C. 455 at 500.

[669] See Lord Hope at [2007] UKHL 39; [2008] A.C. 281 [52], Lord Mance at [104]. In contrast, Lord Hoffmann at [32] thought it was not likely to give rise to difficulties if confined to the situations which the court had in mind in the case; and in *Corr v IBC Vehicles Ltd* [2008] UKHL 13; [2008] A.C. 884 Lord Walker remarked at [40] that, "it provides a much simpler test for judges trying personal injury cases, even if it sometimes results in compensation for damage in the form of psychiatric sequelae which might not, on their own, have been reasonably foreseeable."

[670] It is clear that there need be no actual injury to B, it is enough that C reasonably believes that B is in peril; but under the Criminal Injuries Compensation Scheme, closely modelled on the common law of tort, there must be an actual injury to B: para.9(b).

[671] Of course C may be in danger as well, see above.

[672] [1992] 1 A.C. 310.

[673] It was assumed for the purposes of deciding the issue of law that damage and causation could be established.

Hillsborough Stadium in Sheffield, in which, because of the admitted negligence of the defendants, some 95 people were crushed to death and over 400 physically injured.[674] None of the appellants had suffered any physical injury, nor been in any danger, indeed most of them were not at the ground, though they saw part of the events on television. All whose appeals were before the House of Lords failed.

The starting point is a clear assumption that there is a real need for the law to place some limitation going beyond reasonable foreseeability and medical proof of causation on the range of admissible claims.[675] This limitation is to be found by reference to three elements: (1) the class of persons whose claims should be recognised; (2) the proximity of those persons to the accident; and (3) the means by which the trauma to the claimant is caused (though in practice heads (2) and (3) are closely related).

As to the first element, the House rejected any arbitrary qualifying test by reference to particular relationships such as husband and wife or parent and child for, as Lord Keith pointed out:

> "[T]he kinds of relationship which may involve close ties of love and affection are numerous, and it is the existence of such ties which leads to mental disturbance when the loved one suffers a catastrophe. They may be present in family relationships or those of close friendship,[676] and may be stronger in the case of engaged couples than in that of persons who have been married to each other for many years."[677]

The question is therefore whether there is a sufficiently close relationship of love and affection in fact between the claimant and the person injured or threatened, subject to the practical qualifications that a sufficiently close relationship will be presumed in the case of the relationship of parent and child or husband and wife and perhaps engaged couples but the claims of remoter relatives will be scrutinised with care.[678] The effect is that those falling outside the

---

[674] There were out-of-court settlements in many of these cases, which generally (but see *Hicks v CC South Yorkshire*, above) raised no issue of law.

[675] Lord Wilberforce's view to this effect in *McLoughlin v O'Brian* [1983] 1 A.C. 410, was endorsed in *Alcock* by Lords Keith, Ackner and Jauncey.

[676] In *Burdett v Dahill*, February 15, 2002, Sheffield CC, the court declined to strike out a claim by a "best friend"; but the standard the claimant must meet to defeat a CPR Pt 24 attack is not high.

[677] [1992] 1 A.C. at 397.

[678] Lord Keith says that, "it is sufficient that reasonable foreseeability should be the guide" but it seems unlikely that he could have meant that the defendant should actually as a reasonable man be able to foresee anything about the myriad relationships in the crowd at Hillsborough. Rather the question seems to be, "given the relationship between the plaintiff and the person injured was shock reasonably foreseeable?" Since the claimant has to prove that he has in fact suffered mental injury as a result of the event, we might just as well ask whether the claimant was unusually susceptible.

narrow category have to show a relationship which is more intense than that usually found. The only claimants in *Alcock* who satisfied this requirement failed on the next ground. The result is that a mere bystander will not be able to sue and the law in effect reflects what Lord Porter said long ago in *Bourhill v Young*:

> "[T]he driver of a car ... is entitled to assume that the ordinary frequenter of the streets has sufficient fortitude to endure such incidents as may from time to time be expected to occur in them, including the noise of a collision and the sight of injury to others, and is not to be considered negligent towards one who does not possess the customary phlegm."[679]

In *Alcock* three judges left open the possibility that a mere bystander might have a claim if the circumstances of the accident were unusually horrific, as where a petrol tanker collided with a school in session.[680] However, the Court of Appeal in *McFarlane v E.E. Caledonia Ltd*,[681] a case arising out of the Piper Alpha oil rig disaster, rejected this extension, on the ground that it ran counter to the general thrust of *Alcock* and would present practical problems since reactions to horrific events are subjective and variable. Even where there is a very close relationship, the thin skull rule does not apply, so a parent who suffers an hysterical and disproportionate reaction to a minor injury to his child may fail.[682]

The second element which must be satisfied is that there must be sufficient proximity of time and place to the event leading to the mental injury.[683] However, there is a considerable extension of this to cover the "immediate aftermath" of the event. Hence in *McLoughlin v O'Brian*[684] a road accident caused by the defendant's negligence killed the claimant's young daughter and caused injuries of varying severity to other of her children and to her husband. At the time the claimant was at home two miles away. An hour later the

5–67

---

[679] [1943] A.C. 92 at 117. See also Lord Bridge in *McLoughlin v O'Brian* [1983] 1 A.C. 410 at 442 (even though he was espousing a basis of liability wider than *Alcock*).

[680] Lord Ackner's example at [1992] 1 A.C. 403. See also Lord Keith at 397 and Lord Oliver at 416.

[681] [1994] 2 All E.R. 1.

[682] *Vanek v Great Atlantic etc. Co of Canada* (1999) 180 D.L.R. (4th) 748; *Mustapha v Culligan of Canada Ltd* [2008] SCC 27; [2008] 2 S.C.R. 114 (bizarre reaction to fly in bottle of water).

[683] The NZCA reserved its position on this requirement in *van Soest v Residual Health Management Unit* [2000] 1 N.Z.L.R. 179. The requirement was rejected by the majority of the High Court of Australia in *Annetts v Australian Stations Pty Ltd* [2002] HCA 35; 211 C.L.R. 37, a claim which would clearly fail under English law.

[684] [1983] 1 A.C. 410. See also *Kelly v Hennessy* [1996] 1 I.L.R.M. 321, SC.

accident was reported to her by a friend, who drove her to the hospital in Cambridge, where she was told of the death and saw the injured members of her family in circumstances which, it was found, were, "distressing in the extreme and were capable of producing an effect going well beyond that of grief and sorrow".[685] Her claim was unanimously upheld by the House of Lords and the decision was approved in *Alcock*.[686] However, in the latter case *McLoughlin* was distinguished because in *Alcock* the interval between the accident and the sight of the bodies by the claimants was longer (nine hours)[687] and (at least according to Lord Jauncey) because the purpose was formal identification, rather than aid and comfort.[688]

5–68   The third element, the means by which the injury is caused, requires that it must be by sight or hearing of the event or its immediate aftermath. Notification by third parties (including newspaper or broadcast reports) will not do.[689] In practical terms, a claimant who fails on the second element will not be able to satisfy this requirement, though it is possible that there could be a case in which the claimant was in the vicinity but failed to satisfy the third requirement. However, in *Alcock* the House of Lords did not altogether rule out the possibility of liability where the mental injury was induced by contemporaneous television transmission of the incident, two members using the example given by Nolan L.J. in the Court of Appeal of a live television broadcast of a ballooning event for children, watched by parents, in which the balloon bursts into flames. In *Alcock* itself the television transmission showed the developing chaos in the stadium and no doubt provided the framework in which the fear of the claimants for their loved ones developed, but it did not show the suffering of identifiable individuals[690]

---

[685] [1983] 1 A.C. 410 at 417.

[686] However, Lord Oliver described the aftermath extension as not wholly free from difficulty. See also *Benson v Lee* [1972] V.R. 879; *Fenn v City of Peterborough* (1976) 73 D.L.R. (3d) 177. In *R. v C.I.C.B., Ex p. Johnson, The Independent*, July 22, 1994, shock at finding the murdered body of the applicant's partner was held to qualify under the "old" Criminal Injuries Compensation Scheme.

[687] See also *Palmer v Tees HA* [2000] P.I.Q.R. P1; *Spence v Percy* [1992] 2 Qd. R. 299.

[688] Cf. *Galli-Atkinson v Seghal* [2003] EWCA Civ 697; [2003] Lloyd's Rep. Med 285 (visit to mortuary not merely for formal identification but for claimant to convince herself of the death; body in very badly disfigured condition). *Froggatt v Chesterfield and North Derbyshire NHS Trust*, December 13, 2002, QB, where the husband recovered damages for shock suffered on seeing his wife unclothed for the first time after an unnecessary mastectomy, is a surprising decision since the operation must have been performed some considerable time before this.

[689] The contrary decision in *Hevican v Ruane* [1991] 3 All E.R. 65 must be regarded as wrongly decided. *Ravenscroft v Rederiaktebolaget Transatlantic* [1991] 3 All E.R. 73 was reversed [1992] 2 All E.R. 470.

[690] The pictures shown conformed with the code of ethics followed by broadcasters in such situations. Had they not so conformed the claimants conceded that this would have broken the chain of causation between the breach of duty and the damage.

and therefore lacked the immediacy necessary to found a claim.[691] The illness must be caused by the, "sudden appreciation by sight or sound of a horrifying event which violently agitated the mind".[692]

We have already seen that mental injury only gives rise to a cause of action if there is a recognised psychiatric illness but it is a logical consequence of the second and third requirements that there can be no recovery even if there is an illness if it is the product of grief at the death of the loved one rather than a reaction to the event causing the death. This may require the court to carry out the very difficult exercise of distinguishing between "post traumatic stress disorder" and "pathological grief disorder".[693]

iv. Participants other than mere bystanders. Where the claim- **5–69** ant is shocked by fear for his own safety the "relationship" require- ment is ex hypothesi irrelevant since he is the direct victim and the requirements of proximity and direct perception are automatically satisfied. In *Alcock* Lord Oliver had placed in the same category (and therefore exempt from the control devices applicable to the case of mere witnesses) persons who suffered mental injury while engaged as rescuers at the incident and employees who, as a result of the employer's negligence, had become unwilling participants in the injury of a workmate[694]: like persons fearful for their own safety they did not need to establish any relationship of love and affection with the person injured. This must now be read in the light of another Hillsborough case, *Frost v CC South Yorkshire*.[695] This time the claimants were police officers who were not in physical danger from the crush in the pens but who tended the victims of the tragedy in various ways and who claimed to have suffered mental injury as a result. Reversing the Court of Appeal, the House of Lords held by

---

[691] "It would be inaccurate and hurtful to suggest that grief is made any the less real or deprivation more tolerable by a mere gradual realisation, but to extend liability to cover injury in such cases would be to extend the law in a direction for which there is no pressing policy and in which there is no logical stopping point": [1992] 1 A.C. at 416 per Lord Oliver. *Palmer v Tees HA*, above, fn.687.

[692] [1992] 1 A.C. at 401. per Lord Ackner. *Ward v Leeds Teaching Hospital NHS Trust* [2004] EWHC 2106 (QB). Cf. *Walters v North Glamorgan NHS Trust* [2002] EWCA Civ 1792; [2003] Lloyd's Rep. Med. 49 and see *Annetts v Australian Stations Pty Ltd* [2002] HCA 35; 211 C.L.R. 37, where the requirement of "sudden shock" was rejected.

[693] See *Vernon v Bosley (No.1)* [1994] 1 All E.R. 577. It seems that if the conclusion is that the illness is a product of both PTSD and PGD there is no discount for the latter element (though only Evans L.J. in the majority deals clearly with the point); and see *Galli-Atkinson v Seghal* [2003] EWCA Civ 697; [2003] Lloyd's Rep. Med 285. However, there may now be a drift towards "apportionment" in this area: see *Rahman v Arearose Ltd* [2001] Q.B. 351 and *Hatton v Sutherland* [2002] EWCA Civ 76. See also para.21–1, below.

[694] *Dooley v Cammell Laird & Co Ltd* [1951] 1 Lloyd's Rep. 271.

[695] [1999] 2 A.C. 455.

a majority that there was no special category of rescuers for this purpose. While it is well established that a rescuer may be owed a duty of care by the person responsible for the danger,[696] that is simply because the fact that he is engaged in a rescue makes his presence foreseeable and negatives the arguments that he has assumed the risk of injury or that his intervention has broken the chain of causation; it is not a reason for equating him with a primary victim (though of course he may fall into that category[697]) and for dispensing with the requirement that he should have a relationship of love and affection with those threatened. The claims of the relatives in the same disaster had failed in *Alcock* and the court was of the view that people in general:

"[W]ould think it wrong that policemen, even as part of a general class of persons who rendered assistance, should have the right to compensation for psychiatric injury out of public funds while the bereaved relatives are sent away with nothing".[698]

Nor could the claims succeed on the alternative basis (which had also been espoused by the Court of Appeal) that the officers were owed a duty of care by their employer[699] who was responsible for the disaster. Certainly the employer's duty of care may extend to cases of psychiatric injury to a worker,[700] but that does not dispense with the *Alcock* "control devices" where the claim is based on the worker's reaction to witnessing the injury or endangerment of a third party on a particular occasion.[701] Had the employment basis of the claims in *Frost* been accepted, the result would have been that the claims of the police officers would have succeeded, whereas those of ambulance crew performing the same function would have failed because their employers would not have been responsible for the disaster. If the employer had reason to believe that a particular worker in an emergency service was susceptible to trauma from witnessing danger to others and took no steps to reduce this risk, that

---

[696] See para.25–14, below.
[697] As did Mr Chadwick, para.5–63, above; cf. *Gregg v Ashbrae Ltd* [2006] NICA 17; [2006] N.I. 300. Claims by officers who worked within the pens seem to have been settled on the basis that they were at personal risk of physical injury: [1999] 2 A.C. at 466.
[698] [1999] 2 A.C. 466 at 510 per Lord Hoffmann.
[699] Strictly the police are not employees, but they are owed the same duty as those who are.
[700] See para.5–71, below (long-term stress at work).
[701] Thus in *Keen v Tayside Contracts* [2003] Scot CS 55; 2003 S.L.T. 500 the claim failed where the pursuer, a road worker, was required to remain at the scene while four burned bodies were removed from a crash. Cf. *Harrhy v Thames Trains Ltd* [2003] EWHC 2286 (QB).

might be a different case and the fact that the employer was responsible for the disaster in question would be irrelevant.[702]

There may still be liability in the other situation envisaged by
Lord Oliver in *Alcock*. In *Dooley v Cammell Laird & Co Ltd*[703] the
claimant, a crane operator, suffered shock when, by the negligence
of his employers, the rope snapped and precipitated the load into the
hold where his colleagues were working.[704] Lord Oliver regarded
this as a case where the negligent act of the defendant had put the
claimant in the position of thinking that he had been the involuntary
instrument of death or injury to another,[705] and in *Frost* Lord
Hoffmann said that there might be reason for regarding such cases
as outside the *Alcock* control mechanisms for secondary
victims.[706]

There can be no doubt in view of *Frost* that rescuers are not to be
treated as a special category and must satisfy the *Alcock* control
mechanisms. However, there is a certain ambiguity running through
the case law in this area. In *Frost* Lord Steyn and Lord Griffiths
(though he dissented on the rescue issue) clearly assume that the
category of primary victim is defined by *Page v Smith*, that is to say
the claimant must be in danger or reasonably believe himself to be
so.[707] Yet this is narrower than the formulation by Lord Oliver in

---

[702] That, however, is more likely if the exposure is frequent (*Hartman v South Essex Mental Health etc. NHS Trust* [2005] EWCA Civ 6; [2005] I.R.L.R. 293) or prolonged (cf. *Harrhy v Thames Trains Ltd* [2003] EWHC 2120 (QB)). There is some tension between *Frost* and the general duty of the employer to safeguard the health and safety of workers. The latter duty has in practice been explored in cases of long-term stress but as a matter of principle it is hard to see why it should not apply to a sudden stressful situation foreseeably causing psychiatric trauma. The focus of the two claims would of course be different. In *Frost* the argument was "You were responsible for the injury to the direct victim and I am a rescuer; so you owe me a duty, too". Here the argument would be "You required me to go participate in this stressful situation (who was responsible for the situation does not matter) and you should have foreseen that I could not cope with it." In *Butchart v Home Office* [2006] EWCA Civ 239; [2006] 1 W.L.R. 1155 the court declined to strike out a claim by a prisoner who was alleged to be psychologically vulnerable and who was placed in a cell with a known suicide risk. However, the claims were struck out in *French v CC Sussex* [2006] EWCA Civ 312. Officers became subject to criminal charges (dismissed) and disciplinary proceedings (largely not pursued) after a shooting incident which, they alleged, had been brought about by management failures. "The appellants' case involves postulating a duty of care on the part of employers towards their employees not to cause or permit an untoward event to occur that could foreseeably lead to proceedings in which the employees' conduct would be in issue. It would not be appropriate for a lower court to make such an extension to the law of negligence and we see no prospect that the House of Lords would be minded to do so": at [34].

[703] [1951] 1 Lloyd's Rep. 271.

[704] In fact none of them was injured.

[705] [1992] 1 A.C. at 408. Contrast *Gregg v Ashbrae Ltd* [2006] NICA 17; [2006] N.I. 300 (not guilt but reaction to ill-informed beliefs of others). See also *W v Essex CC* [2000] 2 W.L.R. 601 at 607.

[706] [1999] 2 A.C. at 508; *Anderson v Christian Salvesen Plc* [2006] CSOH 101; 2006 SLT 815. Cf. *Robertson v Forth Road Bridge* 1996 S.L.T. ; *Hunter v British Coal* [1999] Q.B. 140; *Monk v P.C. Harrington Ltd* [2008] EWHC 1879 (QB); [2009] P.I.Q.R. P3.

[707] [1999] 2 A.C. at 496 and 464

Alcock, which distinguished between witnesses and those actively involved.[708] *Page v Smith* was essentially concerned with extending liability via the thin skull rule but the effect of this approach is also to restrict the category of primary victims. The view is sometimes taken[709] that in all psychiatric trauma cases claimants must be placed in one or other category, but the distinction was created around the case where there is sudden danger to the claimant or a third party and there are situations of liability (or possible liability) which bear no resemblance to that. These are considered after we have looked at the situation where D puts himself in danger and thereby causes shock to C.

5–70   **v. Claimant shocked by defendant's exposure of himself to danger.** In *Greatorex v Greatorex*[710] the defendant was seriously injured in a road accident due to his own fault. The claimant, a fire officer and the defendant's father, attended at the scene and contended that he had suffered post-traumatic stress disorder from seeing the defendant's injuries. The defendant was uninsured, so the claim was in reality one against the Motor Insurers' Bureau.[711] The claimant, given the rather extraordinary circumstances, fulfilled the *Alcock* requirements for a secondary victim, but Cazalet J. dismissed the claim on the ground that the defendant, as the primary victim, did not owe a duty of care to others not to inflict shock upon them by the self-infliction of his injuries. Given that the "relationship" requirement in *Alcock* would confine such claims to cases between close family members, to admit a duty of care would open up the possibility of undesirable litigation arising from domestic accidents or deliberate self-harm[712]; furthermore, a duty to take care of oneself so as not to shock others would impinge upon the defendant's right of self-determination.[713] Most people would probably be surprised if, on such facts, the general body of motorists, via the MIB, were made to bear the full, tort law cost of the injury inflicted by the defendant on his father. Nevertheless, the result may not be entirely just where another defendant is involved. If the accident is caused by the combined fault of the defendant and another person, the

---

[708] See para.5–62, above.

[709] *Organ Retention Group Litigation, Re*, [2004] EWHC 644 (QB); [2005] Q.B. 506. The claimants, parents of deceased children from whom organs had been taken without authority for research, could only be primary victims because the children, being already dead, could have been owed no duty of care. There can be no question of applying the thin skull rule in such a case.

[710] [2000] 1 W.L.R. 1970.

[711] See para.1–30, above. In its turn the Bureau was seeking an indemnity against the owner of the vehicle for allowing the defendant to drive whilst uninsured: para.7–9, below.

[712] Note there is no bar on a claim where one family member injures another, nor where member A endangers member B in the presence of member C.

[713] Note that it seems to be accepted that if D negligently gets himself into danger and C is physically injured trying to rescue him, D may be liable to C: para.25–17, below.

defendant's own personal injury claim against the other would be reduced for contributory negligence,[714] whereas the other would be liable in full to the shock claimant[715] and, because the defendant would not be liable to the claimant, the other would be unable to recover any contribution[716] from him.[717]

vi. Other situations. At one time the vast majority of reported **5–71** cases on psychiatric injury arose from accidents caused by the defendant's negligence and injuring or threatening the claimant or, more usually, a third party but other situations are possible.[718] Liability has, for example, been imposed for mental trauma caused by long drawn out exposure to stress,[719] usually at work, and this is a growing area of litigation. Plainly here there is no requirement that the injury must be a response to a sudden event.[720] In these cases there are no special control mechanisms, the issue is simply whether the employer has fulfilled the general duty (which is a matter of contract as well as tort) which he owes not to injure the health of his workers.[721] The duty to workers is owed to them as individuals and must take account of their individual weaknesses where these ought to be known to the employer[722] so one cannot apply the test of "persons of normal fortitude" which is used in respect of secondary victims of accidents, with whom the defendant will have had no prior connection; but the duty is still one of reasonable care and an employer is usually entitled to assume that the employee can withstand the normal pressures of the job unless he knows of some

---

[714] See para.6–43, below.

[715] Where A and B cause indivisible harm to C, each is liable in full to him. Cf. the approach of s.30(3) of the Civil Liability Act 2002 (NSW): "Any damages to be awarded to the plaintiff for pure mental harm are to be reduced in the same proportion as any reduction in the damages that may be recovered from the defendant by or through the victim on the basis of the contributory negligence of the victim."

[716] Under the Civil Liability (Contribution) Act 1978, para.21–4, below. Cazalet J. referred to the German decision *I.S. Hu. w. Ha.*, 11 May 1971, Bundesgerichtshof (Sixth Civil Division), in which the court held that even though the defendant could not be liable to the shock claimant, the latter's damages against the other could be reduced in proportion to the defendant's fault.

[717] Of course, in a motor case all liabilities would end up with motor insurers collectively whichever line one adopts.

[718] *Hall v Gwent Healthcare NHS Trust* [2005] EWCA Civ 919 is a truly extraordinary claim, which defies classification. D, by way of a malicious joke, tells lies to X. By a roundabout route, this causes X to kill his daughter Y and his wife C suffers psychiatric trauma by coming upon the aftermath. Had C had any prospect of proving that D had the requisite knowledge of X's state of mind that might have raised a triable issue but on the facts she did not.

[719] *Hatton v Sutherland* [2002] EWCA Civ 76; [2002] I.C.R. 613; *Walker v Northumberland CC* [1995] I.C.R. 702; *Cross v Highlands and Islands Enterprise* [2001] I.R.L.R. 336.

[720] Cf. *Chief Adjudication Officer v Faulds* [2001] 1 W.L.R. 1035 (personal injury by accident under industrial injuries scheme).

[721] *Hatton v Sutherland* above, fn.719 at [22].

[722] See para.5–84, below.

particular problem or vulnerability.[723] It has also been said that the employer will not incur liability if, having done what is reasonable[724] to reduce the risk, he declines to dismiss an employee who is willing to continue.[725] However, there may no longer be any absolute rule to this effect.[726] Similar issues may arise in other relationships, for example that of a school and pupil.[727] In *Leach v CC Gloucestershire*[728] the claimant had agreed to act as the "responsible adult" required under the Police and Criminal Evidence Act 1984 where the police interview a person who may be mentally disordered, and she claimed that she suffered psychiatric injury and a stroke as a result of her involvement and that the police ought to have been aware that she was susceptible to this. The majority of the Court of Appeal struck out the claim on the basis that if the police owed a duty to safeguard the claimant's mental well-being that might impede their investigation of the offence; however, that aspect of her claim which was based on failure to offer counselling was allowed to go forward because that was offered to police officers in the case and would not have interfered with the investigative process.[729] Another case which does not fit easily into the tidy categories created in the accident cases is *W v Essex County Council*[730] in which the House of Lords refused to strike out a claim based on parents' reaction to the discovery that they had taken into their home a foster child who had a history of abusing other children and had taken the opportunity to abuse their children. It was not a case of witnessing a sudden event threatening their children, nor were the parents in any danger; but the case had some affinity with those where claimants had felt guilt at thinking themselves responsible for an accident and on the pleaded facts the defendants had

---

[723] *Hatton v Sutherland* at [29]. And what must be foreseeable is psychiatric injury, not just anger or resentment: *Fraser v State Hospitals Board for Scotland* 2001 S.L.T. 1051. Despite some criticism of Hale L.J.'s judgment in *Hatton* by Lord Walker in *Barber v Somerset CC* [2004] UKHL 13; [2004] 1 W.L.R. 1089 (an appeal from one of the four decisions in *Hatton*) it remains the central authority in this area: *Hartman v South Essex Mental Health etc. NHS Trust* [2005] EWCA Civ 6; [2005] I.R.L.R. 293.

[724] In the light of the terms of the contract, which is an essential part of the picture, though the relationship of the contract and the tort has not been explored much in the cases: *Barber* at [35] per Lord Rodger; *Koehler v Cerebos (Aust) Ltd* [2005] HCA 15; 222 C.L.R. 44; *New South Wales v Fahy* [2007] HCA 20.

[725] *Hatton v Sutherland* at [43].

[726] See *Coxall v Goodyear Great Britain Ltd* [2002] EWCA Civ 1010; [2003] 1 W.L.R. 536 and para.8–16, below.

[727] See *Bradford-Smart v West Sussex CC* [2002] EWCA Civ 7 (bullying).

[728] [1999] 1 W.L.R. 1421.

[729] In *Swinney v CC Northumbria* [1997] Q.B. 464 the claimants claimed that they were suffering from psychiatric illnesses because they had been threatened with violence and arson after some confidential information furnished by the first claimant to the police had been stolen from a police vehicle broken into by criminals. The claim was allowed to proceed and as Brooke L.J. pointed out in *Leach* at 1435 the court did not pay any particular attention to the fact that the claims were for damages for psychiatric illness.

[730] [2001] 2 A.C. 592.

knowingly sent a child with a history of abuse even though the parents had made it clear that they would not take a child of that type.

Claims may arise where psychiatric trauma is caused by damage **5–72** to property. In *Attia v British Gas Plc*[731] the Court of Appeal declined to strike out a claim for psychiatric illness arising from the defendant's negligent destruction of the claimant's house by fire (whether because of any direct rule of law forbidding such a claim or because shock resulting from damage to property was so unlikely as to be beyond the contemplation of the reasonable man). In the majority of property damage cases the issue of psychiatric harm may not arise in quite the same form, for where the property is in the ownership or possession of the claimant there will have been a breach of duty in respect of the property damage itself and the nature of any further consequential loss might be regarded as a matter of remoteness of damage. In *Attia* at least two of the judges appear to have treated the case in terms of remoteness rather than duty.[732] However, the current acceptance of the proposition that a duty of care may be confined to a particular type of damage[733] may block this approach. In *Attia* the claimant witnessed the fire. What would have happened if she had been abroad, had been told of it on the telephone and suffered the same trauma? It would be strange if she could recover when a person told of the death of his child cannot recover under the *Alcock* principles and even with regard to its facts it must be borne in mind that the case was decided before *Alcock* and *Frost*. Yet a person may recover damages for mental distress falling well short of psychiatric illness in certain types of claim for breach of a contract, e.g. to provide a holiday[734] or damages for inconvenience consequent on a negligent survey,[735] where peace of mind is an important element in the obligation undertaken, so it would be hard to support a principle which automatically rejected the claim of a householder whose home and possessions were destroyed before his eyes.[736] Or even perhaps one who suffered shock by hearing of

---

[731] [1988] Q.B. 304.

[732] [1988] Q.B. 304, Dillon L.J. at 312 and Bingham L.J. at 319. Perhaps also Woolf L.J. at 315–316. A complicating factor is that the property damage claim had already been settled.

[733] See para.6–27, above.

[734] *Jarvis v Swans Tours Ltd* [1973] 1 QB 233.

[735] *Farley v Skinner* [2001] UKHL 49; [2002] 2 AC 732

[736] It is difficult to know how to classify the strange case of *Owens v Liverpool Corp* [1939] 1 K.B. 394, where mourners recovered damages when they witnessed a collision involving the hearse, the overturning of the coffin and the threat that the contents might fall out. It seems unrealistic to treat it as a case of a threat to property (there is no property in a corpse). It does not fall within *Alcock* since no "third person" was endangered, yet one can imagine that such an event would be traumatic for the widow. Lord Oliver in *Alcock* doubted whether the case could any longer be relied on. Cf. *Mason v Westside Cemeteries Ltd* (1996) 135 DLR (4th) 361 (where, however, there was a bailment of urns containing ashes).

it. In *Yearworth v North Bristol NHS Trust*[737] some of the claimants claimed to have suffered psychiatric trauma from hearing of the destruction of sperm samples which they had deposited for storage before treatment which affected their fertility. Others suffered a lesser degree of mental distress. The Court of Appeal found it unnecessary to decide the fate of their claims in tort because there was a bailment[738] which, although non-contractual, involved a specific promise to the claimants and should therefore be treated as akin to a claim in contract for this purpose. Accordingly, all the claimants would be able to recover if they showed that their loss was foreseeable.

5–73   Damages have been recovered for psychiatric illness where a spouse's children were kidnapped as a result of the negligence of a solicitor engaged in the matrimonial proceedings,[739] where organs were removed from deceased children without the parents' consent[740] and where the claimant was falsely informed of the death of her child soon after birth.[741] Such cases bear some resemblance to those concerning stress during employment in that there is some prior relationship between the parties, though of a more transitory nature.[742] It is unlikely that a court will find that mental trauma is the foreseeable[743] result of a solicitor mishandling a commercial transaction but the Court of Appeal has declined to strike out a claim where the alleged negligence of the defendants brought about loss of liberty.[744] It has been held overseas that there may be liability where the claimant was falsely informed that her husband had been detained in a mental asylum,[745] though a contrary result was reached in the case of a false death notice in a newspaper.[746] Shock may be

---

[737] [2009] EWCA Civ 37; [2009] 3 W.L.R. 118.

[738] See para.1–12, above.

[739] *Al-Kandari v J.R. Brown & Co* [1988] Q.B. 665 (not the sole type of damage).

[740] *Organ Retention Group Litigation, Re,* [2004] EWHC 644 (QB); [2005] Q.B. 506.

[741] *Allin v City & Hackney HA* (1996) 7 Med. L.R. 91 (but the duty issue was conceded). Cf. *Halech v South Australia* [2006] SASC 29 (mis-identification of bodies; but even if there was a duty and breach the chain of causation was broken).

[742] i.e. one can say there is an "assumption of responsibility". See also *Swinney v CC Northumbria,* above, fn.729.

[743] For a discussion of foreseeability and its relationship with medical evidence, see *McLoughlin v Grovers* [2001] EWCA Civ 1743; [2002] Q.B. 1312 at [40].

[744] *McLoughlin v Grovers,* above, fn.743. Can it be argued that the loss of liberty is analogous to the foreseeable personal injury in *Page v Smith* so as to attract the thin skull rule? See Hale L.J. at [57].

[745] *Barnes v Commonwealth* (1937) 37 S.R.N.S.W. 511; *Johnson v State* 334 N.E. 2d 590 (N.Y. 1975). Compare *Molien v Kaiser Foundation Hospital* 616 P. 2d 813 (Cal. 1980) (false diagnosis of disease which led to collapse of marriage and mental trauma).

[746] *Guay v Sun Publishing Co* [1953] 4 D.L.R. 577. The court was divided and the reasoning is somewhat diverse. However, requiring an official sender of a private communication to take steps to get it right is one thing; to impose liability on the press would seem to go a step too far.

caused by the communication of true facts[747] and it has been said that there is no duty to break bad news gently,[748] but this may possibly go too far if the circumstances are such that the impact of the news is needlessly exacerbated.[749]

vii. The future. It is clear that psychiatric injury presents the law 5–74 with the most profound problems and it has only kept it under control by drawing a series of arbitrary lines. The problems are in fact so profound that voices have been heard to suggest that it was an error to have recognised this type of loss at all.[750] In 1998 the Law Commission produced a series of proposals for law reform.[751] The full report will repay careful study but the following is an outline of the proposals.

1. No general codification of the law on liability for psychiatric illness is proposed and save in so far as it was inconsistent with legislation arising from the proposals, the common law would continue to be developed by the courts if they thought it necessary.
2. A major change would be made in the *Alcock* approach to the situation where D causes psychiatric injury to C by injuring or imperilling X. It would no longer be necessary to show that C was close to the accident in time or space, nor that he perceived it or its aftermath by his own unaided senses. The result would be that people in the position of the *Alcock* claimants would be able to recover, as would the spouse who succumbs to pathological grief after the death of his partner.
3. However, it would remain necessary that there should be a close tie of love and affection between the claimant and the person injured or imperilled. The law would, nevertheless, be modified so that a statutory list would provide automatic qualification for this purpose (spouse, parent, child, sibling, cohabitant for at least two years), leaving persons outside the list to establish the requisite tie by evidence (as of course is now the

---

[747] We are concerned now with the position of the news bearer. If A negligently kills B and C suffers shock when this news is brought to him by D, A escapes liability because C did not directly perceive the event or its immediate aftermath.

[748] *Mount Isa Mines Ltd v Pusey* (1970) 125 C.L.R. 383 at 407 per Windeyer J.

[749] Cf. *Furniss v Fitchett* [1958] N.Z.L.R. 396. See Mullany and Handford, *Tortious Liability for Psychiatric Damage*, 2nd edn, pp.183. In *A v Tameside and Glossop HA* (1996) 35 B.M.L.R. 77 the defendants conceded that they owed patients a duty of care in respect of the manner in which they informed them that they had been treated by one of the defendants' servants who was HIV positive, though on the facts the Court of Appeal held that there had been no negligence; but in *Tame v New South Wales, Annetts v Australian Stations Pty Ltd* [2002] HCA 35; 211 C.L.R. 37 Gummow and Kirby JJ. thought that only a malign intention would do.

[750] See Stapleton, "In Restraint of Tort" in Birks (ed.) *Frontiers of Liability* (1994).

[751] Law Com. No.249. See also Scot Law Com. No.196 (2004).

position where the claimant is not a "close relative"). Mere
bystanders would continue not to qualify. The position of
rescuers and "involuntary participants" would be left to the
common law.
4. Potentially of equal importance with head 2 above is the
proposal whereby the requirement that the psychiatric illness
be traceable to "sudden shock" would be removed. The long-
term carer who succumbs to the strain of looking after the
injured victim of the defendant's negligence would be able to
recover.
5. The liability for psychiatric harm suffered by reason of injury
or imperilment of another is based on an independent duty to
the person who suffers the psychiatric harm[752] but it is conceivable that it would be undesirable to impose liability upon
the defendant in at least some cases where there would be no
liability to the person injured or imperilled. Hence it is proposed that there should be no duty of care to the person
suffering the psychiatric harm if the court is satisfied that its
imposition would not be just and reasonable, an example given
being that where the person injured or imperilled was *volens*.
However, the application of this would be for the court on a
case-by-case basis.
6. Perhaps of less practical, but nonetheless considerable theoretical, importance is the situation where it is the defendant's
injuring or imperilling of himself which causes the psychiatric
harm to the claimant. There is no liability in such a case under
the present law[753] but the Commission proposes that a duty of
care should be owed by the defendant, again with power in the
courts to decide that no duty should be owed if it was not fair,
just and reasonable (for example where the defendant chose to
engage in a dangerous activity or decided to refuse medical
treatment).

Clearly only Parliament can undertake radical reform of the law
in this area. However, the Commission's proposals would involve a
not inconsiderable extension of liability (though nothing like as
much as some would wish[754]) and the majority view in *Frost v CC
South Yorkshire* is distinctly hostile to that. There cannot be a high
likelihood of the implementation of the proposals in the present
climate. If, however, they were implemented, they would bring the
law closer to that stated by the High Court of Australia, where the

---

[752] There will be no tort against the person who is imperilled but not injured. Hence the Law
Commission's warning about the potentially misleading nature of the expressions "primary" and "secondary" victim.
[753] See para.5–70, above.
[754] See, e.g. Mullany and Handford, *Tortious Liability for Psychiatric Damage*, 2nd edn.

emphasis was very much upon the foreseeability of psychiatric injury without rigid categories of primary and secondary victim or a requirement of sudden shock.[755] The Australian position is now largely governed by more or less uniform state legislation but this is not dissimilar to the position stated at Australian common law. Thus s.32 of the Civil Liability Act 2002 (NSW) provides that a:

> "[P]erson ('the defendant') does not owe a duty of care to another person ('the plaintiff') to take care not to cause the plaintiff mental harm unless the defendant ought to have foreseen that a person of normal fortitude might, in the circumstances of the case, suffer a recognised psychiatric illness if reasonable care were not taken."

Matters like the relationship between the plaintiff and the person imperilled and whether there was a sudden shock are then part of the "circumstances of the case". However, a person who is not a close relative of the person injured or imperilled must have, "witnessed, at the scene, [that person] being killed, injured or imperilled"[756] and that does not include the immediate aftermath, thereby excluding liability to rescuers who come on the scene after the event has happened.[757]

3. BREACH OF DUTY

A. Criterion of "The Reasonable Man"
The defendant must not only owe the claimant a duty of care, he must be in breach of it. The test for deciding whether there has been a breach of duty is laid down in the oft-cited dictum of Alderson B. in *Blyth v Birmingham Waterworks Co.*[758] Negligence is the omission to do something which a reasonable man, guided upon those considerations which ordinarily regulate the conduct of human affairs, would do, or doing something which a prudent and reasonable man would not do.

5–75

---

[755] *Tame v New South Wales, Annetts v Australian Stations* [2002] HCA 35; 211 C.L.R. 37. For New Zealand (where the matter is relevant since recovery for mental injury under the Accidents Compensation Scheme is limited) see *van Soest v Residual Health Management Unit* [2001] 1 N.Z.L.R. 179.

[756] Section 30 of the NSW Act.

[757] *Sheehan v State Rail Authority* [2009] NSWCA 261. But the legislation is less uniform on mental injury than on other matters. Thus the Tasmanian Act includes the aftermath and the Queensland Act does not deal with mental injury at all.

[758] (1856) 11 Ex. 781 at 784.

The general characteristics of the reasonable man have already been described.[759] Since he is an abstraction, the standard of reference he provides can be applied to particular cases only by the intuition of the court. The standard is objective and impersonal in the sense that it eliminates the personal equation and is generally independent of the idiosyncrasies of the particular person whose conduct is in question, but it cannot eliminate the personality of the judge.

"It is . . . left to the judge to decide what, in the circumstances of the particular case, the reasonable man would have in contemplation, and what, accordingly, the party sought to be made liable ought to have foreseen."[760]

In the following pages we describe some of the factors taken into account by the judges in reaching their conclusions.

B. "Reasonable" Varies With The Circumstances

5–76   There can be no doubt that the general standard is objective and the question is not "did the defendant do his best?" but "did he come up to the standard of the reasonable man?" Nevertheless, the law cannot be understood unless we bear in mind that it judges conduct by the particular circumstances in which the defendant finds himself and in some circumstances actually modifies the objective standard. An example of the latter category is *Goldman v Hargrave*[761] where, in dealing with the liability of the defendant for failing to extinguish a fire started on his land by natural causes, the Privy Council held that the standard was what it was reasonable to expect of him in his individual circumstances.

"Less must be expected of the infirm than of the able-bodied . . . [and the defendant] should not be liable unless it is clearly proved that he could, and reasonably in his individual circumstances should, have done more."[762]

This, however, was a case in which the defendant was making no unusual use of his land and had a risk thrust upon him: the test

---

[759] See para.3–6, above, where the point is made that despite the traditional language, he is intended to be gender neutral.

[760] *Glasgow Corp v Muir* [1943] A.C. 448 at 457 per Lord Macmillan.

[761] [1967] 1 A.C. 645 at 663, para.14–21, below.

[762] The case does not mean that the court has to engage in a detailed assessment of financial resources: *Leakey v National Trust* [1980] Q.B. 485.

would be unsuitable for a case in which the danger arose from the defendant's activity,[763] even where the activity is a public service operating under straitened circumstances.[764] Generally speaking, if the defendant embarks on an activity he must ensure that he has the skill and resources to carry it on without unnecessary risk to others. Unlike a number of European systems, the law does not recognise the concepts of "gross" or "slight" negligence: the defendant has come up to a single required standard or he has not.[765] No reasonable person handles a stick of dynamite and a walking stick in the same way, but that is not an admission that there are different degrees of negligence in the law of torts but simply a reflection of the fact that precautions must be in proportion to the risk. However, the character of the defendant's fault may be relevant if it is sought to reduce the claimant's damages on account of contributory negligence on his part,[766] for then it may be necessary to compare the conduct of the two parties.

It might be expected that the particular circumstances of the relationship between the claimant and the defendant might lead the courts to modify the content of the defendant's duty as, for example, where the claimant submitted himself to treatment by someone whom he knew to be of limited competence. However, in *Nettleship v Weston*[767] the Court of Appeal came to the rather remarkable conclusion that a learner driver was required, even vis-à-vis his instructor, to come up to the standard of an ordinary, competent driver. The Court of Appeal was heavily influenced by the presence of compulsory insurance,[768] as was the High Court of Australia in coming to the same conclusion[769] (though it had earlier held the contrary).[770] A similar problem is raised by a passenger who knowingly takes a lift with a drunken driver: English courts have tended

---

[763] See, e.g. the cases on professional negligence, para.5–79, below.

[764] *P.Q. v Australian Red Cross Society* [1992] V.R. 19 (where charity required to test blood for HIV); cf. *Knight v Home Office* [1990] 3 All E.R. 237, para.5–86, below.

[765] See *Caswell v Powell Duffryn Associated Collieries Ltd* [1940] A.C. 152 at 175 per Lord Wright: "Generally speaking in civil cases 'gross' negligence has no more effect than negligence without an opprobrious epithet". *Palmer v Tees HA* [2000] P.I.Q.R. P1.

[766] See para.6–53, below.

[767] [1971] 2 Q.B. 691. Cf. *Phillips v William Whiteley Ltd* [1938] 1 All E.R. 566 (jeweller piercing ears is not bound to take the same precautions as a surgeon, but such as may reasonably be expected of a jeweller; but in the AIDS era, high standards should be required even of a jeweller).

[768] See Lord Denning M.R. at 700. Salmon L.J., however, would have come to the opposite conclusion but for a prior conversation about insurance between the parties.

[769] *Imbree v McNeilly* [2008] HCA 40.

[770] *Cook v Cook* (1986) 68 A.L.R. 353. A volunteer referee from the crowd at an amateur rugby match cannot be expected to have the skill of one who professes to be a referee nor even necessarily to be fully conversant with the laws of the game: *Vowles v Evans* [2003] EWCA Civ 318; [2003] 1 W.L.R. 1607 at [28]. Neither *Nettleship* nor *Imbree* necessarily applies outside the motor context.

to adopt the objective standard and reduce the damages for contributory negligence.[771] On the other hand, it has been said that if a person chooses to submit himself to treatment by an alternative medical practitioner that is something which must be taken into account in determining the standard of care, though the impact of this is somewhat diminished by the fact that the alternative practitioner should take steps to keep himself informed of knowledge in conventional medicine which relates to the safety of the treatments he prescribes.[772]

It does not follow from the objective standard that every error of judgement or mistake amounts to negligence. There must be a falling below the standard of care called for by the circumstances and these may allow for an excusable "margin of error", particularly where the defendant has to deal with an emergency[773] or take quick decisions[774] or deal with a problem which has not arisen before[775] or exercise judgment on a matter on which opinions may differ.[776] For example, "serious and dangerous foul play" on the football field amounts to negligence but it does not follow that the same is true of every infringement of the technical rules of the game, nor can the claimant, who has entered voluntarily into the game, expect other players to behave as if they were taking a walk in the countryside.[777] Similarly, what will be demanded by way of care in a domestic situation is not to be equated with the standards of business.[778] In the case of valuation of a building a group of competent valuers are likely to come up with a range of figures[779] and no valuation within that range will amount to professional negligence. The phrase "error of judgement" is ambiguous, it may signify a failure to come up to the professional standard required[780] or excusably taking the wrong course in complex circumstances.[781]

---

[771] See para.25–13, below.

[772] *Shakoor v Situ* [2001] 1 W.L.R. 410.

[773] *Greene v Sookdeo* [2009] UKPC 31.

[774] *Smoldon v Whitworth* [1997] P.I.Q.R. P133.

[775] *A v Tameside and Glossop HA* (1996) 35 B.M.L.R. 77 (how to inform patients that they had been treated by HIV positive members of staff).

[776] On matters of opinion and judgment see *Luxmore-May v Messenger May Baverstock* [1990] 1 W.L.R. 1009 (valuation and attribution of works of art).

[777] *Condon v Basi* [1985] 1 W.L.R. 866. In accepting (1) that the claimant's voluntary participation is a factor in determining the content of the duty of care and (2) that a higher degree of care may be required in the First Division than in a local league (see *Watson v Gray, The Times*, November 26, 1998) this case appears to depart from *Nettleship v Weston*, though that decision is not mentioned. For the relationship between the standard of care and the defence of volenti non fit injuria, see para.25–13, below.

[778] *Surtees v Kingston on Thames BC* [1991] 2 F.L.R. 559.

[779] See, e.g. *Banque Bruxelles Lambert SA v Eagle Star Insurance Co Ltd* [1997] A.C. 191, where the range was between £630,000 and £770,000. Where there is an overvaluation, the damages are based on the difference between the valuation given and the "true" value. The latter will be taken to be the mean of the competent valuations: as above.

[780] *Whitehouse v Jordan* [1981] 1 W.L.R. 246.

[781] As in *Caldwell v Maguire* [2001] EWCA Civ 1054; [2002] P.I.Q.R. P6 (jockey).

Since the standard is that of the hypothetical reasonable man, in **5–77**
applying this standard it is necessary to ask what, in the circumstances, the reasonable man would have foreseen.[782] This question is
not always susceptible of only one possible answer. "What to one
judge may seem far-fetched may seem to another both natural and
probable"[783] but the legal concept of foreseeability, "incorporates
the idea that the event is not only imaginable, but that there is some
reasonable prospect or expectation that it will arise."[784] The application of this standard probably became more predictable when trial
by jury was replaced by trial by judge alone, though it has to be said
that in recent years tort cases have become triable by a much wider
range of judges than was the case.

In some cases the question of the foreseeability of an event will
depend upon whether or not a particular item of knowledge is to be
imputed to the reasonable man and in these cases it is of particular
importance to remember that what is in question is foreseeability,
not probability. The probability of a consequence does not depend
upon the knowledge or experience of anybody, but its reasonable
foreseeability can only be discovered if it is first decided what
knowledge and experience is to be attributed to the reasonable man
in the circumstances.[785] In *Roe v Minister of Health*[786] R was, in
1947, a patient in a hospital and Dr G, an anaesthetist, administered
a spinal anaesthetic to him in preparation for a minor operation. The
anaesthetic was contained in a glass ampoule which had been kept
before use in a solution of phenol and unfortunately some of the
phenol had made its way through an "invisible crack" into the
ampoule. It thus contaminated the anaesthetic, with the result that R
became permanently paralysed from the waist down. Dr G was
aware of consequences of injecting phenol, and he therefore subjected the ampoule to a visual examination before administering the
anaesthetic, but he was not aware of the possibility of "invisible
cracks". Had he been aware of this possibility, the danger to R could
have been eliminated by adding a powerful colouring agent to the
phenol so that contamination of the anaesthetic could have been
observed. It was held that he was not negligent in not causing the

---

[782] As we have already seen, this question is also of importance in determining whether a duty
is owed to the claimant (para.5–21, above). It may again be of critical importance to the
problem of remoteness of damage: para.6–17, below.
[783] *Glasgow Corp v Muir* [1943] A.C. 448 at 457 per Lord Macmillan. For a high degree of
prescience see *Bohlen v Perdue* [1976] 1 W.W.R. 364. On "hindsight bias" see *Shire of
Gingin v Coombe* [2009] WASCA 92.
[784] *Fullowka v Royal Oak Ventures Inc* [2008] NWTCA 4; [2008] 7 W.W.R. 411 at [53]
[785] In construing the word "likely" in the Factories Act 1961 s.72, the CA in *Bailey v Rolls
Royce Ltd* [1984] I.C.R. 688 put the emphasis on probability; but in *Whitfield v H.&R.
Johnson (Tilers) Ltd* [1991] I.C.R. 109 the same court held that likelihood must be judged
by references to the employee's apparent characteristics, i.e. there is a shift to
foreseeability.
[786] [1954] 2 Q.B. 66.

phenol to be coloured because the risk of invisible cracks had not been drawn to the attention of the profession until 1951 and:

"[C]are has to be exercised to ensure that conduct in 1947 is only judged in the light of knowledge which then was or ought reasonably to have been possessed. In this connection the then-existing state of medical literature must be had in mind."[787]

However, the then-existing state of medical literature did not make R's injury any less probable than it would have been after 1951.

C. "Abnormal" Defendants

5–78   Although the objective standard eliminates the personal abilities of the defendant, the law has never taken this to the ultimate conclusion[788]: for example, no one would ever have suggested that a tiny baby could be liable for negligence. There is not a great deal of case law, but it is now clear that a child is to be judged by the standard of what would be reasonable to expect of a child of that age[789] and some allowance is also probably to be made for physical disability, for example in judging whether a blind person took reasonable care as a pedestrian where a driver was injured trying to avoid him. Disabled people must be allowed to live in the world and if they take what precautionary steps are open to them[790] and do not engage in activities which are unavoidably perilous given their condition, the resulting risk is one we must all put up with.

D. Professional and Industry Standards

5–79   The proposition that the defendant must have failed to behave reasonably in the circumstances means that a passer-by who renders emergency first aid after an accident is not required to show the skill of a qualified surgeon[791] and when the driver of a car suddenly

---

[787] [1954] 2 Q.B. 66 at 92 per Morris L.J.; *Gunn v Wallsend Slipway & Engineering Co, The Times*, January 23, 1989; *Pinder v Cape Plc* [2006] EWHC 3630 (QB). See also *Dwan v Farquhar* [1988] 1 Qd. R. 234 (journal article in March 1983 adverting to possible transmission of AIDS by blood transfusions transfusion in May 1983; no negligence). Compare the standard under the Consumer Protection Act 1987, para.10–23, below.
[788] As to contributory negligence in these cases, see para.6–50, below.
[789] *Mullin v Richards* [1998] 1 W.L.R. 1304; *Orchard v Lee* [2009] EWCA Civ 295; [2009] P.I.Q.R. P16. Is the paucity of case law to be explained by the rarity of incidents or does the lack of liability insurance cover make suits futile? Many acts by children would be covered by the add-on public liability element in a standard household policy.
[790] As to insane persons, who cannot appreciate the need to take these precautions, see para.24–26, below.
[791] A ship's master who diagnoses insanity in a crew member is required to act only as a prudent master armed with the ship's medical guide: *Ali v Furness, Withy* [1988] 2 Lloyd's Rep. 1.

collapsed the incompetent best efforts of the non-driver passenger to bring the vehicle to a halt did not amount to negligence.[792] Perhaps less obviously, a householder who does some small job of repair or replacement about his house is not required to show the skill which might be required of a professional carpenter working for reward—he need only do his work with the skill of a reasonably competent carpenter doing the work in question.[793] Where, however, anyone practices a profession or is engaged in a transaction in which he holds himself out as having professional skill, the law expects him to show the amount of competence associated with the proper discharge of the duties of that profession, trade or calling, and if he falls short of that and injures someone in consequence, he is not behaving reasonably.[794] Thus, where a brewing company owned a ship which was regularly used for the carriage of their stout from Dublin to Liverpool and Manchester, it was held that the board of directors of the company must exercise the same degree of care and skill in the management of the ship as would any other shipowner.[795]

> "The law must apply a standard which is not relaxed to cater for their factual ignorance of all activities outside brewing: having become owners of ships, they must behave as reasonable shipowners."[796]

The rule *imperitia culpae adnumeratur* (inexperience is counted as fault) is just as true in English law as in Roman law.[797]

The objective standard therefore appears to make no allowance for the fact that everyone must learn to some extent by practical experience of the job, a point which was pressed upon the Court of Appeal in *Wilsher v Essex Area Health Authority*,[798] where one of the doctor defendants was junior and of limited experience. The majority of the court, however, rejected the argument that what was expected of an individual doctor was what was reasonably to be

---

[792] *Phillips v John*, Unreported, CA, July 11, 1996.

[793] *Wells v Cooper* [1958] 2 Q.B. 265. Even this, however, is an objective standard, which may be higher than the defendant's "best." Cf. *Moon v Garrett* [2006] EWCA Civ 1121 (not mere DIY work).

[794] He is not to be expected to travel outside the scope of his instructions and hold a watching brief for the client's general welfare: *Pickersgill v Riley* [2004] UKPC 14; [2004] P.N.L.R. 31 (solicitor).

[795] *The Lady Gwendolen* [1965] P. 294 ("actual fault" under the Merchant Shipping Act 1893 s.503); *Griffiths v Arch Engineering Co Ltd* [1968] 3 All E.R. 217; *Cardy & Son v Taylor* [1994] N.P.C. 30.

[796] [1965] P. 294 at 350 per Winn L.J.

[797] Buckland and McNair, *Roman Law and Common Law*, 2nd edn, pp.259–260.

[798] [1987] Q.B. 730. The case was reversed by the House of Lords but not on this point: [1988] A.C. 1074.

required of a person of his qualifications and experience, for that would entail that, "the standard of care which the patient is entitled to demand [would] vary according to the chance of recruitment and rostering."[799] Rather, the standard was to be set by reference to the post held by the defendant in the unit in which he operated.[800] A junior member of the team could not be expected to show the skill of a consultant, but subject to that no allowance would be made for the inexperience of the individual any more than for his domestic circumstances or his financial worries, either of which might equally contribute to an error.[801] A "general practitioner" (whether in medicine, law, the valuation of pictures or any other trade or profession) cannot be expected to have the expertise of a specialist but he should possess a sense of when it is necessary to take appropriate specialist advice.[802] It follows that a specialist will be held to the higher standard of those practising within that specialism.[803]

5–80 The content of the duty of professional people is a large subject and must be sought in specialised works[804] but it is necessary to say something about the courts' approach to the setting of standards. There is no reason in principle why a professional person should not by contract promise to produce a result rather than merely exercise skill and care to do so,[805] but in the absence of an express promise the courts will be reluctant to hold that he has impliedly given such

---

[799] [1987] Q.B. 730 at 750 per Mustill L.J. Unlike the situation in *Nettleship v Weston* there is no voluntary relationship here.

[800] The case was not presented on the basis that the hospital authority had failed in its duty (see para.20–6, below). This might cover some cases in which the individual doctor was not liable. It has been held that a barrister, "must conduct himself in his professional work with the competence (care and skill) of a barrister of ordinary skill who is competent to handle that type of and weight of work and a breach of that duty occurs when the error is one which no reasonably competent member of the profession possessing those skills should have made": *McFaddens v Platford* [2009] EWHC 126 (TCC) at [49]; cf. *Williams v Leatherdale & Francis* [2008] EWHC 2574 (QB) at [67] (taking account of seniority).

[801] "If this test appears unduly harsh ... the inexperienced doctor called on to exercise a specialist skill will, as part of that skill, seek the advice and help of his superiors when he does or may need it. If he does seek such help, he will often have satisfied the test, even though he may himself have made a mistake": [1987] Q.B. 730 at 774 per Glidewell L.J. Despite the headnote it is not entirely clear that Glidewell L.J. was not imposing an even more severe standard than Mustill L.J.

[802] *Luxmore-May v Messenger May Baverstock* [1990] 1 W.L.R. 1009. No doubt the effect of compulsory continuing education, the setting of official practice standards and the "licensing" of specialist forms of practice in law will mean that the general practitioner (if he can survive at all) will need an ever more acute sense of when he is getting "out of his depth".

[803] There will of course in many cases be a contract. The Supply of Goods and Services Act 1982 s.13 implies a term of reasonable care and skill, but "reasonable", in contract as in tort, varies with the circumstances.

[804] Jackson and Powell, *Professional Liability*, 6th edn; Charlesworth and Percy, *Negligence*, 11th edn.

[805] *Greaves & Co v Baynham Meikle* [1975] 1 W.L.R. 1095.

an undertaking.[806] In practice, however, many claims brought against professional people are based on failure to carry out fairly simple, even mechanical, functions and proof of the failure itself will virtually guarantee success in these cases whether the action is framed in contract or tort: there must be a very limited range of circumstances in which a solicitor could show that failing to issue proceedings within the limitation period was "not his fault".[807] Nevertheless, in theory the standard is one of reasonable care.

There is no doubt that the question of what amounts to reasonable care is to be determined by a legal standard framed by the court,[808] not by the profession or industry in question. "Neglect of duty does not cease by repetition to be neglect of duty"[809] and the courts have not hesitated to hold that a general practice amounts to negligence in law though the cases in which they have done so have been overwhelmingly in an industrial[810] rather than a professional context.[811] Considerable deference is, however, paid to the practices of the professions (particularly the medical profession) as established by expert evidence and the court should not attempt to put itself into the shoes of the surgeon or other professional person.[812] This means that if it is shown that the defendant did comply with professional standards the court is very likely indeed to find for him,[813] for:

---

[806] *Thake v Maurice* [1986] Q.B. 644 (vasectomy; statement of irreversibility did not amount to warranty of permanent sterility; but note that on the facts the trial judge came to the opposite conclusion (at 658) and Kerr L.J. thought he was entitled to do so).

[807] Cf. *X v Woollcombe Young* [2001] Lloyd's Rep. P.N. 274 (promptness over making of will).

[808] On a judge's duty to give reasons for his decision see *Flannery v Halifax Estate Agencies Ltd* [2000] 1 W.L.R. 377.

[809] *Bank of Montreal v Dominion Guarantee, etc. Co Ltd* [1930] A.C. 659 at 666 per Lord Tomlin; *The Herald of Free Enterprise, Re, The Independent*, December 18, 1987 (not a tort case).

[810] *Lloyd's Bank Ltd v Savory* [1933] A.C. 201; *Markland v Manchester Corp* [1934] 1 K.B. 566; *Barkway v South Wales Transport Co Ltd* [1950] A.C. 185; *Paris v Stepney BC* [1951] A.C. 367; *General Cleaning Contractors v Christmas* [1953] A.C. 180; *Morris v West Hartlepool Steam Navigation Co Ltd* [1956] A.C. 552; *Cavanagh v Ulster Weaving Co Ltd* [1960] A.C. 145; *MacDonald v Scottish Stamping & Engineering Co* 1972 S.L.T. (Notes) 73.

[811] In *Edward Wong Finance Co Ltd v Johnson Stokes & Master* [1984] A.C. 296 the Privy Council held that following the customary "Hong Kong" style of conveyancing completion amounted to negligence, though the risk could have been avoided by changes in practice which would not wholly undermine the institution; and in *Organ Retention Group Litigation, Re*, [2004] EWHC 644; [2005] Q.B. 506 the evidence was that it was the universal practice, when seeking consent for a post mortem on a child, not to tell parents of the possibility of organ removal and retention but the practice was nevertheless held to be negligent towards the parents.

[812] See, e.g. *Sidaway v Bethlehem Royal Hospital and Maudsley Hospital* [1985] A.C. 871, para.25–4, below, dealing with the giving of information to patients.

[813] *Vancouver General Hospital v McDaniel* (1934) 152 L.T. 56 at 57 per Lord Alness (methods of preventing infection in hospital); *Whiteford v Hunter* [1950] W.N. 533; *Wright v Cheshire CC* [1952] 2 All E.R. 789; *Rich v L.C.C.* [1953] 1 W.L.R. 895; *Simmons v Pennington & Sons* [1955] 1 W.L.R. 183.

"[W]hen the court finds a clearly established practice 'in like circumstances' the practice weighs heavily in the scale on the side of the defendant and the burden of establishing negligence, which the plaintiff has to discharge, is a heavy one".[814]

Where the defendant has not so complied that is not of itself negligence for, "otherwise all inducement to progress ... would then be destroyed"[815] and in any event a professional body cannot set or change the law of the land,[816] but it may raise an inference of negligence against him and it has been held that it reverses the burden of proof and requires him to justify his conduct.[817] "Keeping up-to-date" is obviously a central element in the attainment of a proper standard of care,[818] for in most professions and trades each generation convicts its predecessor of ignorance and there is a steady rise in the standard of competence incident to them, and what is due care in one generation may be negligence in the next.[819] This was given detailed consideration in the context of an employer's duty to guard his workers against the risk of deafness in *Thompson v Smiths Shiprepairers (North Shields) Ltd*.[820] Basing himself upon the proposition that the employer should take reasonable care to keep up-to-date with devices available to protect hearing but must not be blamed for failing to plough a lone furrow, Mustill J. held that even though the availability of effective ear protectors had been announced in *The Lancet* in 1951, the defendants were not in breach of their duty until the publication in 1963 of a government pamphlet on the subject.[821] However, in a later decision on deafness, the Northern Ireland Court of Appeal, while accepting the "ploughing

---

[814] *Morris v West Hartlepool Steam Navigation Co Ltd* [1956] A.C. 552 at 579 per Lord Cohen; *Brown v Rolls-Royce Ltd* [1960] 1 W.L.R. 210; *Gray v Stead* [1999] 2 Lloyd's Rep. 59. Lord Dunedin in *Morton v Dixon (William) Ltd* 1909 S.C. 807 said: "where the negligence of the employer consists of what I may call a fault of omission, I think it absolutely necessary that the proof of that fault of omission should be one of two kinds—either to show that the thing which he did not do was a thing which was commonly done by other persons in like circumstances, or to show that it was a thing which was so obviously wanted that it would be folly in anyone to neglect to provide it."

[815] *Hunter v Hanley* 1955 S.C. 200 at 206 per Lord Clyde.

[816] *Johnson v Bingley, The Times*, February 28, 1995.

[817] The Statements of Standard Accounting Practice drawn up by the professional bodies are strong evidence of proper standards and consequently a departure from them requires to be justified: *Lloyd Cheyham & Co Ltd v Littlejohn & Co* [1987] B.C.L.C. 303.

[818] In the case of a lawyer advising on a settlement this may involve considering possible changes as a result of an appeal in other litigation: *Williams v Thompson Leatherdale* [2008] EWHC (QB) 2574.

[819] See, e.g. *Newell v Goldenberg* [1995] 6 Med.L.R. 371 (warnings on reversibility of vasectomy); *King v Smith* [1995] I.C.R. 339 (instructions to window cleaner about safety).

[820] [1984] Q.B. 405.

[821] See also *N. v UK Medical Research Council* [1996] 7 Med. L.R. 309 (failure to undertake thorough reappraisal of human growth hormone programme after the discovery of Creutzfeldt-Jakob disease risk); *Armstrong v British Coal, The Times*, December 6, 1996; *Bowman v Harland & Wolff Plc* [1992] I.R.L.R. 349 (vibration white finger).

the lone furrow" point, considered that the information available to employers justified an earlier date for the imposition of a duty and emphasised that it was necessary for an employer to apply his mind to matters of safety and not merely to react to directions or union complaints.[822]

One further problem arises on "general and approved practice", **5–81** as it is often known, namely, that there may be no uniformity within the profession as to what is proper. The law here is clearly that the defendant is not negligent if he acts in accordance with a practice accepted at the time as proper by a responsible body of professional opinion skilled in the particular type of activity,[823] even though there is a body of competent professional opinion which might adopt a different technique.[824] It is not the court's function to choose between the schools of professional thought.[825] Though originating in the context of medical negligence,[826] this test is of general application to professional people,[827] and in the medical context it is not confined to "therapeutic" treatment. Hence in *Gold v Haringey Health Authority*[828] a doctor was not negligent in failing to warn the claimant of the failure rate for female sterilisation when the expert witnesses testified that although they would have given such a warning a substantial body of doctors (perhaps as many as 50 per cent) would not have done so.[829] However, since in the last resort even a universal professional practice is not beyond the reach of the law,[830] it must follow that a court may reject a body of professional

---

[822] *Baxter v Harland & Wolff* [1990] I.R.L.R. 516.

[823] It is not necessary that the defendant has made a conscious choice between the two schools: *Adams v Rhymney Valley DC* [2000] Lloyd's Rep. P.N. 777.

[824] *Bolam v Friern Hospital Management Committee* [1957] 1 W.L.R. 582 at 587 (the direction to the jury in this case has become known as the "*Bolam* test"); *Sidaway v Bethlem Royal Hospital* [1985] A.C. 871; *Shaw v Redbridge LBC* [2005] EWHC 150 (QB).

[825] However, "evidence which really amounts to no more than an expression of opinion by a particular practitioner of what he thinks that he would have done had he been placed, hypothetically and without the benefit of hindsight, in the position of the defendants, is of little assistance to the court": *Midland Bank Trust Co Ltd v Hett Stubbs & Kemp* [1979] Ch 384 at 402; *J. D. Williams & Co Ltd v Michael Hyde & Associates Ltd* [2000] Lloyd's Rep. P.N. 823.

[826] Even in a medical context, *Bolam* is concerned with liability to the patient and it does not follow that a course of action which would not be a breach of duty to the patient cannot therefore be a breach of duty to a staff member to whom the patient presents a risk: *Buck v Nottinghamshire Health Care NHS Trust* [2006] EWCA Civ 1576; 93 B.M.L.R. 28.

[827] *Gold v Haringey Health Authority* [1988] Q.B. 481; *Luxmoore-May v Messenger May Baverstock* [1990] 1 W.L.R. 1009; *Adams v Rhymney Valley DC* [2000] Lloyd's Rep. P.N. 777; *Levicom International Holdings BV v Linklaters* [2009] EWHC (Comm) 812.

[828] Above, fn.827. On the scope of the duty to warn of risks of treatment, see further para.25–4, below.

[829] The *Bolam* test applies to the question whether the conduct is negligent it does not apply to proof of causation. If some or even a majority of experts believe that omission of a treatment did not cause the damage that does not preclude the court from concluding that it did: *Cavanagh v Weston HA* [1992] 3 Med.L.R. 49.

[830] See above.

opinion in the very rare case where it can be shown that the opinion in question is not logically supportable at all.[831]

5-82   Many matters other than general practice may be adverted to for guidance on the standard which the court should adopt as the measure of reasonable care. For example, the Highway Code does not of itself give rise to any liability but it is specifically provided that a failure to observe it may be relied upon to establish (or negative) any liability which is in question in a civil action.[832] As to criminal law, it may be said that (putting aside cases where statute gives rise to a direct civil liability, which are dealt with in Ch.7) failure to comply with it is normally good evidence of negligence but it is not possible to lay down any hard and fast rule. There are circumstances for example, in which it would not be negligent to exceed the statutory speed limit. Equally, it is not difficult to imagine a case in which statutory requirements are met but the court would find that there is common law negligence. With regard to the latter type of case, however, a distinction must be drawn between activities like driving, or operating a factory, where there must be room for varying standards to meet varying circumstances, and matters such as the legally permissible level of toxic materials in products. For example, if statutory regulations lay down the amount of an ingredient which may be incorporated in petrol, it has been held that the court cannot hold it negligent to incorporate this amount even in the face of evidence that this amount is harmful: to do so would be tantamount to declaring that if the speed limit on a stretch of road were 30mph it was nonetheless always (and not merely in unusual conditions like ice or fog) negligent to exceed 20mph.[833]

E. Factors of the Objective Standard

5-83   The standard of reasonable care is set by law but its application in a particular case is sometimes described as a "question of fact" in the sense that propositions of good sense which are applied by one judge in one case should not be regarded thereafter as propositions of law.[834] If that were the case, the system would collapse under the

---

[831] *Bolitho v City and Hackney HA* [1998] A.C. 232, particularly at 243B and C. Note the slightly different formulation of the burden of persuasion at 243A.

[832] Road Traffic Act 1988 s.38(7); *Powell v Phillips* [1972] 3 All E.R. 864; Fire Safety and Safety of Places of Sport Act 1987 s.6. There are also codes of practice under the Health and Safety at Work (etc.) Act 1974, see Ch.8.

[833] See *Albery and Budden v BP Oil* [1980] J.P.L. 586. Cf. Consumer Protection Act 1987, para.10–25, below.

[834] *Qualcast (Wolverhampton) Ltd v Haynes* [1959] A.C. 743; *Foskett v Mistry* [1984] R.T.R. 1. So a decision in one case that a warning sign about submerged rocks was required does not dictate that such a sign is necessarily required at another place: *Vairy v Wyong Shire Council* [2005] HCA 62; 223 C.L.R. 422.

weight of accumulated precedent. On the other hand situations do tend to repeat themselves, even if not exactly, and it is permissible to look at decisions of the courts to see how the legal standard[835] of the reasonable man should be applied.[836] The result is that in each case a balance must be struck between the magnitude of the risk and the burden to the defendant in doing (or not doing) what it is alleged he should (or should not) have done. "The law in all cases exacts a degree of care commensurate with the risk."[837] In some cases, where there is only a remote possibility of injury, no precautions need be taken for, "one must guard against reasonable probabilities, not fantastic possibilities",[838] but this means no more than that if the risk is very slight the defendant may have behaved reasonably though he did nothing to prevent the harm.[839] If his act was one for which there was in any case no justification he may still be liable so long only as the risk of damage to the claimant is not such that a reasonable man would brush it aside as far-fetched.[840] Theoretically at least, in every case where a duty of care exists the courts must consider whether the risk was sufficiently great to require of the defendant more than he has actually done.

i. Magnitude of the risk. Two elements go to make up the magnitude of the risk, the likelihood that injury will be incurred[841] and the seriousness of the injury that is risked. In *Bolton v Stone*[842] the claimant was standing on the highway in a road adjoining a cricket ground when she was struck by a ball which a batsman had hit out of the ground. Such an event was foreseeable and, indeed, balls had to the defendant's knowledge occasionally been hit out of

5–84

---

[835] "The evaluation of the various factors involved in making these decisions does not take place as a matter of the possibly idiosyncratic opinion of the judge who makes the decision. Any court's decision about whether there has been a failure to exercise reasonable care takes place in a context where there has been an articulation by courts over decades, of what does, or does not, amount to taking reasonable care in a particular situation" : *Certain Lloyds Underwriters v Giannopoulos* [2009] NSWCA 56 at [106] per Campbell JA. Nor is it proper to describe such a process as the exercise of a discretion.

[836] *Hazell v British Transport Commission* [1958] 1 W.L.R. 169.

[837] *Read v J. Lyons & Co Ltd* [1974] A.C. 156 at 173 per Lord Macmillan. "As the danger increases, so must the precautions increase": *Lloyds Bank Ltd v Ry Executive* [1952] 1 All E.R. 1248 at 1253 per Denning L.J.

[838] *Fardon v Harcourt-Rivington* (1932) 146 L.T. 391 at 392 per Lord Dunedin; *Jones v Whippey* [2009] EWCA Civ 452.

[839] *Bolton v Stone* [1951] A.C. 850 at 886–889 per Lord Radcliffe. Thus in the absence of telling indications to the contrary a bank handling a corporate customer's account is entitled to assume that a director of the customer is not attempting to defraud it: *Barclays Bank v Quincecare & Unichem* [1988] F.L.R. 166; and the risk of a police officer watching the crowd at a match being hit by a player impelled off the pitch can be ignored: *Gillon v CC Strathclyde, The Times*, November 22, 1996. So also a gaoler is not obliged to treat every person in custody as a suicide risk: *Orange v CC West Yorkshire* [2001] EWCA Civ 611; [2002] Q.B. 347.

[840] *The Wagon Mound (No.2)* [1967] 1 A.C. 617, 643–644 per Lord Reid.

[841] i.e. the foreseeable, not the objective, likelihood. See para.5–77, above.

[842] [1951] A.C. 850. Cf. *Miller v Jackson* [1977] Q.B. 966, on somewhat similar facts.

the ground before. Nevertheless, taking into account such factors as the distance from the pitch to the edge of the ground, the presence of a seven-foot fence and the upward slope of the ground in the direction in which the ball was struck, the House of Lords considered that the likelihood of injury to a person in the claimant's position was so slight that the cricket club was not negligent in allowing cricket to be played without having taken additional precautions such as increasing the height of the fence. As Lord Reid said:

> "I think that reasonable men do in fact take into account the degree of risk and do not act upon a bare possibility as they would if the risk were more substantial."[843]

So also in *Harris v Perry* parents at a party were not required continuously to supervise children engaged in boisterous play.[844]

On the other hand, in *Hilder v Associated Portland Cement Manufacturers Ltd*[845] the claimant's husband was riding his motorcycle along a road outside a piece of open land, occupied by the defendants, where children were permitted to play football, when a ball was kicked into the road and caused him to have an accident. The conditions were such that the likelihood of injury to passers-by was much greater than in *Bolton v Stone* and accordingly the defendants were held liable for having permitted football to be played on their land without having taken any additional precautions. A very high degree of care indeed is likely to be required over the testing of medicines and vaccines.[846]

The relevance of the seriousness of the injury was recognised by the House of Lords in *Paris v Stepney Borough Council*.[847] The claimant, a one-eyed man employed by the defendants, was working in conditions involving some risk of eye injury, but the likelihood of injury was not sufficient to call upon the defendants to provide goggles to a normal two-eyed workman. In the case of the claimant, however, goggles should have been provided for, whereas the risk to a two-eyed man was of the loss of one eye, the claimant risked the much greater injury of total blindness.[848] In assessing the magnitude of the risk it is important to notice that the duty of care is owed to

---

[843] [1951] A.C. 850 at 865; cf. *The Wagon Mound (No.2)* [1967] 1 A.C. 617 at 642 per Lord Reid.

[844] [2008] EWCA Civ 907; [2009] 1 W.L.R. 19.

[845] [1961] 1 W.L.R. 1434. For different views on indoor cricket, see *Wood v Multi-Sport* (2002) 186 A.L.R. 145.

[846] *Best v Wellcome Foundation* [1994] 5 Med. L.R. 81 (Ir.S.C.). For liability under the Consumer Protection Act 1987 see para.10–18, below.

[847] [1951] A.C. 367; *Pentney v Anglian Water Authority* [1983] I.C.R. 464.

[848] Of course standards change and 50 years later even the risk to a two-eyed man might require the provision of goggles.

the claimant himself and therefore if he suffers from some disability
which increases the magnitude of the risk to him that disability must
be taken into account so long as it is or should be known to the
defendant.[849] If it is unknown and could not reasonably have been
known to the defendant then it is, of course, irrelevant.[850]

ii. The importance of the object to be attained. Asquith L.J. **5–85**
summed it up by saying that it is necessary to balance the risk
against the consequences of not taking it.

"As has often been pointed out, if all the trains in this country
were restricted to a speed of five miles an hour, there would be
fewer accidents, but our national life would be intolerably slowed
down. The purpose to be served, if sufficiently important, justifies
the assumption of abnormal risk."[851]

In *Watt v Hertfordshire CC*,[852] W, a fireman, was injured by the
movement of a heavy jack when travelling with it in a lorry not
specially equipped for carrying it. A woman had been trapped under
a heavy vehicle and the jack was urgently required to save her life.
It was held that the fire authorities had not been negligent, for the
risk involved to W was not so great as to prohibit the attempt to save
life; but if the same accident had occurred in a commercial enterprise W could have recovered. "The commercial end to make profit

[849] *Paris v Stepney Borough Council*, above, fn.847; *Haley v London Electricity Board* [1965]
A.C. 778; *Baxter v Woolcombers* (1963) 107 S.J. 553 (claimant's low intelligence relevant
to standard of care due to him but not to question of contributory negligence); *Johnstone
v Bloomsbury HA* [1992] Q.B. 333; *Morrell v Owen, The Times*, December 14, 1993
(coach of disabled athletes); *Walker v Northumberland CC* [1995] I.C.R. 702; *Hatton v
Sutherland* [2002] EWCA Civ 76; [2002] I.C.R. 613 (susceptibility to stress).
[850] *Bourhill v Young* [1943] A.C. 92 at 109–110 per Lord Wright.
[851] *Daborn Bath Tramways* [1946] 2 All E.R. 333 at 336 (left-hand drive ambulance during
emergency period of war not negligent in turning right without giving a signal); *Brisco v
Secretary of State for Scotland* 1997 S.C. 14 (small risk of injury justified in training of
prison officers). Cf. *Quinn v Scott* [1965] 1 W.L.R. 1004 (National Trust negligent in not
felling dangerous tree near highway. Safety of public must take precedence over preservation of the amenities). The fact that the defendants in *Bolton v Stone* were playing cricket
must have had some influence upon the decision. It by no means follows that the same risk
could be taken for a less worthy end.
[852] [1954] 1 W.L.R. 835; *King v Sussex Ambulance NHS Trust* [2002] EWCA Civ 953. In the
latter case at [47] Buxton L.J. said: "Why should . . . men of courage, who are the persons
who run the risk on behalf of the public, suffer if the risk eventuates? If, as this court held
in *Kent v Griffiths*, the public interest obliges the service to respond to public need, why
should it not be equally in the public interest to compensate those who are foreseeably
injured in the course of meeting that public need? If the furniture mover [faced with a risky
task] . . . decided to go on with the job, for whatever reason, he would do so at his peril
if workers were injured . . . . It is difficult to see why . . . if employees required to run
risks to advance private interests can recover if doing their employer's bidding leads to
injury, so employees required to run risks to advance public interests should [not] by the
same token be able to recover."

is very different from the human end to save life or limb."[853] A fire
authority has been held liable for damage caused by a fire engine
which went through a red light on the way to a fire[854] for there is no
special exemption from the law of negligence for them, the police or
other emergency services.[855] However, the question of whether the
defendant behaved like a reasonable man admits of a flexible
response which may take account of the emergency in which the
defendant acts.[856]

All this is not to say that some risk can be taken only in an
emergency: tea and coffee are only palatable when they are made
with hot water, people generally want them to be served hot and a
person who caters for that is not negligent merely because there is
some risk of scalding.[857] If the law goes too far in setting the
standard of care required the legitimate activities of people in
general will be curtailed.

"There have been occasions when judges appear to have forgotten that the response of prudent and reasonable people to many
of life's hazards is to do nothing. If it were otherwise, we would
live in a forest of warning signs."[858]

The point is made with great force by the House of Lords in
Tomlinson v Congleton BC.[859]

The particular context was the liability of an occupier in respect
of obvious, natural risks on his premises,[860] the claimant having
been seriously injured by taking a standing dive into shallow water
in a perfectly unexceptional lake and hitting his head on the bottom.
However, what is said in rejecting the argument that the occupier

---

[853] *Watt* (fn.852) at 838 per Denning L.J. That is not to say, of course, that an increased
element of risk in a change of practice automatically makes a commercial enterprise
negligent: *Nilson v Redditch BC*, Unreported, CA, October 31, 1994 (change from
"wheely bin" to "black bag" rubbish collection system increased risk of cutting
injuries).

[854] *Ward v L.C.C.* [1938] 2 All E.R. 341; *Wardell-Yerburgh v Surrey CC* [1973] R.T.R. 462;
Purdue v Devon Fire and Rescue Service [2002] EWCA Civ 1538.

[855] Even though they may be exempt from criminal liability for, e.g. exceeding the speed limit.
Gaynor v Allen [1959] 2 Q.B. 403; *Griffin v Mersey Regional Ambulance* [1998] P.I.Q.R.
P34.

[856] *Marshall v Osmond* [1983] Q.B. 1034; *Scutts v MPC* [2001] EWCA Civ 715; cf. *Rigby v
CC Northamptonshire* [1985] 1 W.L.R. 1242, where, on the facts, the defendants were
negligent even allowing for the emergency. See the extraordinary case of *Craggy v CC
Cleveland* [2009] EWCA Civ 1128 (collision between fire engine and police car at
controlled junction).

[857] *Bogle v McDonald's Restaurants Ltd* [2002] EWHC 490 (QB).

[858] *New South Wales v Fahy* [2007] HCA 20 at [6] per Gleeson C.J. See *Alexis v Newham LBC*
[2009] EWHC 1323; [2009] I.C.R. 1517 (no reason to anticipate poisoning of teacher by
allowing child access to room).

[859] [2003] UKHL 47; [2004] 1 A.C. 46.

[860] See para.9–17, below.

should have taken effective steps to keep people away from the water is clearly of general application. As Lord Hoffmann put it:

"I think that there is an important question of freedom at stake. It is unjust that the harmless recreation of responsible parents and children with buckets and spades on the beaches should be prohibited in order to comply with what is thought to be a legal duty to safeguard irresponsible visitors against dangers which are perfectly obvious. The fact that such people take no notice of warnings cannot create a duty to take other steps to protect them ... A duty to protect against obvious risks or self-inflicted harm exists only in cases in which there is no genuine and informed choice, as in the case of employees whose work requires them to take the risk, or some lack of capacity, such as the inability of children to recognise danger ... or the despair of prisoners which may lead them to inflict injury on themselves ...

It is of course understandable that organisations like the Royal Society for the Prevention of Accidents should favour policies which require people to be prevented from taking risks. Their function is to prevent accidents and that is one way of doing so. But they do not have to consider the cost, not only in money but also in deprivation of liberty, which such restrictions entail. The courts will naturally respect the technical expertise of such organisations in drawing attention to what can be done to prevent accidents. But the balance between risk on the one hand and individual autonomy on the other is not a matter of expert opinion. It is a judgment which the courts must make and which in England reflects the individualist values of the common law."[861]

iii. Practicability of precautions. The risk must be balanced   **5–86**
against the measures necessary to eliminate it, and the practical measures which the defendant could have taken must be considered.[862] In *Latimer v AEC*[863] a factory floor became slippery after a flood. The occupiers of the factory did everything possible to get rid of the effects of the flood, but nevertheless the claimant was

---

[861] At [46]. *Keown v Coventry Healthcare NHS Trust* [2006] EWCA Civ 39; [2006] 1 W.L.R. 953 at [17]
[862] See *Haley v London Electricity Board* [1965] A.C. 778; *Stokes v Guest, Keen and Nettleford (Bolts and Nuts) Ltd* [1968] 1 W.L.R. 1776.
[863] [1953] A.C. 643. Cf. *Bolton v Stone* [1951] A.C. 850 at 867 per Lord Reid: "I think that it would be right to take into account not only how remote is the chance that a person might be struck but also how serious the consequences are likely to be if a person is struck but I do not think that it would be right to take into account the difficulty of remedial measures." The risk involved in taking a precaution may actually outweigh the advantages of taking it: *Morris v West Hartlepool Steam Navigation Co Ltd* [1956] A.C. 552; *Bolam v Friern Hospital Management Committee* [1957] 1 W.L.R. 582.

injured and then sought to say that the occupiers should have closed
down the factory. The House of Lords held that the risk of injury
created by the slippery floor was not so great as to justify, much less
require, so onerous a precaution.[864] The greater the risk, the less
receptive a court is likely to be to a defence based simply upon the
cost, in terms of money, of the required precautions[865] and there may
be situations in which an activity must be abandoned altogether if
adequate safeguards cannot be provided. However, it must always
be borne in mind that there may be costs other than financial ones,
such as the restriction on the freedom of others which has been
referred to above, and therefore a measure may be unjustifiable on
that ground even if it would not cost very much.[866] The courts in
England have certainly not shown overt attachment to the theory
that negligence is merely an economic cost/benefit equation,[867] but
at the end of the day the cost of a precaution and the ability of a
socially useful activity to bear that cost have to be brought into
account.[868] In *Knight v Home Office*[869] a mentally disturbed prisoner
who was known to have suicidal tendencies hanged himself despite
being observed every 15 minutes by staff in the prison hospital
wing. In coming to the conclusion that the defendants were not in
breach of their duty of care, Pill J. said that (a) it was not correct to
demand of a prison hospital the same facilities and the same level of
staffing as could be expected in a specialised psychiatric hospital (to
which the deceased would have been transferred a few days later)

---

[864] In *Gough v Upshire Primary School* [2002] E.L.R. 169 the fact that a child might slide
down a banister was perfectly foreseeable but that did not require alteration of the
staircase. Countervailing disadvantages are not confined to financial ones: *Searby v
Yorkshire Traction Ltd* [2003] EWCA Civ 1856.

[865] See, e.g. *Morris v Luton Corp* [1946] 1 All E.R. 1 at 4 per Lord Greene M.R. (the report
of this case at [1946] K.B. 116 is incomplete); *Christmas v General Cleaning Contractors*
[1952] 1 K.B. 141 at 149 per Denning L.J. (affirmed [1953] A.C. 180).

[866] *Tomlinson v Congleton BC* [2003] UKHL 47; [2004] 1 A.C. 46. "Negligence is not an
economic cost/benefit equation. Immeasurable 'soft' values such as community concepts
of justice, health, life and freedom of conduct have to be taken into account": *Western
Suburbs Hospital v Currie* (1987) 9 N.S.W.L.R. 511 at 523 per McHugh J.A.

[867] For this approach see, e.g. Posner, *Economic Analysis of Law*, 2nd edn, Ch.6. See also
Learned Hand J.'s algebraic formula in *US v Carroll Towing Co* 159 F. 2d 169, 173 (1947).
Speaking in a case where a barge had broken adrift, he said: "the owner's duty ... is a
function of three variables: (1) The probability that she will break away (2) the gravity of
the resulting injury if she does (3) the burden of adequate precautions. Possibly it serves
to bring that notion into relief to state it in algebraic terms: if the probability be called D
the injury L, and the burden B liability depends on whether B is less than L multiplied by
P." As Posner J. admitted in *McCarty v Pheasant Run Inc* 826 F 2d 1554 at 1557 (1987)
the court rarely has the information required to quantify all the variables and the Hand
formula therefore has greater analytical than operational utility.

[868] The leading case on breach of duty at common law in Australia is *Wyong Shire Council
v Shirt* [1980] HCA 12; 146 C.L.R. 40. There has been disagreement in the High Court as
to whether it tends to produce an assumption that because something *could* be done
without great expense, it follows that it *should* be done: see *New South Wales v Fahy*
[2007] HCA 20. The position may be affected by legislation in all states comparable to
s.5B of the Civil Liability Act 2002 (NSW).

[869] [1990] 3 All E.R. 237. See also *Cekan v Haines* (1990) 21 N.S.W.L.R. 296.

and (b) while lack of funds was no more a defence per se for a public body than for a private trader, yet he had to bear in mind that, "resources available for the public service are limited and that the allocation of resources is a matter for Parliament".[870] It has been said that:

"[I]t is not open to a statutory authority that has responsibility for administering some field of endeavour conferred on it by statute, to withdraw from that field if it lacks resources to carry out some particular activity that is within its powers. It would ignore reality for a court to proceed on the basis that a statutory authority should be taken to have sufficient resources to carry out all its statutory duties, powers and discretions. An effect of this is that the standard by which one decides whether a statutory authority has acted negligently is not the same as that applicable to a private individual or corporation, but rather is the standard of what a reasonable authority, with its powers and resources, would have done in all the circumstances of the case."[871]

4. PROOF OF NEGLIGENCE

The burden of proof of the defendant's negligence on a balance of probabilities is upon the claimant, but it should not be thought that the claimant necessarily has to establish this by direct testimony. **5–87**

A. Criminal Convictions

First, in many cases (especially road accident cases) there may have been criminal proceedings which have led to the conviction of the defendant. The Civil Evidence Act 1968 reversed the common law rule that a conviction might not be used as evidence in civil proceedings[872] and provides in s.11 that if a person is proved to have been convicted of an offence then he shall be taken to have committed that offence unless the contrary is proved.[873] So if the defendant has been convicted of careless driving in respect of the incident which led to the claimant's injury that is likely to be **5–88**

---

[870] [1990] 3 All E.R. 237 at 243. Where a danger arises on the defendant's property and he is obliged to take steps to abate it, account is taken of his personal circumstances, including his resources (para.5–76, above). While one could not argue that the provision of a public service can be equated with this situation they share the characteristic that in both cases the defendant has no choice but to act and the size of the demand on him is beyond his control.

[871] *Roads and Traffic Authority of NSW v Refrigerated Roadways Pty Ltd* [2009] NSWCA 263 at [265].

[872] *Hollington v F. Hewthorn & Co Ltd* [1943] K.B. 587.

[873] See *Wauchope v Mordecai* [1970] 1 W.L.R. 317.

powerful evidence that he is guilty of civil negligence.[874] Of course
the defendant may, if he can, show that he did not in fact commit the
offence[875] or that for some reason his conduct did not amount to
civil negligence[876]; and the criminal conviction may not determine
issues in the civil case (for example causation of damage) because
they were simply not relevant in the earlier proceedings. When it
applies, however, the Act shifts the legal burden of proof on to the
defendant once his conviction is proved.[877] The defendant may find
it very difficult to discharge this burden, but the fact that it is open
to him to seek to do so may deprive the claimant of summary
judgment.[878]

B. Res Ipsa Loquitur

5–89   It is open to the court to infer negligence from the circumstances
in which the accident occurred. This has traditionally been described
by the phrase res ipsa loquitur—the thing speaks for itself. Nowadays we are going through a phase of aversion from Latin,[879] but the
phrase is a convenient shorthand and will be used here, though it is
no longer possible to regard it as a special principle, nor even as a
maxim. Its nature was admirably put by Morris L.J. when he said
that it:

> "[P]ossesses no magic qualities, nor has it any added virtue, other
> than that of brevity, merely because it is expressed in Latin. When
> used on behalf of a plaintiff it is generally a short way of saying:
> 'I submit that the facts and circumstances which I have proved
> establish a prima facie case of negligence against the defendant
> . . . ' There are certain happenings that do not normally occur in
> the absence of negligence and upon proof of these a court will
> probably hold that there is a case to answer."[880]

---

[874] An acquittal is of no evidential relevance to civil liability. The criminal standard of proof
is higher.

[875] This does not infringe the rule against collateral attacks on issues decided in criminal
proceedings (*Hunter v CC West Midlands* [1982] A.C. 529): *McCauley v Hope* [1999]
P.I.Q.R. P 185; *J v Oyston, The Times*, December 11, 1998. Care must be taken to
distinguish s.11 from s.13, which makes proof of a conviction *conclusive* evidence of guilt
for the purposes of defamation: para.12–29, below.

[876] Thus a conviction for speeding is evidence of civil negligence but speeding is not
necessarily negligence.

[877] *Stupple v Royal Insurance Co Ltd* [1971] 1 Q.B. 50.

[878] CPR Pt 24.

[879] See *Fryer v Pearson, The Times,* April 4, 2000.

[880] *Roe v Minister of Health* [1954] 2 Q.B. 66 at 87. See also Hobhouse L.J. in *Ratcliffe v
Plymouth and Torbay HA* [1998] P.I.Q.R. P170. The judgment of Brooke L.J. in this case
contains a helpful survey and analysis of modern medical negligence cases in this
context.

In the past there was a tendency to elevate this to a special rule of the law of negligence and the older cases should be read with this in mind. One had disputes as to whether res ipsa loquitur "could" apply to complex matters like surgery or the operation of an aircraft,[881] but to modern eyes these controversies are misplaced, because matters of drawing inferences from particular facts cannot be subject to rules of law and it is not possible to identify in advance the categories of fact situations to which res ipsa loquitur will be applicable. It would be impossible to argue that if a patient dies during surgery or a child is born with brain damage that necessarily establishes a prima facie case of negligence against the doctors or the theatre staff. On the other hand, if the procedure is simple and regarded as unattended by serious risk, an adverse outcome may well justify an inference of negligence. Even in such a case, however, the claimant will probably[882] need to lay a foundation with expert evidence about the procedure, whereas a court is not likely to require expert evidence before it concludes that a car veering across the carriageway suggests negligence on the part of the driver.[883] It has been said that in medical negligence cases the essential function of res ipsa loquitur is not so much to prove the claimant's case as to enable him, when he is not in possession of all the material facts:

"[T]o be able to plead an allegation of negligence in an acceptable form and to force the defendant to respond to it at the peril of having a finding of negligence made against the defendant if the defendant does not make an adequate response."[884]

The cases on res ipsa loquitur are no more than illustrations of the way in which the courts infer negligence from circumstantial evidence so that the Supreme Court of Canada was clearly correct to say it should no longer be treated as a "separate component" of the law of negligence.[885] Nonetheless, the student should have some idea of how cases are decided where there is no direct evidence.

The essential element is that the mere fact of the happening of the accident should tell its own story so as to establish a prima facie case against the defendant. This is commonly divided into two parts on

---

[881] It was held that in suitable circumstances res ipsa loquitur could be applied to air crashes in *George v Eagle Air Services* [2009] UKPC 21. Normally no such issue can arise because commercial carriage of passengers is governed by an international convention regime outside general tort law.

[882] Cf. *Ludlow v Swindon Health Authority* [1989] 1 Med.L.R. 104.

[883] In the case of a head-on collision in the middle of the road there may be no pointer one way or the other as to whose fault it was and the correct inference will often be that both drivers were to blame: *Bray v Palmer* [1961] 1 W.L.R. 1455; *Baker v Market Harborough Co-operative Society* [1953] 1 W.L.R. 1472.

[884] Hobhouse L.J. in *Ratcliffe v Plymouth and Torbay HA*, above, fn.880, at P189.

[885] *Fontaine v British Columbia* [1998] 1 S.C.R. 424.

the basis of Erle C.J.'s famous statement in *Scott v London and St. Katherine Dock Co*[886]:

> "There must be reasonable evidence of negligence, but when the thing is shown to be under the management of the defendant or his servants, and the accident is such as in the ordinary course of things does not happen if those who have the management use proper care, it affords reasonable evidence, in the absence of explanation by the defendants, that the accident arose from want of care."

So the elements are (a) control and (b) an accident of a type which does not normally occur without the defendant's fault. In reality, however, the two parts are closely interconnected: "control" is required because the absence of control by the defendant makes it less likely that the accident arose from *his* fault. That is why, in *Easson v L.N.E.Ry.*[887] where the claimant, aged four, fell through the door of a corridor train about seven miles from its destination, res ipsa loquitur did not apply. On the journey from Edinburgh to London there was so much opportunity for the doors to be interfered with by passengers that their action could as well have been the cause of the door coming open as the fault of the railway company. On a modern train with electrically locked doors the incident might point to a fault in the system. Again, if a barrel falls from an upstairs opening on to a passer-by that is unlikely to happen if those in charge take proper care[888]; but if an armchair falls from an unidentified window in a tall hotel, that points to some act of malice or madness on the part of a guest, not to the fault of the hotel.[889] On the other hand, it is not difficult to imagine cases which might raise an inference of negligence even though the defendant was not in control at the time of the accident. If A borrows a car from B and A runs into C, that suggests negligence on A's part; but if it is shown that the cause was the sudden failure of the brakes that would exonerate A, but not necessarily B, for it is rare for the brakes on a well-maintained car to fail without warning. If of course B produces evidence that the car was properly maintained, C's claim fails altogether: even if the defendant cannot explain how the defect came to occur he succeeds if he shows that there was no breach of duty in

---

[886] (1865) 3 H. & C. 596 (six bags of flour fell on claimant while he was walking past the defendant's warehouse, claim should have been left to the jury).

[887] [1944] 2 K.B. 421. Cf. *Gee v Metropolitan Ry* (1873) L.R. 8 Q.B. 161 (door opened soon after train left station).

[888] *Byrne v Boadle* (1863) 2 H. & C. 722. It could of course be the fault of a malicious person who had gained entry and was lying in wait for the claimant, but that is sufficiently unlikely to be discounted unless the defendant produces evidence.

[889] *Larson v St. Francis Hotel* 188 P. 2d 513 (1948).

the matter as far as he was concerned.[890] As to the other element, the nature of the accident, one cannot lay down any hard and fast rules, for the inference arises from all the evidence before the court. If a car strikes a pedestrian on the pavement that suggests negligence on the driver's part,[891] nor does it help the driver to show that the car skidded, for an unexplained skid is itself evidence of negligence[892]; but if a car leaves a dirt road in unexplained circumstances in very bad weather that does not necessarily support the same inference.[893] No doubt it will commonly be true that experience shows that a fire may escape from a domestic grate without negligence on anyone's part[894] and that losses occur in commodities futures trading without any fault by brokers[895]; but that does not rule out all possibility of an inference of negligence arising from the circumstances. As has been pointed out above, past cases cannot be regarded as precedents in this area but even if one regards them as having a persuasive or "educative" value one must be aware of the fact that experience may show that an activity which years ago was regarded as fraught with inherent danger is in fact rather safe if conducted with proper care.

There was often said to be a third requirement for the application of res ipsa loquitur, namely that there must be no evidence of the actual cause of the accident. In a sense this is true—the drawing of inferences is only necessary to meet an evidentiary gap; but even when the immediate cause is known (as in the brake failure example above) the question may still remain whether negligence causing this is to be inferred or not.[896] Of course, when enough is known about the circumstances of the accident the question ceases to be one of drawing inferences about what the defendant did or did not do and becomes one of the characterisation of his conduct. In *Barkway v South Wales Transport Co Ltd*[897] the claimant was killed when the defendants' bus veered off the road down an embankment and it was established that the accident occurred because of a defect in one of

---

[890] *Woods v Duncan* [1946] A.C. 401.
[891] *Ellor v Selfridge & Co Ltd* (1930) 46 T.L.R. 236. For a fairly generous decision see *Widdowson v Newgate Meat Corp* [1998] P.I.Q.R. P138 (claimant walking on dual carriageway at midnight wearing dark clothing).
[892] *Richley v Faull* [1965] 1 W.L.R. 1454.
[893] *Fontaine v British Columbia* [1998] S.C.R. 424.
[894] *Sochaki v Sas* [1947] 1 All E.R. 344.
[895] *Stafford v Conti Commodity Services* [1981] 1 All E.R. 691; *Merrill Lynch Futures Inc v York House Trading* (1984) 81 L.S. Gaz. 2544.
[896] The mere fact that the claimant has tried and failed to prove some specific act of negligence on the part of the defendant does not prevent him inviting the court to draw an inference of negligence in the alternative: *Anchor Products Ltd v Hedges* (1966) 115 C.L.R. 493.
[897] [1950] 1 All E.R. 392.

the tyres. It was shown that the defect might have been discovered beforehand if the defendants had required drivers to report incidents which could give rise to "impact fractures" and the House of Lords held that the negligence of the defendants in failing to institute such a system was established.

C. Rebutting the Inference

5–90   If the defendant chooses not to respond by offering an explanation consistent with due care, then the claimant will win. This was not necessarily so in the days of trial by jury, for the question then was whether there was sufficient evidence to leave the case to the jury and if the judge did so a verdict for the defendant was not necessarily perverse.[898] A judge sitting alone, however, cannot separate his functions as tribunal of law and fact in this way and sensibly say in one breath that it is a case of res ipsa loquitur and then go on to find for the defendant.[899] If he is not prepared to say that, in the absence of evidence from the defendant, the claimant has proved his case by pointing to the circumstances of the accident he will not hold that it is a res ipsa loquitur case in the first place. In most cases where the claim gets as far as trial, however, the defendant will have something to say in response and the question arises of what he has to do to rebut the prima facie case. At one time there was support for the view that once res ipsa loquitur applied the legal burden of proof shifted to the defendant, i.e. he was liable unless he proved on a balance of probabilities that the event was due to no fault on his part. This is inconsistent with he current view of the nature and operation of res ipsa loquitur. There is no shift in the formal burden of proof, which remains throughout on the claimant,[900] so that at the end of the day the court must ask itself what is the effect of the rebutting evidence by the defendant upon the cogency of the initial inference of negligence which arose from the mere happening of the accident.

---

[898] Indeed, the jury in the second trial in *Scott v London and St. Katherine Docks*, above, fn.886, found for the defendant. Even where the claimant has supported his case by direct evidence the defendant may, at the close of the claimant's case, submit that there is no case to answer. The traditional approach has been to consider such a submission if the defendant elects to call no evidence since it is inconvenient to ask the trier of fact for an opinion when the evidence is incomplete: *Alexander v Rayson* [1936] [1936] 1 K.B. 169. There is, however, a discretion and this is probably rather broader under the CPR: *Blinkhorn v Hall*, April 13, 2000, CA.

[899] See Lord Pearson in *Henderson v Henry E. Jenkins & Sons* [1970] A.C. 282 at 310: "the issue will be decided in the claimant's favour unless the defendants by their evidence provide some answer which is adequate to displace the prima facie inference."

[900] *Ng v Lee* [1988] R.T.R. 296 (PC).

"The *res*, which previously spoke for itself, may be silenced, or its voice may, on the whole of the evidence, become too weak or muted."[901]

The explanation offered by the defendant must be at least a plausible one, not a mere theoretical or speculative possibility, but at the end of the day the court must ask itself whether, taking the evidence as a whole, it is more likely than not that the accident is attributable to the defendant's fault. If the defendant cannot offer any explanation of how the accident occurred but seeks to show that he has exercised all due care in any event his evidence must be a complete answer to the claim. In *J v North Lincolnshire CC*[902] the claimant, a ten-year-old boy with arrested global development, escaped from school and was injured by a car without any fault on the driver's part. There was no evidence as to how he had left the school, there being five entrances with varying degrees of security or insecurity. Conceivably he might have left by a gate which was reasonably secure (the defendants not being required to provide absolute security) in which case, the defendants argued, their proven fault in relation to another gate was not causative. The Court of Appeal rejected this argument: the circumstances of the child getting on to the road called for an explanation by the defendants which was consistent with their having taken proper care and this would be emasculated if they were able to throw the issue of causation on to the claimant. In *Henderson v Henry E. Jenkins & Sons*,[903] where the claimant's husband was killed by a heavy lorry whose brakes failed on a steep hill, the defendants pleaded that the brake failure was due to a latent defect in the main brake fluid pipe. They proved that they had cleaned and carried out visual inspections of the pipe at the proper intervals and that the cause of its failure was corrosion in a part of the pipe which could only be inspected by removing the pipe itself from the vehicle. Notwithstanding that neither the manufacturers of the vehicle nor the Ministry of Transport recommended removal of the pipe for inspection in normal circumstances, it was held by a majority of the House of Lords that the defendants had not done sufficient to rebut the inference that they had been negligent: they should have gone on to show that nothing had occurred in the life of the vehicle which would cause abnormal corrosion or call for special inspection or treatment. The strength of the inference of

---

[901] *Lloyde v West Midlands Gas Board* [1970] 1 W.L.R. 749 at 755, approved in *Ng v Lee* above, fn.900. However, one should not exaggerate the burden on the claimant. If he slips on yoghurt on a supermarket floor he wins unless the store shows there was a system of frequent inspections and that it was operated: *Ward v Tesco Stores Ltd* [1976] 1 W.L.R. 810; *Hall v Holker Estate Co Ltd* [2008] EWCA Civ 1422
[902] [2000] P.I.Q.R. P84.
[903] [1970] A.C. 282.

negligence raised by the extensive corrosion of the pipe, and the extremely high standard of inspection and maintenance required of a person who sends a heavy lorry on a journey involving the descent of a steep hill justified the heavy burden placed on the defendants in this case.

5. Consequent Damage

5–91 The third ingredient of the tort of negligence is that the claimant's damage must have been caused by the defendant's breach of duty and must not be too remote a consequence of it. Discussion of this ingredient thus involves consideration of causation and (if it be different) remoteness of damage, topics relevant in all torts and not only in the tort of negligence. It is in cases of negligence, however, that these problems most commonly arise, and they can only be dealt with against the background of the tort of negligence as a whole. The next chapter will deal with these issues and with the often closely associated matter of the contributory fault of the claimant.

CHAPTER 6

NEGLIGENCE: CAUSATION, REMOTENESS (SCOPE OF LIABILITY) AND CONTRIBUTORY NEGLIGENCE

THE claimant must show a causal link on the usual civil standard of **6–1** a balance of probabilities between the loss he has suffered and the defendant's wrong; he must also show that the loss in respect of which he claims is within the range of that for which it is just to make the defendant responsible (though this element, too, is to some extent expressed in the language of "causation"); and if the claimant has contributed to the occurrence of that loss his damages may be reduced (or even extinguished). These issues arise in connection with other torts, too, but most of the case law involves claims for negligence, so they are dealt with here, though it will be necessary to consider them again at various later points.

1. CAUSATION AND REMOTENESS (SCOPE OF LIABIITY): INTRODUCTION

6–2   Even if the claimant proves every other element in tortious liability he will lose the action or, in the case of torts actionable per se, fail to recover more than nominal damages, if what the defendant did is not treated as a legally effective cause of his loss. This issue is logically distinct from and anterior to the question of measure of damages, which is concerned with the amount of the pecuniary compensation which the defendant must pay in respect of those items of the claimant's loss for which he is legally responsible.[1] Thus in one of the leading cases, the issue was whether the defendants were liable for fire damage to a wharf which arose from a rather unusual chain of events after the defendants spilled oil into a harbour.[2] If they had been liable (in fact they were not) the prima facie measure of damages would have been the cost of repairing the wharf plus consequential losses like loss of business, but a number of other, subsidiary issues might have been raised, for example the effect on the defendant's liability of payments made by the claimants' fire insurers, or the position if the cost of repairs had exceeded the value of the wharf. Matters like this will be dealt with at a later stage,[3] though it may as well be admitted now that the line between "causation/remoteness" and "measure" is not always easy to draw,[4] for measure of damages is not merely a matter of mathematical calculation.

A. Terminology and Classification

6–3   Although the general principles of the law dealt with in this chapter are clear enough, the topic is difficult to expound because, as is so often the case, our terminology is not consistent. The first part of this chapter, "Causation in Fact", is concerned with a

---

[1] See *The Argentino* (1881) 13 P.D. 101 at 196.
[2] *The Wagon Mound* [1961] A.C. 388, para.6–17, below.
[3] See Ch.22, below.
[4] Furthermore, "measure of damages" is sometimes used by judges when causation/remoteness is meant. See, e.g. *The Wagon Mound (No.2)* [1967] 1 A.C. 617 at 638 per Lord Reid.

question which arises (at least in theory) in every case, that is to say, whether the defendant's act (or omission) should be excluded from the events which contributed to the occurrence of the claimant's loss. If it is so excluded, that is the end of the case, for if there is no connection between the defendant's act and the loss there is no reason for a private law system of liability to operate with regard to him. It is conceivable that in another society or another time or in a different context it might be regarded as a good reason for saying that A must pay for damage suffered by B, that A was rich and B was poor, or that A was head of B's clan; or we might, as to some extent we do, via social security, decide that society as a whole should pay for B's loss. However, to our way of thinking the necessary bedrock[5] of tort liability as a general rule is at least a causal connection between A's act and B's loss,[6] and if what A did made no contribution to the situation in which B now finds himself the connection is absent, whatever other legal sanctions (the criminal law, professional discipline) may be directed at A's *behaviour.* At this stage we are not concerned with whether the defendant's act was the cause (or even an important cause) but whether it was *a* cause, whether it is relevant to B's loss. This stage is primarily[7] a matter of historical mechanics (though it necessarily involves hypothetical questions about what would have happened in different circumstances—"but for the defendant's act would the damage have occurred?"). If we conclude that it was a cause, we move on to consider whether it was a sufficiently legally effective cause among the complex of other causes (and there may be many) to justify imposing tort liability on the defendant. Suppose D leaves a loaded shotgun in an unlocked cupboard, X steals it and uses it to murder C (D knowing nothing of X's murderous intentions). D's breach of duty in failing to lock up the gun was a cause of C's death in the sense used at this first stage because had the gun not been available X would not have used it to kill C (though he might of course have done so at another time with another weapon), but a court is quite likely to say that if X is an adult of sound mind, then X, not D, is responsible for C's death and it may do so by speaking in terms of X's act being "the cause" or of X's act having "broken the chain of

---

[5] Any other view would be irrational: *Kuwait Airways Corp v Iraqi Airways Co (Nos 4 and 5)* [2002] UKHL 19; [2002] 2 A.C. 883 at [127] per Lord Hoffmann.
[6] *Sindell v Abbot Laboratories* 607 P. 2d 924 (1980), where a Californian court imposed a "market share proportion" liability upon manufacturers of a generic drug when the claimant could not show which manufacturer produced the batch in question may be regarded either as extreme modification of private law principles to cope with damage done by one of a group, or as an ad hoc, judicially created and industry based compensation system.
[7] Though not entirely, see below.

causation"[8] between D's negligence and C's death.[9] This is the second stage of the inquiry. On the other hand, if a little child had taken the gun in our example and shot C while playing with it, we would probably readily agree that C's death was well within the risk created by D's negligence in leaving it about, and that D ought to be responsible, even though what D did was just as much an "historical" or "mechanical" cause in one case as in the other. So if we are going to distinguish between the two cases at the second stage and still speak in the language of causation we are now using a different concept and despite a tendency even at this stage to use mechanical metaphors about chains and links, the issue is much more obviously[10] one of fairness and of legal policy, about setting limits to the responsibility which D bears for his negligence.[11]

6–4   None of this is controversial, the problem lies in expressing it in the shorthand way we need for easy reference (especially in a student book). The first stage is described in this chapter by the well-established term "causation in fact". However, that may give the false impression that the process of determining cause is akin to using a litmus paper to establish acidity. Admittedly, the basic test of "but-for" causation comes somewhere near that but it does involve a hypothetical inquiry into what would have happened if the defendant had not been at fault and the answers to hypothetical questions can never be entirely certain; furthermore, there are cases in which it produces a result which offends our intuitive "common sense" or sense of justice and we abandon it. A good example is the situation discussed below where an agency for which the defendant is responsible may have been a cause of the harm but the claimant is unable to prove that it operated, rather than one or more identical agencies for which other persons were responsible. The real difficulties of

---

[8] Lord Bingham has said that it is "perhaps equally accurate to say that the . . . independent act forms no part of a chain of causation beginning with the tortfeasor's breach of duty": *Corr v IBC Vehicles Ltd* [2008] UKHL 13; [2008] A.C. 884 at 15.

[9] See also Lord Hoffmann's illustration of the theft of a car radio in *Environment Agency v Empress Car Co (Abertillery) Ltd* [1999] 2 A.C. 22 at 29, where he points out that the meaning of "cause", like that of most words, depends on the context in which it is used. While at the trial of the thief we would unhesitatingly say that his act caused the loss of the radio, the owner's spouse might also properly say, by way of complaint, that the owner's negligence in leaving it in the car had caused its loss. This is not to say, of course, that a negligent D can never be liable in tort for wilful harm inflicted by another: para.6–38, below. Where the defendant's liability is not based on fault we may create a defence of "act of a third party" but we are not consistent about this: compare paras 15–15 and 16–8, below.

[10] The usual distinction between "factual" and "legal" causation is criticised by Hoffmann, "Causation" (2005) 121 L.Q.R. 592. It is of course true that the requirements of the first are set by law as much as the second and sometimes we depart from "historical mechanics" but it is still the case that there are major practical differences between the issues considered in sections 2 and 3 of this chapter.

[11] "A value judgment ('*ought* to be held liable')": *Kuwait Airways Corp v Iraqi Airways Co (Nos 4 and 5)* [2002] UKHL 19; [2002] 2 A.C. 883 at [70] per Lord Nicholls; *Corr v IBC Vehicles Ltd* [2008] UKHL 13; [2008] A.C. 884 at 15.

terminology arise, however, at the second stage. Traditionally, English lawyers would probably have used the phrase "remoteness of damage" to describe this (though some would have continued to speak of our example of X and the shotgun in terms of causation[12]) and their American counterparts would have said that not only must the defendant's act have been a cause in fact of the damage, it must have been a "proximate cause". So in the wharf fire case we have referred to[13] we would say that the fire was "too remote" because it was unforeseeable and they would have said (assuming that they would have reached the same conclusion, for these things are not governed by precise, scientific laws) that the spilling of the oil on the water was not the "proximate cause" of the fire (for the same reason). To the layman, however, neither expression would seem very apt to describe the process of reasoning. The oil was dumped just across the bay from the site of the fire and while, admittedly, a couple of days passed before it ignited, the decision did not turn on this but upon the fact that the fire was unforeseeable.[14] Some would say that "proximate cause" is even worse because it is liable to produce confusion with the first stage and to give the erroneous impression that the defendant's act has to be the factor closest in time to the damage. This has led the American Law Institute in the draft *Third Restatement of Torts* to abandon "proximate cause" in favour of "scope of liability",[15] though the fact that old habits die hard has compelled it to use "proximate cause" in parentheses after the new expression.

There is no doubt that "scope of liability" is a better expression **6–5** than either remoteness or proximate cause because it immediately conveys the idea that we are concerned with setting limits to the defendant's responsibility after the first stage has been passed. It

---

[12] See, e.g. Staughton L.J. in *Wright v Lodge* [1993] 4 All E.R. 299 at 309 (which is plainly a case about whether the gross negligence of the second defendant broke the chain of causation): "Causation is not the same as remoteness of damage. Foreseeability may be a useful guide, but it is by no means the true criterion." See also the same judge in the context of contract in *Total Transport Corp v Arcadia Petroleum Ltd, The Times*, December 16, 1997: "the word 'remoteness' is often used to refer both to causation and to the question whether loss was foreseeable or within the reasonable contemplation of the parties. It was so used by Rix J. in the present case at [1996] 2 Lloyd's Rep. 423, following McGregor on *Damages* (1988), para.131. Without entering upon the rights and wrongs of the matter, I propose to use remoteness to describe only the issue whether loss is outside the scope of recovery because it was not within the reasonable contemplation of the parties."

[13] Para.6–2, above.

[14] All legal systems grapple with this sort of problem. "Remoteness" might be a more apt word to use in order to reject liability in the German case in [1952] N.J.W. 1010 (C suffered leg injury by D's fault in a traffic accident in 1936; claim based on C's having been killed in an artillery bombardment eight years later because he could not get to the bunker fast enough; however, the German court did not answer the question directly).

[15] Ch.6, proposed Final Draft, 2005. See also the *Principles of European Tort Law* (2005), which uses the same expression, though under the section heading of "Causation".

also accords very well with those cases where it has been held that the nature of the duty undertaken by the defendant limits the range of the consequences for which he is liable.[16] However, it may not quite accord with our natural way of thinking about some aspects of this area. Although it is perfectly clear that we accept that more than one act or event or condition may be the cause of a loss, there is something (perhaps the fact that the causation inquiry is, after all, concerned with attributing responsibility) that makes us link causation and responsibility and makes us look for *the* cause. To adapt a well-known example, if I set fire to a piece of paper and we ask what was the cause of the paper being burned, everyone would say, "He set fire to it". Not even a combustion engineer would also refer to the presence of oxygen in the air as a cause, though that is just as necessary a condition of the paper being burned as my striking the match. To go back again to X and the shotgun (though that is not such a clear-cut case) our notions of individual responsibility would lead us to say that X caused the claimant's death, not D or (which amounts to the same thing) that what X did overwhelms D's fault and renders it part of the history. To say that D's conduct was a cause in fact of the death but that wilful interventions by a third party to exploit a danger produced by D's conduct are not within the scope of D's potential liability produces the same result but perhaps looks "over-scientific" compared with using the language of "responsibility-causation".[17]

The variations in classification and terminology in this area were described by Lord Nicholls as follows:

"The law has to set a limit to the causally connected losses for which a defendant is to be held responsible. In the ordinary language of lawyers, losses outside the limit may bear one of several labels. They may be described as too remote because the wrongful conduct was not a substantial or proximate cause, or because the loss was the product of an intervening cause. The

---

[16] See para.6–27, below.
[17] The *Restatement 3d* deals with harm directly caused by an intervening act in s.34: "When . . . an independent act is also a factual cause of physical harm, an actor's liability is limited to those harms that result from the risks that made the actor's conduct tortious." Illustration 4 involves an unguarded excavation caused by D and X deliberately pushing C into the excavation and the conclusion is that it is for the factfinder (in practice there, the jury) to determine whether the appropriate characterisation of the harm to C "is falling into an unguarded excavation site or being deliberately pushed into an unguarded excavation site and, if the latter, whether it is among the risks that made [D] negligent." One cannot say that this is necessarily *inconsistent* with English law (remember that in our shotgun example D knew nothing of X's intentions) but it is likely that we would lean more firmly towards "no liability". Section 442B of *Restatement 2d* provided that an intervening criminal act insulated D from liability as a matter of law.

defendant's responsibility may be excluded because the plaintiff failed to mitigate his loss. Familiar principles, such as foreseeability, assist in promoting some consistency of general approach. These are guidelines, some more helpful than others, but they are never more than this."[18]

2. Causation in Fact

As a first—but not, it must be emphasised, conclusive—step it must   **6–6** be decided whether the defendant's breach of duty was, as a matter of fact, a cause of the damage. Although the question of factual causation has exercised philosophers and more than one approach is possible,[19] for the practical purposes of the law that most generally mentioned by the courts is the so-called "but-for" test, or in Latin, causa (or conditio) sine qua non.[20] If the result would not have happened but for a certain event then that event is a cause; contrariwise, if it would have happened anyway, the event is not a cause.[21] Of course this test will produce a multitude of causes which are not legally effective from the point of view of allocating responsibility,[22] but as has been emphasised above the but-for test merely acts as a preliminary filter to eliminate the irrelevant. The application of the but-for approach is neatly illustrated by *Barnett v Chelsea and Kensington Hospital Management Committee*.[23] The claimant's husband, a night watchman, called early in the morning at the defendants' hospital and complained of vomiting after drinking tea. He was told to go home and consult his own doctor later, which amounted to a breach of the hospital's duty of care. Later that day the claimant's husband died of arsenical poisoning and the coroner's verdict was of murder by persons unknown. The hospital's breach of

---

[18] *Kuwait Airways Corp v Iraqi Airways Co (Nos 4 and 5)* [2002] UKHL 19; [2002] 2 A.C. 883 at [70].

[19] Hart and Honoré, *Causation in the Law*, 2nd edn, Part I; Honoré, "Necessary and Sufficient Conditions in Tort Law" in Owen (ed.) *Philosophical Foundations of Tort Law* (1995).

[20] i.e. "a cause without which [the event would] not [have happened]". A legally effective cause is known as a *causa causans*.

[21] "Subject to the question of remoteness, causation is a question of fact. If the damage would not have happened but for the particular fault, then that fault is a cause of the damage; if it would have happened just the same, fault or no fault, the fault is not the cause of the damage. It is to be decided by the ordinary plain common sense of the business": *Cork v Kirby Maclean Ltd* [1952] 2 All E.R. 402 at 406.

[22] *Rahman v Arearose Ltd* [2001] Q.B. 351 at 367.

[23] [1969] 1 Q.B. 428. See also *Deloitte Haskins & Sells v National Mutual Life Nominees Ltd* [1993] A.C. 774 and *Chittock v Woodbridge School* [2002] EWCA Civ 915; [2003] P.I.Q.R. P6.

duty[24] was held not to be a cause of the death because, even if the deceased had been examined and treated with proper care, the probability was that it would have been impossible to save his life by the time he arrived at the hospital. The claimant's claim therefore failed.[25] However, despite the seemingly mechanical nature of the but-for approach, care must be taken to make the correct inquiry in the light of the nature of the tort in question. Thus the tort of conversion[26] protects a person's rights in his goods and any person who wrongfully takes them is treated as under a continuing duty to restore them or their value. If, therefore, D converts C's goods it is irrelevant that if he had not done so it is inevitable that they would have been converted instead by X.[27]

A. Multiple Causation

6–7   Although the but-for test is a useful rule of thumb,[28] its application leads to results which appear to defy common sense where there is more than one cause which alone would be sufficient to produce the result, as where A and B at the same moment inflict fatal injuries

---

[24] Even in a case of strict liability, care must be taken to determine the scope of the issue of causation. Thus under the Consumer Protection Act 1987 (see para.10–12, below) the defendant is strictly liable for damage caused by a defect in a product made by him, but this is not quite the same as being liable for damage caused by the defective product. To take the example of counsel in *A v National Blood Authority* [2001] 3 All E.R. 289 at 360, if a product is defective because it does not carry an adequate warning and the claimant is injured because, on the facts, he could not and would not have been able to heed a warning, the damage is not caused by the defect.

[25] See also *McWilliams v Sir William Arrol & Co Ltd* [1962] 1 W.L.R. 295, (death by falling; breach of employer's duty to provide safety harness; evidence showed that deceased would not have used it).

[26] Ch.17.

[27] *Kuwait Airways Corp v Iraqi Airways Co (Nos 4 and 5)* [2002] UKHL 19; [2002] 2 A.C. 883. So also if C's consent to a trespass to his person is obtained by a misrepresentation by D which is sufficient to vitiate C's consent, it is irrelevant that C would have consented had he known the truth: *Chatterton v Gerson* [1981] Q.B. 432. Trespass to the person is actionable per se, but it seems that the hypothetical issue is irrelevant even to a claim for actual damage suffered.

[28] "Although it often yields the right answer, [it] does not always do so": Lord Steyn in *Smith New Court Securities Ltd v Scrimgeour Vickers (Asset Management) Ltd* [1997] A.C. 254 at 285. "In very many cases this test operates satisfactorily, but it is not always a reliable guide": *Kuwait Airways Corp v Iraqi Airways Co (Nos 4 and 5)*, above, fn.27, at [83], per Lord Nicholls. However, the restrictions imposed on tort liability in Australia at the beginning of the century have affected the position there. Thus under the Civil Liability Act 2002 (NSW) s.5D(1) the negligence must be a necessary condition of the harm, subject to s.5D(2) under which, "in determining in an exceptional case, in accordance with established principles, whether negligence that cannot be established as a necessary condition of the occurrence of harm should be accepted as establishing factual causation, the court is to consider (amongst other relevant things) whether or not and why responsibility for the harm should be imposed on the negligent party." Whatever the qualification covers, it does not cover a case where action by the defendant *might* have prevented harm inflicted by a third party: *Adeels Palace Pty Ltd v Moubarak* [2009] HCA 48.

upon C.[29] In such a case, there is no doubt that, however we justify it,[30] each wrongdoer is liable in full for the loss, subject to the right of contribution against the other (a matter which does not concern the claimant).[31] The position is the same where the injury is produced by a combination of the defendant's tort and some innocent cause, as where the claimant contracted a lung condition from the combination of dust which the defendants had created in breach of safety regulations and other dust which was an inevitable accompaniment of the activity.[32] The same approach to multiple causes underlies the law where the claimant is partly to blame for his own loss, save that there the damages are reduced in proportion to his share of the blame.[33] In all these cases we can say that the defendant's act made a material[34] contribution to the claimant's loss and that is all that is required.[35] There may now be a greater willingness than in the past to accept that an injury is divisible and that a

---

[29] On one view of the facts *Roberts v J.W. Ward & Son* (1981) 126 S.J. 120 involved two errors by the defendants which were both fatal to the claimant's contract but only one of which was negligent. The CA said that in this event the defendants would not be allowed to set up their innocent error to escape the consequences of their negligence. Nor can a defendant say that his breach of duty A was not a cause of the claimant's injury because anyway he would have committed breach of duty B which would have had the same effect: *Bolitho v City and Hackney HA* [1997] A.C. 232 at 240. In *Beart v Prison Service* [2005] EWCA Civ 467 the defendant committed the statutory wrong of discrimination, which does give rise to damages for injury to health; it then unfairly dismissed the claimant, a wrong which does not give rise to such damages. It could not say that the second wrong broke the chain of causation in respect of consequences stemming from the first.

[30] See Wright, "Causation in Tort Law" (1985) 73 Cal. L.Rev 1735 and "Once More into the Bramble Bush: Duty, Causal Contribution, and the Extent of Legal Responsibility" (2001) 53 Vanderbilt L.R. 1071; Honoré, fn.19, above; Stapleton, "Unpacking Causation" in *Relating to Responsibility*, Cane and Gardner (eds) (2001).

[31] See Ch.21, below.

[32] *Bonnington Castings Ltd v Wardlaw* [1956] A.C. 613.

[33] See para.6–43, below. So if C contracts lung cancer and this was produced both by a toxic agent for which D is responsible and by C's smoking, C's damages are to be reduced but if the second agent is one for which C is not responsible he recovers in full.

[34] "More than negligible": *Bailey v MoD* [2008] EWCA Civ 883; [2009] 1 W.L.R. 1052 at [46]. See also *Thames Water Utilities Ltd v London Regional Transport* [2004] EWHC 2021 (TCC); 95 Con. L.R. 127 (fracture of water main; argument that very slight movement could have been produced at any time by other sources), where it is suggested that a "but-for" cause which was simply the straw that broke the camel's back is not legally effective. An alternative approach leading to much the same practical result in such a case might be to say that the defendant's liability is very small because of the vulnerability of the claimant's property.

[35] "If the defendant's breach has 'materially contributed' to the loss or damage suffered, it will be regarded as a cause of the loss or damage, despite other factors or conditions having played an even more significant role in producing the loss or damage. As long as the breach materially contributed to the damage, a causal connection will ordinarily exist even though the breach without more would not have brought about the damage.": *Henville v Walker* [2001] HCA 52; 206 CLR 459 at [106] per McHugh J; but it is a material contribution to the loss, not to the *risk* of the loss happening: *Clough v First Choice Holidays and Flights Ltd* [2006] EWCA Civ 15; [2006] P.I.Q.R. P22. *Bonnington Castings* is a case of a disease made worse by continuing exposure and where there could be no doubt that both sources of dust contributed. It does not fit so easily the case where the condition *might* have been triggered by either of two causes. In *Cookson v Novartis Grimsby Ltd* [2007] EWCA Civ 1261 the CA held that the judge had been entitled to prefer

defendant is liable to the claimant only for that portion of the harm that he caused and this is discussed in Ch.21. However, as a matter of principle no one denies that an indivisible loss may have two sufficient causes.

"While the law does not expect tortfeasors to pay for damage that they have not caused, it regards them as having caused damage to which they have materially contributed."[36]

One distinction must, however, be drawn between the case of two cumulative torts and that where there is a tort and some factor for which no one is to blame. Where A and B both inflict injuries on C and either would have been fatal, we are compelled to say that both caused the death because otherwise we would have the absurd result that neither did, but it seems that where the force generated by A's tort combines with a natural force which the evidence shows would in itself have been sufficient to cause all the damage,[37] A is not liable.[38]

It may be that the claimant is affected by two successive events or the act of the defendant precludes the operation of some other cause which would otherwise have taken effect. If D injures or kills C then it is of course obvious that C would have one day died anyway and the law therefore limits the damages recoverable by C or his dependants by reference to C's pre-accident life expectancy: if D kills a person who is very old or who is suffering from a terminal disease he is undoubtedly liable for the death, but the damages will be much

expert evidence that exposure to aromatic amines for which D was responsible was twice as likely to cause bladder cancer as C's smoking and that this amounted to proof on a balance of probabilities that the amines had caused it. There should have been no liability if the figures had been reversed. In *Amaca Pty Ltd v Ellis* [2010] HCA 5 the claim failed when the epidemiological evidence was that, despite the possibility of synergistic effect, the relative risk of developing the cancer from asbestos fibres was much lower than the relative risk from his smoking. "Knowing that inhaling asbestos *can* cause cancer does not entail that in this case it probably *did*": at [68]. See also para.6–9, below.

[36] *Dickins v O2 Plc* [2008] EWCA Civ 1144; [2009] I.R.L.R. 58 at [53] per Sedley L.J. Applied, "literally, or as if the two words ['but for'] embody the entire principle, the words can mislead. They may convey the impression that the claimant's claim for damages for personal injuries must fail unless he can prove that the defendant's negligence was the only, or the single, or even, chronologically the last cause of his injuries. The authorities demonstrate that such an impression would be incorrect": *Clough v First Choice Holidays* [2006] EWCA Civ 15; [2006] P.I.Q.R. P22 at [44].

[37] Cf. *Bailey v MoD* [2008] EWCA Civ 883; [2009] 1 W.L.R. 1052, where the judge was entitled on the evidence to conclude that the weakness leading to brain damage was the result of lack of care and other factors.

[38] *Bailey* at [46]. Compare *Anderson v Minneapolis etc Ry* 179 N.W. 45 (Minn 1920) (railway fire combining with natural fire; liable).

lower than they would be in the case of a young, healthy victim.[39] So also if D seriously injures C and, before C's action comes to a trial, C dies from some wholly unrelated cause, the damages payable by D will be limited to those representing the loss incurred before the death.[40] In other cases it may not be so easy to determine whether the later event obliterates the causative effect of the defendant's act.

In *Baker v Willoughby*,[41] as a result of the defendant's negligence, the claimant suffered an injury to his left leg and, taking both past and future losses into account, the judge assessed his damages, on the basis of full liability,[42] at £1,600. Before the trial, however, and while the claimant was working at a new job he had taken up after his accident, he was the victim of an armed robbery in the course of which he suffered gunshot wounds to his left leg of such severity that the leg had to be amputated. The defendant therefore argued that his liability was limited to the loss suffered before the date of the robbery: all loss suffered thereafter was merged in and flowed from the robbery.[43] This argument was rejected by the House of Lords because it produced a manifest injustice. Even if the robbers had been successfully sued to judgment,[44] they would only have been liable to the claimant for depriving him of an already damaged leg[45] and the claimant would therefore have been left uncompensated in the period after the robbery for the "difference" between a sound leg and a damaged one. The defendant's argument was said to contain a fallacy in its assertion that the injury to the leg was

---

[39] *Smith v Cawdle Fen Commissioners* [1938] 4 All E.R. 64 at 71; *Dillon v Twin State Gas and Electric Co* 163 A. 111 (N.H. 1932)..

[40] A well-known conundrum is the following: D injures C in a road accident while C is on the way to the airport, crippling him for life. The aircraft on which C was booked crashes, killing all on board. We cannot, without a degree of fiction, escape by saying that C might not have taken the flight, but there is a reluctance to accept that D escapes liability for losses after the notional death.

[41] [1970] A.C. 467.

[42] The claimant was 25 per cent contributorily negligent.

[43] Note that in a purely factual sense the accident was a cause of the injury in the robbery since the claimant changed his job as a result of the accident, but it could not possibly be contended that the defendant was liable in law for the shooting: *Carslogie SS Co Ltd v Royal Norwegian Government* [1952] A.C. 292, and para.6–35, below.

[44] The speeches do not disclose whether the claimant made any claim under the Criminal Injuries Compensation Scheme.

[45] *Performance Cars Ltd v Abraham* [1962] 1 Q.B. 33; *Baker v Willoughby* [1970] A.C. 467 at 495. An argument that the robbers would in theory be liable for the whole of the claimant's loss because they had reduced the value of his right of action against the defendant was rejected: at 496. Cf. *Griffiths v Commonwealth* (1983) 50 A.C.T.R. 7. However, an award of this nature was made in the fatal accident case of *Singh v Aitken* [1998] P.I.Q.R. Q37, though *Baker v Willoughby* is not mentioned in the judgment. In any event, to have held that the claimant had a complete remedy against the robbers would have brought him little comfort, though it would increase a criminal injuries compensation claim on such facts.

obliterated by the subsequent amputation because, as Lord Reid put it,[46] a person:

> "[I]s not compensated for the physical injury: he is compensated for the loss which he suffers as a result of the injury. His loss is not in having a stiff leg: it is his inability to lead a full life, his inability to enjoy those amenities which depend on freedom of movement and his inability to earn as much as he used to earn or could have earned if there had been no accident. In this case the second injury did not diminish any of these. So why should it be regarded as having obliterated or superseded them?"

In other words, the claimant's loss after the removal of the leg was regarded as having two concurrent causes, though it is clear that if the robbers had shot him dead the defendant's liability would not have extended beyond that point.[47]

6–8   The decision in *Baker v Willoughby* received a hard knock in *Jobling v Associated Dairies Ltd*.[48] The defendants' breach of duty caused the claimant to suffer injury to his back and this left him with a continuing disability. Three years later, and before trial, the claimant was diagnosed as suffering from a condition (myelopathy), unrelated to the accident and arising after the accident,[49] which of itself rendered him totally unfit for work. The defendants naturally contended that the onset of the myelopathy terminated the period in respect of which they were liable for the effects of the back injury; in reply, the claimant argued that the case should be governed by *Baker v Willoughby*. A unanimous House of Lords found for the defendants. The myelopathy was one of the "vicissitudes of life" for the chance of which the courts regularly made discounts in the assessment of damages for future loss of earnings[50] and it followed

---

[46] [1970] A.C. at 492.

[47] The robbers would (in theory) have been liable to his dependants under the Fatal Accidents Act, but the damages would take account of any reduction in earning capacity attributable to the accident. If the claimant had died of natural causes before the trial the liability of neither the defendant nor the robbers would have extended beyond that point.

[48] [1982] A.C. 794.

[49] It had been conceded that if the myelopathy had been existing but dormant at the time of the accident it would have to be taken into account in assessing damages.

[50] See Ch.22, below. If the case had come on quickly or been settled without anyone knowing about the impending illness then recovery for the injury would of course have been much more substantial and the matter could not have been reopened. See also *Dudarec v Andrews* [2006] EWCA Civ 256; [2006] 1 W.L.R. 3002; *Whitehead v Searle* [2008] EWCA Civ 285; [2009] 1 W.L.R. 549 where alleged negligence caused the delay of settlement of an action for support of a child. Had the matter been dealt with promptly liability would have been on the basis of lifetime care but in fact the claimant unexpectedly died, cutting short her responsibility. The CA held that the "actual truth" that the death had curtailed the loss must prevail over the "hypothetical truth" that would have been assumed at the time of prompt settlement.

inevitably that it must be taken into account in full when it had actually occurred before the trial.

"When the supervening illness or injury which is the independent cause of the loss of earning capacity has manifested itself before trial, the event has demonstrated that, even if the plaintiff had never sustained the tortious injury, his earnings would now be reduced or extinguished. To hold the tortfeasor, in this situation, liable to pay damages for a notional continuing loss of earnings attributable to the tortious injury, is to put the plaintiff in a better position than he would be in if he had never suffered the tortious injury."[51]

This approach is totally inconsistent with the theory of the concurrent effect of consecutive causes advanced in *Baker v Willoughby*[52] and that case can no longer be regarded as a general authority on causation.[53] How far it is an authority on successive *tortious* injuries is less clear. Lord Russell was prepared to suggest that it might have been correctly decided on the basis that a subsequent tortious injury was not to be regarded as within the "vicissitudes" principle, and hence should not be regarded as removing the effects of the first injury,[54] and Lord Keith, though not for the same reasons, drew a distinction between tortious and non-tortious injuries.[55] However, Lord Bridge, while recognising the force of the argument that the claimant should not be under-compensated by reason of the chance that he is the victim of two torts rather than one, pointed out that the distinction between tortious and non-tortious causes was implicitly rejected in *Baker*.[56] It would be a fiction to say that a second tortious injury was necessarily more

---

[51] [1982] A.C. at 820 per Lord Bridge.

[52] Is it also inconsistent with the proposition that simultaneous sufficient causes may have concurrent effect? But there is no sign in *Jobling* that anyone intended anything so revolutionary.

[53] [1982] A.C. at 802, 809, 815, 821. However, in *Rahman v Arearose Ltd* [2001] Q.B. 351 at 367 Laws L.J. saw "no inconsistency whatever between the two cases", though the matter was not pursued.

[54] [1982] A.C. at 810. See also *Penner v Mitchell* [1978] 4 W.W.R. 328.

[55] [1982] A.C. at 815.

[56] [1982] A.C. at 819. Lord Edmund Davies would seem to have agreed with Lord Bridge, for he said that he could "formulate no convincing juristic or logical principles supportive of the decision" in *Baker*. Lord Wilberforce in *Jobling* paid a good deal of attention to the fact that compensation is not merely a matter of tort damages and that the claimant's position with regard to other sources of money may determine whether he is under-or over-compensated. With respect, however, this is the general problem of offsets and deductions of collateral benefits (Ch.22 below) and raises no more issues in multiple causation cases than in those where the issue of causation is clear.

318 Negligence: Causation, Remoteness (Scope of Liability) etc

unlikely than an illness: in the case of a police officer, for example, it might be a good deal more likely.[57]

The illness in *Jobling* was not produced by the initial injury. If it had been the defendant might have been liable for it if the requirements of remoteness had been satisfied. So in *Corr v I.B.C. Vehicles*[58] the defendants were liable for the suicide of the victim of the accident brought about by depression induced by the initial injury, whereas if he had died in, say, a road accident before trial that would have terminated the period during which the defendant would have been liable to his family for loss of support. Equally if he had failed in his suicide attempt and had suffered further injuries the defendant would have been liable to him for those. However, in *Gray v Thames Trains*[59] the defendants were not liable for the detention of the claimant following a conviction for an offence of manslaughter brought about by the effect on him of the initial accident. That was because of two related principles of public policy, first that to award the claimant damages would be for the civil court to act inconsistently with the decision of the criminal court that he was responsible for his actions and secondly that the defendant's act is not to be regarded in law as the cause of an act for which the claimant is criminally responsible.[60]

B. Proof, Uncertainty and Causation

6–9   **i. What happened?** In the cases we have considered so far we have essentially been concerned with what the outcome for the claimant would have been had it not been for the defendant's tort

---

[57] It is hard to see the justification for dissecting the "accident" side of life's vicissitudes but not the "illness" side. In *Heil v Rankin* [2001] P.I.Q.R. Q16 (not to be confused with the case of the same name [2001] Q.B. 272 on damages for non-pecuniary loss, para.22–22, below) the CA held that the claimant's damages against the defendant were to be reduced to take account of the fact that some other incident might have occurred which would have triggered an aggravation of the claimant's low grade PTSD condition and rendered him incapable of continuing in the police service. *Baker v Willoughby* was explained as a case where it was necessary to ignore the *occurrence* of the second tort to prevent the claimant being caught between the two propositions that (a) the first tortfeasor could argue that the damage inflicted by him was now to be attributed to another cause and (b) the second tortfeasor could argue that he took the devalued claimant as he found him. That was necessary to avoid under-compensation, whereas in *Heil* to ignore the risk of future disabling tortious conduct would lead to over-compensation. These matters are clearly to be decided on the basis of pragmatism rather than logic but from an intuitive point of view it looks odd to ignore what we know has happened and take into account what might have happened.
[58] [2008] UKHL 13; [2008] A.C. 884, para.6–41, below.
[59] [2009] UKHL 33.
[60] See further para.25–20, below.

and we have assumed that we can determine the answer to that question. We return later to the position where there is uncertainty about that, but there may, of course, be a preliminary question of whether what the defendant did had any impact on the claimant at all, as in the classic case of the two hunters who fire simultaneously in the claimant's direction and one bullet hits him but it cannot be shown which. According to traditional principles the claimant fails since he cannot prove on a balance of probabilities[61] that either of them shot him,[62] but the law is no longer as simple as that.

The problem of proof of causation is particularly acute in disease cases, particularly those arising from asbestos, now very frequent in the employment context.[63] Even bearing in mind that the defendant's wrong need not have been the sole cause of the claimant's condition, it being enough that it made a material contribution to it,[64] the court is concerned with causation in the particular case, whereas epidemiological evidence, which is likely to be critical in these cases, can speak only in terms of the increase in risk which has been found to apply taking known[65] relevant factors into account. It has been said that if the claimant proves a doubling of the risk from the agent for which the defendant is responsible he has succeeded in proving causation in the traditional sense[66] but the claimant may not be in a position to pass even that threshold. In *Fairchild v Glenhaven Funeral Services Ltd*[67] the essential facts may be summarised[68] by saying that the claimant worked for differing periods for a number of employers, each of whom exposed him, in breach of duty, to asbestos dust. He contracted a mesothelioma as a result of the exposure.[69] The evidence before the court (which may not accord

---

[61] It has been said that, "where only two possibilities are under consideration, both of which seem unlikely, if one seems much less likely than the other the less likely can be discounted thus making the first likely to happen on the balance on probabilities": *Kiani v Land Rover Ltd* [2006] EWCA Civ 880 at [30].

[62] *Cook v Lewis* 1951] S.C.R. 830. But the Canadian court held the opposite on the basis that where two defendants have committed acts of negligence in circumstances that deprive the claimant of the ability to prove which of them caused his damage, the burden is cast upon each of the defendants to exculpate himself, and if both fail to discharge this burden, then both are liable.

[63] The problem is by no means confined to he workplace: many schools and public buildings contained large quantities of asbestos: see *Willmore v Knowsley MBC* [2009] EWCA Civ 1211.

[64] Diseases often have multiple causes. See Coggon and Taylor, "Causation and Attribution of Diseases in Personal Injury Cases: A Scientific Perspective" [2009] J.P.I. Law 12.

[65] Some factors may be unknown or even unknowable: [2009] J.P.I. Law 12 at 14.

[66] *Sienkiewicz v Greif (UK) Ltd* [2009] EWCA Civ 1159; [2010] 2 W.L.R. 951 at [23], applying *Cookson v Novartis Grimsby Ltd* [2007] EWCA Civ 1261.

[67] [2002] UKHL 22; [2003] 1 A.C. 32.

[68] There were three appeals, which differed in many matters of detail.

[69] There was no doubt about this since the disease is very rare and those occupationally exposed have a 1,000 times greater incidence than the general population.

with current opinion,[70] but we have to consider the case on the basis on which it was decided) was that whereas asbestosis is influenced by the total amount of dust inhaled, a mesothelioma may be produced by the inhalation of a single fibre, though the risk of contracting it is increased by constant exposure. It was, therefore, scientifically impossible to identify the source of the fibre or fibres which had produced the tumour. Nevertheless, the House of Lords held that the claimant was entitled to succeed. As Lord Nicholls put it:

> "Any other outcome would be deeply offensive to instinctive notions of what justice requires and fairness demands. The real difficulty lies in elucidating in sufficiently specific terms the principle being applied in reaching this conclusion. To be acceptable the law must be coherent. It must be principled. The basis on which one case, or one type of case, is distinguished from another should be transparent and capable of identification. When a decision departs from principles normally applied, the basis for doing so must be rational and justifiable if the decision is to avoid the reproach that hard cases make bad law."[71]

The starting point was the decision in *McGhee v NCB*,[72] where the pursuer developed dermatitis and alleged that it had been caused by the defenders' failure to provide washing facilities at the workplace. The defenders admitted negligence in failing to provide these facilities but medical knowledge about the causes of dermatitis was such that it was not possible to say that had washing facilities been provided the pursuer would have escaped the disease. All that could be said was that the defenders' failure had materially increased the risk of dermatitis but no figure could be put on that contribution to the risk. On these facts the pursuer was held entitled to succeed in the absence of proof by the defenders that their breach of duty was not causative and there seems little doubt that the decision was motivated as much by policy as by logic for, as Lord Wilberforce candidly said:

> "[I]f one asks which of the parties, the workman or the employers, should suffer from this inherent evidential difficulty, the answer as a matter of policy or justice should be that it is the creator of the risk who, ex hypothesi, must be taken to have

---

[70] See para.6–11, below.
[71] At [36].
[72] [1973] 1 W.L.R. 1.

foreseen the possibility of damage, who should bear its consequences."[73]

In *Fairchild* the case was said to be more than a "robust and pragmatic" decision that it was legitimate to infer from the primary facts that the defenders' breach of duty probably made some contribution to the development of the disease[74] but to stand for the proposition that proof of a material increase in a risk could be sufficient to satisfy the causal requirements for liability:

"[I]n the particular circumstances, a breach of duty which materially increased the risk[75] [of the disease] should be treated *as if* it had materially contributed to the disease".[76]

Lord Bingham stated six conditions which must be satisfied to attract the principle[77]:

"(1) C was employed at different times and for differing periods by both A and B, and (2) A and B were both subject to a duty to take reasonable care or to take all practicable measures to prevent C inhaling asbestos dust because of the known risk that asbestos dust (if inhaled) might cause a mesothelioma, and (3) both A and B were in breach of that duty in relation to C during the periods of C's employment by each of them with the result that during both periods C inhaled excessive quantities of asbestos dust, and (4) C is found to be suffering from a mesothelioma, and (5) any cause of C's mesothelioma other than the inhalation of asbestos dust at work can be effectively discounted, but (6) C cannot (because of the current limits of human science) prove, on the balance of probabilities, that his mesothelioma was the result of his inhaling asbestos dust during his employment by A or during his employment by B or during his employment by A and B taken together."

However, Lord Bingham was speaking in the context of the facts of the case and he did not deny that the matter was capable of

[73] [1973] 1 W.L.R. at 6.
[74] Its description in *Wilsher v Essex Area Health Authority* [1988] A.C. at 1090 per Lord Bridge. See also *Freidin v St Laurent* [2007] VSCA 16 (if the defendant's negligence did increase the risk of the consequence the trier of fact may be *entitled* to conclude that it probably did cause it).
[75] Compare *Wootton v J.Docter Ltd* [2008] EWCA Civ 1361 (no increase in risk).
[76] [2002] UKHL 22; [2003] 1 A.C. 32 at [65] per Lord Hoffmann.
[77] At [2] and [34].

"incremental and analogical development".[78] For example, although occupational disease is by far the most likely situation to raise the problem, there seems no reason why the principle should be confined to employment[79]; nor, given the reliance on *McGhee*, where there was only one defendant responsible for the dust which caused the injury (though he was not at fault with regard to the mere presence of that in the workplace), can it be applicable only to cases of multiple tortfeasors. So in *Barker v Corus (UK) Ltd*[80] the House of Lords applied *Fairchild* to a case where the claimant had been exposed to asbestos dust as a result of breach of duty by the employer-defendant but had also been exposed by his own neglect of precautions during a period of self-employment. As Lord Hoffmann put it:

> "The purpose of the *Fairchild* exception is to provide a cause of action against a defendant who has materially increased the risk that the claimant will suffer damage and may have caused that damage, but cannot be proved to have done so because it is impossible to show, on a balance of probability, that some other exposure to the same risk may not have caused it instead. For this purpose, it should be irrelevant whether the other exposure was tortious or non-tortious, by natural causes or human agency or by

---

[78] Cf. the more general formulation of Lord Rodger at [170]:
"First, the principle is designed to resolve the difficulty that arises where it is inherently impossible for the claimant to prove exactly how his injury was caused. It applies, therefore, where the claimant has proved all that he possibly can, but the causal link could only ever be established by scientific investigation and the current state of the relevant science leaves it uncertain exactly how the injury was caused and, so, who caused it . . . . Secondly, part of the underlying rationale of the principle is that the defendant's wrongdoing has materially increased the risk that the claimant will suffer injury. It is therefore essential not just that the defendant's conduct created a material risk of injury to a class of persons but that it actually created a material risk of injury to the claimant himself. Thirdly, it follows that the defendant's conduct must have been capable of causing the claimant's injury. Fourthly, the claimant must prove that his injury was caused by the eventuation of the kind of risk created by the defendant's wrongdoing . . . . By contrast, the principle does not apply where the claimant has merely proved that his injury could have been caused by a number of different events, only one of which is the eventuation of the risk created by the defendant's wrongful act or omission . . . . Fifthly, this will usually mean that the claimant must prove that his injury was caused, if not by exactly the same agency as was involved in the defendant's wrongdoing, at least by an agency that operated in substantially the same way. A possible example would be where a workman suffered injury from exposure to dusts coming from two sources, the dusts being particles of different substances each of which, however, could have caused his injury in the same way . . . . Sixthly, the principle applies where the other possible source of the claimant's injury is a similar wrongful act or omission of another person, but it can also apply where, as in *McGhee*, the other possible source of the injury is a similar, but lawful, act or omission of the same defendant."
[79] One defendant in one of the actions was sued as an occupier. Presumably it should apply to the "two hunters" case, above, though cf. Lord Walker in *Barker v Corus*, below, fn.80, at [114].
[80] [2006] UKHL 20; [2006] 2 A.C. 572.

the claimant himself. These distinctions may be relevant to whether and to whom responsibility can also be attributed, but from the point of view of satisfying the requirement of a sufficient causal link between the defendant's conduct and the claimant's injury, they should not matter."[81]

Of course if we extend the scope of *Fairchild* to cases where an exposure by one person is non-tortious or arises from natural causes we have to accept that the injustice which prompted the decision to some extent "loses its edge"[82] for it is no longer the case that we can say "This harm *must* have been caused by defendant A or defendant B, even though we cannot determine which it was."

The *Fairchild* principle is not, however, a recipe for the relaxation **6–10** of the usual standards of proof wherever the claimant faces evidentiary difficulties on causation,[83] for the House of Lords approved its decision in *Wilsher v Essex Area Health Authority*.[84] The claimant, born prematurely, succumbed to RLF, a retinal condition causing serious damage to his sight. A possible cause, or contributing cause, of this was an excess of oxygen caused by a mistaken placing of a catheter[85] but the conflicting expert evidence at the trial identified a number of other possible causes which were not attributable to the fault of the defendants and the failure of the trial judge to find that the mistake was more likely as a cause than these others[86] meant that there had to be a retrial on the causation issue. Here there were a number of different agents operating in entirely different ways. Although the point was not in issue both Lord Scott and Lord Walker in *Barker v Corus* took the view that *Fairchild* was confined to "single agent" cases.[87] Lord Hoffmann in *Fairchild* would seem to go marginally further:

"What if [the claimant] had been exposed to two different agents —asbestos dust and some other dust—both of which created a material risk of the same cancer and it was equally impossible to

---

[81] At [17]. Lord Rodger at [97] accepted that his reservation of opinion in *Fairchild* at [170] on the case where one exposure was non-tortious was too cautious.

[82] Lord Walker at [117].

[83] *Clough v First Choice Holidays and Flights Ltd* [2006] EWCA Civ 15; [2006] P.I.Q.R. P22 (unexceptional accident arising from single incident). Nor of course does it assist the claimant in establishing a breach of duty: *Brett v University of Reading* [2007] EWCA Civ 88.

[84] [1988] A.C. 1074.

[85] A further point on breach of duty is discussed in the Court of Appeal but not dealt with by the House of Lords: para.5–79, above.

[86] Indeed, he had placed the onus squarely onto the defendants to show that it was probably not a cause.

[87] [2006] UKHL 20; [2006] 2 A.C. 572 at [64] and [114].

say which had caused the fatal cell mutation? I cannot see why this should make a difference."[88]

Even where there is only a single agent at work it does not follow that the *Fairchild* principle will apply. In *Hull v Sanderson*[89] the claimant worked for the defendant as a turkey packer and contracted campylobacter enteritis from contact with turkeys. The negligence established against the defendant was failure to warn the claimant of the risk of touching her mouth without thorough washing after handling carcases. However, on the evidence it was possible that the claimant, even if warned, might have inadvertently touched her mouth while working or might have picked up the infection on her hands from a surface which could not practicably have been rendered sterile. It would have been open to the judge to make findings of fact that if the claimant had been warned of the risk she would have taken enough care to avoid touching her mouth or that contamination from another surface was unlikely but he had not done so. In the circumstances it was not the sort of case, at which *Fairchild* was aimed, where it was "scientifically impossible" to establish the likely cause and the judge should not have fallen back on the principle as a way avoiding making such findings.[90]

Furthermore, the *Fairchild* principle does not impose liability merely for contribution to creation of a risk, there must be an injury which eventuates from that risk: if D exposes C to a toxic agent C's cause of action is generally not complete until the agent affects C's physical health,[91] though he may be able to sue if he foreseeably suffers a psychiatric disorder from fear of the risk.[92]

6–11   The *Fairchild* appeals were conducted on the basis that if the defendants before the court were liable at all, each was liable for all the damage suffered by the claimant in accordance with the normal rule about contributing causes of indivisible injuries (joint and several liability).[93] Each defendant is, of course, entitled to seek contribution from any other persons liable (whether they have been sued by the claimant or not)[94] but under the normal rule the claimant

---

[88] At [71]. See also Lord Rodger's reference to "an agency that operated in substantially the same way".

[89] [2008] EWCA Civ 1211.

[90] Compare *Sienkiewicz v Greif (UK) Ltd* [2009] EWCA Civ 1159; [2010] 2 W.L.R. 951.

[91] An insurer under the standard forms of employers' liability policy must pay if a successful suit is eventually brought if it was on risk at the time fibres were inhaled: *Durham v BAI (Run Off) Ltd* [2008] EWHC 2692 (QB) (which is a mine of information on insurance and the history of employers' liability).

[92] *Rothwell v Chemical and Insulating Co Ltd* [2007] UKHL 39; [2008] A.C. 281, para.5–64, above.

[93] See para.21–1, below.

[94] See para.21–3, below.

is entitled to enforce the whole judgment against any of them and in cases of this type, where breaches of duty may be spread over decades, there must be a high risk of some tortfeasors having gone into liquidation or no longer having effective insurance cover, rendering the right of contribution of a solvent defendant futile. Where *Fairchild* is applied the court is in effect making a defendant liable even though on a balance of probabilities he did *not* cause harm to the claimant and therefore when this issue was squarely raised in *Barker v Corus (UK)* the majority of the House of Lords departed from the normal rule and imposed "proportionate" liability, that is to say liability based in amount on the extent to which the defendant contributed to the risk of the harm. If there would be unfairness in sending the claimant away empty-handed in such a case because he cannot establish causation on a balance of probabilities, there would be a countervailing unfairness in applying the ordinary rule of joint and several liability. In practice, in an employment disease case, the starting point (though not necessarily the finishing point) in apportioning liability is likely to be the periods of time to which each employer exposed the claimant to the noxious agent. In *Barker* itself the Court of Appeal had dealt with the period when the claimant had exposed himself to asbestos during self-employment by making a reduction for contributory negligence; on the approach taken by the House of Lords this is unnecessary because the defendant is simply not liable in respect of the increase in risk caused by the self-exposure, though on the facts the final result is much the same.[95]

Lord Rodger dissented in *Barker* and the basis of the disagreement is the interpretation of what *Fairchild* decided. In Lord Rodger's view *Fairchild* decided that by showing that the defendant materially increased the *risk* of the disease he had in effect shown that the defendant had made a material contribution to it and the normal rule should apply. In the view of the majority, however, *Fairchild* proceeded on the different basis that the claimant had failed to prove causation of harm but succeeded on the different basis that he had shown a material increase in the risk of his succumbing to the disease. In any event, Parliament's view of what is fair does not accord with that of the House of Lords and the decision in *Barker* was swiftly reversed (and with retrospective effect, so as to apply to cases which had not come to judgment or been settled) by s. 3 of the Compensation Act 2006 so that in claims for mesothelioma induced by exposure to asbestos where the defendant is found liable on the basis of *Fairchild* the rule of joint and

---

[95] The results produced by the two approaches would be different if the self-exposure had not been blameworthy.

several liability applies again.[96] However, the Act has no effect at all on any other type of damage to which the *Fairchild* principle is held to apply.[97] It seems that the proposition that mesothelioma may be contracted from ingestion of a single fibre is now discredited in medical circles,[98] which may be regarded as lending some support to the application of the ordinary rule of joint and several liability (though it may be noted that there has been some shift towards apportioned liability in the context of other asbestos related conditions where it has always accepted that the causative effect was cumulative).[99]

6–12   **ii. What would have happened?** As we have seen, the "but-for" approach involves a hypothetical inquiry into what the situation would have been if the defendant had not committed a tort. This is not really a matter of historical fact like "when did the accident occur?" or "how fast was the defendant going?"; but the basic approach is to treat it in the same way for purpoes of proof. The burden of proving that the harm would not have occurred if the tort had not been committed rests, as a general rule, upon the claimant.[100] If he succeeds in showing this on a balance of probabilities then the hypothetical non-occurrence of the harm is treated as being conclusively established even though there may be a substantial chance that it would have happened just the same; and the claimant recovers all the damages flowing from the wrong, not a proportion of them discounted by that chance.[101] We must contrast with this the issue of what may happen in the future, or what would have

---

[96] Hence on facts like *Barker*, where there is self-exposure, we revert to making a reduction for contributory negligence. The Act applies to mesothelioma claims in general, even though *Fairchild* was a case where it was impossible for the claimant to show the sort of doubling of the risk that now seems to be regarded as sufficient proof of traditional causation (para.6–9, above): *Sienkiewicz v Greif (UK) Ltd* [2009] EWCA Civ 1159; [2010] 2 W.L.R. 951. However, it remains the law that to make the defendant liable there must be a *material* increase in the risk by reason of his actions, something more than de minimis: *Cox v Rolls Royce Industrial Power (India) Ltd* [2007] EWCA Civ 1189. Nevertheless, provided the exposure is not of very short duration, it may be that a level not very much more than that found in the air and the general environment will do: see *Willmore v Knowsley MBC* [2009] EWCA Civ 1211. The Compensation Act 2006 (Contribution for Mesothelioma Claims) Regulations SI 2006/3259 allow an insurer who is held liable in full to make a claim against the Financial Services Compensation Scheme.

[97] Burton J. in *Durham v BAI (Run Off) Ltd* [2008] EWHC 2692 (QB) at [54] remarked that we could be said to have a special "mesothelioma jurisprudence".

[98] [2008] EWHC 2692 (QB) at [31].

[99] See para.21–1, below.

[100] "There is no inherent uncertainty about what caused something to happen in the past or about whether something which happened in the past will cause something to happen in the future. Everything is determined by causality. What we lack is knowledge and the law deals with lack of knowledge by the concept of the burden of proof.": *Gregg v Scott* [2005] UKHL 2; [2005] 2 A.C. 176 at [79] per Lord Hoffmann.

[101] For an example see *Athey v Leonati* (1996) 140 D.L.R. (4th) 235 (road accident: claimant having history of back trouble; subsequently developed herniated disc; trial judge's finding interpreted as meaning that the accident made a 25 per cent causal contribution to the

happened in the future had it not been for the defendant's wrong, both of which have obvious relevance to the quantification of the claimant's damages. Here the balance of probabilities is irrelevant and:

"[T]he court must make an estimate as to what are the chances that a particular thing will or would have happened and reflect those chances, whether they are more or less than even, in the amount of damages which it awards".[102]

In such cases, where proof:

"[I]s necessarily unattainable, it would be unfair to treat as certain a prediction which has a 51 per cent probability of occurring, but to ignore altogether a prediction which has a 49 per cent probability of occurring".[103]

The general "vicissitudes of life" are usually simply allowed for in the general discount on damages which also takes account of the fact that if the claimant will be receiving a lump sum that will generate income[104] but if there is evidence that the claimant was in some way at greater risk of loss from some other cause (for example if he has a weak heart or is in insecure employment) the discount may be greater. Equally, the damages may in a suitable case be increased to allow for contingencies[105]—for example it has been commonplace in cases of head injury to award something for the risk that epilepsy may develop.[106] If, however, the claimant fails to show on a balance of probabilities that the harm was caused by the defendant's tort he recovers nothing, even though there may be a possibility that it was.

This issue has figured prominently in medical negligence cases. A doctor owes a patient a duty to inform him of significant risks attached to treatment.[107] If he fails to do so and the patient can show that he would not have consented to the treatment if he had been told

---

herniation; claimant recovered in full; had the finding meant that there was a 25 per cent chance that the accident made a causal contribution to the herniation, claimant would have failed).

[102] *Mallet v McMonagle* [1970] A.C. 166 at 176 per Lord Diplock.

[103] *Malec v J.C. Hutton Pty Ltd* (1990) 92 A.L.R. 545 at 549.

[104] See para.22–26, below.

[105] For an example of very difficult facts see *Langford v Hebran* [2001] P.I.Q.R. Q13 (career prospects of kick-boxer).

[106] Though since the Administration of Justice Act 1982 such a case would probably be more suitable for the award of provisional damages: para.22–23, below. Periodical payments awards can help with the "what will happen" problem but not the "what would have happened" one: para.22–26, below.

[107] See para.25–3, below.

then the doctor is liable for adverse effects relating to the failure to warn even though the treatment has been carried out with all due care and skill. In *Chester v Afshar*[108] the defendant, in breach of duty, failed to warn the claimant of a 1 or 2 per cent unavoidable risk of cauda equina syndrome in surgery on her spinal column and this eventuated. The trial judge found that if the claimant had been properly warned the operation would not have taken place when it did but he was unable to find whether if the claimant had been duly warned she would, after further medical advice, have given or refused consent to surgery at some later date. If she had so consented the risk would have been the same because it was a random one, not related to any known feature of the method of performing the surgery. A majority of the House of Lords held that she was entitled to recover damages in respect of the worsening of her position by the adverse outcome. One might have thought that this result was a simple, straightforward application of the standard combination of "but-for" causation and proof on a balance of probabilities.[109] There was a finding of fact that if she had been informed she would not have had the surgery on that day, the adverse outcome was exactly within the risk about which the defendant had failed to warn her and even if it could have been positively shown that she would have had it on another day a random risk of 1 or 2 per cent would have come nowhere near establishing that the adverse outcome would have been suffered on the later occasion: if I win on particular number at the casino on Monday that does not make it likely that I would win on the same number on the following Tuesday.[110] Nevertheless, even the majority of the court who found in the claimant's favour felt compelled to say that they were modifying the standard principles of causation, albeit in a "narrow and modest"[111] way, in order to vindicate the claimant's autonomy, her freedom to make an informed choice over the treatment she was to receive.[112] Although there is no doubt that in a "historical" sense the failure to warn was a cause of the injury, the reason for the failure on the traditional test seems to have been that the court regarded the defendant's breach of duty as exposing the claimant to

---

[108] [2004] UKHL 41; [2005] 1 A.C. 345. See also *Chappel v Hart* (1998) 195 CLR 232 and *Elbourne v Gibbs* [2006] NSWCA 127.

[109] As the CA had held: [2002] EWCA Civ 724; [2003] Q.B. 356 at [40].

[110] Cf. Lord Hoffmann's use of the roulette analogy to the opposite effect at [31].

[111] Lord Steyn at [24].

[112] This right goes unvindicated where the evidence shows that she would have gone ahead there and then even if she had been informed. Is it enough to say that the matter was not important to her? Cf. *Rees v Darlington Memorial Hospital NHS Trust* [2003] UKHL 52; [2004] 1 A.C. 309 (para.24–15, below) where, in a different context, the award of a fixed, conventional sum was regarded as the proper way to deal with the violation of the right to autonomy.

the *risk* of the injury and that was in no way increased on the later occasion when she underwent the treatment.[113]

iii. Loss of a chance. An attempt to apply the same approach to causation as is applied to quantification (i.e. assessment of the chance rather than all-or-nothing balance of probabilities) was rejected by the House of Lords in *Hotson v East Berkshire Health Authority*.[114] The defendants failed correctly to diagnose the claimant's condition after a fall and there developed a serious disability of the hip joint. On the facts there was, statistically, a 75 per cent risk that this disability would have developed even if the claimant had been treated properly[115] but the trial judge (and the Court of Appeal) held that he was entitled to damages representing 25 per cent of his full loss. This was reversed by the House of Lords: the judge's findings of fact amounted to a conclusion that on a balance of probabilities the disability would have occurred anyway and that the fall was therefore the sole cause of the loss. On this basis there was no foundation for awarding damages for loss of the chance of recovery.[116] As we have seen, had the claimant shown on a slight balance of probability that he would have been cured if given proper treatment, then he would have recovered his damages in full.

The issue was revisited in *Gregg v Scott*.[117] There was a blameworthy delay in the diagnosis of the claimant's cancer and when treatment began he had (in similar statistical terms to those in *Hotson*) only a 25 per cent chance of recovery, whereas if it had been diagnosed promptly his chance would have been 42 per cent. Even on the latter assumption it was still more likely than not that he would not have survived with treatment. The majority of the

6–13

---

[113] In other words, the case is like *Carslogie SS Co Ltd v Royal Norwegian Government* [1952] A.C. 292, para.6–35, below.

[114] [1987] A.C. 750. On this case and its ramifications, see Stapleton, "The Gist of Negligence, Part II" (1988) 104 L.Q.R. 389.

[115] To say that the claimant had such a chance is a considerable over-simplification. It seems to have represented a conclusion that of a sample of 100 people with a similar injury 25 would have recovered with prompt treatment, but the precise degree of blood vessel damage suffered by C before he entered the hospital was not known, nor will the figure be known for any of the sample. Some of the 100 would inevitably have suffered the disability whatever was done and the claimant might have been one of those. The point is made by Lord Mackay in *Hotson*. In principle one must look at the chances of this individual claimant rather than the statistical group (*Wardlaw v Farrar* [2003] EWCA Civ 1719; [2004] P.I.Q.R. P19) but how far one can dissociate the two in practice must be debatable.

[116] It will be observed that there is some difficulty in drawing the line between the two categories of case. If C is killed by D and it is shown that C had a weak heart, C's dependants will recover damages but they will be less than if C had been fit. Yet the question is a hypothetical one of the same general nature as that in *Hotson*: what would have happened to the victim but for D's wrong? The only difference appears to be that in *Hotson* the claimant is unable to show any loss at all, whereas in our example his difficulty will lie in being able to show how long the loss would have lasted.

[117] [2005] UKHL 2; [2005] 2 A.C. 176.

House of Lords rejected his claim that the delay in treatment had caused the damage of which he complained. The case was different from *Hotson* in that the immediate spread of the cancer would probably not have occurred had there been prompt diagnosis[118] but the basis of the claim was that the claimant had been deprived of the chance of a *cure*. It also differed from *Hotson* in the fact that in that case the outcome was predetermined by the (unknown) amount of blood vessel damage which had been caused by the fall (so that, strictly speaking, the question of loss of a chance was never before the court) whereas now the developments which reduced his life expectancy were subsequent to the negligence. Nevertheless, for Lord Hoffmann and Baroness Hale the claim was an attempt to reformulate the basis of the law in terms of lost chances rather than causal outcomes and should be rejected.

> "In effect, the appellant submits that the exceptional rule in *Fairchild*'s case should be generalised and damages awarded in all cases in which the defendant may have caused an injury and has increased the likelihood of the injury being suffered."[119]

Among the minority, Lord Nicholls would have allowed recovery based upon the loss of a chance in those cases of medical negligence relating to the treatment of an existing illness[120] where there was significant uncertainty about the outcome at the time of the negligence.[121] However, as we have seen in connection with *Fairchild*, it is difficult for the common law to create and maintain special pockets of causation rules for particular types of litigation.[122] Although Lord Hope agreed with Lord Nicholls, the emphasis in his speech seems to be on the view that this was really a case of a proved physical injury (the enlargement of the tumour) which simply had to be *quantified*.[123] The claim:

> "[I]s, in essence, a claim for the loss and damage caused by the enlargement of the tumour due to the delay in diagnosis. It is for

---

[118] At [70].

[119] At [85] per Lord Hoffmann.

[120] And not, therefore, to the *Fairchild* situation: at [51].

[121] He would also, therefore, exclude the *Hotson* situation: at [38]. Quaere how realistic this is. To say that there was "no uncertainty" in that case is only true in so far as we assume that the "but-for/balance of probabilities" approach gives us the correct answer but we know that there is a one in four chance that it is incorrect. Cf. Porat and Stein, *Tort Liability under Uncertainty* (2001) who would award the *Hotson* claimant 25 per cent of his loss on the basis that the defendants' negligence in not examining him has deprived him of the chance of showing that they were responsible for his physical condition.

[122] Lord Phillips said at [172] that, "there is a danger, if special tests of causation are developed piecemeal to deal with perceived injustices in particular factual situations, that the coherence of our common law will be destroyed."

[123] Lord Nicholls thought this approach was only "superficially attractive": at [58].

the loss and damage caused, in other words, by a physical injury which the appellant would not have suffered but for the doctor's negligence. The fact that there was a physical injury has been proved on a balance of probabilities. So too has the fact that, in addition to pain and suffering, it caused a reduction in the prospects of a successful outcome. I would hold that, where these factors are present, the way is open for losses which are consequential on the physical injury to be claimed too."[124]

Lord Phillips, who agreed in rejecting the claim, analysed the evidence closely and emphasised the difficulty of deciding cases about individual claimants on the basis of statistical evidence based on groups.[125] However, he contemplated that the law might allow a "chance-based" claim where the adverse outcome which due care might have averted had actually occurred.[126]

The general question of loss of a chance has been widely debated **6–14** in other jurisdictions and systems.[127] The American case law is divided[128] with some courts denying such recovery, others allowing it on the basis of the value of the chance lost and yet others going so far as to allow the jury to give damages on the basis that the loss *would* have occurred. The last seems to give the claimant the best of all possible worlds. Indeed, even if one adopts the second position it seems logical that one could no longer maintain the position of the claimant who can show causation on a balance of probabilities and who now recovers damages in full. Hence if the court had taken the opposite line in *Hotson* many currently successful claimants would receive less.[129] Although the effect of the loss of a chance approach would mean that fewer cases would fail altogether, it does not follow that the global liability bill would be any greater, for the reduction in the claims which now succeed in full might offset (or

---

[124] At [118].

[125] Although the case had been treated below in terms of loss of the chance of a "cure" the medical definition of this was survival for 10 years. The trial took place five years after the negligence and the claimant was still alive at the time of the appeal decision, a little over 10 years after the negligence.

[126] At [188].

[127] After making some progress in Australia the doctrine appears to have been blocked for the time being in *Gett v Tabett* [2009] NSWCA 76. French law recognises the *perte d'une chance* as damage (see Khoury, (2008) L.Q.R. 103) though it must be borne in mind that, in common with some other European systems, it requires that proof of conventional causation be "certain". While the Supreme Court of Canada rejected loss of a chance in *Laferrière v Lawson* [1991] 1 S.C.R. 541, the decision in *Resurfice Corp v Hanke* [2007] SCC 7; [2007] 1 S.C.R. 333 contains passages which can be read as supporting liability in a limited class of cases based on increase in risk but it does not seem to have made any difference in the typical "loss of a chance of a better medical outcome" situation: *Bohun v Segal* [2007] BCCA 23; 289 D.L.R. (4th) 614.

[128] See Dobbs, *Torts* (2000) §178.

[129] The claimant in *Gregg v Scott* accepted that any change to a "chance-based" system would have to "cut both ways": [2005] UKHL 2; [2005] 2 A.C. 176 at [225].

even exceed) the amount payable to claimants like *Hotson*. Since under the present law there is no reason for a judge to put any figure on the probability of causation, whether or not it passes the point of balance, there is no way of accumulating the data from which we could know what the effect would be. In any event, it would certainly make the negotiation and adjudication of claims a great deal more complicated. "Almost any claim for loss of an outcome could be reformulated as a claim for loss of a chance of that outcome"[130] and despite the fact that it is difficult to counter the argument that to make the success or failure of a case turn on whether a risk is, say, 45 per cent or 55 per cent is "irrational and indefensible",[131] it seems right to say that the effects of such a shift would be incalculable, crude as the present system may appear to be.

6–15   **iv. Cases where outcome dependent on action of a third party.** There were cases before *Hotson* in which the claimant appeared to have recovered damages for "loss of a chance" and these were little considered in the House of Lords in that case. Some of them were cases of contract[132] but it now appears that the explanation of them does not rest on the distinction between contract and tort and that it would be going too far to say that loss of a chance is wholly outside the scope of tort law. Damages for loss of a chance will be recoverable where the claimant's loss depends upon what action would have been taken by a third party.[133] In *Allied Maples Group Ltd v Simmons & Simmons*[134] the facts assumed for the purpose of a preliminary issue were that the defendants had been negligent in advising the claimants, who were acquiring the shops of a furnishing group, on the consequences of liabilities of that group as tenants, which liabilities fell on the claimants. The Court of Appeal held that in order to establish liability on the part of the defendants it was not necessary for the claimants to show that if they had been properly advised they would have succeeded in persuading the group to grant them protection or indemnity against these liabilities but merely that there was a substantial, rather than merely speculative, chance of success, the damages then being discounted to allow for the chance.[135] The same approach would have been taken even if it was

---

[130] At [224] per Baroness Hale.

[131] Lord Nicholls at [3].

[132] Such as *Chaplin v Hicks* [1911] 2 K.B. 786.

[133] It is not clear why it was necessary to rely on this in *Doyle v Wallace* [1998] P.I.Q.R. Q146, since that was a pure case of quantification. Nor does it apply where C's ship would probably have earned profits and there is evidence of the market: *The Vicky I* [2008] EWCA Civ 101; [2008] 1 Lloyd's Rep 45.

[134] [1995] 1 W.L.R. 1602.

[135] It would, however, be necessary for the claimants to prove on a balance of probabilities that they would have taken steps to persuade the group. The principle in *Allied Maples* does not apply if the issue is what the claimant would have done if properly advised.

more likely than not that the protection would have been obtained,[136] until it becomes a "near certainty"[137] when the chance that it would not have been obtained can be ignored. As it has been succinctly put in the context of loss of opportunity to pursue a case:

"[T]he court has to decide whether [the claimant] lost something of value, in the sense that the prospects were better than negligible. If the answer to that is 'yes', then it has to put a figure on what [the claimant] has lost."[138]

Examples of other situations where this approach will be adopted are failure by a solicitor to proceed with a claim within the limitation period[139] and an inaccurate reference which deprives the claimant of an opportunity of employment.[140]

In view of the common assumption that personal well-being deserves a higher level of protection than property or money, it may be asked why we are more ready to admit a claim based on loss of a chance in these cases, which may often in practice involve financial loss.[141] The question is not easy to answer and it hardly seems

---

[136] Thus in *Kitchen v Royal Air Force Association* [1958] 1 W.L.R. 563 the claimant recovered two-thirds of the damages she would have received if successful in the action which had never been pursued because of the defendants' negligence.

[137] [1995] 1 W.L.R. at 1614. *Charles v Hugh James Jones & Jenkins* [2000] 1 W.L.R. 1278.

[138] *Dixon v Clement Jones Solicitors* [2004] EWCA Civ 1005 at [53] per Carnwath L.J. The chance, "can in theory range across the whole spectrum from some non-fanciful albeit rather meagre chance to something approaching certainty": *Equitable Life Assurance Society v Ernst & Young* [2003] EWCA Civ 1114; [2004] P.N.L.R. 16 at [83].

[139] *Kitchen v Royal Air Forces Association*, above, fn.136; *Hanson v Bloom Camillin (No.2)* [2000] Lloyd's Rep. P.N. 89; *Pearson v Sanders Witherspoon* [2000] Lloyd's Rep. 151. Cf. *Otter v Church, Adams, Tatham & Co* [1953] Ch. 280, where it was probably wrong to apply a discount of 10 per cent for the chance that the deceased would not have disentailed, because in effect that was a case of what the claimant, not a third party, would have done and should be governed by the "all-or-nothing" balance of probability rule. Some American courts have accepted a tort of "spoliation" of evidence but even on a loss of a chance basis this would seem to present formidable problems in proving loss: Dobbs, *Torts* (2000), para.451.

[140] This was the view of Lord Lowry in *Spring v Guardian Assurance Plc* [1995] 2 A.C. 296 at 327. See also *Davies v Taylor* [1974] A.C. 207, where although the House of Lords dismissed the claim on the ground that the chance was merely speculative, it accepted that for the purposes of establishing her claim under the Fatal Accidents Act the claimant did not have to prove that a reconciliation with her deceased husband was more probable than not.

[141] Consider *Gouldsmith v Mid-Staffordshire etc NHS Trust* [2007] EWCA Civ 397. D was negligent in failing to refer C for specialist treatment and C lost fingers. The evidence was that "most" specialists would have operated and the fingers would have been saved. The majority of the CA treated this as amounting to evidence that on a balance of probabilities the surgery would have been carried out and the claimant therefore succeeded, but Maurice Kay L.J. dissented on the basis that there was no evidence of to whom the claimant would have been referred and that the evidence clearly implied that a respectable body of specialists would not have operated. He suggested that the case was essentially one of loss of a chance but this was not a route pursued by either party.

enough to call in aid, "the subtle distinction between deterministic events in the natural world and indeterministic events involving the unfathomable actions of human agents".[142]

3. REMOTENESS OF DAMAGE (SCOPE OF LIABILITY)

6–16   The principles contained in the previous section may have led to the conclusion that the defendant's wrong was a cause of the claimant's loss in the sense that it was (or is to be treated as if it was) a necessary condition to produce that loss or made a material contribution to it. We have it on the authority of two members of the House of Lords that although the failure of the farrier in the old rhyme to shoe the horse properly contributed to the loss of the Kingdom the farrier would not have been liable in damages for the defeat.[143] No defendant is responsible ad infinitum for all the consequences of his wrongful conduct, however remote in time and however indirect the process of causation, for otherwise human activity would be unreasonably hampered. The law must draw a line somewhere, some consequences must be abstracted as relevant, not on grounds of pure logic, but simply for practical reasons.[144] Nor is the law of tort (or even the private law of obligations) unique in this way: a social security or "no fault" compensation scheme has, for the same practical reason, to find a formula which will limit the reach of compensation.[145]

The dominant (though by no means conclusive or all-embracing) question in the determination of the scope of the defendant's liability is whether the harm in respect of which he is sued was a foreseeable consequence of his negligent act.

A. The Wagon Mound

6–17   In the hundred years or so until the middle of the last century two competing views of the test of "legal" causation or remoteness of

---

[142] *Gregg v Scott* [2005] UKHL 2; [2005] 2 A.C. 176 at [220] per Baroness Hale, referring to Reece, "Losses of Chances in the Law" (1996) 59 MLR 188.

[143] *Smith v Littlewoods Organisation Ltd* [1987] A.C. 221 at 251 per Lord Griffiths; *Banque Keyser Ullmann SA v Skandia (UK) Insurance Co Ltd* [1991] 2 A.C. 249 at 279 per Lord Templeman.

[144] *Liesbosch Dredger v Edison SS* [1933] A.C. 449 at 460 per Lord Wright.

[145] Thus industrial injury benefit is payable in respect of an accident, "arising out of and in the course of employment", an expression which has attracted a good deal of case law. In *Augusto v Board of Territory Insurance Office* (1990) N.T.R. 1 the court had to decide whether burns to a child caused by playing with a cigar lighter in a stationary vehicle "arose out of the use" of the vehicle within the Northern Territories Motor Accident Compensation Scheme. A Frenchman, in celebrating the restoration of Alsace to France in 1919, fired a revolver which burst and injured him. His claim that his injuries were due to the outbreak of war in 1914 was rejected by the Metz Pensions Board as too remote: *The Times*, February 6, 1933.

consequence were current in the law. According to the first, consequences are too remote if a reasonable man would not have foreseen
them[146]; according to the second, if a reasonable man would have
foreseen any damage to the claimant as likely to result from his act,
then he is liable for the direct consequences of it suffered by the
claimant, whether a reasonable man would have foreseen them or
not. To put the second view another way, reasonable foresight is
relevant to the question, "Was there any legal duty owed by the
defendant to the claimant to take care?" It is irrelevant to the
question, "If the defendant broke a legal duty, was the consequence
of this breach too remote?" What ought to have been reasonably
contemplated "goes to culpability, not to compensation".[147]

In 1921, in the case known as *Re Polemis*,[148] the Court of Appeal
apparently settled English law in favour of the second rule. A
chartered vessel was unloading in Casablanca when stevedores, who
were servants of the charterers, negligently let a plank drop into the
hold. Part of the cargo was a quantity of benzine in tins, which had
leaked, and a rush of flames at once followed, totally destroying the
ship. The charterers were held liable for the loss[149]—nearly
£200,000—the Court of Appeal holding that they were responsible
for all the direct consequences of the negligence, even though they
could not reasonably have been anticipated. None of the court
except Scrutton L.J. defined "direct" consequences. He said that
damage is indirect if it is, "due to the operation of independent
causes having no connection with the negligent act, except that they
could not avoid its results".[150] It is important to note that in *Re
Polemis* it was foreseeable that the ship would suffer some damage
from the dropping of the plank and the initial breach of duty was
therefore established. The case was no authority on the "unforeseeable claimant",[151] despite some passages which might suggest the
contrary.

In *The Wagon Mound*[152] the Judicial Committee of the Privy
Council, through Viscount Simonds, expressed its unqualified disapproval of *Re Polemis* and refused to follow it. O.T. Ltd were
charterers by demise[153] of *The Wagon Mound*, an oil-burning vessel
which was moored at the C. Oil Co's wharf in Sydney harbour for
the purpose of taking on fuel oil. Owing to the carelessness of O.T.

---

[146] First propounded by Pollock C.B. in *Rigby v Hewitt* (1859) 5 Ex. 240 at 243; *Greenland
v Chaplin* (1850) 5 Ex. 243 at 248.
[147] *Weld-Blundell v Stephens* [1920] A.C. 956 at p.984 per Lord Sumner.
[148] [1921] 3 K.B. 560.
[149] A fire exception clause in the charter did not help them because it did not cover
negligence.
[150] [1921] 3 K.B. at 577.
[151] See para.5–21, above.
[152] [1961] A.C. 388.
[153] That is, they were in full possession of it with their own crew.

Ltd's servants a large quantity of fuel oil was spilt on to the water, and after a few hours this had spread to M.D. Ltd's wharf about 600 feet away where another ship, the *Corrimal*, was under repair. Welding operations were being carried out on the *Corrimal*, but when M.D Ltd's manager became aware of the presence of the oil he stopped the welding operations and inquired of the C. Oil Co whether they might safely be continued. The result of this inquiry, coupled with his own belief as to the non-inflammability of fuel oil in the open, led him to give instructions for the welding operations to continue, though with all precautions to prevent inflammable material from falling into the oil. Two days later the oil caught fire and extensive damage was done to M.D. Ltd's wharf.

6–18   Two findings of fact are important: (1) It was unforeseeable that fuel oil spread on water and would catch fire[154] (2) some foreseeable damage was caused to M.D. Ltd's wharf from the spillage of the oil in that the oil had got on to the slipways and interfered with their use. The case was dealt with, therefore, on the footing that there was a breach of duty and direct damage, but that the damage caused was unforeseeable. The Privy Council, reversing the decision below in favour of the claimants, held that *Re Polemis* should no longer be regarded as good law.

> "It is the foresight of the reasonable man which alone can determine responsibility. The *Polemis* rule by substituting 'direct' for 'reasonably foreseeable' consequence leads to a conclusion equally illogical and unjust."[155]

Notwithstanding the fact that *Re Polemis* was a decision of the Court of Appeal, the technical point of precedent was side-stepped or ignored and *The Wagon Mound* was immediately accepted as the law in England. However, whether this made very much difference to the results of cases is debatable in view of the subsequent decisions. The essence of *The Wagon Mound* is that in negligence foreseeability is the criterion not only for the existence of a duty of care but also for remoteness of damage, and the Privy Council clearly attached importance to the supposed illogicality of using different tests at different stages of the inquiry in any given case:

> "If some limitation must be imposed upon the consequences for which the negligent actor is to be held responsible—and all are agreed that some limitation there must be—why should that test

---

[154] In *Overseas Tankship (UK) Ltd v Miller Steamship Co Pty Ltd (The Wagon Mound) (No.2)* [1967] A.C 617, an action by the owners of the *Corrimal* for damage caused to their ship by the same fire, the Privy Council, on somewhat different evidence, held that the damage was foreseeable.

[155] [1961] A.C. at 424.

(reasonable foreseeability) be rejected which, since he is judged by what the reasonable man ought to foresee, corresponds with common conscience of mankind, and a test (the 'direct' consequence) be substituted which leads to nowhere but the never-ending and insoluble problems of causation."[156]

It might have been thought from this that the effect of *The Wagon Mound* was restricted to actions for negligence, or at least to cases in which foreseeability of damage is relevant to liability. In *The Wagon Mound (No.2)*,[157] however, the Privy Council held that foreseeability is the test for remoteness of damage in cases of nuisance also, and, though they pointed out that liability in many cases of nuisance depends on fault and thus on foreseeability, they stated that the same test must apply even where this is not so.[158] If the "foresight of the reasonable man" is to be used as a test of remoteness in torts of strict liability some adjustment will have to be made. If a person may be liable notwithstanding that he neither could nor should have foreseen any harmful consequences of his act whatever, it is meaningless to say that the extent of his liability is limited to what he ought reasonably to have foreseen. In *Galashiels Gas Co Ltd v O'Donnell*,[159] for example, the defendants had a lift at their gas works and the lift, so far as anyone could discover, was in perfect condition both before and after the accident. Nevertheless, on a single isolated occasion something went wrong for reasons no one could ascertain and as a result the claimant's husband was killed. The defendants were held liable for breach of an absolute statutory duty, but how can it realistically be said that they could have foreseen the death of the deceased? What can be said—and this seems now to be the meaning of "reasonably foreseeable" in such cases—is that a reasonable man, told of the way in which the lift went wrong, would not be surprised to learn that the deceased had been killed.[160]

However, the test of reasonable foreseeability is not a universal one: it is a rational policy to impose a more extensive liability upon **6–19**

---

[156] [1961] A.C. at 423.

[157] [1967] 1 A.C. 617.

[158] Although not couched in terms of remoteness of damage, it has since been held that the test of liability under the rule in *Rylands v Fletcher* is whether some damage was to be anticipated from the thing: see para.15–19, below.

[159] [1949] A.C. 275.

[160] See Dias, [1967] C.L.J. 62. at 68, 77–82. Cf. *Millard v Serck Tubes Ltd* [1969] 1 W.L.R. 211 where the Court of Appeal held that once a part of machinery was found to be "dangerous" within s.14(1) of the Factories Act 1961, which meant that it was a foreseeable cause of injury, and was unfenced in breach of the section, it mattered not that the claimant's injury occurred in an unforeseeable way, so long as the injury would not have occurred if the duty to fence had been fulfilled. The judgments, which refer to no decisions on remoteness of damage, provide admirable, if unintentional, examples of the operation of the rule in *Polemis, Re* at its most straightforward.

an intentional wrongdoer for reasons of both deterrence and morality[161] and so a fraudster will be held liable for direct consequences of his wrong even though they are unforeseeable.[162]

B. Application of Foreseeability

6–20   The test of foreseeability involves the assessment of facts against a legal standard and, because all the facts of the particular case have to be brought into account it is generally undesirable to engage in extensive citation of authority.[163] Nevertheless, the student will want to be given some idea of how in practice judges approach these matters. The test was from the beginning heavily qualified by the fact that neither the precise extent of the damage nor the precise manner of its infliction need be foreseeable. As Lord Denning M.R. put it:

> "It is not necessary that the precise concatenation of circumstances should be envisaged. If the consequence was one which was within the general range which any reasonable person might foresee (and was not of an entirely different kind which no one would anticipate) then it is within the rule that a person who has been guilty of negligence is liable for the consequences."[164]

In *Hughes v Lord Advocate*[165] employees of the Post Office opened a manhole in the street and in the evening left the open manhole covered by a canvas shelter, unattended and surrounded by warning paraffin lamps. The claimant, a boy aged eight, took one of the lamps into the shelter and was playing with it there when he stumbled over and it fell into the manhole. A violent explosion followed and the claimant himself fell into the hole, sustaining terrible injuries from the burns. It was quite unpredictable that a lamp might explode, but the Post Office men were in breach of duty leaving the manhole unattended because they should have appreciated that boys might take a lamp into the shelter and that, if the lamp fell and broke, they might suffer serious injury from burning. So the lamp, a known source of danger, caused injury through an

---

[161] *Smith New Court Securities Ltd v Scrimgeour Vickers (Asset Management) Ltd* [1997] A.C. 254 at 279.

[162] *Smith New Court*, above, fn.161; *Doyle v Olby (Ironmongers) Ltd* [1969] 2 Q.B. 158. See para.11–14, below. As to conversion, see para.17–28, below. The statutory wrong of direct racial discrimination has been held not to require foreseeability: *Essa v Laing Ltd* [2004] EWCA Civ 2; [2004] I.C.R. 746.

[163] *Jolley v Sutton LBC* [2000] 1 W.L.R. 1082.

[164] *Stewart v West African Terminals Ltd* [1964] 2 Lloyd's Rep. 371 at 375; *Bradford v Robinson Rentals Ltd* [1967] 1 W.L.R. 337 at 344–345 per Rees J.

[165] [1963] A.C. 837. Cf. *Doughty v Turner Manufacturing Co Ltd* [1964] 1 Q.B. 518.

unforeseeable sequence of events, but the defendants were nevertheless held liable. In *Jolley v Sutton London Borough*[166] the defendants had failed to take steps to remove an old, abandoned boat from land of theirs to which the public had easy access. The obvious risk (indeed the defendants conceded the point) was that a child might suffer injury from climbing on the boat and falling through the rotten planking; in fact the claimant and a friend embarked on a futile project to restore the boat and, while he was working underneath it, it fell on him, breaking his back. The House of Lords restored the decision for the claimant by the trial judge, who had been entitled to conclude that the accident which occurred was within the range of what was foreseeable, given the ingenuity of children, "in finding unexpected ways of doing mischief to themselves and others".[167] It is, however, not easy to accept Lord Hoffmann's view that the result could be justified by the fact that, given the defendants' exposure to potential liability for the lesser risk, they would have had to incur no additional expense to eliminate the more serious risk. "They would only have had to do what they admit they should have done anyway."[168] The same is true of *The Wagon Mound*.[169]

The Wagon Mound contains the requirement that the foreseeable **6–21** damage must be of the same "kind" as the damage which actually occurred. In point of fact even under *Re Polemis* it was probably necessary to distinguish between three very broad "kinds" of damage, namely injury to the person, damage to property and pure financial loss, but *The Wagon Mound* certainly demands a more elaborate classification of "kinds" of damage than that: in the case itself damage to the claimants' wharf was foreseeable and damage to the claimants' wharf occurred. It follows that, in the Privy Council's judgment, a distinction must be taken between damage by fouling, which was foreseeable, and damage by fire, which occurred. The difficulty is to know how narrowly the kind of damage in question in any given case must be defined. In *Tremain v Pike*[170] the rat population on the defendant's farm was allowed to become unduly large and the claimant, a herdsman on the farm, contracted leptospirosis, otherwise known as Weil's disease, in consequence. Even on the assumption that the defendants had been negligent in failing to

---

[166] [2000] 1 W.L.R. 1082.
[167] [2000] 1 W.L.R. at 1093 per Lord Hoffmann; and see *Jebson v MoD* [2000] 1 W.L.R. 2055 (drunken person).
[168] [2000] 1 W.L.R. at 1092.
[169] Cf. *Darby v National Trust* [2001] EWCA Civ 189; [2001] P.I.Q.R. P27 (drowning accident; risk of drowning obvious to claimant; could not rely on failure to warn of less obvious risk of Weil's disease).
[170] [1969] 1 W.L.R. 1556; cf. *Bradford v Robinson Rentals Ltd* [1967] 1 W.L.R. 337; *Malcolm v Broadhurst* [1970] 3 All E.R. 508.

control the rat population,[171] Payne J. held that the claimant could not succeed. Weil's disease is extremely rare and is caused by contact with rat's urine, and in the learned judge's opinion it was therefore both unforeseeable and "entirely different in kind" from such foreseeable consequences as the effect of a rat bite or food poisoning from contaminated food: the claimant could not simply say that the rat-induced disease was foreseeable and rat-induced disease occurred.[172]

Tremain v Pike requires a rather high degree of precision in classifying kinds of damage, but there do not seem to be very many personal injury[173] cases since *The Wagon Mound* where the claim has failed on the basis of remoteness.[174] The House of Lords, in emphasising the difference between the rules of remoteness in contract and tort has given to the word "foreseeable" a meaning which is very far removed from "probable" or "likely". The rule in tort imposes a much wider liability than that in contract:

> "[T]he defendant [in tort] will be liable for any type of damage which is reasonably foreseeable as liable to happen, *even in the most unusual case*, unless the risk is so small that a reasonable man would in the whole circumstances feel justified in neglecting it".[175]

However, "reasonable foreseeability must imply *some* understanding of the chain of events which is putatively foreseen; otherwise we are looking not at foresight, but divination."[176] In addition to this broad approach to foreseeability, it is clear that three other principles survived *The Wagon Mound*: that the defendant is not relieved of liability because the damage is more extensive that might have been foreseen[177]; that foreseeability is not required of the pecuniary

---

[171] The defendant's negligence in this respect was not actually made out.

[172] His Lordship's suggested method of avoiding the question about what is meant by difference in kind by asking instead the direct question whether on the facts leptospirosis was reasonably foreseeable, succeeds only by assuming one particular answer to the question: [1969] 1 WLR 1556 at 1561. Cf. the opinion of Edmund Davies L.J. in *Draper v Hodder* [1972] 2 Q.B. 556 that the foreseeable risk of the infant claimant being injured by being bowled over by the dogs would justify the imposition of liability where the dogs attacked him.

[173] A "broad brush" approach is also discernible with regard to property damage: see *The Carnival* [1994] 2 Lloyd's Rep. 14.

[174] Though see *Pratley v Surrey CC* [2003] EWCA Civ 1067; [2004] ICR 159 (employer aware of risk of injury to health from over-work but not of the sudden collapse which occurred as a result of disappointment at non-implementation of palliative measures; not enough to categorise the risk as "risk of psychiatric illness").

[175] *C. Czarnikow Ltd v Koufos* [1969] 1 A.C. 350 at 385 per Lord Reid (emphasis added). See also at 411, 422.

[176] *Arscott v The Coal Authority* [2004] EWCA Civ 892; [2005] Env L.R. 6 at [58] (a nuisance case).

[177] See para.6–31, below.

amount of the damage[178]; and that the defendant takes the victim as he finds him, including weaknesses which exacerbate the damage in an unforeseeable way—the so-called egg-shell skull rule.[179] The last principle in particular means that a defendant who can show an unforeseeable kind of damage may get little comfort from the principles of remoteness, as where a motorist who was responsible for a minor collision was held liable to the other driver for long-term unemployability caused by a psychiatric condition which was dormant but which was revived by the accident.[180] As Lord Lloyd put it:

"The test in every case ought to be whether the defendant can reasonably foresee that his conduct will expose the plaintiff to risk of personal injury. If so, then he comes under a duty of care to that plaintiff . . . There is no justification for regarding physical and psychiatric injury as different 'kinds' of injury. Once it is established that the defendant is under a duty of care to avoid causing personal injury to the plaintiff, it matters not whether the injury in fact sustained is physical, psychiatric or both."[181]

These words are, of course, spoken in context of the egg-shell skull rule, or they would efface *The Wagon Mound* altogether but provided the accident occurs in a broadly foreseeable way unforeseeably serious consequences will commonly be attributable to some characteristic of the victim.

Foreseeability is a relative, not an absolute, concept. In *The* **6–22** *Wagon Mound* the Privy Council accepted and based its reasoning on the trial judge's finding that the defendant did not know and could not reasonably be expected to have known that furnace oil was capable of being set afire when spread on water. In *The Wagon Mound (No.2)*, however, somewhat different evidence was presented[182] and in the Privy Council the trial judge's finding to similar effect, not being a primary finding of fact but an inference from other findings, was rejected. There was, it was held, a real risk of fire such as would have been appreciated by a properly qualified and alert chief engineer and this, given the fact that there was no justification for discharging oil into Sydney Harbour in any case, was sufficient to fix liability on the defendants. In other words, the mere fact that the damage suffered was unlikely to occur does not relieve the defendant of liability if his conduct was unreasonable—a

---

[178] See para.6–30, below.
[179] See para.6–32, below.
[180] *Page v Smith* [1996] A.C. 155. See para.5–63, above.
[181] [1996] A.C. 155 at 190.
[182] See Lord Reid's explanation of this [1967] 1 A.C. 617 at 640–641, and Dias, [1967] C.L.J. at pp.63–65.

proposition very little different from that contained in *Re Polemis* itself. On the facts of that case, notwithstanding the arbitrator's finding that the spark which caused the explosion was not reasonably foreseeable, there was, surely, a "real risk" that the vapour in the hold might be accidentally ignited and there was, of course, no justification for dropping the plank into the hold.

C. Competing Rules Compared

6–23   It seems, therefore, that *The Wagon Mound* has made little difference to the law in terms of practical result, and, indeed, Viscount Simonds indicated that this would probably be so in *The Wagon Mound* itself.[183] That case, however, undoubtedly produced a change of principle and it is right, therefore, to conclude with some brief discussion of its merits as compared with those of *Re Polemis*. Much has been written on this subject but two points only can be considered here:

6–24   **i. Simplicity.** The Privy Council laid much stress upon the difficulties of the directness test, but it is difficult to see how the foreseeability test is any easier. Not only does the change from the one to the other raise the question of the meaning of "kind" of damage but it:

> "[G]ets rid of the difficulties of determining causal connection by substituting the difficulty of determining the range and extent of foresight of the hypothetical reasonable man."[184]

The fact is that the issue of remoteness of damage is not susceptible to short cuts.

> "There is no substitute for dealing with the particular facts, and considering all the factors that bear on them, interlocked as they must be. Theories . . . have not improved at all on the old words 'proximate' and 'remote' with the idea they convey of some reasonable connection between the original negligence and its consequences, between the harm threatened and the harm done".[185]

6–25   **ii. Fairness.** According to the Privy Council the test of directness works unfairly:

---

[183] [1961] A.C. at 422.
[184] Walker, "Remoteness of Damage and Re Polemis" 1961 S.L.T. 37.
[185] Prosser, "Palsgraf Revisited" (1953) 52 Michigan L.Rev 1 at 32.

"It does not seem consonant with current ideas of justice or morality that for an act of negligence, however slight or venial, which results in some trivial foreseeable damage the actor should be liable for all consequences however unforeseeable and however grave, so long as they can be said to be 'direct'."[186]

It is no doubt hard on a negligent defendant that he should be held liable for unexpectedly large damages, but it is not clear that the final outcome is any fairer if the claimant is left without redress for damage which he has suffered through no fault of his own. Bearing in mind that negligence involves the creation of an unreasonable risk of causing some foreseeable damage to the claimant it might be thought that even though "justice" may be impossible of achievement where unforeseeable damage occurs,[187] greater injustice is produced by *The Wagon Mound* than by *Re Polemis*.

D. Further Principles as to Remoteness

The preceding account of *The Wagon Mound* should not mislead **6–26** one into thinking that foreseeability is all there is to the law of remoteness: the task of determining the scope of the defendant's responsibility has too many strands for that. The starting point is that a defendant:

"[I]s not liable for a consequence of a kind which is not reasonably foreseeable; it does not follow that he is liable for all damage that was reasonably foreseeable."[188]

As was stated at the beginning of this chapter remoteness is an aspect of causation in a broader sense than that of simply "but-for" and frequently the courts will speak in the language of causation because although the defendant's act is a cause in the "but-for" sense some subsequent act or event is regarded as eclipsing it. Sometimes policy comes to the surface and a loss is dismissed as too remote simply because the court does not think it reasonable or desirable to impose it on the defendant. Thus in *Pritchard v J.H. Cobden Ltd*,[189] it was held that where the claimant's marriage broke up as a result of his injuries, orders for financial provision made against him by the divorce court could not be the subject of a claim against the tortfeasor: quite apart from the point that redistribution of assets on divorce could not be regarded as a "loss", acceptance

---

[186] [1961] A.C. at 422.
[187] Prosser, loc. cit. at 17.
[188] *British Steel Plc v Simmons* [2004] UKHL 20; [2004] I.C.R. 585 at [67] per Lord Rodger.
[189] [1988] Fam. 22. See also para.25–18, below.

of such claims would risk confusion in the judicial process and be open to abuse. There are also a number of commonly recurring situations in which principles have developed which are qualifications of foreseeability and which we must consider in more detail.

6–27   **i. Scope of liability limited by scope of duty of care.** The House of Lords has emphasised that in deciding the scope of the defendant's liability for the consequences of his wrong it is necessary to consider the nature of the loss against which the legal rule in question is designed to keep the claimant harmless.

> "One cannot separate questions of liability from questions of causation. They are inextricably connected. One is never simply liable; one is always liable *for* something and the rules which determine what one is liable for are as much part of the substantive law as the rules which determine which acts give rise to liability."[190]

> "Damage is of the essence of a cause of action for negligence, and the critical question in a particular case is a composite one, that is whether the scope of the duty of care[191] in the circumstances of the case is such as to embrace damage of the kind which the claimant claims to have suffered."[192]

The point is more obvious in the tort of breach of statutory duty, so that, for example, a claim in respect of the loss of unpenned livestock from a ship in a storm failed because the purpose of the statute requiring penning was to prevent the spread of disease[193]; but

---

[190] *Kuwait Airways Corp v Iraq Airways Co* [2002] UKHL 19; [2002] 2 A.C. 883 at [128] per Lord Hoffmann.

[191] This language is open to criticism because the "scope of the duty of care" is to prevent the damaging event (see Hoffmann, "Causation" (2005) 121 L.Q.R. 592) but the point is clear enough.

[192] *Calvert v William Hill Ltd* [2008] EWCA Civ 1427; [2009] Ch 330 at [54] per May P. See the extraordinary case of *Bhamra v Dubb* [2010] EWCA Civ 13. D catered at a Sikh wedding. Sikhs do not eat eggs for religious reasons but it was found that D had obtained additional supplies of a dish (sometimes made with eggs) when food began to run short and had not taken steps to check that it did not contain eggs. C, a guest, died from an allergic anaphylaxic reaction. Egg allergy is so rare that it is not necessary to warn of the presence of eggs when the provider has no reason to expect the presence of an egg-allergic person and Sikhs presumably have no higher incidence of the allergy than anyone else. The CA was of the view that D was "under a duty" to take care not to offend guests' religious susceptibilities (though it is not obvious what tort that would be, even if would clearly be a breach of contract against the person who engaged D) and that he was liable for the death because, whereas persons with egg allergy would normally be expected to take their own precautions, C had reason to expect that at a Sikh wedding any food served would be free of eggs. The court clearly thought that the case was very close to the line.

[193] *Gorris v Scott* (1874) L.R. 9 Exch. 125, para.7–14, below. This has obvious affinities with the notion of the "protective purpose of the norm" which is found in Austrian and German law. See van Gerven, Lever and Larouche, *Tort Law (Common Law of Europe Casebooks)* Ch.4.1.1.

the same principle is applicable at common law and liability is generally limited to those consequences, factually caused by the defendant and not otherwise too remote, which are attributable to that which makes the act complained of wrongful. It is, "the scope of the tort which determines the extent of the remedy to which the injured party is entitled".[194]

The cases generally involve a contract between the parties, but in the professional negligence context contract and tort are interchangeable. In *Banque Bruxelles Lambert SA v Eagle Star Insurance Co Ltd*[195] the issue in a number of consolidated appeals was whether a valuer who had negligently overvalued a property on which a lender advanced money on mortgage was liable not merely for the difference between the valuation figure and the amount which would have been realised on sale of the property at the time but for the further loss attributable to a general fall in the property market. The lender would not have entered into the transaction if he had known the truth and it could hardly be denied that falls in markets are foreseeable as a general rule. Nevertheless, the answer given by the House of Lords was "No", for in the case of liability for information provided to enable the claimant to decide on a course of action, liability for negligence[196] was limited to the consequences of the information being wrong.[197] So, suppose property is valued at £500,000 when a true valuation would have been £400,000. When, on default, the property is sold, it realises only £300,000 because of a general fall in the market. In a purely causative sense the lender's loss is £200,000[198] but the valuer's liability is only £100,000 because the balance represents the risk

---

[194] *Platform Home Loans Ltd v Oyston Shipways Ltd* [2000] 2 A.C. 190 at 209 per Lord Hobhouse.

[195] [1997] A.C. 191 (reported in [1996] 3 All E.R. 365 sub nom. *South Australia Asset Managment Corp v York Montague Ltd* and commonly known as the "SAAMCO principle"); *Nykredit Mortgage Bank Plc v Edward Erdman Group Ltd (No.2)* [1997] 1 W.L.R. 1627; *Bank of Tokyo-Mitsubishi UFJ Ltd v Baskan Gida etc AS* [2009] EWHC 1276 (Ch). Cf. *Kenny & Good Pty Ltd v MGICA (1992) Ltd* (1999) 163 A.L.R. 611.

[196] The position is different if the defendant is guilty of fraud, for then he is liable for all losses flowing from the fraudulently induced transaction: *Smith New Court Securities Ltd v Scrimgeour Vickers (Asset Management) Ltd* [1997] A.C. 254 at 283. Indeed, he is liable even for unforeseeable consequences.

[197] Cf. *Caparo v Dickman* [1990] 2 A.C. 605, para.5–9, above, where the purpose of the rule infringed went to whether a duty was owed to the claimant. Lord Hoffmann in *Banque Bruxelles* at [1997] A.C. 213 explains *The Empire Jamaica* [1955] P. 259 on a somewhat similar basis (negligence by mate whom owners knew to be uncertificated but whom they reasonably believed to be competent: damage not done with their "actual fault and privity").

[198] In one of the cases reported as *Bristol and West BS v Fancy & Jackson* [1997] 4 All E.R. 582 the defendants incorrectly represented to the mortgagees that they had an official search certificate, without which the mortgagees would not have proceeded. The mortgagor defaulted. The breach was not causative of the mortgagees' loss.

which the claimant would have taken on himself even if the transaction had been sound.[199]

6–28   This case concerned an obligation to provide information on the basis of which the claimant could take a decision. The position is different where the defendant undertakes to advise generally upon the wisdom of entering into a transaction, for he will then be liable for all the foreseeable consequences of it.[200] The line between the two categories may be hard to draw. In *Aneco Reinsurance Underwriting Ltd v Johnson & Higgs Ltd*[201] the defendant brokers, acting on behalf of the claimant reinsurers, negligently failed to disclose certain facts on a proposal for further reinsurance of a US$10 million portion of a risk to be carried by the claimants. This meant that the re-reinsurers, who would have refused cover had they known the full facts, lawfully repudiated the claim. However, the claimants lost US$35 million on the risk as a whole. The majority of the House of Lords held that the brokers were liable for the full amount. Had the brokers carried out their duty properly they would have become aware that cover was not obtainable in the market on commercially sensible terms and the claimants would therefore have declined the main risk and suffered no loss, and in the view of the majority the duty of the brokers was not merely to seek to obtain valid cover and report on having done so, but to advise on the market's estimation of the risk.[202] For Lord Millett, dissenting, it was not enough that the brokers might have volunteered their estimation of the state of the market, the question was whether such an estimation was within the scope of the duty they had undertaken and he thought that they had not done so.

It is not wholly obvious why responsibility for risks like market forces should be imposed on the defendant even where his function is to advise the claimant as to the wisdom of a transaction, at least where those risks are as apparent to the claimant as to the defendant. In *Banque Bruxelles* Lord Hoffmann gave an example[203] of a doctor giving negligent advice to a mountaineer about the fitness of his knee. If the mountaineer were to be injured on an expedition because his knee gave way, the doctor might be liable; but if the mountaineer were injured by a foreseeable risk of mountaineering unconnected with his knee (for example, being hit by a rock fall) the doctor would not be liable for that. That conclusion is plainly correct, though it is debatable whether it is correct to say that this is because the injury "would have occurred even if the advice had

[199] *Nykredit Mortgage Bank Plc v Edward Erdman Group Ltd (No.2)*, above, fn.195, at 1631 per Lord Nicholls.
[200] *Banque Bruxelles Lambert* at [1997] A.C. 214.
[201] [2001] UKHL 51; [2002] 1 Lloyd's Rep. 157.
[202] Cf. *Intervention Board for Agricultural Produce v Leidig* [2000] Lloyd's Rep. P.N. 144.
[203] [1997] A.C. at 213.

been correct",[204] since the mountaineer would not have gone on the
expedition if he had known the truth. It seems better to say that the
rock fall is a mere coincidence (like the victim of a road accident
being injured in another road accident while in the ambulance on the
way to hospital) or (which amounts to the same thing) that it is not
within the risk created by the doctor's negligence. However, suppose the doctor is consulted by a patient with a history of heart
trouble and the doctor negligently advises him that the best way to
improve his fitness is to take up again the climbing activities of his
youth. It is not difficult to say that the doctor could be liable if the
patient suffers a heart attack, but is he now to be responsible for
death in the rock fall? That is just as much a coincidence as in the
other case. Perhaps the answer lies in what the doctor's duty is, that
is to say to advise the mountaineer about his health, not his physical
safety.

ii. Intended consequences and intentional wrongdoers. 6–29
Intended consequences are never too remote. "The intention to
injure the plaintiff ... disposes of any question of remoteness of
damage."[205] However, the liability of an intentional wrongdoer is
not limited to the intended consequences and it will extend at least
to such as are foreseeable. *Scott v Shepherd*[206] may be regarded as
a classical instance of this. D throws a squib into a crowd. A, in
alarm, throws it away and B does likewise. The squib ends its
journey by falling upon C, exploding and putting out his eye. D
certainly intended to scare somebody or other. With equal certainty
he did not, in common parlance, "intend" to hurt C, much less to
destroy his eye, but he was nevertheless held liable to C, because the
law insists, and insists quite rightly, that fools and mischievous
persons must answer for consequences which common sense would
unhesitatingly attribute to their wrongdoing.[207] Indeed, the intentional wrongdoer's liability may extend beyond the foreseeable
because intentional torts have not necessarily been affected by *The
Wagon Mound*. A fraudster is liable for unforeseeable consequences[208] and an intentional departure from the terms of a bailment
may make the bailee subject to the liability of an insurer.[209]

---

[204] [1997] A.C. at 213.
[205] *Quinn v Leatham* [1901] A.C. 495 at 537 per Lord Lindley.
[206] (1773) 2 W.Bl. 892.
[207] See also para.3–2, above.
[208] See para.11–14, below.
[209] A trespasser to land is not liable for unintended, indirect and unforeseen damage: *Mayfair Ltd v Pears* [1987] 1 N.Z.L.R. 459 (fire in wrongfully parked car). The draft *Restatement of Torts*, 3d, s.33 provides that, "an actor who intentionally causes physical harm is subject to liability for that harm even if it was unlikely to occur" but that he is not liable for harm the risk of which was not increased by his conduct. Illustration 3 has the claimant running away from the defendant muggers and being struck by lightning: not liable.

iii. Unintended consequences

(a) *Existing states of affairs*

6–30   (I) PECUNIARY AMOUNT OF THE DAMAGE. If the defendant injures a high income earner or a piece of property with a high intrinsic value (such as an antique vase) he cannot argue that he had no reason to expect the amount of the loss to be so great.[210] Such an issue is treated as belonging to the realm of assessment of damages rather than of remoteness, so that foreseeability is irrelevant.[211] The law is not, however, so clearly committed to this stand where the loss claimed is not "intrinsic" but arises from the fact that the damage to the claimant's goods renders him unable to earn profits with them.[212] Support can be found in the cases (none of them decisive, at least for the purposes of negligence[213]) for both views: on the one hand that foreseeability is irrelevant,[214] on the other, that the defendant's liability is limited to "ordinary" or "foreseeable" losses.[215]

6–31   (II) EXTENT OF THE DAMAGE. If the accident occurs in a foreseeable way the defendant will be liable even though the damage is much greater in extent that would have been anticipated.[216] Where the loss is economic, this is in practical terms indistinguishable from the previous principle.[217] It has sometimes been said that the "egg-

---

[210] The point is perhaps so obvious that the only express authority for it appears to be the celebrated dictum of Scrutton L.J. in *The Arpad* [1934] P. 189 at 202, though that case had nothing to do with negligence and the judgment was a dissenting one.

[211] However, in *B.D.C. Ltd v Hofstrand Farms Ltd* (1986) 26 D.L.R. (4th) 1 the Supreme Court of Canada said, obiter, that if D were liable in tort for failure to deliver C's package and had notice that C would suffer some loss, he would not be liable for a loss of extraordinary magnitude, of the risk of which he had no notice. The contract rule is applied even though the action is in tort: what goes for damage does not necessarily apply to economic loss.

[212] The case of a claimant who is disabled from performing particular contracts (e.g. a musician) is perhaps analogous: see *The Arpad*, above, fn.210, at 221 per Greer L.J.

[213] *The Arpad*, denying lost profits on the sale of a cargo, was a case of conversion.

[214] *The Star of India* (1876) 1 P.D. 466; *Liesbosch Dredger v SS Edison* [1933] A.C. 449 at 463–464 ("The measure of damages is the value of the ship to her owner as a going concern at the time and place of the loss. In assessing that value regard must naturally be had to her pending engagements, either profitable or the reverse"). This case is, of course, best known on the different point relating to the claimant's impecuniosity, para.6–33, below.

[215] *The Argentino* (1899) 14 App. Cas. 519 at 523; *The Arpad*, above, fn.210; *The Daressa* [1971] 1 Lloyd's Rep. 60.

[216] *Holbeck Hall Hotel Ltd v Scarborough BC* [2000] Q.B. 836 at 858 (where, however, the court declined to apply the principle because the case was one of a limited duty in face of a natural disaster). One of the few clear examples of this is *Vacwell Engineering v B.D.H. Chemicals* [1971] 1 Q.B. 88 (minor explosion foreseeable; huge explosion took place because claimants put a number of ampoules in the same sink). See also *Bradford v Robinson Rentals Ltd* [1967] 1 W.L.R. 337 (exposure causing frostbite) and *Richards v State of Victoria* [1969] V.R. 136 (blow causing brain damage).

[217] See *Brown v K.M.R. Services Ltd* [1994] 4 All E.R. 385 (a contract case).

shell skull" rule (see below) is an example of this,[218] though that would involve saying that the law regarded personal injury as indivisible and that damage from cancer triggered by a burn[219] was damage of the same kind as the burn.[220] At any rate, the principles are obviously closely related.

(III) THE "EGG-SHELL SKULL" PRINCIPLE. *The Wagon Mound* did **6–32** not displace the principle that the defendant must take his victim[221] as he finds him.[222] It has for long been the law that if a person is:

"[N]egligently run over or otherwise negligently injured in his body, it is no answer to the sufferer's claim for damages that he would have suffered less injury . . . [223] if he had not had an unusually thin skull or an unusually weak heart."[224]

This principle is as applicable to "nervous shock" as to any other sort of personal injury[225] and applies where the foreseeable danger is of physical trauma but the claimant is shocked, because of his susceptible personality, into mental illness, even though no physical injury has in fact occurred.[226] It has also been applied where the immediate cause of the loss is voluntary conduct by the claimant to

---

[218] The suggestion seems to be made by Lord Wright in the *Liesbosch* case, above, fn.214, at 461 and by Lord Parker C.J. in *Smith v Leech Brain & Co Ltd* [1962] 2 Q.B. 405 at 415.

[219] As in *Smith v Leech Brain*.

[220] Though this may be the implication of *Page v Smith* [1996] A.C. 155, below and para.5–63, above: *Margereson v J.W. Roberts Ltd* [1996] P.I.Q.R. P154 (on appeal [1996] P.I.Q.R. P358).

[221] But not his family: *McLaren v Bradstreet* (1969) 113 S.J. 471, cf. *Nader v Urban Transport Authority* [1985] 2 N.S.W.L.R. 501 and *Kavanagh v Akhtar* (1998) 45 N.S.W.L.R. 588.

[222] *Smith v Leech Brain & Co Ltd* [1962] 2 Q.B. 405; *Warren v Scruttons* [1962] 1 Lloyd's Rep. 497; *Lines v Harland and Wolff* [1966] 1 Lloyd's Rep. 400; *Boon v Thomas Hubback* [1967] 1 Lloyd's Rep. 281; *Wieland v Cyril Lord Carpets Ltd* [1969] 3 All E.R. 100.

[223] The missing words are "or no injury at all". Kennedy J. went too far here, for there must be a breach of duty owed to the claimant and if no damage at all could have been foreseen to a person of normal sensitivity and the claimant's abnormal sensitivity was unknown to the defendant, then he is not liable: *Bourhill v Young* [1943] A.C. 92 at 109; *Cook v Swinfen* [1967] 1 W.L.R. 457.

[224] *Dulieu v White* [1901] 2 K.B. 669 at 679 per Kennedy J. On the burden of proof of whether the greater injury was caused by the susceptibility see *Shorey v P.T. Ltd* [2003] HCA 87; 197 A.L.R. 410.

[225] Does it apply to property damage? In *The Sivand* [1998] 2 Lloyd's Rep. 97 the unusual ground conditions at the claimants' harbour meant that unexpected delay and expense was incurred in effecting repairs to damage to moorings caused by the defendants' vessel. The defendants were liable for this and, although he regarded the problem as foreseeable, Pill L.J. said at 100 that the, "liability of the defendants is founded on one aspect of the principle that a tortfeasor takes his victim as he finds him"; but note that in the context of nuisance we tend to say that a landowner cannot increase the liabilities of a neighbour by putting his property to unusually sensitive use: see para.14–9, below.

[226] *Page v Smith* [1996] A.C. 155, para.5–63, above; contra Lord Goff dissenting in *Frost v CC South Yorkshire* [1999] A.C. 455 at 476.

which his personality may have predisposed him but which would not have occurred but for his injury,[227] but the conduct in question in the case was the commission of a crime and in such a case the claim would now be barred by public policy.[228] The claimant's weakness cuts both ways, however: his damages are likely to be less than those of a "normal" person suffering the same overall injury in order to reflect the greater risk to which he was exposed by the normal vicissitudes of life.[229]

Since the egg-shell skull principle seems to be based either on the great difficulty that would arise if the court had to determine in detail what were the foreseeable physical consequences of an injury or on the view that all sorts of individually unlikely consequences are foreseeable in a general way,[230] the same (or a similar[231]) principle operates when the claimant's injury is exacerbated by a combination of his abnormality and some external force which foreseeably and naturally intervenes after the accident, for example medical treatment to which he is allergic.[232]

6–33   (IV) CLAIMANT'S IMPECUNIOSITY. In *Liesbosch Dredger v Edison SS*[233] the House of Lords held that where the claimant, whose dredger had been sunk and who could not afford to purchase a substitute, incurred extra expense in hiring one in order to complete his contracts he could not recover that extra expense, which was an extraneous matter and too remote. The then leading case of *Re Polemis* was distinguished on the ground that it was concerned with the, "immediate physical consequences of the negligent act".[234] It was never very clear why a distinction was drawn between the claimant's physical weakness, in which context the defendant took his victim as he found him, and his financial weakness.[235] Indeed, from a different point of view the defendant *did* take the claimant's financial position as he found it, for the claimant was always entitled to base his claim for lost earnings upon his actual pre-accident

---

[227] *Meah v McCreamer* [1985] 1 All E.R. 367, though the point is only referred to in subsequent proceedings: *Meah v McCreamer (No.2)* [1986] 1 All E.R. 943.

[228] *Clunis v Camden and Islington HA* [1998] Q.B. 978 and para.25–20, below. Indeed the claim in *Meah v McCreamer (No.2)* was dismissed on this basis.

[229] Apparently known in Canada as the "crumbling skull" doctrine: *Athey v Leonati* (1996) 140 D.L.R. (4th) 235. The damages in *Page v Smith* [1996] A.C. 155 were reduced by some 40 per cent on account of this.

[230] See *The Sivand*, above, fn.225.

[231] It has been said that it is a logical corollary of the egg-shell skull principle: *Stephenson v Waite Tileman Ltd* [1973] N.Z.L.R. 152.

[232] *Robinson v Post Office* [1974] 1 W.L.R. 1176. As to whether negligent treatment amounts to a novus actus interveniens, see para.6–37, below.

[233] [1933] A.C. 448.

[234] [1933] A.C. 448 at 461.

[235] The rule may have had some connection with the former rule that damages are not recoverable for non-payment of money. Where special loss is within the contemplation of the parties this is no longer the law: *Wadsworth v Lydall* [1981] 1 W.L.R. 598.

income, not some sort of national average. Furthermore, although the claimant is required to mitigate his loss and cannot recover damages for losses which he could have avoided, it is up to the defendant to show that the claimant failed to take such steps as were reasonable in his circumstances. While there is undoubtedly a theoretical distinction between the concepts of remoteness and mitigation,[236] judges have admitted that no one has ever satisfactorily shown where the line between the two is to be drawn.[237] If the failure of a personal injuries claimant to take medical treatment is a failure to mitigate loss, why was not the failure to buy a replacement dredger in *The Liesbosch* in the same category? For a good many years this principle was criticised and frequently distinguished and the House of Lords finally departed from it in *Lagden v O'Connor*.[238] The claimant's car was damaged by the defendant's negligence. On normal principles the claimant was entitled to the costs of repairs and the hire of a substitute vehicle while those were done.[239] However, being unable to afford the outlay on the hire of a car in the ordinary way, the claimant had contracted with a credit hire company, on terms that the company would take over the prosecution of his claim, he would receive a hire car on credit while his was repaired and the charges would be paid out of the damages recovered from the defendant. Due to the cost of handling the claim and the element of risk the charge for hire was about 30 per cent more than the standard "spot rate" for car hire in that area.[240] The House of Lords unanimously held that there should no longer be any hard and fast rule that additional losses attributable to the claimant's impecuniosity were irrecoverable. However, the court was divided on whether the particular claim should succeed. For the majority this was a case where the defendant had failed to show that the claimant had behaved unreasonably in using the credit hire company. His financial position was such that he had no choice but to do so if he wished to obtain a car. That would not necessarily be so in other cases where the claimant had greater resources. The effect therefore is that we have replaced a rule which is mechanical and "efficient" in terms of the disposition of claims with a test that is somewhat

---

[236] See *Geest Plc v Lansiquot* [2002] UKPC 48; [2002] 1 W.L.R. 3111.
[237] See in particular Oliver J. in *Radford v De Froberville* [1977] 1 W.L.R. 1262 at 1268; the caustic remarks of the Court of Appeal in *Compania Financiera "Soleada" SA v Hamoor Tanker Corp Inc* [1981] 1 W.L.R. 274; and *The Sivand* [1998] 2 Lloyd's Rep. 97.
[238] [2003] UKHL 64; [2004] 1 A.C. 1067.
[239] *Bee v Jenson* [2007] EWCA Civ 923; [2007] 4 All E.R. 791.
[240] Before the advent of the credit hire system, private motorists whose cars were damaged comparatively rarely obtained hire cars and charged the costs to defendants. Although the sums involved in individual cases were small, motor insurers naturally became concerned when the new system produced many more claims for this item and bitterly fought the issue on a number of legal fronts. See, e.g. *Giles v Thompson* [1994] 1 A.C. 142; *Dimond v Lovell* [2002] 1 A.C. 384.

open-ended and therefore more likely to be productive of dispute.[241] This was the basis of the dissents. As Lord Scott said:

> "What is to be the test of sufficient impecuniosity? The sugges-
> tion has been made that lack of possession of a credit card or a
> debit card might be taken as an indication of sufficient impecu-
> niosity. But there are still many people in this country who keep
> cash in their houses, would be accounted quite well-off by most
> standards, but who do not have credit or debit cards. Some people
> have bank accounts and overdraft facilities. Their accounts may
> be consistently overdrawn but within the facility. They have no
> spare cash but the facility to borrow. How, sensibly, can their
> position be distinguished from that of those like Mr Lagden who,
> similarly, have no spare cash but have no bank overdraft facility?
> If Mr Lagden is to be entitled to reimbursement of Helphire's
> financing charge, why should the others not be entitled to re-im-
> bursement of their bank's financing charge? In each case it could
> be said that without the financing the replacement vehicle could
> not have been hired."

While the majority recognised this risk, they thought it exaggerated because it would be in the interests of motor insurers to keep
down the costs of small claims. A further complication is the fact
that in so far as the claimant was entitled to the claims handling
element of the hire charges the law is in effect allowing him to evade
the normal rule that the expense of asserting a claim is not recoverable as damages but only as costs.

Lagden v O'Connor illustrates the continuing lack of clarity on
the distinction between remoteness and mitigation.[242] The majority
of opinions are couched, as was *The Liesbosch*, mainly in terms of
remoteness but the placing of the burden on the defendant to show
that the claimant had a realistic choice between taking an ordinary
hire car and using credit hire matches the approach to mitigation.[243]
So also does the rejection of the argument that the claimant had to
bring into account against the damages the additional benefits (the
credit, the claims handling service and the waiving of charges if the
claim were unsuccessful) received from the agreement. For Lord
Hope in the majority the position was analogous to that of a
claimant whose property is damaged and which ends up more
valuable after repairs than before (e.g. because new parts have been

---

[241] Judging by LAWTEL, this seems to be a fairly frequent source of dispute at county court
level.
[242] *Lagden* at [96].
[243] The claimant must show that the damage is not too remote; the defendant must show that
the claimant failed to take reasonable steps in mitigation: *Geest Plc v Lansiquot* [2002]
UKPC 48; [2002] 1 W.L.R. 3111.

fitted, there being no equivalent used ones available).[244] The wrong-doer cannot call for a deduction on account of this "betterment" because the claimant has no choice but to accept it. If the evidence shows:

"[T]hat the claimant had no other choice available to him, the betterment must be seen as incidental to the step which he was entitled to take in the mitigation of his loss and there will be no ground for it to be deducted."[245]

For Lord Walker the case was not one of mitigation at all. If the claimant had used his car for business and stood to lose £1,000 by not having its use, then the expenditure of £460 in spot hiring (or indeed the £659 spent on credit hire) could sensibly be regarded as expenditure to mitigate that consequential loss, but the claimant kept a car solely for convenience and while he was certainly entitled to hire a reasonable substitute this could not be regarded as mitigating some greater loss. If he had not hired a car at all he would have been entitled to general damages for loss of its use and as a practical matter the law simply uses the cost of hire as a measure[246] for the otherwise unquantifiable inconvenience he suffers.[247] It is difficult to see how the measure of the inconvenience to the wealthy claimant can be only £460 whereas that to the poor claimant is £695.

(b) *Intervening acts or events.* Here it is common to return to the language of causation.[248] Everyone agrees that a consequence is too remote if it follows a "break in the chain of causation" or is due to a nova causa interveniens.[249] This means that although the defendant's breach of duty is a cause of the claimant's damage in the sense that it satisfies the "but-for" test of causation in fact, nevertheless in the eyes of the law some other intervening event is

6–34

---

[244] See para.22–45, below. However, rather than any iron rule about the claimant having no choice, it may be that the fundamental issue in such a case is whether he gets any real benefit.

[245] [2003] UKHL 64; [2004] 1 A.C. 1067 at [34].

[246] It may use a smaller measure. At the time of *Lagden* it seems that the more-or-less routine going rate in the county court where no car was hired was £10 a day: at [101].

[247] See *Lagden* at [101]. See also Lord Hobhouse in *Dimond v Lovell* [2002] 1 A.C. 384 at 406. Compare Lord Scott, also in the minority, who was prepared to accept that the hire cost can be regarded as the measure of general damages but thought it more accurately classified as an item of special damage suffered as a result of the defendant's negligence: *Lagden* at [81].

[248] "Unfortunately in this area of the law the same issues can be formulated in a number of different ways . . . It would, so I may confidently assert, surprise a newcomer to this area that there is considerable overlap even between [the questions of foreseeability and causation]": *Corr v I.B.C. Vehicles* [2006] EWCA Civ 331; [2007] Q.B. 46 at [85] per Wilson L.J. (for the appeal to the HL see para.6–41, below).

[249] If a human act is involved novus actus is often substituted.

regarded as the sole effective cause of that damage. Three classes of case fall to be considered, namely (1) where a natural event occurs independently of the act of any human being; (2) where the event consists of the act or omission of a third party; and (3) where the event consists of the act or omission of the claimant himself. It should not be thought, however, that in any of these cases the law will be particularly astute to attribute the claimant's damage to a single cause. There is no objection to a finding that the separate torts of two independent actors were both causes of the damage, and where this is so the claimant may recover in full from either of them.[250] Nor is there any objection to a finding that the defendant's breach of duty and the claimant's own fault were both causes of the claimant's damage. On the contrary, such a finding is a condition precedent to the operation of the law of contributory negligence.[251]

6–35   (I) INTERVENING NATURAL EVENT. It is, of course, impossible for anything to happen in the physical world without the operation of natural forces, but sometimes the claimant suffers damage as the immediate result of a natural event which occurs independently of the defendant's breach of duty but which would have caused the claimant no damage if the breach of duty had not occurred. In such a case, if the breach of duty has neither increased the likelihood that the claimant will suffer damage nor rendered him more susceptible to damage, it will not be treated as a cause of the damage. Thus, in *Carslogie Steamship Co Ltd v Royal Norwegian Government*[252] the claimant's ship was damaged in a collision for which the defendant's ship was wholly responsible. After temporary repairs which restored the ship to a seaworthy condition she set out on a voyage to the United States, a voyage which she would not have made had the collision not occurred. During her crossing of the Atlantic she suffered extensive damage due to heavy weather, and on her arrival in the United States the collision damage was permanently repaired at the same time that the heavy weather damage was dealt with. It was held in the House of Lords that the claimants were not even entitled to damages for the loss of the use of the ship while the collision damage was being repaired because that time was used also for the repair of the heavy weather damage. There was no question of the defendants being liable for the heavy weather damage itself—that damage:

---

[250] See para.6–7, above. For contribution between tortfeasors, see, Ch.21, below.
[251] See para.6–43, below.
[252] [1952] A.C. 292.

"[W]as not in any sense a consequence of the collision, and must be treated as a supervening event occurring in the course of a normal voyage".[253]

It was true that with the benefit of hindsight it was possible to say that if the collision had not taken place the storm damage also would not have taken place because the vessel would not have been there at that time, but no reasonable man would have said that such damage was within the likely or foreseeable risk created by the defendant's negligence.[254]

The effect of market falls in cases of negligent valuation has already been considered.[255]

(II) INTERVENING ACT OF A THIRD PARTY. If the defendant's breach **6–36** of duty has done no more than provide the occasion for an entirely independent act by a third party and that act is the immediate cause of the claimant's damage, then it will amount to a nova causa interveniens and the defendant will not be liable.[256] This, however, may not be the case if the act of the third party was not truly independent. In *The Oropesa*[257] a collision occurred between the ship of that name and another ship, the *Manchester Regiment*, for which both ships were to blame. The *Manchester Regiment* was severely damaged and her master decided to cross to the *Oropesa* in one of the ship's boats to discuss salvage arrangements with the master of the *Oropesa*. The boat overturned in heavy seas before reaching the *Oropesa* and nine of the men on board, one of whom was the claimant's son, were drowned. The question was whether his death was caused by the negligence of the *Oropesa*,[258] or whether the master's action in taking to the boat constituted a nova causa interveniens. It was held that action could not be severed from the circumstances affecting the two ships, that the "hand of the casualty lay heavily" upon the *Manchester Regiment*, and so that it was caused by and flowed from the collision.[259]

---

[253] [1952] 1 All E.R. 20 per Viscount Jowitt. Not all of his Lordship's speech is reported in the Law Reports. It seems that if the supervening event had been detention caused by an outbreak of war, the defendants would have been liable: *Monarch SS Co v Karlshamns Oljifabriker* [1949] A.C. 196.

[254] Distinguish the situation where the vessel is rendered less able to ride out the storm because of the damage inflicted on it by the defendant. See also *Chester v Afshar*, para.6–12, above.

[255] See para.6–27, above.

[256] *Weld-Blundell v Stephens* [1920] A.C. 956; *Harnett v Bond* [1925] A.C. 669; *SS Singleton Abbey v SS Paludina* [1927] A.C. 16.

[257] [1943] P. 32.

[258] It is irrelevant to this question that the negligence of the *Manchester Regiment* leading to the collision may also have been a cause of the death.

[259] [1943] P. 32 at 37 per Lord Wright.

"To break the chain of causation it must be shown that there is something which I will call ultroneous,[260] something unwarrantable, a new cause which disturbs the sequence of events, something which can be described as either unreasonable or extraneous or extrinsic."[261]

In *The Oropesa*, the action of the master was not itself tortious: he was not guilty of a breach of duty to the deceased in ordering him into the boat, but that fact is not itself decisive one way or another. A wholly unpredictable but non-tortious intervention may break the chain of causation in one case while in another even deliberate tortious conduct may not do so, though as a general proposition it is probably correct to say that the further along the scale from innocent mistake to wilful wrongdoing the third party's conduct moves the more likely it is to terminate the defendant's liability.[262] The matter is what in former times would have been regarded as a jury question[263] (though according to modern practice on appeal from trial by judge alone it is a question which the appellate court considers itself in as good a position to answer as the trial judge) and there have been calls for "common sense rather than logic"[264] and a "robust and sensible approach".[265] The student is only likely to get a "feel" for the current application of the law by reading cases, but some multiple collision cases, on each side of the line, may be used for illustration. In *Rouse v Squires*[266] D1, driving negligently, jack-knifed his lorry across a motorway; a following car collided with the lorry, and some minutes later D2's lorry, also being driven negligently, collided with the other vehicles, killing C, who was assisting at the scene. The Court of Appeal, reversing the trial judge, held that D1's negligence was an operative cause of C's death,[267] for if:

"[A] driver so negligently manages his vehicle as to cause it to obstruct the highway and constitute a danger to other road users, including those who are driving too fast or not keeping a proper lookout, but not those who deliberately or recklessly drive into

---

[260] "So Lord Wright found it necessary to go outside the dictionary, or at least to explore its furthest corners, in order to identify the kind of circumstances in which the defendant might cease to be liable for what could otherwise be regarded as the consequences of his act": *The Sivand* [1998] 2 Lloyd's Rep. 97 at 102 per Evans L.J.

[261] [1943] P. 32 at 39 per Lord Wright.

[262] *Knightley v Johns* [1982] 1 W.L.R. 349 at 365.

[263] *Wright v Lodge* [1993] 4 All E.R. 299 at 307.

[264] *Knightley v Johns*, above, fn.262, at 367.

[265] *Lamb v Camden LBC* [1981] Q.B. 625 at 647 and see Sir Robin Cook, "Remoteness of Damages and Judicial Discretion" [1978] C.L.J. 288.

[266] [1973] Q.B. 889; *Lloyds Bank Ltd v Budd* [1982] R.T.R. 80. For an example in a wholly different context see *Clarke v CC Northamptonshire, The Times*, June 14, 1999.

[267] For which D1 was held 25 per cent to blame under the Law Reform (Married Women and Tortfeasors) Act 1935.

the obstruction, then the first driver's negligence may be held to have contributed to the causation of an accident of which the immediate cause was the negligent driving of the vehicle which because of the presence of the obstruction collides with it."[268]

In contrast, in *Wright v Lodge*[269] D1's vehicle broke down and she negligently failed to take steps to remove it from the highway. D1 was liable to her passenger C1, who was injured when D2's lorry struck the car, but not to C2 and C3, who were injured by colliding with the lorry in the opposite carriageway, where it had come to rest after the collision. The effective cause of the lorry being in the other carriageway was the reckless manner in which D2 had been driving when he collided with the car.[270] The chain of causation was broken by intervening events though there was no recklessness in *Knightley v Johns*.[271] D1's negligent driving caused the blocking of a busy tunnel. After a good deal of confusion as to the location of the accident, D2, a police inspector, took charge but did not immediately close the tunnel as he should have done. He then ordered C, a constable, to drive back against the traffic for that purpose. While doing so C was struck and injured by D3, who was driving too fast into the tunnel. The Court of Appeal set aside a judgment for C against D1.[272] While it might be natural, probable and foreseeable that the police would come to deal with the accident in the tunnel and that there might be risk-taking[273] and even errors on their part, there had in fact been so many errors before the claimant was ordered to ride back down the tunnel[274] that the subsequent collision with D3 was too remote a consequence of D1's original negligence.

It is not too difficult to say that if C is knocked down and injured **6–37** by D1 and a few moments later is struck and further injured by D2, also driving negligently, D1 may bear some responsibility for the further injury. It is perhaps less intuitive to conclude that D1 might be liable for the consequences of negligent medical treatment of the injury directly inflicted by him, but he will be unless the treatment

---

[268] [1973] Q.B. at 898 per Cairns L.J.

[269] [1993] 4 All E.R. 299..

[270] D2 was of course liable to C2 and C3 (and to C1). The issue was whether D2 could claim contribution from D1. D1's share in the liability to C1 was only 10 per cent. It will be observed that both of these cases could equally well be analysed in terms of duty of care to the particular claimant, indeed *Wright v Lodge* has some affinities with *Palsgraf v Long Island Railroad* (para.5–18, above).

[271] [1982] 1 W.L.R. 349.

[272] However, D2 and D3 were liable to C. In many cases, provided all defendants are claim-worthy, these issues will essentially be related to contribution among defendants and will be of no direct concern to the claimant.

[273] Taking risks to save others from danger does not normally break the chain of causation: see para.25–16, below.

[274] See in particular [1982] 1 W.L.R. 349 at 365–366.

is completely inappropriate.[275] Generally, of course, the matter will be one of contribution between the two defendants in respect of the second injury.[276]

6–38   Most difficulty arises in the case of acts of a third party which are wilfully wrong towards the claimant, for it is especially here that the straightforward and literal application of the test of reasonable foreseeability (at least as it has been applied to personal injury cases) leads to an unacceptably wide-ranging liability.

> "In general . . . even though A is in fault, he is not responsible for injury to C which B, a stranger to him, deliberately chooses to do. Though A may have given the occasion for B's mischievous activity, B then becomes a new and independent cause."[277]

Much of the case law in this area analyses the problem in terms of the existence of a duty of care to prevent wilful injury by a third party and the problem has already been considered in that context.[278] It has been suggested that:

> "[T]he question of the existence of duty and that of whether damage brought about by the act of a third party is too remote are simply two facets of the same problem"[279]

but where the defendant has caused some initial injury to the claimant before the intervention of the third party the cases have continued to look at the question as one of remoteness. Not surprisingly, however, there is the same reluctance to find the defendant liable for the wilful wrongdoing of others. It has been said that the conduct of the third party must be something very likely to happen if it is not to break the chain of causation[280] but if anything, this formulation, whether it is to be regarded as a separate test to be applied after that of reasonable foreseeability,[281] or as representing

---

[275] *Webb v Barclays Bank Plc* [2001] EWCA Civ 1141; [2002] P.I.Q.R. P8, following *Mahony v Kruschich (Demolitions) Pty* (1985) 59 A.L.R. 722. In *Prendergast v Sam & Dee Ltd, The Times*, March 14, 1989, D1, a doctor, wrote an unclear prescription; D2, a pharmacist misread it, though he should have been put on inquiry. D2's act did not break the chain of causation and the relative responsibility was assessed as 75 per cent to D2. Cf. *Horton v Evans* [2006] EWHC 2808 (QB); [2007] P.N.L.R. 17 (pharmacist liable for failing to question prescription, doctor prescribing repeat prescription not at fault).

[276] Cf. the difficult case of *Rahman v Arearose Ltd* [2001] Q.B. 351, where it was conceded that the medical treatment was the sole cause of the loss of the eye.

[277] *Weld-Blundell v Stephens* [1920] A.C. 956 at 986 per Lord Sumner.

[278] See para.5–31, above.

[279] *Perl v Camden London Borough* [1984] Q.B. 342 per Oliver L.J.

[280] *Home Office v Dorset Yacht Co Ltd* [1970] A.C. 1004 per Lord Reid. Note, however, that the majority of the House of Lords regarded this case as about duty, not causation.

[281] *Lamb v Camden London Borough* [1981] Q.B. 625 at 647 per Watkins L.J.

what the hypothetical reasonable man would contemplate[282] probably understates the burden on the claimant and:

> "[T]here may be circumstances in which the court would require
> a degree of likelihood amounting almost to inevitability before it
> fixes the defendant with responsibility for the act of a third party
> over whom he had and can have no control."[283]

In *Lamb v Camden London Borough*[284] the defendants' negligence caused the claimant's house to be damaged and become
unoccupied but they were not liable for the further damage done by
the depredations of squatters, notwithstanding a finding by the
Official Referee that squatting was "foreseeable". On the other
hand, in *Ward v Cannock Chase DC* on rather similar facts, but
where the defendants had been guilty of wilful delay in effecting
repairs and where the risk of vandal damage was rather higher, they
were found liable for the further loss.[285] The consequence of all of
this may be, of course, that precisely the same physical act may or
may not break the chain of causation depending on the mental state
of the actor: further negligence may be within the risk created by the
defendant when wilful conduct may not.[286] So also, the intervening
deliberate act of a child may not break the chain when that of an
adult would.

The above principles are applicable where there are no special **6–39**
circumstances imposing upon the defendant a duty to take care to
guard against the wrongdoing of the third party. If such a duty exists,
it would be futile to classify the damage as too remote merely
because it was wilfully inflicted. A driver who knocks down a
pedestrian would not be liable for theft of the pedestrian's wallet
while he was lying injured, but a bailee, who is under a duty
(normally, but not necessarily, arising from a contract) to safeguard
his bailor's goods, is just as much liable where, by his default, they
are stolen by a burglar as he is where they are destroyed in a fire.[287]

---

[282] [1981] Q.B 625 at 644, 647 per Oliver L.J. Lord Mackay in *Smith v Littlewoods Organisation Ltd* [1987] A.C. 241, would appear to agree, despite the remark at 263E.

[283] *Lamb v Camden London Borough*, above, fn.281, at 647 per Oliver L.J. Cf. *Alexis v Newham LBC* [2009] EWHC 1323 (QB) (prank by school child; but no breach).

[284] [1981] Q.B. 625.

[285] [1986] Ch. 546. But the defendants were not liable for theft of the claimant's goods, perhaps because he could have taken steps himself to secure those. Note that this case shows (at 558) that Lord Denning M.R. was wrong in *Lamb*'s case to assume that claimants will have insurance against these losses.

[286] *Environment Agency v Empress Car Co Ltd* [1999] 2 A.C. 22 at 30. A good example is *Watson v Kentucky & Indiana Bridge R.R.* 126 S.W. 146 (1916). D negligently derailed a petrol tanker. X struck a match and caused an explosion. New trial ordered for failure to leave to jury issue of D's liability upon conflicting testimony that X acted negligently or maliciously. See also *Philco Radio, etc. Corp v J. Spurling Ltd* [1949] 2 K.B. 33.

[287] In *Lockspeiser Aircraft Ltd v Brooklands Aircraft Co Ltd, The Times*, March 7, 1990, the intruder started a fire which destroyed the goods.

In *Stansbie v Troman*[288] a decorator was at work in a house and left it for two hours to get wallpaper. He was alone and had been told by the householder to close the front door whenever he left the house. Instead of doing so he left the door unlocked and during his absence a thief entered the house and stole a diamond bracelet and some clothes. The Court of Appeal held that the decorator was liable for the loss.[289] Similarly, in *Haynes v Harwood*[290] the defendants were held liable when the claimant was injured by their horses which had been left unattended in the street and caused to bolt by a mischievous boy. It was negligent to leave the horses unattended precisely because children might interfere.[291]

6–40   (III) INTERVENING ACT OF THE CLAIMANT. Where it is the claimant's own act or omission which, in combination with the defendant's breach of duty, has brought about his damage, then the problem is generally seen as one of contributory negligence. Before there can be any question of contributory negligence, however, it is necessary that both the claimant's lack of care and the defendant's breach of duty shall be found to have been causes of the claimant's damage and in some cases, especially those in which the claimant seeks to recover for damage suffered in a second accident, the defendant has been exonerated on the ground that the claimant's conduct amounted to a nova causa interveniens. In *McKew v Holland & Hannen & Cubitts (Scotland) Ltd*[292] the pursuer had suffered an injury in an accident for which the defenders were liable and as a result he occasionally lost control of his left leg which gave way under him. Some days after this accident he went to inspect a flat which was approached by a steep stair between two walls and without a handrail. On leaving the flat he started to descend the stair holding his young daughter by the hand and going ahead of his wife

---

[288] [1948] 2 K.B. 48, criticised by Lord Denning M.R. in *Lamb*'s case, above, fn.284, at 638 but approved by Lord Goff in *Smith v Littlewoods*, above, fn.282, at 272. The defendant was not a bailee.

[289] Even in these cases the loss must be within the ambit of the duty. Would the defendant have been liable for malicious damage? For the seizure of the house by squatters? In *Royscot Trust Ltd v Rogerson* [1991] 2 Q.B. 297, D, a dealer, misrepresented to a finance company that a customer taking a car on hire purchase had paid the minimum deposit required by the finance company (the representation was not alleged to be fraudulent). The customer wrongfully sold the vehicle and this was held, for the purposes of the statutory cause of action under the Misrepresentation Act 1967 s.2(1) to be a reasonably foreseeable act which did not break the chain of causation. The purpose of requiring a minimum deposit was to reduce the risk of placing cars with customers who might default and wrongful disposition was just one variety of default.

[290] [1935] 1 K.B. 147.

[291] [1935] 1 K.B. 147 at 153 per Greer L.J. Would the defendant have been liable if an adult had caused the horses to bolt? Cf. *Topp v London Country Bus* [1993] 1 W.L.R. 976, where the matter was considered in terms of duty.

[292] [1969] 3 All E.R. 1621 (H.L.Sc.). *The San Onofre* [1922] P. 243. Cf. *Wieland v Cyril Lord Carpets Ltd* [1969] 3 All E.R. 1006.

and brother-in-law who had accompanied him. Suddenly he lost control of his left leg, threw his daughter back in order to save her, and tried to jump so as to land in an upright position instead of falling down the stairs. As a result he sustained a severe fracture of his ankle. The House of Lords agreed that the pursuer's act of jumping in the emergency in which he found himself did not break the chain of causation, but that it had been broken by his conduct in placing himself unnecessarily in a position where he might be confronted by just such an emergency, when he could have descended the stair slowly and carefully by himself or sought the assistance of his wife or brother-in-law.

The basis of the decision of the House of Lords in this case was that the pursuer's conduct amounted to a nova causa interveniens because, even though it may have been foreseeable, it was unreasonable in the circumstances.[293] If he had no reasonable alternative to acting as he did his conduct would not have broken the chain of causation.[294] The threshold of unreasonableness set by *McKew* is a high one, though there is no basis for saying that it must involve deliberate or reckless risk-taking.[295] The rationale of nova causa interveniens is fairness between the parties[296] and the court should be slow to stigmatise the claimant's behaviour as unreasonable merely because he does not take the course which is cheapest for the defendant. In *Emeh v Kensington and Chelsea and Westminster Health Authority*[297] the defendants negligently performed a sterilisation operation on the claimant and she became pregnant again, though she did not discover this until 20 weeks into the pregnancy. The Court of Appeal rejected the argument that her refusal to have an abortion broke the chain of causation between the negligence and the child's birth.[298] As Slade L.J. put it:

---

[293] [1969] 3 All E.R. 1621 at 1623 per Lord Reid.

[294] For a strong example, where there was not even contributory negligence, see *NSW v Nominal Defendant* [2009] NSWCA 255. A rescuer will not be regarded as acting unreasonably because he takes a risk, para.25–17, below.

[295] *Spencer v Wincanton Holdings Ltd* [2009] EWCA Civ 1404. Aikens L.J. at [45] thought that the, "line between a set of facts which results in a finding of contributory negligence and a set of facts which results in a finding that the "unreasonable conduct" of the claimant constitutes a novus actus interveniens is not, in my view, capable of precise definition." In *Smith v Youth Justice Board* [2010] EWCA Civ 99 D was at fault in taking a complacent attitude to the dangers of a method of restraint of persons in custody. This led to the death of X, and C, who had participated in using the method on X, claimed to have suffered psychiatric trauma as a result. The claim failed, because, even assuming that a review would have led to the abandonment of the method, its use on that occasion was in breach of the rules and excessive and prevented any causative link between the fault of D and the injury of C.

[296] *Corr v IBC Vehicles Ltd* [2008] UKHL 13; [2008] A.C. 884 at [15].

[297] [1985] Q.B. 1012.

[298] This was at a time when the courts allowed damages for the cost of upbringing of an unwanted child in such cases, but see now para.24–15, below. However, the child was born with abnormalities so some of the claim might still succeed.

"[S]ave in the most exceptional circumstances, I cannot think it right that the court should ever declare it unreasonable for a woman to decline to have an abortion, in a case where there is no evidence that there were any medical or psychiatric grounds for terminating the particular pregnancy."[299]

6–41   We have seen that the wilful conduct of a third party is more likely to break the chain of causation than negligence on his part but that the defendant may be liable in respect of wilful acts the guarding against which is the very foundation of his duty. There is a close analogy in the case of wilful conduct by the claimant. In *Reeves v Metropolitan Police Commissioner*[300] the claimant committed suicide while in police custody. The case was fought on the basis that he was sane at the time. A majority of the House of Lords held that since the defendants owed the claimant a duty of care to prevent him inflicting harm on himself[301] it would be futile at the next step to go on to hold that his voluntary decision to die broke the chain of causation.[302] There was, however, a reduction of damages under the Law Reform (Contributory Negligence) Act 1945.[303]

Another possibility is that the defendant injures the claimant and the latter, because of depression brought about by the accident, commits suicide.[304] Can the defendant be liable for his death? An affirmative answer was given by the House of Lords in *Corr v IBC Vehicles Ltd*[305] even though the deceased was not insane in the legal sense. Whether or not suicide could be regarded as "reasonably foreseeable" at the time of the initial injury the defendant had to take his victim as he found him, his psychological weaknesses as well as physical ones.[306] There was, however, a difference of opinion as to whether the facts warranted a reduction in damages under the Law Reform (Contributory Negligence) Act 1945. The deceased

---

[299] [1985] Q.B. 1012 at 1024. See also *The Calliope* [1970] P. 172, maritime collision caused by negligence of claimant and defendant; claimant vessel sustaining further damage in turning because of Chief Officer's negligence turning; manoeuvre difficult but not unreasonable and did not break chain of causation; defendant liable for further damage, subject to further apportionment for contributory negligence: para.6–53, below.

[300] [2000] 1 A.C. 360.

[301] The duty was conceded: see para.5–33, above.

[302] Nor was *volenti* applicable (para.25–8, below); nor was the claim against public policy (para.25–20, below).

[303] See para.6–45, below.

[304] Cf. the extraordinary case of *AMP General Insurance Ltd v Roads and Traffic Authority of NSW* [2001] NSWCA 186, where the trigger of the depression leading to suicide was the deceased's cross-examination during his pursuit of his claim and this was held to break the chain of causation.

[305] [2008] UKHL 13; [2008] A.C. 884. A similar answer had been given in *Pigney v Pointer's Transport Services* [1957] 1 W.L.R. 1121, even though suicide was then a crime.

[306] There is some difference of opinion as to which it was because some members of the court did not wish to rely on the controversial decision in *Page v Smith* (para.5–63, above). However, it is not clear this concern was well founded. Page was not physically injured in the accident, Corr was and very severely.

was not legally irresponsible and would have been liable if he had killed a passer-by when he jumped from the high building and Lord Scott would have made a reduction of 20 per cent to reflect a degree of responsibility for his own death. Lords Mance and Neuberger did not rule out a reduction in principle but were not prepared to make one because the issue had not been pressed and explored in detail below; and Lords Bingham and Walker would not have made a reduction in any event on the facts.[307]

4. CONTRIBUTORY NEGLIGENCE[308]

If the claimant's injuries have been caused partly by the negligence of the defendant and partly by his own negligence,[309] then, at common law, the claimant could recover nothing. This rule of "contributory negligence" first appeared at the beginning of the 19th century, though the general idea is traceable much earlier. The courts modified the defence of contributory negligence by the so-called rule of last opportunity. This enabled the claimant to recover notwithstanding his own negligence, if upon the occasion of the accident the defendant could have avoided the accident while the claimant could not. The authorities were confused, and confusion was made worse confounded by the extension of the rule, in *British Columbia Electric Ry v Loach*,[310] to cases of "constructive last opportunity". This meant that if the defendant would have had the last opportunity but for his own negligence, he was in the same position as if he had actually had it, and the claimant again recovered in full. Apportionment of the loss between claimant and defendant became possible in cases of maritime collision under the Maritime Conventions Act 1911. The Law Reform (Contributory Negligence) Act 1945[311] applied the principle on which the Maritime Conventions act 1911[312] was based to contributory negligence on land and today, therefore, the claimant's damages may be

6–42

---

[307] There is probably less distance between the members of the court than might be thought. The deceased was undoubtedly suffering from serious depression but Lord Bingham seems to have been prepared to contemplate that a truly voluntary suicide based on the deceased's assessment that his life was not worth living might break the chain of causation altogether: at [15].

[308] Williams, *Joint Torts and Contributory Negligence*. The expression should not be used to describe the situation where the combined negligence of D1 and D2 inflicts injury on C (see Ch.21).

[309] The burden of proving the claimant's negligence lies with the defendant: *Heranger (Owners) v SS Diamond* [1939] A.C. 94 at 104 per Lord Wright; *Fitzgerald v Lane* [1989] A.C. 328.

[310] [1916] 1 A.C. 719.

[311] The common law rule of "all or nothing" was more tenacious in the USA, but there was a fundamental shift after the 1960s and now nearly all states have some form of apportionment. In American terminology a regime which allows reduction of damages is generally called "comparative negligence". See Dobbs, *Torts* (2000) §201.

[312] The Act of 1911 was unaffected by the Act of 1945.

reduced wherever both parties have been negligent and both have contributed to the damage.[313] It is still open to the court to conclude that the fault of only one party was the sole effective cause of the loss[314] but all the refinements of "last opportunity" have gone. The relevant provisions of the Maritime Conventions Act 1911 have been re-enacted in s.187 of the Merchant Shipping Act 1995. A reduction for contributory negligence will generally[315] mean a loss for the claimant which he will have to bear, whereas in most cases the defendant will be insured against liability. Nevertheless, where liability is based on fault it would be difficult to ignore the contributory fault of the claimant. We also generally[316] apply contributory negligence in cases of strict liability, where the defendant's responsibility may be regarded as based on "risk"; the argument is that claimants, like defendants, need some incentive to avoid accidents.[317]

A. Present Law—the Act of 1945

6–43   Section 1(1) of the Act of 1945 provides as follows:

> "Where any person suffers damage as the result partly of his own fault and partly of the fault of any other person or persons, a claim in respect of that damage shall not be defeated by reason of the fault of the person suffering the damage, but the damages recoverable in respect thereof shall be reduced to such extent as the court thinks just and equitable having regard to the claimant's share in the responsibility for the damage."[318]

By s.4, damage includes loss of life and personal injury. It also includes economic loss[319] and injury to property. By the same section "fault" means negligence, breach of statutory duty or other

---

[313] Apportionment for contributory negligence came rather later in Australia. Now, in one context, the complete defence is back with a bang. See the Civil Liability Act 2002 (NSW) Pt 6 (no recovery for intoxicated claimant unless proved that injury was likely to have occurred even if he had not been intoxicated).

[314] See para.6–46, below.

[315] But not necessarily: in some cases the claimant may be covered by loss insurance, to which the claimant's fault (depending on the terms of the policy) will be irrelevant.

[316] For an exception, see the Nuclear Installations Act 1965.

[317] Cf. the French road accident regime, which attenuates contributory fault in claims by non-driver victims. See van Gerven, Lever and Larouche, *Tort Law (Common Law of Europe Casebooks)* Ch.6.2.1.B.

[318] The section does not operate to defeat any defence arising under a contract (though such defences will be limited in scope after the Unfair Contract Terms Act 1977), nor can the amount of damages recoverable exceed the limit fixed by any contract or enactment applicable to the claim: s.1(2) and (6). The court must find and record the total damages which would have been recoverable had the claimant not been at fault. The Act binds the Crown: Crown Proceedings Act 1947 s.4(3). The Act must be pleaded: *Fookes v Slaytor* [1978] 1 W.L.R. 1293.

[319] See, e.g. *Platform Home Loans Ltd v Oyston Shipways Ltd* [2000] 2 A.C. 190.

act or omission which gives rise to a liability in tort or would, apart from the Act, give rise to the defence of contributory negligence.

B. The Scope of the Act

The proper construction of the definition of fault in s.4 is that the **6–44** words, "negligence, breach of statutory duty or other act or omission which would give rise to liability in tort" apply to the "original" liability-creating fault of the defendant, and the contributory fault of the claimant is negligence, breach of statutory duty or other act or omission which gave rise at common law to a defence of contributory negligence.[320] The scope of the Act is therefore wide, but not unlimited, for there were a number of torts where at common law the defendant could not escape liability by showing "contributory negligence" on the part of the claimant and this is carried over into the statutory regime. Thus the 1945 Act is inapplicable to intentional interference with goods,[321] to deceit[322] or to other claims based upon dishonesty, whether framed as conspiracy, inducing breach of contract or in some other way.[323] A fraudster cannot say that his victim should have been more cautious in relying on what he said. However, it must be borne in mind that with regard to a particular item of loss, failure by the claimant to act with common prudence when he has reason to know about the dishonesty may lead to the conclusion that he is the author of his own misfortune.[324] After some hesitation, the courts seem now to accept that the Act may be applicable to cases of intentional trespass to the person, given sufficiently serious conduct on the part of the claimant.[325] The

---

[320] *Standard Chartered Bank v Pakistan National Shipping Corp (Nos 2 and 4)* [2002] UKHL 43; [2003] 1 A.C. 959 at [11].

[321] Torts (Interference with Goods) Act 1977 s.11; but under the Banking Act 1979 s.47, a collecting banker sued for conversion of a cheque in circumstances in which the Cheques Act 1957 s.4, would be applicable has "a defence of contributory negligence". It is thought that this means that the 1945 Act applies. Cf. the position in New Zealand: *Dairy Containers v NZI Bank* [1995] 2 N.Z.L.R. 30.

[322] *Standard Chartered Bank v Pakistan National Shipping Corp (Nos 2 and 4)*, above, fn.320.

[323] *Corporacion Nacional de Cobre de Chile v Sogemin Metals Ltd* [1997] 1 W.L.R. 1396. The identical New Zealand statute was held not to apply to the economic torts in *Dellabarca v Storemen and Packers Union* [1980] 2 N.Z.L.R. 734.

[324] *Corporacion Nacional de Cobre de Chile*, above, fn.323; *Doyle v Olby (Ironmongers) Ltd* [1969] 2 Q.B. 158 at 168.

[325] *Murphy v Culhane* [1977] Q.B. 96; *Barnes v Nayer, The Times*, December 19, 1986; *Wasson v CC, R.U.C.* (1987) 6 B.N.I.L. 140; *Tumelty v MoD* (1988) 4 B.N.I.L. 140; *Parmer v Big Security Co Ltd* [2008] EWHC 1414 (QB); contra, *Horkin v Melbourne Football Club* [1983] V.R. 153. See Hudson, "Contributory Negligence as a Defence to Battery" (1984) 4 L.S.332. Cf. *Lane v Holloway* [1968] 1 Q.B. 379 and see para.25–18, below. In *Standard Chartered Bank v Pakistan National Shipping Corp (Nos 2 and 4)*, above, fn.320, Lord Rodger at [45] reserved his opinion on *Murphy v Culhane*. In *Bici v MoD* [2004] EWHC 786 (QB) Elias J. at [111] expressed the view that it would be a very rare case in which the negligence of the claimant could be set up against the deliberate wrongdoing of the defendant.

Act does not apply to claims for breach of contract where the
defendant's liability arises from some contractual provision which
does not depend on negligence on his part[326] (for example, the
implied terms to be found in ss.12 to 15 of the Sale of Goods Act
1979) or from a contractual obligation which is expressed in terms
of taking care but which does not correspond to a common law duty
to take care which would exist in the given case independently of
contract.[327] Where, however, the defendant's liability, though
framed in contract, is the same as his liability in the tort of negligence independently of the existence of any contract, the Act is
applicable.[328] This would be the case, for example, in a claim for
personal injuries by a patient against a doctor giving private treatment, by passenger against carrier or by visitor against occupier,[329]
and in a claim against a solicitor or valuer.[330] What if the defendant
is liable in tort to the claimant but the claimant has committed a
breach of contract which cannot be framed as a liability in tort (for
example, breach of a strict repairing covenant in a lease)? The 1945
Act is inapplicable because the claimant's conduct is not "contributory negligence", but it has been held that the court has power to
apportion, based on causation.[331] The difference in principles applicable to contributory fault in contract and tort has, like limitation of
actions, been a significant source of litigation over the boundary
between those two heads of liability, particularly where economic
loss is in issue,[332] and the position worked out by the courts does go
some way towards preventing a purely tactical approach to cases.
However, it is difficult to see why a regime of apportionment should
be inapplicable to a duty to take care which arises in contract only,
and the Law Commission recommended legislation on similar lines

[326] *Barclays Bank v Fairclough Building Ltd* [1995] Q.B. 214.
[327] *Forsikringsaktieselskapet Vesta v Butcher* [1988] 3 W.L.R. 565 (affirmed [1989] A.C.
852); *Raflatac Ltd v Eade* [1999] 1 Lloyd's Rep. 506. It seems that in contract the matter
is to be dealt with as one of causation, so that the claimant recovers his whole loss unless
his fault is the substantial cause of the accident, in which case he recovers nothing. In
Lambert v Lewis [1982] A.C. 268 a party's negligence was held to be the effective cause
of his loss rather than the breach of warranty of the dealer who had supplied him, thus
preventing recovery of a contractual indemnity. See also para.26–11, below, "negligence"
in the Limitation Act 1980 s.14A.
[328] *Forsikringsaktieselskapet Vesta v Butcher*, above, fn.327; *Youell v Bland Welch & Co Ltd
(No.2)* [1990] 2 Lloyd's Rep. 431.
[329] *Sayers v Harlow UDC* [1958] 1 W.L.R. 623. Hence the claimant guilty of a small degree
of contributory negligence cannot avoid a reduction by pleading his claim only in contract.
Cf. *Astley v Austrust Ltd* (1999) 161 A.L.R. 155. In *Pilmer v Duke Group Ltd* [2001] HCA
31; 180 A.L.R. 249 the court declined to apply the contributory negligence legislation to
breach of fiduciary duty.
[330] *UCB Bank Plc v Hepherd Winstanley & Pugh* [1999] Lloyd's Rep. P.N. 963.
[331] *Tennant Radiant Heat Ltd v Warrington Development Corp* [1988] 11 E.G. 71. In *Bank of
Nova Scotia v Hellenic Mutual War Risks Association* [1990] 1 Q.B. 818 it was said that
the, "scope and extent of this . . . case will have to be a matter of substantial argument"
in a future case.
[332] See, e.g. *Barclays Bank v Fairclough Building Ltd (No.2)* [1995] I.R.L.R. 605.

for such contractual duties.[333] However, notwithstanding the applicability of the 1945 Act to some instances of "strict" liability in tort, it was not proposed that the new provisions should extend to strict contractual duties, for example those arising under s.14 of the Sale of Goods Act 1979.

Turning to the conduct of the claimant to which the Act applies, **6–45** it is not confined to contributory *negligence*. Where the claimant intends to do harm to himself and that does not break the chain of causation entirely, the Act is applicable, so that in *Reeves v Metropolitan Police Commissioner*,[334] where the defendants were in breach of duty to prevent the sane deceased killing himself, the damages were reduced by 50 per cent. Some may think it odd that his death was not wholly his own fault[335]; it would certainly have been very odd to say that his decision played no part at all in his death,[336] even if the result does look like a rather unprincipled compromise.[337] There was intentional wrongdoing by the claimant in *Standard Chartered Bank v Pakistan National Shipping Corp (Nos 2 and 4)*[338] but, unlike in *Reeves*, it was not intentional as to the *loss suffered.* Shipowners knowingly presented to the claimant bank an incorrectly dated bill of lading and the bank (not having noticed the falsity) paid the seller of the goods under a letter of credit issued by a Vietnamese bank. The claimant bank then presented the various shipping documents to the Vietnamese bank, concealing the fact that some of these did not conform with the letter of credit. The Vietnamese bank noticed discrepancies and refused to pay the claimant bank on the letter of credit. When the claimant bank sued the shipowners for deceit the latter contended that since the claimant bank had themselves unsuccessfully attempted to deceive the Vietnamese bank, their loss[339] was at least partly their own fault under the 1945 Act. However, while the claimants intended to deceive the Vietnamese bank, they did not intend to lose their payment under the credit; with regard to that, they were "negligent" and the case was governed, without reference to *Reeves*, by the ordinary rule that a fraudster cannot rely on the contributory negligence of his victim.[340]

---

[333] Law Com. No.219 (1993).

[334] [2000] 1 A.C. 360.

[335] See para.6–41, above.

[336] This is a robust interpretation, but given the way the Act looks back to what the common law would have said before 1945 (when such matters had probably never been considered) the court must indulge in some creative history.

[337] Another "compromise" may be *Revill v Newberry* [1996] Q.B. 567, where the defence of illegality (para.25–18, below) was rejected in a claim by a burglar shot by the landowner but there was a two thirds reduction under the 1945 Act.

[338] [2002] UKHL 43; [2003] 1 A.C. 959.

[339] i.e. the amount of the payment under the credit, less whatever was realised by the sale of the cargo.

[340] Cf. Sir Anthony Evans in the CA [2001] 1 Q.B. 167.

The relationship between negligence and deceit arose in a curious form in *Barings Plc v Coopers & Lybrand*.[341] A, an auditor, failed to detect fraud by B, an employee of the company being audited. A relied without proper investigation on representations made by B. When sued by the company, A contended that since the company was liable for the deceit of B, A therefore had a defence to the company's claim on the ground of circuity of action. This was rejected. The case was different from the simple one where the fraudster cannot raise the contributory fault of the representee because it was A's function to look for things like B's fraud. The cause of the loss was not B's fraud but A's failure to detect it:

> "[B's] employer can say 'it was your job to check the truth of what [B] said. You cannot sue me for being deceived [by B] when, if you had done your job, you would not have been' ".[342]

In such a case B's fraud neither extinguishes nor reduces A's liability.

C. Causation of Damage

6–46   In the majority of cases the claimant's negligence will have contributed to the *accident* which led to his injury (as where a driver or pedestrian fails to keep a proper look-out or an employee omits to turn off a machine before cleaning it) but this is not necessary for a finding of contributory negligence: what is essential is that the claimant's conduct contributes to his *damage*. Thus there may be a reduction where a motorcyclist fails to wear a crash helmet,[343] where a passenger in a car does not wear his seat belt,[344] or where a man rides in a dangerous position on the outside of a dust cart,[345] or rides with a driver whom he knows to have taken substantial quantities of alcohol.[346] It is, however, essential that the claimant's

---

[341] [2003] EWHC 1319 (Ch); [2003] PNLR 34.

[342] At [733].

[343] *O'Connel v Jackson* [1972] 1 Q.B. 270; *Capps v Miller* [1989] 2 All E.R. 333. See also *Smith v Finch* [2009] EWHC 53 (QB) (pedal cyclist not wearing helmet).

[344] *Froom v Butcher* [1976] Q.B. 286, para.6–48, below.

[345] *Davies v Swan Motor Co* [1949] 2 K.B. 291. The fact that the contributory negligence need not contribute to the accident means that it may be very difficult to distinguish it from the duty to mitigate damage. Before the Act, the courts seem to have regarded contributory negligence as something that related to the occurrence of the initial injury and mitigation as relating to the time after that occurrence. Failure to mitigate would debar the claimant from any recovery for additional loss suffered by reason of that failure but would have no effect on his other loss. The Act probably does not apply to failure to mitigate, but for a powerful argument that it should see Williams, Ch.11. For an account of the confusion which prevails in this area see *Ackland v Commonwealth* [2007] NSWCA 250.

[346] *Owens v Brimmel* [1977] Q.B. 859. See also *Gregory v Kelly* [1978] R.T.R. 426 (knowledge of defective brakes).

lack of care should be a contributory factor to his damage, and this means not only that his fault should be a cause in fact of his loss, but that the loss is within the broad scope of the risk created by his fault. In *Jones v Livox Quarries Ltd*,[347] the claimant was riding on the towbar at the back of a "traxcavator" vehicle in order to return from his place of work to the canteen when the driver of another vehicle negligently drove into the back of the traxcavator and caused him injury. Though the obvious danger arising from riding on the towbar was that of being thrown off, it was held that the risk of injury from the traxcavator being run into from behind was also one to which the claimant had exposed himself and his damages were reduced accordingly. The result would have been otherwise if, for example, he had been hit in the eye by a shot from a negligent sportsman.[348] In that case his presence on the towbar would have been only part of the history.[349] Similarly, if a person suffering from a disease caused by smoking dies because of the failure to provide medical treatment which would have saved him, damages in respect of the death are not to be reduced by his fault in smoking.[350] One word of warning should be added here. While it always seems to have been accepted that only causative fault has any role to play in cases of contributory negligence, the Court of Appeal has held that under the similar regime of contribution by multiple tortfeasors under the Civil Liability (Contribution) Act 1945[351] non-causative fault may be taken into account. The limits (or indeed the validity) of that proposition are not clear and it would probably be difficult to convince the court that the same should apply in the context of contributory negligence.

The power to apportion damages under the Act certainly meant that we were freed from some of the artificiality of the old law and there is no longer the same temptation to avoid finding a small element of contributory negligence on the part of the claimant.[352] However, we should guard against the assumption that merely because the acts of the claimant and the defendant combine in a

---

[347] [1952] 2 Q.B. 608.

[348] For a somewhat more colourful example, see *Moor v Nolan* (1960) 94 I.L.T.R. 153. In *Monie v Australia* [2007] NSWCA 230 an employer's perfunctory inquiries on hiring a worker may have been fault in relation to his economic interests but not in relation to violence by the worker.

[349] [1952] 2 Q.B. at 616 per Denning L.J. See also, at 612 per Singleton L.J., at 618 per Hodson L.J.

[350] *St George v Home Office* [2008] EWCA Civ 1068; [2008] 4 All E.R. 1039 (prisoner falling from bunk because of drug addiction seizure). In this and the example in the text the "fault" goes far back into the past but it is submitted that the same is true of a person brought into hospital after an accident which is his fault: the hospital must take him as it finds him and cannot go back into his pre-admission history. See also *Calvert v William Hill Credit Ltd* [2008] EWCA Civ 427; [2009] Ch. 330.

[351] See para.21–5, below.

[352] *Boy Andrew (Owners) v St Rognvald (Owners)* [1948] A.C. 140 at 155 per Lord Porter; *Sayers v Harlow UDC* [1958] 1 W.L.R. 623 at 630 per Lord Evershed M.R.

factual sense to cause the injury that the case is one for apportionment, for the intention of the Act was to alter only the legal
consequences of contributory negligence and not the general rules
for determining whether a case of contributory negligence exists.[353]
What was the legal cause of the event involves an enquiry of the
same nature as existed before the Act.[354] Thus it is still perfectly
possible for a court to come to the conclusion that as a matter of
legal cause the fault of the claimant is so overwhelming that he must
bear the whole loss.[355] This is typified in a series of cases where
employers were guilty of breaches of strict statutory duty but the
breaches were brought about solely by the failure of the claimants,
experienced workmen, to carry out clear safety procedures in which
they had been properly instructed.[356]

D. Duty of Care

6–47   The existence of a duty of care is, of course, essential to a cause
of action for negligence, but for contributory negligence it is quite
unnecessary that the claimant should owe a duty of the defendant.[357]
All that is required is that the claimant should have failed to take
reasonable care for his own safety.[358] One sometimes comes across
references to the claimant owing himself a duty to take care of his
own safety,[359] but strictly speaking this, like the "duty" to mitigate,
is a contradiction in terms. The fact that the defendant is under a
duty of care to guide and supervise the claimant does not necessarily
exclude contributory negligence if the claimant fails to warn the
defendant that he is "getting out of his depth".[360]

---

[353] *Davies v Swan Motor Co* [1949] 2 K.B. 291 at 310 per Bucknill L.J., at 322 per Denning
L.J.

[354] *Stapley v Gypsum Mines Ltd* [1953] A.C. 663 at 677, 681, 684, 687 (two miners abandoned
attempt to bring down unsafe part of roof; one of them killed in subsequent fall; widow
suing employers as vicariously responsible for fault of other miner). This case provoked
much judicial disagreement during its passage. The decision that the fault of both men
contributed to the accident was followed on somewhat similar facts in *I.C.I. Ltd v Shatwell*
[1965] A.C. 565 but the House of Lords in that case was able to come to a different
conclusion by the application of the defence of volenti non fit injuria: para.25–9, below.

[355] See para.6–53, below.

[356] *Rushton v Turner Bros* [1960] 1 W.L.R. 96; *Ginty v Belmont Building Supplies Ltd* [1959]
1 All E.R. 414; *Horne v Lec Refrigeration Ltd* [1965] 2 All E.R. 898; cf. *Ross v Associated
Portland Cement Manufacturers Ltd* [1964] 1 W.L.R. 768. For civil liability for breach of
statutory duty in factories, etc. see Chs 7 and 8, below.

[357] Nevertheless, it will often be the case, as where there is a collision between two vehicles,
that the claimant does owe a duty of care to the defendant. A duty is essential if the
defendant wishes to counterclaim against the claimant in respect of his own damage. In the
unusual case of *La Plante v La Plante* (1995) 125 D.L.R. (4th) 569, C was jointly and
severally liable with A to B but was not guilty of contributory negligence in relation to his
claim against A.

[358] *Nance v British Columbia Electric Ry* [1951] A.C. 601 at 611 per Viscount Simon; *Davies
v Swan Motor Co* [1949] 2 K.B. 291 for a full discussion.

[359] e.g. *Langley v Dray* [1998] P.I.Q.R. P314 at 320.

[360] *Anderson v Lyotier* [2008] EWHC 2790 (QB).

E. Standard of Care

If what is alleged is negligence by the claimant, the standard of **6-48**
care expected of him for his own safety is in general the same as that
in negligence itself[361] and is in the same sense objective and impersonal,[362] though, as there, some concession is made towards children[363] and probably towards other persons suffering from some
infirmity of disability[364] rendering them unable to come up to the
normal standard.[365] Putting aside such exceptional cases, a:

> "[P]erson is guilty of contributory negligence if he ought reason-
> ably to have foreseen that, if he did not act as a reasonable,
> prudent man, he might be hurt himself and in his reckonings he
> must take into account the possibility of others being
> careless."[366]

The degree of want of care which will constitute contributory
negligence varies with the circumstances[367]: the law certainly does
not require the claimant to proceed on his way like a timorous
fugitive constantly looking over his shoulder for threats from others.[368] For example, it is not the law that a pedestrian is guilty of

[361] *Billings & Sons Ltd v Riden* [1958] A.C. 240. "Fault" in the Act of 1945 does not include
some fault falling short of negligence: *Jones v Price* [1963] C.L.Y. 2316.

[362] See para.5-75, above.

[363] See below.

[364] Not self-induced intoxication: *Owens v Brimmell* [1977] Q.B. 859.

[365] *Daly v Liverpool Corp* [1939] 2 All E.R. 142; *M'Kibbon v Glasgow Corp* 1920 S.C. 590;
cf. *Baxter v Woolcombers* (1963) 107 S.J. 553. The proposition is, indeed, implicit in
Haley v London Electricity Board [1965] A.C. 778 since a sighted person would have had
no difficulty in avoiding the danger. On the other hand, an infirm person may act in such
an unpredictable way that there is no breach of duty by the defendant: *Bourhill v Young*
[1943] A.C. 92 at 109; *Barnes v Flucker* 1985 S.L.T. 142.

[366] *Jones v Livox Quarries Ltd* [1952] 2 Q.B. 608 at 615 per Denning L.J. See also *Grant v
Sun Shipping Co* [1948] A.C. 549 per Lord du Parcq. Cf. *Hawkins v Ian Ross (Castings)
Ltd* [1970] 1 All E.R. 180. Equally, however, the defendant should bear in mind the
possibility that his activity may distract persons from looking after their own safety. A
bizarre example is *Edwards v Tracy Starr's Shows (Edmonton) Ltd* (1984) 13 D.L.R. (4th)
129 (patron of "burlesque show" falling over unseen obstruction).

[367] Phillips J. in *Banque Bruxelles Lambert SA v Eagle Star Insurance Co Ltd* [1995] 2 All
E.R. 769 at 820, held that the fact that the claimant was insured against loss was not to be
taken into account in determining whether he had behaved with reasonable prudence. The
contrary view of Steyn J. and the Court of Appeal in *Banque Keyser Ullman SA v Skandia
(UK) Insurance Co Ltd* [1990] 1 Q.B. 665 at 721, 815, was based on a concession.
Contributory negligence was not in issue in the appeals reported as *Banque Bruxelles*
[1997] A.C. 191.

[368] A worker is not normally put on inquiry as to whether his employer has fulfilled his duties
under statutes and regulations governing industrial safety: *Westwood v Post Office* [1974]
A.C. 1. So also a person is prima facie entitled to take the advice of his professional adviser
at its face value: *Banque Bruxelles*, above, fn.367, at [1995] 2 All E.R. 824; *Henderson v
Merrett Syndicates (No.2)* [1996] 1 P.N.L.R. 32. The judgment of Phillips J. in *Banque
Bruxelles* contains an extended discussion of the process of determining contributory
negligence in relation to commercial risks.

contributory negligence if he crosses the road without using an "authorised" crossing.[369]

As with any other aspect of the law of negligence the standard of care demanded may be adjusted to meet changing conditions[370]; for example, in *Froom v Butcher*[371] the Court of Appeal held that non-use of a car seat belt generally constituted contributory negligence some seven years before Parliament made the wearing of belts compulsory.[372] Now that there is legislation requiring belts to be worn the correctness of this decision becomes even more obvious, though the incidence of criminal liability and contributory negligence may not be entirely coterminous.[373] For many years there has been increasing public awareness of the dangers of smoking and a reduction was made under the Act for the claimant's failure to give up where this had made a material contribution to his lung cancer, which was also caused by the defendants' exposure of him to asbestos.[374] However, although public attitudes towards drinking and driving have become more severe in recent years, a person who accepts a lift from a person whom he has not seen consuming large quantities of alcohol is not obliged to interrogate him on his consumption.[375]

F. Dilemma Produced by Negligence

6–49   Where the defendant's negligence has put the claimant in a dilemma, the defendant cannot escape liability if the claimant, in the agony of the moment, tries to save himself by choosing a course of

---

[369] *Tremayne v Hill* [1987] R.T.R. 131.

[370] For consideration of how far it may be contributory negligence not to fit modern fire control devices, see *Oakville Storage and Forwarders Ltd v Canadian National Ry* (1991) 80 D.L.R. (4th) 675.

[371] [1976] Q.B. 286. As to apportionment in such cases see para.6–53, below.

[372] In 1976 the position as to a seat belt was that, "everyone is free to wear it or not, as he pleases. Free in this sense, that if he does not wear it, he is free from any penalty by the magistrates. Free in the sense that everyone is free to run his head against a brick wall, if he pleases . . . But it is not a sensible thing to do. If he does it it is his own fault and he has only himself to thank for the consequences": [1976] Q.B. 286 at 293. See also *Smith v Finch* [2009] EWHC 53 (QB) (pedal cyclist not wearing helmet).

[373] In *Froom v Butcher* the court said that it is no excuse that the claimant sincerely believes that wearing a belt is more dangerous than not wearing one, but that an unduly fat man or pregnant woman might be spared a finding of contributory negligence. However, the last two categories are not exempted as such from the criminal law, though they might obtain a medical certificate of exemption. It is thought that, e.g. a pregnant woman who had no certificate might still escape a finding of contributory negligence. A taxi driver (exempt) who followed police advice not to wear a belt because of the risk of attack by passengers was held not guilty of contributory negligence in *Pace v Culley* 1992 S.L.T. 1073. It has been held that where a vehicle is not required by law to be fitted with belts it is a question of fact whether failure to fit them amounts to contributory negligence: *Hoadly v Dartford DC* [1979] R.T.R. 359.

[374] *Badger v MoD* [2005] EWHC 2941 (QB). Cf. on proof of causation, *McTear v Imperial Tobacco Ltd* [2005] CSOH 69.

[375] *Booth v White* [2003] EWCA Civ 1708.

conduct which proves to be the wrong one, provided the claimant acted in a reasonable apprehension of danger and the method by which he tried to avoid it was a reasonable one.[376] If those conditions are satisfied he committed no contributory negligence.[377] A famous illustration of the principle is *Jones v Boyce*,[378] where the claimant was a passenger on the top of the defendant's coach and, owing to the breaking of a defective coupling rein, the coach was in imminent peril of being overturned. The claimant, seeing this, jumped from it and broke his leg. In fact the coach was not upset. Lord Ellenborough C.J. directed the jury that if the claimant acted as a reasonable and prudent man would have done, he was entitled to recover, although he had selected the more perilous of the two alternatives with which he was confronted by the defendant's negligence and the jury gave a verdict for the claimant. However, where all that the claimant is threatened with is mere personal inconvenience of a trifling kind, he is not entitled to run a considerable risk in order to get rid of it; so, for example, where the door of a railway-carriage was so ill-secured that it kept flying open, but the claimant could avoid the draught by sitting elsewhere, it would be his own fault if he fell out in trying to shut it (after several earlier unsuccessful attempts) while the train was in motion.[379]

G. Children

While it is not possible to specify an age below which, as a matter of law, a child cannot be guilty of contributory negligence,[380] the age of the child is a circumstance which must be considered in deciding whether it has been guilty of contributory negligence.[381] In *Yachuk v Oliver Blais Co Ltd*, Y,[382] a boy aged nine years, bought

6–50

---

[376] Glanville Williams, pp.360–364.

[377] The rule is equally applicable in favour of the defendant where there is contributory negligence on the part of the claimant which has forced the dilemma upon him instead of upon the claimant: *Swadling v Cooper* [1931] A.C. 1 at 9; *McLean v Bell* (1932) 147 L.T. 262 at 263.

[378] (1816) 1 Stark. 493; *The Bywell Castle* (1879) 4 P.D. 219; *United States of America v Laird Line Ltd* [1924] A.C. 286; *Admiralty Commissioners v SS Volute* [1922] 1 A.C. 129 at 136; *Sayers v Harlow UDC* [1958] 1 W.L.R. 623.

[379] *Adams v L. & Y. Ry* (1869) L.R. 4 C.P. 739. Cf. *Sayers v Harlow UDC* [1958] 1 W.L.R. 623.

[380] Cf. *Gough v Thorne* [1966] 1 W.L.R. 1387 at 1390 per Lord Denning M.R. and *Ducharme v Davies* [1984] 1 W.W.R. 699. "The descending line measuring reasonable expectation of care rapidly approaches zero as the age diminishes, but the line is apparently asymptotic": *Beasley v Marshall* (1977) 17 S.A.S.R. 456 at 459 per Bright J.; in South Australia a reduction has been made against a child as young as 6: *Bye v Bates* (1989) 51 S.A.S.R. 67.

[381] A comparison of *Jones v Lawrence* [1969] 3 All E.R. 267 with *McKinnel v White* 1971 S.L.T. (Notes) 61 suggests that standards were at that time more severe north of the border.

[382] [1949] A.C. 386; *French v Sunshine Holiday Camp (Hayling Island) Ltd* (1963) 107 S.J. 595.

from O. B. Co some gasoline, falsely stating that his mother wanted it for her car. In fact, he used it to play with, and, in doing so, was badly burnt by it. It was held by the Judicial Committee that O. B. Co were negligent in supplying gasoline to so young a boy and that Y had not been guilty of contributory negligence for he neither knew nor could be expected to know the properties of gasoline. Although Lord Denning M.R. said that a child should not be found guilty of contributory negligence "unless he or she is blameworthy",[383] it is not thought that the characteristics of the particular child other than its age are to be considered. The question is whether an "ordinary" child of the claimant's age—not a "paragon of prudence" nor a "scatterbrained" child—would have taken any more care than did the claimant.[384]

H. Identification

6–51   If the injury is due partly to the negligence of the child's parent or guardian in failing to look after it and partly to the negligence of the defendant the child may still recover his whole loss against the defendant, for he is not "identified" with the negligence of his parent or guardian[385] and the case follows the normal rule that a claimant may sue and execute judgment against either of two concurrent tortfeasors for the whole sum.[386] In practice, however, the impact of this rule was substantially changed by the introduction of contribution between concurrent tortfeasors,[387] for the defendant may now join the negligent parent or guardian as a third party and hold him responsible for a proportion of the damages.[388] If the parent or guardian is insured[389] this may be a matter of indifference, but if he is not, the result, for obvious practical reasons, is likely to be a settlement which makes a deduction for his share in the blame for the accident. In a fatal accident case the dependants of the deceased are identified with his contributory negligence.[390] In *Gorham v British Telecommunications Plc*[391] the defendant insurers

---

[383] *Gough v Thorne*, above, fn.380, at 1390. *Jones v Lawrence*, above, refers to the need for culpable want of care by the child for his own safety.

[384] [1966] 1 W.L.R. 1387 at 1391 per Salmon L.J. Cf. *Beasley v Marshall* (1977) S.A.S.R. 456 at 458.

[385] The contrary view was exploded in *Oliver v Birmingham, etc. Omnibus Co Ltd* [1933] 1 K.B. 35, following *The Bernina* (1888) 13 App.Cas. 1. Cf. the position of master and servant, below. A minor exception to the non-identification rule is found in the Congenital Disabilities (Civil Liability) Act 1976: para.24–14, below.

[386] See Ch.21, below.

[387] See Ch.21, below.

[388] *Jones v Wilkins* [2001] P.I.Q.R. Q12; *McCallion v Dodd* [1966] N.Z.L.R. 710. For the parental duty of care, see para.5–29, above.

[389] As where the claimant is a passenger in his parent's car.

[390] See para.23–17, below.

[391] [2000] 1 W.L.R. 2129.

were held to owe a duty of care to the family of the deceased with regard to pension provision which he made with them[392] and to have been in breach of that duty. The majority of the Court of Appeal held that the failure of the deceased to take corrective action after he discovered the truth broke the chain of causation. What would have been the result if the conduct of the deceased had been only contributory negligence? The fatal accidents legislation does not apply because the defendants have not caused the death of the deceased and the 1945 Act only allows a reduction for the contributory fault of the claimants, that is to say the members of the family. Sir Murray Stuart-Smith thought that the court would be entitled to make a reduction at common law.

As between the claimant and the defendant each is identified with any third person for whom he is vicariously responsible. The rule that the negligence of a servant in the course of his employment is imputed to his employer applies whether the latter is the claimant or the defendant, but the contributory negligence of an independent contractor for whom the claimant is not responsible does not affect the claimant's action. If X has charge of the person or property of C, C is not for that reason identified with X, hence if an accident happens owing to the negligence of X and a third person, D, C may sue D and recover in full, even though X could not.[393]

I. Work Accidents

It has been suggested that in actions by workers against their **6–52** employers for injuries sustained at work the courts are justified in taking a more lenient view of careless conduct on the part of the claimant than would otherwise be justified, and that it is not for every risky thing which a worker in a factory may do that he is to be held to have been negligent. Regard must be had to the dulling of the sense of danger through familiarity, repetition, noise, confusion, fatigue and preoccupation with work.[394] Where, however, the operation leading up to the accident is divorced from the bustle, noise and repetition that occurs in such places as factories these considerations cannot apply and, indeed, it may be that they are only relevant where the worker's cause of action is founded upon his employer's breach

---

[392] On this aspect of the case, see para.5–38, above.
[393] *The Bernina*, above, fn.385; *France v Parkinson* [1954] 1 W.L.R. 581.
[394] *Flower v Ebbw Vale Steel, Iron and Coal Co Ltd* [1934] 2 K.B. 132 at 139–140 per Lawrence J., cited with approval by Lord Wright, [1936] A.C. 206 at 214; *Caswell v Powell Duffryn Collieries Ltd* [1940] A.C. 152 at 166 per Lord Atkin, at 176–179 per Lord Wright; *Grant v Sun Shipping Co* [1948] A.C. 549 at 567 per Lord du Parcq; *Hawkins v Ian Ross (Castings) Ltd* [1970] 1 All E.R. 180.

of statutory duty.[395] Where the claimant's case rests upon an unsafe system of work it would be rare for the claimant's acquiescence in this to amount to contributory negligence.[396]

It was settled by the House of Lords in 1939 that contributory negligence is a defence to an action for breach of statutory duty,[397] and the general principles of contributory negligence are the same as where the cause of action is founded upon negligence. In practice, however, especially where the statute creates an absolute obligation to secure the existence of a certain state of affairs, questions of contributory negligence may be treated rather differently. It has often been stated that safety legislation exists to protect workers from the consequences of their own carelessness,[398] and the courts will therefore be slow to hold a worker guilty of contributory negligence where the defendant is in breach of his statutory duty.[399] Furthermore, even if the worker's negligence involves him in breach of his own statutory duty[400] his claim is not defeated by the maxim ex turpi causa non oritur actio.[401] On the other hand, given the nature of some statutory duties, it can happen that the defendant's breach is brought about wholly and exclusively by the claimant's own breach of his duty, and in such a case the claimant can recover nothing.[402]

J. Apportionment of Loss

6–53   In a case of contributory negligence the damages recoverable by the claimant are to be reduced: "to such extent as the court thinks

---

[395] *Staveley v Iron & Chemical Co v Jones* [1956] A.C. 627 at 642 per Lord Reid, at 647–648 per Lord Tucker; *Hicks v British Transport Commission* [1958] 1 W.L.R. 493; *Quintas v National Smelting Co* [1961] 1 W.L.R. 401 at 411 per Willmer L.J. Cf. at 408–409 per Sellers L.J. Disobedience is not necessarily contributory negligence: *Westwood v Post Office* [1974] A.C. 1.

[396] *State Ry Authority v Wiegold* (1991) 25 N.S.W.R. 500. For the court's attitude to a plea of volenti non fit injuria in this context, see para.25–11, below.

[397] *Caswell v Powell Duffryn Associated Collieries Ltd* [1940] A.C. 152 (Factories Act); *Sparks v Edward Ash Ltd* [1943] K.B. 223 (Pedestrian Crossing Places Regulations). For the action for breach of statutory duty, see Ch.7, below.

[398] *Staveley Iron & Chemical Co v Jones* [1956] A.C. 627 at 648 per Lord Tucker; *Hutchinson v L & NE Ry* [1942] 1 K.B. 481. Cf. *Mullard v Ben Line Steamers Ltd* [1970] 1 W.L.R. 1414.

[399] See, e.g. *John Summers & Sons Ltd v Frost* [1955] A.C. 740. Nevertheless, cases in which workers are held partly and even substantially to blame for their own injuries are common. See, e.g. *Cork v Kirby Maclean Ltd* [1952] 2 All E.R. 402; *Jones v Richards* [1955] 1 W.L.R. 444; *Hodkinson v H. Wallwork & Co Ltd* [1955] 1 W.L.R. 1195 (claimant 90 per cent to blame); *Uddin v Associated Portland Cement Manufacturers Ltd* [1965] 2 Q.B. 582; *Thornton v Swan Hunter (Shipbuilders) Ltd* [1971] 1 W.L.R. 1759; *King v Smith* [1995] I.C.R. 339; *Jebson v MoD* [2000] 1 W.L.R. 2055 (far removed from the typical employment case).

[400] For examples of statutory duties imposed directly on workers see Management of Health and Safety at Work Regulations 1999 reg.14, Personal Protective Equipment at Work Regulations 1992 reg.10, Manual Handling Regulations 1992 reg.5.

[401] *National Coal Board v England* [1954] A.C. 403. See para.25–20, below.

[402] See para.7–16, below.

just and equitable having regard to the claimant's share in the responsibility for the damage."[403] This may seem simple enough at first sight, though the problem may be complex when there are successive accidents which are causally connected with one another,[404] and in the majority of cases the judges give little by way of reason for their assessments of the extent to which the claimant's damages should be reduced. The matter is commonly treated as one of fact, and appellate courts will only vary an assessment in extreme cases unless the trial judge can be said to have erred in principle or failed to take some relevant factor into account.[405]

Broadly speaking, two principal criteria of "responsibility" suggest themselves, causation and blameworthiness or culpability and there is high authority for the view that both causation and blameworthiness must be taken into account.[406] It would seem, however, that no hard-and-fast rule can be laid down, for the exercise is not a science.[407] Degrees of causation may be impossible of rational assessment, but concentration exclusively upon comparative blameworthiness will tend in some cases to defeat the purpose of the Contributory Negligence Act. Where the defendant's liability is based upon breach of a strict common law or statutory duty he may have been guilty of no blameworthy behaviour at all, in which case if comparative blameworthiness were the sole criterion, even slight contributory negligence would prevent the claimant from recovering any damages. Naturally the courts have been unwilling to reach such a conclusion; on the contrary, as has been stated, the protection

---

[403] Law Reform (Contributory Negligence) Act 1945 s.1(1). The equivalent provision in the Merchant Shipping Act 1995 s.187(1) lays down that, "the liability to make good the damage or loss shall be in proportion to the degree in which each vessel was in fault". For apportionment between defendants under the Civil Liability (Contribution) Act 1978, see Ch.21, below.

[404] In *The Calliope* [1970] P. 172 Brandon J. held that where the first accident is caused partly by the negligence of the defendant and partly by the negligence of the claimant and then the claimant suffers further, consequential, damage which is caused partly by the first accident and partly by his own further negligence, there must be a sub-apportionment of responsibility for that consequential damage.

[405] Of the many authorities, see *The Macgregor* [1943] A.C. 197 at 200–201 per Lord Wright; *Brown v Thompson* [1968] 1 W.L.R. 1003 at 1009–1011 per Winn L.J.; *The Jan Laurenz* [1973] 1 Lloyd's Rep. 329; *Hannam v Mann* [1984] R.T.R. 252 (only when "clearly wrong"). Nevertheless appellate courts, and especially the House of Lords, have from time to time varied apportionments of damages quite freely: *Stapley v Gypsum Mines Ltd* [1953] A.C. 663; *National Coal Board v England* [1954] A.C. 403; *Quintas v National Smelting Co* [1961] 1 W.L.R. 401; *Barrett v MoD* [1995] 1 W.L.R. 1217; *Brannan v Airtours Plc, The Times*, February 1, 1999.

[406] *Davies v Swan Motor Co* [1949] 2 K.B. 29 at 326 per Denning L.J.; *Stapley v Gypsum Mines Ltd* [1953] A.C. 663 at 682 per Lord Reid; *The British Aviator* [1965] 1 Lloyd's Rep. 271; *The Miraflores and The Abadesa* [1967] 1 A.C. 826, especially per Lord Pearce at 845; *Brown v Thompson*, fn.405, above at 1008 per Winn L.J.; *Pride Valley Foods Ltd v Hall & Partners* [2001] EWCA Civ 1001; (2001) 76 Con. L.R. 1 at [51].

[407] *Pride Valley Foods*, above, fn.406, at [53].

intended to be given by strict statutory duties must not be emasculated by the "side-wind of apportionment".[408] It has been persuasively argued, therefore, that once the liability of the defendant has been established, regard should be had only to the claimant's conduct in assessing the extent to which the damages should be reduced.[409] Comparative blameworthiness cannot be assessed when the defendant's liability is not based upon moral fault, but, "the legal effects of contributory negligence follow only from morally culpable conduct".[410] This may, in fact, very possibly explain the way in which judges often approach the problem of apportionment, but it is not in truth always possible to ignore the nature of the defendant's liability. In *Quintas v National Smelting Co* Devlin J.[411] held that the defendants had not been guilty of negligence but had broken their statutory duty and assessed the claimant's contributory negligence at 75 per cent. The Court of Appeal, by a majority, held that the defendants were not guilty of breach of statutory duty but had been guilty of negligence and therefore reduced Devlin J.'s assessment to 50 per cent:

> "The respective responsibilities of the parties, and what is just and equitable having regard thereto, can only properly be assessed when it has been found what the plaintiff in fact did and what the defendants failed in their duty to do. The nature and extent of the defendants' duty is, in my view, highly important in assessing the effect of the breach of failure of duty on the happening of the accident giving rise to the plaintiff's claim and on the conduct of the plaintiff. There is an interaction of factors, acts and omissions to be considered."[412]

Comparative blameworthiness becomes even more difficult where the claimant's conduct in no way contributes to the accident but consists in failure to take some safety precaution which would have eliminated or reduced his damage, for example failing to wear a car safety belt. What the courts have done here is to lay down a "ready made" range of reductions which will operate regardless of whether the defendant's driving was slightly or grossly negligent and of whether the failure to wear the belt was "entirely inexcusable

---

[408] *Mullard v Ben Line Steamers Ltd* [1970] 1 W.L.R. 1414 at 1418 per Sachs L.J.; *McGuinness v Key Markets Ltd* (1973) 13 K.I.R. 249; *Reeves v MPC* [2000] 1 A.C. 360 at 371.

[409] Payne "Reduction of Damages for Contributory Negligence" (1955) 18 M.L.R. 344.

[410] (1955) 18 M.L.R. 344 at 347. Cf. the view of "morally culpable" in *Pennington v Norris* (1956) 96 C.L.R. 10.

[411] [1960] 1 W.L.R. 217 [1961] 1 W.L.R. 401. See also the example given by Lord Pearce in *The Miraflores and The Abadesa* [1967] 1 A.C. 826 at 845.

[412] [1961] 1 W.L.R. 401 at 408 per Sellers L.J.

or almost forgivable".[413] If the claimant's injuries would have been altogether avoided by wearing the belt there should be a reduction of 25 per cent, but if he would still have been injured, but less severely, the reduction should be only 15 per cent.[414] The court will not encourage attempts to reduce these figures by speculative evidence as to what injuries would have been suffered if the claimant had been wearing a belt.[415] While these are guidelines, not absolutely rigid figures,[416] they will apply in the vast majority of cases and remain valid today even though they were established over thirty years ago.[417]

A finding of "100 per cent contributory negligence" is a contradiction in terms. Whether the claim is for negligence or breach of statutory duty it is possible for the court to conclude that the claimant's own fault is the sole cause of his injury but in that event there is no initial liability for his fault to "contribute to".[418] In practice the court will not attempt a minute assessment of responsibility and even a finding of contributory negligence of 10 per cent is apparently unusual.[419]

We saw earlier in this chapter how a valuer's liability to a secured lender is limited to the difference between his valuation and the true value of the property and that he is not liable for losses attributable to falls in the market.[420] In *Platform Home Loans Ltd v Oyston Shipways Ltd*[421] the total loss suffered by the lender was £611,000 but the amount of the overvaluation was £500,000. The trial judge held that the lenders were guilty of twenty per cent contributory

6–54

---

[413] *Froom v Butcher* [1976] Q.B. 286 at 296. These are not rigid rules (*Salmon v Newland, The Times*, May 16, 1983) but they should generally be followed: *Capps v Miller* [1989] 2 All E.R. 333.

[414] Note that the reduction is to be made only in respect of the category of injury causally related to the lack of a belt. If head injuries would have been avoided by wearing a belt there should be a reduction of 25 per cent in respect of them, but no reduction in respect of a broken leg which would have occurred anyway. There is a powerful public interest in avoiding expensive inquiries into fine degrees of contributory negligence and it is therefore legitimate to take the line that, "absent something exceptional, there should be no reduction in a case where the injury would not have been reduced 'to a considerable extent' by the seat belt": *Stanton v Collinson* [2010] EWCA Civ 81 at [26]. See also *Owens v Brimmell* [1977] Q.B. 859 and *Smith v Finch* [2009] EWHC 53 (QB).

[415] *Patience v Andrews* [1983] R.T.R. 447.

[416] *Jones v Wilkins* [2001] P.I.Q.R. Q12.

[417] *Gawler v Raettig* [2007] EWHC 373 (QB) (permission to appeal refused because in view of the agreement between the parties the issue was academic: [2007] EWCA Civ 1560); *Stanton v Collinson* [2010] EWCA Civ 81; *Gleeson v Court* [2007] EWHC 2397 (QB); [2008] R.T.R. 10 (travelling in boot, knowledge driver drunk, 30 per cent).

[418] *Anderson v Newham F.E. College* [2002] EWCA Civ 505; [2003] I.C.R. 212, disapproving *Jayes v I.M.I. (Kynoch)* [1985] I.C.R. 155.

[419] *Cooper v Carillion Plc* [2003] EWCA Civ 1811. The lowest allocation of responsibility traced is 5 per cent to the claimant in *Laszczyk v NCB* [1954] 1 W.L.R. 1426. A figure of 5 per cent was agreed in *Stringman v McArdle* [1994] 1 W.L.R. 1653. Most cases seem to be within the range 25 per cent/75 per cent either way.

[420] See para.6–27, above.

[421] [2000] 2 A.C. 190.

negligence in making an imprudently large advance.[422] Was the twenty per cent reduction to be applied to the overall loss or to the "capped" sum? The House of Lords held that the first was the correct course, leaving an award of £489,000 rather than £400,000.[423]

The result is, therefore, that there is no single principle for the apportionment of damages in cases of contributory negligence, and certainly no mathematical approach is possible.

> "The law of torts is not just a matter of simple morality but contains many strands of policy, not all of them consistent with each other, which reflect the complexity of life. An apportionment of responsibility 'as the court thinks just and equitable' will sometimes require a balancing of different goals."[424]

No doubt the extent of the claimant's lack of care for his own safety must be a major factor in all cases, but since the court is directed by the statute to do what is "just and equitable" the matter is thus one for the discretion of the court,[425] and, though the discretion must be exercised judicially, it is both unnecessary and undesirable that the exercise of the discretion be fettered by rigid rules requiring the court to take some aspects of the given case into account and to reject others.

K. Multiple Defendants

6–55   Where the acts of two or more defendants combine to injure the claimant each is liable to the claimant for the whole amount of the loss, though as between the defendants the court has a statutory power to apportion liability.[426] Both matters are usually settled in the same proceedings, but there are two stages. First the court must determine liability and decide what deduction if any is to be made for the claimant's contributory negligence. This is done by comparing the claimant's conduct on the one hand with the totality of the tortious conduct on the other: the question at this stage is not "what is the relative share of responsibility of each and every party?" but "how far is the claimant the author of his own loss?" The respective

---

[422] See also *Mortgage Corp Plc v Halifax (SW) Ltd (No.2)* [1999] Lloyd's Rep. P.N. 159.

[423] Cf. Lord Cooke, dissenting at [2000] 2 A.C. 199: "the 'damage' referred to four times in section 1(1) of the Act of 1945 is the damage for which, but for the Act, the claimant's action would be defeated by reason of his own fault: it does not extend to damage for which his claim would be defeated by reason of a limit upon the other person's duty of care".

[424] *Reeves v MPC* [2000] 1 A.C. at 372 per Lord Hoffmann.

[425] Where there is a jury it is a question for the jury: s.1(6) of the Act of 1945. Nowadays this would only be likely in the case of certain intentional torts.

[426] See Ch.21, below.

shares of the resulting liability are then determined in the contribution proceedings, which are no concern of the claimant's.[427] Hence if, at the first stage, the court concludes that the claimant is 50 per cent responsible there is judgment against both defendants for 50 per cent of the damage. If the defendants' responsibility inter se is equal then, assuming both to be solvent, each one will finally bear 25 per cent of the loss. If, however, the court concludes that the claimant is only one-third to blame, then the correct judgment is for two-thirds of the damage against both defendants, even though the claimant is as much at fault as either defendant.[428]

---

[427] The position is different under the Merchant Shipping Act 1995, formerly Maritime Convention Act 1911: see *The Miraflores and The Abadesa* [1967] 1 A.C. 826, as explained in *Fitzgerald v Lane* [1989] A.C. 328.

[428] *Fitzgerald v Lane*, above, fn.427.

CHAPTER 7

BREACH OF STATUTORY DUTY[1] AND MISFEASANCE IN A PUBLIC OFFICE

1. BREACH OF STATUTORY DUTY: EXISTENCE OF LIABILITY

THIS chapter is not concerned with statutes which have as their **7–1** principal objective the imposition of tort liability,[2] nor with the circumstances in which the courts may pay regard to a statutory requirement or standard in deciding whether the defendant's conduct amounts to negligence.[3] What it is concerned with is when a court will conclude that a statute which is primarily regulatory or criminal in its purpose should be treated as giving rise to a civil action for damages at the suit of a person who is injured as a result of non-compliance with it. Fundamentally, the question is one of interpretation of the particular statute, but enough case law has accumulated around the subject to require treatment in a book on torts.

---

[1] Stanton et al, *Statutory Torts*; Buckley, "Liability in Tort for Breach of Statutory Duty" (1984) 100 L.Q.R. 204; Stanton, "New Forms of the Tort of Breach of Statutory Duty" (2004) 120 L.Q.R. 324; Williams, "The Effect of Penal Legislation in the Law of Tort" (1960) 23 M.L.R. 233.

[2] e.g. the Occupiers' Liability Act 1957 (Ch.9) and the Consumer Protection Act 1987 Pt I (Ch.10).

[3] See para.5–82, above.

Before looking at the approach of the courts to this question of interpretation something should be said about the nature of the action for breach of statutory duty. In purely numerical terms, the most important area of operation of the tort of breach of statutory duty is that concerned with work injuries[4] and there is, of course, no doubt that an employer owes his employee a duty of care for the purposes of the tort of negligence. The English view is that liability for breach of statutory duty is a wholly separate tort superimposed on this, but this is not the approach of all common law countries. In the majority of jurisdictions in the United States, in accident cases, breach of a statute is "negligence per se" and this is tantamount to saying that the statute "concretises" the common law duty by putting beyond controversy the question whether reasonable care in the circumstances required that a particular precaution be taken. Other American states adopt the view that the statutory standard is compelling evidence of what reasonable care demands but in the last resort does not bind the court, a view taken since 1983 in Canada.[5] There are attractions in these views where a common law duty exists, for they relieve the court of the task of searching for a legislative intention on civil liability, but where there is no common law duty it would amount to rejecting statutes as a source of civil liability, a view which is inconsistent with English law as it stands. In any event, even where there is a common law duty, the overwhelming weight of authority is to the effect that the action for breach of statutory duty is a separate tort. As Lord Wright put it in *L.P.T.B. v Upson*:

"A claim for damages for breach of a statutory duty intended to protect a person in the position of the particular plaintiff is a specific common law right which is not to be confused in essence with a claim for negligence ... I have desired before I deal specifically with the regulations to make it clear how in my judgment they should be approached, and also to make it clear that a claim for their breach may stand or fall independently of negligence. There is always a danger if the claim is not sufficiently specific that the due consideration of the claim for breach of statutory duty may be prejudiced if it is confused with the claim in negligence."[6]

---

[4] Much of the statute law in this area has undergone radical amendment (see para.8–4, below) but the proposition in the text remains true. See *Ziemniak v ETBM Deep Sea Ltd* [2003] EWCA Civ 636.

[5] *R. v Saskatchewan Wheat Pool* (1983) 143 D.L.R. (3d) 9. However, US federal law does recognise the concept of breach of statutory duty as a distinct tort. The implication of tort causes of action from the Constitution and civil rights legislation has been particularly important since *Bivens v Six Unknown Agents*, 403 U.S. 388 (1971).

[6] [1949] A.C. 155 at 168–169.

Thus, where the statute imposes strict liability it is possible for the defendant to be acquitted of negligence but still held liable for breach of the statute; contrariwise, the defendant may have fulfilled his statutory duty but is still nevertheless liable for negligence because the statute is not inconsistent with a common law duty broader in extent. Furthermore, it does not seem satisfactory or even sensible to describe as a failure to take care the breach of such duties as the unqualified obligation that dangerous parts of machinery shall be "securely fenced".[7]

In the industrial safety cases it would have been impossible to   7–2
deny a general common law duty of care to workers, but in the modern law many claims for breach of statutory duty have been advanced on the basis of legislation concerned with child protection, education and other matters of social welfare. They have generally failed because the nature of the legislation did not support the inference of a Parliamentary intention to confer a civil right of action.[8] It may also be the case that the statutory framework is inconsistent with a common law duty of care, in which case there is no liability at all, but if this is not so, there is no reason why the common law of negligence should not operate.[9] It is wrong to assume that because a statute in the area in question does not give rise to civil liability it therefore excludes a common law duty: the two questions are entirely separate.[10] Any common law duty must be sought in the principles of the law of negligence, not in the non-actionable statute.[11]

The question, then, is when a private right of action in tort[12] will   7–3
be inferred from the existence of the statutory duty. When Parliament has clearly stated its intention one way or the other no difficulty arises,[13] but all too often this is not the case. Until the 19th century the view seems to have been taken that whenever a statutory

---

[7] Factories Act 1961 s.14(1). See *John Summers Ltd v Frost* [1955] A.C. 740. This particular statutory duty has been modified, but the various industrial safety regulations still contain absolute obligations: para.8–5, below.

[8] See para.7–4, below.

[9] *X (Minors) v Bedfordshire CC* [1995] 2 A.C. 633 at 765; *Barrett v Enfield London Borough Council* [2001] 2 A.C. 550; *Phelps v Hillingdon LBC* [2001] 2 A.C. 619. An obvious example is road accidents: road traffic legislation hardly ever gives rise to an action for breach of statutory duty but road accidents are a major source of negligence cases.

[10] *Gorringe v Calderdale MBC* [2004] UKHL 15; [2004] 1 W.L.R. 1057 at [3].

[11] [2004] UKHL 15; [2004] 1 W.L.R. 1057 at [32]; *Neil Martin Ltd v Revenue and Customs Comrs* [2007] EWCA Civ 1041; [2007] S.T.C. 1802.

[12] The action is properly an action in tort, even though the duty arises from statute: *American Express Co v British Airways Board* [1983] 1 W.L.R. 701 (action "in tort" within the Post Office Act 1969 s.29(1)); *Philip Morris Ltd v Ainley* [1975] V.R. 345.

[13] See, e.g. Health and Safety at Work etc Act 1974 s.47; Guard Dogs Act 1975 s.5; Safety of Sports Grounds Act 1975 s.13; Building Act 1984 s.38; Telecommunications Act 1984 s.18(6)(a); Fire Safety and Places of Sport Act 1987 s.12; Copyright Designs and Patents Act 1988 s.103; Financial Services and Markets Act 2000 s.71; Railways Act 2005 s.44. The European Convention on Human Rights, via the Human Rights Act 1998, of course gives rise to the possibility of an award of damages. However, there is no *right* to damages

duty is created, any person who can show that he has sustained harm from its non-performance can bring an action against the person on whom the duty is imposed.[14] During the first half of that century, however, a different view began to be taken, and in *Atkinson v Newcastle Waterworks Co*[15] the Court of Appeal's doubts about the old rule were so strong as to amount to disapproval of it. With the vast increase in legislative activity, the old rule was perceived to carry the risk of liability wider than the legislature could have contemplated, particularly in relation to public authorities. Since that time, therefore, the claimant has generally been required to point to some indication in the statute that it was intended to give rise to a civil action. If there is no such indication, the claimant is thrown back on such common law right of action as he may have. Although, as we have seen, a common law duty of care may coexist with a statutory duty (whether or not the latter gives rise to a civil action) there is no common law tort of "careless performance of a statutory duty". Either there is a duty of care under the common law, or the statute gives rise to liability in its own right, or both; but if there is no common law duty and the statute only operates in the public law sphere then the fact that the duty under the statute is carried out carelessly does not avail the claimant seeking damages.[16]

On the question whether the statute gives rise to a civil right of action:

"[T]he only rule which in all circumstances is valid is that the answer must depend on a consideration of the whole Act and the circumstances, including the pre-existing law, in which it was enacted."[17]

Where the civil right of action is alleged to arise from subordinate legislation an intention to confer such a right (or at least authority to

and one would not describe such a claim as one for breach of statutory duty, nor even for tort.

[14] "Where-ever a statute enacts anything, or prohibits anything, for the advantage of any person, that person shall have remedy to recover the advantage given him, or to have satisfaction for the injury done him contrary to the law by the same statute for it would be a fine thing to make a law by which one has a right, but no remedy in equity": *Anon* (1704) 6 Mod. 26 per Holt C.J. Com.Dig.tit. "Action upon Statute," F; *Ashby v White* (1703) 2 Ld.Raym. 938; *Couch v Steel* (1854) 3 E. & B. 402.

[15] (1877) 2 Ex.D. 441.

[16] *X (Minors) v Bedfordshire CC* [1995] 2 A.C. 633. Dicta which might, on a superficial reading, indicate the contrary (most particularly Lord Blackburn in *Geddis v Proprietors of the Bann Reservoir* (1878) 3 A.C. 430 at 435) are concerned with a different question: whether, when D, acting under statutory authority, does something which, without that authority, would be a tort against C, D's "negligence" loses him the protection of the authority.

[17] *Cutler v Wandsworth Stadium Ltd* [1949] A.C. 398 at 407 per Lord Simonds, at 412 per Lord Normand; *Ministry of Housing v Sharp* [1970] 2 Q.B. 223 at 272 per Salmon L.J.

confer it) must be found in the enabling legislation.[18] Unfortunately, statutes all too rarely contain very much in the way of a clear indication on legislative intent and various presumptions have been developed by the courts.

A. The Protection of a Class

First, it is said that an indication that the intention of Parliament   **7–4** was to provide a civil action is that the statute was passed for the protection of a limited class of the public, rather than for the benefit of the public as a whole. This was criticised many years ago by Atkin L.J. on the ground that:

> "[I]t would be strange if a less important duty, which is owed to a section of the public, may be enforced by action, while a more important duty owed to the public at large cannot."[19]

Furthermore, the concept of a "class of persons" lacks clear definition[20]: road users are not treated as a class of persons for this purpose since traffic legislation has generally not been interpreted so as to give rise to a civil action, but workers have been, the opposite conclusion having been consistently reached under industrial safety legislation. Nevertheless, this factor has been repeated in modern statements of the law.[21] Perhaps it is more helpful to put the matter negatively: it is not so much that the identifiability of a protected class is a particularly powerful pointer towards liability, as that, where there is no such class, it is inherently unlikely that Parliament would have intended a duty, sounding in damages, to the public as a whole in the absence of plain words.[22] This has some affinity with the "floodgates" argument that we encounter so frequently in the

---

[18] *R. v Deputy Governor of Parkhurst Prison, Ex p. Hague* [1992] 1 A.C. 58 per Lord Jauncey. Lord Bridge at 160 does not seem to be disagreeing with the proposition, he merely seems to be taking a rather wider view of the regulation-making power under the Act in question. See also *Olotu v Home Office* [1997] 1 W.L.R. 328 at 339; *The Maraghetha Maria* [2002] EWCA Civ 509; [2002] 2 Lloyd's Rep. 293.

[19] *Phillips v Britannia Hygienic Laundry Co* [1923] 1 K.B. 832 at 841. The oddness of such a conclusion is illustrated by *Cullen v CC Royal Ulster Constabulary* [2003] UKHL 39; [2003] 1 W.L.R. 1763, where the majority held that there was no action for breach of a duty which went to, "a quasi-constitutional right of fundamental importance in a free society": at [67].

[20] It seems the class must be definable by reference to their type or status or in some analogous way. "Victims of this offence" is not enough: *Issa v Hackney LBC* [1997] 1 W.L.R. 956.

[21] *X (Minors) v Bedfordshire CC* [1995] 2 A.C. 633 at 731; *O'Rourke v Camden LBC* [1998] A.C. 188 at 194; *Thames Trains v H.S.E.* [2003] EWCA Civ 720.

[22] Thus in *Mid Kent Holdings Plc v General Utilities Plc* [1997] 1 W.L.R. 14, a literal interpretation of the Fair Trading Act 1973 s.93A, would have led to the extraordinary result of allowing any of the whole population to bring proceedings to enforce an undertaking to the Minister.

context of negligence.[23] In *Atkinson v Newcastle Waterworks Co*[24] an Act requiring a water company to keep pipes, to which fire plugs were fixed, charged with a certain pressure of water, was construed as in the nature of a bargain between the company and Parliament for the supply of water to the city rather than as creating a duty actionable by householders. The court regarded it as startling that the water company should virtually become insurers of the safety from fire, so far as water can produce that safety, of all the houses in the district. A modern example is the refusal by the Court of Appeal to find that the duty owed by a fire authority to take reasonable measures to ensure an adequate supply of water for fire-fighting gave rise to civil liability.[25] In any event, the mere fact that the statute intends to confer some benefit upon an identified group of persons is not conclusive. In one case it was contended that book-makers were a class of persons intended to be benefited by a provision in the Betting and Lotteries Act 1934 requiring the owner of a dog track to provide space for them, but the action failed, for the purpose of the statute was not the conferring of private rights but the regulation of dog racing.[26] At the end of the day the question of the existence or nonexistence of an identifiable class does not provide an easy substitute for the fundamental question of what purpose the legislature intended to achieve by the particular legislation, taken as a whole.[27]

B. Nature of the Legislation

7–5   Closely related to the "class" issue is the nature of the legislation. While a private law duty may be fairly readily inferred from legislation prescribing safety standards,[28] it is unlikely to be found in legislation on "social welfare", especially when that confers a wide discretion upon the body responsible for administering it. The proper remedy for maladministration is judicial review, not an action for damages. Not surprisingly, a New Zealand court rejected

---

[23] Also with the "special damage" requirement in public nuisance: para.14–3, below.

[24] (1877) 2 Ex.D. 441. Note that "the inhabitants of Newcastle" could easily be described as a class: there are certainly far less of them than "workers". "The ratepayers of Bingley" were regarded as an identifiable class in another fire plug decision, *Dawson & Co v Bingley UDC* [1911] 2 K.B. 149, though the case is of no importance since the *Capital and Counties* case, below, fn.25.

[25] *Capital and Counties Plc v Hampshire CC* [1997] Q.B. 1004. See also para.5–33, above.

[26] *Cutler v Wandsworth Stadium Ltd* [1949] A.C. 398.

[27] *R. v Deputy Governor of Brixton Prison, Ex p. Hague* [1992] 1 A.C. 58 at 171; *Morrison Sports Ltd v Scottish Power* [2009] CSIH 92 (electricity supply regulations).

[28] *Roe v Sheffield CC* [2003] EWCA Civ 1; [2004] Q.B. 653; *Morrison Sports Ltd,* above, fn.27, at 47. Cf. *The Maraghetha Maria* [2002] EWCA Civ 509; [2002] 2 Lloyd's Rep 293 (safety of trawlers; designed to protect crew but indications that to be enforced by administrative means); and *Souter v P & O Resorts Pty Ltd* [1999] 2 Qd. R. 106 (injury to guest at club by drunken patron; legislative duty too vague to found a civil action).

a civil action based upon breach of an amorphous statutory duty imposed upon an electricity undertaker to, "exhibit a sense of social responsibility by having regard to the interests of the community in which it operates"[29] and in England the House of Lords has rejected claims based upon child protection legislation,[30] the duty to provide sufficient and appropriate education under the Education Acts[31] and the duty to house homeless persons under the housing legislation.[32] As Lord Hoffmann put it in relation to the last issue:

"[T]he Act is a scheme of social welfare, intended to confer benefits at the public expense on grounds of public policy. Public money is spent on housing the homeless not merely for the benefit of people who find themselves homeless but on grounds of general public interest: because, for example, proper housing means that people will be less likely to suffer illness, turn to crime or require the attention of other social services. The expenditure interacts with expenditure on other public services such as education, the National Health Service and even the police. It is not simply a private matter between the claimant and the housing authority."[33]

In the child protection case it will be recalled that the House of Lords had rejected a common law duty of care because of the delicate nature of the local authority's function in investigating allegations of child abuse[34] and it was not, therefore, surprising that a private law action under the statute (which would not necessarily even have required proof of negligence) was also rejected. However, the European Court of Human Rights has subsequently held[35] that the failure to intervene constituted a breach of art.3 of the Convention (torture or inhuman or degrading treatment) and that the failure of domestic law to afford a remedy for this was a violation of art.13. The consequence seems to be that now in such a case there is a common law duty of care (at least to the child who is not adequately protected)[36] or damages may be awarded by an English court (since the Human Rights Act 1998) for breach of the Convention, but there

---

[29] *Auckland Electric Power Board v Electricity Corp of New Zealand Ltd* [1993] 3 N.Z.L.R. 53 (on appeal on another point, sub nom. *Mercury v Electricity Corp* [1994] 1 W.L.R. 521).

[30] *X v Bedfordshire CC* [1995] 2 A.C. 633.

[31] *Phelps v Hillingdon LBC* [2001] 2 A.C. 619.

[32] *O'Rourke v Camden LBC* [1998] A.C. 188. See now the Housing Act 1996. Such duties may not involve individual civil rights so as to attract art.6(1) of the European Convention on Human Rights: *Ali v Birmingham CC* [2010] UKSC 8; [2010] 2 W.L.R. 471.

[33] [1998] A.C. at 193.

[34] See para.5–52, above.

[35] *Z v UK* (2002) 34 E.H.R.R. 3. See para.5–53, above.

[36] See para.5–53, above.

seems to be no direct impact on the actionability of the breach of statutory duty.

C. Remedy Provided by the Statute

7–6   An important factor in deciding whether there is a civil action is the nature of the remedy, if any, provided by the statute. If the statute provides no remedy for its breach and there is an intention to protect a limited class,[37] that is an indication that Parliament intended a civil action, "since otherwise there is no method of securing the protection the statute was intended to confer".[38] In the great majority of cases, however, some machinery or sanction, whether administrative or criminal, will be contained in the statute and it has been said that:

> "[W]here an Act creates an obligation, and enforces the performance in a specified manner, we take it to be a general rule that performance cannot be enforced in any other manner."[39]

Where the statute provides its own administrative machinery for redress (for example, by appeal to the Minister) the court is likely to adopt this approach.[40] It now seems that on the parallel issue of whether there is a common law duty of care attaching to the performance of a statutory function, the court must take into account how far, if at all, the availability of an alternative remedy enables the claimant to gain financial redress,[41] but there is no indication that the principles applicable to breach of statutory duty are affected. The existence of the general remedy of judicial review may be an indication that no private law action for damages is available, though it is not conclusive.[42]

D. Criminal Penalties

7–7   Statutes which are silent on civil liability frequently impose criminal penalties. In principle the starting point is said to be the

---

[37] This element is important: in practice the most likely case in which a statute will not provide a sanction is where it imposes a general duty owed to the public.

[38] *X (Minors) v Bedfordshire CC* [1995] 2 A.C. 633 at 731; *Doe d Murray v Bridges* (1831) 1 B. & Ad. 847 at 859; cf. *Poulton's Trustee v Ministry of Justice* [2010] EWCA Civ 392.

[39] *Doe d Murray v Bridges,* above, fn.38.

[40] *Wyatt v Hillingdon LBC* (1978) 76 L.G.R. 727; *Scally v Southern Health and Social Services Board* [1992] 1 A.B. 294; *X (Minors) v Bedfordshire CC,* above, fn.38.

[41] *Phelps v Hillingdon LBC* [2001] 2 A.C. 619 at 672.

[42] *Calveley v CC Merseyside* [1989] A.C. 1228. The possibility of judicial review of a complaints procedure was regarded as pointing away from a civil action because it reduced the possibility of damage being suffered by the person being investigated. So also in *Cullen v CC Royal Ulster Constabulary* [2003] UKHL 39; [2003] 1 W.L.R. 1763 the majority relied on the availability of judicial review to deny a claim for damages for being refused access to a lawyer; the minority adverted to the "formidable practical problems" in applying for judicial review when access to a lawyer is refused.

same as in the case of administrative remedies, that is to say the criminal penalty is presumed to be the sole means of enforcement but it has to be pointed out that in the area where breach of statutory duty is of most importance (safety at work) the express provisions of the legislation in question were, for over a century and almost without exception, based solely on criminal penalties.[43]

E. Other Statutory Indications

Sometimes an indication of an intention on civil liability may be 7–8 found in the wording or structure of the statute. In *Keating v Elvan Reinforced Concrete Ltd*[44] the fact that the Public Utilities Street Works Act 1950 contained provisions creating civil liabilities in favour of public authorities was regarded as a reason for holding that it gave no right of action to individuals. On this basis the decision in *Groves v Wimborne*[45] is rather surprising. The statute made the occupier of a factory who did not properly fence dangerous machinery liable to a fine of £100 and it provided that the whole or any part of the fine might be applied, if the Secretary of State should so determine, for the benefit of the person injured by the occupier's neglect. A boy employed in the factory of the defendant was caught by an unfenced cog wheel and his arm had to be amputated. The Court of Appeal held that he was entitled to recover damages for breach of the statute in a civil action. The court reasoned that there was no certainty that any part of the fine would be awarded to the victim[46] and, even if it were awarded, its upper limit of £100,[47] it was said, made it incredible that Parliament would have regarded that as a sufficient and exclusive compensation for mutilation or death. Nevertheless, since Parliament had expressly adverted to the matter of compensation and the law of negligence applied as between employer and employee,[48] there was some force in the argument that no civil claim was intended. Nevertheless, *Groves v Wimborne* was the progenitor of hundreds of reported cases (and no doubt thousands of others) giving a civil remedy for breach of industrial safety legislation.

---

[43] Thus the Factories Act 1961 and its predecessors contained no mention of civil liability. Now the Health and Safety at Work etc. Act 1974 provides that the successor regulations give rise to civil liability unless the contrary is stated: para.8–4, below.

[44] [1968] 1 W.L.R. 722.

[45] [1898] 2 Q.B. 402.

[46] Cf. *Richardson v Pitt-Stanley* [1995] Q.B. 123, where there was no such power to divert the penalty and where its potential quantum militated against the victim's chances of recovery of damages in an action for negligence.

[47] Perhaps £8,000 today.

[48] Though then restricted by the doctrine of "common employment": para.8–2, below.

A common form of words in statutes creating offences is that:

"[N]othing in this Act shall be taken to prejudice any liability or remedy to which a person guilty of an offence thereunder may be subject in civil proceedings,"

but such words do not create civil liability, they merely preserve whatever liability (for example, for negligence or trespass) may exist apart from the statute.[49] It has also been said, though the point is far from decisive, that it is easier to spell out a civil right of action if Parliament has expressly stated that something is unlawful and then provided a penalty, rather than merely saying, "it is an offence to do such-and-such",[50] but this seems a very tenuous basis upon which to decide this issue.[51]

F. Relationship with the Common Law

7–9   The fact that the loss likely to be suffered as a result of the breach of statutory duty is of a type not recoverable (or recoverable only on a restricted basis) under the general law of tort is, it seems, a factor pointing away from the implication of a civil right of action. In *Pickering v Liverpool Daily Post and Echo Newspapers Plc*[52] the statutory provision related to the publication of information about an application to a Mental Health Review Tribunal. This gave rise to no civil right of action because although the publication might be said to be against the applicant's interest in the sense that it involved the disclosure of information he would prefer not to have ventilated in public, that was not then[53] any form of damage known to the civil law. The court will more readily imply a civil action where the damage inflicted by the breach is physical harm, rather than economic loss, reflecting the common law's more restrictive approach to the latter.[54] However, this is not a universal rule,[55] for in *Monk v*

---

[49] *McCall v Abelesz* [1976] Q.B. 585.

[50] *Rickless v United Artists Corp* [1988] Q.B. 40 at 51 (civil action found nonetheless); *Richardson v Pitt-Stanley* [1995] Q.B. 123 (action rejected).

[51] See the dissent of Sir John Megaw in *Richardson v Pitt-Stanley*.

[52] [1991] 2 A.C. 370; and see *Cullen v CC Royal Ulster Constabulary* [2003] UKHL 39; [2003] 1 W.L.R. 1763 (no damage at all, not even substantial distress; it is not clear what the position would have been if there had been damage of a type generally recognised by the common law).

[53] Nowadays there might of course be claims under the law of misuse of private information or under the data protection legislation: see Ch.12, below.

[54] *Richardson v Pitt-Stanley* [1995] Q.B. 123.

[55] That there may be liability for breach of statutory duty causing economic loss is expressly accepted by Lord Bridge in *Pickering v Liverpool Daily Post and Echo Newspapers Plc*, above, fn.52, at 420. The main thrust of a claim based on breach of EC law (see below) is likely to be economic loss.

Warbey[56] the court imposed civil liability upon the owner of a vehicle who allowed an uninsured driver (who was destitute of means) to use it, and thereby committed an offence under s.35 of the Road Traffic Act 1930.[57] The owner, who had no reason to doubt the driver's competence, had not in any legally relevant sense caused the claimant to be *injured*,[58] but he had caused the claimant to be in a position whereby his claim against the driver was worthless.[59]

An indication that a civil action does not arise from the statute may be the fact that the common law and other statute law already contain adequate remedies to enforce private rights in the area in question. Thus in *McCall v Abelesz*[60] the Court of Appeal, in denying that the crime of harassment of tenants in s.30 of the Rent Act 1965[61] gave rise to civil liability, laid stress upon the fact that many acts of harassment by a landlord must inevitably involve trespass or breach of contract. That, of course, leaves the question of what is "adequate": Atkin L.J. in *Phillips v Britannia Hygienic Laundry Co*,[62] in rejecting the contention the regulations governing the construction and use of motor vehicles gave rise to civil liability,

---

[56] [1935] 1 K.B. 75. *Richardson v Pitt-Stanley*, above, fn.54, involved a rather similar situation, failure to comply with the Employers' Liability (Compulsory Insurance) Act 1969. However, the majority of the CA rejected a civil claim against the directors (the company was in insolvent liquidation) for breach of statutory duty. The reason was that to allow an action for breach of statutory duty against it would add nothing to the (worthless) claims against it for breach of the Factories Act 1961 and negligence, and without an action lying against the company there could be none against the directors.

[57] See now the Road Traffic Act 1988 s.143(1)(b).

[58] But the claim is still one for damages for personal injuries for limitation purposes: *Norman v Ali* [2000] R.T.R. 107. A permits B to drive A's car while uninsured. There is an accident caused by the combined fault of B, and C driving another vehicle (the proportions of fault being 25 per cent and 75 per cent) in which A is injured. A sues C and recovers in full. C's counterclaim against A under *Monk v Warbey* will fail because the Act requires insurance only against personal injury and property damage and C's counterclaim is economic loss: *Bretton v Hancock* [2005] EWCA Civ 404; [2005] R.T.R. 22 (s.143(1)(a) rather than (b) was in issue but the point is the same).

[59] It has been held that the court must look at the realities of the matter, and it is not necessary to show that the driver can never pay: *Martin v Dean* [1971] 2 Q.B. 208; but in *Norman v Ali* the court left open how far it was necessary to establish impecuniosity. The uninsured driver situation is now rather more complicated than it was when *Monk v Warbey* was decided. Under s.151 of the Road Traffic Act 1988 where there is a policy of insurance in respect of a vehicle, the insurer must satisfy (subject to a financial limit in the case of property damage) a judgment against any person who drives it while uninsured, subject to a right of recourse against him or any person who causes or permits the driving. In other words, the "permitter" remains answerable, but to the insurer rather than to the victim under *Monk v Warbey*. Where there is no insurance at all, the claimant may proceed against the MIB but it will require the claimant to obtain and assign to it a judgment against the driver and any person who permitted the driving (see *Norman v Ali*, fn.58).

[60] [1976] Q.B. 585.

[61] Replaced by the Housing Act 1988 Pt I Ch.IV, which does give rise to civil liability. See also the more general statutory crime and tort of harassment under the Protection from Harassment Act 1997, para.4–38, above.

[62] [1923] 2 K.B. 832.

spoke of highway accidents being "already well provided for" by
the common law, but that is a view that would not necessarily
command widespread assent today. In any event, the fact that the
general law of tort and the law of contract are applicable to the
relationship between employer and employee has not prevented the
courts from holding that an action lies for breach of industrial safety
legislation. More convincing (though once again industrial accident
cases may have to be treated as an exception) is the view that the
courts, in the absence of clear words, will tend to lean against a
civilly actionable statutory duty which would contradict the general
pattern of liability in a particular area of activity, but will tend to find
one which will support or supplement it. This would explain why
the courts have consistently[63] rejected road traffic legislation as a
direct source of civil liability, for the effect would have been to
introduce isolated pockets of strict liability into an area generally
governed by negligence. At the same time, however, it would
support the decision in *Monk v Warbey* because that case made it
more likely that a victim of actionable negligence would recover.[64]
Again, in *Issa v Hackney London Borough*[65] an attempt to bring a
civil action on the basis of the "statutory nuisance" provisions of the
Public Health Act 1936[66] was rejected. In the normal case of
activities on land A causing disturbance to the occupiers of land B,
the common law of nuisance would give an adequate remedy for
harm suffered if that was still necessary after the operation of the
statutory enforcement procedures and the exercise of the court's
power to make a compensation order; but on the facts, the statute
was being used in an attempt to outflank established principles
governing the responsibility of a landlord for the upkeep of premises. Those principles were seriously deficient because of legislative
inaction,[67] but the solution was to be sought in direct legislative
amendment, not by the side-wind of straining the law of breach of
statutory duty.

[63] *Phillips v Britannia Hygienic Laundry Co*, above, fn.62; *Badham v Lambs Ltd* [1946] K.B.
45; *Clark v Brims* [1947] K.B. 497; *Coote v Stone* [1971] 1 W.L.R. 279; *Exel Logistics Ltd
v Curran* [2004] EWCA Civ 1249. A rare exception is *L.P.T.B. v Upson* [1949] A.C. 155
(breach of the Pedestrian Crossing Regulations). See also *Roe v Sheffield CC* [2003]
EWCA Civ 1; [2004] Q.B. 653, though that related to the condition of the highway rather
than the manner of using it. Conversely, the fact that the common law afforded no remedy
to a highway user for injury caused by straying animals (but see now the Animals Act
1971, para.16–2, below) did not lead the courts to grant a civil remedy for the statutory
offence of allowing animals to stray on to the highway: *Heath's Garage Ltd v Hodges*
[1916] 2 K.B. 370.
[64] *Richardson v Pitt-Stanley*, above, fn.54, certainly does not support the policy of *Monk v
Warbey*, but the decision is based more on the wording of the statute than on policy.
[65] [1997] 1 W.L.R. 956.
[66] See now Pt III of the Environmental Protection Act 1990, para.14–1, below.
[67] As is devastatingly demonstrated in the judgment of Brooke L.J.

G. Public Rights and Special Damage

In *Lonrho Ltd v Shell Petroleum Co Ltd (No.2)*[68] Lord Diplock,   **7–10**
having referred to the cases on statutes for the protection of particular classes of persons, such as those dealing with industrial safety,
said that there was a further exception to the general rule (that a
statute was to be enforced only by the means prescribed in it)
namely:

"[W]here the statute creates a public right (i.e. a right to be
enjoyed by all those of Her Majesty's subjects who wish to avail
themselves of it) and a particular member of the public suffers
what Brett J. in *Benjamin v Storr*[69] described as 'particular, direct
and substantial' damage 'other and different from that which was
common to all the rest of the public'."

Benjamin v Storr was in fact a case on whether an individual can
bring an action for damages in respect of a public nuisance[70] but the
principal authority relied on by Lord Diplock in the context of
statutory duty was not an action for damages but concerned the
question whether a member of the public could, without the assistance of the Attorney-General, seek an injunction to restrain an
interference with public rights.[71] However, it was said in *Lonrho*
that a, "mere prohibition on members of the public generally from
doing what it would otherwise be lawful for them to do is not
enough" to create a public right for this purpose. It will not therefore
be enough for the claimant to point to the commission of a crime and
say that he has been damaged by it and he cannot escape by this
route from the fundamental question of whether the statute is
intended to give rise to a civil action.[72]

---

[68] [1982] A.C. 173.
[69] (1874) L.R. 9 C.P. 400 at 407.
[70] See para.14–3, below. However, the connection is obvious. Public nuisance, like breach of
statutory duty, is an example of civil liability arising out of what is primarily a crime,
though in this case a common law crime.
[71] *Boyce v Paddington BC* [1903] 1 Ch. 109.
[72] *Mid Kent Holdings Plc v General Utilities Plc* [1997] 1 W.L.R. 14 (whether the claim is
for damages, an injunction or a declaration). Another of the law's mysteries is the case of
Emperor of Austria v Day and Kossuth (1861) 3 De G. & J. 217. The claimant obtained
an injunction to restrain the printing of false Hungarian bank notes here on the ground of
an "injury to property". The HL has said that a cause of action in private law which
attracted only an injunction against future harm but no damages for loss already suffered,
would be "wholly novel" (*Garden Cottage Foods v Milk Marketing Board* [1984] A.C.
130) but it is not obvious what the cause of action in the *Emperor of Austria* case was.
Browne-Wilkinson V.C. followed the case in *Kingdom of Spain v Christie Manson &
Woods Ltd* [1986] 1 W.L.R. 1120, but Hoffmann J. in *Associated Newspapers v Insert
Media Ltd* [1988] 1 W.L.R. 509 declined to accept that it could extend to restrain "unfair
competition" which was not actionable as one of the economic torts. See also *Mbasogo v
Logo Ltd* [2006] EWCA Civ 1370; [2007] Q.B. 846.

7–11   The law on inferring civil actions from statutory duties is not very satisfactory and Lord Denning M.R. commented with perhaps a little pardonable exaggeration that the legislature:

"[H]as left the courts with a guess-work puzzle. The dividing line between the pro-cases and the contra-cases is so blurred and so ill-defined that you might as well toss a coin to decide it."[73]

As Lord du Parcq pointed out[74] the draftsmen of Acts of Parliament are aware of the principles—and lack of principles—applied by the courts to fill the gaps left in legislation, and it can be argued, therefore, that the silence of a statute on the question of civil remedies for its breach is a deliberate invitation to the courts to decide the question for themselves. Certainly it should not be assumed that where the statute is silent this is because its promoters have not adverted to the point—much more likely that it would be politically inconvenient to attempt to answer the question one way or the other. If this is so, then the pretence of seeking for the nonexistent intention of Parliament should be abandoned. Not only does it involve an unnecessary fiction, but it may lead to decisions being made on the basis of insignificant details of phraseology instead of matters of substance. If the question whether a person injured by breach of statutory duty is to have a right of action for damages is in truth a question to be decided by the courts, then it should be acknowledged as such and some useful principles of law developed, if that is possible.[75] It is, however, debatable whether a clear overall presumption might help.[76] At least it can be said that there are numerous decisions on particular statutes so that in many cases it is already settled that a right of action does or does not exist.[77] Even where a right of action has been held to exist, however, it is not enough for the claimant simply to prove breach of the statute. There are other elements in the tort which we must now consider. We may, however, note that where the statute creates a criminal offence the victim may choose to seek a compensation

---

[73] *Ex p. Islands Records* [1978] Ch. 132 at 134–135. See also Schiemann J. in *R. v Knowsley MBC, Ex p. Maguire* (1992) 90 L.G.R. 224.

[74] *Cutler v Wandsworth Stadium Ltd* [1949] A.C. 398 at 411; *Solomons v R. Gertzenstein Ltd* [1954] 2 Q.B. 243 at 267 per Romer L.J.

[75] For a case decided by reference to principle and policy rather than the supposed intention of Parliament, see *Hargreaves v Bretherton* [1959] 1 Q.B. 45 (no action in tort for perjury).

[76] The Law Commission suggested a general presumption in favour of actionability: Law Com. No.21 (1969).

[77] Professor Glanville Williams, writing in 1960, concluded that, as a very broad and oversimplified conclusion, legislation concerning industrial safety gave rise to civil liability but other legislation did not. The actionability of current and future safety legislation is now covered by a specific statutory provision: see para.8–4, below. It is also the case that many statutory duties are less than absolute: para.8–5, below.

order from the criminal court, a procedure which is not dependent upon the establishing of a civil right of action. Though applicable to all criminal offences outside the road traffic field, this mechanism has so far been of limited importance in the type of case considered in this chapter but its role in compensating losses may increase.[78]

H. European Legislation

The general reluctance to find an actionable breach of statutory duty in cases brought against public authorities reflects the general principle that an ultra vires act does not of itself give rise to a claim for damages—there must be some tort,[79] breach of contract or other actionable wrong. However, one has to take account of the inter-action of English private law remedies with European law, a matter of which only a bare outline can be attempted here. The House of Lords in *Garden Cottage Foods Ltd v Milk Marketing Board*[80] held that directly applicable provisions of the Treaty of Rome might give rise to a civil action for damages in an English court.[81] The Court of Appeal in *Bourgoin SA v Ministry of Agriculture, Fisheries and Food*[82] later held that this was not the case where the legislation in question imposed obligations only on the State and not on private persons but since then another element has entered the picture, for the European Court of Justice in *Francovich v Italy*[83] held that a Member State may be liable to make good damage suffered by individuals as a result of the State's failure to implement a Directive and the Court spoke in rather broader terms of a principle of Community Law:

> "[A]ccording to which a Member State is obliged to make good the damage to individuals ... by a breach of Community law for which it is responsible."

This is apt to cover direct breaches of the Treaty provisions as well as failure to implement Directives. The subsequent case law indicates that the following conditions must be satisfied to give rise to such a liability: (1) the law infringed must be intended to confer rights on individuals; (2) (in cases where the State has any element of discretion) the breach by the Member State must be sufficiently serious; and (3) there must be a direct causal link between the breach

7–12

---

[78] For the powers of the criminal court, see para.4–2, above.
[79] As to misfeasance in a public office, see para.7–20, below.
[80] [1984] A.C. 130.
[81] Article 86 (now art.82) abuse of a dominant market position.
[82] [1986] Q.B. 716.
[83] (C–6/90) [1995] I.C.R. 722.

and the damage sustained by the claimant.[84] This is plainly wider than the common law notion of breach of statutory duty, most obviously in that it allows an action where the legislation itself is in breach of Community law. However, the first requirement is not wholly dissimilar from the underlying question in claims for breach of statutory duty, for Community law may be intended to confer benefits on a particular group without granting them rights enforceable by action in municipal courts. Thus in *Three Rivers DC v Bank of England (No.3)*[85] the House of Lords held that the 1977 Banking Directive[86] was intended as a measure to harmonise the regulation of banking but did not create a right to damages for depositors who suffered loss by reason of the failure of supervisory mechanisms. There has been some dispute as to the nature of the State's liability under this head for the purposes of English law, but in *R. v Secretary of State, Ex p. Factortame Ltd (No.7)*,[87] where the issue arose in the context of limitation of actions, it was held that it was in the nature of a breach of statutory duty and therefore an action in tort.[88]

2. ELEMENTS OF THE TORT

A. Duty Must be Owed to the Claimant

7–13   Some statutory duties are so expressed as to limit the classes of person for whose benefit they exist, and where this is so it is a question of the construction of the statutory provision in question whether the claimant is a member of the protected class. If he is not, then his action for breach of statutory duty cannot succeed. In *Hartley v Mayoh & Co*,[89] for example, a fireman was electrocuted while fighting a fire at the defendants' factory. His widow relied, inter alia, upon a breach by the defendants of their obligations under certain statutory regulations, but these existed only for the protection of "persons employed", and firemen did not come within this description. The claim for breach of statutory duty therefore failed. In *West Wiltshire DC v Garland*[90] it was held that the statutory duty of a district auditor gave rise to a civil cause of action in the local

---

[84] See the summary in *R. v Secretary of State, Ex p. Factortame Ltd (No.5)* [2000] 1 A.C. 524 at 538.
[85] [2001] UKHL 16; [2003] 2 A.C. 1.
[86] Directive on the co-ordination of laws, regulations and administrative provisions relating to the taking up and pursuit of the business of credit institutions (EEC) 77/80.
[87] [2001] 1 W.L.R. 942.
[88] The inadequacy of the implementation may not be apparent to the claimant until his claim has been adjudicated but the limitation period runs from the date of the injury: see *Spencer v Secretary of State for Work and Pensions* [2008] EWCA Civ 750; [2009] Q.B. 358.
[89] [1954] 1 Q.B. 383.
[90] [1995] Ch. 297.

authority, the accounts of which were audited by him, but there was no duty to an individual officer of the authority.

B. Injury Must be of the Kind which the Statute is Intended to Prevent

If the object of the statute was to prevent mischief of a particular **7–14** kind, one who suffers from its non-observance loss of a different kind cannot twist its remedy into an action for his own recoupment. In *Gorris v Scott*[91] the defendant, a shipowner, was under a statutory duty to provide pens for cattle on his ship in order to lessen the risk of murrain among them. The claimant's sheep were swept overboard in consequence of lack of such pens. The defendant was held not liable, because it was not part of the purpose of the statute to protect cattle against the perils of the sea.[92] The modern tendency is, however, not to apply this decision too strictly, and it has been said that if the claimant's damage is of the kind that the statute was designed to prevent, then it does not matter that it occurred in a way not contemplated by the statute.[93] On the other hand the House of Lords held that a workman who was injured by a dangerous part of machinery which flew out of a machine and hit him could not base a claim on the statutory obligation that dangerous parts of machinery "shall be securely fenced".[94] The object of this provision, it was said, was, "to keep the worker out, not to keep the machine or its product in".[95] It was only if he came into contact with the dangerous part of the machine, therefore, that the workman could rely upon breach of the obligation to fence, and an injury caused in a different way was not covered.[96]

---

[91] (1874) L.R. 9 Exch. 125. *Larrimore v American National Insurance Co* 89 P.2d 340 (1939).

[92] This decision may easily be misunderstood unless it is realised that the claimants made no claim whatever apart from the statute. If, quite apart from this statutory duty, the defendant had been negligent so that the sheep would have been washed overboard, pens or no pens, then the claimants could have recovered either for breach of contract or for the tort of negligence. As it was, they relied on the statutory obligation and on nothing else. Yet even in a case of negligence, the defendant's liability may be limited by an approach similar to that in *Gorris v Scott*: *Banque Bruxelles Lambert v Eagle Star Insurance*, para.6–27 above.

[93] *Donaghey v Boulton & Paul Ltd* [1968] A.C. 1 at 26 per Lord Reid. Note the similarity to the development at common law subsequent to *The Wagon Mound*, para.6–20, above.

[94] Factories Act 1961 s.14; *Close v Steel Co of Wales Ltd* [1962] A.C. 367; *Sparrow v Fairey Aviation Co Ltd* [1964] A.C. 1019.

[95] *Nicholls v F. Austin (Leyton) Ltd* [1946] A.C. 493 at 505 per Lord Simonds. See also *Fytche v Wincanton Logistics Ltd* [2004] UKHL 31; [2004] I.C.R. 975 (steel toe-capped boot; purpose of provision under regulations to protect from impact injury not wet and cold).

[96] Cf. *Young v Charles Church (Southern) Ltd* (1997) 39 B.M.L.R. 146 (regulation designed to prevent electrocution covered nervous shock at seeing workmate electrocuted).

C. Defendant Must be Guilty of a Breach of His Statutory Obligation

7–15   Two points must be noted here. In the first place, many statutes and statutory regulations have strictly defined spheres of application, and outside their proper sphere they are irrelevant. For example, many actions for injury caused by acts or omissions which would have amounted to breaches of the Factories Act had they occurred in a factory failed on the ground that the place where they in fact occurred was not a factory as defined.[97] The modification of much safety legislation so that it applies to workplaces in general will reduce the likelihood of such cases[98] but the general point remains valid. In *Chipchase v British Titan Products Co*,[99] a workman was injured when he fell from a platform nine inches wide and six feet above the ground. Statutory regulations then required that:

> "[E]very working platform from which a person is liable to fall more than six feet and six inches shall be . . . at least 34 inches wide"

and it was argued that the case was so nearly within the regulations that the court ought to take them into account. The argument was rejected and the defendants were held not liable either for breach of statutory duty, for there was none, or for negligence at common law.

The second point which it is necessary to make is that the measure of the defendant's obligation in every case must be found in the statute itself and that no single standard of conduct exists.[100] In some cases the statute imposes an unqualified obligation, i.e. an absolute duty, that a certain state of affairs shall exist, and in such cases the nonexistence of that state of affairs constitutes the breach.[101] Historically, the best-known example was the provision of s.14 of the Factories Act 1961 requiring that, "every dangerous part of any machinery . . . shall be securely fenced."[102] This has been replaced by more complex regulations which create a less than absolute obligation[103] but there continue to be many examples in

---

[97] An example is *Longhurst v Guildford, etc. Water Board* [1963] A.C. 265.

[98] See para.8–5, below.

[99] [1956] 1 Q.B. 545.

[100] In Germany para.823(2) of the BGB has some similarities to breach of statutory duty but the liability arises from the Code, with a uniform standard of fault.

[101] *Galashiels Gas Co v Millar* [1949] A.C. 275.

[102] See, e.g. *John Summers & Sons Ltd v Frost* [1955] A.C. 740. In *MacMillan v Wimpey Offshore Engineers & Contractors* 1991 S.L.T. 514 a statutory duty was held to make the employer liable for something the cause of which was the wilful act of a worker outside the course of employment.

[103] See para.8–6, below.

industrial safety legislation of duties to secure a result, not merely to take care to do so. Sometimes a duty is imposed "so far as is reasonably practicable", which is has some similarity to the standard of common law negligence, though it is by no means identical and the burden is on the defendant to show that the thing was not reasonably practicable.[104] Duties to secure something "so far as practicable" or to "take such steps as may be necessary" are more onerous but still not absolute.[105] There is no substitute for an analysis of the particular provision in its context.

D. Breach of Duty Must have Caused the Damage

In an action for breach of statutory duty, as in an action for common law negligence, the claimant bears the burden of proving the causal connection between the breach of duty and the damage.[106] There is, however, one rather special kind of case, peculiar to actions for breach of statutory duty, which must be mentioned, namely that in which the act or omission of the claimant himself has the legal result that both claimant and defendant are in breach of the same duty. **7–16**

In *Ginty v Belmont Building Supplies Ltd*[107] the claimant was an experienced workman in the employment of the defendants, who were roofing contractors. Statutory regulations binding upon both parties required that crawling boards should be used for work done on fragile roofs and, although boards had been provided by the defendants, the claimant neglected to use them and fell through a roof in consequence. In law both claimant and defendants were in breach of their statutory duties, but Pearson J. held that the claimant's claim failed altogether because the defendants' breach consisted of and was coextensive with his own wrongful act.[108] In other words, there was no wrongful act but the claimant's own, and:

"[I]t would be absurd if, notwithstanding the employer having done all he could reasonably be expected to do to ensure compliance, a workman, who deliberately disobeyed his employer's orders and thereby put the employer in breach of a regulation,

---

[104] See para.8–6, below.
[105] See para.8–6, below.
[106] *Bonnington Castings Ltd v Wardlaw* [1956] A.C. 613; *McWilliams v Sir William Arrol & Co* [1962] 1 W.L.R. 295. These cases concern "factual causation"; factors which go to "legal causation" such as acts of a third party, may be relevant (*Horton v Taplin Contracts Ltd* [2002] EWCA Civ 1604; [2003] I.C.R. 179) but everything finally depends on the words of the statute.
[107] [1959] 1 All E.R. 414.
[108] [1959] 1 All E.R. 414 at 424.

could claim damages for injury caused to him solely by his own wrongdoing".[109]

Although the result reached in *Ginty* has been judicially described as "obvious",[110] the scope of the decision is restricted. If the claimant establishes the defendant's breach of duty and that he suffered injury as a result, he establishes a prima facie case against the defendant. The defendant will escape liability only if he can rebut that prima facie case by proof that the only act or default of anyone which caused the breach was that of the claimant himself.[111] It follows that where some fault is to be attributed to the defendant, as where an employer calls upon a worker to do a job beyond his proper competence,[112] fails to provide adequate instructions or supervision,[113] is responsible for some independent fault,[114] or encourages him in his own breach of statutory duty,[115] then the claimant is entitled to recover some damages, even though they may be substantially reduced on account of his contributory negligence.

E. Volenti Non Fit Injuria[116]

7–17   It was long thought that this defence was not available in actions for breach of statutory duty and perhaps this is still generally so, though the law needs to be clarified. It is obviously open to Parliament to create a statutory duty and to provide that this defence does not apply; but where, as is often the case, the actionable duty is conjured up by a process of construction somewhat akin to divination it is not easy to see why there should be any hard and fast rule. In 1964 the House of Lords held that the defence was available where a worker engaged with a colleague in flagrant breach of safety rules and sued the employer on the basis that there was a breach of

---

[109] *Boyle v Kodak Ltd* [1969] 1 W.L.R. 661 at 665–666 per Lord Reid. "To say you are liable to me for my own wrongdoing is neither good morals nor good law": at 673 per Lord Diplock.

[110] *Donaghey v Boulton & Paul Ltd* [1968] A.C. 1 at 24 per Lord Reid.

[111] *Boyle v Kodak Ltd* [1969] 1 W.L.R. 661 at 672–673 per Lord Diplock.

[112] *Byers v Head Wrightson & Co Ltd* [1961] 1 W.L.R. 961; *Ross v Associated Portland Cement Manufacturers Ltd* [1964] 1 W.L.R. 768.

[113] *Jenner v Allen West & Co Ltd* [1959] 1 W.L.R. 554; *Ross v Associated Portland Cement Manufacturers Ltd*, above, fn.112; *Boyle v Kodak Ltd* [1969] 1 W.L.R. 661; *McCreesh v Courtaulds Plc* [1997] P.I.Q.R. P421.

[114] *McMath v Rimmer Bros (Liverpool) Ltd* [1962] 1 W.L.R. 1; *Leach v Standard Telephones & Cables Ltd* [1966] 1 W.L.R. 1392; *Donaghey v Boulton & Paul Ltd* [1968] A.C. 1; *Keaney v British Railways Board* [1968] 1 W.L.R. 879. It appears that the fault for which the employer is responsible need not be such as to suffice as an independent ground of action.

[115] *Barcock v Brighton Corp* [1949] 1 K.B. 339; *Laszczyk v National Coal Board* [1954] 1 W.L.R. 1426.

[116] See para.25–15, below.

statutory duty only via the vicarious liability for the other worker's acts.[117] That was not a case where the employer was in breach of a duty directly imposed on *him*, and the case is consistent with a position whereby in that event the defence is still inapplicable.[118] It is certainly true that the courts are much less willing than they once were to accept, even at common law, that a worker has voluntarily run a known risk without access to a claim for damages and that there are often other routes (for example causation) to denying liability. However, a blanket rule of exclusion based on the public policy of recognising the will of Parliament is in the nature of a fiction.

F. Contributory Negligence

Before the Law Reform (Contributory Negligence) Act 1945 the **7–18** contributory negligence of the claimant was a complete defence to an action for breach of statutory duty[119] and now, therefore, it is a reason for reducing the damages which he may recover. This matter has already been considered.[120]

G. Delegation

It is clear that in the ordinary way it is no defence for a person **7–19** subjected to a statutory duty to claim that he has delegated the duty or its performance to another person.[121] In some cases, however, it seems to have been thought that delegation may be a defence where performance of the tasks necessary to secure compliance with the statutory obligation has been delegated to the claimant himself.[122] Nevertheless, although some specific requirements for the defence

---

[117] *Imperial Chemical Industries Ltd v Shatwell* [1965] A.C. 656.

[118] However, the dicta on the point are not perhaps entirely consistent: compare Lord Reid at 674 referring to, "an employer who is himself at fault in persistently refusing to comply with a statutory rule"; Lord Pearce at 687, seeming to accept a general rule of non-applicability of the defence; Lord Donovan at 693, referring to unequal bargaining strength.

[119] *Caswell v Powell Duffryn Associated Collieries* [1940] A.C. 152.

[120] See para.6–52, above. A possible technical explanation of the result in *Ginty v Belmont Building Supplies Ltd*, above, fn.107 (if one be needed), is that in that case the odd situation prevailed that the accident was caused wholly by the fault of the claimant and wholly by the (identical) fault of the defendant while the Act of 1945 governs the case where, "any person suffers damage as the result partly of his own fault and partly of the fault of any other person". So the Act did not apply and at common law a person whose own fault was a cause of his injury can recover nothing: [1959] 1 All E.R. 414 at 424 per Pearson J.

[121] *Gray v Pullen* (1864) 5 B. & S. 970; *Whitby v Burt, Boulton & Hayward Ltd* [1947] K.B. 918. See para.20–27, below.

[122] See, e.g. *Vincent v Southern Ry* [1927] A.C. 430; *Smith v Baveystock & Co* [1945] 1 All E.R. 531.

of delegation were laid down,[123] in no case did the claimant clearly fail in his action on the express ground that the defendant's statutory duty had been delegated to him[124] and the doctrine has now fallen into disrepute. In *Ginty v Belmont Building Supplies Ltd*,[125] in a passage subsequently approved by the Court of Appeal,[126] Pearson J. doubted its soundness:

> "There has been a number of cases ... in which it has been considered whether or not the employer delegated to the employee the performance of the statutory duty. In my view, the law which is applicable here is clear and comprehensible if one does not confuse it by seeking to investigate this very difficult and complicated question whether or not there was a delegation. In my view, the important and fundamental question in a case like this is not whether there was a delegation, but simply the usual question: Whose fault was it? ... If the answer to that question is that in substance and reality the accident was solely due to the fault of the claimant, so that he was the sole author of his own wrong, he is disentitled to recover."[127]

It is submitted, therefore, that there is no special defence of delegation of a statutory duty and, indeed, that any other view would conflict with the general principle that no duty can be delegated.[128]

3. Misfeasance in a Public Office

7–20   This is a convenient point at which to outline the tort of misfeasance in a public office.[129] It is not based upon breach of statutory duty, but a claim for it is not infrequently coupled with a claim for breach of statutory duty in an action against a public authority. The tort is traceable back to the 17th century,[130] and was described in modern

---

[123] See, e.g. *Beale v Gomme Ltd* (1949) 65 T.L.R. 543; *Manwaring v Billington* [1952] 2 All E.R. 774.

[124] However, the judgments of Lord Goddard in *Smith v Baveystock & Co* [1945] 1 All E.R. 531 at 533–534 and Hilbery J. in *Barcock v Brighton Corp* [1949] 1 K.B. 339, could be taken as supporting this view.

[125] [1959] 1 All E.R. 414 at 423–424.

[126] *McMath v Rimmer Bros. Ltd* [1962] 1 W.L.R. 1 at 6. See also *Jenner v Allen West & Co* [1959] 1 W.L.R. 554.

[127] "Fault is not necessarily equivalent in this context to blameworthiness. The question really is whose conduct caused the accident": *Ross v Associated Portland Cement Manufacturers Ltd* [1964] 1 W.L.R. 768 at 777 per Lord Reid.

[128] [1964] 1 W.L.R. 768 at 776 per Lord Reid.

[129] There is a comparable common law crime of misbehaviour in a public office: *R. v Bowden* [1996] 1 W.L.R. 98. In s.9(5) of the Anti-Social Behaviour Act 2003 the tort is called "misfeasance in public duty".

[130] *Turner v Sterling* (1671) 2 Vent. 24.

times by the Privy Council as "well-established" in *Dunlop v Woollahra Municipal Council.*[131] The law was comprehensively reviewed by the House of Lords in *Three Rivers DC v Bank of England (No.3).*[132] The purpose of the tort is to give compensation to those who have suffered loss as a result of improper abuse of public power,[133] it being based on the principle that such power may be exercised only for the public good and not for ulterior and improper purposes.[134] It applies to an unlawful (that is to say, unauthorised) act[135] by a person holding a public office[136] (which includes a public body such as a local authority,[137] a government department[138] or the Bank of England[139]) provided it is done with the requisite mental element. Where a claim is brought against a public body or institution it will be necessary to show that the mental element was possessed by an identifiable human agent.[140] Although the mental element is restricted to intention or "recklessness" the tort has a considerable reach, for there is no requirement that the conduct should be actionable in damages in its own right[141]:

[131] [1982] A.C. 158. See also *David v Abdul Cader* [1963] 1 W.L.R. 834.

[132] [2001] UKHL 16; [2003] 2 A.C. 1. This is an amalgam of two hearings, the first (judgment given on May 18, 2000—[2003] 2 A.C. at 187) examining the law and the second applying it to the application to amend the particulars of claim (judgment given on March 22, 2001—[2003] 2 A.C. at 237). The second has the now usual paragraph numbers, the first does not.

[133] Since *Kuddus v CC Leicestershire* [2001] UKHL 29; [2002] 2 A.C. 222 exemplary damages may be available for this tort: para.22–11, below. On damages see also para.7–23, below. It is capable of applying to personal injury: *Akenzua v Secretary of State for the Home Dept* [2002] EWCA Civ 1470; [2003] 1 W.L.R. 741.

[134] *Three Rivers* at [2003] 2 A.C. 190 per Lord Steyn, citing Nourse L.J. in *Jones v Swansea CC* [1990] 1 W.L.R. 54 at 85.

[135] In principle the tort is equally applicable to an omission by a public officer, provided there is a decision not to act (see *Three Rivers* at [2003] 2 A.C. 228 per Lord Hutton, at 230 per Lord Hobhouse; see also Clark J. at first instance, [1996] 3 All E.R. at 583) or at least the ignoring of obvious risks (*Three Rivers* at 254); but liability for mere inadvertence or oversight is precluded by the mental element of bad faith.

[136] It has been held in New Zealand and Victoria that this may include a judicial office (*Rawlinson v Rice* [1998] 1 N.Z.L.R. 454; *Cannon v Tahche* [2002] V.R. 317) though other torts such as false imprisonment might arise from a malicious judicial act without jurisdiction. On judicial officers see para.24–8, below.

[137] *Jones v Swansea CC* [1990] 1 W.L.R. 1453.

[138] *Bourgoin SA v Ministry of Agriculture, Fisheries and Food* [1986] Q.B. 716. Including a vicarious liability for an individual officer: *Racz v Home Office* [1994] 2 A.C. 45.

[139] The *Three Rivers* case; but not the governing body of Lloyd's: *Society of Lloyd's v Henderson* [2007] EWCA Civ 930; [2008] 1 W.L.R. 2255. The tort is also applicable to the police (*Darker v CC W Midlands* [2001] 1 A.C. 435; *Kuddus v CC Leicestershire* [2001] UKHL 29; [2002] 2 A.C. 222; *L v Reading BC* [2001] EWCA Civ 346; [2001] 1 W.L.R. 1575; *Garrett v Att Gen* [1993] 3 N.Z.L.R. 600) and the Crown Prosecution Service (*Elguzouli-Daf v MPC* [1995] Q.B. 335) but it has been held that it does not apply to an independent prosecutor or lawyer representing Government: *Cannon v Tahche* [2002] V.R. 317; *Leerdam v Noori* [2009] NSWCA 90.

[140] *Chagos Islanders v Att Gen* [2004] EWCA Civ 997; *Southwark LBC v Dennett* [2007] EWCA Civ 1091; [2008] L.G.R. 94.

[141] One category of case, the unnecessary release of embarrassing information, may now be directly actionable under the Human Rights Act 1998 or at common law: para.12–80, below.

it covers non-actionable breach of statutory duty and a decision which is taken contrary to the requirements of natural justice. The mental element relates both to the validity of the act and its effect upon the claimant.[142] As to the first, the officer must act in bad faith, that is to say he must either be aware that his act is unlawful or be consciously indifferent as to its lawfulness—mere negligence is not enough. As to the effect on the claimant, there are two situations. The first is what has been called "targeted malice", that is to say, the case where the defendant acts with the *purpose* of causing harm to the claimant.[143] An example of this category is *Roncarelli v Duplessis*[144] (though the case was actually decided under the civil law of Quebec) where the defendant, Prime Minister and Attorney-General of Quebec, deprived the claimant of his restaurant licence as an act of revenge for standing bail for members of the Jehovah's Witnesses sect, against whose activities there had been a campaign. Alternatively, the defendant will be liable if he is aware that his act will probably (or in the ordinary course of things[145]) cause damage of the type in fact suffered by the claimant[146] or he is consciously indifferent to that risk.[147] So, turning a blind eye to either invalidity or consequences will do, but not failure to appreciate the risk of those matters. This:

---

[142] In *Beaudesert S.C. v Smith* (1966) 120 C.L.R. 145, the High Court of Australia had laid down that: "independently of trespass, negligence or nuisance but by an action for damages upon the case, a person who suffers harm or loss as the inevitable consequence of the unlawful, intentional and positive acts of another is entitled to recover damages from that other." This was rejected in England in *Lonrho Ltd v Shell Petroleum Co Ltd (No.2)* [1982] A.C. 173 and overruled by the High Court in *Northern Territory v Mengel* (1995) 129 ALR 1.

[143] As Lord Millett (who, however, did not agree with the "two limb" analysis of the tort) points out in *Three Rivers* at [2003] 2 A.C. 235 the claimant in this case does not have to show independently that the official exceeded his power, for, "his deliberate use of the power of his office to injure the plaintiff takes his conduct outside the power". The tort is, "an exception to the general rule that, if conduct is presumptively unlawful, a good motive will not exonerate the Defendant, and that, if conduct is lawful apart from motive, a bad motive will not make him liable": Lord Steyn at 190.

[144] (1959) 16 D.L.R. (2d) 698. For the current law in Canada see *Odhavji Estate v Woodhouse* [2003] SCC 69; [2003] 3 S.C.R. 263.

[145] The former expression is used by Lord Steyn (at [2003] 2 A.C. 191) and Lord Hutton (at 228), the latter by Lord Hobhouse (at 230) who adds a requirement that the loss must be such as to arise "directly". Cf. Lord Millett at 236: "I do not think that it is sufficient that he should foresee that it will probably do so. The principle in play is that a man is presumed to intend the natural and probable consequences of his actions . . . it should be calculated (in the sense of likely) in the ordinary course of events to cause injury. But the inference cannot be drawn unless the official did foresee the consequences." In the second decision Lord Hope refers to awareness of "a serious risk of loss" (at 247).

[146] *Three Rivers* at [2003] 2 A.C. 196 per Lord Steyn. So in *Tang Nin Mun v Secretary for Justice* 2000–2 H.K.C. 749, HKCA, a claim against a police officer was struck out because he could not have contemplated that his interference with evidence would cause psychiatric harm to the claimants. Compare the narrower test which now seems to apply in the economic torts—the defendant must intend to harm the claimant as an end in itself or as a means to some other end: Ch.18, below.

[147] See *Muuse v Secretary of State for the Home Dept* [2010] EWCA Civ 453 at [56]. **See Preface**.

"[R]epresents a satisfactory balance between the two competing policy considerations, namely enlisting tort law to combat executive and administrative abuse of power and not allowing public officers, who must always act for the public good, to be assailed by unmeritorious actions."[148]

In some circumstances the public officer may be exposed to an action for negligence[149] but the tort of misfeasance is wider: for example, a claim against the police for negligence in allowing a murderer to remain at large would be likely to fail on the grounds that there was insufficient proximity between them and the next, unidentifiable victim and for the policy reason of a fear of "defensive policing", but if they procured his release for some corrupt purpose a claim for misfeasance would not be defeated on that ground.[150] Judicial review is, of course, available on the basis of the invalidity of the act in question and without reference to fault, but there is no claim for damages unless there is a tort or some other wrong.[151]

The *Three Rivers* litigation arose out of allegations that the Bank of England had acted wrongfully in granting a banking licence (or failing to revoke the existing licence) to the Bank of Credit and Commerce International, thereby causing loss to over 6,000 depositors.[152] The amended particulars of claim were held sufficiently to set out the elements of the tort and the majority of the House of Lords held that the question of whether the pleaded particulars could be established was a question which could not be determined on the pleadings but required the case to go to trial.[153] However, after further interlocutory sparring (leading to an important decision on legal professional privilege[154]) the claim collapsed in November 2005, with costs reported to be £100 million.[155]

---

[148] [2003] 2 A.C. at 196.

[149] See para.5–45, above.

[150] *Akenzua v Secretary of State for the Home Dept* [2002] EWCA Civ 1470; [2003] 1 W.L.R. 741. In *Carter v CC Cumbria* [2008] EWHC 1072 (QB) a misfeasance claim was brought in connexion with police disciplinary proceedings. Tugendhat J. remarked at [66] that it was, "essential that before this action for misfeasance is allowed to be pursued through the courts, anxious scrutiny should be made of it to ensure that the Defendant's immunity against actions for negligence is not circumvented by the pleading device of converting what is in reality no more than allegations of negligence into claims for misfeasance in public office."

[151] See generally Law Commission, *Administrative Redress: Public Bodies and the Citizen*, C.P. No. 1897 (2008) and para.5–55, above.

[152] Section 1(4) of the Banking Act 1987 precluded any argument that there could be liability for negligence. Another argument based on European law failed: para.7–12, above.

[153] The claimant's contention was that the pleaded case showed the Bank running away from its supervisory function (the tort): [2003] 2 A.C. at 254. The defendants' contention was that it showed the Bank never getting to grips with the problem of supervision (not the tort): at 293.

[154] *Three Rivers DC v Bank of England* [2004] UKHL 48; [2005] 1 A.C. 610.

[155] *The Times*, November 3, 2005.

7–21   The claimant must obviously have sufficient legal standing to sue,[156] so that if for example, the defendant were alleged to have improperly refused the claimant's vote in an election (at a time when this was remediable by an action for damages) the claimant must necessarily show that he had the right to vote[157]—there must be some damage which, "completes the special connection between him and the official's act".[158] But normally it will not be necessary to show that the claimant has some legal "right" peculiar to him and it is enough that the defendant causes him injury with the requisite state of mind.[159] Thus in a case like *Roncarelli v Duplessis* it would not matter that the claimant had no absolute right to a licence.

7–22   The misfeasance must be *in* the public office so that a malicious act done by the defendant solely in his private capacity falls outside this tort, but if the officer acts out of motives of personal profit or spite those are plain examples of the abuse of power which underlies the tort. In the case of a public body the tort is not confined to things done in the direct exercise of functions which can only be carried on by a public body, so that a local authority would be liable in this way if, for example, it acted maliciously in refusing consent to a change of use of premises of which it was landlord, even though the source of its power to refuse was contract, not statute.

> "It is not the nature or origin of the power which matters. Whatever its nature or origin, the power may be exercised only for the public good. It is the office on which everything depends."[160]

Where a local authority passes a resolution with the object of damaging the claimant the authority is liable for the tort where, "a majority of the councillors present, having voted for the resolution, did so with the object of damaging the plaintiff".[161] It is clear that one member may be "infected" with the malice of another where he knows of it and merely follows the party whip, but such a case is likely to raise extremely difficult evidential issues.[162]

---

[156] *Three Rivers* at [2003] 2 A.C. 193.
[157] The subject matter of some of the older cases. However, this situation is now entirely governed by the Representation of the People Act 1985.
[158] *Three Rivers* at [2003] 2 A.C. 231 per Lord Hobhouse.
[159] See *Three Rivers* at [2003] 2 A.C. 230.
[160] *Jones v Swansea CC* [1989] 3 All E.R. 162 at 186 per Nourse L.J. The decision was reversed by the HL, [1990] 1 W.L.R. 1453, but on the facts. Lord Lowry (at 1458), with whom the other members of the House concurred, said that he was, "inclined to agree with the [CA] on the question of the nature of the power exercised". So also Lord Steyn in *Three Rivers* at [2003] 2 A.C. 191.
[161] *Jones v Swansea CC* [1990] 1 W.L.R. 1453 at 1458 per Lord Lowry.
[162] No individual councillor was sued in *Jones*. Cf. *Barnard v Restormel BC* [1998] 3 P.L.R.27 (allegation merely that other committee members deceived).

Historically, misfeasance in a public office is an action on the **7–23** case, for which the general rule is that there is no cause of action unless the claimant has suffered damage. Usually this will be economic damage,[163] but the tort is capable of extending to personal injury[164] or loss of liberty.[165] However, the House of Lords has rejected an attempt to make it actionable per se in the case of infringement of rights of a "constitutional" nature: it would be, "entirely novel to treat the character of the right invaded as determinative . . . of whether material damage need be proved."[166] In *Watkins v Home Office*[167] prison officers had interfered with the claimant's correspondence in contravention of the Prison Rules. At that time the Human Rights Act 1998 was not in force, but for the future that is where redress for such conduct should be sought.

Claims or misfeasance in a public office have been brought **7–24** frequently in recent years but they have rarely succeeded, probably because of the difficulty of proving the requisite state of mind in the public officials involved. The Law Commission has provisionally proposed that the tort be abolished as part of a wider project on claims for damages against public bodies where there would be a new liability for "serious fault" when the claim involved a "truly public" function.[168] These proposals are outlined above.[169]

---

[163] As an action on the case it should not cover "mere" loss of reputation without proof of financial loss though such damages have been awarded in Canada: *Uni-Jet Industrial Pipe Ltd v Canada (Attorney General)* (2001)198 D.L.R. (4th) 577. In *Odhavji Estate v Woodhouse* [2003] S.C.C. 69; [2003] 3 S.C.R. 263 at [32] it is said that the loss must be such as is "compensable in tort law" and *Uni-Jet* is referred to without disapproval. On the other hand, if some material loss is established damages should be available for worry and distress.

[164] *Akenzua v Secretary of State for the Home Dept* [2002] EWCA Civ 1470; [2003] 1 W.L.R. 741.

[165] *Karagozlu v MPC* [2006] EWCA Civ 1691; [2007] 1 W.L.R. 1881.

[166] *Watkins v Home Office* [2006] UKHL 17; [2006] 2 A.C. 395 at [25] per Lord Bingham.

[167] Above, fn.166. *Hussain v CC West Mercia* [2008] EWCA Civ 1205.

[168] *Administrative Redress: Public Bodies and the Citizen*, LCP No.187.

[169] Para.5–55, above.

EMPLOYERS' LIABILITY

1. INTRODUCTION

SINCE 1948, when the National Insurance (Industrial Injuries) Act **8–1**
1946[1] came into force, there has been in operation a national
insurance system under which benefits are payable to the victims of
industrial accidents and to sufferers from certain prescribed industrial diseases. Both employer and worker make national insurance
contributions and, generally speaking, any person employed under a
contract of service or apprenticeship is entitled to the benefits
provided by the Act. Since 1948 the scheme of benefits provided for
industrial injuries has to some extent been assimilated with the
general social security system, but disablement benefit remains
special to this area. This is paid when as a result of an accident, the
claimant suffers disablement amounting to at least a 14 per cent loss
of physical or mental faculty. Benefit is payable in respect of
personal injury by accident, "arising out of and in the course of
insurable employment". An accident arising in the course of the
employment is deemed in the absence of evidence to the contrary, to
have arisen out of that employment.[2] If the employee was, at the
time of the accident, disobeying any statutory or other regulations
applicable to his employment, or disobeying his employer's order,
the accident is nevertheless deemed to arise out of and in the course
of the employment, provided (1) the accident would be deemed so

---

[1] The principal Act is now the Social Security (Contributions and Benefits) Act 1992.
[2] Social Security (Contributions and Benefits) Act 1992 s.94(3).

to have arisen if there had been no disobedience, and (2) the act was done for the purpose of, and in connection with, the employer's trade or business.[3] The employee is insured against injuries sustained while travelling to and from work in transport provided by his employer[4] or while acting in an emergency (actual or supposed) on his employer's premises, for instance, averting damage by fire. The legislation is administered on behalf of the Dept of Work and Pensions and not by the ordinary courts. Claims under the Act are not a matter for the employer, they are made against the State, and their validity depends in no way upon proof of the fault or breach of duty of the employer.

The Act of 1946 replaced the Workmen's Compensation Acts, the first of which was enacted in 1897, and these Acts too, though in a different way, provided compensation to an injured worker without requiring him to prove the fault or breach of duty of his employer. It has thus been possible since 1897 for an injured worker to receive some compensation independently of the ordinary law governing the civil liability of his employer. Under the law now in force the worker is entitled to retain his benefits under the scheme and also to bring an action for damages against his employer.[5] There has thus always been a strong incentive for a worker whose case offers reasonable prospects of success to bring an action against his employer, and those prospects were considerably enhanced by the abolition of the rule that contributory negligence is a complete defence[6] and of the doctrine of common employment.[7] Actions by workers against their employers are, in fact, amongst the most numerous to be dealt with by the courts.[8] In earlier times cases nearly always concerned physical injury by accident; nowadays a much greater proportion of claims against employers arise from illness and disease. Many cases now concern mental illness caused by stress[9] and this presents formidable problems of risk assessment for employers and of adjudication for the courts.

---

[3] Social Security (Contributions and Benefits) Act 1992 s.98.

[4] Social Security (Contributions and Benefits) Act 1992 s.99.

[5] However, since 1990 there has existed a "clawback" system whereby certain benefits payable in the first five years are deductible from damages with a concomitant obligation on the defendant to reimburse the Secretary of State (para.22–24, below). There is no such deduction in fatal accident cases in respect of benefits payable on death.

[6] Law Reform (Contributory Negligence) Act 1945, para.6–43, above.

[7] See below.

[8] Under the Employers' Liability (Compulsory Insurance) Act 1969 all employers other than the nationalised industries, local authorities and the police are compelled to maintain insurance against their liability to their workmen. Such insurance was, of course, extremely common before the Act. Directors are not personally liable in damages for failure to comply: *Richardson v Pitt-Stanley* [1995] Q.B. 123.

[9] See para.5–71, above.

The recorded history of employers' liability does not start until 1837, and then it began by denying the worker a remedy. *Priestley v Fowler*,[10] decided in that year, is generally regarded as the *fons et origo* of the doctrine of common employment, which held that the employer was not liable to his employee for injury caused by the negligence of another employee, but the case really went further than that. It came close to denying that an employer might be liable to his workmen on any grounds,[11] and there can be no doubt that the judges of the first half of the 19th century viewed with alarm the possibility of widespread liability for industrial accidents.[12] Nevertheless, by 1858, if not earlier, common employment was recognised to be an exception to the ordinary principle that an employer is liable for the tort of his servant done in the course of the servant's employment.[13] It was said to rest upon the theory that the contract of service contained an implied term to the effect that the servant agreed to run the risks naturally incident to the employment, including the risk of negligence on the part of his fellow employees, but it did not follow that he agreed to take the risk of negligence on the part of the employer himself. If the employer had been negligent the worker's claim was still defeated if he had been guilty of contributory negligence, or even if he merely knew of the danger,[14] but something of a general principle had emerged. If the worker was injured by the employer's own negligence he could recover, but if he was injured by the negligence of a fellow employee he could not.[15]

During the second half of the 19th century judicial opinion veered in favour of the worker, and efforts began to be made to limit the scope of common employment. The doctrine was not finally abolished, however, until 1948[16] and, though much restricted in scope before that date,[17] the harshness of the law was chiefly modified by the evasion of common employment through the development of the rule that an employer was liable for an injury to his worker caused

8–2

---

[10] (1837) 3 M. & W. 1; *Farwell v Boston and Worcester Railroad Corp* (1842) 4 Metcalf 49 149 R.R. 262.

[11] "The mere relation of the master and the servant can never imply an obligation on the part of the master to take more care of the servant than he may reasonably be expected to do of himself": per Lord Abinger C.B., at 6.

[12] Striking instances are the judgments of Pollock C.B. in *Vose v Lancs & Yorks Ry* (1858) 27 L.J. Ex. 249 and of Bramwell B. in *Dynen v Leach* (1857) 26 L.J.(N.S.) Ex. 221.

[13] Ch.20, below.

[14] In *Smith v Baker & Sons* [1891] A.C. 325 the House of Lords finally held that mere knowledge did not defeat the workman's claim: para.25–11, below.

[15] The negligent employee was, of course, liable, but he was seldom worth suing.

[16] Law Reform (Personal Injuries) Act 1948 s.1(1). Contracting out of the Act is forbidden: s.1(3). The abolition of the doctrine extends only to personal injuries and Lord Denning M.R. suggested that it survives for the purposes of defamation: para.12–22, below.

[17] See, e.g. *Radcliffe v Ribble Motor Services* [1939] A.C. 215; *Graham v Glasgow Corp* [1947] A.C. 368; *Lancaster v L.P.T.B.* [1948] 2 All E.R. 796, HL.

by his own negligence or breach of statutory duty.[18] So far as the latter is concerned, no particular difficulty existed: if a duty is placed directly upon the employer by statute, then he does not discharge that duty by entrusting its performance to another.[19] Nonetheless, how can an employer be personally negligent unless he actually takes a hand in the work himself, a physical impossibility where the employer is not a human individual but, as was increasingly the case during the 19th century and is now the general rule, a company with independent legal personality? Such an employer could only act through its servants, and if they were negligent the doctrine of common employment applied and relieved the employer of liability.[20]

8–3   The answer to this difficulty was found in the concept of duties personal to the employer, for the careful performance of which the employer remained responsible even though the tasks necessary to discharge the duties were entrusted to a servant: "It is quite clear," said Lord Herschell[21]:

> "[T]hat the contract between employer and employed involves on the part of the former the duty of taking reasonable care to provide proper appliances, and to maintain them in a proper condition, and so to carry on his operations as not to subject those employed by him to unnecessary risk. Whatever the dangers of the employment which the employed undertakes, amongst them is certainly not to be numbered the risk of the employer's negligence and the creation or enhancement of danger thereby engendered."

Later, in the famous case of *Wilsons and Clyde Coal Co v English*,[22] Lord Wright redefined the employer's duty as threefold: "the provision of a competent staff of men, adequate material, and a proper system and effective supervision." The duty is not absolute, for it is fulfilled by the exercise of due care and skill. "But it is not fulfilled by entrusting its fulfilment to employees, even though selected with due care and skill."[23]

Before the abolition of common employment, therefore, it was important to maintain carefully the distinction between a breach of

---

[18] It was settled in *Groves v Wimborne* [1898] 2 Q.B. 402 that common employment afforded no defence in an action brought against the employer for breach of his statutory duty. The Employers' Liability Act 1880 (repealed by the Law Reform (Personal Injuries) Act 1948 s.1(2)) also excluded the defence in a limited number of defined cases.

[19] See para.7–19, above.

[20] Subject to the Employers' Liability Act 1880 it was no answer to the defence of common employment that the negligent servant was the claimant's superior: *Wilson v Merry* (1868) L.R. 1 H.L.(Sc.) 326.

[21] *Smith v Baker* [1891] A.C. 325 at 362.

[22] [1938] A.C. 57.

[23] [1938] A.C. 57 per Lord Wright.

the employer's personal duty, for which he was liable, and the mere negligence of a fellow employee, for which he was not:

"There is a sphere in which the employer must exercise his discretion and there are other spheres in which foremen and workmen must exercise theirs. It is not easy to define these spheres, but where the system or mode of operation is complicated or highly dangerous or prolonged or involves a number of men performing different functions, it is naturally a matter for the employer to take the responsibility of deciding what system shall be adopted. On the other hand, where the operation is simple and the decision how it shall be done has to be taken frequently, it is natural and reasonable that it should be left to the foreman or workmen on the spot."[24]

With the abolition of the doctrine of common employment in 1948,[25] the employer became liable as much for the negligence of a fellow servant of the claimant acting in the course of his employment as for breach of his personal duty, and it thus became unnecessary always to distinguish between the two kinds of wrongdoing. Nevertheless the concept of the employer's personal duty was not destroyed, and the employer is today liable either vicariously or for breach of his personal duty.[26] Additionally, there are numerous and detailed statutory duties which are imposed directly upon employers and these have the effect of increasing his overall liability for injury suffered by his workers. Vicarious liability is the subject of a separate chapter and here we shall consider the employer's personal duty to his employees, but in view of the mass of statutory duties in existence, to consider the common law alone would give a false picture of the present law of employer's liability. We shall also, therefore, consider first some of the more significant of these duties and their effect upon employer's liability as a whole. Very many claims are presented on the basis of both common law negligence and breach of statutory duty and it is perfectly possible for the claimant to succeed on one and fail on the other or succeed on both.

2. Statute Law[27]

The Health and Safety at Work, etc., Act 1974 was passed as a result **8–4** of the report of a Royal Commission which recommended a thorough review of the then existing patchwork of industrial safety

[24] *Winter v Cardiff RDC* [1950] 1 All E.R. 819 at 822–823 per Lord Oaksey.
[25] Law Reform (Personal Injuries) Act 1948 s.1(1).
[26] See *Staveley Iron & Chemical Co v Jones* [1956] A.C. 627.
[27] *Encyclopaedia of Health and Safety at Work, Law and Practice.*

legislation.[28] The Act contains a generalised duty upon employers to ensure, so far as is reasonably practicable, the health, safety and welfare at work of all employees. This duty is in some respects reminiscent of the employer's common law duty of care towards his workers, but the duty is supported only by penal sanctions and does not give rise to any civil liability.[29] However, the Act also gave power to repeal existing statutes governing safety and replace them with regulations which would continue to give rise to civil liability unless they provided otherwise.[30] This process made comparatively slow progress until the arrival on the scene of European Community legislation. As a result of a series of EC Directives,[31] implemented by a number of important Regulations, there was a radical reform of the statutory law in this area. It would be entirely out of place in a book of this kind to attempt to consider these provisions in detail but they are an important source of civil liability and without some sketch it is not possible to see the general common law in its wider context. As a result of the Regulations, most of the once familiar provisions of the Factories Act 1961 and the Offices, Shops and Ry Premises Act 1963 (major sources of case law) disappeared.[32]

The Management of Health and Safety at Work Regulations 1999[33] are, from an administrative point of view, the central element in the scheme and implement the so-called "framework" EC Directive[34] in so far as the general provisions of the Health and Safety at Work, etc., Act do not already incorporate the principles of the Directive into English law. Perhaps the most significant feature of these Regulations is the duty of every employer to make a "suitable and sufficient assessment" of the risks to the health and safety of workers and of other persons likely to be affected. These Regulations, unlike the others, did not at first generally give rise to civil liability, but now they do.[35]

8–5   Broadly speaking, the scheme was to replace the old system of legislating separately for each type of trade by a unified set of regulations governing particular aspects of employment, so that, for example, the Workplace (Health, Safety and Welfare) Regulations[36] deal with ventilation, cleanliness and working facilities in offices

---

[28] Cmnd. 5034.
[29] 1974 Act s.47(1).
[30] 1974 Act s.47(2). Is the liability created by s.47(2) confined to personal injury? Not answered in *Polestar Jowetts Ltd v Komori UK Ltd* [2005] EWHC 1674 (QB) where s.47(2) did not, anyway, apply.
[31] Directives 89/391, 89/654, 89/655, 89/656, 90/269, 90/270, 91/383.
[32] For a sketch of the previous law, see the 13th edn of this work, p.197 et seq.
[33] SI 1999/3242 (replacing SI 1992/2051).
[34] Directive 89/391.
[35] As a result of SI 2003/2457. Cf. the regulations governing working time: *Sayers v Cambridgeshire CC* [2006] EWHC 2029; [2007] I.R.L.R. 29.
[36] SI 1992/3004.

and shops as well as in factories.[37] As was previously the case, the regulations impose a mixture of unqualified, or absolute, obligations and obligations which are qualified in some way. An example of the first category is reg.19 of the Workplace Regulations, which provides that "escalators and moving walkways shall [inter alia] function safely". On the other hand, the duty to keep floors free from obstructions or substances which may cause a fall (reg.12(3)) must be complied with "so far as is reasonably practicable".[38] In some cases one obligation may be absolute and another one, in relation to the same risk, may be qualified.[39] There is a substantial amount of case law under the existing and previous legislation on the meaning of "reasonably practicable" and not all of it is wholly reconcilable (apart from the fact that in any case what is in issue is the construction of the particular regulation). It is clear that the burden of pleading and proving that something was not reasonably practicable rests on the defendant[40] and therefore a worker who proves that he has suffered injury because the statutory requirement has not been met establishes at least a prima facie case—he is not required to aver what measures the defendant should have taken to comply with the regulation. It is true that after all the evidence has been produced the initial burden of proof is rarely of importance,[41] but the claimant is in a stronger position when attempting to negotiate an agreed settlement of his claim and in the early stages of litigation if he can rely upon the legislative provision than if he has to shoulder the burden of proving negligence at common law. However, even as a matter of substance, failure to do what is reasonably practicable cannot be exactly equated with negligence at common law. The matter has been put in the following way:

"The hallmark of liability at common law is that the employer must be shown not to have acted reasonably. Reasonableness pervades the whole concept of common law liability. If the

[37] However, the coverage is not universal: e.g. SI 1992/3004 does not apply to ships, building sites or mines and quarries.
[38] Regulation 12(1) and (2), which deal with unevenness and slipperiness, appear to be unqualified. It has been said that the regulations preserve the old distinction under the Factories Act between the state of the workplace and obstructions: *Craner v Dorset CC* [2008] EWCA Civ 1323; [2009] I.C.R. 563.
[39] See *Dugmore v Swansea NHS Trust* [2002] EWCA Civ 1689; [2003] I.C.R. 574 (Control of Substances Hazardous to Health Regulations 1988—now SI 1999/437; exposure of employee to substance to be prevented so far as reasonably practicable or, where not reasonably practicable, to be adequately controlled).
[40] *Nimmo v Alexander Cowan & Sons Ltd* [1968] A.C. 107; *Larner v British Steel Plc* [1993] I.C.R. 55; *Egan v Central Manchester etc NHS Trust* [2008] EWCA Civ 1424; [2009] I.C.R. 585.
[41] *Dorman Long (Steel) Ltd v Bell* [1964] 1 W.L.R. 333 at 335 per Lord Reid; *Jenkins v Allied Ironfounders Ltd* [1970] 1 W.L.R. 304 at 312 per Lord Guest.

employer has acted reasonably, he will avoid common law liability. It might be reasonable for an employer to conclude that a particular risk is so slight or of such little consequence if it occurs that he can properly do nothing to eliminate or reduce it. He might reasonably decide to do nothing because a responsible body of professional or official opinion has suggested that the degree of risk in question is acceptable.

However, under the statute, the adjective 'reasonably' serves only to qualify the concept of practicability. Reasonableness of conduct does not stand as the hallmark by which statutory liability is avoided as it does at common law. The focus of the defence by which liability is avoided, once it has been shown that the place of work was unsafe, is practicability—qualified by reasonableness. Under the statute, the employer must first consider whether the employee's place of work is safe. If the place of work is not safe (even though the danger is not of grave injury or the risk very likely to occur) the employer's duty is to do what is reasonably practicable to eliminate it. Thus, once any risk has been identified, the approach must be to ask whether it is practicable to eliminate it and then, if it is, to consider whether, in the light of the quantum of the risk and the cost and difficulty of the steps to be taken to eliminate it, the employer can show that the cost and difficulty of the steps substantially outweigh the quantum of risk involved. I cannot see how or where the concept of an acceptable risk comes into the equation or balancing exercise. . . . In that respect, it appears to me that there is a significant difference between common law liability where a risk might reasonably be regarded as acceptable and statutory liability where the duty is to avoid *any* risk within the limits of reasonable practicability."[42]

However, some duties are imposed "so far as practicable" without the qualifying epithet of "reasonably" and under the old law it was established that something might be "practicable" without being "reasonably practicable" (though it might be "impracticable" without being actually impossible[43]); it was also held that a precaution might be practicable even though it was unnecessary and inconvenient on any cost-benefit analysis and even though the risks involved in setting it up exceeded the probable benefit to be gained

[42] *Baker v Quantum Clothing Group* [2009] EWCA Civ 499 at [88]–[89] per Smith L.J. Premises or a process may be objectively unsafe even though the employer has no reason to be aware of the risk but if he is in that position it will not be reasonably practicable for him to take any measures to counter it: *Abraham v G. Ireson & Son (Properties) Ltd* [2009] EWHC 1958 (QB).

[43] *Jayne v National Coal Board* [1963] 2 All E.R. 220.

from it.[44] Logic might therefore suggest a (possibly over-elaborate) four-stage system: (1) to ensure a result, an absolute obligation[45]; (2) next down, to do what is practicable; (3) then what is reasonably practicable; (4) and finally the common law "floor" standard of reasonable care under the law of negligence.

One of the best known provisions of the old law was s.14 of the **8–6** Factories Act 1961, which required that every dangerous part of machinery should be securely fenced and which was construed as imposing an absolute duty in the sense that difficulty or even impossibility of complying and at the same time leaving the machine in a usable condition afforded no defence. The new equivalent is reg.11 of the Provision and Use of Work Equipment Regulations 1998[46] and this adopts a different approach in the form of safety measures in a graded hierarchy according to practicability. First, if practicable, there must be fixed guards; if that is not practicable, then "other guards or protection devices" must be provided; if that is not practicable then the employer must provide jigs, or holders or similar protection for use in conjunction with the machinery; finally, failing all else, he must at least provide information, training and supervision. There has probably therefore been some degree of reduction in the strictness of the employer's liability in this area but it should be noted that under the regulation the condition for a step down the hierarchy of protective measures is that the more onerous measure is not practicable. The fencing requirements of the old law did not apply to cases where the claimant was struck by something ejected from the machine, whether part of the material on which the machine was working or part of the machine itself.[47] This is still so since the measures required by reg.11 must be effective to "prevent access to" the

[44] *Boynton v Willment Bros* [1971] 1 W.L.R. 1625; *Sanders v F.H. Lloyd & Co Ltd* [1982] I.C.R. 360.
[45] In *Bruce v Ben Odeco* 1996 S.L.T. 1315 "so maintained as to ensure" was held to create an absolute obligation to keep in repair.
[46] SI 1998/2306 (replacing SI 1992/2932). The Regulation applies to, "any dangerous part of machinery or to any rotating stock bar". Although the Regulation now applies to other premises as well as factories it seems that "dangerous part of machinery" should be given the same meaning as under the Factories Act. There it was held that there was no duty to fence parts of machinery being constructed in the factory rather than forming part of the equipment used in its processes (*Parvin v Morton Machine Co* [1952] A.C. 515), nor to fence vehicles moving around the premises (*Mirza v Ford Motor Co* [1981] I.C.R. 757). In deciding whether a part of machinery was dangerous, the basic question was whether it was foreseeably likely to cause injury and in assessing this not only the careful but the careless and inattentive worker had to be borne in mind. However, it was held that if a part of machinery was a foreseeable cause of injury, and was unfenced, then it was irrelevant that the claimant's accident occurred in an unforeseeable way: *Millard v Serck Tubes Ltd* [1969] 1 W.L.R. 211.
[47] *Nicholls v Austin (Leyton) Ltd* [1946] A.C. 493; *Carroll v Andrew Barclay & Sons* [1948] A.C. 477.

dangerous part of machinery[48] but reg.12 requires the taking of measures to ensure[49] that risks to safety from certain specified hazards are either prevented or, where that is not reasonably practicable, adequately controlled,[50] and ejection of material[51] or disintegration of machinery are among the specified hazards.

The specific obligations under reg.11 are to be contrasted with what might be regarded as the basic provisions of the Equipment Regulations, which are that the employer must, "ensure that work equipment is so constructed as to be suitable for the purpose for which it is used or provided"[52] and that it is, "maintained in an efficient state, in efficient working order and in good repair".[53] In *Galashiels Gas Co Ltd v O'Donnell*[54] a provision of the Factories Act requiring lifts to be of "good mechanical construction . . . and . . . properly maintained" was held to give rise to liability merely on the basis that it failed to function properly and the same has been held under the 1998 Regulations.[55] Work equipment means, "any machinery, appliance, apparatus, tool or installation for use at work (whether exclusively or not)" and the requirements of the Regulations apply to, "such equipment provided for use or used by an employee at his work". The Regulations present formidable problems in determining how far they extend beyond the "direct sphere of the employer's undertaking or control"[56] since they plainly do not require that the equipment should have been provided by the employer or even specifically approved by him.[57] Although the law of employer's liability has large elements of liability without fault it is not a social insurance scheme for work injuries[58] and it could hardly be the law that a solicitor's firm was liable for an injury to a

---

[48] Regulation 11(1)(a). In the alternative under reg.11(1)(b) they may be to stop the movement of the dangerous part before the worker's entry into a danger zone.

[49] Whereas "shall ensure" seems to create an absolute obligation, to "take measures to ensure" has some affinities with the requirement to "take such steps . . . as may be necessary" in the Mines and Quarries Act s.48(1), which in *Brown v NCB* [1962] A.C. 574 was held to be satisfied where all relevant information had been obtained and acted on with due care and skill.

[50] The rather Delphic reg.12(4) provides that " 'adequate' means adequate having regard only to the nature of the hazard and the nature and degree of exposure to the risk". "Adequate" is not defined in reg. 9 (training): *Allison v London Underground Ltd* [2008] EWCA Civ 71.

[51] Emissions of certain toxic substances and noise are governed by other regulations, see reg.12(5).

[52] Regulation 4(1). In determining suitability the employer has to bear in mind that workers may be inattentive: *Robb v Salamis (M & I) Ltd* [2006] UKHL 56; [2007] I.C.R. 175.

[53] Regulation 5(1).

[54] [1949] A.C. 275.

[55] *Stark v Post Office* [2000] I.C.R. 1013 (bicycle; dealing with the 1992 Regulations, which are identical in this respect); *Ball v Street* [2005] EWCA Civ 76.

[56] *Smith v Northamptonshire CC* [2009] UKHL 27; [2009] I.C.R. 734 at [64].

[57] Cf. the wording of para.3(1) of the underlying Directive.

[58] There is clearly a substantial difference of view between Baroness Hale at [41] and Lord Mance at [69] on the "starting point" for the role of strict liability.

clerk by falling from a defective chair at a court hearing which he was attending, even though it could fairly be said that the chair was being used at his work.[59] In *Smith v Northamptonshire County Council*[60] the claimant was injured when a ramp at the house from which she was collecting a person confined to a wheelchair collapsed. Her employers knew of the ramp, indeed they had inspected it properly and that had revealed no defect. A majority of the House of Lords held that there had been no breach of the Regulations. There had to be "some specific nexus (beyond the mere fact of use) . . . . between the equipment and the employer's undertaking"[61]; the equipment had to be:

"[I]ncorporated into and adopted as part of the employer's business or other undertaking, whether as a result of being provided by the employer for use in it or as a result of being provided by anyone else and being used by the employee in it with the employer's consent and endorsement".[62]

The position where the employer's business is to deal with equipment submitted for repair by third parties is unclear.[63] In deciding whether equipment is "suitable" it has been held that there must be some element of balancing of risk against countervailing factors, it is not enough that altering the equipment would have prevented the damage[64]; but a Scots decision denies that the cost of alternative equipment plays any role in this.[65]

The old legislation was always primarily regulatory in its nature, **8–7** that is to say it provided an administrative mechanism, backed by the enforcement powers of bodies like the Factory Inspectorate and the Health and Safety Executive, and, if necessary, by criminal

---

[59] Cf. *PRP Architects v Reid* [2006] EWCA Civ 1119; [2007] P.I.Q.R. P4 (lift in shared office building) on which Lords Carswell and Mance in *Smith v Northamptonshire* reserved their opinion.

[60] Above.

[61] At [63] per Lord Mance.

[62] At [65]. Cf. Lord Hope, who thought that control was enough; but Lord Mance thought it unrealistic to say there was control of the ramp. See also *Spencer-Franks v Kellogg Brown and Root* [2008] UKHL 46; [2008] I.C.R. 863; *PRP Architects v Reid* [2006] EWCA Civ 1119; [2007] ICR 78; *Couzens v T. McGee & Co Ltd* [2009] EWCA Civ 95.

[63] In *Spencer-Franks v Kellogg Brown and Root*, above, fn.62, Lord Hoffmann at [26] doubted whether the Regulations would make an employer liable for defects in equipment submitted by a third party for repair but thought that, since the Regulations extended the scope of the liability to persons having "control" of the equipment, the third party might be liable. It seems extraordinary that a person taking his car to a garage for repair could incur liability without fault for a vehicle about which he has no expertise to a mechanic with whom he has no relationship whatever.

[64] *Searby v Yorkshire Traction Ltd* [2003] EWCA Civ 1856.

[65] *Skinner v Scottish Ambulance Service* [2004] S.L.T. 834, IH.

prosecution,[66] to promote safety by preventing accidents and disease. That remains true under the present regime.[67] There is therefore a tension between the regulatory and compensatory roles: the Regulations are not designed as a code of compensation under the civil law, that is merely their incidental effect as a result of the long tradition in this country of treating industrial safety legislation as giving rise to a civil cause of action. Indeed, the background European legislation comes from a legal tradition in which compensation for work injury is exclusively or predominantly dealt with under various forms of workers' compensation schemes. We do not, therefore, have a coherent system of employer's civil liability but a patchwork of statutory duties overlaying general common law liability for negligence. There do seem to be differences of approach to the balance of these elements of liability, one seeking to reconcile them with the common law approach, the other emphasising compensation. In *Fytche v Wincanton Logistics Ltd*[68] the claimant was a tanker driver who had been issued with steel-toed boots by his employers because there was a risk of heavy things falling on his feet. During freezing weather in which the claimant had had to dig to extricate his tanker, some water got into one of the boots through a tiny hole and he suffered mild frostbite to a toe. The employers were not negligent in failing to provide weatherproof boots because as a rule he would not be exposed to freezing conditions: a travelling salesman might conceivably get stuck in a snowdrift but no one would suggest that his employers should provide equipment to guard against that risk. However, because the boots had been provided as a precaution against the risk of falling objects they were safety equipment under the Personal Protective Equipment at Work Regulations[69] and had to be, "maintained ... in an efficient state, in efficient working order and in good repair." So, it was argued, the tiny hole meant that they were not in this state and this had caused his injury, leading to liability. The majority of the House of Lords regarded such a result as "very strange and arbitrary"[70] and they rejected it: the equipment only had to be efficient and in good repair in respect of the risk against which it was provided. For the minority,

---

[66] The regulations themselves say nothing about criminal penalties, those are to be found in the 1974 Act, s.33. See the remarks of Ormrod L.J. in *Mirza v Ford Motor Co Ltd* [1981] I.C.R. 757 at 761, on the tension between the penal purposes and the compensatory effect of the Factories Act 1961.

[67] The various regulations, "are there primarily to promote a culture of good practice with a view to preventing injury": *Smith v Northamptonshire CC* [2009] UKHL 27; [2009] I.C.R. 734 at [4] per Lord Hope.

[68] [2004] UKHL 31; [2004] I.C.R. 975.

[69] SI 1992/2966. These Regulations were held to require the provision of body armour in *Henser-Leather v Securicor Cash Services Ltd* [2002] EWCA Civ 816.

[70] [2004] UKHL 31; [2004] I.C.R. 975 at [7] per Lord Hoffmann.

however, this involved reading a restriction into the legislation which was not there. In the view of Baroness Hale[71]:

> "The issue in this case ... is who should bear the risk that the boots supplied for a particular reason turn out to have an incidental defect which causes the employee injury while he is at work. I have no difficulty with the conclusion that the employer rather than the employee should bear that risk. There are good policy reasons for imposing strict liability on employers for many of the injuries which their employees suffer at work. The overall object of the legislation is to protect the health and safety of workers: if this fails and they suffer injury, strict liability means that they are compensated for that injury without the need for slow and costly litigation such as this. I appreciate that we have not yet reached the point where there is strict liability for every injury suffered by a worker in the course of his employment, but I see no need to bring in limitations which are not in the statutory language."

Of course as the majority accepted, it cannot be wholly true that the ultimate issue of liability turns on whether the equipment is suitable to guard against the risk in respect of which it is provided. Thus a pair of boots might offer the most excellent protection against falling objects but for that very reason might be so stiff and heavy that they were unsuitable for driving and there is no doubt that the employer would then be liable for a crash in which the driver was injured. But that would be a new or positive risk created by the boots and there would be liability for negligence quite independently of the Regulations.

However expansively the Regulations are interpreted, for the foreseeable future we shall have the familiar dual liability system. It has always been possible to rely on statutory infringements as evidence of common law negligence but the statutory framework will grow in relative importance in relation to civil actions for damages. In the first place, the statutory obligations are now more wide-ranging in their scope since they apply, subject to specified exceptions, to all types of employment, rather than to employment in a factory, in an office, on a building site and so on. Secondly, in some cases the regulations (and their associated Codes of Practice) may come very close in practice to being treated as the standard measure of what is required under the common law so that the

---

[71] At [70].

distinction between statutory and common law liability will become to some extent blurred.[72]

8–8 The various regulations have been made to implement the EC Directives[73] in pursuance of this country's treaty obligations. As in any such case there must be a possibility of conflict between the local legislation and the Directives, even allowing for the clear principle that the local legislation is to be construed so far as is reasonably possible so as to give effect to the Directive. This is a complex question which should be pursued elsewhere but there is a possibility[74] that a claimant damnified by failure to implement one of the Directives may have an action against the Crown.[75] What is certain is that the regulations are fast acquiring an overlay of interpretative case law which equals or even exceeds that under the old law.

3. COMMON LAW

8–9 Since, as we have seen, the employer is now liable to his employee for an injury caused by a fellow employee, it might be thought that there is no longer value in retaining the concept of the employer's personal duty.[76] The enormous majority of workers are in the service of corporate employers who are in reality not capable of negligence, or anything else, so why not treat every case as one of vicarious liability? One answer to this may be that habits of thought acquired under the rule of common employment have survived its abolition, but in fact the concept of the personal duty continues to serve a

---

[72] The Manual Handling Regulations 1992 (SI 1992/2793) may provide an example because the Regulations themselves are (necessarily, given their subject matter) rather less precise than the others. On the application of these Regulations see *Koonjul v Thameslink Healthcare Services NHS Trust* [2000] P.I.Q.R. P123; *King v R.C.O. Support Services Ltd* [2001] I.C.R. 608; *O'Neill v D.S.G. Retail Ltd* [2002] EWCA Civ 1139; [2003] I.C.R. 222. At common law an employer certainly owes his workers a duty to give adequate information about the operation of equipment. This is also required by the Provision and Use of Work Equipment Regulations 1998 reg.9 (SI 1998/2306). The associated Code of Practice, para.88, spells this out by referring to factors (workers' command of English, learning or reading disabilities, experience) which would obviously be taken into account at common law.

[73] In fact the Management of Health and Safety at Work Regulations only implement part of Directive 89/391, because the view has been taken that some of it had already been anticipated by the general provisions of the Health and Safety at Work, etc., Act 1974.

[74] Before the Management of Health and Safety at Work Regulations became civilly actionable, unsuccessful attempts were made to argue that they could be directly relied on in *Cross v Highlands and Islands Enterprises* [2001] I.R.L.R. 336, OH and *Millward v Oxfordshire CC* [2004] EWHC 455 (QB). Note, however, that in the latter case liability was imposed at common law in respect of failure to undertake and implement an adequate risk assessment.

[75] *Francovich v Italy* [1995] I.C.R. 722, para.7–12, above. As to employees of "emanations of the state" see also *Foster v British Gas Plc* [1991] 2 A.C. 306.

[76] See *Sullivan v Gallagher & Craig* 1960 S.L.T. 70 at 76 per Lord Justice-Clerk Thomson.

useful purpose. In many cases it is obviously much more convenient to say that a given state of affairs or a given event proves a breach by the employer of his personal duty than to say that some employee must somehow have been negligent for that state of affairs to exist or for that event to come about. If a worker is injured because no one has taken the trouble to provide him with an obviously necessary safety device, it is sufficient and in general satisfactory to say that the employer has not fulfilled his duty,[77] even if the employer is a company.[78] It is unnecessarily complicated to say that someone whose duty it was to provide the device in question, or someone whose duty it was to see that there was someone else to consider what safety devices were required and to provide them, must have been negligent and therefore that the employer is liable. Again, in many cases the only person involved in the sequence of events leading up to the accident is the claimant himself and yet his employer is liable, for example because the claimant should not have been left alone to do the job. In terms of vicarious liability this would have to be explained by saying that some other employee had somehow failed in his duty of organising the work. It is simpler, and no less accurate, to say that the employer himself was in breach of his duty.[79]

It is not only for its convenience, however, that the continued use of the employer's personal duty is justified. True vicarious liability exists only where a servant has committed a tort in the course of his employment,[80] but the employer's liability is not so restricted, so that there are cases in which the worker's injury is attributable to the negligence of an independent contractor and yet the employer is liable for breach of his personal duty to the worker.[81] Moreover, though employer's liability is most commonly dealt with as a matter of tort, it is also a matter of contract,[82] and the worker's contract of service is made with his employer, not with his fellow employees. Duties which exist by virtue of express or implied terms in the contract of employment must, therefore, be duties owed by the

---

[77] See *Commonwealth v Introvigne* (1982) 41 A.L.R. 577 (accident at school).

[78] Cf. the criminal law, where there must be an act of an identifiable human being: *Att Gen's Reference (No.2 of 1999)* [2000] Q.B. 796.

[79] *McCafferty v Metropolitan Police Receiver* [1977] 1 W.L.R. 1073 is a good example of this approach. In Australia it has been held that if a Minister is aware of a health hazard to workers the Crown may be in breach of duty even though the department responsible for the work has no such knowledge: *Western Australia v Watson* [1990] W.A.R. 248.

[80] See Ch.20, below. Potential problems with very small companies where the directors are also the workers are illustrated by *Nicol v Allyacht Spars Pty Ltd* (1987) 75 A.L.R. 1.

[81] See para.8–16, below.

[82] *Matthews v Kuwait Bechtel Corp* [1959] 2 Q.B. 57; *Reid v Rush & Tompkins* [1989] 3 All E.R. 228; *Johnstone v Bloomsbury HA* [1992] Q.B. 333; *Scally v Southern Health & Social Services Board* [1992] 1 A.C. 294 and see para.1–8, above. One employer's tort liability may pass to his successor under the legislation governing transfer of undertakings because it "arises in connection with" a contract of employment: *Martin v Lancashire CC* [2000] I.C.R. 197.

employer himself. Theoretically at least, the employer's vicarious liability for his servant's negligence, which is a liability in tort, must be distinct.[83]

A. Nature of Employer's Duty

8–10   We have already noticed Lord Wright's threefold division of the employer's duty—"the provision of a competent staff of men, adequate material and a proper system and effective supervision"[84] —and, making due allowance for its being expressed in terms contemplating industrial work, it is convenient to adhere approximately to this in an exposition of the law. In truth, however, there is but one duty, a duty to take reasonable care so to carry on operations as not to subject the persons employed to unnecessary risk[85]:

> "In case there is any doubt about the meaning of 'unnecessary' I would ... take the duty as being a duty not to subject the employee to any risk which the employer can reasonably foresee, or, to put it slightly lower, not to subject the employee to any risk which the employer can reasonably foresee and which he can guard against by any measure, the convenience and expense of which are not entirely disproportionate to the risk involved."[86]

The majority of the reported cases concern accidents, but that is only because in earlier times there was less awareness of the risks to health (as opposed to safety) presented by employment. The development of knowledge about matters like the effects of asbestos,[87] noise,[88] vibration[89] and the effects of repetitive manual movements,[90] coupled with a relaxation of the former strict provisions on limitation of actions,[91] has produced litigation in recent years, sometimes on a very large scale indeed. Furthermore, it is now recognised

---

[83] See Jolowicz [1959] C.L.J. 163 at 164–165.

[84] *Wilsons and Clyde Coal Co v English* [1938] A.C. 57 at 78, para.8–3, above.

[85] i.e. risk of injury: it is not the employer's duty to insure his employee nor to advise him to insure himself (*Reid v Rush & Tompkins*, above, fn.82) nor, in the absence of some specific assumption of responsibility, to take steps to safeguard the employee's economic well-being: *Crossley v Faithful & Gould Holdings Ltd* [2004] EWCA Civ 293; [2004] I.C.R. 1615.

[86] *Harris v Brights Asphalt Contractors* [1953] 1 Q.B. 617 at 626 per Slade J. What is necessary is related to the job. It may be legitimate to ask police officers or firemen to take risks which could not be expected of other workers: *Mullaney v CC West Midlands* [2001] EWCA Civ 700.

[87] See, e.g. *Jameson v C.E.G.B.* [2000] 1 A.C. 455.

[88] See, e.g. *Thompson v Smith's Shiprepairers (North Shields) Ltd* [1984] Q.B. 405.

[89] See, e.g *Bowman v Harland & Wolff* [1992] I.R.L.R. 349. However, "vibration white finger" or "Reynaud's phenomenon" figured in the reports as far back as 1946: *Fitzsimmons v Ford Motor Co* [1946] 1 All E.R. 429 (workmen's compensation).

[90] "Repetitive strain injury". See, e.g. *Pickford v I.C.I. Plc* [1998] 1 W.L.R. 1189.

[91] See Ch.26.

that the employer's duty may extend to the effect of working conditions[92] on the mental health of his employees.[93]

In many respects, therefore, the duty is similar to the duty of care in the tort of negligence generally, but expressed in terms appropriate to the relationship of employer and employee.[94] The same general duty will be owed in relationships which are not, strictly speaking within the category of contracts of employment but which are closely analogous, such as that between a police officer and a chief constable,[95] though in that case the operational requirements of the job may mean that the *content* of the duty is very different from that which is normally imposed. As we shall see, the duty of the employer cannot, as can an ordinary duty of care, always be discharged by the employment of an independent contractor,[96] but it is nevertheless a duty of care, not an absolute duty,[97] and it is for the claimant to prove its breach. If a worker cannot prove negligence, whether by direct evidence or with the aid of res ipsa loquitur, an action based upon breach of the employer's personal duty must fail. With this in mind we can consider the various branches of the employer's common law duty to his workers.

i. Competent staff. The duty to take reasonable care to provide a **8–11** competent staff is still extant, but it is of comparative little importance since the abolition of common employment. If, however, an employer engages a person with insufficient experience or training for a particular job and as a result a worker is injured, it may well be that there is a breach of this branch of the employer's duty.[98]

In one situation of a slightly different kind, however, this branch of the employer's liability retains its importance. If one employee is

---

[92] i.e. long-term conditions, not merely in respect of "nervous shock" caused by being threatened by an accident.

[93] *Hatton v Sutherland* [2002] EWCA Civ 76; [2002] I.C.R. 613. See para.5–71, above.

[94] The special relationship of employer and worker may impose positive duties of assistance or protection: thus an employer may be obliged to provide medical assistance in cases of illness or injury in no way attributable to him (*Kasapis v Laimos* [1959] 2 Lloyd's Rep. 378) or to warn his workers to be medically examined if he learns that past working conditions, which were then regarded as proper, have caused a danger of disease (*Wright v Dunlop Rubber Co* (1971) 11 K.I.R. 311). As to the employer's duty in respect of giving a reference, see *Spring v Guardian Assurance* [1995] 2 A.C. 296, para.11–33, below.

[95] *Mullaney v CC West Midlands* [2001] EWCA Civ 700; *Waters v MPC* [2000] 1 W.L.R. 1607.

[96] See para.8–16, below.

[97] *Winter v Cardiff RDC* [1950] 1 All E.R. 819 at 823 per Lord MacDermott; *Davie v New Merton Board Mills* [1959] A.C. 604.

[98] See *Butler v Fife Coal Co* [1912] A.C. 149. So regarded, a case of this kind would not give rise to the question whether negligence is to be judged subjectively or objectively. If a worker who has never previously operated a crane is put in charge of one and an accident results, despite the exercise by him of all the care of which he is, subjectively, capable, there might be difficulties in saying that the employer is vicariously liable for his negligence. In a question whether the employer is personally in breach of his duty no such difficulty exists.

injured by the violent horseplay of another, or is actually assaulted by him, it is unlikely that the employer will be liable vicariously, for the horseplay or the attack will not have been done in the course of the employment.[99] It may be, however, that the employer should have known of his employee's playful or vicious propensities and have taken steps to prevent them from resulting in injury to another. In that case he may be liable for breach of his personal duty.[100]

8–12   **ii. Adequate plant and equipment.** The employer must take reasonable care to provide his workers with the necessary plant and equipment,[101] and is therefore liable if an accident is caused through the absence of some item of equipment which was obviously necessary or which a reasonable employer would recognise to be needed.[102] He must also take reasonable care to maintain the plant and equipment in proper condition, and the more complex and dangerous that machinery the more frequent must be the inspection.[103] What is required in each case, however, is reasonable care according to the circumstances, and in some cases it may be legitimate to rely upon the worker himself to rectify simple defects in the plant he is using.[104] The duty extends to the installation of necessary safety devices on dangerous machinery[105] and the provision of protective equipment when required,[106] but the employer does not warrant the safety of plant and equipment. At common law, therefore, he is not liable if an accident is caused by some latent defect

---

[99] *O'Reilly v National Rail and Tramway Appliances Ltd* [1966] 1 All E.R. 499. Cf. *Harrison v Michelin Tyre Co Ltd* [1985] I.C.R. 696, doubted in *Aldred v Nacano* [1987] I.R.L.R. 292.

[100] *Hudson v Ridge Manufacturing Co* [1957] 2 Q.B. 348; *Veness v Dyson Bell & Co* [1965] C.L.Y. 2691. Cf. *Smith v Crossley Bros* (1951) 95 S.J. 655; *Coddington v International Harvester Co of Great Britain Ltd* (1969) 6 K.I.R. 146. The principle may extend to victimisation or bullying where there is sufficient injury: *Waters v MPC* [2000] 1 W.L.R. 1607. For an extreme example where one worker shot another see *Gittani Stone Pty Ltd v Pavkovic* [2007] NSWCA 355.

[101] While a defendant who engages a contractor is generally entitled to look to the contractor to safeguard the latter's employees, he may owe the employees a duty if he in some way assumes some responsibility, for example by providing some unsuitable piece of equipment: *McGarvey v Eve N.C.I. Ltd* [2002] EWCA Civ 374.

[102] *Williams v Birmingham Battery and Metal Co* [1892] 2 Q.B. 338; *Lovell v Blundells & Crompton & Co* [1944] 1 K.B. 502; *Ross v Associated Portland Cement Manufacturers Ltd* [1964] 1 W.L.R. 768. It is not always necessary, however, for the employer to adopt the latest improvements: *Toronto Power Co v Paskwan* [1915] A.C. 734 per Sir Arthur Channell. See also *O'Connor v B.T.C.* [1958] 1 W.L.R. 346.

[103] e.g. *Murphy v Phillips* (1876) 35 L.T. 477; *Baxter v St Helena Hospital Management Committee, The Times*, February 14, 1972. Even inspection may not always be sufficient: *Barkway v S Wales Transport Co* [1950] A.C. 185; *Pearce v Round Oak Steel Works Ltd* [1969] 1 W.L.R. 595.

[104] *Bristol Aeroplane Co v Franklin* [1948] W.N. 341; *Richardson v Stephenson Clarke Ltd* [1969] 1 W.L.R. 1695.

[105] *Jones v Richards* [1955] 1 W.L.R. 444; *Lovelidge v Anselm Odling & Sons Ltd* [1967] 2 Q.B. 351. See also *Naismith v London Film Productions* [1939] 1 All E.R. 794.

[106] *Qualcast Ltd v Haynes* [1959] A.C. 743 per Lord Denning; but see *Brown v Rolls-Royce* [1960] 1 W.L.R. 210. See also *McGhee v NCB* [1973] 1 W.L.R. 1 (washing facilities).

in equipment which could not have been discovered by the exercise of reasonable care on the part of the persons for whose negligence he is answerable.[107] By the Employer's Liability (Defective Equipment) Act 1969,[108] however, if an employee is injured in the course of his employment in consequence of a defect in equipment provided by his employer and the defect is due to the fault of a third party, whether identified or not, then the injury is deemed to be also attributable to the negligence of the employer. Today, therefore, if a worker can show, for example, that a tool he was using was defective in such a way that there must, on a balance of probabilities, have been negligence or other fault in its manufacture, and that his injury was caused by that defect, then the employer as well as the manufacturer will be liable to him, whether or not the employer was in any way to blame.[109] The principal advantage of this from the worker's point of view is that he is relieved of any need to identify and sue the manufacturer of defective equipment provided by his employer. Since the coming into force of the Consumer Protection Act 1987,[110] the manufacturer is subject to a stricter liability not dependent on proof of negligence. Since "fault" is defined in the 1969 Act as, "negligence, breach of statutory duty or other act or omission which gives rise to liability in tort"[111] it seems that in such a case the employer may be liable even if there is no real fault on anyone's part.

The provisions of the Provision and Use of Work Equipment Regulations 1998 have been referred to above.[112] Under reg.4 every employer is required to, "ensure that work equipment is so constructed or adapted as to be suitable for the purpose for which it is used or provided" and by reg.5 he must, "ensure that work equipment is maintained in an efficient state, in efficient working order and in good repair". Regulation 4 may make the common law liability and that under the 1969 Act less significant, though the Regulations would not cover the case where the complaint is that there has been a failure to provide necessary equipment. Although the Regulations are primarily directed at employers, they are extended to persons who have control of the equipment but it is

---

[107] *Davie v New Merton Board Mills* [1959] A.C. 604..

[108] The Act came into force on October 25, 1969, its main purpose being to reverse on its facts the result of *Davie v New Merton Board Mills Ltd*, above, fn.107. "Equipment" has been held to include a 90,000-ton ship: *Coltman v Bibby Tankers Ltd* [1988] A.C. 276. The word extends to material which is used in the employment and is not confined to tools with which that material is processed: *Knowles v Liverpool CC* [1993] 1 W.L.R. 1428.

[109] *Clarkson v Jackson, The Times*, November 21, 1984. The employer is entitled to raise the defence of contributory negligence against the worker and may seek to recover indemnity or contribution from the person to whose fault the defect is attributable. He cannot, however, contract out of the liability imposed by the Act.

[110] See para.10–12, below (strict liability of manufacturer).

[111] 1969 Act s.1(3).

[112] See para.8–5, above.

specifically provided that they do not apply to a person supplying equipment by way of sale or hire purchase.[113] Although a manufacturer may incur liability under the Consumer Protection Act 1987 for injury caused by a defect in equipment it is thought that he does not fall under the Regulations because he does not have "control".

8–13   **iii. Safe place of work.** Though not expressly mentioned by Lord Wright in *Wilsons and Clyde Coal Co v English*,[114] it is clear that the employer's duty of care extends to the place of work[115] and in some cases may even also apply to the means of access to the place of work.[116] No particular difficulty exists where the place of work is in the occupation or control of the employer, but it must be recalled that the duty is one of reasonable care only and thus the employer is not obliged to take unreasonable precautions even against foreseeable risks.[117] At one time, however, it was thought that because an employer had no control over premises in the occupation of a third party he could owe no duty in respect of those premises, but it is now clear that this is wrong.[118] The duty of care remains, but what is required for its performance may well be different where the place of work is not under the employer's control[119]:

> "The master's own premises are under his control: if they are dangerously in need of repair he can and must rectify the fault at once if he is to escape the censure of negligence. But if a master sends his plumber to mend a leak in a private house, no one could hold him negligent for not visiting the house himself to see if the

---

[113] Regulation 3(5).

[114] [1938] A.C. 57.

[115] e.g. *Cole v De Trafford (No.2)* [1918] 2 K.B. 535 per Scrutton L.J.; *Davidson v Handley Page* [1945] 1 All E.R. 235 at 236 per Lord Greene M.R. At the lowest, the employer's duty to his employee in respect of premises occupied by the employer must be the common duty of care under the Occupiers' Liability Act 1957, but probably it is stricter than that duty: para.8–16, below. Most workplaces are now likely to be covered by the Workplace (Health, Safety and Welfare) Regulations 1992: para.8–5, above. See in particular reg.5.

[116] *Ashdown v Samuel Williams & Sons* [1957] 1 Q.B. 409 at 430–432 per Parker L.J.; *Smith v National Coal Board* [1967] 1 W.L.R. 871. The employer can be subject to no duty of maintenance so far as the means of access consists of a public highway, but if the employee has to cross private property, whether the employer's own or that of a third party, the duty should exist.

[117] *Latimer v A.E.C.* [1953] A.C. 643; *Thomas v Bristol Aeroplane Co* [1954] 1 W.L.R. 694. Nor is he liable for a defect which would not have been revealed by inspection: *Bevan v Milford Haven Dry Dock Co* [1962] 2 Lloyd's Rep. 281; *O'Reilly v National Rail and Tramway Appliances Ltd* [1966] 1 All E.R. 499.

[118] *Wilson v Tyneside Window Cleaning Co* [1958] 2 Q.B. 110; *Smith v Austin Lifts* [1959] 1 W.L.R. 100; *Clay v A.J. Crump & Sons Ltd* [1964] 1 Q.B. 533.

[119] It is likely of course that the occupier of the premises will owe a duty to the worker and even if the claimant does not sue him, if the employer of the worker is held liable he may seek a contribution from the occupier: see *Andrews v Initial Cleaning Services Ltd* [2000] I.C.R. 166, where it was conceded that both the employer and the owner of the premises were occupiers of the room.

carpet in the hall creates a trap. Between these extremes are countless possible examples in which the court may have to decide the question of fact: Did the master take reasonable care so to carry out his operations as not to subject those employed by him to unnecessary risk? ... So viewed, the question whether the master was in control of the premises ceases to be a matter of technicality and becomes merely one of the ingredients, albeit a very important one, in a consideration of the question of fact whether, in all the circumstances, the master took reasonable care."[120]

Even if the employer is not responsible for defects in someone else's premises under this heading, he may be under a duty to give advice, instructions or orders about commonly encountered hazards (a matter which would fall under the next heading). Thus it has been held that in modern conditions[121] the employer of a window cleaner should place an embargo on cleaning upper floor windows by standing on the sill unless there are anchorage points for safety harness.[122]

iv. Safe system of working. This, the most frequently invoked **8–14** branch of the employer's duty,[123] is also the most difficult to define, but it includes:

" ... [T]he physical lay-out of the job—the setting of the stage, so to speak—the sequence in which the work is to be carried out, the provision in proper cases of warnings and notices and the issue of special instructions. A system may be adequate for the whole course of the job or it may have to be modified or improved to meet the circumstances which arise; such modifications or improvements ... equally fall under the head of system."[124]

The employer's duty in respect of the system of working is most evident where the work is of regular or routine nature, but its application is not limited to such cases. The concept is a flexible one, which can be applied as much to a police operation as to work

---

[120] *Wilson v Tyneside Window Cleaning Co* [1958] 2 Q.B. 110 at 121–122 per Pearce L.J.; *Kilbride v Scottish & Newcastle Breweries* 1986 S.L.T. 642.
[121] Cf. *General Cleaning Contractors Ltd v Christmas* [1953] A.C. 180, where the HL was not prepared to go so far.
[122] *King v Smith* [1995] I.C.R. 339..
[123] It is obvious that the classic quadripartite approach is based on accidents and cannot be applied to illness caused by work stress; but this one may have some analogical application.
[124] *Speed v Thomas Swift & Co* [1943] K.B. 557 at 563–564 per Lord Greene M.R. For the relevance of general practice in industry, see para.5–79, above.

in a factory.[125] Even where a single act of a particular kind is to be performed, the employer may have an obligation to organise the work, for example if it is of a complicated or unusual kind or if a large number of people are involved.[126] In each case it is a question of fact whether a reasonable employer would have left it to his workers to decide for themselves how the job should be done.[127]

In devising a system of working the employer must take into account the fact that workers are often heedless of their own safety,[128] and this has two consequences. First, the system should so far as possible minimise the danger of a worker's own foreseeable carelessness. Secondly, the employer must also exercise reasonable care to see that his system of working is complied with by those for whose safety it is instituted and that the necessary safety precautions are observed.[129] Lord Denning said in one case,[130] however, (and others have agreed[131]) that this is not a proposition of law but a proposition of good sense, so that proof that a worker was never actually instructed to wear necessary protective clothing is not of itself proof of negligence. As a practical matter, however, now that there is, for most employments, an unqualified statutory duty to take all reasonable steps to ensure that any protective equipment is properly used,[132] any failure to instruct (and to check) is likely to lead to liability, subject to contributory negligence.[133] The employer's personal duty is not confined to devising a safe system, it

---

[125] *Mullaney v CC West Midlands* [2001] EWCA Civ 700; *French v Sussex CC* [2006] EWCA Civ 312 (claim failed on other grounds). See also *Lloyd v Ministry of Justice* [2007] EWHC 2475 (QB) (warning of violent character of prisoner necessary).

[126] *Winter v Cardiff RDC* [1950] W.N. 193 at 200 per Lord Reid; *Byers v Head Wrightson & Co* [1961] 1 W.L.R. 961; *Boyle v Kodak Ltd* [1969] 1 W.L.R. 661. The fact that an untrained young man with indifferent English is a member of a team may call for special precautions by the employer: *Hawkins v Ian Ross (Castings) Ltd* [1970] 1 All E.R. 180 at 186. Cf. *Brennan v Techno Constructions* [1962] C.L.Y. 2069; *Vinnyey v Star Paper Mills Ltd* [1965] 1 All E.R. 175.

[127] Since the abolition of common employment the employer is liable vicariously for the negligence of the person in charge of the operation, but this cannot assist the claimant if he was himself in charge or if no worker was guilty of negligence.

[128] *General Cleaning Contractors v Christmas* [1953] A.C. 180 at 189–190 per Lord Oaksey; *Smith v National Coal Board* [1967] 1 W.L.R. 871 at 873 per Lord Reid; *Kerry v Carter* [1969] 1 W.L.R. 1372; *Bus v Sydney CC* (1989) 85 A.L.R. 211.

[129] *General Cleaning Contractors v Christmas* [1953] A.C. 180; *Clifford v Charles H. Challen & Son* [1951] 1 K.B. 495; *Crookall v Vickers-Armstrong Ltd* [1955] 1 W.L.R. 659; *Nolan v Dental Manufacturing Co* [1958] 1 W.L.R. 936. Cf. *Woods v Durable Suites* [1953] 1 W.L.R. 857; *Bux v Slough Metals Ltd* [1973] 1 W.L.R. 1358; *Pape v Cumbria CC* [1992] I.C.R. 132.

[130] *Qualcast (Wolverhampton) Ltd v Haynes* [1959] A.C. 743 at 760.

[131] "I depreciate any tendency to treat the relation of employer and skilled workman as equivalent to that of a nurse and imbecile child": *Smith v Austin Lifts* [1959] 1 W.L.R. 100 at 105 per Viscount Simonds. In *Smith v Scot Bowyers* [1986] I.R.L.R. 315 it was held to be enough to inform workers about the availability of replacement boots it was not necessary to inspect boots in use from time to time. *Osarak v Hawker Siddeley Water Engineering Ltd, The Times*, October 28, 1982, is an entertaining case.

[132] Personal Protective Equipment at Work Regulations 1992 reg.10(1).

[133] It is the employee's duty to use the equipment: reg.10(2).

extends to its implementation, so that the employer is liable even if the system itself is safe but A fails to follow it and causes injury to B.[134]

B. Scope of Duty

The employer's duty of care concerns not only the actual work of his employees, but also all such acts as are normally and reasonably incidental to a day's work,[135] and the mere fact that an employee disobeys an order does not necessarily deprive him of the protection of his employer's duty, though he may, of course, be guilty of contributory negligence.[136] The special duty we are now considering arises only when the relationship of employer and servant exists[137] and so an independent contractor employed to do work in a factory, or a visitor, cannot rely upon it. Such a person will, however, generally be owed some other duty of care.[138] It is important to notice that although the employer's duty springs from the relationship of employment, the duty is owed individually to each worker, so that circumstances concerning the particular worker which are known or which ought to be known to the employer will affect the precautions which the employer must take in order to fulfil his duty. Thus in *Paris v Stepney Borough Council*[139] the claimant had only one eye and it was therefore held that he should have been provided with goggles even though the risk involved in his work was not so great as to require the provision of goggles to a normal two-eyed man doing a similar job. Conversely:

"[A]n experienced man dealing with a familiar and obvious risk may not reasonably need the same attention or the same precaution as an inexperienced man who is likely to be more receptive of advice or admonition."[140]

This point is particularly important in the context of mental harm caused by stress.

8–15

[134] *McDermid v Nash Dredging and Reclamation Co Ltd* [1987] A.C. 906.
[135] *Davidson v Handley Page Ltd* [1945] 1 All E.R. 235.
[136] *Rands v McNeil* [1955] 1 Q.B. 253 (but no breach of duty on the facts).
[137] The importance of safety may lead the court to emphasise the substance rather than the form of the relationship: *Lane v Shire Roofing (Oxford) Ltd* [1995] I.R.L.R. 493; see *Mullaney v CC West Midlands* [2001] EWCA Civ 700 (police—"quasi-employment").
[138] e.g. under the Occupiers' Liability Act 1957.
[139] [1951] A.C. 367. Cf. *Hatton v Sutherland* [2002] EWCA Civ 76; [2002] I.C.R. 613 (stress; employer's legitimate expectations about capacity).
[140] *Qualcast (Wolverhampton) Ltd v Haynes* [1959] A.C. 743 at 754 per Lord Radcliffe. But the employer cannot necessarily accept at face value the servant's assertion of previous experience: *Tasci v Pekalp of London Ltd* [2000] I.C.R. 633. Cf. *Makepeace v Evans Bros (Reading), The Times*, June 13, 2000.

"Unless he knows of some particular problem or vulnerability, an employer is usually entitled to assume that his employee is up to the normal pressures of the job. It is only if there is something specific about the job or the employee or the combination of the two that he has to think harder. But thinking harder does not necessarily mean that he has to make searching or intrusive enquiries."[141]

C. Strictness of the Duty

8–16   As has been emphasised in the foregoing paragraphs and has been constantly reiterated by the courts, the employer's duty is a duty of care only and, though a high standard is required, there are limits to the protection which the employer must provide, even against foreseeable risk to his employee.[142] In *Withers v Perry Chain Co*[143] the claimant had previously contracted dermatitis from contact with grease in the course of her work and was therefore given by her employers the driest work they had available. This work she accepted without protest but nevertheless she again contracted dermatitis and sued her employers on the ground that, knowing that she was susceptible to dermatitis, they should not have permitted her to do work carrying a risk of causing that disease. Her action was dismissed by the Court of Appeal because the employers had done everything they reasonably could have done to protect the claimant short of refusing to employ her at all.

"In my opinion there is no legal duty on an employer to prevent an adult employee from doing work which he or she is willing to do. If there is a slight risk . . . it is for the employee to weigh it against the desirability, or perhaps the necessity, of employment. The relationship of master and servant is not that of a schoolmaster and pupil[144] . . . It cannot be said that an employer is bound to dismiss an employee rather than allow her to run a small risk."[145]

There is a tension here between the stance of the common law in giving primacy to the worker's personal autonomy and the expanding responsibility of employers. While what is said in *Withers* is probably still the starting point, there is no absolute rule that an employer may expose a willing worker to *any* risk by continuing to

---

[141] *Hatton v Sutherland* [2002] EWCA Civ 76; [2002] ICR 613. See para.5–71, above.
[142] See, e.g. *Latimer v A.E.C.* [1953] A.C. 643 and *Coates v Jaguar Cars Ltd* [2004] EWCA Civ 337. For the standard of care in negligence generally see Ch.5, above.
[143] [1961] 1 W.L.R. 1314.
[144] See, e.g. *Rozario v Post Office* [1997] P.I.Q.R. P15 (simple lifting task).
[145] [1961] 1 W.L.R. 1314 at 1320 per Devlin L.J.

employ him: it has been said that to employ someone known to suffer from vertigo as a "spiderman" would be a plain breach of the employer's duty.[146] That is not necessarily good news from the worker's point of view, for it follows that dismissal may be fair for the purposes of employment protection or discrimination legislation.[147] In the case of stress, even where the risk to health is substantial, it has to be for the employee to decide whether or not to carry on[148]: it should not be for the law to say that the employer must sack a worker to protect his mental health.

The general defence of voluntary assumption of risk is rarely available in cases of employers' liability because the courts are unwilling to infer an agreement by the worker to run the risk of his employer's negligence merely because he remains in unsafe employment.[149] However, in *Johnstone v Bloomsbury Health Authority*,[150] where the claimant was contractually committed to work up to an average of 88 hours a week if the employer so required, it was contended that the express term of the contract limited or overrode the employer's duty of care not to injure his health. On a striking-out application, this was accepted in principle by Browne-Wilkinson V.C. and Leggatt L.J.[151] but the majority of the court (Stuart-Smith L.J. and Browne-Wilkinson V.C.) held that the contractual right to call for long hours was, on the proper construction of the contract of employment, limited to calling for work that was compatible with the employer's duty of care. Such a case will also raise issues under the Unfair Contract Terms Act 1977.[152]

D. Independent Contractors

It might be supposed that an employer who entrusts some task to **8–17** a third party (not a servant), whose competence he has taken reasonable care to ascertain, has thereby discharged his own duty of reasonable care. To state the law in this way, however, would be to

---

[146] *Coxall v Goodyear Great Britain Ltd* [2002] EWCA Civ 1010; [2003] 1 W.L.R. 536 at [26].
[147] *Lane Group Plc v Farmiloe* [2004] P.I.Q.R. 22. As the defendant's safety officer put it, "You cannot opt out of Health and Safety". Cf. *Canterbury CC v Howletts* [1997] I.C.R. 925 (duty under the Health and Safety at Work etc. Act 1974 s.2, to ensure safety to employees was duty to do what could be done in the context of the job and did not prohibit work—entering tiger's cage—which could not be done without danger; but on the civil liability in such a situation, see the Animals Act 1971 s.6(5), para.16–8, below).
[148] *Hatton v Sutherland* [2002] EWCA Civ 76; [2002] I.C.R. 613.
[149] See para.25–11, below.
[150] [1992] Q.B. 333.
[151] In fact, Stuart-Smith L.J. also accepted that what he called an "express term of *volenti non fit injuria*" would exclude the employer's duty.
[152] See para.25–6, below.

deny the ratio decidendi of *Wilsons and Clyde Coal Co v English*[153] that the employer's duty is personal and is not discharged simply by the appointment of a competent person to carry out the necessary tasks. In that case the defendant employers were held liable in respect of an injury sustained by a miner because the system of working was not reasonably safe. The system had been devised by the manager of the mine, a fellow servant of the claimant, to whom the employers were obliged by statute to leave the matter, but yet, despite the existence of common employment and despite the fact that the employers personally had done everything they possibly could, they were held to be in breach of their duty to the claimant. Their duty was:

> "[T]he employer's personal duty, whether he performs or can perform it himself, or whether he does not perform it or cannot perform it save by servants or agents. A failure to perform such a duty is the employer's personal negligence."[154]

The employer's liability, therefore, not being a vicarious liability, was not defeated by the doctrine of common employment.

Although the concept of the employer's personal duty was developed to avoid the now defunct doctrine of common employment, its practical effect goes beyond cases formerly covered by that doctrine because it involves the proposition that the employer's duty is not so much a duty to take care but a duty that care be taken and therefore the employer may be liable for damage caused by independent contractors. A person can only be vicariously liable for the torts of his servants committed in the course of employment, but a duty that care will be taken is not fulfilled if there is fault on the part of anyone to whom the employer entrusts its performance.[155] This view of the law is confirmed by *McDermid v Nash Dredging and Reclamation Co Ltd.*[156] The defendants were a wholly owned subsidiary of S, a Dutch company, and their function was to employ British staff engaged in S's dredging work in Sweden. While the claimant, an employee of the defendants, was aboard a tug owned by S he was seriously injured as a result of the negligence of the skipper (an employee of S) in putting the engines astern without warning to the claimant. The defendants were liable because they had delegated the performance of their duty to take care for the claimant's safety to S and its employees on the tug and could not escape liability

---

[153] [1938] A.C. 57, para.8–9, above.
[154] [1938] A.C. 57 at 83–84 per Lord Wright. See also per Lord Thankerton at 64–65, per Lord Macmillan at 75, per Lord Maugham at 87–88; per Lord Woolf in *Spring v Guardian Assurance Plc* [1995] 2 A.C. 296 at 354.
[155] See para.20–1, below.
[156] [1987] A.C. 906..

when that duty was not fulfilled.[157] Given the close connection between the defendants and S the decision is not surprising,[158] for if the law were otherwise the claimant's rights would be at risk from the chances of corporate organisation.[159] One Court of Appeal decision in which liability was not imposed upon the employer for injury suffered by an employee working in Saudi Arabia distinguished *Nash* on the basis that it was confined to cases where there was some sort of "joint venture"[160] but this seems an unsatisfactory distinction and the principle of *Nash* has been applied at first instance[161] and by the Court of Appeal[162] to cases where the employer was a "labour only" contractor and in one of which[163] the injury took place abroad.[164] However, it has been said that the, "suggestion that the homebased employers have any responsibility for the daily events of a site in [another country] has an air of unreality"[165] and it may be that the question of how far the employer has control of the distant site is a critical factor in such cases.[166] Where no actual fault is attributable to the employer, that may justify awarding him a complete indemnity in contribution proceedings against the person at fault.[167] This does not, of course, mean

---

[157] It was not regarded as important whether the case was one of failing to devise a safe system of work or failing to operate a safe system.

[158] The tug was skippered turn and turn about by an employee of S and an employee of the defendants. Had the accident occurred on the next shift there could have been no disputing the defendants' liability.

[159] No proceedings were brought against S because of the difficulties of effecting service against a Dutch company in respect of a claim arising in Sweden and because of a practice of the legal aid authorities not to support claims against a foreign defendant in respect of a foreign tort. Had S been sued, they might have been entitled to limit their liability under the merchant shipping legislation. In *Johnson v Coventry Churchill International Ltd*, below, fn.161, the persons on whose premises the claimant was working were not liable under German law unless there was a wilful act by them but under English law one would expect that in such a situation there would have been a duty of care. Where the claimant has a contract with one member of a group it may be that on the facts other members of the group have assumed responsibility for his safety: *Newton-Sealey v Armor Group Services Ltd* [2008] EWHC 233 (QB).

[160] *Cook v Square D. Ltd* [1992] I.C.R. 262. The accident arose from the defective state of the premises but the condition of the premises is clearly something within the scope of the employer's duty under *Wilsons & Clyde Coal v English*.

[161] *Johnson v Coventry Churchill International Ltd* [1992] 3 All E.R. 15.

[162] *Morris v Breaveglen Ltd* [1993] I.R.L.R. 350. This despite the fact that the court was prepared to accept that the claimant was sufficiently under the control of the site occupiers for them to be vicariously liable for damage he did to others.

[163] *Johnson v Coventry Churchill International Ltd*, above, fn.161.

[164] Cf. *A v MoD* [2004] EWCA Civ 641; [2005] Q.B. 183 (no liability on Army where it arranged medical facilities in German hospital for wife of a soldier; note that in this case there was no reason to believe that either the liability of the hospital or its quantum under German law would have been any less than liability under English law).

[165] *Cook v Square D. Ltd*, above, fn.160, at 271. However, it was accepted that in some cases it might be incumbent on the employer of someone working abroad to inspect the site and satisfy himself that the occupiers were conscious of safety obligations.

[166] See *DIB Group Pty Ltd v Cole* [2009] NSWCA 210, in which the use of the concept of non-delegable duty is criticised.

[167] *Nelhams v Sandells Maintenance Ltd, The Times*, June 15, 1995.

that the employer is liable whenever his employee is injured at work as a result of the negligence of a third party: the employer is only responsible if it can be fairly said that he has delegated the performance of his duty of care to the third party. Thus if a lorry driver delivering goods to a factory were negligently to run down a worker, the worker's employer would not be liable—the negligence of the lorry driver (and the vicarious responsibility of his employer) does not negative the exercise of care in the employer's personal duty for it is unrelated to any aspect of that duty, and the employer has delegated nothing to him. Similarly, although the effect of the case has been reversed by the Employer's Liability (Defective Equipment) Act 1969,[168] the underlying ratio of *Davie v New Merton Board Mills*,[169] denying the liability of the employer for a latent defect in a tool, was that the employer had discharged rather than delegated his duty by buying from a reputable supplier. If, on the other hand, a gas fitter negligently installs a gas appliance at the employer's premises with the result that a worker is injured by an explosion, it is submitted that the employer's personal duty with regard to the safety of the place of work has not been fulfilled and he is liable, whether or not the worker is entitled to rely on the Act of 1969.[170]

---

[168] See para.8–12, above.

[169] [1959] A.C. 604, para.8–12, above.

[170] In *Knowles v Liverpool CC* [1993] 1 W.L.R. 1428 *Davie* is given a broad interpretation so as to include material with which the employee is working. However, this is done for the purpose of justifying an equally wide meaning of "equipment" in the 1969 Act. It is accepted in *Coltman v Bibby Tankers Ltd* [1988] A.C. 276 that the Act does not extend to the factory premises themselves.

CHAPTER 9

LIABILITY FOR LAND AND STRUCTURES[1]

1. INTRODUCTION

THE greater part of this chapter concerns the liability of an occupier **9–1** of premises for damage done to visitors on the premises[2] and the main source of the law is the Occupiers' Liability Act 1957. Where things done on the premises affect other premises, that is the province of the law of nuisance, which is dealt with in Ch.14. "Liability for premises", though it would be a neat antithesis to the "liability for products" in the next chapter would not, however, be an exact description, for the rules now to be discussed are not limited to immovable property like open land, houses, railway stations and bridges, but have been extended to movable structures like ships, gangways and scaffolding. Technically, a claim by a passenger in a

---

[1] North, *Occupiers' Liability* (1971) is the leading treatment.
[2] i.e. persons who have entered the premises. It is conceivable that an occupier may "assume responsibility" at common law in respect of the safety of the approach to the premises, which may be the explanation of *Dodkins v West Ham Utd* [2000] C.L.Y. 4226, Cty Ct. (season ticket holder fell on broken manhole cover outside gate to ground).

vehicle against its owner[3] in respect of a collision caused by the defective condition of the vehicle[4] could be framed as one falling within the scope of this chapter, though most lawyers would probably conceive it more as a case of common law negligence. No real difficulties arise over the borderline between these two heads of liability because the duty under the Act is for most purposes identical to the ordinary duty in negligence and the courts are in any event quite ready to accept that the law of negligence can operate concurrently with the statutory liability.[5] Henceforth we shall use the expression "premises" because that does cover the vast majority of cases.

A. Common Law before the Occupiers' Liability Act 1957[6]

9–2   At common law the duties of an occupier were cast in a descending scale to four different kinds of persons and a brief account is necessary to gain a full understanding of the Act. The highest degree of care was owed by the occupier to one who entered in pursuance of a contract with him (for example a guest in a hotel): in that case there was an implied warranty that the premises were as safe as reasonable care and skill could make them.[7] A lower duty was owed to the "invitee", that is to say, a person who (without any contract) entered on business of interest both to himself and the occupier (for example a customer coming into a shop to view the wares): he was entitled to expect that the occupier should prevent damage from unusual danger, of which he knew or ought to have known.[8] Lower still was the duty to the "licensee", a person who entered with the occupier's express or implied permission but without any community of interest with the occupier: the occupier's duty towards him was to warn him of any concealed danger or trap of which he actually knew.[9] Finally, there was the trespasser, to whom under the original common law there was owed only a duty to abstain from

---

[3] If the defect was caused by the manufacturer or a previous owner the case would fall under the principles considered in Ch.10. The present chapter deals with cases where the defendant has control of the structure when the damage occurs.

[4] Before the Act of 1957 is was clear that at common law the special rules of occupiers' liability had no relevance to the way the vehicle was driven: *Haseldine v Daw* [1941] 2 K.B. 343 at 353, 373.

[5] See para.9–3, below.

[6] The common law could still be relevant in asbestos cases over 40 years after the Act: *Fairchild v Glenhaven Funeral Services Ltd* [2001] EWCA Civ 1881.

[7] Where the use of the premises was merely ancillary to the main purpose of the contract the occupier warranted that he, and perhaps his independent contractor, had taken reasonable care to see that the premises were safe.

[8] *Indermaur v Dames* (1866) L.R. 1 C.P. 274; affirmed (1867) L.R. 2 C.P. 311.

[9] The later cases held that if the occupier knew the factual situation the test of his appreciation that it constituted a danger was objective. This blurred the distinction between invitees and licensees.

deliberate or reckless injury.[10] With regard to lawful visitors the tripartite classification into contractual entrants, invitees and licensees did not provide a complete picture of the law for the courts sometimes showed themselves willing to confine these categories to cases arising from the static condition of the premises, and to treat accidents arising from an activity on the premises as governed by the general law of negligence. As Denning L.J. graphically put it:

> "If a landowner is driving his car down his private drive and meets someone lawfully walking upon it, then he is under a duty to take reasonable care so as not to injure the walker and his duty is the same, no matter whether it is his gardener coming up with his plants, a tradesman delivering his goods, a friend coming to tea, or a flag seller seeking a charitable gift."[11]

The law was widely thought to be unsatisfactory and to have ossified in the form in which it was stated in *Indermaur v Dames*[12] at a time when the general law of negligence was undeveloped. It was, therefore, referred to the Law Reform Committee in 1952 and as a result of the Committee's Report[13] the Occupiers' Liability Act 1957 was passed.

2. MODERN LAW: THE OCCUPIERS' LIABILITY ACT 1957

A. Scope of the Occupiers' Liability Act 1957

The Act abolished the common law distinction between invitees **9–3** and licensees and substituted for it a single common duty of care owed by the occupier to his "visitors".[14] The definition of "occupier" remains the same as at common law, and "visitors" are those persons who would at common law have been treated as either invitees or licensees.[15] The law therefore continues to treat contractual entrants as a separate category, but this is now of less significance than formerly: if there is an express provision in the contract warranting the safety of the premises, that will govern the

---

[10] *Robert Addie & Sons (Collieries) Ltd v Dumbreck* [1929] A.C. 358.
[11] *Slater v Clay Cross Co Ltd* [1956] 2 Q.B. 264 at 269.
[12] Above, fn.8.
[13] Cmnd. 9305, 1954. The principal criticisms and recommendations of the Committee are summarised in the 12th edition of this work, pp.204–206.
[14] In the United States, a trend towards the same "unitary" approach to occupiers' liability began with *Rowland v Christian* 443 P. 2d 561 (1968). By 1998 about half the states had adopted a single standard for invitees and licensees and some of these had also assimilated trespassers: Dobbs, *Torts* (2000) §237. In Australia the law was restated in terms of general negligence law in *Australian Safeway Stores Pty Ltd v Zaluzna* (1987) 162 C.L.R. 479.
[15] 1957 Act s.1(2).

case,[16] but if, as is usual, the contract is silent on the matter, the Act provides that there shall be implied into the contract a term that the occupier owes the entrant the common duty of care.[17] There may, of course, be obligations under a contract which are wholly outside the scope of the law of occupiers' liability: if, for example, a lease requires the landlord to maintain a lift, failure to do so, so that it becomes inoperative, would be a breach of contract but it would not be a breach of the common duty of care,[18] except in the unlikely event that there was no other reasonably safe access to accommodation in the building.

We saw how the courts utilised the concept of the "activity duty" to blur the distinction between invitees and licensees at common law and it may be asked whether this concept has survived the Act. On the one hand, it is enacted that the rules provided by the Occupiers' Liability Act:

> "[S]hall have effect, in place of the rules of the common law, to regulate the duty which an occupier of premises owes to visitors in respect of dangers due to the state of the premises or to things done or omitted to be done on them."[19]

On the other hand, it is also enacted that those rules, "shall regulate the nature of the duty imposed by law in consequence of a person's occupation or control of premises",[20] and the "activity duty" does not seem to be aptly described in this way. It arises, generally speaking, by the application of the ordinary principles of negligence and applies equally to occupiers and non-occupiers.[21] It seems that the first provision is not to be read literally as covering all conduct of an occupier on his own premises so that, for example, the Act was regarded as irrelevant when the defendant failed to warn his children against playing with lighted candles,[22] and in *Ogwo v Taylor*[23] a claim arising out of the defendant's negligence in setting fire to his

---

[16] In the majority of personal injury cases an express provision can now only be effective if it favours the entrant: a term reducing the occupier's duty below the common duty of care will usually be void under the Unfair Contract Terms Act 1977 s.2, para.9–19, below.

[17] 1957 Act s.5(1). *Maguire v Sefton MBC* [2006] EWCA Civ 316; [2006] 1 W.L.R. 2550. A contractual entrant may frame his claim in the alternative as a non-contractual visitor: *Sole v W.J. Hallt* [1973] Q.B. 574. The defendant in the famous case of *The Moorcock* (1889) 14 P.D. 64 was not occupier of the area where the vessel grounded but the implied term as to its safety was essentially the same as that under the Act: *George v Coastal Marine 2004 Ltd* [2009] EWHC 816 (Admlty); [2009] 2 Lloyds Rep 356.

[18] *Berryman v Hounslow LBC, The Times*, December 18, 1996.

[19] 1957 Act s.1(1).

[20] 1957 Act s.1(2).

[21] *Riden v Billings & Sons* [1957] 1 Q.B. 46 at 56 per Denning L.J., affirmed [1958] A.C. 240; *Ogwo v Taylor* [1988] A.C. 431 at 434 per Dillon L.J., affirmed at 441.

[22] *Jauffar v Akhbar, The Times*, February 10, 1984.

[23] [1988] A.C. 431. The case was in fact pleaded in the alternative under both heads: see the decision of the Court of Appeal at 434.

house was decided on the basis of common law negligence.[24] Defects in the premises which were not created by the occupier but which he has failed to remedy must be within the Act and the Act alone if there is no other relationship between him and the claimant,[25] for it is then only his role as occupier that puts the defendant under any duty to make the premises safe. The intermediate case is where the defendant by some positive act creates a danger affecting the condition of the premises and here the matter is probably covered both by the Act and by the law of negligence. The issue is not very often likely to be of very much practical significance[26] for there will typically be little if any difference between the duty of care in negligence and the common duty of care as applied to current activities.[27] From a pleading point of view the answer would seem to be to plead the Act and negligence as alternatives wherever there is any doubt. The Act may also overlap with other statutory liabilities: for example, it is quite possible to hold that the occupier/employer is not negligent in a claim by a worker for an injury caused by the state of the premises but that he is liable on the basis of some stricter liability in employment safety regulations.[28]

As before, the occupier's duties apply not only to land and buildings but also to fixed and movable structures,[29] and they govern his liability in respect of damage to property as well as injury to the person, including the property of persons not themselves visitors.[30] The Act also made certain alterations in the liability of a

---

[24] See also *Fowles v Bedfordshire CC, The Times*, May 22, 1995; *Revill v Newberry* [1996] Q.B. 567 (Occupiers' Liability Act 1984).

[25] If there is (e.g. employer and employee), the claimant may rely upon both the Act and any duty incidental to that relationship; but where A is carrying out operations at B's property and the conduct of those causes injury to C, any liability of B for failing to protect C is governed by the general law rather than the Act: *Fairchild v Glenhaven Funeral Services Ltd* [2001] EWCA Civ 1881; [2002] 1 W.L.R. 1052.

[26] *Tomlinson v Congleton BC* [2003] UKHL 47; [2004] 1 A.C. 46 (on the Occupiers' Liability Act 1984, where the same words appear) does not really advance the matter. The essential point there was that any danger presented by the premises was obvious and the defendants were not doing anything at all. The issue arose in a curious form in *New Zealand Insurance Co v Prudential Insurance Co* [1976] 1 N.Z.L.R. 84 where an indemnity policy set different limits for occupiers' liability and general public liability. Though the court discussed the various academic views on the scope of the Act, it declined to give any firm opinion.

[27] However, in *Bottomley v Todmorden Cricket Club* [2003] EWCA Civ 1575; [2004] P.I.Q.R. P18 it was said that the fact that the case turned on an extra-hazardous activity rather than the state of the premises meant that the common law rule (now in some doubt) making a principal liable for the negligence of an independent contractor in such cases (para.20–25, below) applied.

[28] See, e.g. *Irvine v MPC* [2004] EWHC 1536 (QB); [2005] P.I.Q.R. P11.

[29] 1957 Act s.1(3)(a). *Bunker v Charles Brand & Son Ltd* [1969] 2 Q.B. 480; *Hollingworth v Southern Ferries* [1977] 2 Lloyd's Rep. 70. Cf. *Wheeler v Copas* [1981] 3 All E.R. 405.

[30] 1957 Act s.1(3)(b). See further para.9–24, below.

landlord to the visitors of his tenants though these have now been replaced by further legislation.[31]

B. Occupier

9–4   The duty under the Act is imposed upon the "occupier," but that is a word which may vary considerably in its meaning according to the context in which it is used. Its meaning in the context of landlord and tenant legislation, for example, is not necessarily the same as in the context of the Occupiers' Liability Act.[32] Here the essential question is "Who has control of the premises?". The word occupier is simply a convenient one to denote a person who has a sufficient degree of control over premises to put him under a duty of care towards those who come lawfully upon the premises.[33] An owner in possession is, no doubt, an "occupier"[34]; an owner who has let the premises to another and parted with possession is not[35]; but an absentee owner may "occupy" through his servant and remain subject to the duty[36] and he may also be subject to it though he has contracted to allow a third party to have the use of the premises.[37] On the other hand, it is not necessary that an "occupier" should have any estate in land[38] or even exclusive occupation.[39] There may thus be more than one "occupier" of the same structure or part of the structure.[40] The foundation of occupier's liability is occupational control, i.e. control associated with and arising from presence in and use of or activity in the premises.[41] Whether this exists is a question

---

[31] See para.9–40, below.

[32] *Graysim Holdings Ltd v P.&O. Property Holdings Ltd* [1996] A.C. 329.

[33] *Wheat v Lacon & Co Ltd* [1966] A.C. 552 at 577 per Lord Denning.

[34] In *Harvey v Plymouth CC*, November 13, 2009 (QBD) the defendants admitted that they were occupiers even though they were not conscious they owned the land.

[35] A landlord may, nevertheless, be liable if the conditions of the Defective Premises Act 1972 s.4, are fulfilled. See para.9–40, below.

[36] *Wheat v Lacon & Co Ltd*, above, fn.33. A company can only occupy through its servants: at 571 per Viscount Dilhorne; *Stone v Taffe* [1974] 1 W.L.R. 1575.

[37] *Wheat v Lacon & Co Ltd*, above, fn.33; *Fisher v C.H.T. Ltd (No.2)* [1966] 2 Q.B. 475. See also, e.g. *Hawkins v Coulsdon & Purley UDC* [1954] 1 Q.B. 319; *Greene v Chelsea Borough Council* [1954] 2 Q.B. 127, where requisitioning authorities were held to occupy requisitioned houses which were being lived in by persons they had placed in them. Cf. *Kearney v Eric Waller Ltd* [1967] 1 Q.B. 29.

[38] *Humphreys v Dreamland (Margate) Ltd* (1930) 144 L.T. 529.

[39] *Hartwell v Grayson Rollo and Clover Docks Ltd* [1947] K.B. 901; *Donovan v Cammell Laird & Co* [1949] 2 All E.R. 82. The concept is therefore a good deal wider than the "possession" which qualifies for the right to sue for a nuisance affecting the land: *Hunter v Canary Wharf Ltd* [1997] A.C. 655. A local authority which has made a compulsory purchase order and served a notice of entry becomes an occupier when the former owner vacates the premises, and it is unnecessary that there should be any actual or symbolic taking of possession: *Harris v Birkenhead Corp* [1976] 1 W.L.R. 279.

[40] *Wheat v Lacon & Co Ltd*, fn.33; *Fisher v C.H.T. Ltd (No.2)*, above, fn.37; *AMF International Ltd v Magnet Bowling Ltd* [1968] 1 W.L.R. 1028; *Andrews v Initial Cleaning Services Ltd* [2000] I.C.R. 166.

[41] *Wheat v Lacon & Co Ltd*, above, fn.33, at 589 per Lord Pearson.

of degree: a contractor undertaking a large building development would be an occupier of the site, but a decorator painting a house would not.[42] Such occupational control may perfectly well be shared between two or more people, but where this is so, though each is under the same common duty of care, it does not follow that what that duty requires of each of them is necessarily itself the same.[43]

C. Visitors

The common duty of care is owed by the occupier to his "visitors" and they are those persons who would at common law have been treated as invitees or licensees.[44] For all practical purposes, therefore, the distinction between invitees and licensees was abolished.[45] A visitor is generally a person to whom the occupier has given express or implied permission to enter and the principal category opposed to visitor is that of trespasser, whose rights are governed not by the Act of 1957 but by the Occupiers' Liability Act 1984.[46] However, the Act of 1957 extends the concept of visitor to include persons who enter the premises for any purpose in the exercise of a right conferred by law, for they are to be treated as permitted by the occupier to be there for that purpose, whether they in fact have his permission or not.[47] The occupier therefore owes the common duty of care to firemen attending a fire, to policemen executing a search warrant and to members of the public entering recreation grounds under rights guaranteed by law.[48] On the other hand, it has been held that despite the wide wording of the Act, a person using a public[49] or private[50] right of way is not a visitor for the purposes of the Act. The user of a private right of way is now owed a duty under the Occupiers' Liability Act 1984,[51] but that

9-5

---

[42] *Page v Read* (1984) N.L.J. 723.
[43] *Wheat v Lacon*, fn.33 at 581, 585–586, 587.
[44] 1957 Act s.1(2).
[45] "It is true that this is not done in so many words, but no significance is to be attached to this omission. A legal distinction is abolished by depriving it of legal consequences": Payne (1958) 21 M.L.R. 359 at 360. Lord Browne-Wilkinson in *McGeown v Northern Ireland Housing Executive* [1995] 1 A.C. 233 attempted to revive it in relation to public rights of way, but see *Campbell v Northern Ireland Housing Executive* [1996] 1 B.N.I.L. 99.
[46] See para.9–25, below.
[47] 1957 Act s.2(6).
[48] The balance of authority at common law was against the existence of a special category of persons entering as of right. The firemen and policemen in our examples were probably to be treated as invitees, the users of the recreation ground as licensees: see further the 6th edition of this work, pp.692–696 and Cmnd. 9305 (1954), paras 37–38.
[49] *Greenhalgh v British Railways Board* [1969] 2 Q.B. 286.
[50] *Holden v White* [1982] 2 Q.B. 679.
[51] See para.9–25, below.

aside, the owner of the highway[52] or servient tenement has no obligation to the user to maintain its safety, as opposed to not creating dangers on it. While it is true that public rights of way pass over so many different types of property and in such varying circumstances that any blanket duty of care would be impracticable[53] the present state of the law may lead to results which the public might consider arbitrary. For example, the owners of shopping malls commonly take steps to ensure that the public do not acquire rights of way through them, but if such a right is acquired by user,[54] or by express dedication, entrants to the property, who may know nothing of this, will lose the protection of the Occupiers' Liability Act which they formerly had, whereas if they were outside on the pavement they would be likely to have the protection of the highway authority's duty of care under the Highways Act 1980.[55] Persons exercising access rights under the National Parks and Access to the Countryside Act 1949 or the Countryside and Rights of Way Act 2000 are not visitors[56] but a duty is owed to them under the Act of 1984.[57]

9–6   Where there is no express permission, it is a question of fact in each case whether the occupier has impliedly given permission to a person to enter upon his premises, and the onus of proving an implied permission rests upon the person who claims that it existed.[58] The simplest example of implied permission is also the commonest in practice. Any person who enters the occupier's premises for the purpose of communicating with him[59] will be treated as having the occupier's tacit permission unless he knows or ought to know that he has been forbidden to enter,[60] for example by a notice "no canvassers, hawkers or circulars".[61] The occupier may, of course, withdraw this licence by refusing to speak or deal with the

---

[52] *McGeown v Northern Ireland Housing Executive* [1995] 1 A.C. 233. A highway authority may have a duty to maintain a highway under the Highways Act 1980: para.14–42, below.

[53] Lord Keith in *McGeown*'s case at [1995] 1 A.C. 243.

[54] As in *Cumbernauld and Kilsyth DC v Dollar Land (Cumbernauld) Ltd* 1993 S.L.T. 1318.

[55] See Lord Browne-Wilkinson in *McGeown*'s case. See generally Barker and Parry in (1995) 15 L.S. 335.

[56] 1957 Act s.1(4), as substituted by s.13 of the Countryside and Rights of Way Act 2000.

[57] See para.9–25, below.

[58] *Edwards v Ry Executive* [1952] A.C. 737.

[59] Not necessarily in connection with business of the occupier: *Brunner v Williams* [1975] Crim.L.R. 250.

[60] *Robson v Hallett* [1967] 2 Q.B. 393; *Christian v Johanesson* [1956] N.Z.L.R. 664 Cmd. 9305 (1954) para.67. Cf. *Dunster v Abbott* [1954] 1 W.L.R. 58 at 59–60 per Denning L.J. and *Great Central Ry v Bates* [1921] 3 K.B. 578. The policeman in the last case, despite some unguarded dicta of Lord Sterndale M.R., was not acting in the execution of his duty: du Parcq J. in *Davis v Lisle* [1936] 2 K.B. 434 at 439–440. Nor would he now be assisted by the Occupiers' Liability Act 1957 s.2(6) (see para.9–5, above).

[61] Quaere as to the effect of "Private" or "Keep Out" in such cases: cf. *Christian v Johanesson*, above, fn.60, at 666.

entrant, but if he does so the entrant has a reasonable time in which to leave the premises before he becomes a trespasser.[62] Other cases depend very much upon their particular facts and it is difficult to state any general rule. This much, however, is clear in principle: the facts must support the implication from the occupier's conduct that he has permitted entry,[63] not merely tolerated it, for knowledge is not tantamount to consent and failure to turn one's premises into a fortress does not confer a licence on anyone who may seek to take advantage of one's inaction.[64] This said, it must, however, be admitted that in some cases the courts have gone to surprising lengths in implying licences in the teeth of the facts.[65] In many cases the court has been astute to find an implied licence because of the severity of the law relating to liability to trespassers. The trespasser's position has now been improved,[66] and it is likely that implied permission will be rather less readily found,[67] but the courts will still have to grapple with the problem of the implied licence, for the duty owed to a trespasser is by no means identical with that owed to a visitor under the Occupiers' Liability Act 1957.[68]

The duty owed to a visitor does not extend to anyone who is injured by going where he is expressly or impliedly warned by the occupier not to go, as where a person falls over a cliff by getting on the wrong side of railings erected by the proprietor who has also put up a notice of the danger of going near the cliff[69] or where a tradesman's boy deliberately chooses to go into a pitch dark part of

---

[62] *Robson v Hallett*, above, fn.60; *Kay v Hibbert* [1977] Crim.L.R. 226. Dismissive words may sometimes be abuse rather than revocation of the licence: *Snook v Mannion* [1982] Crim.L.R. 601.

[63] *Edwards v Ry Executive* [1952] A.C. 737; *Phipps v Rochester Corp* [1955] 1 Q.B. 450 at 455; *Faulkner v Willetts* [1982] R.T.R. 159. It is what may properly be inferred that counts, not the occupier's actual intention. Where O licenses A to enter his land to do work, A may have ostensible authority to invite B to enter as a sub-contractor even though the contract between O and A forbids this: *Ferguson v Welsh* [1987] 1 W.L.R. 1553.

[64] "Repeated trespass of itself confers no licence; the owner of a park in the neighbourhood of a town knows probably only too well that it will be raided by young and old to gather flowers, nuts or mushrooms whenever they get an opportunity, but because he does not cover his park wall with a chevaux de frise or post a number of keepers to chase away intruders how is it to be said that he has licensed that which he cannot prevent?": *Edwards v Ry Executive*, above, fn.63, at 746 per Lord Goddard C.J.

[65] See, e.g. *Lowery v Walker* [1911] A.C. 10 and *Cooke v Midland G.W. Ry of Ireland* [1909] A.C. 229 (the facts must be supplemented from the report of the case in the lower courts: [1908] 2 Ir.R. 242). More easily supportable are the decisions in: *Oldham v Sheffield Corp* (1927) 136 L.T. 681; *Coleshill v Manchester Corp* [1928] 1 K.B. 776; *Purkis v Walthamstow BC* (1934) 151 L.T. 30; *Phipps v Rochester Corp* [1955] 1 Q.B. 450.

[66] See para.9–25, below.

[67] "The 'licence' treated as having been granted in such cases was a legal fiction employed to justify extending to meritorious trespassers, particularly if they were children, the benefit of the duty which at common law an occupier owed to his licensees . . . ": *British Railways Board v Herrington* [1972] A.C. 877 at 933 per Lord Diplock.

[68] However, if what is in issue is a breach of statutory duty there is no universal rule that the claimant is disentitled to recover if he is a trespasser, for everything depends on the construction of the statute in question: *Westwood v Post Office* [1974] A.C. 1.

[69] *Anderson v Coutts* (1894) 58 J.P. 369.

the premises not included in the invitation and falls downstairs there.[70] Further, the duty does not protect a visitor who goes to a part of the premises where no one would reasonably expect him to go.[71] A person who has two pieces of land and invites the public to come on one of them, can, if he chooses, limit the invitation to that one of the two pieces but if the other piece is contiguous to the first piece, he may be held to have invited the public to come to both pieces.[72] Again the claimant cannot succeed if, although rightly on the structure, he makes a use of it alien to the invitation.

> "When you invite a person into your house to use the staircase you do not invite him to slide down the bannisters."[73]

So, where a stevedore in loading a ship was injured by making use of the hatch covers for loading, although he knew that a statutory regulation forbade this practice in his own interests, it was held that he had no remedy.[74] In fact, in all these cases the claimant ceases to be a visitor and becomes a mere trespasser.[75] Where, however, the negligence of the occupier causes the visitor to take an involuntary step outside the area in which he is permitted to be, he does not thereby cease to be a visitor to whom a duty of care is owed,[76] and the position is probably the same even if the involuntary step is not caused by the occupier's negligence.[77] A person may equally exceed his licence by staying on premises after the occupier's permission has expired but the limitation of time must be clearly brought home to him. Thus a person on licensed premises who remained there when drinks were being consumed long after closing time was held to continue to be a visitor in the absence of evidence that he knew of instructions from the brewers to their manager forbidding this practice.[78]

---

[70] *Lewis v Ronald* (1909) 101 L.T. 534 distinguished in *Prole v Allen* [1950] 1 All E.R. 476.

[71] *Mersey Docks and Harbour Board v Procter* [1923] A.C. 253, where there was a great difference of opinion as to the application of this principle to the facts; *Lee v Luper* [1936] 3 All E.R. 817; *Gould v McAuliffe* [1941] 2 All E.R. 527; *Periscinotti v Brighton West Pier* (1961) 105 S.J. 526.

[72] *Pearson v Coleman Bros* [1948] 2 K.B. 359 at 375 per Lord Greene M.R.

[73] Scrutton L.J. in *The Carlgarth* [1927] P. 93 at 110. In any case, the common duty of care only applies where the visitor is using the premises for the purpose for which he is invited or permitted to be there: s.2(2), below and *Keown v Coventry Healthcare NHS Trust* [2006] EWCA Civ 39; [2006] 1 W.L.R. 953.

[74] *Hillen v I.C.I. (Alkali) Ltd* [1936] A.C. 65.

[75] [1936] A.C. 65 at 69–70 per Lord Atkin.

[76] *Braithwaite v S. Durham Steel Co* [1958] 1 W.L.R. 986.

[77] This provoked a difference of opinion in the High Court of Australia in *Public Transport Commission (NSW) v Perry* (1977) 137 C.L.R. 107. Quaere as to the claimant whose initial entry is involuntary. He cannot be sued for trespass, but that does not necessarily make him a visitor.

[78] *Stone v Taffe* [1974] 1 W.L.R. 1575. The manager, as agent of the brewers, had authority to invite the claimant on to the premises in the first place.

The above principles have been applied with some degree of   **9–7**
allowance for the proclivities of young children. The common duty
of care, like the common law before it, requires that the occupier
must be prepared for children to be less careful than adults[79] but the
special characteristics of children may be relevant also to the question of whether they enjoy the status of visitor. In *Glasgow Corp v
Taylor*[80] it was alleged that a child aged seven had died from eating
poisonous berries which he had picked from a shrub in some public
gardens under the control of the corporation. The berries looked like
cherries or large blackcurrants and were of a very tempting appearance to children. They thus constituted an "allurement" to the child.
The corporation was aware of their poisonous nature, but nevertheless the shrub was not properly fenced from the public nor was
any warning given of its deadly character. It was held that these facts
disclosed a good cause of action. Certainly the child had no right to
take the berries nor even to approach the bush, and an adult doing
the same thing might well have become a trespasser, but since the
object was an "allurement" the very fact of its being left there
constituted a breach of the occupier's duty. That, however, was a
case where entry into the general area was permitted[81]: it does not
follow that the same would have applied if the park had been
private,[82] nor if the danger had been obvious. Very young children,
however, may be incapable of appreciating even the most obvious
danger. In determining whether the occupier has fulfilled his duty to
them there must be taken into account his reasonable expectations of
the habits of prudent parents in relation to their children. This is
dealt with below.[83] It must, however, be said that since the Occupiers' Liability Act 1984 there is likely to be very little practical
difference between the duties owed to a very young child who is a
trespasser and one who is a lawful visitor.

D. Common Duty of Care
The common duty of care, owed to all visitors and also where the   **9–8**
duty of the occupier depends upon a term to be implied in a contract,
is defined as:

"[A] duty to take such care as in all the circumstances of the case
is reasonable[84] to see that the visitor will be reasonably safe in

---

[79] 1957 Act s.2(3)(a). See para.9–11, below.
[80] [1922] 1 A.C. 44.
[81] See also *Jolley v Sutton LBC* [2000] 1 W.L.R. 1083.
[82] *Edwards v Ry Executive* [1952] A.C. 737.
[83] See para.9–11, below.
[84] i.e. not necessarily as safe as it could possibly be made: see, e.g. *Phillis v Daly* (1988) 15
N.S.W.L.R. 65; *Unger v City of Ottawa* (1989) 58 D.L.R. (4th) 98; *Romeo v Conservation
Commission of the Northern Territory* (1998) 152 A.L.R. 263.

using the premises for the purposes for which he is invited or permitted to be there."[85]

The question whether the occupier has fulfilled his duty to the visitor is thus dependent upon the facts of the case,[86] and, though the purpose of the visit may be a relevant circumstance, it can no longer be conclusive as it so often was before when it governed the status of the entrant. All the circumstances must be taken into account.[87] If, for example, the owner of an inn permits the resident manager to accept paying guests, both are "occupiers" in relation to such guests, but while the owner may be liable for injury caused to them by a structural defect such as the collapse of a staircase, the manager alone would be liable for injury caused by a defect in his own furnishings, such as a dangerous hole in the carpet of the living room.[88]

9–9   The Act itself gives some guidance on the application of the common duty of care but we have been forcefully reminded that this must be set in the context of the "threshold" question of the scope of the 1957 Act. Whatever the precise relationship between the Act and general negligence law with regard to activities on the premises[89] the heart of the Act is liability for "dangers due to the state of the premises".[90] In *Tomlinson v Congleton BC*[91] the claimant was injured when he dived from a standing position into the shallow water of a lake occupied by the defendants in a country park in Cheshire. Because swimming was forbidden by notices it was held by the majority of the House of Lords (indeed, the point had been conceded) that he was a trespasser,[92] but the same words appear in the Occupiers' Liability Act 1984 dealing with trespassers, it is clear that the same decision in favour of the defendants would have been reached even if he had been a lawful visitor[93] and the case is as relevant to the Act of 1957 as it is to the later Act. The risk, such as

---

[85] 1957 Act s.2(2). *Ferguson v Welsh* [1987] 1 W.L.R. 1553. Where premises are hired for a purpose about which the hirer knows more than the occupier, the latter may be entitled to leave it to the hirer's judgment whether the premises are suitable: *Wheeler v St Mary's Hall, The Times*, October 10, 1989.

[86] For a case in which the House of Lords gave full consideration to the application of the duty to the facts before them, see *Wheat v Lacon & Co Ltd* [1966] A.C. 552. The similarity of the duty to the common law duty of care is demonstrated in *Simms v Leigh Rugby Football Club Ltd* [1969] 2 All E.R. 923.

[87] Including the era when the building was constructed: *Hogg v Historic Buildings and Monuments Commission* [1988] 3 C.L. 285 (Cty Ct.).

[88] *Wheat v Lacon & Co Ltd*, above, fn.86, at 585–586 per Lord Morris, at 587 per Lord Pearce.

[89] para.9–3, above.

[90] 1957 Act s.1(1).

[91] [2003] UKHL 47; [2004] 1 A.C. 46..

[92] See para.9–26, below.

[93] See at [1] (Lord Nicholls agreeing with Lord Hoffmann), [50], [67], [92] (Lord Scott, who thought the claimant was not a trespasser).

it was, was obvious to any sensible person.[94] There was no concealed hazard or trap and the lake presented no dangers other than
those (in particular drowning) inherent in any substantial body of
water. In the view of the majority of the House of Lords the injury
could not fairly be said to have been due to the state of the
premises.[95] It would be a misuse of language on facts like those in
Tomlinson to describe obvious natural features like cliffs, trees,
rivers and lakes as "the state of the premises", otherwise any
premises would be dangerous to those prepared to encounter risks.[96]
Nor is there liability in respect of some artificial thing like a building
which is in good repair if the claimant chooses to use it in order to
carry out some hazardous activity.[97] That does not of course mean
that the occupier cannot be liable in respect of a natural feature: one
could not rent out an hotel room with a balcony overlooking a cliff
without incorporating an adequate guard rail. The underlying idea,
vague as it may be, seems to be "Was there something wrong with
the premises, given the purposes for which visitors were invited[98]?"
No one could deny that there would be something wrong with the
hotel room; but it could hardly be said that there was something
wrong with Beachy Head. Many cases of this type might be dealt
with by saying that it was not reasonable to require the occupier to
take protective steps, or the claimant voluntarily assumed the risk or
that his own fault was so great as to be the sole effective cause of his
loss; but that is not necessary: it seems the proper analysis is that the
Act is simply not engaged.[99]

---

[94] Even a commercial operator of a climbing wall is not obliged to point out to users that
matting does not provide security in the event of a fall or to train him before allowing
access: *Poppleton v Portsmouth Youth Activities Committee* [2008] EWCA Civ 646;
[2009] P.I.Q.R. P1. Cf. *Radclyffe v MoD* [2009] EWCA Civ 635 (non-occupier defendant
had assumed responsibility). As to children, who may lack powers of discernment, see
para.9–11, below.

[95] At [1], [28] and [69]. Lord Scott does not address the state of the premises issue directly
but he agreed with Lord Hoffman, save as to whether the claimant was a trespasser. Contra,
Lord Hutton at [53].

[96] Nor can it be said that failure to remove the natural condition which may be a temptation
to some is a "thing omitted to be done thereon". "The trouble with the island of the Sirens
was not the state of the premises. It was that the Sirens held mariners spellbound until they
died of hunger. The beach, give or take a fringe of human bones, was an ordinary
Mediterranean beach. If Odysseus had gone ashore and accidentally drowned himself
having a swim, Penelope would have had no action against the Sirens for luring him there
with their songs. Likewise in this case, the water was perfectly safe for all normal
activities": Lord Hoffmann at [28].

[97] *Keown v Coventry Healthcare NHS Trust* [2006] EWCA Civ 39; [2006] 1 W.L.R. 953
(another trespasser case; climbing up underside of fire escape); *Siddorn v Patel* [2007]
EWHC 1248 (QB). The issue seems to have been rather passed over in *Maloney v Torfaen
CBC* [2005] EWCA Civ 1762.

[98] The last phrase is important. The murky condition of natural waters presents an obvious
hazard. A municipal swimming pool with water so murky one could not see the bottom
might be a different matter.

[99] One might say that this case provided the classic example of the overlap of the duty and
breach issues: para.5–23, above.

9–10   The Act provides[100] that the relevant circumstances in applying the common duty of care include the degree of care and of want of care that may be looked for in the particular visitor,[101]

> "[S]o that (for example) in proper cases:
>
> (a) an occupier must be prepared for children to be less careful than adults and
>
> (b) an occupier may expect that a person, in the exercise of his calling, will appreciate and guard against any special risks ordinarily incident to it, so far as the occupier leaves him free to do so."

9–11   As to paragraph (a), we have seen above that one cannot say there is a danger due to the state of the premises simply because a visitor may choose to take obviously hazardous risks, but children may lack the awareness of danger which can be expected of an adult: an ordinary, well-maintained staircase may present a hazard to a toddler. Even where children are involved it is not right to take no account of someone's choice to ignore a danger simply because he is a child[102] but even where there is no capacity for discernment at all it would be unrealistic to expect that all land must be made safe enough for unaccompanied toddlers. A person who owns a mountain in the vicinity of a town is not obliged to fence it off in case small children come there.[103] What Lord M'Laren said a hundred years ago about the Scots common law remains true under the Occupiers' Liability Act.

> "In a town, as well as in the country, there are physical features which may be productive of injury to careless persons or to young children against which it is impossible to guard by protective measures. The situation of a town on the banks of a river is a familiar feature; and whether the stream be sluggish like the Clyde at Glasgow, or swift and variable like the Ness at Inverness, or the Tay at Perth, there is always danger to the individual who may be so unfortunate as to fall into the stream. But in none of these places has it been found necessary to fence the river to prevent children or careless persons from falling into the water. Now, as the common law is just the formal statement of the results and conclusions of the common sense of mankind, I come

---

[100] 1957 Act s.2(3).

[101] In some cases the occupier may be required to take account of the risk of wrongful conduct by other visitors: *Cunningham v Reading FC, The Independent*, March 20, 1991 (hooligans using lumps of rubble as weapons).

[102] *Keown v Coventry Healthcare NHS Trust* [2006] EWCA Civ 39; [2006] 1 W.L.R. 953 (a trespasser case, but the same must apply to visitors).

[103] *Simkiss v Rhondda BC* (1983) 81 L.G.R. 460.

without difficulty to the conclusion that precautions which have been rejected by common sense as unnecessary and inconvenient are not required by the law."[104]

That is not "harsh", it simply reflects the fact that the law of occupiers' liability is not an insurance scheme to compensate people for any misfortune which may occur on another's land.

The reason for saying that there is no relevant danger due to the state of the premises in such cases no doubt reflects the fact that society expects parents to take care of their children. That is the basis of the decision in *Phipps v Rochester Corp.*[105] The claimant, a boy aged five, was out blackberrying with his sister, aged seven, and they walked across a large open space which formed part of a housing estate being developed by the defendants. The defendants had dug a long deep trench in the middle of the open space, a danger which was quite obvious to an adult. The claimant fell in and broke his leg. On the facts it was held that a prudent parent would not have allowed two small children to go alone on the open space in question or, at least, he would have satisfied himself that the place held no dangers for the children. The defendants were entitled to assume that parents would behave in this way and therefore, although the claimant was a licensee, the defendants were not in breach of their duty to him. Devlin J.'s judgment squarely placed the primary responsibility for the safety of small children upon their parents:

"It is their duty[106] to see that such children are not allowed to wander about by themselves, or at least to satisfy themselves that the places to which they do allow their children to go unaccompanied are safe for them to go to. It would not be socially desirable if parents were, as a matter of course, able to shift the burden of looking after their children from their own shoulders to those who happen to have accessible bits of land."[107]

The occupier will have discharged his duty if the place is reasonably safe for a child who is accompanied by the sort of guardian whom the occupier is in all the circumstances entitled to expect him to have with him. If the child is in fact accompanied by a guardian, then the question will be whether the occupier ought to have foreseen that the source of the child's injury would be a danger to the child, bearing in mind the guardian's responsibility for the child's safety. There seems no reason, at least in theory, why the child's injury should not in an appropriate case be attributed both to the occupier's breach of

---

[104] *Stevenson v Glasgow Corp* 1908 SC 1034 at 1039.
[105] [1955] 1 Q.B. 450.
[106] This is not necessarily in all cases an actionable duty: see para.5–29, above.
[107] [1955] 1 Q.B. at 472.

his common duty of care and to the negligence of the guardian. In such a case the occupier would be liable in full to the child, but presumably could recover contribution from the guardian.[108] However, it is not the case that either one or both of the occupier and the parents must be liable: if a danger to a small child is obvious to accompanying parents the occupier will have discharged his duty, but as far as the parents are concerned a child may be "gone in an instant".[109]

9–12   Paragraph (b) clearly preserves such decisions as *Bates v Parker*,[110] to the general effect that:

> "[W]here a householder employs an independent contractor to do work, be it of cleaning or repairing, on his premises, the contractor must satisfy himself as to the safety or condition of that part of the premises on which he is to work."[111]

In *Roles v Nathan*[112] two chimney sweeps were killed by carbon monoxide gas while attempting to seal up a "sweep hole" in the chimney of a coke-fired boiler, the boiler being alight at the time, but the occupier was not held liable for their deaths, partly at least on the ground that paragraph (b) applied.[113] As Lord Denning M.R. said:

> "When a householder calls in a specialist to deal with a defective installation on his premises, he can reasonably expect the specialist to appreciate and guard against the dangers arising from the defect."[114]

Nonetheless, the result might no doubt have been different if, for example, the stairs leading to the cellar where the boiler was had given way,[115] for that would not have been a special risk ordinarily

---

[108] Civil Liability (Contribution) Act 1978, para.21–5, below

[109] *Marsden v Bourne Leisure Ltd* [2009] EWCA Civ 671 at 17.

[110] [1953] 2 Q.B. 231; *Christmas v General Cleaning Contractors* [1952] 1 K.B. 141, affirmed [1953] A.C. 180; Cmd. 9305 (1954), para.77(iii); *Roles v Nathan* [1963] 1 W.L.R. 1117 at 1123 per Lord Denning M.R.

[111] [1953] 2 Q.B. 231 at 235 per Lord Goddard C.J.

[112] Above, fn.110.

[113] [1963] 1 W.L.R. 1117 at 1123–1125 per Lord Denning M.R. Pearson L.J. dissented on the interpretation of the evidence but not on the law. Harman L.J., while not differing from Lord Denning, preferred to base his judgment in favour of the defendant upon the fact that the sweeps had been actually warned of the danger. See also *Phillips v Perry* [1997] C.L.Y.

[114] [1963] 1 W.L.R. 1117 at 1123; *Clare v Whittaker & Son (London) Ltd* [1976] I.C.R. 1; *Kealey v Heard* [1983] 1 W.L.R. 573. For an unsuccessful attempt by the servant of an insolvent contractor to turn health and safety regulations against the occupier see *Kmiecic v Isaacs* [2010] EWHC 381 (QB).

[115] [1963] 1 W.L.R. 1117; *Bird v King Line* [1970] 2 Lloyd's Rep. 349; *Rae v Mars (UK)* [1990] 3 E.G. 80; *Eden v West & Co* [2002] EWCA Civ 991; [2003] P.I.Q.R. Q2.

incidental to the calling of a sweep. In any case, it is important to note that the fact that the claimant is an expert is only a factor to be taken into account in determining whether there has been a breach of duty: his calling is not in itself a defence. Thus an occupier who negligently starts a fire may be liable to a fireman injured by even an ordinary risk of fighting it if that risk is one which remains even when all proper skill is used.[116] Furthermore, the fact that there is someone else whose duty it is to safeguard the visitor, for example his employer, does not of itself insulate the occupier from liability, though the occupier may be able to seek contribution from the other.[117]

E. Specific Aspects

Two specific aspects of the common duty of care are also dealt   **9–13**
with. Regard is to be had to all the circumstances in the case, so that
(for example):

i. Warning.

"(a) Where damage is caused to a visitor by a danger of which he   **9–14**
had been warned by the occupier, the warning is not to be treated
without more as absolving the occupier from liability, unless in all
the circumstances it was enough to enable the visitor to be
reasonably safe."[118]

In most cases, probably, a warning of the danger will be sufficient
to enable the visitor to be reasonably safe and so amount to a
discharge by the occupier of his duty of care, but if, for some reason,
the warning is not sufficient then the occupier remains liable.[119]
There are, after all, some situations in which a reasonable person
incurs a known risk and the question now, therefore, is whether such
a situation existed on the particular facts of the case. It is clear too,

---

[116] *Ogwo v Taylor* [1988] A.C. 431; *Salmon v Seafarers Restaurant Ltd* [1983] 1 W.L.R. 1264. As to the position of "rescuers" generally, see para.25–14, below, but where there is no negligence by the defendant in starting the fire, then he will only be liable for failing to call attention to unusual risks in the premises: *Bermingham v Sher Bros* (1980) 124 S.J. 117 (no duty on occupier of warehouse to provide means of egress which would remain safe throughout fire). Strictly, perhaps, only the second type of case falls within the Act, the other involving the common law, but if the claimant pleads both the Act and the common law nothing turns on the point.

[117] *Intruder Detection etc Ltd v Fulton* [2008] EWCA Civ 1009.

[118] The warning may be given by the occupier's agent: *Roles v Nathan*, above, fn.110.

[119] See the different opinions expressed in the Court of Appeal about the warning given in *Roles v Nathan*, above.

since a warning of the danger is not necessarily sufficient to constitute performance of the occupier's duty, that the decision in
London Graving Dock Co v Horton[120] is no longer good law.[121] In
that case, the House of Lords held that an invitee could not succeed
if he had full knowledge of the nature and extent of the danger. Now,
however, as in cases where he has actually received a warning, the
question is whether a visitor with knowledge of the danger reasonably incurred it.[122]

ii. Independent contractor.

9–15   "(b) where damage is caused to a visitor by a danger due to the
faulty execution of any work of construction, maintenance or
repair[123] by an independent contractor employed by the occupier,
the occupier is not to be treated without more[124] as answerable for
the danger if in all the circumstances he had acted reasonably in
entrusting the work to an[125] independent contractor and had taken
such steps (if any) as he reasonably ought in order to satisfy
himself that the contractor was competent[126] and that the work
had been properly done."[127]

This is designed to afford some protection for the occupier who
has engaged an independent contractor who has done the work in a
faulty manner and was intended to reverse the decision of the House
of Lords in *Thompson v Cremin*[128] in so far as that laid down that an
invitor was responsible for the shortcomings of his contractor. The
paragraph therefore makes the law under the Act accord with the
general law, under which, as a rule, there is no vicarious liability for
independent contractors.[129]

[120] [1951] A.C. 737.
[121] *Roles v Nathan*, above, fn.110, at 1124 per Lord Denning M.R.
[122] *Bunker v Charles Brandt & Son Ltd* [1969] 2 Q.B. 480 at 489 per O'Connor J. For
contributory negligence in relation to the occupier's liability, see para.9–18, below.
[123] A broad, purposive interpretation is required which will embrace demolition: *Ferguson v
Welsh* [1987] 1 W.L.R. 1553.
[124] For possible meanings of this cryptic phrase see North, *Occupiers' Liability* (1971),
p.144.
[125] How can it ever be unreasonable to employ *a* (as opposed to *the*) contractor?
[126] On the content of this duty see para.9–16, below.
[127] 1957 Act s.2(4)(b). *O'Connor v Swan & Edgar* (1963) 107 S.J. 215; *Gibson v Skibs A/S.
Marina, etc.* [1966] 2 All E.R. 476. The burden of proving that the danger was due to the
fault of an independent contractor rests with the occupier: *Christmas v Blue Star Line*
[1961] 1 Lloyd's Rep. 94; *A.M.F. International Ltd v Magnet Bowling Ltd* [1968] 1 W.L.R.
1028 at 1042–1043.
[128] [1953] 2 All E.R. 1181.
[129] *A.M.F. International Ltd v Magnet Bowling Ltd* [1968] 1 W.L.R. 1028. See para.20–21,
below.

The operation of the paragraph is illustrated by two cases from the period before the Act. In *Haseldine v Daw*[130] H was going to visit a tenant in a block of flats belonging to D and was injured when the lift fell to the bottom of its shaft as a result of the negligence of a firm of engineers employed by D to repair the lift. It was held that D, having employed a competent firm of engineers to make periodical inspections of the lift, to adjust it and report on it, had discharged the duty owed to H, whether H was an invitee or licensee. As Scott L.J. observed:

"[T]he landlord of a block of flats, as occupier of the lifts, does not profess as such to be either an electrical or, as in this case, a hydraulic engineer. Having no technical skill he cannot rely on his own judgment, and the duty of care towards his invitees requires him to obtain and follow good technical advice. If he did not do so, he would, indeed, be guilty of negligence. To hold him responsible for the misdeeds of his independent contractor would be to make him insure the safety of his lift. That duty can only rise out of contract . . . "[131]

In *Woodward v Mayor of Hastings*,[132] on the other hand, a pupil at a school for which the defendants were responsible fell and was injured on an icy step which had been negligently left in a dangerous condition by a cleaner. Even assuming that the cleaner was an independent contractor, it was held that the defendants were liable and *Haseldine v Daw* was distinguished. Technical knowledge was required in the maintenance and repair of a lift, but such considerations were not relevant in *Woodward*'s case.

"The craft of the charwoman may have its mysteries, but there is no esoteric quality in the nature of the work which the cleaning of a snow-covered step demands."[133]

Where an independent contractor has been employed, therefore, **9–16** the question today is whether the occupier himself has done all that reasonable care requires of him. He must take reasonable steps to satisfy himself that the contractor he employs is competent, and, if the character of the work permits, he must take similar steps to see

[130] [1941] 2 K.B. 343.
[131] [1941] 2 K.B. 343 at 356. See also per Goddard L.J. at 374.
[132] [1954] K.B. 174.
[133] [1954] K.B. 174 at 813 per du Parcq L.J.

that the work has been properly done. In fact, where the work is especially complex, as with the construction of a large building or a ship, he may even have to cause the independent contractor's work to be supervised by a properly instructed architect or other professional person.[134] As the dictum of Scott L.J. indicates, there are many cases in which the technical nature of the work to be done will require the occupier to employ an independent contractor and he will be negligent if he attempts to do it himself. This does not mean, however, that a householder must not himself undertake some ordinary domestic repair such as the fixing of a new door handle. Provided that he does the work with the care and skill of a reasonably competent carpenter he has fulfilled his duty.[135]

One justification for a general rule of non-liability for independent contractors is that the contractor (who is of course personally liable) is more likely to be claim-worthy than an individual servant of the occupier. That prompts the question, "Is the occupier therefore obliged to investigate the liability insurance position of the contractor?". Some statements in *Gwilliam v West Hertfordshire NHS Trust*[136] might be taken as supporting that but in *Payling v T. Naylor (Trading as Mainstreet)*[137] the court rejected any such general, free-standing duty. The claimant suffered injury by the fault of a doorman when he was ejected from a club. The doorman was the servant of W, who carried no liability insurance and could not satisfy a judgment. The occupier of the club was held not liable because W had been licensed by the local authority to carry out such activities and that knowledge was sufficient to give the occupier reasonable cause to be satisfied as to his competence. Not only would the contrary rule be difficult to reconcile with the wording of the statute, which refers to "competence" rather than "suitability", it would also, it is submitted, be rather impracticable—consider, for example,

---

[134] *A.M.F. International Ltd v Magnet Bowling Ltd* [1968] 1 W.L.R. 1028 at 1044, 1045–1047 per Mocatta J.; *Kealey v Heard* [1983] 1 All E.R. 973. Mocatta J. also held that the negligence of the architect or other supervisor would not itself involve the occupier in liability for otherwise, in technical cases, the common duty of care would become equivalent to the obligation of an insurer. Negligence in supervision would not fall under s.2(4)(b), but it must be remembered that the purpose of s.2(4) is to insist that in determining whether the common duty of care has been discharged, regard is to be had to all the circumstances. Paragraphs (a) and (b) are introduced by the words "so that (for example)" and there is no reason for saying that an occupier is necessarily liable for the negligence of his independent contractor except when s.2(4)(b) applies. Thus an omission by a contractor called in to advise on safety may not literally fall within the paragraph, but that does not make the occupier liable when he has taken due care in selecting the contractor: *Wattleworth v Goodwood Racing Co Ltd* [2004] EWHC 140; [2004] P.I.Q.R. P25.

[135] *Wells v Cooper* [1958] 2 Q.B. 265.

[136] [2002] EWCA Civ 1041; [2002] Q.B. 443.

[137] [2004] EWCA Civ 560; [2004] P.I.Q.R. P36.

the position of the householder who engages a contractor to do a job around the house or garden.[138] It has been said that:

"[I]f D had no duty to protect C against the *physical* consequences of an accident caused by the negligence of T, I would not regard it as just and reasonable to impose on D the more remote duty to protect C against the *economic* consequences of C being unable to enforce a judgment against T."[139]

Where an occupier engages a contractor to do work on his premises and the claimant suffers injury not from the condition in which the contractor leaves the premises but from the manner in which the operation is carried out,[140] any liability arises under the general law and not under the Act.

"It would not ordinarily be reasonable to expect an occupier of premises having engaged a contractor whom he has reasonable grounds for regarding as competent, to supervise the contractor's activities in order to ensure that he was discharging his duty to his employees to observe a safe system of work."[141]

However, there may be circumstances where the occupier is required to intervene where he has failed to take care in selecting a competent contractor[142] or if it is obvious that the contractor is using an unsafe system of work.

F. Personal Responsibility: *Tomlinson*'s Case
It must be emphasised that the provisions dealt with in the preceding paragraphs are no more than explanations or illustrations of the fundamental rule, which is that the occupier must do what is reasonable in the circumstances of the case and that standard, as in any other case of negligence, will be arrived at by the court's

9–17

---

[138] It is also submitted that the fact that the employer of the contractor is required to carry liability insurance should not lead to the contrary conclusion. To take an example outside the area of occupiers' liability, the owner of a vehicle is required to have liability insurance in respect of its use and that would have to cover, inter alia, accidents caused by defects in the vehicle; but that should not mean that the owner should have to inquire into the garage's liability insurance cover when he took the car to be serviced.

[139] *Glaister v Appleby in Westmorland Town Council* [2009] EWCA Civ 1325; [2010] P.I.Q.R. P6 at [63] per Toulson L.J.

[140] e.g. removing asbestos lagging without taking the recognised precautions.

[141] *Ferguson v Welsh* [1987] 1 W.L.R. 1553 at 1560. *Fairchild v Glenhaven Funeral Services Ltd* [2001] EWCA Civ 1881; [2002] 1 W.L.R. 1052.

[142] *Bottomley v Todmorden Cricket Club* [2003] EWCA Civ 1575; [2004] P.I.Q.R. P18.

weighing the relative risks and burdens.[143] The burdens are not only those that would be directly imposed on the particular occupier if he were required to take the action contended for by the claimant, they include the restrictions on the freedom of the majority of people which will be imposed[144] if what is required of the occupier is set at a level which will prevent the foolhardy[145] encountering obvious risks.[146] This is the basis of *Tomlinson v Congleton BC*[147] and even though that case was, strictly, concerned with the question of whether there was a danger within the meaning of the Act rather than breach of the occupier's duty, the point is the same. As Lord Hobhouse said:

"It is not, and should never be, the policy of the law to require the protection of the foolhardy or reckless few to deprive, or interfere with, the enjoyment by the remainder of society of the liberties and amenities to which they are rightly entitled.[148] Does the law require that all trees be cut down because some youths may climb them and fall? Does the law require the coastline and other beauty spots to be lined with warning notices? Does the law require that attractive waterside picnic spots be destroyed because of a few foolhardy individuals who choose to ignore warning notices and indulge in activities dangerous only to themselves? The answer to all these questions is, of course, no. But this is the road down which your Lordships, like other courts before, have been invited to travel and which the councils in the present case found so inviting. In truth, the arguments for the claimant have involved an

---

[143] See, e.g. *Lewis v Six Continents Plc* [2005] EWCA Civ 1805 (no need to make upper storey hotel window unopenable). "Not all people live, or can afford to live, in premises that are completely free of hazards. In fact, nobody lives in premises that are risk-free. Concrete pathways crack. Unpaved surfaces become slippery, or uneven. Many objects in dwelling houses could be a cause of injury. People enter dwelling houses for a variety of purposes, and in many different circumstances. Entrants may have differing capacities to observe and appreciate risks, and to take care for their own safety": *Neindorf v Junkovic* [2005] HCA 75; 222 A.L.R. 631 at [8].

[144] See *Hampstead Heath Winter Swimming Club v London Corp* [2005] EWHC 713 (Admin); [2005] 1 W.L.R. 2930, where an attempt was made by the defendants to ban unsupervised swimming on Hampstead Heath on the ground of risk to the participants.

[145] Of course the fudge of the Law Reform (Contributory Negligence) Act 1945 is always available. The CA in *Tomlinson* made a two-thirds reduction.

[146] Indeed, even where the risk is not obvious and the claimant is not foolhardy there is a danger of inhibiting ordinary activities if the standard of care is set too high: *Cole v Davis-Gilbert* [2007] EWCA Civ 396.

[147] [2003] UKHL 47; [2004] 1 A.C. 46, para.9–9, above. *Donoghue v Folkestone Properties Ltd* [2003] EWCA Civ 231; [2003] Q.B. 1008; *Staples v West Dorset DC, The Times*, April 28, 1995; *Cotton v Derbyshire Dales DC, The Times*, June 20, 1994; *Darby v National Trust* [2001] EWCA Civ 189; [2001] P.I.Q.R. P27. The reasoning of *Tomlinson* applies to cases under the Package Travel, Package Holidays and Package Tours Regulations SI 1992/3288: *Evans v Kosmar Villa Holidays Plc* [2007] EWCA Civ 1003; [2008] 1 W.L.R. 297.

[148] See *Keown v Coventry Healthcare NHS Trust* [2006] EWCA Civ 39; [2006] 1 W.L.R. 953 at [17].

attack upon the liberties of the citizen which should not be countenanced. They attack the liberty of the individual to engage in dangerous, but otherwise harmless, pastimes at his own risk and the liberty of citizens as a whole fully to enjoy the variety and quality of the landscape of this country. The pursuit of an unrestrained culture of blame and compensation has many evil consequences and one is certainly the interference with the liberty of the citizen."[149]

G. Contributory Negligence

In view of some doubts which existed as to whether the scheme **9–18** of the Law Reform Contributory Negligence Act 1945[150] applied where an invitee was guilty of lack of care for his own safety it is perhaps surprising that the Occupiers' Liability Act does not expressly incorporate the Act of 1945. However, the point is probably implicit[151] and judges have in numerous cases applied the 1945 Act without hesitation to reduce damages.[152] Where the claimant's fault is extreme it may, of course, amount to the sole legal cause of his loss.[153]

H. Exclusion of Liability

We have seen that the occupier may be able to discharge his duty **9–19** by warning the visitor of the danger if the warning is enough to make the visitor reasonably safe. If he chooses to impose on the visitor's permission to enter a condition excluding or restricting his duty the answer will turn on whether or not the Unfair Contract

---

[149] At [81]. See also Lord Hoffmann at [46]. *Vairy v Wyong SC* [2005] HCA 62; 223 C.L.R. 422 and *Mulligan v Coffs Harbour CC* [2005] HCA 63; 223 C.L.R. 486, both claims based on diving into natural waters and which failed. The reasoning is by no means on all fours with *Tomlinson* and *Vairy* was a divided decision. But there is an emphasis on individual responsibility and the impracticability of draping miles of coastline with warnings. "It is only reasonably to be expected that people will conduct themselves according to dictates of common sense, which must include the observation of, and an appropriately careful response to what is obvious. Courts in deciding whether that response has been made are bound to keep in mind that defendants have rights and interests too. A tendency to see cases through the eyes of plaintiffs only is to be avoided": *Mulligan* at [80] per Callinan and Heydon JJ. See also *Roads and Traffic Authority of NSW v Dederer* [2007] HCA 42. Legislation in most Australian states provides that there is no liability for the materialisation of an obvious risk of a dangerous recreational activity (see *Dederer* at [253]).
[150] See the 12th edn of this work, p.217.
[151] The statement of Diplock L.J.: "My neighbour does not enlarge my duty of care for his safety by neglecting it himself" (*Wheat v Lacon & Co Ltd* [1966] 1 Q.B. 335 at 372) which was approved by Viscount Dilhorne in the House of Lords [1966] A.C. 552 at 576, is not inconsistent with this. The point is that a person cannot, by carelessness of his own safety, thereby put an occupier in breach of the common duty of care.
[152] See, e.g. *Woolins v British Celanese Ltd* (1966) 1 K.I.R. 438; *Stone v Taffe* [1974] 1 W.L.R. 1575.
[153] See, e.g. *Brayshaw v Leeds CC* [1984] 2 C.L. 234.

Terms Act 1977 applies to the case. This Act, despite its short title, extends much further than the control of contractual exemption clauses. Section 2 provides that:

> "(1) A person cannot by reference to any contract term or to a notice[154] exclude or restrict his liability for death or personal injury resulting from negligence;
>
> (2) in the case of other loss or damage, a person cannot so exclude or restrict his liability for negligence except in so far as the term or notice satisfies the requirement of reasonableness."[155]

The definition of "negligence" expressly includes the breach of the common duty of care imposed by the Occupiers' Liability Act 1957[156] but the prohibition on exclusion of liability applies only where the duty arises from things done in the course of a business or from the occupation of premises used for the business purposes of the occupier. A business probably requires at least some degree of regularity, so that an isolated transaction whereby access to land was granted for payment would probably not fall within the ban, but the Act contains an extended definition which makes the concept cover some activities which would not ordinarily be thought of as a business.[157] Activities in aid of charity are an obvious example which would present the court with difficult questions of degree.[158] Since the owner of a farm or a commercial forest is clearly occupying his land in the course of a business, the effect of the Act as originally formulated was to cause restriction of public access and it was amended by s.2 of the Occupiers' Liability Act 1984, which provides that:

> "[T]he liability of an occupier of premises for breach of an obligation or duty towards a person obtaining access to the premises for recreational or educational purposes, being liability for loss or damage suffered by reason of the dangerous state of the premises, is not a business liability of the occupier unless granting

---

[154] Defined in s.14, e.g. a sign at the entry to the premises.

[155] See s.11.

[156] The Act does not prevent exclusion of a stricter duty: s.1(1)(b). By virtue of s.1(4) it is immaterial whether liability "arises directly or vicariously". This would probably cover any situations where the occupier is liable for the negligence of an independent contractor.

[157] By s.14 " 'business' includes a profession and the activities of any government department or local or public authority". The concept of business liability is relevant for various other purposes under the Unfair Contract Terms Act. For a full survey, see *Benjamin's Sale of Goods*.

[158] See, e.g. *White v Blackmore* [1972] 2 Q.B. 651.

that person such access for the purposes concerned falls within the business of the occupier."

Hence if a farmer has on his land a ruinous castle he may allow access on condition that he is not liable for death or personal injury caused by the state of the premises,[159] but the ancient monuments body English Heritage may not impose such a condition because admission for recreation or education is (probably) its business within the meaning of the Act. The liberty to exclude liability is, however, confined to damage suffered by reason of the dangerous state of the premises, so that if the visitor is knocked down by the farmer's tractor the exclusion, no matter how widely drawn, is ineffective. The Unfair Contract Terms Act does not abolish the defence of volenti non fit injuria but provides that a person's agreement to or awareness of an exempting condition or notice, "is not of itself to be taken as indicating his voluntary acceptance of the risk".[160]

Where the Unfair Contract Terms Act does not apply because the premises are not occupied for business purposes the matter is still governed by s.2(1) of the 1957 Act, which provides that the occupier owes the common duty of care, "except in so far as he is free to and does extend, restrict, modify or exclude his duty ... by agreement or otherwise". No contract is necessary for this purpose, for s.2(1) gives statutory force to the decision of the Court of Appeal, shortly before the Act, in *Ashdown v Samuel Williams & Sons*[161] though the actual decision would now go the other way, since the defendants were business occupiers. The claimant was a licensee on land belonging to the defendants when she was knocked down and injured by railway trucks which were being negligently shunted along a railway line on the land. Various notices had been posted by the defendants to the effect that every person on the land was there at his own risk and should have no claim against the defendants for any injury whatsoever, and it was found as a fact that they had taken reasonable steps to bring the conditions contained in the notices to the claimant's attention. It was held, therefore, that the claimant could not recover. Despite criticism that the absence of a contract should have been fatal to the defence,[162] the decision seems to accord with general principle. If I can exclude you from my property altogether, why can I not permit you to enter upon any terms that I like to make? The result might, indeed, be construed as a contract whereby you give up what would otherwise be your legal rights in

9–20

---

[159] If the farmer charges the public even a small sum for admission there is likely to be a business occupation.
[160] UCTA s.2(3). See further para.25–6, below.
[161] [1957] 1 Q.B. 409; *White v Blackmore* [1972] 2 Q.B. 651.
[162] See Gower (1956) 19 M.L.R. 536.

return for my allowing you to enter, but this construction is not essential to the validity of the conditions.[163] The occupier can (or at least could, as the law then stood) say simply:

> "You have your choice: stay out of my premises or enter them on my terms. You will be a trespasser unless you have my permission. I give it subject to your agreeing that I owe you no duty. If later you claim to have entered without so agreeing you must admit you have entered without my permission and you will indeed be a trespasser."[164]

9–21   It will be noticed that *Ashdown*'s case was concerned not with the static condition of the land on which the claimant was a licensee but with the current activities of the occupier. Clearly, therefore, the power to exclude liability is not restricted to the static condition of the structure, but it is less easy to justify the existence of that power with regard to current activities.

> "There is much to be said for an occupier who is prepared to grant a gratuitous licence provided he is not put to trouble or expense in inspecting or maintaining his property: there is less to be said for one who claims a right to shoot, drive, shunt or blast without taking reasonable care."[165]

The occupier's power to exclude the common duty of care is, however, governed by the words "in so far as he is free to" do so. Clearly, therefore the Occupier's Liability Act does not enlarge the power which existed at common law. It is submitted, for example, that there could be no exclusion of liability to a person entering in exercise of a right conferred by law. Furthermore, the law's original level of duty to trespassers (not to injure them deliberately or recklessly) represented a minimum standard of conduct which could not be excluded, for A cannot lawfully license B to inflict a wilful injury upon him. However, the duty owed to trespassers is now much higher[166] and in practice in some cases approaches the level of

---

[163] It was rejected by Lord Greene M.R. in *Wilkie v L.P.T.B.* [1947] 1 All E.R. 258 at 260. Cf. *Gore v Van Der Lann* [1967] 2 Q.B. 31. Odgers, "The Strange Case of Mrs. Gore" (1970) 86 L.Q.R. 69.

[164] On the other hand, as Lord Denning M.R. forcefully points out in *White v Blackmore* [1972] 2 Q.B. 651 at 665–666, this approach derogates severely from the purpose of s.2(4)(a) of the Act. Further, the duty to trespassers has risen since *Ashdown*'s case: below.

[165] Odgers [1957] C.L.J. 39, 54.

[166] See para.9–26, below.

the common duty of care. To make this the minimum standard would largely remove by the back door the freedom to exclude liability which Parliament has conferred. Perhaps there is much to be said for allowing non-business occupiers to exclude liability for all injury except that inflicted wilfully or recklessly; if it be objected that a lawful visitor may therefore be worse off than a trespasser entering without notice of the occupier's terms[167] it may be replied that at least the visitor is, or ought to be, aware of these terms.

I. Effect of Contract on Occupier's Liability to Third Parties

It was the opinion of the Law Reform Committee[168] that where a **9–22** person contracts with the occupier for the use of premises on the footing that he is to be entitled to permit third persons to use them, the duty owed by the occupier to those third persons is the same as that owed to the other party to the contract. This could lead to a person being deprived of his rights by a contract to which he was not a party and of whose provisions he was unaware. It is therefore provided by the Act that:

> "[W]here an occupier of premises is bound by contract to permit persons who are strangers to the contract[169] to enter or use the premises, the duty of care which he owes to them as his visitors cannot be restricted or excluded by that contract, but (subject to any provision of the contract to the contrary) shall include the duty to perform his obligations under the contract, whether undertaken for their protection or not, in so far as those obligations go beyond the obligations otherwise involved in that duty."[170]

Furthermore, where a tenancy, including a statutory tenancy which does not in law amount to a tenancy, requires either the landlord or the tenant to permit persons to enter premises of which he is the occupier, the section applies as if the tenancy were a contract between the landlord and the tenant.[171]

This section has a twofold effect. The occupier cannot by contract reduce his obligations to visitors who are strangers to the contract to

---

[167] Cf. Clerk and Lindsell, *Torts*, 19th edn, para.12–74, where it is argued that the statutory duty to a trespasser may be excluded by an adequate notice.
[168] On the authority of *Fosbroke-Hobbes v Airwork Ltd* [1937] 1 All E.R. 108. Cmd. 9305 (1954), para.55. See, too, para.79.
[169] Defined in s.3(3).
[170] Section 3(1).
[171] 1957 Act s.3(4).

a level below that imposed by the common duty of care.[172] If, however, the contract requires him to take some precaution not required in the circumstances by that duty, the visitor shall have the benefit of that precaution. If, for example, A contracts with B to allow B and C to use his premises and the contract provides that the premises shall be lit during the hours of darkness, C has a right of action against A for injury due to A's failure to light the premises, whether or not such a failure would amount to a breach of the common duty of care. It is provided, however, that the section shall not have the effect, unless the contract so provides, of making an occupier who has taken all reasonable care liable for dangers due to the faulty execution of any work of construction, maintenance or repair or other like operation by persons other than himself, his servants or persons acting under his direction and control.[173]

9–23   There will now be cases where the visitor may be able to rely on the general provisions of the Contracts (Rights of Third Parties) Act 1999 in order to enforce a term in the contract between the occupier and another under which the visitor is allowed entry and which imposes a higher duty than the common duty of care.[174] Like the Occupiers' Liability Act, this right is subject to the contrary agreement of the contracting parties.[175] However, in practice the 1957 Act may continue to be relied on, if only because it is unnecessary to establish that the term in question "purported to confer a benefit"[176] on the third party.

It was formerly an open question whether the occupier, though unable to restrict his duty to third parties by a provision in the contract itself, could do so by publishing a notice as in *Ashdown v Samuel Williams & Sons.*[177] Where the occupation is of a business nature it is now clear that such a notice is caught by the Unfair Contract Terms Act[178] and in other situations it is submitted that the case is one where the occupier is not "free to" restrict or exclude his

---

[172] It may be that as far as personal injuries are concerned much the same effect is achieved by the Unfair Contract Terms Act 1977 s.2(1), above. According to Law Com. No.69, p.133 "contract term" bears, "its natural meaning of any term in any contract (and is not limited to the terms in a contract between the instant parties)". However, the provisions of the Occupiers' Liability Act are more favourable to the claimant since (1) they are not confined to business occupation and (2) they extend to all types of loss or damage whereas the Unfair Contract Terms Act prohibition is a qualified one with regard to property damage.

[173] 1957 Act s.3(2). The wording of this subsection differs from that of s.2(4)(b), para.9–15, above, but the effect of the two subsections is probably the same and if s.2(4)(b) includes demolition (*Ferguson v Welsh* [1987] 1 W.L.R. 1153) so should s.3(2).

[174] However, the 1999 Act would not apply if the obligation to admit the third party was an implied one, because the third party would not then be expressly identified in the contract: s.1(3).

[175] Contracts (Rights of Third Parties) Act 1999 s.1(2).

[176] 1999 Act s.1((1)(b).

[177] [1957] 1 Q.B. 409, above.

[178] See para.9–19, above.

duty of care, for the alternative view would tend to defeat the object of s.3 of the Occupiers' Liability Act.[179]

J. Damage to Property

The Act provides[180] that the rules which it enacts shall apply: **9–24**

" ... [I]n like manner and to the like extent as the principles applicable at common law to an occupier of premises and his invitees or licensees would apply to regulate ... the obligations of a person occupying or having control over any premises or structure in respect of damage to property, including the property of persons who are not themselves his visitors."[181]

Clearly, therefore, where property lawfully on the premises is damaged by a structural defect of the premises,[182] whether it actually belongs to a visitor or not, the question in each case is whether the occupier has discharged the common duty of care. Where there has been a bailment, however, as where goods are deposited in a warehouse, the liability of the warehouse-keeper will not depend upon the common duty of care but upon his duty under the bailment or special contract. The rules contained in the Occupiers' Liability Act replace only the principles of the common law formerly applicable between the occupier and his invitee or licensee. They do not affect the relationship of bailor and bailee.[183] Where there is no bailment, the common law rule was that there was no duty on the occupier to protect the goods of his visitors from theft by a third party[184] and the Act has not changed this. A mere licence

---

[179] Cf. Clerk & Lindsell, *Torts*, 19th edn, para.12–55; North, *Occupiers' Liability* (1971), pp.151–152. It must be admitted, however, that the Law Reform Committee seem to have been concerned only with the position of a person affected by an exempting term unknown to him: Cmnd. 9305 (1954), para.55.

[180] Section 1(3)(b). North, *Occupiers' Liability* (1971), pp.94–112 (based on the author's article, "Damage to Property and the Occupiers' Liability Act 1957" (1966) 30 Conv (N.S.) 264).

[181] The last phrase would seem to allow an action by an owner who is not a visitor, as in *Drive Yourself Lessey's Pty Ltd v Burnside* [1959] S.R.(NSW) 390: but cf. North, *Occupiers' Liability* (1971), pp.101–105.

[182] e.g. if, with your permission, I leave my car in the drive outside your house and a tile falls off the roof and damages it: *A.M.F. International Ltd v Magnet Bowling Ltd* [1968] 1 W.L.R. 1028. Damages may be recovered not only in respect of actual damage to the property but also in respect of consequential financial loss: at 1049–1051 per Mocatta J.

[183] Cf. *Fairline Shipping Corp v Adamson* [1975] Q.B. 180.

[184] *Tinsley v Dudley* [1951] 2 K.B. 18. See also *Ashby v Tolhurst* [1937] 2 K.B. 242; *Deyong v Shenburn* [1946] K.B. 227; *Edwards v West Herts Group Hospital Management Committee* [1957] 1 W.L.R. 418.

to put goods on land (as in the case of most car parks) does not make the occupier a bailee.[185]

3. LIABILITY TO TRESPASSERS AND OTHER NON-VISITORS

9–25 The duty of an occupier to a trespasser was unaffected by the Occupiers' Liability Act 1957.[186] The original common law rule was that the occupier was only liable to a trespasser in respect of some wilful act, "done with deliberate intention of doing harm ... or at least some act done with reckless disregard of the presence of the trespasser",[187] but the law underwent substantial alteration and development by the House of Lords in 1972 in *British Railways Board v Herrington*.[188] As a result of that case the occupier owed to the trespasser a "duty of common humanity" which, generally speaking, was lower than the common duty of care but substantially higher than the original duty. *Herrington*'s case was applied by the Court of Appeal on a number of occasions without undue difficulty[189] but on a reference to the Law Commission that body decided that no sufficiently clear principle emerged from the case and recommended legislative action. After a long delay, this was done by the Occupiers' Liability Act 1984.[190]

Though in this section we shall continue to speak of trespassers, for that is the commonest case, the Act in fact covers a rather wider field, for it applies to liability to persons other than the occupier's visitors. It applies, for example, to persons exercising private rights of way,[191] and persons exercising access rights under National Parks legislation[192] but not to persons using a public right of way,[193] whose rights, if any, must be sought in the highways legislation.[194] Section 1(3) provides that a duty is owed to the trespasser in relation

---

[185] *Tinsley v Dudley*, above, fn.184; *Hinks v Fleet* [1986] 2 E.G.L.R. 243; *Chappell v National Car Parks, The Times,* May 22, 1987; *John C. Dogherty v Drogheda Harbour Commissioners* [1993] 1 I.R. 315.
[186] Contrast the Occupiers' Liability (Scotland) Act 1960. See *McGlone v British Railways Board,* 1966 S.C.(H.L.) 1.
[187] *Robert Addie & Sons (Collieries) Ltd v Dumbreck* [1929] A.C. 358 at 365. This is the position under the Irish Occupiers' Liability Act 1995 s.4(1). However, s.4(2) then directs the court to have regard, in determining whether there has been reckless disregard, to the factors specified in the English Act of 1984 s.1(3) (below).
[188] [1972] A.C. 877.
[189] See, e.g. *Pannett v P. McGuinness & Co Ltd* [1972] 2 Q.B. 599; *Melvin v Franklins (Builders) Ltd* (1973) 71 L.G.R. 142; *Harris v Birkenhead Corp* [1976] 2 W.L.R. 279.
[190] Law Com. No.75.
[191] *Vodden v Gayton* [2001] P.I.Q.R. P4 (owners of servient tenement across which fenced track ran occupiers of the track; no breach of duty on facts).
[192] See para.9–5, above. As to persons exercising rights under the Countryside and Rights of Way Act 2000, see below.
[193] Section 1(7).
[194] See para.14–42, below.

to the risk of their suffering injury by reason of any danger due to the state of the premises or things done or omitted to be done thereon[195] if:

> "(a) [The occupier] is aware of the danger or has reasonable grounds to believe that it exists;
> (b) he knows or has reasonable grounds to believe that the [trespasser] is in the vicinity of the danger concerned or that he may come into the vicinity of the danger ... and
> (c) the risk is one against which, in all the circumstances of the case, he may reasonably be expected to offer the other some protection."

The expression "has reasonable grounds to believe" in paragraphs (a) and (b) requires actual knowledge of facts which would lead a reasonable person to be aware of the danger or the presence of the trespasser[196] and simple ignorance, though blameworthy, is not enough, though it would be under the 1957 Act.[197]   **9–26**

The duty is to take such care as is reasonable in all the circumstances to see that the entrant does not suffer injury[198] on the premises by reason of the danger concerned[199] and it may, in appropriate circumstances, be discharged by taking such steps as are reasonable to give warning of the danger concerned or to discourage persons from incurring the risk.[200] The defence of volenti non fit injuria is expressly preserved.[201] On the face of it, the standard appears to be objective and not conditioned by the occupier's own resources, which was not true of the duty of common humanity,[202] but in *Ratcliffe v McConnell*[203] the Court of Appeal treated the Act as largely a restatement of what Lord Diplock had said in *Herrington*, citing a passage which had referred to the occupier's resources.

---

[195] See s.1(1)(a).

[196] *Swain v Puri* [1996] P.I.Q.R. P442. See also *White v St Alban's District CC, The Times*, March 12, 1990; *Rhind v Astbury Water Park Ltd* [2004] EWCA Civ 756. The question is whether the occupier has reason to expect the trespasser at that time: *Donoghue v Folkestone Properties Ltd* [2003] EWCA Civ 231; [2003] Q.B. 1008.

[197] Consciously closing one's eyes to an obvious risk should suffice. However, it is suggested in *Young v Kent CC* [2005] EWHC 1342 (QB) that in the case of premises like a school a risk assessment exercise is necessary even with regard to dangers to trespassers. The actual decision is called into question in *Keown v Coventry Healthcare NHS Trust* [2006] EWCA Civ 39; [2006] 1 W.L.R. 953.

[198] 1984 Act s.1(9).

[199] 1984 Act s.1(4).

[200] 1984 Act s.1(5). In some cases there may be specific, statutory provisions aimed at preventing access: *Mann v Northern Electric Distribution Ltd* [2010] EWCA Civ 141.

[201] 1984 Act s.1(6).

[202] [1972] A.C. 877 at 899, 920–921, 942. It might be argued that the occupier's resources are to be taken into account as part of "all the circumstances of the case", but the same words appear in s.2(2), the 1957 Act and it has not been suggested that the occupier's "personal equation" forms part of the standard of care owed to visitors.

[203] [1999] 1 W.L.R. 670 at 680.

However, it is submitted that the nature or character of the trespass is a matter which is very relevant in determining what the occupier may reasonably be expected to do: the very same precautions which should be taken for the benefit of a lawful visitor may in some cases be required to protect young trespassing children but it would be wholly unacceptable that they should be required for the benefit of a burglar or entrant intent on criminal damage. Furthermore, while the giving of a prominent warning will not necessarily in all cases discharge the occupier's duty[204] it is more likely to do so than with regard to lawful visitors. The latter may have no choice but to encounter the risk and the warning must therefore in itself make them reasonably safe; the trespasser who continues to intrude after passing a prominent warning notice has himself to blame for any injury he may suffer. Even where no effective warning is given, an adult trespasser or even a child with sufficient understanding[205]) who takes a risk which should be obvious to him cannot complain that the occupier did not take more rigorous steps to discourage his folly.[206] The leading case of *Tomlinson v Congleton BC*[207] has been considered above in the context of the 1957 Act. In fact the majority of the House of Lords considered that the claimant was a trespasser in the lake and if they were not liable under the 1957 Act then a fortiori this was true under the 1984 Act. The latter uses the same formula as the former in relation to defining its scope and some members of the House were of the view that the injury suffered could not even be said to be, "due to the state of the premises or things done or omitted to be done thereon."[208] In such a case it is therefore unnecessary to rely on volenti non fit injuria as an answer to the claim.

9–27   Although the 1984 Act is in terms as ambiguous as that of 1957 on the relationship between the "occupancy" and "activity" duties, it has been said that it is confined to the liability of "an occupier as occupier".[209] On this basis it does not therefore apply to a case where the occupier negligently[210] shoots a trespasser.[211] However, both the wording of the statute and history show that it must apply to some activities carried on on the land—some of the leading cases

---

[204] For example, where the likely trespassers are young children; but the principle that the occupier must be entitled to look to parents to take principal responsibility for the safety of their children (para.9–11, above) must apply here, too.

[205] *Keown v Coventry Healthcare NHS Trust* [2006] EWCA Civ 39; [2006] 1 W.L.R. 953.

[206] *Ratcliffe v McConnell*, above, fn.203.

[207] [2003] UKHL 47; [2004] 1 A.C. 46, para.9–9, above; and see *Donoghue v Folkestone Properties Ltd* [2003] EWCA Civ 231; [2003] Q.B. 1008.

[208] para.9–9, above.

[209] *Revill v Newberry* [1996] Q.B. 567 per Neill L.J. Evans L.J. did not feel it necessary to come to a conclusion on the scope of the 1984 Act.

[210] If the injury is inflicted deliberately or recklessly the question will not be one of occupiers' liability but of what force may be used in the defence of property.

[211] *Revill v Newberry*, above, fn.209.

on the common law involved activities, such as operating winding gear[212] or running trains.[213] These cases are perhaps distinguishable from that of the shooting since the pursuit of the activity was the very reason for the occupation of the land.[214] Where the common law is applicable it should, as a matter of precedent, be that stated by the House of Lords in *Herrington*'s case[215]—in summary, the occupier was not obliged to institute checks for the presence of trespassers or dangers but a duty arose if on the facts of which he knew there was a likelihood of serious harm to the trespasser sufficient to make it inhumane to fail to take steps against it. Putting aside the point that *Herrington*'s case made some allowance for the ability and resources of the individual occupier and that the Act may not do that,[216] this is very similar indeed to the approach of the Act and in *Revill v Newberry*[217] Neill L.J. suggested that the Act might provide useful guidance on the nature of the duty owed at common law. If this is so, then where the precautions required do not involve significant effort or expenditure there will be little, if any, practical difference between the Act and the common law.[218]

The Act is plainly inapplicable to damage to the property of the trespasser. If therefore, C trespasses on D's property and he suffers injury when his car falls down a disused and concealed mine shaft, he may well be able to recover damages for his personal injuries but not for the loss of his car. However, the Act seems to leave the common law untouched on this point.[219] There can be little doubt that where an occupier is in breach of his duty of common humanity at common law his liability would extend beyond the personal injuries suffered by the trespasser to, say, the destruction of his clothing and it has been said, obiter, that there can be liability even where no personal injury is involved—on the facts where the claimant's bees were foraging across land sprayed by the defendant with a poisonous chemical.[220] It is not, however, easy to apply the

---

[212] *Robert Addie and Sons (Collieries) Ltd v Dumbreck* [1929] A.C. 358.

[213] *Videan v British Transport Commission* [1963] 2 Q.B. 650; *British Railways Board v Herrington* [1972] A.C. 877.

[214] Consider the case of the trespasser shot on a grouse moor by its owner. In *Revill* Neill L.J. admitted that if the case were framed as the negligent organisation of a shooting party by the owner of the estate, it would plainly fall within the 1984 Act.

[215] [1972] A.C. 877. See the 12th edn of this work.

[216] Above.

[217] Above, fn.209.

[218] So it seems that the common law is to be looked at to interpret the Act (*Ratcliff v McConnell*, above, fn.203) and the Act is to be looked at to decide the common law!

[219] Section 1(1) provides that the Act is to replace the rules of the common law in respect of personal injury. s.1(8), preventing recovery in respect of "loss of or damage to property", applies only to breaches of duty under s.1.

[220] *Tutton v A.D. Walter Ltd* [1986] Q.B. 61. The judge's decision, however, was that the categories of "visitor" and "trespasser" were inapt terms to be applied to the bees and the ordinary law of negligence applied.

concept of "common humanity" to a situation where there is no personal injury or even no threat of personal injury.

9–28   One more situation appears to be governed by the common law. Suppose the defendant is not the occupier but the occupier's contractor or guest, a situation to which the 1984 Act is plainly inapplicable. There was authority that, as between the trespasser and the non-occupier, trespassory status as such[221] was irrelevant,[222] but the balance of the dicta in *Herrington*'s case pointed towards the removal of any sharp distinction between occupiers and others in this respect,[223] and in *Revill v Newberry* it was assumed that a non-occupier would be in the same position as the occupier.

9–29   The Countryside and Rights of Way Act 2000 introduced a general right of public access to open land for recreational purposes. Persons exercising this right, like those taking advantage of the access agreements under the more limited National Parks and Access to the Countryside Act 1949, are not visitors of the occupier[224] but they are owed a duty under the 1984 Act. However, the occupier's duty to them is specifically excluded in respect of:

> "(a) [A] risk resulting from the existence of any natural feature of the landscape, or any river, stream, ditch or pond whether or not a natural feature, or (b) a risk of [the entrant] suffering injury when passing over, under or through any wall, fence or gate, except by proper use of the gate or of a stile."[225]

This restriction does not apply to dangers arising from anything done by the occupier with the intention of creating the risk, or reckless as to whether the risk is created.[226] At first sight these provisions are curious, for their purpose appears to be to impose a more restricted liability than that to trespassers.[227] The answer may be that their purpose was to head off any argument that, the duty under the 1984 Act being a flexible one, it should embrace such hazards in relation to the lawful entrant exercising his statutory

---

[221] On the facts, a trespasser might of course be unforeseeable when a lawful visitor would not.

[222] *Buckland v Guildford Gas Light and Coke Co* [1949] 1 K.B. 410; *Davis v St Mary's Demolition and Excavation Co Ltd* [1954] 1 W.L.R. 592; *Creed v McGeogh & Sons Ltd* [1955] 1 W.L.R. 1005.

[223] Lord Wilberforce [1972] A.C. at 914 and Lord Pearson at 929. Cf. Lord Diplock at 943. See also the *Restatement, Torts* (2d), ss.383–386.

[224] Occupiers' Liability Act 1984 s.1(4)(a) as substituted by s.13(1) of the Countryside and Rights of Way Act 2000.

[225] Occupiers' Liability Act 1984 s.1(6A) as inserted by s.13(2) of the Countryside and Rights of Way Act 2000. Plants, shrubs and trees "of whatever origin" are regarded as natural features: s.1(6B). See also s.306 of the Marine and Coastal Access Act 2009.

[226] Section 1(6C).

[227] Which the entrants will become if they abuse their privilege: Countryside and Rights of Way Act 2000 s.2.

"right to roam". However, in the light of *Tomlinson*'s case[228] in 2003 it is not very likely that these matters would attract liability under either the 1957 or 1984 Acts. It is also provided that in determining the duty owed to an entrant under the Act of 2000 regard is to be had to the fact that the existence of that right ought not to place an undue burden (whether financial or otherwise) on the occupier, and to the importance of maintaining the character of the countryside.[229]

4. Liability of Vendors and Lessors

A. Contractors
If D is working on B's land and causes injury to a visitor C it is the ordinary principles of negligence which apply, and not the Occupiers' Liability Act 1957. This was established as the law before the Act in *A. C. Billings & Sons Ltd v Riden*[230] but now the distinction between a duty at common law and the common duty of care under the Act will rarely be of importance.

9–30

B. Vendors and Lessors
We are concerned here with the position of a vendor or lessor who creates a danger or defect in his premises and then sells or lets them to another who (or whose successor) suffers damage from that danger or defect. The common law was at first solicitous to the vendor or lessor then, in the 1970s, it swung sharply in favour of the purchaser or tenant but at the price of getting into a quite extraordinary state of complexity and uncertainty. At this stage a complicating strand in the story was the imposition of liability on local authorities for faulty exercise of their statutory functions of approval and inspection; indeed, since the builder had commonly gone into liquidation by the time the problem became apparent, local authorities usually ended up with the bill. One of the main characteristics of the cases in this period was to blur the distinction between contract and tort. From 1988 there was a sharp reaction, culminating

9–31

---

[228] para.9–9, above.
[229] Occupiers' Liability Act 1984 s.1A as inserted by s.13(3) of the Countryside and Rights of Way Act 2000. Also to Codes of Conduct to be issued under that Act. Cf. *Dept of Natural Resources v Harper* [2000] V.R. 1.
[230] [1958] A.C. 240. The case arose before the Act. It is, of course, possible for a contractor to be an occupier within the meaning of the Act: *A.M.F. International Ltd v Magnet Bowling Ltd* [1968] 1 W.L.R. 1028.

in the decision in *Murphy v Brentwood DC*[231] and scores of cases in the middle period must now be regarded as wrongly decided.

i. Vendor

9–32   (a) *Common law.* There is, of course, a contract between vendor and purchaser of land but the implied contractual obligations as to quality are very much less extensive than they are in contracts for the sale of goods even if the vendor is a builder or developer, and hence "in the business" of selling houses. The basic rule is caveat emptor though this may be displaced by express terms in the contract or misrepresentations. In one situation, however, there is a limited implied obligation, namely, when there is a contract for the sale of a house to be built or completed by the vendor.[232] There is then a threefold implied warranty: that the builder will do his work in a good and workmanlike manner,[233] that he will supply good and proper materials and that it will be reasonably fit for human habitation.[234] This warranty avails only the first purchaser from the builder and the limitation period (six years) will start to run when the defective work is done, not when it comes to the purchaser's notice. The latter rule is, however, somewhat mitigated by the fact that if the builder knowingly covers up defective work this will constitute concealment of the cause of action so that time will not run until the purchaser discovers, or could with reasonable diligence have discovered, the defect.[235] In practical terms, the NHBC insurance scheme, which is considered below, is a good deal more important than the implied contractual warranties. While the law of contract may be of limited importance in the context of dwellings it may have a larger role to play in respect of defects in commercial buildings and in such cases recovery by, or for the benefit of, a subsequent transferee may be possible, either by the transferee if the original contracting party's claim is assigned to him[236] or by the contracting party for the benefit of the transferee.[237]

9–33   As for the law of tort, the original position was that if the builder was not himself the vendor he was liable for injury caused by

---

[231] [1991] 1 A.C. 398.

[232] Thus there is no implied warranty if the house is already completed before sale.

[233] The Supply of Goods and Services Act 1982 s.13, seems to apply but not to add anything of substance.

[234] *Hancock v B.W. Brazier (Anerley) Ltd* [1966] 1 W.L.R. 1317.

[235] Limitation Act 1980 s.32(1)(b); *King v Victor Parsons & Co* [1973] 1 W.L.R. 29.

[236] *Darlington BC v Wiltshier Northern* [1995] 1 W.L.R. 68.

[237] See *Linden Gardens Trust Ltd v Lenesta Sludge Disposal* [1994] 1 A.C. 85 and *Alfred McAlpine Construction Ltd v Panatown Ltd* [2001] 1 A.C. 518. As the latter case shows, the builder may give some direct undertaking to the third party. In some cases, the Contracts (Rights of Third Parties) Act 1999 may also be applicable.

negligent work, but if he was also vendor he enjoyed an immunity from suit once the property had been transferred. The rule, which may have been based on an unwillingness to allow contractual and tortious duties to exist concurrently, was established before *Donoghue v Stevenson* and survived that decision.[238] This immunity has now disappeared from the common law and in any event was firmly buried from January 1, 1974 by s.3 of the Defective Premises Act 1972 which provides that:

"[W]here work of construction, repair, maintenance or demolition or any other work[239] is done on or in relation to premises any duty of care owed because of the doing of the work, to persons who might reasonably be expected to be affected by defects in the state of the premises created by the doing of the work shall not be abated by the subsequent disposal of the premises."

However, the question which has given rise to difficulty is "for what type of loss is the builder liable at common law?". Personal injuries caused by structural defects in premises, though not unknown,[240] are rare in comparison with complaints that the premises are inadequately built and are deteriorating, perhaps with a long-term threat of collapse. It was to just such cases that the courts in the 1970s extended the liability of the builder, even though a house which threatens to collapse (or even one which does collapse, causing no injury to person or other property) is surely analogous to a manufactured article which is fragile and inferior in quality, matters which have traditionally been looked on as the province of contract rather than tort. In other words, the loss, though having physical symptoms in the form of, for example, cracks in walls, is in its nature economic. Orthodoxy was restored by the House of Lords in *Murphy v Brentwood DC*.[241] The case concerned only the liability of a local authority in connection with the approval of the plans of a

---

[238] *Otto v Bolton* [1936] 2 K.B. 46. Winfield in (1936) 52 L.Q.R. 313 suggested that if no one had ever sued in tort for injury arising from a ruinous house until after *Donoghue v Stevenson* the "jerry-builder" would then have been held to be the "neighbour" of the injured person.

[239] To be construed *ejusdem generis*?

[240] See, e.g. *Otto v Bolton*, above, fn.238; *Sharpe v E.T. Sweeting & Son Ltd* [1963] 1 W.L.R. 605.

[241] [1991] 1 A.C. 398. Cooke, "An Impossible Distinction" (1991) 107 L.Q.R. 46; Giles and Szyzczak, "Negligence and Defective Buildings: Demolishing the Foundations of *Anns*?" (1991) 11 L.S. 85; Howarth, "Negligence after Murphy: Time to Re-think" [1991] 50 C.L.J. 58; Markesinis and Deakin, "The Random Element in their Lordships' Infallible Judgment" (1992) 55 M.L.R. 619; Wallace, "Anns Beyond Repair" (1991) 107 L.Q.R. 228.

house[242] but the reasoning is inescapably applicable to the builder's liability for defective premises—indeed much of the discussion is couched directly in terms of the builder's liability.[243] It is now clear that in the absence of a special relationship of proximity such as existed in *Junior Books v Veitchi*[244] (and which, it appears, does not normally exist between the builder and even the first purchaser of a standard house[245]) there is no liability in tort for defects in quality in the building. In fact, even the previous case law had not gone so far as to impose such liability in all cases[246] but had done so only where the defect in the premises presented an imminent danger to the health or safety of the persons occupying it.[247]

9–34   Essentially, the basis of this approach was that because, if the defect had not been discovered and someone had been injured, the defendant would have been liable for that injury on the principle of *Donoghue v Stevenson*, therefore it would be absurd to deny liability for the cost of preventing that injury arising.[248] However, this reasoning is now held to be fallacious because once, it is said, the defect becomes apparent (which is, ex hypothesi, the first point at which any claim can be made) it no longer presents a danger.

> "The injury will not now ever occur unless the claimant causes it to do so by courting a danger of which he is aware and his expenditure [in removing the danger] is incurred not in preventing

---

[242] The plans had been prepared by apparently competent consulting engineers, but since the authority was under no duty in respect of the loss in question the HL did not find it necessary to consider how far the authority was entitled to rely on the engineers.

[243] *DoE v Thomas Bates & Son Ltd* [1991] A.C. 499, decided on the same day, is a direct authority applying *Murphy* to a builder.

[244] See para.5–44, above.

[245] It is not entirely clear why this should be so with regard to the first purchaser. If even in the absence of a contract there may be a special relationship of proximity sufficiently akin to contract to attract liability for economic loss (*Junior Books*), should there not be such liability where there is a contract? Despite occasional wistful looks in that direction (para.1–8, above) we do not have a doctrine of *non cumul des obligations*. Where the house was yet to be constructed there would, after all, be a more extensive contractual warranty. Nevertheless, in *Lancashire and Cheshire Association of Baptist Churches Inc v Howard & Seddon Partnership* [1993] 3 All E.R. 467 liability in tort was denied even though there would seem to have been a clear contractual duty (the right of action for which was assumed to be statute-barred for the purpose of the proceedings). Since the case concerned "business" premises and the defendants acted as both architects and builders it seems to make *Junior Books* even harder to explain. Cf. the majority in *Bryan v Maloney* (1995) 182 C.L.R. 609, who point out that it appears to be the classic instance of assumption of responsibility and actual reliance.

[246] At least after *Anns v Merton LBC* [1978] A.C. 728.

[247] [1978] A.C. 728 at 760. The logic of this requirement lies in the fact that the local authority's duty of care (with which the cases were primarily concerned) originated in its functions under the public health legislation. Though the measure of damages is not much discussed in the case law, it seems that liability would only have been in such an amount as was necessary to avert the danger.

[248] See Lord Oliver in *Murphy*, above, fn.241, at 488. In *Dutton v Bognor Regis UDC* [1972] 1 Q.B. 373 at 396 (overruled in *Murphy*) Lord Denning M.R. described any attempted distinction between the two cases as "impossible".

an otherwise inevitable injury but in order to enable him to continue to use the property."[249]

The argument that the loss is in truth economic and that the "averting of danger" does not change its nature is logically compelling,[250] though it raises severe difficulties for an owner who simply cannot afford to abandon his house.[251] The justification that if the claimant does not abandon the property and suffers injury he is the author of his own loss may, however, mislead if it is divorced from the underlying nature of his complaint. Suppose, for example, that the claimant owns property which is initially sound and the defendant by negligence causes it damage which renders it dangerous. It may well be that if the claimant chooses to remain in the property (unrepaired because he cannot immediately afford to repair it) rather than move into temporary accommodation, he is the author of his own loss if the property collapses on him,[252] but no one would suggest that he was therefore precluded from recovering the cost of repairs from the defendant. In such a case he had something which was perfect and which was rendered imperfect by what the defendant did; in *Murphy* the essence of the complaint was that the property was imperfect from the beginning, it was not "damaged", it was simply worth less than he paid for it. The argument that if the house owner remained and suffered injury he would be the author of his own loss was advanced in a slightly different context in *Targett v Torfaen Borough Council*[253] where the claimant was a weekly tenant of a council house and was aware of the defect and the danger presented by it, but had failed to persuade the council to repair it. The Court of Appeal, in finding for the claimant, distinguished *Murphy* on the ground that the House of Lords was there concerned with the nature of the loss and could not be taken to have intended to lay down any absolute rule to the effect that a claimant suffering personal injury from a defective building was automatically barred by his knowledge of the defect.[254] So to hold would be absurdly

---

[249] *Murphy*, above, fn.241, at 488 per Lord Oliver. See also *DoE v Thomas Bates & Son Ltd* [1991] 1 A.C. 499 (building safe if used below design loading).

[250] In fact, to impose a requirement of imminent danger leads to absurdity, as Lord Bridge points out at 480. Assume that the building is not at present a danger, that the defect can be cured at a cost of £1,000 now, but that it will gradually get worse and become a danger, at which point the cost of cure is likely to be £5,000. The requirement appears to make the owner wait until the later time in order to have a claim.

[251] It is suggested in *Murphy* at 472 that many householders will have loss insurance (subsidence is the standard problem). *Murphy* itself was said to be "largely" a contest between loss insurers and the local authority's liability insurers; but nowadays loss insurance in respect of subsidence commonly excludes cases where it is caused by a structural defect, as opposed to, e.g. ground movement.

[252] The case is more obvious with continued use of a chattel, e.g. an unroadworthy car.

[253] [1992] 3 All E.R. 27.

[254] The CA pointed out that its own decision in *Rimmer v Liverpool CC* [1985] Q.B. 1, which was inconsistent with this view, had not been referred to in *Murphy*.

unrealistic[255] for many householders and the question should rather be determined by asking whether in all the circumstances it was reasonable, in the light of the danger, to remain in the house.[256]

9–35   *Murphy v Brentwood* in no way casts doubt upon the proposition that if a negligently constructed building causes damage to other property, whether of the claimant or a third party, the defendant is liable for that.[257] So if the claimant's house collapses he can, at least on the assumption that he was unaware of imminent danger, recover damages for loss of the contents. However, a certain amount of obscurity still remains on the question of what is "other property". In *D.&F. Estates Ltd v Church Commissioners*[258] (which had anticipated many of the issues in *Murphy*) Lord Bridge had, to use his words in *Murphy*[259]:

> "[M]ooted the possibility that in complex structures or complex chattels one part of a structure or chattel might, when it caused damage to another part of the same structure or chattel, be regarded in the law of tort as having caused damage to 'other property' for the purpose of the application of *Donoghue v Stevenson* principles."

This theory of the complex structure was not embraced with any enthusiasm in the *D.&F. Estates* case, rather it was offered as a possible explanation of the line of cases centring on *Anns v Merton*, which the House of Lords was at that stage unwilling to overrule without further argument. It is clear as a result of *Murphy* that these cases cannot be supported in this way. When a single builder builds a house from the foundations upwards he is creating a single, integrated unit and it is completely unrealistic to argue that the foundations (the usual source of problems) are one piece of property and, when they fail, they cause damage to "other" property—the walls, floors, etc. of the house.[260] However, some difficult and perhaps arbitrary lines will still have to be drawn. If, for example, something ancillary to the building (say, the central heating boiler) malfunctions and sets the building on fire then the manufacturer of the boiler (or the negligent installer) would be liable for the damage

---

[255] Nicholls V.C. at [1992] 3 All E.R. 37.

[256] Both *Targett* and *Rimmer* concern lettings but no distinction can be drawn between tenants and purchasers. If anything, the former are likely to be in a better position to find alternative accommodation than the latter.

[257] Illustrated by *Bellefield Computer Services v E Turner & Sons* [2000] BLR 97 and [2002] EWCA Civ 1823; [2003] Lloyd's Rep. P.N. 53.

[258] [1989] A.C. 177.

[259] [1991] 1 A.C. at 476.

[260] However, the position was held to be different where the defendants inserted underpinning (itself defective) to cure an existing defect: *Jacobs v Morton & Partners* (1996) 72 B.L.R. 92.

to the building. Lords Keith and Bridge would be willing to extend this to the electrical system of the building[261] and Lord Jauncey would even go so far as to bring within this principle a case where a separate contractor had negligently installed the steel frame on which the structure of the building depended.[262]

Even where no physical damage has been done there remains the possibility that the cost of "pre-emptive repairs" may be recoverable in one situation. Lord Bridge suggested[263] that:

> "[I]f a building stands so close to the boundary of the building owner's land that after discovery of the dangerous defect it remains a potential source of injury to persons or property on neighbouring land or on the highway, the building owner ought, in principle, to be entitled to recover in tort from the negligent builder the cost of obviating the danger."

His Lordship did not set out the reasoning behind this possible exception, but it could perhaps be justified on the basis that the building would constitute a nuisance in respect of which the adjoining landowner[264] would be able to obtain an injunction requiring repair or demolition.[265] Alternatively, it may represent a rather broader principle whereby the claimant may recover the cost of removing a danger which threatens others[266] (for example members of his family, visitors and even trespassers) and for which the defendant is responsible. If this is confined to the cost of demolition where that is less than the cost of repairs it does not represent too serious a derogation from the reasoning upon which *Murphy* is based.

While *Murphy v Brentwood* certainly clarified the law, it has been **9–36** the subject of widespread criticism and three major Commonwealth courts have declined to accept it. In *Winnipeg Condominium Corp v*

---

[261] [1991] 1 A.C at 470–478.
[262] [1991] 1 A.C. at 497. In this case it is clearly essential to insist on the defendant being a separate contractor, otherwise we would be a long way back towards *Anns v Merton*; but if a sole builder negligently instals something which is clearly not a fixture he would surely be liable for resulting damage to the building. Where is the line to be drawn? The suggestions in *The Orjula* [1995] 2 Lloyd's Rep. 395 and *Payne v John Setchell Ltd* [2002] P.N.L.R. 146 that *Murphy* "disapproves" the complex structure theory is, with respect, something of an over-simplification.
[263] [1991] A.C. at 475.
[264] Or the local authority under the "statutory nuisance" procedure: para.14–1, below.
[265] Though the builder may be said to have created the nuisance, no injunction could be obtained against him because he is not in occupation. Though the building owner's loss is still "economic", it seems just that the builder should have to pay the cost, imposed on the house owner by law, of averting the threatened collapse.
[266] See *The Orjula* [1995] 2 Lloyd's Rep. 395, where Mance J. held it arguable that it could apply to the cost of decontamination work on a cargo ordered by harbour authorities.

Bird Construction Co[267] the Supreme Court of Canada held that a remote purchaser might recover in negligence against a builder the cost of remedying dangerous defects in the building. In *Bryan v Maloney*[268] the majority of the High Court of Australia held that such a purchaser might recover in respect of defects in quality which rendered a house less valuable even though they presented no danger.[269] In the New Zealand case of *Invercargill CC v Hamlin*,[270] as in *Murphy* itself, the liability of the builder was not directly in issue because he had gone out of business, but the New Zealand Court of Appeal rejected the whole line of English development leading up to *Murphy* by imposing liability upon the local authority for negligence in inspection during construction.[271] The decision was upheld by the Privy Council[272] on the bases that (1) New Zealand courts were entitled to develop their version of the common law in accordance with local policy considerations and community expectations, of which they were the best judge[273] and (2) there were differences in the statutory backgrounds, in particular the existence in England of the Defective Premises Act 1972, which had been an important factor lying behind the decision in *Murphy*.[274]

As we have seen, *Murphy v Brentwood*, like most of the earlier building cases, was a claim against the local authority. The House of Lords in *Murphy* agreed with the reasoning in *Anns v Merton* in so far as it had held that any liability of the local authority could not be more extensive than that of the builder, who is, after all, primarily responsible. If the duty of the local authority is co-extensive with that of the builder then the authority would be liable in the comparatively rare case where there is personal injury or damage to other property. However, the House of Lords did not have to decide whether the local authority's liability extended even this far and the

[267] (1995) 121 D.L.R. (4th) 193 (thereby reviving the reasoning in the dissent in *Rivtow Marine v Washington Iron Works* (1973) 40 D.L.R. (3d) 530).

[268] (1995) 182 C.L.R. 609. See, however, the criticism by Clarke J.A. of the assumptions upon which this case is based in *Woolahra M.C. v Sved* (1996) 40 N.S.W.L.R. 101 (in which the majority found an absence of reliance on the facts); *Fangrove Pty Ltd v Tod Group Holdings Pty Ltd* [1999] 2 Qd. R. 236.

[269] Brennan J., dissenting, would have imposed liability, in line with the *Winnipeg* case, if the expenditure had been to remove a danger. Cf. *Woolcock St Investments Pty Ltd v CDG Pty Ltd* [2004] HCA 16; 216 C.L.R. 515 (no duty because no duty in circumstances to initial purchaser).

[270] [1994] 3 N.Z.L.R. 513.

[271] The position is different with commercial buildings: *Te Mata Properties Ltd v Hastings DC* [2008] NZCA 446; [2009] 1 N.Z.L.R. 460; *Queenstown Lakes DC v Charterhall Trustees Ltd* [2009] NZCA 374.

[272] [1996] A.C. 624.

[273] A fortiori this is the case for Canadian and Australian courts, since there was no appeal from those jurisdictions. Lord Lloyd referred to the majority view in the High Court of Australia in *Bryan v Maloney* as "a possible and indeed respectable view".

[274] Note, however, that the litigation in *Invercargill* had commenced 18 years after the construction of the house, and any such claim under the Defective Premises Act would have been long barred.

decision should not therefore be taken as approval of *Anns* even to this very limited extent.[275] This issue is part of the wider question of how far statutory functions which do not attract an action for breach of statutory duty can nevertheless be the basis of a common law duty of care.[276]

Finally, what of the house owner himself? If he does work on his house in a negligent manner and this injures a subsequent owner then there would be liability in negligence.[277] If, however, he has not created the danger by his own action but knew or ought to have known about it at the time of sale it is unlikely that any liability would be imposed upon him. It is true that such a liability has been imposed upon a trader disposing of goods[278] but such a great departure from the principle of caveat emptor would, in the case of realty, be open only to the House of Lords[279] or the legislature.[280]

(b) *Statute.* A recurrent theme of the speeches in *Murphy v* **9–37** *Brentwood* is the need for the courts not to trespass upon ground already covered by parliamentary action. Some years before the decision in *Dutton v Bognor Regis Urban DC* started the short-lived revolution in the common law the issue of liability for defective premises was referred to the Law Commission and the result was the Defective Premises Act 1972, which was passed more or less contemporaneously with *Dutton*'s case and which came into force on January 1, 1974.[281] It cannot be pretended that the development of the law in this area provides a model in law reform techniques. As Roskill L.J. remarked in one of the earlier cases[282]:

"[I]n the [early 1970s] law reform was being pursued through two different channels—the Law Commission and Parliament on the one hand, and the courts on the other—without either apparently

---

[275] Lord Bridge said [1991] 1 A.C. at 479: "I am content for present purposes to assume, though I am by no means satisfied that the assumption is correct, that where the local authority ... have in fact approved the defective plans or inspected the defective foundations and negligently failed to discover the defect, their potential liability in tort is co-extensive with that of the builder."

[276] See para.5–46, above.

[277] *Hone v Benson* (1978) 248 E.G. 1013; Defective Premises Act 1972 s.3. For mere defects of quality there is of course no liability because of *Murphy v Brentwood*. The law is the same in New Zealand (where *Murphy* is not followed) because of the importance of encouraging socially useful do-it-yourself activity: *Willis v Castellein* [1993] 3 N.Z.L.R. 103.

[278] *Andrews v Hopkinson* [1957] 1 Q.B. 229 (dealer selling goods to a finance company to be let by it to the claimant on hire-purchase terms).

[279] See *Rimmer v Liverpool CC* [1985] Q.B. 1 (a landlord-tenant case).

[280] It may be of some significance that the Defective Premises Bill, cl.3, would have made the "mere" vendor liable in respect of defects of which he knew, but this was rejected by Parliament.

[281] See Law Com. No.40 (1970).

[282] *Sparham-Souter v Town and Country Developments (Essex) Ltd* [1976] Q.B. 858 at 876.

appreciating what developments the other was seeking to make."

The common law developments had the effect of making the Act something of a dead letter but *Murphy v Brentwood* has now restored it to primacy. The provisions of the Act cannot be excluded or restricted by any agreement.[283]

9–38   Section 1 of the Defective Premises Act 1972 imposes upon persons who undertake work for, or in connection with, the provision[284] of a dwelling[285] a statutory duty to see that the work taken on is done[286] in a workmanlike or professional manner, with proper materials and so that as regards that work the dwelling will be fit for habitation when completed.[287] The range of persons on whom the duty is imposed therefore goes beyond the builder himself and includes the architect[288] and surveyor and any sub-contractors involved,[289] though the manufacturer of standard components is not covered.[290] The duty is owed not only to the persons ordering the work but also to every person who then or later acquires an interest (whether legal or equitable) in the dwelling. The duty is therefore a statutory hybrid, having characteristics of both contract and tort: on the one hand, it covers mere defects of quality (provided they make the house unfit for human habitation) without any necessity for imminent danger of personal injury; on the other hand it may pass

---

[283] Section 6(3).

[284] This does not include work of rectification on an existing building: *Jacobs v Morton & Partners* (1996) 72 B.L.R. 92.

[285] Industrial and commercial premises are therefore outside the scope of this section. Such premises are also outside the scope of the NHBC scheme.

[286] The Act applies as much to failing to do necessary work as to doing work badly: *Andrews v Schooling* [1991] 1 W.L.R. 783.

[287] This is in some ways stricter than a duty of care. It corresponds closely with the implied warranty at common law in a contract for the construction of a house (see para.9–32, above) and in that context it has been held that the warranty in relation to materials is strict: *Hancock v B.W. Brazier (Anerley) Ltd* [1966] 1 W.L.R. 1317; see also Supply of Goods and Services Act 1982 s.4. A sub-contractor may now also owe a duty of care at common law in respect of defects of quality in the very limited circumstances in which *Junior Books Ltd v Veitchi Co Ltd* applies: para.5–40, above.

[288] *Payne v John Setchell Ltd* [2002] P.N.L.R. 146 (structural engineer).

[289] See also s.2(4) (developers), but note the important provisions of s.1(2), (3), which will generally relieve a person of liability if he does the work properly in accordance with instructions given by another. This would appear to cover not only the builder on whom the client imposes detailed specifications, but also the sub-contractor who receives instructions from the builder. However, "a person shall not be treated ... as having given instructions for the doing of work merely because he has agreed to the work being done in a specified manner".

[290] He may, however, be liable under the Consumer Protection Act 1987 Pt I (para.10–16, below) and if he were negligent he might be in breach of a common law duty. A builder held liable under s.1 might anyway seek a contractual indemnity from him. A local authority exercising powers of inspection probably cannot be said to, "take on work for or in connection with the provision of a dwelling"; but cf. the doubts of Lord Denning M.R. and Roskill L.J. in *Sparham-Souter v Town and Country Developments (Essex) Ltd* [1976] Q.B. 858 at 870, 877.

along a chain of purchasers notwithstanding the lack of privity between them and the builder.[291]

For many years the operation of the Act was very substantially restricted because it has no application to houses protected by an "approved scheme".[292] In practice this was the scheme operated by the National House-Building Council (NHBC), which covers the great majority of newly-constructed dwelling-houses. The NHBC scheme, though by no means unlimited, generally provides superior cover in comparison with the Act because claims for major structural defects may be made for up to 10 years and, although the primary responsibility for defects in the initial period lies upon the builder, his liability is underwritten by the scheme. However, the NHBC no longer submits the scheme for approval[293] and the Act now has a much wider field of operation. However, it is still very much less favourable to the claimant than the common law cases struck down by *Murphy v Brentwood* because the six-year limitation period begins to run when the dwelling is completed[294] whereas at common law time might start to run at a later date, when some physical symptoms appeared (though they might not then necessarily be observable by the owner).[295] Indeed, Parliament by the Latent Damage Act 1986 sought to improve the claimant's position still further by providing, in actions for negligence, an alternative limitation period of three years running from the time when the claimant could reasonably have known about the damage (subject to a "long-stop" of 15 years from the last act of negligence) and specifically providing for the case where the property was acquired by a subsequent purchaser.[296] The Act is not confined to building cases but they were undoubtedly the prime cause of its enactment and *Murphy v Brentwood* removed most of them from the ambit of the Act by declaring that there is simply no cause of action in the

---

[291] "The analogy is not with the common law of tort but with the rule contained in the Bills of Lading Act 1855 that a subsequent purchaser of goods carried by sea succeeds to the rights of the person who contracted with the carrier thereof": Weir, *Casebook on Tort*, 3rd edn, p.24.

[292] See s.2.

[293] This seems to have begun with the 1988 amendments and for some years appears not to have been widely known: see Wallace, "*Anns* Beyond Repair" (1991) 107 L.Q.R. 228.

[294] Section 1(5).

[295] The reach of the common law is illustrated by *Dennis v Charnwood BC* [1983] Q.B. 409. Barrow-upon-Soar UDC in 1955 negligently passed plans for the claimant's house. The defendants succeeded to their liabilities in 1974 under the local government reorganisation. An action commenced in 1978 succeeded. Lawton L.J. commented that, "a compulsory insurance scheme for builders of houses might provide better justice than the uncertainties of litigation", but the claim in *Dennis* would have been far outside the time limits of the NHBC scheme or the Latent Damage Act (below) and it must be doubted whether such long-term cover would be actuarially acceptable.

[296] See para.26–11, below.

first place.[297] It is one of the curiosities of this area that, just as *Anns v Merton* contained no mention of the Defective Premises Act 1972, so *Murphy v Brentwood* is silent on the Latent Damage Act 1986.[298]

Finally, there are the Building Regulations,[299] which impose detailed obligations on builders. In *Anns v Merton* Lord Wilberforce thought that the builder might be liable for breach of statutory duty by reason of non-compliance with building byelaws, the then equivalent of the building regulations,[300] though this was doubted even before *Murphy v Brentwood*.[301] It seems inconceivable that Lord Wilberforce's view can represent the law after *Murphy,* especially bearing in mind that there has existed since 1974 a statutory provision creating just such a cause of action but which has never been brought into force.[302]

ii. Lessor

9–39   (a) *Common law.* A lease is a contract as well as an estate in land, but at common law the range of implied terms relating to the fitness of the premises is very limited. There is an implied warranty in the letting of furnished premises that they are fit for occupation at the commencement of the tenancy[303] and the House of Lords has held that in the case of a "high rise" block, obligations may be implied with regard to the maintenance of such necessary things as stairs and lifts.[304] These obligations sound in contract and hence avail only the tenant, unless the Contracts (Rights of Third Parties) Act 1999 applies.[305] As for tort, the lessor's position was equated with that of the vendor and he was immune from liability for negligence in

[297] Where there is damage to other property or personal injury time will run under the general law of limitation from the date when that injury or damage occurs.
[298] However, the two cases are not on all fours. The HL in *Anns* can fairly be said to have ignored a legislative scheme introduced into Parliament when there was no clear liability at common law and which might thereby have been regarded as "pre-empting" the area. At the time of the Latent Damage Act the common law liability seemed fairly solidly established and Parliament may be taken to have intended to deal with the ancillary problems thrown up by it without necessarily giving it positive legislative approval.
[299] Now SI 2000/2531.
[300] [1978] A.C. 728 at 759. Cf. *Solomons v R. Gertzenstein Ltd* [1954] 2 Q.B. 243 (London Building Acts).
[301] *Worlock v S.A.W.S.* (1982) 26 E.G. 774; *Perry v Tendring DC* (1984) 30 Build. L.R. 118.
[302] Building Act 1984 s.38 (formerly Health and Safety at Work, etc. Act 1974 s.71). Is there another example of a provision which has lain dormant for 26 years? If it were brought into force it is very arguable that the definition of "damage" would lead to the same result as under *Murphy.*
[303] *Collins v Hopkins* [1923] 2 K.B. 617.
[304] *Liverpool CC v Irwin* [1977] A.C. 239. As to licences for occupation of business premises, see *Wettern Electric Ltd v Welsh Development Agency* [1983] Q.B. 796.
[305] Which will require that the contract (a) purports to confer a benefit on the third party and (b) sufficiently "identifies" him.

respect of defects created by him before the demise.[306] This immunity has now died along with that of the vendor,[307] subject to the
point that the range of damage recoverable is restricted by *Murphy
v Brentwood.*

(b) *Statute.* Sections 1 and 3 of the Defective Premises Act, which **9–40**
have been discussed above in relation to vendors, apply equally to
lessors.[308] Statute, however, also imposes certain non-excludable
obligations during the currency of the lease. By s.8 of the Landlord
and Tenant Act 1985 there is implied into contracts for the letting of
a house at a very low rent an undertaking by the landlord that it is,
and will be kept, fit for human habitation, but the rent limits are so
low that the section is never in practice applicable.[309] By s.11 of the
same Act[310] there is imposed upon the landlord in relation to leases
for less than seven years an obligation to carry out certain repairs to
the structure and to installations for sanitation and the supply of
water, gas and electricity. Though primarily designed to allow the
tenant to compel the landlord to do repairs, these provisions would
also avail the tenant if, for example, he suffered personal injury as
a result of the landlord's breach of obligation, but being contractual
covenants their breach gave rise to no liability towards the tenant's
family or visitors. This was first changed by s.4 of the Occupiers'
Liability Act 1957, which imposed on the landlord a tortious duty of
care in respect of dangers arising from default in his repairing
obligations under the lease.[311] This was replaced and carried very
much further by s.4 of the Defective Premises Act 1972. Where
premises are let under a tenancy which puts on the landlord an
obligation to the tenant for the maintenance or repair of the premises, the landlord owes to all persons who might reasonably be
expected to be affected by defects in the state of the premises a duty

---

[306] *Robbins v Jones* (1863) 15 C.B.(N.S.) 221. "Fraud apart, there is no law against letting a
tumbledown house": at 240 per Erle C.J.
[307] *Anns v Merton London Borough* [1978] A.C. 728 was a case of a long lease, but where the
landlord did not create the defect, only the House of Lords can impose a duty: *Rimmer v
Liverpool CC* [1985] Q.B. 1; *McNerny v Lambeth BC* [1989] 19 E.G. 77; *Boldack v East
Lindsey DC* (1999) 31 H.L.R. 41.
[308] See para.9–38, above.
[309] *Quick v Taff-Ely BC* [1986] Q.B. 809 at 817. For an update, see Law Com. No.238, s.4.3.
In the original legislation of 1885 the rental figure in London was £20 per annum, now it
is £80. The 1885 figure was 222 per cent of the average rent. In 1995 the statutory figure
was less than 4 per cent of the average council house rent.
[310] Extended by the Housing Act 1988 s.116, to cover parts of the building and installations
outside the demised premises.
[311] Whether those obligations arose from express covenants in the lease or from the equivalent
statutory obligations existing before the Landlord and Tenant Act 1985. Care should be
taken to note that we are now concerned with dangers arising on the premises which the
landlord has demised. If he retains part in his own occupation (e.g. staircases and lifts in
a block of flats), he is liable for that *qua* occupier under the general provisions of the
Occupiers' Liability Act: above.

to take such care as is reasonable in all the circumstances to see that they are reasonably safe from personal injury or damage to their property caused by a defect within the maintenance or repairing obligation.[312] The duty of care is not limited by requirements of notice which might be relevant to the contractual obligation.[313] Most significant of all, a landlord who has a power, express or implied, to enter and repair is to be treated for the purposes of the section (but no other[314]) as if he were under an obligation to the tenant to repair.[315] The obvious beneficiaries of s.4 are the tenant's family and visitors, but other persons who might reasonably be expected to be affected include trespassers,[316] neighbours and passers-by[317] and even the tenant himself, not withstanding the existence of a contractual obligation to him.[318] The tenant, however, is not owed any duty in respect of a defect arising from, or continuing because of, a failure to carry out an obligation expressly imposed on the tenant by the tenancy.[319]

---

[312] "Safety" is narrower than "fitness for habitation": Law Com. No.238, s.5.28. Nor is the landlord required to make safe an existing "design" defect: *Alker v Collingwood Housing Association* [2007] EWCA Civ 343; [2007] 1 W.L.R. 2230.

[313] *Sykes v Harry* [2001] EWCA Civ 167; [2001] Q.B. 1014. In relation to gas appliances the landlord is under what appears to be an absolute duty to maintain in safe condition under the Gas Safety (Installation and Use) Regulations 1994, SI 1886.

[314] Thus the tenant could not compel such a landlord to repair under the Landlord and Tenant Act 1985 s.17.

[315] Section 4(4). *Smith v Bradford Metropolitan Council* (1982) 44 P.&C.R. 171; *Barrett v Lounova Ltd* [1989] 1 All E.R. 351. Such a power is said to exist in the case of small houses let on periodic tenancies (*Mint v Good* [1951] 1 K.B. 517, para.14–27, below).

[316] Cf. the position of the tenant-occupier himself: para.9–25, above.

[317] In other words the section creates liability in nuisance, though it probably adds nothing to the common law in this respect: para.14–27, below.

[318] *Sykes v Harry*, above, fn.313.

[319] Section 4(4).

CHAPTER 10

LIABILITY FOR DEFECTIVE PRODUCTS[1]

THIS chapter is primarily concerned with the liability in tort of **10–1** manufacturers (and certain other transferors) of defective products but since transfers of products normally take place pursuant to a contract, a realistic picture of the incidence of liability can only be obtained by bearing the relevant contractual principles in mind. Where a claimant is injured by a product transferred to him under a contract of sale[2] he may rely, subject to any valid exemption clause,[3] upon the seller's implied undertakings as to compliance with

---

[1] Miller, *Product Liability and Safety Encyclopaedia*; Miller and Goldberg, *Products Liability*, 2nd edn; Howells, *Law of Product Liability*; Stapleton, *Product Liability* (1994).

[2] The duties of the creditor under a contract of hire-purchase are for practical purposes the same as those of a seller: see the Supply of Goods (Implied Terms) Act 1973, as amended by the Consumer Credit Act 1974. The Supply of Goods and Services Act 1982 implies similar terms into other contracts for the transfer of goods (e.g. exchange) and hire of goods. Most material used in medical treatment here will not be "supplied" under contract. However, the Supreme Court of Canada has declined to imply an absolute warranty of fitness where there is a contract: *ter Neuzen v Korn* (1995) 127 D.L.R. (4th) 577.

[3] If the purchaser is a "consumer" the clause will be void under the Unfair Contract Terms Act 1977, s.6(2). Otherwise it will be subject to a test of reasonableness: s.6(3).

description, satisfactory quality,[4] fitness for purpose and compliance with sample under the Sale of Goods Act 1979.[5] These undertakings give rise to absolute obligations, i.e. the seller is liable if the goods do not come up to the standard required by the Act even though he has taken all possible care that they should do so and is in no way to blame for the defect.[6] Though the purpose of these undertakings when they were being developed at common law[7] was probably to allow the buyer a remedy for the financial loss he suffered in acquiring goods of inferior quality,[8] it has been accepted for many years that they also allow recovery for consequential damage to other property and, most significantly, for personal injuries.[9] The existence of this strict liability in the seller (often, in modern conditions, a much larger organisation than the manufacturer[10]) means that as far as the purchaser is concerned his right of action in tort, dependent on proof of negligence, is often of academic interest and may only be utilised where the seller is insolvent or cannot, for some other reason, be successfully sued.[11] Where a contractual action is successfully pursued then, in theory, the implied terms in the chain of contracts between manufacturer and retailer will lead to the manufacturer bearing the ultimate responsibility, but in practice this chain may be broken by the insolvency of a "middleman" or by some valid exemption clause.[12] The contractual liability outlined above is of no assistance to persons injured by the product who have

[4] By s.14(2D) of the Sale of Goods Act (inserted by the Sale and Supply of Goods to Consumers Regulations 2002 SI 3045/2002) the relevant circumstances in determining whether goods are of satisfactory quality may include public statements (e.g. in advertisements) made by the manufacturer.

[5] Directive 1999/44/EC required the UK to modify the law of contract governing consumer sales. This was done by the Sale and Supply of Goods to Consumers Regulations 2002 (SI 3045/2002) inserting Pt 5A in the Sale of Goods Act. However, this is more concerned with remedies like repair and cancellation than with substantive questions of breach and does not derogate from any existing rights under the Sale of Goods Act.

[6] He may, of course, have an indemnity under the contract of sale between him and his supplier, and so on up the chain to the manufacturer.

[7] The Sale of Goods Act 1893 (the fundamental structure of which is repeated in the 1979 Act) was a restatement of the common law.

[8] The use of "merchantable quality" (until the 1994 amendment, which substituted "satisfactory quality") to describe one of the obligations under the Sale of Goods Act, s.14, is revealing.

[9] *Godley v Perry* [1960] 1 W.L.R. 9 is an excellent example. See also *Grant v Australian Knitting Mills Ltd* [1936] A.C. 85.

[10] Some retailers (e.g. Marks & Spencer, British Home Stores) affix their own brand name to all or some of their goods, though the goods are of course manufactured by specialist manufacturers. For the tort implications of this, see para.10–15, below.

[11] There is nothing to prevent the claimant suing both seller (in contract) and manufacturer (in tort): *Grant v Australian Knitting Mills Ltd* [1936] A.C. 85. Furthermore, in the present state of the law (para.1–8, above) there is nothing to prevent the claimant suing the seller in tort. In *Nitrigin Eireann Teoranta v Inco Alloys Ltd* [1992] 1 All E.R. 854 this gave the claimants the important advantage of a later starting point for the limitation period.

[12] Or even as in *Lambert v Lewis* [1982] A.C. 225, by a simple lack of records. These intermediate contracts will not be consumer transactions so that the exception clauses will be valid if shown to be reasonable under the Unfair Contract Terms Act 1977.

not acquired any interests in it by contract—members of the purchaser's family,[13] passers-by[14] or donees from the buyer[15] and they
will not generally be assisted by the Contracts (Rights of Third
Parties) Act 1999.[16] It is this class of "ultimate consumers" who are
most likely to seek to rely on tort.

1. LIABILITY AT COMMON LAW

Before *Donoghue v Stevenson*[17] was decided in 1932, it was doubtful whether the transferor of a product owed any duty to the ultimate
transferee (in the absence of a contractual relationship between
them) unless it belonged to the class of "dangerous chattels"[18] or
was actually known to the transferor to be dangerous.[19] The classification of products into those which are dangerous and those which
are not is, however, an unsatisfactory one and Scrutton L.J. confessed that he did not understand the difference:

10–2

> "[B]etween a thing dangerous in itself, as poison, and a thing not
> dangerous as a class, but by negligent construction dangerous as
> a particular thing. The latter, if anything, seems to me the more
> dangerous of the two; it is a wolf in sheep's clothing instead of an
> obvious wolf."[20]

Donoghue v Stevenson finally established, by a majority of three to
two, that apart from contract and without reference to any special
rule about dangerous chattels, there are circumstances in which a

[13] *Evans v Triplex Safety Glass Co* [1936] 1 All E.R. 283.
[14] *Stennett v Hancock* [1939] 2 All E.R. 578.
[15] *Donoghue v Stevenson* [1932] A.C. 562; *Fisher v Harrods* [1966] 1 Lloyd's Rep. 500.
Where the original buyer has resold the product to the claimant there will be no implied
condition of satisfactory quality or fitness for purpose in that contract unless the sale was
in the course of a business: Sale of Goods Act 1979 s.14(2), (3).
[16] Because a third party seeking to enforce a term in a contract to which he is not a party must
show (a) that the contract purported to confer a benefit on him and (b) that he was
identified by name, class or description in the contract. Nor will the Act generally be of
assistance to the buyer from the retailer seeking to establish a contractual right against the
manufacturer. However, art.6 Directive 1999/44/EC required that manufacturers' guarantees should be legally enforceable and the Sale and Supply of Goods to Consumers
Regulations 2002 SI 3045/2002 made them so. They probably were already (as a collateral
contract) where the buyer knew he would get one before he entered into the sale contract
with the retailer.
[17] [1932] A.C. 562, para.5–5, above.
[18] The "privity of contract fallacy" held that because the manufacturer (A) had a contract
with the retailer (B) he could not owe a tort duty to the consumer (C).
[19] If the fraud of the transferor could be proved he would be liable for that: *Langridge v Levy*
(1837) 2 M. & W. 519; (1838) M. & W. 337.
[20] *Hodge v Anglo-American Oil Co* (1922) 12 Ll.L. Rep. 183 at 187.

person owes a duty of care in respect of products. Lord Atkin laid down the following principle[21] for both Scots and English law:

"A manufacturer of products, which he sells in such a form as to show that he intends them to reach the ultimate consumer in the form in which they left him with no reasonable possibility of intermediate examination and with the knowledge that the absence of reasonable care in the preparation or putting up of the products will result in an injury to the consumer's life or property, owes a duty to the consumer to take that reasonable care."[22]

The category of dangerous chattels lingered on for some years but had expired by the 1950s. Now, apart from statute, there is no liability in tort for damage caused by products unless there is negligence and there is no class of product in respect of which there is no liability for negligence. There is simply the ordinary rule that the greater the risk the greater the precautions that must be taken to obviate it.[23] It is true that the law expects a great deal more care in the handling of a pound of dynamite than a pound of butter, but that is the result of the general law of negligence, not of the application of a special rule of law concerning dangerous things.

The liability under *Donoghue v Stevenson* stands completely untouched by the enactment of the principle of strict liability in the Consumer Protection Act 1987[24] but in practice claimants will be much more likely to rely upon the latter than upon the former and the existence of the Act may be a reason for not extending the common law liability.[25] However, recourse to the common law will remain necessary in some cases, for example where the loss takes the form of damage to property not intended for private use[26] or where the special limitation period under the Act has expired.[27]

A. Persons Liable

10–3   The principle has been extended from manufacturers to include repairers,[28] fitters, erectors,[29] and assemblers.[30] Where a manu-

---

[21] This is sometimes known as the "narrow rule" in *Donoghue v Stevenson*. The "wide rule" about the duty of care in general has been considered, para.5–5, above.

[22] [1932] A.C. at 599. An American court had anticipated this by 16 years: *MacPherson v Buick Motor Co* (1916) 111 N.E. 1050.

[23] *Read v J. Lyons & Co* [1947] A.C. 156 at 172–173 per Lord Macmillan, at 180–181 per Lord Simonds.

[24] para.10–12, below.

[25] Simon Brown L.J. in *Hayes v Leo Scaffolding Ltd*, Unreported, CA, December 3, 1996.

[26] See para.10–17, below.

[27] See para.10–28, below.

[28] *Stennett v Hancock* [1939] 2 All E.R. 578; *Haseldine v Daw* [1941] 2 K.B. 343.

[29] *Brown v Cotterill* (1934) 51 T.L.R. 21.

[30] *Howard v Furness-Houlder Argentine Lines Ltd* [1936] 2 All E.R. 296.

facturer of a finished article (such as a motor car) buys in components from another he is under a duty to consider their suitability and cannot rely blindly on the other to produce a good design.[31] The manufacturer's duty extends to taking steps (for example, warnings) concerning dangers which are discovered only after the product has gone into circulation.[32] A mere distributor or supplier has not actively created the danger in the same way as a manufacturer but he, too, may be under a duty to make inquiries or carry out an inspection of the product and if it is dangerous for some reason of which he should have known, his failure to warn of it will then amount to negligence.[33] In *Andrews v Hopkinson*,[34] by arrangement with the claimant the defendant sold a second-hand car to a finance company and the company hired the car to the claimant under a hire-purchase agreement.[35] The car was some 18 years old, and the defendant, who was a dealer in second-hand cars, had taken no steps to see that it was in a roadworthy condition although the car had been in his possession for a week. In fact the car had a defective steering mechanism which caused the claimant to have an accident a week after he took delivery of the car. Evidence showed that in an old car the danger spot is the steering mechanism and that the defect in question could have been discovered by a competent mechanic if the car had been jacked up. McNair J. held that the defendant was liable and said[36]:

"Having regard to the extreme peril involved in allowing an old car with a defective steering mechanism to be used on the road, I have no hesitation in holding that the defendant was guilty of negligence in failing to make the necessary examination, or at

---

[31] *Winward v T.VR. Engineering* [1986] B.T.L.C. 366.

[32] *E. Hobbs v Baxenden Chemical Co* [1992] 1 Lloyd's Rep. 54; *Hamble Fisheries Ltd v Gardner* [1999] 2 Lloyd's Rep. 1; *Hollis v Dow Corning* (1996) 129 D.L.R. (4th) 609. See also *Carroll v Fearon* [1998] P.I.Q.R. P416.

[33] In the case of a gratuitous transfer, it is true that older authorities held that, unless the product was in the class of dangerous things, the transferor was liable only for wilful or reckless conduct, i.e. when he actually knew of the danger: *Gautret v Egerton* (1867) L.R. 2 C.P. 371 at 375; *Coughlin v Gillison* [1899] 1 Q.B. 145. The validity of these cases is now very doubtful (see *Griffiths v Arch Engineering Co Ltd* [1968] 3 All E.R. 217 at 220; Marsh (1950) 66 L.Q.R. 39) and it is submitted that in the modern law the gratuitous nature of the transfer is simply a factor to be taken into account in assessing what is reasonable care by the transferor. Cf. *Chaudhury v Prabhakar* [1989] 1 W.L.R. 29 (gratuitous agent inspecting property liable to principal, though the existence of a duty of care was conceded).

[34] [1957] 1 Q.B. 229. See, too, *White v John Warwick & Co* [1953] 1 W.L.R. 1285; *Griffiths v Arch Engineering Co Ltd* [1968] 3 All E.R. 217.

[35] The finance company in a hire-purchase agreement gives the same implied warranties (now non-excludable) as to the condition of the goods as does a seller in a sale: see above.

[36] [1957] 1 Q.B. 229 at 237. Cf. *Rees v Saville* [1983] R.T.R. 332 (duty of private purchaser; MOT certificate).

least in failing to warn the plaintiff that no such examination had been carried out."[37]

10–4 Similarly, suppliers may be liable if they carelessly represent the goods to be harmless[38] without having made any adequate tests,[39] but it should not be thought that these cases impose a general duty on suppliers to subject all their goods to an exhaustive examination. The duty to examine will only arise if in all the circumstances they could reasonably be expected to carry out an examination. A second-hand car dealer may be expected to discover a patent defect in the steering mechanism of one of his cars, and a manufacturer and supplier of chemicals must take reasonable care to discover and give warning of industrial hazards arising out of the chemicals he supplies,[40] but a retail grocer, for example, cannot be expected to institute inspections to discover whether his tinned food is contaminated. He may be obliged to satisfy himself as to the reputation of his supplier[41] and he must certainly follow proper practices in keeping his wares but otherwise, unless the contamination was caused by his negligence or he actually knew of it, his only liability is to the actual purchaser under the contract of sale. If a third party becomes ill on eating the contaminated food, his remedy, if any, is against the manufacturer.

Given the potential liability for negligence of a supplier of goods (particularly second-hand goods) for failing to trace defects is there any way in which he can protect himself other than by carrying out an adequate inspection? It is clear that any exclusion clause in the contract of sale or otherwise will generally be void under the Unfair Contract Terms Act 1977,[42] but a suitable warning of possible defects may be regarded not as an attempt to exclude liability but as a discharge of the duty of care. In this respect, *Hurley v Dyke*,[43] a claim arising before the Act, suggests that the supplier will be treated fairly leniently. The defendant, a garage owner, sold an old three-wheeler car by auction on terms that it was sold, "as seen and

---

[37] He was also prepared to hold the dealer liable on a collateral contract with the claimant.

[38] Those who test and certify goods may incur liability for negligence: *N v Medical Research Council* (1997) 7 Med. L.R. 309; *Perrett v Collins* [1998] 2 Lloyd's Rep. 255. See further, para.5–13, above.

[39] *Watson v Buckley, Osborne, Garrett & Co* [1940] 1 All E.R. 174 (distributors of a dangerous hair dye held liable because they advertised it as positively harmless and requiring no tests); *Devilez v Boots Pure Drug Co* [1962] C.L.Y. 2015; *Goodchild v Vaclight* [1965] C.L.Y. 2669.

[40] *Vacwell Engineering Co Ltd v B.D.H. Chemicals Ltd* [1971] 1 Q.B. 88. An appeal from the judgment of Rees J. was settled: [1971] 1 Q.B. 111n.

[41] *Fisher v Harrods* [1966] C.L.Y. 8148.

[42] See para.25–6, below.

[43] [1979] R.T.R. 265.

with all its faults and without warranty". It was then resold by the purchaser to one Clay and eight days later it crashed because of corrosion in the chassis, injuring the claimant passenger. It was conceded before the House of Lords that the defendant's duty would be satisfied by giving adequate warning to his purchaser[44] and that if the defendant knew only that the car might be dangerous but had no knowledge of the specific defect the "all faults" terms on which it was sold would provide such a warning. The House seems to have thought these concessions rightly made and, no specific knowledge having been established, the claimant's claim failed. No concluded opinion was expressed on what the position would have been if the defendant had had knowledge of the defect but two judges said that it should not be assumed that on such facts he would be in breach of duty.[45]

B. Extension of Subject Matter

The principle has been extended from articles of food and drink **10–5** and has been applied to, inter alia, kiosks,[46] tombstones,[47] hair dye,[48] industrial chemicals,[49] lifts,[50] motor cars[51] and pants.[52] Likewise the term "consumer" includes the ultimate user of the article[53] or anyone who is within physical proximity to it.[54] The significance of *Donoghue v Stevenson* in the context of liability for defective buildings has already been considered.[55]

The duty of reasonable care extends not only to the manufacture, erection or repair of the product itself but also to any container,[56]

---

[44] Cf. *Goodwear Treaders Ltd v D.&B. Holdings Ltd* (1979) 98 D.L.R (3d) 59 (suppliers of tyre held liable to third party when they knew that purchaser would ignore their warning of its unsuitability for his purpose).

[45] Viscount Dilhorne and Lord Scarman. Cf. Lord Hailsham who thought (at 303) that the old decision in *Ward v Hobbs* (1878) 4 App. Cas. 13 might have to be reconsidered in the light of developments in the law of negligence.

[46] *Paine v Colne Valley Electricity Supply Co* [1938] 4 All E.R. 803.

[47] *Brown v Cotterill* [1934] 51 T.L.R. 21.

[48] *Watson v Buckley* [1940] 1 Al E.R. 174.

[49] *Vacwell Engineering Co Ltd v B.D.H. Chemicals Ltd* [1971] 1 Q.B. 88.

[50] *Haseldine v Daw* [1941] 2 K.B. 343.

[51] *Herschtal v Stewart & Ardern* [1940] 1 K.B. 155; *Andrews v Hopkinson* [1957] 1 Q.B. 229.

[52] *Grant v Austalian Knitting Mills* [1936] A.C. 85.

[53] *Grant v Australian Knitting Mills*, above, fn.52; *Griffiths v Arch Engineering Co Ltd* [1968] 3 All E.R. 217; *Cassidy v Imperial Chemical Industries Ltd, The Times*, November 2, 1972.

[54] *Brown v Cotterill*, above, fn.47 (child injured by falling tombstone); *Stennett v Hancock* [1939] 2 All E.R. 578 (pedestrian hit by flange of lorry wheel). In *Lambert v Lewis* [1978] 1 Lloyd's Rep. 610 manufacturers were held liable for a design defect in a vehicle coupling which caused a trailer to come adrift and injure the claimant. This was not challenged on appeal: [1982] A.C. 225.

[55] Ch.9, above.

[56] *Donoghue v Stevenson* [1932] A.C. at 585.

package or pipe[57] in which it is distributed, and to the labels, directions or instructions for use that accompany it.[58]

C. Burden of Proof

10–6   The duty owed is that of reasonable care[59] and the burden of proving negligence is on the claimant. Although in *Donoghue v Stevenson*[60] itself Lord Macmillan said that in a case such as that there was no justification for applying res ipsa loquitur,[61] the practice of the courts is to draw inferences of negligence in suitable product liability cases as much as in any other. The question in each case is whether the claimant has given sufficient evidence to justify the inference of negligence against the defendant and he is not necessarily required to specify what the defendant did wrong[62] and, indeed, any other rule would stultify the principle of *Donoghue v Stevenson*, for normally it will be impossible for a claimant to bring evidence of particular negligent acts or omissions occurring in the defendant's manufacturing processes. In *Mason v Williams & Williams Ltd*[63] the claimant was injured while using a cold chisel manufactured by the defendants and which was too hard for its purpose. Finnemore J. held that since the claimant had established that nothing had happened to the chisel after it left the defendants' factory which could have caused the excessive hardness, the defendants' negligence was established. It is suggested that the claimant will generally discharge his burden of proof by showing that the article was defective and that, on a balance of probabilities, the defect arose in the course of manufacture[64] by the defendant. In many cases in practice this comes very close to the imposition of a strict liability, for even if the defendant gives evidence that the quality control system in his factory complies with approved practice, there is still the possibility—indeed it perhaps becomes stronger by this very evidence—that one of his servants was careless

---

[57] *Barnes v Irwell Valley Water Board* [1938] 2 All E.R. 650.

[58] *Watson v Buckley* [1940] 1 All E.R. 174; *Holmes v Ashford* [1950] 2 All E.R. 76; *Vacwell Engineering Co Ltd v B.D.H. Chemicals Ltd* [1971] 1 Q.B. 88; *Thompson v Johnson & Johnson* [1991] 2 VR. 449. Macleod (1981) 97 L.Q.R. 550. For a claim concerning instructions which was based on contract see *Wormell v R.H.M. Agriculture (East) Ltd* [1987] 1 W.L.R. 1091.

[59] A manufacturer is not liable on the ground only that an independent contractor employed by him had been negligent: *Taylor v Rover Co Ltd* [1966] 1 W.L.R. 1491.

[60] [1932] A.C. 585 at 622.

[61] See para.5–89, above.

[62] In *Grant* the claimant succeeded because if excess sulphites were left in the garment, that could only be because someone was at fault. "The appellant is not required to lay his finger on the exact person in all the chain who was responsible, or to specify what he did wrong. Negligence is found as a matter of inference from the existence of the defects taken in conjunction with all the known circumstances": at 101 per Lord Wright.

[63] [1955] 1 W.L.R. 549.

[64] Or repair, etc. according to the business of the defendant.

and prevented that system operating correctly, in which case he remains liable, though vicariously rather than for breach of his personal duty.[65]

D. Possibility of Alternative Cause

In *Grant v Australian Knitting Mills Ltd*,[66] the Judicial Committee held that the defendants were liable to the ultimate purchaser of some pants which they had manufactured and which contained a chemical that gave the claimant a skin disease when he wore them. It was argued for the defendants that as they dispatched the pants in paper packets of six sets there was greater possibility of intermediate tampering with the goods before they reached the user than there was with the sealed bottle in *Donoghue*'s case, but the court held that:

10–7

"[T]he decision in that case did not depend on the bottle being stoppered and sealed; the essential point in this regard was that the article should reach the consumer or user subject to the same defect as it had when it left the manufacturer."[67]

Mere possibility of interference did not affect their liability. There must, however, be sufficient evidence that the defect existed when the article left the manufacturer's hands and that it was not caused later. In *Evans v Triplex Safety Glass Co Ltd*,[68] the claimant bought a motor car fitted with a "Triplex Toughened Safety Glass" windscreen of the defendants' manufacture. A year later, when the car was being used, the windscreen suddenly and for no apparent reason broke into many fragments and injured the occupants of the car. The defendants were held not liable for the following reasons: (1) the lapse of time between the purchase and the accident; (2) the possibility that the glass may have been strained when screwed into its frame; (3) the opportunity of intermediate examination by the intermediate seller; and (4) the breaking of the glass may have been caused by something other than a defect in manufacture. By contrast, in *Carroll v Fearon*,[69] although the tyre, the bursting of which caused the accident, was seven years old and three-quarters worn, there was evidence of a manufacturing defect and the action against the manufacturer succeeded.

---

[65] See *Grant v Australian Knitting Mills Ltd* [1936] A.C. 85 at 101; *Smedley's Ltd v Breed* [1974] A.C. 839 (a criminal prosecution under food hygiene statutes). *Daniels v White & Sons* [1938] 4 All E.R. 258 is hard to reconcile with *Grant*'s case and MacKenna J. refused to follow it in *Hill v J. Crowe (Cases)* [1978] 1 All E.R. 812.

[66] [1936] A.C. 85.

[67] [1936] A.C. 85 at 106–107.

[68] [1936] 1 All E.R. 283. Cf. *Mason v Williams & Williams Ltd* [1955] 1 W.L.R. 549.

[69] [1998] P.I.Q.R. P416.

The use of the article by the claimant for a purpose materially different from that for which the maker designed it or which he might reasonably be taken to have contemplated will also defeat a claim, but use for a different but similar purpose does not ipso facto absolve him from liability. The question here is one of fact and degree,[70] and it is suggested that the right thing to ask is whether the cause of the claimant's injury was the defect in the article or the claimant's own misuse of it.[71]

E. Intermediate Examination

10–8   As originally formulated by Lord Atkin the principle applies where there is, "no reasonable possibility of intermediate examination". These words have been the subject of much analysis, "almost as if they formed part of a statute"[72] but the better view is that they do not constitute an independent requirement which the claimant must satisfy but rather are to be taken into account in determining whether the injury to the claimant was foreseeable.[73] Even a probability of an intermediate examination will not exonerate the defendant unless it gives him reason to expect that it will reveal the defect and that this will result in the elimination of the defect or at least the claimant's being warned of it in such a way as to make him safe.[74] In *Griffiths v Arch Engineering Co Ltd*[75] the claimant borrowed from the first defendants a portable grinding tool which had been lent to them by its owners, the second defendants. The tool was in a dangerous condition because an incorrect part had been fitted to it at some time by a servant of the second defendants, and the claimant was injured in consequence. Although the first defendants had an opportunity of examining the tool, the second defendants had no reason to suppose that an examination would actually be carried out

[70] *Davie v New Merton Board Mills Ltd* [1957] 2 Q.B. 368 at 378–379 per Ashworth J. The manufacturers' liability was not in issue on appeal: [1959] A.C. 604.

[71] If both are causes, then damages should be reduced under the Law Reform (Contributory Negligence) Act 1945, as in *Griffiths v Arch Engineering Co Ltd* [1968] 3 All E.R. 217.

[72] *M/S Aswan Engineering Establishment Co v Lupdine Ltd* [1987] 1 W.L.R. 1 at 22 per Lloyd L.J.

[73] [1987] 1 W.L.R. 1 at 23.

[74] The, "duty does not cease to exist because there is a possibility or probability of inspection by an intermediary or by the neighbour himself before the article is taken into use. If an inspection is certain and will reveal the defect and the person making the inspection will appreciate the danger, then no doubt a risk to the neighbour is not reasonably foreseeable": *McIlveen v Charlesworth Developments* [1982] N.I. 216 at 221; *Pearson Education Ltd v Charter Partnership Ltd* [2007] EWCA Civ 130; [2007] B.L.R 324. It may not be so much a matter of intermediate examination as of intermediate treatment. In *Regal Pearl Pty Ltd v Stewart* [2002] NSWCA 291 it would have been practically impossible for the importer to test frozen prawns for hepatitis A virus and he was entitled to rely on their being properly cooked.

[75] [1968] 3 All E.R. 217. *Lambert v Lewis* [1978] 1 Lloyd's Rep. 610 (point not involved on appeal [1982] A.C. 225). Cf. *Taylor v Rover Co Ltd* [1966] 1 W.L.R. 1491.

and they were liable to the claimant. The fact that the first defendants were also liable to the claimant meant not that the second defendants had a defence to the claimant's claim but that the case was one for ultimate apportionment of liability between the defendants.[76] On the other hand, in *Kubach v Hollands*[77] a manufacturer sold a chemical to an intermediary with an express warning that it had to be tested before use. The intermediary was liable for the resulting injury, but the manufacturer was not and it would be difficult to do business on any other basis.[78] Prescription drugs will commonly have untoward side-effects upon a minority of users and a manufacturer will normally fulfil his duty under *Donoghue v Stevenson* by giving adequate warning to the prescribing physician (who is far more likely than is the patient to be able to understand the warning)[79]: if the physician fails to heed the warning his default may properly be regarded as the sole cause of injury to the patient.[80]

F. Nature of the Loss

Liability under *Donoghue v Stevenson* clearly covers personal **10–9** injury and damage to other property: if, for example, a defectively wired heater causes a fire which burns down the consumer's house he could sue for the value of the house. It does not, however, normally cover the financial loss caused by the failure of a product to fulfil the function for which it was acquired. Such loss is properly claimable only in an action by the buyer against the seller under the Sale of Goods Act. In other words, *Donoghue v Stevenson* is about dangerous products, not merely defective ones and a modern Mrs Donoghue could not sue Stevenson if her bottle of "ginger beer" contained pure water. These matters have already been discussed in

---

[76] See now the Civil Liability (Contribution) Act 1978, para.21–4, below. If the claimant himself neglects an opportunity of examination it may be a case for reduction of damages under the Law Reform (Contributory Negligence) Act 1945. If his default is so extreme as to break the chain of causation there may be a complete defence: *Nitrigin Eireann Teoranta v Inco Alloys Ltd* [1992] 1 All E.R. 854 at 862.

[77] [1937] 3 All E.R. 970.

[78] Similarly, one may well sell an unroadworthy vehicle for scrap and if it is then used on the road that will be the purchaser's responsibility. See also *Hurley v Dyke*, para.10–4, above. *Viridian Inc v Bovar Inc* (2002) 216 D.L.R. (4th) 122 (product supplied to the "sophisticated intermediary" was standard part supplied for no disclosed purpose; manufacturer entitled to expect examination; no liability).

[79] *Hollis v Dow Corning* (1996) 129 D.L.R. (4th) 609 (breast implants).

[80] See *Hollis v Dow Corning*, above, fn.79, but what if there is no warning? In *Hollis v Dow Corning* the SCC held that in such a case the manufacturer cannot escape liability by giving evidence tending to show that the doctor would not have passed the information on. That would leave the claimant in the position of failing against the doctor (who is not negligent because he received no warning) and against the manufacturer. Cf. *Walker Estate v York Finch General Hospital* [2001] SCC 23; [2001] 1 S.C.R. 647.

the context of the duty of care and economic loss[81] and the related area of defective premises.[82] In so far as *Junior Books v Veitchi Co Ltd*[83] remains an authority on economic loss it may no doubt be applicable to chattels where the requisite special and unusual relationship subsists between the parties,[84] but that will not normally be so between manufacturer and ultimate consumer, even if the manufacturer is aware of the destination of his product.[85]

10–10   However, the undoubted proposition that *Donogue v Stevenson* applies where the product causes damage to other property of the claimant causes some difficulty where failure of a component in a complex product causes damage to the product itself.[86] This is essentially the same issue as that of the "complex structure" which has been discussed earlier in connection with *Murphy v Brentwood DC*.[87] It is clear that if the negligently manufactured component is a replacement or added[88] part the manufacturer is liable for damage to the rest of the article[89] whether or not he was the manufacturer of the article in its original state.[90] The discussion of complex structures in *Murphy v Brentwood* is somewhat inconclusive but members of the House of Lords did not rule out the possibility that sub-contractors constructing or installing elements of a building which then caused damage to the building as a whole might be liable for this damage. The problem in the case of chattels may be considerably more complex: in the case of a motor vehicle, for example, there may be hundreds of component parts by dozens of different manufacturers and the "manufacturer" of the vehicle may in reality be no more than a designer and assembler. On the basis of what is

---

[81] See para.5–44, above.

[82] See para.9–33, above.

[83] [1983] 1 A.C. 520.

[84] See para.5–44, above.

[85] See *Simaan General Contracting Co v Pilkington Glass Ltd (No.2)* [1988] Q.B. 758 where C ordered building components from D via a contract between A and B because the building owner required use of D's components. C's claim against D failed. See also *Man B & W Diesel etc Ltd v PT Bumi International Tankers* [2004] SGCA 8; [2004] 2 S.L.R. 300, where the decision against liability rests on the absence of sufficient proximity rather than any general rule of law.

[86] See Tettenborn [2000] L.M.& C.L.Q. 333.

[87] See para.9–35, above.

[88] For the case where the part is a component of a new product produced by the claimant, see *Bacardi-Martini Beverages Ltd v Thomas Hardy Packaging Ltd* [2002] EWCA Civ 549; [2002] 2 Lloyd's Rep. 379, para.5–44, above.

[89] For example a replacement tyre on a car which bursts and causes a crash damaging the car. In *Andrew Weir Shipping Ltd v Wartsila UK Ltd* [2004] EWHC 1284 (Comm); [2004] 2 Lloyd's Rep. 377 (fire starting in ship's engine) there was no dispute that there was physical damage, the contest being whether the defendants were under a duty to warn the owners of the risk. However, the question of assumption of responsibility or "special relationship" may be relevant both to the existence of liability for economic loss and to the existence of a duty to speak: at [59].

[90] The defendants in *Nitrigin Eireann Teoranta v Inco Alloys Ltd* [1992] 1 All E.R. 854 were manufacturers of the original and replacement material, though the case concerned only limitation.

said in *Murphy v Brentwood* we may, at one end of the spectrum, fairly safely say that if an engine component made by the assembler of the vehicle fails and causes damage to the rest of the engine[91] a claim for damage to "other property" caused by the failure of the component would be hopeless. The same is almost certainly true even if the failed component is manufactured by B and installed into the engine by the manufacturer of the car, A. At the other end of the spectrum is the case in which a car radio negligently manufactured by B and installed in a car assembled by A causes a fire which destroys the car. B may be liable to the owner for that,[92] since the radio is "accessory to the car", but not perhaps where the failed component is a tyre manufactured by B and fitted (not as replacement) to a car assembled by A.[93] The question of liability for defects in packaging was considered in *M/S Aswan Engineering Establishment Co v Lupdine Ltd.*[94] The claimants lost a quantity of waterproofing compound when the pails in which it was contained collapsed because of the high temperatures to which they were exposed in Kuwait. An action against the manufacturer of the pails failed[95] on the ground that the circumstances in which the damage occurred were outside the range of what was reasonably foreseeable, but Lloyd L.J.[96] expressed the provisional view that had that not been the case the loss of the compound would have been damage to the property of the claimants for which the manufacturer would have been liable. Nicholls L.J., on the other hand, inclined to the view that *Donoghue v Stevenson* should not extend to making a container manufacturer liable for loss of contents,[97] not so much because the contents are not in strict legal analysis "other property of the claimant" but because such a liability would be unreasonable. Difficult lines have to be drawn here but as the law now stands we must guard against the natural assumption that because the defect manifests itself in some external, physical form or by sudden catastrophe it is necessarily "damage to property" for the purposes of tort. In

---

[91] Cf. the facts of *Bernstein v Pamson Motors (Golders Green) Ltd* [1987] 2 All E.R. 220 where (1) the action was against the seller and (2) the problem arose from the process of assembly rather than a failure of a component. However, the fact that the damage was repaired under the manufacturer's warranty shows why the issue is of limited practical importance in the case of vehicles.

[92] Not for the value of the radio itself: *Aloe Coal Co v Clark Equipment Co* 816, F. 2d 110, cited with approval by Lord Keith in *Murphy v Brentwood DC* at [1991] 1 A.C. 469.

[93] Yet a car radio, while easily detachable, can only be used in a car; and tyres can be removed and put on another car.

[94] [1987] 1 W.L.R. 1.

[95] An action in contract against other defendants who had sold the compound and pails to the claimants also failed.

[96] With whose judgment Fox L.J. agreed.

[97] Mance J. in *The Orjula* [1995] 2 Lloyd's Rep. 395 thought that the view of Nicholls L.J. gained some support from *Murphy v Brentwood DC* [1991] 1 A.C. 398.

both *D.&F. Estates Ltd v Church Commissioners*[98] and *Murphy v Brentwood*[99] the House of Lords referred approvingly to the United States Supreme Court decision in *East River Steamship Corp v Transamerica Delaval Inc*[100] denying a claim by tanker charterers against the manufacturer of turbines which caused the tankers to malfunction, in which the court remarked that:

> "[W]e [do not] find persuasive a distinction that rests on the manner in which the product is injured. We realise that the damage may be qualitative, occurring through a gradual deterioration or internal breakage. Or it may be calamitous . . . But either way, since by definition no person or other property is damaged, the resulting loss is purely economic. Even when the harm to the product itself occurs through an abrupt, accident-like event, the resulting loss due to repair costs, decreased value and lost profits is essentially the failure of the purchaser to receive the benefits of its bargain—traditionally the core concern of contract law."[101]

10–11   A further possibility is that a dangerous defect is discovered in a product before it has the opportunity to cause harm and is then repaired. There was once some support for the view that the claimant in such a case could recover the costs of repair but this approach was flatly rejected in the *D.&F. Estates* case:

> "If the hidden defect in the chattel is the cause of personal injury or of damage to property other than the chattel itself, the manufacturer is liable. But if the hidden defect is discovered before any such damage is caused, there is no longer any room for the application of the *Donoghue v Stevenson* principle. The chattel is now defective in quality, but is no longer dangerous.[102] It may be valueless or it may be incapable of economic repair. In either case the economic loss is recoverable in contract by a buyer or hirer of the chattel entitled to the benefit of a relevant warranty of quality, but is not recoverable in tort by a remote buyer or hirer of the chattel."[103]

---

[98] [1989] A.C. 117.
[99] [1991] 1 A.C. 398.
[100] 476 U.S. 858 (1986).
[101] See further Prosser and Keeton, *Torts*, 5th edn, p.708.
[102] If a badly made fire alarm fails to function and a building is burned down the manufacturer is in principle liable for the damage. But if the defect is discovered before any fire has occurred he is not liable for the cost of replacing it. The law may be different in Canada: *Hughes v Sunbeam Corp (Canada) Ltd* (2002) 219 D.L.R. (4th) 467.
[103] [1989] A.C. 177 per Lord Bridge.

These propositions are reaffirmed in *Murphy v Brentwood DC*[104] where it is said that where the property is used with knowledge of the danger the user is likely to be treated as the author of his own loss. This causes some difficulty in the case of defects in buildings but less in the case of chattels.[105]

The post-*Junior Books* cases are part of a general pattern of restriction on the reach of negligence law and represent an attempt to keep separate the spheres of tort and contract law. In none of them, however, is there very much discussion of the practical impact of placing upon the manufacturer a liability for defects of quality and performance and it must be borne in mind that if the claimant is a purchaser of the article and the usual chain of contractual indemnities functions fully it is the manufacturer, as the originator of the defect, who carries responsibility, even if he is not negligent. Certainly, the creation of a direct liability from manufacturer to consumer might raise formidable difficulties. For example, how would a standard of "defectiveness of quality" be set, since that is something which must be related to the terms of the contract (in particular, the price) between the manufacturer and the intermediary (the seller or some more remote person in the distribution chain)? Further, what would be the effect of exclusions or limitations of liability in the contract between the manufacturer and the intermediary?[106] Perhaps these problems would be far from insuperable in the context of standard form transactions with little room for bargaining and judicial control of exemption clauses.

2. LIABILITY UNDER THE CONSUMER PROTECTION ACT 1987

Looked at against the background of the general law of tort the level of protection given to victims of dangerous goods by *Donoghue v Stevenson* may be thought not unreasonable, though it may be hard to justify the strict liability in respect of death or personal injury[107] which the purchaser acquires by virtue of his contract of sale. Such a view is, however, out of accord with the spirit of a time in which consumer interest has become one of the most important pressures for law reform. In the United States, liability for negligence was overtaken by judicial reform in favour of the consumer. The first

10–12

---

[104] [1991] 1 A.C. 398.
[105] See para.9–34, above.
[106] e.g. in *Junior Books v Veitchi* Lord Fraser thought that the claimant in tort could be in no better position than the purchaser from the manufacturer: [1983] 1 A.C. 520 at 534.
[107] As opposed to the liability for financial loss caused by the failure of the goods to function.

step was liability for express warranty, shorn of the restriction of privity of contract and based on advertising claims,[108] but this was soon overtaken by the idea of the implied warranty of safety.[109] The culmination was *Greenman v Yuba Power Products Inc*[110] in which the court abandoned the idea of warranty and imposed a straightforward strict liability in tort.[111] Various arguments have been advanced in favour of these developments[112] but the most commonly occurring ones are that the manufacturer, as creator of the risk, should bear its consequences[113]; that he is in the best position to insure that risk and to cover the cost of that insurance in his price[114]; that strict liability is even more of an incentive than fault to the taking of adequate precautions; and that strict tort liability only achieves in one action what the law of contract achieves in many cases by the chain of indemnities stretching back from the consumer-purchaser to the manufacturer.

In numerical terms the problem of injuries caused by product defects is small when compared with those attributable to other risks[115] and the difficulty of establishing a case under the law of negligence can be exaggerated,[116] but there was a powerful tide in favour of change in the 1970s, prompted in part by the Thalidomide tragedy[117] and given impetus by pressure for harmonisation of laws within the EEC. The adoption by the Council of the EEC of a Directive on liability for defective products[118] meant that the UK was required, by virtue of its treaty obligations, to legislate to make

---

[108] *Baxter v Ford Motor Co* 12 P. 2d 409 (1932). This has obvious affinities with the collateral contract.

[109] *Henningsen v Bloomfield Motors* 161 A 2d 69 (1960). Cf. the alternative forms of the Uniform Commercial Code, art.2–318.

[110] (1963) 27 Cal. Rptr. 697.

[111] See now the 3d *Restatement of Torts, Product Liability*, on this topic (1998).

[112] See, e.g. Law Com. No.82, Liability for Defective Products (1977), para.38.

[113] This argument proves too much—it would suggest strict liability for any injury caused in the production and distribution process, e.g. an accident to a worker in the factory or a crash caused by the driving of a delivery van. Liability under the Consumer Protection Act 1987 is confined to injuries caused by a defect in the product, which is by no means the same thing as injuries caused by the product.

[114] A sufficiently bad claims record should raise his premium costs to such a level that he is driven off the market.

[115] On the basis of its personal injury survey the Pearson Commission in 1978 estimated that between 30,000 and 40,000 injuries per year (about 1 per cent of all injuries) might be attributable to defective products other than drugs and that the risk of death was lower than for other categories of risk: Cmnd. 7054, Vol.1, para.1201. The 1987 Act hardly figured in case law for 12 years but there have been some important decisions since 2000.

[116] See para.10–6, above; but tort compensation was recovered in only 5 per cent of cases (half the rate for work accidents and one-fifth of the rate for road accidents) and the average payment was only half that for all personal injury accidents.

[117] See Teff and Munro, *Thalidomide: The Legal Aftermath* (1976).

[118] A draft version of the Directive (different in a number of significant respects) was considered by the Law Commission (Law Com. No.82 (1977)) and the Pearson Commission.

our law accord with the Directive and this was done by Pt I of the Consumer Protection Act 1987[119] which came into force on March 1, 1988,[120] and which expressly states that it is to:

"[H]ave effect for the purpose of making such provision as is necessary in order to comply with the . . . Directive and shall be construed accordingly".[121]

The Act is too complicated to summarise accurately in one sentence and it is necessary to look at particular provisions in some detail, but very broadly its effect is to make the producer of a product (and certain others dealing with it) liable in damages for personal injury and some property damage caused by a defect in the product, without the necessity for the claimant to show fault, though certain defences may be raised by the producer. Liability is by no means absolute, how far it is properly described as "strict" is debatable but judgment on that must be suspended until the Act has been looked at more closely.

Article 13 of the Directive provided that it should not: **10–13**

"[A]ffect any rights which an injured person may have according to the rules of contractual or non-contractual liability or a special liability system existing at the moment when"

the Directive was notified. It was widely thought that this meant that the Directive merely set a minimum standard and left it open to the local law to impose a stricter or more extensive liability. However, the European Court of Justice has ruled that this is incorrect in the light of the fact that divergences in liability law may distort competition and "maximal" rather "minimal" harmonisation is imposed.[122] Hence the French transposition of the Directive, which put the liability of the supplier on the same level as the manufacturer (whereas under the Directive the supplier is liable only if the

---

[119] Miller, *Product Liability and Safety Encyclopaedia*, Division III; Fairest, *The Consumer Protection Act 1987*; Howells, *Comparative Product Liability* (1993). For a highly critical account of the changes produced by the Directive, see Stapleton, "Products Liability Reform—Real or Illusory" (1986) 6 O.J.L.S. 392 and Stapleton, *Product Liability* (1994).

[120] The Act applies if the product was supplied to any person by the producer on or after that date. Hence it did not apply in *Carroll v Fearon* [1998] P.I.Q.R. P416, even though the accident took place after the commencement of the Act.

[121] Section 1(1). Surprisingly, perhaps, the Directive (85/374) is not annexed to the Act. It can be found in the *Official Journal of the European Communities*, No.L 210/29.

[122] *Gonzalez Sanchez v Medicina Asturiana SA* [2002] E.C.R. I–3901.

manufacturer is unidentified) was struck down.[123] However, art.13 allows the imposition of liability on some other ground such as fault or warranty[124] so in English law the general liability for negligence and breach of contract operate in parallel with the Directive regime.

A. Who is Liable?

10–14   Subject to a point discussed below, the Act does not impose liability on persons who merely supply goods, though it must again be emphasised that the supplier usually has a contractual liability which is more onerous than that imposed by the Act, albeit only to his immediate purchaser. The three principal categories of persons liable under the Act are listed in s.2(2) and the first is the producer of the product,[125] who is further defined in s.1(2) as:

"(a) the person who manufactured it;
  (b) in the case of a substance which has not been manufactured but has been won or abstracted, the person who won or abstracted it;
  (c) in the case of a product which has not been manufactured, won or abstracted but essential characteristics of which are attributable to an industrial or other process having been carried out (for example, in relation to agricultural produce), the person who carried out that process."

The first class within s.1(2) is self-explanatory, but it is important to note that if a product causes damage as a result of failure of a component part (for example, an aircraft which crashes because of a defective altimeter) then both the manufacturer of the component part and the final manufacturer/assembler are treated as producers and are liable under the Act.[126] Their liability is joint and several,[127] that is to say, each is liable in full to the claimant, though as between themselves the liability may be apportioned under the contribution legislation[128] and there may, of course, be contractual rights of indemnity. Paragraph (b) covers minerals and raw materials (oil, coal, cement). Paragraph (c), which covers things not falling within

---

[123] *Commission v France* [2002] E.C.R. I–3827.
[124] At [31].
[125] Section 2(2)(a).
[126] This is the effect of the definition of "product" in s.1(2), though this very important point could, perhaps, have been stated more clearly.
[127] Section 2(5).
[128] Ch.21, below.

either of the two previous categories,[129] will raise some awkward questions of degree as to what is an "essential characteristic": the packing of vegetable crops does not, presumably, bring this paragraph into play but the processing and freezing of poultry probably do.[130]

The second category in s.2(2) is the "own brander" or, as the Act **10–15** puts it:

"[A]ny person who by putting his name on the product or using a trade mark or other distinguishing mark in relation to the product, has held himself out to be the producer of the product"

("presents himself as the producer" in the words of the Directive). This provision may be of narrower effect than it has often been assumed to be, for it is not enough to put your name on the goods, you must do so in such a way as to hold yourself out as the producer: does anyone really believe that, for example, Marks & Spencer Plc actually makes the products marketed under the "St Michael" brand? The matter is, of course, fundamentally a question of fact but labelling which clearly states that the product is made for and not by the store will presumably exclude s.2(2).[131]

Vast quantities of consumer goods are imported from abroad and the third category in s.2(2) goes some way towards relieving the claimant from the problems of suing a foreign producer, for it imposes liability upon the person who has imported the product into Europe, from a place outside Europe.[132] Hence, if A, a Belgian company, imports goods into Belgium from China and then sells them to B, who imports them into the UK, where they are sold to C, A (but not B) is liable under this head.[133]

---

[129] If X extracts oil and Y refines it into petroleum, X falls within paragraph (b). Does Y fall within paragraph (a) or paragraph (c)? If (c), it is presumably irrelevant that it has been abstracted in another form.

[130] A cup of coffee is served in a restaurant. Is the restaurant a producer under para.(a) or para.(c)? It must be one or the other but in *Bogle v McDonalds Restaurants Ltd* [2002] EWHC 490 (QB) the defendants seem to have conceded it was (a).

[131] A similar issue may arise over franchised outlets but in *Bogle v McDonalds Restaurants Ltd*, above, fn.130, the defendants accepted responsibility for franchisees.

[132] Section 2(2)(c) (since 1994 all EU and most former EFTA). However, the importing must be, "in order to supply it to another". An airline which brings an American airliner to England to use it here is not liable under this paragraph: s.46(9).

[133] The conflict of laws is outside the scope of this book but it should be noted that under the current rules C could sue A either here or in Belgium. If the latter, the Belgian judgment would be enforceable here. Fears were expressed in Parliament about the prospect of nominally capitalised "front" companies being used to import goods into the EEC. Such a company could be sacrificed and a judgment against it would exhaust the Act. However, the control of this sort of activity is a matter for company law, not tort.

This part opened by saying that the mere supply of goods to another did not of itself attract the operation of the Act, but under s.2(3) a supplier[134] who receives a request from the injured person to identify the producer (or other person liable under s.2(2)) is liable under the Act if he does not within a reasonable time either comply with the request or identify his supplier. The idea is to enable the claimant to trace "anonymous" goods back along the chain of distribution to a producer or importer who carries primary liability under the Act and anyone who breaks this chain[135] by his inability to identify his supplier is made liable as if he were the producer. Since in this way a wholesaler who is contractually remote from the claimant and who is in no way at fault with regard to the goods may incur heavy damages without hope of recourse, the importance of adequate record keeping can hardly be overemphasised.

B. Products

10–16   A product is any goods or electricity[136] and "goods" is further defined as including, "substances,[137] growing crops[138] and things comprised in land by virtue of being attached to it and any ship, aircraft or vehicle".[139] Components of a building are, therefore, covered, so that a manufacturer of defective steel joists would be liable for injury caused by the collapse of a block of flats but it is thought that the building as a whole is not "goods" and that a builder is not therefore responsible under the Act for shoddy workmanship,[140] though the law of negligence and the Defective Premises Act 1972 of course apply to these cases. It seems that information is not within the Act even though it is incorporated in

---

[134] "Supply" is defined in s.46(1) and extends a good deal more widely than supply under a sale. But a finance company is not a supplier for the purposes of this Act; the "effective supplier" (e.g. the garage in a car hire-purchase transaction) is: s.46(2).

[135] The request may be made to any supplier, not merely the one who directly supplied the goods to the claimant.

[136] Section 1(2).

[137] It was conceded in *A v National Blood Authority* [2001] 3 All E.R. 289 that blood and blood products for transfusion were within the Act. Contrast American law, where this category of liability has been uniformly rejected and is rejected by *Restatement* 3d §19.

[138] Until 2000 the producer of primary agricultural produce and game (the farmer or fisherman) was exempt from liability under the 1985 Directive if he supplied them before they had undergone an industrial process. This exemption was removed by the Consumer Protection Act 1987 (Product Liability) (Modification) Order 2000, SI 2000/2771, implementing Directive 1999/34/EC. While there is no doubt as to the legislative intention, it must be observed that the farmer does not fall easily into any of the definitions of producer in s.1(2). With a little strain he could be described as the "producer of . . . raw material" under art.3(1) of the 1985 Directive.

[139] Section 45(1).

[140] Even if this view is wrong, the same result will be reached in cases where the builder sells the house as a result of the combined effect of ss.4(1)(b), 46(3), 46(4).

tangible form in a book[141] but the same may not be true of computerised information, where the line between "software" and "hardware" may be difficult to draw sensibly. If an airliner crashes because a component in an automatic landing device fails above a certain temperature there is clearly a defective product within the Act. Can the position really be any different if it is programmed so that it simply does not operate in certain, foreseeable conditions or if it gives the pilot a misleading indication?[142] It has been said that while software as such is not "goods" within the Sale of Goods Act, a disk containing a programme is, and when that is sold[143] the statutory implied terms apply to the software as well as the disk itself.[144] Misleading instructions for use of a product are clearly not to be equated with "pure" information, for they may themselves render an otherwise perfect product defective.[145]

C. Damage

The Act applies to death or personal injury no matter how large **10–17** or small the loss[146] but the position with regard to property damage is more restricted. First, there is no liability in respect of loss of or damage to the product itself or the whole or any part of any product which has been supplied with the product in question comprised in it.[147] If, therefore, my car radio catches fire as a result of faulty components and burns out the car, neither the car assembler nor the radio manufacturer is strictly liable,[148] but if the same thing were to happen with a replacement radio liability would be imposed on the manufacturer of that. Secondly, no liability arises unless the damages (apart from interest) would be at least £275.[149] Thirdly, the Act is inapplicable unless the property is of a description ordinarily

---

[141] This was certainly the Government's intention, though two remarkably opaque sub-clauses in the Bill which were designed to make this clear were removed. Cf. Whittaker, "European Product Liability and Intellectual Products" (1989) 105 L.Q.R. 125. American courts have generally declined to apply products liability theory to information. A book contains tangible elements like paper and intangible ideas expressed therein: *Winter v G.P. Putnam's Sons* 938 F. 2d 1033 (C9, 1991).

[142] It must, however, be confessed that the distinction between this and the book which contains misleading information is not easy to discern, still less to state. Cf. *Brocklesby v US* 767 F. 2d 1288 (C9,1985), para.11–28, below.

[143] Or hired: Supply of Goods and Services Act 1982.

[144] *St Albans DC v I.C.L.* [1996] 4 All E.R. 481 at 493.

[145] See s.3(2)(a).

[146] The Act did not adopt the provisions of the Directive, art.16, whereby liability for death or personal injury caused by identical items with the same defect might be limited to 70 million ECU. There would be formidable practical difficulties in the application of such a provision.

[147] Section 5(2).

[148] Compare the rather uncertain position at common law: para.10–9, above.

[149] Section 5(4). It seems that the Directive, art.9(2), from which this curious limit stems, is mandatory. It is a curiosity in English conditions, being well below the level at which most lawyers would probably advise embarking on litigation.

intended for private use and is mainly so intended by the claimant.[150] The Act would, therefore, have no application to the *Muirhead* and *Aswan* cases.[151]

D. Defect
10–18   This is the core of the Act, the proposition that the damage must be caused wholly or partly by a defect in the product.[152] Defect[153] is defined in s.3 as being present where, "the safety of the product is not such as persons generally are entitled to expect".[154] Section 3 goes on to provide that that all the circumstances are to be taken into account in determining whether the product is as safe as persons generally are entitled to expect, specifically drawing attention to the following:

> "(a) [T]he manner in which, and the purposes for which, the product has been marketed, its get-up, the use of any mark in relation to the product and any instructions for, or warnings with respect to, doing or refraining from doing anything in relation to the product;
> (b) what might reasonably be expected to be done with or in relation to the product and
> (c) the time when the product was supplied by its producer to another; and nothing . . . shall require a defect to be inferred from the fact alone that the safety of a product which is supplied after that time is greater than the safety of the product in question."

10–19   **i. Non-standard products.** It is crucial to note that the standard is what persons generally are entitled to expect, a standard to be set by the court and which may be lower than what they do expect: public expectations may be unreasonably high, especially in a litigation-conscious society. On the other hand, the standard may be *higher* than what they do expect: the public may be stoically aware that some examples of a particular product will turn out to be defective, but this does not necessarily mean that they are not entitled to expect them to be perfect.[155] American product liability

---

[150] Section 5(3).
[151] See paras 5–40 and 10–9, above.
[152] Although the burden of proof is on the claimant, it is possible that the existence of the defect and its causal relationship may be established merely by inference: *Ide v ATB Sales Ltd* [2008] EWCA Civ 424.
[153] Stoppa, "The Concept of Defectiveness in the Consumer Protection Act 1987" (1992) 12 L.S. 210.
[154] It is further provided that, "safety, in relation to a product, shall include safety with respect to products comprised in the product and safety in the context of risks of damage to property, as well as in the context of risks of death or personal injury."
[155] *A v National Blood Authority* [2001] 3 All E.R. 289.

law has generally drawn a distinction between the "production or manufacturing defect" (the case where, despite quality controls, the production line turns out a sub-standard article) and the "design defect" (the case where the danger is inherent even in standard products of that type).[156] In *A v National Blood Authority*[157] Burton J. rejected this categorisation as alien to the structure of the Product Liability Directive and the Act. Nevertheless there are differences between the two situations of the product which is dangerous only because it is non-standard and the product every example of which carries a risk. In the case of the non-standard product (that is to say, one which is not in the condition in which the manufacturer intended it to be distributed to the public) the claimant will succeed by showing the non-standard nature of the article and that that made it dangerous and caused his damage. Although in many cases the mere existence of the defect would provide powerful indirect evidence of negligence the claimant is no longer required to rely on this and will succeed even if there is no fault. In the *National Blood Authority* case the claims arose from hepatitis C infections from blood products at a time when no reasonable and effective methods of screening for the virus were available—indeed, in the case of the earlier claims the products had been administered before the virus had even been identified. In concluding that the products were defective within the meaning of the Act, Burton J. held that the focus was upon the individual item which caused the damage and that the cost and practicability of eliminating the "rogue product" were not elements in the "circumstances of the case" in determining what the user was entitled to expect in the way of safety. Even if (which was not the case) the public had been generally aware of the risk of untraced infected samples of blood, the individual user was entitled to expect that his bag of blood was infection-free and was not to be taken to be participating in a form of Russian roulette.[158]

ii. Standard products. Turning to inherent dangers in standard **10–20** products, some of them will not work effectively unless there is an element of risk to everyone in their design—carving knives which cut meat well are also more efficient at lopping off users' fingers. In other cases, the product—medicines, for example—will be harmless and even beneficial to most but will present a danger to a minority. Yet other products could be made safer only by the expenditure of amounts of money which would be incompatible with the price

---

[156] A distinction maintained by *Restatement, Torts, Product Liability* 3d §2.
[157] [2001] 3 All E.R. 289.
[158] At [65]. Cf. *Richardson v LRC* [2000] P.I.Q.R. P164. In *Pollard v Tesco Stores Ltd* [2006] EWCA Civ 393 where a child-resistant cap did not quite conform to its design standards, it was held that the public could reasonably expect such a cap to be difficult to open but not to be compliant with design standards (about which they would know nothing).

range in the market at which the product is aimed—if all cars were required to be fitted with ABS brakes and four-wheel drive there would be no cheap cars available to the public. The relationship of the Act with the law of negligence in these cases has not been fully explored but it must surely be that the court is required to come to a judgment on whether the risks associated with the product in its present form are outweighed by the benefits that it brings, otherwise there would be liability for injuries caused by products rather than for injuries caused by defects in products, which would be neither socially acceptable nor within the scope of the Directive. While scientific evidence is no doubt relevant and often helpful there is no escaping the fact that in the last resort the judgment is a "value" one: there is no scientific formula which will tell us whether the risk of allowing cars to be made without advanced safety systems is greater or less than the benefits obtained by having cheaper cars. "Benefit" should not be taken too narrowly for this purpose because it may include elements that are completely unquantifiable. The dangers of alcohol are well known but in our society it is a generally accepted source of pleasure and even if some may think that the (very roughly quantifiable) cost still outweighs the (wholly unquantifiable) benefit, it is important that we respect people's right to self-determination, so even if alcohol could be said to be defective in any sense of the word, it is not so within the meaning of the Act. The necessity of adopting a cost-benefit approach was candidly admitted by the DTI explanatory note on the Directive, which commented, in relation to drugs:

> "The more active the medicine, and the greater its beneficial potential, the more extensive its effects are likely to be, and therefore the greater the chances of an adverse effect. A medicine used to treat a life threatening condition is likely to be much more powerful than a medicine used in the treatment of a less serious condition, and the safety that one is reasonably entitled to expect of such a medicine may therefore be correspondingly lower."[159]

10–21   The ultimate question for the common law of negligence in such cases would be, "was it reasonable to market this design in the light of the risks and benefits?" (not that that is necessarily the same as "do the measurable financial costs of the risks exceed the measurable benefits?"). No doubt under the Act (where the safety of the

---

[159] A different view is taken in the *National Blood Authority* case, that there is no weighing of risks and benefits but rather that the general knowledge of the inherent danger is a factor in the standards persons are entitled to expect. The distinction is probably only significant where the inherent danger comes to light after the product has been used for some time.

product rather than the conduct of the defendant is the point of focus) we have to modify the question so that it becomes "can the public legitimately expect a greater degree of safety from the product?", but there is clearly a substantial overlap between the two. However, it has been denied that the two issues are identical and in *Iman Abouzaid v Mothercare (UK) Ltd*[160] the claim under the Act succeeded even though the common law claim failed because the risk was not one, which, at the time of distribution, the manufacturer could reasonably have been expected to have in contemplation as a serious one—though how, precisely, the court is to determine legitimate public expectations in such cases remains unclear.[161] Furthermore, in the *National Blood Authority* case Burton J. regarded the question of what the defendant could have done to reduce or eliminate the danger as just as irrelevant in this type of case as in that of the non-standard product. Referring to the fact that s.3(2) requires that a product is not to be considered defective for the sole reason that a better product is subsequently put into circulation, he continued[162]:

"In the comparative process, the claimant may point to a product which is safer, but which the producer shows to be produced five years later. Particularly if no other contemporary product had these features, this is likely to be capable of being established, and insofar as such product has improved safety features which have only evolved later in time, they should be ignored, as a result of [section 3(2)].[163] The claimant might however want to allege that the later safety features *could* have been developed earlier by the producer. That would obviously amount to the *claimant* running the evidence of 'should have done', to which the producer would no doubt respond 'could not have done'. This would however once again go to the issue of *avoidability*, which I have concluded to be outside the ambit of [section 3], and so once again if the claimant really wanted to do so he could run the point, but only in negligence."

However, it is unclear how the court is to determine legitimate expectation without taking into account how, if at all, the product could have been improved.

The proposition in s.3(2) that the safety of a product is to be judged by reference to standards prevailing when it was put into circulation (so that a 2002 car is not defective merely because

---

[160] December 21, 2000, CA (design of pushchair strap).
[161] Pill L.J. contented himself with saying, at [27], "members of the public were entitled to expect better from the appellants".
[162] At [72].
[163] Throughout his judgment Burton J. refers to the Directive rather than the Act.

subsequent models are produced with more advanced safety features) seems to be an inevitable concomitant of the concept of "defect"[164] and if the rule were otherwise there might be a positive disincentive to an industry to introduce safety improvements. The "product" in question for this purpose is, of course, the individual item which causes the damage, not the product "line" or design —one cannot go on forever producing cars to 2002 standards when everyone else's safety standards have improved—but except in cases where legislative requirements are imposed (for example, as to the fitting of safety belts) it may be very difficult for the court to decide at what point a development becomes necessary to satisfy the requirement of safety, as opposed to being merely desirable. Again, too, we have the problem, if the *National Blood Authority* case is correct, of the apparent exclusion of what the manufacturer should have done from the "defect" issue.

10–22   **iii. Warnings and instructions.** A standard product may be perfectly safe if used properly but unsafe if used in an improper way or for an improper purpose. To take from the demonology of American product liability law the (apocryphal) case of the claimant who attempted to dry her dog in a microwave oven, the oven would not for that reason be defective. However, where a risk is not obvious to the user,[165] the product may be defective because it is not accompanied by adequate warnings or instructions. The standard here would seem to be similar to that for negligence but circumstances of danger are so infinitely various that very little can be said in general about instructions and labelling[166] beyond the general

---

[164] Stapleton, *Product Liability* (1994) (writing from the standpoint that the Act is a misguided and ineffective compensation measure which sticks much too closely to common law concepts, a proposition perhaps now less easy to defend than when it was put forward) argues that reformers are illogical in readily accepting this proposition while at the same time rejecting (as many of them do) the "development risks" defence now enshrined in s.4(1)(e): "It is odd that risks discovered after circulation should be taken into account to show that a product was defective all along, but the development of better products after circulation should not be taken into account to demonstrate that the benefits of the product were all along less than supposed."

[165] In New Zealand on the basis of negligence liability it was held that although there are now statutory requirements for warnings on cigarette packets a manufacturer was not under a duty in tort to warn in the 1960s because the danger to health was common knowledge by that time: *Pou v British American Tobacco (NZ) Ltd* [2006] NZHC 451.

[166] See *Worsley v Tambrands Ltd*, December 3, 1999, QBD. These matters are obviously intimately connected with foreseeable use. By way of example—(1) most perfume is highly inflammable, but should a manufacturer have to give warning of this? Yes, according to an American court in *Moran v Faberge*, 332 A. (2d) 11 (1975)—claimant dowsing candle in perfume. (2) Sealing compounds are inflammable and contain warnings not to expose to naked flame. Should this extend to a warning to extinguish the pilot light on a stove? Yes, according to the Supreme Court of Canada, reversing an appeal court in *Lambert v Lastoplex Chemicals* (1971) 25 D.L.R. (3d) 121, decided on a negligence standard.

proposition that the manufacturer should err on the side of action.[167]

E. The Development Risks Defence

By s.4(1)(e) it is a defence for the defendant to prove that: **10–23**

"[T]he state of scientific and technical knowledge at the relevant time[168] was not such that a producer of products of the same description as the product in question might be expected to have discovered the defect if it had existed in his products while they were under his control."

This defence proved highly controversial during the passage of the Act but the Government insisted on its inclusion. The first point is that the Directive merely allows the inclusion of such a defence[169] and the policy among Member States has not been uniform: Germany, for example, allows such a defence generally, but not for pharmaceuticals. Secondly, the terms of s.4(1)(e) do not accord completely with art.7(e) of the Directive, which provides:

"[T]hat the state of scientific and technical knowledge at the time when [the producer] put the product into circulation was not such as to enable the existence of the defect to be discovered,"

and it is certainly arguable that the Directive speaks in terms of scientific possibility, whereas s.4(1)(e), with its references to comparable producers and what might have been expected, comes closer to a traditional negligence formula. The European Commission challenged s.4(1)(e) before the European Court of Justice. The challenge was rejected[170] on the grounds that the provision did not plainly and irremediably fail to comply with art.7(e) and that the English court would have to interpret it in the light of the Directive. The Court said that art.7(e) was not directed at the state of knowledge in the industrial sector on which the producer is operating but at the state of knowledge in general; on the other hand it was

---

[167] Provided, that is, he does not put in so much information that consumers are likely not to bother to read it! There is no blanket rule that the manufacturer may safely ignore a danger which is "obvious", for the product may foreseeably get into the hands of children or other incompetents and if a simple design change will reduce the danger to them, the law may require it: see Miller, op. cit., Division III. But warnings of obvious dangers may detract from safety by diminishing the significance of warnings about non-obvious risks.

[168] The time of the supply by the producer: s.4(2).

[169] See generally, Newdick, "The Development Risks Defence of the Consumer Protection Act 1987" [1988] C.L.J. 455 and Newdick, "Risk, Uncertainty and 'Knowledge' in the Development Risk Defence" (1992) 20 Anglo-American L.R. 309.

[170] *European Commission v UK* [1997] All E.R. (EC) 481.

implicit in art.7(e) that the knowledge in question must be accessible.[171] Although as a matter of language both s.4(1)(e) and art.7(e) of the Directive could be read as allowing the defence to operate where there is no known method of discovering the defect in an individual product (the non-standard product), this is not so: the defence only applies if there is no knowledge of the existence of the risk in a generic sense, and once this knowledge has been acquired, the manufacturer produces at his own risk, even if it is impossible to identify the individual, non-standard products in which that risk is present.[172] Hence, "development risks defence" is a better shorthand than "state of the art defence".[173]

The argument in favour of s.4(1)(e), at least in so far as it applies to unknown design risks, is succinctly put in the DTI Consultative Document on the Directive.

> "Manufacturers . . . have argued that it would be wrong in principle, and disastrous in practice, for businesses to be held liable for defects that they could not possibly have foreseen. They believe that the absence of this defence would raise costs and inhibit innovation, especially in high risk industries. Many useful new products, which might entail a development risk, would not be put on the market, and consumers as well as businesses might lose out."

On the other hand, there is no such defence in contract law,[174] and it has been suggested that another thalidomide-type tragedy might slip through the liability net under the Act, for which reason both the Law Commission and the Pearson Commission rejected any exemption for development risks.[175]

F. Other Defences

10–24 Section 4 contains other defences which, like s.4(1)(e), are defences in the proper sense of that term, i.e. matters which must be raised and proved by the defendant. To the common law mind some of them are matters which might more naturally be regarded as

---

[171] Advocate-General Tesauro in his opinion had given the example of an article published only in Chinese in Manchuria. In *A v National Blood Authority*, above, at [49] Burton J. regarded as a more realistic example results which had not been published and were held within the research department of a company.

[172] *A v National Blood Authority* [2001] 3 All E.R. 289.

[173] The decision of the German Supreme Court in NJW 1995, 1262 can be read as holding that the defence can *never* apply to non-standard products. However, Burton J, in the *National Blood Authority* case thought that this would not be so if the very possibility of the existence of the non-standard product were unknown.

[174] *Henry Kendall & Sons v William Lillico & Sons Ltd* [1969] 2 A.C. 31; *Ashington Piggeries Ltd v Christopher Hill Ltd* [1972] A.C. 441.

[175] See Law Com. No.82, para.105; Cmnd. 7054, Vol.1, para.1259.

casting a burden on the claimant but the Act is a consumer protection measure and the allocation of the burden is deliberate. Section 4 will, therefore, come into play if we postulate that the claimant has proved, directly or by getting the court to draw inferences:

1. damage
2. attributable to a defect
3. in an article for which the defendant is responsible under the Act, as producer or otherwise.

The defences are—   **10–25**

1. That the defect is attributable to compliance with any requirement imposed by law

Suppose that the law required all wine to contain sulphur dioxide. Suppose also that the ingredient was then found to be harmful. The producer would have a defence without reference to the "development risks" defence of s.4(1)(e). This defence does not mean that compliance with minimum legal standards automatically provides a defence.[176] The hypothetical wine law forbids the addition of ingredients A, B and C. The producer adds ingredient X, widely thought to be beneficial, but then discovered to be harmful. Subject to s.4(1)(e), the producer is liable. Perhaps a more likely state of affairs is one where an ingredient is expressly permitted by law even though it is believed, or even known, to carry some risk of injury. Section 4(1)(a) would seem not to provide a defence, though it might be very difficult to establish a case of negligence in such circumstances.[177]

2. That the defendant did not at any time supply the product to another

Being a supplier does not involve liability under the Act unless the "tracing" provision of s.2(3) comes into play. But even a producer is not liable if he has not supplied[178] the article to another. "Supply" is widely defined to include hiring out or lending but it does not cover merely putting goods in someone's hands for him to use, so if D produces a machine for internal use in the factory and it has a defect which injures workman C the Act does not apply.[179]

---

[176] Nor does it under *Restatement* (3d), s.3(d).
[177] Cf. *Albery and Budden v B.P. Oil*, para.5–82, above, a claim in negligence.
[178] See s.46.
[179] Miller, op. cit., points out that for the same reason the Act would have no application to an incident like the Bhopal disaster; but see *Veedfald v Arhus Amtskommune* [2001] E.C.R. I–3569.

3. That any supply by the defendant was a "non-commercial" one within s.4(1)(c).[180]

4. That the defect did not exist in the product when he put it into circulation.[181]

The producer is not liable for defects which have arisen from interference, misuse or fair wear and tear but once the claimant has shown that the product was defective in the s.3 sense and has caused damage it is up to the producer to raise and prove such matters. Of course he may do so by indirect evidence (for example, by showing that a weakness in the wall of a burst tyre is reasonably consistent only with impact damage in use) but where the court is left in doubt the claimant should win.

It should be noted that where the defect does exist when the product leaves the hands of the producer, the possibility or probability of intermediate examination does not insulate him from liability.[182]

5. Section 4(1)(e) provides:

"That the defect

   (i) constituted a defect in a product ('the subsequent product') in which the product in question had been comprised and

   (ii) was wholly attributable to the design of the subsequent product or to compliance by the producer of the product in question with instructions given by the producer of the subsequent product."

A Co orders a consignment of standard tyres from B Co and fits them to a high-speed sports car model for which they are wholly

---

[180] This reads as follows:

> "(i) that the only supply of the product to another by the person proceeded against was otherwise than in the course of a business of that person's and
>
> (ii) that section 2(2) . . . does not apply to that person or applies to him by virtue only of things done otherwise than with a view to profit."

Hence a person donating a home-made pie to a church fete escapes liability, but if he sold it he would be liable if the cooking made him a "producer" within s.1(2)(c). A private seller of second-hand goods would escape the "tracing' liability under s.2(3) because s.2(2) does not apply to him.

[181] This is the position of defendants falling within s.2(2). There are, however, special provisions as to the relevant time in relation to electricity and to s.2(3) defendants.

[182] Cf. the common law, para.10–8, above. In *Hayes v Leo Scaffolding Ltd*, CA, December 3, 1996, where the employers of the claimant had submitted to judgment in respect of a fall caused by a defective plank, their claim for contribution against the producer of the plank failed because, in the court's view, the likelihood of intermediate examination insulated the producer from liability to the claimant and therefore the producer was not a person "liable to" the claimant for the purposes of the Civil Liability (Contribution) Act 1978. However, the employers did not rely upon the Consumer Protection Act, which, in the words of Simon Brown L.J.: "on the face of it, would have provided them with a well nigh impregnable argument."

unsuitable. The car is therefore "defective". If, as this paragraph seems to assume,[183] the tyre is also thereby defective, B Co. has a defence to an action by an injured consumer. Where the component producer knows or ought to know that the final assembler intends, through inexperience, to make an unsuitable use of the component then an action in negligence might lie against the component producer at the suit of an injured consumer,[184] quite apart from any liability in contract to the assembler. The position is less clear where the assembler is aware of the danger and presses on regardless but it is submitted that the component manufacturer must be entitled, after due warning to the assembler, to act on assurances by the latter and is not obliged to investigate compliance with those assurances.

G. Contributory Negligence

The Consumer Protection Act applies the Law Reform (Contributory Negligence) Act 1945[185] by providing that when damage is caused partly by a defect in a product and partly by the fault of the person suffering the damage then the defect is to be treated as if it were the fault of every person liable for it under the Act.[186] In "deeming" fault to exist in the producer the Act recognises the difficulty of balancing blameworthy against non-blameworthy conduct, though it does not really solve the problem. However, there is plenty of experience under acts and regulations on industrial safety of applying apportionment of liability to strict liability situations and the courts should have no difficulty with this. Where the claimant's fault is extreme then it may amount to the sole cause in law and deprive him of damages altogether; in many cases, exactly the same result may be reached by concluding that the claimant's use of the product is so unusual that it is not defective, even if it has caused damage.

10–26

H. Exclusion of Liability

Section 7 enacts a simple rule invalidating any limitation or exclusion of liability, "by any contract term, by any notice or by any other provision", no matter what the nature of the damage.[187] Of course, care must be taken to distinguish substance from form:

10–27

---

[183] Oddly, perhaps.

[184] Whether the Act also applies in this situation would not seem to matter.

[185] See para.6–43, above.

[186] Section 6(4). Various other Acts are also applied by s.6, e.g. the Fatal Accidents Act 1976 and the Congenital Disabilities (Civil Liability) Act 1976.

[187] Contrast s.2 of the Unfair Contract Terms Act 1977, para.25–6, below, which makes exclusion of liability for property damage caused by negligence subject to a reasonableness test.

"manufacturers will not be responsible unless this product is earthed" is not an exclusion of liability but a warning which goes to the safety of the product under s.3. Nor does s.7 invalidate the terms of contracts between, say, an assembler and component manufacturers allocating ultimate responsibility among themselves, though those contracts may be subject to judicial control under the Unfair Contract Terms Act 1977.

I. Limitation

10–28   This is dealt with in Ch.26. At this stage, however, it is worth noting the "cut-off" provision whereby any liability is extinguished 10 years after the product has been put into circulation, thus smothering to some extent the risk of mass disaster litigation arising from defects which come to light only after many years.[188] This does not, however, affect the common law of negligence.

3. CONCLUSION

10–29   From a theoretical point of view, the Consumer Protection Act is one of the most important developments in English tort law for many years. However, liability is by no means absolute: the Act has affinities with the common law in some respects and only time will tell, especially in relation to development risks, how far it will effect a substantial change in practice. One matter of great controversy is the cost of implementation. There is no doubt that in the United States strict product liability judgments became a serious burden on some sectors of manufacturing industry[189] but the cause of this may have lain as much in American practice on the use of juries, contingency fees and other matters as in strict liability.[190] One estimate was that the implementation of the Directive would lead to an increase of no more than 25 per cent in liability insurance premiums, which means, on average, an increase in unit costs of the order of 0.02 per cent,[191] though there might be huge variations from one trade to another. However, the European Commission in its review of the operation of the Directive was wholly unable to make any assessment of the cost of strict liability in Europe after 13

---

[188] e.g. asbestosis. On when a product is put into circulation, see *O'Byrne v Sanofi Pasteur MSD Ltd* [2006] 1 W.L.R. 1606 (ECJ) and *O'Byrne v Aventis Pasteur SA* [2010] UKSC 23.

[189] There has been widespread state legislation in an effort to stem the tide: reduced limitation periods and "caps" on non-pecuniary—loss damages have been popular devices.

[190] There has been a similar crisis (or perceived crisis) in medical malpractice, which remains governed by the law of negligence.

[191] See North (1978) 128 New L.J. 315, 318 (based on the Law Commission/Pearson proposals, i.e. with no development risks defence).

years.[192] In any event, greater "litigation consciousness" could wholly falsify early estimates.[193]

It should also be noted that there is a further, modest element of strict liability in the consumer protection field. Since 1961 the Secretary of State has had power to make regulations imposing safety requirements for classes of goods and to make orders prohibiting the supply of goods which are not safe.[194] This power is now contained in Pt II of the Consumer Protection Act 1987 (s.11) and contravention of the regulations is actionable[195] (as a breach of statutory duty) by any person affected thereby.[196] Part II is, however, primarily concerned with the enforcement of safety by criminal sanctions.

[192] COM/2000/0893. See p.8. Apart from the fact that no uniform statistics are kept, many cases will be based on negligence and contract law as well as on strict tort liability.
[193] Curiously, the UK has had a very low rate of cases arising from the Directive, even though there is a common view in Europe that the English legal system has a more "American" culture than others. Of course, many claims may have been settled out of court.
[194] Originally in the Consumer Protection Act 1961, succeeded by the Consumer Safety Act 1978. See also General Product Safety Regulations 2005, SI 2005/1803.
[195] Except in so far as safety regulations provide otherwise.
[196] Section 41.

CHAPTER 11

LIABILITY FOR STATEMENTS

THE title of this chapter raises the difficulty of arranging a general account of tort law, for a good deal of the law about liability for damage done by statements will be found elsewhere in this book. Statements may cause harm even if true, as where they involve invasions of a person's privacy or breach of his confidences. Liability for untrue statements has a wider canvas. (1) A statement may injure a person's reputation, if defamatory and published to a third party; (2) it may cause direct injury by shock to the person to whom it is addressed; (3) it may cause him to act in reliance on it and suffer loss as a result; (4) or it may cause him loss because it is addressed to other persons who, in reliance on it, act (perhaps perfectly lawfully) to his detriment. The first is covered by the tort of defamation, the subject of a separate chapter, which also looks at privacy and confidence.[1] The second is the liability under *Wilkinson v Downton*, which has been considered in connection with intentional

11–1

---

[1] Ch.12.

wrongs to the person.[2] This chapter is concerned with the third category and part of the fourth; only part of the fourth, because that category includes malicious falsehood, which is considered with defamation because it often overlaps with it. However, even on this basis the arrangement is still to a certain extent arbitrary. Deceit typically involves deliberate interference with economic interests in a business or contractual context[3] and could be placed in the chapter on the economic torts.[4] "Negligent misstatement" is certainly not a tort in its own right (though deceit is) and liability is often (though not wholly—after all, *Caparo v Dickman*[5] was a "statement" case) based upon a broader concept of assumption of responsibility, which we have examined in the context of the duty of care in negligence[6]: if a professional person undertakes a task in respect of which he owes a duty to the claimant he is liable whether he performs that task incompetently or negligently advises the claimant on the action he should take.

The fact that merely because there is a "statement" we do not move outside the general principles of negligence may be illustrated by *West Bromwich Albion Football Club v El-Safty.*[7] The defendant regularly treated footballers referred to him by the claimant club. On this occasion he advised reconstructive surgery on X's knee which was unsuccessful and led to the end of X's playing career; the correct course would have been conservative treatment. The club brought a claim for damages for the loss it suffered from not having X's services. There was held to be no contractual relationship between the defendant and the club. This was not a case where the defendant had undertaken to advise the club on anything and the defendant's concern was with the medical condition of his patient, not with the financial situation of the club and the case could not be equated with those where financial advice is given to X and it is known that this will be relied on by third parties, nor with those where X seeks a service from D in order to confer a benefit on others.[8] Nor would it be fair, just and reasonable to impose a duty to the club. As the trial judge had put it[9]:

---

[2] [1897] 2 Q.B. 57, para.4–36, above.
[3] Not always. Liability for deceit has been found in cases of false claims of paternity: *P v B (paternity: damages for deceit)* [2001] 1 F.L.R. 1041; *A v B* [2007] EWHC 1246 (QB); [2007] 2 F.L.R. 1051. Cf. *Magill v Magill* [2005] HCA 51, 231 A.L.R. 277; but the principle in *McFarlane v Tayside Health Board* [2000] 2 A.C. 59 (para.24–15, below) blocks any claim for expenditure on the maintenance of the child even though the cause of action is different.
[4] Ch.18.
[5] [1990] 2 A.C. 605, para.5–9, above.
[6] See para.5–34, above.
[7] [2006] EWCA Civ 1299; [2007] P.I.Q.R. P7.
[8] *White v Jones*, para.5–37, above.
[9] [2005] EWHC 2866 (QB).

"Should a consultant for example advising a Rooney or a Beckham or a Flintoff[10] have a potential tortious liability to their club/county or England for negligent treatment—a liability running to many millions of pounds? What about negligent treatment of a resident conductor of an orchestra or a leading player in a rock band or the managing director of a major company? The consultant would probably know each patient was a valuable asset.

Should the consultant take steps to ascertain their value so as to evaluate his potential liability? Should he seek to put in hand a disclaimer or limitation of his liability? How would he do this? How would insurance premiums be affected?

In my judgement, one only has to pose these questions to conclude that it would not be fair, just and equitable for there to be liability in such cases."

The result seems entirely correct: if the defendant had knocked down X with his car it is clear that he would not have been liable to the club for its loss[11]; the same must be true if he had caused X's injury by the negligent performance of the operation; it can hardly make a difference that his fault lay in the advice he gave to X.

Nevertheless, "statement" cases throw up enough commonly recurring features (legitimacy of reliance and the range of persons to whom a duty is owed) to justify some further, separate treatment.

1. DECEIT

Since *Pasley v Freeman*[12] in 1789, it has been the rule that A is **11–2** liable in tort to B if he knowingly or recklessly (i.e. not caring whether it is true or false) makes a false statement to B with intent that it shall be acted upon by B, who does act upon it and thereby suffers damage. This is the tort of deceit (or "fraud"), and for liability in deceit the defendant must make the statement with knowledge of its falsity or at least reckless whether it is true or false.[13] It was for long thought that this meant that there could be no liability in tort for a false statement honestly made, however negligent its maker may have been and however disastrous its consequences: a careless person is not a dishonest one. Eventually

---

[10] A duty to the patient is undeniable and it must be pointed out that in these cases the potential liability would be many millions of pounds.

[11] See para.5–40, above.

[12] (1789) 3 T.R. 51.

[13] *Derry v Peek* (1889) 14 App.Cas. 337. In one instance, the law allows (but does not compel) the making of a false statement: Rehabilitation of Offenders Act 1974 s.4(2).

however, the House of Lords held that there may in certain circumstances be a duty of care upon the maker of a statement,[14] and thus that a person may be liable for a false statement honestly but negligently made. Such liability cannot be brought under the tort of deceit—it is liability for negligence and not for fraud—but its existence has a profound bearing on liability for statements as a whole. If there may be liability in negligence it may be of little more than academic interest that absence of fraudulent intent is fatal to a claim founded on deceit. Nevertheless, the tort has not been abolished (indeed it seems to be arising with greater frequency) and the claimant may have good reason for seeking to establish a case of deceit (for example, there is no need to establish a duty based on a special relationship,[15] it may enable him to avoid a disclaimer which would otherwise be valid,[16] his claim cannot be met by an allegation of contributory negligence[17] and the rules on damages will be more favourable to him[18]). However, a case based on deceit should not be advanced without clear instructions and credible material to support it[19] and it must be unequivocally pleaded[20] and distinctly proved,[21] for fraud is inherently less likely than negligence.[22] Summary judgment is now in principle available in a case of deceit[23] but is rather unlikely in practice.

2. ESSENTIALS OF DECEIT

11–3   The five things that the claimant has to establish in a common law action of deceit may be summarised as follows[24]:

[14] *Hedley Byrne & Co Ltd v Heller & Partners Ltd* [1964] A.C. 465. See, too, the Misrepresentation Act 1967 s.2.

[15] *Noel v Poland* [2001] B.C.L.C 645 at [48.

[16] It should be noted that "fraud" is sometimes used in equity in a broader sense than the common law tort of deceit: see *Armitage v Nurse* [1998] Ch. 241.

[17] See para.6–44, above.

[18] See para.11–14, below. Oddly, however, the effect of *Royscott Trust v Rogerson* [1991] 2 Q.B. 297 is to apply the deceit rule on damages to the statutory cause of action under the Misrepresentation Act 1967 s.2(1).

[19] Though not necessarily admissible evidence at the pleading stage: *Medcalf v Weatherill* [2002] UKHL 27; [2003] 1 A.C. 120.

[20] "Knew or ought to have known" is not taken as two alternative allegations, the first of which imputes fraud: *Armitage v Nurse*, above, fn.16, at 257.

[21] *Hornal v Neuberger Products Ltd* [1957] 1 Q.B. 247.

[22] *H (Minors), Re* [1996] A.C. 563 at 586, but on principle it would not seem necessary for the claimant to establish damage to the same elevated standard: *G.E. Commercial Finance Ltd v Gee* [2005] EWHC 2056 (QB) at [122].

[23] CPR 24.

[24] There is no general liability for "fraud" in the sense of dishonesty unless it amounts to the tort of deceit or to equitable fraud. *Amalgamated Metal Trading Ltd v D.T.I., The Times,* March 21, 1989. However, a principal may recover damages for "fraud" in respect of a transaction into which his agent is bribed (*Mahesan v Malaysia Government Officers' Co-operative Housing Society* [1979] A.C. 374) although there will not usually be any representation to the principal. This has been described as, "not . . . deceit, but a special form of fraud": *Petrotrade Inc v Smith* [2001] 1 Lloyd's Rep. 486 at 490. The Fraud Act

1. There must be a representation of fact made by words or conduct.
2. The representation must be made with knowledge that it is or may be false. It must be wilfully false, or at least made in the absence of any genuine belief that it is true.
3. The representation must be made with the intention that it should be acted upon by the claimant, or by a class of persons which includes the claimant, in the manner which resulted in damage to him.
4. It must be proved that the claimant has acted upon the false statement.
5. It must be proved that the claimant suffered damage by so doing.[25]

A. A False Statement of Fact

i. Representations. The statement may, of course, be oral or **11–4** written. It may also be implied from conduct. If the defendant deliberately acts in a manner calculated to deceive the claimant and the other elements of the tort are present, the defendant is as much liable for deceit as if he had expressly made a false statement of fact.[26] Deliberate concealment, too, amounts to deceit,[27] but subject to what is said below mere silence, however morally wrong, will not support an action for deceit.[28]

ii. Promises and other statements of intention. It is commonly **11–5** said that mere promises are not statements of fact, but this is misleading, for every promise involves a statement of present intention as to future conduct.

2006 for the first time create a general *criminal offence* of fraud, replacing a number of offences of obtaining by deception. Tort and crime overlap here but they are not identical in their requirements.

[25] The damage is the gist of the action: *Smith v Chadwick* (1884) 9 App. Cas. 187 at 196 per Lord Blackburn; *Briess v Woolley* [1954] A.C. 332. See *Renault UK v Fleetpro Technical Services Ltd* [2007] EWHC 2541 (QB).

[26] *Ward v Hobbs* (1878) 4 App. Cas. 13 at 16 per Lord O'Hagan; *Bradford Building Society v Borders* [1942] 1 All E.R. 205 at 211 per Lord Maugham; *Advanced Industrial Technology Corp Ltd v Bond Street Jewellers Ltd* [2006] EWCA Civ 923. For a criminal case, see *R. v Barnard* (1837) 7 C. & P. 784.

[27] *Gordon v Selico* (1984) 275 E.G. 899. But there is a difference between the concealing of a serious defect and doing minor acts to make a property more attractive to a purchaser.

[28] *Bradford Building Society v Borders*, above, fn.26, at [1942] 1 All E.R. 205 at 211 per Lord Maugham, citing *Peek v Gurney* (1873) L.R. 6 H.L. 377 at 390 per Lord Chelmsford, at 403 per Lord Cairns. Cf. the rule in s.551 of the *Restatement* 2d.

"There must be a misstatement of an existing fact: but the state of a man's mind is as much a fact as the state of his digestion."[29]

If, then, I make a promise believing that I shall fulfil it, the reason that I am not liable for deceit if I do not fulfil it is not that my promise was not a statement of fact but that the statement of fact involved in the promise was true.[30] If at the time I made it I had no intention of fulfilling my promise, I may be liable for deceit. So in *Edgington v Fitzmaurice*[31] directors of a company were held liable for deceit in procuring the public to subscribe for debentures by falsely stating in a prospectus that the loan secured by the debentures was for the purpose of completing buildings of the company, purchasing horses and vans and developing the trade of the company; in fact the directors intended to use it for paying off pressing liabilities.[32]

11–6   **iii. Opinion.** A statement of opinion frequently carries within itself a statement of fact. A person who says "I believe X to be honest" is making a statement of fact as to his state of mind, and if it is untrue there is no reason why, if the other requirements of the tort are met, he should not be held liable for deceit. Often also an expression of opinion carries the implication that the person expressing it has reasonable grounds for it, and where this is not the case he may be guilty of a misstatement of fact.[33] On the other hand, there must be some latitude for "sales talk" and a seller's imprecise commendations of his wares do not give rise to liability merely because even the seller might, on careful reflection, think them exaggerated.[34]

11–7   **iv. Statements of law.** As a matter of general principle a misstatement of law ought to be a sufficient misstatement of fact for the

---

[29] *Edgington v Fitzmaurice* (1885) 29 Ch.D. 459 at 483 per Bowen L.J.; *Clydesdale Bank Ltd v Paton* [1896] A.C. 381 at 394 per Lord Herschell: cf. at 397 per Lord Davey.

[30] Cf. *British Airways Board v Taylor* [1976] 1 W.L.R. 13 (Trade Descriptions Act; statement false because maker concealed risk that he might be unable to fulfil his promise).

[31] (1885) 29 Ch.D. 459.

[32] There is said to be an exception to this, namely, that a purchaser may freely state his intention to pay no more than a certain sum or a vendor his intention to accept no less than a certain sum: Rolle Abr. 101, pl. 16 (1598); *Vernon v Keys* (1810) 12 East 632 affirmed, sub. nom. *Vernon v Keyes* (1812) 4 Taunt. 488. The exception (which seems perfectly sensible, for such conduct in bargaining would surely not be regarded as improper) must not, however, be carried too far: Pollock in 11 R. R. Pref. vi–vii, and *Torts*, 15th edn, p.213, n.6; *Haygarth v Wearing* (1871) L.R. 12 Eq. 320.

[33] *Brown v Raphael* [1958] Ch. 636, a case of innocent misrepresentation in contract. For a discussion in the context of insurance, see *Economides v Commercial Union Assurance Co* [1998] Q.B. 587.

[34] See the comments of Learned Hand J. in *Vulcan Metals Co v Simmons Mfg. Co* 248 F. 853 (1918). Yet everything depends on the circumstances: see the words which were held to amount to the "higher" legal category of warranty in *Andrews v Hopkinson* [1957] Q.B. 229.

purposes of deceit provided at least that the parties are not on equal footing with respect to knowledge of the law or to general intelligence.[35] A great many statements which we should not hesitate to describe as statements of fact involve inferences from legal rules[36] and the distinction between law and fact is by no means as precise as might at first appear. So, in *West London Commercial Bank Ltd v Kitson*,[37] where directors of a company, knowing that the private Act of Parliament which incorporated the company gave them no legal power to accept bills of exchange, nevertheless represented to the claimant that they had such authority there was held to have been deceit:

"Suppose I were to say I have a private Act of Parliament which gives me power to do so and so. Is not that an assertion that I have such an Act of Parliament? It appears to me to be as much a representation of a matter of fact as if I had said I have a particular bound copy of 'Johnson's Dictionary'."[38]

If the representation is of a pure proposition of law and not a deduction from a rule of law there may be greater difficulty in treating it as a statement of fact, but there is no reason for holding that a solicitor, for example, can never be liable in deceit for a misstatement of law to his client.[39] It is not easy to see what argument can be produced the other way. To urge that everyone is presumed to know the law is to carry into the law of deceit a distinction between law and fact which, artificial enough in any event, was never invented for the purpose of shielding swindlers.[40] On the other hand, professional lawyers dealing with each other at arm's length would doubtless be deemed equal and if one falsely alleged to the other something purporting to be a pure proposition of

[35] Direct authority for this propositon is lacking but the view stated in the text is shared by Clerk & Lindsell, *Torts*, 19th edn, para.18–13, pointing out a tendency in other areas like mistake and misrepresentation to bring matters of law within the scope of legal responsibility. A deliberate false statement of law is sufficient for the crime of fraud under s.2(3) of the Fraud Act 2006.
[36] "There is not a single fact connected with personal status that does not, more or less, involve a question of law. If you state that a man is the eldest son of a marriage, you state a question of law, because you must know that there has been a valid marriage, and that that man was the firstborn son after the marriage .... Therefore, to state it is not a representation of fact seems to arise from a confusion of ideas. It is not the less a fact because that fact involves some knowledge or relation of law": *Eaglesfield v Marquis of Londonderry* (1876) 4 Ch.D. 693 at 703 per Jessel M.R.
[37] (1884) 13 Q.B.D. 360.
[38] (1884) 13 Q.B.D. 360 at 363 per Bowen L.J.
[39] There is, of course, a contract between solicitor and client, and a solicitor may be liable for a negligent misstatement: *Otter v Church, Adams, Tatham & Co* [1953] Ch. 280.
[40] Furthermore, money may now be recovered for mistake of law as well as fact (*Kleinwort Benson v Lincoln CC* [1999] 2 A.C. 349) and it has been held that a statement of law can fall within the Misrepresentation Act 1967 (*Pankhania v Hackney LBC* [2002] EWHC 2441 (Ch)).

law, there might be serious difficulty in establishing a claim for deceit.[41]

11–8   v. Half-truths. The general rule is that there must be a statement or representation by words or conduct.[42] This does not mean that there must be a direct lie: *suppressio veri* may amount to *suggestio falsi* if it is:

> "[S]uch a partial and fragmentary statement of fact, as that the withholding of that which is not stated makes that which is stated absolutely false".[43]

For example, where a husband whose income is £80,000 a year is under agreement to pay half to his wife and writes to her saying, "I send £30,000, half my income"—that would be a lie. It makes no difference if he sends her £30,000 and says nothing, for it would be an implied statement that it is half his income and he is guilty of deceit.[44] Sometimes, however, a person is under a legal duty to disclose facts and Lord Blackburn said that in such a case if he deliberately held his tongue with the intention of inducing the other party to act on the belief that he did not speak because he had nothing to say, that would be fraud.[45]

11–9   vi. Statements which prove to be false. Related to the above is the situation where D makes a true statement to C and then discovers, before C acts upon it, that it has become false. Does the law permit D to remain silent or does it compel him to correct C's false impression under pain of an action of deceit? It is submitted that the latter answer is in general correct. The tort of deceit is not complete when the representation is made. It only becomes complete when

---

[41] One professional lawyer would not normally act in a professional capacity in reliance upon another's statement of law in an adversarial situation. Statements made in connexion with judicial proceedings may anyway fall within the different principle of witness immunity: *Walsh v Sprecher Grier Halberstam LLP* [2008] EWCA Civ 1324.

[42] See above. In *Ward v Hobbs* (1878) 4 App. Cas. 13, a failure to warn of a dangerous defect in goods sold was not deceit, though the result may have turned on the fact that the sale was "with all faults". Cf. Mummery L.J. in *Hamble Fisheries Ltd v L. Gardner & Sons Ltd* [1999] 2 Lloyd's Rep. 1 at 9. But now it might amount to negligence: *Hurley v Dyke* [1979] R.T.R. 265.

[43] *Peek v Gurney* (1873) L.R. 6 H.L. 377 at 403 per Lord Cairns. "Half the truth will sometimes amount to a real falsehood": at 392 per Lord Chelmsford. *Arkwright v Newbold* (1881) 17 Ch.D. 301 at 317–318; *Briess v Woolley* [1955] A.C. 333. "A cocktail of truth, falsity and evasion is a more powerful instrument of deception than undiluted falsehood": *Smith New Court Securities Ltd v Scrimgeour Vickers (Asset Management) Ltd* [1997] A.C. 254 at 274 per Lord Steyn.

[44] *Legh v Legh* (1930) 143 L.T. 151 at 152 per MacKinnon L.J.

[45] *Brownlie v Campbell* (1880) 5 App. Cas. 925 at 950; *Conlon v Simms* [2006] EWCA Civ 1749; [2008] 1 W.L.R. 484 at [130]. For the criminal law see s.3 of the Fraud Act 2006.

the misrepresentation—not having been corrected in the mean-
time—is acted upon by the representee.[46] The proper question in
any case, therefore, is whether the statement was false when it was
acted upon, not when it was made, and so a person whose true
statement becomes false to his knowledge before it is acted upon
should be liable in deceit if he does not correct it.[47]

Closely akin to this is another problem. Suppose that D's statement was false from the very beginning, but that when he made it he
honestly believed it to be true and then discovers later and before C
has acted upon it that it is false. Must he acquaint C with this? Here
equity has a decided answer, whereas the common law is short of
any direct decision. In *Reynell v Sprye*[48] a deed was cancelled by the
Court of Chancery because D had not communicated the falsity of
his belief. As to the wider liability to an action of deceit, it might be
inferred from a dictum of Lord Blackburn that it exists.[49]

However we treat the question, there is no substantial difference
between the two problems just put,[50] so that D is guilty of deceit in
both of them if he withholds from C the further information. This
certainly ought to be the law where there is plenty of time to retract
the statement and where the result of not doing so is certain to result
in widespread loss or damage (as in the case of a company prospectus) or in physical danger or serious business loss to even one
person; but it must not be taken too far. As we have seen, a false
statement of intention is a sufficient misrepresentation of fact to
support an action of deceit, and the difference between a false
statement of intention and a breach of a promise is that in the latter
case the promisor believes what he says about his intention. The
subsequent breach of promise shows, however, that at some time his
intention must have changed, but it does not follow that his failure
to inform the promisee of his change of intention is fraudulent.
Suppose that C has booked (but not paid for) a seat on D's coach at
9am, and that D tells him correctly that he intends to start the
journey at 11am. Suppose that D, finding it more convenient to start
at 10.30, starts then without informing C of his change of plans,
because it would take nearly half an hour to find C. Here, D has

---

[46] *Briess v Woolley* [1954] A.C. 33 at 353 per Lord Tucker, at 349 per Lord Reid; *Diamond v Bank of London & Montreal* [1979] Q.B. 333 (service out of jurisdiction); *Lindsay v O'Loughnane* [2010] EWHC 529 (QB).

[47] See *Incledon v Watson* (1862) 2 F. & F. 841; *With v O'Flanagan* [1936] Ch. 575 at 584 per Lord Wright; *Bradford Building Society v Borders* [1941] 2 All E.R. 205 at 220; *Jones v Dumbrell* [1981] V.R. 199. Cf. *Arkwright v Newbold* (1881) 17 Ch.D. 301 at 325, 329.

[48] (1852) 1 De G.M. & G. 660 at 708–709.

[49] *Brownlie v Campbell* (1880) 5 App. Cas. 925 at 950. It was not necessary to decide the point in *Henry Ansbacher & Co Ltd v Brinks Stern, The Times*, June 26, 1997.

[50] Except that in the latter case the statement was false from the moment it was made, while in the former it was not. Since it is impossible for a person to make a false statement of his intention while believing it to be true, it would appear that the qualification stated below has no application to the solution of the second problem put.

certainly committed a breach of contract, but it is wrong to style his silence as to the changed circumstances deceit, even though it is admittedly intentional. It is really no more than a churlish indifference to a breach of contract. On the other hand where D induced C to embark on the development of a shopping centre by representing that it proposed to restrict the "tenant mix" at a nearby development by X and then made a secret agreement with X to relax that, D was liable in deceit for loss suffered by C when, a few months later, C irrevocably committed itself to the work. In fact, there were further, positive misrepresentations of D's intention after the secret agreement, but it seems that the result would have been the same if D had kept silent. Certainly it seems realistic in this situation to treat D as making a continuing representation up to the time when C acts in reliance.[51]

One more possible case of silence raises no difficulty. If D knowingly makes a false statement to C, but before C acts upon it subsequent events have turned the statement into a true one, this is not deceit. Thus in *Ship v Crosskill*,[52] a false allegation in a prospectus, that applications for more than half the capital of the company had been subscribed, had become true before the claimant made his application for shares, and it was held that there was no misrepresentation for which relief could be given to him. "If false when made but true when acted upon there is no misrepresentation."[53]

B. The Statement Must be Made Without Belief in its Truth

11–10   This rule is the result of the decision in *Derry v Peek*,[54] where the House of Lords made it clear that blundering but honest belief in an allegation cannot be deceit. In Lord Herschell's classic formulation,

> "[F]raud is proved when it is shewn that a false representation has been made (1) knowingly,[55] or (2) without belief in its truth, or (3) recklessly, careless whether it be true or false. Although I have treated the second and third as distinct cases, I think the third is

---

[51] *Slough Estates Plc v Welwyn Hatfield DC* [1996] 2 P.L.R. 50.
[52] (1870) L.R. 10 Eq. 73.
[53] *Briess v Woolley* [1954] A.C. 333 at 353 per Lord Tucker.
[54] (1889) 14 App. Cas. 337.
[55] "A man may be said to know a fact when once he has been told it and pigeonholed it somewhere in his brain where it is more or less accessible in case of need. In another sense of the word a man knows a fact only when he is fully conscious of it. For an action of deceit there must be knowledge in the narrower sense and conscious knowledge of falsity must always amount to wickedness and dishonesty": *Armstrong v Strain* [1951] 1 T.L.R. 856 at 871 per Devlin J. For recklessness, see *Angus v Clifford* [1891] 2 Ch. 449 at 471 per Bowen L.J.; *Derry v Peek* (1889) 14 App. Cas. 337 at 371 per Lord Herschell.

but an instance of the second, for one who makes a statement under such circumstances can have no real belief in the truth of what he states. To prevent a false statement being fraudulent, there must, I think, always be an honest belief in its truth."[56]

The facts of *Derry v Peek* were that the directors of a tramway company issued a prospectus in which they stated that they had parliamentary powers to use steam in propelling their trams. In fact the grant of such powers was subject to the consent of the Board of Trade. The directors honestly but mistakenly believed the giving of this consent to be a merely formal matter; it was, however, refused. The company was wound up in consequence and the claimant, who had bought shares in it on the faith of the prospectus, instituted an action for deceit against the directors. The House of Lords, reversing the decision of the Court of Appeal, gave judgment for the defendants, holding that a false statement made carelessly and without reasonable ground for believing it to be true could not be fraud, though it might furnish evidence of it. A careless person is not a deceitful one and no amount of argument will prove he is one. However, dishonesty[57] in the criminal law sense is not necessary,[58] so the defendant is not excused by a belief that such a misrepresentation is common practice or will facilitate the transaction.[59] It must be noted that Lord Herschell's formulation of the law as requiring an honest belief in the truth of the statement was made in the context of a statement by promoters, who had a completely free choice as to what they said. It has been suggested that it does not necessarily follow that an employee is personally guilty of deceit where he makes a statement on the instruction of a senior officer and has some uncertainty as to its accuracy.[60]

C. Intent

The statement must be made with intent that the claimant shall act **11–11** upon it. So long as that is satisfied, it need not be made to him either

---

[56] At 14 App. Cas. 374. "Recklessness" in the third situation is a species of dishonest knowledge: *AIC Ltd v ITS Testing Services (UK) Ltd* [2006] EWCA Civ 1601; [2007] 1 Lloyd's Rep 555 at [257].

[57] However, the word "dishonest" is frequently used in the civil cases. It should be understood as simply meaning knowledge or recklessness as to untruth.

[58] *Society of Lloyd's v Jaffray* [2002] EWCA Civ 1101 at [66].

[59] *Standard Chartered Bank v Pakistan National Shipping Corp* [2000] 1 Lloyd's Rep. 218 (on appeal on other issues, [2002] UKHL 43, [2003] 1 A.C. 959); *Brown Jenkinson & Co Ltd v Percy Dalton (London) Ltd* [1957] 2 Q.B. 621.

[60] *G.E. Commercial Finance Ltd v Gee* [2005] EWHC 2056 (QB); [2006] 1 Lloyd's Rep 337. However, if there is the requisite state of mind the fact that a person purports to speak on behalf of a company does not insulate him from personal liability: para.24–23, below.

literally[61] or in particular. In *Langridge v Levy*,[62] the seller of a defective gun which he had falsely and knowingly warranted to be sound, was held liable to the claimant who was injured by its bursting, although it was the claimant's father to whom the gun had been sold, but who had acquainted the seller with the fact that he intended his sons to use it. The claimant need not be individually identifiable[63] but if the statement is made to a limited class of persons, no one outside that class can sue upon it. Thus a company prospectus was at common law ordinarily confined in its scope to the original shareholders. For false statements in it they could sue, but purchasers of the shares from them could not do so[64]; but circumstances might quite possibly make the prospectus fraudulent with respect even to them, as where it was supplemented by further lying statements intended to make persons who were not original allottees of the shares buy them in the market.[65] The intent need not be to cause damage to the claimant: it is enough that the claimant was intended to act on it and did act on it in the manner contemplated. The defendant is liable whether he actually intended damage to ensue or not.[66]

D. Claimant Must Rely on the Statement

11–12   The claimant must be "taken in" by the misrepresentation,[67] in other words, it must induce him to enter into the transaction[68]: attempted fraud may be a crime, but it is not a tort.[69] If, however, the

---

[61] It has been held that a fraudulent misrepresentation may be made to a machine acting on behalf of the claimant, rather than to an individual, if the machine was set up to process certain information in a particular way in which it would not process information about the material transaction if the correct information were given: *Renault UK v Fleetpro Technical Services Ltd* [2007] EWHC 2541 (QB).

[62] (1837) 2 M. & W. 519 4 M. & W. 337. See Clerk & Lindsell, *Torts*, 19th edn, para.18–29.

[63] *Abu Dhabi Investment Co v H. Clarkson & Co* [2008] EWCA Civ 699.

[64] *Peek v Gurney* (1873) L.R. 6 H.L. 377. But the statutory remedy under the Financial Services and Markets Act 2000 s.90, is not so limited. As to the position in common law negligence, see para.11–25, below. The question of to whom it was contemplated the false statement would be communicated is one of fact and if A makes a false statement to B with the intention that C will hear of it and act upon it, he cannot escape liability by telling B that it is for B's private use only: *Commercial Banking Co of Sydney Ltd v R.H. Brown & Co* [1972] 2 Lloyd's Rep. 360.

[65] *Andrews v Mockford* [1896] 1 Q.B. 372.

[66] *Polhill v Walter* (1832) 3 B. & Ad. 114; *Edgington v Fitzmaurice* (1885) 29 Ch.D. 459 at 482; *Brown Jenkinson & Co Ltd v Percy Dalton (London) Ltd* [1957] 2 Q.B. 621.

[67] It has been held in Australia that there may be fraud even though the victim is aware to some extent of the untruth of the statement, so long as he is not aware of the full extent of the untruth: *Gipps v Gipps* [1978] 1 N.S.W.L.R. 454.

[68] *Downs v Chappell* [1997] 1 W.L.R. 426.

[69] For this purpose the knowledge of the claimant's agent is not to be imputed to the claimant, e.g. where a house-agent acting for the claimant knew that a prospective tenant of the claimant's house was a woman of immoral character, but the claimant was unaware of this: *Wells v Smith* [1914] 3 K.B. 722. However, it is pointed out in Spencer, Bower &

claimant does rely on the defendant's statement it is no defence that he acted incautiously and failed to take those steps to verify its truth which a prudent person would have taken[70] and since 1945 the Law Reform (Contributory Negligence) Act has no application to cases of deceit.[71] In *Central Ry of Venezuela v Kisch*[72] directors of a company made deceitful statements in a prospectus and were held liable to a shareholder defrauded thereby, although the prospectus stated that certain documents could be inspected at the company's office and, if the shareholder had taken the trouble to do so, he would have discovered the fraud.[73] If the fraud is not obvious, it will not help that he inserted an express clause in a contract with the claimant that he must verify all representations for himself and not rely on their accuracy, for, "such a clause might in some cases be part of a fraud, and might advance and disguise a fraud".[74]

It is rare for a person to enter upon a transaction solely on the basis of one factor and it is no bar to a claim for damages for deceit that the claimant was influenced by other things beside the defendant's misrepresentation.[75] Nor need the misrepresentation be even the decisive factor, so long as it has a real or substantial effect on the claimant's decision.[76] It is wrong to ask what the claimant would have done if he had known the truth[77]: if he proves that he was induced by the lie he has made out his case on liability.[78]

In the case of an ambiguous statement the claimant must prove (1) **11–13** the sense in which he understood the statement, (2) that in that sense it was false, and (3) that the defendant intended him to understand it in that sense or deliberately made use of the ambiguity with the

---

Turner, *Actionable Misrepresentation*, 3rd edn, p.216, that the rule can hardly be applied in this unqualified form to a corporation.

[70] It is sometimes said that there is no actionable deceit when the defect in what is sold is so obvious that any sensible purchaser would have discovered the untruth of the representation upon inspection (see Prosser & Keeton, *Torts*, 5th edn, p.750). It is doubtful if the English cases support such a proposition as a rule of law, as opposed to a common sense matter of evidence pointing to the conclusion that the claimant was not in fact misled.

[71] *Standard Chartered Bank v Pakistan National Shipping Corp (Nos 2 and 4)* [2002] UKHL 43; [2003] 1 A.C. 959. See para.6–44, above.

[72] (1867) L.R. 2 H.L. 99.

[73] So too, *Dobell v Stevens* (1825) 3 B. & C. 623.

[74] *S. Pearson & Son Ltd v Dublin Corp* [1907] A.C. 351 at 360 per Lord Ashbourne; Cf. *Diamond v Bank of London & Montreal* [1979] Q.B. 333 at 347.

[75] *Edgington v Fitzmaurice* (1885) 29 Ch.D. 459.

[76] *J.E.B. Fasteners Ltd v Marks Bloom & Co* [1983] 1 All E.R. 583 at 589 per Stephenson L.J.

[77] In the sense that one should not allow the fraudster to say "you would still have acted in the same way", but there is no reason why the claimant should not be allowed to prove that he would have acted differently as cogent evidence of inducement: *Parabola Investments Ltd v Browallia Cal Ltd* [2009] EWHC 901 (Comm).

[78] *Downs v Chappell* [1997] 1 W.L.R. 426; *Smith v Kay* (1859) 7 H.L. Cas. 750 at 759. See also *Bristol and West B.S. v Mothew* [1998] Ch. 1 (negligent misrepresentation, but see *Hagen v I.C.I.* [2002] I.R.L.R. 31).

express purpose of deceiving him.[79] It does not follow because the defendant uses ambiguous language that he is conscious of the way in which the claimant will understand it. Unless the defendant:

> "[I]s conscious that it will be understood in a different manner from that in which he is honestly though blunderingly using it, he is not fraudulent. An honest blunder in the use of language is not dishonest."[80]

An ambiguous statement must therefore be taken in the sense in which the defendant intended it to be understood, and however reasonable a claimant may be in attaching the untrue meaning to the statement, there is no deceit unless the defendant intended his words to be taken in that sense.

> "The question is not whether the defendant in any given case honestly believed the representation to be true in the sense assigned to it by the court on an objective consideration of its truth or falsity, but whether he honestly believed the representation to be true in the sense in which he understood it, albeit erroneously, when it was made."[81]

In *Smith v Chadwick*,[82] the prospectus of a company alleged that, "the present value of the turnover or output of the entire works is over £1,000,000 sterling per annum." Did this mean that the works had actually turned out in one year produce worth more than a million, or at that rate per year? If so, it was untrue. Or did it mean only that the works were capable of turning out that amount of produce? If so, it was true. The claimant failed to prove that he had interpreted the words in the sense in which they were false, so he

---

[79] *Smith v Chadwick* (1884) 9 App. Cas. 187 at 201 per Lord Blackburn; *Arkwright v Newbold* (1881) 17 Ch.D. 301 at 324 per Cotton L.J.; *AIC Ltd v ITS Testing Services (UK) Ltd* [2006] EWCA Civ 1601; [2007] 1 Lloyd's Rep 555 at [253].

[80] *Angus v Clifford* [1891] 2 Ch. 449 at 472 per Bowen L.J.; *Smith v Chadwick* (1892) 20 Ch.D. 27 at 79 per Lindley L.J.; *Gross v Lewis Hillman Ltd* [1970] Ch. 445.

[81] *Akerhielm v De Mare* [1959] A.C. 789 at 805 per Lord Jenkins. This proposition is subject to the limitation that the meaning placed by the defendant on the representation may be so far removed from the sense in which it would be understood by any reasonable person as to make it impossible to hold that the defendant honestly understood the representation to bear the meaning claimed by him and honestly believed it in that sense to be true; *Henry Ansbacher & Co Ltd v Brinks Stern, The Times,* June 26, 1997. Note that where liability for a negligent, as distinct from a fraudulent, misstatement is in issue, the important question concerns the sense in which the claimant, not the defendant, understood it: *W.B. Anderson & Sons Ltd v Rhodes (Liverpool) Ltd* [1967] 2 All E.R. 850 at 855–856 per Cairns J.

[82] (1884) 9 App. Cas. 187.

lost his action. On the question of the actual meaning of the statement, the court was evenly divided, but there is no doubt that if an allegation is deliberately put forth in an ambiguous form with the design of catching the claimant on that meaning of it which makes it false, it is fraudulent and indeed is aggravated by a shabby attempt to get the benefit of a fraud without incurring the responsibility.[83]

E. Damage

The damage which the claimant must prove that he has suffered **11–14** in consequence of acting upon the statement will usually be financial but it may consist of personal injury[84] or mental distress[85] or damage to property; and it has also been held that loss of possession of a regulated tenancy under the Rent Acts, even without actual financial loss, will suffice.[86]

In principle the claimant is entitled, so far as money can do it, to be put into the position in which he would have been if the fraudulent statement had not been made and the defendant must make reparation for all the actual losses which flow from his deceit. The rule thus differs from that governing the damages recoverable for breach of contract[87] in that the claimant cannot recover the gains he would have made from that transaction (his expectation loss). He may recover for the loss of opportunity to lay out his money in other, more profitable ways which he is unable to pursue as a result of the tort,[88] but a decision that he may recover on the basis of what his deal with the defendant would have been had the latter told him the truth seems almost to elide the difference between the two measures of damages.[89] Where the claimant has been induced to buy property by a fraudulent representation the normal assessment of damages is the difference between the price he paid and the real value of the property, but this is only a method of giving effect to the overriding

---

[83] (1884) 9 App. Cas. 187 at 201 per Lord Blackburn.
[84] *Langridge v Levy* (1837) 2 M. & W. 519 (1838) 4 M. & W. 337; *Burrows v Rhodes* [1899] 1 Q.B. 816. See also *Graham v Saville* [1945] 2 D.L.R. 489; *Beaulne v Ricketts* (1979) 96 D.L.R. (3d) 550 (bigamy); *Allan v Ellis & Co* [1990] 11 E.G. 78 (misdescription in survey causative of claimant's subsequent fall); *Banks v Cox* [2002] EWHC 2166 (Ch) (depression).
[85] *Shelley v Paddock* [1979] Q.B. 120, affirmed [1980] Q.B. 348; *Saunders v Edwards* [1987] 1 W.L.R. 1116; *A v B* [2007] EWHC 1246 (QB); [2007] 2 F.L.R. 1051; *Kinch v Rosling* [2009] EWHC 286 (QB). In *F. v Wirral MBC* [1991] Fam. 69 it is suggested that deceit leading to loss of parental "rights" could be actionable.
[86] *Mafo v Adams* [1979] 1 Q.B. 548.
[87] *McConnel v Wright* [1903] 1 Ch. 546 at 554–555 per Collins M.R.
[88] *East v Maurer* [1991] 1 W.L.R. 461; *4Eng Ltd v Harper* [2008] EWHC 915; [2009] Ch 91. The claimant does not need to identify a specific alternative transaction: *Parabola Investments Ltd v Browallia Cal Ltd* [2009] EWHC 901 (Comm), affirmed [2010] EWCA Civ 486.
[89] *Clef Aquitaine S.A.R.L. v Laporte Materials (Barrow) Ltd* [2001] Q.B. 488.

principle of compensation.[90] Thus if a fraud does not come to light
for some time the claimant is not necessarily barred from recovering
his full loss because the property might have been disposed of at its
"false" value immediately after the sale.[91] As an intentional wrongdoer the fraudster is not entitled to the benefit of the reasonable
foreseeability test of remoteness commonly applicable in tort,[92] but
has to pay for all actual loss directly flowing from the transaction he
induced.[93] In *Smith New Court Securities Ltd v Scrimgeour Vickers
(Asset Management) Ltd*[94] C was induced to bid 82p a share for a
parcel of 28 million-odd Ferranti shares by a fraudulent misrepresentation that there were other buyers in the market. At that time
the shares had a market value of 78p. Unknown to D, Ferranti had
itself been defrauded on a massive scale by one G, and when this
came out the shares fell in value to 44p. The House of Lords
restored the trial judge's decision that C was entitled to damages
based on the difference between 82p and 44p and did not have to
give credit for the "value" of the shares at the time of purchase.[95]
The shares in *Smith New Court* were "fatally flawed" or "pregnant
with loss"[96] at the time of acquisition. If D induced C to buy a
racehorse by representing that it had a good record as a winner and
then it died as a result of some latent disease it already had, C would
be able to recover all he had paid for it.[97] The case would have been
different if the slump in value had been caused by a subsequent
fraud, for then the fraud practised by D would have been a cause of
C's loss only in the sine qua non sense, not an effective cause: it
would have been like a case where a person buys a horse for 200 per
cent of its true value as the result of a fraudulent misrepresentation
about its record and then it *later* catches a disease (wholly unrelated

[90] *Smith New Court Securities Ltd v Scrimgeour Vickers (Asset Management) Ltd* [1997]
A.C. 254 at 284.
[91] *Peek v Derry* (1887) 37 Ch. D. 541 at 591 (reversed on a different point (1889) 14 App.
Cas. 337). For an extreme application of this in a case of innocent misrepresentation, see
Naughton v O'Callaghan [1990] 3 All E.R. 991, though quaere whether it is consistent
with *Banque Bruxelles Lambert SA v Eagle Star Insurance Co Ltd* [1997] A.C. 191.
[92] See para.6–29, above.
[93] *Doyle v Olby (Ironmongers) Ltd* [1969] 2 Q.B. 158; *Smith New Court*, above, fn.90.
[94] Above, fn.90.
[95] In fact the HL said that the correct figure was the rather larger loss produced by the
difference between the price paid and sums actually realised by their sale. However, C
asked only for restoration of the trial decision. Note that if C had been able to rescind the
contract he would have recovered the price in exchange for the shares and the quantum of
loss would have been irrelevant. A claim to rescind seems to have been abandoned because
the shares had been sold, but Lord Browne-Wilkinson was of the tentative opinion that C
might have rescinded by tendering an equivalent quantity of other Ferranti shares.
[96] Lord Browne-Wilkinson at [1997] A.C. 267.
[97] Cockburn C.J.'s example in *Twycross v Grant* (1877) 2 C.P.D. 469 at 544–545. See also
MAN Nutzfahrzeuge A.G. v Freightliner Ltd [2005] EWHC 2347 (Comm) at [242] ("bad
apple" financial controller within acquired company, on appeal on other issues [2007]
EWCA Civ 910; [2008] P.N.L.R. 6).

to the fraud) from which it dies.[98] It may be, however, that the fraudster bears the risk of subsequent general falls in the market where, by the nature of the transaction, the claimant will be "locked into" the property[99] or where it is acquired with the intention of retaining it. In *Banque Bruxelles Lambert SA v Eagle Star Insurance Co Ltd*[100] the House of Lords held that a negligent valuer did not bear this risk because his liability was confined to the consequences of the information which he gave being wrong, but the position in a case of fraud, where the law looks to the consequences of the transaction, was left open.[101]

The claimant must, of course, give credit for any benefit he may have received from the transaction into which he entered as a result of the deceit, provided it may fairly be said to be causally related to the transaction.[102] Further, the law:

11–15

"[S]trict though it is, still requires the plaintiff to mitigate his loss once he is aware of the fraud. So long as he is not aware of the fraud, no question of a duty to mitigate can arise. But once the fraud has been discovered, if the plaintiff is not locked into the asset and the fraud has ceased to operate on his mind, a failure to take reasonable steps to sell the property may constitute a failure to mitigate his loss requiring him to bring the value of the property into account as at the date when he discovered the fraud or shortly thereafter."[103]

---

[98] The other example in *Twycross v Grant*, approved by Lord Steyn in *Smith New Court*. Both he and Cockburn C.J. plainly thought that D would be liable for the difference between the price paid and the "true" value, but should D be liable at all in such a case? Has the supervening event prevented his fraud having damaging effect? The view that D is liable for the difference between the price paid and the true value can of course be defended by reference to a mechanical rule based on assessment of damages at the time of the sale but such a rule is rejected in *Smith New Court*. *Naughton v O'Callaghan*, above, fn.91, is a difficult case. The horse "as was" would have been worth, at the time of sale, a very large proportion of the price paid. Its value fell sharply because it turned out not to be a winner; but there was no evidence that it would have been a winner "as represented".
[99] As where he lends money on an over-valued security.
[100] [1997] A.C. 191, para.6–27, above.
[101] In *Downs v Chappell* [1997] 1 W.L.R. 426, Hobhouse L.J. in a case of fraud applied what seems to be essentially the negligence principle and Lord Steyn (and perhaps Lord Browne-Wilkinson) in *Smith New Court* said that this was wrong. May J. in *Slough Estates Plc v Welwyn Hatfield DC* [1996] 2 P.L.R. 50 imposed liability in deceit for losses attributable to a general fall in the market. "A windfall is an unexpected piece of good fortune. The expression does not necessarily imply that it is undeserved. Damages may be undeserved as a windfall if they amount to or include sums which the injured plaintiff ought not in fairness to receive. If, as I conceive, the policy of the law is to transfer the whole foreseeable risk of a transaction induced by fraud to the fraudulent defendant, and if, as I conceive, the court does not speculate what, if any, different transaction the plaintiff might have done if the fraudulent representation had not been made, damages on this basis are not to be regarded as a windfall, but the proper application of the policy of the law."
[102] Cf. *Hussey v Eels* [1990] 2 Q.B. 227 (not a case of fraud).
[103] *Smith New Court* [1997] A.C. 254 per Lord Browne-Wilkinson.

Subject to this the claimant may also[104] recover consequential loss which is directly caused by the fraud, for example liabilities reasonably incurred in seeking to run a business[105] or damage to other property caused by a fraudulently concealed danger.[106]

3. Liability for Negligent Misstatement[107]

11–16 *Derry v Peek* settled that liability for deceit is liability for fraudulent and not for careless statements, but for many years the case was treated as authority for more than that, for the House of Lords was taken to have held that there could be no tortious liability of any kind for a misstatement so long only as it was not fraudulent.[108] However, the House itself in *Nocton v Lord Ashburton*[109] in 1914 pointed out that *Derry v Peek* had not ruled out every form of liability (independent of statute) but that for fraud. Not only would there be liability in contract[110] but it could exist in equity as well, for a fiduciary relationship, such as that of solicitor and client, although based upon loyalty, could in certain circumstances lead to equitable compensation for advice which was not "dishonest" in the common law sense. Fifty years later, in *Hedley Byrne & Co Ltd v Heller & Partners Ltd*,[111] the House was able to rely on *Nocton v Lord Ashburton* as showing that *Derry v Peek* governed only liability for deceit so that they were not precluded from holding that a tortious duty of care in making statements might exist. In the period between these cases it was also recognised that there could be liability for physical damage caused by a misleading statement.[112] Many cases which are primarily thought of in terms of acts also contain elements of misstatement: no harm would have come to the pursuer in *Donoghue v Stevenson*, for example, if there had been no implied representation that the ginger beer was fit for human consumption.

---

[104] As to exemplary damages, see para.22–8, below.

[105] *Doyle v Olby (Ironmongers) Ltd* [1969] 2 Q.B. 158; *Downs v Chappell* [1997] 1 W.L.R. 426. In *Hornal v Neuberger Products Ltd* [1957] 1 Q.B. 247, the claimant was induced to buy a lathe by a fraudulent representation that it was fit for immediate use. Although it was worth what he paid for it, he was put to seven weeks delay in preparing it for use and recovered damages for this delay.

[106] See, e.g. *Mullett v Mason* (1866) L.R. 1 C.P. 559; *Nicholls v Taylor* [1939] V.L.R. 119.

[107] Witting, *Liability for Negligent Misstatement* (2004).

[108] However, the year after *Derry v Peek*, Parliament imposed liability for false statements in prospectuses by the Directors Liability Act 1890.

[109] [1914] A.C. 932.

[110] Which sometimes led to the artificial finding of contracts: *De La Bere v Pearson* [1908] 1 K.B. 280.

[111] [1964] A.C. 465.

[112] See, e.g. *Watson v Buckley, Osborne, Garrett & Co Ltd* [1940] 1 All E.R. 174; *Devillez v Boots Pure Drug Co* (1962) 106 S.J. 552. See also *Clayton v Woodman & Son (Builders) Ltd* [1962] 2 Q.B. 533 (reversed on the facts [1962] 1 W.L.R. 585) and *The Apollo* [1891] A.C. 499.

Indeed, in some cases the distinction between word and deed is for all practical purposes nonexistent. Quite apart from contract, a doctor is as much liable for negligently advising his patient to take a certain drug as he is for negligently injecting the drug himself. However, in *Hedley Byrne* the loss was unquestionably pecuniary or economic.

The facts of *Hedley Byrne* were that the claimants, who were advertising agents, were anxious to know whether they could safely give credit to a company, Easipower, on whose behalf they had entered into various advertising contracts, and they therefore sought bankers' references about Easipower. For this purpose the claimants' bankers approached the defendants, who were Easipower's bankers, and on two occasions the defendants gave favourable references. These were passed on to the claimants by their bankers and, although the defendants did not know who the claimants were and had in fact marked their communications to the claimants' bankers "Confidential. For your private use ... ", they did know the inquiry was made in connection with an advertising contract. They must also have known that the references were to be passed on to a customer.[113] In reliance on these references the claimants incurred expenditure on Easipower's behalf and, when Easipower went into liquidation, they suffered substantial loss. This loss they sought to recover from the defendants in an action based upon the defendants' alleged negligence in giving favourable references concerning Easipower. At first instance McNair J. held that the defendants owed no duty to the claimants, and this decision was affirmed in the Court of Appeal[114] both on the ground that the case was covered by authority and also on the ground that it would not be reasonable to impose upon a banker an obligation to exercise care when informing a third party of the credit-worthiness of his client. In the House of Lords the decision in favour of the defendants was affirmed, but none of their Lordships based his decision on a general rule of non-liability for negligent misstatement. On the contrary, Lords Reid, Devlin and Pearce held that, assuming the defendants to have been negligent, the only reason for exonerating them was that the references had been given "without responsibility".[115] Lord Hodson and, perhaps, Lord Morris considered that even without this denial of responsibility there was no duty of care on the facts, but nevertheless agreed that a duty of care in making statements was a legal possibility.[116]

---

[113] [1964] A.C. 465 at 482, 503.

[114] [1962] 1 Q.B. 396.

[115] See para.11–30, below.

[116] See, too, *Royal Bank Trust Co (Trinidad) Ltd v Pampellone* [1987] 1 Lloyd's Rep. 218, which also provoked a difference of opinion as to whether a duty was owed on the facts.

A. A Special Relationship

11–17 We have seen that *Hedley Byrne* has been regarded as the progenitor of the principle of "assumption of responsibility", which has now been extended beyond liability for statements. In that broader context the decision has really become part of the background to the House of Lords cases in the 1990s concerning services to be performed for the claimant or a third party.[117] However, we are now concerned with *Hedley Byrne* in the particular context of statements and advice and it should not be assumed that all cases based upon assumption of responsibility have common characteristics: for example, in the situations dealt with in this section it is always necessary that the claimant should have relied on the statement, whereas reliance is not always necessary in the broader context.[118]

It is clear from *Hedley Byrne* that for a duty of care to arise in respect of speech or writing, something more is required than in the straightforward case of physical damage caused by an act where, generally speaking, foreseeability of harm will be sufficient. This is very largely because a statement is likely to cause economic loss rather than physical harm and the risk of crushing liability is exacerbated by the fact that information is likely to be disseminated among a large number of persons even if it was originally addressed only to a small group. In some activities, for example auditing or financial advice, the potential liability is so great that it is beyond the capacity of the insurance market.[119] Their Lordships in *Hedley Byrne* were in general agreement that *Donoghue v Stevenson* had little, if any, direct bearing on the problem of negligent misstatement and that a duty of care would exist in relation to statements only if there is a "special relationship" between the parties, a relationship (to use the currently fashionable terminology) of close "proximity". Indeed, Lord Devlin spoke in terms of a relationship "equivalent to contract"[120] and in a later case where liability was imposed on a valuer engaged by a mortgagee for loss incurred by the mortgagor as a result of a negligent report, the relationship between the valuer and mortgagor was described as "akin to contract".[121] While expressly disclaiming any intention to lay down conditions which were either conclusive or exclusive, Lord Oliver in *Caparo Plc v Dickman*[122]

---

[117] See para.5–34, above.

[118] See para.5–37, above.

[119] See para.5–14, above.

[120] [1964] A.C. at p.530. Lord Devlin's formulation does not, however, mean that the defendant must have intended to make a contract: *McInerny v Lloyd's Bank Ltd* [1973] 2 Lloyd's Rep. 389 at 400 (on appeal [1974] 1 Lloyd's Rep. 246).

[121] *Smith v Eric S. Bush* [1990] 1 A.C. 831 at 846 per Lord Templeman. However, the situation here was different: the recipient had paid for the advice but he had paid a third party, who was the direct recipient.

[122] [1990] 2 A.C. 605 at 638.

described the necessary relationship as typically having four characteristics:

"(1) the advice is required for a purpose, whether particularly specified or generally described, which is made known, either actually or inferentially, to the adviser at the time when the advice is given; (2) the adviser knows, either actually or inferentially, that his advice will be communicated to the advisee, either specifically or as a member of an ascertained class, in order that it should be used by the advisee for that purpose; (3) it is known, either actually or inferentially, that the advice so communicated is likely to be acted upon by the advisee for that purpose without independent inquiry[123]; and (4) it is so acted upon by the advisee to his detriment."

B. Professional Advisers

There is a view that liability is further restricted to professional **11–18** advisers or those claiming equivalent skills. This is based on the majority view in the Privy Council in *Mutual Life and Citizens' Assurance Co Ltd v Evatt*.[124] The claimant, a policyholder in the defendant company, sought advice from it as to the financial soundness of another company, "Palmer", with which it was closely associated. The information he was given was incorrect and he lost his money. It was held by the majority that the omission from the claimant's declaration of any allegation that the defendant was in the business of supplying information or advice or had claimed to possess the necessary skill to do so was fatal. However, the broader approach of the minority that:

"[O]ne must assume a reasonable man who has that degree of knowledge and skill which facts known to the inquirer (including statements made by the adviser) entitled him to expect of the adviser, and then inquire whether a reasonable man could have given the advice which was in fact given if he had exercised reasonable care"[125]

---

[123] See *Patchett v Swimming Pool and Allied Trades Association Ltd* [2009] EWCA Civ 717 (trade association website; advice to seek further information). Cf. *HSBC Bank Plc v So* [2009] EWCA Civ 296 (no reason to investigate matter where other party had made unqualified statement about matter within its own knowledge.

[124] [1971] A.C. 793. The appeal was on the defendants' demurrer to the claimant's declaration in accordance with the old form of procedure then still current in New South Wales.

[125] [1971] A.C. 793 at 812 per Lords Reid and Morris.

has recommended itself to judges at first instance,[126] in the Court of Appeal[127] and in the High Court of Australia,[128] though strictly perhaps it has not been necessary for them to choose between the majority and minority views in *Evatt*'s case.[129] The issue was also really irrelevant when the House of Lords considered *Hedley Byrne* in *Smith v Eric S. Bush*[130] and in *Caparo Industries Plc v Dickman*.[131] In fact, the extent of the practical difference between the two camps very much depends upon the way in which the court interprets the majority test in *Evatt* and its qualifications.[132] Thus it seems clear that the expression "business or profession" is not meant to confine liability to those engaged in private enterprise or the pursuit of profit, but may extend to a public authority supplying information and in *Spring v Guardian Assurance Plc*,[133] where the claim arose from an incorrect reference, Lord Goff, having referred to the criticisms of *Evatt*, said that in any event it did not stand in the way of a decision in favour of the claimant, for the skill of preparing a reference in respect of an employee falls as much within the expertise of an employer as the skill of preparing a bank reference fell within the expertise of the bank.

C. Voluntariness

11–19   There is a clear thread running through *Hedley Byrne* that the duty arises from an "undertaking", express or implied, to use due care, a voluntary assumption of responsibility, but it is plain that these expressions should not be understood as requiring any actual or subjective acceptance of legal liability by the defendant. In *Smith v Eric S. Bush*, Lord Griffiths said that:

> "[T]he phrase 'assumption of responsibility' can only have any real meaning if it is understood as referring to the circumstances in which the law will deem the maker of the statement to have

---

[126] *Argy Trading Development Co Ltd v Lapid Developments Ltd* [1977] 1 W.L.R. 444.

[127] *Esso Petroleum Co Ltd v Mardon* [1976] Q.B. 801 at 827; *Howard Marine and Dredging Co Ltd v A. Ogden (Excavations) Ltd* [1978] Q.B. 574. As a decision of the Privy Council, *Evatt*'s case does not, of course bind an English court (though cf. the *Wagon Mound* saga).

[128] *Shaddock v Parramatta CC* (1981) 36 A.L.R. 385, which contains a very full account of the problem.

[129] See, in particular, the differing views expressed in *Shaddock*'s case about the extent to which the facts could be covered by the *Evatt* formula.

[130] [1990] 1 A.C. 831.

[131] [1990] 2 A.C. 605.

[132] Namely, that a duty may arise if the defendant holds himself out as possessing a skill equivalent to that of a "professional" or if he has a financial interest in the transaction. The former case in particular seems capable of almost infinite expansion.

[133] [1995] 2 A.C. 296. Note that this case does not represent a straightforward *Hedley Byrne* situation since the statement was made by D to X about C. See para.11–33, below. See also *Lennon v MPC* [2004] EWCA Civ 130; [2004] 1 W.L.R. 2594.

assumed responsibility to the person who acts upon the advice."[134]

Indeed, where a surveyor carried out a valuation of an ordinary dwelling house on the instructions of a building society he thereby "assumed responsibility" to the intending purchaser who, as he knew, would rely upon his skill, even though in fact he attempted (unsuccessfully) to exclude his liability.[135] The test is an objective one applied to the context and what passes between the claimant and the defendant.[136]

"Because the question of whether a defendant has assumed responsibility is a legal inference to be drawn from his conduct against the background of all the circumstances of the case, it is by no means a simple question of fact. Questions of fairness and policy will enter into the decision."[137]

The assumption of responsibility is certainly voluntary in the sense that at common law the defendant can normally displace the duty by disclaimer, but this escape route is often barred by the Unfair Contract Terms Act 1977.[138]

D. Public Officers and Bodies

We have already seen that a certification or inspection authority may incur liability for personal injury to a member of the public even without any direct communication or reliance.[139] Even where there is a direct statement, however, matters are not so simple with regard to economic loss, even though a public authority has no "immunity".[140] For example, a person who alleges that an inspection authority has told him to spend too much money on safety precautions may have difficulty in establishing a duty of care

11–20

---

[134] [1990] 1 A.C. at 862. "The phrase means simply that the law recognises that there is a duty of care. It is not so much that responsibility is assumed as that it is recognised or imposed by the law": Lord Slynn in *Phelps v Hillingdon LBC* [2001] 2 A.C. 619 at 654.

[135] *Smith v Eric S. Bush*, above, fn.130. Note that the building society does not assume responsibility for the accuracy of the report of an independent valuer: its duty is to take care in selecting the valuer. Cf. *Harris v Wyre Forest DC* [1990] 1 A.C. 831 (appeal heard with *Smith v Bush*) where the valuer was a servant of the lender and the lender was vicariously liable for his negligence and *Beresford v Chesterfield BC, The Times*, August 14, 1989 (lender presenting independent valuer's report as its own).

[136] *Williams v Natural Life Health Foods Ltd* [1998] 1 W.L.R. 830 at 835; *Electra Private Equity Partners v K.P.M.G. Peat Marwick* [2001] B.C.L.C. 589.

[137] Lord Hoffmann in *Customs and Excise Commrs v Barclays Bank Plc* [2006] UKHL 28; [2007] 1 A.C. 181 at [36].

[138] See para.11–30, below.

[139] See para.5–33, above.

[140] So in *Gooden v Northamptonshire CC* [2001] EWCA Civ 1744 it was accepted that a local authority could owe a duty in answering search enquiries.

because such a duty might encourage untoward cautiousness in the performance of the statutory function.[141] In one of the early American cases liability was imposed upon a public weigher whose negligent notification caused a purchaser of goods to pay too much for them[142] and Lord Oliver in *Caparo* implied that the result would be the same here. A local land registry was held liable when its answer to an inquiry caused an incumbrancer to lose his rights.[143] Although this was not a "standard" statement case in that the loss was suffered by a third party rather than the recipient of the statement, it does show that voluntary assumption of responsibility cannot, even in an attenuated sense, be the universal solvent—it was the defendant's statutory function to respond to search requests. It will be recalled that a local authority owes no duty of care to prospective owners of houses in respect of statutory inspections during construction.[144] In principle, however, it has been said that a clear, subsequent assertion, in response to an inquiry, that an inspection had proved satisfactory could attract liability under *Hedley Byrne*.[145] Persons undertaking development of land must, perforce, rely on planning authorities to perform their functions and may make inquiries before embarking on the project. It has been held that:

> "[T]he ordinary process of giving routine advice to an applicant for planning permission and answering such questions as he or she may raise, especially when the applicant is one known to have her own professional advisers,"

does not give rise to any duty of care.[146] Further, it is no doubt the case, as has been held in Australia, that it would normally be unreasonable for a property developer to rely upon a city development plan as an assurance that the level of development specified therein was feasible and that therefore there was no assumption of

---

[141] *Harris v Evans* [1998] 1 W.L.R. 1285. In fact the case involved not advice but the making of a prohibition notice, which brought into play the statutory appeal process. In *Welton v North Cornwall DC* [1997] 1 W.L.R. 570, where the defendants' environmental health officer imposed wholly excessive hygiene requirements upon the claimants' guest house, the claim was described as "well within" *Hedley Byrne* and "incontrovertible". The court in *Harris* was able to distinguish *Welton* because there the "advice" was directly given to the claimant, whereas in *Harris* the officer caused the local authority to impose the prohibition notice, but it clearly had doubts about *Welton*.

[142] *Glanzer v Shepherd* 135 N.E. 275 (1922).

[143] *Ministry of Housing and Local Government v Sharp* [1970] 2 Q.B. 223.

[144] See para.9–33, above.

[145] *King v North Cornwall DC*, February 8, 1995, CA, where, however, the authority's response amounted to no more than a statement that an inspection had been made.

[146] *Haddow v Secretary of State for the Environment* [2000] Env L.R. 212; *Tidman v Reading BC* [1994] E.G.C.S. 180; *Fashion Brokers Ltd v Clarke Hayes* [2000] Lloyd's Rep. P.N. 398. See also *R. v Customs and Excise, Ex p. F & I Services Ltd* [2000] S.T.C. 364 (VAT advice).

responsibility in respect of it; in any event, a public authority owes a duty to the public to ensure that its discretionary powers are exercised in the general interest, which must be allowed to prevail over the expectations of developers, except in so far as the plan is given effect by statute or by contract.[147]

E. Hedley Byrne and Contract Relations

Negligent misstatement very often takes place in the context of a **11–21** contract or the negotiations for a contract. It was established in *Henderson v Merrett Syndicates Ltd*[148] that a duty of care in tort could coexist with a contractual obligation where there had been an assumption of responsibility in relation to the provision of services and the same is true in relation to a statement.[149] However, in relation to negotiations the importance of *Hedley Byrne* was very much diminished by s.2(1) of the Misrepresentation Act 1967. This provides that where a person has entered into a contract after a misrepresentation has been made to him by another party to the contract then, if the representor would have been liable in damages if the representation had been made fraudulently, he shall be so liable unless he proves that he had reasonable grounds to believe that the statement was true.[150] This is more favourable to the claimant than *Hedley Byrne* because there can be no argument about duty and the defendant bears the burden of proof.[151] However, there may still be cases where no contract is concluded (but the claimant has still suffered loss)[152] or where it is sought to impose liability

---

[147] See *San Sebastian Pty v Minister Administering the Environmental Planning, etc. Act* (1986) 162 C.L.R. 340. In *Unilan Holdings Pty Ltd v Kerin* (1992) 107 A.L.R. 709 the court refused to strike out a claim based on a categorical assurance by a minister in a speech. But it would be surprising if even the firmest electoral pledge could be relied upon.

[148] [1995] 2 A.C. 145, para.1–8, above.

[149] *Esso Petroleum Co Ltd v Mardon* [1976] Q.B. 801; *Howard Marine and Dredging Co Ltd v A. Ogden & Son (Excavations) Ltd* [1978] Q.B. 574; *Hagen v I.C.I.* [2002] I.R.L.R. 31.

[150] Since the liability created by s.2(1) is, ex hypothesi, non-contractual (a misrepresentation is not a term) the measure of damages is tortious, not contractual, but it was some time before the case law settled to this view in *Royscott Trust v Rogerson* [1991] 2 Q.B. 297. However, the application in that case of the deceit rule of remoteness in that case is regrettable.

[151] See also Bridge L.J. in *Howard Marine and Dredging*, above, fn.149, who points out that, quite apart from the burden of proof, the "fault" required under the Act is not necessarily the same as common law negligence.

[152] In *Holman Construction Ltd v Delta Timber Co Ltd* [1972] 1 N.Z.L.R. 1081, a sub-contractor mistakenly bid at too low a price and the head contractor relied on this in fixing his bid for the contract, which he won. But the sub-contractor discovered the error and withdrew before the head contractor could bind him. It was held that to impose a duty of care would subvert the law of contract formation. In *Blackpool Aero Club v Blackpool BC* [1990] 1 W.L.R. 1195 a tort duty to take reasonable care in considering a bid was advanced but the CA did not find it necessary to decide the issue. See also *Design Services Ltd Canada* [2008] SCC 22; [2008] 1 S.C.R. 737.

upon an agent.[153] Where there is a contract between the parties there is no reason in principle why there should not be a tort duty of care, during the currency of the contract, which involves a matter outside the scope of the contract[154] but the fact that the proposed duty is inconsistent with the terms of the contact is, of course, reason for rejecting it.[155]

The fact that D, in relation to the statement which causes damage to C, is performing a task under contract for X does not mean that D may not owe a duty of care to C—this is, after all, the "statement" equivalent of *Donoghue v Stevenson*.[156] A valuer engaged to value an ordinary dwelling on behalf of the mortgagee owes a duty of care to the mortgagor (purchaser) to whom he knows the report will be shown[157] and where accountants or financial advisers provide information to persons contemplating a transaction with their client they may owe a duty to those persons.[158] However, the nature of the contractual arrangements between the various parties[159] or the nature of the transaction may lead to the conclusion that no special relationship arises. Thus the valuer for the mortgagee may not owe a duty to the purchaser where the sale involves a commercial or industrial property or an expensive residential property[160] and the same will apply where for other reasons it is legitimate to expect that the claimant will undertake his own inquiries.[161] Although it has been said that once a case falls:

[153] See below.
[154] *Holt v Payne Skillington* (1995) 49 Con LR 99 (where, however, there was no sufficient pleaded case).
[155] *J. Nunes Diamonds Ltd v Dominion Electric Co* (1972) 26 D.L.R. (3d) 699. Though not a *Hedley Byrne* case, *Tai Hing Cotton Mill Ltd v Liu Chong Hing Bank Ltd* [1986] A.C. 80 is another example of the principle (para.1–9, above). It may not be easy to discern the distinction between (1) a duty going beyond the contract and (2) a duty inconsistent with the contract. The first category is plainly not confined to matters which have nothing to do with the subject matter of the contract (e.g. being knocked down by the careless driving of your accountant).
[156] See *White v Jones* [1995] 2 A.C. 207.
[157] *Smith v Eric S. Bush* [1990] A.C. 831.
[158] See the dissenting judgment of Denning L.J. (which was approved in *Hedley Byrne*) in *Candler v Crane Christmas & Co* [1951] 2 K.B. 164; *Morgan Crucible v Hill Samuel Bank Ltd* [1991] Ch. 295; *Electra Private Equity Partners v K.P.M.G. Peat Marwick* [2001] B.C.L.C. 589.
[159] As in *Pacific Associates Inc v Baxter* [1990] 1 Q.B. 993 and *Galliford Try Infrastructure Ltd v Mott MacDonald Ltd* [2008] EWHC 1570 (TCC). But there is certainly no rule that the fact that the parties have arranged their relationships so that there is no direct contractual link precludes a duty of care: *Henderson v Merrett Syndicates Ltd* [1995] 2 A.C. 181; *Riyad Bank v Ahli United Bank (UK)* [2006] EWCA Civ 780; [2006] 2 Lloyd's Rep 292.
[160] *Smith v Eric S. Bush*, above, fn.157. In *McCullagh v Lane Fox & Partners Ltd* [1996] 1 E.G.L.R. 35 the estate agent was at the time of the statement entitled to assume that the buyer would take independent advice.
[161] *James McNaughton Paper Group Ltd v Hicks Anderson & Co* [1991] 2 Q.B. 295 (draft accounts requested as quickly as possible for use in negotiation; buyers aware of poor state of client's affairs).

"[W]ithin the *Hedley Byrne* principle, there should be no need to embark upon any further inquiry whether it is fair, just and reasonable to impose liability for economic loss",[162]

cases of this type sometimes show an inclination to test the issue of duty against the *Caparo* tripartite factors, even if assumption of responsibility is the starting point.[163]

F. Agents

The statement may be made by the agent of one party to a transaction, in the sense of representing that party in the matter. The principal will incur liability for what the agent says if that is within the scope of his authority (and, depending on the terms of any contract between the agent and the principal) the principal will in turn have recourse against the agent, but the question of the agent's personal liability in tort to the recipient of the statement[164] may arise, for example if the principal is insolvent. In *Williams v Natural Life Health Foods Ltd*[165] the House of Lords held that a director of a company did not owe a duty of care to its customers merely because he worked on the fulfilment of the contract which they made with the company—there must be something in his conduct to justify a finding of assumption of personal responsibility. However, it was never doubted in earlier cases that a valuer was (in theory) personally liable to the house buyer whose intended house he surveyed and in *Merrett v Babb*[166] the Court of Appeal held that this was so, notwithstanding *Williams*,[167] even though the house buyer had never had any communication with him and his employer was insolvent and uninsured.[168] On the other hand, in *Gran Gelato Ltd v Richcliff (Group) Ltd*[169] (which was not referred to in *Merrett*) Nicholls V.C. declined to impose a duty of care upon the vendor's solicitor in answering inquiries before contract because the vendor's liability for the acts of his agent done on his behalf was a reasonable

11–22

---

[162] Lord Goff in *Henderson v Merrett Syndicates Ltd* [1995] 2 A.C. 181

[163] *Electra Private Equity Partners v K.P.M.G. Peat Marwick* [2001] B.C.L.C. 589; *Bank of Credit and Commerce International (Overseas) Ltd v Price Waterhouse (No.2)* [1998] PNLR 564. However, if the assumption of responsibility is clear such questions may tend to answer themselves: *Customs and Excise Commrs v Barclays Bank* [2006] UKHL 28; [2007] 1 A.C. 181 at [85].

[164] The agent will generally not be party to any contract with the recipient. Nor will the agent incur a personal liability under the Misrepresentation Act 1967 s.2(1): *Resolute Maritime v Nippon Karji Kyokai* [1983] 1 W.L.R. 857.

[165] [1998] 1 W.L.R. 830. See para.24–23, below.

[166] [2001] EWCA Civ 214; [2001] Q.B. 1174. See also *McCullagh v Lane Fox & Partners Ltd* [1996] 1 E.G.L.R. 35.

[167] Which May L.J. at [45] regarded as turning on the fact that it involved a director.

[168] The trustees in bankruptcy had cancelled the principal's insurance without run-off cover. Did they owe a duty of care to the valuer?

[169] [1992] Ch. 560.

and sufficient legal protection for the purchaser, even though that liability would become worthless in the event of the vendor's insolvency, which seems difficult to reconcile with *Merrett*. What was being done in *Gran Gelato* was not concerned with an adversarial matter, where there is no doubt that one should deny a duty of care in the agent to the third party,[170] but on the other hand it cannot be described as a merely ministerial act. Perhaps the case represents a general rule only for solicitors who are doing no more than representing their clients in conveyancing transactions[171] or transactions of a similar nature. Certainly it does not rule out the possibility that even in such a transaction there may be facts to support a direct assumption of responsibility[172]; and in *Dean v Allin & Watts*[173] the Court of Appeal held that a solicitor acting for a borrower on a loan transaction owed a duty of care to the lender to create the effective security which was fundamental to the transaction and which the borrower was willing to grant to the lender.

G. Failure to Speak

11–23   Failure to speak raises the same issues as omissions generally in the law of negligence and misrepresentation. There is no general duty to volunteer information for the protection of others, even between contracting parties,[174] and even where there is a duty to disclose, that primarily relates to the avoidance of the contract, though it seems that in a suitable case there may be damages for deceit.[175] However, everything turns on the responsibility which the defendant has assumed towards the claimant: if, as is clear, D may be liable for an omission if he has undertaken the management of C's affairs,[176] there is no reason why he should not be equally liable if he fails to perform an undertaking to warn C of hazards or

[170] See the position of lawyers in connection with litigation, para.5–60, above. See also *Sulzinger v C.K. Alexander Ltd* (1971) 24 D.L.R. 137 (insurance adjuster) and *Huxford v Stoy Hayward, The Times*, January 11, 1989 (person advising on appointment of receiver; no duty to company's guarantors).
[171] The view of Hobhouse L.J. in *McCullagh v Lane Fox & Partners Ltd*, above. See also Lord Goff in *White v Jones* [1995] 2 A.C. 207 at 256, though the point was not in issue there.
[172] See the approval of *Allied Finance and Investments Ltd v Haddow* [1983] N.Z.L.R. 22 at [1992] Ch. 571.
[173] [2001] EWCA Civ 758; [2001] 2 Lloyd's Rep 249; cited with approval by Lord Bingham in *Customs and Excise Commrs v Barclays Bank Plc* [2006] UKHL 28; [2007] 1 A.C. 181 at [22]. Cf. *Brownie Wills v Shrimpton* [1998] 2 N.Z.L.R. 320.
[174] Still less on the part of those who play no active part in the transaction: *Bentley v Wright* [1997] V.R. 175. The relationship between banker and customer is not fiduciary and in the absence of some positive assumption of responsibility the bank does not owe a duty to advise the customer on the wisdom of a transaction in respect of which he seeks a loan: *Williams & Glyns Bank Ltd v Barnes* [1981] Com. L.R. 205; *Murphy v HSBC Plc* [2004] EWHC 467 (Ch).
[175] See para.11–8, above.
[176] *Henderson v Merrett Syndicates* [1995] 2 A.C. 145 at 181.

problems.[177] If a statement is made in circumstances where there is a duty of care which at the time is fulfilled (because the statement is true or the maker has reasonable cause to believe it to be true) then, by analogy with the law on rescission for misrepresentation and fraud there should be a duty to take steps to bring a change of circumstances to notice of the recipient where this occurs before he acts upon it.[178] The defendant may, however, make it clear that he is not undertaking to inform of any future developments.[179]

H. Advice Informally Given

It is universally agreed that no duty arises in respect of advice requested and given[180] on a purely social occasion, for it is then neither reasonably foreseeable to the defendant that the claimant will rely upon it nor reasonable for the claimant to do so. The boundaries of this type of case, where the informality of the transaction leads to a denial of duty, cannot be drawn with precision. In *Chaudhry v Prabhakar*[181] liability was imposed upon a friend making an assessment of a used car for the claimant. The friend had some knowledge about cars and the task undertaken was related to a specific purchase but the existence of a duty was conceded and one judge doubted the correctness of that concession. In *Howard Marine and Dredging Co Ltd v A. Ogden (Excavations) Ltd*[182] the defendant answered an inquiry as to the carrying capacity of barges on the basis of his (accurate) recollection of the Lloyd's Register figure, which was incorrect, and without checking the barge's papers. The actual decision went on s.2(1) of the Misrepresentation Act 1967 but

11–24

---

[177] *Holt v Payne Skillington* (1995) 49 Con. L.R. 99 (no duty on facts). Cf. *Van Oppen v Bedford School* [1989] 1 All E.R. 273 and *Reid v Rush & Tompkins Group Plc* [1990] 1 W.L.R. 212 where, despite an existing relationship, there was no implied undertaking to advise about insurance and *Tai Hing Cotton Mill Ltd v Liu Chong Hing Bank Ltd* [1986] A.C. 80 (no duty to check bank statements to check against fraud). In *Hamble Fisheries Ltd v L. Gardiner & Sons Ltd* [1999] 2 Lloyd's Rep. 1 there was no relationship at all, simply the fact that C owned an engine made by D's predecessor. Cf. *Andrew Weir Shipping Ltd v Wartsila UK Ltd* [2004] EWHC 1284 (Comm), [2004] 2 Lloyd's Rep 377.

[178] In *McCullagh v Lane Fox & Partners Ltd* [1996] 1 E.G.L.R. 35 D was not under a duty when the statement was made because he expected C to verify the postion. Before C acted upon it, it became clear that he would not be doing so. Sir Christopher Slade (Nourse L.J. concurring) held that D was not liable unless he had knowledge of C's reliance at that time (which he did) and of the untruth of the statement (which he did not). Contra, Hobhouse L.J.

[179] *IFE Fund SA v Goldman Sachs International* [2007] EWCA Civ 811; [2007] 2 Lloyds Rep 449.

[180] No doubt the sort of situation the courts have had in mind is that of a claimant "cadging" free advice from a professional person at a party. However, if, say, an investment adviser were officiously to seek out someone in such a situation and suggest the purchase of particular shares, the "social occasion" factor might not help him.

[181] [1989] 1 W.L.R. 29.

[182] [1978] Q.B. 574.

as far as the common law was concerned, two members of the court were of the view that, given the impromptu, "off the cuff" circumstances of the response, the defendant's only duty was to give an honest answer.[183]

The fear of imposing an unreasonably onerous duty in respect of responses to comparatively informal inquiries may, in the alternative, be met by manipulation of the standard of care required. If it is unreasonable to expect a banker answering a query about a customer to spend time and trouble in searching records and so on, then a duty to take such care as is reasonable in all the circumstances of the case does not require him to do so. The duty of care is not a duty to take every possible care still less is it a duty to be right. Similarly, a surveyor conducting a valuation for mortgage purposes is not expected to go to the lengths required in an expensive structural survey; but if his inspection reveals grounds for suspicion he must take reasonable steps to follow the trail, even though he is working to a standard fee-he must "take the rough with the smooth" or decline to proceed.[184]

I. Range of Persons to Whom Duty is Owed and Purpose of the Communication

11–25   It is clearly not necessary that the defendant should know the identity of the claimant, for in *Hedley Byrne* itself the inquiry was made and the response received via an intermediary bank[185] but the inquiry was clearly on behalf of a particular individual or company. What is the position where information is foreseeably relied on by a larger group of persons? Most of the cases have concerned accountants and auditors and all the earlier decisions must be read in the light of *Caparo Industries Plc v Dickman*,[186] which concerned the statutory audit of the accounts of a public company, which, it

---

[183] See also *Titan Steel Wheels Ltd v Royal Bank of Scotland Plc* [2010] EWHC 211 (Comm) (mere sales conversation). There was a difference of opinion in *Hedley Byrne* as to the outcome of the case in the absence of the disclaimer. See also the disclaimer in *Royal Trust Co (Trinidad) Ltd v Pampellone* [1987] 1 Lloyd's Rep. 218 (where, even though there was no duty to consider the advisability of the claimant's investment, there was, it seems, a duty to convey accurately the information the defendants held).

[184] *Roberts v J. Hampson & Co* [1990] 1 W.L.R. 94; *Smith v Eric S. Bush* [1990] 2 A.C. 831. Cf. *Cross v Davis Martin & Mortimer* [1989] 10 E.G. 110.

[185] Lord Reid (at 482) and Lord Morris (at 493) regarded it as sufficient that it was obvious that the inquiry was being made by someone thinking of doing business with Easipower, but the later cases suggest that some more specific knowledge of the nature of the transaction is necessary.

[186] [1990] 2 A.C. 605. See also the decisions of the High Court of Australia in *Esanda Finance Corp Ltd v Peat Marwick Hungerfords* (1997) 188 C.L.R. 241 and the Supreme Court of Canada in *Hercules Management Ltd v Ernst & Young* (1997) 146 D.L.R. (4th) 577.

was alleged, was performed negligently and gave a misleading impression of the company's financial position and upon which the claimants relied to make a successful bid to acquire the company's shareholding. The House of Lords held that the claim failed. While it was perfectly true that it was foreseeable that the accounts of a public company (which are public documents) might be relied upon by a vast range of persons in an almost infinite variety of dealings with the company, the liability of the auditors had to be considered against the background of the statutory purpose of the audit and this was to enable shareholders to exercise their rights in the management of the company, it was not to provide information to investors, least of all predators. Accordingly, a duty of care was owed neither to persons investing in the company for the first time in reliance on the accounts, nor to existing shareholders who acquired further shares.[187] The auditors are, of course, liable to the company (which engages them on the basis of a contract) for losses caused by a negligent audit, (for example failure to expose an employee who has been defrauding the company)[188] but an over-valuation (as in *Caparo*) is not likely to cause the company damage[189] in a takeover situation. Given the decision in *Caparo*, it is inevitable that there is no duty on the part of the auditors to the creditors of the company even though they are far fewer in number than potential investors and are easily identified,[190] for the purpose of the audit is not to provide information for them. However, this situation presents legal issues of some difficulty and complexity. Suppose that X is sole beneficial owner of the company and has sole managerial control of

[187] On the policy factors, see para.5–11, above. The majority of the CA ([1989] Q.B. 653), though accepting the arbitrariness of the result, would have allowed existing shareholders to sue in respect of further acquisitions. The HL did not decide whether shareholders who, in reliance on an under-valuation, sold existing holdings could sue, but since the basis of the decision is that any duty is owed to the shareholders as a whole it is thought the answer should be "No." So also where a shareholder sues for diminution in value of retained shares because of loss of opportunity to "turn the company round". The purpose of the audit is still to inform the collective process of management, not to protect individual holdings: *Hercules Managements Ltd v Ernst & Young* (1997) 146 D.L.R. (4th) 577.

[188] However, ss.534 to 538 of the Companies Act 2006 now allows auditors to enter into a fair and reasonable agreement for limitation of liability with the audited company. In June 2008 the European Commission issued a recommendation on limiting liability of auditors (2008/473/EC). However, one of optional methods proposed is via limitation agreements.

[189] According to *The Independent*, March 26, 1991, further proceedings by the audited company in *Caparo* were contemplated on the basis that the company had suffered damage by becoming part of a group that had paid too much for it!

[190] *Al Saudi Banque v Clarke Pixley* [1990] Ch. 313, approved in *Caparo*. Cf. *R. Lowe Lippmann Figdor & Franck v A.G.C. (Advances) Ltd* [1992] 2 V.R. 671. Similarly (though it was a case of reliance by a third party) in *South Pacific Mfg. Co v NZ Consultants & Investigations* [1992] 2 N.Z.L.R. 282 it was held that even if an insurer's investigator could owe a duty to the insured he would not do so to a creditor or shareholder of the insured.

it (the so-called "one man company"). X uses the company as a vehicle to defraud C, something which the auditors of the company fail to detect. In accordance with the normal principles of attribution this fraud by X, the "directing mind", would be regarded as also the fraud of the company.[191] The company is therefore liable to C but is probably by now insolvent. Can the liquidator (acting as the company) sue the auditors for the damages for which the company is liable to C? The majority of the House of Lords in *Stone & Rolls Ltd v Moore Stephens*[192] held that he cannot, largely because they viewed it as a de facto reversal of the effect of *Caparo*. The decision is expressly limited to the situation where there is no person involved in the management and ownership of the company other than those implicated in the fraud, the position where there is an "innocent constituency"[193] being left for a future case.

To be contrasted with *Caparo* is another "auditing" situation, that in *Law Society v K.P.M.G. Peat Marwick*.[194] The defendants supplied to a firm of solicitors, D.F., a report required by the Solicitors Act 1974 to the effect that the firm had complied with the professional accounting rules and, as the defendants knew, this report was to be sent to the Law Society. It was subsequently discovered that two partners in D.F. had taken large amounts of clients' money and this led to payments of £8.5 million out of the compensation fund administered by the Law Society. On a preliminary issue based on an allegation that the report was insufficiently qualified, the Court of Appeal held that the defendants owed a duty of care to the Society: although the report was obtained and paid for by D.F., the whole purpose of the reporting system was to allow the Law Society to intervene in the running of a firm in order to protect the compensation fund.[195]

11–26   The purpose of a statement is not necessarily therefore equivalent to the reliance which may foreseeably be placed on it. Thus a marine surveyor or certifier does not owe a duty to a potential purchaser of

---

[191] See para.24–22, below.

[192] [2009] UKHL 39; [2009] 3 W.L.R. 455.

[193] Lord Mance at [228]. His Lordship's powerful dissent is based on the claimed inconsistency of the majority view with some elementary principles of company law and denies that recovery by the company would be inconsistent with *Caparo* because the loss of the company and the creditors are not the same, though there may be an overlap.

[194] [2000] 1 W.L.R. 1921. Cf. *Stringer v Peat Marwick Mitchell & Co* [2000] 1 N.Z.L.R. 450; but a claim by a person who provides a bond to the audited firm for the fulfilment of its duties to the regulatory body would be, "at or near the margin of existing decisions": *Independents' Advantage Insurance Co Ltd v Cook* [2003] EWCA Civ 1103; [2004] P.N.L.R. 3.

[195] Cf. also *Royal Bank of Scotland v Bannerman Johnstone Maclay* [2005] CSIH 39; [2005] P.N.L.R. 43 (overdraft facility supplied by C; business plan prepared by D; monthly management accounts and annual accounts audited by D required by C; duty of care arguable).

the vessel surveyed,[196] even if he is aware that it may be sold.[197] However, the purpose test is not easy to apply, for it may often be arguable that there is a further, superadded purpose beyond the primary purpose for which the information is given and *Caparo*, it will be recalled, turned on the court's interpretation of the statutory scheme underlying the audit. A clear example of a secondary purpose giving rise to a duty of care is *Smith v Eric S. Bush*,[198] where the immediate purpose of the valuation was to enable the mortgagees to decide whether the property valued provided adequate security for the loan. The knowledge that the report would probably be passed on to the mortgagor, who would use it to confirm his decision to buy the house, was sufficient to impose on the valuer a duty of care to him. This was so even though the report contained a notice that it was given without any assumption of responsibility to the purchaser, this being held unreasonable under the Unfair Contract Terms Act 1977.[199] The pointers towards a finding in favour of the claimant were, however, very strong in this case: the sum at stake was modest because the house was at the lower end of the market and liability in such cases would not place an unmanageable burden on valuers; it was virtually certain that the purchaser would have no form of independent advice[200]; and the purchaser was in effect paying the valuer's fee because he was reimbursing the mortgagees in respect of it.[201] Even here, however, a line is drawn at the purchaser in pursuance of whose application the report is prepared—the duty does not extend to subsequent purchasers of the house.[202]

A narrow view of the purpose of the statement was taken in *Al Nakib Investments (Jersey) Ltd v Longcroft*.[203] Directors issued a prospectus inviting shareholders of CT to subscribe for shares in CT and in M (a new company). While it was conceded that a duty was owed to shareholders who accepted the invitation, that part of the statement of claim which related to "after-market" purchases[204] was

[196] *Reeman v DoT* [1997] 2 Lloyd's Rep. 648.
[197] *Mariola Marine Corp v Lloyd's Register of Shipping* [1990] 1 Lloyd's Rep. 547. See also *Marc Rich & Co A.G. v Bishop Rock Marine Co Ltd* [1996] A.C. 211, para.5–13, above.
[198] [1990] 1 A.C. 831, para.11–21, above.
[199] See para.11–30, below.
[200] Building societies commonly advise purchasers to have their own surveys done, but at the lower end of the market very few do. See *Yianni v Edwin Evans & Sons* [1982] Q.B. 438.
[201] Compare the audit situation, where the claimant is relying on something paid for by someone else. In *Preston v Torfaen BC* (1993) Con. L.R. 48 a surveyor engaged to do a site survey for a housing development was held not to owe a duty to the purchasers of houses.
[202] [1990] 1 A.C. at 865.
[203] [1990] 1 W.L.R. 1390.
[204] i.e. purchases in the market from persons to whom shares had been allotted in the issue.

struck out, for the purpose of the prospectus was to invite participation in the rights issue, not market dealings in the shares.[205] Nonetheless, market practices (and hence reasonable expectations) may change and it may be that *Al Nakib* represents too narrow a view in modern conditions. In *Possfund Custodian Trustee Ltd v Diamond*[206] the claimants proposed to produce expert evidence that the current perception of the function of a prospectus in the unlisted securities market was that it was intended to influence after-market purchases as well as applications for allotment and Lightman J. accordingly held that the issue of liability was arguable and could only be determined at trial. This was so even though the statutory liability in this area, which extends to after-market purchasers as well as allottees, applied only to listed securities.[207] Another example of a refusal to strike out[208] is *Morgan Crucible Co Plc v Hill Samuel Bank Ltd*[209] where the claimants were bidders for FCE and the defendants had issued profit forecasts in circulars to shareholders in FCE advising them to reject the bid.[210] Although this was the primary or immediate purpose of the circulars it would be unrealistic in the normal take-over situation to deny that the circulars were also intended to persuade the bidders to increase the amount of their bid[211] and this was, arguably, another purpose of the circulars.[212]

11–27 If the reliance by the claimant takes place outside the relevant purpose, the defendant's knowledge of the reliance is irrelevant: it would have made no difference in *Caparo* if at the time of the audit a partner in the defendant firm had been aware, as a result of a conversation in the pub, that his next-door neighbour was interested in acquiring Fidelity shares. At the opposite extreme, a bidder for a company may extract from the auditors a warranty that the accounts are an accurate view of the company's financial health, in which

---

[205] The result is the same as in the deceit case of *Peek v Gurney* (1873) L.R. 6 H.L. 377. See also Denning L.J. in *Candler v Crane Christmas* [1951] 2 K.B. 164 at 183: "for the guidance of the very person in the very transaction in question."

[206] [1996] 1 W.L.R. 1351.

[207] For the somewhat complicated statutory background see [1996] 1 W.L.R. 1351 at 1359.

[208] It would of course be wrong to treat refusals to strike out as decisions in favour of liability and such cases are often compromised without a trial. Note, however, that from the defendant's point of view failure on a striking-out application is a serious matter because he has to prepare for trial. Courts are now even more reluctant to strike out: see para.5–3, above.

[209] [1991] Ch. 295.

[210] The claim was brought against (1) the directors of FCE, who had issued the circulars, (2) a merchant bank, FCE's advisers, and (3) FCE's auditors. The claims against (2) and (3) were allowed to go to trial, even though they were at one step removed from those against the directors.

[211] In which the circulars were successful. An increased bid was made and a further circular recommended acceptance. The action was brought after the claimants had acquired FCE and, so they alleged, discovered the forecasts to have been exaggerated.

[212] At first instance Hoffmann J. had referred to "the knowledge, intention and purposes" of the parties as "an impoverished set of concepts" to determine the issue of duty. The CA said it was not sure what he meant by this.

case there can be no possible defence to a claim if they are not. However, something less may do, as where the defendant is aware of the claimant's interest in the transaction and supplies information relating to it directly to the claimant[213] or expressly or impliedly confirms information he has supplied before for another purpose. In principle a duty may arise even where an auditor simply repeats what he has said in his audit report, provided it can be said that in the circumstances the defendant can be taken to have assumed responsibility to an identified person, which may be possible where he is aware that that person contemplates a transaction with the client and makes no qualification or disclaimer.[214] However, every case will require detailed examination of the facts to see if, at the end of the day, the provider of the information can fairly be said to have behaved in such a way as to indicate that he is assuming responsibility to the person relying on it. In *Precis (521) Plc v William M. Mercer Ltd*[215] the defendant actuaries prepared a valuation report on the pension fund of the SG company and this turned out to have seriously underestimated the deficit of the fund. Later the claimants made a successful offer for SG and sued the defendants when they discovered the size of the deficit. The defendants were held not liable. They had prepared the valuation for the information of SG (it expressly declared that its purpose was to enable SG to review its contribution rate) and even though they had provided a copy of the valuation for SG to pass to the claimants that could just as well have been done by SG, in which case there would have been no shadow of a claim. There was no direct contact between the claimants and the defendants and the knowledge that there was some sort of "corporate transaction" on foot between SG and the claimants was not enough to justify treating them as having assumed any responsibility to the claimants.[216] In *MAN Nutzfahrzeuge AG v Freightliner Ltd* auditors might have been under a duty to the purchaser of a company in respect of losses arising from statements in the accounts used in the share-purchase agreement but they could not foresee what was the true cause of the loss, namely fraudulent statements about the accounts made (on behalf of the

---

[213] See the dissenting judgment of Denning L.J. in *Candler v Crane Christmas* [1951] 2 K.B. 164.

[214] *Andrew v Kounis Freeman* [1999] 2 B.C.L.C. 641. Cf. *Peach Publishing Ltd v Slater & Co* [1998] P.N.L.R. 364; and *R. Lowe Lippmann Figdor & Franck v A.G.C. (Advances) Ltd* [1992] V.R. 671 at 682, approved in *Esanda Finance Corp v Peat Marwick Hungerfords* (1997) 188 C.L.R. 241. See also *Galoo Ltd v Bright Grahame Murray* [1994] 1 W.L.R. 1360.

[215] [2005] EWCA Civ 114; [2005] P.N.L.R. 28.

[216] The claimants had chosen to ignore legal advice to obtain their own actuarial assessment, which was at least contributory negligence. Furthermore, SG had supplied the valuation report on the basis that neither SG nor its advisers had any responsibility for its accuracy and the defendants had "accepted" the benefit of this for the purposes of the Contracts (Rights of Third Parties) Act 1999.

parent company) during the negotiations by the company's financial controller; and even if they had been able to foresee that, to:

> "[H]old that the auditors assumed responsibility for the use which a dishonest employee of the audited company might make of the accounts in the context of the parent company's negotiations for the sale of the company would . . . be to impose on them a liability greater than they could reasonably have thought they were undertaking."[217]

D may be instructed to prepare a report by X in circumstances in which a duty of care is clearly owed (probably by contract) to X, but the report may also be relied on by C. If it is clear that X is acting with, or on behalf of, others, the fact that C is not identified by name should not prevent a duty of care being owed to him[218] but if D has no reason to know of C's involvement it may be that C cannot sue: D is entitled to know who his client is,[219] even if, where C is merely a joint purchaser or lender, D's liability is not then increased beyond what he could have expected.[220] It is true that there may be a duty to each member of an ascertained class, but that begins from the assumption that the defendant has reason to know there *is* a class. When this condition is fulfilled is a question of fact, so probably not a great deal by way of general application can be said. However, it has been held (not surprisingly) that where a person acting on behalf of a vendor of property engages an architect to certify the progress of conversion work (being done by the vendor) the architect should contemplate that the certificate may be shown to the purchaser, though it does not follow that he necessarily assumes responsibility to the purchaser if the latter takes the decisive step of completing the purchase.[221]

Even if the adviser has a particular person in mind as likely to rely on his statement he will not be liable if the reliance takes place in the context of a transaction different from that which the adviser contemplated. However, it is thought that the law should not require too

---

[217] [2007] EWCA Civ 910; [2008] P.N.L.R. 6 at [56].

[218] This was, after all, essentially the position in *Hedley Byrne*.

[219] The point was left undecided in *Omega Trust Co Ltd v Wright Son & Pepper* (1997) 75 P. & C.R. 57 since the case turned on the disclaimer, but Henry L.J.'s judgment seems sympathetic to this submission.

[220] In *Smith v Carter* 1995 S.L.T. 295 the point is made that it is not uncommon for one person to instruct a report as the undisclosed agent of others whose interest in a property transaction might not be fully known at the early stages.

[221] *Machin v Adams* (1997) 59 Con. L.R. 14. The majority held that there was no duty. Why, precisely, is not clear, perhaps because he might believe that the purchaser had his own expert (though the contract—unfulfilled in this respect and unknown to the architect —between vendor and purchaser had provided for the appointment of a *joint* architect!).

literal a congruence between the transaction contemplated and that which in fact takes place, so long as this does not increase the liability to which the adviser would be exposed. Where, for example, a valuer provides a report knowing that it will be shown to a particular intending purchaser of a property it ought not to matter that, say, the recipient eventually takes a long lease rather than buying the freehold.[222] Even if the transaction is exactly what was contemplated, one must also bear in mind that the defendant only owes a duty of care in respect of a type of damage arising from it which he ought to have in contemplation, so that if, for example, a local authority receives from a potential purchaser an inquiry about the maintenance obligations governing a way fronting a property, it does not follow that if its answer is incorrect it is responsible for losses which are attributable to the impact on the development value of the site.[223]

J. Physical Damage

Liability for physical damage is plainly much wider than for economic loss. Nevertheless, some intriguing questions remain to be explored by the courts on the extent of liability for physical damage caused by negligent misstatements. Cases like *Caparo* effectively block liability for economic loss caused by generally published information. However, in *Candler v Crane Christmas & Co* Denning L.J. gave his opinion that a marine hydrographer would not be liable for omitting a reef and causing the wreck of an ocean liner.[224] Though the matter has not been much discussed here, cases in other jurisdictions seem not to have adopted a blanket rejection of liability in all cases arising from generally published material[225] and it would seem unreasonable to deny liability where, say, a handbook on

11–28

---

[222] Cf. *Restatement*, 2d, s.552, "or in a substantially similar transaction". In *J.E.B. Fasteners Ltd v Marks, Bloom & Co* [1981] 3 All E.R. 289 it was held that a duty was owed by accountants to a person whom they believed might be approached by the company for financial support even though in fact he effected a takeover rather than making a loan. The claim failed for lack of causative reliance (on appeal [1983] 1 All E.R. 583). It was said in *Caparo* that the case might have been correctly decided on its facts and it seems that the accountants had in fact been aware of developments right up to the acquisition.

[223] *Gooden v Northamptonshire CC* [2001] EWCA Civ 1744 (where there was a difference of opinion on what the authority ought to have foreseen).

[224] [1951] 2 K.B. 164 at 182. Lord Brown appears to have agreed in *Sutradhar v National Environmental Research Council* [2006] UKHL 33; [2006] 4 All E.R. 490.

[225] In the *Willemstad* (1976) 136 C.L.R. 529 producers of a navigation plotting chart were held liable at first instance. There was no appeal on the issue of duty by these defendants. In *Brocklesby v US* 767 F.2d 1288 (C9,1985) the publisher of an inaccurate instrument approach chart for aircraft was held liable on strict product liability and negligence theories.

edible mushrooms[226] or a book on DIY electrics gave dangerously misleading instructions.

K. Immunity

11–29 As with any other head of negligence, there may be reasons of public policy which prevent a duty of care arising. *Hedley Byrne* has not affected the immunity from suit of a judge[227] but there is no reason for extending that immunity to a person appointed as a valuer[228] or to an architect granting certificates of completion of work under a building contract[229]: there is a difference between the judicial function and a duty to act fairly. Although there was some doubt about the position of an arbitrator at common law, s.29 of the Arbitration Act 1996 provides that:

> "[A]n arbitrator is not liable for anything done or omitted to be done in the discharge or purported discharge of his functions as arbitrator unless the act or omission is shown to have been in bad faith".

L. Disclaimer of Responsibility

11–30 It must not be overlooked that, in the result, judgment in *Hedley Byrne* went to the defendants and this, at least in the opinion of the majority, was because they had supplied the information "without responsibility".[230] In effect, therefore, the liability created by the House of Lords would exist only if the defendant has been too careless of his own interests or too proud to protect himself by such a declaration or was unable for some reason (such as professional conduct rules) to do so. However, this situation was radically altered by the Unfair Contract Terms Act 1977.[231] By s.2(2) of the Act, a person cannot by means of any contract term or notice restrict his liability for loss or damage other than personal injury[232] caused by negligence in the course of a business unless he shows that the term or notice is reasonable and s.1(1)(b) defines "negligence" as including the breach of any common law duty to take reasonable care or

---

[226] See the decision of a French court on such facts cited by Whittaker, "European Product Liability and Intellectual Products" (1989) 105 L.Q.R. 125. On instructions accompanying products, see para.10–5, above.

[227] See para.24–8, below. A sequestrator, though an officer of the court, is not immune from suit: *I.R.C. v Hoogstraten* [1985] Q.B. 1007.

[228] *Arenson v Casson Beckman Rutley & Co* [1977] A.C. 405.

[229] *Sutcliffe v Thackrah* [1974] A.C. 727.

[230] Lord Hodson and, perhaps, Lord Morris would have reached the same conclusion even in the absence of the disclaimer.

[231] The Unfair Terms in Consumer Contracts Regulations 1999 apply only to a "term in a contract". They might be relevant where liability was being asserted concurrently in contract and tort.

[232] Personal injury is governed by s.2(1), which is still more onerous on the defendant.

exercise reasonable skill. It may be objected that this is not apt to catch a statement given "without responsibility" since the defendant is then making it clear that he does not undertake a duty in the first place but this objection is met by the provision in s.13 that s.2 also prevents, "excluding or restricting liability by reference to terms and notices which exclude or restrict the relevant obligation or duty".[233] However, there is a distinction between such a case and one where there cannot fairly be said to be any assumption of responsibility at all and this is a matter of substance rather than form.[234] Of course, even where the case falls under the Act the disclaimer may still be effective if it is reasonable in all the circumstances and the inquirer may not be able to expect the same standard of care in response to a gratuitous inquiry as he could expect if paying for the service.[235] Furthermore, while it will generally be unreasonable for a surveyor conducting a valuation for the purchase of a dwelling on mortgage to disclaim liability,[236] the more "commercial" the transaction becomes the more likely it is that a disclaimer or limit of liability will be found reasonable. Thus in a valuation of commercial property a clause which has the effect of restricting the duty to the client and excluding liability to any unknown participants is valid,[237] as is a disclaimer by an estate agent made to a prospective purchaser of property at the upper end of the housing market.[238]

Whether or not the Unfair Contract Terms Act is applicable, the following qualifications under the common law would appear to apply to the power to disclaim responsibility:

1. A person guilty of deceit will remain liable whatever he may have said by way of disclaimer,[239] though the same does not

---

[233] *Smith v Eric S. Bush* [1990] 1 A.C. 831; but cf. Nourse L.J. in *First National Commercial Bank v Loxleys* [1997] P.N.L.R. 211.

[234] *IFE Fund SA v Goldman Sachs International* [2007] EWCA Civ 811; [2007] 2 Lloyds Rep 449.

[235] Note, however, that the disclaimer will commonly be a "notice" rather than a "contract term" and by s.11(3): "in relation to a notice ... the requirement of reasonableness ... is that it should be fair and reasonable to allow reliance on it, having regard to all circumstances obtaining when the liability arose or (but for the notice) would have arisen." Cf. s.11(1), in relation to contract terms, which fixes the point of time as that when the contract was made.

[236] *Smith v Eric S. Bush*, above, fn.233.

[237] *Omega Trust Co Ltd v Wright Son & Pepper* [1997] 75 P. & C.R. 57.

[238] *McCullagh v Lane Fox & Partners Ltd* [1996] 1 E.G.L.R. 35; and see *Bank of Scotland v Fuller Peiser* 2002 S.L.T. 574 (survey commissioned by purchaser of hotel; disclaimer reasonable against lending bank). Note that under the Property Misdescriptions Act 1991 an estate agent may incur criminal liability, subject to a defence of due diligence, for false or misleading statements about property; but this does not give rise to civil liability: s.1(4).

[239] *H.I.H. Casualty and General Insurance Ltd v Chase Manhattan Bank* [2003] UKHL 6; [2003] 2 Lloyd's Rep. 61.

necessarily apply to a clause excluding liability for the fraud of his agent.[240]

2. Clear language should be used to disclaim liability. For example, it is submitted that the letters "E. & O.E." (errors and omissions excepted) which are printed on many documents should not necessarily be regarded as sufficient in themselves to exclude a duty of care. However, a disclaimer should not be treated to that sort of strained interpretation which once (though no longer) was applied to contractual exclusion clauses: subject always to s.2 of the Unfair Contract Terms Act, the ultimate question is not whether the defendant has excluded his liability but whether it is legitimate for the recipient of the advice to regard the defendant as having assumed responsibility for his statement.[241]

3. Given that the liability is non-contractual and that reliance by the claimant is an essential element of it,[242] it is thought that it should be sufficient that the defendant makes it known that he disclaims responsibility before the claimant acts on the information or advice and he need not necessarily do so when the statement is made.[243]

M. Reliance and Contributory Negligence

11–31   Although reliance by the claimant is not necessary in all cases based upon assumption of responsibility,[244] it is plainly required where the damage arises from a statement by the defendant to the claimant and this reliance must be a cause of the loss.[245] Although here, as in the case of deceit, the law allows for mixed motives, if

---

[240] This was the view of the CA in *H.I.H. Casualty and General Insurance Ltd v Chase Manhattan Bank* [2001] EWCA Civ 1250; [2001] 2 Lloyd's Rep. 483. However, the HL did not have to decide the point since the clause did not cover such a situation. It is probably "extraordinarily unlikely" that parties to a contract will agree such a term, "with sufficient clarity to raise squarely the question of whether it should be lawful to do so": Lord Hoffmann [2003] UKHL 6; [2003] 2 Lloyd's Rep. 61 at [81]. Cf. *Frans Maas (UK) Ltd v Samsung Electronics (UK) Ltd* [2004] EWHC 1502 (Comm); [2004] 2 Lloyd's Rep. 251 (wilful wrongdoing of servants in performance of contract).

[241] See the judgment of Hobhouse L.J. in *McCullagh v Lane Fox & Partners Ltd* [1996] 1 E.G.L.R. 35.

[242] See below.

[243] This is perhaps supported by *McCullagh v Lane Fox & Partners Ltd*, above, fn.241, though the point there was different, there being no duty at the time the statement was made and the disclaimer being made before it became known that the statement would be acted on without verification.

[244] See para.5–37, above.

[245] So also where there is a statement about C to X, X must act in reliance on it in relation to C: *Spring v Guardian Assurance* [1995] 2 A.C. 296. A case which falls within neither pattern is *Wildgust v Norwich Union* [2006] IESC 19; [2006] 1 I.R. 570. C has a policy with D on the life of X, assigned to Y as security for a loan; because of industrial action a premium is missed. Y becomes aware of this but is told incorrectly by D that C has paid. X dies and D refuses to pay C on the lapsed policy. Liable to C.

the claimant, though aware of the defendant's statement, did not believe it[246] or was uninfluenced by it, there is no liability. As to contributory negligence, Woolf J. in *J.E.B. Fasteners v Marks, Bloom & Co*[247] (where the issue did not in fact arise) commented that in the case of negligent auditing of accounts:

"[I]f it is reasonable to rely on the accounts, it is difficult to envisage circumstances where as a matter of fact it would be negligent to do so without taking further steps to protect yourself from the consequences of relying on the auditor's certificate".

However, perhaps because of the modern emphasis on assumption of responsibility as the basis of liability, the case law shows that there are situations in which the claimant's failure to look after his own interests justifies a reduction in damages[248] (though it has been said that only in a "very special case" would the court be justified in reducing the damages of a claimant who has done what the defendant intended him to do by way of reliance on the misrepresentation[249]). If the fault alleged against the claimant was subsequent to the point at which he had irrevocably committed himself to a transaction in reliance on the defendant's advice,[250] that might be a case of failure to mitigate rather than contributory negligence properly so called.

N. Lord Tenterden's Act

By the Statute of Frauds 1677 promises that are guarantees to answer for another's debts must be in writing and signed by the party to be charged or his agent in order to make them actionable. The Statute of Frauds Amendment Act 1828 (commonly called Lord Tenterden's Act), s.6, was passed (providing, in effect, that a false representation as to credit cannot be sued upon unless it is made in writing and signed by the party to be charged[251]) to prevent the Statute being evaded by utilising the comparatively new action of deceit. The section clearly covers fraudulent representations as to a

11–32

---

[246] *Rushmer v Smith* [2009] EWHC 94 (QB).

[247] [1981] 3 All E.R. 289 at 297.

[248] See *Platform Home Loans Ltd v Oyston Shipways Ltd* [2000] 2 A.C. 190 (imprudent to make large loan on "non-status" basis; however, the issue was the impact on contributory negligence of *Banque Bruxelles v Eagle Star* [1997] A.C. 191, para.6–54, above); *Precis (521) Plc v William M. Mercer Ltd* [2005] EWCA Civ 114; [2005] P.N.L.R. 28 (where, however, there was held to be no duty).

[249] *Gran Gelato Ltd v Richcliff (Group) Ltd* [1992] Ch. 560. Contributory negligence is inapplicable to a claim for deceit: para.6–44, above.

[250] e.g. C buys a house on D's negligently conducted survey but C then negligently fails to notice warning signs so that the damage is greater than it would otherwise have been.

[251] See *Contex Drouzhba Ltd v Wiseman* [2006] EWCA Civ 2708; *Lindsay v O'Loughnane* [2010] EWHC 529 (QB).

person's credit but it does not apply to an action between contracting parties in respect of advice negligently given.[252] The section was not considered in *Hedley Byrne* and rightly so, for it has no more place in actions for tortious negligence than it has in actions founded upon contract.[253] Nevertheless it is strange that what would be a defence in an action for fraud should not be one in an action for negligence.[254] It would be even stranger if a defendant against whom negligence is alleged could affirmatively set up his own fraudulent intent and plead the statute. Presumably, however, such a plea could be struck out on the general ground that no one should be allowed to take advantage of his own wrongful act.[255]

4. Injury to Persons not Relying on the Statement

11–33 Reliance on a statement made by D to X may cause X to act in a manner detrimental to C, but in respect of which C has no redress against X, and the question then arises whether D is liable to C. Putting aside the case where the statement is defamatory of C there is no doubt that D incurs liability where the statement was made with "malice" and causes damage[256] to C, as where D knowingly published a false story that C had ceased to trade.[257] This is the tort of malicious falsehood, which is outlined at a later point.[258] It is also possible that D may incur liability to C for damage caused by lies to X under the head of unlawful interference with trade[259]; but neither of these wrongs is committed by mere negligence. That there may, however, be liability for negligence in some such situations is established by the decision of the House of Lords in *Spring v Guardian Assurance Plc*.[260] The claimant had been employed by A and had been a "company representative" of G, selling G's policies. He was dismissed by G when G took over A. The claimant then went into business and sought to gain authority to sell SA policies. In accordance with the rules of the regulatory body under the Financial Services Act 1986, SA sought a reference on the claimant and this was very uncomplimentary, asserting inter alia that the claimant was, "of little or no integrity and could not be regarded as honest".[261] SA thereupon declined to authorise the claimant to sell

---

[252] *Banbury v Bank of Montreal* [1918] A.C. 626.
[253] *W.B. Anderson & Sons Ltd v Rhodes (Liverpool) Ltd* [1967] 2 All E.R. 850.
[254] It does apply to the Misrepresentation Act 1967 s.2(1), because of the form of that provision: *U.B.A.F. Ltd v European Banking Corp* [1984] Q.B. 713.
[255] Cf. *Alghussein v Eton College* [1988] 1 W.L.R. 587.
[256] Damage is now sometimes presumed.
[257] *Ratcliffe v Evans* [1892] 2 Q.B. 525.
[258] See para.12–72, below.
[259] See para.18–9, below.
[260] [1995] 2 A.C. 296.
[261] [1995] 2 A.C. 296 at 306.

its policies. The trial judge held that while the claimant had certainly been guilty of incompetence he had not been dishonest and that the sources in G who had supplied information to the compiler of the reference had failed to exercise reasonable care, although they were not malicious.[262] There was some dispute as to whether the claimant's status was that of employee or independent contractor but nothing was thought to turn upon that and for convenience the judgments were largely couched in terms of the former status.[263] The words were plainly defamatory but the provision of a reference at the request of a prospective employer is the classic occasion of qualified privilege[264] and the finding of lack of malice was therefore fatal to the claimant's libel claim, as it was to the alternative claim for malicious falsehood. However, a majority of the House of Lords[265] held that if causation of loss could be established[266] the claimant had a cause of action in negligence. The argument (which had convinced the Court of Appeal) that the imposition of liability for negligence would subvert the protection which the law of defamation had deliberately cast around referees was rejected by the House of Lords because there were significant differences between the two heads of liability: on the one hand, negligence required proof of fault and damage; on the other, an inaccurate statement might be damaging without being defamatory, in that it reflected on a person's suitability for employment without being defamatory of him.[267] It was, of course, accepted that the introduction into this area of liability for negligence would significantly affect for the worse the position of the referee, but this was said to be a necessary change in the law in view of developments in the relationship between employer and employee.

"There would be no purpose in extending the tort of negligence to protect the subject of an inaccurate reference if he was already adequately protected by the law of defamation . . . The result of [the requirement of malice in such cases] is that an action for defamation provides a wholly inadequate remedy for an employee who is caused damage by a reference which due to negligence is inaccurate. This is because it places a wholly disproportionate

---

[262] The above is a somewhat simplified account, since the reference was in fact compiled by an employee of GRE, the parent company of G, on the basis of information supplied by other employees of GRE and an employee of A (which was itself two associated companies) but this was treated as the responsibility of G. Lord Goff did not think GRE were under any duty of care to the claimant but the other members of the majority treated all four companies as one unit.

[263] See, e.g. [1995] 2 A.C. at 340 and at 341.

[264] See para.12–46, below.

[265] Lord Keith dissenting.

[266] For which purpose the case had to be remitted to the Court of Appeal.

[267] e.g. that a student got a lower class of degree than was in fact the case.

burden on the employee. Malice is extremely difficult to establish . . . If the law provides a remedy for references which are
inaccurate due to carelessness this would be beneficial. It would
encourage the adoption of appropriate standards when preparing
references."[268]

11–34   The duty extends to not making misleading (as opposed to simply
untrue) statements[269] but does not extend to an obligation to write a
"full" reference.[270] The majority of the judges in *Spring* were of the
view that there would be a parallel liability based on the (terminated) contract between the former employer and the claimant.[271]
As far as the tort liability is concerned, there is some difference in
the reasoning employed: Lord Goff's speech rests primarily upon
the principle of assumption of responsibility, but the other members
of the minority base their reasoning upon the general tripartite
approach to the duty of care in *Caparo v Dickman*.[272] Looked at as
a case of assumption of responsibility, the decision may be said to
stand between *Hedley Byrne*[273] and the fullest extension of the
principle in *White v Jones*.[274] In the latter case there was no reliance
at all by the claimants. In *Spring* the direct reliance on the statement
was by the new employer who rejected the claimant but there is
commonly an element of reliance by the claimant, who will have
asked for the reference or will at least know that it is likely to be
given. It seems, however, that there would be liability in such a case
even if the claimant is entirely unaware that the reference is being
written.[275]

11–35   It is clear from the case that because a former employer is liable
to the subject of a reference it by no means follows that the same
applies to a reference written by a social acquaintance.[276] The
speeches concentrate very heavily upon the "reference situation"
and emphasise the close degree of proximity between the parties and
it therefore seems most unlikely that the law will be developed so as
to create liability for damaging but non-malicious and non-defamatory statements which are published generally (for example that a

---

[268] [1995] 2 A.C. at 346 per Lord Woolf. Similar reasoning applies to malicious falsehood,
which is wider than defamation in that the statement need not be defamatory, but it still
requires malice.

[269] *Bartholomew v Hackney LBC* [1999] I.R.L.R. 246.

[270] *Kidd v Axa Equity and Law* [2000] I.R.L.R. 301.

[271] There is some discussion in the case of whether there could be a duty on the employer to
provide a reference (as opposed to taking care when he does provide one).

[272] See para.5–9, above.

[273] This was also, of course, a case about a reference but it involved liability to the recipient,
not to the subject.

[274] See para.5–37, above.

[275] Cf. *Wade v State of Victoria* [1999] 1 V.R. 121. However, *Spring* may not be the law in
Australia: *Cornwall v Rowan* [2004] SASC 384; 90 S.A.S.R. 269.

[276] [1995] 2 A.C. 296 at 319, 336, 345.

company has ceased to trade or that its sales are lower than in fact they are).[277] However, there are obvious relationships which are as "proximate" as those of referee and subject.[278] Consider, for example, the case of a doctor who is commissioned by an insurer to report on the health of a proposer or by an employer on the health of a prospective employee. Both cases seem very similar to the case of a reference, save that they are carried out under contract with a person other than the claimant.[279] However, in *X v Bedfordshire CC*,[280] Lord Browne-Wilkinson, in rejecting the argument that a social worker and psychiatrist investigating a case of suspected child abuse owed a duty of care to the child said:

"The social workers and the psychiatrists were retained by the local authority to advise the local authority, not the plaintiffs. The subject matter of the advice and activities of the professionals is the child . . . But the fact that the carrying out of the retainer involves contact with and relationship with the child cannot alter the extent of the duty owed by the professionals under the retainer from the local authority. The Court of Appeal[281] drew a correct analogy with the doctor instructed by an insurance company to examine an applicant for life insurance. The doctor does not, by examining the applicant, come under any general duty of medical care to the applicant. He is under a duty not to damage the applicant in the course of the examination: but beyond that his duties are owed to the insurance company and not to the applicant."[282]

Since then it has been held that a doctor employed by a company owed no duty of care to a prospective employee in reporting on his health.[283] However, it may be unsafe to conclude that there is necessarily a simple rule of non-liability in all these cases. First, matters have moved on somewhat in the context of child abuse investigations and it is now held that there may be a duty of care to

---

[277] See, e.g. *Midland Metals Overseas Pte. Ltd v Christchurch Press Co Ltd* [2001] NZCA 321; [2002] 2 N.Z.L.R. 289.

[278] See *Young v Bella* [2006] SCC 3; [2006] 1 S.C.R. 108 (student reported to authorities as suspected child abuser).

[279] Even this is not necessarily true: a family doctor may receive an inquiry from an insurer which is to be answered briefly on the basis of the patient's records.

[280] [1995] 2 A.C. 633 at 752–753. See para.5–52, above.

[281] See [1995] 2 A.C. at 651.

[282] This view is supported by Denning L.J. in *Candler v Crane Christmas* [1951] 2 K.B. 164. Staughton L.J. in the CA had said the same would be true of a police surgeon called to examine a suspected drunken motorist: [1995] 2 A.C. at 673–674.

[283] *Kapfunde v Abbey National* [1999] I.C.R. 1. Of course even if one took the alternative view the purpose of the examination has to be borne in mind. It is one thing to say that the doctor should be liable for causing the claimant to lose his job; it is another to say that he should be liable for failing to warn of abnormalities, at least so long as they are not life-threatening. See *R. v Croydon HA* (1997) 40 B.M.L.R. 40.

the child, though still not to the parents.[284] Secondly, the denial of duty in *X v Bedfordshire* rested primarily upon the view that a duty of care would cut across and interfere with the statutory framework of child care, a matter which is hardly relevant to the case of the insurance company or the employer's doctor.[285] Thirdly, it has since been held in *Phelps v Hillingdon London Borough Council*[286] that where an educational psychologist was asked to assess a child in circumstances where it was clear that others would act on the assessment, a duty of care was owed to the child despite the fact that the psychologist had been engaged to report to the education authority. "The duty to the pupil would march hand in hand with the professional's responsibilities to his own employer."[287] It is hard to see why the same could not be said of the insurer's or employer's doctor.[288]

---

[284] *D v East Berkshire Community NHS Trust* [2003] EWCA Civ 1151; [2004] Q.B. 558 and [2005] UKHL 23; [2005] 2 A.C. 373, para.5–53, above.

[285] A case where denial of a duty seems amply justified on policy grounds is *Mortensen v Laing (sub nom. South Pacific Manufacturing Co v New Zealand Security Consultants & Investigations)* [1992] 2 N.Z.L.R. 282 (insurer's claims investigator owed no duty to the insured in respect of the investigation report, which led to the insured suffering a conviction—subsequently set aside—for arson; to impose a duty would not only cut across the law of qualified privilege in respect of defamation—not in itself enough after *Spring* —but would also provide a means of bypassing the law of malicious prosecution, the absolute privilege which might attach to the investigator's report as prepared with a view to potential litigation between his client and the insured and the procedural privilege of the insurer to produce the report in such litigation. In any event, the insured still had his claim on the contract against the insurer).

[286] [2001] 2 A.C. 619.

[287] [2001] 2 A.C. at 666 per Lord Nicholls.

[288] In *Farah v British Airways, The Times*, January 26, 2000, the CA, referring to *Spring*, declined to strike out a claim alleging that a Home Office immigration liaison officer negligently and wrongly advised an airline that the claimants did not have the required documentation to obtain access to this country, with the result that they lost their flights.

CHAPTER 12

DEFAMATION, PRIVACY AND RELATED MATTERS

12–1 MOST legal systems confer some protection on the related interests of reputation, dignity and privacy, though this may be via the criminal law.[1] In England libel,[2] one of the two forms of defamation, was a common law crime, though for many years it was almost moribund and quite eclipsed in practical importance by tort liability. The crime was abolished by s.73(b) of the Coroners and Justice Act 2009.[3] Until almost the end of the 20th century the emphasis of the law was very much on the protection of reputation and there was certainly no general wrong of invasion of privacy. Technically that is still so but the wrong of misuse of private information, having grown out of the law of breach of confidence, comes very close to being a general privacy tort. There have always been restrictions on obtaining an injunction against the publication of defamatory material so the almost exclusive remedy is damages awarded after the event. Reputation is rarely an asset in respect of which damage can be calculated in financial terms (indeed, evidence of actual financial loss is rarely given) but damages in defamation cases may be substantial,[4] no doubt because awards reflect juries'[5] ideas of the value of dignity and honour as well as reputation strictly so called. There is a more powerful flavour of punishment and deterrence in

---

[1] Students of conflicts of laws will recall that *Machado v Fontes* [1897] 2 Q.B. 231 arose because the Brazilian law of defamation was criminal only. The criminal law plays a significant role in the protection of reputation in a number of European countries and many cases coming before the European Court of Human Rights in this area have arisen from criminal prosecutions.

[2] i.e. a statement damaging reputation couched in a permanent form: see para.12–4, below. Slander (e.g. spoken words) was not criminal on the same basis.

[3] However, there are a number of statutory crimes penalising statements likely to cause disorder or hatred. These are not founded on protection of reputation but may be applicable where formerly there would have been an offence of defamatory libel.

[4] Though not so high as they were a few years ago: below, para.12–71.

[5] Trial by jury is still the "default" mode of trial for defamation, though a quite high proportion of cases now seem to be heard by judge alone.

defamation than one commonly finds in the law of torts. Even where a claim for defamation fails the claimant may have a remedy under some other part of the law, most particularly the law of negligence[6] and the law of malicious falsehood[7] but in these torts damages follow more conventional lines and are not recoverable for injury to reputation as such. There is more scope for obtaining an injunction to restrain disclosure of private information but where damages are sought after the event they have some similarities with damages for defamation in that, for example, they are much concerned with assuaging the claimant's hurt feelings (though overall they are lower).

The European Convention on Human Rights. We saw earlier 12–2 that the general position now is that the common law and the Convention (breaches of which are actionable here under the Human Rights Act 1998) have rather different roles and that it is quite possible that on a particular set of facts the Convention may impose liability and the common law may not, or vice versa.[8] However, in the context of defamation the most prominent aspect of the Convention is the guarantee of freedom of expression in art.6 and that sort of "peaceful co-existence" is hardly possible where traditional principles of defamation would infringe that guarantee. Accordingly, certain defences, notably that of qualified privilege, have been extended by the courts in response to the Convention. However, the Convention is by no means only "restrictive" in the areas with which this chapter is concerned. Article 8 provides a qualified guarantee of respect for, "private and family life, [the] home and . . . correspondence". Contraventions of that by a public authority may be actionable under the Human Rights Act 1998 but there is no doubt that art.8 has been the prime mover in the development of the common law wrong of misuse of private information, which extends beyond public authorities. Furthermore, it is now accepted that reputation can be an interest protected by art.8[9] and it may be that the requirement of proportionality set by that article, if interference is to be treated as defensible, requires reconsideration of some common law defences designed to protect freedom of expression but which, if effective, are absolute.[10] At any rate we can safely say that here, as with other areas of tort law, the advent of Convention rights makes the picture more complex.

---

[6] See above, para.11–33.
[7] See below, para.12–72.
[8] See para.2–8, above.
[9] *Pfeiffer v Austria* App. No. 12556/03; [2007] ECHR 935; *Greene v Associated Newspapers Ltd* [2004] EWCA Civ 1462; [2005] Q.B. 972.
[10] *Clift v Slough BC* [2009] EWHC 1550; [2009] 4 All E.R. 756; *LNS v Persons Unknown* [2010] EWHC 119 (QB). However, that will require radical rewriting of the law: *Underhill v Corser* [2009] EWHC 3058 (QB).

1. Defamation: Definition and Elements[11]

12–3 *Defamation is the publication of a statement which reflects on a person's reputation and tends to lower him in the estimation of right-thinking members of society generally or tends to make them shun or avoid him.*

For historical reasons defamation takes the form of two separate torts, libel and slander, the former being generally more favourable to the claimant because it is actionable per se and injury to reputation will be presumed. However, whether the case is one of libel or slander the following elements must be proved by the claimant:

1. The statement must be defamatory.
2. It must refer to the claimant, i.e. identify him.
3. It must be published, i.e. communicated to at least one person other than the claimant.

In practice the statement ("imputation" is the technically correct description) is almost always in the form of words but it can take any form which conveys meaning, for example a picture, a cartoon or a statue.

A. Libel and Slander

12–4 Once upon a time the fundamental distinction was between written (including printed) words, which were libel, and spoken words which were slander. Nowadays the general view is that the test of libel is whether the publication is in a "permanent" form,[12] other cases being slander. However, by statute certain forms of publication are made libel even though they are not necessarily very permanent at all. Examples of libel are a writing, printed material, or other mark or sign exposed to view, or a picture, waxwork, statue or effigy. On the other hand, defamation in the sign language of the deaf and dumb, and mimicry and gesticulation generally (e.g. holding up an empty purse to indicate that the claimant has been robbed by the defendant[13]) would be slander, because the movements are more transient.[14] However, some arbitrary lines have to be drawn: it

---

[11] Gatley, *Libel and Slander*, 11th edn; Duncan and Neill, *Defamation*, 3rd edn; Carter-Ruck, *Libel and Privacy*, 6th edn; Price, *Defamation*, 4th edn. The law of defamation rests mainly upon the common law, but there are important statutes, notably the Defamation Acts of 1952 and 1996.

[12] The main reason being that Parliament, in dealing with broadcasting in the Defamation Act 1952, took this as the test at common law: "shall be deemed to be publication in a permanent form".

[13] *Cook v Cox* (1814) 3 M. & S. 110 at 114.

[14] These example show that it is only broadly true to say that libel is addressed to the eye, slander to the ear.

is thought that chalk marks on a wall would be libel even though they may be quickly washed away by the rain. Far more important in practice are the statutory provisions whereby broadcasting, both radio and television,[15] and theatrical performances,[16] are libel. The Court of Appeal in *Youssoupoff v Metro-Goldwyn-Mayer Pictures Ltd* had no doubt that the showing of defamatory matter embodied in a film with a soundtrack was libel:

> "There can be no doubt that, so far as the photographic part of the exhibition is concerned, that is a permanent matter to be seen by the eye, and is the proper subject of an action for libel, if defamatory. I regard the speech which is synchronised with the photographic reproduction and forms part of one complex, common exhibition as an ancillary circumstance, part of the surroundings explaining that which is to be seen".[17]

That, of course, does not deal with the position where there is nothing defamatory in the visual part of the film, but it is submitted that that case, too, should be libel: the distinction between libel and slander is anachronistic (indeed over-ripe for abolition) and fine distinctions should not be encouraged. Other borderline cases which should also, it is submitted, be libel are the playing of a video tape,[18] or a record or audio tape or disc,[19] or the calling up of defamatory material on a computer screen or its distribution on the Internet.[20]

Obviously if an oral utterance is communicated to a person it is a slander which is published and if a written statement is shown it is libel, but an oral statement by A may be written down by D and shown by D to B. In that case D publishes a libel. No doubt A's original uttering of the words to D was slander, but the communication to B is not by word of mouth.[21] Conversely, if A writes to D

---

[15] Broadcasting Act 1990 s.166, replacing a similar provision in the Defamation Act 1952. For a consideration of television broadcasting in the absence of any statutory provision, see *Wainer v Rippon* [1981] V.R. 129.

[16] Theatres Act 1968 s.4. This does not apply to performances given on domestic occasions in private dwellings: s.7.

[17] Slesser L.J. (1934) 50 T.L.R. 581 at 587.

[18] The only difference between this and a film is that the image cannot be viewed in any way unless the tape is played in a machine.

[19] Winfield thought, however, that playing a record should be slander on the ground that although the matter was embodied in a permanent form, its publication was transient and appealed to the ear. In practice of course most publications of defamatory sound recordings giving rise to complaint will be in broadcasts. Is it libel or slander when defamatory material is imparted to a parrot and it repeats it? See *Chicken v Ham*, Herbert, *Uncommon Law*, p.75.

[20] Although there have now been a number of defamation cases about the Internet here, in the United States and the Commonwealth it has not been necessary to pay much attention to the libel/slander issue. A purely aural Internet transmission was held slander in *Mickelberg v 6 P.R. Southern Cross Radio Pty Ltd* [2001] WASC 150. On the Internet in general see Collins, *Law of Defamation and the Internet*, 2nd edn.

[21] On liability for repetition see below, para.12–24.

something defamatory of C and D reads it aloud to B, that ought logically to be slander, but the balance of authority (though there is little reasoning to support it) is the other way.[22] If I dictate a defamatory letter to a typist I publish a slander in doing so,[23] but when the typist reads or hands it back to me it seems that there is no publication at all by him[24] and although I can be liable for a publication by my agent I can hardly publish it to myself.

12–5   **i. Consequences of the distinction.** Now that there is no longer a crime of defamatory libel the consequence of the distinction between libel and slander is that libel is always actionable per se, whereas in most cases of slander "special damage" must be shown.

"Special damage" is a phrase which has been rightly criticised as either meaningless or misleading and "actual" damage has been suggested as a more accurate expression,[25] but whatever adjective is used, the wrong is not actionable unless the claimant proves loss of money or of some temporal or material advantage estimable in money. If there is only loss of the society of one's friends, even ostracism, that is not enough. Hence, while loss of your friend's hospitality is special damage, exclusion from the religious congregation to which you belong is not, for a dinner has a temporal and material value, while spiritual communion has none in this connection.[26] In contrast, in cases of libel (and in some cases of slander) the claimant can recover general damages for the injury to his reputation without adducing any evidence that it has in fact been harmed, for the law presumes that some damage will arise in the ordinary course of things. If, of course, the claimant in a libel case contends that actual damage has been suffered he can plead it and prove it if he can, but even if he breaks down on this point he may still be able to recover general damages. The proposition that libel is actionable per se should not, however, be pressed too far. The presumption of damage has been defended as pragmatic good sense[27] and it is not inconsistent with the European Convention on Human Rights because it does not mean that the judge or jury has to award damages in excess of the loss likely to have been suffered, for where

---

[22] *Forrester v Tyrrell* (1893) 9 T.L.R. 257; *Robinson v Chambers* [1946] N.I. 148. In *Osborne v Boulter* [1930] 2 K.B. 226 Scrutton and Slesser L.JJ. were of the view that reading back a dictated statement in the presence of a third party was slander; contra Greer L.J. *Forrester v Tyrrell* was not cited.

[23] It may of course be a publication on a privileged occasion: below, para.12–52.

[24] *Eglantine Inn Ltd v Smith* [1948] N.I. 29 at 33. Compare the situation where a third party is present, the situation with which the dicta in *Osborne v Boulter* are concerned.

[25] Bower, *Actionable Defamation*, 2nd edn, art.13. See, too, Bowen L.J. in *Ratcliffe v Evans* [1892] 2 Q.B. 524. For other meanings of the phrase see Jolowicz in [1960] C.L.J. 214.

[26] *Roberts v Roberts* (1864) 5 B. & S. 384; *Davies v Solomon* (1871) L.R. 7 Q.B. 112.

[27] *Jameel (Yousef) v Dow Jones & Co Inc* [2005] EWCA Civ 75; [2005] Q.B. 946.

it is apparent that there has been no damage in fact, it is open to the court to award nominal damages. Indeed, under present practice the court may strike out a trivial claim as an abuse of process because if such a claim is allowed to proceed the cost of the exercise may be out of all proportion to what has been achieved. The presumption of damage is justified where a serious accusation is published to a significant number of people, but where either or both of those elements is lacking striking out may be justifiable because the, "game will not merely not have been worth the candle, it will not have been worth the wick".[28]

The special damage must not be too remote a consequence of the slander. It was once held that if D slandered C so that C was wrongfully dismissed from employment by X, D was not liable to C because the damage was not the "legal and natural consequence" of the words spoken: X's wrongful act was regarded as breaking the chain of causation.[29] It is not the law now that this is necessarily so, though no doubt the court's conclusion that it would be too remote if the neighbours, on hearing the slander, put the claimant in the duck pond, is still correct. In *Lynch v Knight*[30] Lord Wensleydale said:

"To make the words actionable by reason of special damage, the consequence must be such as, taking human nature as it is, with its infirmities and having regard to the relationship of the parties concerned, might fairly and reasonably have been anticipated and feared would follow from the speaking of the words."[31]

In other words, if D slanders C, the chain of causation may possibly be broken by the unlawful act of X, but it does not follow that it must necessarily be severed thereby.[32] What may be "reasonably anticipated and feared" will no doubt be affected by changes in social attitudes and customs. In *Lynch v Knight* itself the husband's turning his wife out on hearing of a relationship before the marriage was held too remote.

Illness arising from worry induced by the slander is too remote,[33] which is at least a theoretical distinction from the position in libel.[34]

---

[28] *Jameel* at [69]. For a strong example where the accusation, made only to two people, was of terrorism, see *Noorani v Calver* [2009] EWHC 561 (QB).

[29] *Vicars v Wilcocks* (1806) 8 East 1.

[30] (1861) 9 H.L.C. 597.

[31] (1861) 9 H.L.C. 597 at 600.

[32] See also *Bowen v Hall* (1881) 6 Q.B.D. 333.

[33] *Allsop v Allsop* (1865) 5 H. & N. 534.

[34] In *Wheeler v Somerfield* [1966] 2 Q.B. 94 it was said that there was no known case of a libel claimant recovering damages for injury to health, but in libel, unlike slander, mere worry and distress is a proper element of damages.

12–6   **ii. Exceptional cases of slander actionable per se.** There are four exceptional cases in which slander is actionable without proof of special damage. Three of them stem from the common law and may have originated in the idea that the nature of the allegation made damage so likely that it should be presumed.

12–7   (a) *Imputation of a criminal offence punishable with imprisonment.* There must be a direct imputation of the offence, not merely of suspicion of it,[35] and the offence must be punishable by imprisonment in the first instance[36] and not merely because, for example, a fine imposed on conviction has not been paid.[37] Technical language need not be used[38] but if the words as a whole in their context do not impute a crime punishable by imprisonment they do not fall within the rule, as in *Jackson v Adams*,[39] where the defendant said to the claimant, a churchwarden, "Who stole the parish bellropes, you scamping rascal?" As the possession of the ropes was vested in the churchwarden, theft of them by him was at that time impossible.[40] It now seems to be established that the basis of this exception is the probability of social ostracism of the claimant and not his jeopardy of imprisonment,[41] though such ostracism may of course arise in the case of conduct not punishable by imprisonment.

12–8   (b) *Imputation of disease.* An imputation of a contagious or infectious disease likely to prevent people from associating with the claimant is actionable per se. There is some uncertainty about the scope of this, not least since the last reported English case was in 1844.[42] It has always included venereal disease and plague and leprosy. It does not arise from the likelihood of moral censure for long ago it was said that it applied whether the condition be, "owing to the visitation of God, to accident, or to indiscretion of the party therewith afflicted".[43] In 1599 it was held not to apply to smallpox, though the decision turned on a rule of interpretation now extinct.[44]

---

[35] *Simmons v Mitchell* (1880) 6 App. Cas. 156.
[36] *Hellwig v Mitchell* [1910] 1 K.B. 609.
[37] *Ormiston v G.W. Ry* [1917] 1 K.B. 598.
[38] *Webb v Beavan* (1883) 11 Q.B.D. 609.
[39] (1835) 2 Bing. N.C. 402.
[40] Perhaps the case would have been differently decided under the modern law of theft.
[41] *Gray v Jones* (1939) 160 L.T. 361. A company cannot be imprisoned but in *D&L Caterers v D'Ajou* [1945] K.B. 210 Stable J. thought that an imputation of a crime to a company which would be punishable by imprisonment in the case of a natural person was actionable per se. The CA left the point open.
[42] *Bloodworth v Gray* (1844) 7 Man. & Gr. 334.
[43] Bacon, Abr, 7th edn, vii, 266–267. The Porter Committee (Cmd. 7536, para.45) thought it might cover, "such contagious skin complaints as are often caused by personal uncleanliness" but in *Villers v Monsley* (1769) 2 Wils. 403 there are obiter dicta that an oral imputation of the itch was not actionable.
[44] *James v Rutlech* (1599) 4 Co. Rep. 17a. Ambiguous words were then interpreted mitiori sensu, i.e. in the sense more favourable to the defendant.

An obvious issue today is whether it covers AIDS. The law is so obscure that it is submitted that either the category should be extended to every serious communicable disease or abandoned altogether.

(c) *Imputation of unchastity to a female.* At common law an **12–9** imputation of unchastity to either sex required special damage, but the Slander of Women Act 1891 made it actionable per se to impute unchastity[45] or adultery to any woman or girl, though the statute provides that, "the claimant shall not recover more costs than damages, unless the judge shall certify that there was reasonable ground for bringing the action."[46] This statute not only sits rather uneasily alongside current conceptions of equality but it would be curious to apply the mores of 1891 to deciding what was now "unchaste" behaviour.

(d) *Imputation of unfitness or incompetence.* This is by far the **12–10** most important exception because it's the most frequently invoked. It is actionable per se to impute to any person unfitness, dishonesty or incompetence in any office, profession, calling trade or business[47] carried on by him at the time when the slander was published. At common law its scope was severely restricted by the rule that the slander must be spoken of the claimant in the way of his office so that it was not, for example, slander actionable per se to say of a schoolmaster that he had committed adultery with one of the school cleaners.[48] Now, however, it is provided by s.2 of the Defamation Act 1952:

> "In an action for slander in respect of words calculated to disparage the claimant in any office,[49] profession, calling, trade or business held or carried on by him at the time of publication, it shall not be necessary to allege or prove special damage, whether or not the words are spoken of the claimant in the way of his office, profession, calling, trade or business."

Though there is no decisive authority, "calculated to" probably means "likely to". What will satisfy this test is of course going to turn on the nature of the office and the nature of the charge: a charge

---

[45] Held in *Kerr v Kennedy* [1942] 1 K.B. 409 to include an imputation of lesbianism.
[46] Section 1.
[47] It matters not how humble the office, etc. may be: Gatley, *Libel and Slander*, 11th edn §4.18, but the exception was held not to apply to performance of a duty imposed on citizens in war time: *Cleghorn v Sadler* [1945] K.B. 325 (fire watching).
[48] *Jones v Jones* [1916] 2 A.C. 481; *Hopwood v Muirson* [1945] K.B. 313 ("the slander was upon the solicitor as a man; not upon the man as a solicitor").
[49] The common law drew a distinction between offices of profit and offices of honour but it has not survived the 1952 Act: *Maccaba v Liechtenstein* [2004] EWHC 1580 (QB).

of uncharitable behaviour against a clergyman may be more likely to be damaging than the same charge against an ordinary person, and to say of a judge that he could not stay awake on the bench would be actionable per se, though to say that he had committed adultery would not be.[50]

The distinction between libel and slander has few friends and many jurisdictions have abolished it[51] either formally or in all but name.[52] The distinction appears to have arisen for historical reasons which are to some extent obscure, though it was firmly set in the law by the end of the 18th century.[53] Even then it was subject to criticism and its abolition was advocated by a Select Committee of the House of Lords in 1843 and rationalisations such as that libel has a greater potentiality for harm or is more likely to be premeditated do not alter the fact that, as Sir James Mansfield C.J. said long ago:

"[A]n assertion made in a public place, as upon the Royal Exchange, concerning a merchant in London, may be much more extensively diffused than a few printed papers dispersed or a private letter."[54]

Had it not been for the intervention of the legislature in the case of broadcasting the distinction would probably have become an absurdity. The Faulks Committee recommended in 1975[55] that the distinction should be abolished and fears that this might lead to a flood of petty actions for spoken words appear not to be borne out by experience in other parts of the world.[56]

B. What is Defamatory

12–11   As we shall see, truth is normally a complete defence to an action for defamation[57] but this is separate from the question of whether the statement is defamatory, which looks solely to the effect of the statement upon the claimant's reputation. Thus the statement "C is

---

[50] Allegations of sexual harassment would now seem to be likely to fall into this category: *Houston v Smith, The Times,* October 26, 1991 (news report).
[51] New Zealand, the Australian states and most Canadian provinces. Ireland moved to this position by s.6 of the Defamation Act 2009. The distinction does not exist in Scots law, though the expressions "libel" and "slander" are in common use there.
[52] e.g. by providing that all cases of slander are actionable per se.
[53] *Thorley v Kerry* (1812) 4 Taunt. 355. See earlier editions of this book and for detail see Holdsworth in (1924) 40 L.Q.R. 302 and (1925) 41 L.Q.R. 13; Kaye, "Libel and Slander—Two Torts or One?" (1975) 91 L.Q.R. 524.
[54] *Thorley v Kerry* (1812) 4 Taunt. 355 at 364.
[55] Cmnd. 5909, Ch.2.
[56] However, some jurisdictions which have abolished the distinction have a special provision allowing the court to dismiss a trivial case.
[57] Below, para.12–26.

a thief" is defamatory of C even if D can show beyond any doubt that C is a thief, but if he can show that, it is not *actionable*.

A comprehensive definition has eluded courts and commentators. Sometimes it is defined simply as the publication of words which tend to bring a person into "hatred, contempt or ridicule"[58] but this is too narrow,[59] for a statement may be defamatory if it excites in reasonable people feelings less strong than that.[60] Often quoted tests are that the words must tend to lower the claimant in the estimation of right-thinking members of society generally[61] or must amount to a false statement about a person to his discredit[62]; but to these we must at least add that words may be defamatory if they tend to cause the claimant to be shunned or avoided, for it is unquestionably defamatory to impute insanity or insolvency to a person, although, far from exciting hatred, contempt or ridicule, it would rouse only pity or sympathy in the minds of reasonable people, who may nevertheless be inclined to shun his society. Slesser L.J. took this view in *Youssoupoff v Metro-Goldwyn-Mayer Pictures Ltd*[63] where a film falsely imputed that the claimant, a Russian princess, had been raped[64] by Rasputin, for that tended, "to make the claimant be shunned and avoided and that without any moral discredit on her part." Whether the hypothetical reasonable person would behave in that way must be open to question but Slesser L.J. thought that it would be, "to shut one's eyes to realities to make these nice distinctions".[65] A statement which disparages a person in his reputation in relation to his office, profession, calling trade or business may be defamatory, e.g. the imputation of some quality which would be detrimental or the absence of some quality which is essential to the successful carrying on of the office, etc. such as want of ability, incompetence, conduct which breaches widely recognised canons of business ethics[66] and of course, fraudulent or dishonest conduct.[67] The fact that an imputation in a business or employment

---

[58] *Parmiter v Coupland* (1840) 6 M. & W. 105.
[59] Words which expose to ridicule are defamatory even if none of the other tests is satisfied: *Berkoff v Burchill* [1996] 4 All E.R. 1008. Compare *Norman v Future Publishing Ltd* [1999] E.M.L.R. 325 (poking gentle fun).
[60] *Drummond-Jackson v BMA* [1970] 1 W.L.R. 691 at 700.
[61] *Sim v Stretch* (1936) 52 T.L.R. 669 per Lord Atkin.
[62] *Youssoupoff v MGM* (1934) 50 T.L.R. 581 at 584 per Scrutton L.J.
[63] (1934) 50 T.L.R. 581.
[64] An alternative interpretation of the film was that she was seduced.
[65] It has been said that the result would have been the same in New South Wales in 1986: *Krahe v T.C.N. Channel Nine News* (1986) 4 N.S.W.L.R. 536 at 546. Cf. *LNS v Persons Unknown* [2010] EWHC 119 (QB), para.12–87, below.
[66] *Mount Cook Group v Johnstone Motors Ltd* [1990] 2 N.Z.L.R. 488. See also *Clark v Express Newspapers* [2004] EWHC 481 (QB) (politician "ratted" on manifesto promise).
[67] For examples see *Turner v MGM Pictures Ltd* [1950] 2 All E.R. 449; *Angell v H.H. Bushell & Co Ltd* [1968] 1 Q.B. 813; *Drummond-Jackson v BMA* [1970] 1 W.L.R. 688.

context cannot be said to reflect on the claimant's *character* does not
necessarily prevent it from being defamatory.[68] An untrue injurious
statement which does not reflect on reputation in this broad sense is
not defamatory, though it will be actionable if made maliciously[69];
thus it is not defamatory to say that a trader has ceased to trade,[70]
though there may be some difficult borderline cases.[71]

The words must tend to give rise to the feelings mentioned above,
though there is no necessity that they actually do so: if you defame
me to my best friend who does not believe a word of it I have still
been defamed,[72] but in whom should they produce this tendency?
The answer is the reasonable person, here transformed into the
reasonable reader or viewer or listener. This rules out on the one
hand those persons who are so cynical that they would think none
the worse of a person whatever was imputed to him, and on the other
hand those who are so censorious as to regard even trivial accusations (if they were true) as lowering a person's reputation. He is the
"right-thinking member of society generally"[73] and in reality of
course he is the personification of the judge's view of the state of
public feelings and opinion. Plainly public views on topics change
over time. In the reign of Charles II it was defamatory to accuse
someone of being a Roman Catholic or a witch but neither would be
defamatory now, because adherence to Catholicism is now wholly
respectable and no sensible person believes in witchcraft. At a
particular point opinion may be in the process of change. Fifty years
ago to say that a man was a homosexual would have been regarded
as a very serious defamation; it may still be defamatory in 2010, but
there is now so much wider an acceptance of homosexuality that the
matter is now nothing like so clear.[74] After all, under the Civil
Partnership Act 2004 a formalised homosexual relationship has
many of the legal incidents of marriage.

12–12   Even where the words on one interpretation are plainly defamatory there may be an issue as to what the words mean. In *Bennison*

---

[68] *John Fairfax Publications Pty Ltd v Gacic* [2007] HCA 28, 235 A.L.R. 402.
[69] See below, para.12–72.
[70] *Ratcliffe v Evans* [1892] 2 Q.B. 524.
[71] See *Sungravure Pty Ltd v Middle East Airlines* (1978) 5 A.L.R. 147 (not defamatory at
common law to say that an airline, without any fault on its part, was peculiarly susceptible
to hijacking); *Dawson Bloodstock Agency v Mirror Newspapers* [1979] 2 N.S.W.L.R. 733
(not defamatory to say stud farm had closed because of virus).
[72] *Hough v London Express Newspaper* [1940] 2 K.B. 507 at 515. In *Morgan v Odhams
Press Ltd* [1971] 1 W.L.R. 1239 at 1246 Lord Reid referred to this as a proposition so
obvious that no one had had the hardihood to dispute it, but in modern practice such a
claim must be at risk of being struck out as an abuse of process: para.12–5, above.
[73] *Sim v Stretch* (1936) 52 T.L.R. 669.
[74] See *Quilty v Windsor* [1999] S.L.T. 346 and for Australia, *John Fairfax Publications Pty
Ltd v Rivkin* [2003] HCA 50; 201 A.L.R. 77 at [140].

v Hulton[75] Scrutton L.J. said that, "suspicious people might get a defamatory meaning out of 'chop and tomato sauce'." Here again the test is the meaning that would be conveyed to the reasonable person. He is neither unusually suspicious nor unusually naive and he does not always interpret the meaning of words as would a lawyer for he, "is not inhibited by knowledge of the rules of construction."[76] However, he is fair-minded and reasonable and will be taken, at least in the case of an article in a popular newspaper, to have read the piece as a whole. Thus where pictures in an article might have given the impression that the claimants had participated in the making of a pornographic video game it was held that the defendants were not liable because the attached article made it plain that they had not and it was irrelevant that many readers of the newspaper might just have seen the "bane" in the photographs and not the "antidote" in the text.[77]

If the words would tend only to disparage the claimant in the eyes of a particular class or group of persons that is not enough, they must have that effect in the eyes of persons "generally".[78] In practice this is not quite so restrictive as it seems because in many cases where a claimant is charged with offending against the tenets of a group to which he belongs there may be an implication of disloyalty or hypocrisy, which is actionable in its own right, even though ordinary people are indifferent to the direct charge against him.[79] To say of a person that he takes alcohol in moderation is not defamatory; but to say it of a temperance crusader may very well be.[80] To say of someone that he has put in motion the proper machinery for suppressing crime, in that he has reported certain acts, wrongful in law, to the police, cannot be defamatory, for the law cannot admit that a reasonable person would think less of the claimant for that (even though in practice where the crime was a

---

[75] *The Times,* April 13, 1926.

[76] *Lewis v Daily Telegraph Ltd* [1964] A.C. 234 at 258 per Lord Reid.

[77] *Charleston v News Group Newspapers Ltd* [1995] 2 A.C. 65. The position would be different if the antidote was in a place where the reader would be unlikely to find it, but *Charleston* is strongly criticised by Kirby J. in *Chakravarti v Advertiser Newspaper* [1998] HCA 37 at [134]; (1998) 193 C.L.R. 519. He said that, "it ignores the realities of the way in which ordinary people receive, and are intended to receive, communications of this kind. It ignores changes in media technology and presentation."

[78] In *Arab News Network v Jihad Al Khazen* [2001] EWCA Civ 118 Keene L.J. said at [30] that, "we are today a much more diverse society than in the past and that the reputation of a person within his own racial or religious community may be damaged by a statement which would not be regarded as damaging by society at large. This is an issue which may need to be addressed at some stage in the future."

[79] *Leetham v Rank* (1912) 57 Sol. Jo. 111; *Myroft v Sleight* (1921) 90 L.J.K.B. 883.

[80] Compare *Peck v Tribune Co* 214 U.S. 185 (1909). It is defamatory of a Muslim to say that he has insulted the Prophet because the reasonable man disapproves of any insult to religious beliefs: *Shah v Akram* (1981) 79 L.S. Gaz. 814.

minor one real people might well do so).[81] An additional comment that he had thereby behaved dishonourably could be.[82]

It is clearly established that what is important is what the words may reasonably be taken as meaning, not what the defendant intended by them,[83] though the defendant's intention may be relevant on damages, on the statutory offer of amends defence[84] or if the occasion is a privileged one.[85] The common law position is illustrated by *Cassidy v Daily Mirror Newspapers Ltd*.[86] The defendants published in their newspaper a photograph of one C and Miss X together with the words, "Mr. C, the race-horse owner, and Miss X, whose engagement has been announced." Mrs. C was, and was known among her acquaintances as the wife of C, although she and C were not living together. The information on which the defendants based their statement was derived from C alone, and they had made no attempt to verify it from any other source. Mrs C sued them for libel. A majority of the Court of Appeal held that the publication might convey to reasonable persons that the claimant was not C's husband, that she had cohabited with him and that this impugned her character.[87]

12–13   **i. Function of judge and jury.** If this and other aspects of defamation law are to be understood we need to outline the relative functions of judge and jury, trial by jury being still the norm for defamation cases. After fierce controversy, Fox's Libel Act 1792, which purported to be a declaratory Act, allotted to the jury in a trial for *criminal* libel the task of deciding whether the words were defamatory or not. The Act has for long been regarded as also applicable to civil actions for defamation, but the jury's power is not unlimited, for the judge acts as a gatekeeper on this issue; he must first rule that the words are capable as a matter of law of being defamatory, i.e. could a reasonable jury come to the conclusion that the statement satisfies the legal criteria for being defamatory? Thus a statement that the claimant had influenza last month would be withdrawn from the jury for that in no way impugns his character or reputation; on the other hand, a statement that he has a venereal disease is plainly capable of being defamatory. If the words are obviously defamatory, the judge, although he cannot directly tell the

---

[81] *Byrne v Deane* [1937] 1 K.B. 818. In *Mawe v Piggott* (1869) L.R. 4 C.L. 54 the potential consequences for the claimant were a good deal more serious, as they might have been in *Williams v MGN Ltd* [2009] EWHC 3150 (QB).

[82] Greer L.J. dissenting in *Byrne v Deane* thought such an imputation could be implied into the libel.

[83] "Trite law": *Berkoff v Burchill* [1996] 4 All E.R. 1008 at 1018.

[84] Below, para.12–66.

[85] *Loveless v Earl* [1999] E.M.L.R. 530 at 538–539.

[86] [1929] 2 K.B. 331.

[87] Followed in *Hough v London Express Newspaper Ltd* [1940] 2 K.B. 507.

jury that they are so, may nevertheless indicate to them that the evidence cannot reasonably bear any other interpretation. In practice the issue is not very likely to be presented in this bald form because there may be a dispute as to what the words mean. Here, too, the judge has a similar role in deciding whether the words are capable of bearing a defamatory meaning. His task is to, "evaluate the words complained of and to delimit the range of meanings of which the words are reasonably capable",[88] excluding meanings which are "fanciful, absurd or factitious".[89] It is then for the jury to decide which, if any, of the meanings held capable of being defamatory the words do in fact bear.[90] The Human Rights Act 1998 does not require a change in approach in favour of defendants on these issues, for:

> "[T]here is no defensible way in which the courts can adjust the meaning of meaning so as to include things which no sensible reading of the words could embrace".[91]

Capital and Counties Bank Ltd v Henty[92] illustrates the difficulties which can arise. Having quarrelled with X, the manager of a branch of the bank used by Hentys, the latter sent a printed circular to a large number of their customers (who knew nothing of the squabble), "Henty & Sons hereby give notice that they will not receive in payment cheques drawn on any of the branches of the Capital and Counties Bank." The circular became known to other persons and there was a run on the bank, which sued Hentys on the ground that the circular imputed insolvency, such an imputation being plainly defamatory of a bank. By a majority of four to one, having had the case twice argued, the House of Lords held that the circular, taken in conjunction with the circumstances of its publication, did not constitute evidence from which any reasonable person would infer such an imputation; that there was no case to go to the jury; and that the defendants were not liable. There were a number of possible innocent explanations for the circular which might suggest themselves to a reader and the court was not willing to seize on the bad one in the absence of any evidence to suggest that readers would not

---

[88] *Mapp v News Group Newspapers Limited* [1998] Q.B. 520 at 526.
[89] *Jeynes v News Magazines Ltd* [2008] EWCA Civ 130 at [20].
[90] As far as the jury is concerned, the words have a single, "right" meaning: *Slim v Daily Telegraph* [1968] 2 Q.B. 157 at 174 (though there may be no way of knowing whether they follow this requirement, which may be thought to be artificial). If the case is tried by judge alone it follows that he must decide what the words mean, not what they are capable of meaning. The same "single meaning" rule does not apply to malicious falsehood: *Ajinomoto Sweeteners Europe SAS v Asda Stores Ltd* [2010] EWCA Civ 609.
[91] *Berezovsky v Forbes Inc* [2001] EWCA Civ 1251; [2001] E.M.L.R. 45 at [14].
[92] (1882) 7 App. Cas. 741.

necessarily have done so.[93] Even if it is the law that where there are a number of possible explanations it is not reasonable to pick on the one defamatory of the claimant,[94] the *Henty* case is perhaps a dubious application of that principle for it might be thought that the first reason that would occur to any reasonable person was that the bank was unsound[95] and the decision has been subjected to considerable criticism. Salmon L.J. said that the principles, never better formulated than in *Henty*'s case, were perhaps never worse applied.[96] Of course, no one would deny that where the statement has only one reasonable meaning, the court should not allow it to be tortured into a defamatory meaning.[97]

12–14   In *Henty*'s case the controversy was whether the words were capable of bearing any defamatory meaning at all, but in *Lewis v Daily Telegraph Ltd*[98] the defendants admitted that the words were defamatory. What they denied was that they were defamatory in the particular sense alleged by the claimants. The defendants had published a paragraph in their newspaper stating that officers of the City of London Fraud Squad were investigating the affairs of the claimant company (which was defamatory but true[99]) and the claimants alleged that these words carried the meaning that the company's affairs were being conducted fraudulently or dishonestly. By a majority the House of Lords held that the words were not capable of bearing that meaning. As Lord Devlin pointed out, one cannot make a rule about the fundamental question—what is the meaning which the words convey to the ordinary person—which anyway depends upon the context of the statement,[100] but the ordinary sensible

---

[93] Lord Selborne L.C. placed some weight on the fact that Hentys had not authorised the showing of the circular to strangers. He (and Lord Blackburn) thought the case might have been different if there had been a general distribution in the first place. Scrutton L.J. in *Tolley v Fry* [1930] 1 K.B. 467 at 476 said that he had difficulty in, "understanding that the circular incapable of a defamatory meaning to a limited audience might be capable of a defamatory meaning if published more widely". For the present law on repetition see below, para.12–24.

[94] In *Stubbs v Russell* [1913] A.C. 386, however, Lord Shaw would have allowed one defamatory meaning to go to the jury when there were three other non-defamatory ones. There are other statements supporting the view that where words are fairly capable of several meanings, some defamatory, others not, the case should be left to the jury: *Cassidy v Daily Mirror Newspapers Ltd* [1929] 1 K.B. 331 at 339; *Newstead v London Express Newspapers Ltd* [1940] 1 K.B. 377 at 396; *Aspro Travel Ltd v Owners Abroad Group* [1996] 1 W.L.R. 132 at 137.

[95] See the dissent of Lord Penzance.

[96] *Slim v Daily Telegraph Ltd* [1968] 2 Q.B. 157 at 187. Scrutton L.J. in *Youssoupoff v MGM* (1934) 50 T.L.R. 581 at 594, thought that the law and the facts got pretty far apart from each other in *Henty*'s case.

[97] *Jones v Skelton* [1963] 1 W.L.R. 1362 at 1370.

[98] [1964] A.C. 234.

[99] Such a statement might bear the meaning that the claimant had behaved in such a way as to give reasonable grounds for suspicion or at least that there were grounds to investigate the matter.

[100] "A man who wants to talk at large about smoke may have to pick his words very carefully if he wants to exclude the suggestion that there is also a fire": [1964] A.C. at 285.

person is not capable of thinking that whenever there is a police inquiry there is guilt. Otherwise it would be almost impossible to report criminal investigations.[101] Nowadays the law recognises that in the context of imputations of wrongdoing by the claimant, for example the commission of a criminal offence, that there may be three possible levels of defamatory meaning in descending order of seriousness: (i) that he has committed the offence, (ii) that there are reasonable grounds to suspect that he has committed the offence, and (iii) that there are grounds for investigation whether he committed the offence. A defendant who has made a direct charge which is only capable of meaning (i) will not be allowed to try to persuade the jury that it only bears meaning (ii) or (iii)[102] but it is frequently held that more than one meaning is possible.[103]

The "ordinary sensible reader" is therefore as artificial a creature as the "reasonable man" of the law of negligence but at the end of the day he is a layman not a lawyer and the judge must therefore try to put himself in the position of someone who may be guilty of a certain amount[104] of loose thinking and who may not reflect fully and carefully upon a newspaper story or a television programme.[105] It has been said that where the judge rules that the words are capable of bearing a defamatory meaning it may be better for him to refrain

---

[101] "A distinction needs to be drawn between the reader's understanding of what a newspaper is saying and judgments or conclusions which he may reach as a result of his own beliefs and prejudices. It is one thing to say that a statement is capable of bearing an imputation defamatory of the claimant because the ordinary reasonable reader would understand it in that sense, drawing on his own knowledge and experience of human affairs in order to reach that result. It is quite another thing to say that a statement is capable of bearing such an imputation because it excites in some readers a belief or prejudice from which they proceed to arrive at a conclusion unfavourable to the claimant. The defamatory quality of the published material is to be determined by the first, not the second proposition": *Mirror Newspapers Ltd v Harrison* (1982) 42 A.L.R. 487 per Mason J.

[102] It is not merely a question of what the jury may find the words mean: if the defendant seeks to prove the truth of the imputation in sense (ii) he must base his case on the conduct of the claimant. But if the imputation is at level (iii) this may not be so, though the consequences have been described as "disquieting": *Jameel v Times Newspapers Ltd* [2004] EWCA Civ 983; [2004] E.M.L.R. 31 at [30].

[103] See e.g. *Jameel v Wall Street Journal Europe Sprl* [2003] EWCA Civ 1694; [2004] E.M.L.R. 6; *Jameel v Times Newspapers Ltd*, above, fn.102. Cf. *Armstrong v Times Newspapers Ltd* [2004] EWHC 2928 (QB) (level (ii) possible but not level (iii); on appeal, but not on this issue, [2005] EWCA Civ 1007).

[104] Not an unlimited amount: see *Charleston v News Group Newspapers*, above, fn.77. Lord Devlin's view in *Lewis v Daily Telegraph* at [1964] A.C. 277 that the, "layman reads in an implication much more freely; and unfortunately, as the law of defamation has to take into account, is especially prone to do so when it is derogatory" has been described as perhaps rather patronising to the modern way of thinking: *Armstrong v Times Newspapers* [2005] EWHC 2816 (QB) at [31].

[105] *Lewis v Daily Telegraph* at [1964] A.C. 259. The approach the court should take to assessing the impact of a broadcast (which offers less opportunity for review and reflection) on viewers or listeners is reviewed by Hunt C.J. at C.L. in *Amalgamated Television Services Pty Ltd v Marsden* (1998) 43 N.S.W.L.R. 158, NSWCA. Statutory provisions deeming broadcasting to be publication in a permanent form have no effect on the way in which the viewer or listener should be taken to understand the broadcast, they are simply designed to make the publication libel rather than slander.

from giving any reasons for that conclusion, lest it be argued that the expressed reasons might influence his summing-up to the jury.[106]

Under CPR PD 53 at any stage after the service of the particulars of claim either party may apply to a judge for a determination whether or not the words complained of are capable of bearing a particular meaning or are capable of being defamatory of the claimant.

12–15   **ii. Innuendo.** The words of which the claimant complains may be either (a) defamatory in their natural and ordinary meaning or (b) defamatory only or in addition to (a), in the light of facts and circumstances known to persons to whom the words were published. The natural and ordinary meaning includes implications: it is as defamatory of C to say that justice miscarried when he was acquitted of murdering X, as it is to say outright that he did murder X.[107]

> "The ordinary and natural meaning may . . . include any implication or inference which a reasonable reader guided not by any special but only by general knowledge, and not fettered by any strict legal rules of construction would draw from the words."[108]

Thus, for example, juxtaposition of material about the claimant with other material may make an otherwise innocent statement defamatory. The most famous instance is *Monson v Tussauds Ltd*.[109] The defendants, who kept a waxwork exhibition, placed an effigy of the claimant, with a gun, in a room adjoining the "Chamber of Horrors". The claimant had been tried for murder in Scotland and released on a verdict of "Not Proven" and a representation of the scene of the alleged murder was displayed in the Chamber of Horrors. The Court of Appeal considered that although in all the circumstances the case was not suitable for the issue of an interlocutory injunction,[110] the exhibition was capable of being found by a jury to be defamatory. On the other hand, the mere fact that an article about the claimant appeared in a newspaper where numerous articles attacking dishonest businessmen had appeared on other occasions was held incapable of carrying a defamatory imputation.[111] If reliance is placed upon juxtaposition it must be shown that

---

[106] *Keays v Murdoch Magazines (UK) Ltd* [1991] 1 W.L.R. 1184.
[107] See, e.g. Lords Reid and Devlin in *Lewis v Daily Telegraph* [1964] A.C. 234 at 258 and 280.
[108] *Jones v Skelton* [1963] 1 W.L.R. 1362 at 1370–1371 per Lord Morris.
[109] [1894] 1 Q.B. 671; *Garbett v Hazell, Watson and Viney Ltd* [1943] 2 All E.R. 359.
[110] Now an interim injunction. See below, para.22–50.
[111] *Wheeler v Somerfield* [1966] 2 Q.B. 94. In *Astaire v Campling* [1966] 1 W.L.R. 34 it was held that a newspaper article identifying by name a "Mr. X" about whom derogatory articles had appeared in other newspapers (but without repeating or adopting them) was not capable of a defamatory meaning.

a reasonable person, seeing the two objects together, would draw from their relative positions an inference defamatory of the claimant.

The modern practice is to require the claimant to say in his **12–16** particulars of claim what meaning he attributes to the statement in order that the defendant may know what case he has to meet and the judge may know upon what meanings he may have to rule.[112] In ordinary English any implied or allusive meanings are called "innuendoes" but the technical legal meaning is narrower.[113] An innuendo in the legal sense arises only when the defamatory nature of the statement depends upon facts or circumstances which are not part of general knowledge but which are known to the persons to whom the statement is published. So to state that the claimant is "no Mother Theresa" might imply to the ordinary reader that she was wanting in kindness or charity because people generally know about Mother Theresa; but to say of a surgeon that he had carried out 10 private operations last week would convey nothing defamatory at all except to people who know that he is contracted full time to the National Health Service, in which case it might carry the implication that he was "moonlighting". In the case of a true innuendo the claimant was always required to give particulars of the special meaning and the facts supporting it, so the present more rigorous practice on pleading "implied ordinary meanings" has brought the legal and the "popular" innuendo closer together. Nevertheless, there are still important distinctions: each innuendo is a separate cause of action[114] and the claimant must identify the persons with knowledge of the special facts to whom he alleges the words were published and prove their knowledge[115] and publication to them.[116]

"If matter which on the face of it is capable of being regarded as defaming a particular person, who is mentioned by name, is proved to have been published to any one whomsoever the tort of libel is committed; but if the matter on the face of it is not capable of being regarded as defamatory, or, if defamatory, it cannot be regarded as defaming a particular person, it cannot be regarded as having been published unless it is proved to have been published

---

[112] CPR PD 53 para.2.3(1).
[113] Lord Devlin in *Lewis v Daily Telegraph* [1964] A.C. 234 at 279 doubted the value of the technical distinction, but it is recognised by PD 53.
[114] *Grubb v Bristol United Press Ltd* [1963] 1 Q.B. 309 at 327.
[115] At the time of the publication: *Grappelli v Derek Block (Holdings) Ltd* [1981] 1 W.L.R. 822. The issue of whether a statement is defamatory must be determined as at the time of publication; but consider a serial publication.
[116] For a possible exception where it may be inferred that some readers of a general publication knew the facts see *Fullam v Newcastle Chronicle* [1977] 1 W.L.R. 651 at 659 and *Grappelli's* case, above, fn.115, at 830.

to someone possessing knowledge which would suffice to enable him to realise that the matter was defamatory or defamatory of the claimant as the case may be." [117]

So if it is stated that the claimant was seen entering a particular house which is a brothel, but the nature of the house is not specified, the words are defamatory only in so far as it is proved that they were published to persons who knew the character of the house. [118] If the claimant fails to establish the supporting facts for the innuendo he may, of course, still fall back on the ordinary meaning of the words if those are defamatory.

The line between the true and the popular innuendo may be very difficult to draw [119] because it turns on the general knowledge possessed by ordinary people and this changes from time to time. Nowadays most people know what the Mafia is and so words alleging that a company is controlled by the Mafia are defamatory in their ordinary meaning, [120] but, "cony catcher" is unlikely to convey much to people today, though once upon a time it was a common word for a swindler [121]; and a knowledge of Biblical allusions and characters is probably far less common than would have been assumed by Victorian judges. [122] In the well-known case of *Tolley v Fry & Sons Ltd* [123] the claimant, a famous amateur golfer, was caricatured by the defendants, without his knowledge or consent, in an advertisement for their chocolate. The claimant alleged in an

---

[117] *Consolidated Trust v Brown* (1948) 49 S.R. (NSW) 86 at 90.

[118] Lord Devlin's example in *Lewis v Daily Telegraph* [1964] A.C. 234 at 278. See also *Cassidy v Daily Mirror* [1929] 2 K.B. 331; *Morrison v Ritchie* (1902) 4 F. 645. It seems that in principle a defendant may contend that words which are defamatory in their ordinary sense are not so because of special knowledge possessed by the persons to whom they were published, but he will have to show that all the persons to whom the words were published knew those facts, which might be very difficult and impossible in the case of a generally circulated libel: *Hankinson v Bilby* (1847) 16 M. & W. 422.

[119] It is often said that a publication in a foreign language necessarily raises a legal innuendo but this is doubtful: Gatley, *Libel and Slander*, 11th edn §34.28. If there is a true innuendo a witness with the requisite special knowledge may be asked how he understood the words, but such evidence is inadmissible where the ordinary meaning is relied on. If a document in French said that the claimant was "une putain" she would be relying on the ordinary meaning of those words. Of course it is necessary to prove that the words were published to persons who understood the language but publication to persons who can read French may be inferred without specific proof: if a newspaper in Serbo-Croat is published in England it seems reasonable to infer that at least some of the purchasers understood Serbo-Croat.

[120] Even Mafia may be used in a non-defamatory, metaphorical sense meaning a close-knit group: *Brooks v Lind, The Times,* March 26, 1997, OH.

[121] "Blackleg" in the 1850s apparently meant a gambler: *Barnett v Allen* (1858) 3 H. & N. 376.

[122] More generally, the suggestion in *Lennon v Scottish Daily Record and Sunday Mail Ltd* [2004] EWHC 359 (QB); [2004] E.M.L.R. 18 that the ordinary reader must now be credited with having achieved a level of education which was not widely accessible to earlier generations must surely be debatable.

[123] [1931] A.C. 333.

innuendo that the defendants thereby meant that he had agreed to appear in the advertisement for gain and that he had thus prostituted his reputation as an amateur golfer. The House of Lords held that the caricature was actionable. It is not, however, clear that the case is an example of a true innuendo at all. The advertisement appeared in two national newspapers and the only evidence which was called was that of two persons associated with amateur golf, who testified to the likely damaging effect of an imputation that the claimant had taken money to appear in it. There was no evidence of the knowledge of persons who saw the advertisement of any practice whereby persons who so appeared commonly gave their consent to it[124] but Viscount Hailsham said that:

> "[T]he question . . . does not depend upon a state of facts known only to some special class of the community, but upon the inference which would be drawn by the ordinary man or woman from the facts of the publication. It is always difficult to determine with precision the amount of judicial knowledge which is permissible to a judge or jury[125]; but I am not satisfied that it would not be open to a jury, acting on their own knowledge as ordinary citizens, to assume that no reputable firm would have the effrontery and bad taste to take the name and reputation of a well known man for an advertisement commending their goods without first obtaining his consent."[126]

The reality appears to be that a case like *Tolley v Fry* is one where the claimant is clearly required to particularise what imputations he says are implied in the publication but that the question whether evidence is required on the other aspects of the case (the claimant's status and notoriety, the practices of advertisers and opinion within the sport) is a matter of degree.

iii. Abuse. It is commonly said that mere vulgar spoken abuse is   **12–17**
not defamation nor indeed any other tort[127] but this needs some explanation. Spoken words which are prima facie defamatory are not actionable if it is clear that they were uttered merely as general

---

[124] Though the correspondence showed that the defendants were aware of the risk of the inference complained of.

[125] Compare the mordant remark of Scrutton L.J. dissenting in the CA: "It is difficult to know what judges are allowed to know, though they are ridiculed if they pretend not to know. A jury is certainly allowed to know something not in the evidence when they are constantly told to use their knowledge as 'men of the world' in interpreting the evidence."

[126] [1931] A.C. at 339.

[127] "For mere general abuse spoken no action lies": Mansfield C.J. in *Thorley v Kerry* (1812) 4 Taunt. 355 at 365. Pollock C.B. and Wilde B. in *Parkins v Scott* (1862) 1 H. & C. 153 at 158, 159. Abuse may of course be a crime under public order or race relations legislation and may lead the speaker to be bound over to keep the peace.

vituperation *and* were so understood by those who heard them[128] and the same applies to words spoken in jest,[129] but the defendant takes the risk on the understanding of his hearers and the burden of proof that they understood them in a non-defamatory sense is on him.[130] This makes the manner and context in which the words were spoken very important, e.g. whether they are used deliberately in cold blood or bawled out at the height of a violent quarrel. It is generally said that written words cannot be protected as abuse because the defendant had time for reflection before he wrote and his readers may know nothing of any dispute or other circumstances which caused him to write as he did—no doubt this is generally true but it is hard to see why there should be any absolute rule[131] and it is submitted that the same should be true where a jest is expressed in writing or in a cartoon.[132]

12–18   **iv. Reputations protected.** Any living human being may be the claimant in a defamation action.[133] There is no doubt that a trading corporation may sue for defamation in respect of words affecting its trading reputation or property[134] and the same is probably true of non-trading corporations in so far as they raise funds and own property.[135] However, in English law a governmental body (whether a local authority or an organ of central government) cannot sue even if the statement in no way concerns its "governing" reputation.[136]

---

[128] For entertaining cases on abuse see *Rambo v Cohen* 587 N.E. 2d 147 (Ind. 1992) and *Ralston v Fomich* [1994] 2 W.W.R. 284 (variations on the theme of "son of a bitch").

[129] *Donoghue v Hayes* (1831) Hayes (Ir. Ex.) R. 265. Given the content of many satirical radio and television shows, there are remarkably few cases on this. Perhaps the reason is that the public figures lampooned have more sense than to sue; but for a case where a radio skit was held capable of imputing drug dealing to a café proprietor see *Entienne v Festival City Broadcasters* [2001] SASC 60.

[130] See, e.g. *Penfold v Westcote* (1806) 2 B. & P. (N.R.) 335.

[131] e.g. words scrawled on a board during a dispute between a lecturer and a member of his class.

[132] Publications on the Internet are technically libel but for this purpose bulletin board exchanges should perhaps be treated as more akin to slander: *Smith v ADVFN Plc* [2008] EWHC 1797 (QB). Of course written or spoken words may be protected on some other ground such as fair comment, which does not have to be "fair" in any meaningful sense, below, para.12–35. See, e.g. *Jameson v BBC* (unreported): newspaper editor described as "the man who thinks erudite is a kind of glue" and "east end boy made bad".

[133] One cannot be liable for defaming the dead: below, para.23–3.

[134] *Metropolitan Saloon Omnibus Co v Hawkins* (1859) 4 H. & N. 87; *South Hetton Coal Co v North Eastern News Association Ltd* [1894] 1 Q.B. 133; *Steel & Morris v UK* [2005] E.M.L.R. 15, ECHR. The underlying action by the McDonald's fast food chain lasted 313 days. The damages and costs (which must have been well over £1,000,000) will have been completely irrecoverable from the litigant in person defendants, but the ECHR found that the lack of legal aid for the defendants contravened art.6.

[135] For trade unions see below, para.18–35.

[136] *Derbyshire CC v Times Newspapers Ltd* [1993] A.C. 534 (management of local authority pension fund). *Ballina SC v Ringland* (1994) 33 N.S.W.L.R. 680. Unlike the CA, the HL in *Derbyshire* found it unnecessary to rely upon the European Convention on Human Rights.

As was said in the context of central government in a South African case,[137] it:

"[W]ould be a serious interference with the free expression of opinion . . . if the wealth of the State, derived from the State's subjects, could be used to launch against those subjects actions for defamation because they have, falsely and unfairly it may be, criticised or condemned the management of the country."

The principle has been applied to a political party[138] and it is probably not necessary that the "governmental body" should be popularly elected,[139] but it remains to be seen whether it will be applied, for example, to public utility suppliers, which in legal form are now generally ordinary trading companies, though regulated in their activities.[140] On the other hand a governmental body can sue for malicious falsehood, which requires proof of malice and actual damage (or, where the words are in writing, likelihood of it)[141] and an attack on a governmental body may be defamatory of individual members or officers and there is no "public figure" privilege as there is in US law.[142]

C. Reference to the Claimant

If the claimant is mentioned by name there is usually no difficulty, **12–19** but he need not be named, for the issue is whether the statement may be understood by reasonable people as referring to the claimant.[143] He may for example be referred to by a nickname or by initials[144] or by his job[145] or by reference to some allegorical or historical character or by a word picture. In *I'Anson v Stuart*[146] a newspaper paragraph stated:

"This diabolical character, like Polyphemus the man-eater, has but one eye, and is well-known to all persons acquainted with the name of a certain noble circumnavigator."

[137] *Die Spoorbond v South African Railways* [1946] A.D. 999 at 1012, cited in *Derbyshire.*
[138] *Goldsmith v Boyruhl* [1998] Q.B. 459.
[139] *New South Wales Aboriginal Land Council v Jones* (1998) 43 N.S.W.L.R. 300.
[140] Cf. *British Coal v NUM*, Unreported, June 28, 1996 (applied to British Coal) and *New South Wales Aboriginal Land Council v Jones* (1998) 43 N.S.W.L.R. 300; *Hong Kong Polytechnic University v Next Magazine Publishing Ltd* [1997] H.K.L.R.D. 514 (university established by statute could sue for libel).
[141] Below, para.12–75.
[142] Below, para.12–53.
[143] If the claimant's picture is published without identifying text does he need to show that it was seen by persons who knew him? For some difference of opinion see *Dwek v Macmillan Publishers Ltd* [2000] E.M.L.R. 284.
[144] See *Heller v Bianco* 244 P. (2d) 757 (Cal. 1952) (Christian name and telephone number on toilet wall).
[145] e.g. "the Prime Minister".
[146] (1787) 1 T.R. 748.

It was clear that the claimant was the person referred to on his giving proof that he had one eye and bore a name similar to that of Anson, the famous admiral. A reference to A may by implication also amount to a reference to B, so that for example a derogatory statement about the conduct of a company may impute wrongdoing or incompetence to its directors or officers. In such a case there are two questions: is the statement capable of referring to the directors? and does it defame them?[147]

In the above cases there is at least some "peg or pointer" in the article itself which points to the claimant but this is not necessary given the fundamental principle. In *Morgan v Odhams Press Ltd*[148] a newspaper article alleged that a girl had been kidnapped by a dog-doping gang. At the relevant time the girl had been staying at the claimant's flat and the claimant produced six witnesses who swore that they understood from the article that he was connected with the gang. A majority of the House of Lords held that these facts constituted sufficient material to leave to the jury. The test of whether the words "refer to the claimant" in this situation is whether a hypothetical, sensible reader, having knowledge of the special circumstances, would believe that the claimant was referred to.[149] In such a case of course it is essential that the claimant shows that the material was published to persons who knew the special facts. Where, on the other hand, the article identifies the claimant on its face, so that no true innuendo is necessary, it seems that the claimant does not need to show that anyone who read it knew him and therefore was actually put in mind of him. Provided there is evidence that the words were published to others, the question is whether ordinary, sensible readers, knowing of the claimant, would be of opinion that the words referred to him (though evidence that people actually did so may of course inflate the damages). Thus in *Shevill v Presse Alliance SA*[150] the court refused to strike out a claim by a claimant in Yorkshire in respect of an issue of *France Soir*, of which perhaps 10 copies had been sold in Yorkshire and 230 in England and Wales.

---

[147] *Aspro Travel Ltd v Owners Abroad Group* [1996] 1 W.L.R. 132. For the reverse case of imputations about officers reflecting on the company see *Jameel v Times Newspapers Ltd* [2004] EWCA Civ 983; [2004] E.M.L.R. 31.

[148] [1971] 1 W.L.R. 1239.

[149] The minority in *Morgan* dissented because they thought that there was no material in the article which a reasonable person could sensibly infer to apply to the claimant; they did not accede to the "key or pointer" argument which had found favour in the court below.

[150] [1992] 1 W.L.R. 1. The case went to the House of Lords and the European Court of Justice on the jurisdiction point: [1995] 2 A.C. 18; [1996] A.C. 959. Article 5(3) of the Brussels Convention giving jurisdiction to the courts of the country where the harmful event occurred was satisfied by the presumption of damage which attaches to libel in English law, but a minimal publication here may lead the court to refuse service out of the jurisdiction or to strike out the claim as an abuse of process: *Jameel (Yousef) v Dow Jones* [2005] EWCA Civ 75; [2005] 2 W.L.R. 1614.

We have seen that the question of whether a publication is defamatory must be determined on the basis of the article itself and the surrounding circumstances and words cannot become defamatory by virtue of later information or events. However, where a defamatory publication does not sufficiently identify the claimant, he may nevertheless rely for identification purposes on a subsequent publication by the same defendant,[151] or on a forthcoming publication by another to which the defendant draws attention.[152] It has been said that were the law otherwise, it would be open to a newspaper to publish a virulent libel without identifying the person defamed but adding a statement that the victim would be identified in a week's time.[153]

As in the case of defamatory meaning, the ultimate question is not what the defendant intended but what the words can reasonably be understood as conveying. Therefore the defendant may be liable at common law even if he intended to write about a wholly fictitious character, if a reasonable reader might think the claimant was referred to. In *Hulton & Co v Jones*[154] H were newspaper proprietors and published a humorous account of a motor festival at Dieppe in which imputations were cast on the morals of one Artemus Jones, a churchwarden at Peckham. This person was intended to be, and was believed by the writer of the article and the editor of the paper to be, purely fictitious. In fact there was a barrister named Artemus Jones, who was not a churchwarden, did not live at Peckham and had taken no part in the Dieppe motor festival. He sued H for libel and friends of his swore that they believed the article referred to him. In affirming a verdict for the claimant the House of Lords held that there was evidence upon which the jury could have come to the conclusion that reasonable people would believe the claimant was referred to and that it was immaterial that the defendants did not intend to defame him.[155] It logically follows from *Hulton v Jones* that if D intends to refer to X, about whom the statement is true, and reasonable people might take it as referring to C, then D has

12–20

---

[151] *Hayward v Thompson* [1982] Q.B. 47, distinguishing *Grappelli v Derek Block (Holdings) Ltd* [1981] 1 W.L.R. 822, where the issue was not identification but the meaning of the words.

[152] *Baltinos v Foreign Language Publications Ltd* (1986) 6 N.S.W.L.R. 85.

[153] *Hayward v Thompson*, above, fn.151, at 72 per Sir Stanley Rees. In *Astaire v Campling* [1966] 1 W.L.R. 34 various disparaging things had been said in newspapers about a "Mr X" in the world of boxing. The defendants' article stated that the claimant was known as "Mr X". This was not actionable by the claimant unless the defendants in some way adopted or repeated what had been said before.

[154] [1910] A.C. 20..

[155] Mere coincidence of name is not of course necessarily enough to lead to this conclusion otherwise it would be impossible to write fiction. *Hulton v Jones* must be on the margins of this type of case and the jury may have been influenced by the fact that the claimant had once worked for the newspaper, even though his counsel accepted that they had forgotten about him.

defamed C, and this was accepted by the Court of Appeal in *Newstead v London Express*,[156] where a report of the conviction of "Harold Newstead, thirty year old Camberwell man" for bigamy was held actionable by another Harold Newstead in Camberwell of about the same age.[157] Both situations may now be affected by s.2 of the Defamation Act 1996, under which the defendant may make an offer of amends,[158] but if the section is not applicable or the defendant chooses not to use it the cases still represent the common law. However, sooner or later this is likely to be challenged under art.10 of the European Convention on Human Rights. A sign of this appears in *O'Shea v MGN Ltd*[159] where the defendants published an advertisement for pornographic Internet services which contained a photograph of a woman, E, who was alleged to be the "spit and image" of the claimant. Morland J. held that under the common law the case would have fallen within the principle of strict liability for unintentional defamation. However, he concluded that such a result would be incompatible with art.10 and the claim was dismissed as having no reasonable prospect of success.

> "It would impose an impossible burden on a publisher if he were required to check if the true picture of someone resembled some-one else who because of the context of the picture was defamed. Examples are legion—unlawful violence in street protest demonstrations, looting, hooliganism at football matches, people apparently leaving or entering Court with criminal defendants and investigative journalism into drug dealing, corruption, child abuse and prostitution."

It remains to be seen whether *Hulton* and *Newstead* can be distinguished, as Morland J. thought, because "theoretically" the existence of the claimants could have been discovered.[160]

12–21   The question whether an individual can sue in respect of words which are directed against a group, or body, or class of persons generally was considered by the House of Lords in *Knuppfer v London Express Newspaper Ltd*,[161] and the law may be summarised as follows: (a) The crucial question is whether the words were published "of the claimant" in the sense that he can be said to be personally pointed at, rather than any arbitrary general rule, subject to exceptions, that liability cannot arise from words published of a

---

[156] [1940] 1 K.B. 377; *Lee v Wilson* (1934) 51 C.L.R. 276.
[157] The jury awarded only one farthing. The case shows the importance of giving the address of the accused in court reports.
[158] See below, para.12–66.
[159] [2001] E.M.L.R. 40.
[160] Quaere, however, as to whether the decision might not have been too generous to the claimant on the common law issue: see fn.155, above.
[161] [1944] A.C. 116.

class[162]; (b) normally where the defamatory statement is directed at a class of persons no individual belonging to the class is entitled to say that the words were published of him[163]:

> "No doubt it is true to say that a class cannot be defamed as a class, nor can an individual be defamed by a general reference to the class to which he belongs"[164];

as Willes J. said in *Eastwood v Holmes*[165]:

> "[I]f a man wrote that all lawyers were thieves, no particular lawyer could sue him unless there was something to point to the particular individual"

what the psalmist said in haste of us all was not defamatory even if it had been untrue; (c) words which appear to apply to a class may be actionable if there is something in the words, or in the circumstances in which they were published,[166] which indicates a particular claimant or claimants[167]; (d) in practice the smaller the group upon which the attack is directed the more likely it is that the claimant will be able to make out a case, so that if the reference is to a limited group like trustees, members of a firm or tenants of a particular building, all will generally be able to sue[168]; (e) it has been said that each member of a body:

> "[N]o matter how large [would be] defamed when the libel consisted in the assertion that no one of the members of a community was elected unless he had committed a murder",[169]

---

[162] Indeed it has been said to be misleading to speak of class defamation: *Orme v Associated Newspapers Ltd, The Times,* February 4, 1981.

[163] We are of course talking only about the civil law. Attacks on groups may be criminally punishable in various ways.

[164] Lord Porter in *Knuppfer's* case at [1944] A.C. 124. A representative action will not assist the claimant in a "class" case: such an action does not get over the problem of identification.

[165] (1858) 1 F.& F. 347 at 349.

[166] See the example in Eldredge, *Law of Defamation* (1978) §10 of a speaker who attacks surgeons while glaring at a surgeon in the audience.

[167] *Le Fanu v Malcolmson* (1848) 11 H.L.C. 637.

[168] *Browne v D.C. Thomson* 1912 S.C. 359. In *Foxcroft v Lacey* (1613) Hob. 89, 17 men were indicted for conspiracy and D said, "These defendants are those that helped to murder Henry Farrer". It was held that each could sue. *Hyams v Peterson* [1991] 3 N.Z.L.R. 648. It must also be borne in mind that where there is a charge of wrongdoing against a group of persons the claimant may be impliedly referred to by association: see above, para.12–19 and *MCormick v John Fairfax* (1989) 16 N.S.W.L.R. 458.

[169] Lord Porter in *Knuppfer's* case at [1944] A.C. 124; *Sauls v Hendrickse* 1992 (3) S.A. 912.

but it is thought that to bring this into play the charge must be very specific indeed[170]; (f) whether there is evidence upon which the words can be regarded as *capable* of referring to the claimant is always a matter for the judge and this case is no different.[171]

A conundrum arises where a charge is made in terms like "one of these people stole my watch". Logically it can be argued that the statement does not impute the wrongdoing to any individual,[172] but it is not clear that this is the law[173] and the statement would seem to impute suspicion, which is itself defamatory, though to a lesser degree.[174]

D. Publication

12–22   There is no actionable wrong of defamation unless the words are communicated to at least one person other than the claimant. Publication in the commercial sense, as in a book or newspaper or broadcast is not necessary, though these are of course likely to attract larger damages.[175] In principle it is still the law that publication to one person will suffice but nowadays this must be read in the light of the court's power to strike out the claim as an abuse of process. In *Duke of Brunswick v Harmer*[176] a libel on the Duke in a newspaper was time-barred so the Duke sent his agent to purchase another copy and that publication to the agent was held to be a new cause of action, the time running from that day. Nowadays, however, the claim would be struck out, for if the agent read the article it is unlikely he would have thought less of the Duke and if he did, the Duke brought it on his own head.[177] On the other hand, the publication of a slander to only one person might have a very damaging effect.[178] Publication is of the essence of libel and slander because the wrong is injury to reputation, not insult, and reputation is what other people think of one, and not one's own opinion of oneself.[179] Where defamatory material is contained in a newspaper or book it will be presumed that a significant number of readers read

---

[170] Thus it obviously would not apply to "all lawyers are thieves", perhaps because no sensible person can take that as anything but general abuse.

[171] *Knuppfer's* case at [1944] A.C. 121, 124.

[172] *MCormick v John Fairfax* (1989) 16 N.S.W.L.R. 458; *Blaser v Krattiger* 195 P. 359 (Or. 1921).

[173] *Farrington v Leigh, The Times,* December 10, 1987; *Pryke v Advertiser Newspapers* (1984) 37 S.A.S.R. 175.

[174] *Lewis v Daily Telegraph* [1964] A.C. 234.

[175] However, commercial publication is of significance for the purposes of the defence of innocent dissemination: below, para.12–23.

[176] (1849) 14 Q.B. 185.

[177] *Jameel (Yousef) v Dow Jones Inc* [2005] EWCA Civ 75; [2005] Q.B. 946 at [56].

[178] *Crossland v Wilkinson Hardware Stores Ltd* [2005] EWHC 481 (QB).

[179] *Bata v Bata* [1948] W.N. 366.

the offending passages but there is no such presumption with regard to material placed on the Internet, though evidence of the number of times the site was accessed may justify a finding that a substantial number of people read the material.[180] At one time the statement of claim would contain an allegation that the words were published "maliciously" but this was purely formal and the practice has ceased. Malice—or "express malice" as it was called to distinguish it from the purely formal allegation in the statement of claim—will, however, defeat the defences of fair comment and qualified privilege.

The handing back by a printer or typist to the author of a defamatory document processed by them on the author's instructions is not a publication by them,[181] but there is, of course, publication *to* the printer or typist when the author hands[182] the document to them. Unless such communication is protected by qualified privilege,[183] it follows that if a manager of a company in the course of his duties dictates to a secretary a memorandum defamatory of a fellow servant, not only has the manager committed libel but the company is also vicariously liable,[184] though it has been suggested that the doctrine of common employment should be used to protect the company in such a case[185] and one imagines that such a case would anyway be very suitable for the application of abuse of process.[186]

Communication of defamatory matter by a husband to his wife or vice versa is not a publication: what passes between them is protected on the ground that any other rule "might lead to disastrous results to social life",[187] though in modern conditions a broader rule based on "domestic relations", however hard to define, might be more apt. Communication by a third party to one spouse of matter defamatory of the other is a publication; even at a time when husband and wife could fairly be said to be one person for legal purposes that was not:

---

[180] *Al Amoudi v Brisard* [2006] EWHC 1062; [2007] 1 W.L.R. 113.
[181] *Eglantine Inn Ltd v Smith* [1948] N.I. 29.
[182] Or, in modern conditions transmits the information to them on a disk or network.
[183] See below, para.12–53. If the claimant comes across the memorandum by disclosure in other proceedings there are restrictions on the use he can make of it outside those proceedings: CPR 31.22.
[184] *Riddick v Thames Board Mills Ltd* [1977] Q.B. 881. Cf. Hunt J. in *Jones v Amalgamated TV Services Pty Ltd* (1991) 23 N.S.W.L.R. 364 and the judgment of Giles J.A. in *State Bank of New South Wales Ltd v Currabubula Holdings Pty Ltd* [2001] NSWCA 47; (2001) 51 NSWLR 399.
[185] *Riddick's* case per Lord Denning M.R. For the abolition of the doctrine in relation to personal injuries see above, para.8–3.
[186] See *Lonzim Plc v Sprague* [2009] EWHC 2838 (QB).
[187] *Wennhak v Morgan* (1888) 20 Q.B.D. 635 at 639.

"[F]or the purpose of having the honour and feelings of the husband assailed and injured by acts done or communications made to his wife."[188]

The statement must be intelligible to the recipient of it. There is no publication if it is in a foreign language which he does not understand[189] or if he is too deaf to hear it or too blind to read it, though in the case of books, newspapers or broadcasts it will of course be inferred that it was intelligible to the majority of recipients. Similarly in the case of postcards there is a presumption that these are published on being sent through the post without proof that anyone did in fact read them. This is based on the practical impossibility of proving that anyone did read them; in theory the presumption is rebuttable but it very difficult to conceive, if the postcard is written in English, how such rebutting evidence could be given.

Normally publication will be an intentional act but this need not necessarily be so. If, for example, D sends a letter to C containing defamatory imputations about C (which would not be actionable if read by C) D will be liable if the letter is not marked "private" (or with some similar expression) and is opened in the ordinary course of business by an employee of C.[190] It is a question of what the defendant should reasonably have foreseen would happen to the letter. It is normal for clerks in offices to open mail addressed to their employers but in *Huth v Huth*[191] there was no publication where the letter was opened by an inquisitive butler, even though it was unsealed.[192] If the defendant leaves his correspondence about, or if he inadvertently puts a letter in the wrong envelope or if he speaks too loudly he will have published the material, but not if a thief breaks in and takes the document.[193]

---

[188] *Wenman v Ash* (1853) 13 C.B. 836 at 844; *Theaker v Richardson* [1962] 1 W.L.R. 151.
[189] If he immediately goes home and deciphers it with the aid of a dictionary is the case governed by *Grappelli v Derek Block (Holdings)*, above, fn.115, para.12–16?
[190] *Pullman v Hill* [1891] 1 Q.B. 524.
[191] [1915] 3 K.B. 32.
[192] Cf. *Theaker v Richardson* [1962] 1 W.L.R. 151 (husband opened sealed letter addressed to wife, jury found publication; the letter looked like an election circular and the CA's decision that the verdict was not perverse should not be taken as authority for the proposition that it is always foreseeable that one spouse will open the other's mail).
[193] *Pullman v Hill* [1891] 1 Q.B. 524 at 527. See the review of the early cases by Palmer J. in *Tom and Bill Waterhouse Pty Ltd v Racing New South Wales* [2008] NSWSC 1013 at [25] (citations omitted): "So, for example, if a man wished to annoy his wife by writing her an insulting letter, he would have published an actionable defamation if he wrote the diatribe on a postcard and mailed it to her, even if he proved positively that no one had ever read the postcard apart from his wife. But he would not have '*published*' the defamation if he had folded the letter and sealed it with a wax seal, even if the servant to whom he gave the letter for delivery opened and read it. He might well have published the defamation if he put the letter in an envelope which he did not seal but gummed its flap down before handing it to his servant. The risk that he had actionably published the letter was increased if he did not lick the gum on the flap. The risk was reduced if he put a penny stamp on the envelope before mailing it, but was increased if he could only afford a half-penny stamp

i. Distributors. The common law spreads the net of liability very **12–23** wide. In the case of an article in a newspaper, for example, not only is the author treated as a publisher, but so is the editor, the printer, the proprietor of the newspaper,[194] indeed anyone who participated in the publication.[195] However, those concerned with the mere mechanical distribution of material—newsagents, libraries,[196] book-sellers—could escape liability if they could prove: (a) that they were innocent of any knowledge of the libel contained in the work; (b) that there was nothing in the work or in the circumstances in which it came to them or was disseminated by them which ought to have led them to suppose that it contained a libel; and (c) that when the work was disseminated by them, it was not by any negligence on their part that they did not know it contained the libel.[197] This is in practice replaced[198] by the defence under s.1 of the Defamation Act 1996.

It is a defence for the defendant to show that he was not the author,[199] editor or publisher (in the commercial sense[200]) of the statement, that he took reasonable care in relation to the publication and that he did not know, and had no reason to believe, that what he did caused or contributed to the publication of a defamatory statement.[201] More specifically, s.1(3) provides that certain persons are not to be considered as author, editor or publisher, though the list is not exclusive for the court may have regard to it by way of analogy in cases falling outside it. Distributors are covered, as they were at common law, but printers[202] are now brought within the statutory

---

because post office officials would have the right, almost never exercised, to open a half-penny stamped letter in the course of delivery. Again, even if he gummed the flap of the envelope down before mailing it, the risk of actionable publication was increased if he did not write '*Private*' on the front of the envelope. However, he was quite safe if he put the letter to his wife in an envelope, did not write "private" on it, did not gum the flap down and mailed it with a half-penny stamp if, in the event, the letter happened to be read on delivery by his wife's curious butler."

[194] In modern conditions newspapers are of course always operated as companies.
[195] Hence there may be many separate publications before it is issued to the public, though it is that which will in practice be sued on. Technically there is a separate publication to each reader. In practice the edition will be sued on as a whole but the issue of separate publications may be significant if a true innuendo is relied on. Now that many newspapers publish Internet editions, we have another example of separate publication: *Green v Times Newspapers Ltd*, January 17, 2001, QBD.
[196] There are special provisions for copyright libraries in the Legal Deposit Libraries Act 2003.
[197] *Vizetelly v Mudie's Select Library Ltd* [1900] 2 Q.B. 170. Though as Scrutton L.J. pointed out in *Sun Life Assurance Co of Canada v W.H. Smith & So Ltd* (1934) 150 L.T. 211 (b) and (c) might be combined in a single question.
[198] The common law defence has not been formally abolished: *Metropolitan International Schools Ltd v DesignTechnica Corp* [2009] EWHC 1765 (QB).
[199] "Author" is defined as the originator of the statement: s.1(2).
[200] i.e. whose business is issuing material to the public or a section of the public: s.1(2)
[201] Section 1(1).
[202] Printers were often sued because they were more claim-worthy than the originators of the material they printed.

defence.[203] Broadcasters could not rely on the distributor's defence at common law, they were regarded as publishing the entire content of their programmes in their own right. Now they may rely on the s.1 defence if the programme is live[204] and in the circumstances they had no effective control over the maker of the statement.[205] Finally comes the:

> "[O]perator or provider of access to a communications system by means of which the statement is transmitted, or made available, by a person over whom he has no effective control."[206]

This is primarily aimed at the providers of Internet services, where the decentralised nature of the information and the quantity of material makes prior control of what goes on to the system difficult or impossible.[207] In determining whether a person took reasonable care or had reason to believe that he was contributing to the publication of a defamatory statement, the court is to have regard to the extent of his responsibility for the content of or the decision to publish the statement, the nature and circumstances of the publication, and the previous conduct or character of the author, editor or publisher.[208] Obvious examples of questions which may arise in litigation are: at what point does a publication acquire a "reputation for libel" and what steps does a distributor have to take to check new issues?; what steps should a radio company running a live phone-in programme take to "vet" potential contributions?[209]; and should the broadcaster in such a case utilise a delay mechanism on transmission? In the case of material of other than a transitory nature the distributor who receives notice of its defamatory nature will of course be liable for further publications if he fails to withdraw it.[210]

---

[203] Section 1(3)(a). There are equivalent provisions for processors and distributors of films or sound recordings (s.1(3)(b) and electronic media (s.1(3)(c)).

[204] Comparatively few programmes are live.

[205] Section 1(3)(d). Presumably "control" means "right of control": it is no more possible to prevent an ad-lib remark by an employee than by a contributor to a programme but it would be surprising if the broadcasting company were not liable for the acts of the former.

[206] Section 1(3)(e).

[207] See *Godfrey v Demon Internet Ltd* [2001] Q.B. 201. If a newsgroup is "moderated" new messages will be examined for content. Presumably whoever does this is an "editor" but it will be extraordinarily difficult to identify all but the most glaring defamatory messages..

[208] See s.1(5).

[209] It is understood that this was done under the old law, e.g. by asking what contributors proposed to say and emphasising to them that they should not make defamatory statements.

[210] *Godfrey v Demon Internet Ltd* [2001] Q.B. 201. Though he must have a reasonable opportunity to make inquiry into the complaint.

Internet service providers have further protection under the Electronic Commerce (EC Directive) Regulations.[211] One acting as a mere conduit (e.g. for the transmission of email or access to the site where the information sought is stored) is simply not liable in damages at all. One who hosts information (e.g. stores on its servers web pages produced by others) is not liable in damages if he is not aware of facts from which it is apparent to him that the information is "unlawful" and acts expeditiously to remove it when he acquires such knowledge.[212] Though not identical with the 1996 Act, this is at least similar to it.

This complex web of municipal and European legislation has not proved easy to apply to Internet publications. Take, for example, a search engine which leads the user to a defamatory publication originated by another. Does the search engine operator publish the communication to which it leads? Does it make any difference if the "snippet" which it shows itself contains defamatory words? Does the search engine operator provide its service "for remuneration" (a requirement of the Regulations) when it obtains its funds from advertising rather than direct charges to users? How is the concept of reasonable care to be applied when the information collected by the search engine is obtained by web-crawling "robots" which simply look for particular words and the ability of the search engine operator to "close off" offending sites without at the same time blocking thousands of innocuous ones is very limited? English courts have so far shown an inclination instead to deal with these problems via the common law concept of publication. Eady J. in *Bunt v Tilley*[213] was prepared to hold that any service provider playing only a passive role in facilitating Internet transactions was not a "publisher" at common law and in *Metropolitan International Schools Ltd v DesignTechnica Corp*[214] the same approach was applied to a search engine.

While the statutory defence gives a distributor a degree of protection, the fact that he is presumptively liable may lead him to refuse to distribute a journal, with or without the threat of legal proceedings. In *Goldsmith v Pressdram*[215] the claimant, considering himself

---

[211] SI 2002/2013. Strangely described in the Directive and Regulations as "information society service providers". See *Bunt v Tilley* [2006] EWHC 407; [2007] 1 W.L.R. 1243.

[212] There is an intermediate category of "caching", which involves temporary storage of information on other sites to make access more efficient. The cacher is not liable in damages if he acts expeditiously to remove it upon becoming aware that it has been removed from the initial source site.

[213] [2006] EWHC 407 (QB); [2007] 1 W.L.R. 1243.

[214] [2009] EWHC 1765 (QB); [2009] E.M.L.R. 27. Email carriers must fall within the "passive role" concept. Carrying email is rather like a telephone service and it has been held in the United States that a telephone company is not a publisher of the words spoken down its lines: *Anderson v New York Telephone Co* 361 N.Y.S. 2d 913 (1974).

[215] [1977] 1 W.L.R. 478.

defamed by *Private Eye*, brought a criminal prosecution (as was then possible) against the magazine in respect of one article and a civil action in respect of two others but he also sued 37 distributors of the magazine. Many settled by an undertaking not to distribute *Private Eye* again, but some sought an order that the actions against them be stayed as an abuse of the process of the court. The majority of the Court of Appeal dismissed this application because, whilst it was undoubtedly an abuse of process to pursue by legal action a collateral advantage which the law would not allow,[216] the claimant believed that the magazine was carrying on a defamatory campaign against him and the terms of the settlements were thus directly related to the grievances which had caused him to sue. His purpose was not to shut down *Private Eye* (though the proceedings might, conceivably, have had that effect[217]) but to protect his reputation.

12–24   **ii. Repetition.** Where a defendant's words are voluntarily repeated or republished by the person to whom he published them (and for whom he is not vicariously liable), the question arises whether he is liable for that repetition or republication.[218] The first point is that if the defendant is so liable the claimant's claim may be approached in two ways. He may sue the defendant both for the original publication and for the republication as separate causes of action[219]; or he may sue in respect of the original publication only but seek to recover damages in that action in respect of the further loss caused by the republication.[220] In either event, the starting point is that a republication by the voluntary act of another will generally break the chain of causation.[221] However, the defendant will be liable where he authorised or intended the republication, as where he sent a letter to a newspaper[222] or spoke at a press conference[223]; or where he must be aware that there is a significant risk that the words will be republished, because of the circumstances in which they are initially published or because the person to whom they are addressed is under a legal or moral duty to repeat them to a third person. The underlying concept may be that there is liability if republication is

---

[216] See below, para.19–14.
[217] The dispute between Sir James Goldsmith and *Private Eye* was eventually compromised.
[218] Distinguish the case where A tells a story to D and D is sued for repeating it: see para.12–27, below.
[219] *Cutler v McPhail* [1962] 2 Q.B. 292 (where there had been a release of the claim in respect of the republication—criticised in *Timms v Clift* [1998] 2 Qd. R. 100).
[220] As in *Slipper v BBC* [1991] 2 Q.B. 283 with regard to the "preview" action. In this situation what counts is not whether the statement is "repeated" but whether the second publication conveys the sting of the first: *McManus v Beckham* [2002] EWCA Civ 939; [2002] 1 W.L.R. 2982. See *Baturina v Times Newspapers* [2010] EWHC 696 (QB).
[221] *Ward v Weeks* (1830) 7 Bing. N.C. 211; *Weld-Blundell v Stephens* [1920] A.C. 945.
[222] *Cutler v McPhail*, above, fn.219.
[223] *Sims v Wran* [1984] 1 N.S.W.L.R. 317.

reasonably foreseeable,[224] but for reasons of clarity it is better not to direct the jury in those terms.[225] Hence where the defendants gave a preview of a television film to press journalists who reviewed the film it was plainly arguable for the purposes of a striking out application that press reviews would be likely to repeat the sting of the alleged libel, for otherwise the reviewers would not be able to deal fairly with the film.[226]

2. DEFENCES

There are a number of specialised defences to defamation. These are: **12–25**

1. Justification (truth)
2. Fair comment
3. Privilege, which may be

   (a) absolute or
   (b) qualified.

4. Offer of amends under the Defamation Act 1996.

A. Justification (or Truth)

The claimant does not need to prove that the statement is false, for **12–26** the law presumes that in his favour,[227] but the defendant can plead justification (the technical name for truth here) and if he can establish it by evidence he has a good defence though he may have been actuated by ill-will or spite. It is not that the law has any special relish for the indiscriminate infliction of truth on other people, but defamation is an injury to a person's reputation, and if people think the worse of him when they hear the truth about him that merely shows that his reputation has been reduced to its proper level. If one introduces a condition that the publication must relate to a matter of public interest[228] one is in effect creating a form of liability for invasion of privacy.[229] At the same time justification may be a

---

[224] *McManus v Beckham,* above, fn.220, at [44]; *Slipper v BBC* [1991] 2 Q.B. 283 at 301.

[225] *McManus v Beckham,* above, fn.220, at [43].

[226] *Slipper v BBC,* above, fn.220.

[227] As a consequence of constitutional restrictions on defamation the claimant now bears the burden of proof of falsity in the USA: *Philadelphia Newspapers v Hepps* 475 U.S. 767 (1986). To put the burden of proof on the defendant is sometimes said to be out of line with tort law in general, but if the defendant says the claimant has misbehaved, should not the claimant be presumed innocent until proven guilty? Consider the problems of rebutting a generalised charge of wrongdoing. The rule survived a challenge (or at least a blanket challenge) in *McVicar v UK* (2002) 35 E.H.R.R. 22, ECtHR.

[228] As was formerly the case for example in New South Wales, Defamation Act 1974 s.15. However, s.25 of the NSW Defamation Act 2005 reverts to the common law defence of truth simpliciter.

[229] See below, para.12–78.

dangerous plea if it is the only one which the defendant decides to adopt, for if he fails in it the jury may regard his conduct as wanton and return a verdict for heavier damages. While there is no doubt that justification is a defence to an action for defamation, it has been held in interlocutory proceedings that it is not a defence if the statement is published as part of a conspiracy the object of which is to injure the claimant, for the tort of conspiracy may be committed without any act which is independently tortious.[230] However, conspiracy does not give rise to a claim for damages for loss of reputation or injury to feelings.

12–27   **i. Must be true in substance.** The defendant need not show that the charge he seeks to justify is precisely true in every particular: what matters is whether it is substantially true and it has been said that journalists, "need to be permitted a degree of exaggeration even in the context of factual assertions".[231] Subject to that, it is a general principle that the justification must be as broad as the charge, and must justify the precise charge. To justify the repetition of a defamatory statement already made, therefore, the defendant must prove that the content of the statement was true, not merely that it was made.[232] If I say to you, "Smith told me that Brown swindled his creditors", I can justify this only by proof that Brown did swindle his creditors; it is idle to show merely that Smith gave me the information or that I have not "adopted" the allegation as my own.[233] This is commonly known as the "repetition rule".[234] It has sometimes been suggested that the rule in its present form is incompatible with the European Convention on Human Rights, at least where the media publish material on matters of public concern. However, in some cases of this type the media may be able to plead privilege, where truth is not necessary.[235] This was applied, for example, where the press reported accusations and counter-accusations by two sides in a political dispute in which the public had a legitimate interest.[236] In this limited sense English law may now

---

[230] *Gulf Oil (Great Britain) Ltd v Page* [1988] Ch. 327, below, para.18–22.

[231] Eady J. in *Turcu v News Group Newspapers Ltd* [2005] EWHC 799 (QB) at [108].

[232] For the detailed application of this in the context of an accusation that there are reasonable grounds to suspect the claimant of wrongdoing see *Musa King v Telegraph Group Ltd* [2004] EWCA Civ 613; [2004] E.M.L.R. 23 (passage not in [2005] 1 W.L.R. 2282).

[233] If I say "Smith told me that Brown swindled his creditors, which shows that Smith is a liar" that is not defamatory of Brown because the antidote counters the bane. It is of course defamatory of Smith.

[234] *Shah v Standard Chartered Bank* [1999] Q.B. 240 (which goes so far as to hold that even if the imputation is only that the defendant is under suspicion it is not enough to show that the imputation came from a reputable source: the defendant must point to conduct by the claimant which justifies the suspicion). Distinguish the situation where the question is whether Smith is liable for the repetition by me: para.12–24, above.

[235] See para.12–53, below.

[236] *Al Fagih v H.H. Saudi Research & Marketing (UK) Ltd* [2001] EWCA Civ 1634; [2002] E.M.L.R. 13.

recognise a limited defence of "neutral reportage", though the limits of this are not yet clear.[237]

Although the defence of justification is distinct from the question whether the words are defamatory, the two are interlinked to some extent. In *Lewis v Daily Telegraph Ltd*,[238] for example, the defendants were clearly able to justify the literal meaning, admittedly itself defamatory, of their statement that the Fraud Squad was investigating the claimant company's affairs, and so once the House of Lords had held that the words were incapable of meaning that the claimants had been guilty of fraud the case was at an end. In *Cadam v Beaverbrook Newspapers Ltd*,[239] the defendants published a statement that a writ had been issued against the claimant for conspiracy to defraud and they sought to justify this by proving that such a writ had indeed been issued. On an interlocutory appeal the Court of Appeal held that it could not be said that proof of the issue of the writ could not justify some defamatory meaning that somebody might say was the ordinary meaning of the words, and the issue of justification must therefore be allowed to go to the jury. It must be for the jury to decide whether proof that the writ had been issued justified the natural and ordinary meaning of the words, whatever the jury itself might decide the natural and ordinary meaning to be. There is of course a privilege for fair and accurate reports of court proceedings (absolute in the case of contemporaneous reports)[240] but this only applies to reports of proceedings in open court and would not apply to a report of the issue of proceedings[241] and if *Cadam*'s case had gone the other way it would have been dangerous to report anything at all until the trial commenced.[242]

The relationship between the claim and the defence of justification was responsible for much of what was fairly called the "artificial minuet"[243] of libel pleading. The courts are now less willing to countenance fine distinctions but the law is still difficult. It may be summarised in the following propositions. **12–28**

---

[237] See further para.12–55, below.
[238] [1964] A.C. 234, above, para.12–13.
[239] [1959] 1 Q.B. 413.
[240] See below, para.12–44.
[241] This is assumed in *Stern v Piper* [1997] Q.B. 123 but it may require reconsideration in the light of the fact that far more of the proceedings are nowadays conducted on paper and under CPR r.5.4(5) most of the documentation is accessible to the public (subject, in some cases, to the court's permission). A report of the contents of a claim form (which is accessible as of right) would seem to be covered by qualified privilege under Pt I, Sch.1, para.5 of the Defamation Act 1996.
[242] Arguably it does not go far enough. Perhaps if the report of the issue of proceedings is accurate the issue should be withdrawn from the jury. In *Stern v Piper* [1997] Q.B. 123 *Cadam*'s case was not applied to a report of the contents of an affirmation made by a party to litigation before trial.
[243] *Polly Peck (Holdings) Plc v Trelford* [1986] Q.B. 1000 at 1020. May L.J. in *Morrell v International Thomson Publishing Ltd* [1989] 3 All E.R. 733 at 734, thought a saraband more apt.

1. Just as the claimant must give particulars of any defamatory meaning which is not the plain, ordinary meaning of the words,[244] so must the defendant make clear and explicit the meaning he seeks to justify.[245] This, it will be observed, is not quite the same as requiring him to specify what the words do mean: he may give notice in his defence of his preparedness to justify two or three different meanings and he is not obliged to pick out one of those as his exclusive defence. He is certainly not tied to the meaning the claimant pleads: the issue is not what the claimant contends the words mean but what meaning or meanings they are reasonably capable of bearing.

2. Where a defamatory statement contains more than one charge, the common law rule was that each must be justified. This was altered by s.5 of the Defamation Act 1952 so that:

> "[I]n an action ... in respect of words containing two or more distinct charges ... a defence of justification shall not fail by reason only that the truth of every charge is not proved if the words not proved to be true do not materially injure the claimant's reputation having regard to the truth of the remaining charges."[246]

To give a simple example: if D were to allege of C, (i) that he had participated in genocide during a war, and (ii) while so serving had made certain dishonest expenses claims, justification of (i) would entitle the jury to bring in a verdict for D on the whole article even if there was no evidence at all to justify (ii).[247] However, s.5 is only applicable where the action is brought in respect of the distinct charges, so if the claimant chooses to sue only in respect of one (and the initiative is his) the defendant cannot adduce evidence of justification relating to the other.[248] "It is no defence to a charge that 'You called me A' to say 'Yes, but I also called you B on the same occasion and that was true'".[249]

3. The claimant is not, however, wholly free to pick and choose those items which he thinks the defendant will be unable to

---

[244] Above, para.12–16.

[245] *Lucas-Box v News Group Newspapers Ltd* [1986] 1 W.L.R. 147.

[246] Applied in *Irving v Penguin Books Ltd* April 11, 2000 (QB).

[247] Compare Lord Denning in *Moore v News of the World Ltd* [1972] 1 Q.B. 441 at 448: "That is a very complicated section, but it means that a defendant is not to fail simply because he cannot prove every single thing in the libel to be true." On the guidance which the judge might give the jury about the relative gravity of the charges see *Jackson v John Fairfax* [1981] 1 N.S.W.L.R. 36.

[248] *Polly Peck (Holdings) Plc v Trelford* [1986] Q.B. 1000; *Bookbinder v Tebbit* [1989] 1 W.L.R. 640. For a clear example see *McKeith v News Group Newspapers Ltd* [2005] EWHC 1162 (QB).

[249] *Cruise v Express Newspapers Plc* [1999] Q.B. 931 at 954.

justify: the question of what is a distinct allegation is one of fact and degree and where a number of defamatory allegations in their context have a common sting the defendant is entitled to justify the sting even though that sting amounts to a charge of more general wrongdoing in respect of which the claimant has not sued.[250] So much depends upon the facts of particular cases that the decision in one is rarely likely to be of assistance in another, but two examples may be helpful. In *Williams v Reason*[251] the allegation was that the claimant had written a book for money and had thereby compromised his amateur status as a Rugby Union player. The defendants obtained leave to allege, by way of particulars of justification, that the claimant had taken money for wearing the boots of a named manufacturer, for the sting of the libel was "shamateurism", not merely the writing of the book. However, in *Bookbinder v Tebbit*,[252] where a local politician was accused of squandering public money by overprinting stationery in support of "nuclear free zones", the defendant was not allowed to introduce, by way of justification, a number of other alleged instances of irresponsibility with public money. Had the charge been made in the context of a broader political attack on maladministration the position might have been different but on the facts to accept the defendant's contention would be tantamount to saying that a particular charge of wrongdoing necessarily included a general charge of that sort of wrongdoing, thereby considerably widening the field in the defendant's favour. Furthermore, where the defendant directly accuses the claimant of misconduct, he will not be allowed to justify a charge of reasonable suspicion of misconduct.[253] To say that C stole the silver is not reasonably susceptible of meaning only that he is suspected of stealing the silver.[254] The defendant is in any event entitled to use the whole publication to provide the context of the words complained of when the jury is considering their meaning, the:

> "[C]laimant is not permitted to use a blue pencil on words published of him so as to change their meaning and then prevent the defendant from justifying the words in their unexpurgated form."[255]

---

[250] *Khashoggi v I.P.C. Magazines Ltd* [1986] 1 W.L.R. 1412.
[251] [1988] 1 W.L.R. 96.
[252] [1989] 1 W.L.R. 640.
[253] Compare *Lewis v Daily Telegraph*, above, para.12–13, where the court held that the words used did not impute the direct charge.
[254] *Berezovsky v Forbes Inc* [2001] EWCA Civ 1251; [2001] E.M.L.R. 45. Nor is s.5 of the 1952 Act relevant.
[255] *Polly Peck (Holdings) Plc v Trelford* [1986] Q.B. at 1023.

4. In many of the cases the defendant might have been inclined to admit privately that it was optimistic to expect the jury to accept his "lesser" or "broader" meaning as a justification of the claim. What he was really concerned to do was to show, if he could not establish that the claimant was "bad" in way A then at least he was "bad" in way B, with a view to reducing the damages. The traditional rule has been that the defendant may adduce evidence of general bad reputation on the issue of damages but not of specific acts of misconduct[256]: the law must prevent the recovery of substantial damages by a person whose reputation is unworthy of protection but it would be oppressive to allow the defendant (perhaps a newspaper with large financial resources) to lengthen a trial with evidence of the claimant's past conduct. On the other hand, the defendant is entitled to rely in mitigation of damages on any evidence which has been properly before the jury and this may include evidence of specific acts of misconduct advanced under an unsuccessful plea of justification.[257] What the court must not countenance is the pleading of such specific acts under the guise of a plea of justification with the sole purpose of mitigation of damages.[258] It is the restriction on evidence which may be given in mitigation of damages which lies at the heart of most of the fencing on justification. As the Neill Committee put it:

> "[T]here is often a feeling of injustice or resentment on the part of defendants when claimants recover large damages from a jury which they would probably have been disinclined to award if they had been permitted to have a fuller picture of the claimant's conduct. It has been said that defendants would be less inclined to go for wide-ranging pleas of justification, sometimes based upon attaching imaginative or ingenious meanings to the words complained of, if it were open to them to bring the disreputable behaviour of the claimant before the court purely for the purpose of reducing damages"[259]

The Committee proposed a new approach whereby the defendant would, subject to certain procedural safeguards and the

---

[256] *Plato Films v Speidel* [1961] A.C. 1090. The restriction on such evidence is commonly known as the rule in *Scott v Sampson* (1882) 8 Q.B.D. 491.
[257] *Pamplin v Express Newspapers Ltd (Note)* [1988] 1 W.L.R. 116.
[258] *Atkinson v Fitzwalter* [1987] 1 W.L.R. 201; *Prager v Times Newspapers Ltd* [1988] 1 W.L.R. 77.
[259] Report of the Supreme Court Procedure Committee (1991).

control of the judge, be allowed to adduce evidence of facts
related to the same sector of the claimant's life and a clause to
this effect was included in the Defamation Bill 1995. In its
passage through the House of Commons the clause was thrown
out as a "muckrakers' charter". However, since then the courts
have at least modified the basic rule. In *Burstein v Times
Newspapers Ltd*[260] the Court of Appeal held that there is
nothing to prevent the admission in evidence of matters,
"which relate to the background context which is directly
relevant to the publication". So even though the defendant
could not justify a charge that the claimant had organised
bands of hecklers to wreck performances of atonal music, it
could give evidence of an incident in which the claimant had
booed after one performance. The principle applies equally to
the situation where the claimant has accepted the defendant's
offer of amends under the Defamation Act 1996[261] and the
court has to assess compensation because the amount of this
has not been agreed[262]—indeed, it is particularly important
that it should apply in such a case because the defendant will
have had no opportunity to raise the claimant's conduct under
a plea of justification or fair comment. It is inevitable that
cases will arise where it is difficult to decide whether the
evidence relates to the "directly relevant background context"[263] and it should be applied with some caution. However,
there is no requirement for any causative effect between the
facts sought to be put forward and the publication of the libel
nor that the defendant should have had those facts in mind at
the time.[264]

ii. Proof of justification. The standard of proof of justification is   **12–29**
the normal civil one of balance of probabilities, but as in other civil
cases the seriousness of the defendant's allegation may be taken into
account in determining whether he has discharged that burden.[265]
Where the defamatory allegation was that the claimant had committed a criminal offence, the rule of the common law was that his
criminal conviction was not even prima facie evidence of guilt for
the purpose of the defamation proceedings, and this meant that the
defendant had to prove the guilt of the claimant all over again if the

[260] [2001] 1 W.L.R. 579.
[261] See para.12–66, below.
[262] *Turner v News Group Newspapers Ltd* [2006] EWCA Civ 540; [2006] 1 W.L.R. 3469.
[263] *Turner* at [56].
[264] *Turner*, above, fn.262, at [53] and [54].
[265] *Laurence v Chester Chronicle, The Times*, February 8, 1986.

defence of justification was to succeed.[266] However, it is provided by s.13 of the Civil Evidence Act 1968 that in an action for libel or slander in which the question whether the claimant[267] committed a criminal offence is relevant, proof that he stands convicted of the offence is conclusive evidence that he did commit it.

12–30   iii. Rehabilitation of Offenders Act 1974. The only qualification in English law to the proposition that truth is a complete defence is to be found in the Rehabilitation of Offenders Act 1974. The Act seeks to rehabilitate convicted offenders by restricting or forbidding the disclosure of "spent convictions", which, broadly speaking, means convictions for offences in respect of which the offender has received a sentence not exceeding 30 months' imprisonment and where a specified time (the rehabilitation period, varying from 5–10 years, depending on the sentence) has elapsed since the conviction. A rehabilitated person is then to:

> "[B]e treated for all purposes in law as a person who has not committed or been charged with or prosecuted for or convicted of or sentenced for the offence ... the subject of that conviction".[268]

However, this is severely limited with respect to proceedings for defamation by s.8(3)[269] which provides that nothing shall prevent a defendant in such an action from:

> "[R]elying on any defence of justification or fair comment or of absolute or qualified privilege which is available to him or restrict matters he may establish in support of any such defence".

At this point, however, the Act introduces a novel concept into English law, for it goes on to provide that a defendant shall not be entitled to rely upon the defence of justification if the publication is proved to have been made with malice.[270] Malice here means that

---

[266] This he did not always succeed in doing: *Hinds v Sparks* [1964] Crim. L.R. 717; *Goody v Odhams Press Ltd* [1967] 1 Q.B. 333.

[267] "Claimant" was substituted for "person" by s.12 of the Defamation Act 1996. The original form inhibited a plea of justification in an action brought by a police officer who had been involved in an investigation leading to a conviction.

[268] Section 4(1).

[269] By s.49 of the Criminal Justice and Immigration Act 2008 the rehabilitation scheme is extended to cautions. However, there is no amendment of s.8 of the 1974 Act so that it seems that there are no circumstances in which the defendant can defeat a claim in respect of a spent caution to which he referred.

[270] Section 8(5).

the publication is made with some spiteful, irrelevant or improper motive,[271] but there are difficulties about applying malice to justification and there must be some question of the compatibility of the Act with art.10 of the European Convention on Human Rights.[272]

B. Fair Comment

It is a defence to an action for defamation that the statement is a **12–31** fair comment on a matter of public interest.[273]

Honest criticism ought to be, and is, recognised in any civilised system of law as indispensable to the efficient working of any public institution or office, and as salutary for private persons who make themselves or their work the object of public interest. The defence has been recognised for a long time in English law, and, although criticism of government and of public functionaries was not always so freely allowed as today, it is now fully recognised as one of the essential elements of freedom of speech which is not to be whittled down by legal refinement. At one time, fair comment and qualified privilege were not clearly distinguished but now they are distinct defences. Fair comment is both wider and narrower than qualified privilege: it is wider in that, provided the matter commented on is of public interest, it is open to anyone, whereas in the case of qualified privilege at common law there must generally be a reciprocal duty or interest in the matter between the giver of the information and the recipient, which may present obstacles to establishing that a statement to the public at large is protected by privilege; it is narrower in that, subject to what is said below, fair comment is not applicable to statements of fact.

---

[271] *Herbage v Pressdram Ltd* [1984] 1 W.L.R. 1160. If the writer wishes to plead non-malicious justification, the provisions of s.13 of the Civil Evidence Act 1968 will still be available to him for the purpose of proving the offence and conviction but will not, of course, be finally conclusive on the issue of liability. The position of the writer of a reference after the Act appears to be that he is not obliged to disclose a spent conviction of which he knows and incurs no liability to the addressee for failing to do so (s.4(2)). If he chooses to disclose he may plead non-malicious privilege or justification but it remains to be seen how far such an answer may be non-malicious. In fact, however, the Rehabilitation of Offenders Act 1974 (Exceptions) Order SI 1974/1023, as amended, has the effect of excluding from the protection of the Act members, or those who wish to be members, of a very wide range of professions and occupations.

[272] *Silkman v Heard*, February 28, 2001, QBD. It is difficult to regard it as buttressing the right to private life under art.8 because until the rehabilitation period has expired the conviction is in the public domain.

[273] That is to say, a comment on the claimant or his conduct. If the defendant writes a critical piece on the state of the law of libel (which he is perfectly entitled to do without relying on fair comment) he cannot use that to repeat allegations of fact about the claimant, the truth of which he has failed to establish in previous proceedings: *Baldwin v Rusbridger* [2001] E.M.L.R. 47.

i. The requisites of fair comment.

12–32   (a) *Matter commented on must be of public interest.* It is a question for the judge, not the jury, whether the matter is of public interest. No principle for decision is laid down, the books contenting themselves with examples, but the public interest is not confined within narrow limits and covers matters in which the public is legitimately interested as well as matters in which it is legitimately concerned. It ranges from the behaviour of a Prime Minister or of a sanitary authority to the conduct of a flower show and includes the conduct of every public person and every public institution but it is not limited to what is sometimes called "public life". The presentation of a new play or the sudden closure of one enjoying a successful run, the quality of a television programme, the publication of a book, the exhibition of a picture, the conduct of a newspaper, the quality of a product offered to the public, the claim of a company to use a pedestrian way for vehicular traffic, and even criticism publicly made may all be the subject of fair comment.

12–33   (b) *An observation or inference from facts, not an assertion of fact.* The very existence of the defence demonstrates that a comment may be defamatory in law, but the proposition that fair comment is confined to statements of opinion is an oversimplification. The borderline between fact and opinion is difficult to draw, which is why a critic should take pains to keep his facts and the comment on them separate from each other, for if it is not reasonably clear that the matter purports to be comment, he cannot plead fair comment as a defence and is thrown back on justification or privilege.[274] To describe the line, "A Mr. Wilkinson, a clergyman,"[275] as the worst in English poetry is obviously comment, for verification of it as exact is impossible, but some cases are much nearer than that to the borderline between comment and fact. In *Dakhyl v Labouchere*[276] the claimant described himself as, "a specialist for the treatment of deafness, ear, nose, and throat diseases." The defendant described him as a "quack of the rankest species". Was this comment or an allegation of fact? It was held by the House of Lords that it might be comment. Again, calling someone a fornicator or a swindler looks like a statement of fact, but what is calling him immoral or a sinner? Are immorality and sin facts or matters of opinion? To this there is no dogmatic answer. Every statement must be taken on its merits. The very same words may be one or the other according to the context. To say that "A is a disgrace to human nature", is a

---

[274] *Hunt v Star Newspaper Co Ltd* [1908] 2 K.B. 309 at 320; *London Artists Ltd v Littler* [1969] 2 Q.B. 375 at 395.
[275] A parody of Wordsworth in Benson's *Life of Fitzgerald*.
[276] [1908] 2 K.B. 325n.

allegation of fact, but if the words were, "A murdered his father and is therefore a disgrace to human nature", the latter words are clearly a comment on the former.[277] The key point is not the nature of the statement standing alone but whether, in the context in which it is published, it can be seen to be a comment upon facts stated or referred to in it. The underlying reason for this, fair comment being more favourable to the defendant than justification, is that to:

> "[S]tate accurately what a man has done, and then to say that such conduct is dishonourable or disgraceful, is comment which may do no harm, as everyone can judge for himself whether the opinion expressed is well-founded or not. Misdescription of conduct, on the other hand, only leads to the one conclusion detrimental to the person whose conduct is misdescribed, and leaves the reader no opportunity for judging for himself the character of the conduct condemned."[278]

It follows from this that the defence of fair comment, although concerned with "evaluation" may embrace certain inferences or deductions or conclusions of fact drawn from other facts stated or referred to. So in *Branson v Bower*[279] a statement that the claimant's motive for his actions was revenge fell within the scope of fair comment. However, the defence will not apply to statements of fact which are verifiable in the ordinary way, such as that there exist reasonable grounds to suspect the claimant of crime.[280]

It is for the judge to rule whether the words are capable of being regarded as comment and for the jury to decide whether they are.[281]

What is a sufficient reference to the facts upon which the comment purports to be made is something upon which no hard and fast rule can be laid down. Certainly it is not necessary that the commentator should set out verbatim in the alleged libel all the facts

---

[277] *Cooper v Lawson* (1838) 8 A. & E. 746 at 752; *Telnikoff v Matusevitch* [1992] 2 A.C. 343 at 358; *Branson v Bower* [2001] EWCA Civ 791; [2001] E.M.L.R. 32.

[278] *Christie v Robertson* (1889) 19 N.S.W.L.R. 157 at 161.

[279] Above, fn.277.

[280] *Hamilton v Clifford* [2004] EWCA Civ 1407. The distinction is not very satisfactory but the reason behind it has some force. A wide extension of fair comment to inferences of fact from other facts would largely subvert the "repetition rule" (see para.12–27, above) if the charge were carefully framed. The charge in *Hamilton* was that there were reasonable grounds to suspect criminality by the claimants. To justify that one would have to show that the claimants had behaved in a way that gave such grounds. What the defendant was trying to do was to frame a plea of fair comment in terms of: "The claimants are being investigated by the Metropolitan Police [fact]; from this I honestly conclude that there must be reasonable grounds to suspect them of criminality." See also *Galloway v Telegraph Group Ltd* [2004] EWHC 2786 (QB); [2005] E.M.L.R. 7 at [185], affirmed [2006] EWCA Civ 17.

[281] See *British Chiropractic Association v Singh* [2010] EWCA Civ 350 where, however, the trial was to be by judge alone and the CA disagreed with his conclusion that it was fact.

upon which he comments. The question is whether there is a sufficient substratum of facts *indicated* in the words which are the subject matter of the action to show that a comment is being made.[282] The substratum of facts or subject matter may be indicated impliedly in the circumstances of the publication, even by their general notoriety. In *Kemsley v Foot*[283] the defendant had published a newspaper article under the heading "Lower than Kemsley". The article was violently critical of the conduct of a newspaper not owned by the claimant and contained no reference to the claimant other than the heading. The House of Lords held that the defence of fair comment was open to the defendant as in the circumstances the conduct of the Kemsley press in its publications was sufficiently indicated as the fact on which the comment was made, and if the jury found that the comment was such as an honest, though possibly prejudiced, person might make the defence of fair comment would be established. This is a very favourable decision for the defence.[284] However, in determining whether a statement is capable of being comment the court may not voyage beyond what is said expressly or by implication in the defendant's words. In *Telnikoff v Matusevitch*[285] it was held that where a defendant writes a letter to a newspaper refuting an article published in it, then in deciding whether statements in the letter are capable of being construed as fact or comment the court is confined to the letter itself because the readers of the letter may include a substantial number of people who have not read the article. The majority of the court denied that this meant that the whole of the material being commented on would have to be repeated in the letter containing the comment (a situation obviously unacceptable to any newspaper editor) as long as some form of words was used which made it plain that the letter was comment and nothing else; but this seems to put an unrealistic burden upon persons who comment (sometimes, with little time for reflection) upon matters of public interest. Furthermore, although the jury is confined to the letter to determine what is comment and what is fact, it will inevitably have to refer to the material on which the matter is based in order to determine whether that comment is "fair".

---

[282] *Lowe v Associated Newspapers Ltd* [2006] EWHC 320 (QB); [2007] Q.B. 580. The commonly stated proposition that the comment must be "on facts truly stated" does not mean that the facts must be stated but that if the facts are stated and are not true the defence is unavailable: at [46].

[283] [1952] A.C. 345..

[284] Compare Lord Nicholls in the Hong Kong Court of Final Appeal in *Cheng v Tse Wai Chun* [2000] 3 H.K.L.R.D. 418 at 425: "The reader or hearer should be in a position to judge for himself how far the comment was well founded." However, in the light of *Kemsley v Foot* this should not be taken as meaning that readers must have before them all the facts on which the comment is based, nor that the defendant is precluded from relying on others: *Lowe v Associated Newspapers Ltd* [2006] EWHC 320 (QB); [2007] Q.B. 580.

[285] [1992] 2 A.C. 343, with a vigorous dissent from Lord Ackner.

For comment to be fair it must first of all be based upon true facts **12–34** in existence when the comment was made.[286] You cannot invent untrue facts about a person and then comment upon them.[287] They must also have been known to the commentator, at least in a general way, when the comment was made.[288] To the proposition that the facts commented on must be true there is, however, one necessary exception, namely, that fair comment may be based upon an untrue statement which is made by some person upon a privileged occasion, e.g. a statement made by a witness in the course of judicial proceedings, and properly attributed to him in a fair and accurate report of those proceedings. Moreover if the comment is upon the statement of another person, even if the statement was not made on a privileged occasion, the statement need not always be proved to be true, for in some cases such proof is impossible. If C publishes a statement that there are men on the planet Mars and D criticises this allegation as unfounded, D's criticism may well be fair comment, for it is based on fact in the sense that it refers to an assertion actually made by C. D is not bound to prove that there are men on Mars—in fact it is the very thing that he denies. Suppose, however, that A's statement were false and defamatory of C, then if D repeats it with some comment of his own, and C sues D for defamation, D cannot successfully plead fair comment unless his comment is a repudiation of the lie; for any other kind of comment of his would be an acceptance of a lie put in circulation by A: i.e. comment based upon what is untrue.

A number of points should be noticed about the relationship between fair comment and justification. First, justification is as much applicable to a comment as to a statement of fact, though in order to succeed on this basis the defendant must of course satisfy the jury that the comment represents the correct view of the matter, a more severe hurdle than showing that the comment is such as an honest person might make.[289] Of course, justification may have to be relied on if for some reason fair comment is not available, for example if the subject of the comment is not a matter of public interest. Secondly, if the facts upon which the comment is made are set out in the article complained of, they may themselves be defamatory and if they are sued on they must be justified[290] (unless they are the subject of privilege): fair comment is not a defence to assertions

---

[286] *Cohen v Daily Telegraph Ltd* [1968] 1 W.L.R. 916.
[287] *Joynt v Cycle Trade Publishing Co* [1904] 2 K.B. 292 at 294; *Hunt v Star Newspaper Co Ltd* [1908] 2 K.B. 309 at 317, 320; *Silkin v Beaverbrook Newspapers Ltd* [1958] 1 W.L.R. 743 at 746; *London Artists Ltd v Littler* [1969] 2 Q.B. 375; *Thornton v Telegraph* [2009] EWHC 2863 (QB).
[288] *Lowe v Associated Newspapers Ltd*, above, fn.284 (see the summary at [74]).
[289] See *Broadway Approvals Ltd v Odhams Press Ltd (No.2)* [1965] 1 W.L.R. 805 at 817–818.
[290] [1965] 1 W.L.R. 805; *Truth (NZ) Ltd v Avery* [1959] N.Z.L.R. 274.

of fact, except in the form of certain inferences. Thirdly, even if there is no claim in respect of the facts adverted to in the article, the position at common law was that each fact stated must be shown to be true to enable the defence of fair comment to succeed. However, this was modified by s.6 of the Defamation Act 1952 so that now the defence of fair comment does not fail by reason only that the truth of every allegation of fact contained in the libel is not proved. It is enough:

"[I]f the expression of opinion is fair comment having regard to such of the facts alleged or referred to in the words complained of as are proved."

Where the facts commented on are merely indicated in the article, the details of the facts will be given in particulars in support of the defendant's plea.

"Twenty facts might be given in the particulars and only one justified, yet if that one fact were sufficient to support the comment so as to make it fair, a failure to prove the other nineteen would not of necessity defeat the defendant's claim."[291]

12–35   (c) *Fair comment and malice.* Finally, the comment must be fair. The adjective is potentially misleading,[292] for it is clear that for comment to be fair it is not necessary that the jury should accept it as correct and therefore the test is not what the ordinary reasonable man would think about the subject matter of the comment. Beyond this, however, the matter becomes more complicated and it is necessary to pay careful attention to the nature of the burden of proof on the different aspects of fair comment.

First, there is the so-called objective question of whether the statement falls within the bounds of what the law regards as fair comment. There have been numerous attempts to formulate a test for this, but the best is probably that of Lord Esher M.R. in *Merivale v Carson*[293] as modified by Lord Porter in *Turner v Metro-Goldwyn-Mayer*[294]: "would any honest[295] man, however prejudiced he might be, or however exaggerated or obstinate his views, have written this criticism?" At this stage it is not necessary to inquire whether the defendant actually held the view put forward, what counts is whether an honest person might hold that view. Mere violence in

[291] *Kemsley v Foot* [1952] A.C. 345 at 358.
[292] Or even "meaningless": Lord Nicholls in *Reynolds v Times Newspapers Ltd* [2001] 2 A.C. 127 at 193.
[293] (1887) 20 Q.B.D. 275 at 281.
[294] [1950] 1 All E.R. 449 at 461.
[295] Lord Esher had said "fair". Lord Porter would substitute "honest" "lest some suggestion of reasonableness . . . should be read in."

criticism does not make it unfair. So, in the case of literary criticism, views which are extravagant and the outcome of prejudice on the part of the writer are not beyond the bounds of fair comment and in *McQuire v Western Morning News Co Ltd*,[296] where a critique of a play indicated that it was dull, vulgar and degrading, the Court of Appeal, in giving judgment for the defendants, said that the case ought not even to have been left to the jury.[297] Nor need comment on a literary production be confined to criticism of it as literature—it can be criticised for its social effect as freely as it can for bad writing.[298]

"The basis of our public life is that the crank, the enthusiast, may say what he honestly thinks as much as the reasonable man or woman who sits on a jury."[299]

It has sometimes been said that a rather stricter rule applies where the claimant is charged with base, dishonourable or wicked motives. For example, in *Hunt v Star Newspaper*,[300] Cozens-Hardy M.R. said that in such a case the true question was whether, "the comment made . . . upon [the] facts was fair and such as *might*, in the opinion of the jury, be *reasonably made*"; and in *Campbell v Spottiswoode*[301] Cockburn C.J. referred to the danger to public affairs if the law, "were to sanction attacks [upon persons taking part in] them, destructive of their honour and character, and made without any foundation".

It is submitted that, whatever may have been the position a century ago, modern experience of the conduct of public figures, both at home and abroad, amply demonstrates that any special protection in respect of charges of base or dishonourable motives is not justified.[302] There are two recent judicial statements against any special rule in these cases[303] and that now probably represents the position.

If the statement is comment in this objective sense the defence **12–36** will succeed unless the claimant is able to show that it was actuated

[296] [1903] 2 K.B. 100.
[297] Unfortunately, the more competent a juror to judge the matter criticised, the harder it will be for him to observe the rule that he should not substitute his views for those of the critic.
[298] *Kemsley v Foot* [1952] A.C. 345 at 356.
[299] *Silkin v Beaverbrook Newspapers Ltd* [1958] 1 W.L.R. 743 at 747.
[300] [1908] 2 K.B. 304 at 317; see also at 320; *Dakhyl v Labouchere* [1908] 2 K.B. 325n at 329n.
[301] (1863) 3 B. & S. 679.
[302] The Faulks Committee recommended that there should be no special rule for case of this type.
[303] Sir Anthony Mason in the Hong Kong Final Court of Appeal in *Eastern Express Publisher Ltd v Mo* [1999] 3 H.K.L.R. D. 530 at 543 and Eady J. in *Branson v Bower* [2001] E.M.L.R. 33.

by malice on the part of the defendant. Now the burden of proof is clearly on the claimant. The judge must not allow the case to go to the jury unless he is satisfied that there is evidence to support a finding that the defendant was malicious, that is to say that there is evidence which is more consistent with the presence of malice than with its absence.[304] In the context of qualified privilege malice means some improper motive for the making of the statement, often established by proof that the defendant did not believe in its truth.[305] Though malice was for long thought to be the same in fair comment, the law now is that the defendant who pleads fair comment is only guilty of malice if he has no belief in what he says. If he has such a belief there is no malice even if he is pursuing his own private agenda or ambitions.[306] While proof that the defendant does not hold the opinion expressed will normally be decisive on malice, that will not, however, be so when the defendant legitimately publishes the opinions of another person which satisfy the "objective" element of the defence. Thus the claimant cannot deprive a newspaper of the defence in respect of a letter published in it by showing that the newspaper's publisher or editor holds diametrically opposed views, nor by showing that the writer of the letter was actuated by malice.[307] Malice is a personal matter which is independent of the issue of whether there is something which satisfies the objective stage of fair comment. No doubt the position would be different if the newspaper was aware of the writer's state of mind, but it does not incur liability by failing to verify the name and address of a correspondent.[308] Where the newspaper is vicariously liable for the acts of the person who wrote the material then, of course, malice on his part would be attributed to the newspaper.[309]

The whole terminology of fair comment is confusing and it must be very difficult to explain it to a jury. It has been suggested that to

---

[304] *Somerville v Hawkins* (1851) 10 C.B. 583; *Turner v MGM* [1950] 1 All E.R. 449 at 455; *Telnikoff v Matusevitch* [1991] 1 Q.B. 102 where (a) the defendant believed passionately in the evil of anti-Semitism and (b) he and the claimant were total strangers, so that no reasonable jury could have held that his dominant motive was to injure the claimant (on appeal, [1992] 2 A.C. 343).

[305] Below, para.12–63.

[306] *Cheng v Tse Wai Chun* [2000] 3 H.K.L.R.D. 418. Although this is a decision of the Hong Kong Final Court of Appeal, the leading judgment is given by Lord Nicholls and it was quickly accepted as stating English law: *Sugar v Associated Newspapers Ltd*, February 6, 2001, QBD; *Branson v Bower* [2001] E.M.L.R. 33.

[307] In *Egger v Viscount Chelmsford* [1965] 1 Q.B. 248 (see below, para.12–65) it was held with regard to qualified privilege that one co-publisher was not "infected" with the malice of another. The view of Davies L.J. that this might not be so with regard to fair comment was, it is submitted, based upon a view of the nature of that defence which cannot stand after *Telnikoff v Matusevitch*.

[308] *Lyon v Daily Telegraph* [1943] K.B. 746.

[309] *Gros v Cook* (1969) 113 Sol. Jo. 408.

rename the defence "honest comment" or "honest opinion"[310] risks losing sight of the first, objective stage[311] but it might be enough if at this stage we simply asked, "Are these words capable of being comment on the facts stated, as opposed to mere abuse or invective"?

ii. Pleading. By analogy with the stance taken on pleading justifi-   **12–37** cation,[312] the defendant should spell out his defence of fair comment with sufficient precision to enable the claimant to know what statements are said to attract the defence.[313] The usual form of pleading is that, "the said words are fair comment on a matter of public interest, namely . . . ", followed by particulars of the facts on which the comment is based. The alternative, the so-called rolled-up plea, often used where the facts relied on were set out in the article, has fallen out of use. This ran:

> "[I]n so far as the words complained of consist of statements of fact, they are true in substance and in fact; and in so far as they consist of expressions of opinion they are fair comment made in good faith and without malice on those acts, which are matters of public interest."

Despite its appearance this was not a combined plea of fair comment and justification,[314] but of fair comment only, so that if any defamatory portion of the article is found to be a statement of fact, it does not protect the defendant. The plea fell out of use when it ceased to be possible in this way to avoid giving particulars.

C. Privilege
In addition to the cases covered by the defence of fair comment   **12–38** the law recognises that there are other occasions on which freedom of communication without fear of an action for defamation is more important than the protection of a person's reputation. Such occasions are said to be "privileged", and the privilege may be either absolute or qualified. The term privilege is apt to be misleading. For the moment it prevails, but in the longer term it might be replaced by "immunity". Absolute privilege covers cases in which complete freedom of communication is regarded as of such paramount importance that actions for defamation cannot be entertained at all: a

---

[310] The Irish Defamation Act 2009 s.20, renames it "honest opinion", but under that it is for the defendant to show that it was his opinion.
[311] Lloyd L.J. in *Telnikoff v Matusevitch* in the CA (above, fn.304).
[312] Above, para.12–28.
[313] *Control Risks Ltd v New English Library Ltd* [1990] 1 W.L.R. 183.
[314] *Sutherland v Stopes* [1925] A.C. 47.

person defamed on an occasion of absolute privilege has no legal redress via the law of defamation, however outrageous the untrue statement which has been made about him and however malicious the motive of the maker of it. Qualified privilege, on the other hand, though it also protects the maker of an untrue defamatory statement, does so only if the maker of the statement acted honestly and without malice. If the claimant can prove malice the privilege is displaced and he may recover damages, but it is for him to prove malice, once the privilege has been made out, not for the defendant to disprove it. It is for the jury to decide whether malice has been proved, but it is for the judge to rule whether or not the occasion is a privileged one.[315]

i. Absolute privilege.

12–39 (a) *Statements in Parliament.* The Bill of Rights 1688 provides that:

> "[T]he freedom of speech and debates or proceedings in Parliament ought not to be impeached or questioned in any court or place out of Parliament."[316]

This confers absolute privilege on statements made in the chamber of either House of Parliament,[317] but the underlying purpose of the Bill of Rights is the wider one of preventing the courts inquiring into the propriety of the conduct of Parliamentary business.[318] Thus while it is clear that if an MP repeats outside the House what he said

---

[315] *Adam v Ward* [1917] A.C. 309.

[316] The Bill of Rights was declared law by 2 W. & M., c.1 (1689). For an unsuccessful challenge under the European Convention on Human Rights see *A v UK* (2003) E.H.R.R. 51. The legislation creating the Scottish Parliament and the Northern Irish and Welsh Assemblies also contains provisions conferring absolute privilege.

[317] What is a "proceeding in Parliament" is not wholly clear. See for example *Parliamentary Privilege Act 1770, Re* [1958] A.C. 331, on a letter written by an MP to a Minister. Section 13(5) of the Defamation Act 1996 makes it clear that the privilege extends to, inter alia, giving evidence before either House or a committee and the presentation or submission of a document to either House or a committee. See also *Hamilton v Al Fayed* [2001] A.C. 395 (proceedings before the Parliamentary Commissioner for Standards); *Erglis v Buckley* [2005] QSC 25; *Adams v Guardian Newspapers Ltd* [2003] ScotCS 131; 2003 S.L.T. 1058; *Stewart v Ronalds* [2009] NSWCA 277.

[318] There may be no objection to proof of what was done in the House as a mere matter of history. *Rost v Edwards* [1990] 2 Q.B. 460 (Member not allowed to call evidence of fact as to his membership of a standing committee) was doubted in *Prebble v Television New Zealand* [1995] 1 A.C. 321. See also *Hyams v Peterson* [1991] 3 N.Z.L.R. 648 (reference to Parliamentary proceedings to show that words refer to claimant) and *Pepper v Hart* [1993] A.C. 593 (use of Parliamentary proceedings as an aid to interpret legislation). For a full review see *Office of Government Commerce v Information Commr* [2008] EWHC 774 (Admin); [2009] 3 W.L.R. 627.

inside it, the second statement is not protected by privilege,[319] it has been held that the claimant may not use statements in Parliament as evidence of malice in respect of statements made outside it.[320] The Bill of Rights may, indeed, have the effect of blocking a libel action *by* a Member, for if a significant element of the defence put forward in such a case turns on what happened in Parliament the inability of the court to inquire into that means that the only just course is to stay the Member's action.[321] However, by s.13 of the Defamation Act 1996 a Member may in such a case waive the privilege for the purposes of the proceedings.[322]

(b) *Reports, papers, votes and proceedings ordered to be pub-* **12–40** *lished by either House of Parliament.* These are the subject of absolute privilege under s.1 of the Parliamentary Papers Act 1840.[323] Command papers do not enjoy absolute privilege.[324] Extracts from or abstracts of Parliamentary papers and reports of Parliamentary proceedings (e.g. in the press) enjoy qualified privilege.[325]

(c) *Judicial proceedings.* Whatever is stated, whether orally or in **12–41** documentary form, in judicial proceedings[326] is absolutely privileged. It does not matter how false or malicious the statement may be, and it does not matter who makes it—the judge,[327] the jury, the parties, the advocates,[328] or the witnesses.[329] The protection is probably limited by some minimal requirement of relevance to the proceedings in hand. So if, for example, in response to counsel's question, "Were you at York on 1st April last year?" the witness

---

[319] Even if he repeats it by reference rather than *in extenso*: *Buchanan v Jennings* [2004] UKPC 36; [2005] 1 A.C. 115. The propriety of the member's behaviour as a Parliamentarian will not be in issue. Nor will his state of mind, motive or intention when saying what he did in Parliament.

[320] *Church of Scientology v Johnson-Smith* [1972] 1 Q.B. 522.

[321] *Prebble v Television New Zealand* [1995] 1 A.C. 321.

[322] *Hamilton v Al Fayed* [2001] A.C. 395. This does not affect his immunity in respect of what was said in the House: s.13(4).

[323] Passed as a result of *Stockdale v Hansard* (1839) 9 A. & E. 1.

[324] The Faulks Committee rejected a proposal by the Law Officers to bring them within the 1840 Act: Cmnd. 5909, para.225.

[325] Below, para.12–58.

[326] The judgment and the reasons for it are part of the proceedings, so neither the judge nor court officials who disseminate the judgment need rely on the reporting privilege (para.12–44, below): *Rogers v Nationwide News Pty Ltd* [2003] HCA 52; 216 C.L.R. 327.

[327] *Glick v Hinchcliffe* (1967) 111 S.J. 927 is a modern example. The privilege appears to be broader than the general immunity of judges for acts done in the execution of their office (below, para.24–8) in that no distinction is drawn between the various steps in the judicial hierarchy.

[328] *Munster v Lamb* (1883) 11 Q.B.D. 588 at 603–604. This is unaffected by the removal of the immunity from suit for negligence enjoyed by advocates in relation to the conduct of a case in court: above, para.5–60.

[329] *Seaman v Netherclift* (1876) 2 C.P.D. 53; *Kennedy v Hilliard* (1859) 10 Irish Common Law Reports 195.

replied, "Yes, and A.B. [who has nothing at all to do with the case] picked my pocket there" that would not be privileged.[330] However, the privilege is to be given the widest application and extends to anything a witness might naturally and reasonably say when giving evidence with reference to the subject matter of the proceedings; it is certainly not limited by technical legal considerations of relevance.[331]

Judicial privilege, in the wide sense explained above, applies not only to an ordinary law court but also whenever there is an authorised inquiry which, though not before a court of justice, is before a tribunal which has similar attributes,[332] e.g. an employment tribunal,[333] a military court of inquiry[334] or the Disciplinary Committee of the Law Society,[335] but an industrial conciliation procedure,[336] a social security adjudication,[337] and an investigation by the Commission of the EU into breaches of the competition provisions of the Treaty[338] have been held not to possess these attributes. In any case it is essential that the tribunal be one "recognized by law"; only qualified privilege applies to things said before a domestic tribunal established by contract.[339]

The absolute privilege is not confined to what is said in the presence of the court or tribunal for otherwise it would be impossible to prepare a case. In *Watson v McEwan* where privilege was held to apply to what was said by a witness to a solicitor taking a proof of his evidence, Lord Halsbury said that:

"[I]f the law were otherwise ... the object for which the privilege exists is gone, because then no witness could be called;

---

[330] *Seaman v Netherclift* (1876) 2 C.P.D. at 56.

[331] (1876) 2 C.P.D. at 60 per Bramwell J.A.; *Samuels v Coole & Haddock*, Unreported, May 22, 1997, CA. An attempt by a witness to introduce a "spent conviction" within the Rehabilitation of Offenders Act 1974 (above, para.12–30) would be privileged, but a report of such an attempt might not be.

[332] Lord Esher M.R. in *Royal Aquarium Society Ltd v Parkinson* [1892] 1 Q.B. 431 at 442. For a modern statement of the law see *Trapp v Mackie* [1979] 1 W.L.R. 377, HL (Sc.). For a modern, statutory example see the Inquiries Act 2005. The Upper Tribunal under the Tribunals, Courts and Enforcement Act 2007 has the same "powers, rights, privileges and authority" as the High Court or Court of Session.

[333] *Wilson v Westney* [2001] EWCA Civ 839.

[334] *Dawkins v Lord Rokeby* (1873) L.R. 8 Q.B. 255, affirmed (1875) L.R. 7 H.L. 744. *Heath v MPC* [2004] EWCA Civ 943 (police disciplinary tribunal).

[335] *Addis v Crocker* [1961] 1 Q.B. 11. That the Committee sits in private makes no difference provided that its functions are similar to those of a court of justice. *Marrinan v Vibart* [1963] 1 Q.B. 234, affirmed [1963] 1 Q.B. 528 (barrister). Compare an organisation or company's internal disciplinary committee: *Gregory v Portsmouth CC* [2000] 1 A.C. 419.

[336] *Tadd v Eastwood* [1985] I.C.R. 132.

[337] *Purdew v Serres-Smith, The Times*, September 9,1992.

[338] *Hasselblad (GB) Ltd Orbinson* [1985] Q.B. 475; but on another aspect of this case, see below.

[339] *Trapp v Mackie* [1979] 1 W.L.R. 377 at 379. See also *Gregory v Portsmouth CC* [2000] 1 A.C. 41 (committee to exercise disciplinary powers over councillors).

no one would know whether what he was going to say was relevant to the question in debate between the parties. A witness would only have to say: 'I shall not tell you anything; I may have an action brought against me tomorrow if I do; therefore I shall not give you any information at all'."[340]

However, this "witness immunity" now goes considerably further than the proof of evidence of a person who is then an intended witness. In *Evans v London Hospital Medical College*[341] Drake J. said that the absolute privilege covered any:

"[S]tatement or conduct [which] is such that it can fairly be said to be part of the process of investigating a crime or a possible crime with a view to a prosecution or a possible prosecution in respect of the matter being investigated"

and this was approved by the House of Lords in *Taylor v Director of the Serious Fraud Office.*[342] Where people answer police questions it may be unclear whether they will be called to give evidence or whether any crime has been committed at all, but it is necessary, in order to ensure that they speak freely, that they should know where they stand when they answer. Similarly, it is necessary for the investigating officers to share information among themselves. This immunity from suit is not confined to defamation—it would extend, for example, to malicious falsehood—but it does not extend to malicious prosecution,[343] nor does it apply to a claim (for example for conspiracy to injure or misfeasance in a public office) involving the fabrication of a case or the "planting" of evidence[344] and it is unlikely that a case will be struck out where such allegations are made.[345] Witness immunity extends beyond criminal proceedings to inquiries made in connection with potential proceedings before any tribunal the proceedings of which are protected by absolute privilege.[346] Traditionally, a mere complaint[347] or the voluntary giving of information[348] attracted only qualified privilege for they were not regarded as a, "step in judicial or quasi-judicial proceedings". Now,

---

[340] [1905] A.C. 480 at 487; *Beresford v White* (1914) 30 T.L.R. 591.

[341] [1981] 1 W.L.R. 184.

[342] [1999] 2 A.C. 177.

[343] *Darker v CC West Midlands* [2001] 1 A.C. 435.

[344] *Darker*, above, fn.343.

[345] *L v Reading BC* [2001] 1 W.L.R. 1575.

[346] *Mahon v Rahn (No.2)* [2000] 4 All E.R. 41; but compare *Daniels v Griffiths* [1998] E.M.L.R. 488 (Parole Board); *S v Newham London Borough Council* [1998] E.M.L.R. 583 (statement to body maintaining child protection index). The latter case suggests a rather open-textured approach.

[347] See *Lincoln v Daniels* [1962] 1 Q.B. 237, especially the judgment of Devlin L.J.

[348] *Shufflebottom v Allday* (1857) 28 L.T. O.S. 292; *Hasselblad (GB) Ltd Orbinson* [1985] Q.B. 475; *Mann v O'Neill* (1997) 145 A.L.R. 682.

however, the absolute privilege of witnesses has been extended to
those who make a complaint to the police.[349] This is a regrettable
development. Of course the old law presented difficulties in drawing
the line between cases which fell within and outwith the witness
privilege and it could be said that the possibility of being sued might
deter honest complaints by persons in need of protection, but the
burden of proving malice to defeat qualified privilege is a heavy
one. A person's life may be ruined by a false accusation of crime but
now any claim against the complainant will be automatically struck
out. Perhaps not all whose good name has been maliciously traduced
would agree that they should be satisfied with the fact that the CPS
has decided not to prosecute them. If a prosecution does take place
and there is an acquittal it is possible in theory to sue the complainant for malicious prosecution but there may be great difficulty in
showing that he is a "prosecutor" for this purpose.[350]

12–42   Communications between solicitor and client in connection with
litigation which is on foot will be protected by privilege. An entirely
separate principle (which is not directly connected with the law of
defamation and which is referred to below[351]) entitles the client to
prevent disclosure of communications between him and his solicitor
on any professional matter. However, the Court of Appeal in *More
v Weaver*[352] was of the view that any professional communication
between solicitor and client was protected by absolute privilege in
the defamation sense, though the House of Lords in *Minter v
Priest*[353] found it unnecessary to decide the issue and preferred to
leave the matter open. On principle there seems to be no strong
reason for treating the privilege as absolute. It ought only to be in
the most exceptional cases that, in the interests of the public,
privilege should be ranked as absolute, and a solicitor and his client
in non-contentious matters would seem to be adequately protected if
they are conceded qualified privilege in their transactions with each
other.[354]

12–43   (d) *Communications between certain officers of State.*[355] In *Chatterton v Secretary of State for India*[356] the Court of Appeal held that

[349] *Westcott v Westcott* [2008] EWCA Civ 818; [2009] QB 407.
[350] See para.19–3, below.
[351] Below, para.12–43.
[352] [1928] 2 K.B. 520.
[353] [1930] A.C. 558. The case illustrates the scope of the professional relationship. Conversations relating to the business of obtaining a loan for the deposit to be paid on the purchase
of land fell under the professional work of a solicitor, but not conversations about
speculation in land to enable the solicitor to share in the profits.
[354] This is the view expressed in *Waple v Surrey CC* [1998] 1 W.L.R. 860.
[355] Various statutes make particular types of communication subject to absolute privilege, e.g.
the Parliamentary Commissioner Act 1967. See Gatley, *Libel and Slander*, 11th edn,
§13.49.
[356] [1895] 2 Q.B. 189.

an action for libel based on a letter from the defendant to the Under-Secretary of State concerning the claimant's removal to the list of half pay officers was rightly dismissed, on the ground that to allow any judicial inquiry into such matters would tend to deprive officers of State of their freedom of action, "in matters concerning the public weal". The decision in *Isaacs & Sons Ltd v Cook*[357] shows that the fact that a report relates to commercial matters does not preclude it falling within this principle.[358] The extent of this head of absolute privilege is, however, somewhat uncertain, though there is certainly no blanket immunity for communications between civil servants. One High Court judge has suggested that it does not extend to officials below the rank of Minister,[359] and in *Merricks v Nott-Bower*[360] the Court of Appeal refused to strike out a claim for libel based on a report on two police officers written by a Deputy Commissioner of the Metropolitan Police to the Commissioner. The position is equally uncertain in relation to military affairs. In *Dawkins v Lord Paulet*[361] a majority of the Queen's Bench held that a report on a lieutenant-colonel made by a major-general to the adjutant-general of the Army was covered by absolute privilege, but Cockburn C.J. delivered a strong dissenting judgment and in *Dawkins v Lord Rokeby*[362] the Exchequer Chamber regarded the matter as open for consideration by the House of Lords.

The argument generally advanced for absolute rather than qualified privilege is to the effect that a person will perform his duties better by being released from the fear of being sued than by being given an easily substantiated defence if he is sued, but this is as true of public services and private concerns as it is of the State. Absolute privilege should be reserved for those cases alone in which complete freedom of communication is so important that it is right to deprive the citizen of his remedy for all defamatory statements made about him including even those made maliciously. No one could claim that this is true of all communications between all servants of the Crown. It is submitted, therefore, that the caution of the Court of Appeal in *Merricks v Nott-Bower* was fully justified and that care should be taken not to extend absolute privilege further than can be shown to be really necessary. It is no less in the interest of the State that justice should be done to the citizen than that the machinery of government should be able to work without fear of legal action.

---

[357] [1925] 2 K.B. 391.
[358] For a comparable principle, based on the comity of nations, whereby a foreign embassy document is subject to absolute privilege, see *Fayed v Al-Tajir* [1988] Q.B. 712.
[359] Henn-Collins J. in *Szalatnay-Stacho v Fink* [1946] 1 All E.R. 303. The CA made no reference to this point: [1947] K.B. 1.
[360] [1965] 1 Q.B. 57; *Richards v Naum* [1967] 1 Q.B. 620.
[361] (1869) L.R. 5 Q.B. 94.
[362] (1873) L.R. 8 Q.B. 255. On appeal the decision was on the basis of witness immunity: (1875) L.R. 7 HL 744.

Distinct from absolute privilege in the law of defamation is evidential privilege. For example, a solicitor cannot be compelled to answer questions about what passed between him and his client seeking legal advice, and is not entitled to do so unless the client consents, whether or not litigation was intended when the advice was given[363]: the confidentiality of the relationship outweighs the interests of justice in ensuring the availability of all relevant evidence.[364] Again, disclosure of documents relevant to an action will be refused where to order the production would be against the public interest.[365] Evidentiary privilege has no direct connection with the law of defamation, though its application may hinder the claimant who brings proceedings for that (or any other) tort by depriving him of vital evidence.[366] However, the concept of "public interest" has been used to bar an action for defamation even though the case did not concern evidential privilege and did not fall within the established heads of absolute privilege. In *Hasselblad (GB) Ltd v Orbinson*[367] the action was founded upon a letter of complaint written by the defendant to X about the claimants' servicing policies and this was disclosed to the claimants during an investigation into the trading practices of the claimants by the Commission of the European Communities. The Court of Appeal held that the Commission's activities were more in the nature of administrative than judicial proceedings and that the absolute privilege attaching to the judicial process did not therefore apply. However, the majority of the court went on to hold that the action failed for the independent reason that there was a public interest in ensuring that the Commission should not be hindered carrying out its duties of enforcing fair competition under the EC Treaty and if complaints to the Commission could be subjected to the law of defamation the supply of information would soon dry up. This was a surprising decision because it was then[368] well established in English law that an informer or complainant outside the context of judicial proceedings enjoyed only qualified privilege,[369] but the court was influenced by the fact that the Commission was required to disclose to the claimants the written evidence upon which it relied.

---

[363] See, e.g. *Sarah Getty Trust, Re* [1985] Q.B. 956.

[364] On the privilege see generally *Three Rivers DC v Bank of England (No.6)* [2004] UKHL 48; [2005] 1 A.C. 610. It is restricted in certain contexts by statute (though not in relation to litigation advice): *Bowman v Fells* [2005] EWCA Civ 226; [2005] 1 W.L.R. 3083.

[365] See, e.g. *R. v CC West Midlands, Ex p. Wiley* [1995] 1 A.C. 274.

[366] As in *Minter v Priest* [1930] A.C. 558. And see the remarks of Mustill L.J. in *Fayed v Al-Tajir* [1988] Q.B. 712.

[367] [1985] Q.B. 475.

[368] But see above as to the present law.

[369] See above, para.12–41. However, Otton L.J. in *Mahon v Rahn* [1998] Q.B. 424 seems to regard the *Hasselblad* case as an example of "witness immunity".

(e) *Reports of UK (and certain other) court proceedings.* By s.14 **12–44**
of the Defamation Act 1996 absolute privilege is accorded to fair
and accurate contemporaneous reports of court[370] proceedings in
public in the UK or of certain supranational tribunals.[371] This
replaces a very similar provision in the Law of Libel Amendment
Act 1888,[372] which was confined to the news media. There is no
such restriction in the 1996 Act but in practice the requirement of
contemporaneity is likely to restrict it to them.[373] "Contemporaneous" probably means at the first reasonable opportunity after the
event (which will vary with the frequency of the journal or broadcast
involved)[374] but if publication is restricted by law[375] time will not
begin to run until that restriction is removed. Though there is no
case law on the meaning of "fair and accurate" under the 1996 Act,
that concept was equally applicable to the privilege under the Act of
1888, and to the common law qualified privilege for reports of
proceedings, and the case law on those will therefore continue to be
relevant. It is not necessary that the report should be verbatim,[376] nor
that it should await the outcome of a trial lasting several days[377] and
a report in the press cannot be judged by the standards of a law
report.[378] Nonetheless, it should be impartial and should not give the
evidence for one side and suppress that of the other.[379] The basis of
the privilege is that the reporter is merely the eyes and ears of the

[370] This, "includes any tribunal or body exercising the judicial power of the state":
s.14(3).
[371] The ECJ or any court attached to it, the European Court of Human Rights and certain
international criminal tribunals: s.14(3)
[372] Regarded as creating an absolute privilege in *McCarey v Associated Newspapers Ltd*
[1964] 1 W.L.R. 855.
[373] It might be regarded as making little sense that a law report in *The Times* the next day was
absolutely privileged but a fuller version in the Weekly Law Reports two months later was
not. However, the original legislation was probably aimed at newspaper reports of things
like crime and divorce cases which involved evidence rather than law. There are both
common law and statutory privileges for non-contemporaneous reports (below,
para.12–57) and it does not seem likely that malice could be established. It is true that
under the statutory qualified privilege the defendant must show that the report was, "of
public concern and for the public benefit" but as far as English proceedings are concerned,
"citizens in this jurisdiction are entitled to know what goes on in public hearings before
any of Her Majesty's courts": *Crossley v Newsquest (Midlands South) Ltd* [2008] EWHC
3054 (QB) at [26].
[374] It is thought that for this purpose "publication" should be treated as the initial issue of the
material. It would be very strange if a report on LAWTEL were absolutely privileged on
the day it was placed on the database but not when it was accessed six months later; but
material from previous hearings will be similarly protected in so far as it is necessary to
explain the case reported: *Crossley v Newsquest (Midlands South) Ltd*, above, fn.373.
[375] See, e.g. Contempt of Court Act 1981 s.4.
[376] *McDougall v Knight* (1886) 17 Q.B.D. 636 at 642.
[377] *Kimber v Press Association Ltd* [1893] 1 Q.B. 65 at 71.
[378] *Hope v Leng Ltd* (1907) 23 T.L.R. 243. On a report containing comment see *Curistan v
Times Newspapers Ltd* [2008] EWCA Civ 432; [2009] Q.B. 231 (a case of qualified
privilege under s.15 of the Defamation Act 1996, but the concept of a "fair and accurate
report" must have common features across the law of privilege).
[379] *Wright v Outram* (1890) 17 R. 596.

public, who have the right to attend and therefore it is said that it is confined to what passes in open court,[380] and does not extend to the publication of the contents of documents such as pleadings and affidavits, which are not brought up in court.[381] However, this may need reconsideration in view of changes in the way litigation is conducted and the provision in rules of court for public access to documents.[382]

12–45   **ii. Qualified privilege.** Until the 1990s the law in this section would have been comparatively simple to explain in outline, though its application in practice would frequently have raised difficult questions of degree. One might have said that there were three basic propositions about the common law. First, where the defendant showed that the statement was made on an occasion of qualified privilege he had a defence unless the claimant could prove that he was guilty of malice: the question was whether the defendant had acted honestly, not whether he had acted responsibly or carefully. Secondly, there were a number of situations where generally published reports were subject to qualified privilege, for example reports of court proceedings or proceedings in Parliament. Some of these were duplicated by statutory provisions. Thirdly, the law accorded qualified privilege to communications between persons who had a common interest or between whom there was a reciprocal duty and interest. This category concerned essentially private communications: there was, except in very exceptional circumstances, no community of interest between a newspaper and its readers, nor did the former have any duty to inform the latter.

Two developments have now rendered this a very incomplete picture. The decision of the House of Lords in *Reynolds v Times Newspapers Ltd*[383] created a category of qualified privilege for the general communication of matters of public concern. It is not confined to the news media but they will in almost all cases be the persons relying on it. Despite sharing the same name (perhaps for want of anything better) this is a completely different animal from traditional privilege for the defendant must show that he acted in conformity with the standards of "responsible journalism". Common law malice is therefore irrelevant, "because "the propriety of the conduct of the defendant is built into the conditions under which the material is privileged".[384]

---

[380] On irrelevant matters such as interruptions see *Hope v Leng Ltd*, above, fn.378, and *Farmer v Hyde* [1937] 1 K.B. 728.
[381] This was common ground in *Stern v Piper* [1997] Q.B. 123.
[382] See para.12–27, above.
[383] [2001] 2 A.C. 127. Para.12–53, below.
[384] *Jameel (Mohamed) v Wall Street Journal Europe Sprl* [2006] UKHL; [2007] 1 A.C. 359 at [46] per Lord Hoffmann.

"*Reynolds* privilege" is a common law doctrine but its creation was largely triggered by the guarantee of freedom of expression in art.10 of the European Convention on Human Rights. However, art.8 is now regarded as protecting reputation as well as privacy and the touchstone of the Convention is proportionality rather than fixed categories defeated only by malice. It is therefore possible, at least where the defendant is a public authority and subject to the Human Rights Act 1998, that there could be a case in which there was an infringement of art.8 even though there was no malice to found a claim of libel at common law (though infringement of the Convention right does not lead to the award of damages unless it is necessary to give just satisfaction).[385] Further complication arises because of the Data Protection Act 1998. This extends beyond computerised data to records held in a readily searchable filing system and among the "data protection principles" which must be obeyed by the data controller at the risk of an action for damages[386] are that data must be accurate and must be processed fairly. This again could potentially give rise to a claim which would be defeated, if brought as libel, by qualified privilege.[387]

If we take the simple case of D supplying X with an employment reference on C (a paradigm example of a privileged occasion) which turns out to be defamatory and inaccurate, only a few years ago the sole issue would have been whether D acted honestly.[388] Now one may also have to consider (i) the law of negligence (applied to such a situation by the House of Lords in *Spring v Guardian Assurance*[389]), (ii) the Data Protection Act, and (iii) where the defendant is a public authority the Convention as given effect here by the Human Rights Act 1998. Furthermore, the concept of recoverable damage differs from one head to another.

With all this in mind we must turn to consider the categories of qualified privilege.

(a) *Qualified privilege at common law.*

(I) DUTY AND INTEREST. The common law has for many years **12–46** conferred qualified privilege upon statements made by D to X about C: (a) which D is under a legal, moral or social duty to communicate to X and which X has a corresponding interest in receiving; or (b) where X has an interest to be protected and D has a corresponding

---

[385] *W v JH* [2008] EWHC 399 (QB).
[386] Under s.13 of the Act.
[387] *Clift v Slough BC* [2009] EWHC 1550 (QB).
[388] The claim might also be brought as one for malicious falsehood (para.12–72, below). Again the issue would be one of malice, though unlike in defamation the claimant would have to prove the statement false.
[389] [1995] 2 AC 296, para.11–33, above.

interest or has a duty to protect the interest of X. The general
approach was put as follows by Parke B. in *Toogood v Spyring*[390] in
terms which remain valid today, save that we no longer generally
speak of the "implied malice" which was once said to arise on the
making of any defamatory statement.

> "In general, an action lies for the malicious publication of state-
> ments which are false in fact, and injurious to the character of
> another, and the law considers such publication as malicious,
> unless it is fairly made by a person in the discharge of some
> public or private duty whether legal or moral, or in the conduct of
> his own affairs, in matters where his interest is concerned. In such
> cases the occasion prevents the inference of malice which the law
> draws from unauthorised communications, and affords a qualified
> defence depending on the absence of actual malice. *If fairly
> warranted by any reasonable occasion or exigency, and honestly
> made, such communications are protected for the common con-
> venience and welfare of society.*"

It is impossible to classify the cases precisely under "duty" or
"interest" and there is a good deal of overlap between the two
categories, so that where the Bar Council issued a circular on the
propriety of accepting instructions from the claimants it was said
that it mattered:

> "[N]ot at all whether the ... Bar Council are properly to be
> regarded as owing a duty to the Bar to rule on questions of
> professional conduct such as arose here, or as sharing with the
> Bar   a   common   interest   in   maintaining   professional
> standards."[391]

What is essential is that there should be reciprocity of duty or
interest and that is normally based on some relationship between the
maker of the statement and the recipient.

> "A privileged occasion is ... an occasion where the person who
> makes a communication has an interest, or a duty, legal, social or
> moral, to make it to the person to whom it is made, and the person
> to whom it is so made has a corresponding interest or duty to
> receive it. This reciprocity is essential."[392]

---

[390] (1834) 1 C.M. & R. 181 at 193.
[391] *Kearns v General Council of the Bar* [2003] EWCA Civ 331; [2003] 1 W.L.R. 1357 at
[39].
[392] *Adam v Ward* [1917] A.C. 309 at 334 per Lord Atkinson.

This does not mean that both parties must have a duty or both an interest: one may have an interest and the other a duty, as in the common case of an employment reference. In *Watt v Longsdon*[393] B was a foreign manager of the X Co. He wrote to the defendant, a director of the company, a letter containing gross charges of immorality, drunkenness and dishonesty on the part of the claimant, who was managing director of the company abroad. The defendant wrote a reply to B in which he stated his own suspicions of the claimant's immorality and asked B to get confirmation of B's own allegations in order that the defendant might communicate them to the claimant's wife whom the defendant stated to be an old friend of his. Then, without waiting for any corroboration of B's statement, the defendant showed B's letter to S, the chairman of the board of directors and largest shareholder in the company and also to the claimant's wife. All the allegations against the claimant were false. He sued the defendant for libel: (a) in writing what he did to B; (b) in communicating B's letter to S; (c) in communicating B's letter to the claimant's wife. The defendant pleaded qualified privilege. The Court of Appeal had little difficulty in holding that: (a) the defendant's letter to B was privileged, because both B and the defendant had a common interest in the affairs of the company, and that entitled them to discuss the behaviour of the claimant as another employee of the company and to collect further information for the chairman of the Company; (b) the defendant's communication of B's letter to S was privileged, because a duty to make it arose both from the fact of employment in the same company and from the possibility that S might be asked by the claimant for a testimonial if the claimant were to seek other situation; but the court held that (c) the communication of the letter to the claimant's wife was not privileged. No doubt she had the strongest possible interest in hearing a statement about the husband's moral conduct; no doubt also there may be occasions on which a friend of the wife is under a duty, or has a corresponding interest, in informing her of statements about her husband—indeed each case must depend on its own circumstances, the nature of the information and the relation of the speaker to the wife.[394] However, here the defendant had no sufficient interest or duty, for the information came from a very doubtful source and he had never consulted the claimant nor obtained any confirmation of the outrageous accusations before passing them to the wife.

a. *What is a duty?* The question of whether there is a duty to **12–47** communicate the matter is one of law for the judge. It is easy

---

[393] [1930] 1 K.B. 130.
[394] Scrutton L.J. at [1930] 1 K.B. 149.

enough where there is a legal duty but in this context "duty" embraces "moral" or "social" duties which could not be enforced by legal means. Lindley L.J. said in *Stuart v Bell*[395]:

> "The question of moral or social duty being for the judge, each judge must decide it as best he can for himself. I take moral or social duty to mean a duty recognised by English people of ordinary intelligence and moral principle, but at the same time not a duty enforceable by legal proceedings, whether civil or criminal."

As "all or, at all events, the great mass of right-minded men in the position of the defendant would have considered it their duty under the circumstances"[396] to give the information, the learned Lord Justice thought that the privilege arose. Scrutton L.J. in *Watt v Longsdon*[397] referred to the difficulties in this area when he asked:

> "Is the judge merely to give his own view of moral and social duty, though he thinks that a considerable portion of the community hold a different opinion? Or is he to endeavour to ascertain what view the great mass of right-minded men would take?"

It is suggested that the answer to this is that the judge's view, if, as is probable, it takes account of the arguments of counsel on each side, as well as of his own personal predictions, is the nearest approach that is possible to the ascertainment of right-minded opinion. You cannot subpoena as witnesses a portion of the community in order to discover what they regard as a moral duty. Of course opinions may differ on the issue of whether there is such a duty as should be recognised by law.[398] The existence of a particular relationship[399] is often a guide to the existence of a privileged occasion —thus the classic example of "duty and interest" is the situation where a former employer gives a reference on a former employee. However, it is wrong to suppose that the mere existence of any relationship will necessarily suffice to raise the duty without weighing all the circumstances of the particular case before the court. In any event, when faced with a novel situation the court must proceed from principle.

---

[395] [1891] 2 Q.B. 341 at 350.
[396] Informing a guest that his servant was suspected by the police of theft.
[397] [1930] 1 K.B. 130 at 144.
[398] As they did in *Coxhead v Richards* (1846) 2C.B. 569, where the court was evenly divided.
[399] What Eady J. in *Komarek v Ramco Energy* [2002] EWHC 2501 (QB) at [46] called the "off the peg" categories.

A distinction has been drawn between a statement which is made in answer to an inquiry and one which is merely volunteered. Certainly, where there has been a request for information, that is useful evidence towards showing that the privilege exists, particularly if the case is on the borderline, but it does not follow that because the information is given unasked there can be no privilege. One is a poor citizen, to say the least, if one is deliberately silent when one sees the safety or property of another person imperilled[400] and it has therefore been held that, "when a person has reason to believe that a crime has been committed it is his duty and his right to inform the police."[401]

b. *What is an interest?* In the majority of the reported cases the   **12–48** interest is a business or financial one, as where a complaint is made about the quality of work done,[402] an employer informs workers about the reason for the dismissal of a fellow worker,[403] an insurance company writes to policyholders about an agent,[404] a creditor informs an auctioneer holding funds from a sale of a suspected act of bankruptcy by the seller,[405] or information is given to hoteliers about the imminent collapse of a travel firm so as to minimise claims on a travel insurance fund[406]; but any legitimate interest worthy of protection by the law[407] will do.

"So long as the interest is of so tangible a nature that for the common convenience and welfare of society it is expedient to protect it, it will come within the rule."[408]

So it was held that a complaint to the Home Secretary that a magistrate had incited breaches of the peace,[409] to a bishop that a clergyman had got into a fight with the schoolmaster[410] and a statement by an invigilator to examinees that one of their number had cheated[411] were privileged, as were (on the basis of legitimate self-defence) a statement by a bishop justifying conduct of his which

---

[400] Compare *Coxhead v Richards*, above, fn.398.
[401] *Croucher v Inglis* (1889) 16 R. 774 at 778. If a person reports a crime against himself he may be regarded as acting in protection of an interest, though nowadays this situation attracts absolute privilege: para.12–41, above.
[402] *Toogood v Spyring* (1834) 1 C.M. & R. 181.
[403] *Hunt v GN Ry* [1891] 2 Q.B. 189.
[404] *Nevill v Fine Art and General Insurance Co* [1897] A.C. 68.
[405] *Baker v Carrick* [1894] 1 Q.B. 838; *Boston v W.S. Bagshaw & Sons* [1966] 1 W.L.R. 1126.
[406] *Aspro Travel v Owners Abroad Group* [1996] 1 W.L.R. 132 (interest arguable).
[407] Which issue, as in the case of a duty, is a matter for the judge.
[408] *Howe v Lees* (1910) 11 C.L.R. 361 at 377. Not a "matter of gossip or curiosity": at 398.
[409] *Harrison v Bush* (1855) E. & B. 355.
[410] *James v Boston* (1846) 2 C. & K. 4.
[411] *Bridgman v Stockdale* [1953] 1 W.L.R. 704.

had been attacked in public[412] and a reply by a daughter to a statement in the press about her father.[413]

12–49   **c. *Reality of interest and duty.*** The question is whether the law recognises an interest or duty, not whether the defendant believes there is one, so that in *Hebditch v MacIlwaine* no privilege was held to exist in respect of a complaint to a body with no jurisdiction in the matter.[414] While the principle remains valid, this case may have taken a rather narrow view of interest on its facts[415] and in any event there must be circumstances in which a person is entitled to act upon what he honestly and reasonably, though wrongly, believes are the facts. Thus if a person receives a request for a reference from someone who represents that he is a prospective employer but in fact is a nosy busybody, the giver of the reference should not lose the protection of privilege because the recipient has no legitimate interest. However, the defendant can only rely on matters which were known to him at the time when he published the statement for the purposes of establishing a duty.[416]

In deciding whether there is a sufficient common interest in respect of a communication it may be important to consider the stage which has been reached in the matter upon which the statement is made. In *De Buse v McCarthy*[417] a committee of the council had been charged to inquire into the loss of petrol from depots and the report of the committee was placed in public libraries in the borough as part of the agenda papers for the meeting of the council at which it was to be considered. The Court of Appeal held that at that stage, the report being still a matter of internal administration upon which no decision or resolution had been made, the council had neither a duty nor an interest in making the contents known to the body of ratepayers. Although it was not necessary to decide the matter, the court accepted that the position might have been different once the council had come to a decision on the matter.[418]

12–50   **d. *Trade protection societies.*** The difficulty of reconciling the protection of legitimate commercial interest and the protection of reputation is illustrated by two decisions. Trade protection societies

---

[412] *Laughton v Bishop of Sodor and Man* (1872) L.R. 4 P.C. 495.
[413] *Bowen-Rowlands v Argus Press, The Times*, March 26, 1926.
[414] [1894] 2 Q.B. 54; *Blagg v Stuart* (1846) 10 C.B. 899.
[415] Compare *Beach v Freeson* [1972] 1 Q.B. 14 (Lord Chancellor having no formal disciplinary powers over solicitors but having a interest in receiving complaints in view of his position in the legal system).
[416] *G.K.R. Karate (UK) Ltd v Yorkshire Post Newspapers Ltd* [2000] 1 W.L.R. 2571; *Loutchansky v Times Newspapers Ltd* [2001] EWCA Civ 536; [2002] Q.B. 321.
[417] [1942] 1 K.B. 156.
[418] Hence the preference of Lord Greene M.R. for, "an interest or duty to make the communication in question" rather than an "interest in the subject-matter".

are often formed for the purpose of supplying information on the
financial stability of traders to inquirers and the law has to steer a
course between allowing third persons to help a trader to protect
himself against dealing with insolvent persons and:

> "[S]afeguarding commercial credit against the most dangerous
> and insidious of all enemies—the dissemination of prejudicial
> rumour, the author of which cannot be easily identified, nor its
> medium readily disclosed."[419]

In *Macintosh v Dun*[420] the defendants carried on business as a trade
protection society under the title, "The Mercantile Agency". X, one
of the subscribers to the agency, asked for information about the
credit of the claimants, who were ironmongers. The agency replied
unfavourably and, as it turned out, untruly. In an action for libel, the
Privy Council held that there was no privilege, for the defendants
were only collectors of information which they were ready to sell to
their customers, and it was immaterial whether the customers
bought the information across the counter or whether they enjoyed
the privilege of being enrolled as a subscriber by paying a fee in
advance. In *London Association etc. v Greenlands Ltd*[421] the facts
were similar except that the defendants did not trade for profit and
the secretary of the association collected and supplied the information about the claimants to X. The House of Lords held that the
communication was privileged on the ground that the secretary, in
supplying the information, was acting, not as the agent of the
association as a whole but as the confidential agent of X; for if X had
the right to make inquiries on his own account (as he undoubtedly
did) he equally had the right to make them through an agent and the
agent had a duty to report to him. However, had the association itself
any such privilege? The question could not be directly decided by
the House of Lords owing to the way the case had been conducted
at first instance, but it may be deduced from the speech of Lord
Buckmaster[422] that the privilege exists if: (a) the association consists
of persons who are themselves involved in trade; and (b) it exercises
control over the person who on their behalf procures the information
and over the manner in which he procures it; and (c) it does not
conduct its business purely for the purposes of gain.[423] In *Macintosh
v Dun* not one of these conditions was satisfied; in the *Greenlands*
case all were.[424] The chances of an action for defamation being

---

[419] *London Association etc. v Greenlands Ltd* [1916] 2 A.C. 15 at 26.
[420] [1908] A.C. 390.
[421] [1916] 2 A.C. 15.
[422] [1916] 2 A.C. 15 at 26.
[423] Quaere whether the last element is always necessary: see [1916] 2 A.C. 15 at 42.
[424] See also *Barr v Mussleburgh* 1912 S.C. 174.

brought in respect of information held by credit bureaux are now increased by the Consumer Credit Act 1974, which gives the consumer the right to the disclosure of the name and address of any bureau to which his creditor has made inquiries and the right to require from that bureau a copy of the file on him.[425] The purpose of these provisions is to enable the consumer to correct wrong information but it is perfectly possible that he may decide to take defamation proceedings against the bureau[426] or against the person who supplied the information to the bureau.[427] Since in practice such information will be held in electronic form or at least a form making individual records readily accessible, the provisions of the Data Protection Act 1998 must also be borne in mind. This gives a right of action, subject to a defence of due care, for loss caused by contravention of the Act.[428]

12–51   **e. *Relevance.*** A statement made on a privileged occasion may contain material which is irrelevant to the purpose for which the law grants the privilege. One view is that this goes only to malice[429] (which is a question for the jury and on which the decisive question is the defendant's honest belief) but the judgments in *Adam v Ward*[430] are to the effect that the inclusion of irrelevant material may take the case outside the protection of privilege altogether. Perhaps the views can be reconciled by saying that it is a question of degree: to exclude from the scope of protection material which is not "logically relevant"[431] would be a dangerous restriction on qualified privilege but to cast the cloak of protection around material which is "quite unconnected with and irrelevant to"[432] the inquiry in hand would seem to strike at the very basis of qualified privilege, which rests, after all, upon the law's assessment of the need for candour, not on what the defendant believes that need to be.[433] If, for example, A were to make an inquiry to D about C's creditworthiness and D were to give a reply on this subject to which was added the imputation that C was a paedophile it is difficult to see why C's irrational but honest belief in that should give him a defence. Thus

---

[425] See ss.157–160. Under s.160 the bureau may be required to provide the Director General of Fair Trading with a copy of the file. The publication to the Director would clearly attract qualified privilege since it would be done in pursuance of a statutory duty.

[426] i.e. in respect of the publication to the creditor.

[427] The original Consumer Credit Bill would have given the protection of qualified privilege to publications by or to a licensed credit bureau. The Faulks Committee thought that privilege should apply to publications by, but not to, a bureau.

[428] Section 13. Replacing the Data Protection Act 1984.

[429] *Horrocks v Lowe* [1975] A.C. 135 at 151 per Lord Diplock.

[430] [1917] A.C. 309 at 318, 339, 340, 348.

[431] Lord Diplock's expression in *Horrocks v Lowe*.

[432] Lord Dunedin in *Adam v Ward* at 327.

[433] Above, para.12–49.

in *Warren v Warren*[434] D wrote a letter to the manager of property in which D and C were jointly interested which was principally about C's conduct in relation to the property but which also contained charges against C in relation to his conduct towards his family. It was held that the latter were not privileged. On the other hand:

"[T]here may be an excess of the privilege in the sense that something has been published which is not within the privileged occasion at all, because it can have no reference to it ... But when there is only an excessive statement having reference to the privileged occasion, and which, therefore, comes within it, then the only way in which the excess is material is as being evidence of malice."[435]

In *Watts v Times Newspapers*[436] the defendant solicitors negotiated, on behalf of their client, an apology in the newspaper for a libel which had arisen from a confusion of identity between their client and C. The apology contained a defamatory reference to C, upon which the defendants insisted. This reference went beyond the bounds of what was objectively necessary as an apology to the client but was still protected by privilege, for, "if you are attacked by a prize fighter you are not bound to adhere to the Queensberry rules in your defence"[437] and the content of the apology was not "unconnected with the theme" and did not include "entirely irrelevant and extraneous material".[438]

f. Range of publication. The requirement of reciprocity between the maker of the statement and the recipient means that a publication which reaches uninterested persons and is therefore wider than is reasonably necessary to serve the interest underlying the protection may take the case outside the protection of privilege,[439] though as in the case of relevance the issue may in some cases be treated as one of malice and it is difficult to lay down any hard and fast rule.[440] A simple example is *Williamson v Freer*[441] where a communication **12–52**

---

[434] (1834) 1 C.M. & R. 250.
[435] *Nevill v Fine Art and General Insurance Co* [1895] 2 Q.B. 156 at 170 per Lord Esher M.R.
[436] [1997] Q.B. 650. On the position of a solicitor speaking in defence of his client's interests see also *Regan v Taylor* [2000] E.M.L.R. 549.
[437] *Turner v MGM Pictures* [1950] 1 All E.R. 449 at 470 per Lord Oaksey.
[438] The newspaper failed on the issue of privilege for its position had to be judged independently of that of the solicitors' client.
[439] See e.g. *Brady v Norman* [2008] EWHC 2481(QB) (union journal with circulation of 18,000; about 130 subscribers not connected with union).
[440] As in *Pittard v Oliver* [1891] 1 Q.B. 474.
[441] (1884) L.R. 9 C.P. 393. See also *De Buse v McCarthy*, fn.417, above.

which would have been privileged if sent by sealed letter was not so protected when sent by telegram. However:

"[I]f a business communication is privileged ... the privilege covers all the incidents of the transmission and treatment of that communication which are in accordance with the reasonable and usual course of business,"[442]

so that, for example, the dictation of a letter to a clerk[443] or the delivery of a company circular to a printer[444] is likely to be protected. Such a privilege may be regarded as ancillary to that which protects the communication to the addressee of the letter.[445] In some cases, of course, there may be an independent, "original" privilege between the sender of the letter and the typist based upon community of interest[446] but the view that an original privilege arises automatically from a contract of employment has been rejected.[447] A further possibility is that D sends a letter to C which is defamatory of C himself[448] and in the usual course of business first dictates the letter to a typist. The "ancillary privilege" explanation will hardly serve here for the only publication apart from that to the typist is to the defamed person himself and that needs no privilege for it is not tortious. Nonetheless, the Court of Appeal in *Osborne v Thomas Boulter & Sons*[449] assumed that there was some sort of privilege in such a situation.

Even where there is no ancillary privilege it may be reasonable to take the risk of the communication coming to the attention of uninterested persons if that is practically necessary in order to publish it, as where a notice about the dismissal of a conductor was posted in the company's private offices, where it was seen by persons not employed by the company.[450]

---

[442] *Edmondson v Birch & Co* [1907] 1 K.B. 371 at 382.

[443] *Boxsius v Goblet Frères* [1894] 1 Q.B. 842.

[444] *Lawless v Anglo-Egyptian Co* (1869) L.R. 4 Q.B. 262.

[445] *Bryanston Finance Ltd v de Vries* [1975] Q.B. 703 at 727, 736, cf. below, para.12–65.

[446] e.g. if A discovers that B, a notorious asset stripper, is seeking to take over A's company, the publication of A's views about B to A's employees may be protected because they have a common interest in the welfare of the company; but even if such a common interest is present, it is hard to see how A can rely on it, since in dictating the letter to the third party A's purpose is not to inform the typist.

[447] *Bryanston Finance Ltd v de Vries*, above, fn.445 per Lord Diplock and Lawton L.J. Contra, Lord Denning M.R. Perhaps the view of Lord Diplock should be discounted as he dissented from the actual decision, but this would seem to be rather a narrow view.

[448] If the intended publication is to a third party but this never in fact takes place (e.g. because it is restrained by injunction) it is, "the use which the author ... intends to make of it ... that attracts whatever ancillary privilege there may be": *Bryanston Finance Ltd v de Vries* [1975] Q.B. at 729 per Diplock L.J.

[449] [1930] 2 K.B. 226.

[450] *Tench v GW Ry* (1873) 33 Up. Can. Q.B. 8.

These issues have been important because the classical common law form of qualified privilege has tended to be confined to communications of a private nature and not those directed at the public. However, there are sometimes situations where a much wider range of communication is necessary and justifiable: the issue of a circular to all members of the Bar was held to be a privileged occasion[451] and it was held arguable that the same was true of the publication of material on a website directed at British Jews and warning them about terrorism—it:

"[C]ould hardly be suggested that the Board [of Deputies] should address their information by individual letters to each and every Jew in the country".[452]

In such cases the fact that the communication is likely to come to the attention of "uninterested" persons is really irrelevant.

(II) "*REYNOLDS*" PRIVILEGE. Due to the requirement of reciprocity **12–53** it would, until recently, be a comparatively rare case in which a publication to the world at large via a book, newspaper or broadcast would attract the protection of qualified privilege. An example of a case where privilege would apply is that where the defendant is replying in the media to a charge or attack made against him in that form.[453] While there were examples of qualified privilege being accorded to general publication of the results of formal investigations and proceedings[454] (many of which would now anyway fall within the privilege accorded by Sch.1 to the Defamation Act 1996[455]) this would not generally be the case at an earlier stage,[456] except perhaps in cases of grave emergency or public danger.[457] However, a newspaper had no special duty or interest with regard to the public and there is no defence of "fair information upon a matter of public interest".[458] Nor was there any general principle that privilege attaches to statements by the media in respect of which they have taken reasonable care. Overall there was a sharp contrast with the law of defamation in the United States where, as a result of

---

[451] *Kearns v General Council of the Bar* [2003] EWCA Civ 331; [2003] 1 W.L.R. 1357.
[452] *Hewitt v Grunwald* [2004] EWHC 2959 (QB) at [74].
[453] *Dwyer v Esmonde* (1873) 2 L.R. Ir. 243. See also the previous para.
[454] *Allbutt v General Council of Medical Education* (1889 23 Q.B.D. 400; *Perera v Peiris* [1949] A.C. 1 (on the Roman-Dutch law of Ceylon, but the PC seems to have thought it was the same as English law in this respect). Contrast *Chapman v Ellesmere* [1932] 2 K.B. 431, though that would now fall under Sch.1 to the Defamation Act 1996.
[455] See below, para.12–60.
[456] See *Blackshaw v Lord* [1984] Q.B. 1 (civil servant alleged to be implicated in wasting taxpayers' money).
[457] [1984] Q.B. 1 at 27.
[458] Despite *Webb v Times Publishing Co* [1960] 2 Q.B. 535.

the First Amendment to the Constitution,[459] a public figure or public official may only recover damages for defamation if he is able to show by clear and convincing evidence that the defendant published with knowledge or reckless disregard as to falsity[460]; and in the case of private persons the most severe standard that state common law[461] can adopt (at least if the matter is one of public concern[462]) is one of negligence.[463]

The law on this subject was transformed by *Reynolds v Times Newspapers Ltd.*[464] A major background factor is art.10 of the European Convention on Human Rights, which in part provides:

"1. Everyone has the right to freedom of expression. This right shall include freedom to hold opinions and to receive and impart information and ideas without interference by public authority . . .

2. The exercise of these freedoms, since it carries with it duties and responsibilities, may be subject to such formalities, conditions, restrictions or penalties as are prescribed by law and are necessary in a democratic society . . . for the protection of the reputation or rights of others . . . "

Now, of course, the Human Rights Act 1998 gives a form of direct effect to the Convention by means of the provision requiring a public authority (which includes a court) not to act in a manner inconsistent with it.[465] This was not in force at the time of *Reynolds*, but the Act had been passed and in any event the Convention had long bound the UK on an international plane. In the view of the House of Lords, reputation (including that of public figures) remains a major value underpinning many activities and functions in society and its protection is for the public good as well as that of the individual defamed; however, modern conceptions of democracy require that the role of the media[466] in informing the public of matters of controversy be more readily recognised than has been the case in the past. The leading speech is that of Lord Nicholls, with whom Lord Cooke and Lord Hobhouse explicitly agreed. Lord

---

[459] "Congress shall make no law . . . abridging the freedom of speech, or of the press".
[460] *New York Times v Sullivan* 376 U.S. 254 (1964).
[461] There is no federal common private law. The issue is therefore the effect of the Constitution upon the state common law.
[462] It may be that in the case of a purely private libel the common law position remains acceptable: *Dun & Bradstreet v Greenmoss Builders* 472 U.S. 749 (1985).
[463] *Gertz v Robert Welch Inc* 418 U.S. 323 (1974).
[464] [2001] 2 A.C. 127.
[465] See above, para.2–9.
[466] The privilege created by *Reynolds* is not confined to the news media, though in practice they will most frequently seek to take advantage of it: *Seaga v Harper* [2008] UKPC 9; [2009] 1 A.C. 1. One can imagine that it could apply to a website drawing attention to fraudulent trading practices.

Nicholls set out a non-exhaustive list of circumstances which would be relevant to the question of whether the media should be regarded as having a duty to convey information and the public a corresponding interest in receiving it.

"1. The seriousness of the allegation. The more serious the charge, the more the public is misinformed and the individual harmed, if the allegation is not true.

2. The nature of the information, and the extent to which the subject-matter is a matter of public concern.

3. The source of the information. Some informants have no direct knowledge of the events. Some have their own axes to grind, or are being paid for their stories.[467]

4. The steps taken to verify the information.

5. The status of the information.[468] The allegation may have already been the subject of an investigation which commands respect.[469]

6. The urgency of the matter. News is often a perishable commodity.

7. Whether comment was sought from the claimant. He may have information others do not possess or have not disclosed. An approach to the claimant will not always be necessary.

8. Whether the article contained the gist of the claimant's side of the story.

9. The tone of the article.[470] A newspaper can raise queries or call for an investigation. It need not adopt allegations as statements of fact.

10. The circumstances of the publication, including the timing.[471]

---

[467] In comparing English and American law it should be borne in mind that in the United States there is pre-trial disclosure of sources, whereas the media here will generally be unwilling to reveal the identity of an informant and the courts will rarely compel them to do so. Since the refusal cannot, therefore, be treated as amounting to evidence that the source is unreliable, an extensive application of privilege can put the claimant in a very difficult position.

[468] Past numbers of a newspaper may now often be accessed on an Internet archive and it may be necessary to draw a distinction between the print and electronic publications. A story in print which later turns out to be untrue may be protected by *Reynolds*, but it does not follow that the same protection extends to the maintenance of the material on the Internet after the truth has come out: *Flood v Times Newspapers Ltd* [2009] EWHC 2375 (QB).

[469] *Miller v Associated Newspapers Ltd* [2004] EWHC 2799; [2004] E.M.L.R. 33; *Flood v Times Newspapers Ltd*, above, fn.468.

[470] *Grobelaar v News Group Newspapers Ltd* [2001] EWCA Civ 33; [2001] 2 All E.R. 437; *Galloway v Telegraph Group Ltd* [2006] EWCA Civ 17; [2006] E.M.L.R. 11.

[471] The decision of the CA had been based on similar factors but the court had subsumed these under a new, additional "circumstantial" element to be added to the tests of interest and duty: [1998] 3 W.L.R. 863. Lord Cooke in the HL thought that the difference between what the House decided and the threefold approach of the CA was largely "a matter of arrangement" ([2001] 2 A.C. at 224).

The list is not exhaustive. The weight to be given to these and any other relevant factors will vary from case to case. Any disputes of primary facts will be a matter for the jury, if there is one. The decision on whether, having regard to the admitted or proved facts, the publication was subject to qualified privilege is a matter for the judge. This is the established practice and seems sound. A balancing operation is better carried out by a judge in a reasoned judgment than by a jury. Over time, a valuable corpus of case law will be built up."[472]

12–54   Unlike the contemporaneous developments in the law in Australia[473] and New Zealand[474] *Reynolds* is not confined to statements about those seeking public office[475] or to "political speech" but covers a much broader range of matters of public concern,[476] though the facts did concern political matters. The claimant was a former Taoiseach of the Irish Republic and sued the *Sunday Times* in respect of an alleged libel in its British mainland edition concerning the circumstances of his resignation as leader of the Fianna Fail/ Labour coalition in 1994. He alleged that the article meant that he had knowingly misled the Dail and his Cabinet colleagues over the handling of a controversial extradition case by the then Attorney General, whom he wished to appoint as President of the High Court. The majority of the House of Lords rejected the plea of privilege because the article had omitted all reference to what the claimant had said in the Dail by way of explanation.

Reynolds was subject to further consideration in *Jameel (Mohamed) v Wall Street Journal Europe Sprl.*[477] This arose out of a story which was capable of meaning either that there were reasonable grounds to suspect the claimants of being involved in the

---

[472] [2001] 2 A.C. at 205.

[473] *Lange v Australian Broadcasting Corp* (1997) 187 C.L.R. 520. However, the actual decision was that s.22 of the Defamation Act 1974 (NSW) complied with the constitutional requirement. Since then the Australian states have enacted uniform defamation legislation. The equivalent provision in NSW is now s.30 of the Defamation Act 2005 (NSW) and this is not confined to matters of government and politics. Indeed, the factors adverted to in s.30 bear some resemblance to those in *Reynolds* so there may be less difference between English and Australian law than at first appears. For Ireland see now s.26 of the Defamation Act 2009 ("fair and reasonable publication on a matter of public interest") which is recognisably from the same stable as *Reynolds*.

[474] *Lange v Atkinson* [2000] NZCA 95, [2000] 3 N.Z.L.R. 385 .

[475] For many years it was thought that the effect of s.10 of the Defamation Act 1952 was that a candidate in a parliamentary or local government election could not rely on qualified privilege. However, this is not so: *Culnane v Morris* [2005] EWHC 2438, QBD; [2006] 1 W.L.R. 2880. The section simply prevents the candidate having any special privilege qua candidate. He might therefore rely on "classical" privilege if for example he was refuting an attack on him and he might rely on *Reynolds* privilege in suitable circumstances.

[476] Canadian law was restated in terms rather similar to *Reynolds* in *Grant v Torstar Corp* [2009] SCC 61. For South Africa see *National Media Ltd v Bogoshi* 1998 (4) S.A. 1196.

[477] [2006] UKHL 44; [2007] 1 A.C. 359.

funding of terrorism or at least that there were grounds to investigate the matter. The House of Lords allowed the defendants' appeal and perhaps the central point from the decision is the emphasis on the fact that Lord Nicholls' ten "points" are not to be seen as a series of hurdles to be negotiated in succession by a defendant with the loss of the defence if he cannot pass one of them.[478] The matter must be approached in a practical and flexible manner and due deference paid to editorial discretion. It is not necessary to show that the editor would be open to criticism for *not* publishing. If that is the case the claim to privilege is beyond dispute; but there may be a valid claim even though in the circumstances other editors would have abstained.[479] In *Jameel* itself it was not *necessary* to name the claimants but the editor was entitled to take the view that doing so would be more effective than merely referring to, "certain Saudi companies". Lord Nicholls in *Reynolds* said that the:

> "[C]ourt should be slow to conclude that a publication was not in the public interest and, therefore, the public had no right to know, especially when the information is in the field of political discussion. Any lingering doubts should be resolved in favour of publication."[480]

However, it has since been said that the recognition that reputation is a right encompassed in art.8 of the European Convention on Human Rights means that in all cases there must be a balancing exercise between the protection of this right and that of freedom of expression and there is no longer a built-in bias in favour of the latter.[481]

There is some disagreement in *Jameel* as to whether this privilege is based on reciprocal duty and interest.[482] Lord Hoffmann thought it, "might more appropriately be called the *Reynolds* public interest defence rather than privilege"[483] and Lord Scott said that:

> "[T]he touchstone of a reciprocal interest and duty between the receiver and the giver of the defamatory statement was a judicial construct of the 20th century designed to produce certainty as to the circumstances in which a defamatory statement made by A to B could be accorded the protection of qualified privilege. It is a

---

[478] [2006] UKHL 44; [2007] 1 A.C. 359 at [53].
[479] *Loutchansky v Times Newspapers Ltd (Nos 2–5)* [2001] EWCA Civ 1805; [2002] Q.B. 783 at [49].
[480] [2001] 2 A.C. at 205.
[481] *Flood v Times Newspapers Ltd* [2009] EWHC 2375 (QB), applying *Re S (A Child)* [2004] UKHL 47; [2005] 1 A.C. 593.
[482] Compare Lords Bingham and Hope at [30], [105]; and Lord Hoffmann and Baroness Hale at [50], [146].
[483] At [46].

touchstone that makes little sense in relation to statements, typically those contained in the pages of newspapers, made to the
world at large. *Reynolds* was not supplanting the duty/interest
touchstone for situations to which that touchstone was intended to
apply and could sensibly be applied. It was supplementing that
touchstone in order to provide the protection of qualified privilege, where the circumstances warranted that protection, to statements published to the world at large."[484]

Certainly it is unlike traditional qualified privilege in that malice
is irrelevant. It is for the defendant to show that he has complied
with what in the news media context have come to be called the
standards of responsible journalism and therefore, "the propriety of
the conduct of the defendant is built into the conditions under which
the material is privileged".[485]

The various factors under *Reynolds* are necessarily imprecise and
fact-sensitive, so it is unlikely that the decision in one case will
provide an easy solution to the next one and the decided cases tend
to be "one-off" illustrations of the application of the principles.
Furthermore, although cases decided before *Jameel* are not necessarily wrong, they must be read bearing in mind that that case did
involve emphasis on the propositions that the defence was not to be
closely restricted and failure by the defendant on one factor was not
necessarily fatal to his case. To take one example, failure to put to
the claimant the charges which are to be made against him will often
be seriously damaging to the defence because not only is doing so
generally simple fairness but it is often the best way to verify a story.
In *Jameel* itself the failure to hold back the story for 24 hours to see
if the human claimant[486] could be contacted was not fatal. The basis
of the story was that the accounts of his business were subject to
intelligence monitoring, the Saudi authorities had declined to make
any comment to the defendants and even if the claimant had been
able to obtain a denial from those authorities it would have meant
very little since the claimant would have had no information of his
own and if the monitoring was going on the authorities were hardly
likely to admit it.

The *Reynolds* privilege has proved difficult to operate under the
regime of trial by jury and it has been said that it is open to question
whether jury trial is desirable at all in such a case.[487] In the typical
case of "classical" qualified privilege the determination of the facts

---

[484] At [137].
[485] *Jameel (Mohamed) v Wall Street Journal Europe Sprl* [2006] UKHL; [2007] 1 A.C. 359
at [46] per Lord Hoffmann.
[486] The other claimant was one of his companies.
[487] *Jameel v Wall Street Journal Europe Sprl (No.2)* [2005] EWCA Civ 74; [2005] Q.B. 904
at [70].

which constitute the privileged occasion, if they are in dispute at all, are likely to be suitable for determination by the jury and if the judge rules that the privileged occasion is made out the jury's function is confined to deciding whether malice has been proved. In a *Reynolds* case the defendant's conduct (what he believed about the veracity of his sources, what he did to check on them, how far he gave the claimant the opportunity to respond) are at the heart of the existence of the privilege. A not unlikely scenario nowadays, therefore, is that at the end of the trial the jury will be presented with a series of questions going first to meaning and reference (if those are in dispute) then to the *Reynolds* factors and then to damages, the *Reynolds* issue then being reserved for ultimate determination by the judge, who has to "evaluate" the effect of the jury's answers to determine whether there was the requisite duty to publish. This is likely to be complicated enough but there is also a problem with the burden of proof on disputed facts going to the existence of the privilege. It is clear that on liability the basic stance of the law is that it is for the defendant to prove that the defamatory sting of the publication is substantially true; but for the purposes of the privilege the fact that the truth of the allegations has not been proved is a "neutral circumstance".[488]

a. Reynolds and reportage. As we have seen, the "repetition rule" says that if D repeats a statement made by X then D is treated as publishing the imputations in it even if D makes it clear that he is only repeating what X said. Since *Reynolds*, however, there has been some modification of this. In *Al-Fagih v H.H. Saudi Research & Marketing (UK) Ltd*[489] privilege was held to apply to the publication in a newspaper circulating among Saudi residents in England of developments in a feud in a group seeking political change in Saudi Arabia. This was so even though it was obvious that an informant had an axe to grind and there were no steps taken to verify the story. The majority of the Court of Appeal held that the defendants had in no way adopted or endorsed the allegation: this was a report of a stage in an ongoing political dispute of legitimate interest to the readership and the failure of the defendants to take steps to verify the allegation did not in such a case exclude the report's being privileged. There:

12–55

"[W]ill be circumstances where, as here, . . . both sides to a political dispute are being fully, fairly and disinterestedly reported

---

[488] *Jameel (Mohammed) v Wall Street Journal Europe Sprl* [2006] UKHL 44; [2007] 1 A.C. 359 at [62]. As the CA pointed out ([2005] EWCA Civ 74; [2005] Q.B. 904 at [61]), "it follows that the jury are required to perform some mental gymnastics". This will be particularly so where there is a concurrent plea of justification.
[489] [2001] EWCA Civ 1634; [2002] E.M.L.R. 13.

in their respective allegations and responses. In this situation . . .
the public is entitled to be informed of such a dispute without
having to wait for the publisher, following an attempt at verification, to commit himself to one side or the other."[490]

The Court of Appeal has subsequently said that this is not inconsistent with the repetition rule, which is concerned with meaning
and justification, and privilege as a whole (of which this is a form)
assumes the existence of the rule and is a qualification of it.

> "To qualify as reportage the report, judging the thrust of it as a
> whole, must have the effect of reporting, not the truth of the
> statements, but the fact that they were made . . . If upon a proper
> construction of the thrust of the article the defamatory material is
> attributed to another and is not being put forward as true, then a
> responsible journalist would not need to take steps to verify its
> accuracy. He is absolved from that responsibility because he is
> simply reporting in a neutral fashion the fact that it has been said
> without adopting the truth".[491]

What remains unclear is how far this is confined to the reporting of
a dispute. It has been said that, "the reportage doctrine . . . cannot
logically be confined to the reporting of reciprocal allegations. A
unilateral libel, reported disinterestedly, will be equally protected"[492]; but if we travel far down this road it will change the
balance between claimants and the media quite dramatically. No one
in *Jameel* seems to have regarded it as a reportage case and it has
subsequently been said that the doctrine has no application to
ordinary investigative journalism:

> "[W]here [the author] was acting as the bloodhound sniffing out
> bits of the story from here and there, from published material and
> unpublished material, not as the watchdog barking to wake us up
> to the story already out there."[493]

12–56   (III) MISCELLANEOUS HEADS OF PRIVILEGE AT COMMON LAW. A
number of heads of qualified privilege at common law are reduced
to minimal practical importance, though they are not wholly abolished, by the Defamation Act 1996.

---

[490] At [52] per Simon Brown L.J.
[491] *Roberts v Gable* [2007] EWCA Civ 721; [2008] Q.B. 502 at [61(3)].
[492] [2007] EWCA Civ 721; [2008] Q.B. 502 at [91] per Sedley L.J.
[493] *Charman v Orion Publishing Ltd* [2007] EWCA Civ 972; [2008] 1 All E.R. 750 at
[49].

a. *Reports of judicial proceedings*. The common law gives the   **12–57**
protection of qualified privilege to fair and accurate reports of public
judicial proceedings. As far as *contemporaneous* reports of UK
proceedings are concerned there has been absolute privilege for
reports in newspapers since 1888,[494] in broadcasts since 1952[495] and
now, without restriction as to medium, under s.14 of the Defamation
Act 1996.[496] Until the 1996 Act the common law privilege remained
significant for non-contemporaneous reports (e.g. in a casebook) or
for reports of foreign proceedings. In the case of the latter a fair and
accurate report was protected if the matter was of legitimate public
interest in this country.[497] Now, however, a fair and accurate report,
contemporaneous or not, of proceedings in public before a court
anywhere in the world is privileged without explanation or contradiction under Sch.1 to the 1996 Act[498] and the common law privilege seems practically redundant.[499]

b. *Reports of Parliamentary proceedings*. Qualified privilege for   **12–58**
fair and accurate reports[500] of Parliamentary proceedings[501] was
established in *Wason v Walter*[502] and was regarded as standing upon
the same footing as reports of judicial proceedings, i.e. the advantage of publicity to the workings of the legislature outweighed any
private injury resulting from publications. It is not confined to any
particular medium and applies to broadcasting of Parliament.[503]
Now, under Sch.1 to the Defamation Act 1996,[504] there is privilege
for a fair and accurate report of proceedings in public of a legislature

---

[494] Law of Libel Amendment Act 1888 s.3.
[495] Defamation Act 1952 s.9(2).
[496] Above, para.12–44 (this applies to certain overseas proceedings).
[497] *Webb v Times Publishing Co* [1960] 2 Q.B. 535.
[498] para.2.
[499] There is a theoretical argument for its continued relevance in that the Schedule does not
apply to matter, "which is not of public concern and the publication of which is not for the
public benefit (below, para.12–60), but it is unlikely that this is practically different from
the legitimate public interest of the common law: see Gatley, *Libel and Slander*, 11th edn,
§14.102.
[500] *Cornwall v Rowan* [2004] SASC 384; 90 S.A.S.R. 269.
[501] The publication of extracts from Parliamentary papers etc. is privileged under s.3 of the
Parliamentary Papers Act 1840, provided the defendant proves he published bona fide and
without malice (this burden of proof is unique). Again, the matter seems largely covered
by Sch.1, para.7 of the 1996 Act.
[502] (1868) L.R. 4 Q.B. 73. For the background to this case see the 14th edn of this book,
p.358.
[503] However, the Joint Committee on Parliamentary Privilege thought it arguable that s.1 of
the Parliamentary Papers Act could be interpreted to confer absolute privilege on the
broadcasting of proceedings: HL Paper 43/HC214-1, 1998–99. The Member whose words
are broadcast of course enjoys absolute privilege under the Bill of Rights. Compare s.13(2)
of the Defamation Act 1992 (NZ) which confers absolute privilege on live broadcasting of
Parliament. See also the Faulks Committee (Cmnd. 5909).
[504] para.1.

anywhere in the world,[505] so that the common law privilege, as with the previous category, seems largely eclipsed.[506]

12–59   **c. Registers.** The publication of a fair and accurate copy of or extract from a statutory register open to public inspection (e.g. the register of county court judgments) is privileged at common law.[507] Once again, the matter is also covered by the 1996 Act.[508]

(b) *Qualified privilege under statute.*

12–60   (I) SCHEDULE 1 TO THE DEFAMATION ACT 1996. This dates back to the Law of Libel Amendment Act 1888,[509] which was updated in the Schedule to the Defamation Act 1952. It confers the protection of qualified privilege upon a very wide range of reports and, though it is not now confined to reports in the news media,[510] it remains of considerable importance to them, notwithstanding *Reynolds*, because it gives clear and predictable answers to issues which might be unclear under that case. However, unlike the common law privilege it is confined to reports of what others have said on public occasions or in statements of an "official" or "quasi-official" nature—it does not cover the newspaper's own conclusions from its inquiries or "reports" which are heavily editorialised with comment.[511] The 1996 Act made many changes of detail and considerably expanded the range of protected reports. However, the basic structure of the previous law is retained and it may be expected that decisions under that will remain authoritative.

The reports and other statements privileged under the Schedule are divided into two categories, the first (Pt I) comprising those which are privileged, "without explanation or contradiction", and the second (Pt II) those which are privileged, "subject to explanation or contradiction". As regards matters in the second category, the defence of qualified privilege is lost if[512] it is proved that the defendant has been requested by the claimant to publish in a suitable manner[513] a reasonable letter or statement by way of explanation or

---

[505] Below, para.12–61. Note, however, that it is suggested in *Wason v Walter* at 93 that the common law privilege would apply to a report of a secret debate or where publication had been forbidden by the House, which would not be so with the statutory privilege.

[506] It is perhaps surprising that fair and accurate reports of Parliamentary proceedings are not subject to absolute privilege.

[507] *Searles v Scarlett* [1892] 2 Q.B. 56.

[508] Sch.1, para.5.

[509] Indeed, as far as reports of public meetings are concerned it can be traced to the Newspaper Libel and Registration Act 1881.

[510] As it was until the 1996 Act.

[511] *Henry v BBC* [2005] EWHC 2787 (QB).

[512] See Defamation Act 1996 s.15(2).

[513] Which means in the same manner as the publication complained of or in a manner that is adequate and reasonable in the circumstances.

contradiction,[514] and has refused or neglected to do so. In other words, in some cases, the defendant must accord the claimant a "right of reply" if he wishes to rely on the defence.[515] Fairness and accuracy are approached in a manner similar to that under the statutory and common law privileges for reports of judicial proceedings, that is to say, the report need not be verbatim (indeed it may be a very brief summary[516]) and need only be substantially accurate. The law should take care not to impose too high a duty upon the press and to transform, "investigative journalism from a virtue to a necessity".[517] Protection is not given to the publication of any matter which is not of public concern and the publication of which is not for the public benefit,[518] nor to the publication of matter which is prohibited by law.[519] "Public concern" and "public benefit" are matters for the jury.[520]

a. Statements privileged without explanation or contradiction. A fair and accurate report of proceedings in public of a legislature[521] anywhere in the world.[522]   **12–61**

A fair and accurate report of proceedings in public before a court anywhere in the world.[523]

A fair and accurate report of proceedings in public[524] of a person appointed to hold a public inquiry by a government or legislature anywhere in the world.[525]

A fair and accurate report of proceedings in public anywhere in the world of an international organisation or an international conference.[526]

---

[514] For discussion of a similar Australian provision see *Chakravarti v Advertiser Newspapers Ltd* [1998] HCA 37; (1998) 93 C.L.R. 519.

[515] Of course, if the defendant does not rely on the Schedule there is no such right.

[516] *Tsikata v Newspaper Publishing* [1997] 1 All E.R. 655 (decided under the 1952 Act).

[517] *Tsikata v Newspaper Publishing* at 671 per Ward L.J.

[518] Defamation Act 1996 s.15(3). These are, at least in theory, distinct requirements: *Kelly v O'Malley* (1889) 6 T.L.R. 62; *Crossley v Newsquest (Midlands South) Ltd* [2008] EWHC 3054 (QB).

[519] Section 15(4).

[520] *Kingshott v Associated Kent Newspapers Ltd* [1991] 1 Q.B. 88. Contrast common law privilege.

[521] By para.16(4) the European Parliament is a legislature (also for the purposes of paras 3 and 7). Without this specific provision it might not be such.

[522] para.1. As to the common law, see above, para.12–58.

[523] para.2. For the avoidance of doubt the International Court of Justice and other judicial or arbitral tribunals deciding matters in dispute between states are expressly included in the definition of court: para.16(3)(d). For absolute privilege see above, para.12–44.

[524] para.3. This includes the report of the inquiry, even though that may be delivered to a government officer and released by him: *Tsikata v Newspaper Publishing* [1997] 1 All E.R. 655, CA. "Common sense informs us that the proceedings of public inquiry begin with the evidence but end with the findings": per Ward L.J. at 669.

[525] The fact that there are doubts about the correctness of the conclusions does not remove the privilege: *Tsikata v Newspaper Publishing* [1997] 1 All E.R. 655, CA.

[526] para.4.

A fair and accurate copy of or extract from any register or other document required by law to be open to public inspection.[527]

A notice or advertisement published by or on the authority of a court, or of a judge or officer of a court, anywhere in the world.[528]

A fair and accurate copy of or extract from matter published by or on the authority of a government or legislature anywhere in the world.[529]

A fair and accurate copy of or extract from matter published anywhere in the world by an international organisation or an international conference.[530]

12–62   **b. *Statements privileged subject to explanation or contradiction.*** A fair and accurate copy of or extract from a notice or other matter issued[531] for the information of the public by or on behalf of: (a) a legislature in any Member State[532] or the European Parliament; (b) the government of any Member State, or any authority performing governmental functions[533] in any Member State or part of a Member State, or the European Commission; (c) an international organisation or international conference.[534]

A fair and accurate copy of or extract from a document made available by a court in any Member State or the European Court of Justice (or any court attached to that court), or by a judge or officer of any such court.[535]

A fair and accurate report of proceedings at any public meeting held in a Member State.[536] A public meeting means a meeting bona fide and lawfully held for a lawful purpose and for the furtherance or discussion of a matter of public concern, whether admission to the meeting is general or restricted.[537] A meeting is public if those who organise it open it to the public or, by issuing a general invitation to the press, manifest an intention or desire that the proceedings of the meeting should be communicated to a wider public. Press representatives may be regarded either as members of

---

[527] para.5. For the common law see above, para.12–59.
[528] para.6.
[529] para.7.
[530] para.8. There were no equivalents of this and the preceding paragraph in the 1952 Act.
[531] i.e. volunteered rather than extracted by questioning: *Blackshaw v Lord* [1984] Q.B. 1.
[532] i.e. of the European Union.
[533] This includes police functions: para.9(2). So, for example, a notice of a reward would be covered: *Boston v W.S. Bagshaw* [1966] 1 W.L.R. 1126, CA.
[534] para.9. There appears to be a very substantial overlap with para.7, which deals with copies or extracts privileged *without explanation or contradiction*. Note, however, that the equivalent provision of the 1952 Act (para.12) applied to a, "copy or fair and accurate report or summary" of the matter issued and, "copy or extract from" would appear to be narrower.
[535] para.10. There was no equivalent provision in the 1952 Act.
[536] para.12(1).
[537] para.12(2).

the public or as the eyes and ears of the public to whom they report. A public meeting does not require any participation or opportunity for participation by those attending it.[538]

A fair and accurate report of proceedings at a general meeting of a UK public company[539]; or a fair and accurate copy of or extract from any document circulated to members of a UK public company: (a) by or with the authority of the board of directors; or (b) by the auditors; or (c) by any member of the company in pursuance of a right conferred by statutory provisions[540]; or a fair and accurate copy of or extract from any document circulated to members of a UK public company which relates to the appointment, resignation, retirement or dismissal of directors of the company.[541] The same protection is conferred in relation to corresponding meetings of or documents circulated to members of a public company formed under the law of any of the Channel Islands or the Isle of Man or of another Member State.[542]

A fair and accurate report of the findings or decision[543] of any of the following associations formed in the UK or another Member State, or of any committee or governing body of such an association[544]:

1. an association formed for the purpose of promoting or encouraging the exercise of or interest in any art, science, religion or learning, and empowered by its constitution to exercise control over or adjudicate upon matters of interest or concern to the association, or the actions or conduct of any persons subject to such control or adjudication;
2. an association formed for the purpose of promoting or safeguarding the interests of any trade, business, industry or profession, or of the persons carrying on or engaged in the same, and empowered by its constitution to exercise control over or adjudicate upon matters connected with the trade, business, industry or profession or the actions or conduct of those persons;
3. an association formed for the purpose of promoting or safeguarding the interests of any game, sport or pastime to the

---

[538] *McCartan Turkington Breen v Times Newspapers Ltd* [2001] 2 A.C. 227. The case concerns Northern Irish legislation identical to the 1952 Act, but there are no material differences from the 1996 Act. The report of the meeting may include a press release issued at it.
[539] para.13(1).
[540] para.13(2).
[541] para.13(3).
[542] para.13(5).
[543] Not, therefore, the proceedings: compare the Defamation Amendment Act (NZ) 1974. It is no longer necessary that the finding or decision should relate to a person who is a member of the association or subject to its rules: cf. para.8 of the 1952 Act.
[544] para.14.

playing or exercise of which members of the public are invited or admitted, and empowered by its constitution to exercise control over or adjudicate upon persons connected with or taking part in the game, sport or pastime[545];

4. an association formed for the purpose of promoting charitable objects or other objects beneficial to the community and empowered by its constitution to exercise control over or to adjudicate on matters of interest or concern to the association, or the actions or conduct of any person subject to such control or adjudication.

In addition, the Lord Chancellor and Secretary of State for Scotland are given power to designate by statutory instrument bodies, officers or persons fair and accurate reports[546] of whose adjudications, reports, statements or notices will be protected by the Sch.1 privilege.[547]

12–63   (c) *Malice.* It is now time to look in more detail at the "malice" which defeats qualified privilege both at common law (except under *Reynolds v Times Newspapers*, where it is irrelevant) and under statute. It was once common to describe this as "express" malice to distinguish it from the (fictitious) implied malice which was pleaded in the statement of claim. Now that this practice has almost entirely ceased,[548] there seems no point in retaining "express" either.

Malice means use of the privileged occasion for some improper purpose.

"If the occasion is privileged it is so for some reason, and the defendant is only entitled to the protection of the privilege if he uses the occasion for this reason. He is not entitled to the protection if he uses the occasion not for the reason which makes the occasion privileged but for an indirect or wrong motive."[549]

Of course people act from mixed motives and to constitute malice in law the improper purpose must be the dominant one: I do not lose the protection of qualified privilege if I receive information that a person I dislike has committed a crime and I take pleasure in reporting it to the police.

---

[545] The publication in *The Times* of the decision of the domestic tribunal in *Chapman v Ellesmere* [1932] 2 K.B. 431 would now be covered.

[546] Copies or extracts from adjudications, etc. are treated in the same way.

[547] para.15.

[548] See Lord Hope in *Reynolds v Times Newspapers Ltd* [2001] 2 A.C. 127 at 229.

[549] *Clarke v Molyneux* (1877) 3 Q.B.D. 237 at 246 per Brett L.J. For a full discussion see *Roberts v Bass* [2002] HCA 57; 212 C.L.R. 1.

"It is only where his desire to comply with the relevant duty or to protect the relevant interest plays no significant part in his motives for publishing what he believes to be true that ... malice can properly be found."[550]

Although a desire to injure the claimant is of course malice, this is not necessary: the defendant's motive might be to advance his own interests or to injure some third person: the issue is whether the defendant used the occasion for the purpose for which it was granted by law. Lack of belief in the truth of what is said is generally conclusive evidence of malice,[551] though not where the defendant is under a duty to pass on defamatory statements made by another, as where he receives a complaint or is under a duty to protect the interest of a third party.[552] Mere carelessness in arriving at a belief, or even belief produced by unreasoning prejudice is not malice:

"[D]espite the imperfection of the mental process by which the belief is arrived at it may still be 'honest'. The law demands no more."[553]

Even an honest belief will not, however, protect the defendant if he uses the occasion for some purpose other than that for which the privilege is accorded by law.

The question of malice is for the jury, provided there is evidence **12–64** of it fit to go before them.[554] Evidence of malice may be found in the publication itself. If the language used is utterly disproportionate to the facts, that may lead to an inference of malice,[555] but the law does not weight words in a hair balance and it does not follow that merely because the words are excessive there is therefore malice[556]: "malice is not established by forensic imagination, however, eloquently and subtly expressed".[557] Similarly, although the defendant is not malicious if he makes a charge in which he believes, even though he

---

[550] *Horrocks v Lowe* [1975] A.C. 135 at 151..

[551] As in the tort of deceit, conscious indifference to the truth is here equivalent to knowledge of falsity, for it equally involves lack of honest belief.

[552] See, e.g. *Stuart v Bell* [1891] 2 Q.B. 341. The same will be true in the case of privileged reports, for otherwise the reporter might have to censor his report, making it inaccurate and losing the privilege that way: *Waterhouse v Broadcasting Station 2 G.B. Pty Ltd* (1988) 1 N.S.W.L.R. 58.

[553] *Horrocks v Lowe* [1975] A.C. at 150.

[554] See *Boston v W.S. Bagshaw & Sons Ltd* [1966] 1 W.L.R. 1126 and *Seray-Wurie v Charity Commission* [2008] EWHC 870 (QB). It is almost inconceivable that summary judgment could be given for the claimant on the issue of the defendant's malice: *Hayter v Fahie* [2008] EWCA Civ 1336.

[555] *Adam v Ward* [1917] A.C. 309 at 327, 330, 335.

[556] *Nevill v Fine Arts and General Insurance Co* [1895] 2 Q.B. 156 at 170.

[557] *Broadway Approvals Ltd v Odhams Press Ltd (No.2)* [1965] 1 W.L.R. 805 at 815 per Sellers L.J.

has arrived at that belief by prejudice rather than rational thought,[558] the unlikelihood that a reasonable person could come to such a conclusion may be evidence from which the jury may infer that the defendant did not in fact hold the belief.[559] Malice may also be inferred from the relations between the parties before or after publication or from the conduct of the defendant in the course of the proceedings themselves, as, for example, where the defendant persisted in a plea of justification while nevertheless making no attempt to prove it.[560] The mere pleading of justification is not of itself evidence of malice even though the plea ultimately fails: on the contrary, it may point more to honesty than to malice.[561]

There may also be evidence of malice in the mode of publication and this is commonly illustrated by wider dissemination of the statement than is necessary, such as circulating it on a postcard instead of in a sealed letter, or saying it at the top of one's voice so that bystanders who have no proper interest in it overhear.[562] However, at least in some such cases the publication to uninterested persons in this way may take the case right outside the ambit of privilege, in which case malice is irrelevant.[563]

12–65   Malice is "individual". When a defamatory communication is made by several persons (for example partners or a committee) on an occasion of qualified privilege, only those against whom malice is proved are liable.[564] However, it was for long thought that where a defamatory communication was published by an agent, for example a clerk or a printer, the agent was necessarily liable if the principal was actuated by malice, for the agent's privilege was "ancillary" to or "derivative" from that of the principal and the malice of the principal therefore destroyed the protection of the agent.[565] However, in *Egger v Viscount Chelmsford*[566] the Court of Appeal declared this to be wrong. The malice of an agent may make the innocent principal liable in some cases on the ordinary principles

---

[558] See above.
[559] See, e.g. *Fountain v Boodle* (1842) 3 Q.B. 5 (statement that C incompetent and ill-tempered; evidence that D had kept C in service for a year without complaint and had recommended her for another position left to jury on question of whether belief genuinely held).
[560] *Simpson v Robinson* (1848) 12 Q.B. 511.
[561] *Broadway Approvals Ltd v Odhams Press Ltd (No.2)* [1965] 1 W.L.R. at 825. A plea of justification should not, of course, be made unless the defendant has evidence of the truth of the statement. Where a plea of justification is evidence of malice for the purposes of privilege it may also be relevant on damages.
[562] *Sadgrove v Hole* [1901] 2 K.B. 1; *Oddy v Paulet* (1865) 4 F. & F. 1009; *Chapman v Ellesmere* [1932] 2 K.B. 421 at 474.
[563] A similar problem arises in relation to the inclusion of irrelevant material: above, para.12–51.
[564] *Longdon-Griffiths v Smith* [1951] 1 K.B. 295; *Meekings v Henson* [1964] 1 Q.B. 472.
[565] *Smith v Streatfield* [1913] 3 K.B. 764.
[566] [1965] 1 Q.B. 248; *Richardson v Schwarzenegger* [2004] EWHC 2422 (QB).

of vicarious liability,[567] but the malice of the principal cannot do the same for the innocent agent: it is *respondeat superior*, not *respondeat inferior*. It may be argued that there are difficulties in a derivative privilege standing alone in this way and that the Court of Appeal in effect created a new head of privilege, namely, publication by an agent in circumstances in which the principal has a prima facie privilege to make the defamatory communication, but the decision accords well with common sense—it would be absurd to hold a typist liable because the employer was malicious.[568]

D. Offer of Amends: The Defamation Act 1996

It is open to the defendant to a claim for defamation, as in the case **12-66** of any other tort, to settle out of court. This may involve an apology, which may be incorporated in a statement in open court (approved by the judge).[569] However, generally speaking, an apology is not, as such, a *defence*, though it may of course reduce the damages if the claimant wins, just as its absence may aggravate[570] them. An apology need not be an abject one, but it should at least withdraw completely the imputation and express regret for having made it. To say that someone has manners not fit for a pig and then to retract that by saying that his manners are fit for a pig would merely aggravate the damages. Under Lord Campbell's Act 1843, as amended by the Libel Act 1845, a newspaper which publishes a libel without malice and without gross negligence may plead in defence the publication of a full apology and payment of money into court.[571] This has fallen into complete disuse because it is more advantageous for the

---

[567] Thus there is no doubt that a newspaper would be vicariously liable for the malice of the journalist who wrote the article, but the position is different if the servant played no part in the creation of the libel but merely distributed it: *Hay v Australasian Institute* (1906) 3 C.L.R. 1002.

[568] Even though the typist could recover a full indemnity under the Civil Liability (Contribution) Act 1978. In some of these cases the agent might have an alternative defence under s.1 of the Defamation Act 1996 (above, para.12–23) but that is narrower than privilege since negligence is in issue.

[569] CPR PD 53, para.6.1. This will come to the attention of the press and will be protected by absolute privilege: *Barnet v Crozier* [1987] 1 W.L.R. 272. These are commonly very briefly reported in the "quality" press (but not in other newspapers) along the lines of, "X accepted substantial damages in the High Court yesterday in settlement of an action for libel against the *Daily Weasel* arising from a report that he had been concerned in wasting public money as an officer of Gloomshire Council. Mr Z for the *Weasel* said that his clients unreservedly withdrew any imputation against Mr X, wished it to be known that the publication had arisen from a regrettable error on their part and apologised for the worry and distress suffered by Mr X."

[570] This has been said to be illogical (*Carson v John Fairfax* (1993) 113 A.L.R. 577) but it seems to be the settled general practice here: *Rantzen v Mirror Group Newspapers (1986) Ltd* [1994] Q.B. 670 at 683.

[571] Section 2 of the 1843 Act; s.1 allows the defendant to offer an apology in mitigation of damages only.

defendant to make a "Pt 36 offer" under the general provisions applicable to all actions for damages.[572]

12–67   An apology is, however, part of the steps which, if followed by the defendant, may constitute a defence in an indirect way under the Defamation Act 1996, s.4. The predecessor of this was s.4 of the Defamation Act 1952,[573] which was aimed at cases of "unintentional defamation", that is to say where the defendant did not intend to refer to the claimant[574] or was not aware of some innuendo which made what he said defamatory. It was not, however, applicable to the more common case where the defendant did intend to refer to the claimant, knew very well that the words were defamatory but believed on reasonable grounds that they were true. Where the section applied, the defendant could make an offer of amends, which involved correction and apology, but not the payment of damages.[575] If this was rejected by the claimant the defendant could raise the offer as a defence to the action. The statutory machinery was cumbersome and was little used.

Under the offer of amends procedure in the 1996 Act the position is as follows. The first point is that it requires the defendant to admit that he was wrong (or partly wrong) so if he is unwilling to do this he must take his chances on justification, fair comment or privilege[576] or whatever other defence he can mount. An offer under the statute must be[577] to make a suitable correction and a sufficient apology, to publish those in a manner that is reasonable and practicable in the circumstances and to pay to the claimant[578] such compensation (if any), and such costs, as may be agreed or determined to be payable.[579] An offer may only be made before service

---

[572] CPR Pt 36. Formerly known as making a payment into court but the payment in is no longer necessary. This is a powerful weapon, particularly so in defamation cases, where the amount of damages is likely to be more unpredictable than in the general run of tort cases. The offer is not revealed to the jury and if they make an award which is less advantageous than the settlement offered the defendant will get costs from the date specified in the offer (being not less than 21 days). Now (but not under the former RSC) the *claimant* may make a formal settlement offer and if this is refused and the claimant recovers a judgment at least as advantageous as the offer, the defendant may be made to pay interest at 10 per cent above base rate and pay costs on an indemnity basis. Under the former procedure it was a simple matter of comparing the amount of the defendant's offer and the verdict. Now the matter of whether the verdict is as advantageous as the offer has to be looked at more generally: *Jones v Associated Newspapers* [2007] EWHC 1489 (QB); [2008] 3 All E.R. 911 (verdict for £1 more than offer one year later not as advantageous).

[573] See further the 14th edn of this book, p.332.

[574] *Hulton v Jones* 1910] A.C. 20, above, para.12–20.

[575] Though the court could award costs on an indemnity basis.

[576] There would, for example, be no point in making an offer of amends if the publication was plainly on an occasion of absolute privilege.

[577] It must be in writing and be expressed to be under the Act: s.2(3).

[578] Strictly, in the words of the statute, "person aggrieved" since no proceedings may have been started when the offer is made.

[579] Section 2(4).

of a defence,[580] though he may still of course offer to settle under the general law. If the offer is accepted the claimant may not of course bring an action for defamation or continue one he has started against the defendant, but it may be that the parties have not agreed the details of what should be done under the offer, even though it has been accepted.[581] If so, there is no question of the court being able to compel the defendant to do anything in particular by way of correction, apology or publication[582]—in the absence of agreement that is a matter for the defendant to decide. If, however, the parties have also failed to agree on the amount of the compensation to be paid, that is something which will be settled by the court (sitting without a jury[583]), "on the same principles as damages in defamation proceedings"[584] and account may be taken in setting the figure of the suitability and sufficiency of what the defendant has done by way of correction and apology. An early and unqualified offer of amends followed by an agreed apology will typically attract a "discount" of 50 per cent on the damages.[585]

If the offer is not accepted the action will proceed but the defendant may use the making of the offer as a defence to the action unless the claimant is able to show[586] that the defendant knew[587] or had reason to believe that the statement referred to the claimant (or was likely to be understood as referring to him) and was both false and defamatory of him.[588] "Had reason to believe" is not to be equated with "failed to take reasonable care"—it is equivalent to the recklessness or conscious indifference as to truth which constitutes malice for the purpose of qualified privilege.[589]

The defendant cannot rely on an offer by way of defence in combination with any other defence.[590] However, since defamatory words are often capable of more than one interpretation, it is open

[580] Section 2(5). Nor can one make an offer before defence, speedily withdraw it and then revive it later. A renewed offer is treated as a new offer: s.2(6).

[581] This may be rather surprising but the effect of s.2 seems to be that, "I make an unqualified offer of amends under s.2 of the Defamation Act 1996" is a valid offer. Of course such an offer might be unlikely to be accepted.

[582] Such a power would have been unacceptable to the press.

[583] Section 3(10).

[584] Section 3(6). This presents problems. The CPR PD 53 envisages offer of amends issues being dealt with under Pt 8 on the basis of written evidence, but factual issues underlying the amount of damages may be hotly contested.

[585] *Nail v News Group Newspapers Ltd* [2004] EWCA Civ 1708; [2005] E.M.L.R. 12. Cf. *Campbell-James v Guardian Media Group Plc* [2005] EWHC 893 (QB).

[586] For the burden of proof see the concluding words of s.4(3). The burden was the other way round under s.4 of the 1952 Act.

[587] i.e. (although the Act does not explicitly say so) at the time of the publication.

[588] Section 4(3). He may therefore rely on the defence if he was aware that the story was defamatory and referred to the claimant but believed on reasonable grounds that it was true. This was not so under s.4 of the 1952 Act.

[589] *Milne v Express Newspapers* [2004] EWCA Civ 664; [2004] E.M.L.R. 24.

[590] Section 4(4); but even if not relied on by way of defence the offer may be relied on in mitigation of damages: s.4(5).

to the defendant to make a qualified offer in relation to a specific defamatory meaning which he accepts that the words bear. So if the allegation against a financial director is that his conduct has caused his company to get into difficulties the defendant might concede that this imputed incompetence and make an offer in respect of that meaning. The claimant, however, might contend that the words in their context carried the implication that he had been dishonest. If the offer of amends in respect of the lesser meaning is not accepted then it will be for the jury at the trial to determine what the words do mean. If, though untrue, they bear only the lesser meaning and the claimant is unable to show that the defendant had reason to believe them to be untrue the defence based upon the offer of amends will succeed; if the jury considers that the words were to be understood in the more serious sense, the claimant will win.[591]

The purpose of the procedure is to encourage settlement by holding a fair balance between the parties. A claimant accepting an offer has his reputation vindicated and obtains compensation without the worry and expense of trial. A defendant who is willing to make an offer gets to put the claimant to the difficult burden of proof of malice if it is not accepted. The Act merely speaks of the consequences of the offer being accepted or not accepted: it contains no concept of the offer being refused. However, the claimant cannot simply sit on the offer and pursue his case, accepting it at the last moment if things go badly, thereby pulling the plug on the statutory defence at the price perhaps of suffering some adverse consequence on costs. Although the matter is not strictly contractual,[592] a claimant cannot accept an offer after a reasonable time.[593]

3. PROCEDURE AND REMEDIES IN DEFAMATION

12–68   The law of defamation has been considered by two committees on the subject in the last 40 years, the Faulks Committee[594] and a Supreme Court Procedure Committee Working Group, under the chairmanship of Neill L.J.[595] The Faulks Report was left to gather dust but many of the Neill proposals were implemented by the Defamation Act 1996. The law has come in for a good deal of criticism in some quarters, primarily because of a number of high

---

[591] The defendant may, however, rely on any other defence in respect of a meaning to which a qualified offer does not relate: s.4(4).

[592] *Warren v Random House Group Ltd* [2008] EWCA Civ 834; [2009] Q.B. 600.

[593] *Tesco Stores Ltd v Guardian News & Media Ltd* [2009] E.M.L.R. 5.

[594] Cmnd. 5909 (1975).

[595] *Report on Practice and Procedure in Defamation* (July 1991) (no command number or other publishing designation).

profile and controversial cases in which very large awards of damages have been made, even though no measurable financial loss was suffered and juries were not (or at least were not supposed to be) exercising the power to punish by way of an award of exemplary damages. Since these cases[596] the Court of Appeal has shown a much greater readiness to interfere in defamation awards if they are extravagant, and damages are now much lower, though they are still high by the standards of other European countries. From the point of view of those who conceive themselves defamed, however, the bonanza image was never the whole story, and if the law of defamation has presented a harsh face to media defendants it can present an even harsher one to claimants, for costs can be very high[597] and legal aid has never been applicable. Most defamation defendants are media corporations and most claimants are individuals and under the traditional system of funding litigation the cards were necessarily stacked in favour of the former. However, the picture has to some extent changed under the system of conditional fees which is now of general application in civil litigation.[598] Provided that the claimant can find lawyers willing to conduct his claim on a no-win/no-fee basis he avoids the risk of having to pay his own legal costs if he loses; if he wins the defendant is liable for the claimant's lawyers' success fee, which may be up to twice normally recoverable costs. In principle the unsuccessful claimant remains liable for the costs of the successful defendant but, as in personal injury actions these may be secured by ATE insurance. If that is not so the defendant may find himself saddled with a large quantity of costs which are irrecoverable because the claimant does not have the funds to pay them.[599] There is no doubt that the use of conditional fees in libel cases enables pursuit of a remedy for the most grievous wrongs[600]; on the other hand it has a potential "chilling effect" on the freedom of expression of the press which is equivalent to the massive awards of damages in the past.[601] It has been held that it is open to the court in such cases to make a "costs-capping" order at an early stage of the litigation[602] but the House of Lords has held the present regime does not offend art.10 of the European Convention on Human

---

[596] Prominent examples are *Archer v Express Newspapers* (1987); *Stark v Mirror Group* (1988); and, most notoriously, *Aldington v Tolstoy* (1989).

[597] It has been suggested that even an award of £30,000 damages against a solvent defendant might leave a claimant out of pocket on irrecoverable costs: *Clarke v Bain* [2008] EWHC 2636 (QB) at [54].

[598] See generally para.1–27, above.

[599] See *Turcu v News Group Newspapers Ltd* [2005] EWHC 799 (QB).

[600] *Lillie v Newcastle CC* [2002] EWHC 1600 (QB) is a good example.

[601] See *Campbell v M.G.N. (No.2)* [2005] UKHL 61; [2005] 4 All E.R. 793, where the successful claimant's costs were over £1 million and the damages were only £3,500. This is a breach of confidence rather than a libel case but the two types of claim are very similar.

[602] *King v Telegraph Group Ltd* [2004] EWCA Civ 613; [2005] 1 W.L.R. 2282.

Rights and that the conditional fee system is open to everyone, even those who could afford to finance the litigation from their own resources.[603] Proposals have been made across the board for the abolition of the ability to recover the successful claimant's success fee and ATE premium[604] but the Government as an interim measure has said that it proposes to limit success fees in defamation cases to 10 per cent.[605] Very occasionally the libel claimant has ample means and the defendant is impecunious, as was the case in *Steel v UK*,[606] where the McDonald's Corp had obtained judgment for £76,000 damages against the unwaged defendants in person (which there was not the remotest hope of enforcing) and had not sought an order for claimants' costs (which must have been a seven-figure sum). The European Court of Human Rights held that the absence of legal aid for the defendants contravened art.6 of the Convention.

It is also argued that the virtually exclusive emphasis of the law on damages as a remedy militates against what a claimant will (or should, according to some conventional wisdom, which is perhaps inclined to underrate the motives of anger and revenge) regard as the major purpose of his claim, the vindication of his good name. The recovery of damages, whether by judgment or settlement, will not necessarily achieve this end unless it is widely publicised.[607] Furthermore, the defences available in a defamation action, while they are undoubtedly necessary to protect freedom of speech, may have the effect that the issue of the truth of the allegations is wholly[608] or partly suppressed and a wholly unfounded and very damaging accusation may still lead to a verdict for the defendant which on its face says nothing about the jury's opinion on the truth of the accusation.[609] Even where the claimant's reputation is vindicated it will only be after protracted litigation, the expense of which is at least in part produced by the necessity to hold the balance between the protection of reputation and free speech. On the face of it,

---

[603] *Campbell v M.G.N. (No.2)*, above, fn.601.

[604] See para.1–27, above.

[605] Ministry of Justice CP1/2010.

[606] [2005] E.M.L.R. 15, ECHR.

[607] For statements in open court on settlement, see above, para.12–66.

[608] The most extreme example is a statement made on an occasion of absolute privilege, which cannot even get to the jury.

[609] It is now rare to instruct the jury to answer a series of questions by way of special verdict, but they sometimes volunteer the information, e.g. "the words were untrue but the defendant was not malicious". However, it has been suggested that now that reputation is regarded as a protected interest under art.8 of the European Convention on Human Rights the court might grant a declaration of falsity under s.7 of the Human Rights Act 1998 even if the common law claim were defeated by privilege: *W v Westminster CC* [2004] EWHC 2866 (QB). However, this would be unworkable in a trial by jury and anyway it might be said that it would require the defendant to deal with the issue of falsity when he has a perfectly good, "cheap" defence on another basis.

therefore, there is much attraction in a system for media defamation whereby there would be a speedy procedure for requiring a correction of a defamatory statement or the publication of a counter-statement by the complainant. Such a "right of reply" exists in the press laws of some European countries[610] and is required in certain circumstances by an EC Directive on approximation of broadcasting laws.[611] It must also be borne in mind that a person aggrieved by inaccurate statements about him may complain to the Press Complaints Commission (a self-regulatory body for the press) or to the Broadcasting Standards Commission (a statutory body) which do not award compensation but which may require the offending newspaper or broadcaster to publish a summary of any adjudication. However, there are some difficulties with such remedies if they are made the exclusive or even the primary form of redress. From the claimant's point of view "mud sticks"[612] and the possibility of being required to publish an apology and correction would not be a very powerful deterrent against the dissemination of the careless or even reckless falsehoods which are undoubtedly from time to time published by the media.[613] As for the defendant, it would be a new and perhaps dangerous step to impose upon a newspaper a legal requirement[614] (which presumably would have to be backed by criminal sanctions) to publish a statement, "extolling the complainant's non-existent virtue".[615] In any event, forced publication might not convince the reader that the smoke really had no underlying fire. The law of torts is not just about compensation and deterrence is undoubtedly an element, even if sometimes a rather covert one,[616] in defamation law; experience suggests that unless there were to be comprehensive criminal sanctions[617] or administrative regulation of the media—neither being likely for historical and constitutional

[610] e.g. Germany. See Braithwaite, *International Libel Handbook* (1995), Ch.7.

[611] See O.J. (L) 298 (1989). This is apparently regarded as satisfied in this country by s.146 of the Broadcasting Act 1990, requiring publication of a summary of an adjudication.

[612] See the remarks in the Supreme Court of Canada in *Hill v Church of Scientology* (1995) 126 D.L.R. (4th) 129 at 176.

[613] See, e.g. *John v Mirror Group Newspapers* [1997] Q.B. 586.

[614] Under Sch.1 to the Defamation Act 1996 certain reports are privileged subject to explanation or contradiction (above, para.12–62) but there is no way of compelling a correction if the defendant is willing to forgo the statutory defence.

[615] The phrase is the Faulks Committee's (Cmnd. 5909, 1975). This was also the view of the Calcutt Committee (Cm. 1102, 1990) and the Neill Committee (1990). The power to compel publication of an adjudication under s.146 of the Broadcasting Act 1990 may be explained by the fact that the broadcast media are regulated in a way that the print media have not been since the end of the 17th century. The Press Complaints Commission is of course a voluntary body.

[616] Lord Hoffmann is quite open about the deterrent function in *The Gleaner Co Ltd v Abrahams* [2003] UKPC 55; [2004] 1 A.C. 628 at [53].

[617] It is difficult to transfer experience in non-common law systems simply because the criminal law plays a much larger part in many of them.

reasons—then the possibility of heavy damages is the only effective deterrent.[618]

12–69   The media (quite understandably) would like as little defamation liability as possible and there is a current highly orchestrated campaign against the supposed phenomenon of "libel tourism", that is to say, persons who are not based in England suing in respect of publications here, a matter made more problematical by publications on the Internet, which will be published here if accessed here. There is not much evidence about the scale of this but it is not difficult to see how, for example, a foreign businessman or corporation might legitimately feel that he has a reputation in London which is worth protecting. The courts already have power to strike out trivial claims unlikely to cause damage as an abuse of process but thought obviously needs to be given to whether some more substantial hurdle ought to be put in place.[619] However, most of the pressure on this comes from the United States and it is perfectly clear that nothing will satisfy Americans except the wholesale Americanisation of defamation law. Several states have passed legislation (bizarrely named in New York the Libel Terrorism Protection Act 2008) refusing any enforcement of foreign libel judgments against their citizens unless the law under which they were given conforms to that in the United States (and it is of course for Americans sued here to decide whether they will come here to defend claims against them). There is room for substantial differences of opinion as to whether English or American law has a "better rule" on liability for defamatory statements about public figures but one point seems to be entirely absent from the discussion, which is largely couched in terms of English law being "archaic" and "complex": that the other major common law courts have over the last few years (Canada as recently as 2009) rejected the American model.[620]

A. Trial by Jury: the "Summary Procedure"

12–70   Some of the criticism of defamation law has been directed at trial by jury. At present either party to a defamation case is entitled to claim trial by jury unless the court is of the opinion that the trial,

---

[618] See the Neill Report, para.XVIII 14. Compare the provisions of the Defamation Act 1992 (NZ) s.24 and the Irish Defamation Act 2009 ss.28 and 30. However, neither removes the sanction of damages as an alternative. The Irish Act provides that the court may require a correction and prescribe its content, the NZ provisions merely allow it to recommend. The Irish Act specifically provides that the applicant for a declaratory order is not required to prove the statement false. For further difficulties with declaratory relief see Young J.A. in *Bracks v Smyth Kirk* [2009] NSWCA 401.
[619] This is considered, among other matters relating to libel and privacy, in the 2010 Report of the House of Commons Culture Media and Sport Committee: HC 362–1, February 9, 2010. See now Preface.
[620] See para.12–54, above.

"requires any prolonged examination of documents or accounts or any scientific or local investigation which cannot conveniently[621] be made with a jury."[622] It has been said that trial by jury is a major reason for high costs in defamation cases because the action must proceed at a slower pace[623] but the institution received a substantial body of support in the evidence given to the Faulks Committee and the arguments most commonly advanced in its favour were that the jury was better placed than a judge to determine the "ordinary meaning" of words and how damaging the words were to the claimant's reputation. The Committee nevertheless recommended that the right to trial by jury be abolished, though a discretion to award one would remain. This has not come about, but s.8 of the Defamation Act 1996 introduced a summary, non-jury procedure which has become the method[624] of dealing with some defamation cases.[625]

First, the court (i.e. a judge sitting without a jury) may dismiss the claimant's claim, "if it appears that it has no realistic prospect of success[626] and there is no reason why it should be tried."[627] It seems unlikely that this can be used against trivial claims: the issue is whether the claimant might get a verdict, not whether the claim is worth pursuing. Secondly, the court may give judgment for the claimant and grant him summary relief if it appears that there is no

---

[621] See *Beta Construction v Channel Four* [1990] 1 W.L.R. 1042.

[622] Supreme Court Act 1981 s.69(1). The mere fact that the trial is likely to be a lengthy one is not a reason for refusing a jury under s.69(1). The formation of an opinion under s.69(1) is not a matter of discretion, though if such an opinion is formed there is still a discretion to order trial by jury: *Viscount de L'Isle v Times Newspapers Ltd* [1988] 1 W.L.R. 1042; *Aitken v Preston* [1997] E.M.L.R. 415.

[623] Faulks Report, Cmnd, 5909, para.490. It should not be assumed that juries are necessarily favoured by claimants and disliked by defendants. If the resources of the defendant are considerable the prospect of a long and costly trial may raise the stakes in favour of the defence.

[624] It also now seems more common for the parties to agree to trial by judge alone even where the summary procedure is not applicable. *Galloway v Telegraph Group Ltd* [2004] EWHC 2786; [2005] E.M.L.R. 7 (affirmed [2006] EWCA Civ 17) is a high profile example. There is nothing to prevent the parties agreeing to settle their differences by other means. It is believed that a High Court judge was awarded £7,500 in 1991 by an arbitrator in respect of a libel in a local newspaper; but the Neill Committee concluded that neither the various forms of alternative dispute resolution nor the Press Complaints/Broadcasting Standards Commissions could become a substitute for the action.

[625] See CPR PD 53 s.5. In fact the position is rather more complicated for CPR Pt 24 now provides an alternative route to summary disposal of a defamation claim. Although the wording is slightly different, the "prospects of success" tests are the same: *James Gilbert v MGN* [2000] E.M.L.R. 680. However, s.8 only enables the whole case to be disposed of, whereas Pt 24 can be used to dispose of a particular issue, e.g. a defence.

[626] See *Swain v Hillman* [2001] 1 All E.R. 91, CA, a Pt 24 case.

[627] Defamation Act 1996 s.8(2). The concept of a reason why a claim should be tried even though it has no realistic prospect of success is at first sight a curious one. Some factors are listed in s.8(5) but in the case of one of them ("the extent to which there is conflict of evidence") it would seem that the court would anyway not be in a position to say that there was no realistic prospect of success.

defence which has a realistic prospect of success[628] and there is no other reason why the claim should be tried.[629] Summary relief is a declaration that the statement was false and defamatory, an order that the defendant publish a suitable correction and apology and damages not exceeding £10,000.[630] This provision may mislead on a superficial reading for the court cannot in fact dictate the terms of any correction and apology: if the defendant is intransigent it can only compel him to publish a summary of the court's judgment.[631] For the claimant who desires a cheaper and speedier vindication of his reputation than is offered by a full trial this provides a "fast track" route,[632] but it should not be looked on solely in this light for the court may force this solution on the claimant and deny him trial by jury if it is satisfied that the summary relief, "will adequately compensate him for the wrong he has suffered".[633] It is therefore clearly contemplated that there is a distinction between "minor" and "serious" libels, the former being suitable for summary disposition even if the claimant wishes to go to trial. It may of course be difficult to predict at what level judges will pitch the boundary line between the two situations.[634] Furthermore, the judicial declaration of falsity under the summary procedure goes some way to meeting that element of libel damages which are concerned with vindicating the claimant's reputation so that the procedure may extend further up the scale than libels which are "worth" £10,000 in damages terms.[635]

B. Awards of Damages and their Control

12–71   The Court of Appeal has always had power to set aside a jury award of damages on the ground that it is excessive[636] but in the past the power was rarely exercised and the standard at which the court would interfere was set very high, where the award was such that it

---

[628] In the past the general Order 14 procedure did not apply to defamation.
[629] Section 8(3).
[630] Section 9(1). The maximum figure may be varied by order.
[631] Section 9(2), which contemplates that the content and venue will normally be agreed by the parties. See also above, para.12–66.
[632] A defendant wishing to take advantage of s.8 may legitimately waive a triable defence: *Milne v Telegraph Group Ltd* [2001] E.M.L.R. 30. The origin of the summary procedure is a Bill drafted by Lord Hoffmann in 1989. The proposal was not supported by the Neill Committee, which doubted whether there were large numbers of "trivial" libels which did not settle anyway: Ch.XVII.
[633] Section 8(3).
[634] See *Milne v Telegraph Group Ltd*, above, fn.632 (newspaper report that C had been called a vindictive liar—£5,000). Compare the maximum figure of £10,000 with the £25,000 the CA thought proper as general damages in *John v Mirror Group Newspapers* [1997] Q.B. 586, below.
[635] *Mawdsley v Guardian Newspapers Ltd* [2002] EWHC 1780 (QB).
[636] In theory at least the same is true if the award is inadequate, but the approach to this has been even more cautious.

was "divorced from reality".[637] In part at least this was because if the court did set aside the award there had to be new trial, with all the attendant expense. Section 8 of the Courts and Legal Services Act 1990 empowered the Court of Appeal to substitute its own figure of damages rather than ordering a new trial. There is no indication in the Act itself that this was intended to alter the "threshold of intervention"[638] but the change coincided with concern about the seemingly endless rise in the level of awards and the Court of Appeal in *Rantzen v Mirror Group Newspapers (1986) Ltd*[639] began a new chapter. The court was influenced by the guarantee of freedom of expression in art.10 of the European Convention on Human Rights[640] and said that in the light of the Convention:

"[I]t seems . . . that the grant of an almost limitless discretion to a jury fails to provide a satisfactory measurement for deciding what is 'necessary in a democratic society' or 'justified by a pressing social need'. We consider therefore that the common law if properly understood requires the courts to subject large awards of damages to a more searching scrutiny than has been customary in the past. It follows that what has been regarded as the barrier against intervention should be lowered. The question becomes: could a reasonable jury have thought that their award was necessary to compensate the claimant and to re-establish his reputation?"[641]

Another very high award in *John v Mirror Group Newspapers Ltd*,[642] which is now the leading case, compelled the Court to reiterate this policy of restraint and to develop the law on the guidance that should be given to juries. Now it is proper to inform the jury by way of guidance of the general range of damages for non-pecuniary loss in personal injury cases,[643] although the loss of a leg cannot of course be directly compared with the loss of a reputation.[644] Furthermore, although the jury may not be told of the figures which have been awarded by other juries, they may be told of figures approved or substituted by the Court of Appeal in cases

---

[637] *McCarey v Associated Newspapers Ltd* [1965] 2 Q.B. 86 at 111.
[638] Indeed the statement by the Lord Chancellor in 516 HL (5th series) cols 170–171 may indicate the contrary.
[639] [1994] Q.B. 670.
[640] Above, para.12–53.
[641] [1994] Q.B. at 692.
[642] [1997] Q.B. 586. The general damages element of the award was reduced from £75,000 to £25,000.
[643] As to other elements in personal injury awards see fn.649, below.
[644] By way of comparison, the £10,000 maximum figure for the use of the summary procedure (above) was, at the time of the 1996 Act, about the mid-range figure for severe facial scarring with permanent disfigurement for males or total loss of the sense of taste, and about two and a half times that for a simple fracture of the tibia.

since the Courts and Legal Services Act[645] and it is permissible for the judge[646] to indicate the sum that might be appropriate.[647] An award of damages for defamation may include elements of aggravated or exemplary damages. These are considered later.[648]

Whether or not it is strictly so as a matter of precedent, the maximum allowable damages for defamation (leaving aside exemplary damages and proved financial loss) seems to be the maximum sum for non-pecuniary loss in personal injury cases (currently something above £250,000).[649] There are plainly differing judicial opinions on this matter[650] but a number of elements differentiate an award of damages for defamation from one for personal injury, which have to be borne in mind when it is contended that it is unacceptable for a libel claimant to be awarded as much as the victim of a catastrophic personal injury: personal injury damages are nearly always awarded for negligence or breach of statutory duty rather than intentional wrongdoing; in global terms such damages have a far greater economic impact on society than those for defamation; a defamation claimant may well in the long term suffer serious financial loss from the attack on his reputation but is commonly unable to prove that (or what its amount may be) to the required legal standard; and there is an undoubted element of deterrence in defamation damages which requires that awards should be substantial and it is not necessarily correct to assume that the *only* purpose of tort law is compensation.[651]

4. Malicious Falsehood[652]

12–72 A false statement may be damaging even though it is not defamatory. It may be relied on by others to their loss, in which case it may

---

[645] These are summarised in Gatley, *Libel and Slander*, 11th edn, Appendix 3 (and Supplement).

[646] According to a press report (*The Times*, January 24, 1998, "A good joke worth sharing") Popplewell J. in *Allason v BBC Worldwide* (description of former MP as "conniving little shit") told the jury that £10,000 (the maximum figure for the summary remedy) might be a proper figure. The claimant lost, though whether because the jury found the statement not to be defamatory or to be fair comment or both, is not clear.

[647] Although it is indicated in *John* that counsel might make suggestions to the jury in practice they do not do so: *Kiam v MGN Ltd* [2002] EWCA Civ 43; [2003] Q.B. 281 at [55].

[648] See below, para.22–8.

[649] Other elements in personal injury awards (loss of earnings and expenses) are of course irrelevant. Libel juries may have been misled in the past by believing that multi-million pound awards in personal injury cases represented non-pecuniary loss.

[650] Compare Lord Hoffmann in *The Gleaner Co Ltd v Abrahams* [2003] UKPC 55; [2004] 1 A.C. 628 and Sedley L.J. in *Kiam v MGN Ltd* [2002] EWCA Civ 43; [2003] Q.B. 281.

[651] "Oil and vinegar may not mix in solution but they combine to make an acceptable salad dressing": *The Gleaner Co Ltd v Abrahams,* above, fn.650, at [54] per Lord Hoffmann.

[652] Injurious falsehood is an alternative name.

be actionable as deceit if made knowingly or recklessly[653] or, if there is a "special relationship", as negligence[654]; but a false, non-defamatory statement may also cause damage by influencing the way in which other persons behave towards the claimant. For example, a newspaper may publish incorrectly that a trader has closed his business, with the result that potential customers do not approach him; or a manufacturer may circulate false information that because of technological development his product is now twice as effective as the claimant's and thereby take business away from him; alternatively, the manufacturer may represent that his goods are in fact the goods of the claimant, which enjoy a good reputation. None of these representations is, on the face of it, defamatory, for they do not impute anything derogatory, indeed in the third case the position is quite the reverse. The third case is covered by the tort of passing off, which is dealt with in a separate part of this book,[655] but the other two may fall within malicious falsehood,[656] which overlaps considerably with defamation.[657] This area shows clearly, if proof were needed, that English law is a law of separate torts: there is no general right to sue in respect of untruths or even to restrain the circulation of untruths.[658]

Malicious falsehood requires the making of false statement, with "malice" to some person other than the claimant, as a result of which the claimant suffers damage.

A. False Statement to some Person other than the Claimant

The statement may be oral or written and even conduct conveying a false impression will be sufficient.[659] It is for the claimant to prove that the statement is false and there is no presumption in his favour.[660]

12–73

The statement usually affects the claimant's trade or business. So, in the leading case of *Ratcliffe v Evans*[661] an action succeeded in respect of a statement by a newspaper that the claimant had ceased to trade; but so long as the statement is made with the requisite

---

[653] Above, para.11–2.
[654] Above, para.11–16.
[655] Below, para.18–44.
[656] The tort has lost most of its importance in Australia and New Zealand because of the enactment of a statutory wrong of engaging in misleading or deceptive conduct in the course of trade or commerce. See, e.g. s.52(1), Trade Practices Act 1974 (Cwth.).
[657] In the case of the representation about greater efficiency that would also be the tort of deceit, *but only against the purchasers of the product who were misled.*
[658] *Kingdom of Spain v Christie, Manson & Woods Ltd* [1986] 1 W.L.R. 1120.
[659] *Wilts United Dairies v Robinson & Sons* [1958] R.P.C. 94.
[660] Cf. the position in defamation.
[661] [1892] 2 Q.B. 524; *Joyce v Motor Surveys Ltd* [1948] Ch. 252.

intent there is no restriction about its subject matter. In one of the earliest cases the false statement was that the claimant was already married, whereby she lost a proposed marriage[662]; in an American case the defendant gave false information that the claimant was not a citizen, subjecting him to deportation proceedings[663]; and in *Kaye v Robertson*[664] the tort was established where a newspaper published what was falsely claimed to be an interview to which a television personality had consented, thereby depriving him of the chance to sell his story as an "exclusive". The tort does not, however, extend to statements which have no connection with the claimant or his property: it is not this tort (though it may be another one) by A against C if A tells B lies to obtain property and thereby deprives C of the opportunity to bid for it.[665] A statement by one trader that his goods are superior to those of a rival (mere "puffing"), even if it is false and known to be so and causes damage is not actionable, for courts of law cannot be converted into agencies for trying the relative merits of rival productions.[666] However, this "privilege" is confined to those imprecise commendations which are a common part of advertising and to which a reasonable person does not attach very much importance. Accordingly, if a defendant chooses to frame his comparison in the form of scientific tests or other statements of ascertainable fact, he will be liable if they are proved untrue.[667]

B. Malice

12–74   This expression is never easy to define in the law of torts, but here it is essentially the same as the malice which defeats qualified privilege in defamation.[668] The requirement is satisfied if the defendant knows that the statement is false or if he is reckless, i.e. makes

---

[662] *Sheperd v Wakeman* (1662) 1 Sid. 79.

[663] *Al Raschid v News Syndicate Co* 191 N.E. 713 (1934). The deportation proceedings were not "judicial proceedings" for the purposes of the tort of malicious prosecution.

[664] [1991] F.S.R. 52.

[665] *Lonrho Plc v Fayed* [1988] 3 All E.R. 464 (though no claim for malicious falsehood appears to have been made). On appeal on another point [1989] 2 All E.R. 65 and [1992] 1 A.C. 448.

[666] *White v Mellin* [1895] A.C. 154 at 164; *Hubbuck & Sons Ltd Wilkinson* [1899] 1 Q.B. 86.

[667] *De Beers Products Ltd v International General Electric Co of New York* [1975] 1 W.L.R. 972; *D.S.G. Retail v Comet Group*, February 8, 2002, QBD (prices). Even imprecise assertions of superiority may be actionable if they denigrate the claimant's wares in a manner which a reasonable person would take seriously: *White v Mellin,* above, fn.666, at 171; *Alcott v Miller's Karri etc. Ltd* (1904) 91 L.T. 722. For the statutory remedy for unfounded claims of patent infringement see Clerk and Lindsell, *Torts,* 19th edn, para.26–99.

[668] *Spring v Guardian Assurance Plc* [1993] 2 All E.R. 273 (reversed on another point, [1995] 2 A.C. 296).

the statement not caring whether it is true or false, but negligence is not enough.[669] "Honest belief," said Scrutton L.J.[670]:

"[I]n an unfounded claim is not malice, but the nature of the unfounded claim may be evidence that there is not an honest belief in it. It may be so unfounded that the particular fact that it is put forward may be evidence that it is not honestly believed."[671]

However, even if the defendant does believe the untrue statement there will still be malice if he is actuated by some indirect, dishonest or improper motive, which seems here to mean the purpose of injuring the claimant rather than defending his own interests or pushing his own business.[672]

C. Damage

Save in cases falling within the provisions of s.3(1) of the Defamation Act 1952 proof of special (i.e. actual, pecuniary) damage is required[673] but this is satisfied by proof of a general loss of business where the falsehood is in its very nature intended, or is reasonably likely, to produce and actually does produce in the ordinary course of things, such loss; for there are businesses, like those of an auctioneer or a publican, where the customers are often so fleeting in their patronage that it would be almost impossible for the claimant to name in particular such of them as have ceased to deal with him as a consequence of the defendant's tort.[674] By s.3(1) of the Defamation Act 1952 it is no longer necessary to allege or prove special damage if (a) the words complained of are published in writing or other permanent form,[675] or if (b) the words are calculated[676] to cause pecuniary damage to the claimant in respect of any office, profession, calling, trade or business carried on by him at the

12–75

---

[669] *Shapiro v La Morta* (1923) 40 T.L.R. 39 and 201; *Balden v Shorter* [1933] Ch. 427; *Loudon v Ryder (No.2)* [1953] Ch. 423 (absence of malice does not preclude declaration of right); *McDonalds Hamburgers v Burgerking (UK) Ltd* [1986] F.S.R. 45.

[670] *Greers Ltd v Pearman & Corder Ltd* (1922) 39 R.P.C. 406 at 417 (assertion of trade mark infringement after years of disclaimer of right to exclusive use).

[671] If there is no belief in the truth of the statement it does not matter that the defendant's motive is only to advance his own interests: *Wilts United Dairies v Robinson & Sons* [1957] R.P.C. 220 (on appeal but not on this point [1958] R.P.C. 94).

[672] *Dunlop v Maison Talbot* (1904) 20 T.L.R. 579.

[673] *White v Mellin* [1895] A.C. 154; *Royal Baking Powder Co v Wright & Co* (1900) 18 R.P.C. 95 at 99.

[674] *Ratcliffe v Evans* [1892] 2 Q.B. 524 at 533. Cf. *Joyce v Sengupta* [1993] 1 W.L.R. 337 at 347.

[675] *Fielding v Variety Inc* [1967] 2 Q.B. 841. Broadcasting is publication in a permanent form: s.3(2).

[676] Which means "likely to": *Customglass Boats v Salthouse Bros* [1976] R.P.C. 589 (equivalent provision of NZ Act).

time of the publication. Distress and injury to feelings do not amount to special damage for the purpose of this tort at common law; but where special damage is established (or where the claimant is entitled to rely on s.3 of the 1952 Act) he may recover aggravated damages for injury to feelings in the same way as he can in an action for defamation and the award may take account of the conduct of the defendant during the litigation, for example in trying to blacken the claimant's name.[677]

D. Varieties of the Tort

12–76   Particular varieties of malicious falsehood have acquired names of their own: slander of goods (where the defendant disparages the claimant's goods) and slander of title (where he questions the claimant's ownership of property). These are not separate torts and have nothing to do with "slander" in the defamation sense. It would be better if the expressions were dropped.

E. Malicious Falsehood and Defamation

12–77   Although malicious falsehood may lie where defamation does not, the two torts nevertheless overlap. In *Joyce v Sengupta*[678] a statement that the claimant had stolen her royal employer's confidential correspondence and sold it to a newspaper was plainly defamatory as well as being malicious falsehood. However, malicious falsehood is both wider and narrower than defamation: it is wider in the sense that the statement need not reflect upon the character or reputation of the claimant; it is narrower in that in defamation the claimant need not prove the falsity of the statement and, broadly speaking, untrue defamatory statements are actionable without proof of actual malice.[679] Furthermore, malicious falsehood does not cover mere loss of reputation without proof of pecuniary loss.[680] Framing a claim as malicious falsehood deprives the defendant of the right to trial by jury which he would have in a case of defamation, but that is not in itself a reason for the court to dismiss as an abuse of process a claim for malicious falsehood which could be run as a claim for defamation.[681] However, where the claimant

---

[677] *Khodaparast v Shad* [2000] 1 W.L.R. 618. On causation of damage see *Palmer Bruyn & Parker v Parsons* [2001] HCA 69; 185 A.L.R. 280.

[678] [1993] 1 W.L.R. 337.

[679] Malice may rebut the defences of fair comment or qualified privilege but those defences only apply to certain types of statements or statements made on certain occasions.

[680] *Joyce v Sengupta*, above, fn.678; *Lonrho v Fayed (No.5)* [1993] 1 W.L.R. 1489 at 1504.

[681] *Joyce v Sengupta*. Until 2000 malicious falsehood claims were eligible for legal aid. It is no longer eligible for the replacement, litigation funded by the Legal Services Commission.

brought concurrent claims for defamation and malicious falsehood and the defendant made an offer of amends under the Defamation Act 1996 in respect of the former, thereby admitting that it had been wrong, the latter claim was stayed.[682]

5. PRIVACY

The English common law does not give any direct action for the invasion of privacy as such.[683] The law in the United States took a different course at the end of the 19th century[684] but, like the law of defamation there, has been affected by the constitutional protection afforded to freedom of speech by the First Amendment.[685] In France and Germany general rights of personal privacy exist (the first by legislation,[686] the second by judicial decision[687]) but damages are modest by English defamation standards.

12–78

However, the technically correct proposition that there is no common law tort of invasion of privacy would be seriously misleading if not substantially qualified. The protection of privacy is a value recognised by the law and underlying certain specific rules of law but it is not a principle of law in itself capable without more of giving a cause of action for its infringement.[688] There is in fact considerable protection for the interest of privacy in a number of ways. First, there is the "incidental" protection afforded by torts like trespass and nuisance which are primarily focused on other interests; secondly, there are various statutory provisions, most particularly those relating to data protection and the behaviour of public authorities under the Human Rights Act 1998; thirdly, the last few years have seen the substantial development of the old law of breach of confidence so that it has developed an offshoot which we are probably now justified in calling the tort of misuse of private information.

A. The Indirect Impact of other Torts

It is perhaps an oversimplification to say that the law of defamation is not concerned with the invasion of privacy: the distress which

12–79

---

[682] *Tesco Stores Ltd v Guardian News & Media Ltd* [2009] E.M.L.R. 5.
[683] *Wainwright v Home Office* [2003] UKHL 53; [2004] 2 A.C. 406.
[684] Largely as a result of a famous article, Warren and Brandeis, "The Right of Privacy" (1890) 4 Harv L.R. 193. The Restatement 2d of Torts, s.652A–I enumerates four forms of invasion (intrusion upon seclusion; appropriation of name or likeness; offensive publicity to private life; publicity placing a person in a false light). Some of these are rather far removed from privacy in the commonly understood sense.
[685] See Bedingfield (1992) 55 M.L.R. 111.
[686] Law of July 17, 1970.
[687] 13 B.G.H.Z. 334, May 25, 1954.
[688] See *Wainwright v Home Office*, above, fn.683, at [31].

is felt by the victim of a libel may be as much due to the torrent of intrusive publicity which descends upon him as to the affront he feels at having untrue things said about him; and the protection which is granted to statements amounting to fair comment is confined to matters of public interest. However, in one fundamental sense defamation and privacy are mutually exclusive in that, almost without exception,[689] truth is a complete defence in English law.[690] Hence, a defeated boxer has no remedy against one who publishes an accurate film of the fight in which he was beaten[691] and there is no control via the law of defamation on the practice of digging up scandalous or ridiculous aspects of a person's past,[692] unless, at least, the statement can be said to impute such matters at present. Even where the statement is untrue there is no defamation unless it can properly be said to reflect on the reputation of the person about whom it is made, whether directly or by way of innuendo.[693] Thus it is not difficult to conceive of statements about, say, a person's health which would be distressing but not defamatory of him.[694]

Where there is a trespass to land it is quite likely that one of the claimant's grievances will be the invasion of his privacy and in a suitable case there is no reason why damages for trespass should not reflect that.[695] However, the law of trespass operates only in favour of the person who is the occupier of the premises entered[696] and,

---

[689] The clear exception, but of limited scope, is the Rehabilitation of Offenders Act 1974, above, para.12–30, but while that may prevent the dragging up of old convictions it is no use if what is revealed is a crime for which the claimant was never convicted. The other exception, whereby truth may not be a defence if the case is framed as conspiracy (below, para.18–22) is perhaps more dubious.

[690] Those legal systems which recognise a wrong of invasion of privacy and make truth a defence only to defamation where the publication is in the public interest therefore have some difficulty in separating the two wrongs. See the discussion in *Independent Newspapers Holdings Ltd v Suliman* [2004] ZASCA 57.

[691] *Palmer v National Sporting Club Ltd* (1906) in MacGillivray's Copyright Cases (1905–1910), p.55; *Sports etc. Agency v "Our Dogs" Publishing Co Ltd* [1916] 2 K.B. 880; [1917] 2 K.B. 125.

[692] Compare in US law, *Melvin v Reid* 297 P. 91 (1931); and see *McDonald v North Queensland Newspaper* [1997] 1 Qd. R. 62.

[693] As in *Tolley v Fry* [1931] A.C. 333, above, para.12–16. There was an arguable defamatory implication in *Kaye v Robertson* [1991] F.S.R. 62, in that the paper which published the purported interview had a notoriously low reputation but the case was not clear enough to obtain the interlocutory injunction which was sought.

[694] Of course there have been occasions when the concept of a statement which would lower the claimant in the estimation of right-thinking people has been stretched: see *Youssoupoff v MGM* (1934) 50 T.L.R. 581, para.12–11, above. In *Ettingshausen v Australian Consolidated Press* (1991) 23 N.S.W.L.R. 443 it is suggested that to publish a nude photograph of the claimant would be defamatory even if it did not convey the imputation that it had been published with his consent. Sed quaere, even though at that time truth was not a defence in New South Wales unless publication was for the public benefit.

[695] *Morris v Beardmore* [1981] A.C. 446 at 464.

[696] Thus in *Kaye v Robertson*, above, fn.693, the defendants probably committed trespass against the Charing Cross Hospital, but the claimant was only a licensee there; but in some cases the impact on the occupier's guests might affect the damages awarded to the occupier: *NSW v Ibbett* [2006] HCA 57; 231 A.L.R. 485.

after a brief flirtation with a wider rule, that has been affirmed to be also the case for the law of nuisance.[697] Further, neither tort is apt to deal with modern means of electronic and optical surveillance, which may be carried on from a great distance.[698] There is no trespass in watching or listening from outside[699] and it is difficult to see how the law of nuisance could be stretched to cover an "interference" of which the occupier was wholly unaware at the time. Thus in *Malone v Metropolitan Police Commissioner*[700] the claimant failed in his action for a declaration that the tapping of his telephone on the authority of the Secretary of State was unlawful because, inter alia, there was no right to "telephonic privacy".[701]

Another actionable form of interference with proprietary rights which may indirectly involve a court in protecting privacy is breach of copyright. In *Williams v Settle*[702] the claimant's father-in-law had been murdered in circumstances which attracted publicity. The defendant, who had taken the photographs at the claimant's wedding two years previously, sold one for publication in the national press. The copyright in the photographs was the claimant's and therefore the court was able to award him heavy damages for the defendant's "scandalous conduct" which was, "in total disregard not only of the legal rights of the claimant regarding copyright but of his feelings and his sense of family dignity and pride."[703] Under current copyright law the rights in such a photograph would probably be in the photographer but, ironically, this is one instance in which the law does address the issue of privacy head on, for under s.85 of the Copyright, Designs and Patents Act 1988, breach of which is actionable as a breach of statutory duty, a person who for private and domestic purposes commissions the making of a photograph or film has the right to prevent the issue of copies to the public.

B. The Human Rights Act 1998 and the Data Protection Act 1998

There is no doubt that the "development" of the law of confidence into a law of misuse of private information has been influenced by the presence of the European Convention on Human

12–80

---

[697] *Hunter v Canary Wharf* [1997] A.C. 655.
[698] Such conduct may contravene the current code of the Press Complaints Commission (above, para.12–67) but that does not give rise to a legal remedy.
[699] Except perhaps against the person from whose land it is done: below, para.13–5.
[700] [1979] Ch. 344.
[701] The matter is now governed by the Interception of Communications Act 1985, but this is criminal, not civil.
[702] [1960] 1 W.L.R. 1072. See the observations on this case by Lord Devlin in *Rookes v Barnard* [1964] A.C. 1129 at 1225.
[703] Compare *Bradley v Wingnut Films* [1994] E.M.L.R. 195 (use of C's family gravestone in "comedy horror" film disclosed no cause of action).

Rights but the effect of the Human Rights Act 1998 is also to some extent to create a free-standing right of privacy in English law. Article 8 of the Convention provides:

"1. Everyone has the right to respect for his private and family life, his home and his correspondence.
2. There shall be no interference by a public authority with the exercise of this right except such as is in accordance with the law and is necessary in a democratic society in the interests of national security, public safety or the economic well-being of the country, for the prevention of disorder or crime, for the protection of health or morals, or for the protection of the rights and freedoms of others."

Section 6 of the Human Rights Act 1998 makes it unlawful for a public authority to act in a way which is incompatible with a Convention and a breach of s.6 gives rise to such remedy as the court considers just and appropriate, including damages if the court considers them necessary to afford just satisfaction.[704] Accordingly, bodies like the police, central and local government departments and statutory regulatory bodies which contravene art.8 in their dealings with a citizen are now exposed to a claim for damages in the English courts, whether or not there is a parallel common law liability based on misuse of private information, and in their case there may fairly be said to be a wrong of "invasion of privacy",[705] though a warning has been sounded against the assumption that this would extend to cases where an intrusion which the victim in fact found offensive was the result of sloppiness rather than malice. It is one thing to wander carelessly into the wrong hotel bedroom and another to hide in the wardrobe to take photographs.[706] The giving effect of art.8 in domestic law in this way may create rights of action which would have been wholly beyond the reach of the common law or they may in practical terms negate the effect of a rule of the common law. Thus a common law claim for nuisance or trespass by a non-occupier will fail but the art.8 right applies to "everyone".[707] A newspaper is clearly not a public authority[708] and is not therefore directly subjected to s.6. Equally, the current view is that the substantive articles of the Convention do not require the common law

---

[704] Section 8.
[705] Of course, art.8 goes well beyond anything that could fairly be described as "privacy". See e.g. *R (Wright) v Secretary of State for Health* [2009] UKHL 3; [2009] 2 W.L.R. 267.
[706] *Wainwright v Home Office* [2003] UKHL 53; [2004] 2 A.C. 406 at [51] per Lord Hoffmann.
[707] Though where damages have been awarded to an occupier it does not follow that a substantial award to others is required: para.14–15, below.
[708] For the meaning of this expression see *Aston Cantlow etc. Parochial Church Council v Wallbank* [2003] UKHL 37; [2004] 1 A.C. 546.

automatically to be modified so long as they can be given effect by the mechanisms in the Act[709] and *Wainwright v Home Office* is consistent with this in rejecting any "high level" right of privacy. The Government in 2004 rejected a call from the House of Commons' Culture Media and Sport Committee for legislation to create such a general right.[710] The absence of a direct right of action for invasion of privacy did not attract European sanction before the Act because the law of confidence and the activities of bodies like the Press Complaints Commission were in general regarded as satisfying the Convention requirement[711] and the former has, as we shall see, been very substantially extended in recent years. It has, therefore, been suggested that particular failures of English law to meet Convention standards would be better dealt with by particular legislation.[712] However, while the Convention itself is directed at conduct by the State and is not a code of private law, it may, on an international plane, require the State to take adequate steps to protect the relevant rights from interference by private persons. As the European Court of Human Rights has said in relation to art.8:

"The essential object of Article 8 is to protect the individual against arbitrary interference by public authorities. There may, however, be positive obligations inherent in an effective 'respect' for family life. Those obligations may involve the adoption of measures designed to secure respect for family life, even in the sphere of relations between individuals, including both the provision of a regulatory framework of adjudicatory and enforcement machinery protecting individual's rights and the implementation, where appropriate, of specific steps".[713]

It is not possible here to give any extended account of the amazingly complex Data Protection Act 1998, most of which is of a regulatory nature but which has very significant civil liability consequences.[714] Although it is by no means confined to privacy, the protection of that right has been described as its "central mission".[715] Unlike its predecessor of 1984 it is not confined to computerised data but extends to sophisticated manual filing systems **12–81**

---

[709] See para.2–11, above.
[710] See HC 213, February 9, 2004. The call was not repeated in its 2010 Report: HC 362–1, February 9, 2010.
[711] See, e.g. *Spencer v UK* (1998) 25 E.H.R.R. C.D. 105. Cf. *Peck v UK* (2003) 36 EHRR 719.
[712] Specific legislation, mostly of a criminal/regulatory nature, deals with "bugging", telephone tapping.
[713] *Glaser v UK* (2001) 33 E.H.R.R. 1.
[714] Tugendhat & Christie (eds), *The Law of Privacy and the Media* (2002)
[715] *Johnson v Medical Defence Union* [2007] EWCA Civ 262 at [1]. The Act also has implications for some aspects of defamation since a very large quantity of information will be held by means falling within the scope of the Act: para.12–45, above.

which enable information to be readily accessed.[716] Section 13 provides for compensation for damage (and in certain cases for distress) suffered by reason of contravention of the Act. The "data protection principles" which must be complied with by the data controller include those that the data must be processed[717] fairly and lawfully,[718] that they be obtained only for the means which the data controller specified,[719] that they be not excessive or retained for longer than is necessary and that they be accurate. There is a very wide-ranging exemption from many requirements of the Act for processing for publication of journalistic material where the data controller reasonably believes that publication would be in the public interest and that compliance with the relevant requirements would be impracticable.[720]

C. Misuse of Private Information

12–82   This stems from the law of confidence. Although the foundation case[721] may fairly be said to have been, in modern terms, one concerned with "privacy", the primary focus of the law of confidence was for many years on commercial (and then governmental) secrets. Even where it was applied to personal information[722] it was typically conceived of in terms of information having been imparted (whether by contract or otherwise) in circumstances which expressly or impliedly created an obligation of confidence. However, it became accepted that an obligation of confidence might arise from wrongful taking of confidential material or from accidentally coming across an obviously confidential document[723] and in 1995 a High Court judge declared that if:

> "[S]omeone with a telephoto lens were to take from a distance and with no authority a picture of another engaged in some private act, his subsequent disclosure of the photograph would . . . as surely amount to a breach of confidence as if he had found

---

[716] See *Durant v Financial Services Authority* [2003] EWCA Civ 1746; [2004] F.S.R. 28.

[717] What this means is difficult and controversial: *Johnson v Medical Defence Union* above, fn.715.

[718] In particular in accordance with the requirements of Sch.2 or, in the case of "sensitive personal data" in accordance with the further requirements of Sch.3.

[719] i.e. in his notification to the data subject or the Information Commissioner, who administers the regulatory scheme of the Act.

[720] See *Campbell v MGN Ltd* [2002] EWCA Civ 1373; [2003] Q.B. 633 (no appeal to the HL on this aspect).

[721] *Prince Albert v Strange* (1849) 1 De G. & Sm. 652 (catalogue of etchings by Queen Victoria and Prince Albert).

[722] As in *Argyll v Argyll* [1967] Ch. 302 and *Stephens v Avery* [1988] Ch. 449 (sexual behaviour).

[723] *Att Gen v Guardian Newspapers Ltd (No.2)* [1990] A.C. 109 at 281.

or stolen a letter or diary in which the act was recounted and proceeded to publish it."[724]

Five years later another judge could say that:

"[O]ne of the inhibiting factors about this aspect of the law, hitherto, has been that it was traditionally necessary to establish a duty of confidence—most frequently associated with a prior relationship of some kind. It is becoming easier now, however, to establish that an obligation of confidence can arise (in equity) without the parties having been in any such prior relationship; the obligation may be more readily inferred from the circumstances in which the information came to the defendant's attention."[725]

Thus was born (after a quite short gestation period) a cause of action which has now come to be described as "misuse of private information". As Lord Nicholls put it in *Campbell v MGN Ltd*[726]:

"This cause of action has now firmly shaken off the limiting constraint of the need for an initial confidential relationship. In doing so it has changed its nature ... Now the law imposes a 'duty of confidence' whenever a person receives information he knows or ought to know is fairly and reasonably to be regarded as confidential. Even this formulation is awkward. The continuing use of the phrase 'duty of confidence' and the description of the information as 'confidential' is not altogether comfortable. Information about an individual's private life would not, in ordinary usage, be called 'confidential'. The more natural description today is that such information is private. The essence of the tort is better encapsulated now as misuse of private information."

Later the same judge said that we now have, "two distinct causes of action, protecting two different interests: privacy and secret ('confidential') information."[727] In *Campbell* the defendant newspaper published information about the claimant's attendance at Narcotics Anonymous and photographs of her leaving the premises, and the photographs and part of the contents of the article were held by the majority of the House of Lords to be actionable. In fact the information must have come to the defendants either from another person at

---

[724] *Hellewell v CC Derbyshire* [1995] 4 All E.R. 473 at 475. Under art.3(1) of the Code of Practice of the Press Complaints Commission the use of long lens photography is only forbidden if the complainant is in a place where he has a reasonable expectation of privacy and not, e.g. in the street or on a beach.

[725] Eady J. in *W.B. v H. Bauer Publishing Ltd* [2002] E.M.L.R. 8.

[726] [2004] UKHL 22; [2004] 2 A.C. 457 at [14].

[727] *Douglas v Hello! Ltd (No 3)* [2007] UKHL 21; [2008] 1 A.C. 1 at [255] (a dissenting speech, but not on this point).

Narcotics Anonymous or from a member of the claimant's entourage so that the case could quite easily have been accommodated within the traditional notion of "imparting",[728] but it is perfectly clear from the decision that the result would have been the same even if the defendants had got the information from their own inquiries and the photographs by a stroke of luck.

It will be noticed that Lord Nicholls described the wrong as a "tort", despite its equitable origins,[729] and a number of other examples of this use of terminology can be found, though in one case at first instance, where the issue was important from a remedial point of view, it has been said to be unsettled.[730] At any rate, it is clear that damages are available (and not simply in lieu of an injunction) and these will cover distress suffered by the claimant, so that they bear some resemblance to damages for defamation, though in practice they have been at a much lower level[731] and, unlike in the case of defamation, exemplary damages are not available.[732]

12–83   It is difficult to define the nature of "private" information for this purpose without a degree of circularity: it is information which the "holder" does not intend to be imparted to the public,[733] information in respect of which he has a reasonable expectation of privacy. Still, if that is the case it is unnecessary to go on and ask whether the disclosure would be "highly offensive".[734] Information about a person's sexual life[735] or health[736] or financial affairs or (at least where disclosure might expose him to some danger) his address or whereabouts[737] qualifies. It should not be assumed that the information must relate to something discreditable or embarrassing to the claimant: for example it has been suggested that a donor to charity

---

[728] It was always clear that if C tells something in confidence to X and D acquires the information from X with knowledge of how X acquired it, the obligation of confidence is fixed on D.

[729] See *Kitechnology B.V. v Unicor GmbH Plastmaschinen* [1995] F.S.R. 765, where the point had practical significance because there was an issue whether a claim for breach of confidence was one in, "tort, delict or quasi-delict" for the purposes of the Brussels Convention. Although "tort" does not necessarily have the same meaning for Convention purposes as at common law, there is no doubt about his Lordship's view of English law.

[730] *Mosley v News Group Newspapers Ltd* [2008] EWHC 1777 (QB); [2008] E.M.L.R. 20.

[731] It was held that breach of confidence might be a "wrongful act" which leads to liability for some tort. Thus in *Ansell Rubber Co v Allied Rubber Industries* [1967] V.R. 37 the defendants were held liable in damages for inducing breach of contract (below, para.18–2) when they persuaded one of the claimant's employees, in breach of his contractual duty of fidelity, to disclose his employer's trade secrets.

[732] *Mosley v News Group Newspapers Ltd*, above, fn.730.

[733] *Douglas v Hello! Ltd (No.3)* [2005] EWCA Civ 595; [2006] Q.B. 125 at [83].

[734] *Campbell v MGN Ltd* [2004] UKHL 22; [2004] 2 A.C. 457 at [94].

[735] *Stephens v Avery* [1988] Ch. 449; *Mosley v News Group Newspapers Ltd*, above, fn.730.

[736] *W v Egdell* [1990] Ch. 359; *Campbell v MGN Ltd* [2004] UKHL 22; [2004] 2 A.C. 457.

[737] *Venables v News Group Newspapers Ltd* [2001] Fam. 430; *Mills v News Group Newspapers Ltd* [2001] E.M.L.R. 41.

might restrain the disclosure of his gifts.[738] Information which is already in the public domain is not protected but this should not be taken too literally—something may still be private even though it could be traced by extensive and determined research[739] and it has been suggested that publication of improperly obtained photographs could be restrained even though they had been widely circulated.[740] Nor does the fact that certain aspects of the information are public knowledge prevent other aspects of it being private and secret. So in *Douglas v Hello! Ltd (No.3)*[741] the upcoming glamorous society wedding of the claimants had received widespread coverage in the tabloid press but that did not mean that they were not entitled to control the taking and use of photographs at the event.[742] The fact that a person is a public figure who speaks out on controversial matters does not deprive him of his right to confidentiality over his thoughts on those matters committed to a private journal, even if that has been circulated among associates,[743] still less to his right of privacy in matters unrelated to his public activities.[744] In contrast, a person who ran a "blog" containing criticisms, made from an insider's point of view, of the management of police services or a journalist who wrote under a pseudonym had no reasonable expectation that their identities might not be revealed when discovered by investigation.[745]

i. Justified disclosure. "There is," it was graphically said in the older cases, "no confidence in iniquity". The terminology may be outdated but the principle remains valid as an aspect of the proposition that there are circumstances in which the public interest in disclosure outweighs the private interest in protecting personal information.[746] So in one of the commercial information cases the court refused to strike out an employee's defence that his disclosure

12–84

---

[738] *Att Gen v Guardian Newspapers Ltd (No.2)* [1990] 1 A.C. 109 at 256.

[739] Information about (non-spent) criminal convictions should probably be regarded as conclusively in the public domain, even though it might be hard to trace without access to police computer records.

[740] *Douglas v Hello! Ltd (No.3)* [2005] EWCA Civ 595; [2006] Q.B. 125 at [105].

[741] [2007] UKHL 21; [2008] A.C. 1.

[742] Even though they had sold the photographic rights to the co-claimant magazine. The defendant magazine had obtained unauthorised photographs to use in a "spoiler". This case straddles "personal" and "commercial" secrets. The successful claimants received modest damages for distress and the inconvenience of having to select new photographs. The co-claimant magazine's much larger claim succeeded in a divided HL on the ground of breach of confidence.

[743] *Prince of Wales v Associated Newspapers Ltd* [2006] EWCA Civ 1776; [2008] Ch. 57.

[744] Even well-known people are entitled to some private life: *X v Persons Unknown* [2006] EWHC 2783 (QB); [2007] E.M.L.R. 10.

[745] *Author of a Blog v Times Newspapers Ltd* [2009] EWHC 1359 (QB); *Mahmood v Galloway* [2006] EWHC 1286; [2006] E.M.L.R. 26.

[746] See *MacCaba v Lichtenstein* [2004] EWHC 1579 (QB); [2005] E.M.L.R. 6 at [7].

had been made to expose price-fixing.[747] This is not altogether easy to apply in cases of personal information but in *Campbell v MGN Ltd*,[748] where it seems clear that the claimant must have committed offences against the control of drugs legislation, this fact is barely mentioned, so it is clear that the mere fact that the claimant has committed a crime does not automatically attract the "iniquity" principle. What that case turned upon was another aspect of the public interest. The starting point of the House of Lords' reasoning was that the claimant's drug addiction was a personal matter which she was entitled to keep private. However, this right fell away in face of the fact that she had publicly represented herself to be a person who did not use drugs and the newspaper was therefore entitled to publish the fact that she was attending Narcotics Anonymous to set the public record straight. The minority of the court thought that the (rather obvious) revelations of the nature of meetings of the group and the publication of photographs of the claimant leaving the premises added nothing hurtful to the basic, lawful disclosure but the majority thought otherwise.

Whether or not "iniquity" is in issue there will be many cases in which an arguable case can be made that there is a legitimate public interest in disclosure which outweighs the right to the protection of private information. It is difficult to generalise because the balancing exercise between privacy and the public interest requires an "intense focus" on the facts of the particular case[749] but the guiding principle is that of proportionality.[750] Will the publication of the material pursue a legitimate aim and will the benefits that will be achieved by its publication be proportionate to the harm that may be done by the interference with the right to privacy?[751] Thus in *Mosley v News Group Newspapers Ltd*[752] if there had been, as the newspaper contended, a "Nazi" or "death camp" element in the claimant's sado-masochistic activities that might have justified at least limited disclosure because it cast doubt on his suitability for his leading role in the organisation of motor racing; but since this element was not established there was no basis for disclosure on the ground that many people might regard his behaviour as immoral. It is:

---

[747] *Initial Services v Putterill* [1968] 1 Q.B. 396, CA. See also now the Public Interest Disclosure Act 1998.
[748] [2004] UKHL 22; [2004] 2 A.C. 457.
[749] *Mosley v News Group Newspapers Ltd* [2008] EWHC 1777, QBD at [10].
[750] *Campbell v MGN Ltd* [2004] UKHL 22; [2004] 2 A.C. 457 at [20], [55], [113], [139].
[751] [2004] UKHL 22; [2004] 2 A.C. 457 at [113]. Is, "the intrusion, or perhaps the degree of the intrusion, into the claimant's privacy . . . proportionate to the public interest supposedly being served by it"?: *Mosley v News Group Newspapers Ltd* [2008] EWHC 1777, QBD at [14]. Section 12(4) of the Human Rights Act 1998 requires the court to have regard to the codes of conduct of the Press Complaints Commission and the broadcasting regulators. For an example see *BKM Ltd v BBC* [2009] EWHC 3151.
[752] Above, fn.751.

"[N]ot for the state or for the media to expose sexual conduct which does not involve any significant breach of the criminal law. That is so whether the motive for such intrusion is merely prurience or a moral crusade. It is not for journalists to undermine human rights, or for judges to refuse to enforce them, merely on grounds of taste or moral disapproval."[753]

On the other hand, we have not yet reached the stage where conduct *must* be unlawful in order to justify its disclosure.

"Freedom to live as one chooses is one of the most valuable freedoms. But so is the freedom to criticise (within the limits of the law) the conduct of other members of society as being socially harmful, or wrong."[754]

Where the claimant seeks an injunction without notice against the media in general he must not expect the court necessarily to fall in with his contention that there is no public interest in disclosure when there has been no opportunity to put the opposing view. It may also be the case (though the point is unclear) that just as in some cases of qualified privilege the belief of the defendant that publication is in the public interest may be a relevant factor in relation to disclosure of private information.[755]

Campbell v MGN raises a more general issue about photographs **12–85** taken in public places. Some legal systems give a person, as part of the general "right of personality", the right to control the use of their "image". Hence, while a person may not object to the publication of a photograph in which he is merely an incidental "face in a crowd" he may object if he is the subject of the photograph, even if it is innocuous and entirely non-derogatory.[756] The general thrust of the speeches in *Campbell* is against any such right[757] in English law[758] but this may be difficult to reconcile[759] with the decision of the European Court of Human Rights in *von Hannover v Germany*,[760] where it was held that the denial by German law of a

---

[753] At [127].
[754] *LNS v Persons Unknown* [2010] EWHC 119 (QB) at [104] per Tugendhat J.
[755] *Mosley v News Group Newspapers Ltd*, above, fn.751, at [135]; *LNS v Persons Unknown*, above, fn.754, at [70].
[756] See, e.g. *Aubry v Editions Vice-Versa Inc* [1998] 1 S.C.R. 591, under the Civil Code of Québec.
[757] Distinguish cases where the image is defamatory (*Dunlop Rubber Co Ltd v Dunlop* [1921] 1 A.C. 367 (ridicule)) or exploits the claimant's valuable image for commercial purposes (para.18–49, below).
[758] Most clearly by Lady Hale. Cf. Lord Hope. The claim succeeded on the facts because the photographs showed the claimant leaving Narcotics Anonymous. Had the article been illustrated with an "identifying" photograph of the claimant taken on another occasion the result would have been different.
[759] *McKennitt v Ash* [2006] EWCA Civ 1714; [2008] Q.B. 73 at [39].
[760] (2005) 40 E.H.R.R. 1.

remedy to the daughter of the Prince of Monaco in respect of
continual publication of innocuous photographs of her taken in
public places amounted to a contravention of art.8 of the Convention. The majority judgment in this case certainly reveals a "high
minded" attitude to the activities of the media which is very much
at odds with our traditions of tabloid journalism.[761] After *von Hannover* the issue arose here in *Murray v Express Newspapers Ltd*[762]
where it was held to be arguable for the purpose of a striking out
application that the right to privacy of the claimant, the young son
of a famous author, had been infringed by publication in the press of
innocuous photographs of him taken in the street.[763] However, the
following points should be noted. First, the claimant was a very
young child; the court did not go so far as to say that it would
necessarily have been wrongful to publish a photograph of his
famous mother taken in such circumstances. Secondly, it was not a
case of a single photograph taken by random chance but was the
product of sustained "paparazzo" interest in the mother.[764] It does
not therefore follow that the result is inconsistent with the view of
Baroness Hale in *Campbell* that if the photograph in that case:

> "[H]ad been, and had been presented as, a picture of Naomi
> Campbell going about her business in a public street, there could
> have been no complaint. She makes a substantial part of her living
> out of being photographed looking stunning in designer clothing.
> Readers will obviously be interested to see how she looks if and
> when she pops out to the shops for a bottle of milk. There is
> nothing essentially private about that information nor can it be
> expected to damage her private life."[765]

12–86   A court may grant an injunction to restrain wrongful disclosure of
personal information, understandably so, since once it is out in the
open the harm is done and the award of damages may be a poor

---

[761] Compare the Code of the Press Complaints Commission, which provides that it is
unacceptable to photograph individuals in private places without their consent, a private
place being defined as, "public or private property where there is a reasonable expectation
of privacy".

[762] [2008] EWCA Civ 446; [2009] Ch 481. Compare the denial of a claim in rather similar
circumstances by the NZCA in *Hosking v Runting* [2004] NZCA 34; [2005] 1 N.Z.L.R.
1.

[763] It still seems to be the law that in the absence of violence or threats the *taking* of a
photograph is not actionable but its improper use may be. This is usually general
publication but in *Wood v MPC* [2009] EWCA Civ 414 it was its retention in police
files.

[764] There could be circumstances in which pursuit of a celebrity by a paparazzo might be
wrongful under the Protection from Harassment Act 1997 (cf. *Thomas v News Group
Newspapers Ltd* [2001] EWCA Civ 1233) but that legislation is aimed at D continually
harassing C, not at the case where C is harassed on many occasions by many different
people.

[765] [2004] UKHL 22; [2004] 2 A.C. 457 at [154].

consolation prize.[766] Here again the law differs radically from that applicable in defamation cases. It is practically impossible to obtain an interim[767] injunction against defamation if the defendant asserts that he will raise one of the standard defences like truth or privilege.[768] However, under s.12(3) of the Human Rights Act 1998, where the court is considering whether to grant any relief which, if granted, might affect the exercise of the right of freedom of expression under art.10 of the European Convention on Human Rights:

"[N]o such relief shall be granted so as to restrain publication before trial unless the court is satisfied that the applicant is likely to establish that publication should be allowed".

This does not lower the threshold in defamation cases[769] but it provides a higher threshold in other "expression" cases than the usual one for an interim injunction, which is simply that there is a serious issue to be tried.[770] It is not, however, a single absolute standard.

"On its proper construction the effect of section 12(3) is that the court is not to make an interim restraint order unless satisfied the applicant's prospects of success at the trial are sufficiently favourable to justify such an order being made in the particular circumstances of the case. As to what degree of likelihood makes the prospects of success 'sufficiently favourable', the general approach should be that courts will be exceedingly slow to make interim restraint orders where the applicant has not satisfied the court he will probably ('more likely than not') succeed at the trial. In general, that should be the threshold an applicant must cross before the court embarks on exercising its discretion, duly taking into account the relevant jurisprudence on article 10 and any countervailing Convention rights. But there will be cases where it is necessary for a court to depart from this general approach and a lesser degree of likelihood will suffice as a prerequisite. Circumstances where this may be so include those . . . where the

---

[766] The award in *Mosley v News Group Newspapers Ltd* above, fn.751, was £60,000. Since it is difficult to think of more damaging revelations which would not justify disclosure on public interest grounds, this must be near the maximum.

[767] i.e. a holding injunction pending trial: see para.22–50, below.

[768] *Bonnard v Perryman* [1891] 2 Ch. 269. Para.22–50, below. In *ABC v O'Neill* [2006] HCA 46; 229 A.L.R. 457 there is a very detailed review of the history of *Bonnard v Perryman* and analysis of its underpinnings and modern justification in the judgment of Heydon J.

[769] *Greene v Associated Newspapers Ltd* [2004] EWCA Civ 1462; [2005] E.M.L.R. 10.

[770] See para.22–50, below.

potential adverse consequences of disclosure are particularly grave, or where a short-lived injunction is needed to enable the court to hear and give proper consideration to an application for interim relief pending the trial or any relevant appeal."[771]

12–87   The fact that it is easier to obtain an interim injunction against misuse of private information than against libel raises an interesting point. Private information may be defamatory and actionable as defamation if it cannot be proved to be true. If faced with threatened disclosure may a claimant say, "I deny that what you are about to say is true but whether it is true or not makes no difference because publication would invade my privacy" and proceed for an injunction on the basis of misuse of private information? Indeed, can he go further and, even when the information has been disclosed, sue for damages for misuse of private information rather than defamation and deprive the defendant of the opportunity to prove that what he said was true? Of course it might require a certain hardihood to do that because many people would no doubt conclude that the unwillingness of the claimant to sue for defamation showed that it *was* true; furthermore, a court assessing damages for misuse of private information would surely have to proceed on the basis that the allegation was true and award lower damages. The point has not been squarely decided but it has been said in the Court of Appeal that the:

> "[Q]uestion in a case of misuse of private information is whether the information is private not whether it is true or false. The truth or falsity of the information is an irrelevant inquiry in deciding whether the information is entitled to be protected".[772]

On the other hand it has been said that:

> "[I]f it could be shown that a claim in [misuse of private information] was brought where the nub of the case was a complaint of the falsity of the allegations, and that that was done in order to

---

[771] *Cream Holdings Ltd v Bannerjee* [2004] UKHL 44; [2005] 1 A.C. 253 at [22]. In *Douglas v Hello! Ltd (No.3)* [2005] EWCA Civ 595; [2005] 3 W.L.R. 881 the CA at the interlocutory stage ([2001] Q.B. 967) had refused an interim injunction on the ground that damages would be an adequate remedy. In the appeal from the trial the court recanted and considered that the facts clearly justified an interim injunction. Certainly the facts were such that there could be no realistic argument that the occasion was not private or that there was a public interest in disclosure.
[772] *McKennitt v Ash* [2006] EWCA Civ 1714; [2008] Q.B. 73 at [86]; see also at [80].

avoid the rules of the tort of defamation, then objections could be raised in terms of abuse of process. That might be so at the interlocutory stage in an attempt to avoid the rule [about interim injunctions in defamation cases]".[773]

It has been said that there are four broad groups of cases:

"The first ... , where there is no overlap [between defamation and misuse of private information], is where the information cannot be said to be defamatory .... It is the law of confidence, privacy and harassment that are likely to govern such cases. There is a second group of cases where there is an overlap, but where it is unlikely that it could be said that protection of reputation is the nub of the claim. These are cases where the information would in the past have been said to be defamatory even though it related to matters which were involuntary, eg disease. There was always a difficulty in fitting such cases into defamation, but it was done because of the absence of any alternative cause of action. There is a third group of cases where there is an overlap, but no inconsistency. These are cases where the information relates to conduct which is voluntary, and alleged to be seriously unlawful, even if it is personal (eg sexual or financial). The claimant is unlikely to succeed whether at an interim application or (if the allegation is proved) at trial, whether under the law of defamation or the law of privacy. The fourth group of cases, where it may make a difference which law governs, is where the information relates to conduct which is voluntary, discreditable, and personal (eg sexual or financial) but not unlawful (or not seriously so). In defamation, if the defendant can prove one of the libel defences, he will not have to establish any public interest (except in the case of *Reynolds* privilege, where the law does require consideration of the seriousness of the allegation, including from the point of view of the claimant). But if it is the claimant's choice alone that determines that the only cause of action which the court may take into account is misuse of private information, then the defendant cannot succeed unless he establishes that it comes within the public interest exception (or, perhaps, that he believes that it comes within that exception)."[774]

---

[773] [2008] Q.B. 73 at [79]. In *P v Quigley* [2008] EWHC 1051, QBD an interim and then a permanent injunction were granted in respect of scandalous fictional matter. Eady J. said at [7], "there is no suggestion that this is a libel claim in disguise and that [the claimants] are seeking to suppress defamatory allegations which [the defendant] would wish to allege were true."

[774] *LNS v Persons Unknown* [2010] EWHC 119 (QB) at [96].

In *LNS v Persons Unknown*[775] an injunction was refused in respect of a story about a sexual relationship of a football star who had what was described as a robust personality and the nub of whose claim was found to be concern about his reputation and the effect of the story on sponsorship deals.

---

[775] Above, fn.774.

CHAPTER 13

TRESPASS TO LAND

1. TRESPASS DEFINED

TRESPASS to land is the name given to that form of trespass which is **13–1** constituted by unjustifiable interference with the possession of land. Contrary to popular belief trespass is not criminal in the absence of some special statute which makes it so.[1] Since the decision in *Fowler v Lanning*,[2] it may be asked whether tortious liability for trespass to land, like that for trespass to the person, requires proof of intention or at least negligence on the part of the defendant. We

---

[1] The familiar notice, "Trespassers will be prosecuted" is thus, normally, no more than a "wooden falsehood". The punitive element which originally attached to trespass finally disappeared in 1694, but it had fallen into obsolescence long before that date: Winfield, *Province of the Law of Tort*, p.11. However, there are a growing number of exceptions to the basic rule. Under the Criminal Law Act 1977, as modified by the Criminal Justice and Public Order Act 1994, it is a crime to (1) trespass with a weapon of offence, (2) trespass on a foreign diplomatic mission, (3) refuse to leave premises on being required to do so by a displaced residential occupier, (4) enter premises by violence except as a displaced residential occupier. The crime of conspiracy to trespass is abolished by s.5(1) of the Act. Under the Criminal Justice and Public Order Act 1994, s.61, it is an offence for two or more persons, having trespassed on land with the common purpose of residing there for any period, to refuse to obey the direction of a police officer to leave the land. For the reasons behind this offence, see *Wilts CC v Frazer* [1986] 1 W.L.R. 109. Under the 1994 Act s.68, there is an offence of "aggravated trespass" where persons trespass on land to disrupt a lawful activity taking place there. Under s.128 of the Serious Organized Crime and Police Act 2005 it is an offence to trespass on a site designated by the Secretary of State.

[2] [1959] 1 Q.B. 426. See para.4–33, above.

must, however, be careful to define what that intention or negligence goes to, for it is clear law that an entry upon another's land is tortious whether or not the entrant knows that he is trespassing.[3] Thus it is no defence that the only reason for his entry was that he had lost his way or even that he genuinely but erroneously believed that the land was his.[4] It follows that the great majority of trespasses to land are, for legal purposes, self-evidently intentional—I intend to enter upon your land if I consciously place myself upon what proves to be your land, even though I neither knew nor could reasonably have known that it was not mine.[5] We are left with those cases where the defendant's entry was involuntary, whether caused by his fault or not. Where he is thrown or pushed on to the land he is not liable for trespass simply because there is no act on his part.[6] As for other situations it is clear that where land adjoining the highway is unintentionally entered, as a result, for example, of a motor accident, the claimant must prove negligence, a proposition established long before *Fowler v Lanning*.[7] In *League against Cruel Sports v Scott*,[8] Park J. had to deal with trespass by hounds in pursuit of a stag and he concluded that the law was that the master of the pack was liable if he intended the hounds to enter the claimant's land or if, knowing that there was a real risk that they would enter, their entry was caused by his failure to exercise proper control of them.[9] The burden of proof of either condition is upon the claimant.[10]

Trespass is actionable per se, i.e. whether or not the claimant has suffered any damage.[11] This rule may seem harsh but in earlier times trespass was so likely to lead to a breach of the peace that even trivial deviations on to another person's land were reckoned unlawful. Whether or not there is now greater respect for the law, the

---

[3] *Conway v George Wimpey & Co Ltd* [1951] 2 K.B. 266 at 273–274; *Jolliffe v Willmett & Co* [1971] 1 All E.R. 478.

[4] Hence the possibility, long appreciated, of using trespass as a means of testing title. In *Costello v City of Calgary* (1997) 152 D.L.R. (4th) 453 the defendants had held the property for nine years under a claim of right.

[5] By the Limitation Act 1623 s.5, if the defendant disclaimed any title to the land and proved that his trespass was involuntary or negligent and that he had tendered sufficient amends before the action was brought, he had a defence to an action for trespass; but *Basely v Clarkson* (1682) 3 Lev 37 excluded from the scope of s.5 an intentional act done in ignorance that it was infringing the claimant's right. Hence the defence was extremely restricted. See Williams, *Liability for Animals*, p.196.

[6] *Smith v Stone* (1647) Style 65. Though he could, no doubt, be required to leave. In real life, such an issue is much more likely to arise out of a claim by the entrant for injury suffered on the land, as in *Public Transport Commission (NSW) v Perry* (1977) 14 A.L.R. 273.

[7] See, e.g. *River Wear Commissioners v Adamson* (1877) 2 App. Cas. 743.

[8] [1986] Q.B. 240.

[9] Despite the reference to "knowing", this is a negligence standard, though it is not the tort of negligence since no damage is required.

[10] Cf. *Fowler v Lanning*, para.4–33, above.

[11] *Entick v Carrington* (1765) 2 Wils. K.B. 275 at 291, per curiam Blackstone, Comm. iii, 209–210. If unintentional trespasses are to be relegated to the tort of negligence, proof of damage would, of course, become essential.

theoretical severity of the rules as to land trespass is rarely exploited in practice. An action will not normally be brought for trespass without damage unless the claimant wishes to deter persistent trespassing or there are disputes over boundaries or rights of way.[12]

2. POSSESSION

Trespass to land, like the tort of trespass to goods which is considered in a later chapter, consists of interference with possession, and it is necessary to say something here of this concept.[13] Our law has, however, not worked out a consistent theory of possession, and its meaning may turn upon the context in which it is used.[14]

Mere physical presence on the land or the use[15] or de facto control of it does not amount to possession sufficient to bring an action of trespass. It is, for example, generally said that a lodger in another's house does not have possession,[16] nor does a servant occupying a room in his employer's house[17] or a guest in an hotel. On the other hand, a lessor of land gives up possession to his tenant so that the tenant alone can bring trespass during the currency of the lease—even against the lessor unless, of course, the lessor's entry was effected in accordance with the provisions of the lease.[18] Most of the cases on the distinction between a tenant and a licensee (who does not have possession) have arisen in the context of security of tenure under the Rent Acts, but it is clear that the matter is to be determined by the substance of the agreement between the parties rather than by the label which they have chosen to attach to their relationship[19] and the hallmark of a tenancy is the right in the tenant to "exclusive

13–2

---

[12] In the modern law an action for a declaration might be used to settle disputed rights.

[13] A more elaborate discussion of possession will be found in the 8th edition of this work. See further Wonnacott, *Possession of Land* (2006); Pollock and Wright, *Essay on Possession in the Common Law*; Harris, "The Concept of Possession in English Law", *Oxford Essays in Jurisprudence*, p.69.

[14] *Towers & Co Ltd v Gray* [1961] 2 Q.B. 351 at 361 per Lord Parker C.J.

[15] A person who has been granted a right to grow crops in another's land has sufficient possession to sue for trespass to land in respect of damage to them: *Monsanto Plc v Tilly* [2000] Env L.R. 313.

[16] *Allan v Liverpool Overseers* (1874) L.R. 9 Q.B. 180 at 191–192 per Blackburn J., adopted by Davies L.J. in *Appah v Parncliffe Investments Ltd* [1964] 1 W.L.R. 1064 at 1069–1970.

[17] *White v Bayley* (1861) 10 C.B.(N.S.) 227.

[18] *Lane v Dixon* (1847) 3 C.B. 776. *Aliter* if there was only an oral contract for a lease, unenforceable by virtue of the Law of Property Act 1925 s.40: *Delaney v T.P. Smith Ltd* [1946] K.B. 393, but a tenant in occupation under an unenforceable contract can certainly bring trespass against a stranger: at 397 per Tucker L.J.

[19] *Street v Mountford* [1985] A.C. 809; *Antoniades v Villers* [1990] A.C. 417; *Aslan v Murphy* [1990] 1 W.L.R. 766.

possession".[20] It is, however, possible that in modern conditions
there may be rare cases in which a person has sufficient possession
to bring trespass against a third party even though he is not a
tenant.[21] The lessor cannot bring proceedings for a wrongful entry
during the currency of the lease except in so far as it has caused
permanent damage to the land, leading to a reduction in the value of
his reversion, such as would result from the cutting of trees or the
pulling down of buildings.[22] It is not necessary that the claimant
should have some lawful estate or interest in the land so that there
is no doubt, for example, that a squatter occupying the land without
any claim of right may have sufficient possession to bring trespass[23]
and, generally speaking, a stranger who enters the land without the
squatter's consent cannot rely in his defence upon another person's
superior right (the *jus tertii*) unless he can prove that he acted with
that person's authority.[24] This is not to say that legal title is irrelevant, for where the facts leave it uncertain which of several competing claimants has possession it is in him who can prove title, i.e.
who can prove that he has the right to possess.[25] What will amount
to possession varies according to the nature of the property, so that
possession of a flat with a front door which can be locked is
obviously different from possession of part of an unfenced moor or
hillside.[26] Possession once acquired is not, however, determined by
sending the defendant a letter demanding delivery-up of the land.[27]
Some estate or interest in the land may also lead the court to find
possession in the claimant in other circumstances. For example, it is
probably still the law that a spouse who is occupying a matrimonial
home along with the other spouse does not have possession so as to

---

[20] That is to say, the right to exclude the landlord during the currency of the term except in
so far as a right of entry is reserved for a limited purpose, e.g. to repair. See *Radaich v
Smith* (1959) 101 C.L.R. 209 at 222 per Windeyer J., adopted in *Street v Mountford*, above,
fn.19.

[21] See Clerk and Lindsell, *Torts*, 19th edn, s.19–20. *Mehta v Royal Bank of Scotland* [1999]
3 E.G.L.R. 153 seems to be an example (very long term occupancy of hotel room).

[22] *Ward v Macaulay* (1791) 4 T.R. 489; *Mayfair Property Co v Johnson* [1894] 1 Ch. 508;
Jones v Llanrwst UDC [1911] 1 Ch. 393.

[23] There is no reason why this proposition should be affected by the upheavals in the law of
acquisition of title to registered land by adverse possession. The ECHR has held that the
law of adverse possession relating to registered land before the Land Registration Act 2002
contravenes art.1 of the First Protocol to the Convention: *J.A. Pye (Oxford) Ltd v UK*
(2005) (Application No.44302/02). Under the 2002 Act there is an entirely new regime
which requires the squatter to give formal notice of his wish to apply to be registered as
the proprietor after 10 years adverse possession.

[24] *Chambers v Donaldson* (1809) 11 East 65; *Nicholls v Ely Beet Sugar Factory* [1931] 2 Ch.
84. As to the jus tertii in relation to trespass to goods, see para.17–18, below.

[25] "If there are two persons in a field, each asserting that the field is his, and each doing some
act in assertion of the right of possession, and if the question is, which of those two is in
actual possession, I answer the person who has the title is in actual possession and the other
is a trespasser": *Jones v Chapman* (1849) 2 Exch. 803 at 821 per Maule J.

[26] *Simpson v Fergus* (1999) 79 P. & C.R. 398. *Ocean Estates Ltd v Pinder* [1969] 2 A.C.
19.

[27] *Mount Carmel Investments Ltd v Peter Thurlow Ltd* [1988] 1 W.L.R. 1078.

maintain trespass,[28] but a spouse who has a share in the ownership (as would normally be the case today) would certainly have it.

Possession may obviously extend to things which are beyond a person's immediate physical control. I do not lose possession of my house and its contents when I leave them to go to the office or even to go away on holiday.

A. Immediate Right to Possess: Trespass by Relation

The immediate right to possess, sometimes also known as constructive possession,[29] signifies the lawful right to retain possession when one has it or to acquire it when one has not. Without possession it is not sufficient to support an action of trespass[30] but, owing to the willingness of the courts to extend the superior protection afforded by the older law to possession as distinct from ownership, it has for long been the law that once a person entitled to immediate possession actually enters upon the land and so acquires possession, he is deemed to have been in possession from the moment that his right to it accrued.[31] This fiction, known as trespass by relation, has the result that he can sue for acts of trespass committed while he was actually out of possession and it also provides the foundation for the claim in respect of "mesne profits", that is, the claim for the damage suffered by a person as a result of having been kept out of the possession of his land.[32]

13–3

3. INTERFERENCE

Interference with the possession of land sufficient to amount to trespass may occur in many ways. The most obvious example is unauthorised walking upon it or going into the buildings upon it, but it is equally trespass if I throw things on to your land[33] or allow my cattle to stray on to it from my land, and even if I do no more than

13–4

---

[28] *Hunter v Canary Wharf Ltd* [1997] A.C. 655, para.14–15, below (a case of nuisance but, it is thought, still in point).

[29] For an explanation of this term, see *Alicia Hosiery Ltd v Brown Shipley & Co Ltd* [1970] 1 Q.B. 195 at 207 per Donaldson J.

[30] It is, however, sufficient for an action of conversion and is explained more fully in connection with that tort, para.17–17, below.

[31] See *Dunlop v Macedo* (1891) 8 T.L.R. 43.

[32] The action for mesne profits is explained, para.13–18, below.

[33] For a modern, power-assisted example, see *Rigby v CC Northamptonshire* [1985] 1 W.L.R. 1242. Discharging water into the flowing watercourse of another is trespass: *British Waterways Board v Severn Trent Water Ltd* [2001] EWCA Civ 276; [2001] 1 W.L.R. 613 at [38].

place my ladder against your wall.[34] If you have given me permission to enter your land and I act in excess of the permission or remain on your land after it has expired, then, again, I am a trespasser.[35] The one restriction is that for trespass the injury must be direct and immediate. If it is indirect or consequential, there may well be a remedy (usually for nuisance or for negligence), but whatever it is it will not be trespass. If I plant a tree on your land, that is trespass, but if the roots or branches of a tree on my land project into or over your land, that is a nuisance.[36]

A. Trespass on Highway

13–5   It is obvious that a person who uses a highway for the purpose of travelling from one place to another commits no trespass against anyone, but at one time it was held that the right of user of the highway was confined to use for passage and matters incidental thereto, like resting. Otherwise there was a trespass against the owner of the subsoil.[37] However, in *Director of Public Prosecutions v Jones*[38] (where the civil law issue arose in the context of a charge of taking part in a trespassory assembly under the Public Order Act 1986) the majority of the House of Lords held that it was not a trespass to participate in a peaceful assembly on the highway so long as it was reasonable and caused no obstruction. Lord Irvine L.C. went to far as to say that any reasonable use of the highway, not involving nuisance or obstruction, was lawful. However, he did not seem to regard as wrongly decided earlier cases in which it had been held to be trespass to use the highway to disrupt shooting[39] or to gain information about racehorse trials[40] on land crossed by the highway. As in all cases of trespass, however, only the person

---

[34] *Westripp v Baldock* [1938] 2 All E.R. 779 affirmed [1939] 1 All E.R. 279; *Gregory v Piper* (1829) 9 B. & C. 591; *Home Brewery Co Ltd v William Davis & Co (Leicester) Ltd* [1987] Q.B. 339.

[35] *Hillen v I.C.I. (Alkali) Ltd* [1936] A.C. 65; *Canadian Pacific Ry v Gaud* [1949] 2 K.B. 239 at 249 per Cohen L.J., at 254–255 per Singleton L.J.; *R. v Jones* [1976] 1 W.L.R. 672; but a lessee holding over after the termination of his lease is no trespasser, for trespass can only be committed against the person in present possession of the land: *Hey v Moorhouse* (1839) 6 Bing. N.C. 52. Cf. *Minister of Health v Bellotti* [1944] K.B. 298 (licensee holding over after termination of licence and after lapse of reasonable time, becomes a trespasser).

[36] *Smith v Giddy* [1904] 2 K.B. 448, 451; *Davey v Harrow Corp* [1958] 1 Q.B. 60. As to removal of the intruding growth, see para.22–47, below.

[37] At common law this is the person whose land abuts upon the highway. Cf. *Tithe Redemption Commission v Runcorn UDC* [1954] Ch. 383, and Highways Act 1980 ss.263–265. Where the top surface is vested in a highway authority, there would seem no reason why that authority could not bring proceedings for trespass: see the comment of Collins L.J. in *DPP v Jones* [1998] Q.B. 563 on the view of Lord Denning M.R. in *Hubbard v Pitt* [1976] Q.B. 142.

[38] [1999] A.C. 240.

[39] *Harrison v Duke of Rutland* [1893] 1 Q.B. 142.

[40] *Hickman v Maisey* [1900] 1 Q.B. 752.

Interference 691

having possession can complain of it and, accordingly, the fact that a person on the highway is a trespasser upon it does not relieve lawful users of the highway of any duty of care they may owe to him in accordance with the ordinary law of negligence.[41]

B. Trespass to Subsoil

Any intrusion upon the subsoil is just as much a trespass as entry **13–6** upon the surface, and subsoil and surface may be possessed by different persons. If A is in possession of the surface and B of the subsoil, and I walk upon the land, that is a trespass against A, but not against B. If I dig holes vertically in the land, that is a trespass against both A and B. If I bore a tunnel from my land into B's subsoil, that is a trespass against B only.[42] Even if the landowner has been deprived of ownership of minerals by statute (as is the case here with oil) intrusions beneath the surface, such as pipelines, in order to obtain them still amount to trespass, though in such a case the quantum of damages will be very limited.[43]

C. Interference with Airspace

Lord Ellenborough once expressed the view that the invasion of **13–7** the air space above a person's land could not be trespass unless there was some actual contact with the land itself.[44] Now, however, it is clear that this is incorrect, and in *Kelsen v Imperial Tobacco Co*[45] NcNair J., after a full review of the authorities, held that an advertising sign erected by the defendants on their own property, which projected into the airspace above the claimant's shop, created a trespass. The issue arises not infrequently as a result of the operation of tower cranes on building sites, which swing over adjoining land. There is no doubt that this amounts to trespass[46] and the claimant will normally be entitled to an injunction[47] even though this state of

---

[41] *Farrugia v G.W. Ry* [1947] 2 All E.R. 565.
[42] *Cox v Glue* (1848) 5 C.B. 533.
[43] *Bocardo SA v Star Energy UK Onshore Ltd* [2009] EWCA Civ 579; [2009] 3 W.L.R. 1010 (permission to appeal [2010] 1 W.L.R. 113).
[44] *Pickering v Rudd* (1815) 4 Camp. 219 at 220–221. Lord Ellenborough considered that if the claimant suffered any damage from such an invasion, his remedy lay in an action on the case.
[45] [1957] 2 Q.B. 334. For the effect of the demise of a top floor, see *Haines v Florensa* (1990) 9 E.G. 70.
[46] *Woollerton & Wilson Ltd v Richard Costain Ltd* [1970] 1 W.L.R. 411; *Anchor Brewhouse Developments v Berkley House (Docklands Developments)* (1987) 284 E.G. 625.
[47] In the *Woollerton & Wilson* case the injunction was suspended for long enough to allow the defendant to complete the works but this cannot be supported: *Jaggard v Sawyer* [1995] 1 W.L.R. 269.

the law allows him to take a "dog in the manger" attitude[48] and force the defendant to pay him a sum in excess of any damage he has suffered.[49]

Although an intrusion into air space at a relatively low height constitutes trespass,[50] it is now settled that the landowner's rights in airspace extend only to such height as is necessary for the ordinary use and enjoyment of the land and structures on it,[51] so that the flight of an aircraft "several hundred feet" above a house is not a trespass at common law[52]; but if an aircraft, or anything from it, falls upon the land or comes into contact with a structure on it, that might be a trespass, no matter the height from which it fell.[53]

Quite apart from the position at common law, it is provided by statute that civil aircraft which fly at a reasonable height (having regard to wind, weather and all the circumstances of the case) do not commit trespass.[54] A landowner is not, however, without protection from persistent aerial surveillance from a height outside his zone of user, for such conduct may constitute a nuisance.[55] The Civil Aviation Act also provides that if material loss or damage[56] is caused[57] to any person or property by, or by a person in, or an article or person falling from an aircraft while in flight, taking off[58] or landing, then, unless the loss or damage was caused or contributed to by the negligence of the person by whom it was suffered, damages are recoverable without proof of negligence or intention or other cause of action as if the loss or damage had been caused by the wilful act, neglect, or default of the owner of the aircraft.[59]

---

[48] *Anchor Brewhouse* case, above, fn.46, at 633.

[49] Entry on neighbouring land to effect repairs may now be justified: para.13–11, below.

[50] *Liaquat v Majid* [2005] EWHC 1305 (QB); 26 E.G. 130 (CS) (75cm projection 4.5m above ground).

[51] *Didow v Alberta Power* [1988] 5 W.W.R. 606 (power lines 50 feet up within zone of user).

[52] *Bernstein v Skyviews & General Ltd* [1978] Q.B. 479. The maxim *cujus est solum ejus est usque ad coelum* is not, therefore, to be taken literally.

[53] Unless the contact were without negligence. In view of the Civil Aviation Act 1982 s.76(2), the matter is largely academic in relation to civil aircraft: see below.

[54] Civil Aviation Act 1982 s.76(1) (replacing the Civil Aviation Act 1949 s.40(1)). It is conceivable that s.76 confers a wider exemption than the common law and might, in certain circumstances, justify an entry even into the zone of normal user.

[55] Or harassment under the Protection from Harassment Act 1997.

[56] Which includes psychiatric trauma, subject to the usual control mechanisms applicable to a claim for negligence in respect of such harm: *Glen v Korean Airlines Co Ltd* [2003] EWHC 643 (QB); [2003] Q.B. 1386.

[57] On the causal scope of somewhat similar legislation see *ACQ Pty Ltd v Cook* [2009] HCA 28.

[58] This expression appears to be confined to the period after the pilot has come to the take-off position: *Blankley v Godley* [1952] 1 All E.R. 436n.

[59] Section 76(2). Hence if a hijacker flies an aircraft into a building the owner of the aircraft is liable. There is a proviso to the effect that if the owner's liability arises only by virtue of the section and if a legal liability to pay damages for the loss in question exists in some other person, then the owner is entitled to be indemnified by that other person.

D. Continuing Trespass

Trespass, whether by way of personal entry or by placing things **13–8** on the claimant's land, may be "continuing" and give rise to actions from day-to-day so long as it lasts. In *Holmes v Wilson*,[60] highway authorities supported a road by wrongfully building buttresses on the claimant's land, and they paid full compensation in an action for trespass. They were nevertheless held liable in a further action for trespass, because they had not removed the buttresses. Nor does a transfer of the land by the injured party prevent the transferee from suing the defendant for continuing trespass.[61]

At one time it may have been the law that trespass did not lie for omission to remove something from the land which was lawfully there to begin with,[62] although if the thing did damage to the land after it ought to have been removed an action on the case would lie. However, more modern authority imposes liability for trespass[63] and there is a close analogy with the situation where a visitor's stay exceeds the duration of his licence. However, there is no trespass if the defendant merely omits to restore land to the same condition (apart from removing anything which he has put on it) in which he found it, for example if he fails to fill up a pit which he has dug on his neighbour's land. He is, of course, liable in trespass for the original digging (but not for continuing trespass in allowing it to remain there) and, no doubt, for negligence if anyone falls into the pit.[64]

4. DEFENCES

A. Licence

For the purposes of trespass, the best definition of licence is that **13–9** given by Sir Frederick Pollock. A licence is:

---

[60] (1839) 10 A. & E. 50.
[61] *Hudson v Nicholson* (1839) 5 M. & W. 437 followed in *Konskier v Goodman Ltd* [1928] 1 K.B. 421.
[62] *Shapcott v Mugford* (1696) 1 Ld. Raym. 187 at 188: trespass *vi et armis* does not apply to non-feasance.
[63] *Konskier v Goodman Ltd*, above, fn.61; *Restatement*, 2d, s.160. Cf. *Penarth Dock Co v Pounds* [1963] 1 Lloyd's Rep. 359 (breach of contract) and see the remarks in *Clearlite Holdings Ltd v Auckland City Corp* [1976] 2 N.Z.L.R. 729 at 734. In *Konskier's* case it was held that there was a continuing trespass though negligence (case) would not lie for lack of a duty to the claimant.
[64] *Clegg v Dearden* (1848) 12 Q.B. 576 at 601; but a tenant who removes fixtures and does not make good may be liable for waste. This is a tort, but not one of much importance, since the landlord will normally rely on covenants in the lease: *Mancetter Developments Ltd v Garmanson Ltd* [1986] Q.B. 1212.

"[T]hat consent which, without passing any interest in the property to which it relates, merely prevents the acts for which consent is given from being wrongful."[65]

In the law of real property it is important to distinguish a licence from interests in land like leases, easements or profits a prendre, existing at law. These confer rights in rem, i.e. rights which avail against persons generally, including, of course, the lessor or grantor himself, whereas a licence normally gives only a right in personam against the licensor; but the distinction seems to have little importance so far as defences to trespass are concerned. A person is not a trespasser if he is on land with the permission, express or implied,[66] of the possessor, and that is all that matters for present purposes.[67] Whether that permission is given is a matter for the possessor, even if the public generally have free access to the property (such as a shopping mall) and whether he has a good reason for exclusion or not.[68] Where a landowner refuses to allow access to such premises to demonstrate or collect signatures for a petition the provisions of the European Convention on Human Rights on freedom of expression or association are not brought into play, at least where there is some other means of bringing the subject to public attention.[69]

13–10   A bare licence, i.e. one granted otherwise than for valuable consideration, may be revoked at any time,[70] and so may many contractual licences, even though revocation may involve the licensor in liability for breach of contract.[71] After revocation the licensee becomes a trespasser, but he must be allowed a reasonable time in which to leave and to remove his goods.[72] Some contractual licences are, however, irrevocable because revocation in breach of contract would be prevented by the grant of an equitable remedy to the licensee. A licence coupled with an interest is irrevocable because,

---

[65] *Torts*, 15th edn, p.284.

[66] See *Robson v Hallett* [1967] 2 Q.B. 939 at 950–951 per Lord Parker C.J.; at 953–954 per Diplock L.J. One cannot rely on an implied licence when one knows that the occupier would object to the entry: *TV3 Network Services v Broadcasting Standards Authority* [1995] 2 N.Z.L.R. 720.

[67] *Armstrong v Sheppard and Short Ltd* [1959] 2 Q.B. 384 at 399 per Lord Evershed M.R.

[68] Exclusion might of course amount to a statutory wrong under one of the pieces of discrimination legislation.

[69] *Appleby v UK* (2003) 37 E.H.R.R. 38.

[70] On a licence granted by one co-occupier and revoked by another, see *Robson-Paul v Farrugia* (1969) 20 CCR 820 and *NSW v Koumdjiev* [2005] NSWCA 247; 63 N.S.W.L.R.353.

[71] *Thompson v Park* [1944] K.B. 408. Cf. *Kerrison v Smith* [1897] 2 Q.B. 445; *King v David Allen & Sons Ltd* [1916] 2 A.C. 54.

[72] *Cornish v Stubbs* (1870) L.R. 5 C.P. 334; *Canadian Pacific Ry v The King* [1931] A.C. 414; *Minister of Health v Bellotti* [1944] K.B. 289; *Robson v Hallett*, above, fn.66.

although the licence itself—the bare permission to enter—is only a right in personam, it confers a right in rem to something when you have entered:

"A licence to hunt in a man's park and carry away the deer killed to his own use to cut down a tree in a man's ground, and to carry it away the next day to his own use, are licences as to the acts of hunting and cutting down the tree, but as to the carrying away of the deer killed and the tree cut down, they are grants."[73]

Until the tree or deer is carried away the licence is irrevocable.[74]

A contractual licence may also be irrevocable even if it is not coupled with an interest, but the circumstances in which this will be so are not finally settled. It seems, however, that the following conclusion is warranted by the cases.[75] Whether a contractual licence is revocable is a question of construction of the contract in the light of relevant and admissible circumstances.[76] It will be irrevocable if such is the intention of the parties, and this may be inferred from the terms of the contract, the character of the transaction, and the attendant circumstances that the licence is intended to endure for a definite or ascertainable period. Where it is granted for a limited period and for a definite purpose, it will be irrevocable until the accomplishment of the purpose.[77] If the licensee is prepared to observe the terms of the contract the licensor may be restrained by injunction from revoking the licence[78] and even where there is no opportunity to seek such a remedy (for example, where the claimant is ejected from the cinema) the equitable right which

---

[73] *Thomas v Sorrell* (1672) Vaughan 330 at 351 per Vaughan C.J.

[74] The court in *Wood v Leadbitter* (1845) 13 M. & W. 838 at 844–845; *Wood v Manley* (1839) 11 A. & E. 34; *Jones & Sons Ltd v Tankerville* [1909] 2 Ch. 440 at 442 per Parker J. Cf. *Frank Warr & Co Ltd v LCC* [1904] 1 K.B. 713; *Clore v Theatrical Properties Ltd* [1936] 3 All E.R. 483.

[75] See especially *Hurst v Picture Theatres Ltd* [1915] 1 K.B. 1; *Winter Garden Theatre (London) Ltd v Millennium Productions Ltd* [1948] A.C. 173; *Bendall v McWhirter* [1952] 2 Q.B. 466; *Hounslow v Twickenham Garden Developments Ltd* [1971] Ch. 233. Cf. *Wood v Leadbitter* (1845) 13 M. & W. 838; *Cowell v Rosehill Racecourse Co Ltd* (1937) 56 C.L.R. 605.

[76] *Winter Garden case* [1946] 1 All E.R. 678 at 680 per Lord Greene M.R.; *Re Spenborough UDC's Agreement* [1968] Ch. 139. Cf. *Winter Garden case* [1948] A.C. 173 at 193, per Lord Porter. Wade, "What is Licence" (1948) 64 L.Q.R. 57 at 69.

[77] *Winter Garden case* [1948] A.C. 173 per Lord Porter; at 189 per Lord Simon. See *Munro v Balnagown Estates Co* 1949 S.L.T. 85.

[78] [1946] 1 All E.R. 678 at 685 per Lord Greene M.R.; *Bendall v McWhirter* [1952] 2 Q.B. 466 at 478–483 per Denning L.J. In a proper case, revocation of the licence may be restrained even though performance has not yet commenced: *Verrall v Great Yarmouth BC* [1981] Q.B. 202.

the licensee has destroys the defence of "trespasser" which the licensor would otherwise plead to an action for assault.[79]

If a licence has been executed, it cannot be revoked in the sense that the licensee can be compelled to undo what he has lawfully done. If I allow you to post bills on my hoarding, I can cancel my permission, but I cannot force you to remove bills that you have already stuck there. So in *Liggins v Inge*[80] where an oral licence had been given to lower a riverbank and make a weir above the licensor's mill, it was held that the licensor could not sue the licensee for continuing the weir which the latter had erected; but the rule that an executed licence is irrevocable applies only where the licence can be construed as authorising the doing of exactly what has been done. It does not apply where there has been mere acquiescence in something which was never authorised before it was done.[81] Nor does it apply if its application would amount to the creation of an easement in favour of the licensee. An easement cannot be granted by parol and therefore, after the licence has been revoked, the claimant is prima facie entitled to an injunction restraining the continuation of the trespass.[82]

The power of a public body to revoke a licence to enter its premises may be restricted by the requirements of public law, for example by requiring it to hear the licensee first,[83] but there is no basis for restricting the power of revocation of occupiers of shopping malls, public utility showrooms or the like on the ground that they are "quasi public" places.[84]

B. Justification by Law

13–11   Acts which would otherwise be trespasses, whether to land, goods or the person, are frequently prevented from being so by the existence of some justification provided by the law. A person entering land in pursuance of arrangements made for the public to have access to open country is not a trespasser so long as he does no damage and complies with the specified restrictions,[85] a landlord

---

[79] Wade, "What is Licence" (1945) 64 L.Q.R. 57, p.76; *Errington v Errington* [1952] 1 K.B. 290 at 297–299 and *Bendall v McWhirter* [1952] 2 Q.B. 466 at 479–483 per Denning L.J. *Bendall v McWhirter* was overruled by *National Provincial Bank Ltd v Ainsworth* [1965] A.C. 1175 but, it is submitted, without affecting the statements in the text.

[80] (1831) 3 Bing. 682; *Davies v Marshall* (1861) 10 C.B.(N.S.) 697. See Wade, "What is Licence" (1945) 64 L.Q.R. 57, pp.68–69.

[81] *Canadian Pacific Ry v The King* [1931] A.C. 414 at 428–429 per Lord Russell.

[82] *Armstrong v Sheppard & Short Ltd* [1959] 2 Q.B. 384. The right to an injunction is not unqualified and an injunction may be refused on the ground that the injury is trivial.

[83] *Wandsworth LBC v A* [2000] 1 W.L.R. 1246 (parent's licence to enter child's school).

[84] *C.I.N. Properties Ltd v Rawlins* [1995] E.G.L.R. 30; *Porter v MPC* October 20, 1999, CA.

[85] Countryside and Rights of Way Act 2000 s.2.

commits no trespass if he distrains for rent.[86] Most importantly there
are innumerable instances in which officers of the law are authorised
to enter land, to take goods or to arrest or restrain a person, but these
belong more to public than to private law and only one or two
illustrations can be given here. The police have no general common
law power to enter private premises without consent or warrant[87] but
their most important statutory powers are those conferred by the
Police and Criminal Evidence Act 1984. Under s.17[88] a constable
may enter[89] and search premises (if need be, by force) for the
purpose of arresting a person for an indictable[90] offence and for
various other purposes (including those of saving life or limb or
preventing serious damage to the property[91]) and under s.18 there is
power to enter premises after an arrest for an indictable offence and
search for evidence of that offence or connected or similar
offences.[92] However, when a constable is lawfully on the premises
(for example, with the consent of the occupier or, it seems, pursuant
to a lawful entry under s.18) he may seize anything which he
reasonably believes to be evidence of any offence provided he has
reasonable grounds to believe it would otherwise be concealed,
destroyed, etc. A police officer also has a power of entry to premises
to prevent a breach of the peace.[93] A bailiff who enters private
premises on civil process (for example to seize property in execution) commits no trespass, provided that he does not gain entry by
breaking in.[94] Indeed a bailiff may even enter the house of a stranger

[86] See Clerk and Lindsell, *Torts*, 14th edn, Ch.16 (not in current edn). The common law of
distress for rent will be replaced by a statutory scheme when the Tribunals, Courts and
Enforcement Act 2007 is fully in force (see para.17–34, below). For distress damage
feasant (the seizure of an animal or chattel by the possessor of land when it is wrongfully
on the land and causing damage to it) see Williams, *Animals*, Chs I–VIII and the 7th edn
of this work, p.383. In respect of animals, there is now a statutory right of detention and
sale: see para.16–11, below.
[87] See *Kuru v New South Wales* [2008] HCA 26.
[88] For search warrants, see ss.8–16. See also the Intelligence Services Act 1994 s.5, as
amended by the Security Service Act 1996.
[89] The officer must, unless the circumstances make it impracticable or undesirable, give the
occupier the reason for exercising the power of entry: *O'Loughlin v CC Essex* [1998] 1
W.L.R. 364. For emergency powers of entry of fire officers see s.44 of the Fire and Rescue
Services Act 2004.
[90] "Indictable" was substituted here and in the other provisions referred to by the Serious
Organized Crime and Police Act 2005 Sch.7.
[91] For the power to enter in pursuit of persons "unlawfully at large" see the Prisoners (Return
to Custody) Act 1995.
[92] Only premises occupied by the arrested person: *Khan v MPC* [2008] EWCA Civ 723
(arrestee giving false address). See also s.32, as amended.
[93] *Thomas v Sawkins* [1935] 2 K.B. 249, but not to investigate a past breach: *Kuru v New
South Wales* [2008] HCA 26.
[94] The bailiff may enter by opening an unlocked door, but may not break open a locked one:
Semayne's Case (1604) 5 Co. Rep. 91a; *Southam v Smout* [1964] 1 Q.B. 308; *Vaughan v
McKenzie* [1969] 1 Q.B. 557.

to the debtor to execute process, but this he does at his peril. If the property of the debtor that he is to take is actually there, then he is justified, but otherwise he is a trespasser.[95] Nor is it only officers of the law who may be thus empowered. A private person may in certain circumstances arrest a criminal, and it is no trespass if he breaks into the house of another person in order to prevent him from murdering his wife,[96] or probably from committing other serious offences.[97]

Under the Access to Neighbouring Land Act 1992 the court may make an order allowing access to land for the purpose of carrying out works which are reasonably necessary for the preservation of adjoining land and which cannot be carried out, or would be substantially more difficult to carry out, without entry upon the land. It is not, however to make the order if it would cause unreasonable interference with the enjoyment of the land sought to be entered or unreasonable hardship. The Act does not permit entry for development or improvement as such but does permit entry for the purpose of work of, "alteration, adjustment or improvement [or] demolition if merely incidental to the work necessary for preservation".[98]

13–12   Where an entry upon land or other prima facie trespass is justified by the authority of the law itself, then, according to an ancient doctrine of the common law, if the actor abuses his authority he becomes a trespasser ab initio and his act is reckoned as unlawful from the very beginning, however innocent his conduct may have been up to the moment of the abuse.[99] The doctrine applies only if the authority is that of the law,[100] not that of the other party concerned,[101] and the abuse must be by a positive act, not a mere omission.[102] The explanations of these restrictions on the doctrine are historical,[103] but they show that its purpose, derived from its origin in the law of distress, was to provide protection against abuses of authority. Seen in this light it would seem to be unduly

[95] *Southam v Smout*, above, fn.94. "It is a case of justification not by faith but by works": at 327 per Harman L.J. Cf. *Chic Fashions (West Wales) Ltd v Jones* [1968] 2 Q.B. 299 but for the proposed new enforcement regime under the Tribunals, Courts and Enforcement Act 2007 see fn.86 above.
[96] *Handcock v Baker* (1800) 2 Bos. & P. 260.
[97] (1800) 2 Bos. 6 P. 260 at 265, per Chambre J. See *Dehn v Att Gen* [1988] 2 N.Z.L.R. 564 at 580. Such cases would now fall under the Criminal Law Act 1967 s.3.
[98] See s.1(5). For the background to the Act, see Law Com. No.151. See also the Party Wall, etc., Act 1996.
[99] *Six Carpenters' Case* (1610) 8 Co. Rep. 146a. The older cases are epitomised in Viner's *Abridgement*, Vol.XX, 2nd edn, pp.499–504.
[100] Where entry takes place by virtue of an access order under the Access to Neighbouring Land Act 1992 the doctrine is excluded by s.3(6) of the Act.
[101] *Delta Holdings Ltd v Magrum* (1975) 59 D.L.R. (3d) 126.
[102] (1975) 59 D.L.R. (3d) 126.
[103] Holdsworth, *H.E.L.*, vii, pp.499–501.

optimistic to suppose that the doctrine has outlived its usefulness,[104] even given the modern limitation that partial abuse of an authority does not render everything done under it unlawful. For example, in *Elias v Pasmore*[105] police had lawfully entered the claimant's premises in order to arrest a man, and while there they seized a number of documents, some of them unlawfully. It was held that this did not render their original entry a trespass. However, in *Chic Fasions (West Wales) Ltd v Jones*[106] though no point involving trespass ab initio was in fact in issue, the three members of the Court of Appeal criticised the doctrine as offending against the principle that subsequent events cannot render unlawful an act which was lawful when it was done. This principle is, in general, a sound one, but it should not be over-stressed. Not only may subsequent events illuminate the intent with which an act was originally done and thus assist in determining its lawfulness or unlawfulness,[107] but there are, and should continue to be, cases in which, in effect, the law withholds judgment on the lawfulness of an act for a time and allows it to depend upon subsequent events.[108] The doctrine of trespass ab initio enables this to be done in the important area of the protection of one's person, goods and land against abuse of official power.[109]

5. REMEDIES

The action for trespass, besides being used to remedy trespass as a pure tort, has also some varieties which are employed for the recovery of land and the profits thereof, and of these we shall speak in the next sections on ejectment and mesne profits.

13–13

---

[104] Pace the Court of Appeal in *Chic Fashions (West Wales) Ltd v Jones* [1968] 2 Q.B. 299.

[105] [1934] 2 K.B. 164; *Harvey v Pocock* (1843) 11 M. & W. 740; *Canadian Pacific Wine Co Ltd v Tuley* [1921] 2 A.C. 417.

[106] [1968] 2 Q.B. 299.

[107] This was one of the explanations of the doctrine of trespass ab initio itself given by Coke: 8 Co. Rep. 146b. Winfield ridiculed it (see the 8th edn of this book, p.346) but even though it contains an element of fiction, it is submitted that it does have some merit.

[108] *Southam v Smout* [1964] 1 Q.B. 308 provides one example, and there are others also. The power of a private person to arrest on reasonable suspicion of an offence exists only if the offence suspected has actually been committed (Police and Criminal Evidence Act 1984 s.24A, para.4–22, above), and this cannot be known until further investigations have been carried out. If a person enters upon land under authority of the National Parks and Access to the Countryside Act 1949 s.60(1) and then commits a breach of the restrictions contained in the Second Schedule, it seems that he becomes a trespasser ab initio: the subsection has effect subject to the provisions of the Schedule (s.60(4)) and the Schedule itself provides that s.60(1) "shall not apply to a person who" does any of the forbidden acts on the land. The effect of s.2 and Sch.2 of the Countryside and Rights of Way Act 2000 may be the same.

[109] Lord Denning M.R., a member of the court in *Chic Fashions*, subsequently referred to the doctrine with approval in *Cinnamond v British Airports Authority* [1980] 1 W.L.R. 582.

A. Re-entry

13–14   The remedies for trespass as a pure tort[110] need no special mention except the right of re-entry. The person entitled to possession can enter or re-enter the premises, but the Criminal Law Act 1977 makes it an offence punishable with imprisonment for anyone (other than a displaced residential occupier) to use or threaten violence for the purposes of securing entry to any premises occupied by another.[111] This replaces earlier criminal legislation in a series of Forcible Entry Acts, beginning in 1381. However, in *Hemmings v Stoke Poges Golf Club*[112] the Court of Appeal held that whatever might be his criminal liability under the Statutes of Forcible Entry, a landowner was not civilly liable if he used no more force than necessary to remove the other party and his property. It is submitted that the law remains the same under the Criminal Law Act[113] and it has been said in the Supreme Court that, "self-help is a remedy still available, in principle, to a landowner against trespassers (other than former residential tenants)."[114]

B. Action for the Recovery of Land (Ejectment)

13–15   By the action of ejectment, or, as it now should be called, the action for the recovery of land, a person dispossessed of land can recover it specifically. The story of this remedy is an old one and neatly exemplifies the use of fictions in the development of a legal system. It was originally a species of the action for trespass to land, and was invented for the benefit of the leaseholder, to whom the remedies of the freeholder were denied because he had mere "possession" of the land and not that blessed and superior "seisin" which gave the freeholder very adequate, if excessively dilatory, protection in the shape of the real actions. Then, by a notable paradox, the action of ejectment was seen to be so quick and efficient compared to the ponderous progress of the real actions that the freeholder adopted it by a series of fictions. If, for example, Smith, a freeholder, were seeking to recover the land from Brown, he was allowed to pretend that he had leased the land to John Doe,

---

[110] As to damages in respect of land, see para.22–44, below. A high-handed trespass may attract aggravated (*Horsford v Bird* [2006] UKPC 3) or, where the requisite conditions are fulfilled, exemplary, damages.

[111] The proposition in the text is a bare summary of a complex provision (the 1977 Act was amended by the Criminal Justice and Public Order Act 1994).

[112] [1920] 1 K.B. 720, where the earlier authorities are considered.

[113] See Clerk and Lindsell, *Torts*, 19th edn, s.31–11. This was the view of Clarke L.J. in *Ropaigealach v Barclays Bank Plc* [2000] 1 Q.B. 263. Nor does s.36 of the Administration of Justice Act 1970 deprive a mortgagee of his power to take possession without court proceedings: *Ropaigealach*. On the Human Rights Act see *Horsham Properties Group Ltd v Clark* [2008] EWHC 2327; [2009] 1 All E.R. (Com) 745

[114] *Secretary of State for Environment etc v Meier* [2009] UKSC 11; [2009] 1 W.L.R. 2780 at [66] per Lord Neuberger.

an imaginary person, and that John Doe had been ejected by another nonexistent person, Richard Roe (the "casual ejector"). Then Smith began his action with Doe as the nominal claimant against Roe as the nominal defendant, but he first served on Brown a notice signed by "your loving friend, Roe", in which Roe informed Brown that Roe claimed no interest in the land and advised Brown to defend the action. The fictitious parties then disappeared and the stage was cleared for the proceedings between Smith and Brown. The title of the action was "John Doe on the Demise [i.e. lease] of Smith v Brown", or, more briefly, "Doe d. Smith v Brown". It was useless for Brown to protest against these fictions: he was not allowed to defend the action unless he acquiesced in them.[115] The remarkable result was that the question of ownership of land was fought under the guise of an action of trespass.

These fictions have been long abolished,[116] and an action for the recovery of land differs in no formal respect from any other action. A special summary procedure has, however, been devised to enable a claimant to obtain an order for possession against persons in occupation of his land if they entered or remained there without his licence or consent, whether or not he is able to identify all, or even any, of those persons.[117]

What is it that a person seeking to recover land under the modern procedure must show? He succeeds if he shows that he has a "better title" than the defendant, as where he is a purchaser from an owner who has been excluded by the defendant. However, nothing approaching a paper title is necessary. Although it was said that for ejectment it was insufficient to set up the mere de facto possession which, as we have seen, will usually enable the claimant to sue for trespass as a tort,[118] this distinction is now very tenuous in view of

13–16

---

[115] Sometimes the fictitious names were more descriptive: e.g. *Fairclaim v Shamtitle* (1762) 3 Burr. 1290.

[116] By the Common Law Procedure Act 1852. For the history of the matter, see Holdsworth, *HEL*, iii, pp.213–217 vii, pp.4–23. The best account is is Maitland, *Equity*, pp.352–355 reprinted separately as *Forms of Action*, pp.56–59. John Doe, however, continues to serve the law in another context: see *Barnett v French* [1981] 1 W.L.R. 848, where his participation was singularly apt, the real defendant being the Dept of the Environment.

[117] CPR Pt 55, replacing the former RSC, Ord.113 and CCR, Ord.24. The court's jurisdiction extends to making an order for possession of the whole premises, not just that part presently under adverse occupation provided an intention to decamp can be inferred: *University of Essex v Djemal* [1980] 1 W.L.R. 1301. Where the defendants are in occupation of land A it is possible to grant an injunction restraining them from going on to other, separate land B to which the claimant fears they may decamp, but the special procedure for possession is not available in such a case. This is inconvenient because in cases of "traveller" or "mass protest" trespass the methods of enforcement of injunctions (sequestration or imprisonment) may not be effective. The reason is that a possession order would require the defendants to do what they cannot then do, surrender possession of land B: *Secretary of State for Environment etc v Meier* [2009] UKSC 11; [2009] 1 W.L.R. 2780.

[118] *Harper v Charlesworth* (1825) 4 B. & C. 574 at 589 per Bayley J., at 592–594 per Holroyd J.

Asher v Whitlock,[119] where it was held that if A takes possession of
wasteland without any other title than such seizure, he could get
possession against B who subsequently enters on the land.[120] When,
therefore, it is said that A's former possession raises only a presumption of title it must be confessed that this presumption is not
easily upset.[121] Indeed, it may now be that the law goes further and
allows the claimant to succeed in a claim for possession where he
would fail in an action of pure trespass. In *Manchester Airport Plc
v Dutton*[122] the airport needed to lop and fell trees in Arthur's Wood
in order to build a new runway. To stop this, the wood was occupied
by protestors and the owner than granted the airport a licence to
"enter and occupy" the site. An order for possession against the
protestors was upheld by the majority of the Court of Appeal. For
Laws L.J., modern proceedings for the recovery of land were no
longer subject to the requirements of ejectment so the fact that that
remedy had not concerned itself with the position of the licensee out
of occupation was not decisive:

> "[A] licensee not in occupation may claim possession against a
> trespasser if that is a necessary remedy to vindicate and give
> effect to such rights of occupation as by contract with his licensor
> he enjoys".[123]

Although the airport would not have been able to sue for damages
for trespass, nevertheless, for the purpose of gaining possession it
had a "superior right" to that of the defendants. However, the same
court has subsequently declined to extend this decision to a situation
where the licence was to enter and carry out work on the land but not
to occupy it.[124]

C. *Jus Tertii*

13–17   The modern cases on recovery of land have not addressed another
question, which has been controversial: if the claimant relies on his
title to the land, how far may the defendant defeat his claim by
showing a superior right in a third party? In an ordinary action of
trespass the defendant cannot as a general rule set up the defence of
jus tertii,[125] but is this rule applicable to the defendant to an action
for the recovery of land? If the claimant must prove his title,[126] it

---

[119] (1865) L.R. 1 Q.B. 1. See, too, *Doe d. Hughes v Dyeball* (1829) Moo. & M. 346.
[120] Approved by the Judicial Committee in *Perry v Clissold* [1907] A.C. 73 at 79.
[121] *Whale v Hitchcock* (1876) 34 L.T. 136.
[122] [2000] Q.B. 133.
[123] At 150.
[124] *Countryside Residential (North Thames) Ltd v Tugwell* [2000] 34 EG 87.
[125] See para.13–2, above.
[126] For example, where he is someone who has purchased or inherited the property.

would seem to be a corollary that if the evidence, whether it appear from the claimant's own case or be produced by the defendant, shows that some third person is entitled to the land, the claimant ought not to succeed: in other words, the defendant ought to be allowed to plead *jus tertii*. The position is, however, not necessarily the same where the claimant relies on prior possession of the land. Although the title of the third party (the lord of the manor) was not directly in issue in *Asher v Whitlock*[127] the reasoning seems inconsistent with the view that the defendant could have raised that title and in *Perry v Clissold*[128] Lord Macnaghten thought that the earlier case of *Doe d. Carter v Barnard*[129] could not stand with *Asher v Whitlock*. Although the matter has been greatly debated[130] and is perhaps not finally settled, the better view seems to be that the *jus tertii* cannot be raised in this case.[131]

Whether or not *jus tertii* is in general a defence in such cases, it cannot be relied upon where the defendant has acquired possession from the claimant himself or from one through whom the claimant claims. The rule that a tenant is estopped from denying his landlord's title is well known, but a licensee is similarly estopped from denying the title of his licensor,[132] and indeed this rule of estoppel extends to anyone who is sued in ejectment by one from whom he derived his interest.

"If a person obtains possession of land, claiming under a will or deed, he cannot afterwards set up another title to the land against the will or deed, though the deed or will did not operate to pass the land in question."[133]

D. Mesne Profits

The action for mesne profits is another species of the action for trespass and lies for the damage which the claimant has suffered through having been out of possession of his land. By Blackstone's

13–18

---

[127] See above, fn.119.
[128] [1907] A.C. 73 at 79.
[129] (1849) 13 Q.B. 945.
[130] For full discussion of the question, see Wiren, (1925) 41 L.Q.R. 139, Hargreaves, "Terminology and Title in Ejectment" (1940) 56 L.Q.R. 376 Holdsworth, "Terminology and Title in Ejectment—A Reply," (1940) 56 L.Q.R. 479.
[131] Winfield was firmly of the contrary view: see earlier editions of this book. He contended that the argument that the law greatly respects possession, "is a two-edged argument, for if the law respects possession which the claimant once had, why should it not equally respect possession which the defendant now has? And it sounds odd to insist that, because C is the real owner of land, B, who is in wrongful (but legally protected) possession of it, ought to give it up to A who once had wrongful possession of it."
[132] *Doe d. Johnson v Baytup* (1835) 3 Ad. & E. 188. A general denial in a pleading by a tenant does not amount to a sufficient denial of the landlord's title to cause a forfeiture of the lease: *Warner v Sampson* [1959] 1 Q.B. 297.
[133] Lopes L.J. in *Dalton v Fitzgerald* [1897] 2 Ch. 86 at 93.

time nothing but a shilling or some trivial sum was usually recoverable in the action of ejectment because it had been "licked into the form of a real action"[134] and its chief purpose had become the trial of the title to land.[135] If the claimant was successful, he got possession of the land but no compensation for having been kept out of it. The action for mesne profits enables the claimant to claim a reasonable rent for the possession of the property by the defendant and damages for deterioration and the reasonable costs of getting possession.[136] The claimant in an action for the recovery of land may join with it a claim for mesne profits, and if he does so it is unnecessary for him to have entered the land before he sues.[137] If he prefers he can still bring the action for mesne profits separately but in that event he must first enter, for the action is one of trespass, trespass is a wrong to possession, and until he enters he has not got it. Once he has entered, however, then, by the fiction of trespass by relation[138] the claimant is deemed to have been in possession during the whole period for which he claims the mesne profits.

---

[134] *Goodtitle v Tombs* (1770) 3 Wils. K.B. 118 at 120 per Wilmot C.J.

[135] Blackstone, Comm, ii, p.205.

[136] It does not matter that the claimant cannot show that he could have let the property while he was out of possession, nor that the defendant has not profited from the property: *Inverugie Investments Ltd v Hackett* [1995] 1 W.L.R. 713. See also *MoD v Ashman* (1993) 66 P. & C.R. 195 at 201.

[137] If the claimant's title to the land has been extinguished by adverse possession, so is his claim for mesne profits: *Mount Carmel Investment Ltd v Peter Thurlow Ltd* [1988] 1 W.L.R. 1078.

[138] See para.13–3, above.

CHAPTER 14

NUISANCE[1]

1. INTRODUCTION

IN modern parlance, nuisance is that branch of the law of tort most   **14–1**
closely concerned with "protection of the environment". Thus nuisance actions have concerned pollution by oil[2] or noxious fumes,[3]
interference with leisure activities,[4] offensive smells from premises

---

[1] Buckley, *Law of Nuisance*, 2nd edn.
[2] *Esso Petroleum Co Ltd v Southport Corp* [1956] A.C. 218.
[3] *St Helen's Smelting Co v Tipping* (1865) 11 H.L.C. 642.
[4] *Bridlington Relay v Yorkshire Electricity Board* [1965] Ch. 436.

used for keeping animals[5] or noise from industrial installations.[6] Three important qualifications must be made, however, to this broad generalisation. First, there are areas of nuisance, such as obstruction of the highway or of access thereto,[7] which have no "environmental" flavour. Secondly, the prevailing stance of nuisance liability is that of protection of private rights in the enjoyment of land,[8] so that control of injurious activity for the benefit of the whole community is incidental.[9] Thirdly, the common law of nuisance has been supplemented and to a large extent replaced by an array of statutory powers designed to control environmental damage. A full account of these would be beyond the scope of a book on tort[10] but a very brief sketch of the principal provisions may help the reader to put the common law in context. The main statute is the Environmental Protection Act 1990, which consolidated and restated much previous law as well as introducing a new administrative system for pollution control. Under Pt III of this Act[11] various matters[12] are "statutory nuisances". A local authority which is satisfied that such a nuisance exists is under a duty to serve an abatement notice requiring the nuisance to be terminated and failure, without reasonable excuse, to comply with the notice is a criminal offence.[13] Part II of the Act contains wide-ranging powers to control the deposit of waste and contravention of these provisions causing damage may give rise to civil liability, which is outlined elsewhere in this book.[14]

---

[5] *Rapier v London Tramways Co* [1893] 2 Ch. 588.

[6] *Halsey v Esso Petroleum Co Ltd* [1961] 1 W.L.R. 683.

[7] See para.14–37, below.

[8] *Hunter v Canary Wharf Ltd* [1997] A.C. 655, para.14–15, below. There is, however, a strong public law element in the shape of the power of public authorities to bring proceedings for an injunction to restrain a public nuisance: see below.

[9] Indeed, there may be circumstances in which the enforcement of private rights by injunction will bring positive hardship on the community at large: see e.g. *Bellew v Cement Co Ltd* [1948] Ir.R. 62. The common law of nuisance has been a prominent topic for analysis by the economic approach to law. There is a large American literature on the topic. For an introduction see Ogus and Richardson, "Economics and the Environment" (1977) 36 C.L.J. 284. See also Campbell, "Of Coase and Corn: a (sort of) defence of private nuisance" (2000) 63 M.L.R. 197.

[10] See *Encyclopedia of Environmental Health Law and Practice*; Garner, *Environmental Law*.

[11] As amended, particularly by the Noise and Statutory Nuisance Act 1993 and the Environment Act 1995. For earlier provisions see the Public Health Act 1936 Pt II. Much of the case law on that Act remains relevant.

[12] Section 79, e.g. premises in a state prejudicial to health or constituting a nuisance; similar states of affairs in relation to smoke, fumes, dust, noise or accumulations or deposits. If the complaint is that the premises constitute a nuisance there must be a nuisance in the common law sense, i.e. the matter has to affect neighbouring land: *National Coal Board v Neath BC* [1976] 2 All E.R. 478; but this is not necessary if, e.g. the premises are in a state prejudicial to health, though even then the statute is concerned with the condition of the premises, not the layout or facilities: *Birmingham CC v Oakley* [2001] 1 All E.R. 385.

[13] If the local authority considers that summary proceedings would afford an inadequate remedy it may proceed in the High Court: s.81(5).

[14] See para.15–26, below.

The statutory nuisance provisions do not, as such, give rise to civil liability,[15] though conviction of the criminal offence would entitle the criminal court in a straightforward case to make a compensation order under the Powers of Criminal Courts (Sentencing) Act 2000.[16] However, the principal remedy sought by most victims of nuisance is an order to prevent its continuance and a complaint to the local authority under the 1990 Act will often be a considerably cheaper and more expeditious way of getting redress than a common law action for an injunction. Indeed, even if the local authority declines to take proceedings in the matter it is possible under s.82 for summary proceedings to be brought by a "person aggrieved."[17] The common law is, therefore, something of a residuary category where, for one reason or another, the statutory provisions are inapt or the victim considers there are advantages in a civil action.[18] The traditional "neighbour dispute nuisance" may also now fall under the Protection from Harassment Act 1997,[19] which contains civil as well criminal sanctions.[20] Civil actions for nuisance certainly continue to be brought[21] and it would be wrong to think that the role of the common law is insignificant[22] but the reader should be aware that some of the older cases[23] in this chapter might now be dealt with by other means.

---

[15] *Issa v Hackney LBC* [1997] 1 W.L.R. 956.

[16] In *R. v Crown Court at Liverpool, Ex p. Cooke* [1997] 1 W.L.R. 700, the CA emphasised that only "simple, straightforward" claims should be entertained and that even within the financial limit of £5,000 the magistrates should not engage themselves in what are essentially civil claims.

[17] Under this procedure there is no abatement notice and it is the court which orders the nuisance to be abated. Since s.82(2) allows for the imposition of a fine in respect of conduct before the hearing the proceedings are criminal in nature (despite the reference to "complaint" in s.82(1)) and there is therefore power to make a compensation order.

[18] Possible reasons include: (1) an injunction may be more effective than a criminal fine (even though there are "topping up" provisions where the nuisance continues) see, e.g. *City of London Corp v Bovis Construction Ltd* [1992] 3 All E.R. 697; (2) the nuisance may fall outside the matters listed in s.79; (3) where damage has been suffered the case may be too complex for a compensation order; (4) under s.80(7) it is in some cases a defence to a prosecution that the "best practicable means" have been used to prevent it. This may be more favourable to the defendant in some cases than the common law (but see *Wivenhoe Port v Colchester BC* [1985] J.P.L. 175).

[19] See para.4–38, above.

[20] See for example *Church of Jesus Christ of Latter Day Saints v Price* [2004] EWHC 3245 (QB) and *Fowler v Jones*, June 10, 2002 (Hayward's Heath CC) where £10,100 damages were awarded for nuisance and harassment.

[21] Sometimes on a large scale. In *Hunter v Canary Wharf Ltd* [1997] A.C. 655 there were 690 claimants.

[22] For example, there were substantial settlements in 1993 of civil claims arising from alleged dioxin pollution in Derbyshire where regulatory action had not been taken.

[23] McLaren, "Nuisance Law and the Industrial Revolution" (1983) 3 O.J.L.S. 155 concludes that deficiencies of the law in dealing with pollution in the 19th century stemmed not from defects in principle (indeed, judges were quite ready to reject the pleas of manufacturers) but from the disinclination of those best able to take action to put the law in motion.

As is so often the case nowadays, there is a European dimension. In 2004 the EU adopted a Directive on Environmental Liability.[24] It rests on the principle that "the polluter must pay" but the "liability" imposed in respect of the cost of preventive and remedial action rests on an administrative mechanism rather than the private law of tort. Indeed, it does not apply to:

> "[C]ases of personal injury, to damage to private property or to any economic loss and does not affect any right regarding these types of damages".[25]

Article 8(1) of the European Convention on Human Rights requires respect for "private and family life, [and the] home"[26] and there are already signs that this may have a significant impact in the context of nuisance law, forming (as we have seen in other contexts) a parallel or alternative system of redress, at least where a public authority is involved.[27] In *Lough v First Secretary of State*[28] the court had to deal with a case arising from a planning decision but the propositions it put forward about the effect of art.8 are of equal relevance to the law of nuisance:

> "1. Respect for the home has an environmental dimension in that the law must offer protection to the environment of the home.
> 2. Not every loss of amenity involves a breach of Article 8.1. The degree of seriousness required to trigger lack of respect for the home will depend on the circumstances but it must be substantial.
> 3. The contents of Art.8.2[29] throw light on the extent of the right in Art.8.1 but infringement of Art.8.1 does not necessarily arise upon a loss of amenity and the reasonableness and appropriateness of measures taken by the public authority are relevant in considering whether the respect required by Art.1 has been accorded.
> 4. It is also open to the public authority to justify an interference in accordance with Art.8.2 but the principles to be applied are

---

[24] 2004/35/EC. See Koch, "European Union" in Koziol and Steininger (eds), *European Tort Law 2004*.
[25] Recital 14. For a discussion of the difficulties of the concept of "environmental damage" see *British Columbia v Canadian Forest Products Ltd* [2004] SCC 38; [2004] 2 S.C.R. 74 (where, however, the claim was limited by the pleadings and evidence).
[26] In addition, art.1 of the First Protocol provides that everyone, "is entitled to the peaceful enjoyment of his possessions".
[27] See para.14–35, below.
[28] [2004] EWCA Civ 905; [2004] 1 W.L.R. 2557.
[29] Which forbids interference by a public authority with the right.

broadly similar in the context of the two parts of the article.
5. When balances are struck the competing interests of the individual, other individuals and the community as a whole must be considered.
6. The public authority concerned is granted a certain margin of appreciation in determining the steps to be taken to ensure a compliance with Art.8."[30]

2. PUBLIC AND PRIVATE NUISANCE

A. Public Nuisance

Nuisances are divided into public and private, although it is quite possible for the same conduct to amount to both. A public nuisance is a crime, while a private nuisance is only a tort. A public or common nuisance is one which materially affects the reasonable comfort and convenience of life of a class of the public who come within the sphere or neighbourhood of its operation[31]; the question whether the number of persons affected is sufficient to constitute a class is one of fact in every case, and it is sufficient to show that a representative cross-section of that class has been so affected for an injunction to issue.[32] This definition is vague and it has been rightly said that nuisance, "covers a multitude of sins, great and small".[33] Public nuisances at common law include such diverse activities as carrying on an offensive trade, keeping a disorderly house, selling food unfit for human consumption, obstructing public highways, throwing fireworks about in the street and holding an ill-organised pop festival.[34] In many cases such conduct will now be covered by a specific statutory offence and where this is so a criminal prosecution should normally be brought for that rather than at common law.[35] Subject to this, however, the common law of public nuisance

14–2

---

[30] At [43].
[31] One cannot add together the effect of numerous acts aimed at individuals and thereby claim that the public is affected. Thus a malicious bomb hoax call may be a public nuisance but not a campaign of hate mail to numerous people: *R v Rimmington* [2005] UKHL 63; [2006] 1 A.C. 459.
[32] *Att Gen v P.Y.A. Quarries Ltd* [1957] 2 Q.B. 169 at 184 per Romer L.J. (quarrying blasting, stones and splinters projected from quarry, dust, noise and vibration). Provided it affects the public it does not matter that only a small number of people in fact use the facility: *Jan de Nul (UK) Ltd v Axa Royal Belge* [2000] 2 Lloyd's Rep. 700 (on appeal, [2002] EWCA Civ 209; [2002] 1 Lloyd's Rep. 583). Denning L.J.'s view in *P.Y.A. Quarries* that a public nuisance is one which is so widespread in its range or so indiscriminate in its effect that it would not be reasonable to expect one person as distinct from the community at large to take proceedings to put a stop to it has been doubted: *R v Rimmington* above, fn.31, at [44].
[33] *Southport Corp v Esso Petroleum Co Ltd* [1954] 2 Q.B. 182 at 196 per Denning L.J.
[34] *Att Gen for Ontario v Orange Productions Ltd* (1971)21 D.L.R. (3d) 257.
[35] *R. v Rimmington*, above, fn.31.

meets the requirement of certainty prescribed by the European Convention on Human Rights.[36]

B. Special or Particular Damage Necessary for Action for Damages for Public Nuisance[37]

14–3   So long as the public only or some section of it is injured no civil action can be brought by a private individual for public nuisance. Where a public highway is obstructed, I cannot sue the obstructor for nuisance if I can prove no damage beyond being delayed on several occasions in passing along it and being obliged either to pursue my journey by a devious route or to remove the obstruction, for these are inconveniences common to everyone else.[38] The reason normally given for the rule is that it prevents multiplicity of actions, for if one were allowed to sue, a thousand might do so and this would lead to harsh results.[39] If, for instance, a public body obstructed a highway temporarily for the purpose of draining, paving or lighting it and it was then discovered that owing to some technical error they had no authority to do so, they would be sufficiently punished by a criminal prosecution.[40] If, for some reason, a criminal prosecution is an inadequate sanction, the Attorney-General may, on the information of a member of the public, bring a civil action for an injunction (known as a "relator" action), but if he refuses to do so the courts are not at liberty to inquire into the propriety of his actions or to grant declarations at the suit of the individual instead of injunctions.[41] By statute, a local authority may bring proceedings for an injunction where they, "consider it expedient for the promotion or protection of the interests of the inhabitants of their area".[42] The provision has been called in aid in support of the criminal law,[43] though it has been said that the relationship between it and the "classic public nuisance case"

---

[36] *R. v Rimmington*, fn.31.
[37] Kodilinye, "Public Nuisance and Particular Damage in Modern Law" (1986) 6 L.S. 182.
[38] *Winterbottom v Lord Derby* (1867) L.R. 2 Ex. 316 at 321–322. "Even if he chose to incur expense to remove it. There must be some damage to himself, his trade or calling": per Kelly C.B.
[39] However, this is not entirely easy to square with the undoubted proposition that the same thing may be both a public nuisance and a private nuisance to persons whose property interests are affected. See *Sutherland v Canada* [2002] BCCA 416, 215 D.L.R. 4th 1.
[40] *Winterbottom v Lord Derby*, above, fn.38.
[41] *Gouriet v Union of Post Office Workers* [1978] A.C. 435 (not a case of public nuisance).
[42] Local Government Act 1972 s.222.
[43] It was used in the "Sunday trading" cases (see, e.g. *Kirklees MBC v Wickes Building Supplies Ltd* [1993] A.C. 227). However, the grant of an injunction in the case of conduct falling within the "ASBO" scheme of the Crime and Disorder Act 1998 would only be justified in an exceptional case: *Birmingham CC v Shafi* [2008] EWCA Civ 1186; [2009] 1 W.L.R. 1961.

requires further consideration.[44] Where, however, any private person is injured in some way peculiar to himself, that is, if he can show that he has suffered some particular or special loss over and above the ordinary inconvenience suffered by the public at large, then he can sue in tort, for example if he falls into a trench unlawfully opened in a street and breaks his leg. Particular damage[45] is not limited to special damage in the sense of pecuniary loss actually incurred, for example in an action for negligence. It may consist of proved general damage, such as inconvenience and delay, provided it is substantial, direct and not consequential and is appreciably different in nature or extent to that in fact suffered by the general public, although in another sense it is "general" and not "special" to him.[46] "Direct" here means damage other or different from the damage caused to the rest of the public. It is narrower than when "direct" is used in determining whether damage is too remote.[47] The distinction between public and private nuisance and the meaning of particular damage is illustrated by *Tate & Lyle Industries Ltd v GLC*.[48] Ferry terminals constructed by the defendants in the Thames caused silting which obstructed large vessels' access to the claimants' jetty and the claimants had to spend large sums in dredging operations. Their claim in private nuisance was dismissed because the jetty itself was unaffected and they had no private rights of property in the river bed, but the silting had caused interference with the public right of navigation which the claimants enjoyed along with all other river users and the expenditure incurred by the claimants was damage sufficient to entitle them to bring an action for public nuisance.[49]

In truth, beyond the fact that both involve "unreasonable" behaviour and both may arise from the same facts, public and private nuisance have little in common. Private nuisance is firmly rooted in

---

[44] *Birmingham CC v Shafi*, above, fn.43 at [42].

[45] *Rose v Groves* (1843) 5 Man. & G. 613 at 616. "It is not necessary to prove special damage in this action. It is sufficient to prove particular damage": per Cresswell J. However, the adjectives seem to be used interchangeably.

[46] *Walsh v Ervin* [1952] V.L.R. 361 at 368–369 per Sholl J. reviewing the English authorities; *Jan de Nul (UK) Ltd v N.V. Royal Belge* [2000] 2 Lloyd's Rep. 700. Particular damage includes injury to claimant's person, loss of custom, depreciation in the actual value of the property by reducing or cutting off the approach to it. *Boyd v GN Ry* (1895) 2 I.R. 555 (doctor held up at level crossing for 20 minutes, recovered).

[47] *Overseas Tankship (UK) Ltd v The Miller Steamship Co Pty* [1967] 1 A.C. 617 at 636.

[48] [1983] 2 A.C. 509.

[49] See also *Jan de Nul (UK) Ltd v Axa Royal Belge* [2002] EWCA Civ 209; [2002] 1 Lloyd's Rep. 583; *Rose v Miles* (1815) 4 M. & S. 101; *Iveson v Moore* (1699) 1 Ld.Raym. 486; *News Group Newspapers Ltd v SOGAT'82* [1986] I.R.L.R. 337 (cost of "bussing-in" employees because of picketing). Note that in these cases the loss is "economic" but though that may be a bar to a claim for negligence (though see *Jan de Nul (UK) Ltd v Axa Royal Belge SA*, above, where a harbour conservation authority was held entitled to sue in negligence as well as public nuisance in respect of siltation) it is not to one for public nuisance. Cf. the position where the claim relates to failure to repair the highway: para.14–42, below.

the protection of landholding rights, whereas public nuisance represents a rather unsuccessful attempt to link the criminal law with compensation for damage. It is questionable whether in a modern system of law there should be any connection between liability for interference with the enjoyment of land and for damage done by a crime (often obstruction of the highway) affecting the public as a whole. At any rate, the rules relating to them are not identical. It has now been reaffirmed that to sue in private nuisance one must have an interest in land but no such interest is necessary in public nuisance. On the other hand, while a private nuisance claimant must generally show some damage,[50] the person who sues for public nuisance must show damage going beyond that suffered by the public as a whole. Although it has long been assumed—and now held[51]—that damages for personal injury may be recovered in public nuisance,[52] this is not now the case in the private variety.[53] The same state of affairs may, of course, constitute both torts, a private nuisance in so far as A suffers interference with the enjoyment of land and a public nuisance in so far as B suffers some special damage.[54]

C. Private Nuisance

14–4   Private nuisance may be described as unlawful interference with a person's use or enjoyment of land, or some right over, or in connection with it.[55] It has been said[56] that the tort takes three forms: encroachment on a neighbour's land[57]; direct physical injury to the land; or interference with the enjoyment of the land. The varieties of the third form are almost infinite but it is still a tort against rights of property and therefore lies only at the suit of a person with a sufficient interest in the land.[58] Generally, the essence of a nuisance is a state of affairs that is either continuous or recurrent, a condition or activity which unduly interferes with the use or enjoyment of land. It is not necessary that there be any *physical* emanation from

---

[50] This is not as onerous a requirement as might appear: para.14–28, below.

[51] *Claimants in Corby Group Litigation v Corby BC* [2008] EWCA Civ 463; [2009] 2 W.L.R. 609. .

[52] See the doubts of Lord Goff in *Hunter v Canary Wharf Ltd* [1997] A.C. 655 at 692.

[53] See para.14–15, below.

[54] *Colour Quest Ltd v Total Downstream UK Plc* [2009] EWHC 640 (Comm); [2009] 2 Lloyd's Rep 1. Indeed, the same person may have a claim for both.

[55] Adopted by Scott L.J. in *Read v Lyons & Co Ltd* [1945] K.B. 216 at 236; by Lord Goddard C.J. in *Howard v Walker* [1947] 2 All E.R. 197 at 199; by Evershed J. in *Newcastle-under-Lyme Corp v Wolstanton Ltd* [1947] Ch. 92 at 107 (his dictum on this point was unaffected by the appeal [1947] Ch. 427 at 467–468); and by Windeyer J. in *Hargrave v Goldman* (1963) 37 A.L.J.R. 277 at 283, affirmed [1967] 1 A.C. 645.

[56] *Hunter v Canary Wharf Ltd* [1997] A.C. 655, 695 per Lord Lloyd.

[57] e.g. by spreading roots or overhanging branches.

[58] See para.14–15, below.

the defendant's premises. Noises and smells can be nuisances, but so, it seems can be otherwise offensive businesses.[59] The mere presence of a building is not, however, a nuisance.[60] Not every slight annoyance is actionable. Stenches, smoke, the escape of effluent and a multitude of different things may amount to a nuisance in fact but whether they constitute an actionable nuisance will depend on a variety of considerations, especially the character of the defendant's conduct, and a balancing of conflicting interests. In fact the whole of the law of private nuisance represents an attempt to preserve a balance between two conflicting interests, that of one occupier in using his land as he thinks fit, and that of his neighbour in the quiet enjoyment of his land.[61] Everyone must endure some degree of noise, smell, etc. from his neighbour, otherwise modern life would be impossible and such a privilege of interfering with the comfort of a neighbour is reciprocal. It is repeatedly said in nuisance cases that the rule is *sic utere tuo ut alienum non laedas*,[62] but the maxim is unhelpful and misleading. If it means that no person is ever allowed to use his property so as to injure another, it is palpably false.[63] If it means that a person in using his property may injure his neighbour, but not if he does so unlawfully, it is not worth stating, as it leaves unanswered the critical question of when the interference becomes unlawful.[64] In fact, the law repeatedly recognises that a person may use his own land so as to injure another without committing a nuisance. It is only if such use is unreasonable that it becomes unlawful.

---

[59] *Thompson-Schwab v Costaki* [1956] 1 W.L.R. 335 (prostitution); *Laws v Florinplace Ltd* [1981] 1 All E.R. 659 (sex shop, interlocutory injunction, triable issue of nuisance independently of risk of undesirable activities by customers). In *Hunter v Canary Wharf Ltd* [1997] A.C. 655, Lord Goff seems to approve *Thompson-Schwab*. No doubt it is generally true that nuisance involves some "emanation" from the defendant's land to the claimant's land but (a) this must sometimes be taken rather metaphorically and (b) there are exceptions, e.g. where works on the defendant's land cause a watercourse on the claimant's land to flood: *Bybrook Barn Centre Ltd and others v Kent CC* [2001] B.L.R. 55, but it is essential that the harmful effect has its origin outside the claimant's land: thus a landlord who complains that his tenant has caused long-term damage to the property may have an action for waste or negligence or breach of contract, but not for nuisance: *BP Oil New Zealand Ltd v Ports of Auckland Ltd* [2004] N.Z.L.R. 208.

[60] *Hunter v Canary Wharf Ltd* [1997] A.C. 655, para.14–10, below. *Bank of NZ v Greenwood* [1984] 1 N.Z.L.R. 525 is a borderline case, but the building was not merely a passive thing in the landscape—it threw off dazzling reflections. Cf. *Wernke v Halas* 600 N.E. 2d 117 (Ind., 1992)—offensive sight.

[61] "A balance has to be maintained between the right of the occupier to do what he likes with his own, and the right of his neighbour not to be interfered with": *Sedleigh-Denfield v O'Callaghan* [1940] A.C. 880 at 903 per Lord Wright.

[62] Use your own property in such a way as not to harm that of others.

[63] *Bamford v Turnley* (1862) 3 B. & S. 66 a 79, 83–84. "Liability is imposed only in those cases where the harm or risk to one is greater than he ought to be required to bear under the circumstances": per Bramwell B.

[64] The maxim was described by Erle J. as an "ancient and solemn imposter": *Bonomi v Backhouse* (1858) E.B. & E. 622 at 643.

D. Nuisance to Servitudes

14–5   We have so far been considering private nuisance as the interference with a person's use or enjoyment of land, and we have seen
that in determining liability, the nature and quality of the defendant's conduct is a factor of great importance. In addition to this
situation, however, the tort of nuisance provides a remedy for the
infringement of a servitude,[65] such as the obstruction of a right of
way or the blocking of an acquired right to light. In *Colls v Home
and Colonial Stores Ltd*,[66] Lord Macnaghten regarded the action for
interference with an easement as sui generis, the function of the
action being to remedy the infringement of a right, not to compensate for the commission of a wrong, so that the nature of the
defendant's conduct would be a less relevant consideration than in
other cases of nuisance. However, while this may be true of a simple
case of obstruction of a right of way, servitude rights may be as
qualified as the general right to enjoyment.[67]

3. REASONABLENESS

14–6   The central issue of the whole law of nuisance is the question of
reasonableness of the defendant's conduct, "according to the ordinary usages of mankind living in ... a particular society".[68] It is
vital to grasp at the outset that reasonableness is being used here in
a sense rather different from that in the law of negligence. It is a
comparatively simple proposition that you are liable for negligence
if you drive a car carelessly against a pedestrian in the street and it
would be ridiculous to say that there are some circumstances in
which you may do so and others in which you may not. In other
words, our attention is concentrated on the relative issue of the
characterisation of the defendant's conduct as foreseeably likely to
injure and once we have determined this in the claimant's favour we
immediately progress to legal liability, treating the claimant's right
to personal security as absolute. Nuisance, however, generally
approaches the issue from the other end and we cannot make such
a proposition as that you may not make a noise which irritates your
neighbour, for common sense tells one that such a rule would be
totally unworkable. Some intrusion by noise (or smells or dust, etc.)
is the inevitable price of living in an organised society in proximity
to one's neighbours, indeed:

---

[65] i.e. easements, profits a prendre and natural rights.

[66] [1904] A.C. 179.

[67] For example the right at common law of a riparian owner to take a reasonable amount of
water for agricultural and domestic purposes; but the right to take water is now subject to
extensive statutory control.

[68] *Sedleigh-Denfield v O'Callaghan* [1940] A.C. 880 at 903 per Lord Wright.

"[T]he very nuisance the one complains of, as the ordinary use of his neighbour's land, he himself will create in the ordinary use of his own and the reciprocal nuisances are of a comparatively trifling character".[69]

Accordingly, the protection of such interests must be approached with an attempt to balance the competing rights of neighbours, a process of compromise, a, "rule of give and take, of live and let live".[70] It is to this issue that we are directing our attention when we talk of the "reasonableness" of the defendant's conduct rather than to whether he took reasonable care in the negligence sense. "Reasonableness" signifies what is legally right between the parties taking account of all the circumstances of the case. The difference between the two approaches is in some ways more apparent than real and is perhaps the product of the fact that the majority of nuisance actions involve deliberate interference by the defendant,[71] but for practical purposes there is still a good deal of truth in the statement that knocking a person down carelessly is a tort simpliciter while making a noise that irritates him is only a tort *sub modo*. This is far short of saying that care is irrelevant to liability for nuisance: lack of care may lead to liability, for it is not reasonable to expect the claimant to put up with interference which could be reduced by the adoption of reasonable proper measures[72]; but if two neighbours live in adjoining properties with sound insulation which does not meet modern construction standards neither is liable for the inevitable noise which is produced by their ordinary activities of living, each acting with reasonable consideration[73] for the other.[74] On the other hand, if after balancing the competing interests of the

---

[69] *Bamford v Turnley* (1862) 3 B. & S. 62 at 83 per Bramwell B. *Kennaway v Thompson* [1981] Q.B. 88 at 94.

[70] *Bamford v Turnley*, above, fn.70, at 83; *Cambridge Water Co v Eastern Counties Leather Plc* [1994] 2 AC 264 at 299.

[71] All the circumstances of the case, including the utility of the defendant's activity must be taken into account in determining whether his conduct is so unreasonable as to amount to a nuisance (see below) but such matters may be equally relevant to determine whether his conduct constitutes legal negligence (para.5–83, above). Indeed, where there is physical damage but no deliberate interference by the defendant one can discern a strong tendency to run nuisance and negligence together: *Bolton v Stone* [1951] A.C. 850; *Goldman v Hargrave* [1967] 1 A.C. 645.

[72] *Southwark London Borough Council v Mills* [2001] 1 A.C. 1 at 16. Compare *Leeman v Montagu* [1936] 2 All E.R. 1677 (750 cockerels crowing between 2 and 7am, no attempt to rearrange farm, held a nuisance) with *Moy v Stoop* (1909) 25 T.L.R. 262 (crying children in day nursery, no lack of care, no nuisance); and see the cases on malicious activity, para.14–12, below. It has been said that once the interference is of sufficient magnitude to be a nuisance the burden then shifts to the defendant to show that he took all proper steps: *Hiscox Syndicates Ltd v The Pinnacle Ltd* [2008] EWHC 145 (Ch).

[73] Cf. *Ball v Ray* (1873) LR 8 Ch. App. 467.

[74] *Southwark London Borough Council v Mills*, above, fn.72.

parties, the court considers that the interference is excessive by any
standards then the fact that the defendant has taken all reasonable
care and reduced it to a minimum provides no defence—the irreduc-
ible minimum is itself the nuisance.[75]

No precise or universal formula is possible to determine reasonableness in the above sense. Whether an act constitutes a nuisance
cannot be determined merely by an abstract consideration of the act
itself, but by reference to all the circumstances of the particular case
the time and place of its commission, the seriousness of the harm,
the manner of committing it, whether it is done maliciously or in the
reasonable exercise of rights and the effect of its commission, that
is whether it is transitory or permanent, occasional or continuous; so
that it is a question of fact whether or not a nuisance has been
committed.[76] Certain of these factors will now be discussed in
greater detail.

A. Extent of the Harm and the Nature of the Locality

14–7   In the leading case of *St Helen's Smelting Co v Tipping*[77] where
trees on the claimant's estate were injured by fumes from a copper
smelter, the House of Lords drew a distinction between matters
producing "sensible injury to the value of property" or "material
injury"[78] on the one hand and those causing personal discomfort on
the other. In assessing whether the latter constitute an actionable
nuisance it is necessary to take into account the nature of the
locality, so that interference which may not be permissible in one
area may be in another; as it was once put, "What would be a
nuisance in Belgrave Square would not necessarily be so in Bermondsey",[79] though it must at once be added that even the inhabitants of Bermondsey are entitled to a measure of legal protection. In
these cases there must be something over and above the everyday
inconveniences which are inevitable in that locality. "The law does
not regard trifling inconveniences; everything is to be looked at from
a reasonable point of view"[80]; but in the other type of case these
considerations are said not to apply: property damage must not be

---

[75] *Rapier v London Tramways Co* [1893] 2 Ch. 588.
[76] *Bamford v Turnley* (1862) 3 B. & S. 66 at 79 per Pollock C.B.
[77] (1865) 11 H.L.C. 642.
[78] (1865) 11 H.L.C. at 651.
[79] *Sturges v Bridgman* (1879) 11 Ch.D. 852 at 865 per Thesiger L.J.; *Polsue and Alfieri v
Rushmer* [1907] A.C. 121; *Andreae v Selfridge & Co* [1938] Ch. 11; *Milner v Spencer*
(1976) 239 E.G. 573. The American equivalents are apparently Palm Springs and Pitts-
burgh: Prosser & Keeton, *Torts*, 5th edn, p.633.
[80] (1865) 11 H.L.C. at 653.

inflicted wherever the defendant is carrying on his activity. The distinction is not free from difficulty and its consequences do not seem to have been fully investigated by the courts,[81] but it was reiterated by Veale J. in *Halsey v Esso Petroleum Co.*[82] It may be that in the course of time Belgrave Square declines and Bermondsey goes up in the world. Nowadays a major factor in such changes in the nature of the locality will be the planning process. A grant of planning permission does not amount to statutory authority and therefore does not directly legalise an activity which amounts to a nuisance, even if that is the inevitable consequence of the activity.[83] However, planning permission was held to be relevant in an indirect way in *Gillingham Borough Council v Medway (Chatham) Dock Co Ltd.*[84] The operators of a commercial dock had been granted planning permission for their activity in 1983 and operated, within that permission and as a matter of commercial necessity, on a "round the clock" basis so that heavy lorries continually passed back and forth and caused serious disturbance in the adjoining residential district. In dismissing a claim for an injunction brought by the local authority[85] in respect of a public nuisance[86] Buckley J. held that planning permission could have the effect of altering the character of the neighbourhood[87] and the question of nuisance would fall to be decided by reference to that character as changed by the permission and not as it was previously.[88] This approach has been questioned, even in the case of a large development, on the ground that for practical purposes it would amount to much the same thing as

---

[81] It seems fairly clear from Lord Westbury's speech that he did have in mind physical damage (including visible deterioration). Noises or smells primarily cause only personal discomfort but they may seriously reduce the selling value of the property affected by them and injure a business (e.g. a hotel) carried on therein. If this is not "injury to property" it may be asked whether the distinction is justified. In *Hunter v Canary Wharf Ltd* [1997] A.C. 655 at 706 Lord Hoffmann emphasises that even in the case of nuisances of the "personal discomfort" variety the damages are awarded for the effect on the amenity value of the land.

[82] [1961] 1 W.L.R. 683 and see *Miller v Jackson* [1977] Q.B. 966 at 986.

[83] *Wheeler v J.J. Saunders Ltd* [1996] Ch. 19; *Hunter v Canary Wharf Ltd* [1997] A.C. 655, CA (not in issue on appeal to HL).

[84] [1993] Q.B. 343; *Hawkes Bay Protein Ltd v Davidson* [2003] N.Z.L.R. 536.

[85] Under the Local Government Act 1971 s.222 (see para.14–3, above).

[86] There is no significance in the nature of the claim. The same state of affairs may be both a public and a private nuisance provided the rights of individuals over land are affected: para.14–3, above.

[87] The planning process of course involves rights of objection and appeal, inquiries and references to the Minister, in certain circumstances.

[88] The local authority was the same body which had granted the planning permission in 1983. It had power to revoke the permission, to impose conditions or to make traffic schemes to reduce the disturbance, but to take these steps might have involved it in paying statutory compensation to the defendants. In view of the authority's continuing powers and certain assurances about access which had been given to the defendants in 1983 Buckley J. would in any event have exercised his discretion to refuse an injunction.

statutory authority,[89] but in any event the concept of a change in the character of the neighbourhood cannot be called in aid for a single grant, such as permission to expand a pig farm.[90]

B. Utility of the Defendant's Conduct

14–8   Since nuisance is the law of give and take the court is inevitably concerned to some extent with the utility or general benefit to the community of the defendant's activity. Thus we must all put up with the rattle of early morning milk deliveries, though probably not with the same amount of noise made by drunken neighbours.[91] This approach, however, will only justify an injurious activity up to a certain point, and that point is reached when serious damage is being done to the claimant's enjoyment of his property or to his livelihood. In such a case the court will not accept the argument that the claimant should put up with the harm because it is beneficial to the community as a whole, for that would amount to requiring him to carry the burden alone of an activity from which many others benefit. Nor have the courts in such cases shown much willingness to adopt the device of awarding damages in lieu of an injunction, for that would amount to expropriation without the sanction of Parliament.[92] Indeed, in one case an Irish court enjoined a nuisance even though the order would have the effect of closing for three months the only cement factory in Ireland at a time when building was an urgent public necessity.[93] However, in *Dennis v Ministry of Defence*[94] the court refused a declaration[95] against the defendants in relation to the flying of Harrier jets in view of the needs of national defence and the enormous inconvenience and cost of relocating the

---

[89] Most particularly by Peter Gibson L.J. in *Wheeler v J.J. Saunders*, above, fn.83. Pill L.J. in *Hunter v Canary Wharf*, above, fn.83; said he agreed with Peter Gibson L.J.'s approach.

[90] *Wheeler v J.J. Saunders*, above, fn.83; *Watson v Croft Promo Sport Ltd* [2009] EWCA Civ 15; [2009] 3 All E.R. 249.

[91] This is demonstrated most clearly where the activity is actuated by malice, for malicious conduct can have no utility: see para.14–12, below.

[92] *Shelfer v City of London Electric Co* [1895] 1 Ch. 287; *Elliott v Islington London Borough* [1991] 10 E.G. 145; *Watson v Croft Promo Sport Ltd*, above, fn.90. In *Miller v Jackson* [1977] Q.B. 966 Lord Denning M.R., dissenting, thought that public interest must prevail over private rights of property whether the issue was the existence of a legal nuisance or the grant of an injunction, but the Court of Appeal has rejected this: *Kennaway v Thompson* [1981] Q.B. 88.

[93] *Bellew v Cement Co* [1948] Ir.R. 61.

[94] [2003] EWHC 793 (QB); [2003] Env L.R. 34.

[95] The claimants pursued a declaration in order to avoid the niceties of the grant of injunctions against the Crown. It is not clear from the transcript how the proposed declaration was framed. It could not have been that the flying constituted a nuisance because that was the basis of the court's decision to award damages. A declaration in the form that the defendants should cease or moderate their activities would have been an injunction in all but name.

airfields in question, though a total of £950,000 damages was awarded.

C. Abnormal Sensitivity

In considering what is reasonable the law does not take account of **14–9**
abnormal sensitivity in either persons or property. If the only reason why a person complains of fumes is that he has an unusually sensitive nose or that he owns an exotic flower, he cannot expect any sympathy from the courts.

In *Heath v Mayor of Brighton*[96] for example, the incumbent and trustees of a Brighton church sought an injunction to restrain noise from the defendants' electrical power station. There was no proof of diminution of the congregation or of any personal annoyance to anyone except the incumbent and he was not prevented from preaching or conducting his services, nor was the noise such as to the distract the attention of ordinary healthy persons attending the church. An injunction was not granted. It seems that no regard should be had to the special needs of invalids, or to special occupational needs, for there is no redress for damage due solely to the exceptionally delicate nature of the operations carried on by an injured party.[97]

Robinson v Kilvert[98] illustrates the point with regard to sensitive property. The defendant began to manufacture paper boxes in the cellar of a house the upper part of which was in the occupation of the claimant. The defendant's business required hot and dry air and he heated the cellar accordingly. This raised the temperature on the claimant's floor and dried and diminished the value of brown paper which the claimant warehoused there but it did not inconvenience the claimant's workmen nor would it have injured paper generally. It was held that the defendant was not liable for nuisance. A person who carries on an exceptionally delicate trade cannot complain because it is injured by his neighbour doing something lawful on his property, if it is something which would not injure anything but an exceptionally delicate trade.[99] You cannot increase the liabilities of your neighbour by applying your property to special uses, whether

---

[96] (1908) 98 L.T. 718.
[97] *Bloodworth v Cormack* [1949] N.Z.L.R. 1058 at 1064; *Murray v Laus* [1960] N.Z.L.R. 126 (noise); cf. *Stretch v Romford Football Club* (1971) 115 S.J. 741.
[98] (1889) 41 Ch. D. 88; *Whycer v Urry* [1955] C.L.Y. 1939 (CA held practice of ophthalmic optician in a business area too specially delicate for protection).
[99] This is one of many problems posed for the law of nuisance and associated areas by genetic modification of crops: although there may be no evidence that migration of GM organisms from one property to another will cause any damage in the sense of making the non-GM crop unfit for consumption, the loss of accredited "non-GM" status may be commercially damaging. How far is the non-GM activity "sensitive"? How far is it unreasonable to carry on GM farming in the vicinity? For various aspects of the problem see *Hoffmann v Monsanto Canada Inc* [2005] SKQB 225.

for business or pleasure[100]; but once the nuisance is established, the remedies by way of damages or an injunction will extend to delicate and sensitive operations such as the growing of orchids.[101] It has been suggested that it is difficult to see any further life in the principle about abnormal sensitivity because of the current general approach to reasonableness in nuisance.[102] With respect, that does not seem correct: to say that C cannot restrict the freedom of action of his neighbour by putting his property to a very sensitive use is part and parcel of the idea of reasonableness. Of course, that is not to say that the law's response to what were once regarded as abnormally sensitive activities may not change over time: for example, the use of sensitive electronic equipment is now part of every-day life and there are detailed regulatory controls for its design designed to minimise interference.[103]

D. Limits to Protection

14–10   Nowadays it is probably unlikely that many people would regard as "unduly sensitive" a claimant who complained that his view was ruined or his sitting room darkened or smoke caused to blow back down his chimney by the erection of neighbouring premises. Never-theless it is well established that there is no natural right to a view[104] or to light or to the free passage of air[105] though the last two at least may be acquired by prescription[106] and may of course be conferred by grant. The cases on the absence of a right to a view or light provided the basis of the decision in *Hunter v Canary Wharf Ltd*[107] in which the House of Lords held that the defendants were not liable in nuisance for constructing a 250-metre high stainless steel-clad tower which interfered with the claimants' television reception: if a landowner has a right, at common law, to build on his land in such

---

[100] *Eastern and SA Telegraph Co v Cape Town Tramways* [1902] A.C. 381 at 383. However, there may be liability if defendant fails to adopt such reasonable and practicable precau-tions as could have avoided the damage without appreciable prejudice to his own interests. *Gandel v Mason* [1953] 3 D.L.R. 65 (road contractors liable in nuisance and negligence, they knew of peculiar sensitivity of mink in whelping season) *Nova Mink v TCA* [1951] 2 D.L.R. 241 distinguished.

[101] *McKinnon Industries Ltd v Walker* [1951] 3 D.L.R. 577 at 581 per Lord Simonds.

[102] *Network Rail Infrastructure Ltd v Morris* [2004] EWCA Civ 172 at [35] per Buxton L.J.

[103] *Network Rail Infrastructure Ltd v Morris*, above, fn.102, at [18].

[104] *Dalton v Angus* (1881) 6 App. Cas. 740 at 824. The planning authority will take account of such matters and is required to notify neighbours of applications, but if it fails to do so it has been held in Australia that there is no private law remedy: *Newcastle CC v Shortland Management Services* [2003] NSWCA 156; cf. *Craig v East Coast Bays CC* [1986] N.Z.L.R. 99, at a time when an expansive approach to negligence prevailed in New Zealand.

[105] *Bryant v Lefever* (1879) 4 C.P.D. 172; *Belfast CC v Irish Football Association Ltd* [1988] N.I. 290.

[106] See further Clerk & Lindsell, *Torts*, 19th edn, para.20–112.

[107] [1997] A.C. 655.

a way as to block sunlight from reaching the claimant's land, the same must apply to a structure which blocks television signals.[108] It does not, however, necessarily follow that the same is true of some activity (for example, the generation of electricity) on the defendant's land which interferes with television signals. In *Bridlington Relay Ltd v Yorkshire Electricity Board*[109] Buckley J. in the 1960s doubted whether interference with such a purely recreational amenity was an actionable nuisance,[110] but the overall result of *Hunter v Canary Wharf* is to leave the matter open[111] and it is thought that in principle receiving television should now be a "protected interest": television is watched by virtually the entire population for both recreational and educational purposes and the "ordinary usages of mankind" must be judged by contemporary standards.

We have seen that the law of negligence protects only against physical damage caused by the interruption of utility supplies.[112] Plainly the law of nuisance has no general requirement of "physical damage" otherwise it would not be possible to complain of noise and smells.[113] However, it has been held that the rule on utility supplies cannot be evaded by framing the claim in nuisance. If D damages the X Co's gas main supplying C then, in the absence of physical damage, C's rights are confined to those, if any,[114] which C has under his supply agreement with X.[115]

The only natural right to support of one's land by one's neighbour's is for the land in its natural state and a right to support of the land with buildings on it must be acquired by grant or prescription.[116] This cannot be evaded by framing a claim for damages as

[108] Especially bearing in mind that the direction of these signals may change and the defendant has no control over that. Cf. *Bank of NZ v Greenwood* [1984] 1 N.Z.L.R. 525 (intolerable reflection of light from surface of building).

[109] [1965] Ch. 436.

[110] The interference was only on one channel and was contributed to by the special nature of the claimants' relay services. The actual reason for the refusal of the injunction was that the defendants proposed to correct the matter.

[111] Lords Goff and Cooke ([1997] A.C. at 684 and 719) seem favourable. Lord Hoffmann leaves the issue open (at 708). Lord Lloyd inclines against. See also *Nor-Video Services Ltd v Ontario Hydro* (1978) 84 D.L.R. (3d) 221 and Kidner [1989] Conv 279.

[112] See para.5–40, above.

[113] For an intermediate case see the claim of Hampshire Wildlife Trust in *Jan de Nul (UK) Ltd v Axa. Royal Belge* [2002] EWCA Civ 209; [2002] 1 Lloyd's Rep. 583 (interference with land by deposit of silt; claimants commissioned survey which showed that no serious damage done; cost of survey recoverable).

[114] They are not likely to amount to much: Gas Act 1986 s.10(9).

[115] *Anglian Water Services Ltd v Crawshaw Robbins Ltd* [2001] B.L.R. 173. If, however, this is treated as resting on the proposition that it is not a nuisance to prevent something coming onto the claimant's land it presents difficulties about saying that interference with television reception caused by an activity can be a nuisance. See also *Colour Quest Ltd v Total Downstream UK Plc* [2009] EWHC 640 (Comm); [2009] 2 Lloyd's Rep. 1 at [467] and *Shell UK Ltd v Total UK Ltd* [2010] EWCA Civ 180 at [151].

[116] See *Dalton v Angus* (1881) 6 App. Cas. 740.

one for negligence, as is shown by the cases on the closely analogous issue of support by underground water. In *Langbrook Properties Ltd v Surrey CC*[117] and *Stephens v Anglia Water Authority*[118]
pumping out of underground water led to withdrawal of support and
collapse of the claimants' properties. Since the House of Lords had
confirmed in *Bradford v Pickles*[119] that there was no interest at
common law in percolating or underground water until appropriation[120] it was said to be an inevitable logical consequence that the
claim should fail even:

> "[I]f the defendant's activities . . . resulted in subsidence of build-
> ings or even personal injury. As the law stands the right of the
> landowner to abstract subterranean water flowing in undefined
> channels appears . . . to be exercisable regardless of the conse-
> quences, whether physical or pecuniary, to his neighbours."[121]

E. Temporary Injury
14–11   Where the claimant seeks an injunction to restrain a nuisance, it
will not be issued, except in extreme cases, if the nuisance is
temporary and occasional only. The reason for this is that an injunction is a remedy depending on the discretion of the court and it will
not be issued where damages would be an adequate remedy. In
Swaine v GN Ry,[122] for example, manure heaps which were ordinarily inoffensive were occasionally rendered offensive by a delay
in their removal and also by the presence of dead cats and dogs. The
Court of Chancery declined to grant an injunction, leaving the
claimant to his common law action for damages. An instance of the
exceptional circumstances in which the court did grant an injunction
was pile-driving carried on by night for building purposes for to do
it at that time was unreasonable.[123]

Where the claim is for damages, as distinct from an injunction,
the duration of the alleged nuisance is one of the relevant factors in
determining whether the defendant has acted unreasonably and is

---

[117] [1970] 1 W.L.R. 161.
[118] [1987] 1 W.L.R. 1381.
[119] [1895] A.C. 587.
[120] In the sense that no one can complain of appropriation by another, but it is tortious to
pollute an underground stratum from which neighbours draw water: *Ballard v Tomlinson*
(1885) 29 Ch.D. 115; *Cambridge Water Co Ltd v Eastern Counties Leather Plc* [1994] 2
A.C. 264.
[121] [1971] 1 W.L.R. 1381 at 1387. The law on support has been modified in other jurisdictions:
see, e.g. *Re National Capital Commission and Pugliese* (1979) 97 D.L.R. (3d) 631;
Bognuda v Upton & Shearer [1972] N.Z.L.R. 741.
[122] (1864) 4 De G.J. & S. 211 at 215–216.
[123] *De Keyser's Royal Hotel Ltd v Spicer Bros Ltd* (1914) 30 T.L.R. 257. For damages in lieu
of injunction, see generally para.22–53, below.

liable.[124] All other circumstances must be taken into account and they may on the one hand make a temporary annoyance a nuisance or, on the other, render it lawful. A person who pulls down his house for the purpose of building another no doubt causes considerable inconvenience to his neighbours and it may well be that he will take some months in the process but if he uses all reasonable skill and care to avoid annoyance, that is not a nuisance, for life could scarcely be carried on if it were.[125] On the other hand, blocking up a highway for no more than a month may well be a nuisance because circumstances will usually make the resulting damage so much more serious.[126]

When it is said therefore that the injury must be, "of a substantial character not fleeting or evanescent",[127] what is signified is that the temporary nature of the injury may be evidence, but certainly not conclusive evidence, that it is too trivial to be considered as a nuisance.[128]

It is often said that a continuing state of affairs is normally necessary in nuisance. The meaning of this was put by Thesiger J. in *S.C.M. (UK) Ltd v W.J. Whittal & Son Ltd* as follows:

> "[W]hile there is no doubt that a single isolated escape may cause the damage that entitles a claimant to sue for nuisance, yet it must be proved that the nuisance arose from the condition of the defendant's land or premises or property or activities thereon that constituted a nuisance."[129]

The frequency of the escape on to the claimant's land (or, in the case of public nuisance, on to the highway)[130] and the gravity of the harm likely to be caused, are important factors in determining

---

[124] Per Pollock C.B. in *Bamford v Turnley* (1862) 3 B. & S. 66 at 79 31 L.J.Q.B. 286 at 292 (a dissenting judgment, but certainly not on this point). Bramwell B.'s expression at 294 is too wide.

[125] Vaughan Williams J. in *Harrison v Southwark and Vauxhall Water Co* [1891] 2 Ch. 409 at 413–414; *Clift v Welsh Office* [1999] 1 W.L.R. 796. Cf. *Andreae v Selfridge & Co Ltd* [1938] Ch. 1 at 6 per Sir Wilfrid Greene M.R.: "Common or ordinary use of land . . . does not mean that the methods of using land and building on it are in some way to be stabilised for ever . . . New methods enable land to be more profitably used, either by digging down into the earth or mounting it up into the skies."

[126] *Iveson v Moore* (1699) 1 Ld.Raym. 486.

[127] Brett J. in *Benjamin v Storr* (1874) L.R. 9 C.P. 400 at 407.

[128] See *Crown River Cruises v Kimbolton Fireworks* [1996] 2 Lloyd's Rep. 533 (15–20 minutes firework display with falling debris a nuisance).

[129] [1970] 1 W.L.R. 1017 at 1031. The learned judge continued: "I am satisfied that one negligent act that causes physical damage to an electric cable does not thereby constitute a nuisance." Nuisance was not considered on appeal by the Court of Appeal: [1971] 1 Q.B. 337.

[130] Compare the facts of *Stone v Bolton* [1950] 1 K.B. 210 (the element of nuisance was not discussed in the House of Lords [1951] A.C.850) with those of *Miller v Jackson* [1977] Q.B. 966.

whether a dangerous state of affairs existed on the defendant's land.[131] On the other hand, it has been said that the:

"[P]osition is that on appropriate facts there can be liability in private nuisance for a single or isolated escape as opposed to a state of affairs where there is both unreasonable or negligent user of land and foreseeability of escape."[132]

What makes the point of limited importance is that where the defendant's activity falls within the rule in *Rylands v Fletcher* (itself very closely related to nuisance) there is no difficulty in saying that an isolated escape is actionable without reference to a "state of affairs"; indeed the rule has been said to be merely a special sub-rule of nuisance applicable to certain isolated escapes.[133]

F. Malice

14–12   Is malice material in nuisance? If A's legitimate use of his own property causes to B annoyance which does not amount to a nuisance, will the fact that A's acts are done solely for the purpose of annoying B convert them into a nuisance?

In *Christie v Davey*,[134] the defendant, exasperated by a considerable number of music lessons given by the claimant,[135] a teacher of music whose residence was separated from that of the defendant only by a party-wall, interrupted the claimant's lessons by knocking on the party-wall, beating on trays, whistling and shrieking. North J. issued an injunction because the defendant had acted deliberately and maliciously for the purpose of annoying the claimant. The learned judge added:

"If what has taken place had occurred between two sets of persons both perfectly innocent, I should have taken an entirely different view of the case."[136]

Two years later, however, the House of Lords in *Bradford (Mayor of) v Pickles*[137] asserted that a bad motive cannot make wrongful an

---

[131] See also *Castle v St Augustine's Links* (1922) 38 T.L.R. 615; *Spicer v Smee* [1946] 1 All E.R. 489; *Hilder v Associated Portland Cement Manufacturers Ltd* [1961] 1 W.L.R. 1434.

[132] *Colour Quest Ltd v Total Downstream UK Plc* [2009] EWHC 640 (Comm); [2009] 2 Lloyd's Rep. 1 at [421].

[133] See para.15–3, below.

[134] [1893] 1 Ch. 316; *Palmar v Loder* [1962] C.L.Y. 2233.

[135] Would this now be an "ordinary use" of a terraced house? *Southwark London Borough Council v Mills* [2001] 1 A.C. 1.

[136] [1893] 1 Ch. at 326–327.

[137] [1895] A.C. 587.

act otherwise legal, and they reaffirmed this principle in *Allen v Flood*[138] but in neither decision was any reference made to *Christie v Davey*.

In *Hollywood Silver Fox Farm Ltd v Emmett*,[139] Macnaghten J. followed *Christie v Davey*. The defendant deliberately caused guns to be fired on his own land near the boundary of the claimant's land in order to scare the claimant's silver foxes during breeding time. The vixens of these animals are extremely nervous during breeding time and much damage was done in consequence of the defendant's act, which was motivated by pure spite. Macnaghten J. considered that the intention of the defendant is relevant in determining liability in nuisance and granted an injunction and awarded damages to the claimant. It is submitted that this is the better view. The courts, in judging what constitutes a nuisance, take into consideration the purpose of the defendant's activity,[140] and acts otherwise justified on the ground of reciprocity, if done wantonly and maliciously with the object of injuring a neighbour are devoid of any social utility and cannot be regarded as "reasonable". The element of unreasonableness in nuisance as a tort had been recognised long before *Bradford v Pickles* and that decision did not affect the principle of nuisances of this type, i.e. those in which the law recognises that a certain amount of discomfort is inevitable in life owing to the activities of one's neighbours, but also expects that neighbours by their mutual forbearance will lessen this discomfort as much as they are reasonably able. The law of private nuisance gives to each party a qualified privilege of causing harm to the other. When the activity of one party is motivated principally by malice, his privilege is at an end and he is liable for the damage he has caused.

In both *Christie v Davey* and *Hollywood Silver Fox Farm Ltd v Emmett* the defendant interfered with a legally protected interest of the claimant and the issue was whether, in doing so, he had acted unreasonably. If, however, the defendant's activity has not infringed any such right or interest, the claimant has no cause of action and the defendant's motive is irrelevant. This was in fact the position in *Bradford v Pickles* itself, where the defendant deliberately drained his land so as to diminish the water supply reaching the land of the claimants. His purpose was to coerce the claimants into purchasing his land.[141] It had previously been established that no interest in

---

[138] [1898] A.C. 1.

[139] [1936] 2 K.B. 468 at 475. Distinguished in *Rattray v Daniels* [1959] 17 D.L.R. (2d) 134 (Alberta SC) (noise of bulldozer damaging mink in whelping season).

[140] *Harrison v Southwark and Vauxhall Water Co* [1891] 2 Ch. 409 at 414 per Vaughan Williams L.J.; *Bamford v Turnley* (1862) 31 L.J.Q.B. 286 at 294 per Bramwell B.; *Grant v Fynney* (1872) L.R. 8 Ch.App. 8 at 12 per Lord Selborne L.C.

[141] For the background, see Simpson, "Victorian Law and the Industrial Spirit", Selden Society Lecture, 1995.

percolating waters exists until appropriation,[142] and as no interest or right could therefore have been infringed, the motive of the defendant was not material.[143] In other words, *Christie v Davey* and the *Hollywood Silver Fox Farm* case represent the normal rule, most rights of enjoyment and use of land being relative, and *Bradford v Pickles* turns on the peculiarity of the law governing percolating water.[144] However, it is not easy to support the view of Lord Cooke in *Hunter v Canary Wharf Ltd*[145] that the construction of a building with the purpose of interfering with a neighbour's television reception[146] would be actionable. The decision in that case rested on the analogy of the absence of a right to a view and that would appear to be as much a "no right" situation as that involving percolating water.

4. Standard of Liability in Nuisance

14–13 The question of the extent to which fault (in the sense of negligence) is necessary to establish liability in damages for nuisance has given rise to great difficulty. There are many judicial statements of various vintages asserting that liability in nuisance is "strict" but there are very few cases in which the meaning of that expression has really been explored. It is impossible to reconcile everything that has ever been said on this subject but it is submitted that the current law may be summarised in the following propositions.[147]

1. Where the claimant seeks an injunction to restrain a nuisance the purpose of the remedy is to protect him from future damage. As the Law Commission has pointed out:

   "[C]onsideration of the strictness of the duty is then out of place—all that the court is concerned with is the question,

---

[142] *Acton v Blundell* (1843) 12 M. & W. 324; *Broadbent v Ramsbotham* (1856) 11 Exch. 602; *Chasemore v Richards* (1859) 7 H.L.C. 349.

[143] See Fridman, "Motive in the English Law of Nuisance" (1954) 40 Va.L.R. 583.

[144] In the case of water flowing in a defined channel a riparian owner can take water only for use on the adjoining land. Water supplies, whether percolating or channelled, are now generally subject to licensing control by regional water authorities under statute.

[145] [1997] A.C. 655 at 721.

[146] Perhaps a somewhat unlikely scenario, given modern planning controls.

[147] This section is concerned with private nuisance. As we have seen above, public nuisance is really a quite different tort but the position on that is even more obscure. The parties in *Claimants in Corby Group Litigation v Corby BC* [2008] EWCA Civ 463; [2009] 2 W.L.R. 609 took the preliminary issue of whether it covered personal injuries to the CA. In fact the claimants were able to establish fault and public nuisance figures hardly at all in the decision on liability, Aikenhead J. contenting himself with saying that, "strictly speaking, negligence or breach of a statutory duty is not essential in public nuisance although, if there is negligence or a breach of statutory duty which causes life or health to be endangered, there will be a public nuisance": [2009] EWHC 1944 (TCC) at [688].

'Should the defendant be told to stop this interference with the claimant's rights?' Whether or not the defendant knew of the noise or smell or the like when it first began to annoy the plaintiff does not matter; he becomes aware of it at the latest when the plaintiff brings his claim before the court."[148]

In such a case, as we have seen in the previous section, the court is concerned with balancing the respective rights of the two parties and determining the permissible extent of an interference which, since the defendant ex hypothesi knows about it, is deliberate. If the stench of my pig farm fouls your air, I am liable because I have knowingly created an intolerable situation for you—and if it is intolerable to you by ordinary, sensible standards it is meaningless to ask whether I was negligent in creating the smell. Accordingly, great care must be taken in transferring statements in injunction cases to the different context of claims for damages for past loss.[149]

2. We must draw a distinction between the creation or adoption of a nuisance by the defendant and the continuance of a nuisance[150] created by a third party or an act of nature. An occupier "continues" a nuisance, for the creation of which he is not responsible, if, once he knows or ought to know of its existence, he fails to take reasonable precautions to abate it and it is clear that he is not liable in damages if these conditions are not satisfied.[151] Here there is a "sort of condominium" with the law of negligence.[152]

3. Even where the defendant has created the situation which interferes with the claimant's land, there is no liability in damages where the possibility of interference of the type

---

[148] Report No.32, "Civil Liability for Dangerous Things and Activities", p.25.
[149] [1994] 2 A.C. at 300; e.g. *Rapier v London Tramways Co* [1893] 2 Ch. 588 at 560 per Lindley L.J.: "If I am sued for nuisance, and the nuisance is proved, it is no defence on my part to say, and to prove, that I have taken all reasonable care to prevent it." In its context, this statement means no more than that if the activity is unreasonably injurious when carried on with all care, it should not be carried on at all; but see how in *Transco Plc v Stockport MBC* [2003] UKHL 61; [2004] 2 A.C. 1 at [97] Lord Walker cites the passage in support of the proposition that, "negligence (in the sense of a demonstrable failure to take reasonable care) has traditionally been regarded as irrelevant".
[150] *Sedleigh-Denfield v O'Callaghan* [1940] A.C. 880 at 904–908 per Lord Wright and at 913 per Lord Romer.
[151] This situation is discussed further, para.14–20, below. The burden of proof would appear to lie upon the claimant (*Sedleigh-Denfield v O'Callaghan* [1940] A.C. 880 at 887, 899, 908) and it is significant that in *Goldman v Hargrave* [1967] 1 A.C. 645 the Privy Council thought it unnecessary to decide whether the cause of action lay in nuisance or negligence. See also *Smith v Littlewoods Organisation Ltd* [1987] A.C. 241 at 274 per Lord Goff.
[152] Lord Walker in *Transco Plc v Stockport MBC* above, fn.149, at [96].

which occurs could not reasonably have been foreseen by a person in the defendant's position when he did the acts which are called in question. This has some significance in cases of what has been called "historic pollution", that is to say, contamination by activities which were thought harmless when they were carried on but which are shown, in the light of subsequent advances in knowledge, to be hazardous. In *Cambridge Water Co v Eastern Counties Leather Plc*[153] the defendants had for some years used PCE (an organochlorine) in their trade in tanning. Continual small spillages had gradually built up a pool of PCE under the land and contaminated the aquifer from which the claimants drew their supply of water, forcing them to find another source at a cost of nearly £1million. PCE evaporates quickly in the air but is not readily soluble in water. When the contamination was taking place it was not foreseeable to a skilled person that quantities of the chemical would accumulate in the aquifer nor, even if this could have been foreseen, was it foreseeable that there would be any significant damage to the claimants' water.[154] The only known hazard of PCE at that time was that someone might be overcome by fumes in the case of a large spillage. A unanimous House of Lords held that the defendants were not liable in damages for the contamination. Strictly speaking, because of the way the litigation had gone below, nuisance was not a live issue but it would be nonsense to dismiss as dicta the view of a unanimous House of Lords, especially where it gains force from being delivered in one speech.[155]

4. Where the defendant has thus innocently created the danger its source may remain on his land after the point at which its nature becomes known. Examples are the PCE in the *Cambridge Water* case, which had formed in pools at the base of the aquifer, or chemical contamination of the soil or removal of spoil which unexpectedly turns out to increase the risk of flooding. In such a case liability in damages will not be imposed for a state of affairs which has passed beyond the control of the defendant. Indeed, Lord Goff said[156] that:

> "[I]n such circumstances, I do not consider that [the defendant] should be under any greater liability than that imposed for negligence. At best, if the case is regarded as one of nuisance, it should be treated no differently from, for exam-

---

[153] [1994] 2 A.C. 264. Perhaps *Dempsey v Waterford Corp* [2008] IEHC 55 is a case of this type (unknown sewer connexion).

[154] Indeed, at no point was it contended that the contaminated water was dangerous to health. The problem arose because EC requirements set very low levels for PCE in water.

[155] That of Lord Goff. See also *Savage v Fairclough* [2000] Env L.R. 183.

[156] [1994] 2 A.C. at 307.

ple, the case of the landslip in *Leakey v National Trust*"¹⁵⁷

(a case of a natural hazard not created by the defendant). In other words, the defendant is expected to do what is reasonable in the circumstances and the duty to remove the danger is not an absolute one, for he is in morally no different a position from the occupier whose land suffers an immediately recognisable nuisance from the act of trespassers or of nature.¹⁵⁸

5. In *Cambridge Water* the risk was unknown at the relevant time. However, what is the position where the defendant is carrying on an activity which presents a known, albeit remote, risk to neighbours but which is carried on with all reasonable care,¹⁵⁹ notwithstanding which some catastrophe occurs for which the defendant is not to blame? It is clearly stated in *Cambridge Water* that where the defendant (or someone for whom he is responsible) has created the nuisance:

> "[I]t is still the law that the fact that [he] has taken all reasonable care will not of itself exonerate him from liability, the relevant control mechanism being found within the principle of reasonable user".¹⁶⁰

However, in the later case of *Transco Plc v Stockport MBC*¹⁶¹ the House of Lords accepted that the rule in *Rylands v Fletcher* was a sub-species of the tort of nuisance (as indeed had been said in *Cambridge Water*) concerned with liability for exceptional risks created by the use of land.¹⁶² Now that rule

---

¹⁵⁷ [1980] Q.B. 485.
¹⁵⁸ *Anthony v The Coal Authority* [2005] EWHC (QB) 1654 (where failure to take steps to prevent foreseeable spontaneous combustion of a spoil tip was actionable; but the defendants would not have been held liable for combustion as a result of fires lit by trespassers). Cf. *Arscott v The Coal Authority* [2004] EWCA Civ 892; [2005] Env L.R. 6, where an increased risk of flooding was not foreseeable when infilling works were done.
¹⁵⁹ Liability for tree root damage depends upon the defendant having means of knowledge of the risk: *Delaware Mansions Ltd v Westminster CC* [2001] UKHL 55; [2002] 1 A.C. 321. The principles of factual causation are the same as in negligence, i.e. it is enough to show that the defendant's roots made a material contribution to the damage: *Loftus-Brigham v Ealing LBC* [2003] EWCA Civ 1490.
¹⁶⁰ [1994] 2 A.C. at 269. But even in this situation remoteness of damage is based on foreseeability: *The Wagon Mound (No.2)*, para.6–18, above.
¹⁶¹ [2003] UKHL 61; [2004] 2 A.C. 1. See Ch.15.
¹⁶² Whether this is entirely reconcilable with the view taken in *Cambridge Water* is another matter. The whole thrust of that case is that *Rylands v Fletcher* is not a category of liability for ultra-hazardous activities and the emphasis is upon its applicability to "isolated escapes". While "exceptional risk" may not be precisely the same thing as "ultra-hazardous" it looks rather similar. The speech of Lord Hobhouse comes closer than the others to equating *Rylands v Fletcher* with the general rule in private nuisance (see at [55]–[57]) and at [64] he refers to a "recognizable" rather than an "exceptional" risk, but despite his criticisms of the use of expressions like "ordinary" and "reasonable" at the end of the day he goes along with the conclusion that a standard water system in a block of flats does not attract the rule.

undoubtedly involves some element of "strict" liability, though it is far from absolute, and the House was concerned at the same time to preserve it and to draw its boundaries fairly narrowly. Nonetheless, if the sub-species represents a special rule of strict liability for foreseeable risks it is difficult to see how the general species itself can also involve strict liability; if it did there would be no point in worrying about the precise definition of the sub-species. Nor does it help to appeal to the idea of "unreasonable user". If the defendant is carrying on his activity with all due precautions and it is not sufficiently fraught with risk to attract the rule in *Rylands v Fletcher*, how can it be said to be unreasonable?

14–14   It does therefore seem difficult to support the proposition that in the modern law nuisance involves any general rule of strict liability for damage done. That is not necessarily to say that this is a desirable rule.[163] If nuisance involves "give and take", "live and let live" it might also be said that it involves reciprocity between benefits and burdens. If D undertakes construction work to improve his property and despite the exercise of all possible care by him damage is caused to the property of his neighbour, C, why should D be able to gain the benefit of improvement at the expense of C? A very long time ago Bramwell B. put such an argument in the context of inevitable damage done by public works such as the construction of railways and the contention that they were for the public benefit:

"It is for the public benefit that there should be railways, but it would not be unless the gain of having the railway was sufficient to compensate the loss occasioned by the use of the land required for its site; and accordingly no one thinks that it would be right to take an individual's land without compensation to make a railway. It is for the public benefit that trains should run, but not unless they pay their expenses. If one of those expenses is the burning down of a wood of such value that the railway owners would not run the train and burn down the wood if it were their own, neither is it for the public benefit if the wood is not their own. If, though the wood were their own, they would still find it compensated them to run trains at the cost of burning the wood,

[163] An intermediate position is suggested in *Hamilton v Papakura DC* [2000] 1 N.Z.L.R. 265 at [74], that liability is prima facie strict subject to a defence of reasonable care in the ordinary use of land. The PC did not deal with this point: [2002] UKPC 9; [2002] 3 N.Z.L.R. 308.

then they obviously ought to compensate the owner of the wood, not being themselves."[164]

In modern economic jargon Bramwell B. was saying that the costs of an enterprise ought to be "internalised".[165] Before he spoke, the legislature in the Lands Clauses Consolidation Act 1845, the ancestor of the modern compulsory purchase legislation, had recognised the right to compensation for compulsory taking and for "injurious affection"; and the Railway Fires Acts[166] imposed limited strict liability in his example of the burnt wood some time later. However, such provisions have not been by any means universal[167] and a shift to this broad approach would involve the rewriting of much of our law.[168]

5. WHO CAN SUE

A. Private Nuisance

"He alone has a lawful claim [for private nuisance] who has   **14–15**
suffered an invasion of some proprietary or other interest in land."[169] This proposition was reaffirmed by the House of Lords in *Hunter v Canary Wharf Ltd.*[170] As far as encroachment on or damage to the land is concerned the proposition is self-evident, but it is equally applicable to nuisances like smells and noise which affect the enjoyment of the land, for what is being remedied by the law is not the personal discomfort of the persons on the land but the diminution in the value of the land. Of course in such cases there may not have been any effect on the capital value of the land, but what may be called the "amenity value" of the land is diminished so

---

[164] *Bamford v Turnley* (1862) 3 B. & S. 66. The case involved the burning of bricks.

[165] *Transco Plc v Stockport MBC* [2003] UKHL 61; [2004] 2 A.C. 1 at [29] per Lord Hoffmann. For a full discussion see Oliphant, "*Rylands v Fletcher* and the Emergence of Enterprise Liability in the Common Law" in Koziol and Steininger (eds), *European Tort Law 2004*.

[166] See para.15–22, below.

[167] See para.14–34, below.

[168] We all benefit from road transport but we do not require those using it to pay for damage caused without fault.

[169] *Read v J. Lyons & Co Ltd* [1947] A.C. 156 at 183 per Lord Simonds. The right to sue for a nuisance derives from the general law; it is not part of a "package of rights" which an estate owner acquires by conveyance from the transferor: *Thornhill v Sita Metal Recycling Ltd* [2009] EWHC 2037 (QB).

[170] [1997] A.C. 655. Lord Cooke's dissent on this point relies in part on art.8 of the European Convention on Human Rights. *Jan de Nul (UK) Ltd v Axa. Royal Belge* [2000] 2 Lloyd's Rep. 700 at 719, on appeal [2002] EWCA Civ 209; [2002] 1 Lloyd's Rep. 583 (contractual mooring rights insufficient; alternative claim for public nuisance); cf. *Crown River Cruises v Kimbolton Fireworks* [1996] 2 Lloyd's Rep. 533 (exclusive occupation of mooring).

long as the nuisance continues.[171] It follows that even in such cases a claim may only be brought by a person with sufficient interest in the land (whom for the moment we shall call the occupier) and not by members of the occupier's family,[172] guests, lodgers or employees. In the majority of cases, where the object of the complaint is to obtain an injunction to put an end to the nuisance, this causes no hardship and a contrary rule might be productive of practical difficulties. If the occupier sues, then the other persons using the premises will benefit from the grant of the injunction[173]; if the others were allowed to sue it would mean that a person on adjoining land who wished to come to an arrangement with the occupier whereby the latter would license some temporary nuisance (for example during repairs or improvements) could not safely rely on it.

Given the premise above about damages for "interference with enjoyment" being granted for what is essentially injury to the property it equally follows that where damages are sought, their quantum is in no way affected by whether the property is inhabited by one person or by a family of 12 and that only the occupier has title to sue. Nor will the damages be any larger if there is more than one person who qualifies as "occupier".

> "The damages for nuisance recoverable by the . . . occupier may be affected by the size, commodiousness and value of his property but cannot be increased merely because more people are in occupation and therefore suffer greater collective discomfort. If more than one person has an interest in the property, the damages will have to be divided among them . . . But the damages cannot be increased by the fact that the interests in the land are divided; still less according to the number of persons residing on the premises."[174]

Although *Hunter* does not perhaps decide the point as a matter of precedent, the reasoning in the case irresistibly suggests that even

---

[171] Hence the CA in *Bone v Seale* [1993] Q.B. 727 was right to award damages for smells caused by a pig farm but wrong to use the analogy of damages in personal injury cases. The "loss of amenity" in those cases and "diminution in amenity value" in nuisance cases are two different things. Where an injunction would be easily obtainable to stop the nuisance, failure to seek one may affect damages for loss of amenity: *Hawkes Bay Protein Ltd v Davidson* [2003] N.Z.L.R. 536. The assessment of diminution in amenity may have to be via expert evidence on a notional rental value. This may be a somewhat artificial exercise but no doubt evidence of the actual impact on persons living in the premises will be relevant: *Dobson v Thames Water* [2009] EWCA Civ 28; [2009] 3 All E.R. 319 at [33], where it is also said that if the premises were empty the damages would be nominal.

[172] Cf. *Khorasandjian v Bush* [1993] Q.B. 727 (overruled in *Hunter*, a situation now within the Protection from Harassment Act 1997).

[173] Lord Lloyd (at 696) was unmoved by the somewhat far-fetched case of the occupier unwilling to sue because he was less sensitive to smoke than members of his family.

[174] [1997] A.C. at 706 per Lord Hoffmann.

the occupier of the land may not frame a claim for personal injuries as one for private nuisance.[175]

Since *Hunter* English courts have become able to give direct effect to the European Convention on Human Rights and art.8 provides that, "*everyone* has the right to respect for his private and family life [and] his home". It is plain that a situation which would give rise to common law liability for nuisance may also constitute an infringement of art.8 and where the defendant is a public authority there is a direct right of action which is not on the face of it constrained by the land-holding qualification set by the common law. However, where an occupier has been awarded damages at common law it is most improbable that any additional sum would be awarded to him for violation of the Convention right; in the case of non-occupying members of his family, who cannot recover at common law, it will be necessary, in determining whether "just satisfaction" requires an award of damages to them, to consider how far the process of assessing the occupier's damages for diminution in amenity have in fact taken account of the impact of the nuisance on the family.[176]

As to the precise nature of the interest required, the "owner occupier" can obviously sue.[177] So can a tenant or a person who has de facto exclusive possession.[178] The position of the reversioner is dealt with below. The owner of an incorporeal hereditament such as an easement or profit can sue for disturbance of his right.[179] A reversioner can bring an action in nuisance if he can show that there is a likelihood that permanent injury will be caused to the property

---

[175] There are statements to this effect by Lord Lloyd [1997] A.C. at 696 and Lord Hoffmann at 706 (but cf. *Ribee v Norrie* [2001] P.I.Q.R. P128, para.15–9, below). As to public nuisance see para.14–3, above. Logically the same might be argued to apply to damage to personal property owned by the occupier but where this is combined with damage to land or buildings that might cause practical complications. Lord Hoffmann thought the occupier could recover damages for chattels or livestock as consequential loss (at 706) but that personal injury was not a consequential loss. See also *Crown River Cruises v Kimbolton Fireworks* [1996] 2 Lloyd's Rep. 533. This assumes of course that even damages for physical injury to the land are recoverable: cf. [1997] A.C. at 692.

[176] *Dobson v Thames Water* [2009] EWCA Civ 28; [2009] 3 All E.R. 319 (see fn.171, above). If such a separate award is made it does not call for a reduction in the occupier's common law damages: at [44], disapproving *Dennis v MoD* [2003] EWHC 793 (QB); [2003] Env L.R. 34 on this point.

[177] Where there is a continuing nuisance (e.g. intrusion of tree roots) an owner may recover damages for remedial work even though some of the damage may have been done before he acquired the property: *Delaware Mansions Ltd v Westminster CC* [2001] UKHL 55; [2002] 1 A.C. 321.

[178] [1997] A.C. at 688; *Foster v Warblington UDC* [1906] 1 K.B. 648; *Pemberton v Southwark LBC* [2000] 1 W.L.R. 672 (where the court relied in part upon art.8 of the European Convention on Human Rights); *Transco Plc v Stockport MBC* [2003] UKHL 61; [2004] 2 A.C. 1 at [92].

[179] *Nicholls v Ely Beet Sugar Factory Ltd* [1936] 1 Ch. 343 (destruction of fish by pollution); *Weston v Lawrence Weaver Ltd* [1961] 1 Q.B. 402 (physical damage to an easement of way without interference with right of passage not actionable).

and his right is then coexistent with that of the occupier.¹⁸⁰ A permanent injury is one which will continue indefinitely unless something is done to remove it,¹⁸¹ for example a building which infringes the right to ancient lights,¹⁸² vibrations causing structural damage,¹⁸³ or the keeping locked a gate across a path over which the reversioner has a right of way¹⁸⁴; but the emission of noise or fumes or other invasions of a temporary nature, even if they cause the tenants to leave, or reduce the letting value, will not suffice.¹⁸⁵

B. Public Nuisance

14–16   As we have seen, if a public nuisance has been committed, any person who has suffered special damage can sue in respect of it. It may, for instance, be the occupier of adjacent property and it may be a user of the highway.¹⁸⁶

6. WHO CAN BE SUED

A. Creator of the Nuisance

14–17   In *Hussain v Lancaster CC*¹⁸⁷ persons engaged in a campaign of racial harassment against the claimants, who were shopkeepers. Various acts of trespass and intimidation were committed which were no doubt torts in their own right. However, the Court of Appeal said that there was no nuisance because the acts did not involve the wrongdoers' use of their land, even though it affected the claimants' enjoyment of theirs.¹⁸⁸ With respect, this seems an unnecessary restriction: to say that nuisance is a tort to the claimant's land does not require the additional proposition that it must involve the defendant's use of his land. Suppose, for example, that D, in pursuit of a vendetta against C, repeatedly disturbs C in his remote farmhouse by parking outside, shining his car headlights through the windows and playing his music system at full volume. That is not a public nuisance because it does not affect a "class" of people. Is there any

¹⁸⁰ The damages will have to be divided according to the relative interests of reversioner and occupier: [1997] A.C. at 707.
¹⁸¹ *Jones v Llanrwst UDC* [1911] 1 Ch. 393 at 404 per Parker J.
¹⁸² *Jesser v Gifford* (1767) 4 Burr. 2141.
¹⁸³ *Colwell v St Pancras BC* [1904] Ch. 707.
¹⁸⁴ *Kidgill v Moor* (1850) 9 C.B. 364.
¹⁸⁵ *Simpson v Savage* (1856) 1 C.B.(N.S.) 347; *Cooper v Crabtree* (1882) 20 Ch.D. 589.
¹⁸⁶ e.g. *Holling v Yorkshire Traction Co Ltd* [1948] 2 All E.R. 662; *Dollman v Hillman Ltd* [1941] 1 All E.R. 355; *Hilder v Associated Portland Cement Manufacturers* [1961] 1 W.L.R. 1434.
¹⁸⁷ [2000] Q.B. 1.
¹⁸⁸ [2000] Q.B. at 23.

reason why it should not be a private nuisance?[189] Of course, such conduct might now be a tort under the Protection from Harassment Act 1997[190] but it is surprising that it was not a nuisance before the Act. Furthermore, the issue in *Hussain* was not the liability in tort of the wrongdoers, but whether their landlord could be held responsible for their actions. A perfectly adequate basis for the negative answer would have been that the relationship of landlord and tenant between the defendant and the wrongdoers had no connexion with what was going on at the claimants' shop.[191] The approach in *Hussain* would insulate from liability persons like independent contractors who may create a nuisance affecting the land of C while working on the land of B but have no possession of the latter. In a later decision the Court of Appeal held that a local authority which had undertaken as the agent of the highway authority to maintain trees was liable for a "nuisance of omission" in allowing encroachment by roots, whether or not it was occupier of the land in which the trees stood and said that there was no authority:

"[F]or the proposition that a person cannot be liable in nuisance unless he is in occupation of the land or has some legal interest in it".[192]

In other cases it has been assumed that the creator of the nuisance is liable even though he has no interest in any relevant land.[193]

B. Occupier

The occupier of the premises where the nuisance exists is in **14–18** general liable during the period of his occupancy.[194] This is simple enough where he himself created the nuisance, but further questions arise where it originated: (1) with someone else lawfully on the

---

[189] In *Hussain* at 24 significance is attached to the fact that in *Page Motors Ltd v Epsom and Ewell BC* (1982) 80 L.G.R. 337 the wrongdoers had been "occupying" the council's land for some years.

[190] See para.4–38, above. This was not in force at the time of *Hussain*.

[191] See Evans L.J. in *Lippiatt v South Gloucestershire Council* [2000] Q.B. 51 at 61. For a similar issue under the Housing Act 1996 see *Enfield LBC v B* [2000] 1 W.L.R. 1141.

[192] *L.E. Jones (Insurance Brokers) Ltd v Portsmouth CC* [2002] EWCA Civ 1723; [2003] 1 W.L.R. 427. It is true that *Transco Plc v Stockport MBC* [2003] UKHL 61; [2004] 2 A.C. 1 is replete with statements like, "interference by one occupier of land with the right in or enjoyment of land by another occupier of land" (at [9]) but (a) this is the position in the vast majority of cases and (b) nothing turned on the defendant's status since it plainly was an occupier.

[193] *Fennell v Robson Excavations Pty Ltd* [1977] 2 N.S.W.L.R. 486 is most directly in point and reviews the authorities. See also *Southport Corp v Esso Petroleum Ltd* [1954] 2 Q.B. 182 at 204; [1956] A.C. 218 at 225; *Thompson v Gibson* (1841) 7 M. & W. 456; *Rosewell v Prior* (1701) 12 Mod. 635 at 639.

[194] *Sedleigh-Denfield v O'Callaghan* [1940] A.C. 880; *Rigby v Sun Alliance & London Insurance Ltd* [1980] 1 Lloyd's Rep. 359 (relationship between insurance policies covering liability as "owner" and as "occupier").

premises; or (2) with a trespasser or as a result of an act of nature; or (3) with someone from whom the occupier acquired the property. In such cases:

"[T]he basis for the liability of an occupier for a nuisance on his land is not his occupation as such. Rather, it is that, by virtue of his occupation, an occupier usually has it in his power to take the measures that are necessary to prevent or eliminate the nuisance. He has sufficient control over the hazard which constitutes the nuisance for it to be reasonable to make him liable for the foreseeable consequences of his failure to exercise that control so as to remove the hazard."[195]

14–19   **i. Persons lawfully on premises.** If a nuisance is caused by the servant of the occupier the latter is liable according to the ordinary rules of vicarious liability. As a general rule, a principal cannot be held liable for the acts or defaults of an independent contractor employed by him, but there are certain exceptions to this rule. In some cases, for instance, the principal is said to be under a "non-delegable" duty to see that care is taken and if, in fact, damage is caused to a third party by the activity of the contractor, the principal will be liable, because he himself is thereby in breach of his duty of care.[196]

Whether or not there is still any special rule that a person who engages in any activity which involves an exceptional danger is under such a non-delegable duty of care[197] there certainly seem to be nuisance cases where the idea of the non-delegable duty has been applied. Thus in *Bower v Peate*[198] the defendant employed a contractor to do construction work on his land in the course of which the contractor undermined the support for the claimant's adjoining house. The defendant was held liable. In *Matania v National Provincial Bank*[199] the occupier of the first floor of a building was liable to the occupier of the higher floors for a nuisance by dust and noise created by his independent contractor. In both cases the nature of the work was such that there was a special danger of a nuisance being caused by it. On the other hand, it may be that it is the general rule in nuisance that the occupier is liable for his contractor's negligence.[200]

[195] *L.E. Jones (Insurance Brokers) Ltd v Portsmouth CC* [2002] EWCA Civ 1723; [2003] 1 W.L.R. 427 at [11].
[196] See para.20–1, below.
[197] *Honeywell and Stein Ltd v Larkin Bros* [1934] 1 K.B. 191; see para.20–25, below.
[198] (1876) 1 Q.B.D. 321; *Dalton v Angus* (1881) 6 App.Cas. 740.
[199] [1936] 2 All E.R. 633; *Duncan's Hotel (Glasgow) Ltd v J.&A. Ferguson Ltd* 1972 S.L.T. (Notes) 84.
[200] This (rather than any general "primary" rule of strict liability in nuisance) is the way that *Spicer v Smee* [1946] 1 All E.R. 489 seems to be explained in *Johnson v B.J.W. Property Developments Ltd* [2002] EWHC 1131 (TCC); [2002] 3 All E.R. 574.

A principal whose contractor interferes with or creates a danger on the highway may be liable to anyone who in consequence suffers special damage. In *Hole v Sittingbourne Ry*,[201] for instance, a railway company had authority to build a bridge across a navigable river provided that they did not impede navigation. The contractors whom they employed constructed it so imperfectly that it would not open to let boats through. The company were held liable to a user of the highway.

There is little authority on the position where the nuisance is created by a person who is licensed to be on the premises for his own purposes rather than to do work for the occupier. It seems that the occupier is not liable unless he had knowledge, or means of knowledge, of the nuisance and failed to take steps to control the licensee.[202]

ii. Nuisances created by a trespasser or resulting from an act 14–20 of nature. An occupier is not liable for a state of affairs either created by a trespasser or resulting from an act of nature unless either he adopts the nuisance by using the state of affairs for his own purposes or he "continues" the nuisance. An occupier continues a nuisance if once he has actual or constructive knowledge of its existence he fails to take reasonably prompt and efficient steps to abate it. He cannot of course be liable unless he is in a position to take effective steps to abate the nuisance.[203] This principle was enunciated by the House of Lords in relation to a nuisance created by a trespasser in the leading case of *Sedleigh-Denfield v O'Callaghan*.[204] The defendant occupied land on which there was a ditch. A trespasser laid a pipe in it with a grating designed to keep out leaves, but placed in such an ill-chosen position that it caused a blockage of the pipe when a heavy rainstorm occurred, and in consequence the claimant's adjacent land was flooded. The storm occurred nearly three years after the erection of the grating and during that period the defendant's servant who was responsible for cleansing the ditch ought to have realised the risk of flooding presented by the obstruction. The defendant was held liable in nuisance. The House of Lords

---

[201] (1861) 6 H. & N. 488; *Gray v Pullen* (1864) 5 B. & S. 970. An employer is never liable for "collateral" negligence on the part of an independent contractor: para.20–28, below.

[202] *White v Jamieson* (1874) L.R. 18 Eq. 303, which contains statements which might be regarded as placing a more onerous liability on the occupier, was in fact an action for an injunction. In *Lippiatt v South Gloucestershire Council* [2000] Q.B. 51 (below) it was regarded as of no importance whether the wrongdoers were licensees or trespassers but it was made plain that there was no question of any liability for acts of which the council had no knowledge: at 56. See also *Winch v Mid Bedfordshire DC*, July 22, 2002 (QB); but as to fire, see para.15–20, below.

[203] *Smeaton v Ilford Corp* [1954] Ch. 450 at 462; *Goldman v Hargrave* [1967] 1 A.C. 645.

[204] [1940] A.C. 880. "An absentee owner or occupier oblivious of what is happening under his own eyes is in no better position than a man who looks after his property:" at 887 per Lord Maugham. *Leanse v Egerton* [1943] K.B. 323.

refused to draw any distinction in this connection between public and private nuisance. The principle of *Sedleigh-Denfield* is not confined to cases where the trespasser interferes with the state of the land itself: a local authority was held liable for failing to take steps to remove from its land gypsies whose objectionable behaviour damaged the claimants' business next door.[205] Indeed, a landowner has been held liable where the wrongdoers used his land as a base from which they made damaging forays on to the *claimant's* land.[206]

14–21   Although it had been held even before *Sedleigh-Denfield v O'Callaghan* that an occupier can be liable for continuing a nuisance created by a third party,[207] until quite recent times it was considered that he was never under a duty to abate a natural nuisance.[208] This rule of immunity was however decisively rejected by the Judicial Committee in the important case of *Goldman v Hargrave,*[209] where the defendant was held liable for his failure to take adequate steps to extinguish a fire in a redgum tree on his land which had been struck by lightning, the fire having spread to his neighbour's property. Lord Wilberforce rejected the traditional policy of regarding occupation of land as a source of privilege and immunity.

> "It is only in comparatively recent times that the law has recognised an occupier's duty as one of a more positive character than merely to abstain from creating, or adding to, a source of danger or annoyance."[210]

The principle of *Goldman v Hargrave* was formally accepted as part of English law by the Court of Appeal in *Leakey v National Trust,*[211] which involved damage done by movement of the land itself on to adjoining land below it. As regards such nuisances of omission, therefore, it is no longer relevant whether the state of affairs was originally created by a third party or by nature.[212] Once the occupier

---

[205] *Page Motors Ltd v Epsom and Ewell BC* (1982) 80 L.G.R. 337.

[206] *Lippiatt v South Gloucestershire Council* [2000] Q.B. 51. Something more, however, is required than a mere foreseeable possibility that intruders may gain access to the land and cause damage to the neighbouring owner: *Smith v Littlewoods Organisation Ltd* [1987] A.C. 241, para.5–32, above.

[207] e.g. *Barker v Herbert* [1911] 2 K.B. 633.

[208] *Giles v Walker* (1890) 24 Q.B.D. 656; *Sparke v Osborne* (1909) 7 C.L.R. 51; *Pontardawe UDC v Moore-Gwyn* [1929] 1 Ch. 656; *Neath R.D.C. v Williams* [1951] 1 K.B. 115. The rule of immunity did not extend to public nuisance: *Noble v Harrison* [1926] 2 K.B. 332.

[209] [1967] 1 A.C. 645.

[210] [1967] 1 A.C. 645 at 657.

[211] [1980] Q.B. 485. Shaw L.J. agreed that *Goldman v Hargrave* represented English Law, but expressed substantial misgivings. See also the use made of this principle in the *Cambridge Water* case, para.14–13, above.

[212] It is therefore no longer the law that a higher occupier owes no duty in any circumstances to prevent the natural, unconcentrated flow of water from his land to lower land: *Green v Somerleyton* [2003] EWCA Civ 198; [2004] 1 P & C.R. 520.

becomes aware of the nuisance and fails to remedy it within a reasonable time, he may be liable for any damage it may cause, either to his neighbour[213] or the user of the highway.

"The basis of the occupier's liability lies not in the use of his land; in the absence of 'adoption' there is no such use; but in the neglect of action in the face of something which may damage his neighbour."[214]

However, in determining the standard of care required the court cannot disregard the fact that the occupier is confronted with a nuisance not of his own creation, and because of this the court is entitled to consider the occupier's individual circumstances. As Lord Wilberforce said in a passage of great clarity:

"The law must take account of the fact that the occupier on whom the duty is cast has, *ex hypothesi*, had this hazard thrust upon him through no seeking or fault of his own. His interest, and his resources, whether physical or material, may be of a very modest character either in relation to the magnitude of the hazard, or as compared with those of his threatened neighbour. A rule which required of him in such unsought circumstances in his neighbour's interest a physical effort of which he is not capable, or an excessive expenditure of money, would be unenforceable or unjust. One may say in general terms that the existence of a duty must be based upon knowledge of the hazard, ability to foresee the consequences of not checking or removing it, and the ability to abate it . . . The standard ought to be to require of the occupier what is reasonable to expect of him in his individual circumstances."[215]

This partly subjective test is an exception to the general rule in negligence[216] and is carefully limited by Lord Wilberforce to cases

---

[213] As a result of this principle the rule that the owner of a servient tenement subject to an easement of support owes no duty to incur expenditure has been outflanked: *Holbeck Hall Hotel Ltd v Scarborough BC* [2000] Q.B. 836 at 856; *Rees v Skerrett* [2001] EWCA Civ 760; [2001] 1 W.L.R. 1541.

[214] [1967] 1 A.C. 645 at 661.

[215] [1967] 1 A.C. 645 at 663.

[216] See para.5–75, above; but in applying this test, "I do not think that, except perhaps in a most unusual case, there would be any question of discovery as to means of the plaintiff or the defendant, or evidence as to their respective resources. The question of reasonableness . . . would fall to be decided on a broad basis, in which on some occasions, there might be included an element of obvious discrepancy of financial resources": *Leakey v National Trust*, above, fn.211, at 527 per Megaw L.J.

where the defendant was not himself responsible for the creation of the source of danger.[217] In these cases it is immaterial whether the cause of action is termed "nuisance" or "negligence": the duty of the defendant is a general duty of care to his neighbours and the standard imposed on him is the same.[218]

The magnitude of the hazards which may be involved in cases of this type is illustrated by *Holbeck Hall Hotel Ltd v Scarborough Borough Council*.[219] The lower part of the South Cliff at Scarborough was vested in the council and the cliff became unstable, leading to the collapse of the claimants' hotel at the top. The Court of Appeal held that *Leakey's* case was in principle applicable[220] but although the problem had been apparent in a general way for years and there had been progressive landslides, which might continue and foreseeably affect the grounds of the hotel, on the facts it was found that the council did not have reason to be aware of the likelihood of a comparatively sudden, catastrophic collapse such as took place and it was held not liable. Despite the general rule that when a defendant could foresee some injury to the claimant he was liable for all damage of that type,[221] it would not be fair, just and reasonable to impose such an onerous requirement in respect of the "measured duty of care" which arose in these cases. This approach rendered it unnecessary to consider other issues which may arise in future, similar cases. For example, what are the implications of the fact that the defect in the soil may be present in both the upper and lower properties?[222] Or that the claimant has considerably more at stake than the defendant, even though the latter may have the greater resources?[223] Should they not at least share the burden? But if that is the law the basis of the allocation is far from clear.[224] Furthermore, if the problem is caused not by an isolated event like a lightning strike, why should the defendant (whose own property may also be under threat) owe *any* duty to put his hand in his pocket

---

[217] It seems that this where there is a public nuisance the ordinary, objective standard applies: *Wandsworth LBC v Railtrack Plc* [2001] EWCA Civ 1236; *The Times*, August 2, 2001, applying *Att Gen v Tod Heatley* [1897] 1 Ch. 560.

[218] See para.14–13, above. Quaere how this fits in with the inability to sue for personal injuries in private nuisance.

[219] [2000] Q.B. 836.

[220] *Leakey* was a case of the collapse of the upper property on to the lower. *Holbeck* involved the collapse of the lower property damaging the upper.

[221] See para.6–31, above.

[222] Counsel for the hotel argued that if both did nothing each would be liable in full for damage to the other's land. Stuart Smith L.J. was inclined to the view that neither would be liable: at 863.

[223] As was the case in *Holbeck*.

[224] In *Holbeck* the trial judge (who had come to a different conclusion on liability) would have awarded damages subject to a deduction for what the hotel *would* have contributed to the cost of remedial works.

to protect the claimant?[225] Although obiter, the Court of Appeal contemplated that it might not necessarily have been incumbent on someone in Scarborough's position to carry out extensive and expensive remedial work to prevent the damage which they ought to have foreseen and that the scope of the duty might have been limited to warning of the risk and sharing information.[226]

The development of the law in this line of cases was thought to **14–22** mean that a public authority engaged in drainage or sewerage could no longer necessarily rely on a principle that it escapes liability if its facilities were adequate when installed and have failed to keep pace with increased demand. However, such activities are carried out under statutory schemes and the position is not the same as it is between two adjoining landowners. In *Marcic v Thames Water Utilities Ltd*[227] (where the claimant's property was repeatedly flooded as a result of overloading of the sewerage system, to which owners of new property had the right of connexion) the House of Lords held that the statutory scheme in question placed the decision on what expenditure to require to increase sewerage provision in the hands of the industry regulator, who also set limits on what the sewerage undertakers could charge for their services and who was better able than the courts to take account of the various competing interests,[228] and that to expose the defendants to liability for nuisance would cut across this structure. This statutory scheme was compatible with the rights of the claimant under the European Convention on Human Rights to respect for his private and family life and home and to the peaceful enjoyment of his possessions. It was open to persons aggrieved by flooding to complain to the regulator, who had power to issue enforcement notices against the sewerage undertaker and his decision in response would be open to judicial review.[229] However, since the claimant had never approached the regulator there was no decision of his which could be challenged in this way or under the Human Rights Act 1998.

iii. Predecessor in title. Where the nuisance existed before the **14–23** occupier acquired the property he will be liable if it can be proved that he knew, or ought reasonably to have known, of its existence

---

[225] Parts of the east coast of England are subject to rapid and continuous erosion. Suppose D has a field half a mile wide on the edge of the sea and this is eaten away by the waves, which then begin to erode C's land. It seems bizarre to suggest that D can be under any liability to C.

[226] [2000] Q.B. at 863.

[227] [2003] UKHL 66; [2004] 2 A.C. 42.

[228] Between the trial and the decision of the HL, remedial work was done to the claimant's property and nine other houses at a cost of £731,000. The estimated cost of remedial work for the defendants' whole area, without taking account of new house building, was £1 billion: at [23].

[229] Cf. *Andrews v Reading BC* [2005] EWHC 256 (QB).

but not otherwise.[230] In *St Anne's Well Brewery Co v Roberts*,[231] C owned an ancient inn, one side of which was bounded by the old city wall of Exeter. D owned part of the wall. On either side of C's kitchen fireplace, recesses had at some time unknown been formed by excavations in the wall. Part of the wall belonging to D collapsed and demolished the inn. C sued D, who was held not liable because he neither knew of the defect nor could have discovered it by reasonable diligence. It is arguable that the special standard of care discussed in *Goldman v Hargrave* should apply also to this situation. If the predecessor in title created the nuisance he may remain liable for injury done by it after he disposes of the land.[232] If, however, he did not create it his liability ceases upon disposal. The duty to remedy a nuisance created by another or by natural causes is part of the price of the occupation of land but there is no reason why it should continue after that occupation has ceased.[233]

C. Landlord

14–24   Since the basic liability for nuisance rests upon the occupier of the land it might be thought that a landlord's liability ceased upon letting the land, except where he created the nuisance by some positive act. However, the law has gone a long way towards displacing this general rule, without of course affecting the liability of the tenant as occupier.

14–25   **i. If he has authorised nuisance.** The landlord is liable if he has expressly or impliedly authorised his tenant to create the nuisance. Where D let a field to B for working it as a lime quarry and B's acts in blasting the limestone and letting kiln smoke escape constituted a nuisance to C, D was held liable, for B's method of working the quarry was the usual way of getting lime and D was taken to have authorised it[234]; and a local authority was liable when it let land for go-karting and a nuisance was a natural and necessary consequence of that activity.[235] Here the liability of the landlord is not different from that of any principal who authorises his agent to commit a tort.

---

[230] *Montana Hotels v Fasson Pty* (1986) 69 A.L.R. 258 (a Privy Council decision where the defendant was lessee of a newly completed building with a latent defect).
[231] (1929) 140 L.T. 1. Followed in *Wilkins v Leighton* [1932] 2 Ch. 106. Cf. *Hall v Duke of Norfolk* [1900] 2 Ch. 165 (present occupier held not liable for "continuing" an excavation made by his predecessor which eventually caused a subsidence).
[232] *Roswell v Prior* (1701) 12 Mod. 635.
[233] This is the position of the vendor/lessor with regard to injuries occurring on the premises: *Rimmer v Liverpool CC* [1985] Q.B. 1 (para.9–36, above).
[234] *Harris v James* (1876) 45 L.J.Q.B. 545. *Pwllbach Colliery Co v Woodman* [1915] A.C. 634 at 639, "But permission to carry on a business is quite a different thing from permission to carry it on in such a manner as to create a nuisance, unless it is impossible in a practical sense to carry it on without committing a nuisance": per Lord Loreburn.
[235] *Tetley v Chitty* [1986] 1 All E.R. 663.

The tenant, of course, is also liable, indeed if the tenant is not liable because his actions are not a nuisance then neither is the landlord liable.[236] A local authority which let a house to a "problem" family was not liable to be enjoined in respect of nuisance created by the family even though the authority could have terminated the lease for breaches of covenant[237]: the authority had not expressly authorised the nuisance and it was caused solely by the acts of the tenants, not by any condition of the premises themselves.[238] A person does not authorise another to do an act merely because he has furnished him with the means of doing it or because he has sufficient control to stop him.[239]

ii. If he knew or ought to have known[240] of the nuisance before the letting. At one time it was the law that even if he was aware of the nuisance at the time of the letting the landlord escaped liability if he had taken from the tenant a covenant to repair[241] but this was finally rejected by the Court of Appeal in *Brew Bros Ltd v Snax (Ross) Ltd*.[242] As Sachs L.J. remarked, there is no reason why liability to a third party should be:

14–26

"[S]huffled off merely by signing a document which as between owner and tenant casts on the latter the burden of executing remedial work. The duty of the owner is to ensure that the nuisance causes no injury—not merely to get someone else's promise to take the requisite steps to abate it."[243]

The tenant is of course liable in this situation, but that is because of his occupation, not because of his covenant[244] and any additional

---

[236] *Southwark London Borough Council v Mills* [2001] 1 A.C. 1.

[237] "Social landlords" (e.g. local authorities) have extensive powers against anti-social behaviour causing nuisance or annoyance, including application for an injunction, under Pt 2 of the Anti-Social Behaviour Act 2003.

[238] *Smith v Scott* [1973] Ch. 314; *Hussain v Lancaster CC* [2000] Q.B. 1. Article 8 of the European Convention on Human Rights was unsuccessfully relied on in this context in *Mowan v Wandsworth LBC* [2001] L.G.R. 228, CA, albeit on facts before the Human Rights Act 1998 came into force.

[239] See *C.B.S. Songs Ltd v Amstrad Consumer Electronics Plc* [1988] A.C. 1013 (not a nuisance case).

[240] *Gandy v Jubber* (1865) 5 B. & S. 485 9 B & S. 15; *St Anne's Well Brewery Co v Roberts* (1929) 140 L.T. 1; *Wilchick v Marks* [1934] 2 K.B. 56 at 67–68; *Brew Bros Ltd v Snax (Ross) Ltd* [1970] 1 Q.B. 612 at 638, 644; *Mistry v Thakor* [2005] EWCA Civ 953. "There appears to be no authority on the case where an owner, who is responsible for property which is in a dangerous condition, has in effect delegated his management of the property to an apparently competent surveyor as an independent contractor, but who in the particular case discharges his duty incompetently and in breach of his duty to his client": *Mistry* at [44].

[241] *Pretty v Bickmore* (1873) L.R. 8 C.P. 401.

[242] [1970] 1 Q.B. 612.

[243] [1970] 1 Q.B. 612 at 638–639.

[244] *Montana Hotels v Fasson Pty* (1986) 69 A.L.R. 258.

obligation he may have undertaken by that covenant cannot affect
his liability to third parties.[245]

14–27   **iii. Where the landlord has covenanted to repair or has the
right to enter and repair.** Liability in this situation extends to
nuisances which arise after the tenancy has commenced. The first
point to make is that the landlord will be liable to persons outside
the premises as well as to visitors on them if he is in breach of s.4
of the Defective Premises Act 1972, which has already been considered in connection with occupiers' liability.[246] The duty under
that section is owed to, "all persons who might reasonably be
expected to be affected by defects in the state of the premises" and
is a duty to:

> "[T]ake such care as is reasonable in all the circumstances to see
> that they are reasonably safe from personal injury or from damage
> to their property"

caused by the defects. Though this largely covers the liability which
already existed at common law, the latter continues to exist concurrently. It was extended from the case where the landlord had
covenanted to do repairs[247] to that where he had reserved a right to
enter and repair (without any obligation to do so) and then to the
situation where the right was implied, as it would be, for example,
in the case of a weekly tenancy.[248] The Landlord and Tenant Act
1985 provides that in any lease of a dwelling house for a term of less
than seven years or any lease which is terminable by the lessor in
less than seven years, there is an implied covenant by the lessor to
keep in repair the structure and exterior and certain installations.[249]
Any provision seeking to place these liabilities on the tenant is
ineffective.

If the landlord has undertaken to repair or has the right to enter
and repair his liability does not affect that of the tenant, who is liable
as occupier.[250] Where the landlord has covenanted to repair the
tenant will, of course, be able to obtain an indemnity if sued.

---

[245] Except in the unlikely event that the Contracts (Rights of third Parties) Act 1999 applies.
The covenant may, of course, entitle the landlord to be indemnified if sued.
[246] See para.9–40, above.
[247] *Payne v Rogers* (1794) 2 H.Bl. 350.
[248] *Mint v Good* [1951] 1 K.B. 517.
[249] Section 11, as extended by the Housing Act 1988 s.116.
[250] *St Anne's Well Brewery Co v Roberts* (1929) 140 L.T. 1; *Heap v Ind Coope & Allsopp Ltd*
[1940] 2 K.B. 476 at 482; but the tenant may not be sued, as in *Heap's* case and *Mint v
Good*, perhaps because he is uninsured and a man of straw, which is the rationale for
imposing liability on the landlord.

7. Damage

If the nuisance is a public one, it has long been settled that the **14–28** claimant must prove damage.[251] In the case of a private nuisance, however, although it is said that damage must be proved, the law will often presume it. In *Fay v Prentice*[252] a cornice of the defendant's house projected over the claimant's garden so that rainwater dripped from it on the garden, and it was held that the law would infer injury to the claimant without proof of it. This inference appears to apply to any nuisance where the damage is so likely to occur that it would be superfluous to demand evidence that it has occurred. The inference cannot be made if the discomfort is purely personal, for personal sensitivity to smells, smoke and the like varies considerably and it is only fair that evidence of substantial annoyance should be required. However, such evidence will suffice and it is not necessary that the claimant should show any loss of trade or diminution in the capital value of the property.[253] Where no damage has yet occurred but it is imminent, a quia timet injunction may be granted.[254]

No present damage need be proved where the nuisance is to an easement or profit a prendre, at any rate where the claim is for damages as distinct from a mandatory injunction.[255] As a series of such acts or the continuation of one particular act is evidence of acquiescence by the claimant in the annoyance, if no remedy were available in these circumstances for merely presumed damage the claimant would be barred by prescription after 20 years from suing at all.[256] If damage were not presumed, it might be difficult to establish that any one act had caused it. In these cases, however, although no present damage need be proved, probability that substantial damage will ensue must be shown otherwise the law would be redressing merely fanciful claims.[257] In *Nicholls v Ely Beet Sugar Factory Ltd*,[258] large quantities of refuse and effluent were alleged to have been discharged from the defendants' beet sugar factory into the river in which the claimant owned two several and exclusive

---

[251] See para.14–3, above.

[252] (1845) 1 C.B. 828.

[253] See *Hunter v Canary Wharf Ltd*, para.14–15, above. As to what constitutes damage where the property is physically affected by the activity, see para.5–39, above.

[254] See para.22–52, below.

[255] There substantial damage must be proved, at any rate in infringement of light: *Colls v Home and Colonial Stores* [1904] A.C. 179. The decision might, however, be interpreted rather as defining the limits of the right of light than as laying down any rule with respect to the necessity of proving damage. It is arguable that what the HL actually decided was that the right exists only with respect to a particular amount of light.

[256] Cf. Kelly C.B. in *Harrop v Hirst* (1868) L.R. 4 Ex. 43 at 45, 46–47; Lord Wright M.R. in *Nicholls v Ely Beet Sugar Factory Ltd* [1936] Ch. 343 at 349–350.

[257] *Kensit v GE Ry* (1884) 27 Ch.D. 122.

[258] [1936] Ch. 343. See also *Pride of Derby and Derby Angling Association Ltd v British Celanese Ltd* [1953] Ch. 149.

fisheries. The Court of Appeal held that there was no need for him to prove pecuniary loss, the injury being one actionable per se, although he lost his action on the ground that he had failed to show that the defendant had caused the injury.[259]

8. DEFENCES

A. Coming to Nuisance No Defence

14–29 It is usually said that it is no defence to prove that the claimant came to the nuisance or that the place is a convenient one for committing it. What this means is that, if the annoyance is unreasonable in that particular district, then the claimant can recover even if it has been going on long before he came there. In *Bliss v Hall*,[260] the defendant had set up a tallow-chandlery which emitted: "divers noisome, noxious, and offensive vapours, fumes, smells and stenches" to the discomfort of the claimant, who had taken a house near it. It was held to be no defence that the business had been in existence for three years before the claimant's arrival, for he, "came to the house . . . with all the rights which the common law affords, and one of them is a right to wholesome air".[261]

However, the principle that coming to the nuisance is no defence has to be qualified by another principle. As we have seen,[262] where the claim does not relate to material damage to property the nature of the locality is an important element in deciding if there is a nuisance at all. If you choose to make your home in the heart of a manufacturing district, you can expect no more freedom from the discomfort usually associated with such a place than any other resident.[263]

B. Usefulness not in Itself a Defence[264]

14–30 The mere fact that a process or business is useful to persons generally, in spite of its annoyance to the claimant, is no defence.

---

[259] Lord Wright M.R., at 349, adopted Sir Frederick Pollock's view (*Torts*, 15th edn, p.283): "Disturbance of easements and the like, as completely existing rights of use and enjoyment, is a wrong in the nature of trespass, and remediable by action without any allegation of proof of specific damage; the action was on the case under the old forms of pleading, since trespass was technically impossible, though the act of disturbance might include a distinct trespass of some kind, for which trespass would lie at the plaintiff's option."

[260] (1838) 4 Bing. N.C. 183 (followed, with some reluctance, by the majority of the Court of Appeal in *Miller v Jackson* [1977] Q.B. 966).

[261] *Per* Tindal C.J., at 186. So too, *Elliotson v Feetham* (1835) 2 Bing. N.C. 134.

[262] See para.14–7, above.

[263] A tenant takes the building as it is in respect of the effects of ordinary use by other tenants (*Southwark LBC v Mills* [2001] 1 A.C. 1) or defects present at the commencement of the lease (*Jackson v J.H. Watson Property Investment Ltd* [2008] EWHC 14 (Ch)).

[264] Usefulness is by no means irrelevant in determining whether a nuisance has been committed, para.14–8, above.

One who keeps a pigsty, a tannery, a limekiln or an iron foundry is pursuing a laudable occupation and possibly one of great benefit to the public, yet that by itself will not excuse him. In *Adams v Ursell*[265] a fried-fish shop was held to be a nuisance in the residential part of a street where it was carried on. It was argued unsuccessfully that an injunction would cause great hardship to the defendant and to the poor people who were his customers. The defendant could engage in his business in an area where it would not constitute a nuisance and indeed the injunction granted did not extend to the whole street. Nor does the need to maintain an airforce for national defence excuse serious and continual noise caused by low flying, though that is a case where damages rather than an injunction is likely to be the proper remedy.[266]

C. No Defence that it is Due to Many

It is no defence that the nuisance was created by independent acts **14–31** of different persons, although the act of any one of them was not per se unlawful; for example where 100 people independently leave 100 wheelbarrows in a place and the obstruction consists in the accumulation of these vehicles and not in the presence of any one of them.[267] It may appear paradoxical that a defendant is held liable although his act alone would not be a tort, but the explanation lies in the fact that the standard of what is reasonable is governed by the surrounding circumstances, including the conduct of the others.[268]

D. Twenty Years' Prescription a Defence

Twenty years' continuance will, by prescription, legalise a private **14–32** nuisance[269] but not a public one. The period will not commence to run until the nuisance is known by the claimant to exist. The secret

---

[265] [1913] 1 Ch. 269.

[266] *Dennis v MoD* [2003] EWHC 793 (QB); [2003] Env L.R. 34.

[267] *Thorpe v Brumfitt* (1873) L.R. 8 Ch.App. 650 at 656; *Lambton v Mellish* [1894] 3 Ch. 163.

[268] Prosser & Keeton, *Torts*, 5th edn, p.354.

[269] The right to commit a private nuisance may be acquired by prescription as an easement in cases where such right is capable of being an easement, e.g. a right to discharge rainwater from your eaves on to your neighbour's land. To acquire a right by prescription there must be certainty and uniformity, "for the measurement and determination of the user by which the extent of the prescriptive rights is acquired": per Eve J. in *Hulley v Silversprings Bleaching Co* [1922] 2 Ch. 281. There are dicta that a right may be acquired by prescription to annoy your neighbour by smoke, smells and noise, although the quantity of the inconvenience is constantly changing. There is no reported case when such a right has arisen by prescription: *Waterfield v Goodwin* (1957) 105 L.J. 332; *Khyatt v Morgan* [1961] N.Z.L.R. 1020 at 1024; *Dennis v MoD* [2003] EWHC 793 (QB); [2003] Env L.R. 34.

Nuisance

discharge of pollution upon his premises cannot be a root of prejudice to his rights until he knows of, or suspects, it.[270] This qualification is of especial importance where the nuisance has been in existence before the claimant came to it. In *Sturges v Bridgman*[271] a confectioner had for more than 20 years used large pestles and mortars in the back of his premises which abutted on the garden of a physician, and the noise and vibration were not felt to be a nuisance during that period. In other words there had been no actionable interference with the physician's enjoyment of his own property. Then, however, the physician built a consulting room at the end of his garden and, for the first time, found that the noise and vibration materially interfered with the pursuit of his practice.[272] He was granted an injunction against the confectioner, whose claim to a prescriptive right failed because the interference had not been an actionable nuisance during the whole preceding period of 20 years.

E. *Jus Tertii*

14–33 In *Nicholls v Ely Beet Sugar Factory*,[273] Farwell J. held that the defendant to an action for pollution of a private fishery could not plead *jus tertii* as a defence, i.e. that some third party had a better title to the land than the claimant, but the learned judge left it open whether this applied to nuisance in general. It is true that at common law *jus tertii* might be pleaded in certain actions for conversion of goods but it was irrelevant where the action was based upon possession, for example trespass.[274] Now that it is established that possession or occupation of the land is necessary to entitle the claimant to sue for nuisance it is clear that *jus tertii* does not afford a defence.[275]

F. Conduct Permitted by Statute[276]

14–34 Many alleged nuisances are caused by public authorities acting under statutory powers and the defence of legislative authority is thus particularly important in this area.[277] Everything of course depends on the construction of the particular statute in question and

[270] *Liverpool Corp v Coghill & Son Ltd* [1918] 1 Ch. 307.
[271] (1879) 11 Ch.D. 852 at 863: "Acts which are neither preventable nor actionable cannot be relied on to found an easement"
[272] See *Bliss v Hall*, above, fn.260.
[273] [1931] 2 Ch. 84.
[274] The position has now been substantially altered by the Torts (Interference with Goods) Act 1977 (para.17–18, below) but this has no application to land.
[275] *Hunter v Canary Wharf Ltd* [1997] A.C. 655 at 688, 703.
[276] As to planning permission, see para.14–7, above.
[277] For a modern (and comprehensive) example, see the Railways Act 1993 s.122.

one must therefore be wary of laying down definite propositions.[278] Broadly, however, the position seems to be as follows:

1. Since we are dealing with statutory powers the primary question where what is complained of is damage arising from the exercise of the powers (as opposed to some "collateral" damage[279]) must be whether that exercise is *intra vires* the statute.[280] If it is, the claimant who suffers damage is left without redress unless the statute makes some provision for compensation.[281]

2. Work causing substantial interference with neighbouring property will not normally be *intra vires* the statute unless that interference is the "inevitable" consequence of the work, i.e. unless it must arise even though the work is carried on with reasonable care and with approved techniques. The burden of showing inevitability is on the defendant.[282] Where the statute contains a "nuisance clause",[283] then if the authority is merely permissive there may be liability even for the inevitable consequences of the works, but this is not so if the undertaker is under a statutory duty to carry them out.[284] A more rational distinction is probably between statutes which require works to be done in a particular place and those which give the undertaker a wide discretion in this respect. In the former case, there

---

[278] The cases draw no clear distinction between liability in nuisance and liability under *Rylands v Fletcher*: but in the light of the *Cambridge Water* case (para.15–3, below) this may be justifiable.

[279] e.g. careless driving of a lorry on the way to the construction site or an industrial accident at the site.

[280] See the speech of Lord Diplock in *Home Office v Dorset Yacht Co Ltd* [1970] A.C. 1004 at 1064–1071.

[281] A major general compensation provision is that for "injurious affection" in s.10 of the Compulsory Purchase Act 1965, which is the successor of Victorian legislation dating back to the construction of railways. It is reviewed in *Wildtree Hotels Ltd v Harrow LBC* [2001] 2 A.C. 1. It covers damage which is (a) caused by the construction of the works (b) caused by the lawful exercise of the statutory power and (c) is such as would have been actionable at common law in the absence of statutory authority. Work carried on without reasonable regard for people living in the area will be outside the scope of the statutory power and therefore in such a case the claimant must rely on the law of nuisance.

[282] *Manchester Corp v Farnworth* [1930] A.C. 171. In *Allen v Gulf Oil Refining Ltd* [1981] A.C. 1001 at 1017, Lord Edmund Davies said this issue was to be determined without regard to expense.

[283] e.g. "Nothing in this Act shall exonerate the undertakers from any indictment, action, or other proceedings for nuisance in the event of any nuisance being caused by them."

[284] See the summary in *Dept of Transport v NW Water Authority* [1983] 3 W.L.R. 105 and in the HL [1984] A.C. 336. It might be argued that even without a nuisance clause the granting of merely permissive powers showed an intention not to take away any private rights, particularly since we are here commonly dealing with private Acts, to which the *contra proferentem* approach may fairly be applied, but this would be inconsistent with the authorities. Similarly, the absence of a provision for compensation in the Act is no more than a weak indication of an intention to preserve private rights: *Allen v Gulf Oil Refining Ltd* [1981] A.C. 1001 at 1016.

is no liability provided that the work is undertaken with reasonable care[285]; in the latter, the undertaker may be liable if he chooses to carry out the works in a place where they cause a nuisance to neighbours when he could have carried them out elsewhere without such consequences.[286] Another type of case is where a power is given to effect a variety of works as and when the undertaker deems it necessary or expedient to do so (for example the powers given to land drainage authorities). While no hard and fast line can be drawn between this and the previous situation it is obvious that if powers of this sort are read subject to an implied limitation that they are not to be exercised so as to cause any avoidable infringement of private rights the object of the legislation will be largely frustrated.[287] Accordingly, the court is not, under the guise of imposing liability for nuisance, to substitute its own discretion for that granted to the statutory undertaker by Parliament.[288]

14–35   All of the above must now be read subject to the European Convention on Human Rights and the Human Rights Act 1998. Article 8 of the Convention requires respect for private and family life and the home and breach of that requirement by a public authority is, under the 1998 Act, directly actionable in damages. Although under the common law the protection of private rights was a value that influenced the court in the interpretation of statutory authority, that was subsidiary to the meaning of the words. However, s.3 of the Human Rights Act 1998 requires legislation to be read and given effect in a way which is compatible with the Convention rights "so far as it is possible to do so", which goes beyond merely relying on the rights to resolve an ambiguity in the statute.[289] If the words of the statute are clear by this standard the court may not strike it down but may make a declaration of incompatibility. However, the right of appeal to the Court in Strasbourg remains after the

---

[285] *Manchester Corp v Farnworth* [1930] A.C. 171. *Allen v Gulf Oil Refining Ltd* [1981] A.C. 1001.

[286] *Metropolitan Asylum District v Hill* (1881) 6 App.Cas. 193; but if Parliament had specified the site there would have been no liability: *Allen v Gulf Oil Refining Ltd*, above, fn.285, at 1014.

[287] *Marriage v East Norfolk Rivers Catchment Board* [1950] 1 K.B. 284 at 308 per Jenkins L.J.

[288] See also *Buley v British Railways Board* [1975] C.L.Y. 2458. Jenkins L.J. in *Marriage's* case, above, speaks of liability in nuisance remaining (1) where the board's exercise of its discretion is capricious (2) where an act of negligence in the course of carrying out the work produces some unintended consequence. Note that in *Marriage's* case the statute contained provision for compensation for persons suffering damage by the exercise of the statutory powers.

[289] *R v A (No.2)* [2001] UKHL 25; [2002] 1 A.C. 45 at [44]. For a tort example, see *Cachia v Faluyi* [2001] EWCA Civ 998; [2002] 1 All E.R. 192.

1998 Act and that body is not hampered by any vestiges of Parliamentary supremacy, as illustrated by *Hatton v UK*.[290] Section 76(1) of the Civil Aviation Act 1982 provides that no action shall lie for nuisance:

> "[B]y reason only of the flight of an aircraft over any property at a height above the ground which, having regard to wind, weather and all the circumstances of the case, is reasonable, or the ordinary incidents of such flight"

provided the relevant regulations made under the Act have been observed. The applicants were residents in the vicinity of Heathrow who complained of night flights and the majority of the European Court of Human Rights held that the 1993 Scheme produced by the Minister for the restriction of such flights failed to give adequate protection to the applicants' rights under art.8. Subsequently the Grand Chamber overturned this decision by a majority of 12 votes to 5[291] on the ground that in preparing the Scheme the Government had not exceeded the margin of appreciation allowed it by the Convention. That decision turned on the particular facts and it does not follow that another claim for aircraft noise would necessarily fail. The claim was not of course an action for nuisance against the airlines or the airport and any such claim would have been doomed to failure by the 1982 Act but that is not determinative where art.8 is in issue. The underlying question was one of the proper balance between the rights of enjoyment of property and the economic well-being of the country (including the role of Heathrow as a major European entry point). That has traditionally been regarded as a political issue, but it has now become also a legal one (at least in the sense that it may be decided by a court).[292]

G. Other Defences

Other valid defences are: consent of the claimant,[293] and contributory negligence subject to the provisions of the Law Reform (Contributory Negligence) Act 1945.[294] Even where it is said that liability does not depend upon negligence, the act of a stranger, act of God and the "secret unobservable process of nature" are accepted as defences.[295]

14–36

---

[290] (2003) 37 E.H.R.R. 28.
[291] There was an infringement of art.13 on the basis of the narrow scope of the English law of judicial review at the time but no damages were awarded.
[292] See the dissenting judgment of Sir Brian Kerr in the initial proceedings in *Hatton*.
[293] *Kiddle v City Business Properties Ltd* [1942] 1 K.B. 269, para.15–13, below.
[294] *Trevett v Lee* [1955] 1 W.L.R. 113 at 122; *Gilson v Kerrier RDC* [1976] 1 W.L.R. 904.
[295] See para.14–40, below.

9. Highways[296]

14–37   "Nuisance may be defined, with reference to highways, as any wrongful act or omission upon or near a highway, whereby the public are prevented from freely, safely, and conveniently passing along the highway."[297]

In considering the general law of public nuisance we have to some extent considered its application to highways. We must now discuss some of the applicable rules in greater detail and also certain other matters which have not yet been mentioned.

A. Which Obstructions are Actionable
14–38   Not every obstacle on the highway constitutes an actionable nuisance, for the highway would be scarcely usable if it were. The law requires of users of the highway a certain amount of "give and take" and each person is deemed to assume the normal risks of passage along the highway by way of inconvenience and even danger.[298] It is only when the defendant does something which in the circumstances is unreasonable that it becomes actionable. For this reason, the repair of the water, gas and electric mains which run under the street, of the surface of the street itself, and the building and alteration of the houses bordering on it, all constitute lawful occasions, either under statutory powers or by the common law, for temporary interference with its free passage and its amenities; and if shops and houses are to get any supplies, vehicles and persons must pause on the highway to deliver them. A temporary obstruction, provided it is reasonable in amount and duration, is permissible.[299] Whether it is so is a question of fact varying with the circumstances of each particular case. Nor is every permanent obstruction a nuisance.[300]

Continuing obstructions are one thing, highway accidents are another. In a number of cases the courts have been faced with accidents arising from the parking or stopping of vehicles on the

---

[296] *Encyclopedia of Highway Law and Practice.* Navigable waters are analogous to highways on land. As to ferries see *Gravesham BC v British Rail* [1978] Ch. 379.

[297] *Jacobs v LCC* [1950] A.C. 361 at 375 per Lord Simonds.

[298] "Traffic on the highways, whether by land or sea, cannot be conducted without exposing those whose persons or property are near to it to some inevitable risk, and . . . those who go on the highway or have their property adjacent to it, may well be held to do so subject to their taking on themselves the risk of injury from that inevitable danger." *Fletcher v Rylands* (1866) L.R. 1 Ex. 265 at 286 per Blackburn J. See also the comments of the same judge in *River Wear Commissioners v Adamson* (1877) 2 App.Cas. 743 at 767.

[299] *Harper v Haden & Sons Ltd* [1933] Ch. 298 at 304.

[300] *Att Gen v Wilcox* [1938] Ch. 934.

highway. If the vehicle is left[301] in such a position that it is a foreseeable source of danger to other road users then there may be liability in nuisance but the defendant's conduct would anyway amount to negligence.[302] It has been said, however, that, quite apart from foreseeability of danger, the defendant will be liable in nuisance if he so leaves his vehicle as to constitute an obstruction of the highway even though it does not constitute a risk to other road users.[303] Whether or not this view represents the law, it may be doubted whether the distinction drawn between nuisance and negligence in relation to a stationary vehicle on the highway has any justification in the modern law. As Professor Newark pointed out,[304] such cases are more conveniently dealt with in negligence.[305] It is only because the factual situation became common before the development of the law of negligence that it was incorporated into public nuisance. Whether or not the framing of a claim in nuisance gives the claimant any advantage, the duplication of action and the difficulty of drawing a line between nuisance on the highway and negligence give rise to confusion. The situation was justifiably criticised by Adams J. in the New Zealand case of *Everitt v Martin*[306]:

"It is well established that a duty rests on all users of the highway to exercise due care for the safety of other users and, in regard to highway accidents arising out of the user of the highway and giving rise to claims for injury to persons or to chattels, the law of negligence is sufficient, and any liability, which can be legitimately founded on nuisance, can be equally well, and I think more conveniently, based on negligence. The breach, by act or

---

[301] It is important to distinguish between one who deliberately parks a vehicle and one who stops temporarily, e.g. to deal with an emergency: *Dymond v Pearce* [1972] 1 Q.B. 496 at 504 per Edmund Davies L.J. Thus if the driver, on finding his lights are out, stops the vehicle, this is not of itself a nuisance, though it may be so if he leaves it on the highway for an unreasonable time or without giving warning of its presence there or if the vehicle became unlit because of some fault on his part: *Maitland v Raisbeck* [1944] K.B. 689, explaining and distinguishing *Ware v Garston Haulage Co Ltd* [1944] K.B. 30.

[302] This is not to say that it makes no difference that the liability is founded on nuisance, for, a "nuisance situation" being shown, it may be that the burden of proof of lack of fault is on the defendant: *Southport Corp v Esso Petroleum Co Ltd* [1954] 2 Q.B. 182 at 197 per Denning L.J. It has been held that the statutory obligations in relation to the lighting of vehicles do not give rise to civil liability: *Clarke v Brims* [1947] K.B. 497.

[303] *Dymond v Pearce* [1972] 1 Q.B. 496; but see the contrary view of Edmund Davies L.J. at 503, and *Mitchell v Tsiros (No.2)* [1982] V.R. 301.

[304] "The Boundaries of Nuisance" (1949) 65 L.Q.R. 480 at p.485. See also Pritchard, "Trespass, Case, and the Rule in Williams v Holland" [1964] C.L.J. 234, 237.

[305] In fact, many cases involving a dangerous obstruction of the highway are not pleaded in nuisance at all: e.g. *Tart v G.W. Chitty & Co Ltd* [1933] 2 K.B. 453; *Baker v E. Longhurst & Sons Ltd* [1933] 2 K.B. 461 (though horse and cart were moving); *Tidy v Battman* [1934] 1 K.B. 319; *Henley v Cameron* (1949) 118 L.J.K.B. 989; *Hill-Venning v Beszant* [1950] 2 All E.R. 1151; *Moore v Maxwells of Emsworth Ltd* [1968] 1 W.L.R. 1077.

[306] [1952] N.Z.L.R. 298 at 300; *Mitchell v Tsiros (No.2)* [1982] V.R. 801.

omission, of the duty to exercise due care is indeed the foundation of the liability."

B. Access To and From Highway

14–39   It is clear that the right of passage along the highway is a public right[307] and that interference with it is remediable by an action for public, not private, nuisance. As we have seen,[308] this means that the claimant can only sue if he has suffered damage over and above that suffered by the rest of the public. However, the owner of property adjoining the highway has a common law right of access to the highway[309] which is a private right remediable by an action of private nuisance, so that anything which prevents his access (as opposed to making it less convenient for his purposes[310]) enables the recovery of at least nominal damages.[311] The private right of access is subject to the public right of passage, which is the higher right,[312] but the right of passage of the public is also subject to the private right of access to the highway and is liable to be temporarily interrupted by the adjoining owner.[313] The conflict of these two rights is resolved on the ordinary principle that a reasonable exercise of both must be allowed.[314]

In some cases the gist of the claimant's complaint has been not so much that his access to and from the highway has been impeded but that the obstruction has prevented other people coming on to his premises and doing business with him. It seems that such a state of affairs is both a private and a public nuisance, though as far as the latter is concerned the loss of trade will amount to special damage.[315] Picketing in pursuance of a trade dispute is, in certain

---

[307] *Boyce v Paddington BC* [1903] 1 Ch. 109 at 114 per Buckley J.

[308] See para.14–3, above.

[309] The right is now heavily qualified by statute.

[310] See *Att Gen v Thames Conservators* (1862) 1 H. & M. 1; *Tate & Lyle Ltd v G.L.C.* [1983] A.C. 509 (siltation prevented large vessels approaching claimants' jetty interference with public right of navigation rather than with private right).

[311] *Walsh v Ervin* [1952] V.L.R. 361. Cf. *Chaplin v Westminster Corp* [1901] 2 Ch. 329 (transfer of goods across pavement into adjoining premises an aspect of public right of passage).

[312] *Vanderpant v Mayfair Hotel Co* [1930] 1 Ch. 138 at 152–154 per Luxmoore J.

[313] *Marshall v Blackpool Corp* [1935] A.C. 16 at 22 per Lord Atkin; *Farrell v John Mowlem & Co Ltd* [1954] 1 Lloyd's Rep. 437 at 439, 440 per Devlin J.; *Trevett v Lee* [1955] 1 W.L.R. 113.

[314] The public right now extends to holding a reasonable assembly: *DPP v Jones* [1999] A.C. 240, para.13–5, above.

[315] *Wilkes v Hungerford Market Co* (1835) 2 Bing. N.C. 281; *Lyons, Sons & Co v Gulliver* [1914] 1 Ch. 631; *Blundy, Clark & Co v L & NE Ry* [1931] 2 K.B. 342 at 352, 362; cf. at 372; *Harper v Haden & Sons Ltd* [1933] Ch. 298 at 306–307. There is, "long standing and consistent authority in support of theproposition that a claimant can recover damages in public nuisance where access to or from his premises is obstructed so as to occasion a loss of trade attributable to obstruction of his customers' use of the highway and liberty of access": *Colour Quest Ltd v Total Downstream UK Plc* [2009] EWHC 640 (Comm); [2009] 2 Lloyd's Rep. 1 at [459].

circumstances, made lawful by statute[316] but otherwise it is certainly capable of amounting to a nuisance if it involves violence or intimidation[317] and perhaps even if it is carried on so as to exert pressure to regulate and control access to and from the claimant's premises.[318] Such conduct may also now fall within the Protection from Harassment Act 1997.[319]

Problems have also arisen with queues. A queue as such is not unlawful even if its occupation of the pavement makes foot passengers deviate or access to shops difficult. It is only when it is unreasonable that the proprietors of the establishment which causes it are liable for nuisance, for example where the queue was at times five deep, extended far beyond the theatre itself and remained there for very considerable portions of time, it was held to be a nuisance to the claimants, whose premises were adjacent to the theatre.[320] The defendant is not liable if, although the queue was one of prospective customers at his shop, he was not responsible for it because other circumstances (for example shortage of supplies in consequence of war) were the primary cause of it nor will he be liable unless the claimant can prove damage.[321] However, the defendant is liable if the obstruction by means of the queue is due to an unusual method of conducting business.[322]

C. Damage on the Highway from Premises Adjoining the Highway

This area deserves special mention because the authorities are not of the clearest. The mere fact that something (for example a tree, a clock, a sign, an awning or a corbel) projects over the highway from land or a building adjacent to it does not per se constitute an actionable nuisance. This must be so, for no conceivable damage is done to anyone and there is scarcely a garden or a building on the edge of the highway which would not have to be altered if the law were otherwise.[323] The rule is different where the projection is over

14–40

---

[316] See para.18–42, below.
[317] *Messenger Newspapers Group Ltd v N.G.A.* (1982) [1984] I.R.L.R. 397; *News Group Newspapers Ltd v S.O.G.A.T. '82* [1986] I.R.L.R. 337; *Animal Liberation (Vic) Inc v Gasser* [1991] 1 V.R. 51; but cf. the view in *Hussain v Lancaster CC*, para.14–17, above, that there can be no private nuisance unless the defendant is making use of his land.
[318] *Mersey Dock & Harbour Co v Verrinder* [1982] I.R.L.R. 152; *Hubbard v Pitt* [1976] Q.B. 142. See also *Church of Jesus Christ of Latter Day Saints v Price* [2004] EWHC 3245 (QB) ("witnessing" by loud preaching outside church).
[319] See para.4–38, above.
[320] *Lyons, Sons & Co v Gulliver* [1914] 1 Ch. 631.
[321] *Dwyer v Mansfield* [1946] K.B. 437.
[322] *Fabri v Morris* [1947] 1 All E.R. 315. See also *Chartered Trust Plc v Davies* [1997] 2 E.G.L.R. 83, which did not involve the highway but where the trader's method of doing business caused inconvenience to others.
[323] *Noble v Harrison* [1926] 2 K.B. 332 at 337.

private property because the rights of the proprietor of it are much
wider than the limited right of the user of a highway.[324] If damage
is done owing to the collapse of the projection on the highway or by
some other mischief traceable to it, the occupier of the premises on
which it stood is liable if he knew of the defect or ought, on
investigation, to have known of it. At any rate that is the rule with
respect to a thing that is naturally on the premises, for example a
tree. In *Noble v Harrison*,[325] a branch of a beech tree growing on
X's land overhung the highway and in fine weather suddenly broke
and fell upon Y's vehicle passing along the highway. Neither X nor
his servants knew that the branch was dangerous and the fracture
was due to a latent defect undiscoverable by any reasonably careful
inspection,[326] and for this reason Y's action against X in nuisance
failed.

With respect to artificial things which fall and do damage it might
be argued that there was no reason to treat the occupier's liability
differently from that in the case of trees and some of the earlier
judicial statements seem to take that view.[327] However, in *Wringe v
Cohen*[328] the Court of Appeal stated the law in the following
terms:

> "If, owing to want of repair, premises on a highway become
> dangerous and, therefore, a nuisance and a passer-by or an adjoin-
> ing owner suffers damage by their collapse, the occupier, or
> owner if he has undertaken the duty of repair, is answerable
> whether he knew or ought to have known of the danger or
> not."[329]

The unforeseeable act of a trespasser is a good defence and the
Court of Appeal also held that the defendant would escape liability
should the damage result from, "a secret and unobservable operation of nature, such as subsidence under or near the foundations of
the premises".

---

[324] [1926] 2 K.B. 332 at 340 and *Lemmon v Webb* [1895] A.C. 1; but the context of these
    statements concerns the right of the neighbour to abate the nuisance by lopping the
    branches. There is less reason to think that the occupier is liable in damages for a collapse
    unless he has knowledge or means of knowledge of the defect. As to liability for
    encroachment by tree roots, see para.14–14, above and for trespass by oversailing struc-
    tures, see para.13–7, above.

[325] Above, fn.323; *Caminer v London and Northern Investment Trust Ltd* [1951] A.C. 99;
    Cunliffe v Bankes [1945] 1 All E.R. 459; *Shirvell v Hackwood Estates Co Ltd* [1938] 2
    K.B. 577; *British Road Services v Slater* [1964] 1 W.L.R. 498.

[326] Cf. *Quinn v Scott* [1965] 1 W.L.R. 1004 (means of knowledge of disease).

[327] Blackburn J. in *Tarry v Ashton* (1876) 1 Q.B.D. 314; Wright J. in *Noble v Harrison* [1926]
    2 K.B. 332 at 343–344.

[328] [1940] 1 K.B. 229.

[329] [1940] 1 K.B. 229 at 233.

"Stylistically" this looks different from the law of negligence   **14–41**
because it states a rule of liability subject to exceptions and in that
respect echoes the special Roman law rule about buildings which
can still be traced into modern civil law systems. However, as
Professor Friedmann pointed out, these exceptions seem to deprive
the rule itself of much of its significance.

> "It can hardly be imagined that any damage caused neither by the
> act of a third person nor by a latent defect could be due to
> anything but knowledge or negligence of the occupier."[330]

In effect, it would seem that *Wringe v Cohen* sets a standard
somewhere between strict liability and ordinary fault liability. The
claimant need only show that the defendant had control over the
defective premises and that the injury resulted from their dangerous
condition.[331] This gives rise to a presumption that the defendant has
failed in his duty of inspection and repair, which can only be
rebutted by proof that the accident was inevitable, i.e. it was not, nor
could have been, avoided by reasonable inspection. As Denning L.J.
said in *Mint v Good*,[332] the defendant:

> "[I]s liable when structures fall into dangerous disrepair, because
> there must be some fault on the part of someone or other for that
> to happen".

From a substantive point of view, *Wringe v Cohen* differs from
ordinary liability in negligence because the occupier is liable for the
default of his independent contractor.[333]

D. Condition of the Highway
At common law a highway authority could not be liable for injury   **14–42**
suffered by a user of the highway and resulting from the authority's

---

[330] "Nuisance, Negligence and the Overlapping of Torts" (1940) 3 M.L.R. 305, 309. Cf.
Stephen J. in *Cartwright v McLaine & Long Pty Ltd* (1979) 24 A.L.R. 97 at 106 ("near
absolute liability"). In other cases attempts have been made to distinguish between
inactivity causing the nuisance and the mere continuance of an inherited nuisance: *Cushing
v Peter Walker & Sons Ltd* [1941] 2 All E.R. 693 at 699 per Hallett J.; *Mint v Good* [1951]
1 K.B. 517 at 524 per Somervell L.J. It is suggested that this is not a valid distinction. The
failure of the occupier to discover and remedy an inherited nuisance is equally the cause
of the damage. It results just as much from the occupier's breach of his duty to inspect and
repair as does, e.g. the negligent failure to discover a defective gable-end.
[331] The evidence must show that the damage has occurred as a result of the want of repair
some structure for which the defendant was responsible: *Cartwright v McLaine & Long
Pty Ltd* (1979) 24 A.L.R. 97.
[332] [1951] 1 K.B. 517 at 526.
[333] *Tarry v Ashton* (1876) 1 Q.B.D. 314. It has been suggested ([1951] 1 K.B. 517 at 526) that
this more onerous liability may be justified by a desire to protect users of the public
highway, but one of the oddities of *Wringe v Cohen* is that the premises fell, not on to the
highway, but on to adjoining premises.

failure to discharge its duty to keep the highway in repair. The remedy for breach of the duty was proceedings on indictment. This civil law immunity did not extend to misfeasance on the highway nor to acts of repair improperly performed. The distinction between misfeasance and non-feasance and the rule of immunity were criticised and eventually the latter was abrogated by s.1 of the Highways (Miscellaneous Provisions) Act 1961 which came into force on August 3, 1964.[334] The law is now to be found in the Highways Act 1980 s.41(1):

"The authority who are for the time being the highway authority for a highway maintainable at the public expense[335] are under a duty . . . to maintain the highway".[336]

In any action against a highway authority for damage resulting from its failure to maintain it is a defence (without prejudice to any other defence such as voluntary acceptance of risk and contributory negligence) to prove that the authority had taken such care as in all the circumstances was reasonably required to secure that the part of the highway to which the action relates was not dangerous for traffic. For the purpose of such a defence the court is in particular to have regard to:

1. the character of the highway, and the traffic which was reasonably to be expected to use it;
2. the standard of maintenance appropriate for a highway of that character and used by such traffic;
3. the state of repair in which a reasonable person would have expected to find the highway;
4. whether the highway authority knew, or could reasonably have been expected to know, that the condition of the part of the highway to which the action relates was likely to cause danger to users of the highway;
5. where the highway authority could not reasonably have been expected to repair that part of the highway before the cause of

---

[334] A majority of the High Court of Australia rejected the immunity rule in *Brodie v Singleton SC* [2001] HCA 29; (2001) 180 A.L.R. 145 but in most states the rule has come back in part by statute unless the highway authority is actually aware of the risk. See. e.g. Civil Liability Act 2002 (NSW) s.45.

[335] See *Gulliksen v Pembrokeshire CC* [2002] EWCA Civ 968; [2003] 1 Q.B. 123.

[336] This provision does not cover a complaint of failure to improve the highway, e.g. by painting or erecting traffic signs or removing obstructions in the line of sight, nor will there be any such liability at common law: *Gorringe v Calderdale MBC* [2004] UKHL 15; [2004] 1 W.L.R. 1057; *Stovin v Wise* [1996] A.C. 923, para.5–47, above. Cf. *Bird v Pearce* [1979] R.T.R. 369 (obliterating existing markings; see the remarks on this case in *Gorringe*).

action arose, what warning notice of its condition had been displayed.[337]

The Act applies whether the claimant is suing in nuisance, negligence or for breach of a statutory duty.[338] It is clear from the wording of the statute that it avails only road users who suffer personal injury or property damage and that it does not give an action to an adjoining owner whose business is ruined because the condition of the highway means that vehicles cannot get to his premises, even though such loss would amount to special damage for the purposes of public nuisance if the highway were obstructed or damaged by misfeasance.[339] The only remedy in such a case is an application to the Crown Court for an order for repair.[340]

The correct approach to the statutory liability was summed up by Steyn L.J. in *Mills v Barnsley Borough Council*[341]:

14-43

"In order for a plaintiff to succeed against a highway authority . . . the plaintiff must prove that: (a) the highway was in such a condition that it was dangerous to traffic or pedestrians in the sense that, in the ordinary course of human affairs, danger may reasonably have been anticipated from its continued use by the public (b) the dangerous condition was created by the failure to maintain or repair the highway and (c) the injury or damage resulted from such a failure. Only if the plaintiff proves these *facta probanda* does it become necessary to turn to the highway authority's reliance on the special defence under section 58(1) of the 1980 Act."

It was held that the duty under the Act was to keep the fabric of the highway in suitable condition for ordinary traffic at all seasons of the year but that it did not extend to a duty to remove ice or snow, because that would not have fallen within the duty of the inhabitants at large, enforceable by indictment, before the 1961 Act.[342] This was despite the fact that s.58 would allow the authority, in a particular case, to show that it had taken reasonable steps to remove the hazard, so that although the basic duty may be "absolute" the

---

[337] Highways Act 1980 s.58.

[338] A claim under the Act may involve concurrent issues against other undertakers, e.g. tramway operators: *Roe v Sheffield CC* [2003] EWCA Civ 1; [2004] Q.B. 653.

[339] *Wentworth v Wilts CC* [1993] Q.B. 654.

[340] Beldam L.J. at 673 suggests that there might be cases where non-repair might create a liability for public nuisance but it is difficult to see how this could be so since the common law gave complete immunity for non-feasance and that immunity is only abolished so far as the statute provides.

[341] [1992] 1 P.I.Q.R. P291 at 292.

[342] *Goodes v E Sussex CC* [2000] 1 W.L.R. 1356. Despite this case the Act does cover failure to keep drains clear: *Mitchell v Dept for Transport* [2006] EWCA Civ 1089; [2006] 1 W.L.R. 3356.

liability is not in fact so. However, s.41(1A) of the Act now provides that the highway authority is under a duty to ensure, so far as is reasonably practicable, that safe passage is not endangered by snow or ice.[343]

14–44   With regard to the condition of the highway, there is an inevitable risk in travelling along the highway of unevenness in the pavement, and a highway is not to be criticised by the standards of a bowling green.[344] In *Littler v Liverpool Corp*[345] Cumming-Bruce L.J. stated that the criterion to be applied in assessing whether any particular length of pavement is dangerous is that of reasonable foreseeability of danger:

> "A length of pavement is only dangerous if, in the ordinary course of human affairs, danger may reasonably be anticipated from its common use by the public . . . It is a mistake to isolate and emphasise a particular difference in levels between flagstones unless that difference is such that a reasonable person who noticed and considered it would regard it as presenting a real source of danger."[346]

In relation to danger to vehicular traffic, it has been held that the highway authority must provide not merely for model drivers, but for the normal run of drivers to be found on the roads and that includes those who make the mistakes which experience and common sense teach us are likely to occur.[347] However, the duty is significantly less stringent than to repair every defect in the highway which might foreseeably cause harm.[348]

Where the statutory defence under s.58 comes into play it is not in all respects equivalent to a plea of "no negligence" at common law. It is provided that it shall not be relevant to prove that the highway authority had arranged for a competent person to carry out or supervise the maintenance of the part of the highway to which the action relates unless it is also proved that the authority had given him proper instructions with regard to the maintenance of the highway and that he carried out the instructions—in other words the authority is liable for the negligence of its contractors. It has also

---

[343] Inserted by s.111 of the Railways and Transport Safety Act 2003. It is not clear what is the relationship between s.41(1A) and the statutory defence under s.58. In the industrial safety context, "reasonably practicable" has generally been held to require the defendant to show what steps could have been taken and that those were not reasonably practicable: para.8–5, above.

[344] *Littler v Liverpool Corp* [1968] 2 All E.R. 343 at 345; *Ford v Liverpool Corp* (1973) 117 S.J. 167.

[345] Above, fn.344.

[346] A tilting manhole cover is plainly a danger: *Atkins v Ealing LBC* [2006] EWHC 2515 (QB).

[347] *Rider v Rider* [1973] Q.B. 505; *Tarrant v Rowlands* [1979] R.T.R. 144.

[348] *Jones v Rhondda Cynon Taff CBC* [2008] EWCA Civ 1497; [2009] R.T.R. 151 at [12].

been said that proof that the accident would have happened even if due care had been taken would not be a defence.[349]

A frontager must take reasonable care to keep safe gratings or flagstones covering a cellar under the street.[350]

---

[349] *Griffiths v Liverpool Corp* [1967] 1 Q.B. 374 at 391, 395. However, Diplock L.J. said at 391 that it: "may be that if the highway authority could show that no amount of reasonable care on its part could have prevented the danger the common law defence of inevitable accident would be available to it."

[350] See *Scott v Green & Sons* [1969] 1 W.L.R. 301, relying on what is now the Highways Act 1980 s.180(6).

CHAPTER 15

STRICT LIABILITY: RULE IN RYLANDS v FLETCHER

HAVING considered the tort of nuisance, we now turn to the rule in **15–1**
Rylands v Fletcher. This had its origins in nuisance but for most of
the 20th century was probably regarded by the majority of lawyers
as having developed into a distinct principle. Now it seems to have
returned to what are regarded as its roots: it is a "sub-species of
nuisance"[1]; but on balance it still merits some separate treatment.
Liability under the rule is strict in the sense that it relieves the
claimant of the burden of showing fault; however, it is far from
absolute since there are a number of wide-ranging defences.

1. THE RULE IN RYLANDS v FLETCHER[2]

The facts of this case were as follows. B, a mill owner, employed **15–2**
independent contractors, who were apparently competent, to construct a reservoir on his land to provide water for his mill. In the

---

[1] *Transco Plc v Stockport MBC* [2003] UKHL 61; [2004] 2 A.C. 1 at [9] per Lord
Bingham.
[2] (1865) 3 H. & C. 774 (Court of Exchequer); (1866) L.R. 1 Ex. 265 (Court of Exchequer
Chamber); (1868) L.R. 3 H.L. 330 (House of Lords). See generally: Simpson, "Legal
Liability for Bursting Reservoirs: The Historical Context of *Rylands v Fletcher*" (1984) 13
J.Leg.Stud. 209. Law Com. No.32 (1970), *Civil Liability for Dangerous Things and
Activities* (1970); Report of the Royal Commission on Civil Liability and Compensation
for Personal Injury, Cmnd. 7054 (1978), Vol.1, Ch.31.

course of the work the contractors came upon some old shafts and passages on B's land. They communicated with the mines of A, a neighbour of B, although no one suspected this, for the shafts appeared to be filled with earth. The contractors did not block them up, and when the reservoir was filled the water from it burst through the old shafts and flooded A's mines. It was found as a fact that B had not been negligent, although the contractors had been. A sued B and the House of Lords held B liable.

The decision of the House affirmed that of the Court of Exchequer Chamber, the judgment of which, delivered by Blackburn J., has become a classical exposition of doctrine.[3]

"We think that the true rule of law is, that the person who for his own purposes brings on his lands and collects and keeps there anything likely to do mischief if it escapes, must keep it in at his peril, and, if he does not do so, is prima facie answerable for all the damage which is the natural consequence of its escape."

This may be regarded as the "rule in *Rylands v Fletcher*", but what follows is equally important:

"He can excuse himself by showing that the escape was owing to the plaintiff's default or perhaps that the escape was the consequence of vis major, or the act of God but as nothing of this sort exists here, it is unnecessary to inquire what excuse would be sufficient. The general rule, as above stated, seems on principle just. The person whose grass or corn is eaten down by the escaping cattle of his neighbour, or whose mine is flooded by the water from his neighbour's reservoir, or whose cellar is invaded by the filth of his neighbour's privy, or whose habitation is made unhealthy by the fumes and noisome vapours of his neighbour's alkali works, is damnified without any fault of his own and it seems but reasonable and just that the neighbour, who has brought something on his own property which was not naturally there, harmless to others so long as it is confined to his own property, but which he knows to be mischievous if it gets on his neighbour's, should be obliged to make good the damage which ensues if he does not succeed in confining it to his own property. But for his act in bringing it there no mischief could have accrued, and it seems but just that he should at his peril keep it there so that no mischief may accrue, or answer for the natural and anticipated consequences. And upon authority, this we think is established to be the law whether the things so brought be beasts, or water, or filth, or stenches."

[3] (1866) L.R. 1 Ex. 265 at 279–280.

In the House of Lords Lord Cairns L.C. rested his decision on the ground that the defendant had made a "non-natural use" of his land, though he regarded the judgment of Blackburn J. as reaching the same result and said he entirely concurred in it.[4] Though Blackburn J. did not use this expression in his statement of the law, he had clearly intended the rule to apply only to things collected by the defendant as opposed to things naturally on the land and it may be that Lord Cairns meant nothing more by non-natural use. However, the subsequent case law has given a rather different interpretation to it and it has been regarded as additional to the requirements set out by Blackburn J.[5] In other words, the rule in *Rylands v Fletcher* must be sought in the judgments of both the Exchequer Chamber and the House of Lords.

A. Genesis and Nature of the Principle

The earlier cases from which Blackburn J. drew his statement of **15–3** the law, concerned cattle trespass (animals having to some extent travelled in a compartment of their own for purposes of tort law[6]), overflowing privies and noisome fumes from alkali works and the last two are clear instances of nuisance. Nevertheless, it was Winfield's view (and probably that of most of the profession) that the case should not be regarded as merely an application of the law of nuisance but as laying down a new principle governing a rather ill-defined category of "exceptional" or "unusual" risks. English courts displayed an ambivalent attitude towards the rule but in the United States it made a contribution (after an initially hostile reception) towards the creation of a category of liability for damage caused by ultra-hazardous or abnormally dangerous activities which present an unavoidable risk even when due care is taken,[7] this being justified on the basis that persons carrying them on should bear all the risks associated with them and not merely those arising from negligence. However, there was another view, advanced by Professor Newark,[8] to the effect that all *Rylands v Fletcher* did was to apply a general rule of strict liability in nuisance to situations where there was a claim for damages for an isolated escape rather than the more usual ongoing state of affairs. Nevertheless, the strictness of the liability was brought into sharper focus because in the normal situation of a trickle from a watercourse or pollution from a factory the interference will be apparent for some time:

---

[4] (1868) L.R. 3 H.L. 330 at 338–340.
[5] See para.15–10, below. Cf. the view in *Porter (J.P.) & Co Ltd v Bell* [1955] 1 D.L.R. 62 at 66, that there are two "rules in *Rylands v Fletcher*".
[6] *Read v J. Lyons & Co* [1947] A.C. 156 per Lord Simonds.
[7] See *Restatement* 3d §20 (Tentative Draft No.1, 2001).
[8] "The Boundaries of Nuisance" (1949) 65 L.Q.R. 480.

"[I]t is the single escape which raises the question of whether or not it was reasonably foreseeable and, if not, whether the defendant should nevertheless be liable".[9]

The continuing connection of the rule with nuisance was demonstrated by the decision of the House of Lords in *Read v J. Lyons & Co*[10] to the effect that there must be an "escape", that is to say that it was only applicable to damage occurring outside the place in which the dangerous thing was kept,[11] and by doubts expressed in the case as to the applicability of the rule to personal injuries. In *Cambridge Water Co v Eastern Counties Leather Plc*[12] the House of Lords firmly accepted Professor Newark's view of the origin of the rule.[13] However, it also accepted that in a number of respects the law had moved on since 1868. The judgment emphasises the close connection between the rule and the law of nuisance and at one point it is said that:

"[I]t would . . . lead to a more coherent body of common law principles if the rule were to be regarded as essentially an extension of the law of nuisance to isolated escapes from land."[14]

The rule in *Rylands v Fletcher* has comparatively rarely been the basis of a successful claim in the English courts since 1900[15] and it has been said that it, "has hardly been taken seriously by the English courts"[16] and that:

"[I]t is hard to escape the conclusion that the intellectual effort devoted to the rule by judges and writers over many years has brought forth a mouse".[17]

---

[9] *Transco Plc v Stockport MBC* [2003] UKHL 61; [2004] 2 A.C. 1 at [27] per Lord Hoffmann.

[10] [1947] A.C. 156.

[11] *Transco Plc v Stockport MBC*, above, fn.9, at [9].

[12] [1994] 2 A.C. 264. For the facts, see para.14–13, above.

[13] Cf. Oliphant, *"Rylands v Fletcher* and the Emergence of Enterprise Liability in the Common Law" in Koziol and Steininger (eds), *European Tort Law 2004*, 81, who supports the view that the case was more than a special application of the law of nuisance and points out that the modern position whereby fault liability is the norm and strict liability the exception would not have been so familiar to mid-nineteenth-century eyes. See also Lord Hobhouse in *Transco* at [57] and the views expressed in *Union of India v Kumar* [2008] INSC 802; [2009] 2 L.R.C. 13.

[14] [1994] 2 A.C. at 306.

[15] See Law Com. No.32 (1970), p.7.

[16] *Att Gen v Geothermal Products (NZ) Ltd* [1987] 2 N.Z.L.R. 348 at 354 per Cooke J.

[17] *Transco Plc v Stockport MBC*, above, fn.9, at [39] per Lord Hoffmann. However, the assertion, that no claimant had successfully relied on *Rylands v Fletcher* since the Second World War is incorrect: see *L.M.S. International Ltd v Styrene Packaging Ltd* [2005] EWHC 2065 (TCC) at [26].

This has been largely because of the defences of act of a third party and statutory authority and, above all, the very restrictive attitude taken by many twentieth century cases to the concept of non-natural use. The tendency was to say that common large scale activities, especially services such as the supply of gas or water, do not constitute a non-natural use of land even though their potential for causing damage is very great. Moreover, in determining whether there is a non-natural use, the courts had regard to the benefit accruing to the public from the activity and this was an important element in the rejection of the rule in some of the leading cases.[18]

The *Cambridge Water* case was, strictly, concerned only with the issue of whether the risk presented by the defendant's activity must be a foreseeable one to attract the rule but the case went beyond this and gives some indication of the likely future role of *Rylands v Fletcher* in the law. It is indicated that non-natural use should perhaps be given a rather broader meaning than had been the case,[19] and this may guard the rule against further atrophy. However, while the rule is an example of strict liability for abnormal risk, it does not now represent a general rule of strict liability for ultra-hazardous activities and the House of Lords declined to convert it to that purpose. It is a rule applicable between adjoining landowners, it requires an escape from one property into another and, even where that has taken place, it is inapplicable to personal injuries. The last point looks odd to the modern way of thinking which tends to place bodily integrity at the top of the tree of protected interests; but it makes sense on the assumption that the rule is an offshoot of the law of private nuisance, which was (and still is) concerned only with the protection of the enjoyment of land. The English common law contains a good deal less in the way of strict liability for physical damage than most other European legal systems,[20] though the most prominent examples—the very widespread strict liability for traffic accidents and the French liability for damage done by things "in one's charge"[21] proceed on an entirely different basis. It would be hard to explain either of those examples on the basis of *exceptional* risk: the former is a scheme of collective insurance for the inevitable risks of a commonplace activity operated through the machinery of

---

[18] *Read v Lyons*, above, fn.6; *Dunne v NW Gas Board* [1964] 2 Q.B. 806.

[19] See para.15–10, below.

[20] See van Gerven, Lever and Larouche, *Tort Law, Common Law of Europe Casebooks* (2000), Ch.7; Koziol and Koch (eds), *Unification of Tort Law: Strict Liability* (2002). See also Reid, "Liability for Dangerous Activities: A Comparative Analysis" (1999) 48 I.C.L.Q. 731.

[21] Developed by imaginative interpretation of art.1384 of the Code Civil. It is almost impossible for the common lawyer to adapt himself to the way of thinking behind this: if D falls on C and injures him that requires fault under art.1382; but if at the time D is carrying a stick and that injures C, art.1384 applies: Cour de cassation, assemblée plenière, May 9, 1984, *affaire Gabillet.*

liability; the latter is a judicial creation from a legislative text (some would say a perversion of it[22]) based upon the seeming premise that if possible no one should be denied the benefit of a favourable compensation regime.[23] There is some disagreement in *Transco Plc v Stockport MBC*[24] on the relevance of insurance to the scope of the rule. For Lord Hoffmann one reason for limiting the scope of the rule is the prevalence of property (loss) insurance, which is relatively cheap and accessible:

> "[P]eople should be encouraged to insure their own property rather than seek to transfer the risk to others by means of litigation".[25]

For Lord Hobhouse, on the other hand, this is to put the cart before the horse:

> "[T]he economic burden of insuring against the risk must be borne by he who creates it and has the control of it [i.e. via liability insurance] . . . The argument that insurance makes the rule unnecessary is no more valid than saying that, because some people can afford to and sensibly do take out comprehensive car insurance, no driver should be civilly liable for his negligent driving."[26]

In the *Cambridge Water* case the House of Lords did not disagree with the proposition that strict liability might be economically or morally or socially justifiable but it inclined to the view that:

> "[A]s a general rule, it is more appropriate for strict liability in respect of operations of high risk to be imposed by Parliament than by the courts. If such liability is imposed by statute, the relevant activities can be identified, and those concerned can know where they stand. Furthermore, statute can where appropriate lay down precise criteria establishing the incidence and scope of such liability."[27]

---

[22] The relevant article of the Code Civil (1384) was probably only intended as a header or introduction to the subsequent articles on liability for animals, buildings and one's employees. See generally, van Gerven, Lever and Larouche, *Tort Law (Common Law of Europe Casebooks)* 551–561.

[23] Larouche, fn.22, at 561.

[24] [2003] UKHL 61; [2004] 2 A.C. 1.

[25] At [46].

[26] At [60]. The argument here is of course an old one. For another aspect of it see para.1–29, above. Lord Hobhouse is correct to say that loss insurance against the risk in *Transco* (flooding) is now much more restricted than was once the case but that is because of environmental factors rather than *direct* human responsibility.

[27] [1994] 2 A.C. at 305. Reference is also made to likely European action on environmental pollution, as to which see para.14–1, above.

Thus, for example, statutory water undertakers are strictly liable by statute[28] for damage (including personal injury) caused by escapes of water from mains but the strict liability does not avail other statutory undertakers, such as gas and electricity suppliers or highway authorities, who presumably have a greater capacity to absorb such risks than members of the public, by loss insurance or otherwise. The approach of the House of Lords in the *Cambridge Water* case bears some resemblance to that of the Pearson Commission,[29] though the terms of reference of that body meant that its recommendations were confined to death and personal injury. The Commission proposed a parent statute which would have empowered a Minister to list dangerous things or activities as giving rise to strict liability, the listing being done on the advice of an advisory committee. The Commission's preference, on the ground of certainty, was for the abolition of the rule in *Rylands v Fletcher* rather than its retention as a "back-up".[30]

These approaches to the problem are open to the objection that **15–4** they would leave without redress (except in so far as it was provided by the law of nuisance) any persons suffering injury from an activity which was not the subject of legislation, whether because of commercial or political pressure on the government of the day or because of simple inaction or lack of foresight: if there is a regime of strict liability for injury caused by a burst water main, why should the victim of a gas explosion be in any different position? Furthermore, civil liability arising from a particular statute, even where directly imposed, tends (at least in our system) to be an adjunct to a criminal/regulatory regime and the statutory requirements may be framed with criminal penalties or administrative controls in mind, allowing defences which are not necessarily appropriate to civil liability based on the idea of risk.[31] The absence of a "general clause" on strict liability in the civil law may unduly hamper the courts in fairly allocating responsibility. Any overlap or potential clash with a specific legislative scheme could easily be avoided, the argument continues, by a provision in the scheme excluding other forms of liability from the particular area: examples are to be found in the current statutory regimes for nuclear accidents and oil pollution at sea.[32] Nevertheless, the introduction of such a general clause

[28] Water Industry Act 1991 s.209, replacing the Water Act 1981 s.6.

[29] Cmnd. 7054 (1978), Vol.1, Ch.31.

[30] The majority of High Court of Australia in *Burnie Port Authority v General Jones Pty Ltd* (1994) 120 A.L.R. 42, cast *Rylands v Fletcher* out from the Australian common law on the ground that adequate protection was afforded by the "non-delegable duty" under developed negligence law (para.20–21, below), but the rule still exists in New Zealand: *Hamilton v Papakura DC* [2000] 1 N.Z.L.R. 265.

[31] See, e.g. industrial safety legislation (Ch.8) and the current waste pollution legislation (para.15–26, below).

[32] See paras 15–24 and 15–25, below.

would present formidable problems of uncertainty in its relationship with the fault regime.[33]

It should be noted that power already exists to utilise delegated legislation to go a good way along the road to statutory strict liability. The purposes of the Health and Safety at Work, etc. Act 1974 go beyond the securing of safety in employment[34] and include:

1. "protecting persons other than persons at work against risks to health or safety arising out of or in connection with the activities of persons at work";
2. "controlling the keeping and use of explosive or highly flammable or otherwise dangerous substances, . . . ".[35]

In order to promote these purposes the Secretary of State has power to make regulations which will give rise to liability except in so far as they provide otherwise.[36] However, the overwhelming majority of regulations are concerned with the safety of employees[37] and even where this is not the case any liability depends on the particular provision, which may impose a duty equivalent to, or only marginally different from, common law negligence.[38]

2. THE PRESENT LAW

15–5   Given the various shifts in the fortunes of *Rylands v Fletcher* over the years earlier cases must be approached with more than usual caution, but with this in mind, we may attempt to state the present law as follows.

A. Dangerous Things
15–6   *Rylands v Fletcher* has been applied (or said to apply, because the cases sometimes turned on other points) to a remarkable variety of

---

[33] It might be argued that American experience has not borne this out, but American courts seemed to have practised a self-denying ordinance over strict liability for dangerous activities.
[34] As to which see Ch.8, above.
[35] Health and Safety at Work etc. Act 1974 s.1.
[36] Health and Safety at Work etc. Act 1974 s.47.
[37] See Ch.8.
[38] Thus reg.4 of the Manufacture and Storage of Explosives Regulations SI 2005/1082 requires the manufacturer to, "take appropriate measures (a) to prevent fire or explosion; (b) to limit the extent of fire or explosion including measures to prevent the spreading of fires and the communication of explosions from one location to another; and (c) to protect persons from the effects of fire or explosion." If the appropriate measures are taken but turn out not to be effective there is no breach.

things: fire[39]; gas[40]; blasting and munitions[41]; electricity[42]; oil and petrol[43]; noxious fumes[44]; colliery spoil[45]; rusty wire from a decayed fence[46]; vibrations[47]; poisonous vegetation[48]; a flag pole[49]; a "chair-o-plane" in a fairground[50]; and even (in a case of very questionable validity) noxious persons.[51] However, there seems little point in seeking to identify the precise characteristics of a *"Rylands v Fletcher* object". What matters is the scale of the risk presented by the defendant's activity: a box of matches or a glass of water do not fall within the rule, a million boxes of matches in a store or a reservoir may do so. The requirement that the thing must be likely to do mischief if it escapes cannot therefore be viewed in isolation from the further requirement of non-natural user, which encapsulates the element of exceptional risk which underlies the rule.[52] The House of Lords in the *Cambridge Water*[53] case held, by analogy with their decision on nuisance,[54] that the rule was inapplicable unless it could be foreseen that damage of the relevant type would occur as the result of an escape. Accordingly, if the possibility of the damage which occurs is scientifically unknown at the time when the escape takes place[55] there is no liability. It is clear that the defendant is liable notwithstanding that he has exercised all due care

[39] See para.15–20, below.

[40] *Batchellor v Tunbridge Wells Gas Co* (1901) 84 L.T. 765.

[41] *Miles v Forest Rock Co* (1918) 34 T.L.R. 500; *Rainham Chemical Works Ltd v Belvedere Fish Guano Co Ltd* [1921] 2 A.C. 465.

[42] *National Telephone Co v Baker* [1893] 2 Ch. 186; *Eastern and South African Telegraph Co Ltd v Cape Town Tramways Companies Ltd* [1902] A.C. 381; *Hillier v Air Ministry* [1962] C.L.Y. 2084 (cows electrocuted by an escape of electricity from high-voltage cables laid under claimant's field).

[43] *Smith v GW Ry* (1926) 135 L.T. 112; *Colour Quest Ltd v Total Downstream UK Plc* [2009] EWHC 540 (Comm); [2009] 1 Lloyds Rep 1.

[44] *West v Bristol Tramways Co* [1908] 2 K.B. 14 (in so far as the case applied the rule to a risk which was not foreseeable it cannot stand with the *Cambridge Water* case).

[45] *Att Gen v Cory Bros Ltd* [1921] 1 A.C. 521.

[46] *Firth v Bowling Iron Co* (1878) 3 C.P.D. 254

[47] *Hoare & Co v McAlpine* [1923] 1 Ch. 167; cf. *Dodd Properties Ltd v Canterbury CC* [1979] 2 All E.R. 118 at 122.

[48] *Crowhurst v Amersham Burial Board* (1878) 4 Ex. D. 5; *Ponting v Noakes* [1894] 2 Q.B. 281.

[49] *Shiffman v Order of St John* [1936] 1 All E.R. 557 (obiter, it was decided on the ground of negligence).

[50] *Hale v Jennings Bros* [1938] 1 All E.R. 579.

[51] *Att Gen v Corke* [1933] Ch. 89 but cf. *Smith v Scott* [1973] Ch. 314, where it is suggested that this case could at least equally well have been decided on the basis that the landowner was in possession of the property and was himself liable for nuisances created by his licensees. A New Zealand court refused to follow *Corke*'s case in *Matheson v Board of Governors of Northcote College* [1975] 2 N.Z.L.R. 106 but accepted that the occupier could be liable for creating a nuisance. Liability in nuisance was imposed in similar circumstances in *Lippiatt v South Gloucestershire Council* [2000] Q.B. 51.

[52] *Transco Plc v Stockport MBC* [2003] UKHL 61; [2004] 2 A.C. 1 at [10], [103].

[53] [1994] 2 A.C. 264.

[54] See para.14–13, above.

[55] As, for example, was for long the position in the case of asbestos.

to prevent the escape occurring[56] for the liability is not based on negligence. Nor does the escape have to be likely: the issue is whether damage is likely if the escape occurs, but perhaps it goes a little too far to say that the risk of escape need not be *foreseeable.* In *Cambridge Water*,[57] the damage which occurred was rather unusual in that the pollution of the claimants' water supply did not render it harmful to health but it was technically unwholesome under regulations made to comply with an EC Directive and could not lawfully be supplied as drinking water. Nevertheless the "harmful" qualities of the chemical as potentially polluting of a water supply must have been known in the sense that even before the regulations came into effect it is unlikely that the owners of the borehole would have cheerfully stood by while someone injected the borehole with it. The critical point, which was determinative of the case, was that no one ever contemplated as a possibility that the spilled chemical would get into the aquifer[58] or, even if it did, that it would be found in detectable quantities downstream at the claimants' borehole. That is different from a situation where, for example, a defendant stores quantities of a chemical known to be highly toxic in containers made to the very best standards of quality and safety. In the *Cambridge Water* case the idea of an escape from the defendants' land would simply never have occurred to anyone; in the other case the possibility would be recognised (which is why the precautions are taken) even if it would be regarded as far-fetched.

B. Escape

15–7   The requirement of escape, which demonstrates the connexion of the rule with nuisance, was firmly set in the law by the House of Lords' decision in *Read v J. Lyons & Co Ltd.*[59] The claimant was employed by the Ministry of Supply as an inspector of munitions in the defendants' munitions factory and, in the course of her employment there, was injured by the explosion of a shell that was being manufactured. It was admitted that high explosive shells were dangerous. The defendants were held not liable. There was no allegation of negligence on their part and *Rylands v Fletcher* was inapplicable because there had been no "escape" of the thing that inflicted the injury. "Escape" was defined as, "escape from a place where the defendant has occupation or control over land to a place which is

---

[56] [1994] 2 A.C. at 302.
[57] For the facts, see para.14–13, above.
[58] See also *Dempsey v Waterford Corp* [2008] IEHC 55.
[59] [1947] A.C. 156; *Transco Plc v Stockport MBC* [2003] UKHL 61; [2004] 2 A.C. 1 at [9], [34], [77].

outside his occupation or control".[60] Viscount Simon stated that *Rylands v Fletcher* is conditioned by two elements which he called (1) "the condition of 'escape' from the land of something likely to do mischief if it escapes", and (2) "the condition of 'non-natural' use of the land".[61] However, the House of Lords emphasised that the absence of an "escape" was the basis of their decision. The rule is probably inapplicable to a deliberate release of the thing, the cause of action in that situation being trespass.[62]

C. Land

The rule is not confined to the case where the defendant is the freeholder of the land on which the dangerous thing is accumulated: the defendant in *Rylands v Fletcher* itself appears to have had only a licence from the landowner to construct the reservoir. Similarly, the rule has been applied in cases where the defendant has a franchise or statutory right, for example to lay pipes to carry gas[63] or cables for electricity.[64] Indeed, there are statements to the effect that anyone who collects the dangerous thing and has control of it at the time of the escape would be liable,[65] even when it is being carried on the highway and escapes therefrom.[66] A landowner who is not in occupation of the land when the thing escapes is probably liable if he has authorised the accumulation.[67] As to the status of the claimant, the position is governed by the fact that the rule is an offshoot or variety of private nuisance and in *Hunter v Canary*

15–8

---

[60] Viscount Simon [1947] A.C. 156 at 168 and at 177 per Lord Porter: "Escape from the place in which the dangerous object has been maintained by the defendant to some place not subject to his control".

[61] [1947] A.C. 167 at 173 per Lord Macmillan, "Escape . . . and non-natural use of the land, whatever precisely that may mean."

[62] *Rigby v CC Northamptonshire* [1985] 1 W.L.R. 1242 (firing of CS gas canister). Doubted, unless the thing is aimed at the claimant, in *Crown River Cruises v Kimbolton Fireworks* [1996] 2 Lloyd's Rep. 533. See also *Smeaton v Ilford Corp* [1954] Ch. 450 at 462.

[63] *Northwestern Utilities Ltd v London Guarantee Ltd* [1936] A.C. 108 at 118. Cf. *Read v Lyons* [1947] A.C. 156 at 183.

[64] *Charing Cross Electricity Supply Co v Hydraulic Power Co* [1914] 3 K.B. 772; but if C has an easement to have e.g. a gas main in D's land and there is an escape from one part of D's land to the part where the easement is located there is no "escape" for the purposes of the rule: *Transco Plc v Stockport MBC* [2003] UKHL 61; [2004] 2 A.C. 1 at [80] (only Lord Scott decided the case on this basis).

[65] *Rainham Chemical Works v Belvedere Fish Guano Co* [1921] 2 A.C. 465 at 479.

[66] *Powell v Fall* (1880) 5 Q.B.D. 597; *Rigby v CC Northamptonshire* [1985] 1 Q.L.R. 1242. See also *Crown River Cruises v Kimbolton Fireworks* [1995] 2 Lloyd's Rep. 533. But as to whether under the general law of nuisance the defendant needs to be the occupier of land from which the invasion comes see para.14–17, above.

[67] See *Rainham Chemical Works* case, above, fn.65, at 476, 489. The point actually at issue was whether the defendants had sufficiently divested themselves of occupation of the premises so as to substitute sole occupation of a company.

Wharf Ltd[68] the House of Lords held that an interest in land or de facto exclusive possession of it was a necessary qualification to bring a claim in nuisance.[69] A number of earlier cases applying *Rylands v Fletcher* should probably therefore be regarded as wrongly decided on this basis alone.[70]

D. Personal Injury

15-9   Cases which have held[71] or assumed[72] that *Rylands v Fletcher* is applicable to personal injuries may have ignored the requirement of landholding status, but it is possible that an adjoining occupier might suffer personal injury,[73] in which case the question of the applicability of the rule to personal injuries has to be directly addressed. Again the relationship with nuisance is decisive and the strong indications in *Hunter v Canary Wharf* that such losses fall outside the scope of that tort[74] indicated that the same result would be reached under *Rylands v Fletcher,*[75] a proposition decisively accepted by the House of Lords in the *Transco* case.[76] However, there are cases which are regarded as falling under *Rylands v Fletcher* (or at least some cognate principle) where the liability is "strict" only in the sense that the defendant is liable for the fault of a wider range of persons than his servants in the course of his employment (liability for fire is an example[77]). Such cases are probably unaffected by *Hunter* and *Transco,*[78] though the fact that the issue has to be raised shows how imprecise are our concepts.

---

[68] [1997] A.C. 655, para.14–15, above.
[69] *McKenna v British Aluminium Ltd* [2002] Env L.R. 30.
[70] e.g. *Shiffman v Order of St John* [1936] 1 All E.R. 557; *Miles v Forest Rock Granite Co Ltd* (1918) 34 T.L.R. 500. Some of them might, however, be regarded as cases of public nuisance. In *Weller v Foot and Mouth Disease Research Institute* [1966] 1 Q.B. 569, Widgery J. held that the claimants, cattle auctioneers who suffered loss when sales of cattle were stopped during an outbreak of foot and mouth, could not sue under the rule because they had no interest in any land to which the virus escaped. However, it would have been sufficient to arrive at this result to apply the general principle that A cannot sue for financial loss which arises because of physical damage to the property of B.
[71] See previous note.
[72] *Perry v Kendricks Transport* [1956] 1 W.L.R. 85.
[73] As happened in *Hale v Jennings Bros* [1938] 1 All E.R. 579 (tenant of fairground stall) and *Benning v Wong* (1969) 122 C.L.R. 249.
[74] See para.14–15, above.
[75] However, the relationship also calls into question Lord Goff's doubts in *Hunter* as to whether nuisance covers damage to the property as opposed to interference with enjoyment of it ([1997] A.C. at 692). If that is the law of nuisance and *Rylands v Fletcher* follows the same principle, the rule in the case would in effect disappear.
[76] [2003] UKHL 61; [2004] 2 A.C. 1 at [9], [35], [52]; but this makes it difficult to accept the assertion in *Transco* that the background to *Rylands v Fletcher* was public concern about disasters causing widespread loss of life such as the Bradfield reservoir burst in 1864: at [28].
[77] See para.15–20, below.
[78] See *Ribee v Norrie* [2001] P.I.Q.R. P128, though the point was not raised.

E. Non-natural User[79]

We have already noted that Blackburn J. in the Court of Excheq- **15–10**
uer Chamber made no mention of this requirement. He did, however, make it plain that the principle he stated applied only to things
which the defendant collected for his own purposes. Hence he
cannot be liable under the rule merely for permitting a spontaneous
accumulation (for example, of water, vegetation or birds) on his
land,[80] or even for inducing a spontaneous accumulation as an
undesired byproduct of the normal working of the land.[81] However,
as a practical matter these principles have been much reduced in
importance by the recognition that an occupier may owe a duty of
care to abate a nuisance arising naturally on his land.[82]

It may well be that Lord Cairns in the House of Lords in *Rylands
v Fletcher* did not intend to add anything to Blackburn J.'s requirement that the defendant should have accumulated the dangerous
thing by positive action but it is recognised in *Cambridge Water Co
v Eastern Counties Leather Plc*[83] that the law has developed so as to
give the expression a meaning which excludes from the rule deliberate accumulations which are brought about by "ordinary" uses of
the land. The most frequently quoted "definition" is that given by
Lord Moulton, speaking for the Privy Council in *Rickards v
Lothian*.[84]

"It must be some special use bringing with it increased danger to
others and must not merely be the ordinary use of the land or such
a use as is proper for the general benefit of the community."

It would be hopeless to contend that all of the case law on this issue
is reconcilable and the *Cambridge Water* case may require that we
reconsider some of the earlier cases. However, the following propositions seem to represent the present state of the law.

1. Lord Porter said in *Read v Lyons*[85] that in deciding the ques- **15–11**
tion of non-natural user:

---

[79] Williams, "Non-Natural Use of Land" [1973] C.L.J. 310.
[80] *Giles v Walker* (1890) 24 Q.B.D. 656 (thistledown); *Pontardawe RDC v Moore-Gwyn*
[1929] 1 Ch. 656 (falls of rocks); *Sparkes v Osborne* (1906) 7 C.L.R. 51; *Seligman v
Docker* [1949] Ch. 53.
[81] *Wilson v Waddell* (1876) 2 App. Cas. 95; *Smith v Kenrick* (1849) 7 C.B. 515. *Giles v
Walker*, above, fn.80, is in fact such a case, since the thistle crop had been produced for
unexplained reasons by the defendant's ploughing of some forest land.
[82] However, they remain relevant where there is a sudden disaster against which the occupier
cannot take steps: *Ellison v MoD* (1997) 81 B.L.R. 101 (flood produced by works at
airfield).
[83] [1994] 2 A.C. at 308.
[84] [1913] A.C. 263 at 279–280. See *Read v Lyons* [1947] A.C. 156 at 169; *Cambridge Water
Co v Eastern Counties Leather Plc* [1994] 2 A.C. at 308.
[85] [1947] A.C. at 176.

"[A]ll the circumstances of time and practice of mankind must be taken into consideration so that what may be regarded as dangerous or non-natural may vary according to the circumstances".

For this reason what may seem extraordinary to one generation may seem ordinary to its successor. At the time of the First World War the Court of Appeal held that keeping a motor car in a garage with petrol in a tank was a non-natural use of land,[86] a decision which may well have been dubious even at that time but, it is submitted, would be inconceivable today notwithstanding the doctrine of precedent.[87]

2. Notwithstanding the refusal to develop *Rylands v Fletcher* into a general principle of strict liability for ultra-hazardous activities, the effect of the case law seems to go some way along this road in its particular nuisance-related context by excluding from the scope of the rule minor or common or domestic uses of things which have some potential for danger. So the following have been regarded as natural or ordinary uses of land: water installations in a house or office[88]; the main water supply to a block of flats[89]; a fire in a domestic grate[90]; electric wiring[91]; gas pipes in a house or shop[92]; erecting or pulling down houses or walls[93]; burning stubble in the normal course of agriculture[94]; the ordinary working of mines or minerals[95]; the possession of trees whether planted or self-sown[96] or generating steam on a ship.[97] These are commonplace risks with which people must put up unless there is fault. There has, however, been a greater willingness to apply the rule to the

[86] *Musgrove v Pandelis* [1919] 2 K.B. 43.
[87] See *Transco Plc v Stockport MBC* [2003] UKHL 61; [2004] 2 A.C. 1 at [107] (even though in *Perry v Kendricks Transport Ltd* [1956] 1 W.L.R. 85 at 92 (coach left on parking ground after emptying tank) Parker L.J. considered *Musgrove v Pandelis* was binding on the CA).
[88] *Rickards v Lothian* [1913] A.C. 263. Cf. *Wei's Western Wear Ltd v Yui Holdings Ltd* (1984) 5 D.L.R. (4th).
[89] *Transco Plc v Stockport MBC* [2003] UKHL 61; [2004] 2 A.C. 1.
[90] *Sochacki v Sas* [1947] 1 All E.R. 344.
[91] *Collingwood v Home and Colonial Stores Ltd* [1936] 3 All E.R. 200.
[92] *Miller v Addie & Sons (Collieries) Ltd* 1934 S.C. 150.
[93] *Thomas and Evans Ltd v Mid-Rhondda Co-operative Society* [1941] 1 K.B. 381. Cf. *Gertsen v Municipality of Metropolitan Toronto* (1973) 41 D L.R. (3d) 646 (landfill project using household waste which generated methane gas, not a natural user).
[94] *Perkins v Glyn* [1976] R.T.R. ix (note). Cf. in the somewhat different climatic conditions of New Zealand, *New Zealand Forest Products Ltd v O'Sullivan* [1974] 2 N.Z.L.R. 80, where, however, negligence was clearly established.
[95] *Rouse v Gravelworks Ltd* [1940] 1 K.B. 489.
[96] *Noble v Harrison* [1926] 2 K.B. 332. Cf. *Crowhurst v Amersham Burial Board* (1878) 4 Ex.D. 5 (poisonous yew tree).
[97] *Howard v Furness Ltd* [1936] 2 All E.R. 781; *Eastern Asia Navigation Co Ltd v Freemantle* (1951) 83 C.L.R. 353 (fuel oil store a natural user); *Miller Steamship Co Pty Ltd v Overseas Tankship (UK) Ltd* [1963] 1 Lloyd's Rep. 402 at 426.

bulk storage or transmission of water[98] or gas or electricity,[99] or to the bulk storage of chemicals,[100] or combustible materials,[101] though the defence of statutory authority has in many cases prevented a decision in the claimant's favour.

3. Blackburn J.'s reference to the defendant collecting the dangerous thing "for his own purposes" does not mean that he must be seeking to profit from the activity; indeed, in one case the phrase was said not to be a sufficient reason to refuse to apply the rule to a local authority which was required by statute to receive sewage into its sewers.[102] However, there has sometimes been a marked tendency to say that a use is natural where it leads to a public benefit, whether by way of the provision of public services[103] or by manufacturing,[104] a course which requires the court either to make very difficult value judgments or to deprive the rule of all practical effect. In *Rainham Chemical Works Ltd v Belvedere Fish Guano Co Ltd*[105] it was assumed without argument that the manufacture of military explosives during the First World War was a non-natural use but on similar facts in the Second World War in *Read v Lyons* Viscount Simon and Lord Macmillan suggested that this might not be so because of the urgent public necessity for munitions in time of war.[106] That seems a utilitarian extension too far[107] and the House of Lords in the *Cambridge Water* case said that the rule would not be excluded merely because the activity was one which provided employment and was

---

[98] *Rylands v Fletcher* itself. Cf. *Transco*, above, fn.89.

[99] *Charing Cross Electricity Supply Co v Hydraulic Power Co* [1914] 3 K.B. 772; *Northwestern Utilities v London Guarantee and Accident Co* [1936] A.C. 108.

[100] *Cambridge Water Co v Eastern Counties Leather Plc* [1994] 2 A.C. 264.

[101] *Mason v Levy Auto Parts of England Ltd* [1967] 2 Q.B. 530; *Hobbs (Farms) Ltd v Baxenden Chemical Co Ltd* [1992] 1 Lloyd's Rep. 54; *L.M.S. International Ltd v Styrene Packaging and Insulation Ltd* [2005] EWHC 2065 (TCC); *Colour Quest Ltd v Total Downstream UK Plc* [2009] EWHC 540 (Comm), [2009] 1 Lloyds Rep 1. At 542 in *Mason* McKenna J. saw a close similarity between the way in which the concept of non-natural use is generally applied by the courts and the idea of unreasonable risk in negligence. Cf. the view of the Munich Court of Appeal in 1861 that, "running a railway using locomotives is necessarily and inevitably fault": Seuffert's *Archiv* 14 (1861) n.208, p.354.

[102] *Smeaton v Ilford Corp* [1954] 1 Ch. 459 at 469, 472.

[103] In *Dunne v NW Gas Board* [1964] 2 Q.B. 806 the CA was reluctant to hold a nationalised industry liable in the absence of fault and see the differing views on local authorities expressed by Lord Evershed M.R. and Denning L.J. in *Pride of Derby and Derby Angling Association Ltd v British Celanese Ltd* [1953] Ch. 149. In *Tock v St John's Area Metro Board* (1989) 64 D.L.R. (4th) 620 the Supreme Court of Canada declined to apply *Rylands v Fletcher* to a municipal drainage system.

[104] *British Celanese Ltd v A. H. Hunt Ltd* [1969] 1 W.L.R. 959 at 963–964: "The manufacturing of electrical and electronic components in the year 1964 . . . cannot be adjudged to be a special use . . . The metal foil was there for use in the manufacture of goods of a common type which at all material times were needed for the general benefit of the community."

[105] [1921] 2 A.C. 465.

[106] [1947] A.C. at 169, 174.

[107] *Transco Plc v Stockport MBC* [2003] UKHL 61; [2004] 2 A.C. 1 at [105].

778   *Strict Liability: Rule in Rylands v Fletcher*

therefore worthy of encouragement. Furthermore, it was said that the storage of substantial quantities of chemicals on industrial premises should be regarded as "an almost classic case of non-natural use" and this would be so even if the use was common or ordinary in the industry in question.[108] One cannot say that these storage activities are unreasonable in the nuisance sense for they may be very necessary, but they do impose an "exceptional risk", as those living in the vicinity of such twentieth century disasters as Rainham and Flixborough would no doubt agree.[109] Despite the fact that the *Cambridge Water* case shows a clear intention to prevent *Rylands v Fletcher* becoming a growing point in the general design of the common law, this aspect of the case may lead to a modest revival of the rule.

3. DEFENCES TO THE RULE

15–12 In *Rylands v Fletcher* possible defences to the rule were no more than outlined and we must look to later decisions for their development.

A. Consent of the Claimant
15–13 Where the claimant has expressly or impliedly consented to the presence of the source of danger and there has been no negligence on the part of the defendant, the defendant is not liable.[110] The exception merely illustrates the general defence, volenti non fit injuria. The main application of the principle of implied consent is found in cases where different floors in the same building are occupied by different persons and the tenant of a lower floor suffers damage as the result of water escaping from an upper floor, though it has to be said that the cases which have discussed this defence have tended to involve perfectly ordinary domestic fittings which would to modern eyes be a natural use of land.[111] In a block of premises each tenant can normally be regarded as consenting to the

---

[108] [1994] 2 A.C. at 309. In *Colour Quest Ltd v Total Downstream UK Plc* [2009] EWHC 540 (Comm); [2009] 1 Lloyds Rep 1 (the Buncefield oil depot explosion in 2005) the defendants conceded liability under *Rylands v Fletcher*, subject to the defence of consent by those within the perimeter of the area,

[109] See *Transco Plc v Stockport MBC* [2003] UKHL 61; [2004] 2 A.C. 1 at [104].

[110] *Gill v Edouin* (1894) 71 L.T. 762 72 L.T. 579; *Att Gen v Cory Bros Ltd* [1921] 1 A.C. 521 at 538, 543, 550. *Ross v Fedden* (1872) L.R. 7 Q.B. 661 and *Kiddle v City Business Properties Ltd* [1942] 1 K.B. 269 are cases of this type.

[111] Kadirgamar, "The Escape of Water from Domestic Premises" (1973) Conv(N.S.) 179. Cf. *Western Engraving Co v Film Laboratories Ltd* [1936] 1 All E.R. 106. In the *Transco* case at [61] Lord Hobhouse equates the cases in this category with the basic "live and let live" approach of ordinary nuisance law.

presence of water on the premises if the supply is of the usual character, but not if it is of quite an unusual kind, or defective or dangerous, unless he actually knows of that. The defendant is liable if the escape was due to his negligence.[112]

B. Common Benefit

Where the source of the danger is maintained for the common benefit of the claimant and the defendant, the defendant is not liable for its escape. This is akin to the defence of consent of the claimant, and Bramwell B. in *Carstairs v Taylor*[113] treated it as the same thing. In *Peters v Prince of Wales Theatre (Birmingham) Ltd*,[114] the Court of Appeal regarded "common benefit" as no more than an element (although an important element) in showing consent. In other judicial dicta the exception has been regarded as an independent one.[115] One passage in the *Cambridge Water* case[116] suggests that the rule may be inapplicable to the provision of services to a defined area such as a business park or an industrial estate, but this statement is made in the context of non-natural use. The view that there is a defence of common benefit among consumers of a generally supplied service like gas or electricity seems inconsistent with that case.[117] On balance, common benefit seems redundant (and indeed misleading) as an independent defence.

15–14

C. Act of Stranger

If the escape was caused by the unforeseeable act of a stranger, the rule does not apply. In *Box v Jubb*[118] the defendant's reservoir overflowed partly because of the acts of a neighbouring reservoir owner and the defendant escaped liability. The claimant also failed in his claim in *Rickards v Lothian*[119] where some third person deliberately blocked up the waste pipe of a lavatory basin in the defendant's premises, thereby flooding the claimant's premises.[120] It

15–15

---

[112] *Prosser v Levy* [1955] 1 W.L.R. 1224 at 1233, CA; *Colour Quest Ltd v Total Downstream UK Plc* [2009] EWHC 540 (Comm); [2009] 1 Lloyds Rep 1 (reviewing previous cases and taking the view that where there is negligence the *Rylands v Fletcher* claim remains and is not simply merged into the tort of negligence).

[113] (1871) L.R. 6 Ex. 217. So too, *Northwestern Utilities Ltd v London Guarantee Co Ltd* [1936] A.C. 108 at 120 and *Gilson v Kerrier RDC* [1976] 1 W.L.R. 904.

[114] [1943] 1 K.B. 73 at 78.

[115] *Gill v Edouin* (1894) 72 L.T. 579; *Anderson v Oppenheimer* (1880) L.R. 5 Q.B.D. 602.

[116] [1994] 2 A.C. at 308.

[117] Cf. *Dunne v NW Gas Board* [1964] Q.B. 806 at 832.

[118] (1879) 4 Ex.D. 76

[119] [1913] A.C. 263.

[120] Also *Perry v Kendricks Transport Ltd* [1956] 1 W.L.R. 85 (child threw a match into an empty petrol tank which exploded and injured the claimant—defendants not liable); but as to personal injury, see, para.15–9, above.

has been suggested that the defence is limited to the "mischievous, deliberate and conscious act of a stranger",[121] and therefore excludes his negligent acts. However, as Jenkins L.J. pointed out in *Perry v Kendricks Transport Ltd*[122] the basis of the defence is the absence of any control by the defendant over the acts of a stranger on his land and therefore the nature of the stranger's conduct is irrelevant. The onus is on the defendant to show that the escape was due to the unforeseeable act of a stranger without any negligence on his own part. If, on the other hand, the act of the stranger could reasonably have been anticipated or its consequences prevented, the defendant will still be liable. In *Northwestern Utilities Ltd v London Guarantee and Accident Co Ltd*,[123] a hotel belonging to and insured by the claimants was destroyed in a fire caused by the escape and ignition of natural gas. The gas had percolated into the hotel basement from a fractured welded joint in an intermediate pressure main situated below street level and belonging to the defendants, a public utility company. The fracture was caused during the construction of a storm sewer, involving underground work beneath the defendants' mains, by a third party. The Privy Council accepted that the defences of act of God and act of third party prevent a claimant from succeeding in a claim based on the rule in *Rylands v Fletcher* but held the defendants liable for negligence. The risk involved in the defendants' operations was so great that a high degree of care was expected of them. They knew of the construction of the sewer, and they ought to have appreciated the possibility of damage to their mains and taken appropriate action to prevent or rectify it.

It is clear that a trespasser is a "stranger" for this purpose.[124] For the defaults of his servants in the course of their employment, the occupier is of course liable; he is also liable for the negligence of an independent contractor[125] unless it is entirely collateral.[126] In the closely related context of liability for fire it has been held that the occupier is liable for the fault of his licensees or guests unless the act is wholly alien to the invitation[127] and this seems to be the general rule.

---

[121] *Perry v Kendricks Transport Ltd*, above, fn.120, at 87 per Singleton L.J. Similarly in *Prosser v Levy* [1955] 1 W.L.R. 1224 by the same judge.

[122] Above, fn.120, at 90. Similarly per Parker L.J. in *Smith v Great Western Ry* (1926) 42 T.L.R. 391 the negligent act of a third party (failing to ascertain a defect in an oil tank) was held to be a good defence, but this case was not brought to the attention of the court in *Prosser v Levy*.

[123] [1936] A.C. 108.

[124] *Mandraj v Texaco Trinidad Inc* (1969) 15 W.I.R. 251.

[125] *Balfour v Barty-King* [1957] 1 Q.B. 496 at 505–506 CA per Lord Goddard C.J. (the defendant has control of his independent contractor in that he chooses him, invites him to his premises to do work, can order him to leave at any moment, although it is left to the contractor how the work is to be done).

[126] See para.20–28, below.

[127] See para.15–20, below.

In connection with this exception to the rule in *Rylands v Fletcher*, we must consider whether the rule applies to a danger created on the premises by the occupier's predecessor in title. It may be inferred from the decision in the *Northwestern Utilities* case[128] that if the occupier knew, or might with reasonable care have ascertained, that the danger existed, he is liable for its escape. If, however, this condition is not satisfied, it is submitted that he ought not to be liable. There is no direct decision on the point, but the rule itself seems to make it essential that the defendant should "bring on his lands" the danger.[129]

It is evident from the *Northwestern Utilities* case that once the defendant proves the act of a stranger, the point is reached when a claim based on the rule in *Rylands v Fletcher* for practical purposes merges into a claim in negligence, so that if there is no fault the claimant will not succeed. By means of the defence of act of a stranger the basis of the liability is shifted from the creation of a risk to responsibility for culpable failure to control the risk. The rule in *Rylands v Fletcher* thus ceases to be available at the very moment when the claimant needs it. One can compare liability under the rule with the liability at common law for dangerous animals which was stricter.[130] It seems that the act of a stranger was not a valid defence in the case of the animal, because it was within the risk that must be accepted by anyone who knowingly chooses to keep a dangerous animal.

D. Statutory Authority

The rule in *Rylands v Fletcher* may be excluded by statute. **15–16** Whether it is so or not is a question of construction of the particular statute concerned. In *Green v Chelsea Waterworks Co*,[131] for instance, a main belonging to a waterworks company, which was authorised by Parliament to lay the main, burst without any negligence on the part of the company and the claimant's premises were flooded; the company was held not liable. On the other hand, in *Charing Cross Electricity Co v Hydraulic Power Co*[132] where the

---

[128] Indeed, from *Goldman v Hargrave* [1967] 1 A.C. 465 and associated cases: para.14–21, above.

[129] See also *Whitmores Ltd v Stanford* [1909] 1 Ch. 427 at 438.

[130] The new statutory liability is similarly strict, para.16–8, below.

[131] (1894) 70 L.T. 547 applied by the House of Lords in *Longhurst v Metropolitan Water Board* [1948] 2 All E.R. 834. Note, however, that since April 1, 1982 statutory water undertakers are strictly liable for damage (including personal injury) caused by an escape of water from a communication pipe or main under what is now the Water Industry Act 1991 s.209. This strict liability does not avail other statutory undertakers such as gas and electricity suppliers or highway authorities.

[132] [1914] 3 K.B. 772. Where there is negligence of the sort occurring in *Northwestern Utilities Ltd v London Guarantee Co Ltd* [1936] A.C. 108, statutory authority will be no defence.

facts were similar, the defendants were held to have no exemption upon the interpretation of their statute. The distinction between the cases is that the Hydraulic Power Co were empowered by statute to supply water for industrial purposes, that is, they had permissive power but not a mandatory authority, and they were under no obligation to keep their mains charged with water at high pressure, or at all. The Chelsea Waterworks Co were authorised by statute to lay mains and were under a statutory duty to maintain a continuous supply of water; it was an inevitable consequence that damage would be caused by occasional bursts and so by necessary implication the statute exempted them from liability where there was no "negligence".[133] Where a statutory authority is under a mandatory obligation to supply a service, whether with a savings or nuisance clause (that nothing shall exonerate it from proceedings for nuisance) or whether without such a clause, the authority is under no liability for anything expressly required by statute to be done, or reasonably incidental to that requirement, if it was done without negligence.[134] Where the statutory authority is merely permissive, with no clause imposing liability for nuisance, the authority is not liable for doing what the statute authorises, provided it is not negligent; but it is liable when there is a clause imposing liability for nuisance, even if it is not negligent.[135] As to the escape of water from reservoirs, even express statutory authority for their construction will not by itself exonerate their undertakers since the Reservoirs (Safety Provisions) Act 1930, now replaced by the Reservoirs Act 1975.[136] The Dolgarrog Dam disaster of 1925 led to the passing of this legislation. A reservoir 1,400 feet above sea level and holding 200 million gallons of water burst and caused great devastation and loss of life.

One important question in this area awaits a final answer: if, on its proper construction, the statutory authority exempts the undertaker from *Rylands v Fletcher* liability and imposes only an obligation to use due care, upon whom does the burden of proof lie? A bare

---

[133] *Smeaton v Ilford Corp* [1954] Ch. 450 at 475–477. "Negligence" in this connection is not a very appropriate word for it means, "adopting a method which in fact results in damage to a third person, except in a case where there is no other way of performing the statutory duty": per Farwell J. in *Provender Millers (Winchester) Ltd v Southampton CC* [1940] Ch. 131 at 140.

[134] *Department of Transport v NW Water Authority* [1984] A.C. 336.

[135] *Dunne v North Western Gas Board* [1964] 2 Q.B. 806 at 833–837.

[136] Section 28, Sch.2. However, things may not now be so simple. The wording is, "Where damage or injury is caused by the escape of water from a reservoir constructed . . . under statutory powers . . . the fact that the reservoir was so constructed shall not exonerate the persons for the time being having the management and control of the reservoir from any indictment, action or other proceedings to which they would otherwise have been liable." In other words, the question seems to turn on what their liability is at common law. At the time of the legislation it would have been widely thought that *Rylands v Fletcher* covered personal injuries, but now this is not so: para.15–9, above.

majority of the High Court of Australia[137] held that the burden lies upon the claimant to prove lack of such care but the contrary arguments of the minority seem more convincing in principle and allow for the grave difficulties facing a claimant with the task of proving negligence against the supplier of a public utility such as gas or electricity.

The potential effect of the European Convention on Human Rights on statutory authority to commit nuisance has been considered.[138] Similar questions could arise in relation to *Rylands v Fletcher*, but with the difference that we are now concerned with damage arising from an event rather than (as is normally the case in nuisance) restraining injurious activity. The answer depends on the position from which one starts: compensation for damage or compensation for damage caused by fault? The wider scope for strict liability in other European legal systems may be a significant factor here.

E. Act of God

Where the escape is caused directly by natural causes without human intervention in, "circumstances which no human foresight can provide against and of which human prudence is not bound to recognise the possibility",[139] the defence of act of God applies. This was recognised by Blackburn J. in *Rylands v Fletcher*[140] itself and was applied in *Nichols v Marsland*.[141] In this case the defendant for many years had been in possession of some artificial ornamental lakes formed by damming up a natural stream. An extraordinary rainfall, "greater and more violent than any within the memory of witnesses" broke down the artificial embankments and the rush of escaping water carried away four bridges in respect of which damage the claimant sued. Judgment was given for the defendant; the jury had found that she was not negligent and the court held that she ought not to be liable for an extraordinary act of nature which she could not reasonably anticipate.

Whether a particular occurrence amounts to an act of God is a question of fact, but the tendency of the courts nowadays is to restrict the ambit of the defence, not because strict liability is thought to be desirable but because increased knowledge limits the unpredictable. In *Greenock Corp v Caledonian Ry*,[142] the House of

15–17

---

[137] *Benning v Wong* (1969) 122 C.L.R. 249.
[138] See para.14–35, above.
[139] *Tennent v Earl of Glasgow* (1864) 2 M. (HL) 22 at 26–27 per Lord Westbury, approved by the House of Lords in *Greenock Corp v Caledonian Ry* [1917] A.C. 556.
[140] (1866) L.R. 1 Ex. 265 at 280.
[141] (1876) 2 Ex.D. 1.
[142] [1917] A.C. 556.

Lords criticised the application of the defence in *Nichols v Marsland*, and four of their lordships cast doubt on the finding of facts by the jury in that case.[143] The defendants constructed a concrete paddling pool for children in the bed of the stream and to do so they had to alter the course of the stream and obstruct the natural flow of the water. Owing to a rainfall of extraordinary violence, the stream overflowed at the pond, and a great volume of water, which would normally have been carried off by the stream, poured down a public street into the town and caused damage to the claimants' property. The House of Lords held that the rainfall was not an act of God[144] and that the defendants were liable. It was their duty:

> "[S]o to work as to make proprietors or occupiers on a lower level as secure against injury as they would have been had nature not been interfered with".[145]

Similar considerations apply to an extraordinary high wind[146] and an extraordinary high tide.[147] Lightning,[148] earthquakes, cloudbursts and tornadoes may be acts of God but there seems to be no English decision in which they have been involved.

In law, then, the essence of an act of God is not so much a phenomenon which is sometimes attributed to a positive intervention of the forces of nature, but a process of nature not due to the act of man[149] and it is this negative side which deserves emphasis. The criterion is not whether or not the event could reasonably be anticipated, but whether or not human foresight and prudence could reasonably recognise the possibility of such an event. Even in such limited form, however, this defence, like the defence of act of a stranger, shifts the basis of the tort from responsibility for the creation of a risk to culpable failure to control that risk. This has been criticised on the ground that an accidental escape caused by the forces of nature is within the risk that must be accepted by the defendant when he accumulates the substance on his land.[150] As

---

[143] [1917] A.C. 556 at 573–574, 575, 580–581.

[144] Or *damnum fatale*, the equivalent in Scottish law; but now it has been held that *Rylands v Fletcher* is not part of Scots law and the suggestion that it is, "is a heresy which ought to be extirpated": *R.H.M. Bakeries (Scotland) Ltd v Strathclyde Regional Council* 1985 S.L.T. 214 at 217 per Lord Fraser.

[145] [1917] A.C. at 579 per Lord Shaw.

[146] *Cushing v Walker & Sons* [1941] 2 All E.R. 693 at 695. "Before wind can amount to an act of God . . . the wind must not merely be exceptionally strong, but must be of such exceptional strength that no one could be reasonably expected to anticipate or provide against it" per Hallett J.

[147] *Greenwood Tileries Ltd v Clapson* [1937] 1 All E.R. 765 at 772 per Branson J.

[148] *Nichols v Marsland* (1875) L.R. 10 Ex. 255 at 260, dictum of Bramwell B.

[149] "Something in opposition to the act of man": Lord Mansfield in *Forward v Pittard* (1785) 1 T.R. 27 at 33.

[150] Particularly, Goodhart, "The Third Man" (1951) 4 C.L.P. 177; "Rylands v Fletcher Today" (1956) 72 L.Q.R. 184.

Scrutton L.J. put it in his strong dissenting judgment in *Att Gen v Cory Bros*, "the fact that an artificial danger escaped through natural causes was no excuse to the person who brought an artificial danger there".[151] Nevertheless, the defence, though rarely or never applied in practice, seems to be rooted in the law and brings the rule in *Rylands v Fletcher* closer to the tort of negligence.[152]

F. Default of the Claimant

If the damage is caused solely by the act or default of the claimant himself, he has no remedy. In *Rylands v Fletcher* itself, this was noticed as a defence.[153] If a person knows that there is a danger of his mine being flooded by his neighbour's operations on adjacent land, and courts the danger by doing some act which renders the flooding probable, he cannot complain.[154] So, too, in *Ponting v Noakes*,[155] the claimant's horse reached over the defendant's boundary, nibbled some poisonous tree there and died accordingly, and it was held that the claimant could recover nothing, for the damage was due to the horse's own intrusion and, alternatively, there had been no escape of the vegetation. Had it been grown there expressly for the purpose of alluring cattle to their destruction, the defendant would have been liable, not on the grounds of *Rylands v Fletcher*, but because he would have been in the position of one who deliberately sets traps baited with flesh in order to attract and catch dogs which are otherwise not trespassing at all.[156] Where the claimant is contributorily negligent, the apportionment provisions of the Law Reform (Contributory Negligence) Act 1945 will apply.

If the injury due to the escape of the noxious thing would not have occurred but for the unusual sensitiveness of the claimant's property, there is some conflict of authority whether this can be regarded as default of the claimant. In *Eastern SA Telegraph Co Ltd v Cape*

15–18

---

[151] (1919) 35 T.L.R. 570 at 574 (fall of refuse in Rhondda Valley probably caused by the saturation of its inferior strata by an extraordinary rainfall). Also *Dixon v Metropolitan Board of Works* (1881) 7 Q.B.D. 418 per Lord Coleridge C.J.

[152] See Buxton, "The Negligent Nuisance" (1966) 8 U. Malaya L.R. 7: the decision in *Nichols v Marsland*, "leaves very few cases where a defendant could be held liable who had not in fact been negligent". "Unless one can visualise the accumulation in circumstances which do not constitute an ordinary user of the land of something likely to do mischief if it escapes, and which does escape from the defendant's land neither by act of God nor of third party, everything that is within *Rylands v Fletcher* could also be negligence": Street (1965) I.C.L.Q. 862, 870. See also the *Transco* case [2003] UKHL 61; [2004] 2 A.C. 1 at [39].

[153] (1868) L.R. 3 H.L. 330 at 340. If the rule applies to a deliberate discharge of the thing (which is unlikely) necessity is as much a defence as in trespass: *Rigby v CC Northamptonshire* [1985] 1 W.L.R. 1242.

[154] *Lomax v Stott* (1870) 39 L.J. Ch. 834; *Dunn v Birmingham Canal Co* (1872) L.R. 7 Q.B. 244.

[155] [1894] 2 Q.B. 281. Cf. *Cheater v Cater* [1918] 1 K.B. 247.

[156] *Townsend v Wathen* (1808) 9 East 277.

Town Tramways Companies Ltd,[157] an escape of electricity stored and used by the defendants in working their tramcars, interfered with the sending of messages by the claimants through their submarine cable. The claimants failed to recover as no tangible injury had been done to their property—no apparatus had been damaged. The defendants' operations were not destructive of telegraphic communication generally, but only affected instruments unnecessarily so constructed as to be affected by minute currents of the escaping electricity. With regard to such instruments it was said, "A man cannot increase the liabilities of his neighbour by applying his own property to special uses, whether for business or pleasure." However, in *Hoare Co v McAlpine*,[158] where vibrations from pile-driving caused structural damage to a large hotel on adjoining land, Astbury J. held it to be a bad plea that the vibrations had this effect only because the hotel was so old as to be abnormally unstable but he found also that the evidence did not establish that it was in such a condition. Thus the question remains an open one, and it can hardly be said that the hotel proprietor had put his property to any special or unusually sensitive use.

4. REMOTENESS OF DAMAGE

15–19   The defendant under *Rylands v Fletcher* cannot be liable ad infinitum and in Blackburn J.'s formulation of the rule he, "is prima facie answerable for all the damage which is the natural consequence of its escape". The Privy Council in *The Wagon Mound (No.1)*[159] stated that their Lordships had not found it necessary to consider the rule in *Rylands v Fletcher* in relation to remoteness of damage but the *Cambridge Water* case, though it does not speak in terms of remoteness of damage, has the effect that reasonable foreseeability is the test.[160] There is no very compelling reason, indeed, why foreseeability should not be utilised as the test of remoteness in cases where it is irrelevant to the initial determination of liability: "granted that an escape takes place, albeit unforeseeably, what would a reasonable man regard as the foreseeable consequences of such an escape?"[161] It will also be recollected that so many qualifications have been placed upon the decision in *The Wagon Mound (No.1)* that the concept of foreseeability is now applied in a very

---

[157] [1902] A.C. 381 at 393; *Western Silver Fox Ranch Ltd v Ross and Cromarty CC* 1940 S.C. 601 at 604–606 (breeding silver foxes not a non-natural use of land).
[158] [1923] 1 Ch. 167.
[159] [1961] A.C. 388 at 427.
[160] See para.14–13, above.
[161] See para.6–18, above. *The Wagon Mound (No.2)* [1967] 1 A.C. 617 seems to support this view.

broad and liberal manner[162] and there is unlikely to be much practical difference between an inquiry whether a consequence is foreseeable or natural. The natural or foreseeable consequences of a dam
bursting are, inter alia, the inundation of subjacent land, damage to
buildings, roads and personal injury (though the last is, as we have
seen, irrecoverable under this rule for different reasons). If the water
flows into the shaft of an adjoining mine, with the result that the
mine cannot be worked for six months, the mine owner may recover
damages, but the miners who lose their wages during that period
have no remedy,[163] not because the loss is "unnatural" or "unforeseeable" but because, (1) they have no sufficient interest in the
mine, or (2), which in effect amounts to the same thing, it is a loss
of a type for which the law restricts recovery.[164] Even if the escaping
water flows into a carbide factory and thereby generates gas which
causes a tremendous explosion it is unlikely that much will be
achieved by seeking to draw distinctions between what is natural
and foreseeable. As in all such cases the issue is finally one of legal
policy.

5. FIRE

A. Common Law

Winfield traced the history of the earlier forms of action available   **15–20**
as remedies for damage caused by the spread of fire.[165] The usual
remedy was the special action of trespass on the case for negligently
allowing one's fire to escape in contravention of the general custom
of the realm which we first hear of in *Beaulieu v Finglam*.[166] The
allegation in the action for fire that the defendant *tam negligenter ac
improvide* "kept his fire that it escaped", referred to negligence in its
older sense—one mode of committing a tort. Centuries later remedies became available under the rule in *Rylands v Fletcher*[167] in

---

[162] See para.6–20, above.
[163] *Cattle v Stockton Waterworks Co* (1875) L.R. 10 Q.B. 453 at 457; *Pride v Institute for Animal Health* [2009] EWHC 685 (QB).
[164] See para.5–40, above and *Shell UK Ltd v Total UK Ltd* [2010] EWCA Civ 180 at [151].
[165] Winfield (1926) 42 L.Q.R. 46–50, or *Select Essays*, pp.25–28 and (1931) 4 C.L.J. 203–206 Newark (1945) 6 N.I.L.Q. 134–141 Ogus, "Vagaries in Liability for the Escape of Fire" [1969] C.L.J. 104.
[166] (1401) Y.B. Pashc. 2 Hen. 4, f. 18, pl. 6, translated in Fifoot, *History and Sources of the Common Law*, p.166.
[167] *Jones v Festiniog Ry* (1866) L.R. 1 Ex. 265, fire included in "things likely to do mischief if they escape" and thus within *Rylands v Fletcher*; *Powell v Fall* (1880) 5 Q.B.D. 597; *Musgrove v Pandelis* [1919] 2 K.B. 43; *Job Edwards Ltd v Birmingham Navigations* [1924] 1 K.B. 341 at 351–352; *Collingwood v Home and Colonial Stores Ltd* [1936] 3 All E.R. 200 at 205; *Balfour v Barty-King* [1957] 1 Q.B. 496 at 505, CA (Lord Goddard C.J. deals with the history of the action on the case from its origin to modern times).

nuisance[168] and in negligence.[169] Although it is repeatedly said that at common law a person must keep his fire "at his peril", research shows that we cannot be sure that at any period in the history of the common law he was absolutely liable for the escape of his fire.[170] He is liable for damage done by his fire if it has been caused wilfully,[171] or by his negligence, or by the escape without negligence of a fire which has been brought into existence by some non-natural user of the land. It has been pointed out that the last type of liability is not quite the same as liability under the rule in *Rylands v Fletcher* in that the thing accumulated on the land does not itself escape. The criterion of liability is:

> "Did the defendants . . . bring to their land things likely to catch fire, and keep them there in such conditions that if they did ignite the fire would be likely to spread to the claimant's land?"[172]

With this qualification liability is the same as under the rule in *Rylands v Fletcher.*

Exactly what "negligenter" meant can only be conjectured, for the old authorities are confused, but it certainly excluded liability where the fire spread or occurred (1) by the act of a stranger[173] over whom he had no control, such as a trespasser,[174] and (2) by the act of nature. He is responsible for the default of his servant,[175] his guest[176] or one entering his house with his leave[177] and for his independent contractor,[178] unless the act done is wholly alien to the

---

[168] *Spicer v Smee* [1946] 1 All E.R. 489.

[169] Bankes L.J. in *Musgrove v Pandelis* [1919] 2 K.B. 43 at 46 per Scrutton L.J.; *Job Edwards Ltd v Birmingham Navigations* [1924] 1 K.B. 341 at 361.

[170] Winfield (1926) 42 L.Q.R. 46–50 or *Select Essays*, pp.26–29

[171] If the damage is intentional it is a trespass or assault, e.g. deliberately throwing a lighted match on a haystack or a lighted firework in a person's face.

[172] *Mason v Levy Auto Parts of England Ltd* [1967] 2 Q.B. 530 at 542 per MacKenna J. If the damage is to persons or goods on the property on which the fire starts the only liability is for negligence: *Johnson v B.J.W. Property Developments Ltd* [2002] EWHC 1131 (TCC); [2002] 3 All E.R. 574 at [32].

[173] *Balfour-King* [1957] 1 Q.B. 496 at 504; *Tuberville v Stamp* (1697) 1 Ld. Raym. 264; *H.N. Emanuel Ltd v GLC* [1971] 2 All E.R. 835

[174] Unless the occupier has knowledge of the fire and fails to take steps to extinguish it within a reasonable time.

[175] A servant acting outside the course of his employment is a stranger: *McKenzie v McLeod* (1834) 10 Bing. 385.

[176] *Crogate v Morris* (1617) 1 Brownl. 197; *Iverson v Purser* (1990) 73 D.L.R. (4th) 33.

[177] *Ribee v Norrie* [2001] P.I.Q.R. P128; *Boulcott Golf Club Inc v Engelbrecht* [1945] N.Z.L.R. 553; *Erikson v Clifton* [1963] NZLR 705.

[178] *Balfour v Barty-King* [1957] 1 Q.B. 496 (defendant was held liable for a fire caused by an independent contractor whom he employed to thaw frozen pipes in an attic which contained large quantities of combustible material. Contractor used blowlamp and caused a fire which spread and destroyed plaintiff's adjoining house); *H.N. Emanuel Ltd v GLC* [1971] 2 All E.R. 835; *Johnson v B.J.W. Property Developments Ltd* [2002] EWHC 1131 (TCC); [2002] 3 All E.R. 574; *Spicer v Smee* [1946] 1 All E.R. 489 (as explained in *Johnson*).

permission to enter. The second exception was established in *Tuber-ville v Stamp*[179] where it was held that liability extended to a fire originating in a field as much as to one beginning in a house, but if the defendant kindles it at a proper time and place and the violence of the wind carry it to his neighbour's land, that is fit to be given in evidence. The common law liability still remains in all cases which are not covered by statutory provision.

B. Statutes

i. Fires beginning accidentally on the defendant's land. The **15–21** common law liability has been modified in respect of fires spreading from the defendant's land by the Fires Prevention (Metropolis) Act 1774,[180] which provides that no action shall be maintainable against anyone in whose building or on whose estate a fire shall accidentally begin. This section of the Act is of general application and is not limited to London.[181] In *Filliter v Phippard*[182] the word "acciden-tally" was interpreted restrictively so as to cover only, "a fire produced by mere chance or incapable of being traced to any cause".[183] In other words a fire caused by negligence[184] or due to a nuisance[185] will give rise to a cause of action.

The immunity of a defendant under the statute is illustrated by *Collingwood v Home and Colonial Stores Ltd.*[186] A fire broke out on the defendants' premises and spread to those of the claimant. It originated in the defective condition of the electrical wiring on the defendants' premises, but as there was no negligence on their part they were held not liable. Nor was the rule in *Rylands v Fletcher* applicable, for the installation of electric wiring, whether for domes-tic or trade purposes, was a reasonable and ordinary use of premises. Even if the fire is lit intentionally, providing it is lit properly, there is no liability if it spreads without negligence and causes damage,

---

[179] (1697) 1 Ld. Raym. 264.

[180] Section 86.

[181] *Filliter v Phippard* (1847) 11 Q.B. 347 at 355. Estate applies to land not built upon. The High Court has said that it is obsolete in Australia: *Burnie Port Authority v General Jones Pty Ltd* (1994) 120 A.L.R. 42 at 50. It was repealed in New Zealand by s.365 of the Law of Property Act 2007, seemingly on the ground that any common law liability stricter than that for negligence had been absorbed into *Rylands v Fletcher*.

[182] Above, fn.181.

[183] (1847) 11 Q.B. 347 at 357 per Denman C.J.

[184] e.g. *Mulholland and Tedd v Baker Ltd* [1939] 3 All E.R. 253 at 255 per Asquith J. (paper lit and inserted in drainpipe to smoke out a rat, fire spread to packing case and exploded drum of paraffin. Liable in negligence and under the rule in *Rylands v Fletcher*).

[185] e.g. *Spicer v Smee* [1946] 1 All E.R. 489 at 495 per Atkinson J. (defective electric wiring negligently installed by contractor caused fire, owner liable in nuisance or negligence; see the comments on this case in *Johnson v B.J.W. Property Developments Ltd* [2002] EWHC 1131 (TCC); [2002] 3 All E.R. 574 at [51]).

[186] (1936) 155 L.T. 550.

for example a spark jumps out of an ordinary household fire and causes it to spread.[187] It would be different, of course, if the fire were made too large for the grate.

However, the statute does not confer protection on one who was not at fault so far as the origin of the fire is concerned but who was negligent in letting it spread. In *Musgrove v Pandelis*,[188] the claimant occupied rooms over a garage and let part of the garage to the defendant who kept a car there. The defendant's servant, who had little skill as a chauffeur, started the engine of the car and without any fault on his part the petrol in the carburettor caught fire. If he had acted like any chauffeur of reasonable competence he could have stopped the fire by turning off the tap connecting the petrol tank with the carburettor. He did not do so and the fire spread and damaged the claimant's property. The defendant was held liable, for the fire which did the damage was not that which broke out in the carburettor but that which spread to the car and this second or continuing fire did not "accidentally" begin.[189] The same principle applies where the fire originated as a consequence of an act of nature so that in *Goldman v Hargrave*,[190] the statute provided no defence: the fire in the tree caused by the lightning strike was not the defendant's fault, but that which spread after his inadequate attempts to extinguish it was. The burden of proving such negligence is on the claimant: it is not for the defendant to prove that the fire was accidental.[191] Even though a claimant cannot prove negligence, if the fire originated from a non-natural user of the defendant's land, the Act of 1774 does not provide a defence and the defendant will be liable.[192]

15–22   **ii. Railway engines.** Practically obsolete, because of the demise of stream traction and the rather low value at the present day of the specified sums, the Railway Fires Acts 1905 and 1923 make a railway liable in a sum not exceeding £3,000 for fire damage to agricultural land and crops caused by the emission of sparks from locomotives, even though the statutory authority under which the railway is operated would exclude any common law strict liability.[193]

---

[187] *Sochacki v Sas* [1947] 1 All E.R. 344. Cf. *New Zealand Forest Products Ltd v O'Sullivan* [1974] 2 N.Z.L.R. 80 at 84.
[188] [1919] 2 K.B. 43.
[189] See also *Sturge v Hackett* [1962] 1 W.L.R. 1257.
[190] [1967] 1 A.C. 645. See para.14–21, above.
[191] *Mason v Levy Auto Parts of England Ltd* [1967] 2 Q.B. 530 at 538.
[192] [1967] 2 Q.B. 530 at 540–541. MacKenna J. after reviewing the authorities felt bound to follow them but did so reluctantly: "In holding that an exemption given to accidental fires, 'any law usage or custom to the contrary notwithstanding,' does not include fires for which liability might be imposed on the principle of *Rylands v Fletcher*, the Court of Appeal (in *Musgrove v Pandelis*) went very far."
[193] See further the 13th edition of this work.

6. STRICT LIABILITY UNDER MODERN LEGISLATION

We saw, when considering nuisance, how that branch of the com-   **15–23**
mon law has been supplemented (indeed, in some respects almost
obliterated) by detailed statutory provisions governing pollution of
the environment. Most of this legislation is of a "regulatory" nature
and does not give rise to liability in damages.[194] The reader should
be aware, however, that recent years have seen the enactment of a
number of important statutory forms of liability in particular areas of
exceptional risk which go a long way towards avoiding the likelihood of protracted litigation inherent in the ill-defined nature of the
rules of strict liability at common law. Full accounts of these Acts
must be sought elsewhere but the following is a summary of the
civil liability aspects of some of the more important of them.[195]

A. Nuclear Incidents[196]

The major factors requiring the enactment of legislation on liabil-   **15–24**
ity for nuclear incidents were the risk of widespread damage, possibly involving losses of millions of pounds, from a single emission of
ionising radiations and the possible injustice in the Limitation Acts
owing to the long periods which might elapse between the impact of
ionising radiations on the claimant and his suffering ascertainable
damage.[197]

By the Nuclear Installations Act 1965 no person other than the
UK Atomic Energy Authority shall use any site for the operation of
nuclear plant unless a licence to do so has been granted in respect of
that site by the Minister. Liability arises only when there is a nuclear
incident which occurs at or in connection with certain nuclear
installations, or in the course of transport of nuclear substances, and
it can arise only in connection with licensed nuclear sites.[198] Section
7(1) enacts:

"It shall be the duty of the licensee to secure that—

---

[194] See para.14–1, above.
[195] See also the Gas Act 1965 s.14, which imposes virtually absolute liability for damage
caused by gas in underground storage and the Water Industry Act 1991 s.209, imposing
strict liability for burst mains (para.15–3, above). The strict liability of an aircraft operator
for ground damage is considered para.13–7, above.
[196] Street and Frame, *Law Relating to Nuclear Energy*; Tromans and Fitzgerald, *The Law of
Nuclear Installations and Radioactive Substances*.
[197] Street and Frame, op. cit., p.38. However, after the first Nuclear Installations Act in 1959,
the Limitation Act 1963 to some extent mitigated this problem in all personal injury cases
and this has been carried further by the Limitation Act 1980: Ch.26.
[198] Section 12.

(a) no such occurrence involving nuclear matter as is mentioned in subsection (2) of this section causes[199] injury to any person or damage to any property of any person other than the licensee, being injury or damage arising out of or resulting from the radioactive properties, or a combination of those and any toxic, explosive or other hazardous properties, of that nuclear matter and

(b) no ionising radiations emitted during the period of the licensee's responsibility—

(i) from anything caused or suffered by the licensee to be on the site which is not nuclear matter or

(ii) from any waste discharged (in whatever form) on or from the site,

cause injury to any person or damage to any property of any person other than the licensee."

The liability of the licensee under s.7(1)(a), once damage within the Act is proved to have resulted, is a strict one. There is no need to prove negligence on the part of anyone. Any person, other than the licensee, may sue provided he can prove "injury" (which means "personal injury"[200] and includes loss of life) or "damage to any property".[201] There is no need that the dangerous matter should "escape" from the site on which it was kept onto other land. The Act creates a statutory right of action for damages, where injury or damage has been caused in breach of a duty.[202] Where liability in respect of the same injury is incurred by two or more persons, both or all of those persons shall be treated as jointly and severally liable in respect of that injury or damage.[203] It is a defence that the breach of duty under the Act is attributable to hostile action in the course of any armed conflict,[204] but it is not a defence that it is attributable to a natural disaster, notwithstanding that the disaster is of such an

---

[199] Radiation injury can present acute problems of proof of causation. A multi-party suit alleging causation of leukaemia failed for this reason in 1993.

[200] Not merely worry, falling short of a psychiatric condition, about the risk of injury: *Magnohard Ltd v UKAEA* [2003] CSOH 362; 2003 S.L.T. 1083.

[201] It was held in *Merlin v B.N.F.L.* [1990] 2 Q.B. 557 that this does not cover radioactive contamination which devalues the property because of a perceived risk of personal injury. Cf. *Magnohard Ltd v UKAEA,* above, fn.200. However, it is wrong to say that the Act, in the field of property damage, applies only to livestock and crops, given the enormous dose that would be required to produce a change in inanimate property. There is "damage" if soil is contaminated and has to be removed: *Blue Circle Industries Plc v MoD* [1999] Ch. 289.

[202] Sections 12, 16.

[203] Section 17(3). i.e. two or more licensees, since only a licensee can be liable under the Act.

[204] Thus most acts of terrorism will not fall within this defence.

exceptional character that it could not reasonably have been fore-seen.[205] The amount of compensation payable may be reduced by reason of the fault of the claimant:

"[B]ut only if, and to the extent that, the causing of that injury or damage is attributable to the act of [the claimant] committed with the intention of causing harm to his person or property or with reckless disregard for the consequences of his act."[206]

Under the Law Reform (Contributory Negligence) Act 1945 both the degree of blameworthiness and the causative potency of the act have to be considered in reducing damages.[207] However, under the 1965 Act once the claimant is found to be intentional or reckless within the meaning of the subsection, the amount of the reduction rests solely on the extent to which the harm is caused by the claimant's act.[208] If after the claimant has been harmed his damages are increased by his failure to have proper medical attention, this failure by him to mitigate his damage would have prevented him from recovering that portion of his loss which is attributable to his omission, and it is doubtful whether s.13(6) of the 1965 Act has a different effect.[209] Section 12(1) provides that, "where any injury or damage has been caused in breach of a duty imposed" by the Act, then subject to certain exceptions, "no other liability shall be incurred by any person in respect of that injury or damage".[210] It seems, however, that there might be some other claim where the damage suffered by the claimant fell outside the scope of the Act.[211] Section 15(1) enacts that:

[205] Section 13(4)(a) and (b). Act of God, e.g. earthquake, is not a defence.
[206] Section 13(6).
[207] See para.6–53, above.
[208] Street and Frame, op. cit., p.60.
[209] Street and Frame, op. cit., p.60.
[210] In other words, all liability is "channelled" to the licensee. Contrast the statutory regime applicable to offshore oil installations, where, although a strict liability is imposed on the site operator, he is not inhibited in pursuing rights of indemnity or subrogation: *Caledonia North Sea Ltd v British Telecommunications Plc* [2002] UKHL 4; 2002 S.C. (HL) 117 at [7]. See Street and Frame, op. cit. pp.61–66. The effect of the subsection may be summarised as follows: "Where ionising radiations are emitted as a result of defective equipment provided under contract with the licensee by a supplier, the section, it seems, prevents a person who suffers personal injury in consequence from suing the manufacturer or supplier, however negligent they might have been. It seems to prevent the supplier from being contractually liable to indemnify the licensee against damages payable to the victim by the licensee. It may prevent licensees from invoking *Lister v Romford Ice and Cold Storage Co Ltd* (para.20–18, below) as a means of claiming an indemnity from the employee whose negligence actually caused the emission." The operation of s.12 if unaffected by the Consumer Protection Act 1987, Pt I.
[211] *Blue Circle Industries Plc v MoD, The Times*, December 11, 1996, where Carnwath J. considered escape of ionising radiation to be a classic example of *Rylands v Fletcher* (on appeal [1999] Ch. 289). Devaluation by contamination was treated as actionable at common law in *Highington v Ontario* (1989) 61 D.L.R. (4th) 190, but with little discussion.

"[N]otwithstanding anything in any other enactment, a claim under the Act shall not be entertained after the expiration of 30 years from the date of the occurrence which gives rise to the claim, or, where that occurrence was a continuing one, or was one of a succession of occurrences all attributable to a particular happening"

on a particular site, the date of the last event in the course of that occurrence or succession of occurrences is the relevant one. The period runs from the defendant's act, not from the infliction of damage. However, the licensee's liability is in fact limited to a period of 10 years.[212] He is required to make such provision (either by insurance or some other means) as the Minister may, with the consent of the Treasury, approve for sufficient funds to be available, currently up to a total of £140 million, to cover compensation during this period. In other cases (where the claim exceeds the statutory limit or after the expiry of 10 years) claims are to be directed to the Government, which satisfies them out of moneys provided by Parliament.[213]

The Act applies in certain circumstances to occurrences outside the UK.[214]

B. Oil Pollution

15–25   Chapter III of Pt VI of the Merchant Shipping Act 1995 imposes civil liability for oil pollution damage by ships and gives effect to the 1969 Convention on the subject and the Protocols thereto. Section 153 imposes liability on tanker owners[215] for damage caused by contamination resulting from the discharge or escape of oil, for the cost of reasonable preventative or clean up measures and for any damage caused by those measures.[216] "Damage" includes "loss"[217] but it is specifically provided that liability for:

"[I]mpairment of the environment shall be taken to be a liability only in respect of (a) any resulting loss of profits and (b) the cost

---

[212] Section 16.
[213] Sections 16, 18. The UK Atomic Energy Authority is not a "licensee" within the Act but the liabilities of a licensee are imposed upon it by s.8. The background international conventions are those of Paris (1960) and Brussels (1963). However, in 2004 Amending Protocols were signed (not yet in force) which would increase operators' liability to €700 million (about £620 million), set a 30-year time limit for claims against them and extend the scope of damage covered.
[214] Section 13(1) Street and Frame, op. cit., pp.74–85.
[215] There are equivalent provisions in s.154 for contamination caused by bunker oil (i.e. fuel) from other ships. Tanker bunkers are covered by s.153.
[216] By s.153(2) liability extends to the cost of emergency measures to prevent threatened contamination.
[217] Section 170(1).

of any reasonable measures of reinstatement actually taken or to be taken."[218]

Hence it seems that hoteliers or fishermen in the vicinity of a spill may sue for loss of livelihood, though this has been assumed rather than decided.[219]

The Act provides three defences,[220] namely, that the discharge or escape—

1. resulted from an act of war, hostilities, civil war, insurrection or an exceptional, inevitable and irresistible natural phenomenon[221] or
2. was due wholly to anything done or left undone by another person, not being a servant or agent of the owner, with intent to do damage[222] or
3. was due wholly to the negligence or wrongful act of a government or other authority in exercising its function of maintaining lights or other navigational aids.

The Act provides a complete code of liability of shipowners for such occurrence and any common law liability is generally abolished.[223] There are also provisions for compulsory insurance[224] and for limitation of liability.[225]

---

[218] Section 156(3).
[219] *Landcatch Ltd v International Oil Pollution Compensation Fund* [1999] 2 Lloyd's Rep. 316, but the statute does not extend to more remote sufferers, like persons who buy and sell on the fisherman's catch: *R.J. Tilbury & Sons (Devon) Ltd v Alegrete Shipping Co Inc* [2003] EWCA Civ 65; [2003] 1 Lloyd's Rep. 327.
[220] Section 155.
[221] Cf. "act of God", para.15–17, above.
[222] Thus the negligent act of a third party provides no defence.
[223] Section 153. This abolition extends to the liability of servants or agents of the owner and of salvors, but such persons may be liable for acts done with intent to cause damage or done recklessly in the knowledge that damage would probably result: s.153(1)(ii). Any existing common law liability would, of course, continue to apply to the owner or master of another ship colliding with the oil carrier.
[224] Section 163. Persons suffering damages who are unable to claim under the Act or who are affected by limitation of liability may receive compensation from the International Fund for Compensation for Oil Pollution Damage under the Act Pt VI Ch.IV. Where the damage exceeds both the shipowner's and the Fund's liability there may now be further recourse to a Supplementary Fund: see the Merchant Shipping (Pollution) Act 2006 and the Merchant Shipping (Oil Pollution) (Supplementary Fund Protocol) Order SI 2006/1265. There have also been various voluntary compensation schemes, known by the endearing acronyms of CRISTAL, PLATO and TOVALOP (considered by the House of Lords in *Esso Petroleum Co Ltd v Hall Russell & Co Ltd* [1989] A.C. 643).
[225] Section 157. The right to limit is lost if the damage, "resulted from anything done or omitted to be done by the owner with intent to cause any such damage . . . or recklessly and in the knowledge that any such damage . . . would probably result". This is along the lines of the general maritime limitation provision in the 1995 Act Sch.7. Cf. the old limitation-breaking formula of "actual fault or privity".

The Law Reform (Contributory Negligence) Act 1945 applies to proceedings under the Act.[226]

C. Waste Pollution[227]

15–26   A significant and controversial aspect of environmental damage is that caused by waste disposal, which has been governed by special legislation in this country since the Deposit of Poisonous Waste Act 1972.[228] The current legislation is Pt II of the Environmental Protection Act 1990. This is a large and complex body of regulatory and criminal law and reference should be made directly to the Act[229] but our concern here is that it imposes a measure of civil liability. Where any damage is caused by waste deposited on land, any person who deposited it, or knowingly caused or permitted it to be deposited is liable for that damage provided that the deposit constituted an offence under the Act.[230] Essentially, an offence will be committed where waste is, (1) deposited otherwise than in accordance with a waste management licence, or (2) kept, treated or disposed of otherwise than in accordance with such a licence, or (3) even if there is no contravention of any licence, the waste is treated, kept, or disposed of "in a manner likely to cause the pollution of the environment or harm to human health".[231] Waste is defined as a substance or object set out in Sch.2B[232] to the Act which the holder discards or intends or is required to discard.[233] The definition is wide enough to include almost anything that might be included within the ordinary meaning of that term and there is no requirement that it be known to represent a hazard when disposed of.[234] For the purpose of civil liability, recoverable damage is defined according to the usual standard formula as including personal injury and there can be no doubt that it also includes physical damage to property. Only one step further and no doubt still within the scope of actionable damage is some ongoing condition such as a foul smell, which might be the basis of an action for common law nuisance.[235] However, dumping

---

[226] Sections 153(8), 154(4). See Ch.6, above.
[227] See also the EC White Paper on Environmental Liability, para.14–1, above.
[228] Accumulation of waste might also be a statutory nuisance under the former Public Health Act, now the Environmental Protection Act 1990 Pt III.
[229] See annotations by Tromans in Current Law Statutes.
[230] Primarily under s.33(1).
[231] These concepts are defined in s.29. Since harm to human health includes "offence to any of [the] senses" this covers situations which would amount to a common law nuisance.
[232] Inserted by the Environment Act 1995, to comply with EC requirements.
[233] See the 1990 Act s.75(2), as amended by the 1995 Act. There are further requirements governing the disposal of "special waste" in regulations made under the 1990 Act s.62.
[234] See, however, the defences, below.
[235] Even an action for damages: *Bone v Seale* [1975] 1 All E.R. 787.

of noxious waste may cause "blight" on the neighbourhood, property values becoming reduced because of the threat of future personal injury or property damage. In a very similar situation under the Nuclear Installations Act 1965 such a state of affairs has been held not to be "damage",[236] though neither the statutory formula nor the background is the same.

Liability is by no means absolute. A defendant escapes if he is able to prove that he took all reasonable precautions and exercised all due diligence to avoid the commission of an offence or that the acts were done in an emergency to avoid danger and the waste regulation authority was informed as soon as was reasonably practicable.[237] It does not, however, follow that this is merely a liability for negligence with a reversed burden of proof: for example, it would seem that civil liability would arise if waste were deposited on a site which was unlicensed even though the circumstances might not present any foreseeable danger to others.[238]

---

[236] See para.15–24, above.
[237] Section 33(7). Under s.33(7)(b) a servant acting under the instructions of his employer and who has no reason to believe an offence is being committed has a defence.
[238] This is because the "reasonable care and due diligence" defence goes to the commission of an offence, not the causing of damage.

CHAPTER 16

ANIMALS[1]

AT common law a person might be liable for damage caused by an **16–1** animal on one or more of three distinct grounds, namely ordinary liability in tort, liability under the strict *scienter* rule[2] and liability for cattle trespass. The law was substantially modified with regard to two of these matters by the Animals Act 1971[3] but its structure is still in large measure the same and it is convenient to retain the common law headings for the purposes of exposition.[4]

1. Ordinary Liability in Tort

There are many possible ways in which one may incur tortious **16–2** liability through the instrumentality of an animal under one's control, but the fact that the agent happens to be animate rather than inanimate is immaterial, for while the common law, like other legal

---

[1] The common law on this topic is covered by the exhaustive monograph of Glanville Williams, *Liability for Animals*. There are believed to be about 10 million dogs and one million horses in the UK.

[2] This expression is properly confined to liability for animals which do not belong to a dangerous species, but is commonly used in the wider sense used here.

[3] The Act came into force on October 1, 1971. The leading study of the modern law is North, *The Modern Law of Animals*. See too Law Commission, Civil Liability for Animals, Law Com. No.13 (1967). The Pearson Commission recommended no change in the law: Cmnd. 7054, Vol. 1, Ch.30.

[4] For the previous law, see the 8th edn of this work, Ch.17, and Law Com. No.13 (1967).

systems, developed special or additional rules of liability for animals, it did not deny the applicability to them of general law. A good example of this is nuisance, for you can be liable for nuisance through the agency of your animals, just as you can be for nuisance through the agency of anything else you own. A person who keeps pigs too near his neighbour's house commits a nuisance, but that is not solely because they are pigs. He would commit a nuisance just as much if what he owned were a manure heap. There is no independent tort called "nuisance by pigs", or "nuisance by animals".[5] Indeed, nuisance may be the only appropriate remedy where there is no "escape" and where the animal is not dangerous, for example obstruction of the highway by large numbers of animals,[6] or stench from pigs[7] or the crowing of cockerels.[8] While at one time there was no liability for the escape of noxious animals on the defendant's land in the ordinary course of nature, such as rabbits, rats or birds,[9] and he only incurred liability for damage by them to neighbouring owners if it was caused by "extra-ordinary, non-natural or unreasonable action",[10] it seems that the modern law follows the principle that a landowner may be required to take steps against a situation which is not attributable to his actions.[11]

Again, if a dog owner deliberately sets his dog on a peaceable citizen he is guilty of assault and battery in the ordinary way just as if he had flung a stone or hit him with a cudgel.[12] So, too, if a person teaches his parrot to slander anyone, that is neither more nor less the ordinary tort of defamation than if he prefers to say it with his own tongue rather than with the parrot's. Similarly, ordinary trespass can be committed by means of animals. Trespass by beasts so often takes the form of "cattle trespass" (with which we deal separately) that one does not meet with many ordinary actions for trespass in the reports. However an indirect example is *Paul v Summerhayes*[13]

---

[5] *Pitcher v Martin* [1937] 3 All E.R. 918 illustrates negligence and nuisance committed through the agency of a dog; *Farrer v Nelson* (1885) 15 Q.B.D. 258 nuisance through the agency of pheasants (distinguished in *Seligman v Docker* [1949] 1 Ch. 53).

[6] *Cunningham v Whelan* (1917) 52 Ir.L.T. 67.

[7] *Aldred's Case* (1610) 9 Co. 57b; *Wheeler v J.J. Saunders Ltd* [1996] Ch. 19.

[8] *Leeman v Montagu* [1936] 2 All E.R. 1677. In *Clarkson v Bransford* (1987, Huddersfield County Court) the claimant recovered damages for nervous shock in nuisance and negligence in respect of the escape of the defendant's non-dangerous snakes from his house into hers. The defendant kept 24 snakes in the attic (Kemp & Kemp, *Quantum of Damages*, June 1987 issue).

[9] *Brady v Warren* [1900] 2 Ir. 636 (rabbits); *Seligman v Docker* [1949] 1 Ch. 53 (wild pheasant increasing in numbers owing to favourable weather conditions).

[10] *Farrer v Nelson* (1885) 15 Q.B.D. 258 at 260 (nuisance by unreasonable number of pheasants brought onto the land); *Peech v Best* [1931] 1 K.B. 1 at 14; *Seligman v Docker* [1949] 1 Ch. 53 at 61–63.

[11] *Wandsworth LBC v Railtrack Plc* [2001] EWCA Civ 1236.

[12] *Roberts v CC Kent* [2008] EWCA Civ 1588 (where the action was justified under s.3 of the Criminal Law Act 1967).

[13] (1878) 4 Q.B.D. 9; *League against Cruel Sports v Scott* [1986] Q.B. 240.

where fox hunters persisted in riding over the land of a farmer in spite of his protests and were held to have committed trespass.

Liability for animals may also be based on negligence:

"Quite apart from the liability imposed upon the owner of animals or the person having control of them by reason of knowledge of their propensities, there is the ordinary duty of a person to take care either that his animal or his chattel is not put to such a use as is likely to injure his neighbour—the ordinary duty to take care in the cases put upon negligence."[14]

In an action based upon the breach of such a duty to take care, the ordinary rules in an action of negligence apply. The action for negligence for harm done through animals was quite distinct from both the cattle trespass rule and the *scienter* rule at common law[15] and now is distinct from the various forms of strict liability imposed by the Animals Act 1971.[16] In one respect, however, the common law failed to extend the principles of negligence to cases involving animals. It was the rule for centuries that if animals (or at least, ordinary tame animals) strayed from adjacent land on to the highway neither the owner of the animals nor the occupier of the land was liable for any ensuing damage even though it could have been prevented by controlling the animal or by fencing.[17] This immunity was abolished by the Animals Act 1971,[18] so that where damage is caused by animals straying on the highway the question of liability is to be decided in accordance with the ordinary principles of negligence. It is provided, however, that if a person has a right to place animals on unfenced land, he is not to be regarded as in breach of a duty of care by reason only of his placing them there, so long as the land is in an area where fencing is not customary or is common land or a town or village green.[19] It is important to note

---

[14] *Fardon v Harcourt-Rivington* (1932) 146 L.T. 391 at 392 per Lord Atkin; *Searle v Wallbank* [1947] A.C. 341 at 359–360.

[15] See *Draper v Hodder* [1972] 2 Q.B. 556 (where a claim based upon *scienter* failed at the trial); *Smith v Prendergast, The Times,* October 18, 1984. Similarly, a claim might in some cases be founded upon the statutory variant of negligence created by the Occupier's Liability Act 1957. See North, *Modern Law of Animals,* p.176.

[16] *Jones v Whippey* [2009] EWCA Civ 452.

[17] *Searle v Wallbank* [1947] A.C. 341. The immunity had no application where the animal was brought on to the highway and then got out of control: *Gomberg v Smith* [1963] 1 Q.B. 25.

[18] Section 8, which Lord Hailsham L.C. referred to as, "the only [section] which it is really worth enacting": *Hansard,* HL, Vol. 312, cols 887–888.

[19] Section 8(2). Like many "by reason only" exceptions, this subsection is a fertile source of difficulties. Even without it, the owner would not be liable by reason only of placing his animals there, for there would have to be sufficient traffic to create a serious danger. For various problems of interpretation, see North, *Modern Law of Animals* pp.157–160. The subsection was applied in *Davies v Davies* [1975] Q.B. 172 but the case turned largely on the right of a commoner to license others to graze animals.

that the Act does not require all landowners to fence against the highway: in moorland areas of Wales and the north of England this would be an intolerable burden and in such areas a motorist must be expected to be on the look out for straying livestock.[20] That is not to say that the burden imposed by s.8 is trivial: the Court of Appeal has held that the duty of care of the farmer extends to guarding against the carelessness of hikers lawfully on his land, and may require the provision of stiles, so enabling a stock gate to be secured.[21] Furthermore, there are situations in which the escape of animals attracts strict liability under s.2(2).[22]

2. Liability for Dangerous Animals

16–3   At common law the keeper of an animal was strictly liable, independently of negligence, for damage done by the animal if (1) the animal was *ferae naturae* (i.e. belonged to a dangerous species) or (2) the animal was *mansuetae naturae* (i.e. did not belong to a dangerous species) and he knew of its vicious characteristics. These forms of strict liability have been retained by the Animals Act 1971 and, though they have been subjected to considerable modification, some of the old learning may continue to be relevant. It is, however, important to remember that the only source of the law is now the words of the Act and these must always prevail.

A. Animals Belonging to a Dangerous Species

16–4   Where any damage is caused by an animal which belongs to a dangerous species, any person who is a keeper of the animal is liable for the damage.[23] A dangerous species is defined as:

> "[A] species[24] (a) which is not commonly domesticated in the British Islands and (b) whose fully grown animals normally have such characteristics that they are likely, unless restrained, to cause severe damage or that any damage they may cause is likely to be severe."[25]

A number of points arise on this definition. First, it seems that as was the case at common law in classifying animals as *ferae naturae*,

---

[20] For statistics on road accidents involving animals, see Law Com. No.13 (1967), paras 49–52. Dogs are in fact the major culprits apart, of course, from car drivers. There appear to be no up-to-date statistics.

[21] *Wilson v Donaldson* [2004] EWCA Civ 972.

[22] See para.16–6, below.

[23] Section 2(1). For the definition of "keeper", see below.

[24] By s.11 "species" includes sub-species and variety: see further para.16–5, below.

[25] Section 6(2).

the question of whether an animal belongs to a dangerous species is one of law for the court. It is therefore to be expected that where an animal had been classified as *ferae naturae* at common law it will be regarded as belonging to a dangerous species under the Act (for example a lion,[26] an elephant[27] and at least certain types of monkeys[28]). In two respects, however, the definition is wider than at common law in that the Act (1) renders a species dangerous if it poses a threat to property[29] and (2) allows for a species to be considered dangerous if it is not commonly domesticated in Britain, even though it may be so domesticated overseas.[30] Secondly it will remain the case that once a species has been judicially classified as dangerous, then, subject to the doctrine of precedent, there is no room for distinctions based upon the fact that some variants or individual animals within the species may not in fact be at all dangerous: in other words, the law continues to ignore:

"[T]he world of difference between the wild elephant in the jungle and the trained elephant in the circus . . . [which] is in fact no more dangerous than a cow".[31]

Furthermore, the Act clearly adopts as the test of danger either "the greater risk of harm" or "the risk of greater harm": an elephant may not in fact be very likely to get out of control and do damage, but if it does so, its bulk gives it a great capacity for harm.

---

[26] *Murphy v Zoological Society of London* [1962] C.L.Y. 68.

[27] *Behrens v Bertram Mills Circus Ltd* [1957] 2 Q.B. 1.

[28] Hale 1 P.C. 101. Cf. *Brooke v Cooke* (1961) 105 S.J. 684. As to other animals see Williams, *Liability for Animals*, pp.292–294. Bees are not *ferae naturae* at common law: *Stormer v Ingram* (1978) 21 S.A.S.R. 93. The Dangerous Wild Animals Act 1976 provides for a system of licensing of keepers of dangerous wild animals. Such animals are those listed in the Schedule to the Act and it is thought that such listing would be almost conclusive on the issue of whether the animal belonged to a dangerous species under the 1971 Act (none of the listed animals appears to be commonly domesticated here). Omission from the list should not, however, be particularly persuasive that the animal is not dangerous under the 1971 Act. Species such as the buffalo and hippopotamus were omitted because it was not thought likely that any attempt would be made to keep them privately (HL Vol. 371 col.1180) and the same presumably applied to the elephant and the camel. Under the 1976 Act the local authority must specify, as a condition of the grant of a licence, that the keeper maintains a liability insurance policy: s.6(a)(iv), (v). There is also compulsory insurance under the Riding Establishments Acts 1964 and 1970.

[29] The definition of "damage" in s.11 is not exhaustive, but does, it is submitted, include damage to property: see Law Com. No.13 (1967), para.15(iii).

[30] Thus a camel is dangerous under the Act, though not *ferae naturae* at common law: *Tutin v Chipperfield Promotions Ltd* (1980) 130 N.L.J. 807, not following *McQuaker v Goddard* [1940] 1 K.B. 687 (which probably applied the wrong test at common law, anyway).

[31] *Behrens v Bertram Mills Circus Ltd*, above, fn.27, at 14. However, it is not clear to what extent the common law was prepared to distinguish among sub-species and the same problem will arise under the Act: see para.16–5, below.

For the purposes of this form of liability a person is a "keeper" of the animal if:

"(a) [H]e owns the animal or has it in his possession or (b) he is the head of a household of which a member under the age of 16 owns the animal or has it in his possession and if at any time an animal ceases to be owned by or to be in the possession of a person, any person who immediately before that time was a keeper thereof . . . continues to be a keeper of the animal until another person becomes a keeper thereof . . . "[32]

B. Other Animals
16–5   Section 2(2) provides:

"Where damage is caused by an animal which does not belong to a dangerous species, a keeper[33] of the animal is liable for the damage if:

(a) the damage is of a kind which the animal, unless restrained, was likely to cause or which, if caused by the animal, was likely to be severe; and

(b) the likelihood of the damage or of its being severe was due to characteristics of the animal which are not normally found in animals of the same species or are not normally so found except at particular times or in particular circumstances; and

(c) those characteristics were known to that keeper or were at any time known to a person who at that time had charge of the animal as that keeper's servant or, where that keeper is the head of a household, were known to another keeper of the animal who is a member of that household and under the age of sixteen."

The purpose of this rather complex subsection is to preserve a liability akin to the old rule of *scienter* liability for tame animals: while you are strictly liable in any case for damage done by your tiger you are only strictly liable for damage done by your dog or

---

[32] Section 6(3). It is provided, however, by s.6(4) that where an animal is taken into and kept in possession for the purpose of preventing it from causing damage or of restoring it to its owner, a person is not a keeper of it by virtue only of that possession.

[33] One keeper may be liable to another keeper: *Flack v Hudson* [2001] Q.B. 698 (owner liable to bailee/rider of horse who did not know of its characteristics).

your horse if you have knowledge of some special dangerous characteristic.[34] This provision has come before the courts more frequently than other parts of the Act and has proved troublesome, as witnessed by the fact that it produces a regular stream of appellate decisions.

> "Unfortunately the language of section 2(2) is . . . opaque. In this instance the parliamentary draftsman's zeal for brevity has led to obscurity. Over the years section 2(2) has attracted much judicial obloquy."[35]

The first problem is the range of animals to which s.2(2) applies. Common experience shows that, say, Rottweilers are a good deal fiercer than spaniels, but it has been stated in the Court of Appeal (though the point was not argued) in a case concerning a bull mastiff that the category is "dogs",[36] the generality of which could not possibly be said to belong to a dangerous species under s.2(1). However, the Act defines "species" as including "sub-species and variety"[37] and it has been held in the rather different context of determining what are "abnormal characteristics" under s.2(2)(b) the proper comparators are other dogs of that breed.[38] However, even in the case of dogs of a breed commonly perceived to be fierce the argument that they are covered by s.2(1) would nearly always be defeated by the condition in that subsection requiring that such animals are not commonly[39] domesticated here.[40]

Once it has been determined whether s.2(2) applies at all, it is **16–6** essential to consider each of the requirements in turn.

Paragraph (a) follows the pattern of s.2(1) in adopting the likelihood (which means the foreseeable likelihood[41]) of injury or likelihood that any injury that may be caused will be severe. The second limb of this is not to be read as imposing any requirement that the

---

[34] The old *scienter* rule might be regarded as a primitive form of negligence under which the defendant was regarded, subject to certain defences, as being irrebutably presumed to be negligent in keeping the animal after he discovered its character. There is now liability for negligence under the general law but there is no doubt that the defendant may be liable under s.2(2) even if he is not negligent (in the modern sense) on the occasion in question: *Curtis v Betts* [1990] 1 W.L.R. 459.

[35] *Mirvahedy v Henley* [2003] UKHL 16; [2003] 2 A.C. 491 at [9].

[36] *Curtis v Betts*, above, fn.34, at 462. A contrary contention was not pursued at the trial.

[37] Section 11. For the common law, see North, *Modern Law of Animals*, pp.36–38.

[38] *Hunt v Wallis*, The Times, May 10, 1991. Indeed, this was in effect the approach to the same issue of the CA in *Curtis v Betts*, above, fn.34.

[39] Presumably, however, the test of whether a breed is commonly domesticated here would not be satisfied by showing that there were a tiny number here all kept as pets.

[40] If it be the case that there is a species (or sub-species or variety) which (a) normally and in all circumstances has dangerous characteristics and (b) is commonly domesticated here there would seem to be an illogical gap in the legislation since such animals fall under neither subsection.

[41] *Curtis v Betts*, above, fn.34, at 469.

likelihood that the injury will be severe must be related to any
abnormality in the animal. Alsatians are powerful dogs and if a
member of that breed does bite someone it is likely that the injury
will be severe[42]: it is unnecessary to show that the particular Alsa-
tian is unusually large or has unusually big teeth.[43] Paragraph (a) has
given rise to comparatively little difficulty but that may only be
because it has not been explored very deeply. It seems plain that
something is "likely" even though it does not reach the level of
being "more likely than not" but it is not clear exactly how far down
the scale of probability we can go: perhaps we can do no better than
say that the damage (or, where relevant, its severity) is something
which "might well happen"[44] or which is "reasonably to be
expected".[45] One might break one's neck by falling downstairs after
tripping over an escaped pet dormouse[46] but no one would suggest
that a dormouse was likely to cause death or injury. On the other
hand, it is probable that the requirement will be satisfied where, say,
horses escape on to a busy road.[47]

Paragraph (b) has been the source of the problems.[48] The first
limb deals with the straightforward case where the animal has
"permanent" characteristics which depart from the norm of the
species, for example a dog which has a propensity to attack humans
in all situations and without discrimination as to persons; the second
limb is a further, alternative basis for a claim and imposes liability
for damage caused by characteristics which may be normal to the
species but only manifest themselves at particular times or in particular circumstances, for example a bitch being aggressive when she
has pups[49] or a breed of dog having a tendency aggressively to
defend its "territory".[50] In other words,

> "[I]n such a case the animal's normal behaviour in abnormal
> circumstances is equated with a more vicious [animal's] abnormal
> behaviour in normal circumstances."[51]

---

[42] Note that the actual injury suffered does not have to be severe.

[43] *Curtis v Betts*, above, fn.34, at 463, 469. The contrary view in North, *Modern Law of
Animals*, p.56, perhaps fits the wording of the paragraph better but would be unduly
restrictive because it would limit its operation to rather unlikely cases.

[44] One of the interpretations offered by Neill L.J. in *Smith v Ainger, The Times*, June 5,
1990.

[45] Lord Scott's preference in *Mirvahedy v Henley* [2003] UKHL 16; [2003] 2 A.C. 491 at
[95]; but he thought this meant much the same as Neill L.J.'s suggestion. He did not accept
Neill L.J.'s alternative of "such as might happen".

[46] Lord Scott's example in *Mirvahedy v Henley*, fn.45, at [95].

[47] This was conceded in *Mirvahedy v Henley* and in *Jaundrill v Gillett, The Times*, January
30, 1996, though Lord Scott in *Mirvahedy* reserved his opinion.

[48] It is not in the same form as the Law Commission's original draft: see *Mirvahedy*, fn.45,
at [37].

[49] *Barnes v Lucille Ltd* (1907) 96 L.T. 680 (common law).

[50] *Curtis v Betts*, above, fn.34. See also *Cummings v Grainger* [1977] Q.B. 397.

[51] *Mirvahedy v Henley*, fn.45, at [142] per Lord Walker.

In *Mirvahedy v Henley*[52] horses owned by the defendants were terrified at night by persons unknown, broke down the fence and galloped onto a dual carriageway where one of them collided with the claimant's car and he suffered injury. Horses are not normally in a state of mindless panic but they will be when they are frightened and, for the majority of the House of Lords, their being frightened was "particular circumstances" for the purposes of the second limb. There is:

"[A]n implicit assumption of fact in section 2(2) that domesticated animals are not normally dangerous. But the purpose of paragraph (b) is to make provision for those that are. It deals with two specific categories where that assumption of fact is falsified. The first is that of an animal which is possessed of a characteristic, not normally found in animals of the same species, which makes it dangerous. The second is an animal which, although belonging to a species which does not normally have dangerous characteristics, nevertheless has dangerous characteristics at particular times or in particular circumstances. The essence of these provisions is the falsification of the assumption, in the first because of the departure of the individual from the norm for its species, in the second because of the introduction of special factors."[53]

The rival, unsuccessful interpretation, that the "second limb" is not an alternative basis of liability but merely explains the basic requirement of abnormality by recognising that in some circumstances even placid animals will react dangerously, is less consistent with the statutory wording but may be thought to reflect better policy, bearing in mind that the law of negligence is available as a fallback. Suppose, for example, that a road accident is caused by a panic-stricken deer which has escaped from a deer park. Despite the fact that there are deer parks, deer are presumably not commonly domesticated in this country, yet it would be impossible to say that deer in general satisfied the requirement of "species dangerousness" in s.6(2)(b). Yet, on the basis that the owner of this particular deer can hardly deny that he knows that deer may panic on the highway at night, we have:

"[T]he paradoxical situation in which on the one hand deer are removed by section 6(2)(b) from being categorised as a 'dangerous species' but on the other hand an individual deer may impose

[52] Above, fn.45.
[53] At [71] per Lord Hobhouse.

strict liability on its keeper under section 2(2)(b) for damage caused by behaviour entirely normal for the species."[54]

As things stand, the owner of the animal is in danger of finding himself in a cleft stick: either the behaviour was abnormal by the general standards of the species or, even if it was normal in that sense, the behaviour was produced by the particular circumstances. Suppose, for example, that the claimant kicks a dog and the dog bites him. The owner can hardly be heard to deny that he knew that dogs are likely to bite when they are kicked, biting is a characteristic found in dogs in the particular circumstances of being kicked and therefore the requirements of paragraph (b) are fulfilled. Of course in such a case the owner would not be *liable*, for it is a defence to show that the damage was wholly due to the fault of the claimant[55] but it seems strange to treat the animal as "dangerous" in the first place.[56] It seems that once one attempts to bring in some cases where the ordinary or average animal[57] of the species would behave in that way, s.2(2) becomes very difficult to operate, even more so when it is held that "normally" in s.2(2)(b) is to be read in the sense of "natural" or "conforming to type" even though on most occasions such animals would have reacted differently.[58] It would be better to abandon it and to make liability for domesticated animals turn on negligence in the keeper—or to have a simple, general rule of strict liability for damage done by animals.[59] The latter might be justified on the ground that, while no one would regard a horse or a dog as presenting the same risk as a tiger, yet they have "minds of their own" and are prone to behave unpredictably.

16–7 The strict liability under s.2(2) only arises if the characteristics of the animal were known to the keeper under paragraph (c). The requirement of knowledge is clearly of "actual" rather than of constructive knowledge,[60] though a person who ought to know of

[54] At [117] per Lord Scott.
[55] See para.16–8, below. *Nelms v CC Avon & Somerset*, February 9, 1993, CA.
[56] *Cet animal est méchant. Si on l'attaque, il se defend.* See Lord Scott's example at [115] in *Mirvahedy* of the police horse attacked by a demonstrator and the horse's defensive kick connecting with someone other than the attacker.
[57] The "reasonable animal"?
[58] *Welsh v Stokes* [2007] EWCA Civ 796; [2008] 1 W.L.R. 1224; cf. *Freeman v Higher Park Farm* [2008] EWCA Civ 1185; [2009] P.I.Q.R. P6.
[59] Such is French law: art.1385, Code Civil; but German law, while imposing strict liability for pets does not apply this to "working" animals.
[60] *Chauhan v Paul* [1998] C.L.Y. 3990, CA. There is nothing in the Act to support the view that he must know, at the time of the incident, of the circumstances which bring the characteristic into play. The damage must be attributable to the characteristics referred to in paragraph (b): if the keeper knows that the animal becomes aggressive in certain conditions he is liable if a bite is inflicted in those conditions, but not for an unexpected attack in quite different conditions: *Curtis v Betts*, above, fn.34, but if a dog is prone to attack other dogs but not humans there may still be a likelihood of injury to a human being, namely the owner of the other dog: *Smith v Ainger*, above, fn.44.

his animal's vicious characteristics may, of course, still be liable for negligence. Where the claim is based on the second limb of s.2(2)(b), the situation where the characteristic is common in the species in particular circumstances, it is sufficient that the keeper knows that animals of that type may react in the way which led to the damage, he does not need to have additional knowledge about the particular animal.[61] However, where the individual animal displays a common characteristic which would not normally be dangerous in such an exaggerated form as to make it so, the defendant will not be liable if he does not know of its propensity to do that.[62] In some cases the knowledge is imputed to the keeper by process of law under para.(c), but this does not mean that knowledge of a person not mentioned in that paragraph will be irrelevant: if, for example, the spouse of the keeper has knowledge of the animal's propensities it may be proper for court to infer as a matter of fact that the keeper also knew of them.[63]

It should be noted with regard to both types of dangerous animals, that the Act, unlike the common law,[64] contains no requirement that the animal must escape from control, nor that there must be any sort of attack.[65] If, therefore, an elephant slips or stumbles or a sheep transmits a virulent disease to another's flock,[66] or, it seems, a cow known to be prone to escape stands stock still in the road and is struck by a car,[67] strict liability will apply.[68]

The definition of "keeper" for this head of liability is the same as that for animals belonging to a dangerous species.[69]

The Guard Dogs Act 1975 governs the keeping of guard dogs and the Dangerous Dogs Act 1991 controls the breeding and keeping of fighting dogs or other dogs appearing to the Secretary of State to

---

[61] *Welsh v Stokes* [2007] EWCA Civ 796; [2008] 1 W.L.R. 1224.

[62] *McKenny v Foster* [2008] EWCA Civ 173 (cow so distressed at being separated from her weaned calf that she was able to leap a six bar gate and a 12-foot cattle grid).

[63] As in *Gladman v Johnson* (1867) 36 L.J.C.P. 153.

[64] *Behrens v Bertram Mills Circus Ltd* [1957] 2 Q.B. 1; *Fitzgerald v A.D. and E.H. Cooke Bourne Farms Ltd* [1964] 1 Q.B. 249 at 270; Williams, *Liability for Animals*, p.341.

[65] *Wallace v Newton* [1982] 1 W.L.R. 375. Cf. *Smith v Ainger*, above, fn.44 (no abnormal characteristic).

[66] The requirement of knowledge means that in practice there is not much risk of liability for the spread of foot and mouth disease.

[67] *McKenny v Foster* [2008] EWCA Civ 173 (though the claim failed for want of knowledge of the relevant characteristic). Compare *Jaundrill v Gillett*, *The Times*, January 30, 1996 and *Mirvahedy v Henley* at [162]. There is an obvious tension with s.8 (para.16–2, above), which is based on negligence.

[68] If you fall into the path of a car because an innocuous dog barks at you the damage has been caused not by the animal but by your excessive reaction: Wall J. in *Chauhan v Paul*, above, fn.60.

[69] i.e. the owner or the person in possession. See the appeal in *Hole v Ross-Skinner* [2003] EWCA Civ 774, which seems to have been pursued solely to absolve the possessor from negligence and allow him to seek contribution against the owner.

have the same characteristics. The first does not impose civil liability.[70] The second is silent on the point. No doubt certain contraventions of either Act would be almost conclusive evidence of negligence.[71]

C. Defences

16–8   The Act provides that it is a defence to an action brought under s.2 that the damage was wholly due to the fault of the person suffering it[72] or that he voluntarily assumed the risk thereof[73] (though a person employed as a servant by a keeper of the animal is not to be treated as accepting voluntarily risks incidental to his employment[74]). Contributory negligence, is, of course, a partial defence.[75]

There is special provision for injury to trespassers by dangerous animals. Section 5(3) provides that a person is not liable under s.2 for any damage by an animal kept on any premises or structure[76] to a person trespassing there, if it is proved either (a) that animal was not kept there for the protection[77] of persons or property or (b) (if the animal was kept there for the protection of persons or property) that keeping it there for that purpose was not unreasonable. It would seem unreasonable to protect your premises with a lion or a cobra, but not, perhaps, with a fierce dog.[78] This subsection does not, of course, affect any liability for negligence which the defendant may incur qua occupier of the premises or keeper of the animal, but it is

---

[70] Section 5(2)(a).

[71] e.g. the condition of muzzling in s.1(2)(d) of the 1991 Act.

[72] Section 5(1). *Nelms v CC Avon & Somerset* February 9, 1993, CA, where the claimant kicked the dog. A person who ignores police warnings to come out and who is then bitten by a police dog brings his injury upon himself: *Dhesi v CC West Midlands, The Times*, May 9, 2000, CA.

[73] Section 5(2). The Unfair Contract Terms Act 1977 does not apply to the strict liability under the 1971 Act. Although the subsection no doubt reflects the common law defence of volenti non fit injuria, it is to be interpreted according to the ordinary meaning of the words: *Freeman v Higher Park Farm* [2008] EWCA Civ 1185.

[74] Section 6(5). See North, *Modern Law of Animals* pp.73–76. So if the lion tamer is eaten by the lion, his dependants can sue. Cf. *Canterbury CC v Howletts & Port Lympne* [1997] I.C.R. 925.

[75] Section 10.

[76] Not necessarily animals owned by or kept by the occupier.

[77] This probably does not have to be a dominant purpose. Thus the old lady who keeps a dog partly for companionship and partly for protection would fail on (a), though her conduct would certainly be reasonable under (b).

[78] So held in *Cummings v Grainger* [1977] Q.B. 397, "True it was a fierce dog. But why not? A gentle dog would be no good. The thieves would soon make friends with him": at 405 per Lord Denning M.R. Since 1975 it is an offence to have a guard dog roaming about the premises unless under the control of a handler: Guard Dogs Act 1975. It has been suggested that contravention might make the keeping unreasonable under the 1971 Act: *Cummings v Grainger*, above.

thought that the keeping of guard dogs is consistent with the occupier's duty to trespassers,[79] provided at least some warning of their presence is given.

3. LIABILITY FOR STRAYING LIVESTOCK

At common law the possessor of "cattle"[80] was strictly liable, **16–9** independently of *scienter*, for damage done by them when they trespassed on the land of his neighbour.[81] Whatever may have been the original rationale of this form of liability, it was certainly not the same as that of *scienter*, for agricultural animals present no peculiar risk. However, the Law Commission recommended the retention of strict liability for this type of harm on the ground that it provided a simple method of allocating liability for what were usually comparatively small damages.[82] The law was, however, in need of considerable modification and the modern form of "cattle trespass" is found in s.4 of the Act, which provides:

"(1) Where livestock[83] belonging[84] to any person strays[85] on to land in the ownership or occupation of another and—

(a) damage is done by livestock to the land or to any property on it[86] which is in the ownership or possession of the other person[87] or

(b) any expenses[88] are reasonably incurred by that other person in keeping the livestock while it cannot be restored to the person to whom it belongs or while it is

---

[79] See para.9–25, above.

[80] "Cattle" or avers was a class virtually identical with livestock under the Act: see fn.83, below.

[81] See Williams, *Liability for Animals*, 2 and 3.

[82] Law Com. No.13 (1967), paras 62–63.

[83] Defined in s.11 as, "cattle, horses, asses, mules, hinnies, sheep, pigs, goats and poultry [which is further defined as the domestic varieties of fowls, turkeys, geese, ducks, guinea-fowls, pigeons, peacocks and quails] and also deer not in the wild state".

[84] By s.4(2) livestock belongs to the person in whose possession it is. Finance companies owning herds under hire-purchase agreements may therefore rest easy in their corporate beds.

[85] The marginal note to s.4 refers to "trespassing", but the enacting words do not. "Stray" is probably wide enough to cover the facts of *Ellis v Loftus Iron Co* [1874] L.R. 10 C.P. 10: *Wiseman v Booker* (1878) 3 C.P.D. 184.

[86] Notwithstanding the general definition of "damage" in s.11, it is submitted that the words of this paragraph make it clear beyond argument that damages are not recoverable for personal injuries under this section and *Wormald v Cole* [1954] 1 Q.B. 614 is no longer law.

[87] The range of potential claimants and their claimable losses is, with regard to property, rather wider than at common law: see North, *Modern Law of Animals*, pp.94–96.

[88] A local authority operating a pound for animals straying on its land may properly impose a standard charge: *Morris v Blaenau Gwent DC* (1982) 80 L.G.R. 793.

detained in pursuance of section 7 of [the] Act,[89] or in ascertaining to whom it belongs;

the person to whom the livestock belongs is liable for the damage or expenses, except as otherwise provided by [the] Act."

A. Defences to Strict Liability for Straying Livestock

16–10   The Act provides that there is no liability under this head for damage which is due wholly to the fault of the person suffering it[90] and that contributory negligence is a partial defence.[91] In this context default of the claimant is often closely bound up with fencing obligations and the Act therefore provides that damage:

" . . . [S]hall not be treated as due to the fault of the person suffering it by reason only that he could have prevented it by fencing but [the defendant] is not liable . . . where it is proved that the straying of the livestock on to the land would not have occurred but for a breach by any other person, being a person having an interest in the land, of a duty to fence."[92]

One other common law defence is preserved by the Act: the defendant is not liable under this form of liability if his livestock strayed on to the claimant's property from the highway and its presence there was a lawful use[93] of the highway.[94] An example of this principle is the decision in *Tillet v Ward*.[95] D owned an ox which, while his servants were driving it with due care through a town, entered the shop of C, an ironmonger, through an open door. It took three-quarters of an hour to get it out and meanwhile it did some damage. D was held not liable to X, for this was one of the inevitable risks of driving cattle on the streets. It would have made no difference if the ironmonger's door had been shut instead of

---

[89] See para.16–11, below.

[90] Section 5(1).

[91] Section 10.

[92] Section 5(6). The law relating to the obligation to fence is notoriously complex and the Law Commission thought it inappropriate to deal with it other than by providing a relatively simple rule: Law Com. No.13 (1967), fn.98. It should be noted that there is no requirement under s.5(6) that the duty in question be owed to the defendant. For a detailed comparison of s.5(6) with the common law position, see North, *Modern Law of Animals*, Ch.4.

[93] Hence the defence is inapplicable if the animals had been allowed to stray on to the highway: *Matthews v Wicks, The Times*, May 25, 1987.

[94] Section 5(5). This does not, of course, remove any liability for negligence in such a case: *Gayler and Pope Ltd v Davies & Son Ltd* [1924] 2 K.B. 75.

[95] (1882) 10 Q.B.D. 17.

open, and the ox had pushed its way through, or had gone through a plate-glass window.[96]

B. Detention and Sale of Straying Livestock

The common law provided a form of self-help remedy to a person **16–11**
harmed by straying livestock by way of distress damage feasant.[97]
The Law Commission concluded that some remedy of this type
should be retained but considered that the old remedy was so hedged
about with limitations (in particular, it provided no power of sale)
and obscurities that it would be better to create a new, statutory
right. This is found in s.7 of the Act, which may be summarised as
follows:

1. The right of distress damage feasant is abolished in relation to
   animals.[98]
2. The occupier of land may detain any livestock which has
   strayed[99] on to his land and which is not then under the control
   of any person.[100]
3. He has, within 48 hours of exercising the right of detention, to
   give notice to the police and if he knows the person to whom
   the livestock belongs, to that person.[101]
4. The right to detain the livestock ceases[102] if:

   (a) the detainer has not complied with the provisions regard-
       ing notice or
   (b) the detainer is tendered sufficient money to satisfy any
       claim he may have for damage and expenses in respect of
       the straying livestock[103] or
   (c) he has no such claim and the person to whom the livestock
       belongs claims it.

---

[96] *Gayler and Pope Ltd v Davies & Son Ltd* [1924] 2 K.B. 75. The driver of beasts which stray without his fault into property adjoining the highway is entitled to enter the property in order to get them out, and for that purpose he must be allowed such time as is reasonable in the circumstances: *Goodwin v Cheveley* (1895) 28 L.J. Ex. 298.

[97] See Williams, op. cit., Pt I.

[98] The right is therefore abolished for all animals and the new remedy applies only to livestock, for the definition of which see fn.83, above. The right of distress damage feasant remains in respect of other property: para.17–10, below.

[99] The word "strayed" may not be wide enough to encompass livestock which have been driven on to the land, though the condition that the animals must not be under the control of any person (see fn.100, below) suggests that the draftsman meant to include such a case.

[100] This was also a condition of the exercise of the common law right and is designed to prevent breaches of the peace.

[101] As to the person to whom livestock belongs, see fn.84, above.

[102] In the absence of a request for the return of the livestock, however, the detainer will not necessarily be liable for conversion.

[103] i.e. under s.4.

5. The detainer is liable for any damage caused to the livestock by failure to treat it with reasonable care and supply it with adequate food and water.
6. Where the livestock has been rightfully detained for not less than 14 days, the person detaining it may sell it at a market or by public auction, unless proceedings are then pending for the return of the livestock or for any claim for damages done by it or expenses incurred in detaining it.
7. Where the net proceeds of sale exceed the amount of any claim the detainer may have for damages and expenses, the excess is recoverable from him by the person who would be entitled to the livestock but for the sale.[104]

4. REMOTENESS OF DAMAGE AND STRICT LIABILITY UNDER THE ACT

16–12   The Animals Act contains no provisions relating to remoteness of damage. At common law both forms of *scienter* liability and cattle trespass had close affinities with *Rylands v Fletcher* and were probably governed by the remoteness principle applicable to that rule—was the consequence a "natural" one, a question of causation. There were, however, at least two exceptions to the generality of this principle. First, in the case of *scienter* liability for animals *mansuetae naturae*, the keeper was only liable if the animal caused some harm of the kind to be expected from its known vicious characteristics[105]; secondly, in the case of cattle trespass, there was a rule that the damage had to be in accordance with the natural characteristics of the animals.[106] The position under the Act is to some extent speculative. The rule in *Rylands v Fletcher* was not considered in *The Wagon Mound (No.1)*, though as has been stated elsewhere in this book it is governed by the principles of foreseeability as developed since *The Wagon Mound*.[107] Those principles should also be applicable to the Animals Act. However, the form of s.2(2) means that with regard to liability for animals not belonging to dangerous species the position will be fundamentally the same as at common

---

[104] Presumably, if the net proceeds are not sufficient to meet the claim the detainer may sue for the excess. Further, the section makes no provision for the case where a detainer with no claim for damages or expenses exercises the power of sale which the section undoubtedly confers on him: the only sensible solution is to make him hold the proceeds on trust for the owner. These solutions, however, involve a fairly robust interpretation of the Act: North, *Modern Law of Animals*, pp.119–120.
[105] See Williams, *Liability for Animals*, p.301. If, however, the animal committed a "direct" wrong of the type to be expected, the keeper was probably liable for other losses stemming from that injury, e.g. a disease caught from the bite of a vicious dog: Williams, p.320.
[106] *Wormald v Cole* [1954] 1 Q.B. 614.
[107] See para.15–19, above.

law, since the damage must be of a kind attributable to the characteristics known to the keeper.[108] As for animals belonging to a dangerous species, a camel has been held to be such because it may cause severe injury by kicking and biting, but strict liability was imposed for injuries suffered by falling off the camel because of its irregular gait.[109] Whether or not any special rule survives for trespassing cattle is not likely to be of any importance now that damages for personal injuries cannot be recovered under that head.[110]

5. PROTECTION OF LIVESTOCK AGAINST DOGS

Liability for Attacks on Livestock

Section 3 of the Animals Act re-enacted, with some modification, **16–13** the form of strict liability formerly found in the Dogs Acts 1906 to 1928 and provides that where a dog causes damage by killing or injuring livestock,[111] any person who is a keeper[112] of the dog is liable for the damage.[113] The Act provides the following defences: that the damage was wholly due to the fault of the person suffering it[114] and that the livestock was killed or injured on land on which it had strayed and either the dog belonged to the occupier or its presence on the land was authorised by the occupier.[115] Contributory negligence is a partial defence.[116]

Killing or Injuring Dogs to Protect Livestock

It may, in certain circumstances, be lawful for a person to kill or **16–14** injure an animal belonging to another if this is necessary for protection of his livestock or crops. The common law rule on this was laid down by the Court of Appeal in *Cresswell v Sirl*[117] but this rule has been modified, so far as the protection of livestock against dogs is concerned,[118] by s.9 of the Animals Act.

---

[108] See para.16–5, above.
[109] *Tutin v Chipperfield Promotions Ltd* (1980) 130 N.L.J. 807.
[110] See fn.86, above.
[111] "Livestock" for this purpose is slightly wider than under s.4, including pheasants, partridges and grouse in captivity: s.11.
[112] "Keeper" has the same meaning as in s.2: see para.16–4, above.
[113] Section 3. See North, *Modern Law of Animals*, Ch.7.
[114] Section 5(1).
[115] Section 5(4).
[116] Section 10.
[117] [1948] 1 K.B. 241.
[118] The rule in *Cresswell v Sirl* continues to govern in the case of animals other than dogs, e.g. pigeons damaging crops, as in *Hamps v Darby* [1948] 2 K.B. 311. See the 8th edn of this work, pp.761–762.

It is a defence[119] to an action for killing or injuring a dog to prove that:

1. the defendant acted for the protection of livestock and was a person entitled so to act and
2. within 48 hours thereafter notice was given to the officer in charge of a police station.

A person is entitled to act for the protection of livestock if either the livestock or the land on which it is belongs[120] to him or to any person under whose express or implied authority he is acting[121] and he is deemed to be acting for their protection if and only if,[122] either:

1. the dog is worrying or is about to worry the livestock and there are not other reasonable means of ending or preventing the worrying or
2. the dog has been worrying livestock, has not left the vicinity and is not under the control of any person and there are no practicable means of ascertaining to whom it belongs.[123]

---

[119] Not the only defence. A defendant who fails to make out the statutory defence (e.g. because he has not informed the police) may presumably fall back on the common law.

[120] For this purpose an animal belongs to a person if he owns it or has it in his possession and land belongs to the occupier thereof: s.9(5).

[121] If the livestock have strayed on to the land of another, there is no right under this section to shoot a dog which is lawfully on that land: s.9(2)(b).

[122] The two following conditions are satisfied by reasonable belief on the defendant's part: s.9(4).

[123] This right to take punitive action in respect of an attack which is over the major difference between s.9 and *Cresswell v Sirl*.

CHAPTER 17

INTERFERENCE WITH GOODS

ENGLISH law governing remedies for interference with goods is **17–1** exceedingly technical, partly because of the long survival and overlap of a number of different heads of liability and partly because the law, though tortious in form, is largely proprietary in function. The Torts (Interference with Goods) Act 1977 made some simplification by abolishing one head of liability but it is only a piecemeal attempt to deal with certain deficiencies in the common law and is in no way a code governing interference with goods.[1] Accordingly, the law must still be sought mainly in the decisions of the courts and it is impossible to give an intelligible account of the developed law without a brief historical sketch.

The most obvious forms of interference, such as removing or damaging the goods, were covered in early law by trespass *de bonis asportatis*, the forerunner of the modern "trespass to goods". Trespass was (and still is) essentially a wrong to possession[2] and the defendant need not have asserted any right to deal with the goods or

---

[1] The Act is based upon the Report of the Law Reform Committee, Cmnd. 4774 (1971). See Bentley (1972) 35 M.L.R. 171. The Report proposed rather more thoroughgoing reforms than the Act in fact produces.

[2] See para.17–4, below.

indulged in any "appropriation" of them.³ Trespass was obviously unsuitable to deal with the case where the owner had voluntarily put his goods into another's possession and the other refused to redeliver them, but this situation was covered by the remedy of detinue.⁴ In neither form of action could the claimant be sure of recovering his goods *in specie* since the judgment in trespass was for damages and in detinue gave the defendant the option of giving up the goods or paying damages, but it is unlikely that this was considered a defect⁵ and it should be noted that the remedy of specific restitution of chattels has remained unusual right up to modern times.⁶ However, detinue was open to the very serious objection from the claimant's point of view that the defendant could insist on the method of trial known as wager of law, i.e. getting compurgators to swear that they believed him to be oathworthy, although they knew nothing of the facts of the case. This was the principal reason for the remarkable development whereby detinue was all but wiped out by the encroachment of trover.⁷ Trover began as an action of trespass upon the case in which it was alleged that the defendant had converted the claimant's goods to his own use.⁸ By the mid-16th century it had emerged as a distinct species of case involving four allegations.⁹ It was alleged: (1) that the claimant was possessed of the goods; (2) that he accidentally lost them; (3) that the defendant found them¹⁰; (4) that the defendant converted them to his own use.¹¹ The losing

---

³ An alternative form of action for unlawful taking was replevin. This was originally a tenant's remedy for wrongful distress by his lord. By the 15th century it had become available for other forms of unlawful taking (Y.B. 19 Henry 6, 65 (Pasch. 5)) but in practice has tended to be used only for unlawful distress.

⁴ Detinue was thus based upon the right to possession and its connection with bailment gave it a strong contractual flavour. However, "the medieval writ lay across the categories of modern analysis, and to force it into one or other of them is to be guilty of anachronism": Fifoot, *History and Sources of the Common Law*, p.25.

⁵ Pollock and Maitland, *History of English Law*, ii, pp.181–182. The attitude of the law seems to have been based partly on the fact that medieval movables were often so perishable that the court could not undertake the responsibility of enforcing their restoration and partly on the view that all things had a legal "price": Maitland, *Forms of Action*, p.48.

⁶ See para.17–29, below.

⁷ Another deficiency of detinue was that if the chattel had been damaged in the bailee's hands he could satisfy the judgment by opting to return the damaged chattel. This was met, however, by allowing an action on the case, the ancestor of the modern "bailee's liability". Accidental damage or destruction was never absorbed into trover.

⁸ See Douglas, "The Nature of Conversion" (2009) 68 C.L.J. 198.

⁹ Holdsworth, *History of English Law*, iii, pp.285–287, 350–351, 450, 581–584 vii, pp.403–513 viii, pp.466–468 ix, p.42; Milsom, "Not Doing is no Trespass" [1954] C.L.J. 105, 114; Simpson, "The Introduction of The Action on the Case for Conversion" (1959) 75 L.Q.R. 364.

¹⁰ This seems to have been borrowed from the earlier form of detinue sur trover which, unlike detinue sur bailment, "had no ancestry in debt, and no trace of contract": Milsom, *Historical Foundations of the Common Law*, p.327.

¹¹ Rastell, *Entries* (1596) 4b–5a.

and finding were soon treated as pure fictions and the defendant was not allowed to deny them.[12] The new remedy rapidly encroached upon the spheres of trespass and replevin, though the law never went quite so far as to say that touching or damaging or moving goods was conversion.

The difficulty in extending trover to cases covered by detinue was   **17–2**
that conversion could only be committed by a positive act—misfeasance as opposed to nonfeasance. Detinue lay where a person was in possession of another's goods and refused to give them up but could it be said that such a mere refusal was a positive act? The line between misfeasance and nonfeasance is apt to be a fine one and the courts after some hesitation took advantage of this and held mere refusal to redeliver to be conversion.[13] Detinue, with its procedural disadvantages, wilted considerably under this treatment though it retained a place in the law because inability to redeliver as a result of loss or destruction of the goods was not regarded as conversion.[14]

Nineteenth-century legislation swept away the fictions upon which trover was based and it became the modern action for conversion, though no change was made in the substance of the law. The abolition of the wager of law in 1833 caused some revival in detinue but in view of the expansion of conversion, detinue only really remained necessary where the defendant was unable to redeliver the goods. The process of simplification was carried a stage further by s.2 of the Torts (Interference with Goods) Act 1977 which abolished detinue and provided that conversion also covered the only case that was probably formerly the exclusive province of detinue—i.e. inability to redeliver goods as a result of their loss or destruction.[15] It may be questioned whether this change achieves very much of a practical nature since, (1) one still needs to look back at the common law of detinue to determine what constitutes the new form of conversion, and (2) there still survive two torts of interference with property which have a considerable overlap with conversion, i.e. trespass to goods and replevin.[16]

---

[12] *Gumbleton v Grafton* (1600) Cro. Eliz. 781 (losing); *Isaack v Clark* (1614) 2 Bulstrode 306 (finding).

[13] Holdsworth, *History of English Law*, vii, pp.405–415.

[14] *Owen v Lewyn* (1673) 1 Ventris 223.

[15] See para.17–14, below.

[16] The Law Reform recommended a new, all-embracing tort of "wrongful interference with chattels" (Cmnd. 4774 (1971)). The Act does use this terminology (see s.1) but only as a convenient label for the various reforms made by it on ancillary matters; it certainly does not merge the three torts of conversion, trespass and replevin. Cf. the assertion in *HSBC Rail (UK) Ltd v Network Rail Infrastructure Ltd* [2005] EWCA Civ 1437; [2006] 1 W.L.R. 643 at [1] that there is a tort of wrongful interference with goods and that trespass and conversion are "now old-fashioned terms".

1. Trespass to Goods

17–3   Trespass to goods is a wrongful physical interference with them.[17] It may take innumerable forms, such as scratching the panel of a vehicle,[18] removing a tyre from it[19] or the vehicle itself from a garage,[20] or, in the case of animals, beating[21] or killing[22] them. Putting out poison for an animal to take[23] is probably not trespass since the interference is not direct, a requirement of all true forms of trespass.[24] A defendant engaging in such conduct would, of course, be liable if injury to the animals ensued but his liability would be in what was classified before the abolition of the forms of action as case rather than trespass. Despite the fact that trespass is actionable per se, there is some authority to the effect that trespass to goods requires proof of some damage or asportation[25] but the general view of textbook writers is to the contrary[26] and there must be many instances where, if mere touching of objects like waxworks or exhibits in a gallery or museum were not trespass, their possessor would be without remedy.[27] Where, however, the touching is not intentional the law may well be otherwise. Diplock L.J. has said that actual damage is an essential ingredient in unintentional trespass to the person[28] (if that tort still exists) and if this is so there is no reason for distinguishing the case of trespass to goods. Certainly, the considerations of policy which point to making intentional meddling

---

[17] As to matters like unauthorised Internet access to computers (which may involve minute alterations to hard disk configuration) see Clerk & Lindsell, *Torts*, 19th edn, para.17–126.

[18] Alderson B. in *Fouldes v Willoughby* (1841) 8 M. & W. 538 at 549.

[19] *G.W.K. Ltd v Dunlop Rubber Co Ltd* (1926) 42 T.L.R. 376 at 593.

[20] *Wilson v Lombank Ltd* [1963] 1 W.L.R. 1294.

[21] *Slater v Swann* (1730) 2 Stra. 872.

[22] *Sheldrick v Abery* (1793) 1 Esp. 55.

[23] As opposed to forcing it down its throat.

[24] Clerk and Lindsell, *Torts*, 19th edn, para.17–123. The American *Restatement* 2d s.217, Comment, while abandoning the distinction between direct and indirect harm, appears to accept that it represents the common law. Earlier editions of this work took the contrary view but it is doubtful if the authorities cited (some of them on the different tort of cattle trespass) really carry the point. This is not, however, to say that the rule now stated in the text is a more desirable one: see the comment of the Law Reform Committee in its 18th Report (fn.16, above) para.21. Chasing animals seems to be a borderline case: on the one hand, there is no physical contact; on the other hand, chasing humans has always been accepted as assault, a variety of trespass. The better view is that chasing animals probably is trespass, and this gains some support from *Farmer v Hunt* (1610) 1 Brownl. 220 and *Durant v Childe* (1611) 1 Brownl. 221.

[25] *Everitt v Martin* [1953] N.Z.L.R. 29; *Slater v Swann* (1730) 2 Stra. 872.

[26] Clerk and Lindsell, *Torts*, 19th edn, para.17–123. See also *Leitch & Co Ltd v Leydon* [1931] A.C. 90 at 106 per Lord Blanesburgh.

[27] Perhaps even an intentional touching is not actionable if it is the sort of trivial interference to which people do not object, like moving a coat on a stand to get at one's own: see *White v Withers LLP* [2009] EWCA Civ 1122. Cf. *Collins v Wilcock* [1984] 1 W.L.R. 1172.

[28] *Letang v Cooper* [1965] 1 Q.B. 232 at 244–245, para.4–33, above.

actionable even without damage have no application to unintended contacts.

Assuming that some damage has been caused, is negligence necessary for liability for unintentional trespass to goods? The answer is clearly yes[29] but the traditional view is that once a direct injury has been proved the defendant bears the burden of proving "inevitable accident"[30] as a defence. However, since the decision in *Fowler v Lanning*[31] which held that in an action for unintentional trespass to the person the claimant must prove negligence on the part of the defendant the same may be true of cases of trespass to goods, though the matter cannot be regarded as finally settled. A more extreme view, but one not without its attractions, is that in the modern law trespass to goods is confined to intentional interference and that negligent interference is remediable only by the tort of negligence.[32] Trespass, however, obviously remains appropriate where one takes another's goods in the mistaken belief that he is entitled to do so, for the act is intentional towards the goods.[33] In *Wilson v Lombank Ltd*[34] the claimant had "purchased" a car from a person who had no title to it and had sent it to a garage for repair. The defendant, believing, wrongly, that the car was his, removed it from the garage. It was held that the defendant was liable in trespass.[35]

A. Possession Essential

As trespass is an interference with possession, it follows that if **17–4** the claimant were not in possession at the date of the alleged meddling, he cannot sue for trespass. He may be able to sue for conversion, but that is a different matter.

---

[29] *National Coal Board v Evans* [1951] 2 K.B. 861.

[30] See generally para.25–27, below.

[31] [1959] 1 Q.B. 426, para.4–33, above.

[32] In *Letang v Cooper*, above, fn.28, Lord Denning at 240 went so far as to say that negligence is the only cause of action for unintended injury to the person and presumably his Lordship would have said the same for unintended damage to goods. Though there are clear authorities the other way on trespass to goods (e.g. Br. Abr. Trespass, 63 (A.D. 1373); *Covell v Laming* (1808) 1 Camp. 497) his Lordship was not hampered by equally clear authorities in relation to trespass to the person. In truth, once it is conceded that the burden of proof of negligence lies on the claimant (a point on which the court in *Letang v Cooper* was unanimous) the traditional distinction between trespass and negligence loses almost all its significance and a classification like Lord Denning's, directed at the defendant's state of mind, is more satisfactory. However, some support for the view that there may still be an unintentional trespass to goods is found in the Torts (Interference with Goods) Act 1977. Section 1(1)(b) refers to "trespass to goods" but s.11(1), dealing with contributory negligence, refers only to "intentional trespass to goods".

[33] As in the case of excessive execution. Proof of malice is unnecessary: *Moore v Lambeth County Court Registrar (No.2)* [1970] 1 Q.B. 560.

[34] [1963] 1 W.L.R. 1294; *Colwell v Reeves* (1811) 2 Camp. 575.

[35] See para.17–19, below, as to the possible effect of the Torts (Interference with Goods) Act 1977 on this case.

"The distinction between the actions of trespass and trover is well settled: the former is founded on possession the latter on property."[36]

17–5   It is said that there are exceptions to this rule and that the following persons can sue for trespass although they had not possession:

1. A trustee against any third person who commits a trespass to trust chattels in the hands of the beneficiary.
2. An executor or administrator for trespasses committed to goods of the deceased after his death but before probate is granted to the executor or before the administrator takes out letters of administration.
3. The owner of a franchise (for example a right to take wreck or treasure trove) against anyone who seizes the goods before he himself can take them.

However, it is questionable whether any of these exceptions is genuine. The language used in the authorities relating to the trustee is none too clear, but it indicates that the trustee has possession of chattels in the hands of the beneficiary, and not merely the right to possess them.[37] It does not follow from this that the beneficiary himself cannot sue, for if he holds the chattels he seems to have joint possession with the trustee. Again, the executor and administrator have long been regarded as having the deceased's possession continued in them; when they assume office their title relates back to his death. They have not merely the right to possess: they are in possession.[38] Similarly, in the case of the franchise, possession is deemed to be with the owner of the franchise.[39]

---

[36] Lord Kenyon C.J. in *Ward v Macauley* (1791) 4 T.R. 489 at 490; but in this case the claimant was a person who had let a furnished property to a tenant and had therefore surrendered even the right to possession. It has been said that it does not follow that D is not liable for trespass to C where X wrongfully takes C's goods and then passes them to D: *White v Withers LLP* [2009] EWCA Civ 1122 at [48]. Cf. *Penfolds Wines Pty Ltd v Elliott* (1946) 74 C.L.R. 204, where X in handing the goods to D was merely in breach of the terms of his bailment. If the goods are damaged or destroyed the owner out of possession will have an action formerly classified as case: *Mears v London & South Western Ry* (1862) 11 C.B. (N.S.) 850; *East West Corp v DKBS AF 1912 A/S* [2003] EWCA Civ 83; [2003] Q.B. 1509; *HSBC Rail (UK) Ltd v Network Rail Infrastructure Ltd* [2005] EWCA Civ 1437; [2006] 1 W.L.R. 643 (where, however, the claim failed, the owner having been indemnified under contract by the bailee). See Tettenborn, "Reversionary Damage to Chattels" [1994] C.L.J. 326.

[37] *White v Morris* (1852) 11 C.B. 1015; *Barker v Furlong* [1891] 2 Ch. 172, a case of conversion, but Romer J. approved *White v Morris*.

[38] *Tharpe v Stallwood* (1843) 5 M. & G. 760 at 770; Pollock & Wright, *Possession*, pp.146–147.

[39] *Bailiffs of Dunwich v Sterry* (1831) 1 B. & Ad. 831 (franchise of wreck; cask taken before franchisee could get it).

In a simple bailment determinable at will the bailor does not lose possession and may sue any wrongdoer other than his bailee[40] in trespass,[41] though the bailee may also have sufficient possession to bring trespass.[42]

2. CONVERSION

Conversion at common law may be committed in so many different **17–6** ways that any comprehensive definition is probably impossible[43] but the wrong is committed by dealing with the goods of a person which deprives him of the use or possession of them (though to "deprive" the owner does not necessarily require that the defendant should himself take the goods from him[44]). Thus it may be committed by wrongfully taking possession of goods, by wrongfully disposing of them, by wrongfully misusing them, by wrongfully destroying them or simply by wrongfully refusing to give them up when demanded. At common law there must be some deliberate act[45] depriving the claimant of his rights: if this element was lacking there was no conversion. Thus if a bailee negligently allowed goods in his charge to be destroyed the claimant's loss is just the same as if the bailee had wrongfully sold them to a third party but there was no conversion. Such conduct is now conversion by statute but this is merely for the draftsman's terminological convenience and has no effect on the concept of conversion at common law: for this reason, it must be kept separate in our analysis.

A. What may be Converted[46]

Any corporeal, movable property may be converted.[47] This **17–7** includes money in the form of coins or notes, though once the taker

---

[40] If the act is licensed by the bailee it seems it is not trespass as against a bailor: Palmer, *Bailment*, 2nd edn, p.206—the general chapter on the chattel torts is not included in the 3rd edn).

[41] *Lotan v Cross* (1810) 2 Camp. 464; *Ancona v Rogers* (1876) L.R. 1 Ex. D. 285 at 292. The authorities are discussed in *Penfolds Wines Pty Ltd v Elliott* (1946) 74 C.L.R. 204 at 214–220, 226–236, 239–244; *USA v Dollfus Mieg et Cie* [1952] A.C. 582 at 605, 611–613; *Wilson v Lombank Ltd* [1963] 1 W.L.R. 1294.

[42] *Nicolls v Bastard* (1835) 2 C.M. & R. 659 at 660 per Parke B., *arguendo*; but cf. *Burnett v Randwick City Council* [2006] NSWCA 196 (conversion).

[43] See *Kuwait Airways Corp v Iraqi Airways Co (Nos 4 and 5)* [2002] UKHL 19; [2002] 2 A.C. 883 at [39]; *Howard Perry & Co Ltd v BRB* [1980] 1 W.L.R. 1375 at 1380; *Hiort v London & North Western Ry Co* (1879) 4 Ex. D. 188 at 194.

[44] *Kuwait Airways Corp*, above, fn.43, at [40].

[45] The defendant may still be liable even if he is motivated by some innocent mistake: para.17–22, below. However, innocently taking goods into one's custody (e.g. to transport them) is not conversion unless one is aware of the owner's rights: para.17–23, below.

[46] Clerk and Lindsell, *Torts*, 19th edn, para.17–33.

[47] Hence not wild animals which have not been reduced into possession (they are not anyone's property) nor land. However, where material is wrongfully severed from land the owner may sue in conversion.

has paid them to another they become currency and the payee and
subsequent recipients cannot be sued for conversion by the original
owner. There can be no conversion of a chose in action, so when
invalidly appointed receivers dealt with a company's contracts they
did not commit this tort.[48] Although the true value of cheques and
other negotiable instruments or share certificates lies in their character as evidence of non-corporeal rights,[49] the owner may sue in
conversion for their face value,[50] though not where a cheque has
been materially altered, for then it ceases to be valid and becomes a
worthless piece of paper.[51] There have been a number of cases about
corpses and body parts, though generally in contexts other than
conversion but where rights of ownership have been in issue. There
is no property in a corpse[52] (as opposed to e.g. a preserved speci-
men[53] or skeleton prepared for anatomical purposes) but in suitable
circumstances a person may have ownership of parts of or products
obtained from his body. Hence a tort claim may lie in respect of the
destruction of sperm stored for potential future use or of a body part
severed in an accident which had been capable of being
reattached.[54]

B. What Constitutes Conversion at Common Law

17–8   **i. Taking possession.** Whether taking another's goods is conversion is a matter of degree. Generally it will constitute the tort but

---

[48] *OBG Ltd v Allan* [2007] UKHL 21; [2008] 1 A.C.1 (though the HL was divided on both
the feasibility and desirability of change). See also *Thunder Air Ltd v Hilmarsson* [2008]
EWHC 355 (Ch) (electronic documents).

[49] In the past the full value of the estate has been awardable for the conversion of title deeds
to land (*Coombe v Sanson* (1822) 1 Dorn. & Ry 201, though such an outcome seems
unlikely nowadays.

[50] *Morrison v London County and Westminster Bank* [1914] 3 K.B. 356.

[51] *Smith v Lloyd's TSB Group Plc* [2001] Q.B. 541.

[52] See Clerk and Lindsell, *Torts*, 19th edn, para.17–39. Cf. *Mason v Westside Cemeteries Ltd*
(1996) 135 D.L.R. (4th) 361, where there was a bailment of urns containing ashes.

[53] See *R. v Kelly* [1999] Q.B. 621and *Doodeward v Spence* (1908) 6 C.L.R. 406. In *Dobson
v N Tyneside HA* [1997] 1 W.L.R. 596 it was held that conversion did not lie in respect of
a brain which had been extracted and preserved for an inquest rather than research. The
claim seems to have been linked to the claimants' action for medical negligence causing
the death. The CA in *Yearworth v North Bristol NHS Trust* [2009] EWCA Civ 37 regarded
Dobson as depending on the fact that the pathologist had never undertaken to preserve the
brain. Where a post-mortem is lawfully carried out the removal of organs is lawful and the
person who does that may have the initial right to possession of them. However, failure to
explain the possibility of removal and retention of organs may give rise to a claim for
negligence or, under art.8 of the European Convention on Human Rights: *Organ Retention
Group Litigation, Re* [2004] EWHC 644 (QB); [2005] Q.B. 506.

[54] *Yearworth v North Bristol NHS Trust* [2009] EWCA Civ 37 (sperm; this was despite the
fact that legislation deprived the "owners" of the prime sign of ownership, to *direct* what
should be done with the material. It would have been possible to decide the case on the
basis that the skill used in preserving the sperm made it analogous to the cases on
anatomical specimens but the CA did not wish to proceed on such a narrow basis). As to
bailment, see para.1–12, above.

there will be no conversion where the interference is merely temporary and is unaccompanied by any intention to assert rights over the goods. Thus in *Fouldes v Willoughby*[55] it was not conversion (though no doubt it was trespass) to remove the claimant's horses from a ferry boat to the shore. If I snatch your hat from your head with intent to steal it or destroy it that is conversion as well as trespass, but if I throw it at another person that is trespass only.[56] It is sometimes said that this is because I am not questioning your title to it but a better explanation seems to be that it is because the interference is temporary and trivial[57] for it is clearly not necessary in cases of conversion that the defendant should assert ownership over the goods. Taking for the purpose of acquiring a lien[58] or even for temporary use[59] have been held to be conversion. On the other hand, some of the cases talk in terms of "exercising dominion"[60] or of "denying the owner's right".[61] These expressions should not be taken too literally but if that is how the defendant's conduct would appear to an observer that is certainly a pointer towards its being conversion rather than trespass.[62] Now that the claimant does not have to choose the correct form of action the distinction between trespass and conversion is of course less important but it may still be significant on the question of remedy. There are essentially two points. First, if there is a conversion the claimant's damages are prima facie measurable by the value of the goods, in other words the judgment is a sort of forced sale. This may be thought a draconian remedy for a temporary deprivation and points towards keeping conversion within narrower bounds than trespass.[63] Yet if goods are destroyed while in the possession of a wrongdoer it would surely be wrong to allow him to escape by showing that it was not his fault,

[55] (1841) 8 M. & W. 540.
[56] *Price v Helyer* (1828) 4 Bing. 597.
[57] Cf. *The Playa Larga* [1983] 2 Lloyd's Rep. 171 (diversion of goods by seller at behest of third party conversion). In *384238 Ontario Ltd v R.* (1984) 8 D.L.R. (4th) 676 a temporary taking for three days without use was held not to be conversion. To be conversion the conduct must be, "so extensive an encroachment on the rights of the owner as to exclude him from use and possession of the goods": *Kuwait Airways Corp v Iraqi Airways Co (Nos 4 and 5)* [2002] UKHL 19; [2002] 2 A.C. 883 at [39]
[58] *Tear v Freebody* (1858) C.B. (N.S.) 228. Unlawful wheelclamping is plainly trespass (*Vine v Waltham Forest LBC* [2000] 1 W.L.R. 2383) is it also conversion? In *Arthur v Anker* [1997] Q.B. 504 the cause of action was described as "tortious interference" with the car.
[59] e.g. "joyriding": Rolle Abr. tit. *Action Sur Case*, p.5 (equine variety); *Aitken v Richardson* [1967] 2 N.Z.L.R. 15. Cf. *Schemmell v Pomeroy* (1989) 50 S.A.S.R. 450.
[60] *Hollins v Fowler* (1875) L.R. 7 H.L. 757 at 766, 782, 787, 790, 792; *Oakley v Lister* [1931] 1 K.B. 148 at 156.
[61] *Lancashire and Yorkshire Ry v MacNicholl* (1919) 88 L.J.K.B. 601 at 605; *Oakley v Lister*, fn.60, at 153.
[62] Is taking a document to read it and copy it conversion? See *White v Withers LLP* [2009] EWCA Civ 1122 at [53].
[63] Of course in another sense conversion is *wider* than trespass. I can commit conversion of goods without touching them or even seeing them, as where I sell them.

for that would be to treat him like a bailee. However, both problems can be solved without taking an artificial approach to what amounts to conversion. Where there is a temporary deprivation and the goods are returned to the claimant there is no doubt that this goes in reduction of the damages. If the claimant should refuse to take the goods back then the court has power to stay the action before judgment, if they are tendered undamaged.[64] As to the second situation, since the law imposes the liability of an insurer upon a person who came lawfully into the possession of another's goods but who deviates from the terms of his permission[65] it must inevitably do the same to a defendant who takes the goods wrongfully.[66]

Where A, without lawful authority, transfers B's goods to C, the mere voluntary receipt of them by C is in general conversion, however innocent C may be. This is abundantly supported by decisions with respect to receipt of goods by a buyer[67] and a receipt of a cheque by a banker.[68]

"Certainly a man is guilty of a conversion who takes my property by assignment from another who has no authority to dispose of it for what is that but assisting that other in carrying his wrongful act into effect".[69]

Some qualifications of this where the defendant acts bona fide are discussed below.[70] It was once held that receipt of goods by way of pledge did not amount to conversion even though the same receipt by way of purchase would have.[71] Whether or not this decision was

---

[64] *Fisher v Prince* (1762) 3 Burr. 1363; *Kuwait Airways Corp v Iraqi Airways Co (Nos 4 and 5)* [2001] 3 W.L.R. 1117 at 1235; on appeal [2002] UKHL 19; [2002] 2 A.C. 883.

[65] See, e.g. *Roberts v McDougall* (1887) 3 T.L.R. 666 and the well-known deviation cases about carriers and warehousemen. *Mitchell v Ealing LBC* [1979] Q.B.1; *Toor v Bassi* [1999] E.G.C.S. 9.

[66] This seems more satisfactory than making the act conversion because the goods are destroyed. Cf. *Schemmell v Pomeroy*, above, fn.59.

[67] *Wilkinson v King* (1809) 2 Camp. 335; *Farrant v Thompson* (1822) 5 B. & Ald. 826; *Dyer v Pearson* (1824) 3 B. & C. 38; *Hilbery v Hatton* (1864) 2 H. & C. 822; *Johnson Matthey (Aust) Ltd v Dascorp Pty Ltd* [2003] VSC 291, 9 V.R. 171.

[68] *Fine Art Society v Union Bank of London* (1886) 17 Q.B.D. 705; *Gordon v London City and Midland Bank* [1902] 1 K.B. 242 at 265; *Morison v London County & Westminster Bank* [1914] 3 K.B. 356 at 364; *Reckitt v Barnett* [1928] 2 K.B. 244 at 263; [1929] A.C. 726; *Lloyds Bank v Chartered Bank* [1929] 1 K.B. 40 at 69; *Orbit Mining & Trading Co Ltd v Westminster Bank Ltd* [1963] 1 Q.B. 794. Under the Cheques Act 1957 s.4, re-enacting and extending the Bills of Exchange Act 1882 s.82, the banker has a defence if he has acted in good faith and without negligence. *Middle Temple v Lloyd's Bank Plc* [1999] 1 All E.R. (Comm) 193 (effect of Cheques Act 1992); *Architects of Wine Ltd v Barclays Bank Plc* [2007] EWCA Civ 239; [2007] 2 Lloyd's Rep 471.

[69] Lord Ellenborough C.J. in *McCombie v Davies* (1805) 6 East 538

[70] See para.17–22, below.

[71] *Spackman v Foster* (1883) 11 Q.B.D. 99.

ever good law it was reversed by the Torts (Interference with Goods) Act 1977.[72]

Involuntary reception of goods is not conversion.[73] Such is the **17–9** case of an innocent person into whose pocket a thief, in order to escape detection, inserts a purse which he has stolen from a third person. Even where the receiver knows that the thing belongs to someone else,[74] he incurs no liability by having it thrust upon him. Indeed, by legislation, where unsolicited goods are sent to a person with a view to his acquiring them he may be able to treat them as a gift to him.[75]

The recipient cannot, without his consent, be made a bailee in the strict sense of that term and mere negligence on his part with respect to the safe custody of the thing will not make him liable. So, in *Howard v Harris*,[76] where a playwright sent the manuscript of a play to a theatrical producer who had never asked for it and who lost it, the producer was held not liable. Similarly, the involuntary bailee does no wrong if he acts reasonably in trying to return the goods. In *Elvin and Powell Ltd v Plummer Roddis Ltd*,[77] X, a swindler, directed the claimants to supply the defendants with £350-worth of coats. X then forged a telegram to the defendants: "Goods dispatched to your branch in error.—Sending van to collect. Elvin and Powell." Then a confederate of X called on the defendants, who delivered the coats to him under the impression that he was the claimants' agent. The confederate disappeared. The claimants sued the defendants for (1) negligence as bailees and (2) conversion. The jury negatived negligence and found that there was contributory negligence on the claimants' part, and Hawke J. held that there was no conversion, for the defendants had acted reasonably.[78]

---

[72] Section 11(2). One must look to the substance of the transaction. If A deposits goods with B for B to sell and the contract provides that B has a lien and a residual right to sell to recover unpaid charges that is not a pledge: *Marcq v Christie Manson & Woods Ltd* [2003] EWCA Civ 731; [2004] Q.B. 286.

[73] See Burnett, "Conversion by an Involuntary Bailee" (1960) 76 L.Q.R. 364; Palmer, *Bailment*, 3rd edn, Ch.13.

[74] It seems that where one receives goods one should ensure that they do not belong to someone else before scrapping them: *A.V.X. v E.G.M. Solders, The Times*, July 7, 1982. According to the CA in *Marcq v Christie Manson & Woods Ltd*, above, fn.72, one cannot be a bailee without some knowledge of the existence of one's bailor but if one mistakenly destroys goods which are self-evidently someone else's one that is negligent whether or not there is a bailment. Where one finds goods in property which one has acquired the nature of them will determine what inquiries one should make before concluding that they have been abandoned: *Robot Arenas Ltd v Waterfield* [2010] EWHC 115 (QB).

[75] Consumer Protection (Distance Selling) Regulations, SI 2000/2344, replacing in this regard the Unsolicited Goods and Services Act 1971.

[76] (1884) Cababe & Ellis 253; *Lethbridge v Phillips* (1819) 2 Starkie 544. Compare the view of Palmer, *Bailment*, 3rd edn, para.13–013.

[77] (1933) 50 T.L.R. 158.

[78] So, too, *Batistoni v Dance* (1908) 52 S.J. 202.

Contrast with this case *Hiort v Bott*,[79] where A mistakenly sent an invoice for barley to B (who had ordered none), which stated that B had bought the barley of A through G as broker and A also sent B a delivery order which made the barley deliverable to the order of A or of B. G then told B there had been a mistake and got B to endorse the delivery order to himself. G thereby got hold of the barley, disposed of it and absconded. Here B was held liable to A for conversion. Had he merely handed the delivery order to G for return to A, the decision might have been otherwise, but by endorsing it to G he had gone far beyond what was necessary to secure the return of it to A.

17–10   The recipient must not wilfully damage or destroy the thing.[80] The law has not, however, been fully explored here. It is simple enough with a small and imperishable article like a book or a fountain pen, but what of a parcel of fish or a piano which is delivered at my house in my absence? What I want to do is to get rid of them and I am certainly not bound to incur the expense of packing and returning them. If the sender is traceable, probably the most sensible thing to do is to notify him that the goods are at his risk and to request him to fetch them and if (as is likely with perishables) the goods become a nuisance, the recipient would surely be justified in abating the nuisance by destroying them, even without notice to the sender, if the emergency were so pressing as to leave him no time to give it.[81] A related question arises if the involuntary bailee wishes to detain the goods as security for the payment of his expenses or for the inconvenience caused to him, a situation exemplified by the modern practice of wheel clamping. The ancient right of distress damage feasant applies only where the landowner has suffered actual damage, though this extends to inconvenience, as well as physical injury to the property.[82] The cost of clamping or of towing to another location is not "damage".[83] However, the display of a

---

[79] (1874) L.R. 9 Ex. 86. Note that the defendant was not, strictly, a bailee since he never had actual possession of the barley.

[80] "I am not bound to warehouse it, nor am I entitled to turn it into the street": Bramwell B., obiter, in *Hiort v Bott* (1874) L.R. 9 Ex. 86 at 90.

[81] The position is rather different when the goods came into the defendant's hands by reason of a genuine, voluntary bailment for then the bailee has a statutory power of sale of the goods if the bailor fails to collect them. See the Torts (Interference with Goods) Act 1977 ss.12, 13, replacing the narrower provisions of the Disposal of Uncollected Goods Act 1952. At common law there was no power of disposal except in cases of real necessity: *Sachs v Miklos* [1948] 2 K.B. 23; *Anderson v Earlanger* [1980] C.L.Y. 133. The 1977 Act does not define "bailment" but it is thought that the provisions on sale would not extend to the "involuntary bailment".

[82] *Arthur v Anker* [1997] Q.B. 564.

[83] [1997] Q.B. 564. Cf. *Jamieson's Tow and Salvage v Murray* [1984] 2 N.Z.L.R. 144. The landowner may remove the car, but that may involve him in other trouble: *Lloyd v DPP* [1992] 1 All E.R. 982.

prominent notice warning of clamping may mean that the car owner consents to the risk.[84]

ii. Abusing possession. Abuse of possession which the defendant **17–11** already has may take many forms, such as sale accompanied by delivery of the claimant's goods or their documents of title to another,[85] pawning them,[86] or otherwise disposing of them, even by innocently delivering them to a fraudster with forged delivery documents.[87] The use of a borrowed car for the transporting of uncustomed watches has been held a conversion of the car, for such conduct if discovered leads to the forfeiture of the car under the Customs and Excise legislation and its consequent loss to the owner.[88] In less extreme cases of unauthorised use by a bailee the question whether his act amounts to conversion probably depends upon the degree of departure from the terms of the bailment,[89] though it must be remembered that in any event the departure will expose the bailee to strict liability for damage or loss. However, at common law an omission on the part of the defendant (for example negligently allowing the goods to be stolen) would not make him liable for conversion[90] though if he were a bailee of the goods he might be liable in detinue in such circumstances.[91] Since this type of detinue is now by statute assimilated to conversion there may now be liability in conversion.[92]

A mere bargain and sale or other attempted disposition of goods by a person without a transfer of possession, i.e. delivery, on the

---

[84] *Arthur v Anker*, above, fn.82; *Vine v Waltham Forest LBC* [2000] 1 W.L.R. 2383. It seems from the latter case that it is not necessarily enough that the notices are sufficiently prominent to bring the matter to the attention of a reasonably alert entrant. There is now extensive control via licensing and the criminal law of those engaging in wheel clamping under the Private Security Industry Act 2001.

[85] *Hollins v Fowler* (1875) L.R. 7 H.L. 757.

[86] *Parker v Godin* (1728) 2 Stra. 813.

[87] *Motis Exports Ltd v Dampskibsselskabet AF 1912 A/S* [2000] 1 Lloyd's Rep. 211.

[88] *Moorgate Mercantile Co Ltd v Finch* [1962] 1 Q.B. 701. The Court of Appeal held that it was at least the probable result of such use of the car that the car would be forfeited and therefore that the defendant must be taken to have intended this result even though, no doubt, he hoped that it would not happen. Cf. *BMW Financial Services (GB) Ltd v Bhagwanani* [2007] EWCA Civ 1230. Did the smuggler convert the airliner in *Customs and Excise v Air Canada* [1991] 2 Q.B. 446?

[89] Palmer, *Bailment*, 3rd edn, para.21–07.

[90] *Ashby v Tolhurst* [1937] 2 K.B. 242; *Tinsley v Dudley* [1951] 2 K.B. 18. Both cases of theft of claimant's vehicle from defendant's car park. The decisions would, of course, have been different if the defendants had actually handed the vehicles over under a mistaken belief: *Hollins v J. Davy Ltd* [1963] 1 Q.B. 844 (where, however, a contractual clause protected the defendants).

[91] It is important to note that there is no bailment where a vehicle is placed in an ordinary car park: *Chappell v National Car Parks, The Times*, May 22, 1987. The cases do not seem to have been affected by the Occupier's Liability act 1957: para.9–24, above; but cf. *Fairline Shipping Corp v Adamson* [1975] Q.B. 180.

[92] See para.17–14, below. Thus a carrier who negligently allows goods to be stolen may now be liable for conversion of the goods as well as negligent breach of bailment.

other hand, is not a conversion: the act is void and does not change the property or the possession.[93] However, in those cases where a person in possession of goods to which he has no title may confer a good title on someone else by selling, pledging, or otherwise disposing of the goods,[94] then, since the true owner is deprived of his title to the goods, such a disposition constitutes conversion whether or not the goods are actually delivered.[95]

The destruction of goods amounts to conversion and so does the alteration of their nature. If I make an omelette of your eggs or a statue out of your block of marble, that is conversion.[96] However, the owner of the original material may wish to assert ownership in the product and that is a different question from that whether the process wrongfully applied to the material constituted conversion. If the materials can still be identified in the new product, which is wholly or substantially composed of them[97] (leather turned into shoes,[98] skins turned into a fur coat[99]) the owner of the materials is owner of the product. Where the property of A is wrongfully mixed with that of B which is of substantially the same nature and quality and they cannot practicably be separated (grain in a bin, oil in a tank) the mixture is owned in common in proportion to the quantity contributed by each[100]; and it has been held that the same is true where the components are of different grades, so as to produce a commercially different mixture.[101]

17–12   **iii. Demand and refusal.** Merely keeping someone else's goods, while it may be a breach of contract,[102] is not a conversion of them for it does not necessarily show an intention to exclude the rights of the owner. In practice, proof of a demand by the claimant for the return of the goods met by a refusal of the defendant is the way in

---

[93] *Lancashire Waggon Co v Fitzhugh* (1861) 6 H. & N. 502.

[94] i.e. the exceptions to the rule *nemo dat quod non habet.*

[95] Though most of the exceptions require a delivery.

[96] The bottling of wine entrusted to a person in cask may be evidence of conversion even if none of the wine is drunk, but much will depend on the circumstances of the bottling. If done to preserve the wine from deterioration it is not conversion. See *Philpott v Kelley* (1835) 3 A. & E. 106.

[97] *Glencore International A.G. v Metro Trading International Inc* [2001] 1 Lloyd's Rep. 284 at 328.

[98] *Case of Leather* Y.B. 5 Hen.VII fol.15.

[99] *Jones v de Marchant* (1916) 28 D.L.R. 561, approved by Lord Millett in *Foskett v McKeown* [2001] 1 A.C. 102 at 132.

[100] *Indian Oil Corp Ltd v Greenstone Shipping SA* [1988] Q.B. 345. In *Jones v de Marchant* above, fn.99, four of the 22 skins of which the coat was made belonged to the defendant, but this was a case where separation was not possible.

[101] *Glencore International A.G. v Metro Trading International Inc,* above, fn.97.

[102] A bailee is not, in the absence of special contract, obliged to return the chattel to his bailor, he must merely allow the bailor to collect it: *Capital Finance Co Ltd v Bray* [1964] 1 W.L.R. 323.

which a claimant will usually establish conversion.[103] Yet it is not the only way. In *Kuwait Airways Corp v Iraqi Airways Co (Nos 4 and 5)*[104] aircraft were seized by Iraqi forces in the invasion of Kuwait and transferred to the defendants, who were held to have converted them by resolving to register them in their name, using them to the limited extent possible in the circumstances and generally treating them as their own.[105] Where there is a demand, the refusal must be unconditional or, if it is conditional, the condition must be an unreasonable one. It is certainly not unreasonable to refuse to give up a banknote which you pick up in the street to the first stranger who alleges it to be his, if you tell him that you must make further inquiries or that he must produce evidence which will authenticate his claim.[106] Whether the length of time spent in making these inquiries and the mode in which they are made are reasonable or not may be nice questions.[107] Where, however, there is no question of pursuing inquiries to see whether delivery to the claimant is proper, the defendant cannot justify a refusal because compliance with the demand may have unpleasant consequences for him. In *Howard E. Perry & Co Ltd v BRB*[108] it was held that the defendants' refusal to allow the claimants to enter their premises to collect goods which belonged to them could not be justified by their fear of intensified industrial action.

iv. Residual forms of conversion. Though most cases of conversion at common law fall within the categories of taking or abusing possession, or refusing to return the goods, such acts on the part of the defendant are not a necessary element in liability provided he has dealt with the goods in a way inconsistent with the claimant's rights, such as signing a delivery order for goods which are delivered under that order.[109] It has even been held that refusing to hand

17–13

---

[103] Which would also have been detinue at common law: see *Schwarzchild v Harrods Ltd* [2008] EWHC 521 (QB) (limitation).

[104] [2002] UKHL 19; [2002] 2 A.C. 883.

[105] The initial seizure by the State of Iraq was not actionable in tort because of sovereign immunity (para.24–6, below). Under the law at the time of the events the usurpation by the defendants was actionable in an English court only if (a) it was a tort in English law and (b) civilly actionable under Iraqi law (see now the Private International Law (Miscellaneous Provisions Act 1995)). The expropriatory decree of the Iraqi Government vesting the aircraft in the defendants was not recognised because it was a gross breach of international law.

[106] *Green v Dunn* (1811) 3 Camp. 215n.; *Alexander v Southey* (1821) 5 B. & Ald. 247; *Clayton v Le Roy* [1911] 2 K.B. 1031.

[107] e.g. *Borroughes v Bayne* (1860) 5 H. & N. 296, where the court was not unanimous.

[108] [1980] 1 W.L.R. 1875.

[109] *Hiort v Bott* (1874) L.R. 9 Ex. 86 (distinguished in *Kitano v The Commonwealth* (1974) 129 C.L.R. 151); *Van Oppen v Tredegars* (1921) 37 T.L.R. 504; *Douglas Valley Finance Co Ltd v S. Hughes (Hirers) Ltd* [1969] 1 Q.B. 738; see also *Ernest Scragg & Sons Ltd v Perseverance Banking and Trust Co Ltd* [1973] 2 Lloyd's Rep. 101.

over the registration book of the claimant's car amounts to conversion of the car since the absence of the book makes it difficult to deal with the car.[110] However, dicta in *Oakley v Lyster*[111] went further and suggested that a bare denial of the claimant's title unaccompanied by any possession of or dealing with the goods constituted conversion. The actual decision did not support such a wide doctrine,[112] which was laid to rest by the Torts (Interference with Goods) Act 1977.[113]

Where the defendant is in possession of the claimant's goods there is no doubt that an unjustified refusal to return them generally constitutes conversion but it has been held that where the claimant has possession there is no conversion if the defendant simply refuses to allow the claimant to remove them. In *England v Cowley*[114] M owed money to both the claimant and the defendant, her landlord. The claimant held a bill of sale over M's furniture and put a man into M's house to take charge of it. When the claimant then attempted to remove the furniture the defendant forbade him to do so and stationed a policeman at the gate to make sure he did not. The defendant was held not liable for conversion. Bramwell B. said:

> "In order to maintain trover, a plaintiff who is left in possession of the goods must prove that his dominion over his property has been interfered with, not in some particular way, but altogether that he has been entirely deprived of the use of it. It is not enough that a man should say that something shall not be done by the plaintiff he must say that nothing shall."[115]

C. Conversion under the Torts (Interference with Goods) Act 1977

17–14   Apart from one or two minor matters[116] this Act did not interfere with the concept of conversion at common law. However, the Act

---

[110] *Bryanston Leasings Ltd v Principality Finance Ltd* [1977] R.T.R. 45; see also the *Douglas Valley* case, above. In *Martin v Norbury*, July 21, 1999, CA, wrongfully registering a car with HPI, rendering it unsaleable, was held to be conversion.

[111] [1931] 1 K.B. 148.

[112] The defendant had in fact not only used some of the claimant's property himself but had interfered with the claimant's right to deal with it by denying, or purporting to deny, him access to it.

[113] Section 11(3): "denial of title is not of itself conversion". Note that a denial of title, if accompanied by malice, may amount to the tort of injurious falsehood: Goodhart (1931) 46 L.R. 168, 171; para.12–72, above.

[114] (1873) L.R. 8 Exch. 126; *Club Cruise etc BV v Department of Transport* [2008] EWHC 2794 (Comm); [2009] 1 Lloyd's Rep 201.

[115] It must be pointed out that Bramwell B.'s examples of a man who hinders his friend from taking a pistol to fight a duel or who blocks the path of a horseman so that he has to turn back are somewhat removed from the facts of the case: the first act would be justifiable as an act in the prevention of crime, the second would at least allow the claimant to take his property in other directions.

[116] Receipt by way of pledge (above) conversion by denial of title (above) co-ownership (below).

abolished detinue,[117] which was wrongful retention of a chattel. In most cases of detinue there would be a concurrent liability in conversion based upon a demand and refusal to return[118] but as we have seen conversion required a positive act and had never lain where the defendant once had the claimant's goods but was unable to return them because they had been lost or negligently destroyed.[119] Accordingly, to deal with this situation, the Act provides[120] that an:

"[A]ction lies in conversion for loss or destruction of goods which a bailee[121] has allowed to happen in breach of his duty to his bailor (that is to say it lies in a case which is not otherwise conversion, but would have been detinue before detinue was abolished)."[122]

D. Conversion and Co-owners
As between co-owners there is unity of possession, each is enti- **17–15** tled to possession and use of the chattel, and the mere enjoyment in one way or another by one co-owner cannot amount to conversion against the other. The assertion of exclusive rights will, however, be actionable in tort. By s.10 of the Torts (Interference with Goods) Act 1977 co-ownership is no defence to an action in conversion[123] where one, without the authority of the other[124]:

---

[117] Section 2(1).
[118] See para.17–2, above. The Law Reform Committee went so far to say that, "conversion will lie in every case in which detinue would lie, save only that detinue lies, but conversion does not lie, against a bailee of goods who in breach of his duty has allowed them to be lost or destroyed": Cmnd. 4774 (1971), para.8. Megarry V.C. (who had been a member of the Law Reform Committee) seems to have agreed in *Howard E. Perry & Co Ltd v BRB* [1980] 1 W.L.R. 1375, though it is not clear what attitude the learned judge would have taken to a long but not indefinite detention. Compare Palmer in (1981) 44 M.L.R. 87 "Title to Goods and Occupation of Land: A Conflict of Interests" (1980) 9 Anglo-American L.R. 279 and in "The Abolition of Detinue" [1981] Conv 62.
[119] See para.17–2, above. In cases where before the Act there was a concurrent liability in conversion and detinue the claimant might claim in detinue because this might enable him to get specific restitution. See now, s.3 of the Act.
[120] Section 2(2).
[121] Not, therefore, in a situation like that in *Ashby v Tolhurst*, para.17–11, above.
[122] The claimant must, therefore, show a right to immediate possession since this was necessary for detinue at common law. As to the jus tertii, see, para.17–18, below.
[123] The same rules apply to trespass.
[124] The position is different where co-ownership arises because the parties are buyers of portions of goods in bulk (e.g. oil in a tank) who have paid in full or in part. If there is delivery in full to one and then there is a shortfall as to the rest, the others are deemed to have authorised the first delivery, though they retain their contractual rights against the seller: Sale of Goods Act 1979 s.20B.

"(a) [D]estroys the goods,[125] or disposes of the goods in a way
     giving a good title to the entire property in the goods[126] or
     otherwise does anything equivalent to the destruction of the
     other's interest in the goods,[127] or

(b) purports to dispose of the goods in a way which would give
    a good title to the entire property in the goods if he was
    acting with the authority of all co-owners of the goods."

Paragraph (a) is by way of restatement of the common law[128];
paragraph (b) extends it so as to make the disposition conversion
even if it does not confer a good title on the disponee.[129]

E. Title of Claimant

17–16   What kind of right to the goods must the claimant have in order
that interference with it may amount to conversion? The answer is
that he can maintain the action if at the time of the defendant's act
he had: (1) ownership and possession of the goods; or (2) possession
of them; or (3) an immediate right to possess them, but without
either ownership or actual possession.[130] Some of the older cases
speak in terms that the claimant must have, "a right of property in
the thing and a right of possession" and that unless both these rights
concur the action will not lie[131] but the Court of Appeal has stated
that an immediate right of possession, even if based on contract, is
sufficient.[132] The fact that ownership is not necessary is demonstrated by the fact that it has never been doubted that a bailee (who
has possession but not ownership) can sue.[133]

---

[125] This does not, presumably, cover acts of the normal user which change the form of the
property as in *Fennings v Grenville* (1808) 1 Taunt. 241 (cutting up and boiling down a
whale).

[126] e.g. not a valid pledge under the Factors Act 1889, s.2, since that does not transfer the
"entire property".

[127] *Adventure Films Ltd v Tully, The Times*, October 14, 1982 (detention of television film).

[128] On which see particularly *Baker v Barclays Bank Ltd* [1955] 1 W.L.R. 822.

[129] The common law rule was regarded as no longer sustainable in New Zealand in *Coleman
v Harvey* [1989] 1 N.Z.L.R. 723. In *Nyberg v Handelaar* [1892] 2 Q.B. 202 A and B were
co-owners of a gold enamel box under an agreement that A was to have possession until
it was sold. A entrusted it to B for a limited purpose but B pledged it to C. In A's
successful action against C, Lopes L.J. gave his opinion that A could have maintained
conversion against B because of the agreement, but B's pledge would not now purport to
dispose of the entire property.

[130] *Rogers v Kennay* (1846) 9 Q.B. 594 at 596: "Any person having a right to the possession
of goods may bring trover in respect of the conversion of them, and allege them to be his
property: and lien, as an immediate right of possession, was held to constitute such a
property": per Patteson J.

[131] *Gordon v Harper* (1796) 7 T.R. 9 at 12; *Bloxam v Sanders* (1825) 9 B. & C. 941 at 950;
Owen v Knight (1837) 4 Bing. N.C. 54 at 57; *Bradley v Copley* (1845) 1 C.B. 685.

[132] *Iran v Barakat Galleries Ltd* [2007] EWCA Civ 1374; [2009] Q.B. 22, explaining *Jarvis
v Williams* [1955] 1 W.L.R. 71.

[133] *Burton v Hughes* (1842) 2 Bing. 173 at 175.

i. Examples of right to possess. There is no need to enlarge upon **17–17** (1) ownership and possession, or (2) possession, for possession was analysed in Ch.13. However, (3), the immediate right to possess, must be briefly examined. A reversionary owner out of possession certainly has not got it, for example in the case of a landlord of premises let together with furniture to a tenant whose term is still unexpired: if the furniture is wrongfully seized by the sheriff, it is the tenant and not the landlord who can sue for conversion.[134] Again, an employee in custody of his employer's goods has not possession of them, for it is constructively in the employer[135]; but if the employer has made him a bailee of them so as to vest him with exclusive possession, then, like any other bailee of this sort, he has it; so, too, if goods are delivered to him to hand to his employer, he has possession of them until he has done some act which transfers it to his employer, for example a shop assistant has possession of money paid to him by a customer until he puts it in the till. Up to that moment the employer has only the right to possess. These examples are tolerably plain, but it must depend to a large extent on the facts of each case whether the law will attribute to a person the immediate right to possess. A bailor had it against a mere bailee at pleasure[136] even if he never himself had actual possession of the goods and only acquired title by virtue of an illegal but completely executed contract of sale.[137] So, too, where furniture dealers transferred furniture on hire-purchase to X with an express proviso that the hiring was to terminate without any notice if the goods were taken in execution for debt, they could sue the sheriff for conversion when he levied execution on them.[138] The wrongful sale of goods subject to a hire-purchase agreement will constitute a repudiation and hence vest a right to immediate possession in the finance company even though the agreement does not expressly provide for this.[139] However, in modern conditions legislation may restrict the

---

[134] *Gordon v Harper* (1796) 7 T.R. 9.

[135] See Holmes, *The Common Law*, pp.227–228; Pollock and Wright, *Possession in the Common Law*, pp.58–60.

[136] *Manders v Williams* (1849) 4 Ex. 339 (brewers could maintain trover against a sheriff in respect of empty barrels in charge of publican). Distinguish *Bradley v Copley* (1845) 1 C.B. 685, where, upon the construction of a bill of sale, demand was held to be necessary to confer the immediate right to possess.

[137] *Belvoir Finance Co Ltd v Stapleton* [1971] 1 Q.B. 210 (claimant finance company buys car from dealer and lets it on HP to defendant's employer. Contracts of sale and HP both illegal. Defendant "sells" car on behalf of employer. Liable for conversion).

[138] *Jelks v Hayward* [1905] 2 K.B. 460, applied in *North General Wagon and Finance Co Ltd v Graham* [1950] 2 K.B. 7, CA; *Alexander v Ry Executive* [1951] 2 K.B. 882; distinguished in *Reliance Car Facilities Ltd v Roding Motors* [1952] 2 Q.B. 844, CA (hiring terminable on notice, but no notice given).

[139] *Union Transport Finance Ltd v British Car Auctions Ltd* [1978] 2 All E.R. 385. It may be necessary to identify the point in time when the conversion takes place since the right to possession must exist then. In *Smith v Bridgend CBC* [2001] UKHL 58; [2002] 1 A.C. 336 D's power of sale of C's plant was void as an unregistered floating charge. D contracted

enforcement of the creditor's rights under a hire-purchase agreement.[140]

In a simple bailment, i.e. one which does not exclude the bailor from possession, an action for conversion against a third person is maintainable by either bailor or bailee[141]: by the bailee because he is in possession, by the bailor because it is said that his title to the goods draws with it the right to possession, that the bailee is something like his servant and that the possession of the one is equivalent to that of the other.[142]

A buyer of goods can sue the seller or a third party for conversion if he has ownership of the goods even though he has not yet got possession of them,[143] but he cannot sue the third party if ownership has passed to such third person by reason of exceptions to the rule *nemo dat quod non habet*, under ss.21 to 25 of the Sale of Goods Act 1979 or under the Factors Act 1889[144]; the seller, however, is liable for conversion to the original buyer.

A person who is entitled to the temporary possession of a chattel and who delivers it back to the owner for a special purpose may, after that purpose is satisfied and during the existence of his temporary right, sue the owner for conversion of it[145]; a fortiori he can sue anyone else.

A person who has a merely equitable right in property and who does not have possession,[146] does not have an immediate right to possession for the purposes of conversion, even though the legal owner is a mere nominee who has to transfer the property to the beneficiary on demand.[147] Though there may in some cases be little practical difference between them, the legal distinction between bailor and bailee on the one hand and beneficiary and trustee on the other hand, is fundamental.[148]

to sell the plant to X at a time when D had a contractual right to retain it to complete the works. This did not prevent the delivery of the plant to X when the works had been completed being a conversion.

[140] See, e.g. *Barclays Mercantile Business Finance Ltd v Sibec Developments Ltd* [1993] 2 All E.R. 195, where the restriction was regarded as only procedural. For hire-purchase transactions by individuals see the Consumer Credit Act 1974.

[141] *Nicolls v Bastard* (1835) 2 C.M. & R. 659.

[142] Williams, *Personal Property*, 18th edn, p.59; *Manders v Williams* (1849) 4 Ex. 339 at 344 per Parke B. As to the avoidance of double liability in such cases, see para.17–19, below.

[143] e.g. *North West Securities Ltd v Alexander Breckon Ltd* [1981] R.T.R. 518. Note that if the goods remain in the seller's possession subject to his lien for their unpaid price, the buyer cannot sue a wrongdoer for conversion: *Lord v Price* (1874) L.R. 9 Ex. 54. *Bolwell Fibreglass Pty Ltd v Foley* [1984] V. R. 97.

[144] See para.17–22, below.

[145] *Roberts v Wyatt* (1810) 2 Taunt. 268.

[146] Cf. *Healey v Healey* [1915] 1 K.B. 938, where the beneficiary had actual possession, which was disturbed by the trustee.

[147] *M.C.C. Proceeds Ltd v Lehman Bros* [1998] 4 All E.R. 675, rejecting a contrary view in *International Factors v Rodriguez* [1979] 1 Q.B. 351.

[148] See further Tettenborn, "Trust Property and Conversion An Equitable Confusion" [1996] C.L.J. 36.

F. Jus Tertii

Once a system of law accepts possession as a sufficient founda-   **17–18**
tion for a claim for recovery of personal property it is faced with the
question of how far the defendant should be allowed to raise the
issue that a third party has a better right to the property than the
claimant—the jus tertii. There are arguments either way. On the one
hand, refusal to admit the jus tertii allows recovery by a claimant
who may have himself wrongfully dispossessed the true owner and
also exposes the wrongdoer to the risk of multiple liability. On the
other hand, it may be argued that a person who has dispossessed
another should have no right to raise such issues concerning the
relationship between the dispossessed and some other party having
a claim over the goods, for there is a serious risk of abuse and of the
interminable prolongation of actions. The common law compromised: if the claimant was in possession at the time of the conversion, the defendant could not set up the jus tertii,[149] unless he was
acting under the authority of the true owner.[150] Where, however, the
claimant was not in possession at the time of the conversion but
relied on his right to possession, jus tertii could be pleaded by the
defendant.[151] To this rule there was an exception where the defendant was the claimant's bailee, for the defendant was regarded as
being estopped from denying the claimant's title unless evicted by
title paramount or defending the action on behalf of the true
owner.[152]

These rules were fundamentally changed by the Torts (Interference with Goods) Act 1977. Since then, in an action for "wrongful interference with goods"[153] the defendant is entitled to show, in

[149] Assumed rather than decided in the famous case of *Armory v Delamirie* (1721) 1 Stra. 505
where a chimney-sweep's boy who had found a jewel recovered in conversion against a
goldsmith who took it for valuation and refused to return it. The rule was the same for
trespass where, of course, the claimant's possession was a pre-condition to his right to
sue.

[150] See further the 10th edn of this work, pp.424–425. However, the fact that he had returned
the property to the owner was not of itself a defence: *Wilson v Lombank Ltd* [1963] 1
W.L.R. 1294.

[151] *Leake v Loveday* (1842) 4 M. & G. 972. Cf. Atiyah (1955) 18 M.L.R. 97 and Jolly's reply,
(1955) 18 M.L.R. 371. The reason seems to be that conversion was regarded as a "denial
of title" and the defendant should therefore be allowed to attack the thing upon which the
claimant based his claim. Where, however, the claimant was in possession at the time of
the conversion the defendant's act was also a trespass. Trespass contained a penal element
of deterrence against breach of the peace, which was no doubt why the jus tertii was not
pleadable. It was natural that the trespass rule should "infect" conversion based on
possession.

[152] See Clerk and Lindsell, *Torts*, 19th edn, para.17–77 and *Anderson Group Pty Ltd v Tynan
Motors Pty Ltd* [2006] NSWCA 22; 65 N.S.W.L.R. 400 (loss of goods by bailee; hire-
purchase agreement under which bailor held them had been terminated for breach). A
bailee subjected to competing claims by the bailor and a third party could escape the
quandary by interpleader proceedings enabling him to drop out of the litigation and leave
the other two to fight it out between themselves.

[153] Defined in s.1 as conversion, trespass, negligence so far as it results in damage to goods
or to an interest in goods and "any other tort so far as it results in damage to goods or to

accordance with Rules of Court,[154] that a third party has a better right than the claimant as respects all or any part of the interest claimed by the claimant or in right of which he sues.[155] The Rules require the claimant to identify any other person whom he knows to have a claim on the goods. The defendant may apply for directions as to whether any third person with a competing claim should be joined and if that person fails to appear on such a successful application the court may deprive him of any right of action against the defendant.[156]

17–19   The general purpose of these provisions is to allow the court so far as possible to settle competing claims in one set of proceedings. Where all the claimants are before the court under s.8, then the relief granted is to be, "such as to avoid double liability of the wrong-doer",[157] which presumably means that the court is to apportion the damages representing the value of the chattel according to the respective interests of the claimants.[158] The Act is perhaps not so clear where only the claimant with a possessory title is before the court, for example, because the true owner does not appear or cannot be found. A literal interpretation of s.8 might suggest that the ability to plead the jus tertii provides the defendant with a defence,[159] but it seems clear that in such a case the provisions of s.7 preserve the common law rule that a claimant relying on a possessory interest may recover the full value of the thing converted.[160] In such a situation the true owner may have been divested of his claim against the wrongdoer under s.8(2)(d) but if not, he might still be entitled to sue by virtue of his title. Two provisions of the Act are aimed at this problem. By s.7(3):

"[O]n satisfaction, in whole or in part, of any claim for an amount

---

an interest in goods". The last phrase clearly includes rescous, pound breach and replevin. Quaere as to injurious falsehood? How far can the change in the law on jus tertii be evaded by framing the claim as breach of bailment or in contract? The courts may be able to block the former (cf. *American Express Co v British Airways Board* [1983] 1 W.L.R. 701) but the latter will be more difficult to deal with. See further Palmer, "The Application of the Torts (Interference with Goods) Act 1977 to Actions in Bailment" (1978) 41 M.L.R. 629.
[154] CPR 19.5A.
[155] Section 8(1). This provision applies even though the third party has disposed of the alleged interest before proceedings are begun: *De Franco v MPC, The Times*, May 8, 1987.
[156] See also s.9, which provides machinery to deal with concurrent claims in different courts.
[157] Section 7(2).
[158] As between finder and true owner, the interest of the finder would presumably be nil.
[159] Or at least reduce the claimant's damages to the value of his interest.
[160] *The Winkfield* [1902] P. 42 (a strong case since the bailee claimant would have been under no liability to the owners for loss of the goods); *Swire v Leach* (1865) 18 C.B.(N.S.) 479; *Chabbra Corp Pte Ltd v Jag Shakti (owners)* [1986] A.C. 337. This was certainly the intention of the Law Reform Committee: Cmnd. 4774 (1971), para.75 and was the view taken in *Costello v CC Derbyshire* [2001] EWCA Civ 381; [2001] 1 W.L.R. 1437 at [15]. Some cases, e.g. *The Winkfield*, are claims for negligence but the position is the same.

exceeding that recoverable if subsection (2) applied [i.e. where both claimants are parties], the claimant is liable to account over to the other person having a right to claim to such extent as will avoid double liability",[161]

and by s.7(4):

"[W]here, as a result of enforcement of a double liability, any claimant is unjustly enriched to any extent, he shall be liable to reimburse the wrongdoer to that extent."

Thus if A loses his goods, which are found by C and then converted by D, both C and A might bring successive claims against D. If C accounts to A under s.7(3), A must then reimburse D. If C does not so account, C is liable to reimburse D. A "double liability" would, however, still exist if both A and C were insolvent.[162] A central difficulty in construing the provisions of the 1977 Act on jus tertii is the position where there is a bailment, which is presumably far and away the commonest source of a "possessory title". The position at common law may be summarised as follows:

1. As we have seen, the bailee could recover the full value of the goods on the basis of his possession. If he did so, he had to account to the bailor for the amount by which the damages exceeded his (the bailee's) interest.[163]
2. In such a case the wrongdoer, having paid full damages to the bailee, had a complete answer to any action by the bailor.[164]
3. Contrariwise, if the bailor sued first and recovered full value,[165] the bailee was equally barred.[166]

---

[161] As to the bailee, see below.
[162] What is the effect of the Act upon *Wilson v Lombank Ltd* [1963] 1 W.L.R. 1294? C purchased a car from a person who had no title, the car in fact belonging to M.C. Co. While the car was at a garage after undergoing repairs, D's agents passed by and, mistakenly thinking it belonged to D, took it away. D discovered the truth and returned the car to M.C. Co. C sued D for trespass to goods and recovered the full value of the car (£470) because, in Hinchcliffe J.'s opinion, D could not set up the title of M.C. Co against C's possessory title. Since it is inconceivable that M.C. Co could have sued D for anything other than nominal damages it seems somewhat strained to talk of a "double liability" under s.7. Cf. Clerk and Lindsell, *Torts*, 19th edn, para.17–82. Could this be a case where s.8(1) is to be taken at its face value?
[163] Among the many statements to this effect see *The Winkfield* [1902] P. 42 at 55; *Eastern Construction Co Ltd v National Trust* [1914] A.C. 197 at 210; *Hepburn v A. Tomlinson (Hauliers) Ltd* [1966] A.C. 451 at 467–468, 480.
[164] *Nicolls v Bastard* (1835) 2 C.M. & R. 659 at 660; *The Winkfield* [1902] P. 42 at 61.
[165] It was held in *Chabbra Corp Pte Ltd v Jag Shakti (Owners)* [1986] A.C. 337 that a person with a mere right to possession might recover full value but this is controversial: Palmer, *Bailment*, 3rd edn, para.4–138
[166] *Nicolls v Bastard*, above, fn.164, at 660; *O'Sullivan v Williams* [1992] 3 All E.R. 385, where there was a non-contractual bailment at will and the bailee therefore had no right to look to the bailor. Complications which might arise from the fact that the bailee might

17–20   These principles might cast some doubt upon the reality of the risk of double liability which lies at the root of ss.7 and 8 of the 1977 Act but the Act might still provide a useful means of enabling the court to apportion the full range of loss which might arise from the conversion or destruction of goods and to avoid the risk that, say, the bailor might have difficulties in getting the bailee to account for part of the judgment sum.[167] Curiously, the common law principles have been applied in a modern case in which the Act is not even mentioned[168] and it is to be hoped that certain statements in the case will not present obstacles to the application of the Act's machinery.[169]

It has been seen above that where the true owner of goods cannot be involved in the proceedings the common law rule that a mere possessory interest entitles the claimant to recover the full value of the goods against a wrongdoer still applies. Does this mean that if there is clear evidence that the goods were stolen by C from X (who has since disappeared) C may nevertheless recover from D, who converted them by taking them from C? In *Costello v CC Derbyshire*[170] the police seized a car in C's possession and refused to return it when their investigations were complete. The trial judge found that the car was stolen (though not by C) and that C was aware of that, though the person from whom it had been stolen remained unidentified. The Court of Appeal held that to refuse to return the car to C was conversion of it: his prior possession gave him a better

---

suffer loss of use damages which were not comprehended within the bailor's claim do not seem to have been fully explored in the cases: Palmer, *Bailment*, para.4–099.

[167] See, e.g. Palmer, *Bailment* para.4–138: "It is submitted that s.7(2) should be construed expansively to enable the court, in all cases where two or more claimants are parties, to divide the damages according to the value of their respective interests, whether this is strictly necessary to save the wrongdoer from a [double liability] or not."

[168] *O'Sullivan v Williams* [1992] 3 All E.R. 385. Perhaps this was because the claim arose from a (very unusual) vehicle collision and these were not then subject to the Rules made under the Act: RSC Ord.15, r.10(A).

[169] e.g. "There cannot be separate claims by the bailor and the bailee arising from loss or damage to the chattel" (at p.379) and the reference at p.388 to the rule in *Brunsden v Humphrey*. Though there is not much in the way of case law it is thought that if either the bailee or the bailor recovered only in respect of the value of his interest the other should have a claim for the balance (see Palmer, *Bailment*, para.4–118). The bailee's claim in *O'Sullivan v Williams* was for "inconvenience" in not having the use of the bailor's vehicle, but the bailor had recovered damages for loss of use from the date of the damage and the bailee's "claim" was presumably subsumed in that. The reference at p.388 to the bailee's claim being "purely for economic loss" is curious since it has always been accepted that economic loss arising from damage to a chattel in one's possession is recoverable: para.5–40, above.

[170] [2001] EWCA Civ 381; [2001] 1 W.L.R. 1437. See also *Webb v CC Merseyside* [2000] Q.B. 427 (even if it could be established on a balance of probabilities that money seized from claimant was the product of drug trafficking, that provided no basis for refusing to return it); *Gough v CC West Midlands* [2004] EWCA Civ 206; and *Jaroo v Att Gen of Trinidad and Tobago* [2002] UKPC 5; [2002] 1 A.C. 871 (where the claim was brought under a Constitutional guarantee of the right to enjoyment of property; cf. the First Protocol to the European Convention on Human Rights).

claim to it than the defendants[171] and he was not required to rely on any illegal transaction to establish that.[172] The only ground for refusing to treat him as entitled to the goods (apart from the case where the owner could be identified) would be that it was inherently unlawful to possess the goods, for example controlled drugs. However, in cases like these consideration will have to be given to the enormously extensive powers of confiscation and forfeiture under the Proceeds of Crime Act 2002[173] and under s.329 it is an offence for a person to be in possession of property which constitutes a benefit from his criminal conduct.

G. Finding[174]

The popular saying that "finding is keeping" is a dangerous half-truth, which needs a good deal of expansion and qualification to make it square with the law.

17–21

A finder of a chattel has such a title as will enable him to keep it against everyone,[175] with two exceptions:

1. The rightful owner. Far from getting any title against him, the finder, if he appropriates the chattel, not only commits the tort of conversion,[176] but is also guilty of the crime of theft unless he appropriates the chattel in the belief that the owner cannot be discovered by taking reasonable steps.[177]
2. The occupier[178] of the land on which the chattel[179] is found may in some cases have a title superior to that of the finder. The Court of Appeal in *Parker v British Airways Board*[180] took

---

[171] There are powers under the Police and Criminal Evidence Act 1984 to retain property for the purposes of investigation or as evidence but the conditions for the exercise of these were not satisfied in these cases. The Police Property Act 1897 gives magistrates power to make orders for the disposition of property in the hands of the police but that does not override civil rights under the general law.

[172] See *Tinsley v Milligan* [1994] 1 A.C. 340 and the general discussion of illegality at para.25–18, below.

[173] Various bodies (see the Serious Crime Act 2007) may take civil proceedings for the recovery by the State (on a civil standard of proof and involving assumptions against the defendant if he has a "criminal lifestyle") of the proceeds of criminal activity.

[174] Palmer, *Bailment*, 3rd edn, Ch.26.

[175] Like the person in possession of stolen goods, the finder's claim is based upon his possession alone.

[176] *Moffatt v Kazana* [1969] 2 Q.B. 152.

[177] Theft Act 1968 ss.1, 2(1)(c).

[178] Not a non-occupying owner: *Hannah v Peel* [1945] K.B. 509. For property found on local authority land and handed in, see the Local Government Miscellaneous Provisions Act 1982 s.41.

[179] Different rules apply where the property is "treasure", as to which, see the Treasure Act 1996, replacing the common law of treasure trove. The Crown's rights in treasure override those of the finder and the landowner, with a discretion in the Secretary of State to compensate either or both of them up to the value of the goods found. Treasure under the Act is a good deal wider than at common law.

[180] [1982] Q.B. 1004.

the opportunity to restate the law in a comprehensive manner and bring order to an area in which there were numerous conflicting precedents. The cases in which the occupier of the land has the superior title[181] are:

(a) where the finder is a trespasser on the land[182];

(b) where the property is in or attached to the land, as in *Waverley Borough Council v Fletcher*[183] where a medieval gold brooch was found embedded nine inches deep in the soil of a park;

(c) where he is the occupier of premises on which the chattels (not attached to the premises) are found and, before the finding, "he has manifested an intention to exercise control over the [premises] and the things which may be upon it or in it".[184]

The burden of proof of this rests upon the occupier, though in some cases the matter speaks for itself:

"If a bank manager saw fit to show me round a vault containing safe deposits and I found a gold bracelet on the floor, I should have no doubt that the bank had a better title than I, and the reason is the manifest intention to exercise a very high degree of control. At the other extreme is the park to which the public has unrestricted access during daylight hours. During those hours there is no manifest intention to exercise any such control. In between these extremes are the forecourts of petrol filling stations, unfenced front gardens of private houses, the public parts of shops and supermarkets as part of an almost infinite variety of land, premises and circumstances."[185]

In *Parker*'s case itself the claimant found a gold bracelet on the floor of the executive lounge at Heathrow Airport and was held entitled to it as against the occupiers. The facts that they restricted entry to the lounge to certain classes of passengers and gave their staff instructions as to what to do with lost property were insufficient

---

[181] It is assumed that the finder is not employed by the possessor of the land, for a servant (and perhaps agent) who finds in the course of his employment must account to his employer.

[182] Where the finder is not a trespasser but dishonestly intends to retain the property even against the true owner, the finder, "probably has some title, albeit a frail one, because of the need to avoid a free-for-all": [1982] Q.B. 1004 at 1010.

[183] [1996] Q.B. 334. See also *South Staffs Water Co v Sharman* [1896] 2 Q.B. 44. The case can also be explained on the ground that the finders were employed by the claimants: [1982] Q.B. 1004 at 1013.

[184] [1982] Q.B. 1004 at 1018 per Donaldson L.J.

[185] [1982] Q.B. 1004 at 1019.

to manifest the intention to exercise the requisite degree of control.[186] It is, of course, open to the occupier to regulate the right to possession of lost property by contract with the entrant; it remains to be seen whether merely putting up notices at the entrance declaring that lost property is to vest in the occupier will be an effective manifestation of the intent to control required by *Parker*'s case.[187]

3. STRICT LIABILITY AND CONVERSION

The first thing to be said, is that mistake does not usually provide a defence,[188] for liability in conversion is strict:

    17–22

> "At common law one's duty to one's neighbour who is the owner . . . of any goods is to refrain from doing any voluntary act in relation to his goods which is a usurpation of his proprietary or possessory rights in them. Subject to some exceptions . . . it matters not that the doer of the act of usurpation did not know, and could not by the exercise of any reasonable care have known of his neighbour's interest in the goods. This duty is absolute; he acts at his peril."[189]

The classic illustration is the position of the auctioneer, who is liable in conversion if he innocently effects the sale of another's goods[190] and of whom it has been said that conversion is one of "the risks of his profession".[191]

This rule was set solidly into our law by the House of Lords in *Hollins v Fowler*.[192] B fraudulently obtained possession of cotton from Fowler. Hollins, a cotton broker who was ignorant of the fraud, bought it from B and resold it to another person, receiving only broker's commission. Hollins was held liable to Fowler for the conversion of the cotton. The justification for such a rule is not at all

---

[186] The much-battered case of *Bridges v Hawkesworth* (1851) 21 L.J.Q.B. 75, in which the occupier of a shop failed against the finder of banknotes on the floor of the shop, was approved in *Parker*'s case.

[187] Even if it is not, a finder who takes lost property in defiance of such a condition in his licence would seem to be a trespasser.

[188] Licence and the exercise of a right of distress are defences to an action for conversion but these have already been touched on in relation to trespass to land.

[189] *Marfani & Co Ltd v Midland Bank Ltd* [1968] 1 W.L.R. 956 at 971 per Diplock L.J. However, an innocent converter will be in a more favourable position with regard to limitation than one who knows the facts: para.26–16, below.

[190] *Consolidated Co v Curtis & Son* [1892] 1 Q.B. 495; *R.H. Willis & Sons v British Car Auctions Ltd* [1978] 1 W.L.R. 438, doubting *National Mercantile Bank Ltd v Rymill* (1881) 44 L.T. 767.

[191] *Sachs v Miklos* [1948] 2 K.B. 23 at 37. It seems that in New Zealand the same may be true of a tow truck operator: *Wilson v New Brighton Panelbeaters Ltd* [1989] 1 N.Z.L.R. 74 at 79.

[192] (1875) L.R. 7 H.L. 757.

obvious, particularly when in the typical case the claimant will have handed his goods over to a rogue on some flimsy excuse while the defendant has acquired the goods not only in good faith but from some reputable dealer who has himself been deceived. One solution which has been suggested would be to apportion the loss between claimant and defendant in such a case[193] but this was rejected as impracticable by the Law Reform Committee.[194] An alternative approach would have been to apply the "ready-made" system of apportionment in the Law Reform (Contributory Negligence) Act 1945 to liability in conversion.[195] There was some authority for this but the matter is now governed by s.11(1) of the Torts (Interference with Goods) Act 1977 which firmly states that contributory negligence is no defence in proceedings founded on conversion, or on intentional trespass to goods.[196]

There are, however, exceptions to the rule that innocent mistake is no defence. The first group consists of what is sometimes known as the exceptions to the rule *nemo dat quod non habet*, whereby a bona fide purchaser of goods from A commits no conversion but actually obtains a good title to them even though the goods really belonged to B and B never intended to allow A to sell them. B's remedy is against A alone. In such cases the law has sought to strike a compromise between the competing principles that ownership of property must be protected and that speedy commerce in goods should be facilitated. Details of this very large topic must be sought elsewhere[197] but the principal exceptions are briefly as follows:

1. Estoppel by representation or by negligent conduct.[198]
2. Sale under a voidable title.[199]

---

[193] By Devlin L.J. in *Ingram v Little* [1961] 1 Q.B. 31 at 73–74.

[194] Twelfth Report, Transfer of Title to Chattels Cmnd. 2958 (1966). The Committee's principal reasons were that a scheme of apportionment would introduce a wide judicial discretion just where predictability is particularly important and that there would be grave practical difficulties in "chain" transactions.

[195] This would not have gone so far as Devlin L.J.'s proposal since the claimant's damages could only have been reduced if he was at fault. Devlin L.J. had proposed that as between a completely innocent claimant and a completely innocent defendant the loss should be apportioned equally.

[196] However, under s.47 of the Banking Act 1979 a "defence of contributory negligence" is available to a banker converting a cheque if the circumstances are such that he would be protected by s.4 of the Cheques Act 1957 if he were not negligent. This presumably means that the 1945 Act is to apply and effectively restores the decision in *Lumsden v London Trustee Savings Bank* [1971] 1 Lloyd's Rep. 114.

[197] Benjamin, *Sale of Goods* and other works on sale. For an exception in the context of insolvency to the rule that mistake is no defence, see the Insolvency Act 1986 s.234.

[198] Such a plea is extremely difficult to establish, no doubt because it would soon eat up all the other exceptions. Carelessness in allowing goods to be stolen or putting the goods in the hands of a third party will not found the estoppel. See *Moorgate Mercantile Co Ltd v Twitchings* [1977] A.C. 890.

[199] e.g. *Lewis v Avery* [1972] 1 Q.B. 198.

3. Disposition in the ordinary course of business by a mercantile agent in possession of the goods or documents of title with the owner's consent.[200]
4. Second sale by seller in possession.[201]
5. Sale by buyer in possession.[202]
6. Private purchaser of vehicle subject to a hire-purchase agreement.[203]

We have seen above that a person commits conversion if he sells **17–23** the goods to another, whether on his own behalf or as an agent (e.g. an auctioneer), but the position is different where the defendant innocently interferes with the claimant's goods whether upon his own initiative or upon the instructions of another, when the defendant's act amounts to nothing more than transport or custody or redelivery of the goods. Blackburn J. in *Hollins v Fowler* said that:

" . . . [O]ne who deals with goods at the request of the person who has the actual custody of them, in the bona fide belief that the custodian is the true owner, should be excused for what he does if the act is of such a nature as would be excused if done by the authority of the person in possession, if he was a finder of the goods or entrusted with their custody . . . A warehouseman with whom goods have been deposited is guilty of no conversion by keeping them, or restoring them to the person who deposited them with him, though that person turns out to have had no authority from the true owner."[204]

So in *Marcq v Christie, Manson & Woods Ltd*[205] a painting was deposited by S with the defendant auctioneers for sale. Unknown to the auctioneers the painting had been stolen some years previously from M. It failed to sell at auction and was eventually returned by the defendants to S. A claim for conversion against the auctioneers in redelivering it failed and it was irrelevant that the terms of contract gave the auctioneers a lien for their charges against S. If, of course, M had demanded the painting from them their refusal by assertion of the lien against him *would* have been conversion. Similarly there is no liability if a railway company, acting upon A's

---

[200] Factors Act 1889 s.2.
[201] Sale of Goods Act 1979 s.24.
[202] Sale of Goods Act 1979 s.25.
[203] Hire Purchase Act 1964 Pt III. See also Twelfth Report of the Law Reform Committee Cmnd. 2958 (1966). Another exception, sale in market overt, was abolished by the Sale of Goods (Amendment) Act 1994.
[204] (1875) L.R. 7 H.L. 757 at 766–767. *Aliter* if the warehouseman has notice of the claim of the true owner: *Winter v Bancks* (1901) 84 L.T. 504.
[205] [2003] EWCA Civ 731; [2004] Q.B. 286. Hudson, 10 *Art, Antiquity & Law* 201.

directions, carries B's goods, honestly believing that A has B's authority to give such directions[206] or, of course, where a finder removes them to a place of safety.[207]

17–24   The test (artificial as it is) would protect all those persons in *Hollins v Fowler* who merely handled the cotton ministerially, such as a carrier who merely received and delivered the goods in the ordinary way[208] and it would not save the person who has sold the cotton to another. A solicitor of an undischarged bankrupt who receives after-acquired property on behalf of his client and transfers it to another agent, even with knowledge that that agent has been instructed to sell, is not liable for conversion at the suit of the trustee in bankruptcy, for the solicitor's act can be described as ministerial within the test laid down by Blackburn J.[209] Unfortunately, as Blackburn J. himself admitted, it is doubtful how far it goes. Does it protect the defendant if A wrongfully gives him B's wheat to grind into flour and he innocently does so? The learned judge thought not (and indeed a mere finder of lost wheat could not authorise the grinding of it), and yet he felt that it would be hard to hold the defendant liable. No doubt a finder of perishable commodities would be justified in taking any reasonable steps to preserve them pending the ascertainment of their owner; for example he would not commit conversion by making jam of strawberries if that were the only mode of preserving them, but cases like these might well be based on the general defence of necessity.[210]

---

[206] See (1875) L.R. 7 H.L. 757 at 767; but in *Wilson v New Brighton Panelbeaters Ltd* [1989] 1 N.Z.L.R. 74 D was held liable for conversion where he was tricked by X into towing away C's car and delivering it to X. A rather different approach was taken in *Maynegrain Pty Ltd v Compafina Bank* (1984) 58 A.L.J.R. 389. The defendants were bailees of barley belonging to X which had been pledged to the Y Bank by means of warehouse receipts. Unknown to the defendants Y Bank was acting as agent for Z Bank, the claimant. On X's order and with Y's tacit consent the defendants dispatched some of the barley to Kuwait. This was done without Z's authority. Z's action for conversion failed: Y Bank was agent for an undisclosed principal, Z Bank, and the defendants were entitled to act on Y's consent. Though consent is undeniably a defence to an action for conversion, there are difficulties in reconciling this result, sensible as it may seem, with general principles of agency, for since Y's act was unauthorised it could only be effective if done within an ostensible authority—but that doctrine is inapplicable to undisclosed agency: see Palmer [1986] L.M.& C.L.Q. at p.224. Cf. *The Pioneer Container* [1994] 2 A.C. 324 (bailee "assumes responsibility" only to person of whose interest he is aware).

[207] *Sorrell v Paget* [1950] 1 K.B. 252.

[208] In *Hollins v Fowler*, Blackburn J. speaks of the delivery as merely "changing the custody" but it is hard to see why, as he suggests, it would be "very difficult, if not impossible" to fix the carrier with knowledge that the goods had been sold to the consignee. Yet to impose liability on the carrier who had such knowledge would seem to be a wholly unreasonable burden. See *Samuel (No.2), Re*, below, fn.209.

[209] *Samuel (No.2), Re* [1945] Ch. 408. "To involve conversion the act, looked at in isolation, must have the effect of depriving the true owner of his property" at 411 per Lord Greene M.R. If A lends B's plough to C without authority and C uses it thinking it is A's, such a use is not a conversion by C: Warren, *Trover and Conversion*, p.101.

[210] See para.25–33, below.

4. REMEDIES FOR INTERFERENCE WITH GOODS

A. Retaking of Goods

Retaking of goods is a species of self-help. It may now be an **17–25** oversimplification to say that if A's goods are wrongfully in B's possession there is no need for A to go to the expense of litigation to recover them.[211] No doubt there are still simple cases where this is so, as where A catches B immediately after he has seized A's property and retakes it.[212] It would be a hard rule (and an unrealistic one) which said that a citizen who seized a bag snatcher had to sue to recover his bag and committed an assault if he laid hands on the thief. In such a case there may anyway be the further justification of preventing crime or effecting an arrest. Beyond that simple case it is not easy to state the law with certainty. Perhaps there is also a right to retake the goods wherever the holder came into possession of them wrongfully (even by an innocent purchase from a thief conferring no title) but there is authority both ways on the situation where the taker initially consented to the possession of the holder but then withdrew it.[213] English criminal cases arising out of wheel clamping have shown a hostile attitude to self-help by the vehicle owner, though on the facts the vehicles were not lawfully on the property where the clamp was applied.[214] Even where the owner is justified in using force it must be no more than is reasonably necessary and that varies with the facts of each case and the view of the court or jury after the event, so self-help is likely to be just as dangerous a remedy here as elsewhere in the law.[215] Moreover, there are other qualifications of A's right to retake goods.[216]

Further difficulty arises over the circumstances in which a person **17–26** can enter premises to retrieve his goods without committing a trespass. There is no doubt that the person entitled to goods may enter and take them from the land of the first taker if the taker himself wrongfully put them there[217]; but it is by no means certain

---

[211] Delay may mean destruction or carrying away of the goods by B, who may be quite incapable of paying damages: Blackstone, Comm., iii, 4.

[212] See, e.g. *Whatford v Carty, The Times*, October 29, 1960.

[213] The matter is reviewed at length in *Toyota Finance Australia Ltd v Dennis* [2002] NSWCA 605, but the court was divided, the majority holding that the right was confined to cases of wrongful appropriation. The case concerned a hire-purchase repossession and s.90 of the Consumer Credit Act 1974 certainly assumes that there is in some circumstances a right to retake the bailed goods.

[214] *Lloyd v DPP* [1992] 1 All E.R. 982 ("no reasonable alternative"); *R. v Mitchell* [2003] EWCA Crim 2188. See also *Arthur v Anker* [1996] 1 W.L.R. 602.

[215] Maiming or wounding are unlikely to be justifiable for simple recaption of property, but they may become justifiable for another reason—self-defence. This may occur when B, in endeavouring wrongfully to resist A's attempt to recapture his goods, commits an assault upon A and so justifies A in using reasonably necessary violence to protect himself.

[216] There are certain important statutory restrictions upon the retaking of goods, the best known of which are in the Consumer Credit Act 1974.

[217] *Patrick v Colerick* (1838) 3 M. & W. 483.

what the law is when the goods are on the premises of one who was not responsible for bringing them there and who has committed no tort with respect to them.[218] The only case of any real assistance is *Anthony v Haney*,[219] and even there the dicta are obiter and, although of considerable weight, do not probe the question of recaption very deeply. Tindal C.J. in that case gave as examples of permissible retaking by A from the land of an innocent person, C: (1) where the goods have come there by accident; (2) where they have been feloniously taken by B and A follows them to C's land; (3) where C refuses to deliver up the goods or to make any answer to A's demand for them.

As to (1) accident, the Chief Justice's examples were A's fruit falling upon C's land, or A's tree falling upon it by decay or being blown upon it by the wind. By "accident" it seems clear that "inevitable accident" was meant. Negligent or intentional placing of goods on the land of another is (technically at least) a tort, for example where a cricket ball is hit by any ordinary stroke out of the ground into another person's premises. The occupier of the premises, far from being put under any obligation to allow the owner of the goods to enter and retake them, is entitled to distrain them damage feasant until the owner of the goods pays for such damage as they have done. Where, however, the entry of the goods was inevitable, not only is there no liability for trespass on the part of their owner, but the view that he can retake them seems to be right, even if there is no direct decision to that effect.

As to (2), the rule that if A's goods are feloniously taken by B, the distinction between felonies and misdemeanours no longer exists[220] but there seems no reason why the rule, if it is a rule at all, should not apply wherever B's taking is criminal.[221]

As to (3), Tindal C.J. thought that where C refused to deliver up the goods or to answer A's demand:

> "[A] jury might be induced to presume a conversion from such silence, or at any rate the owner might in such case enter and take his property subject to the payment of any damage he might commit",[222]

---

[218] "The decisions tell too uncertain a story for [the owner] to be properly advised to take the law into his own hands": Lawson, *Remedies of English Law*, 2nd edn, p.28.

[219] (1832) 8 Bing. 186.

[220] Criminal Law Act 1967 s.1(1).

[221] There are practical difficulties here, too, for B's criminality might depend upon B's state of mind, of which A was ignorant: for example, B might have taken the property under a claim of right.

[222] (1832) 8 Bing. 186 at 192–193. The report in 1 L.J.C.P. 81 at 84 omits the passage about the right to enter, subject to payment of damages; the report in 1 Moo. & Sc. 300 at 308 omits any reference to the obligation to pay for the damage done. Since Tindal C.J. had already dealt with accidental entry and wrongful appropriation it is not wholly clear what type of case he had in mind.

though there are cases suggesting that mere refusal to allow collection would not be conversion.[223] As a matter of policy it may be argued on the one hand that where the owner of goods was under no tortious liability for their appearance on the occupier's land, he ought to be able to retake them in any event, provided he does no injury to the premises or gives adequate security for making good any unavoidable injury. On the other hand, it may be urged that self-help ought to be strictly limited even against a wrongdoer and forbidden altogether against one who is not a wrongdoer, except that retaking might be permitted in circumstances of inevitable accident or of necessity (for example where the goods are perishable or are doing considerable damage to the land and it is impossible to communicate speedily enough with the occupier or his agent). It has been held that the owner of a swarm of bees has no right to follow it onto another person's land,[224] but this is of no general assistance for, once the bees get onto that land they become again *ferae naturae*[225] and the property of no one.

Tindal C.J. did not profess to make an exhaustive list of the cases in which recaption is permissible, but be the extent of this justification of trespass and conversion what it may, one thing is clear. The retaker, before he attempts to retake, must, if required to do so, explain to the occupier of the land or the person in possession of the goods the facts upon which his proposed action is based. A mere allegation that the goods are his, without any attempt to show how they came on the premises, will not do, for:

"[T]o allow such a statement to be a justification for entering the soil of another, would be opening too wide a door to parties to attempt righting themselves without resorting to law, and would necessarily tend to breach of the peace."[226]

B. Judicial Remedies

It may be surprising in view of the proprietary nature of the tort,   **17–27**
but in practice damages are, as in the case of other torts, the primary

---

[223] *British Economical Lamp Co Ltd v Empire Mile End Ltd* (1913) 29 T.L.R. 386. Maule J. in *Wilde v Waters* (1855) 24 L.J.C.P 193 at 195 thought that if a former tenant of a house left a picture on a wall and the new tenant refused to admit him and merely said "I don't want your chattel, but I shall not give myself any trouble about it", that would not be conversion. This seems to be a sort of permanent legal stand-off, though since the former tenant undoubtedly remains the owner of the picture he must surely be able to obtain an order allowing collection. See also *Moffatt v Kazana* [1969] 2 Q.B. 152 at 156–157 and Palmer, "Title to Goods and Occupation of Land: A Conflict of Interests" (1980) 9 Anglo-American L.R. 279.

[224] *Kearry v Pattinson* [1939] 1 K.B. 471.

[225] In the property law sense, not the sense of animals belonging to a dangerous species: para.16–3 above.

[226] Tindal C.J. in *Anthony v Haney* at (1832) 8 Bing. 191–192.

remedy. This is necessarily so where the defendant is no longer in possession because he has destroyed the goods or disposed of them or they have been returned, but even where the defendant is still in possession it is comparatively rare for him to be ordered specifically to return them, though he may be given the option of returning them or paying their value.

In most cases the judgment for damages will be for the value[227] of the goods at the time of the conversion[228] together with any consequential loss which is not too remote, because that represents what the claimant has lost. Value is prima facie the market price of such goods, though where they cannot be obtained in the market the cost of replacement may be allowed where the claimant has replaced the goods or will do so.[229] If there is doubt as to the value of the chattel the claimant will get the benefit of it for, *omnia praesumuntur contra spoliatorem,*[230] though this cannot be pressed too far because it would negate the fundamental proposition that it is for the claimant to prove his loss.[231] However, damages for conversion are subject to the normal rule that they are assessed on the basis of what is necessary to give the claimant just compensation for his loss[232] and the test of the value of the goods will have to give way to that where the claimant's loss is smaller. Thus a finance company letting goods on hire-purchase is limited to recovering the amount owing under the agreement[233]; a person who uses raw materials for processing rather than trading in them and who does not replace them during the period they are wrongfully detained cannot recover damages by reference to the fall in the market price during that period[234]; and where by statute ownership of eggs vested immediately on production in the claimant marketing board and the defendant farmers converted them by selling them to others, the

---

[227] For the value of documents such as negotiable instruments, see para.17–7, above. Exemplary damages may be awarded where the defendant calculates to make a profit exceeding compensatory damages: *Borders (UK) Ltd v MPC* [2005] EWCA Civ 197 and para.22–10, below.

[228] This is the general rule and reflects the claimant's duty to mitigate his loss, but the position would be different if the claimant were unaware of the conversion until later: *Sachs v Micklos* [1948] 2 K.B. 23; *B.B.M.B. Finance (Hong Kong) Ltd v Eda Holdings Ltd* [1990] 1 W.L.R. 409: but *Scheps v Fine Art Logistic Ltd* [2007] EWHC 541 (QB) simply allows the claimant to add on any subsequent notional rise in value to judgment as consequential loss.

[229] *Hall v Barclay* [1937] 3 All E.R. 620; *Wilson v Robertsons (London) Ltd* [2006] EWCA Civ 1088; and see para.22–42, below (damage and destruction).

[230] Everything is presumed against a wrongful taker. *Armory v Delamirie* (1721) 1 Stra. 505.

[231] *Zabihi v Janzemini* [2009] EWCA Civ 851; *Malhotra v Dhawan* [1997] Med.L.R. 319; *Colbeck v Diamanta (UK) Ltd* [2002] EWHC 616 (QB).

[232] *Kuwait Airways Corp v Iraqi Airways Co (Nos 4 and 5)* [2002] UKHL 19; [2002] 2 A.C. 883 at [67].

[233] *Wickham Holdings Ltd v Brooke House Motors Ltd* [1967] 1 W.L.R. 295. For the position of the claimant with a possessory interest, see para.17–19, above.

[234] *Brandeis Goldschmidt & Co Ltd v Western Transport Ltd* [1981] Q.B. 864.

board's damages were not the value of the eggs but the difference between what it would have made by selling them and what it would have had to pay the farmers.[235]

Where the goods (or an exact equivalent) are returned, one plainly cannot ignore the value of what the claimant receives. In *B.B.M.B. Finance (Hong Kong) Ltd v Eda Holdings Ltd*[236] D converted C's share certificates by selling the shares for $HK5.75 each. D later replaced these with equivalent shares at $HK2.40 each. On the basis that both these figures represented the market value of the shares at the relevant time, the Privy Council held that C was entitled to the value of the shares sold at the time of conversion, less the value of the replacements, though it has been suggested that in such cases the damages are "gain-based".[237]

The recovery of consequential losses is illustrated in a very simple way by *Bodley v Reynolds*,[238] where a carpenter's tools were converted and he was thereby prevented from working: £10 above the value of the tools was awarded as special damage. Such loss may include personal inconvenience, such as loss of a hobby.[239] On a rather grander scale, when a fleet of airliners was converted during the Gulf War damages for consequential losses such as repairs, chartering substitutes and lost operating profits ran into hundreds of millions of US dollars.[240] Generally, however, loss incurred as a result of the claimant's inability to deliver the goods under a lucrative contract of sale is too remote unless the defendant is aware of the contract.[241]

C. Causation and Loss

It is a general requirement of tort that the defendant must have caused the loss of which the claimant complains. However, damages for conversion are not governed by the application of the simple "but-for" test. Property may be successively converted by A and B and C and the claimant may sue all or any of them for the value of the goods. It has never been suggested that B or C might seek to **17–28**

---

[235] *Butler v Egg and Egg Pulp Marketing Board* (1966) 114 C.L.R. 185.

[236] [1990] 1 W.L.R. 409, PC. See also *Solloway v McLaughlin* [1938] AC 247.

[237] *Kuwait Airways Corp v Iraqi Airways Co (Nos 4 and 5)* [2002] UKHL 19; [2002] 2 A.C. 883 at [88]; *Blue Sky One Ltd v Mahan Air* [2009] EWHC 3314 (Comm). However, it does not seem to be suggested that there should be an inquiry into the gain the defendant *actually* made (in *BBMB* for some obscure reason he seems never to have cashed the cheque for the converted shares) so this is arguably saying the same thing in a different way.

[238] (1846) 8 Q.B. 779. Cf. *Chubb Cash Ltd v John Crilley & Son* [1983] 1 W.L.R. 599 (market value recoverable, not higher sum claimant owed on the goods).

[239] *Graham v Voigt* (1989) 89 A.C.T.R. 11.

[240] *Kuwait Airways Corp v Iraqi Airways Co (Nos 4 and 5)*, above, fn.237. Detention of a stallion turned out to be expensive in *Cash v CC Lancashire* [2008] EWHC 396 (Ch).

[241] *The Arpad* [1934] P. 189; *Saleslease Ltd v Davis* [1999] 1 W.L.R. 1664. Cf. *France v Gaudet* (1871) L.R. 6 Q.B. 199, distinguished in *The Arpad*.

reduce or extinguish the damages because A had already deprived the claimant of his goods or by showing that if A had not transferred them to B he would probably have transferred them to someone else.

> "By definition, each person in a series of conversions wrongfully excludes the owner from possession of his goods. This is the basis on which each is liable to the owner. That is the nature of the tort of conversion. The wrongful acts of a previous possessor do not therefore diminish the plaintiff's claim in respect of the wrongful acts of a later possessor."[242]

In *Kuwait Airways Corp v Iraqi Airways Co (Nos 4 and 5)*[243] the Iraqi Government seized 10 aircraft belonging to the claimants and the defendants subsequently converted them by incorporating them in their fleet pursuant to a decree which was not recognised by English law. Four were then destroyed on the ground by Allied bombing during the Gulf War, something which would probably have happened even if the defendants had not taken them over. Six were spirited away to Iran and eventually recovered by the claimants. As the law then stood,[244] the matters were only actionable in England if they (a) amounted to a tort in English law and (b) were civilly actionable under the law of Iraq. The claim failed in regard to the first four aircraft because in a case of destruction Iraqi law applied a "but-for" test, though the Court of Appeal (this matter was not considered in the House of Lords) thought there was liability in conversion in English law, unless perhaps it could be shown that the destruction was inevitable.[245] However, in the case of the other six the requirements of Iraqi law were no more stringent than those of the English law of conversion and accordingly it was no answer to the claim that if the defendants had not taken them the Iraqi Government would have retained them and probably flown them to Iran anyway.

The question may also arise, especially in relation to consequential losses, whether the damage suffered is too remote. In the *Kuwait Airways* case Lord Nicholls expressed the view that where the defendant converts the goods knowingly the test in deceit applies

---

[242] *Kuwait Airways Corp v Iraqi Airways Co (Nos 4 and 5)*, above, fn.237, at [82] per Lord Nicholls.
[243] Above, fn.237.
[244] See para.17–12, above.
[245] See [2001] 3 W.L.R. 1251 at [606]. Suppose that a week after the conversion of an aircraft a design defect in the type was discovered and all such aircraft had to be scrapped. Is the defendant to be liable for their full market value at the date of the conversion?

—was the loss the "direct and natural consequence" of the conversion?[246] Yet, where the conversion is innocent, although *liability* may be strict, the defendant is liable only for consequences which would be foreseeable on the basis of knowledge that the goods had been misappropriated.[247] On the facts, on any view the cost of hiring substitute aircraft and loss of business were to be expected; but when the claimants went into the market to buy replacement aircraft they did more than seek the most equivalent substitutes, they made significant changes in the structure of their fleet and although this was a commercially reasonable decision they were unable to recover the finance costs associated with it.[248]

D. Defendant Detaining Goods

The only remedy for conversion at common law was the purely **17–29** personal one of damages. However, when the defendant was in possession of the goods and refused to deliver them up on demand his act was not only conversion but also detinue and the form of judgment in detinue might include an order for the delivery up of the goods.[249] Detinue has now been abolished but the remedies for conversion where goods are detained by the defendant[250] are now found in s.3 of the Torts (Interference with Goods) Act 1977, which is modelled on the common law remedies available for detinue.[251] The relief available is in one of the following forms[252]:

1. an order for the delivery of the goods, and for payment of any consequential damages,[253] or

---

[246] See para.11–14, above.

[247] [2002] UKHL 19; [2002] 2 A.C. 883 at [100]–[104].

[248] See also *Sandeman Coprimar SA v Transitos y Transportes Integrales SL* [2003] EWCA Civ 113; [2003] Q.B. 1270 (loss of cartons; carrier unaware of consequent liability of consignor for customs duty).

[249] See the full discussion by Diplock L.J. in *General and Finance Facilities Ltd v Cook Cars (Romford) Ltd* [1963] 1 W.L.R. 644 at 650–651. There were in fact three forms: (1) for the value of the chattel and damages for detention (2) for the return of the chattel or recovery of its value as assessed and damages for detention (3) for the return of the chattel and damages for detention.

[250] Except perhaps in the case of a "one man company", a director is not "in possession or control" of goods in the possession or control of the company: *Thunder Air Ltd v Hilmarsson* [2008] EWHC 355 (Ch); *Joiner v George* [2002] EWHC 90 (Ch). See also *Burnett v Randwick City Council* [2006] NSWCA 196, where the issue was title to sue.

[251] *I.B.L. Ltd v Coussens* [1991] 2 All E.R. 133 at 141. The section applies if the defendant ceases to be in possession between issue of proceedings and judgment: *Hillesden Securities Ltd v Ryjack Ltd* [1983] 1 W.L.R. 959.

[252] Section 3(2).

[253] See *Brandeis Goldschmidt Ltd v Western Transport Ltd* [1981] Q.B. 864, a case of detinue before the Act.

2. an order for delivery[254] of the goods, but giving the defendant
   the alternative of paying damages by reference to the value of
   the goods, together in either alternative[255] with payment of any
   consequential damages, or
3. damages.[256]

Relief under 1. is at the discretion of the court, but the claimant may
choose between 2. and 3.[257] If the claimant chooses 3., the defendant
cannot satisfy the judgment by returning the goods.[258]

It has traditionally been said (though there is nothing in s.3 to
compel a court to take this line) that option 1., specific restitution, is
apt only for rare articles or articles having a special value to the
claimant and not for "ordinary articles of commerce".[259] Option 2.
is said to be the commonest order in practice[260] but the value of the
goods may have changed between wrong and the judgment and the
statute contains no guidance as to the time at which the goods
should be valued for the purpose of quantifying the damages which
the defendant may choose to pay.[261] It was held in *I.B.L. Ltd v
Coussens* (which concerned cars which appreciated in value up to
the time of trial) that it is inappropriate to lay down any hard and fast
rule on this point and the value should be calculated by reference to
such date as will fairly compensate the claimant for his loss if the

---

[254] At common law the form of judgment for detinue was that the claimant "do have delivery
up" of the goods and while the defendant might have to facilitate their collection (*Metals
& Ropes Co Ltd v Tattersall* [1966] 1 W.L.R. 1500) it was up to the claimant to go and get
his goods. Quaere whether the rule is the same under the Act. Manchester (1977) 127
N.L.J. 1219 suggests that the court could order an actual redelivery by virtue of its power
to impose conditions (s.3(6)) and it seems to be implied in *Howard E. Perry & Co Ltd v
British Railways Board* [1980] 1 W.L.R. 1375, that a delivery could be ordered. Nonetheless, the wording of s.3(6) seems more apt for the imposition of conditions on the
claimant.

[255] In *Tanks and Vessels Industries Ltd v Devon Cider Co Ltd* [2009] EWHC 1360 (Ch)
consequential loss of use damages were only allowed if the defendant returned the goods,
only interest being awarded if he chose to pay their value.

[256] i.e. assessed by reference to the value and the consequential loss. There is no reason to
think the Act has changed the common law on consequential loss: *Trafigura Beheer BV v
Mediterranean Shipping Co SA* [2007] EWCA Civ 794; [2007] 2 Lloyd's Rep 622 at
[41].

[257] Section 3(3)(b).

[258] Section 3(5). Where there has been no fall in value it is thought that the court would still
stay the action before judgment upon return of the goods: *Fisher v Prince* (1762) 3 Burr.
1363.

[259] See *Tanks and Vessels Industries Ltd v Devon Cider Co Ltd* [2009] EWHC 1360 (Ch); *Blue
Sky One Ltd v Mahan Air* [2009] EWHC 3314 (Comm).

[260] If the defendant is in financial difficulties a judgment for damages alone is obviously
unattractive to the claimant but this form of order if made for a specific date protects him:
Blue Sky One above, fn.259, at [323].

[261] At common law it was said that in conversion the value was taken at the time of the
conversion, in detinue at the time of the judgment.

defendant chooses to pay damages rather than return the goods,[262] though it has been said that the "general prima facie rule" is of assessment at the date of conversion.[263] There may be cases in which it will be found that the claimant could and should have replaced the converted goods at the time of the wrong or that he would have disposed of them at some later time, facts which would point towards taking the value at the time of the conversion or some intermediate time.[264] If, however, the claimant does not trade in the goods in question and acts reasonably[265] in seeking their return[266] it may be proper to take the value at the time of the trial.[267]

E. Improvement of Goods

The problem of a converter improving goods is illustrated by **17–30** *Munro v Willmott*.[268] The claimant was given a temporary licence to leave her car in the defendant's yard. After the car had been there for some years the defendant wished to convert the yard into a garage but was unable to communicate with the claimant. Accordingly, he "did up" the car (then worth £20) at a cost of £85 and then sold it for £100. In proceedings for conversion Lynskey J. felt obliged to assess the value of the car at the date of judgment (£120) but he gave credit for the sum expended by the defendant, leaving £35 as the damages recoverable by the claimant.[269] The matter is now governed by s.6 of the Torts (Interference with Goods) Act 1977 which provides that if the improver acted in the mistaken but honest belief that he had a good title, an allowance is to be made for the extent to which the value of the goods, at the time at which it falls to be

---

[262] [1991] 2 All E.R. 133; *Trafigura Beheer BV v Mediterranean Shipping Co SA* [2007] EWHC 944 (Comm); [2007] 2 All E.R. (Com) 149 (affirmed on this point [2007] EWCA Civ 794; [2007] 2 Lloyd's Rep 622).

[263] *Kuwait Airways Corp v Iraqi Airways Co (Nos 4 and 5)* [2002] UKHL 19; [2002] 2 A.C. 883 at [67]; *B.B.M.B. Finance (Hong Kong) v Eda Holdings* [1990] 1 W.L.R. 409.

[264] In *Irving v Keen*, Unreported, March 3, 1995, CA, P was "incredibly lackadaisical" about getting his classic car back from D, a repairer, and settling the bill. D detained it for some years, during which it increased in value, but finally sold major parts of it and returned the remainder as scrap. Since there was no conversion until the sale of the parts, that was the earliest point at which damages could be set. Cf. *Sachs v Micklos* [1948] 2 K.B. 23.

[265] Cf. *Radford v De Froberville* [1977] 1 W.L.R. 1262, another example of a general drift away from a general "breach date" rule.

[266] If the claimant replaces the goods and goes for damages only he takes a risk in respect of the defendant's solvency when the matter comes to trial.

[267] In *I.B.L. Ltd v Coussens* the issue was remitted to the master.

[268] [1949] 1 K.B. 295; *Reid v Fairbanks* (1853) 13 C.B. 692.

[269] It is submitted that the correct approach on the conversion count (there was an alternative count for detinue) would have been to assess the value at the date of conversion. On the basis of *Greenwood v Bennett* [1973] Q.B. 195 it seems that the defendant committed two acts of conversion (beginning work on the car and selling it) and that the claimant could rely on either. It has been held at first instance that where a series of acts of conversion constitute a continuous course of conduct the claimant can only claim the value at the beginning: *Highland Leasing v Paul Field* [1986] 2 C.L. 276; but cf. *The Saetta* [1994] 1 All E.R. 851 at 859.

assessed, is attributable to the improvement.[270] The requirement of good faith would seem to make the law somewhat narrower than it was before.[271]

F. Effect of Judgment

17–31   Where damages for wrongful interference are assessed on the basis that the claimant is being compensated for the whole of his interest in the goods[272] (including a case where judgment is subject to a reduction for contributory negligence[273]) payment of the damages or of any settlement[274] in full extinguishes the claimant's title to that interest in the goods.[275] Until payment of the damages, however, the claimant retains his property in the goods and may exercise all his rights as owner even after judgment has been given in his favour. In *Ellis v John Stenning & Son*[276] A sold land to B, reserving to himself the right to cut and sell the uncut timber on the land. He then sold the timber to E. B wrongfully removed some of the timber and E obtained judgment against him for conversion but took no steps to enforce his judgment, because B was insolvent. B sold the timber to S. E then sued S for conversion of the timber. It was held that S was liable because, the judgment against B not having been satisfied, title to the timber remained with E.[277]

---

[270] Section 6(1). Under the Copyright Act 1956 a victim of copyright infringement was the notional owner of an infringing article and could sue for conversion damages based on the value of the article without deduction of the cost of production: *Infrabrics Ltd v Jaytex Ltd* [1982] A.C. 1. However, the Copyright, Designs and Patents Act 1988 abolished conversion damages for breach of copyright.

[271] See, however, Palmer, *Bailment*, 3rd edn, para.4–156, arguing that s.6 is in addition to rather than a replacement of the common law. It must also be pointed out that under s.12 of the 1977 Act the defendant in *Munro v Willmott* might now have a lawful power of sale though this does not help with the cost of improvement. The Act also provides for an allowance in favour of a defendant who is a bona fide purchaser of the car from the improver (who in this instance need not act bona fide), since though not an improver he will normally have paid a price reflecting the improved value (s.6(2)). See also s.6(3) (allowance in action for recovery of purchase price on total failure of consideration).

[272] e.g. where the defendant's trespass or negligence has destroyed them or where they have been wrongfully disposed of. A judgment in respect of mere damage has no effect upon title.

[273] As where the defendant has negligently destroyed the goods. Contributory negligence is no defence to conversion or intentional trespass: para.17–22, above.

[274] See s.5(2). Where a claimant settles with one of two or more defendants the onus is upon him to establish that the settlement was not one which compensated him for the whole of his interest in the goods: *Macaulay v Screenkarn Ltd* [1987] F.S.R. 257.

[275] Section 5. This provision has no application, however, where the damages paid are limited to some lesser amount by virtue of any enactment or rule of law (e.g. under the Merchant Shipping Act 1995 or under the Carriage by Air Act 1961). The claimant's title is, therefore, presumably extinguished where there is a valid limitation of liability clause in a contract not governed by such statutory codes.

[276] [1932] 2 Ch. 81.

[277] E could not then enforce the judgment in full against both B and S: Clerk and Lindsell, *Torts*, 19th edn, para.17–120.

5. OTHER CAUSES OF ACTION FOR WRONGFUL INTERFERENCE WITH GOODS

A. Replevin

As we have seen,[278] replevin is an ancient cause of action which   **17–32**
is theoretically applicable to any trespassory taking[279] of goods but
in practice is limited to taking by wrongful distress. The modern
procedure in the action is for the claimant to apply to the county
court, which will see that the goods alleged to have been wrongfully
taken are restored to the claimant on his giving security to prosecute
an action of replevin in the county court or in the High Court. The
claimant thus recovers his goods without having to await the outcome of the action while the defendant is protected by the security
given by the claimant.

Replevin is therefore now a form of interim relief. Section 4 of
the Torts (Interference with Goods) Act 1977 added a new and more
important form of interim relief, available in the county court and
High Court, whereby goods the subject of present or future proceedings for wrongful interference may be ordered to be delivered up to
the claimant, or a person appointed by the court, on such terms and
conditions as may be specified. The procedure is particularly apt if
there is a risk that the goods may be destroyed or disposed of before
trial of the action but it is not confined to such situations. An order
was made under it in *Howard E. Perry & Co Ltd v British Railways
Board*[280] even though the goods were in no danger and the defendants recognised the claimants' title: the shortage of stock caused by
industrial action was acute and damages would not adequately
compensate the claimants for the injury to their business.

B. Distress and Related Matters

Distress is a remedy given by the common law, whereby a party   **17–33**
in certain cases is entitled to enforce a right or obtain redress for a
wrong in a summary manner, by seizing chattels and retaining them
as a pledge until satisfaction is obtained.[281] Illegal, irregular and
excessive distress are actionable at the suit of the owner of the
chattels[282] but interference by him with a distress may in its turn be
actionable as rescous or pound breach.[283]

---

[278] See para.17–1, above.
[279] Thus it does not lie against a carrier who detains them, for he did not obtain possession by
    trespass though he may be liable in conversion: *Galloway v Bird* (1827) 4 Bing. 299;
    Mennie v Blake (1856) 6 E. & B. 842.
[280] [1980] 1 W.L.R. 1375.
[281] For distress damage feasant and the modern, statutory remedy replacing distress damage
    feasant in respect of straying livestock, see paras 16–11 and 17–10, above.
[282] Clerk and Lindsell, *Torts*, 14th edn, Ch.16 (distress is not treated in later edns).
[283] Clerk and Lindsell, *Torts*, 14th edn, Ch.16. Note the right to claim treble damages under
    2 Will. & Mar. c.5, s.3.

17–34   All of this old learning (and much else) will be replaced when Pt 3 of the Tribunals, Courts and Enforcement Act 2007 comes into force. The common law power to distrain for rent will be abolished (though there will still be a limited form of non-court enforcement for commercial leases) and the various "writs of execution" such as *fi. fa.* will be renamed "warrants of control". Sch.12 will initiate a new code of procedure to be followed by enforcement agents (known to most people as bailiffs) and this will replace replevin among other things. The reader is referred to the Act and the regulations when made.

CHAPTER 18

INTERFERENCE WITH CONTRACT OR BUSINESS[1]

IN this chapter we are concerned with a group of torts the function **18–1** of which is to protect some of a person's intangible interests—those which may loosely be called his business interests—from unlawful interference. As we have already seen, the law has been less ready to protect these interests from negligently inflicted harm than it has been to protect persons and tangible property,[2] but we are now in the main[3] concerned only with liability for intended harm.[4] It is not

---

[1] Carty, *An Analysis of the Economic Torts* (2000); Weir, *The Economic Torts*, (1997); Heydon, *Economic Torts*, 2nd edn; Clerk and Lindsell, *Torts*, 19th edn, Ch.25.

[2] See the discussion of "economic loss", para.5–39, above.

[3] Except in the case of passing off, though here, too, the harm is usually intended.

[4] The criminal law has now entered the arena in connection with acts interfering with contractual relationships so as to harm animal research organisations: Serious Organised Crime and Police Act 2005 s.145.

possible, however, to say simply that whenever one person intentionally causes harm to another that is a tort for, as we have also seen, the mere fact that my motive in performing an otherwise lawful act is to cause damage to another will not of itself make the act tortious.[5] This is so even if my motive is malevolence and it is a fortiori so if my motive is to advance my own interests even at the inevitable cost of harming my competitor's. There is more truth in the proposition that it is tortious intentionally to cause damage to a person's economic interests by an *unlawful* act, though even that would go a good deal too far as an unqualified statement. The law has developed around four situations which we must keep separate. First, it is a tort for the defendant D to induce or procure the breach of A's contract with the claimant C: that is a form of "secondary liability" for A's breach of contract and requires nothing independently unlawful on A's part. Secondly, D may be liable to C if, with the intention of injuring C, he uses unlawful means against A in order to affect A's ability to deal with C. Thirdly, D may be liable to C if, with the intention of injuring C, he uses unlawful means directly against C even if those unlawful means are not in themselves some other tort. Fourthly, where two persons, D1 and D2 combine to injure C they may be liable for the tort of conspiracy. This tort has two forms: where unlawful means are used or where the predominant purpose of the conspirators is to injure C (e.g. out of motives of revenge), in the latter case no unlawful means being required. Under all of these heads two difficulties have constantly recurred: the meaning of "intention" and that of "unlawful". A good deal of welcome clarity was brought to the first and second heads of liability by the decision of the House of Lords, *OBG Ltd v Allan*[6]; and to some extent to the fourth head by *Revenue and Customs Commisioners v Total Network SL*[7] (though in such a way as to produce a questionable distinction between this and the first two heads). The scope of the third head remains obscure. These cases substantially reinterpret many of the earlier decisions and are the basis of the present structure of the law.

Three further prefatory remarks are necessary. First, a great many of the cases in this area of the law are concerned with industrial strife of one kind or another and where this is so the common law has been excluded or modified since 1906 by statutory immunities granted to persons acting in a "trade dispute". The scope of this immunity was subject to repeated change from the 1970s to the 1990s. Since the legislation assumes the existence of the common

[5] See para.3–9, above.
[6] [2007] UKHL 21; [2008] 1 A.C.1.
[7] [2008] UKHL 19; [2008] A.C. 1174. On these cases see Carty, "The Economic Torts in the 21st Century" (2008) 124 L.Q.R. 641 and Deakin and Randall, "Rethinking the Economic Torts" (2009) 72 M.L.R. 519.

law background we must first endeavour to ascertain the general principles governing this area of tort and then see shortly how it is affected when there is a trade dispute.

Secondly, the torts considered in this chapter may also come into question in cases of alleged unlawful competition between traders,[8] but in practice they are of limited significance because of the common law's refusal to adopt any principle of "fair competition" other than the prohibition of obviously unlawful acts like torts and breaches of contract. Any full study of "unfair competition" would have to take account of the legislation (now with a major European dimension) protecting intangible business property like trade marks and patents,[9] and of the statutory controls over restrictive trading agreements and monopolies. The last two for long had little or nothing to do with anything resembling the law of tort. However, one of the most significant sources of competition law is the EC Treaty and the relevant provisions are directly applicable in England. Article 81 (formerly 85) prohibits agreements which have the effect of restricting or distorting competition and art.82 (formerly 86) prohibits the "abuse of a dominant [market] position". These provisions give rise to a civil right of action here for breach of statutory duty or something very like it and damages may therefore be obtained.[10] However, the Competition Act 1998 remodelled municipal competition law along the lines of the Treaty. The Act as enacted was silent on its private law consequences and if standing alone would perhaps not be of the type which gave rise by implication to a private law action, but it would be strange if there were different remedial consequences between two systems which were substantively very similar, and the Government thought that it would give rise to civil actions in the same way and to the same extent as the Treaty provisions do.[11] Now, s.47A[12] makes express reference to claims for damages in connection with appeals to the Competition Appeal Tribunal. These are matters well outside the scope of a general book on tort law.

---

[8] One of the "foundation" cases, *Mogul SS Co Ltd v McGregor Gow & Co* [1892] A.C. 25 arose from attempts by a cartel to monopolise the China tea trade.

[9] See specialist works, such as Kerly, *Trade Marks and Trade Names*, 15th edn; Terrell, *Patents*, 16th edn; Copinger and Skone James, *Copyright*, 15th edn. There is a substantial outline of these areas in Clerk and Lindsell, *Torts*, 19th edn, Ch.26.

[10] See para.7–12, above. *Garden Cottage Foods Ltd v Milk Marketing Board* [1984] A.C. 130; *Courage Ltd v Crehan* Case C–453/99 [2002] QB 507. The European Commission in December 2005 issued a Green Paper on Damages for Breach of EC Anti-Trust Rules (Com (2005) 672 Final) remarking at 1.2 that in all Member States this area of the law represented a state of "total underdevelopment".

[11] See Lord Simon of Highbury, *Hansard*, HL, March 5, 1998: col. 1325. In *Network Multi-Media Television Ltd v Jobserve Ltd*, April 5, 2001, Ch D, it was not contested that an injunction could be obtained by a competitor for breach of s.18 of the Act (the equivalent of art.81).

[12] Inserted by the Enterprise Act 2002. This applies whether the determination of infringement has been made under the domestic legislation or under the EC treaty.

Finally, the common law contained areas of tortious liability for interference with family and service relationships which were based upon the archaic idea that a man had a proprietary interest in the services of his family and his servants. For example, a husband whose wife[13] was incapacitated by the defendant's negligence had his own action against the defendant for the value of the domestic services which she had formerly rendered and for the loss of her "consortium" (or society) and a master had a remedy for "enticement" against one who wrongfully persuaded his servant to leave his employment. Some of these causes of action were restricted by judicial decision[14] and by legislation in 1970.[15] The Administration of Justice Act 1982[16] swept away the remaining ones without putting anything in their place.[17] The Act does not as a matter of law preclude a court from holding that an action for negligence lies in favour of a person who could formerly have brought an action based on loss of services but in view of the current law on economic loss it seems most unlikely that such a development will occur.[18] Where the death of a person causes financial loss to members of the family there is a special statutory regime of liability.[19]

In *F. v Wirral Metropolitan Council*[20] an unsuccessful attempt was made to fashion a new tort of interference with parental rights. The case concerned the retention of a child in local authority care,

---

[13] Still, a wife had no claim in respect of injury to her husband.

[14] e.g. a master's cause of action for loss of services of his servant was restricted to servants living as part of his household: *Inland Revenue Commissioners v Hambrook* [1956] 2 Q.B. 641.

[15] Law Reform (Miscellaneous Provisions) Act 1970 ss.4, 5, abolishing most claims for loss of services of children and for "enticement" and "harbouring" of wives and for damages for adultery. See the 11th edition of this work.

[16] Section 2:
"No person shall be liable in tort . . .
   (a) to a husband on the ground only of his having deprived him of the services or society of his wife;
   (b) to a parent (or person standing in the place of a parent) on the ground only of his having deprived him of the services of a child or
   (c) on the ground only—
      (i) of having deprived another of the services of his menial servant;
      (ii) of having deprived another of the services of his female servant by raping or seducing her or
      (iii) of enticement of a servant or harbouring a servant."

[17] The only cause of action of much significance in modern times was the husband's for loss of his wife's services, for though archaic in form, its function in enabling the recovery of the cost of substitute domestic help was perfectly reasonable. However it became virtually redundant when the courts held that the wife could recover such losses in her own claim: *Daly v General Steam Navigation Ltd* [1981] 1 W.L.R. 120.

[18] Scots common law has never had the actions based on loss of services and the House of Lords in *Robertson v Turnbull*, 1982 S.L.T. 96 refused to allow a relative's claim for financial loss based on breach of duty to the relative. See also *Propaczy v Truitt* (1990) 73 D.L.R. (4th) 712, rejecting a claim by a child for loss of parental guidance where the parent was injured (cf. such claims in death cases, para.23–12, below).

[19] See para.23–9, below.

[20] [1991] Fam. 69.

where there is of course a complex statutory scheme containing safeguards for the position of parents, and that was regarded as a sufficient reason for dismissing the alternative claim for negligence[21]; but the reason for rejecting the intentional tort was more fundamental: since the old common law actions had all been based on the narrow idea of loss of services and Parliament had abolished them it would be quite inconsistent to declare the existence of a more broadly based wrong.[22] However, it does not follow that there are no legal remedies in this situation: where there is fraud or malice there may be liability for deceit or for misfeasance in a public office.[23] These may be very difficult to establish, but art.8 of the European Convention on Human Rights requires respect for, inter alia, family life, and since the Human Rights Act 1998 interference by a public authority which is not necessary and proportionate will be actionable under that head.[24]

1. Inducing or Procuring a Breach of Contract: The "Lumley v Gye Tort"

D commits a tort against C if, without lawful justification, he induces or procures A to break A's contract with C. The origin of this form of liability lies in the mid-19th century in *Lumley v Gye*.[25] The claimant's declaration alleged that he was owner of the Queen's Theatre, that he had contracted with Johanna Wagner,[26] a famous operatic singer, for her to perform exclusively in the theatre for a certain time and that the defendant, owner of a rival theatre, wishing himself to obtain Miss Wagner's services, "knowing the premises and maliciously intending to injure the plaintiff . . . enticed and persuaded [her] to refuse to perform". The claim succeeded on demurrer[27] on the basis, according to the majority of the court, that

18–2

---

[21] See para.5–52, above.

[22] This was so even though the principle of *Lumley v Gye* considered in the next section goes beyond contractual rights. Whether the parent's legal claims in relation to the child are properly described as "rights" at all is a difficult question (the current legislation talks in terms of parental responsibilities). They are certainly not rights like property or contractual rights, but Ralph Gibson L.J. was not prepared to say that they were unprotected by tort law merely because they yield in all cases to the child's welfare.

[23] Or in certain circumstances for breach of contract: *Hamilton-Jones v David & Snape* [2003] EWHC 3147; [2004] 1 W.L.R. 924.

[24] See *T.P. v UK* (2002) 34 E.H.R.R. 2; *Hinds v Liverpool County Court* [2008] EWHC 665 (QB) at [20].

[25] (1853) 2 Bl. & Bl. 216.

[26] Students of contract will be familiar with *Lumley v Wagner* (1852) 1 De G.M. & G. 604, in which the claimant obtained an injunction against Miss Wagner.

[27] Lumley eventually lost, the trial jury finding that Gye believed that Wagner's contract was not binding: Waddams, "Johanna Wagner and the Rival Opera Houses" (2001) 117 L.Q.R. 431.

the action for enticement could be extended beyond the strict relation of master and servant to embrace other contracts for personal
services, but support was also given in varying degrees to a broader
view that a claimant might sue for the knowing violation of any
contractual right.

In *Bowen v Hall*,[28] on rather similar facts, the Court of Appeal
accepted the broader proposition and doubted whether *Lumley v Gye*
could in fact be based upon the narrower ground of enticement. The
rule that inducing or procuring another to break his contract could be
actionable at the suit of the other contracting party who suffered
damage thereby was only accepted in the face of strong dissent
because it appeared to outflank privity of contract.[29] While it was
argued in *Lumley v Gye* that the claimant ought to be satisfied with
his action for breach of contract against the party induced, Crompton J. said that the latter might be incapable of paying all the
damages.[30] Of course, every contractor accepts the risk of insolvency in his co-contractor, but at least in the case of a contract for
services he does not accept it in combination with the procurement
of a breach by a third party. It has sometimes been said to rest on a
property analogy[31] and commercial contractual relations had
become valuable rights which could be regarded as entitled to at
least some of the protection given by the law to property, but the
requirements of knowledge and intent make this tort considerably
more restrictive than conversion or trespass. However this may be,
the current view is that it is a form of "accessory" liability, that is
to say the person who induces the breach incurs an additional
liability in tort for the effects of the "primary" breach of
contract.[32]

A. A Breach of Contract

18–3   Since this is a form of accessory liability it is necessary for D to
be liable that there must have been a breach of contract by A against
C.[33] One, "cannot be liable for inducing a breach unless there has

---

[28] (1881) 6 Q.B.D. 333.

[29] By Coleridge J. in *Lumley v Gye*, above, fn.25, and Lord Coleridge C.J. in *Bowen v Hall*,
above, fn.28.

[30] At 230; *OBG Ltd v Allan* [2007] UKHL 21; [2008] 1 A.C.1 at [32]. Erle J. (at 234) also
refers to the fact that the contractual damages may be limited by factors which ought not
to avail the wilful interferer.

[31] See Bagshaw (1998) O.J.L.S. 729 and the discussion in *Zhu v Treasurer of NSW* [2004]
HCA 56; 218 C.L.R.530 beginning at [123].

[32] *OBG Ltd v Allan* [2007] UKHL 21; [2008] 1 A.C. 1 at [3], [172], [320]. In the CA ([2005]
Q.B. 762 at [42]) it was said that the procurer "makes himself as it were directly privy to
the breach".

[33] The claimant may, of course, obtain a quia timet injunction to restrain a threatened
inducement.

been a breach. No secondary liability without primary liability."[34] Hence in *Allen v Flood*[35] the defendant, an official of the boilermakers' trade union, told shipyard owners that his members would not work unless Flood, a non-member who had done ironwork, was discharged. Flood was dismissed but since he was engaged by the day the owners committed no breach of contract and this tort was not therefore committed by Allen.[36] At one time there was a view that there was a wider liability, even if no unlawful means were used, of "interference" with the performance of a contract short of procuring a breach[37] at least if the interference was "direct" (though it was never very clear what that meant). That view is exploded by *OBG Ltd v Allan*.[38] No one suggests that, without the use of unlawful means, it is a tort for D to persuade A not to contract with C, for that is what competitors in business do every day (and are encouraged to do). It cannot be different if there is an existing contract between A and C and without unlawful means D persuades A to terminate it by proper notice. It would be a strange law which said that if A could terminate his maintenance contract with C on a month's notice, D could be liable for persuading A to do so and hand the task to him.[39]

Where it is clear that the contract-breaker would have taken the same steps anyway the inducement is not an effective cause of the loss.[40] If the contract between A and C is void for contravention of the law there can be no action for inducing breach of it.[41] If the contract between A and C is voidable and D persuades A to exercise his right to avoid contract with C it is thought that this should

---

[34] *OBG Ltd v Allan*, fn.32, at [44].
[35] [1898] A.C. 1. The last case in which the judges were summoned to give their advice to the House of Lords in its judicial capacity.
[36] Nor was there any unlawful means (see the next section) by a threat of breach of contract by the boilermakers since they, too, were employed by the day. In any event, the Trade Disputes Act 1906 (para.18–36, below) later made threats of breaches of contract in such cases non-actionable.
[37] See, e.g. Lord Denning M.R. in *Torquay Hotel Co Ltd v Cousins* [1969] 2 Ch. 106 at 138.
[38] See, e.g. Lord Nicholls at [2007] UKHL 21; [2008] 1 A.C. 1 [185].
[39] In the *Torquay Hotel* case, which arose from the "blacking" by unions of fuel supplies to the hotel, there was a force majeure clause in Esso's contract with the hotel. As Lord Nicholls points out in *OBG*, if a contracting party chooses to succumb to persuasion not to perform, such a clause will not be applicable and there will be a breach. Consider, however, a case where A's contract excuses performance for inability to obtain supplies and D, in order to strike at C, corners the market and refuses to supply A. There is no breach of contract induced nor any unlawful means for the purposes of the tort in the next section.
[40] See *Jones Bros (Hunstanton) Ltd v Stevens* [1955] 1 Q.B. 275.
[41] *De Francesco v Barnum* (1890) 45 Ch.D. 430; *Joe Lee Ltd v Dalmeny* [1927] 1 Ch. 300; *Said v Butt* [1920] 3 K.B. 497; *Associated British Ports Ltd v TGWU* [1989] 3 All E.R. 796 at 816.

plainly not be actionable by C[42] and it has been held that D is equally not liable where he induces A not to perform the voidable contract without any formal avoidance.[43] If, on the other hand, it is C who has the right to avoid the contract there seems no reason why D should be allowed to set up its voidability in a claim by C.

B. Knowledge and Intention of the Defendant

18–4   All are agreed that there is no liability under this tort for negligently interfering with a person's rights under contract (though the law of negligence may give limited protection in certain circumstances[44]). The tort presupposes knowledge of the contract but that does not mean knowledge of all its details. As Lord Denning M.R. said in *Emerald Construction Co Ltd v Lowthian*[45]:

> "Even if [the union officials] did not know the actual terms of the contract, but had the means of knowledge—which they deliberately disregarded—that would be enough. Like the man who turns a blind eye. So here, if the officers deliberately sought to get this contract terminated, heedless of its terms, regardless whether it was terminated by breach or not, they would do wrong. For it is unlawful for a third person to procure a breach of contract knowingly, or recklessly, indifferent whether it is a breach or not."

This state of mind of conscious indifference is not the same as negligence,[46] though of course the required state of mind may be inferred as a matter of evidence from circumstances which would have caused suspicion to a reasonable person. There is no general duty actively to inquire about contracts with others[47] and a supplier of services is not obliged to infer, from the fact that the services are obviously already being supplied by another, that there is a continuing contract, breach of which he must be careful not to induce.[48] In

---

[42] So assumed in *Greig v Insole* [1978] 1 W.L.R. 302.

[43] *Proform Sports Management Ltd v Proactive Sports Management Ltd* [2006] EWHC 22903 (Ch); [2007] 1 All E.R. 542.

[44] See para.5–39, above.

[45] [1966] 1 WLR 691 at 700; *Greig v Insole* [1978] 1 W.L.R. 302.

[46] *OBG Ltd v Allan* at [41]; *Kallang Shipping SA Panama v Axa Assurances Senegal* [2008] EWHC 2761 (Comm); [2009] 1 Lloyd's Rep 124.

[47] *Leitch & Co v Leydon* [1931] A.C. 90.

[48] *Schindler Lifts Australia Pty Ltd v Debelak* (1989) 89 A.L.R. 275; *Unique Pub Properties Ltd v Beer Barrels and Minerals (Wales) Ltd* [2004] EWCA Civ 586; [2005] 1 All E.R. (Comm.) 181.

Mainstream Properties Ltd v Young, one of the three appeals reported as *OBG Ltd v Allan*,[49] the defendant had provided finance for a development venture by A and B, employees of the claimant development company. The risk that this was in conflict with their duties to the company was obvious and the defendant raised this issue with them but it was held that he was entitled to accept their assertion that the land had been offered to the company and it had declined.[50] At one time the view was taken that there would be liability if the defendant intended to bring about a situation where there would as a matter of law be a breach of contract even though he mistakenly believed there would not.[51] The contrary view is taken in clear terms in *OBG Ltd v Allan*.

"It is not enough that you know that you are procuring an act which, as a matter of law or construction of the contract, is a breach. You must actually realize that it will have this effect. Nor does it matter that you ought reasonably to have done so."[52]

The defendant must intend to bring about a breach of the contract but that is not necessarily the same thing as saying that he must intend to cause damage to the claimant. In *South Wales Miners' Federation v Glamorgan Coal Co Ltd*[53] it did not help the union, when it induced breaches of employment contracts by calling a strike, to argue that its intention, "was, OPEC-like, to restrict production of coal and thereby raise its price"[54] thereby benefiting the coal owners as well as the workers. The meaning of intention does not give rise to much difficulty in this tort (intentionally causing loss by unlawful means is a rather different matter[55]) since, given knowledge that your non-performance of your contract with C will be a breach of it, I can hardly persuade you not to perform it without intending to bring about a breach.[56] However, it certainly does not

---

[49] [2007] UKHL 21; [2008] 1 A.C. 1.
[50] The claimants were not allowed to raise at a late stage the alternative argument that the defendant had induced A and B to be in breach of their obligations to give their full time to the claimants' service.
[51] See e.g. *Solihull MBC v National Union of Teachers* [1985] I.R.L.R. 211.
[52] [2007] UKHL 21; [2008] 1 A.C. 1 at [39] per Lord Hoffmann. See also Lord Nicholls at [202]. *Meretz Investments NV v ACP Ltd* [2007] EWCA Civ 1303; [2008] Ch. 244.
[53] [1905] AC 239.
[54] *OBG Ltd v Allan*, fn.32, at [8] per Lord Hoffmann.
[55] See para.18–13, below.
[56] Persuasion directed at a third party lawfully to decline to deal with A does not give rise to liability to C where this foreseeably brings about a breach of A's contract with C: *Middlebrook Mushrooms Ltd v TGWU* [1993] I.C.R. 612 (leafletting and picketing of supermarkets, persuasion directed at customers, exhorting them not to buy C's mushrooms sold in supermarket).

matter that I have no *desire* to injure C and am doing this simply in order to benefit myself.[57]

C. The Inducement

18-5   There must be persuasion directed at[58] a party to the contract. Doing something which has the inevitable consequence of causing that party to be in breach is not this tort, though it may lead to liability if unlawful means are used.[59] A distinction may be taken between persuasion and mere advice, and advice in the sense of, "a mere statement of, or drawing of the attention of the party addressed, to the state of facts as they were",[60] is not actionable.[61] However, it has been said that advice which is intended to have persuasive effect is not distinguishable from inducement.[62] Further:

> "[T]he fact that an inducement to break a contract is couched as an irresistible embargo rather than in terms of seduction does not make it any the less an inducement".[63]

It is submitted that the issue is really one of intention and causation. If D's words were intended to cause and did cause A to break his contract with C, then they are actionable by C whatever their form.[64] If so, bearing in mind that intention in this context is not the same as motive and that the tort may be committed without any ill will towards the claimant, it is likely to be a rare case in which D's words have had a causative effect on A's conduct and yet

---

[57] "Mr Gye would very likely have preferred to be able to obtain Miss Wagner's services without her having to break her contract. But that did not matter": *OBG Ltd v Allan*, fn.32, at [42] per Lord Hoffmann.

[58] There need be no individual contact between A and B: *Greig v Insole* [1978] 1 W.L.R. 302 (resolutions and press statement by cricket governing body).

[59] *Meretz Investments NV v ACP Ltd* [2007] EWCA Civ 1303; [2008] Ch 244.

[60] *D.C. Thomson & Co Ltd v Deakin* [1952] Ch. 646 at 686.

[61] A direction to do something which may be done lawfully or unlawfully cannot be said to induce wrongs committed by those who respond unlawfully, even if the person giving it harbours a secret desire that it be done unlawfully: *Sanders v Snell* (1998) 157 A.L.R. 491; and see *C.B.S. Songs Ltd v Amstrad Consumer Electronics Plc* [1988] A.C. 1013 (provision of machines capable of being used for breach of copyright).

[62] *Camden Nominees Ltd v Forcey* [1940] Ch. 352 at 366; *D.C. Thomson & Co Ltd v Deakin*, above, fn.60, at 686. Cf. the difficult case of *Stocznia Gdanska SA v Latvian Shipping Co* [2002] EWCA Civ 889; [2002] 2 Lloyd's Rep. 436, where the passage at [107] might be thought to question whether persuasion (as opposed to instruction) is sufficient. However, the case is best regarded as turning on the fact that the claim had been pleaded as one of instruction.

[63] *J. T. Stratford & Co Ltd v Lindley* [1965] A.C. 269 at 333 per Lord Pearce; *Greig v Insole* [1978] 1 W.L.R. 302.

[64] The relative positions of the persons involved and the degree of anxiety to achieve his ends shown by the alleged inducer are both factors to be taken into account: *Square Grip Reinforcement Co Ltd v Macdonald* 1968 S.L.T. 65.

D escapes liability on the ground that they were only "advice".[65] If the inducement of A takes the form of wrongful threats against him there will be an overlap with the tort of intentionally causing damage by unlawful means (considered in the next section) this form being commonly known as intimidation.

Liability under this head may arise from D's entering into a contract with A knowing that the contract is inconsistent with a prior contract of A's with C as in *B.M.T.A. v Salvadori*[66] where D bought a car from A knowing that the sale constituted a breach by A of his contract with C that he would not sell the car within a year. However, while statements of principle are often couched in terms that merely knowingly entering into the transaction amounts to the tort,[67] it is not wholly clear that this is so where the defendant merely accedes to an initiative of the contracting party.[68] Where the prior contract of A and C is specifically enforceable it would create an equitable interest in the subject matter in favour of C, which C could enforce against D even if D had only constructive notice of C's rights.[69] In many cases this would render consideration of D's tort liability in a case of actual knowledge otiose, but it seems possible to assert such a claim where there is some additional loss.[70]

If my servant, acting bona fide within the scope of his authority, **18–6** procures or causes me to break a contract which I have made with you, you cannot sue the servant for interference with the contract (despite the principle that the servant is generally liable as well as his employer) for he is my alter ego here, and I cannot be sued for inducing myself to break a contract, although I may be liable for breaking the contract. In *Said v Butt*[71] the claimant wished to get a ticket for X's theatre. He knew that X would not sell him one because they had quarrelled. He therefore persuaded a friend to procure him a ticket without disclosing his identity. When the claimant presented himself at the theatre, the defendant, who was X's manager of the theatre, detected the claimant and refused to admit him. He sued the defendant for procuring a breach of his

---

[65] The defence of justification (para.18–7, below) might be relevant in a case of disinterested advice. Where members of a union have already expressed willingness to take industrial action and instruct a union official to determine what form it shall take the official has "procured" what follows: *Ansett v Australian Federation of Airline Pilots* (1989) 95 A.L.R. 211, applying *S Wales Miners' Federation v Glamorgan Coal Co Ltd*, above, fn.53.

[66] [1949] Ch. 556.

[67] *D.C. Thomson & Co Ltd v Deakin* [1952] Ch. 646 at 694; *Law Debenture Trust Ltd v Ural Caspian Oil Corp Ltd* [1993] 1 W.L.R. 138 at 151.

[68] *Batts Combe Quarry Ltd v Ford* [1943] Ch. 51 and Carty, fn.1, above, p.56.

[69] That is to say, unless D was a bona fide purchaser for value without notice.

[70] See *Pritchard v Briggs* [1980] Ch. 338, though on the facts the majority of the court rejected a claim for damages.

[71] [1920] 3 K.B. 497 at 506.

contract with X. The action was dismissed because there was no contract, since the identity of the claimant was, in the circumstances, material to the formation of the alleged contract; and alternatively, even if there had been a valid contract, the principle stated above would prevent the action from lying.[72] If the servant does not act bona fide, he is liable on the ground that he has ceased to be his employer's alter ego.[73] It is true that even then he might still be acting in the course of his employment, but we must take it that this curious piece of metaphysics exempts the employer from vicarious liability for this particular tort.

D. Defence of Justification

18–7   It is certain that justification is capable of being a defence to this tort, but what constitutes justification is incapable of exact definition.[74] It has been said that regard must be had to the nature of the contract broken, the position of the parties to the contract, the grounds for the breach, the means employed to procure it, the relation of the person procuring it to the person who breaks the contract, and the object of the person procuring the breach.[75] The advancement of one's own interests will not suffice, nor will that of the interests of one's own group[76] and the defendant cannot escape by showing that his motives are impersonal, disinterested and altruistic.[77] However, in *Brimelow v Casson*,[78] persuasion of theatre proprietors by a theatrical performers' protection society to

---

[72] Approved by Greer L.J. in *Scammell Ltd v Hurley* [1929] 1 K.B. 419 at 443. Cf. Scrutton and Sankey L.JJ. at 436, 449. This principle will protect company directors who vote to cause a breach of contract: *Crystalens Ltd v White*, July 7, 2006, QBD; *O'Brien v Dawson* (1942) 66 C.L.R. 18. See also *Welsh Development Agency v Export Finance Co Ltd* [1992] BCLC 148, CA (receivers). Cf. *Ansett v Australian Federation of Air Pilots* (1989) 95 A.L.R. 211—union official not alter ego of all his members.

[73] *D.C. Thomson & Co Ltd v Deakin* [1952] Ch. 646 at 681 per Evershed M.R.: "The difficulty is avoided if the act which the servant is procured to do is not an act in accordance with or under his contract, but is in breach or violation of it.".

[74] Cf. the more definite privileges in defamation.

[75] *Glamorgan Coal Co Ltd v S Wales Miners' Federation* [1903] 2 K.B. 545 at 574–575 per Romer L.J.

[76] *S Wales Miners' Federation v Glamorgan Coal Co Ltd* [1905] A.C. 239; *Camden Nominees Ltd v Forcey* [1940] Ch. 352; *Greig v Insole* [1978] 1 W.L.R. 302. The broader view taken in New Zealand in *Pete's Towing Services Ltd v N.I.U.W.* [1970] N.Z.L.R. 32 was rejected in Australia in *B.W.I.U. v Odco Pty Ltd* (1991) 99 A.L.R. 735, but the protection of health and safety is arguably of a different order from raising wages: *Ranger Uranium Mines v F.M.W.U.A.* (1987) 54 N.T.R. 6.

[77] *Greig v Insole*, above, fn.76; *Posluns v Toronto Stock Exchange* (1964) 46 D.L.R. (2d) 210 at 270 (affirmed (1968) 67 D.L.R. (2d) 165) (where, however, justification arose from the claimant's implied submission to the discipline of the Exchange); *Slade & Stewart Ltd v Haynes* (1969) 5 D.L.R. (3d) 736.

[78] [1924] 1 Ch. 302.

break their contracts with a theatrical manager was justified on the grounds that the wage paid by the manager to chorus girls was so low that they were obliged to supplement it by resort to prostitution.[79] It has been suggested that pressure of a moral[80] obligation as justification is the basis of *Brimelow v Casson*, though the case has been said to stand alone[81] and there are conflicting dicta on moral obligation.[82] Presumably there is justification when a doctor urges[83] his patient to give up fixed-term employment because it is a danger to his health,[84] but what of the tutor who insists that his student give up a vacation job because it will interfere with his studies?[85]

The question of justification may also arise where D seeks to assert rights under a contract with A which is inconsistent with another contract between A and C. The question here is whether D has a right equal or superior to that of C and if he has he is justified in persuading A to break his contract with C. So if A enters into a contract on Monday to sell to D for £10,000 and then next day to sell the same property to C for £15,000, D, by persuading A to perform the first contract commits no wrong against C.[86] D will also be justified in reaching an accommodation with A rather than exercising his strict legal rights under the contract. In *Edwin Hill & Partners v First National Finance Corp*[87] a finance company which had a legal charge over A's property to secure a loan came to an arrangement with A whereby they would develop the property themselves rather than exercise their power of sale under the charge. A condition in this arrangement whereby the claimant was to be replaced as architect for the scheme did not constitute inducing breach of contract.[88] However, after a detailed examination of the cases the High Court of Australia took the view that justification had

---

[79] Cf. *Stott v Gamble* [1916] 2 K.B. 504 (banning of film under statutory powers).

[80] *Pritchard v Briggs* [1980] Ch. 338 at 416 per Goff L.J.

[81] *Camden Nominees Ltd v Forcey* [1940] Ch. 352 at 366 per Simmonds J.; *Pritchard v Briggs* [1980] Ch. 338 at 416 per Goff L.J.; *Timeplan Education Group v NUT* [1996] I.R.L.R. 457 at 460 and see *Zhu v Treasurer of NSW* [2004] HCA 56; 218 C.L.R. 530.

[82] e.g. *South Wales Miners' Federation v Glamorgan Coal Co Ltd* [1905] A.C. 239 at 245, 246, 249, 255; *Crofter Hand-Woven Harris Tweed Co v Veitch* [1942] A.C. 435 at 443, where the example is given of a man inducing his daughter not to marry a "scoundrel" (but engagement is no longer a contract).

[83] It is assumed that the advice is "persuasive" in the sense explained in para.18–5, above.

[84] Might not this give the patient lawful justification for withdrawing from the contract?

[85] The *Restatement* 2d., ss.770 and 772 treat as justification (1) unrequested advice from a person charged with responsibility for the welfare of the other and (2) all other honest advice if requested.

[86] *Smithies v National Association of Operative Plasterers* [1909] 1 K.B. 310 at 337.

[87] [1989] 1 W.L.R. 225.

[88] It appears that the claimant had succeeded in an action against A for breach of contract: (1984) 272 E.G. 63 at 179. It was common ground that if the claimants had appointed a receiver or sold the property a new architect could have been appointed.

to be found in a superior right of a proprietary nature[89] and that competing contractual rights, even if prior in time, would not do.[90]

E. Inducing Breaches of Other Obligations

18–8		Although the principle of *Lumley v Gye* commonly appears under the heading of inducing breach of contract it has been regarded as a wider principle covering violation of legal rights.[91] It has been said that there is no need to call up the tort where the wrong procured is itself a tort against the claimant, for the procurer is then himself liable as a joint tortfeasor,[92] but the courts have recognised a cause of action for inducing breach of statutory duty where the statutory duty gives rise to a private right on behalf of the claimant[93] actionable by him in the courts.[94] There is no tort of inducing breach of trust because a person who procures such an act becomes himself, by the doctrines of equity, liable as a trustee and it is said that is sufficient to protect the beneficiary under the trust.[95] The tort liability probably extends to procuring breaches of equitable obligations such as that of confidence but the readiness of the courts to restrain the use of confidential information by the third party who acquires it makes the point of limited importance in most cases.[96] However, these issues are not discussed in *OBG Ltd v Allan* and Lord Nicholls said that he left:

---

[89] Suggesting that in the example above drawn from the *Smithies* case of two sales, it is real property that is referred to and the first contract would give rise to an equitable interest.

[90] *Zhu v Treasurer of NSW* [2004] HCA 56; 218 C.L.R. 530. That leaves an apparent conundrum. If A makes two inconsistent contracts, one with D and then one with C (C not being then aware of D's) it cannot be that D commits a tort against C in persuading A to perform in his favour and C commits a tort against D in persuading A to perform in *his* favour. The court suggested at [151] that such action might simply not be regarded as an inducement, but is this not simply putting two cross-justification defences in different words?

[91] "A violation of a legal right committed knowingly is a cause of action, and . . . it is a violation of a legal right to interfere with contractual relations recognised by law if there be no sufficient justification for the interference": *Quinn v Leathem* [1901] A.C. 495 at 510 per Lord Macnaghten; *F. v Wirral Metropolitan Council* [1991] Fam. 69 at 107.

[92] *C.B.S. Songs Ltd v Amstrad Consumer Electronics Plc* [1988] A.C. 1013 at 1058; cf. *Belegging, etc. B.V. v Witten Industrial Diamonds Ltd* [1979] F.S.R. 59 at 66.

[93] *Meade v Haringey London Borough* [1979] 1 W.L.R. 637; *Associated British Ports v TGWU* [1989] 3 All E.R. 822 (reversed on other grounds, at 822). See Ch.7, above.

[94] *Wilson v Housing Corp* [1997] I.R.L.R. 345 (no tort of inducing unfair dismissal).

[95] *Metall und Rohstoff A.G. v Donaldson Lufkin & Jenrette Inc* [1990] 1 Q.B. 391 (where it was sought to found the claim on tort in order to get service outside the jurisdiction). However, liability for "knowing assistance" in a breach of trust (as opposed to receipt of trust property) requires dishonesty: *Twinsectra Ltd v Yardley* [2002] UKHL 12; [2002] 2 A.C. 164; *Barlow Clowes International Ltd v Eurotrust International Ltd* [2005] UKPC 37; [2006] 1 W.L.R. 1476.

[96] See Clerk and Lindsell, *Torts*, 19th edn, para.25–41.

"[O]pen the question of how far the *Lumley v Gye* principle applies equally to inducing a breach of other actionable obligations such as statutory duties or equitable or fiduciary obligations."[97]

2. INTENTIONALLY CAUSING LOSS BY UNLAWFUL MEANS

This tort was the source of much confusion in the 20th century but its nature and its relationship with inducing breach of contract have been considerably clarified by *OBG Ltd v Allan*, at least in the case where it is deployed in a "three party situation". D commits a tort against C where, intending to cause loss to C, he uses unlawful means against A which affect A's liberty to deal with C. It is a good deal older than the liability under *Lumley v Gye* and an early example is to be found in *Tarleton v M'Gawley*.[98] D, master of the *Othello*, was trading on the coast of West Africa and when people (A) put off from the shore to trade with another vessel, the *Bannister*, belonging to C, D fired his guns at them, driving them away. C's action against D succeeded. The very short judgment is largely taken up with refuting the argument that C should fail because he had no licence from the local ruler but looked at in the light of *OBG Ltd v Allan* the wrongful act (assault or battery) directed at A and driving A away made D's conduct tortious against C even though C had no subsisting contract with A. In any event even if there had been a contract between A and C, A's retreat under artillery fire could hardly have been a breach of that contract: it was rather as if Johanna Wagner had been kidnapped by Gye rather than enticed away. This is a tort based on the primary liability of D for his wrongdoing and is in no sense, unlike *Lumley v Gye*, accessory to a liability of A. Both torts, it is true, have the common characteristic that they involve D's striking at C through acts directed at a third party, A,[99] but that does not make them the same. Of course the two torts may overlap: if A had had a contract with C and D's threats to A had not been serious enough to justify his non-performance then D would no doubt have committed the *Lumley v Gye* tort and this one.

In earlier cases the relationship between the two torts became very confused. In *GWK Ltd v Dunlop Rubber Co Ltd*[100] C made tyres and had a contract with A, motor manufacturers, that all new cars would be fitted with tyres of C's manufacture and displayed with them at shows. D, a rival tyre company, surreptitiously

18–9

[97] [2007] UKHL 21; [2008] 1 A.C. 1 at [189].
[98] (1793) 1 Peake NPC 270. See also *Garret v Taylor* (1620) Cro Jac 567.
[99] Baroness Hale at [2007] UKHL 21; [2008] 1 A.C. 1 [306].
[100] (1926) 42 T.L.R. 376.

removed the C tyres at the Glasgow motor show and substituted its own. D was held liable to C but on the basis that D had interfered without justification with the contractual relationship between A and C, thereby making it at least an offshoot, though not a direct application, of *Lumley v Gye*. In fact of course it was a simple case falling under the *Tarleton v M'Gawley* principle: D committed trespass to A's goods when it removed the tyres and used that as a means to inflict damage on C. Lord Hoffmann in *OBG Ltd v Allan* suggests that one reason for the confusion is that situations like *Tarleton* had been labelled "intimidation" because they commonly involved threats and this label did not easily fit the case where the unlawful means had been fully implemented.[101] If in *Tarleton* D had warned A that he would sink him if he approached C that would have been "intimidation"; if he had simply sunk A with his broadside before A could become aware of any threat it is inconceivable that the result of the case would have been different or even that it would have been a different tort against C. It is an irresistible inference from the existence of liability for intimidation that there is liability on the same basis where the threat is carried out.[102] In the latter part of the 20th century we saw a process[103] whereby the *Lumley v Gye* tort was regarded as extending beyond simple inducement to (a) "prevention" (the *GWK* situation), (b) "indirect" procurement of a breach (as where D persuaded X to break his contract with A so that A could not perform his contract with C[104]) or even (c) interference short of breach, though all these situations were generally regarded as requiring some independently unlawful means. Now, it seems, after *OBG Ltd v Allan*, we can dispense with these complexities: the *Lumley v Gye* tort is confined to the simple situation where D persuades A to break his contract with C and all the others fall into the "unlawful means" tort we are now considering. It is true that even before *OBG Ltd v Allan* it was recognised that some varieties of "interference with contract", where unlawful means were involved could be regarded as species of a wider "genus" tort of interference with business by unlawful means[105] but this recognition was befogged by the insistence on classifying the categories described above as offshoots or variants of the *Lumley v Gye* tort, even though it was impossible to bring that tort within the genus: it might be possible to describe persuading A to break his contract with C as an "unlawful act" but there was certainly no requirement of independently unlawful means. The persuasion:

---

[101] [2007] UKHL 21; [2008] 1 A.C. 1 at [25].

[102] See *Rookes v Barnard* [1964] A.C. 1129 at 1168.

[103] The leading authority was *D.C. Thomson & Co Ltd v Deakin* [1952] Ch 646.

[104] Exemplified by *J.T. Stratford & Son Ltd v Lindley* [1965] A.C. 269.

[105] *Merkur Island Shipping Corp v Laughton* [1983] 2 A.C. 581 at 610; *J.T. Stratford & Son Ltd v Lindley* above, fn.104, at 324, 329.

"[W]as only wrongful because the court in *Lumley v Gye* said that inducing a breach of contract was tortious. It is circular then to say that it was tortious because it involved a wrongful act."[106]

A. Unlawful Means

The restructuring of the law in *OBG Ltd v Allan* means that we now have two torts where before we had at least five: direct inducement of breach and causing loss by unlawful means (as we shall see below, we still need to treat conspiracy separately). Unlawful means are necessary for the second of these but not the first and the case has brought some measure of clarity into the meaning of this concept. We are now concerned with the situation where, in our customary notation, D directs the unlawful means against A in order to strike at C.

18–10

One view has been that unlawful means embraces anything, "a defendant is not permitted to do, whether by the civil law or the criminal law" and this is supported by Lord Nicholls in *OBG Ltd v Allan*[107] but the majority view is narrower: it covers only acts or threats[108] of acts which are or would be civilly wrongful against and actionable by A (or would be actionable by him if he suffered loss[109]).[110] It does not therefore include criminal breaches of statutory duty which do not give rise to a civil action[111] nor does it cover common law crimes, though many of them will be torts in their own right and "unlawful" under that head. However, even those who would extend the law beyond matters actionable in their own right would not go so far as to include all incidental infringements of the criminal law. The example often given is of a pizza delivery business which manages to gain a larger share of the market by constant infringement of the traffic regulations. For Lord Nicholls that would not amount to a tort actionable by its competitor because it would not be an, "offence committed against the rival company in any

---

[106] *OBG Ltd v Allan* [2007] UKHL 21; [2008] 1 A.C. 1 at [18] per Lord Hoffmann.
[107] At [162].
[108] i.e. the form of this wrong traditionally known as intimidation. Threats of unlawful means are probably commoner in practice than their actual implementation.
[109] *National Phonograph Co Ltd v Edison-Bell Consolidated Phonograph Co Ltd* [1908] 1 Ch 335 and *Lonrho Plc v Fayed* [1992] 1 A.C. 448 seem to be examples of this situation (fraudulently inducing A to act to C's detriment).
[110] Lord Walker (with some hesitation), Baroness Hale and Lord Brown agreed with Lord Hoffmann in this respect.
[111] See Ch.7, above. Lord Hoffmann, at [57], supporting this aspect of *Lonrho Ltd v Shell Petroleum Co Ltd (No.2)* [1982] A.C. 173 (breach of sanctions order in Southern Rhodesian rebellion). Lord Walker in *Revenue and Customs Commisioners v Total Network SL* [2008] UKHL 19; [2008] A.C. 1174 at [95] is critical of the reasoning even though he concurred with Lord Hoffmann in *OBG*. However, *Revenue and Customs* involves the different tort of conspiracy.

meaningful sense of that expression."[112] Perhaps the most significant point in practice is that the concept of unlawful means includes breaches, and threats of breaches, of contract, that being the means of coercion most commonly used. That a threat of a breach of contract was unlawful means was established in the narrower context of intimidation in the pre-*OBG* law in *Rookes v Barnard*.[113] C was employed by BOAC(A) in their design office and the three defendants (D) were officials of the AESD Union, two of them also being employees of BOAC.[114] C had been but was no longer a member of the Union. In order to preserve 100 per cent union membership in the design office and notwithstanding the fact that a strike would have involved the men in breaches of their contracts of employment,[115] D notified A of the resolution passed by members of the union that if C was not dismissed, "a withdrawal of labour of all AESD Membership will take place". A yielded to this threat and lawfully terminated C's contract of employment. Owing to the provisions of the Trade Disputes Act 1906[116] C could not rely upon a simple conspiracy to injure but in the House of Lords it was held that he was entitled to succeed on the ground of intimidation. The House held, agreeing with the Court of Appeal,[117] that there was a tort of intimidation, but they also held, reversing the Court of Appeal, that the tort extended to threats by D to break his contract with A and was not confined to threats of tortious conduct.

18–11   The criticism has been made (and this indeed was the opinion of the Court of Appeal) that if intimidation is extended to threats to break contracts "it would overturn or outflank some elementary principles of contract law",[118] notably the doctrine of privity of contract, which holds that one who is not a party to a contract cannot found a claim upon it or sue for breach of it. Two answers have been made to the privity of contract objection. First, it can be said not merely that C does not sue for breach of contract between D and A, but that his cause of action actually depends upon the contract not having been broken. It is only because A yields to D's threat that it might be broken that C suffers damage at all. If A does not yield and the contract is broken, then D's threat has not caused C to suffer loss[119]; and if it be objected that D may act first (against A) and

---

[112] [2007] UKHL 21; [2008] 1 A.C. 1 at [160].

[113] [1964] A.C. 1129. The general thrust of the speeches in *OBG v Allan* seems to be that *Rookes* is essentially about the causing loss by unlawful means tort considered in *OBG*.

[114] Silverthorne, who was not employed by BOAC, was a party to an unlawful conspiracy to threaten breaches of contract: *Rookes v Barnard*, above, fn.113, at 1210–1211.

[115] An unusual feature of the case is that, as the defendants admitted, the men's contracts of employment contained an express undertaking that no strike would take place.

[116] Section 1. See para.18–36, below.

[117] [1963] 1 Q.B. 623.

[118] [1963] 1 Q.B. at 695 per Pearson L.J.

[119] This is the line of reasoning that seems to be preferred by Lords Evershed, Hodson and Devlin: [1964] A.C. 1129 at 1187–1188, 1200–1201, 1207–1208.

explain why afterwards, whereupon A acts to C's detriment, the answer is that it is not D's act which has caused C's loss but the implied threat that it will be repeated.[120] Alternatively it may be said bluntly that in all cases of intimidation, whatever the nature of the threatened act, C's cause of action is wholly independent of A's. C founds not upon the wrong, if any, done to A but on the fact that D has set out to injure him by the use of an unlawful weapon:

"I can see no difference in principle between a threat to break a contract and a threat to commit a tort. If a third party could not sue for damage caused to him by the former I can see no reason why he should be entitled to sue for damages caused to him by the latter. A person is no more entitled to sue in respect of loss which he suffers by reason of a tort committed against someone else than he is entitled to sue in respect of loss which he suffers by reason of breach of a contract to which he is not a party. What he sues for in each case is loss caused to him by the use of an unlawful weapon against him—intimidation of another person by unlawful means."[121]

The second approach does more than answer the privity of contract objection: it refutes its basic premise. The point is:

"[T]hat the 'weapon', i.e. the means, which the defendant used to inflict loss on the claimant, may be unlawful because it involves conduct wrongful towards a third party.[122] There is no reason in principle why such wrongful conduct should include torts and not breaches of contract. One might argue about whether it is expedient for the law to forbid the use of such acts as a means of causing loss, but the privity doctrine is a red herring."[123]

If one asks why the law should draw the line at threats of breach of contract and not include within the tort some threats against B even though the acts threatened are not strictly unlawful, the answer can lie only in the structure of the law which has been accepted since

---

[120] [1964] A.C. 1129 at 1187–1188, 1208–1209. However, there may be cases where C suffers loss intended by D even though it cannot be said that A acts in response to any implied threat by D, as where D simply fails, in breach of contract, to deliver goods to A which he knows A has sold on to C (see Wedderburn (1964) 27 M.L.R. 257, 265). Such conduct would certainly not then have been actionable as intimidation but, provided the requisite intention to harm C by this means can be shown, it would seem to fall within the current broad tort of intentionally causing loss by unlawful means.

[121] *Rookes v Barnard* [1964] A.C. 1129 at 1168 per Lord Reid. See also Lord Pearce at 1234–1235.

[122] "The wrong done to others reaches him": Lord Lindley in *Quinn v Leathem* [1901] A.C. 495 at 535.

[123] Hoffmann, *"Rookes v Barnard"* (1965) 81 L.Q.R. 116 at p.125.

Allen v Flood.[124] There is a legal "chasm"[125] between, for example, not entering into a contract and breach of an existing contract, which will not easily be bridged.

Furthermore, the second approach extends further than intimidation by threats of breach of contract, which the Court was concerned with in *Rookes v Barnard*, but which we are now told is only a variant of the broader tort of causing loss by unlawful means. If, as now seems to be the case, the commission of a tort against A, and not merely the threat of a tort, in order to harm C may be a tort against C,[126] it is very difficult to see why a breach of contract (as opposed to the threat of a breach) with that purpose should not have the same effect[127]—though it is not clear that the court in *Rookes v Barnard* would have taken that view.[128]

18–12   The majority in *OBG Ltd v Allan* impose a further requirement beyond the fact that there must be a wrong actionable or potentially actionable by A: the wrong (or the threat of it) must hinder A in his ability to deal with C.[129] In an earlier case approved on this basis by the majority,[130] C had an exclusive licence to exploit A's registered design and D sold articles alleged to infringe the design right. The relevant legislation gave A, but not C, the right to sue D and C's claim against D was said to have been rightly struck out for although C's sales may have been less than they would otherwise have been the performance of the contractual relations between A and C were unaffected. As we have seen, Lord Nicholls took a broader view of unlawful means but he agreed with the result in the registered design case on the basis that a wider common law liability would be inconsistent with the statutory scheme of remedies.[131]

B. Intention

18–13   This tort requires that D strikes intentionally at C through A. So if Gye had kidnapped Johanna Wagner in order to damage Lumley's theatre she would no doubt have had a defence to any action for

---

[124] [1898] A.C. 1.
[125] The word is Lord Herschell's: *Allen v Flood* [1898] A.C. 1 at 121.
[126] See para.18–9, above.
[127] See *Mennell v Stock* [2006] EWHC 2514 (QB).
[128] See [1964] A.C. at 1187, 1200, 1208. As to cases where D acts directly against C, see para.18–15, below.
[129] Lord Walker is, however, rather equivocal in his approval: Lord Hoffmann's, "test . . . of whether the defendant's wrong interferes with the freedom of a third party to deal with the claimant, if taken out of context, might be regarded as so flexible as to be of limited utility. But in practice it does not lack context. The authorities demonstrate its application in relation to a wide variety of economic relationships. I would favour a fairly cautious incremental approach to its extension to any category not found in the existing authorities" (at [270]).
[130] *Oren v Red Box Toy Factory Ltd* [1999] FSR 785. See also *RCA Corporation v Pollard* [1983] Ch 135.
[131] [2007] UKHL 21; [2008] 1 A.C. 1 at [157].

breach of contract by Lumley but Gye would (according to current thinking) have been liable to Lumley for causing loss by unlawful means; if on the other hand, Gye had injured Johanna Wagner in a street accident so that she could not sing he would not be liable to Lumley, even though he knew the identity of the person he ran down and was aware of her contract with Lumley, because the latter's only claim would be for negligence and that does not generally cover "relational" economic loss.[132] The mere fact that D's wrong is intentional towards A does not mean that he has the necessary intention to injure C. In *Millar v Bassey*[133] the facts which were required to be assumed to be provable for the purposes of a striking-out application were that D, a popular singer, entered into a contract with A, a recording company, to produce an album and C and others, the claimants, contracted with A to perform various services in connection with the album. D, in breach of contract, failed to turn up for rehearsals and then withdrew from the project. Since her services were irreplaceable this inevitably caused A to be in breach of its contract with C. The House of Lords in *OBG Ltd v Allan* regarded the Court of Appeal's decision to allow the action to proceed as wrong. Although it may have been obvious to D that her action would prevent the performance of the A-C contract she did not intend to cause injury to C:

> "[A] defendant's foresight that his unlawful conduct may or will probably damage the claimant cannot be equated with intention for this purpose ... Miss Bassey did not breach her recording contract with the intention of thereby injuring any of the plaintiffs".[134]

On the other hand:

> "[T]he master of the *Othello* in *Tarleton v M'Gawley* may have had nothing against the other trader. If he had gone off to make his fortune in other waters, he would have wished him well. He simply wanted a monopoly of the local trade for himself. But he nevertheless intended to cause him loss."[135]

---

[132] See para.5–40, above.
[133] [1994] E.M.L.R. 44.
[134] [2007] UKHL 21; [2008] 1 A.C. 1 at [166] per Lord Nicholls. Similarly Lord Hoffmann thought that she did not intend to procure a breach of that contract for the purpose of the first tort: see at [43]; but it is difficult to see how one could bring her conduct within the first tort anyway. See also *Barretts & Baird (Wholesale) Ltd v Institution of Professional Civil Servants* [1987] IRLR 3.
[135] Lord Hoffmann at [63].

So disinterested malice towards the claimant is not necessary: the defendant's purpose may be to advance his own interests by diverting business from the claimant to himself but in that case the claimant's loss and the defendant's gain are two sides of the same coin and in law he intends to injure the claimant.[136] On the other hand, a defendant is not liable where he believes that he is entitled to act as he does in protection of his own interests.[137]

C. Trade or Business

18–14   It has long been customary to call this tort interference with business (or trade) by unlawful means and *OBG Ltd v Allan* is replete with references to that or a similar formula.[138] This may simply be because the overwhelming majority of cases are likely to arise in a business context, but it is hard to see why the tort should be so confined.[139] If it is actionable to use unlawful means to drive away C's prospective customers[140] why should it not equally be actionable to use such means against a person who proposes to buy his house but has not yet signed a contract to do so?[141]

D. "Two party" Cases

18–15   If there is no third party, A, and D uses unlawful means to inflict harm directly on C, then in very many cases D will have committed one of the specific intentional torts dealt with in this book—deceit, conversion, assault and so on—and there seems little point in seeking for any generalised liability for causing loss by unlawful means, indeed, it might be thought positively confusing to erect such a parallel liability. Nonetheless, there may be cases in which C succumbs to the *threat* of unlawful action in which there is no completed, independent tort. In the past such cases have been discussed on the basis that "intimidation" amounted to a separate tort but after *OBG Ltd v Allan* it seems to be a variety (perhaps the most common variety) of causing loss by unlawful means. If, for example, D

---

[136] *OBG v Allan* at [167]; *Sorrell v Smith* [1900] A.C. 700 at 742.
[137] *Meretz Investments NV v ACP Ltd* [2007] EWCA Civ 1303; [2008] Ch 244. The proposition is made in the context of a claim for unlawful means conspiracy but it must equally apply to the unlawful means tort which may be committed by an individual.
[138] e.g. [2007] UKHL 21; [2008] 1 A.C. 1 at [139], [141], [180], [247], [261].
[139] Lord Walker in *Revenue and Customs Commissioners v Total Network SL* [2008] UKHL 19; [2008] 1 A.C. 1174 at [100] seems to be of the view that it is so confined but conspiracy (see para.18–27, below) is not.
[140] *Tarleton v M'Gawley* (1793) Peake N.P. 270, para.18–9, above.
[141] Cf. Deakin and Randall, "Rethinking the Economic Torts" (2009) 72 M.L.R. 519. Most cases of inducing a breach of contract will also occur in a business context, but it seems to be assumed that the tort could apply to a non-commercial property transaction (*Smith v Morrison* [1974] 1 W.L.R. 659) though the result may be affected by the statutory provisions on registration of land charges.

threatens C that he will do him grievous bodily harm unless he pays him money the threat may not be immediate enough to constitute an assault. Certainly C may recover his money by action because the transfer is voidable for duress, but C may have suffered further damage as a result. If D tells lies to A in order to prevent C getting a licence, it seems that this is the tort of inflicting loss by unlawful means.[142] Why should it not be a tort for D to extract money from C by threatening to tell such lies to A in the future? *OBG Ltd v Allan* is not much help on these issues since the House of Lords did no more than barely mention the point and Lord Hoffmann warned that he did:

> "[N]ot intend to say anything about the question of whether a claimant who has been compelled by unlawful intimidation to act to his own detriment, can sue for his loss. Such a case of 'two-party intimidation' raises altogether different issues".[143]

The Court of Appeal accepted two-party intimidation as part of the law in a case where a young girl was kept in coercive and exploitative conditions as a domestic servant.[144] However, Lord Reid warned in *J.T. Stratford & Son Ltd v Lindley*,[145]:

> "A case where a defendant presents to the claimant the alternative of doing what the defendant wants him to do or suffering loss which the defendant can cause him to incur is not necessarily *in pari casu* and may involve questions which cannot arise where there is intimidation of a third person."

The problems centre round the effect in the two-party situation of a threat of a breach of contract.[146]

18–16 First, in the two-party situation there is normally a contractual remedy already available to C, while in the three-party situation, if C cannot sue in tort, he cannot sue at all, because D's threat of breach is made to A.[147] If C is threatened with a breach of contract by D he may be able to treat the contract as repudiated and sue for anticipatory breach or, of course, he may await the breach and then

---

[142] A reasonable inference from the facts of *Lonrho Plc v Fayed* [1992] 1 A.C. 448, approved in *OBG Ltd v Allan*.
[143] See [2007] UKHL 21; [2008] 1 A.C. 1 at [61].
[144] *Godwin v Uzoigwe* [1993] Fam. Law 65. See also *News Group Newspapers Ltd v S.O.G.A.T. '82* [1986] I.R.L.R. 337 at 347, with reference to the seventh claimant.
[145] [1965] A.C. 269 at 325.
[146] The unlawful acts are not very explicitly classified in *Godwin v Uzoigwe*, above, fn.144, but they included acts which were torts and crimes and may have been breaches of contract.
[147] Hoffmann, (1965) 81 L.Q.R. 116 at pp.127–128.

sue for damages. In fact, the balance of advantage would seem to lie in holding that where D threatens C with a breach of his contract with C, C should be restricted to his contractual remedies. The law should not encourage B to yield to the threat but should seek to persuade him to resist it.[148] In some cases he may be able to obtain an injunction to restrain the breach and in any case he will be adequately compensated by his remedy in damages for breach of contract as his damage can scarcely be other than financial. If C is threatened with a tort it is, of course, equally true that he may bring an action for damages if the tort is committed or bring an action for a *quia timet* injunction first, but, especially where the threat is of violence, it is perhaps less realistic to say that these legal remedies afford him adequate protection against the consequences of resistance.[149] From the point of view of policy, therefore, there is much to be said for the view that no independent tort is committed when all that is threatened, in the two-party situation, is a breach of contract.

18–17   Secondly, since threatened breaches of contract were brought within the fold of unlawful means in *Rookes v Barnard* there has been considerable development in the contractual context of the doctrine of "economic duress", and in this context it is clear that although a threat to break a contract is "illegitimate" it will not amount to duress unless it goes beyond commercial pressure and amounts to "coercion of the will".[150] In *Pao On v Lau Yiu*[151] D threatened that unless C agreed to vary an existing contract between them by giving D a guarantee against loss, D would not fulfil his side of the agreement. D's action on the guarantee succeeded because, although C had acceded to the demand because of fears of delay in litigation and loss of public confidence, the pressure fell short of coercion. Though intimidation was not discussed in the case it cannot be that C could have avoided the binding nature of the contract by the simple device of counter-claiming for damages for intimidation and it seems therefore that for the purposes of intimidation the claimant should be required to show unlawful coercion at least of such a degree as would enable him to avoid a contract.[152] If there are any cases in which the victim of unfair pressure may avoid

---

[148] See the example given by Hoffmann, (1965) 81 L.Q.R. 116.

[149] A point demonstrated clearly by *Godwin v Uzoigwe*, above, fn.144.

[150] There is, however, some controversy about the theoretical basis of duress: see *Dimskal Shipping Co SA v I.T.W.F.* [1992] 2 A.C. 152 at 166 per Lord Goff.

[151] [1980] A.C. 614.

[152] Another problem is that the right to avoid a contract for economic duress may be lost by affirmation: *North Ocean Shipping Co Ltd v Hyundai Construction Co Ltd* [1979] Q.B. 705. It is not easy to see on what basis the right to sue for intimidation could be similarly lost: cf. *Neibuhr v Gage* (1906) 108 N.W. 884.

a contract even though the threat is not of unlawful action,[153] there seems no possibility of any concurrent tort liability.[154]

It has been suggested above that in the three-party situation an **18–18** actual breach of contract by D against A is as much unlawful means as a threatened breach in the context of D's liability in tort to C. Is it therefore the law that if D deliberately *breaks* his own contract with C that he is liable in tort as well as in contract? It is thought that the answer is plainly "No". The remedies provided to C by the law of contract are as effective, if not more so, than in the case where D threatens to break the contract; and there would be something very odd in turning every profit-motivated breach of contract into a tort.[155] English law is not unfriendly to concurrent liability[156] but this would be taking it a step too far.

A further difficulty arises from the decision of the House of Lords **18–19** in *Revenue and Customs Commisioners v Total Network SL*[157] on unlawful means conspiracy, the law on which is outlined below. It differs from causing loss by unlawful means in that a crime is capable of being unlawful means. Conspiracy inevitably involves at least three persons (two conspirators and the victim) but since it does not (or does not necessarily) involve the defendants working through acts against a third party, it may for our purposes be regarded as a "two-party" tort. Lord Hoffmann's brief reference to two-party cases in *OBG v Allan*[158] is couched in terms of the simple case where D threatens C, but in the *Revenue and Customs* case there are passages which tend (one can be no more categorical) towards regarding two-party liability as being generally broader in its scope than that in the threeparty cases.[159]

It should be noted that the Protection from Harassment Act 1997 **18–20** created a tort (and crime) of "harassment" by conduct (which includes speech) on at least two occasions which a reasonable

---

[153] Some of the cases on "unconscionable bargains" might be regarded as at least akin to duress.

[154] In *Universe Tankships Inc of Monrovia v I.T.W.F.* [1983] A.C. 366 at 400, Lord Scarman, dissenting (but on another point) said: "It is, I think, already established law that economic pressure can in law amount to duress and that duress, if proved, not only renders voidable a transaction into which a person has entered under its compulsion but is actionable as a tort, if it causes damage or loss". Cf. Lord Diplock, at 385: "The use of economic duress to induce another person to part with property or money is not a tort *per se* ; the form that the duress takes may, or may not, be tortious".

[155] The remedy of requiring the defendant to account for his profits from the breach to the claimant is very restricted and this is no accident: *Att Gen v Blake* [2001] 1 A.C. 268. Exemplary damages for profit-motivated torts go wider (para.22–10, below). The fact that it would suit the claimant to dress up his claim as tort rather than contract is not necessarily a reason for allowing him to do so.

[156] See para.1–8, above.

[157] [2008] UKHL 19; [2008] A.C. 1174

[158] See para.18–15, above.

[159] See at [43], [99], [124] and [223].

person would think amounted to harassment.[160] While this is plainly wider than two-party intimidation in that it is not confined to threats of wrongful acts and allows damages for anxiety as well as financial loss, it would seem to overlap with it to a considerable degree.

3. CONSPIRACY

18–21   Though our early law knew a writ of conspiracy, this was restricted to abuse of legal procedure and the action on the case in the nature of conspiracy, which came into fashion in the reign of Elizabeth I, developed into the modern tort of malicious prosecution. Conspiracy as a crime was developed by the Star Chamber during the 17th century and, when taken over by the common law courts, came to be regarded by them as not only a crime but also as capable of giving rise to civil liability provided damage resulted to the claimant. As a tort, however, it was little developed until the second half of the 19th century[161] and the law remained obscure until the decision of the House of Lords in *Crofter Hand-Woven Harris Tweed Co Ltd v Veitch*.[162] Conspiracy remains a crime as well as a tort, but the scope of the crime has been curtailed by statute[163] so that, broadly speaking, the only conspiracies which are now indictable are those to commit a substantive criminal offence, to defraud or to corrupt public morals or outrage public decency.[164] The Act, however, has no effect on civil liability. In fact, even aside from the Act the tort and the crime have cut loose from whatever common origin they had.[165]

The tort takes two forms according to whether or not unlawful means are used.

A. Conspiracy to Injure—"Crofter" Conspiracy

18–22   It was firmly established in *Crofter Hand-Woven Harris Tweed Co Ltd v Veitch*[166] that if there is a combination of persons whose purpose is to cause damage to the claimant, that purpose may render unlawful acts which would otherwise be lawful and which would be lawful if committed by one person even with the purpose of causing injury. The production of Harris Tweed is an industry of the Isle of Lewis and other islands of the Outer Hebrides. Originally the yarn

---

[160] See para.4–38, above.
[161] It "is a modern invention altogether": *Midland Bank Trust Co Ltd v Green (No.3)* [1982] Ch. 529 at 539 per Lord Denning M.R.
[162] [1942] A.C. 435.
[163] Criminal Law Act 1977.
[164] The last two may be offences even when committed by one person.
[165] *Midland Bank Trust Co Ltd v Green (No.3)*, above, fn.161, at 541.
[166] [1942] A.C. 435.

for the cloth was hand-spun from wool by the crofters of Lewis and was wholly produced in the Isle. By 1930, hand-spinning of wool had become commercially impracticable and thenceforth many weavers in Lewis imported yarn from the mainland. Five mill owners in Lewis nevertheless spun yarn woven by the crofters. These mill owners alleged that cloth woven on Lewis from mainland yarn could be sold much more cheaply than cloth made from yarn spun in Lewis. It was therefore in their interest to get a minimum price fixed for the cloth. Of the workers in their mills 90 per cent belonged to the TGWU and the Lewis dockers were also members of it. The union, with the object of getting all mill workers to be members and of increasing wages, approached the mill owners, who replied that they could not raise the wages because of the competition of the crofters who wove imported yarn. The union officials then put an embargo on the importation of yarn by ordering Lewis dockers not to handle such yarn. They obeyed (without breaking any contract) and thus injured the trade of seven small producers of tweed who used imported yarn and who sued the officials for conspiracy.[167]

It must be stressed at the outset, lest the importance of this form of liability be exaggerated, that the claimants lost their case because the predominant purpose of the embargo was to promote the interests of the union members rather than to injure the claimants,[168] but their Lordships made it clear that if the predominant purpose of a combination is to injure another in his trade or business[169] or in his other legitimate interests[170] then, if damage results, the tort of conspiracy exists. The *Crofter* principle was applied by the Court of Appeal in *Gulf Oil (Great Britain) Ltd v Page*[171] in granting an interlocutory injunction against a combination to publish a statement defamatory of the claimants even though the statement was admitted to be true and there would, therefore, have been an absolute defence to an action for libel; but this is confined to cases where the claimant suffers actual pecuniary loss: if the claim is for general loss of reputation or injured feelings the law of defamation cannot be sidestepped in this way.[172]

---

[167] Now by the Harris Tweed Act 1993 (c. xi) s.7, it means a tweed, "which has been handwoven by the islanders at their homes in the Outer Hebrides, finished in the Outer Hebrides, and made from pure virgin wool dyed and spun in the Outer Hebrides".

[168] See also *Mogul S.S. Co Ltd v McGregor Gow* [1892] A.C. 25; *Sorrell v Smith* [1925] A.C. 700.

[169] This, so their Lordships held, had really been settled in *Quinn v Leathem* [1901] A.C. 495, notwithstanding earlier doubts about the meaning of that case.

[170] [1942] A.C. 435 at 446-447, 451, 462, 478.

[171] [1988] Ch. 327.

[172] *Lonrho Plc v Fayed (No.5)* [1993] 1 W.L.R. 1489. See also *Oyston v Blaker* [1996] 1 W.L.R. 1326.

18–23   **i. Purpose.** The object or purpose of the combination must be to cause damage to the claimant. The test is not what the defendants contemplated as a likely or even an inevitable consequence of their conduct, it is, "what is in truth the object in the minds of the combiners when they acted as they did?"[173] Malice in the sense of malevolence, spite or ill will is not essential for liability,[174] nor is it sufficient if merely superadded to a legitimate purpose[175]; what is required is that the combiners should have acted in order that (not with the result that, even the foreseeably inevitable result) the claimant should suffer damage. If they did not act in order that the claimant should suffer damage but to pursue their own advantage, they are not liable, however selfish their attitude and however inevitable the claimant's damage may have been.[176] Thus the principle applicable in the tort of causing loss by unlawful means[177] (or indeed the unlawful means variety of conspiracy) that a defendant who intends to advance his own interests by diverting business from the claimant to himself intends to injure the claimant because the claimant's loss and the defendant's gain are two sides of the same coin is inapplicable here. At common law an agreement between D1 and D2 to fix prices so that C is driven out of the market and his share passes to them is not an actionable wrong even though the agreement is invalid as in restraint of trade[178] (though it is likely to be so under the Competition Act 1998).[179] It is not, however, essential that the interest promoted be a material one.[180] In *Scala Ballroom (Wolverhampton) Ltd v Ratcliffe*[181] the claimants refused to admit black people to their ballroom[182] but they did allow black musicians to play in the orchestra. The defendants were members of the Musicians' Union, a union with many black members, and they gave notice to the claimants that members of the union would not be permitted to play at the ballroom so long as the colour bar was in operation. An injunction to restrain them from persuading their members not to play there was refused. Although malevolence is not necessary, where that state of mind is what motivates the defendants they may be liable even though precisely the same acts would be

---

[173] [1942] A.C. 435 at 445 per Viscount Simon L.C.
[174] [1942] A.C. 435 at 450, 463, 469–471.
[175] "I cannot see how the pursuit of a legitimate practical object can be vitiated by glee at the adversary's expected discomfiture": per Lord Wright.
[176] As may be expected from this, successful actions for conspiracy are rare.
[177] See para.18–13, above.
[178] *Mogul S.S. Co Ltd v McGregor Gow & Co* [1892] A.C. 25.
[179] See para.18–1, above.
[180] Lord Wright, at 478, implies that a combination of parishioners to withhold subscriptions from the incumbent is not unlawful if the object is the promotion of the religious interests of the parish. Cf. *Bear v Reformed Mennonite Church* 341 A. (2d) 105 (1975).
[181] [1958] 1 W.L.R. 1057.
[182] See now the Race Relations Act 1976.

lawful in pursuit of their interests. In *Huntley v Thornton*[183] damages were awarded against union officials whose object in keeping the claimant out of work was, as Harman J. found, to uphold:

> "[T]heir own ruffled dignity . . . It had become a question of the district committee's prestige; they were determined to use any weapon ready to their hand to vindicate their authority, and grossly abused the quite frightening powers at their command."[184]

Of course even individuals rarely act from a single motive but in these cases the question must be asked what was the predominant purpose of the combination and if that is the pursuit of the defendant's interests their conduct is not actionable because they are also pleased by the claimant's loss.[185] There is no liability where the participants act in pursuance of different forms of self-interest.[186] If one participant has the object of causing injury to the claimant and the others do not there is no conspiracy because there is no common purpose to injure; but if the others are aware of the intention of the one bent on injury it may be that they are all liable.[187] The fact that the damage is disproportionate to the purpose sought to be achieved does not itself render the conspiracy actionable[188] nor is the court concerned with the expediency or otherwise of the policy adopted by the combiners.[189]

The *Crofter* case contains a number of statements to the effect that **18–24** a combination to injure another without the use of unlawful means is not actionable where it is designed to pursue the "legitimate" or "lawful" interests of the defendants. Thus Viscount Simon said that if the:

> "[P]redominant purpose is to damage another person and damage results, that is tortious conspiracy. If the predominant purpose is the lawful protection or promotion of any lawful interest of the

---

[183] [1957] 1 W.L.R. 321; *Hutchinson v Aitchison* (1970) 9 K.I.R. 69.
[184] [1957] 1 W.L.R. 321 at 341 per Harman L.J. Such a case was foreshadowed by Lord Wright in the *Crofter* case, above, fn.166, at 445. The position was not perhaps so clear in *Quinn v Leathem* [1901] A.C. 495 but according to Lord Sumner in *Sorrell v Smith* [1925] A.C. 700 at 736 that case is to be explained on the basis that there was evidence from which the jury could find that the defendants', "real object was to punish Leathem for his conduct in harbouring non-unionists and was not simply to advance their own interests in the future by bringing those non-unionists into their fold". Cf. Lord Lindley in *Quinn v Leathem* at 536.
[185] [1942] A.C. at 471 per Lord Wright.
[186] Thus in the *Crofter* case the interests of the mill owners and the trade unionists were by no means identical.
[187] [1942] A.C. at 495.
[188] Though it may cast doubt upon the defendants' bona fides.
[189] *Crofter* case at [1942] A.C. 447.

combiners (no illegal means being employed), it is not a tortious conspiracy, even though it causes damage to another person."[190]

Clearly therefore there is no actionable conspiracy where the defendants act to improve their share of the market at the claimant's expense[191] or to strengthen the position of a trade union or its members[192] or to maintain prices in the trade to the common benefit of members.[193] However, what if the defendants' activity does not involve "trade" or "business" in any meaningful sense at all but is simply a scheme to cheat others of money? In *Revenue and Customs Commissioners v Total Network SL*[194] the defendants engineered a complex "carousel fraud" involving fictitious supplies of goods and based upon the facts that, (a) a trader in a chain who pays VAT on the supply of goods to him is entitled to reclaim it from the Revenue, and (b) that export transactions between EU countries are not subject to VAT. In its simplest form, A in country X contracts to sell goods to B in country Y. B then sells the goods (in country Y) to C, C paying VAT. B then ceases to trade and disappears without accounting to the Revenue for the tax. Before the Revenue discovers B's disappearance C then resells the goods to A in country X and reclaims the VAT he has paid. The whole scheme was criminal and in such a case it seems extraordinary to say that the parties are merely "advancing their interests" at the expense of the Revenue. Nevertheless in the case the Revenue abandoned a claim based upon conspiracy to injure, seemingly on the basis that causing damage to the Revenue was not the primary aim of the carousel fraud[195] and instead advanced a case based solely on unlawful means conspiracy. That raised questions, which are explored below, about how far a criminal offence may be unlawful means for the purposes of that tort. However, as Lord Neuberger pointed out, on such facts:

"[T]here is little, if any, difference between the conspirators' intention to make money and their intention to deprive the commissioners of money: each is the obverse of the other. On that basis, it may well be that it could be said that the predominant purpose of Total and the other conspirators was indeed to inflict

---

[190] [1942] A.C. at 445; see also at 469.
[191] *Mogul S.S. Co* case above, fn.178.
[192] The *Crofter* case itself. In *Giblan v National Amalgamated Labourers' Union* [1903] 2 K.B. 600, long before *Crofter* and perhaps dubious for that reason, a combination to obtain payment of a debt to the union was held actionable. Certainly the law provides machinery for recovery but this had been tried and had proved ineffective.
[193] *Ware and de Freville Ltd v Motor Trade Association* [1921] 3 K.B. 40.
[194] [2008] UKHL 19; [2008] 1 A.C. 1174.
[195] See at [226].

loss on the [Revenue] just as much as it was to profit the conspirators, and hence the claim in tort is made out in conspiracy to injure."[196]

ii. Combination. There must be concerted action between two or more persons, which includes husband and wife.[197] It seems that there can be no conspiracy between an employer and his employees, at least where they merely go about their employer's business[198] and it is submitted that directors who resolve to cause their company to break its contract do not commit conspiracy by unlawful means[199] against the other contracting party, for they are identified with the company for this purpose[200]; if that were not so there would be an easy way to outflank the denial of liability for inducing breach of contract in such circumstances.[201] On the other hand, there might be circumstances where an employer would be vicariously liable for a conspiracy involving his servants provided the other requirements of that form of liability are met and there may be a conspiracy between a company and its directors, where the latter act so as to incur personal liability in circumstances where their knowledge may be imputed to the company.[202]

18–25

iii. Overt act causing damage. In contrast with the crime of conspiracy, an overt act causing damage is an essential element of liability in tort. If, therefore, the acts relied on are incapable of being made part of any cause of action—for example evidence given by witnesses in a court of law—then the tort cannot be made out.[203] A sufficient element of damage is shown where expenses are necessarily incurred by the claimant in investigating and counteracting the machinations of the defendants.[204] Though the claimant is required

18–26

---

[196] At [228]. Lord Hope, too, thought at [44] that the, "case as a subspecies of unlawful means conspiracy [was] virtually indistinguishable from the tort of conspiracy to injure", and see the CA at [34] of its judgment in the same report. Cf. para.18–13, above.

[197] *Midland Bank Trust Co Ltd v Green (No.3)* [1982] Ch. 529. This is a clear difference between the tort and the crime.

[198] Clerk and Lindsell, *Torts*, 19th edn, para.25–119.

[199] See below (though it is not clear that a breach of contract is unlawful means for this purpose).

[200] *Normart Management Ltd v West Redhill Redevelopment Co* (1998) 155 D.L.R. (4th) 627. See also para.24–23, below; but in *De Jetley Marks v Greenwood* [1936] 1 All E.R. 863 at 871 Porter J. thought that some of the directors could conspire before the meeting.

[201] See para.18–6, above.

[202] *Belmont Finance Corp Ltd v Williams Furniture Ltd (No.2)* [1980] 1 All E.R. 393; *Taylor v Smyth* [1991] I.R. 158. Cf. *Belmont Finance Corp Ltd v Williams Furniture Ltd* [1979] Ch. 250 (knowledge not to be imputed where company claimant).

[203] *Marrinan v Vibart* [1963] 1 Q.B. 234, affirmed, at 528. Cf. *Darker v Chief Constable of West Midlands* [2001] 1 A.C. 435 and *Surzur Overseas Ltd v Koros* [1999] 2 Lloyd's Rep. 611.

[204] *B.M.T.A. v Salvadori* [1949] Ch. 556. Quaere when there is no other financial loss: *Lonrho Plc v Fayed (No.5)* [1993] 1 W.L.R. 1489. These and a number of other cases are examined in *R & V Versicherung AG v Risk Insurance and Reinsurance Solutions SA* [2006] EWHC 42 (Comm).

to prove some actual pecuniary loss, once that is done damages are
not limited to the amount so proved.[205]

B. "Unlawful means" Conspiracy
18–27   This tort:

> "[I]nvolves an arrangement between two or more parties,
> whereby they . . . agree that at least one of them will use 'unlaw-
> ful means' against the claimant, and, although damage to the
> claimant need not be the predominant intention of any of the
> parties, the claimant must have suffered loss or damage as a
> result."[206]

The elements of combination[207] and overt act causing damage are
the same as under *"Crofter"* conspiracy, but we need to look at the
mental element and, of course, at the notion of unlawful means.

18–28   **i. Intention of the defendant.** After a period of uncertainty
caused by *Lonrho Ltd v Shell Petroleum Ltd (No.2)*[208] the House of
Lords in *Lonrho Plc v Fayed*[209] reaffirmed that this form of the tort,
unlike the *Crofter* variety, does not require a predominant purpose to
injure the claimant and *Revenue and Customs Commissioners v
Total Network SL*[210] also proceeds on this basis. However, the tort
still requires an intention to injure: it is not enough that the defendants combine to do an unlawful act which has the effect of causing

---

[205] *Lonrho Plc v Fayed (No.5)*, above, fn.204. When actual pecuniary loss has been proved,
damages are said to be at large, but not to the extent of allowing damages for loss of
reputation. Loss of orders or loss of trade is actionable but not, "airy-fairy general
reputation in the business or commercial community", nor a decline in the share value of
a corporate claimant: *Lonrho Plc v Fayed (No.5)*, fn.204, at 1496.
[206] Said to be "common ground" between the parties in *Revenue and Customs Commissioners
v Total Network SL* [2008] UKHL 19; [2008] 1 A.C. 1174 at [213] per Lord Neuberger.
[207] The knowledge of an "accessory" conspirator may not be the same as that of the principal
actor and it may be necessary to analyse the extent to which the accessory shared a
common objective with the primary actor and the extent to which the achievement of that
objective was to his knowledge to be achieved by unlawful means intended to injure the
claimant, his liability being limited to that common extent: *Bank of Tokyo-Mitsubishi UJF
Ltd v Baskan Gida Sanayive Pazarlama AS* [2008] EWHC 659 (Ch) at [847]; *IS Innovative
Software Ltd v Howes* [2004] EWCA Civ 275; cf. *Kuwait Oil Tanker Co SAK v Al Bader*
[2000] 2 All E.R. Comm. 271.
[208] [1982] A.C. 173.
[209] [1992] 1 A.C. 448, overruling *Metall und Rohstoff v Donaldson Lufkin & Jenrette Inc*
[1990] 1 Q.B. 391 and explaining *Lonrho Ltd v Shell Petroleum Ltd (No.2)* [1982] A.C.
173.
[210] [2008] UKHL 19; [2008] 1 A.C. 1174. See, e.g. at [40], [56], [82], [115], [213].

damage to the claimant. The concept means the same as it does in the tort of intentional infliction of harm by unlawful means: if the damage to the claimant is not an end in itself it must at least be a necessary means to some other end and it is not enough that it is a foreseeable consequence of the unlawful means used.[211] The intentional harm tort (at least in its usual "three-party" form) involves unlawful conduct directed at a third party but with the intention of causing harm to the claimant by interfering with the business relationship between the third party and the claimant. Here, too, although there need be[212] no third party involved, the purpose of the combination must be to strike at the claimant. To take an example loosely based on *Lonrho Ltd v Shell Petroleum Ltd (No.2)*,[213] if D1 and D2 combine to evade legislation prohibiting trade with a country in which C has oil interests and the effect of this is to damage C's interests then even if the evasion of the legislation is unlawful means[214] they do not intend to harm C—that is simply a byproduct, even if an inevitable one, of what they do. That is not to say that it will necessarily be easy to draw the line between this situation and the "means to an end" intention which does fall within the tort. If the correct analysis of the facts is that the conspirators wanted to get hold of the oil market for themselves in that country by destroying C's share,[215] that must be a classic example of using illegal means to achieve some ulterior end. After all, in a conspiracy by D1 and D2 to defraud C, D1 and D2 plainly intend to deprive C of his property so that they can get it.[216]

ii. Unlawful means. There has been an understandable desire in some quarters to give unity to the concept of unlawful means in the economic torts.[217] As we have seen above, the majority in *OBG Ltd v Allan* regarded the tort of intentionally causing loss by unlawful means as essentially one in which D strikes at C by using unlawful

18–29

---

[211] "It is . . . a sub-species of the tort of conspiracy to injure, in which the ordinary requirement that such intent be predominant in the mind of the defendant is replaced by the requirement to show that unlawful conduct has been the means of the intentional infliction of harm to the claimant": *Bank of Tokyo-Mitsubishi UJF Ltd* above, fn.207, at [825].

[212] There may be a third party. If D threatens A that he will break his contract with A unless A ceases to trade with C that is inflicting harm on C by unlawful means. So also is it if D1 and D2 combine so to threaten A, but this time it is also unlawful means conspiracy.

[213] [1982] A.C. 173.

[214] See para.18–29, below.

[215] As far as can be judged from the CA transcript in *Lonrho*, that is not the way the points of claim in the arbitration were framed.

[216] *Kuwait Oil Tanker Co SAK v Al Bader* [2000] 2 All E.R. Comm. 271. Indeed, as has been seen above, Lord Neuberger in the *Revenue and Customs Commissioners* case regarded that as a predominant purpose to injure.

[217] The best discussion of the state of the law in the pre-*OBG/Revenue and Customs Commissioners* period is the judgment of Davis J. *Mbasogo v Logo Ltd* [2005] EWHC 2035 (QB).

means directed against a third party (A)[218] and in that context unlawful means covers only acts or threats of acts which are or would be civilly wrongful against and actionable by A (or would be actionable by A if he suffered loss).[219] The equivalent proposition in a case of conspiracy where the unlawful means were not directed at a third party[220] would be that the means would have to be independently actionable by C.[221] However, the result of *Revenue and Customs Commissioners v Total Network SL*[222] is that in unlawful means conspiracy it also covers acts which are criminal but which would not be civilly actionable if done by one person. Hence on the facts the common law offence of cheating the Revenue, if established, would lead to liability in tort.[223] It would be difficult to say that this conclusion was very closely reasoned. Indeed, as Lord Walker admits, the common assumption in many of the earlier dicta that a crime is unlawful means perhaps rests on a quasi-lay assumption that criminality is so obviously at the top of the tree of unlawfulness that its inclusion hardly needs justification,[224] and it is certainly true that a great deal more judicial effort has been devoted to breach of contract in the context of the economic torts than to crime. For Lord Scott, the imposition of tort liability is justified where the:

> "[C]ircumstances [are] such as to make the conduct sufficiently reprehensible to justify imposing on those who have brought about the harm liability in damages for having done so. Bearing that in mind, the proposition that a combination of two or more people to carry out a scheme that is criminal in its nature and is intended to cause economic harm to some person does not, when carried out with that result, constitute a tort actionable by that person is, in my opinion, unacceptable. Such a proposition is not only inconsistent with the jurisprudence of tortuous conspir-

---

[218] As to "two-party" cases see para.18–15, above.
[219] See para.18–10, above.
[220] As to which see fn.212, above.
[221] See *Powell v Boladz* [1998] Lloyd's Rep Med 116, overruled in *Revenue and Customs Commissioners.*
[222] [2008] UKHL 19; [2008] 1 A.C. 1174.
[223] The case, like so many others in this area, was an appeal against a decision on a preliminary issue. The case is complicated by the statutory background. It was unsuccessfully argued that the claim was bad as an attempt to levy tax without the grant by Parliament (Bill of Rights, art.4) but Lord Hope and Lord Neuberger, dissenting, were of the view that any claim in tort was barred by the existence of the statutory scheme for recovery in the Value Added Tax Act 1994. There was in fact an alternative claim for conspiracy based upon the making of fraudulent misrepresentations. That of course would on the face of it have presented no problems because it would have involved means civilly actionable by the claimant, but the CA was of the view that it would fall foul of the "complete statutory code argument" because that would prevent the Revenue having an ordinary civil fraud claim and thus prevent the unlawful means being actionable by it. The alternative claim was not before the HL.
[224] See at [90]–[94].

acy, . . . but is inconsistent also with the historic role of the action on the case."[225]

All this, however, does not explain why a conclusion which seems obvious in the context of conspiracy is rejected in the context of causing loss by unlawful means. One reason may be that if we confine unlawful means to civilly actionable conduct the tort of unlawful means conspiracy almost disappears because the conspirators will generally be joint tortfeasors anyway.[226] If D1 and D2 conspire to defraud C by making fraudulent misrepresentations to him they jointly commit deceit. The same result may be reached if the means used are not tortious but, say, a breach of contract, the joint tort this time being intentionally causing loss by unlawful means.[227] The clear message of *Revenue and Customs Commissioners* is that unlawful means conspiracy is not merely a form of secondary liability, joint tortfeasance dressed up in other clothes.

The point has been made above that although the *Revenue and Customs Commissioners* case was presented only as one of unlawful means conspiracy, some members of the House of Lords had doubts whether it might not better have been regarded as a straightforward conspiracy to injure.[228] If it was not, that, for Lord Neuberger, was strong reason for including criminality within the scope of unlawful means.

18–30

"In my judgment, given the existence of [conspiracy to injure], it would be anomalous if an unlawful means conspiracy could not found a cause of action where, as here, the means 'merely' involved a crime, where the loss to the claimant was the obvious and inevitable, indeed in many ways the intended, result of the sole purpose of the conspiracy, and where the crime involved, cheating the revenue, has as its purpose the protection of the victim of the conspiracy."[229]

---

[225] At [56]. Earlier in the paragraph he had said: "We were taught at law school that the action on the case was the means whereby our judicial forbears allowed tortious remedies in damages where harm had been caused in circumstances where the conduct of the authors of the harm had been sufficiently reprehensible to require the conclusion that they ought to be held responsible for the harm."

[226] Counsel for the claimants contended that on the defendants' argument unlawful means conspiracy would become a "barren iteration of joint tortfeasance": at [66]; but even where the unlawful means involve a tort actionable directly by the claimant there is no doctrine that the conspiracy is "merged" in the substantive tort and it has been said that the conspiracy claim may express "the true nature and gravamen of the case": *Kuwait Oil Tanker Co SAK v Al Bader* [2000] 2 All E.R. Comm. 271 at [119] (where the conspiracy claim was significant for the then-applicable conflict of laws rules).

[227] Nonetheless, the reader may think twice before accepting that if D1 and D2 have a joint contract with C their decision to break it may be the tort of conspiracy.

[228] See para.18–24, above.

[229] [2008] UKHL 19; [2008] 1 A.C. 1174 at [221].

18-31   It is not, however, in every case that the use of criminal means gives rise to unlawful means conspiracy. It is not enough that there is a crime somewhere in the story. We have already seen in the context of intentionally inflicting harm by unlawful means how even the minority who would have included crimes as unlawful means would not go so far as to say that the tort is committed by the infringement of road traffic rules by a pizza delivery company eager to take trade from its rivals because the crime is not directed at the rivals and is not in a real sense the instrumentality of the harm.[230] The same is true if the claim is framed as a conspiracy.[231] In the *Revenue and Customs Commissioners* case, in contrast, the claimants were the direct target of the offence of cheating and the offence existed, "in its very nature to protect the Revenue".[232] We have seen that the commission of a crime which is not a common law tort in its own right does not give rise to civil liability unless an intention to accord a civil action can be found in the legislation creating the offence.[233] That has been used a reason for rejecting crime as unlawful means in the tort of intentionally causing harm by unlawful means.[234] It is unclear exactly how this principle stands in the context of unlawful means conspiracy, Lord Walker in *Revenue and Customs Commissioners* being content to say that:

> "[T]he sort of considerations relevant to determining whether a breach of statutory duty is actionable in a civil suit . . . may well overlap, or even occasionally coincide with, the issue of unlawful means in the tort of conspiracy. But the range of possible breaches of statutory duty, and the range of possible conspiracies, are both so wide and varied that it would be unwise to attempt to lay down any general rule."[235]

C. Place of Conspiracy in the Law

18-32   *Crofter* conspiracy to injure is widely regarded as anomalous,[236] though it has attracted more controversy among academic writers than success in practical application.[237] The central issue has been why the "magic of plurality" should make something unlawful if it

---

[230] See para.18–10, above.
[231] See [2008] UKHL 19; [2008] 1 A.C. 1174 at [95].
[232] At [120] per Lord Mance.
[233] See Ch.7, above.
[234] *OBG Ltd v Allan* [2007] UKHL 21; [2008] 1 A.C. 1 at [57] per Lord Hoffmann. However, Lord Hoffmann relies on *Lonrho v Shell (No.2)* for this and in the view of Lord Walker in *Revenue and Customs Commissioners* that case turned solely on the lack of intention to injure the claimants: at [95].
[235] [2008] UKHL 19; [2008] 1 A.C. 1174 at [96].
[236] *Lonrho Ltd v Shell Petroleum Ltd (No.2)* [1982] A.C. 173 at 188; *Lonrho Plc v Fayed* [1992] 1 A.C. 448 at 463.
[237] *Lonrho Ltd v Shell Petroleum Co Ltd (No.2)* [1982] A.C. at 188.

is not unlawful when done by one person alone. Numbers may, of course, bring increased power and in the *Crofter* case Viscount Maugham said that he had never felt any difficulty in seeing, "the great difference between the acts of one person and the acts in combination of two or of a multitude",[238] but, as Viscount Simon L.C. remarked in the same case:

"The view that the explanation is to be found in the increasing power of numbers to do damage beyond what one individual can do is open to the obvious answer that this depends on the personality and influence of the individual. In the play, Cyrano de Bergerac's single voice was more effective to drive the bad actor Montfleury off the stage than the protests of all the rest of the audience to restrain him. The action of a single tyrant may be more potent to inflict suffering on the continent of Europe than a combination of less powerful persons."[239]

The argument from numbers continues to have some appeal in the criminal law but there are now few situations in which there may be an indictment for conspiracy in respect of acts which would not be criminal if done by one person.[240] One day the law may (perhaps under the influence of the idea of abuse of rights) re-examine the place in our law of combination and of the "chasm" between lawful and unlawful acts which exists in the case of an individual, but at the moment there is no sign of a move towards a principle that the intentional infliction of harm without justification is actionable.[241]

4. TRADE DISPUTES

A general textbook on the law of tort is not the place for an extended **18–33** discussion of the specialised law relating to trade disputes. Nevertheless these disputes have provided much of the "raw material" for the development of the law of economic torts and some of the leading cases can only be fully understood against the background of the legislative intervention since 1906, so some account is necessary. Unfortunately it cannot be as brief as one might like.

---

[238] [1942] A.C. 435 at 448.
[239] [1942] A.C. 435 at 443. See also Lord Diplock's rather less colourful example of the street-corner grocers and a chain of supermarkets in single ownership in the *Lonrho* case: [1982] A.C. 173 at 189.
[240] Conspiracy to commit a substantive offence has great practical significance in the criminal law because it allows the police to "nip crime in the bud".
[241] Cf. *Bradford Corp v Pickles* [1895] A.C. 151 with *Tuttle v Buck* (1909) 119 N.W. 946. See art.826 of the German Civil Code, discussed in Weir, *Economic Torts*, Ch.3: "A person is liable in damages if he deliberately causes harm to another in a manner repugnant to good morals".

A. History

18–34   The Trade Disputes Act 1906, passed as a result of the *Taff Vale* case,[242] made trade unions immune from actions in tort and conferred protection on individuals, such as union officials, against liability for conspiracy to injure and inducing breach of contract where the acts were done in contemplation or furtherance of a trade dispute. The Trade Disputes Act 1965 extended this immunity to the tort of intimidation after *Rookes v Barnard.* After a brief and unsuccessful experiment by the Conservative Government of 1970–1974 with a new, statutory regime of civil remedies in trade disputes the Trade Union and Labour Relations Act 1974 restored the former position. After 1979 another Conservative Government passed a series of Acts which imposed liability on unions as well as individuals,[243] required ballots as a preliminary to industrial action and withdrew the immunity of unions and individuals in respect of action taken for certain purposes or directed at "secondary targets". The law is now consolidated in Pts II and V of the Trade Union and Labour Relations (Consolidation) Act 1992 (hereafter "the 1992 Act") as amended.

B. The Present Law[244]

18–35   **i. Trade unions.** A trade union is not a body corporate[245] but the 1992 Act gives it certain attributes of a body corporate. It can make contracts and sue and be sued in its own name and, indeed, be prosecuted. Though the Act does not say so in so many words, it seems that where the claim does not concern a trade dispute the union's liability in tort is exactly the same as that of a natural person or corporate body[246] and its liability for the acts of individuals is to be determined by the general law of master and servant and agency. Where, however, the claim relates to one of the economic torts likely to be involved in a trade dispute[247] a different test of vicarious liability applies. The act of an individual or group is taken to have been done by the union if it is authorised or endorsed by it and it is taken to have done so if the act was done or was authorised or

---

[242] *Taff Vale Ry Co v Amalgamated Society of Ry Servants* [1901] A.C. 426.
[243] In fact the Trade Union and Labour Relations Act 1974 imposed liability on unions (where there was no trade dispute) for certain torts causing personal injury or breaches of duty connected with the union's property.
[244] See Clerk and Lindsell, *Torts,* 19th edn, Ch.26, Pt 6.
[245] Trade Union and Labour Relations (Consolidation) Act 1992 s.10(1). A consequence of this is that a trade union does not have sufficient personality to maintain an action for defamation: *E.E.T.P.U. v Times Newspapers Ltd* [1980] Q.B. 585.
[246] There are restrictions on enforcement of judgments against certain property, no matter what the source of the claim: s.23.
[247] For the full statutory formula see s.20(1).

endorsed by any person empowered by the union rules so to act, by the executive or president or general secretary, or by any committee of the union or any official (whether employed by the union or not).[248] Furthermore, action by an official is deemed to be the action of the union for this purpose notwithstanding anything in the rules of the union.[249] These provisions represent a very considerable extension of union responsibility when compared with the legislation which first imposed liability on the union itself.[250] The only escape route for the union is to repudiate the actions under s.21 but this is not necessarily easy to do for not only must notice of the repudiation be given to the persons calling the action but the union must "do its best" to give written notice in prescribed form to every member of the union who the union has reason to believe is taking part, or might otherwise take part, in industrial action. Furthermore, any subsequent conduct by the executive, president or general secretary which is inconsistent with the repudiation renders it ineffective.[251] The stringent requirements of effective repudiation may be expensive for a union but may also face it with "political" difficulties in making the unequivocal statement required.[252]

If the individual act is the union's responsibility under these provisions the union has the same protection against liability for acts done, "in contemplation or furtherance of a trade dispute"[253] as the individuals concerned, though this protection is withdrawn in a number of situations, including that where the action is not supported by a ballot,[254] a point of considerable importance given the

---

[248] Section 20(2). An act is taken to have been done, authorised or endorsed by an official if it was done, etc., "by, or by any member of, any group of persons of which he was at the material time a member, the purposes of which included organising or co-ordinating industrial action": s.20(3)(b). Read literally this would mean that the union was responsible where a works committee of which a shop steward was a member had been established to co-ordinate a "work to rule" but the committee had decided, against the vote of the shop steward, to call a strike.

[249] Section 20(4).

[250] The present law derives from the Employment Act 1990. Under the Employment Act 1982 the union was responsible only for the acts of employed officials and shop stewards were hardly ever union employees. Furthermore, action was not taken to have been authorised or endorsed if it was forbidden by union rules. See Unofficial Action and the Law (Cm. 821). The rules in the 1992 Act apply to a union's responsibility for contempt by disobedience to an injunction as well as to the initial liability in tort.

[251] Section 20(5). See *Express and Star Newspapers v NGA* (1982) [1985] I.R.L.R. 455 ("nods, winks, turning of blind eyes and similar clandestine methods of approval").

[252] In particular, if the union repudiates the action it is "unofficial" and by s.237 the employer may dismiss any persons taking part in it. Of course, the basic rule of the common law is that a strike is a fundamental breach of contract justifying dismissal but under the 1992 Act as enacted where the action was official the employer could not dismiss "selectively". Now even non-selective dismissal is restricted where the action was supported by the requisite ballot: s.238A, inserted by the Employment Relations Act 1999. For a full account see Clerk and Lindsell, *Torts*, 19th edn, para.25–159.

[253] See para.18–36, below.

[254] See para.18–41, below.

width of the union's responsibility for action at local level which is not effectively repudiated in accordance with the Act.

In practice the remedy sought in trade dispute cases has tended to be an injunction because it is far better from the employer's point of view to stop the strike than to seek compensation after the event. In addition, the fact that for many years liability was imposed only on individuals, probably of modest means,[255] made damages claims unattractive. Now that liability is directly imposed on the union, damages may become more attractive but the union's liability is limited on a scale geared to the size of the union and the maximum award of £250,000 is low in relation to the damage that may be suffered.[256] The very large fines (on which there is no limit) imposed for contempt by disobedience to an injunction are probably a more powerful sanction.[257] Where a union's liability arises in respect of personal injury caused by negligence, nuisance or breach of duty, or in respect of the ownership or occupation of property or under Pt I of the Consumer Protection Act 1987[258] there is no limit on damages.[259] There is no limit on the award of damages against an individual in any case.

18–36   **ii. Protection from liability in trade disputes.** If the matter were left to the common law it would be virtually impossible to call a strike because the persons doing so would commit one or more of the torts of inducing breach of contract, intentional infliction of harm by unlawful means and conspiracy. Since 1906, therefore, Parliament has granted a degree of protection (commonly called "immunity") to those engaged in trade disputes. The present law is contained in s.219(1) and (2) of the 1992 Act, which reads as follows:

"(1) An act done by a person in contemplation or furtherance of a trade dispute is not actionable in tort on the ground only—

(a) that it induces another person to break a contract or interferes or induces another person to interfere with its performance, or

---

[255] There was, of course, nothing to prevent the union indemnifying its officials. Under s.15 of the 1992 Act it is unlawful for a union to indemnify an individual against penalties for a crime or a contempt, but this has no application to civil damages. No doubt unions generally conducted and paid the costs of actions brought against individuals.

[256] This is a great deal less in real terms than the £23,000 awarded in the *Taff Vale* case.

[257] When liability was imposed only on individuals the only effective sanction for breach of an injunction was often imprisonment, which, as the events of 1971 showed, was likely to create martyrs.

[258] The last seems an unlikely contingency.

[259] The restrictions on execution against certain types of property apply to all awards of damages.

(b) that it consists in his threatening that a contract (whether one to which he is a party or not) will be broken or its performance interfered with, or that he will induce another person to break a contract or interfere with its performance.

(2) An agreement or combination by two or more persons to do or procure the doing of an act in contemplation or furtherance of a trade dispute is not actionable in tort if the act is one which if done without any such agreement or combination would not be actionable in tort."

It will be observed that the law speaks in terms of rendering certain acts not actionable in tort rather than conferring a "right to strike".[260] Far from there being a right to strike it remains the general rule of contractual employment law that the withdrawal of labour will be a breach of contract, though there are now restrictions on the right to dismiss for it.[261]

(a) *Trade disputes.* In order to gain the protection of s.219, the act done by the defendant must be, "in contemplation or furtherance of a trade dispute". This concept, the so-called "golden formula", is defined in great detail in s.244 but essentially it means a dispute[262] between workers[263] and their employer[264] and which relates wholly or mainly[265] to matters about the employment[266] of workers, such as terms and conditions of employment, engagement and dismissal, allocation of work, discipline, union membership or machinery for negotiation.[267] The central difficulty is to determine when the dispute "relates" to the relevant matters. To be protected the dispute **18–37**

---

[260] See *Metrobus Ltd v UNITE* [2009] EWCA Civ 829; [2009] I.R.L.R. 851 at [118].

[261] See para.18–35, above.

[262] But by s.219(4) pressure which is so effective that the employer succumbs immediately to it is deemed to have been exerted in contemplation or furtherance of a dispute.

[263] Including former workers whose employment was terminated in connection with the dispute or whose dismissal was one of the circumstances giving rise to the dispute: s.244(5).

[264] An inter-union dispute is not, as such, within the protection but such a dispute is likely to involve an employer.

[265] Before 1982 the dispute had merely to be "connected with" the relevant matters and older cases should be read with this in mind. Since the Government has extensive statutory powers to alter and approve conditions of employment in various areas, it is provided in s.244(2) that a dispute between workers and a Minister of the Crown is to be treated for the purposes of protection as a dispute between the workers and their employer. For an example see *Wandsworth London Borough v NASMUWT*, [1994] I.C.R. 81.

[266] "Employment" in this context has a wider meaning than the technical one of master and servant because it includes, "any relationship whereby one person personally does work or performs services for another": s.219(5). Note also s.245, which deems Crown servants to have a contract of employment even though under the general law their relationship with the Crown may not be contractual at all.

[267] For more detail see the Act.

must relate to current contracts of employment and not to potential contracts of employment with another person to whom the employer may at some time transfer the enterprise.[268] Subject to that:

> "[A] dispute about what workers are obliged to do or how the employer is obliged to remunerate them, at any level of generality or particularity, is about terms and conditions of employment."[269]

A dispute arising out of the validity of an order given by an employer can be a trade dispute; and it cannot be the law that protection is confined to disputes about the interpretation of existing terms, for strikes about pay scales or the frequency of rest breaks, for example, involve attempts to change the terms of the existing contracts. Particular difficulty arises when it is contended that the strike is politically motivated. In *BBC v Hearn*[270] the defendants, in order to protest against apartheid, threatened to instruct the members of their union to commit breaches of contract in relation to a broadcast by satellite to South Africa of the 1977 Cup Final. In proceedings for an interlocutory injunction the Court of Appeal held that it was unlikely that it could be established at the trial that there was a trade dispute but it was suggested that the position might well have been different if, instead of simply threatening to "black" the broadcast, the defendants had gone to the BBC and said:

> "We wish it to be established as part of our conditions of employment that we are not required to work on broadcasts to South Africa."[271]

However, it has since been remarked in the House of Lords that a:

> "[T]rade union cannot turn a dispute which in reality has no connection with terms and conditions of employment into a dispute connected with terms and conditions of employment by insisting that the employer inserts appropriate terms into the contracts of employment into which he enters."[272]

---

[268] *UCL Hospitals NHS Trust v UNISON* [1999] I.C.R. 204. Some degree of protection for transferred workers is provided by the Transfer of Undertakings (Protection of Employment) Regulations 2006 (SI 2006/246), replacing earlier legislation.

[269] *P v NASMUWT* [2003] UKHL 8; [2003] 2 A.C. 663 at [28].

[270] [1977] 1 W.L.R. 1004.

[271] This was approved by Lord Diplock in *N.W.L. Ltd v Woods* [1979] 1 W.L.R. 1294.

[272] Lord Cross in *Universe Tankships Inc of Monrovia v I.T.W.F.* [1983] 1 A.C. 366 at 392. However, that was an economic duress case in which there was no dispute between employer and workers and the union was an "interloper" waging a campaign against "flags of convenience".

These propositions are not logically inconsistent because the first does not assert that protection is to be given to what is in reality a political campaign merely dressed up as relating to employment and the second does not deny that a group of workers might demand that their contracts should contain provisions about matters on which they had strong beliefs. However, the dispute must be about what workers are employed to *do* and it has been suggested that even if the demand in *Hearn* had been couched in the above terms it would have made no difference because they would have been required to perform the same services whether or not the broadcast had been beamed to South Africa.[273] *Wandsworth London Borough v NAS-MUWT*[274] concerned a boycott by a teaching union of testing under the national curriculum. The court held that on the evidence there was clearly a trade dispute because the union's predominant concern was with the workload imposed by the tests, even though there was also objection to the methods of testing on educational grounds. However, by implication the result would have been different had the union said:

"Our members believe that the methods proposed are bad methods and we believe we would be in breach of our professional duty to safeguard the welfare of children if we operated them."[275]

An act is "in furtherance" of a trade dispute when the doer genuinely believes that it will assist the cause in support of which it is done: the House of Lords has emphatically rejected the addition of any requirement that the act be "not too remote" or "reasonably likely to succeed".[276]

(b) *Inducing breach of contract and causing loss by unlawful means.* The legislation was of course passed before the decisions in the *OBG* and *Revenue and Customs Commissioners* cases. If it were passed now it would undoubtedly be very differently drafted but we have to do the best we can to fit the present structure of the law into it. Calling a strike would be the *Lumley v Gye* tort at common law because it would involve inducing the workers to break their contracts of employment but it is clearly protected by the opening words   **18–38**

---

[273] *P v NASMUWT* at [31].

[274] [1994] I.C.R. 81.

[275] In *Mercury Communications Ltd v Scott-Garner* [1984] Ch. 37, even though there was a potential threat to jobs of union members with BT because of the Government's policy of allowing Mercury to compete with BT, the court concluded that the action was mainly in support of an ideological campaign against the break up of nationalised industries. Cf. *Westminster CC v Unison* [2001] EWCA Civ 443; [2001] ICR 1046.

[276] *Express Newspapers Ltd v McShane* [1980] A.C. 672; *Duport Steels Ltd v Sirs* [1980] 1 W.L.R. 142.

of s.219(1)(a). It is now clear that there is no tort of "interference" with the performance of a contract[277] and any claim other than in respect of the direct procurement of breaches of the employment contracts is likely to be couched in terms of causing loss by unlawful means. Since the existence of this tort (even if not in precisely its present form) was recognized well before 1992 it is unfortunate that it was not dealt with directly in the statute but in *Hadmor Productions Ltd v Hamilton*[278] the House of Lords held that an act which was "not actionable" under an earlier equivalent of s.219(1) did not amount to unlawful means for the purposes of the tort of intimidation (hence the references to "threatening" in s.219(1)) and we now know that that tort may be only a variant of the general tort of causing loss by unlawful means. It seems therefore that there is immunity whether the strike caller is sued on the basis of, (a) an actual procurement of breaches of the contracts of employment, (b) threatening such breaches, or (c) causing loss by bringing about the non-performance of the employer's contract with a third party. So also the immunity extends to a claim based on causing loss by unlawful means brought by the third party against the strike-caller,[279] though in the normal case it would now seem that the tort would not be committed at common law anyway since there would not be the requisite intention to harm the third party, even if that harm was an obviously likely consequence.[280]

18–39   The protection is conferred where the claim is on the ground *only* of the inducement or threat of breach: if therefore the defendant procures a strike by telling lies he is liable for deceit (and/or defamation).[281] Though the matter is not beyond doubt, it is probably the case that the defendant retains his immunity for the economic tort in question. That may be significant on the issue of damages (though damages are rarely sought in trade dispute cases) where the "other" tort is merely incidental (e.g. a trespass to land committed by a union official while persuading workers to strike) but where the other tort is the essential means of inflicting the harm this may make little difference.

18–40   (c) *Conspiracy.* Section 219(2) removes "conspiracy to injure" from the field of trade disputes because it involves a combination to do an act which would not be actionable in tort if done without any

---

[277] See para.18–3, above.
[278] [1983] 1 A.C. 191.
[279] [1983] 1 A.C. 191.
[280] See para.18–13, above.
[281] Nor was there any trade disputes issue in *Iqbal v Prison Officers Association* [2009] EWCA Civ 1310, though the claim for false imprisonment caused by the action failed on the facts: para.4–22, above.

agreement or combination.[282] The scope of "unlawful means" conspiracy may also be restricted by this provision because of the
requirement that the act should be one which would be actionable *in
tort* if done by an individual. Thus an agreement to break a contract
may not be actionable.[283] An agreement to induce a breach of
contract might be thought to fall outside this provision because
inducement is a tort if committed by one person, but this is not so
if the inducement is protected by s.219(1) because the means are not
then to be regarded as unlawful.[284] Despite the *Revenue and Customs Commissioners* case it also removes tort liability for conspiracy to commit a crime from this field.

iii. Unprotected acts. The protection of s.219 is withdrawn from   **18–41**
industrial action in the following cases.

1. Action taken to enforce union membership.[285] The attempts to
   enforce the "closed shop" which were the source of many
   earlier trade dispute cases would now be exposed to legal
   liability.[286]
2. Action designed to impose union recognition requirements.
   Sections 186 and 187 of the Act prevent commercial discrimination against a person (for example refusing to award him
   contracts or excluding him from tendering) on the ground that
   the work should be done by union labour. This is backed up by
   s.225(1), which withdraws trade dispute protection from action
   taken against an employer to induce him to contravene ss.186
   and 187. In addition, by s.225(2), protection is withdrawn from
   action interfering with employment contracts which disrupts
   the supply of goods and services to the employer from a
   supplier and the reason for the action is the supplier's failure
   to accord recognition to a union.
3. By s.223 there is no protection for action taken because an
   employer has dismissed a worker for taking part in unofficial
   industrial action.

---

[282] The protection is really unnecessary: if the defendants are acting in contemplation or
furtherance of a trade dispute they have a "legitimate purpose" at common law and they
do not "intend to injure" the claimant: *Hadmor Productions Ltd v Hamilton* [1983] 1 A.C.
191 at 228.
[283] The point is of hardly any practical importance since collective agreements between
employers and unions are rarely contracts.
[284] See para.18–38, above.
[285] See s.222.
[286] So there would again be liability on the facts of *Rookes v Barnard* [1964] A.C. 1129, even
though the Trade Disputes Act 1965 brought intimidation within the protection of the trade
disputes immunity.

4. Protection is withdrawn from "secondary action" (other than lawful picketing). Special provision was first made for secondary action by the exceedingly complex s.17 of the Employment Act 1980. This is replaced by s.224 of the 1992 Act,[287] which is a great deal simpler but also more restrictive of union activities. Secondary action is defined in s.224(2) as occurring when:

> "[A] person—
>
> (a) induces another to break a contract of employment or interferes or induces another to interfere with its performance, or
> (b) threatens that a contract of employment under which he or another is employed will be broken or its performance interfered with, or that he will induce another to break a contract of employment or to interfere with its performance,
>
> and the employer under the contract of employment is not the employer party to the dispute."

So protection is withdrawn when, say, there is a dispute with employer A and the union, to put pressure on A, calls out its members at employer B, a supplier of A.[288] A business may be an economic unit but have a corporate structure consisting of a number of companies under a holding company. In that event under the previous legislation the House of Lords held that one could not pierce the corporate veil and the companies were separate "employers" for this purpose.[289] The law seems to be the same under the 1992 Act which, indeed, provides that even if there are disputes with each of the companies within the group each one has to be treated as separate for this purpose.[290] The action must involve interference with contracts of employment[291]: if the action against A has the effect of disrupting the

---

[287] Re-enacting the Employment Act 1990 s.4.

[288] It would seem that the protection is withdrawn whether the claimant is A or B. This was the case under the 1980 Act: *Merkur Island Shipping Corp v Laughton* [1983] 2 A.C. 570 at 609.

[289] *Dimbleby & Sons Ltd v NUJ* [1984] 1 W.L.R. 427.

[290] Section 224(4). The somewhat mysterious s.224(5) provides that: "primary action in relation to [one trade] dispute may not be relied on as secondary action in relation to another trade dispute." This seems to contemplate two trade disputes at employer A and employer B where, say, inducing breaches of contracts at A has the effect of interfering with the employment contracts at B, in which case B cannot complain of unlawful secondary action. This is the only purpose for which primary action is defined and it means action such as is described in s.224(2) directed against A. This seems to ignore the fact that the action against A might be something other than interference with A's contracts of employment.

[291] Given a somewhat extended meaning: see fn.266, above.

commercial contract between A and B then even though B is in a sense a "secondary victim" of the action there is no secondary action for the purposes of the Act and the union is protected against action by B as well as by A.[292]

5. Protection is withdrawn from action which does not have the support of a majority in a ballot.[293] The voting paper must contain a question requiring the union member to state whether he is willing to take part in a strike or action short of a strike and contain a warning that what is proposed may be a breach of his contract of employment. Although there is provision for ignoring inconsequential errors, the requirements on balloting must be strictly complied with.[294] A ballot ceases to be effective after four weeks but there are two qualifications to this. First, so long as the action has begun within the four-week period it may continue thereafter without further ballot[295]; secondly, where there has been an injunction restraining the action but subsequently that is discharged or set aside by the court, then the court may extend the period up to a maximum of 12 weeks from the date of the ballot.[296] The "action" referred to by s.226 is collective action, not the particular action by the person induced. Where, therefore, additional persons join the union after the ballot the immunity is not lost in respect of inducements of breaches of contract by them.[297]

iv. Picketing. Picketing in various forms has shown itself to be one of the most effective forms of industrial action. At common law it may be unlawful as amounting to a trespass to the highway, or a public or private nuisance,[298] or as involving the inducement or   **18–42**

---

[292] The core immunity provisions of s.219 are not confined to interference with contracts of employment. It might be of course that now there would be no tort against B at common law: para.18–13, above.

[293] Section 226. Further amendments to the balloting procedure were are made by the Trade Union Reform and Employment Rights Act 1993, the Employment Relations Act 1999 and the Employment Relations Act 2004, inserting or substituting provisions in the 1992 Act. See s.226, 226A–C, 228, 228A, 231, 231A–B, 232A–B, 234, 234A–E.

[294] *NURMTW v Midland Mainline Ltd* [2001] EWCA Civ 1206; [2001] I.R.L.R. 813. Cf. *English, Welsh and Scottish Ry v NURMTW* [2004] EWCA Civ 1539.

[295] A further ballot is not necessary to reimpose industrial action which has been suspended during negotiations: *Monsanto Plc v TGWU* [1987] 1 W.L.R. 617; but if, as a matter of substance, the first action has ended and the union embarks on a new campaign then a fresh ballot is needed: *Post Office v Union of Communication Workers* [1990] 1 W.L.R. 981.

[296] Section 234.

[297] *London Underground Ltd v NURMTW* [1996] I.C.R. 170. Millett L.J. said that there, "has never been any identity between the constituency of those to be balloted and the constituency of those whom in contemplation or furtherance of a trade dispute the union may with impunity induce to break their contracts ... A union may in contemplation or furtherance of a trade dispute with impunity induce non-members to break their contracts."

[298] See para.14–39, above.

procuring of a breach of contract. However, under s.220 of the 1992 Act it is lawful for a person in contemplation or furtherance of a trade dispute to attend at or near his own place of work,[299] "for the purpose of peacefully obtaining or communicating information, or peacefully persuading any person to work or abstain from working". Immunity for acts done in the course of picketing (for example inducing breaches of contract) exists only if the picket is lawful under s.220.[300] Despite the general withdrawal of protection from secondary action interfering with a contract of employment, such action (for example persuading a supplier's lorry driver not to deliver[301]) is protected when done in the course of lawful picketing,[302] but what used to be known as "secondary picketing", i.e. attendance at the premises of the employer's supplier or customer is not of course protected, given the fundamental requirements of s.220.

18–43　　**v. Injunctions and restraining action by individuals.** Where an employer is the victim of industrial action, his primary purpose in embarking on litigation is usually to obtain an injunction. Since an injunction may be granted on an interim basis pending trial (which may not take place for many months) and, in cases of great urgency, without notice to the other party,[303] it is clear that there is a serious possibility of the union side being robbed of the initiative in an industrial dispute. Section 221 of the 1992 Act contains two provisions which go some way to meeting this point. First, where an application for an injunction is made without notice and the defendant claims, or in the opinion of the court would be likely to claim, that he acted in contemplation or furtherance of a trade dispute, the court shall not grant the injunction unless satisfied that all reasonable steps have been taken to secure that notice of the application and an opportunity of being heard have been given to him. This reduces the risk of the defendants in a "labour injunction" case being taken unawares but it contains nothing about how the court should proceed once the parties are before it. Under the general law, according to *American Cyanamid Ltd v Ethicon Ltd*,[304] the claimant, in order to obtain an interim injunction, must show that there is a

---

[299] Or, where he is a union official, at or near the place of work of a member of the union whom he is accompanying and whom he represents. Where a person's employment was terminated because of a trade dispute or the termination is a cause of the trade dispute then he may attend his former place of work. Cf. *J.&R. Kenny Cleaning Services v TGWU, The Times*, June 15, 1989 (business transferred by former employer, no trade dispute).

[300] Section 219(3).

[301] In modern times this function of picketing has probably been more important than preventing "blackleg" labour.

[302] Section 224(1), (3).

[303] Formerly ex parte.

[304] [1975] A.C. 396. See further para.22–50, below.

"serious question to be tried", something which is fairly easily established given the uncertainty of many issues about economic torts. What is now s.221(2) was enacted in 1976 in response to the *Cyanamid* case and provides that where an application is made for an interim injunction and the party against whom it is sought claims that he acted in contemplation or furtherance of a trade dispute, the court shall, in exercising its discretion whether or not to grant the injunction, have regard to the likelihood of that party's succeeding at the trial of the action in establishing a defence under ss.219 or 220. It is clear that it was intended to be more difficult to obtain an interim injunction in trade dispute cases than in others, but beyond this it is not easy to say what effect the provision has. Under the *American Cyanamid* decision the court must ask itself whether the claimant has shown, (1) a serious question to be tried and, (2) a "balance of convenience" in his favour. It is unclear whether s.221(2) adds a third element or is subsumed in (2) or what practical difference it makes which view is taken.[305] It has been suggested that now that unions (and not merely officials) may in certain circumstances be liable in damages for unlawful industrial action it is more likely that the employer will pursue a claim to a full trial and there is less reason to refuse an interim injunction in trade dispute cases[306] but it has also been said that the "right to strike" is a valuable (indeed essential) element in the system of collective bargaining and that it:

"[S]hould not be rendered less valuable than parliament intended by too fanciful or ingenious a view of what might develop into a serious issue to be tried".[307]

Some strikes are likely to cause widespread inconvenience to the public or even economic damage to the nation as a whole and there are some judicial statements to the effect that the public interest in these cases may be a factor to be taken into account in the exercise of the judicial discretion, independently of the justice of the case between the parties.[308]

The Trade Union Reform and Employment Rights Act 1993 introduced a novel and highly unusual restraint on industrial action

---

[305] For a detailed account see Clerk and Lindsell, *Torts*, 19th edn, para.25–188. See also Wedderburn, "The Injunction and the Sovereignty of Parliament" in *Employment Rights in Britain and Europe* (1991).

[306] *Dimbleby & Sons Ltd v NUJ* [1984] 1 W.L.R. 427 at 431–432.

[307] *Barretts & Baird (Wholesale) Ltd v I.P.C.S.* [1987] I.R.L.R. 3 at 11 per Henry J. However, on the facts, (1) the judge thought there was little likelihood of the action going to trial and, (2) the claimants failed to establish a serious question to be tried.

[308] *Duport Steels Ltd v Sirs* [1980] 1 W.L.R. 142; *Associated British Ports v TGWU* [1989] 3 All E.R. 796 (reversed on appeal on other grounds [1989] 3 All E.R. 822).

which falls outside the trade dispute protection. An individual[309] who claims that a trade union[310] or other person has done or is likely to do an unlawful act[311] to induce any person to take part in industrial action and that the effect or likely effect of the action is to prevent or delay the supply of goods or services to the individual (or reduce their quality) may apply to the High Court for an order requiring him to desist from the inducement and to take steps to terminate the effect of any prior inducement.[312] There is no claim for damages. The effect of this is that a member of the public likely to be affected by industrial action may intervene even though he might be unable to show the requisite interest to found a claim at common law and even though he has no contractual claim to the delivery of the goods or services affected by the dispute.[313] If the claimant makes out the matters required by the section the court may make such order as it considers appropriate to require the defendant to desist, etc. but it appears that the court has no discretion simply to refuse relief.[314]

5. PASSING OFF[315]

18–44   The tort of passing off is part of a much wider canvas of legal remedies controlling unfair competitive practices and we have already said that "unfair competition" would be beyond the scope of this book, so that such matters as copyrights, trade marks and patents must be sought elsewhere. However, a brief account of passing off may be justified since it is, (1) a tort, (2) is based entirely on the common law, and (3) may in some respects be capable of development.[316] The importance of the law of passing off was reduced by the Trade Marks Act 1994, particularly in so far as the Act allowed a trade mark to be registered in respect of a container

---

[309] The term is not defined, but clearly excludes a corporation. There are said to have been instances of apparently private suits financed by pressure groups or parties to the dispute.

[310] The responsibility of the union under these provisions is in accord with s.20, see para.18–35, above.

[311] i.e. one which is actionable in tort.

[312] See s.235A of the 1992 Act as inserted by s.22 of the 1993 Act.

[313] See s.235A(3).

[314] This seems to be the effect of s.235A(4).

[315] See Carty, *An Analysis of the Economic Torts* (2000), Ch.8; Wadlow, *Passing Off*, 3rd edn.

[316] The other matters mentioned above depend almost entirely on statute. Other common law torts which may be relevant in this area include deceit and malicious falsehood. In *United Biscuits (UK) Ltd v Asda Stores Ltd* [1997] R.P.C. 513 there was jocular press comment about seven days in the High Court being devoted to a contest between the "Penguin" and "Puffin" biscuit brands, but as the judge pointed out, the claimants' annual sales of the Penguin brand exceeded £30 million a year and their advertising expenditure was in excess of £4 million a year.

or the "get-up" of the goods. Nevertheless, even where there appears to be a strong case of trade mark infringement it remains common to run a parallel claim for passing off and it will be the only remedy where the law of trade marks is inapplicable or the registration is invalid[317] or, of course, where there has been no attempt at registration.[318]

The action arose in the 19th century and depended upon the simple principle that a person is not to sell his goods or his services under the pretence that they are those of another.[319] It has five elements: (a) a misrepresentation; (b) made by a trader in the course of trade; (c) to prospective customers of his or ultimate consumers of goods or services supplied by him; (d) which is calculated to injure the business or goodwill of another trader (in the sense that this is a reasonably foreseeable consequence); and (e) which causes or threatens actual damage to a business or goodwill of the trader by whom the action is brought.[320]

A. Varieties of Passing Off

The representation must be such as to cause confusion in the **18–45** public mind between the claimant's goods or business and the defendant's goods or business: false statements disparaging the claimant's goods are actionable as malicious falsehood or libel and statements falsely exaggerating the worth of the defendant's wares

---

[317] In *United Biscuits*, above, fn.316, some of the marks relied on were revoked on the ground of non-use.

[318] A trade mark is not to be registered in so far as its use is liable to be prevented by the law of passing off: Trade Marks Act 1994, s.5(4)(a). Similarly, passing off claims may be brought in parallel to claims for infringement of copyright. The gist of passing off is deceptive resemblance; but in the case of copyright, although there typically is resemblance, the gist of the complaint is that the defendant's work is derived from the claimant's: *Designers Guild Ltd v Russell Williams (Textiles) Ltd* [2001] 1 W.L.R. 2416.

[319] *Perry v Truefitt* (1842) 6 Beav 66 at 73 per Lord Langdale M.R.; *Spalding & Bros v A.W. Gamage Ltd* (1915) 84 L.J. Ch. 449 at 450 per Lord Parker. If the defendant does so he is appropriating the effort of the claimant. In French law the equivalent liability is known as "concurrence déloyale et *parasitaire*" (emphasis added): *Kirkbi AG v Ritvik Holdings* [2005] SCC 65 at [55].

[320] *Erwen Warnink B.V. v J. Townend & Sons (Hull) Ltd* [1979] A.C. 731 at 742 per Lord Diplock. This formulation is quoted without criticism by Lord Jauncey in *Reckitt & Colman Products Ltd v Borden Inc* [1990] 1 W.L.R. 491 at 511. Lord Oliver at 499 states three elements: (1) a goodwill or reputation attached to and recognised by the public as distinctive of the claimant's goods or services; (2) a misrepresentation by the defendant leading the public to believe that his goods or services are those of the claimant; (3) damage or likely damage. Nourse L.J. in *Consorzio del Prosciutto di Parma v Marks & Spencer Plc* [1991] R.P.C. 351 at 368–369, expressed a preference for Lord Oliver's formulation. In any event, it is clear that although there are certain differences between the requirements stated by Lords Diplock and Fraser in the *Erwen Warnink* case, they are not to be treated as cumulative sets of requirements.

are not, as such, actionable by a competitor even though he has suffered damage thereby.[321] Nor is passing off committed by using the claimant's name or trade mark in such a way that the public are not deceived about the provenance of the defendant's goods.[322] It is essential that the defendant should have made a representation[323] calculated to deceive,[324] though in the modern law no form of fraud or even negligence is essential to establish liability.[325]

A common form of passing off involves copying or imitating the claimant's registered trade mark, in which case there has always been the possibility of claims both under the trade mark statute and at common law. A modern version of this activity against which passing off has been successfully invoked is registering Internet domain names as variations around the names of well-known companies and then offering the names to the companies at high prices with the express or implied threat of allowing them to be used for deception or as "blockers" to legitimate registration.[326] An example of passing off by imitating the get-up of the claimant's goods (now also covered by the law of trade marks) is *Reckitt & Colman Products Ltd v Borden Inc.*[327] The claimants had for a good many years sold lemon juice ("Jif") in the UK in a "squeezy container"

---

[321] See *BBC v Talksport Ltd* [2001] F.S.R. 6 (false claims that broadcasts were live; no interference with claimants' goodwill); *Schulke & Mayr UK Ltd v Alkapharm UK Ltd* [1999] F.S.R.161. Under the Control of Misleading Advertisement Regulations 1998 (SI 1988/915) as amended by the Control of Misleading Advertisements (Amendment) Regulations 2000 (SI 2000/914) there is a mechanism for administrative complaint to the Director of Fair Trading in respect of unfair comparative advertising.

[322] *Arsenal Football Club Plc v Reed* [2001] R.P.C. 46. There were further proceedings in this case before the European Court of Justice and an appeal to the CA, but these concerned trade marks. At the end of his judgment ([2003] EWCA Civ 696; [2003] R.P.C. 39 at [70]) Aldous L.J. said that he was not convinced that the reasoning below on passing off had been correct. However, the cases referred to did involve confusion as to provenance, though not in the sense that the goods were claimed to be the defendant's. See *Mars UK Ltd v Burgess Group Plc* [2004] EWHC 1912.

[323] Where there is no misrepresentation by the defendant it is not enough that, "people make assumptions, jump to unjustified conclusions, and put two and two together to make five": *HFC Bank Plc v Midland Bank Plc* [2000] F.S.R. 176. On the position of the producer of a new product in a market where there is a de facto monopoly see *British Sky Broadcasting Group Plc v Sky Home Services Ltd* [2006] EWHC 3165 (Ch); [2007] 3 All E.R. 1066.

[324] In *Perkins v Shone* [2004] EWHC 2249 (Ch) C owned the goodwill in the "Pentathlon" name for darts flights as successor to X and these had formerly been supplied exclusively to X by D. D ceased to supply Pentathlon flights to C and supplied them to Y and Z. C's claim for passing off failed. A customer getting Pentathlon flight darts from Y would be getting exactly what he ordered and would not be misled into thinking he was getting darts with flights originating with C or "quality-assured" by C. Had the Pentathlon mark been registered by C the result under the trade mark legislation would have been different because a trade mark is much closer to a monopoly right.

[325] The customer need not know or care about the identity of the manufacturer, provided the customer knows there is such a person and cares that the goods he buys are made by that person: *United Biscuits (UK) Ltd v Asda Stores Ltd* [1997] R.P.C. 513.

[326] *British Telecommunications Plc v One in a Million Ltd* [1999] 1 W.L.R. 903.

[327] [1990] 1 W.L.R. 491.

in the form of a small plastic lemon. They obtained an injunction against the defendants' attempt to sell lemon juice in a similar but not identical container. The difference in the labelling of the products was such as to prevent any risk of confusion in the mind of a careful shopper but the evidence showed that most shoppers did not read labels with any care and that plastic lemons containing lemon juice had become strongly associated in the public mind with the claimants' product.[328] It was no answer that the confusion would not have occurred if the shoppers had been, "more careful, more literate or more perspicacious. Customers have to be taken as they are found".[329] Certainly no person can, except under the patent legislation, claim a monopoly in selling a particular article and the law of passing off would not prevent other people selling plastic lemons; but the claimants' case was not that the defendants were selling plastic lemons but that they were selling lemon juice in a lemon shaped container which had become associated with the claimants.[330] Though the dispute in this case concerned a container rather than the substance of what was sold, it seems that the law of passing off may protect part of the design or structure of the article itself and this is so even if it serves a utilitarian purpose.[331] This is not to say that as a matter of principle or theory the claimant can use the law of passing off to gain a monopoly in the shape of an article[332] for it is always open to the defendant sufficiently to differentiate his product, by labelling, colouring or otherwise, to avoid the risk of confusion: it is simply that it was very difficult and perhaps impossible[333] to do this on the facts of *Reckitt & Colman*, where the goods

---

[328] In this as in other cases differences between package designs which are obvious when they are laid side by side are not apparent when only one line of the article of the type in question is on sale.

[329] [1990] 1 W.L.R. at 508. See also *R. Johnston & Co v Archibald Orr Ewing & Co* (1882) 7 App. Cas. 219 and *White Hudson & Co Ltd v Asian Organisation Ltd* [1964] 1 W.L.R. 1466 ("red paper cough sweets") in both of which the parties were trading in the Far East where customers might have a limited command of English and hence the effect of different labels or names might be limited. In the case of magazines, the modern practice of selling from a rack has made general appearance more important than names: *Advance Magazine Publishing v Redmond Publishing* [1997] F.S.R. 449. Actual confusion on the part of a member of the purchasing public need not be proved as a matter of law (*Lee Kar Choo v Lee Lian Choon* [1967] 1 A.C. 602) but proof that it has occurred will obviously assist the claimant's case, especially if substantial damages are claimed and not merely an injunction.

[330] There was nothing to prevent the defendants selling lemon juice in bottles (as, indeed they were doing) or in plastic carrots, but as a matter of marketing reality if not bottles it was lemons or nothing.

[331] *William Edge & Sons Ltd v William Niccolls & Sons Ltd* [1911] A.C. 693 (dye in cloth bags fitted with a stick which could be used for stirring); and see Lord Jauncey's example in *Reckitt & Colman* at 519.

[332] This is allowed on a limited and temporary basis by the Registered Designs Act 1949 and the Copyright Designs and Patents Act 1988 s.213.

[333] See Lord Bridge's remarks in his reluctant concurrence.

were unlikely to be subjected to close inspection by purchasers,[334] without abandoning the key element of the plastic lemon.

18–46   Had the claimants in *Reckitt & Colman* been for many years the sole producers of lemon juice in the country, selling it in bottles labelled "Lemon Juice" it is clear that they could not have restrained a competitor from entering the market and doing the same thing for no one is entitled to fence off and monopolise descriptive words of the English language.[335] However, long usage may have had the effect that the descriptive words have become distinctively attached to the claimant's goods[336] as opposed to merely saying what they are.[337] The leading case is *Reddaway v Banham*[338] where it was held that "camel hair belting", which originally signified nothing more than belting made of camel hair, had come to signify belting made by the claimants.[339]

As a general rule a person can freely use his own name, or one which he has acquired by reputation, although the use of it inflicts damage on someone else who has the same name.[340] This, however, is qualified to some extent by the law of passing off. In *Parker-Knoll Ltd v Parker-Knoll International Ltd*,[341] both parties were manufacturers of furniture, the claimants being a company well known in

---

[334] Cf. *Hodgkinson & Corby Ltd v Wards Mobility Services Ltd* [1994] 1 W.L.R. 1564 (only likely purchasers professionals, who would be unlikely to be deceived). In *Bostick Ltd v Sellotape GB Ltd* [1994] R.P.C. 556 the similarity was concealed by packaging. The only possible deception was therefore in relation to repeat orders (not shown on the facts).

[335] *Marcus Publishing Plc v Hutton-Wild Communications Plc* [1990] R.P.C. 576 at 579. Note that the risk of confusion in the public's mind might be just as great where the claimant was an established de facto monopolist.

[336] Equally, though once so attached, they may become so public and in such universal use as to be again open to others to use: *Lazenby v White* (1871) 41 L.J. Ch. 354; *Ford v Foster* (1872) L.R. 7 Ch. 611 at 628 per Mellish L.J.; *Gramophone Co's Application* [1910] 2 Ch. 423.

[337] Thus "vacuum cleaner" was held to mean simply a cleaner working by suction and not necessarily one manufactured by the British Vacuum Cleaner Co: *British Vacuum Cleaner Co Ltd v New Vacuum Cleaner Co Ltd* [1907] 2 Ch. 312.

[338] [1896] A.C. 199.

[339] In 1931 it was held, upon the facts, that a Belgian manufacturer did not sufficiently distinguish his goods from the claimants' by describing them as "Lechat's camel hair belting": *Reddaway & Co Ltd v Hartley* (1930) 48 R.P.C. 283. The question of whether goodwill has been established in a trade name is not the same as whether it is sufficiently distinctive to be registered as a trade mark: *Phones4U Ltd v Phone4u.co.uk Internet Ltd* [2006] EWCA Civ 244; [2007] R.P.C. 5.

[340] *Brinsmead v Brinsmead* (1913) 30 R.P.C. 493; *Jay's Ltd v Jacobi* [1933] Ch. 411; but as to nicknames see *Biba Group v Biba Boutique* [1980] R.P.C. 413; *NAD Electronics Inc v NAD Computer Systems Ltd* [1999] F.S.R. 380. "A new company with a title of which the name 'A,' for instance, forms part has none of the natural rights that an individual born with the name 'A' would have": *Fine Cotton Spinners v Cash* (1907) 24 R.P.C. 533 at 538; *Asprey & Garrard Ltd v WRA (Guns) Ltd* [2001] EWCA Civ 1499 at [43]. In *Dent v Turpin* (1861) 2 J&H 139 Dent had two clock shops, one in the City, the other in the West End. He bequeathed one to each son—which resulted in two clock businesses each called Dent. "Neither could stop the other; each could stop a third party . . . from using 'Dent' for such a business": *Phones4U Ltd v Phone4u.co.uk Internet Ltd* [2006] EWCA Civ 244; [2007] R.P.C. 5 at [22].

[341] [1962] R.P.C. 265.

the UK and the defendant an American company which had only recently begun to trade in England. Notwithstanding that the defendant company did no more than use its own name on its furniture, the House of Lords, by a majority, granted an injunction to restrain it from continuing to do so without distinguishing its goods from those of the claimant. The claimant had established that its name had come to denote goods made by it alone and not goods made by anyone else possessing or adopting that name, and the use by the defendant of a similar name did, in the opinion of the majority, amount to the false representation that its goods were the claimant's goods.[342] The central question in each case is, therefore, whether the name or description given by the defendant to his goods is such as to create a likelihood that a substantial section of the purchasing public will be misled into believing that his goods are the goods of the claimant.[343] That the defendant used his own name with no intention to deceive anybody does not mean that such a likelihood has not been created,[344] but proof that the defendant did intend to deceive[345] will materially assist the claimant's case. As has often been pointed out, if it was the defendant's object to deceive people into thinking that his goods were the goods of the claimant, the court will not be reluctant to infer that he achieved his object.[346] Similarly, whatever tolerance is shown to the use of a person's own name will not be extended to altering it—"garnishing" it, as the expression is—so as to be likely to mislead; thus a firm of wine merchants, "Short's Ltd", obtained an injunction against one Short, who set up a similar business and styled it "Short's".[347]

Imitation of an address[348] may be part of conduct amounting to a scheme of passing off, but there is no property in an address as such. In *Day v Brownrigg*[349] the house of X had been known for over 60 years as "Ashford Lodge", and his neighbour Y changed the name of his house (previously known as "Ashford Villa") to "Ashford Lodge". This caused much inconvenience and annoyance to X, who claimed an injunction to restrain Y from such alteration of the name.

---

[342] Cf. *Habib Bank Ltd v Habib Bank A.G. Zurich* [1981] 1 W.L.R. 1265.

[343] *Parker-Knoll*, above, fn.341, at 278–279, 285, 289–290.

[344] *Reed Executive Plc v Reed Business Information Ltd* [2004] EWCA Civ 159; [2004] R.P.C. 40 at [110]: "the English law of passing off abounds with cases where people have been prevented from using their own name."

[345] See James L.J.'s example, in *Massam v Thorley* (1880) 14 Ch. D. 748 at 757, of somebody finding a man named Bass and setting up a brewery at Burton as Bass & Co.

[346] *Brinsmead & Son Ltd v Brinsmead*, above, fn.340, at 507 per Buckley L.J.; *Parker-Knoll*, above, fn.341, at 290 per Lord Devlin.

[347] *Short's Ltd v Short* (1914) 31 R.P.C. 294; *Parker & Son (Reading) Ltd v Parker* [1965] R.P.C. 323.

[348] Or the acquisition of a similar telephone number: *Law Society v Griffiths* [1995] P.C.R. 16.

[349] (1878) 10 Ch.D. 294.

It was held on demurrer that he had no cause of action.[350] Perhaps the result would have been different if the defendant had had the purpose of deceiving others and thereby causing harm to the claimant in his profession.[351]

18–47   The classic form of the tort involves A representing his goods to be those of B, but the basis of the liability is the wider one of injury to the claimant's goodwill ("the benefit and advantage of the good name, reputation and connection of a business . . . the attractive force which brings in custom"[352]) by misrepresentation to customers. Goodwill may attach to the description of a product so that it is shared by all persons making that product and they have a cause of action against a defendant who falsely attributes that description to his own goods even though he does not represent them to be produced by anyone else. In *Erwen Warnink B.V. v Townend & Sons (Hull) Ltd*,[353] the claimants were the main producers of advocaat, a drink of Dutch origin compounded of eggs and spirits, enjoying substantial sales in England. The defendants manufactured a drink, properly known as "egg flip", made from sherry and eggs and marketed under the name of "Keelings Old English Advocaat". Due to it attracting a lower rate of duty than the spirit-based drink it could be sold more cheaply and captured an appreciable share of the English market for advocaat. On the basis of a finding of fact that advocaat was a distinct and recognisable species of beverage based on spirits,[354] the House of Lords held that the defendants were guilty of passing off.[355] In doing so they approved the decision in *J. Bollinger v Costa Brava Wine Co Ltd*[356] (the Champagne case) and

---

[350] Liability was also denied, but this time in a business context, in *Street v Union Bank of Spain and England* (1885) 30 Ch.D. 155.

[351] Cf. *National Phonograph Co v Edison Bell Consolidated Phonograph Co* [1908] 1 Ch. 335 (deception as unlawful means in tort) and *Lonrho Plc v Fayed*, para.18–10, above.

[352] *IRC v Muller & Co's Margarine Ltd* [1901] A.C. 217 at 223–224 per Lord Macnaghten. In modern conditions it may be the reputation of the carefully nurtured brand name rather than the inherent quality of the product which is the basis of goodwill: *Chocosuisse v Cadbury Ltd* [1998] R.P.C. 117 (affirmed [1999] R.P.C. 826).

[353] [1979] A.C. 731. In *C.I.V.C. v Whitworths Group Ltd* [1991] 2 N.Z.L.R. 432 it is said that this form of passing off, as opposed to outright counterfeiting, is characterised by, "inconspicuous attachment, and invalid sharing, or partaking, of a reputation built by another and rightfully belonging to that person".

[354] This is vital: to take an example of counsel for the defendants, the manufacturers of tomato chutney could not restrain someone from marketing "tomato chutney" containing mangoes simply because mangoes had not been used in tomato chutney before. "Tomato chutney" is as vague as "brown bread".

[355] Cf. *Consorzio de Prosciutto di Parma v Marks & Spencer Plc* [1991] R.P.C. 351 (sliced and packaged Parma Ham still "Parma Ham" even though it could not be sold in that way in Italy and might be of lesser quality).

[356] [1960] Ch. 262; *Vine Products Ltd v Mackenzie & Co Ltd* [1969] R.P.C. 1 (sherry); *John Walker & Sons Ltd v Henry Ost & Co Ltd* [1970] 1 W.L.R. 917 (Scotch whisky). Cf. *Institut national etc. v Andres Wines Ltd* (1990) 71 D.L.R. (4th) 575 ("Canadian champagne" had built up a reputation as a different product).

made it clear that the principle was not confined to goods produced in a particular locality.[357] In these cases the common law has in effect produced something akin to the system of *appellation controlée* protection, though care must be taken not to give protection to merely descriptive words.[358]

The broad principle underlying the liability is also demonstrated by the fact that there can be liability for what has been called "reverse (or inverse) passing off", that is to say a case where the defendant shows the customer the claimant's goods intending to fill the resulting contract with goods of his own manufacture.[359] It is obviously unfair for the defendant to increase his trade by claiming credit for the claimant's achievements.

As most of the cases did involve the defendant literally passing off his goods as the claimant's it is not surprising that the older decisions tended to speak in terms of a requirement for a common field of activity between the parties. However, this is now regarded as too narrow a view and the issue of common field of activity is a factor relevant in deciding whether there is a misrepresentation likely to deceive and whether damage is likely to result, rather than an independent requirement.[360] For example, in *Granada Group Ltd v Ford Motor Co Ltd*[361] the claimants, a major publishing and entertainment company failed (not surprisingly on the facts) to restrain the defendants from attaching the name "Granada" to a new car; and in *Fortnum & Mason Plc v Fortnam Ltd*[362] there was no serious risk of confusion between the activities of the claimants (a high class food store) and the defendants (importers and re-exporters of cheap, plastic goods). If, however, the public might think that there was some association between the activities of the parties the claimant is likely to succeed if, for example, the defendant is

18–48

---

[357] There would, of course, be nothing to prevent the defendants in *Warnink* from marketing an English-made egg and spirit drink as advocaat. In the Champagne case the defendants could only have joined the class enjoying the goodwill by setting up in Champagne as well as using Champagne grapes and the "champenoise" method. In *Taittinger v Allbev Ltd* [1993] F.S.R. 641 even the use of "elderflower champagne" was successfully prevented. See also *Matthew Gloag v Welsh Distillers* [1998] F.S.R. 718. Nowadays producers may apply for registration of a Protected Geographical Indication under EC Council Regulation 2081/92/EEC: *Northern Foods Plc v DEFRA and Melton Mowbray Pork Pie Association* [2005] EWHC 2971 (Admin).

[358] *Chocosuisse v Cadbury Ltd* [1999] R.P.C. 826 ("Swiss chocolate").

[359] *Bristol Conservatories Ltd v Conservatories Custom Build Ltd* [1989] R.P.C. 380.

[360] *Harrods Ltd v Harrodian School* [1996] R.P.C. 697; *Nice and Safe Attitude v Flook (t/a Slaam! Clothing)* [1997] F.S.R. 14. Even where the parties are in the same line and there is similarity between their products the court may of course conclude that there is no real risk of the public being deceived: *Financial Times v Evening Standard* [1991] F.S.R. 7 (ES publishing business section on pink paper).

[361] [1972] F.S.R. 103; *Stringfellow v McCain Foods* [1984] R.P.C. 501.

[362] [1994] F.S.R. 438; *Box TV v Haymarket* (1997) 147 N.L.J. 601.

engaged in some activity which might harm the claimant's reputation even though they are in no sense competitors.[363] In this form the action is less "passing off" than "injurious association".[364] In *Associated Newspapers Plc v Insert Media Ltd*,[365] the defendants' practice of placing advertising inserts in the claimants' newspapers after they had been sold to newsagents was held to involve a representation that the defendants were associated with the claimants' business. There was a risk of damage to the goodwill of that business because while the claimants accepted only carefully vetted advertisements and took steps to protect readers against dishonest or insolvent advertisers, some members of the public might conclude that the claimants were responsible in the same way for the insert advertisers, over whom they had no control.[366] Though dishonesty is not a requirement of a successful claim for passing off, it is a relevant consideration in deciding whether the case has been established that the defendant intends to exploit the claimant's goodwill.[367]

18–49   In the *Insert Media* case the defendants could at least be said to be risking damage to the claimants' goodwill in respect of their central activity as newspaper publishers. In modern conditions, sportsmen, performers, film makers and so on actively engage in turning their public images or their creations to profit by granting endorsements or licences to persons manufacturing goods. An early case in Australia allowed an action to a dancing partnership whose picture had been used without consent to advertise a record[368] but the trend of the English cases was at first hostile to granting such protection against "misappropriation of business reputation". This

---

[363] See, e.g. *Annabel's (Berkeley Square) Ltd v G. Schock* [1972] F.S.R. 261 (night club and escort agency); *Harrod's Ltd v R. Harrod Ltd* (1923) 41 R.P.C. 74. See also *Hilton Press v White Eagle Youth Holiday Camp* (1951) 68 R.P.C. 126. Note, however, that in the *Fortnum & Mason* case, above, fn.362, Harman J. remarked of the *Annabel's* case that, "it would be astonishing if there was not in the mind of the ordinary person a close connection between the provision of girls to go out dancing with a man and a place where men may dance with girls.".

[364] Megarry J. in *Unitex Ltd v Union Texturing Co Ltd* [1973] R.P.C. 119. See also *Taittinger v Allbev Ltd* [1993] F.S.R. 64 (insidious dilution of reputation of champagne); *Associated Newspapers Ltd v Express Newspapers* [2003] EWHC 1322; [2003] F.S.R. 51; and Carty (1996) 112 L.Q.R. 632.

[365] [1991] 1 W.L.R. 571. *Lego Systems A/S v Lego Lemelstrich* [1983] F.S.R. 155 seems to reduce the requirement of damage almost to vanishing point.

[366] However, it would not be enough that people might think the claimants were providing "sponsorship" for the defendants: *Harrods Ltd v Harrodian School* [1996] R.P.C. 697. Cf. *Dawnay Day & Co Ltd v Cantor Fitzgerald International* [2000] R.P.C. 669 at 705.

[367] *Stringfellow v McCain Foods* [1984] R.P.C. 501 at 546; *Associated Newspapers Plc v Insert Media Ltd* [1991] 1 W.L.R. 571.

[368] *Henderson v Radio Corp Pty Ltd* [1960] N.S.W.R. 576 followed in *Krouse v Chrysler Canada Ltd* (1971) 25 D.L.R. (3d) 49, reversed on the facts (1973) 40 D.L.R. (3d) 15. Unauthorised use of name or likeness for advertising was one of the earliest forms of the tort of invasion of privacy in the United States. See Frazer, "Appropriation of Personality" (1983) 99 L.Q.R. 281.

approach was reversed in *Irvine v Talksport Ltd*,[369] where a Formula 1 racing driver recovered damages for unauthorised advertisements which implied that he had given his endorsement to the defendants' sports radio station. Although many passing off cases arose from a claimant's fear that the sale of inferior goods under his name would damage his goodwill by associating him with those goods, the law was not confined to that situation. It was well known that in modern marketing conditions famous people made a substantial income from the endorsement of products and services and the law should vindicate their exclusive rights in their reputation or goodwill in that respect.[370]

The *Irvine* case is not intended to state the law for the situation where the defendant sells goods which exploit a demand produced by the artistic creation of the claimant—toys associated with film themes or cartoon characters,[371] for example, what is known as "character merchandising".[372] Since the artistic creator will commonly have authorised exploitation of this type or even be engaged in it, there is no reason of principle why the law of passing off should not apply. In *Mirage Studios v Counter-Feat Clothing*[373] Browne-Wilkinson V.C. granted an injunction[374] restraining unlicensed use of the "Teenage Mutant Ninja Turtle" image on clothing. Certainly the claimants were not in the clothing business but the financial significance in modern conditions of character merchandising meant that neither were they solely in the business of producing cartoon films. The public were now aware in a general way of the practice and the claimants would suffer damage in, (1) losing licensing fees and (2) losing the ability to control the quality of products

---

[369] [2002] EWHC 367 (Ch); [2003] 1 W.L.R. 2355. There was no appeal on the decision of law, though the CA clearly approved of it. It substantially increased the damages awarded: [2003] EWCA Civ 423; [2003] 2 All E.R. 881.

[370] The claimant was in a line of activity where endorsement is a standard part of his business. It does not follow that this development would provide ammunition for the Chancellor of the Exchequer whose image was used in various advertising campaigns nor for the Health Minister who found herself featured in an Easter egg promotion (*The Times*, July 25, 1990), though it is unlikely any sensible person would have thought there was an endorsement anyway. The advertising codes of conduct allow unlicensed use of the images of persons with "a high degree of public exposure". As to whether there is a general right to control the use of one's image, see para.12–84, above.

[371] The law of copyright may be relevant with regard to cartoon characters (see *King Features v Kleeman* [1940] 1 Ch. 523—Popeye; *BBC Worldwide Ltd v Pally Screen Printing Ltd* [1998] F.S.R. 665—Teletubbies).

[372] Indeed, this might arise with regard to a real person. An advertiser might use the image of an actor in a film which had some association in the public mind with the type of product in question, but in such a way as not to imply any endorsement. Cf. *Pacific Dunlop Ltd v Hogan* (1989) 87 A.L.R. 14: the defendant did not use the claimant's image but an actor (who bore little resemblance to the claimant) in a take-off of a role with which the claimant was associated.

[373] [1991] F.S.R. 145.

[374] It was interim but the claimants' case was regarded as more than merely arguable.

marketed with the "Turtle" image, with consequent damage to their goodwill with the public. However, it should certainly not be assumed that we have reached the stage where a celebrity has an exclusive right to exploit the valuable aspects of his own character[375] and in the case of the exploitation of fictional characters it has been suggested that it is difficult to prove confusion because the public may not generally care in these cases whether the product is "genuine" or not.[376]

B. Goodwill

18–50   Mere confusion in the mind of the public is not enough to establish a case of passing off unless there is a risk of damage to the claimant's goodwill and it therefore follows that the tort is not committed if that goodwill has not been established. Hence an action failed where the claimant planned to bring out a leisure magazine and had spent money promoting it but the defendant launched a scheme to publish a magazine with the same name[377]; and it seems that the result would have been the same even if the defendant's act had been a mere "spoiling" operation.[378] Goodwill cannot exist in a vacuum so if a business has been abandoned there is no longer any legally protected goodwill attached to it; but a temporary cessation of business is a different matter.[379] However, there may be damage to goodwill even though there is no evidence of diversion of sales.[380]

A matter of some significance in modern conditions of trade is the "locality" of the goodwill. There is no doubt that an action only lies if the claimant has goodwill here but whether or not that is so can be a difficult question of fact or inference.[381] It is not enough that the claimant has a reputation in the sense that he is known here (for

---

[375] *Elvis Presley Trade Mark* [1999] R.P.C. 567, CA.

[376] *BBC Worldwide Ltd v Pally Screen Printing Ltd* [1998] F.S.R. 665 at 674.

[377] *Marcus Publishing Plc v Hutton-Wild Communications Ltd* [1990] R.P.C. 576. However, there may be cases in which pre-launch publicity suffices to establish goodwill: *Labyrinth Media Ltd v Brave World Ltd* [1995] E.M.L.R. 38.

[378] [1990] R.P.C. 576 at 580, 585. Cf. *Bradford Corp v Pickles* [1895] A.C. 587, para.3–9, above.

[379] *Pink v Sharwood & Co Ltd* (1913) 30 R.P.C. 725; *Star Industrial Co Ltd v Yap Kwee Kor* [1976] F.S.R. 256; *Ad-Lib Club Ltd v Granville* [1972] R.P.C. 673; cf. *Minimax GmbH & Co KG v Chubb Fire Ltd* [2008] EWHC 1960 (Pat).

[380] *Chelsea Man v Chelsea Girl* [1987] R.P.C. 189; *Phones4U Ltd v Phone4u.co.uk Internet Ltd* [2006] EWCA Civ 244; [2007] R.P.C. 5.

[381] There is an exhaustive review of the law throughout the Commonwealth by Lockhart J. in *Conagra Inc v McCain Foods (Aust) Pty Ltd* (1992) 106 A.L.R. 465. The fact that many of the cases involve interlocutory proceedings in which the issue is whether the claimant's contention is arguable means that they are of limited value as precedents.

example from advertising in publications which circulate here as well as abroad),[382] so that in *Bernardin & Cie v Pavilion Properties Ltd*[383] the proprietors of the "Crazy Horse Saloon" nightclub in Paris failed in an action against defendants who set up a similar establishment in London. On the other hand, while the claimant must have business with people here there is no necessity for him to have "a business" here in the sense of a physical presence or even direct sales relationships.[384]

C. The Limits of Passing Off

The law of passing off seems to be adaptable to changing trading **18–51** practices and conditions and has had some notable extensions, particularly in the Champagne case and its successors and in the recognition of endorsement rights of "personalities"; but it has not generalised into a tort of "unfair competition".[385] Thus it is no tort for the defendant to exploit the claimant's advertising campaign so as to seize a share of the market which the claimant has created. In *Cadbury-Schweppes Pty Ltd v Pub Squash Co Pty Ltd*,[386] the claimants launched a lemon drink ("Solo") supported by an extensive advertising campaign evoking an idealised memory of soft drinks of the past. The defendants then launched a lemon drink ("Pub Squash") with a get up and advertising theme closely related to that for "Solo". The dismissal of the claimants' claim for damages and an injunction on the ground of passing off was upheld by the Privy Council for the defendants had sufficiently distinguished their goods from those of the claimants to prevent any likely confusion in the public mind. The alternative claim of "unfair competition" was not even pursued before that court and the High Court of Australia

---

[382] *Athlete's Foot Marketing Associates Inc v Cobra Sports Ltd* [1980] R.P.C. 43; *Anheuser-Busch Inc v Budejovicky Budvar N.P.* [1984] F.S.R. 413; *Jian Tools for Sales v Roderick Manhattan Group* [1995] F.S.R. 924. The Canadian case of *Orkin Exterminating Co Inc v Pestco of Canada Ltd* (1985) 19 D.L.R. (4th) 90 perhaps crosses the line between reputation and goodwill since the claimants had no business in Canada and the services could only be provided at the customer's premises.

[383] [1967] R.P.C. 581 (the claimants had in fact aimed advertising at England).

[384] Thus in *SA etc. Panhard et Levassor v Panhard Levassor Motor Co Ltd* [1901] 2 Ch. 513 the claimants sold no cars in England but English people bought their cars in France and imported them. This was sufficient goodwill. Presumably had the claimants in the *Crazy Horse* case been able to show that a significant amount of their trade was in the form of English tourists attracted by their advertising their case would have been stronger. See also *Tan-Ichi Co Ltd v Jancar Ltd* [1990] F.S.R. 151 (claimants operated Japanese restaurants; no establishments within the jurisdiction—Hong Kong—but goodwill in HK Japanese residents).

[385] *Pace* the suggestion of Aldous L.J. in *Arsenal Football Club Plc v Reed* [2003] EWCA Civ 696; [2003] R.P.C. 39 at [70] that unfair competition would be a better name for it.

[386] [1981] 1 W.L.R. 193.

subsequently delivered a categorical rejection of such a tort.[387] We
have seen that in *Associated Newspapers Group Plc v Insert Media
Ltd* the newspaper publishers succeeded on the basis of passing off,
but in earlier proceedings Hoffmann J. rejected a cause of action
alleging unfair competition by debasing or devaluing the claimants'
goods without misrepresentation.[388] The balance of authority is
similarly against a general liability where A appropriates B's valuable idea, design or information and exploits it without payment.[389]
Nonetheless, there are modern examples of claims being held arguable which are extremely difficult to fit within traditional ideas of
the tort[390] so further development cannot be ruled out.

The setting of passing off is normally trade. However, trade in the
narrow sense is not essential, even if it is difficult to say precisely
how far the law goes. A fundraising charity has succeeded in an
action in respect of conduct which tended to appropriate its goodwill[391] and a religious organisation may also be able to sue.[392] An
author may sue for a false representation that a book is his work[393]
and a professional person or a professional association[394] may have
a cause of action in respect of unauthorised use of their names in a
manner likely to cause harm to their professional activities—for
example, the use of a doctor's name to promote a quack medicine or
cure.[395] It has even been held that a political organisation may
obtain an injunction to restrain a person standing at an election in its
name.[396]

[387] *Moorgate Tobacco Co Ltd v Phillip Morris Ltd* (1984) 56 A.L.R. 193; but see s.52 of the
Australian Trade Practices Act 1974. An American doctrine of unfair competition enunciated in *International News Services v Associated Press* 248 U.S. 215, (1918) has never
gained ascendancy in the face of what are thought to be conflicting statutory rights, but
broad principles against unfair competition may exist in European countries (see, e.g. the
German Law at issue in *Theodore Kohl K.B. v Ringelhaan & Rennett SA* [1985] 3
C.M.L.R. 340).
[388] [1988] 1 W.L.R. 509.
[389] *Lever Bros v Bedingfield* (1896) 16 R.P.C. 3; *Wortheimer v Stewart, Cooper* (1906) 23
R.P.C. 48; *Victoria Park Racing Co v Taylor* (1937) 58 C.L.R. 479; *Conan Doyle v London
Mystery Magazine Ltd* (1949) 66 R.P.C. 246. The law of copyright generally protects the
form of a work, not the idea behind it, but the author of a work who does not have the
copyright may have the right to be identified as the author under the Copyright, Designs
and Patents Act 1988 s.77.
[390] See Carty, *An Analysis of the Economic Torts* (2000), p.222.
[391] *British Diabetic Association v Diabetic Society Ltd* [1995] 4 All E.R. 812.
[392] *Holy Apostolic etc. Church v Att Gen (NSW), ex rel. Elisha* (1989) 18 N.S.W.L.R. 291,
approved in *British Diabetic*, above, fn.391.
[393] *Lord Byron v Johnson* (1816) 2 Mer. 29; *Clark v Associated Newspapers Ltd* [1998] R.P.C.
261. See also Copyright, Designs and Patents Act 1988 s.84.
[394] *Society of Accountants and Auditors v Goodway* [1907] 1 Ch. 489; *Law Society v Society
of Lawyers* [1996] F.S.R. 739. On goodwill and unincorporated trade associations see
Artistic Upholstery Ltd v Art Forma (Furniture) Ltd [1999] 4 All E.R. 277.
[395] See *Dockrell v Douglas* (1899) 80 L.T. 556 at 557, 558; *Walter v Ashton* [1902] 2 Ch. 282
at 293.
[396] *Burge v Haycock* [2001] EWCA Civ 900; [2002] R.P.C. 28.

D. Remedies

The injunction is an important remedy in passing off cases and an interim injunction may well determine the final outcome since the delay before trial may mean that the loser at the interim stage cannot resume production.[397] It may be made in qualified form, i.e. restraining the defendant from disposing of his goods without sufficiently distinguishing them from the claimant's.[398] In addition, damages may be granted in respect of losses to the claimant or, in the alternative, an account of profits made by the defendant from the passing off.[399] It has been held at first instance that damages may be recovered against an innocent defendant, though the alternative of an account of profits is not available in such a case.[400]

18–52

---

[397] See, e.g. *Mirage Studios v Counter-Feat Clothing*, para.18–49, above. The *American Cyanamid* principles (para.22–50, below) are as applicable to passing off as to other torts: *County Sound v Ocean Sound* [1991] F.S.R. 367. However, s.12 of the Human Rights Act 1998 may be relevant: *Blandford Goldsmith & Co Ltd v Prime UK Properties Ltd* [2003] EWHC 3265 (Ch).

[398] "It has been said many times that it is no part of the function of this court to examine imaginary cases of what the defendant could or could not do under this form of injunction. The best guide, if he is an honest man, is his own conscience and it is certainly not the business of this court to give him instructions or limits as to how near the wind he can sail": *Wright, Layman & Unney v Wright* (1949) 66 R.P.C. 149 at 152 per Lord Greene M.R.

[399] There may be circumstances in which a person, e.g. a printer of labels, who facilitates a passing off without actual knowledge, may be liable for negligence, but such a case would be very unusual and a person who receives such orders in the ordinary course of trade is not to be expected to institute inquiries about the lawfulness of the intended use. *Paterson Zochonis & Co Ltd v Merfarken Packaging Ltd* [1986] 3 All E.R. 522.

[400] *Gillette UK Ltd v Eden West Ltd* [1994] R.P.C. 297.

CHAPTER 19

ABUSE OF LEGAL PROCEDURE

1. MALICIOUS PROSECUTION

THE history of this tort[1] can be traced back to the writ of conspiracy   **19–1**
which was in existence as early as Edward I's reign. This fell into
decay in the 16th century, partly because the writ of maintenance
supplanted it. However, this was probably confined to officious
intermeddling in civil suits.[2] The gap was filled by an action on the
case which appeared in Elizabeth I's reign and eventually became
known as the action for malicious prosecution. It was put on a firm
footing in 1698 in *Saville v Roberts*.[3]

Liability for malicious prosecution has always had to steer a path
between two competing principles—on the one hand the freedom of
action that everyone should have to set the law in motion and to
bring criminals to justice and on the other hand the necessity to
check lying accusations against innocent people[4] and the burden
which has to be undertaken by the claimant in a case of malicious

---

[1] See Winfield, *History of Conspiracy and Abuse of Legal Procedure* and Winfield, *Present Law of Abuse of Legal Procedure*.
[2] Maintenance as a tort survived until 1967 but has now been abolished: para.19–15, below.
[3] 1 Ld. Raym. 374.
[4] *Glinski v McIver* [1962] A.C. 726 at 741, 753; *Gregory v Portsmouth CC* [2000] 1 A.C. 419 at 426.

prosecution is a heavy one,[5] so heavy that no honest prosecutor is likely to be deterred from doing his duty. One reason for the complexity of the law in this area is that a number of other torts and principles come into play where the defendant is involved in the events leading up to a prosecution. First, the claimant may have been arrested on the basis of information given by the defendant. As we have seen, in modern conditions the exercise of a discretion by the police officer carrying out the arrest[6] is likely to deprive the claimant of any claim against the defendant for false imprisonment.[7] Secondly, the information given by the defendant is likely to be defamatory, but not only will any evidence given by him in court be subject to absolute privilege, it has now been held that the same applies to a mere complaint to the police.[8] If, however, the defendant is a prosecutor the essence of the complaint is that he has abused the process of the court[9] and the fact that for other legal purposes he is immune from suit is irrelevant. The application of the law of negligence in this area would be inconsistent with the restrictions imposed by the law of malicious prosecution. There is no liability in negligence in respect of the conduct of a prosecution[10] nor the investigation of a charge made against the claimant.[11] There might be liability for misfeasance in a public office[12] but that requires a form of malice and this is not satisfied by negligence, however crass. However, it should be noted that the majority of the Supreme Court of Canada has accepted a liability for "negligent investigation", though the minority view was that the new liability would "effectively subsume" existing torts in this area, "and risk

---

[5] There are two schemes for compensation where a conviction is reversed or a pardon granted on the ground of miscarriage of justice: a statutory scheme under s.133 of the Criminal Justice Act 1988 where there is a new or newly discovered fact and an ex gratia one. However, they operate in the same way. The process of assessment (by an independent assessor) involves substantial analogy with tort damages principles: *R (Miller) v The Independent Assessor* [2009] EWCA Civ 609.

[6] Still more of a magistrate remanding the claimant in custody.

[7] See, para.4–32, above.

[8] *Westcott v Westcott* [2008] EWCA Civ 818; [2009] E.M.L.R. 2. The same would apply to a claim for malicious falsehood. Even before this case it was held that the absolute privilege extended to preliminary statements or the preparation of reports outside court which can fairly be said to be part of the process of investigation However, the immunity in respect of pre-trial matters does not extend to the fabrication of evidence to be used in court: *Darker v CC West Midlands* [2001] A.C. 435. In that case the claims were for conspiracy to injure and misfeasance in a public office. The claimants alleged that the defendants had conspired to cause them to be charged with offences which they knew or believed to be false, but there was no claim for malicious prosecution.

[9] *Martin v Watson* [1996] A.C. 74 at 88.

[10] *Elguzouli-Daf v MPC* [1995] Q.B. 335, para.5–60, above.

[11] *B v Reading BC* [2009] EWHC 998 (QB). Mackay J. thought that the decision of the CA in these proceedings at [2001] EWCA Civ 346; [2001] 1 W.L.R. 1575 could not stand with later developments.

[12] See para.7–20, above.

upsetting the necessary balance between the competing interests at play".[13]

The majority of actions for malicious prosecution nowadays are probably brought against the police, but the House of Lords has reaffirmed that a private person who sets the law in motion may still incur liability.[14] However, the law was largely shaped in an era when there was no formal, state system for investigation and prosecution and care must be taken in applying broad principles established under the old regime to present circumstances.

The action for malicious prosecution being an action on the case **19–2** it is essential for the claimant to prove damage, and in *Saville v Roberts*[15] Holt C.J. classified damage for the purpose of this tort as of three kinds, any one of which might ground the action: malicious prosecution might damage a person's fame (i.e. his character), or the safety of his person, or the security of his property by reason of his expense in repelling an unjust charge.[16] A moral stigma will inevitably attach where the law visits an offence with imprisonment, but there are today innumerable offences which are punishable only by fine. In such cases the claimant can only rely upon damage to his fame if the offence with which he is charged is necessarily and naturally defamatory of him,[17] and in effect the question is the converse of the question of law which is involved in actions for defamation: Is the statement that the claimant was charged with the offence capable of a non-defamatory meaning?[18] Thus a charge of wrongly pulling the communication cord in a railway train does not necessarily affect the fair fame of the accused and will not ground an action for malicious prosecution under Holt C.J.'s first head,[19] but it is otherwise where, for example the claimant is charged with deliberately travelling on a train without having paid his fare.[20] On the other hand, unless the claimant was awarded the equivalent of the taxed costs which he has incurred in defending himself, the difference between the costs awarded in the criminal proceedings, if

---

[13] *Hill v Hamilton-Wentworth Regional Police Services Board* [2007] SCC 41; [2007] 3 S.C.R. 129 at [182].

[14] *Martin v Watson*, above, fn.9.

[15] (1698) 1 Ld. Raym. 374; 5 Mod. 394.

[16] Where the successful claimant is of bad character it may be proper to discount the first element to some extent, but this may be offset by the risk of heavier punishment to which his record exposes him if convicted: *Manley v MPC* [2006] EWCA Civ 879.

[17] *Berry v British Transport Commission* [1961] 1 Q.B. 149 at 166, following *Wiffen v Bailey and Romford UDC* [1915] 1 K.B. 600. This was not the original meaning intended by Holt C.J. (*Berry v British Transport Commission* at 160–163 per Diplock J.) and it has been criticised: *Berry v British Transport Commission* [1962] 1 Q.B. at 333 per Devlin L.J., at 335–336 per Danckwerts L.J.

[18] *Berry v British Transport Commission* at 166 per Diplock J.

[19] [1961] 1 Q.B. 149; *Wiffen v Bailey and Romford UDC* [1915] 1 K.B. 600.

[20] *Rayson v South London Transport Co* [1893] 2 Q.B. 304.

any, and the costs actually incurred is sufficient to ground the action under Holt C.J.'s third head.[21]

Assuming there is damage as explained above, the claimant must prove, (1) that the defendant prosecuted him, and (2) that the prosecution ended in the claimant's favour, and (3) that the prosecution lacked reasonable and probable cause, and (4) that the defendant acted maliciously. We can take these point by point.

A. Essentials of the Tort

19–3   **i. Prosecution.** A person who brings a private prosecution is obviously a prosecutor for this purpose and so is one who swears an information[22] or who is bound over to act as a prosecutor.[23] However, in *Martin v Watson*[24] the House of Lords held that it is not necessary that the defendant should be the prosecutor in any technical sense: what matters is that he should in substance be the person responsible for the prosecution being brought. The defendant made various charges to the police that the claimant had indecently exposed himself to her and this led to a prosecution of the claimant at which no evidence was offered against him. Distinguishing the case of *Danby v Beardsley*[25] in which the defendant had been held not to be a prosecutor when he told the police that goods which he mistakenly believed to have been stolen from him had been found in the claimant's possession, on the ground that in that case there was no malice against the claimant, Lord Keith continued:

> "Where an individual falsely and maliciously gives a police officer information indicating that some person is guilty of a criminal offence and states that he is willing to give evidence in court of the matters in question, it is properly to be inferred that he desires and intends that the person he names should be prosecuted. When the circumstances are such that the facts relating to the alleged offence can be within the knowledge only of the complainant,[26] as was the position here, then it becomes virtually impossible for the police officer to exercise any independent discretion or judgment, and if a prosecution is instituted by the

---

[21] *Berry v British Transport Commission* [1962] 1 Q.B. 306, where *Wiffen v Bailey and Romford UDC* [1915] 1 K.B. 600 was held not binding on this point. It is otherwise where costs incurred in a civil action are concerned: *Quartz Hill Consolidated Gold Mining Co v Eyre* (1883) 11 Q.B.D. 674.

[22] *Watters v Pacific Delivery Service Ltd* (1963) 42 D.L.R. (2d) 661.

[23] *Fitzjohn v Mackinder* (1861) 9 C.B.(N.S.) 505.

[24] [1996] A.C. 74.

[25] (1880) 43 L.T. 603.

[26] Liability for malicious prosecution is not necessarily confined to such cases: *Scott v Ministry of Justice* [2009] EWCA Civ 1215 at [38], [51].

police officer the proper view of the matter is that the prosecution has been procured by the complainant."[27]

Martin v Watson was a strong case because the defendant conducted a campaign against the claimant by making repeated complaints which the police were reluctant to pursue. In contrast in *AH v AB*,[28] where the claimant's conviction for rape of the defendant had been set aside, the defendant had made no complaint to the police, the prosecution arising from a report to them several years after the event and originating with a person in whom the defendant had confided at the time, and it was only under pressure from the police that the defendant had given evidence in the criminal proceedings. She was not a prosecutor because it was impossible to say that she fulfilled the first requirement, which was that she should have "intended or desired" a prosecution.[29]

The difficulties arise in cases lying between *Martin* and *AH*. As **19-4** we have seen, the tort developed at a time when private prosecutions were much more common than now. After the middle of the 19th century most prosecutions were conducted by the police and nowadays the decision to prosecute and the conduct of the proceedings are normally in the hands of the Crown Prosecution Service,[30] which will exercise an independent discretion as to whether to proceed, taking account of the strength of the evidence and relevant guidelines. In *AH* it is said that even a person who initiates the process of investigation and prosecution by making a false complaint[31] is not to be regarded as a prosecutor unless he does something to "manipulate" the prosecuting authorities into doing something they would not otherwise have done[32] and that where the decision to prosecute is taken by the CPS it will be a rare case in which the complainant can be regarded as a prosecutor. No doubt this has merits in the case of a complainant but many prosecutions are brought mainly on the basis of police investigation and evidence, though the decision to prosecute is still made by the CPS. Is the same dispensation to apply to a police officer who concocts such a convincing false story that he does not need to take any further steps

---

[27] [1996] A.C. at 86.
[28] [2009] EWCA Civ 1092.
[29] *Mahon v Rahn (No.2)* [2000] 1 W.L.R. 2150.
[30] See Prosecution of Offences Act 1985, Criminal Justice Act 2003.
[31] Some passages in *Martin v Watson* may be thought to run together the issues of whether the defendant is a prosecutor and whether he is guilty of malice. According to *AH* the true position is that knowledge of the falsity of the charge is relevant on the "prosecutor" issue in so far as it provides evidence of an intention that to procure a prosecution. In the view of Moore-Bick LJ this makes the matter unsuitable to be dealt with as a preliminary issue.
[32] [2009] EWCA Civ 1092 at [47], [58], [84].

to influence the prosecution? If so the position of a falsely accused
person has been seriously weakened. However, very soon after *AH*
a differently constituted Court of Appeal in *Scott v Ministry of
Justice*[33] held that where five prison officers had made clear and
consistent statements accusing the claimant of assault on them there
was an arguable case that they had procured the ensuing prosecution
even though there had been no manipulation or overbearing by them
of the responsible crown prosecutor's view.[34]

19–5   **ii. Favourable termination of the prosecution.** The claimant
must show that the prosecution ended in his favour,[35] but so long as
it did, it is of no moment how this came about, whether by a verdict
of acquittal, or by discontinuance of the prosecution by leave of the
court,[36] or by quashing of the indictment for a defect in it,[37] or
because the proceedings were *coram non judice*.[38] The effect of a
nolle prosequi (staying by the Attorney-General of proceedings on
an indictment) was left open to question in an old case which
indicated that it was not a sufficient ending of the prosecution
because it still left the accused liable to be indicted afresh on the
same charge.[39] Yet, this seems inconsistent with the broad interpretation put upon "favourable termination of the prosecution"
which signifies, not that the accused has been acquitted, but that he
has not been convicted.[40] In New Zealand it has been held that the
key element is the absence of any incriminating finding or plea and
that the claimant does not have to go further and show a favourable
outcome in a positive sense, as after a defended hearing.[41] The
reason for the favourable termination requirement has been said to

---

[33] [2009] EWCA Civ 1215.
[34] Longmore L.J. remarked at [47] that the question of who is a prosecutor, "is in danger of
becoming a little over-complicated".
[35] *Parker v Langly* (1713) 10 Mod. 145 and 209. This was not always the law: Winfield,
Present Law, pp.182–183. The logical result is that the limitation period runs from the time
of the acquittal, not the charge: *Dunlop v Customs and Excise, The Times*, March 17, 1998;
Baker v MPC, June 24, 1996, QBD.
[36] *Watkins v Lee* (1839) 5 M. & W. 270. Under the Prosecution of Offences Act 1985 the
Director of Public Prosecutions may discontinue proceedings in the magistrates' court
without leave. Withdrawal of the charge, even if without prejudice to the right to
recommence, has been held in Canada to be sufficient: *Romegialli v Marceau* (1963) 42
D.L.R. (2d) 481; *Casey v Automobiles Renault Canada Ltd* (1965) 54 D.L.R. (2d) 600.
[37] *Jones v Gwynn* (1712) 10 Mod. 148 at 214.
[38] *Attwood v Monger* (1653) Style 378. See also *Goddard v Smith* (1704) 1 Salk. 21 (non
suit).
[39] *Goddard v Smith*, above, fn.38.
[40] The question has been much litigated in America: Dobbs, *Torts* (2000) §434. See, too,
decisions of the Supreme Courts of NSW (*Gilchrist v Gardner* (1891) 12 N.S.W. Law Rep.
184) and of British Guiana (*Khan v Singh* (1960) 2 W.I.R. 441). See also *Romegialli v
Marceau* (1963) 42 D.L.R. 2d. 481.
[41] *Van Heeren v Cooper* [1999] 1 N.Z.L.R. 731, N.Z.C.A.

be the risk of diverse determinations by different courts on the same facts and between the same parties.[42]

It was held in *Reynolds v Kennedy*[43] that no action could lie if the claimant had been convicted, even if his conviction was later reversed on appeal, the reason apparently being that the original conviction showed conclusively that there was foundation for the prosecution. In a number of modern cases, however, it was the fact that the proceedings had terminated in the claimant's favour only as the result of an appeal, but nothing was made of this.[44] The question of reasonable and probable cause for the prosecution is an independent question and should not be regarded as finally answered in the defendant's favour on the ground only that a conviction was secured in a court of first instance. *Reynolds v Kennedy* should no longer be regarded as good law.

On the other hand, if a conviction stands, then the claimant cannot **19–6** succeed in an action for malicious prosecution, and this is so even if the conviction is one against which there is no right of appeal and which has been obtained by the fraud of the prosecutor. In *Basébé v Matthews*,[45] Byles J. thought that if the rule were otherwise every case would have to be retried on its merits, and Montague Smith J. feared that they would be turning themselves into a Court of Appeal where the legislature allowed none. The rule rests upon the more general principle that the court will strike out as an abuse of process a suit which is a collateral attack on the decision of a competent criminal court for otherwise there is a risk of inconsistent decisions.[46] *Basébé v Matthews* was followed in *Everett v Ribbands*[47] where the claimant had been bound over to find sureties to be of good behaviour. He failed in an action for malicious prosecution, for the proceedings complained of had actually been determined against him.

If the prosecution has terminated in the claimant's favour and he sues for malicious prosecution, may the prosecutor seek in his defence to show that the claimant was in fact guilty? For example,

---

[42] However, it has been pointed out that the issues before the courts are not the same—the issue for the civil court is whether the prosecutor had reasonable and probable cause, which is not the same as whether the claimant was guilty: *Van Heeren* at 738. There is no inconsistency in the criminal court finding that C was not guilty and then the civil court finding that D had reasonable and probable cause for the prosecution. On the relevance of the guilt of the claimant see below, para.19–6.

[43] (1784) 1 Wils. 232.

[44] *Herniman v Smith* [1938] A.C. 305; *Berry v BTC* [1962] 1 Q.B. 306; *Abbott v Refuge Assurance Co Ltd* [1962] 1 Q.B. 432; *Blaker v Weller* [1964] Crim. L.R. 311.

[45] (1867) L.R. 2 C.P. 684.

[46] The general principle may be subject to exception if there is decisive fresh evidence: *Smith v Linskills* [1996] 1 W.L.R. 763.

[47] [1952] 2 Q.B. 198; *Bynoe v Bank of England* [1902] 1 K.B. 467.

the prosecution may have presented a weak case but afterwards there may come to light much stronger evidence against the claimant.[48] Some cases hold that the prosecutor may not do this, or even use the evidence of guilt in mitigation of damages[49] relying either upon the "inconsistency" argument mentioned above or at least upon the undesirability of relitigation of the issue of guilt. However, if D states that C has committed a criminal offence and C, having been acquitted of that offence, then sues D for defamation, we do not prevent D from justifying by trying to show that C was in fact guilty, rash as that plea may perhaps be; and while there may be a general principle which treats as an abuse of process any attempt to mount a collateral attack on the decision of a competent court,[50] that is directed at the initiation of proceedings, not at the formulation of a defence. It has been held in New Zealand that proof of the guilt of the claimant is in itself a defence to a claim for malicious prosecution where the favourable termination of the proceedings was otherwise than by an acquittal on the merits, the position in that case being left open.[51]

19–7   iii. Lack of reasonable and probable cause.[52] There does not appear to be any distinction between "reasonable" and "probable". The conjunction of these adjectives is a heritage from the redundancies in which the old pleaders delighted,[53] and although it has been said that reasonable cause is such as would operate on the mind of a discreet man, while probable cause is such as would operate on the mind of a reasonable man,[54] this does not help us much, for it is difficult to picture a reasonable man who is not discreet.

The principal difficulty, and it is no minor one, in stating the law as to reasonable and probable cause arises from the division of function between judge and jury,[55] cases of malicious prosecution being still, typically, tried by jury. It has been recognised for centuries[56] that once a person has been acquitted by a criminal court,

---

[48] At common law there were no circumstances in which he might be tried again. This can now happen where the conditions of Pt 10 of the Criminal Justice Act 2003 are fulfilled.

[49] *Commonwealth Life Assurance Society Ltd v Smith* (1938) 59 C.L.R. 527.

[50] See para.5–60, above.

[51] *Van Heeren v Cooper* [1999] 1 N.Z.L.R. 731, NZCA. The *Restatement*, 2d §657 makes guilt a defence in all cases, with a civil standard of proof.

[52] There is a valuable review of both reasonable and probable cause and malice in *A v New South Wales* [2007] HCA 10; 233 A.L.R. 584.

[53] Winfield, *Present Law*, p.192.

[54] *Broad v Ham* (1839) 5 Bing. N.C. 72 at 725 per Tindal C.J.

[55] *Glinski v McIver* [1962] A.C. 726 at 742 per Viscount Simonds.

[56] See *Pain v Rochester and Whitfield* (1599) Cro. Eliz. 871, cited by Denning L.J. in *Leibo v Buckman* Ltd [1952] 2 All E.R. 1057 at 1062.

juries are too ready to award him damages against his prosecutor,[57] and therefore it is for the judge to decide whether the defendant had reasonable and probable cause for launching the prosecution,[58] but it is for the jury to decide any incidental questions of fact necessary for the judge's determination.[59] Moreover, this branch of the law is unusual in requiring the claimant to undertake the difficult task of proving a negative. It is for him to prove that the prosecutor did not have reasonable and probable cause, and not for the prosecutor to prove that he had.[60]

In *Herniman v Smith*[61] the House of Lords approved and adopted **19–8** the definition of reasonable and probable cause given by Hawkins J. in *Hicks v Faulkner*[62] as:

"[A]n honest belief in the guilt of the accused based upon a full conviction, founded upon reasonable grounds, of the existence of a state of circumstances, which, assuming them to be true, would reasonably lead any ordinarily prudent and cautious man placed in the position of the accuser, to the conclusion that the person charged was probably guilty of the crime imputed".

On this basis there are two elements, one subjective and one objective. The:

"[M]aterial available to the prosecutor must be assessed in two ways. What did the prosecutor make of it? What should the prosecutor have made of it?"[63]

---

[57] e.g. *Abrath v North Eastern Ry* (1886) 11 App. Cas. 247 at 252 per Lord Bramwell; *Leibo v Buckman Ltd,* above, fn.56, at 1063 per Denning L.J.; *Glinski v McIver,* above, fn.55, at 741–742 per Viscount Simonds, at 777–778 per Lord Devlin. Cf. per Lord Radcliffe at 754.

[58] *Johnstone v Sutton* (1786) 1 T.R. 510; *Herniman v Smith* [1938] A.C. 305; *Reynolds v Metropolitan Police Comr* [1985] Q.B. 881. It is doubtful whether the question is one of fact or law. Probably it is best regarded as a question of fact, but one which is to be treated in the same way as if it were a question of law: *Glinski v McIver,* above, fn.55, at 768 per Lord Devlin.

[59] The judge need put to the jury only questions on the salient issues of fact, for otherwise the questions would have no end: *Dallison v Caffery* [1965] 1 Q.B. 348 at 368 per Lord Denning M.R.

[60] *Abrath v NE Ry* (1883) 11 Q.B.D. 440; *Stapeley v Annetts* [1970] 1 W.L.R. 20. *Green v De Havilland* (1968) 112 S.J. 766, to the contrary, cannot be relied on. Cf. the rule in false imprisonment, para.4–19, above. If, when the principles of malicious prosecution were being laid down, the courts had been acquainted with the idea, now familiar, of a judge himself determining a disputed question of fact, the whole question of reasonable and probable cause would have been left to the judge, but it is now too late to achieve this result without legislation: *Glinski v McIver,* above, fn.55, at 778 per Lord Devlin.

[61] [1938] A.C. 305 at 316 per Lord Atkin.

[62] (1878) 8 Q.B.D. 167 at 171, affirmed (1882) 46 L.T. 130.

[63] *A v New South Wales* [2007] HCA 10, 233 A.L.R. 584 at [58]. *Glinski v McIver* [1962] A.C. 726 at 768 per Lord Devlin; *Abbott v Refuge Assurance Co* [1962] 1 Q.B. 432 at 453 per Upjohn L.J.

If the prosecutor knew, or, rather, thought he knew, certain facts, it matters not that those facts turn out to be false.

> "The defendant can claim to be judged not on the real facts but on those which he honestly, and however erroneously, believes; if he acts honestly upon fiction, he can claim to be judged on that."[64]

The judge's concern is essentially with the objective aspect of the question—whether there was reasonable and probable cause in fact—but the overall question is a double one, both objective and subjective: did the prosecutor actually believe and did he reasonably believe that he had cause for prosecution?[65] Not only must there be reasonable and probable cause in fact, but:

> "[I]t would be quite outrageous if, where a party is proved to believe that a charge is unfounded, it were to be held that he could have reasonable and probable cause",[66]

and the prosecutor himself must also honestly believe that he has reasonable and probable cause. His belief is a matter for the jury, not the judge, to determine, but the burden of proving lack of honest belief is on the claimant[67] and the question should only be put to the jury:

> "[I]n the highly unlikely even that there is cogent positive evidence that, despite the actual existence of reasonable and probable cause, the defendant himself did not believe that it existed".[68]

In principle the fact that the prosecutor has received advice should be regarded as no more than one of the facts to be taken into account, for if the prosecutor did not himself have an honest belief in the case he put forward it is irrelevant that he received advice

---

[64] *Glinski v McIver* [1962] A.C. 726 at 776 per Lord Devlin.

[65] [1962] A.C. 726 at 768 per Lord Devlin; *Abbott v Refuge Assurance Co* [1962] 1 Q.B. 432 at 453 per Upjohn L.J.

[66] *Haddrick v Heslop* (1848) 12 Q.B. 268 at 274 per Lord Denman C.J.; *Broad v Ham* (1839) 8 Scott 40 at 50 per Erskine J.

[67] On requests for further information (formerly further and better particulars or interrogatories) see *Stapley v Annetts* [1970] 1 W.L.R. 20 and *Gibbs v Rea* [1998] A.C. 786 at 794.

[68] *Dallison v Caffery* [1965] 1 Q.B. 348 at 372 per Diplock L.J., at 368 per Lord Denning M.R.; *Glinski v McIver* [1962] A.C. 726 at 743–744 per Viscount Simonds, at 745 per Lord Radcliffe, at 768 per Lord Devlin. For a disagreement as to the inference to be drawn in a case where the defendant elected to call no evidence see *Gibbs v Rea* [1998] A.C. 768 (maliciously procuring a search warrant).

before doing so.[69] In practice, however, if the prosecutor believes in the facts of the case and is advised by competent counsel before whom the facts are fairly laid that a prosecution is justified, it will be exceedingly difficult to establish lack of reasonable and probable cause.[70] An opinion of counsel favourable to the prosecutor is not conclusive, but it is a potent factor to be taken into account when deciding whether to prosecute.[71]

However, in considering all this it must be borne in mind that **19–9** *Hicks v Faulkner* was a private prosecution and in *Herniman v Smith* the prosecution was initiated by an information sworn by the defendant. To require such an "honest belief" in guilt, while perhaps still an apt test for the private prosecutor or an informant who is treated as a prosecutor, would be unrealistic if applied to a member of the CPS taking a decision on the basis of evidence placed before him by the police. It is the function of the court and jury at the criminal trial to determine the accused's guilt; the function of the prosecutor is to apply his professional judgement to the evidence before him and determine whether, as Dixon J. once put it, "the probability of the accused's guilt is such that upon general grounds of justice a charge against him is warranted".[72] He has not even:

"[G]ot to test the full strength of the defence; he is concerned only with the question of whether there is a case fit to be tried."[73]

Indeed, if the public prosecutor personally harboured serious doubts about the guilt of the accused even though the evidence was strong enough to warrant a charge, it could be said that to desist from prosecuting would be a breach of his duty as a minister of justice.[74]

---

[69] *Glinski v McIver*, above, fn.68, at 756–757 per Lord Radcliffe, at 777 per Lord Devlin.

[70] *Abbott v Refuge Assurance Co Ltd* [1962] 1 Q.B. 432, where Davies L.J. dissented on the facts. See also *Ravenga v Macintosh* (1824) 2 B. & C. 693 at 697 per Bayley J.; *Glinski v McIver*, above, fn.68, at 744–745 per Viscount Simonds. A similar result will follow where a private citizen is advised by the police that the facts which he has reported constitute a particular offence: *Malz v Rosen* [1966] 1 W.L.R. 1008. It is respectfully submitted, however, that Diplock L.J. overstates the strength of the defendant's position in such a case: at 1013.

[71] *Abbott v Refuge Assurance Co Ltd*, above, fn.70, at 450 per Ormerod L.J.

[72] *Commonwealth Life Assurance Society Ltd v Brain* (1935) 53 C.L.R. 343, at 382.

[73] Lord Devlin in *Glinski v McIver* [1962] A.C. 726 at 766; *Coudrat v Revenue and Customs Commissioners* [2005] EWCA Civ 616; [2005] S.T.C. 1006 at [41]. Of course, matters other than the strength of the evidence may be relevant to the overall decision of whether a prosecution would be in the public interest.

[74] In the Canadian context the *Report of the Attorney General's Advisory Committee on Charge Screening, Disclosure, and Resolution Discussions* (1993) remarked at 71: "Crown counsel need not and ought not to be substituting his or her own views for those of the trial judge or jury, who are the community's decision makers. It cannot be forgotten that much of the public's confidence in the administration of justice is attributable to the trial court process that ensures that justice is not only done, but is seen to be done . . . Granting Crown counsel the power to initiate or discontinue prosecutions based on a

The private prosecutor has no basis for making a charge in which he does not believe; the same cannot be said for a public prosecutor. It has therefore been persuasively argued that in such a case this third stage should be regarded as a purely objective one.[75]

19–10   If there are several charges in the indictment, the rule as to reasonable and probable cause applies to all of them,[76] but where there is reasonable and probable cause for a prosecution on a lesser charge than that actually preferred, a question of degree may arise:

> "Where there is a charge of theft of 20s. and reasonable and probable cause is shown as regards 19s. of it, it may well be that the prosecutor, when sued for malicious prosecution, is entitled to succeed, because he was in substance justified in making the charge, even though he did so maliciously. But the contrary must surely be the case if the figures are reversed and reasonable and probable cause is shown as to 1s. only out of the 20s."[77]

19–11   **iv. Malice.** Judicial attempts to define malice have not been completely successful. "Some other motive than a desire to bring to justice a person whom he [the accuser] honestly believes to be guilty"[78] seems to overlook the fact that motives are often mixed. Moreover, anger is not malice, indeed it is one of the motives on which the law relies in order to secure the prosecution of criminals,[79] and yet anger is much more akin to revenge than to any desire to uphold the law. Perhaps we are nearer the mark if we suggest that malice exists where the predominant purpose of the accuser is something other than the vindication of the law.[80] The

---

subjective assessment of whether or not the accused is guilty would, in some circumstances, be tantamount to replacing these open, impartial, and community-based processes with the unexplained, unreviewable decisions of prosecutorial officials who have no direct accountability to the public."

[75] *Miazga v Kvello* [2009] SCC 51; [2009] 3 S.C.R. 339.

[76] *Reed v Taylor* (1812) 4 Taunt. 616; cf. *Johnstone v Sutton* (1786) 1 T.R. 510.

[77] *Leibo v Buckman Ltd* [1952] 2 All E.R. 1057 at 1071 per Jenkins L.J., at 1073 per Hodson L.J. Cf. the dissenting judgment of Denning L.J. at 1066–1067.

[78] Cave J. in *Brown v Hawkes* [1891] 2 Q.B. 718 at 723; *Glinski v McIver* [1962] A.C. 726 at 766 per Lord Devlin.

[79] [1891] 2 Q.B. 722, but if the prosecutor's anger is aroused, not by his belief in the claimant's guilt but by some extraneous conduct of the claimant, then there may be evidence of malice: *Glinski v McIver* [1962] A.C. 726 (claimant gave evidence for X on a criminal charge which the defendant, a police officer, believed to be perjured, and X was acquitted. If this was the reason for the claimant's prosecution on a charge of fraud, the prosecutor would have been malicious). See too *Heath v Heape* (1856) 1 H. & N. 478.

[80] *Stevens v Midland Counties Ry* (1854) 10 Ex. 352 at 356 per Alderson B. "Not only spite or ill-will but also improper motive": *Gibbs v Rea* [1998] A.C. at 797. A rare example of such an improper purpose in the case of a professional prosecutor is *Proulx v Québec (Attorney General)* 2001 SCC 66; [2001] 3 S.C.R. 9.

question of its existence is one for the jury[81] and the burden of proving it is on the claimant.[82]

At one time malice was not always kept distinct from lack of reasonable and probable cause,[83] but a cogent reason for separating them is that, however spiteful an accusation may be, the personal feelings of the accuser are really irrelevant to its probable truth. The probability or improbability of X having stolen my purse remains the same however much I dislike X, and it has long been law that malice and lack of reasonable and probable cause must be separately proved. Want of reasonable and probable cause may be evidence of malice in cases where it is such that the jury may come to the conclusion that there was no honest belief in the accusation made.[84] If there was such an honest belief, the claimant must establish malice by some independent evidence, for malicious motives may co-exist with a genuine belief in the guilt of the accused.[85] For the reasons explained above, however, it seems again necessary to draw a distinction between private and professional prosecutors, the question of "honest belief" being arguably irrelevant to the latter. If it is correct that lack of reasonable cause can only be established against the latter by showing that there were no objective grounds for the proceedings then to allow malice to be inferred from lack of cause would entail the risk that it would be established by proof of negligence.[86] In all cases, however, if want of reasonable and probable cause is not proved by the claimant, the defect is not supplied by evidence of malice.[87] "From the most express malice, the want of probable cause cannot be implied."[88]

2. MALICIOUS PROCESS

For malicious prosecution the defendant must have "prosecuted", **19–12** but there may also be liability if the defendant has maliciously and without reasonable and probable cause instituted some process short of actual prosecution, of which the most important example is the procuring of a warrant for the claimant's arrest. In *Roy v Prior*[89] the defendant, a solicitor, was acting for the defence of a man charged

---

[81] *Mitchell v Jenkins* (1833) 5 B. & Ad. 588; *Hicks v Faulkner* (1878) 8 Q.B.D. 167 at 175 per Hawkins J.
[82] *Abrath v NE Ry* (1886) 11 App. Cas. 247.
[83] Winfield, *Present Law*, at p.189.
[84] *Brown v Hawkes* [1891] 2 Q.B. 718 at 722 per Cave J.; *Hicks v Faulkner* (1878) 8 Q.B.D. 167 at 175 per Hawkins J.; *Gibbs v Rea* [1998] A.C. at 798.
[85] *Brown v Hawkes*, above, fn.84, at 726 per Lord Esher.
[86] *Miazga v Kvello* [2009] SCC 51; [2009] 3 S.C.R. 339.
[87] *Turner v Ambler* (1847) 10 Q.B.D. 252; *Glinski v McIver*, above, fn.79.
[88] *Johnstone v Sutton* (1786) 1 T.R. 510 at 545; *Glinski v McIver*, above, fn.79, at 744 per Viscount Simonds.
[89] [1971] A.C. 470.

with a criminal offence. The claimant was a doctor who had attended the accused and the defendant issued a witness summons requiring him to be present to give evidence at the trial. According to the claimant, this summons was never served on him, but in any case he was not present at the trial and, on the defendant's instructions, the accused's counsel applied for a warrant for his arrest. In support of the application the defendant himself gave evidence to the effect that the claimant had been evading service of the summons. As a result the warrant was issued and the claimant was arrested at 1am and kept in custody until 10.30am on the same day, when he was brought before the court. The House of Lords held that if the claimant could prove that the defendant had acted maliciously and without reasonable and probable cause, as he alleged, then he was entitled to succeed.[90] On similar principles a person is also liable for procuring the issue of a search warrant.[91] In that context the European Court of Human Rights has held that to confine liability to cases where there is malice is an insufficient protection of a person's rights under art.8 of the Convention because it prevents the courts examining issues of proportionality and reasonableness.[92] Whether that has any implications for the basic tort of malicious prosecution remains to be seen.[93]

3. MALICIOUS CIVIL PROCEEDINGS

19–13 Historically, there was no reason why the old action upon the case for conspiracy should not be extended to malicious civil proceedings as well as to malicious criminal proceedings,[94] and it was in fact held to apply (inter alia) to malicious procurement of excommunication by an ecclesiastical court,[95] to bringing a second writ of *fi. fa.*

---

[90] It matters not that the arrest was procured in the course of civil rather than criminal proceedings, though arrest on civil process is now exceptional. See, e.g. *Daniels v Fielding* (1846) 16 M. & W. 200; *Melia v Neate* (1863) 3 F. & F. 757. The point decided by the House of Lords in *Roy v Prior*, above, fn.89, was that the immunity from suit of a witness in respect of his evidence does not protect him from an action for maliciously procuring the issue of a warrant of arrest. The claimant is not suing on or in respect of the evidence. He is suing because he alleges that the defendant procured his arrest by means of judicial process which the defendant instituted both maliciously and without reasonable and probable cause: [1971] A.C. 470 at 477 per Lord Morris. See also *Surzur Overseas Ltd v Koros* [1999] 2 Lloyd's Rep. 611 (freezing injunction).

[91] *Gibbs v Rea* [1998] A.C. 786; *Reynolds v MPC* [1985] Q.B. 881; *Keegan v CC Merseyside* [2003] EWCA Civ 936; [2003] 1 WLR 2187.

[92] *Keegan v UK* Application No.28867/03 (2007) 44 E.H.R.R. 83.

[93] Cf. *Hill v Hamilton-Wentworth Regional Police Services Board* [2007] SCC 41; [2007] 3 S.C.R. 129, para.19–1, above.

[94] Winfield, *Present Law*, pp.199, 202.

[95] *Hocking v Matthews* (1670) 1 Vent. 86; *Gray v Dight* (1677) 2 Show. 144.

against a man when one had already been obtained[96] and to malicious arrest of a ship.[97] In more modern times it has been laid down that it is available whenever the civil proceedings attack a person's credit in scandalous fashion, for example, malicious bankruptcy proceedings against him, or malicious winding-up proceedings against a company.[98] The same requisites must be satisfied as for malicious prosecution.[99]

However, does the law go still farther and make the malicious institution of any civil proceedings[100] actionable? The matter has never formally been decided but the general opinion has been that it does not, and this has gained considerable strength by being repeated in the House of Lords in *Gregory v Portsmouth CC.*[101] No doubt this stance has something to do with a wish to have finality in litigation but a reason commonly given has been the absence of legal damage in the great majority of cases. As Bowen L.J. put it in *Quartz Hill Gold Mining Co v Eyre*[102]:

"[T]he bringing of an ordinary action does not as a natural and necessary consequence involve any injury to a man's property, for this reason, that the only costs which the law recognises . . . are the costs properly incurred in the action itself. For these the successful defendant has already been compensated."

Now this is, of course, simply untrue, for the assessed costs may not amount to the total costs of the defence,[103] and it is noteworthy that any deficiency in costs awarded to the accused in a criminal case

---

[96] *Waterer v Freeman* (1617) Hob. 205 at 266.

[97] *The Walter D. Wallet* [1893] P. 202.

[98] *Quartz Hill Gold Mining Co v Eyre* (1883) 11 Q.B.D. 674 at 683, 689; *Brown v Chapman* (1762) 1 W.Bl. 427. For a modern example, where, however, the claimant failed, see *Beechey v William Hill* [1956] C.L.Y. 5442. See also *Little v The Law Institute* [1990] V.R. 257 (proceedings to stop a solicitor practising).

[99] Thus in a claim for malicious bankruptcy there is no cause of action (and hence time does not run) until the adjudication is annulled: *Radivojevic v L.R. Industries Ltd*, Unreported, May 14, 1982, CA; *Tibbs v Islington BC* [2002] EWCA Civ 1682; [2003] B.P.I.R. 743.

[100] i.e. beyond the limited range of situations outlined above.

[101] [2000] 1 A.C. 419. See also *Metall und Rohstoff A.G. v Donaldson Lufkin & Jenrette Inc* [1990] 1 Q.B. 391; *Johnson v Emerson* (1871) L.R. 6 Ex. 329 at 372; *Quartz Hill Gold Mining Co v Eyre* (1883) 11 Q.B.D. 674 at 684.

[102] (1883) 11 Q.B.D. 674 at 690.

[103] That "taxed" costs (the former expression) will equal actual costs is recognised as a fiction by Devlin L.J. in *Berry v BTC* [1962] 1 Q.B. 306 at 323 and by Clarke J.A. in *Hanrahan v Ainsworth* (1990) 22 N.S.W.L.R. 73 at 113. There is no reason to believe that the position is any different under the CPR. No doubt the fact that the proceedings are brought maliciously would be a ground for awarding costs on an indemnity basis but in the suit itself the successful claimant may have limited opportunity to prove this. In the United States the provision for recovery of costs in civil litigation is generally a good deal more restricted and this is a major reason for the more extensive liability for malicious civil proceedings there. See *Restatement* 2d, §§674–675; but a substantial minority of courts require some "special harm" going beyond the costs and reputational harm from the suit: see Dobbs, *Torts* (2000) §437.

does amount to damage.[104] Further, the argument does not explain why an action will not lie in respect of a civil action which blemishes the claimant's character, such as one based on fraud. In modern conditions it is not always true that the suit will receive less publicity than a criminal charge and it will not do to say that the claimant's reputation will be cleared by his successful defence of the action,[105] for exactly the same may be said of the successful defence of a criminal charge. Furthermore, the protection afforded by other torts such as defamation, malicious falsehood or conspiracy is limited by the fact that the immunity cast around the giving and preparation of evidence in criminal cases also attaches to civil litigation,[106] so that unless there is something like the fabrication of physical evidence[107] there will be no remedy. However, the legislature has intervened in outrageous cases, for litigious monomaniacs may be muzzled under s.42 of the Senior Courts Act 1981.[108] The case for extending malicious prosecution to disciplinary proceedings is weaker and what *Gregory* decided as a matter of precedent is that this step should not be taken.[109] In such cases there is no absolute immunity and the law of defamation and malicious falsehood[110] will come into play if malice can be proved.[111]

4. ABUSE OF PROCESS

19–14 Aside from liability for malicious civil proceedings the law also recognises a related tort sometimes called "abuse of process". This lies where a legal process, not itself without foundation, is used for an improper, collateral purpose, for example as an instrument of extortion in a matter not connected with the suit.[112] It is then:

---

[104] *Berry v BTC* [1962] 1 Q.B. 306.
[105] *Quartz Hill Gold Mining Co v Eyre*, above, fn.101 per Bowen L.J. It might be argued that the position of the civil defendant is rather like that of the criminal defendant in the heyday of the private prosecution when the law of malicious prosecution was formed, whereas now the control of the prosecution process by the state provides at least some degree of check on false accusations.
[106] [2000] 1 A.C. at 432; *Surzur Overseas Ltd v Koros* [1999] 2 Lloyd's Rep. 611. Para.12–41, above.
[107] See *Darker v CC West Midlands* [2001] A.C. 435.
[108] Formerly known as the Supreme Court Act. The legislation, which originated in the Vexatious Actions Act 1896, was needed, for in *Chaffers, Re* (1897) 45 W.R. 365 a person had within five years brought 48 civil actions against the Speaker of the House of Commons, the Archbishop of Canterbury, the Lord Chancellor and others; 47 of them were unsuccessful. See also CPR 3.11.
[109] The case concerned disciplinary action taken by a local authority against a councillor.
[110] Also, in a suitable case, misfeasance in a public office.
[111] Yet it is only defamation which provides damages for loss of reputation as such.
[112] *Grainger v Hill* (1838) 4 Bing. N.C. 212; *Speed Seal Products Ltd v Paddington* [1985] 1 W.L.R. 1327. See Preface.

"[M]erely a stalking horse to coerce the defendant in some way entirely outside the ambit of the legal claim upon which the court is asked to adjudicate".[113]

The original case is *Grainger v Hill*[114] where the claimant, having been sued for debt, was arrested on a *capias ad respondendum* obtained by the defendant with the purpose of getting the claimant to surrender the ship's register of the *Nimble*, which was mortgaged to the defendant. The claimant surrendered the register to escape arrest and lost trade as a result of not having the register. The claimant's action succeeded even though the original proceedings for debt had not been terminated. The cases have involved the abuse of ancillary process in suits already in progress (such as the arrest in *Grainger v Hill*) but there seems no reason why the same rule should not apply to the initiation[115] of the original proceedings as a similar instrument of extortion.[116] However, this is by no means the same thing as a general tort of malicious issue or use of civil proceedings. If a person presents a claim for damages in the knowledge that it is completely unfounded he is amenable to penalties for perjury[117] and perhaps to heavy costs but he does not commit the tort of abuse of process because he is using the law, albeit corruptly, for its assigned purpose, namely to recover damages against the defendant in that suit. The position is the same even if the defendant has some further purpose which will be achieved or assisted by success in the suit, for his object is still to succeed in the litigation. So if D were to launch a prosecution against C, a rival for political office, in order to procure a conviction which would disqualify C from the office[118] that would be no more abuse of process than it would be for, say, a rich man to launch a civil action against a poor man with the object of ruining him because the rich man had been worsted in love by the poor man. In neither of these cases is there any element of extorting any advantage or concession from the other party. Furthermore, the tort may be committed even where the claim is in fact well founded,

---

[113] *Varawa v Howard Smith Co* (1911) 13 C.L.R. 35 at 91 per Isaacs J.

[114] Above, fn.112.

[115] Not the threat of proceedings: *Pitman Training Ltd v Nominee UK* [1997] F.S.R. 797. Sed quaere, in view of the logic behind the cause of action.

[116] This seems to be accepted by Clark J.A. in *Hanrahan v Ainsworth* (1990) 22 N.S.W.L.R. 73 at 112 (a judgment which contains an extensive review of the law in this area) and see *Q.I.W. Retailers Ltd v Felview Pty Ltd* [1989] 2 Qd. R. 245. In fact, the *capias* in *Grainger v Hill*, though technically *mesne* process, was the first formal step in the suit, the original writ of debt having disappeared from the process before 1829: see the account by Priestley J.A. in *Spautz v Gibbs* (1990) 21 N.S.W.L.R. 230 at 271–275.

[117] Not to a civil action by his opponent in respect of the perjury: *Hargreaves v Bretherton* [1959] 1 Q.B. 45. Cf. *United Telecasters Sydney Ltd v Hardy* (1991) 23 N.S.W.L.R. 323.

[118] The example given by the majority of the HCA in *Williams v Spautz* (1992) 174 C.L.R. 509.

for a valid claim may be used as an instrument of extortion just as much as an invalid one.[119] The debt in *Grainger v Hill* seems not to have been due so the whole proceedings were fundamentally flawed but the validity of the claim was not in issue and there is no indication that the court regarded it as significant.[120] This is why it is irrelevant in this tort, unlike malicious prosecution, that the proceedings have not been terminated in the claimant's favour. The issue is not whether the principal suit is well founded and there is therefore no risk of infringing the principle that the court seized of an issue should be the one to decide it[121] nor of getting inconsistent results. It seems clear in principle that it is not enough that the defendant issues proceedings in the hope of getting the illegitimate advantage, there must be some overt act demonstrating that improper purpose, as for example a demand on the claimant. It is the abuse of the process to effect the improper purpose that is the gist of the tort.[122]

A related point, but one that goes well beyond the law of torts, is that the court may stay an action as an abuse of process where the claimant is using the process to obtain a collateral advantage in the above sense. The existence of such a power has been asserted on a number of occasions,[123] though it will probably be rarely exercised because the defendant's purpose is likely to be disputed.[124] Nowadays, however, abuse of process is used in a broader sense as a result of the fact that part of the overriding objective of the Civil Procedure Rules is to deal with cases in ways which are proportionate to the importance of the issues and the amounts involved. A claimant may find that what is technically a perfectly good claim that he seriously intends to pursue to judgment is dismissed as an abuse of process because in the court's view the "game is not worth the candle", something particularly prominent in defamation proceedings.[125]

---

[119] Just as a blackmailer threatens what he has a perfect "right" to do, namely expose his victim; but Fleming, *Torts*, 9th edn, p.688 points out that there can hardly be an abuse of process when the holder of a valid claim uses it to gain a settlement on terms more advantageous than a judgment could impose. Note that in *Grainger v Hill* the defendant had something to be said on his side: he had heard rumours that the claimant was a smuggler and was no doubt afraid of losing his security.

[120] See also *Rajski v Bainton* (1990) 22 N.S.W.L.R. 125 at 131.

[121] "No one shall be allowed to allege of a still depending suit that it is unjust": *Gilding v Eyre* (1861) 10 C.B.N.S. 592 at 604.

[122] *Hanrahan v Ainsworth*, above, fn.116, at 120 per Clark J.A; but cf. Dobbs, *Torts* (2000) §438. The point is likely to be of significance in practice on the issue of whether the pleading states a cause of action.

[123] See *Goldsmith v Sperrings* [1977] 1 W.L.R. 478; *Lonrho Plc v Fayed (No.5)* [1993] 1 W.L.R. 1489; *Broxton v McLelland* [1995] E.M.L.R. 485; *Williams v Spautz* (1992) 174 C.L.R. 509.

[124] It was exercised in *Williams v Spautz*, above, fn.123, against a party who had commenced over 30 sets of proceedings in 11 years arising out of one issue.

[125] See para.12–5, above.

5. MAINTENANCE AND CHAMPERTY[126]

Maintenance means the improper stirring up of litigation by giving **19–15** aid to one party to bring or defend a claim without just cause or excuse,[127] while champerty is the particular form of maintenance which exists when the person maintaining the litigation is to be rewarded out of its proceeds. At common law a person guilty of either committed both a crime and a tort, but in modern times the defences became so numerous and the reasons for imposing liability so outdated that the law ceased to serve any useful purpose. As crimes and as torts, maintenance and champerty have now been abolished,[128] but a champertous agreement is still void.[129] Where A supports B's action against C and C wins that action, the court has power to order A to pay C's costs,[130] but C cannot recover those costs as damages in a separate action, for example for conspiracy.[131] In modern times the principal practical importance of champerty has been to invalidate contingency fee arrangements in litigation. Section 58 of the Courts and Legal Services Act 1990 gives recognition to arrangements for conditional fees but apart from the Act, an arrangement between a solicitor and client for the payment of fees only if the client wins the case is still against public policy, even if the payment is not to exceed his ordinary profit costs and disbursements.[132]

---

[126] For the history and former law, see Winfield, *History of Conspiracy and Abuse of Legal Procedure*, pp.131–160, *Present Law*, pp.1–116 ; Bodkin, *Maintenance and Champerty*, and the 8th edn of this work, pp.585–592.

[127] *Trepca Mines Ltd (No.2), Re* [1963] Ch. 199 at 219 per Lord Denning M.R.

[128] Criminal Law Act 1967 ss.13(1)(a), 14(1).

[129] Criminal Law Act 1967 s.14(2). As to assignment of tort claims, see para.26–27, below. Not all arrangements for payment out of the proceeds of litigation are champertous: *Giles v Thompson* [1994] 1 A.C. 142.

[130] *Lonrho Plc v Fayed (No.5)* [1993] 1 W.L.R. 1489; *Hamilton v Fayed*, July 13, 2001, QBD.

[131] *Lonrho Plc v Fayed (No.5)*, above, fn.130. It would not, however, be true to say that costs can never be recovered as damages: e.g. a buyer of goods may recover against the seller unrecovered costs in litigation with a sub-buyer.

[132] *Awwad v Geraghty & Co* [2001] Q.B. 570, disapproving *Thai Trading Co v Taylor* [1998] Q.B. 781.

CHAPTER 20

VICARIOUS LIABILITY[1]

1. The Nature and Basis of Vicarious Liability

THE expression "vicarious liability" signifies the liability which D **20–1**
may incur to C for damage caused to C by the negligence or other
tort of A. The fact that D is liable does not, of course,[2] insulate A
from liability,[3] though in most cases[4] it is unlikely that he will be

---

[1] Atiyah, *Vicarious Liability in the Law of Torts*.
[2] We have tended to regard this as obvious, if somewhat theoretical. However, it is not so
in the case of Federal employees in the United States, nor can the employer recover an
indemnity (as to which, see para.20–18 below) from the Federal servant. In France the
Cour de cassation has held, following the rule of public law, that an employee does not
incur personal liability for negligence committed within the limits of the task which has
been assigned to him: A.P., 25.02.2000, J.C.P. 2000, II, 10295.
[3] *Standard Chartered Bank v Pakistan National Shipping Corp* [2002] UKHL 43; [2003] 1
A.C. 949, para.24–23, below; but statute may provide differently. Thus in New South
Wales only the Crown and not the individual officer, is liable for torts by the police: Law
Reform (Vicarious Liability) Act 1983 (NSW) s. 9B(2).
[4] See *Merrett v Babb* [2001] Q.B. 1174 (where the employer was insolvent) and *Shapland
v Palmer* [1999] 1 W.L.R. 2068.

sued or that judgment will be enforced against him. It is not necessary for vicarious liability to arise that D shall have participated in
any way in the commission of the tort nor that a duty owed in law
by D to C shall have been broken. What is required is that D should
stand in a particular relationship to A and that A's tort should be
referable in a certain manner to that relationship. D's liability is
truly strict, though for it to arise in a case of negligence, there has
to be fault on the part of A.[5] The commonest instance of this in
modern law is the liability of an employer for the torts of his
servants done in the course of their employment. The relationship
required is the specific one, that arising under a contract of service,
and the tort must be referable to that relationship in the sense that it
must have been committed by the servant in the course of his
employment. It is with this instance of vicarious liability that the
first part of this chapter is concerned, but there are other instances
which cannot be followed in detail in a work of this kind. Such are
the liability of partners for each other's torts and, perhaps, the
liability of a principal for the torts of his agent.[6] Although the great
majority of the cases involve common law torts, the principle of
vicarious liability is a general one which will be applied to statutory
wrongs sounding in damages unless the statute indicates the contrary, expressly or by implication.[7]

The traditional terminology used to describe the relationship
under a contract of service was "master and servant". The phrase is
now anachronistic.[8] On the other hand, there are difficulties in
finding suitable alternatives for terms of art.[9] In this chapter a
compromise position is adopted. "Master" has generally[10] been
replaced by "employer"; but "servant" has generally been retained:
it is still in use in ordinary speech in relation to some types of

---

[5] One finds occasional traces of an alternative theory, that the employer is in breach of his
own duty via the act of the servant: *Twine v Bean's Express* (1946) 175 L.T. 131; *Broom
v Morgan* [1953] 1 Q.B. 597; but this approach has now been "firmly discarded":
Majrowski v Guy's and St Thomas's NHS Trust [2006] UKHL 34; [2007] 1 A.C. 224 at
[15]. There are, however, echoes of the "employer's tort" theory in the reasoning of Lord
Hobhouse in *Lister v Hesley Hall Ltd* [2001] UKHL 22; [2002] 1 A.C. 215 in the context
of employers who enter into a voluntary relationship with others (for example schools and
pupils, occupiers and visitors). The general view requires that the servant be personally
liable to the claimant. Hence in *Commonwealth v Griffiths* [2007] NSWCA 370 the
servant's witness immunity availed the employer.

[6] Atiyah, *Vicarious Liability in the Law of Torts*, pp.99–115. See also para.20–19, below.

[7] *Majrowski v Guy's and St Thomas's NHS Trust,* above, fn.5 (Protection from Harassment
Act 1997), but had there not been a clear indication in the Scots provisions that there was
to be vicarious liability (and the law could hardly be different north and south of the
border) a number of members of the HL would have inclined to the view that the particular
statutory context impliedly excluded it.

[8] *Mahmud v B.C.C.I.* [1998] A.C. 20 at 45.

[9] "Employer" and "worker" are the most commonly used terms in employment
legislation.

[10] Except where the historical context justified it and, of course, in quotations.

employment, it is etymologically connected with the core idea of the contract of service and it is still in widespread legal use.[11]

It is important that we should not confuse vicarious liability with the primary liability of D for damage caused to C by the act of A. This arises where D is in breach of his own duty to C, for example where D is at fault in selecting A for the task or allowing him to continue in employment or where D has not given adequate consideration to a safe system of work: many of the cases concern the liability of an employer for injury caused to one of his servants by a fellow servant.[12] The fact that there is no vicarious liability does not necessarily mean that there is no breach of the personal duty.[13] Another category of case is rather more difficult to classify. Sometimes, even though D is not in fact guilty of any negligence, he is said to be liable because the negligence of A, to whom he has entrusted a task, puts D in breach of a "non-delegable duty". This does not mean that D commits any wrong by delegating the performance of the task to an apparently competent person, nor that he is an insurer of the safe completion of the task, but simply that he stands answerable for the fault of that person in carrying it out. Such duties arise for example, where an employer is held liable for damage caused by the act of an independent contractor, for the general rule is that there is no vicarious liability for independent contractors. However, unlike the case of employer and servant, nothing in particular turns on the precise relationship between the employer and the contractor for what is said to matter is the duty owed by the employer to the claimant. It is not very clear why we are reluctant simply to say that there is a vicarious liability in these cases, for that seems to be the practical effect.[14] To say, as we commonly do, that there is a duty "to ensure that care is taken" hardly distinguishes the case from ordinary vicarious liability: although the person who is under the non-delegable duty need not be personally at fault, there must be fault in the person to whom the

---

[11] e.g. in contracts. "Servant or agent" is a time-honoured apposition.

[12] See para.8–9, above. For examples outside this area see *Nahhas v Pier House Management (Cheyne Walk) Ltd* (1984) 270 E.G. 328 (failure to inquire into background of porter) though there was also a true vicarious liability on the facts; *Hartwell v Att Gen* [2004] UKPC 12; [2004] 1 W.L.R. 1273 (personal fault but no vicarious liability); *Colour Quest Ltd v Total Downstream UK Plc* [2009] EWHC 540 (Comm); [2009] 1 Lloyds Rep 1 (failure to design safe system as well as vicarious liability); *Maga v Birmingham Archdiocese* [2010] EWCA Civ 256 (also a true vicarious liability). As *Maga* shows, the "personal" breach of duty by D to C may arise from D's vicarious liability for the failure of X, another employee of D, to carry out his duties.

[13] *Maga*, above, fn.12, at [74].

[14] In *NSW v Lepore* [2003] HCA 4; 212 C.L.R. 511. Gummow and Hayne JJ. at [257] describe it as a "species of vicarious liability"; and see *Leichhardt Municipal Council v Montgomery* [2007] HCA 6; 233 A.L.R. 200 at [155]. Now by statute it is equated with vicarious liability in a number of Australian states, see, e.g. Civil Liability Act 2002 s.5Q (NSW).

task is delegated.[15] In the law of contract, on the other hand, if D promises to do something for C it is generally, and always subject to the construction of the contract,[16] no answer for D in a claim by C to say that the failure of performance was brought about by the act of D's agent, A, and such an assumption of personal responsibility may exist in some cases of tort; but there is no general rule and the assumption must be determined from the circumstances of the case.[17]

20–2   The shape of the modern law is recognisable by the middle of the 19th century. At one time liability seems only to have arisen if the employer had expressly commanded the wrong, which is not a true vicarious liability at all, for one who orders a wrong to be committed is, in the modern law, a direct participant in the tort and an employment relationship is, as such, unnecessary.[18] At the beginning of the 18th century it was accepted that the employer was liable not only for acts done at his express command but also for those done by his implied command, this to be inferred from the general authority he had given his servant in his employment. By the end of the 18th century, however, the idea began to grow up that some special importance attached to the relationship of master and servant as such, something more than the fact that it might supply evidence of implied authority, and by the middle of the next century it was finally accepted that the existence of that relationship was necessary for vicarious liability[19] and sufficient to make the employer liable, provided the act was done in the course of the employment. At the

---

[15] It is true that the vicarious liability of D generally requires that the claimant show that A, the actor, would be personally liable to him and this is not necessarily so where D's personal duty is in issue. Thus there may be cases in which the claimant can establish a breach of D's duty by showing that although the actual wrongdoer cannot be identified, someone in D's organisation must have blundered (see para.8–9, above), but where the identity of the wrongdoer is known, there still seems no practical difference between the non-delegable duty and the vicarious liability.

[16] e.g. at common law in the case of provision of a package holiday it may be a very difficult question how far the tour operator is responsible for defaults of hoteliers and carriers. For an example of a case where it was held at common law that the tour operator was undertaking to supply services rather than merely acting as agent to effect contracts with others, see *Wong v Kwan Kin Travel Services* [1996] 1 W.L.R. 39. However, under the Package Travel, Package Holidays and Package Tours Regulations 1992 (SI 1992/3288) (implementing EC Directive 90/314) the "organiser" of the package is, subject to certain exceptions, liable to the customer for, "the proper performance of the obligations under the contract, irrespective of whether such obligations are to be performed by [the organiser] or by other suppliers of services": but the question will still remain of what are the "obligations under the contract" and it is an oversimplification to say that the regulations necessarily impose a "strict liability" upon the organiser: see *Hone v Going Places Leisure Travel Ltd* [2001] EWCA Civ 947.

[17] See *Esso Petroleum Co Ltd v Hall Russell & Co Ltd* [1988] 3 W.L.R. 730 at 759 per Lord Jauncey. Cf. *Rogers v Night Riders* [1983] R.T.R. 324 (approved in *Wong v Kwan Kin Travel*, above, fn.16) and *Aiken v Stewart Wrightson Members Agency Ltd* [1995] 1 W.L.R. 1281. See para.20–21, below.

[18] See para.21–2, below.

[19] *Reedie v London and North Western Ry* (1849) 4 Exch. 244.

same time the phrase "implied authority" which had been the cornerstone of the master's primary liability gives way gradually to the modern "scope of employment", though the former phrase survives in the context of misrepresentation.

Vicarious liability is a frequent feature of legal systems and those which do not have in its "pure" form, but which in theory require some fault in the employer, have tended to go to considerable lengths to create a liability without fault in practice.[20] Nevertheless, given the fact that most of tort law is formally based on fault, it requires some explanation or justification. The traditional phrases *respondeat superior* and *qui facit per alium facit per se* have been criticised, the former because it, "merely states the rule baldly in two words, and the latter merely gives a fictional explanation of it."[21] However, even if they are not explanations, they probably do represent the expression of a rather deep-seated and intuitive idea that someone who, generally for his own benefit, sets a force in motion should have responsibility for the consequences even if he chooses others to carry out the task. Of course this logically leads on to a full-blown theory of enterprise liability under which an activity should bear its own costs.[22] This is not the law now because there must be some tort and that generally involves fault, but the present position is a compromise, perhaps because pure enterprise liability removes incentives from the victim to take care to avoid accidents. At any rate, if there were no vicarious liability, the employer's incentive to minimise the risks created by his activity would be reduced. Many years ago it was observed that the employer has the deeper pocket[23] and if there were no vicarious liability much of tort law would be stultified, for it would be impracticable (and wasteful) for many employees to insure themselves against liability incurred in employment. A variant of this, though in a more sophisticated form, is that of "loss distribution". An "employer" today is normally not an individual but a substantial enterprise or undertaking, and, by placing liability on the enterprise, what is in fact achieved is the distribution of losses caused in the conduct of its business over all the customers to whom it sells its services or products. Knowing of its potential liability for the torts of its servants, the enterprise insures against this liability and the cost of this insurance is reflected in the price it charges to its customers. In the result, therefore, losses caused by the torts of the enterprise's servants are borne in small and

---

[20] See for example German law, where §831 B.G.B. makes the employer liable unless he shows that he exercised due care in choosing and supervising the servant. No such exculpation is possible in contract under §278 B.G.B. Hence the courts have tended to extend contractual liability.

[21] *Staveley Iron and Chemical Co Ltd v Jones* [1956] A.C. 627 at 643 per Lord Reid.

[22] See Keating, "The Idea of Fairness in the Law of Enterprise Liability" (1997) 95 Mich. L.R. 1266.

[23] *Limpus v L.G.O. Co* (1862) 1 H. & C. 526 at 539 per Willes J.

probably unnoticeable amounts by the body of its customers, and the injured person is compensated without the necessity of calling upon an individual, whose personal fault may be slight or even non-existent, to suffer the disastrous financial consequences that may follow liability in tort. Like many things in the law, the institution is probably to be explained not by reference to any single reason but by the cumulation of several. It is inconceivable that a serious proposal for the abolition of vicarious liability will be made so long as the law of tort as we know it remains alive. Indeed, the trend towards "privatisation" of activities formerly carried on by an organisation's internal, integrated work force and the increasing use of casual and part-time workers[24] may require modification of the present distinction between servants and independent contractors.

2. THE CONTRACT OF SERVICE RELATIONSHIP

20–3 Since vicarious liability generally arises from a contract of service ("servant") but not from a contract for services ("independent contractor") it is necessary to determine the indicia of a contract of service. At the outset it should be noted that this task has to be performed for purposes totally unconnected with vicarious liability[25] and most of the modern cases have arisen in these other contexts. However, it seems to be assumed that the question "who is a servant?" should receive the same answer almost regardless of the context in which it is asked,[26] which is now giving rise to difficulty. Changes in employment practices (for example, the increasing casualisation of the workforce and the growing numbers of "home workers") may produce a situation in which, for employment protection purposes, it becomes difficult to continue to regard people as servants who would once routinely have been such. However, without suggesting for a moment that an employer should

[24] See below.
[25] e.g. the liability of an employer to pay national insurance contributions is generally dependent on the existence of a contract of service and certain duties under industrial safety legislation operate only in favour of "persons employed". For most purposes (including vicarious liability) a contract of apprenticeship is equated with a contract of service.
[26] See Atiyah, *Vicarious Liability in the Law of Torts*, pp.32–33. *Calder v H. Kitson Vickers & Sons (Engineers) Ltd* [1988] I.C.R. 232 at 254. In *Jones v BBC*, June 22, 2007, QBD, there are references to a person being a servant, "for the purposes of health and safety". No doubt the first defendants may have assumed responsibility to the freelance claimant, but that cannot be deployed in support of the vicarious liability which was imposed in respect of freelance defendant R. Of course it does not follow that because, say, the Inland Revenue has decided to treat the claimant as self-employed for tax purposes that the court is precluded from finding that he is a servant. In any event there may be a specific statutory provision applicable only to one context. For example, casual workers are treated as employed for tax purposes but this does not necessarily mean that they are always servants for the purposes of vicarious liability.

always be vicariously liable for the torts of his independent contractors (a course which would be impracticable and probably economically inefficient) it is questionable whether a tort claimant should necessarily be affected by internal changes in the employer's employment structure[27] which have nothing to do with the nature of his activities or the risk presented by them.[28] It is perfectly sensible to say that if Company D has its goods delivered to customers by a carrier, Company A, responsibility for accidents caused in the distribution process should fall on Company A alone, for that is a specialist function which is not "characteristic" of D's business (however necessary it may be to enable that business to function) and it is reasonable to expect that Company A will make proper liability insurance provisions against that risk[29]; it by no means follows that the same result should follow, to take the facts of one Australian case, where D sets up a "bicycle courier" business and engages a number of individuals to carry out deliveries for him.[30] However, short of statutory intervention, the "central conception" of distinguishing between contractors and servants is, "now too deeply rooted to be pulled out".[31]

It may be thought that the starting point in the inquiry about the nature of the relationship should be to ask whether the parties themselves have expressly assigned it to one category or the other, but such a declaration can in fact never be conclusive as to the legal classification of the relationship, though it is one factor to be taken into account by the court.[32] Thus a building worker who rendered services on the express oral understanding that he was a "labour only sub-contractor"[33] was nonetheless held to be a party to a

---

[27] Or in the case of state activities, privatisation: *Quaquah v Group 4 Securities Ltd (No.2)*, *The Times*, June 27, 2001.

[28] See Kidner, "Vicarious Liability: For Whom Should the Employer be Liable" (1995) 15 L.S. 47, instancing *O'Kelly v Trusthouse Forte* [1984] Q.B. 90 and McKendrick, "Vicarious Liability and Independent Contractors—a Re-examination" (1990) 53 M.L.R. 770.

[29] If only because such insurance is required by law.

[30] The majority of the HCA, reversing the NSWCA, held that the couriers were servants in *Hollis v Vabu Pty Ltd* [2001] HCA 44; 207 C.L.R. 21. The defendant had made deductions from fees for liability insurance, but this only covered him.

[31] *Sweeney v Boylan Nominees Pty Ltd* [2006] HCA 19; 226 C.L.R. 161 at [33].

[32] *Ferguson v John Dawson & Partners (Contractors) Ltd* [1976] 1 W.L.R. 1213; *Ready Mixed Concrete (South East) Ltd v Minister of Pensions and National Insurance* [1968] 2 Q.B. 497; *Global Plant Ltd v Secretary of State for Social Services* [1972] 1 Q.B. 139; *Davis v New England College at Arundel* [1977] I.C.R. 6; *Young & Woods Ltd v West* [1980] I.R.L.R. 201; *Calder v H. Kitson Vickers Ltd* [1988] I.C.R. 232; *Johnson v Coventry Churchill International Ltd* [1992] 3 All E.R. 14; *Lane v Shire Roofing Co* [1995] I.R.L.R. 493. Megaw L.J. in the *Ferguson* case at 1222 would have been prepared to go further and say that the parties' declaration ought to be wholly disregarded. There may of course be an issue of whether the parties intended any contractual relationship at all: *New Testament Church of God v Stewart* [2007] EWCA Civ 1004; [2008] I.C.R. 282.

[33] This practice, known as "the lump", grew up mainly to avoid payment of income tax under the PAYE system. Tax legislation now attempts to meet the point by special provisions for the building trade.

contract of service for the purposes of the Construction (Working Places) Regulations 1966 since the remainder of the contractual relationship was indistinguishable from that prevailing between employer and servant.[34] Although it has been held that where the nature of the relationship turns solely on the interpretation of documents the question is one of law,[35] it has been said repeatedly that in the generality of cases the decision is one with which an appellate court will not interfere unless the lower tribunal has misdirected itself or come to a conclusion which is plainly insupportable.[36]

20–4 At one time it was generally accepted that the test of the relationship of master and servant was that of control,[37] and a contract of service was thought to be one by virtue of which the employer, "can not only order or require what is to be done, but how it shall be done".[38] The control test probably retains a good deal of importance in cases to which it can be applied,[39] but in modern conditions the notion that an employer has the right to control the manner of work of all his servants, save perhaps in the most attenuated form,[40] contains more of fiction than of fact. It is clearly the law that such professionally trained persons as the master of a ship, the captain of an aircraft and the house surgeon at a hospital are all servants for whose torts their employers are responsible, and it is unrealistic to suppose that a theoretical right in an employer, who is likely as not to be a corporate and not a natural person, to control how any skilled worker does his job, can have much substance.[41] It has, therefore,

---

[34] *Ferguson v Johan Dawson*, above, fn.32; cf. Lawton L.J., dissenting, at 1226: "I can see no reason why in law a man cannot sell his labour without becoming another man's servant even though he is willing to accept control as to how, when and where he will work." In *Massey v Crown Life Insurance Co* [1978] 1 W.L.R. 676, Lawton L.J. thought that the case was distinguishable from *Ferguson* because there was a written contract with detailed terms. Lord Denning M.R. was content to say that *Ferguson* "turned on its facts".

[35] *Davies v Presbyterian Church* [1986] 1 W.L.R. 323.

[36] See, e.g. *O'Kelly v Trusthouse Forte* [1984] Q.B. 90; *Lee v Cheung* [1990] 2 A.C. 374; *Kapfunde v Abbey National* [1999] I.C.R. 1.

[37] For an early statement of the control test, see *Yewens v Noakes* (1880) 6 Q.B.D. 530 at 532–533 per Bramwell B. For its development see Atiyah, *Vicarious Liability in the Law of Tort*, pp.40–44.

[38] *Collins v Hertfordshire CC* [1947] K.B. 598 at 615 per Hilbery J.

[39] *Argent v Minister of Social Security* [1968] 1 W.L.R. 1749 at 1759 per Roskill L.J.; *Jennings v Forestry Commission* [2008] EWCA Civ 581; [2008] I.C.R. 988.

[40] Although it has been said that, "what matters is lawful authority to command so far as there is scope for it. And there must always be some room for it only in incidental or collateral matters" (*Zuijs v Wirth Brothers Pty Ltd* (1955) 93 C.L.R. 561 at 571) if this is pressed too far the independent contractor who works with others could hardly exist. As the Special Commissioner said in *Hall v Lorimer* 1992 S.T.C. 599: "in the production of a play you must pay attention to the stage directions and the producer's directions. That applies to the leading actor and actress, but they do not for that reason become 'employees'."

[41] Kahn-Freund, "Servants and Independent Contractors" (1951) 14 M.L.R. 504. On ministers of religion and the distinction between employment and spiritual matters see *Percy v Church of Scotland* [2005] UKHL 73; [2006] 2 A.C. 28.

now been recognised that the absence of such control is not conclusive against the existence of a contract of service[42] and various
attempts to find a more suitable test have been made.

In an often cited statement[43] Lord Thankerton said that there are   **20–5**
four indicia of a contract of service: (1) the employer's power of
selection of his servant; (2) the payment of wages or other remuneration; (3) the employer's right to control the method of doing the
work; and (4) the employer's right of suspension or dismissal. It is
respectfully suggested, however, that this does not carry the matter
much further: the first and last, and perhaps also the second, are
indicia rather of the existence of a contract than of the particular
kind of contract which is a contract of service,[44] and some judges
have preferred to leave the question in very general terms. Somervell L.J. thought that one could not get beyond the question whether
the contract was, "a contract of service within the meaning which an
ordinary person would give under those words".[45] Nowadays it is
common to take a "composite" approach in which the various
elements of the relationship are considered as a whole. The Privy
Council said[46] that the matter had never been better put than by
Cook J. in *Market Investigations Ltd v Minister of Social
Security*[47]:

> "The most that can be said is that control will no doubt always
> have to be considered, although it can no longer be regarded as
> the sole determining factor; and that factors which may be of
> importance are such matters as whether the man performing the
> services provides his own equipment, whether he hires his own
> helpers, what degree of financial risk he takes,[48] what degree of
> responsibility for investment and management he has, and

---

[42] *Morren v Swinton and Pendelbury Borough Council* [1965] 1 W.L.R. 576; *Whittaker v
Minister of Pensions and National Insurance* [1967] 1 Q.B. 156; *Ready Mixed Concrete
(South East) Ltd v Minister of Pensions and National Insurance* [1968] 2 Q.B. 497; *Market
Investigations Ltd v Minister of Social Security* [1969] 2 Q.B. 173. Nor is it conclusive
who has control over hours of work: compare *W.H.P.T. Housing Association Ltd v
Secretary of State for Social Services* [1981] I.C.R. 737 and *Nethermere (St Neots) Ltd v
Taverna* [1984] I.C.R. 122.

[43] *Short v J.&W. Henderson Ltd* (1946) 62 T.L.R. 427 at 429.

[44] *Ready Mixed Concrete (South East) Ltd v Minister of Pensions and National Insurance*
[1968] 2 Q.B. 497 at 524 per MacKenna J

[45] *Cassidy v Ministry of Health* [1951] 2 K.B. 343 at 352–353; *Argent v Minister of Social
Security* [1968] 1 W.L.R. 1749 at 1760 per Roskill J.

[46] *Lee v Cheung* [1990] 2 A.C. 374. See also *671122 Ontario Ltd v Sagaz Industries Canada
Ltd* [2001] SCC 59; [2001] 2 S.C.R. 483.

[47] [1969] 2 Q.B. 173 at 185. See also the judgment of MacKenna J. in *Ready Mixed Concrete
(South East) Ltd v Minister of Pensions and National Insurance* [1968] 2 Q.B. 497.

[48] An independent contractor will commonly be paid "by the job" whereas a servant will
generally receive remuneration based upon time worked; but a piece-worker will still be
a servant and a building contract is a contract for services notwithstanding that it may
contain provisions for payment by time.

whether and how far he has an opportunity of profiting from sound management in the performance of his task."[49]

On this basis in *Lee v Cheung*, although the claimant worked for a number of persons the picture that emerged was:

> "[O]f a skilled artisan earning his living by working for more than one employer as an employee and not as a small businessman entering into business on his own account with all its attendant risks."[50]

Denning L.J. once said that:

> "[O]ne feature which seems to run through the instances is that, under a contract of service, a man is employed as part of a business, and his work is done as an integral part of the business whereas under a contract for services, his work, although done for the business, is not integrated into it but is only accessory to it."[51]

Employment protection cases have emphasised that there must be "mutuality" in the contractual arrangement, i.e. an obligation on the employer to provide work and on the other party to perform it when required,[52] but here is perhaps the point at which we are compelled to take into account the context in which the issue arises. In the employment cases the issue will normally be whether there was a contract of service with a degree of continuity, but in the context of vicarious liability the question is whether A is working as D's servant at the time when he injures C. It would certainly be odd if, for example, A did work for D in circumstances where A was subject to direct orders and close control over his manner of work and yet D was not liable for A's acts simply because A had the right to decline work when it suited him to do so.[53] It is perfectly possible

---

[49] Nowadays factors like performance-related pay, commission and bonuses tend to blur the distinction in this respect.

[50] The case concerned a Hong Kong workmen's compensation ordinance which recognised "casual workers" but it is thought the reasoning is applicable to vicarious liability.

[51] *Stevenson, Jordan and Harrison Ltd v Macdonald and Evans* [1952] 1 T.L.R. 101 at 111. His Lordship gave as examples: a ship's master, a chauffeur and a staff reporter are servants but a ship's pilot, a taxi driver and a newspaper contributor are independent contractors. The Pilotage Act 1987 s.16, makes the pilot the servant of the shipowner for the purposes of damage to third parties, but he is not the servant of the port authority for the purposes of damage to the piloted ship: *The Cavendish* [1993] 2 Lloyd's Rep. 292.

[52] *Carmichael v National Power Plc* [1999] 1 W.L.R. 2042; *Stevedoring and Haulage Services Ltd v Fuller* [2001] I.R.L.R. 62.

[53] Similar problems have arisen in an employment protection context in the case of persons who are engaged by an employment agency as purportedly self-employed and then "contracted out" for short-term tasks. See *Dacas v Brook Street Bureau (UK) Ltd* [2004] EWCA Civ 217; [2004] I.C.R. 1437; *James v Greenwich LBC* [2008] EWCA Civ 35; [2008] I.C.R. 545.

to say that, while there is no ongoing relationship between D and A amounting to a contract of service, A is D's servant, at least for the purposes of vicarious liability, while he is actually working.[54] After all, as *Lee v Cheung* shows, it is perfectly possible for a person to be a servant on a casual basis for a number of employers. A factor which, however, is likely to point away from a contract of service is the fact that the person engaged is not required to perform personally but may delegate to others if he chooses.[55]

A. Hospitals

It was to a substantial extent a consequence of developments in the liability of hospitals for the negligence of their staffs that dissatisfaction with the test of control developed, for while it was originally held that a hospital authority could not be liable for negligence in matters involving the exercise of professional skills,[56] this view has not been accepted since 1942. Since then it has been held that radiographers,[57] house-surgeons,[58] whole time-assistant medical officers[59] and, probably, staff anaesthetists are the servants of the authority for the purposes of vicarious liability.[60] In fact, the arrangements for the payment of damages in clinical negligence cases operate on the basis that the net of responsibility is cast wider than it might in fact be under the common law, covering for example staff working for the NHS under contracts for services, locum staff and students.[61] Until 1990 the cost of paying judgments and settlements in hospital cases was shared under an arrangement between health authorities and the medical protection societies. They are now paid entirely by the National Health Service Litigation Authority under "NHS Indemnity", which operates a pooling system known as the Clinical Negligence Scheme for Trusts and no recovery will be sought from individuals. However, in some of the cases there has been a tendency to treat the question of a hospital authority's liability not as one of vicarious liability only but also as one of the primary liability of the authority for breach of its own duty to the

20–6

---

[54] See *Muscat v Cable & Wireless Plc* [2006] EWCA Civ 220 at [27].
[55] *Express and Echo Publications Ltd v Tanton* [1999] IRLR 367; cf. *McFarlane v Glasgow CC* [2001] I.R.L.R. 7.
[56] *Hillyer v St Bartholomew's Hospital* [1909] 2 K.B. 820. Note that the hospital in this case was a charitable body.
[57] *Gold v Essex CC* [1942] 2 K.B. 293.
[58] *Collins v Hertfordshire CC* [1947] K.B. 598; *Cassidy v Ministry of Health* [1951] 2 K.B. 343.
[59] *Cassidy v Ministry of Health*, above, fn.58.
[60] *Roe v Minister of Health* [1954] 2 Q.B. 66.
[61] *NHS Indemnity, Arrangements for Clinical Negligence Claims in the NHS.*

patient.[62] However, while this may save the court the task of determining whether the negligent individual is a servant of the hospital authority it will not relieve the claimant of the burden of showing negligence. In most cases his complaint will be that Dr A was negligent in his treatment and if this is so then (assuming Dr A to be a servant) to say that the hospital authority was in breach of its duty via him is to state a proposition the practical effect of which is the same as saying that it is vicariously liable for his negligence. If, however, he is not negligent (because, for example, he is given a task which is beyond the competence of a doctor holding a post of his seniority) then there is still a possibility that the hospital authority is negligent in failing to secure adequate staffing.[63] Alternatively, if A is at fault but is not a servant it may well be the case now that, having accepted responsibility for treatment, the hospital owes a non-delegable duty to ensure that proper care is taken.[64] However, while this applies to treatment it does not apply to the delegation of the testing of samples where the claimant has been referred to the hospital by a third party.[65] Modern developments in the organisation of health care may produce more complex problems. For example, a public health agency may send a patient into the private sector or even abroad for treatment. Of course the actual provider of the treatment may incur liability for any damage resulting therefrom,[66] but what is the position of the Health Trust that "sends" the patient? In *A v Ministry of Defence*[67] the Ministry ceased to provide direct hospital care for British forces in Germany and their families and entered into an arrangement whereby an English NHS Trust was to procure it from local hospitals. When the claimant suffered brain damage at birth the Court of Appeal held that the Ministry was not liable[68] for the fault of the doctor in the German hospital. It was the

---

[62] See, e.g. *Gold v Essex CC*, above, fn.57, at 301 per Lord Greene M.R. *Cassidy v Ministry of Health*, above, fn.58, at 362–365 per Denning L.J.; but even on this basis one must distinguish the case which may arise in the private sector where the patient makes direct arrangements with the surgeon and the hospital merely provides facilities: *Ellis v Wallsend District Hospital* (1989) 17 N.S.W.L.R. 555.

[63] See *Wilsher v Essex Area Health Authority* [1987] Q.B. 730 where both Glidewell L.J. and Browne-Wilkinson V.C. accepted that there might be a direct liability in the hospital authority but differed as to the measure to be applied to the individual doctor's conduct. Yet a claim that staffing is inadequate may face a formidable obstacle in the court's refusal to interfere with the authority's discretion over the allocation of resources: *Ball v Wirral HA* (2003) 73 B.M.L.R. 31.

[64] *X v Bedfordshire CC* [1995] 2 A.C. 633 at 740; *A v MoD* [2004] EWCA Civ 641; [2005] Q.B. 183 at [63]; and see *Farraj v Kings Healthcare NHS Trust* [2009] EWCA Civ 1203 at [88].

[65] *Farraj v Kings Healthcare NHS Trust,* above, fn.64.

[66] Which, in the case of treatment abroad, may involve conflict of laws issues.

[67] Above, fn.64.

[68] The trial judge had held that the English NHS Trust was not liable and there was no appeal on this. There was no doubt that the claimant would be able to recover against the German hospital in the German courts and that the damages would be at least at the English level.

case that the Ministry was bound to take care to ensure that proper facilities were available in Germany but no non-delegable duty making it liable for individual acts of negligence arose because it was not providing treatment itself. This case is not quite on all fours with the standard arrangement whereby a NHS Trust, having been approached by a patient in England procures treatment abroad and the decision is not perhaps decisive on that issue.[69] The suggestion in some cases that there may be liability for breach of statutory duty under the National Health Service Act 1977 (duty of the Secretary of State to secure effective health provision) must now be regarded as incorrect.[70] However, in many cases, although the patient will be treated in a facility run by a third party, the treatment will be administered by staff working under NHS contracts and there will be the normal NHS liability. Furthermore, independent sector providers of treatment can now benefit, via the Primary Care Trust which refers the patient, from the risk-pooling arrangements.[71]

B. Police

Until 1964 no person or body stood in the position of "master" to a police officer,[72] and accordingly anyone injured by the tortious conduct of the police could have redress only against the individual officers concerned. Now, however, it is provided by s.88 of the Police Act 1996, replacing earlier legislation, that the chief officer of police for any police area shall be liable for torts committed by constables[73] under his direction and control in the performance or purported performance of their functions.[74] This statutory liability is equated with the liability of an employer for the torts of his servants committed in the course of their employment, but the Act does not create a relationship of employer and servant, nor one of principal and agent.[75] The chief officer of police does not, of course, have to

20–7

---

[69] See *A v MoD*, above, fn.64, at [50]–[54].

[70] *A v MoD*, above, fn.64, at [42]. Although this was one basis of the decision in *M v Calderdale and Kirklees HA* [1998] 4 Lloyd's Rep. Med. 157, the defendants appear to have been negligent in failing to make checks on the private hospital in which they arranged the treatment.

[71] *Independent Treatment Centres and CNST* (2006).

[72] Under the Crown Proceedings Act 1947 the Crown is only liable in respect of persons who are paid wholly out of moneys provided by Parliament (s.2(6)) and this excludes the police. Nor are the police servants of the police authority: *Fisher v Oldham Corp* [1930] 2 K.B. 364. For practical purposes a police officer is treated as an employee for the purposes of duties owed to *him* by the chief constable: para.8–10, above. There is no difficulty about applying the general law of vicarious liability to members of the armed forces, though in practice what is regarded as the course of employment may extend beyond matters which are strictly in the course of duty in the military sense: *Radclyffe v MoD* [2009] EWCA Civ 635.

[73] The police authority, not the chief constable, is vicariously liable for police cadets: s.17(3); *Wiltshire Police Authority v Wynn* [1981] Q.B. 95.

[74] As amended by the Police Reform Act 2002. See para.20–14, below.

[75] *Farah v MPC* [1998] Q.B. 65.

956   Vicarious Liability

bear the damage personally. Any damages or costs awarded against
him are paid out of the police fund.[76]

C. Lending a Servant[77]

20–8   D may be the general employer of A but X, by agreement with D
(whether contractual or otherwise), may be making temporary use of
A's services.[78] If A injures some third party who bears the vicarious
liability for his acts? For long it was assumed that it must be one or
the other but it could not be both.[79] This proposition was probably
connected with the idea that there was an actual transfer of the
contract of employment but in reality this was never the case: an
employee cannot be transferred in this sense without his consent and
the "transfer" was simply a device to impose vicarious liability.[80]
The Court of Appeal rejected the proposition in *Viasystems (Tyneside) Ltd v Thermal Transfer (Northern) Ltd.*[81] Ducting was being
fitted by sub-contractor X, who was making use of "labour-only"
services provided by D. The negligence of A, an employee of D,
caused a flood, for which the court held that both X and D were
liable to the factory owner, with equal contribution between themselves under the Civil Liability (Contribution) Act 1978. It does not
follow that such dual vicarious liability will arise in every case. In
Viasystems A was part of a team consisting of his superior and
another skilled worker contracted to X: it was a situation of shared
control of the organisation of A's work. Where, on the other hand,
A's services are supplied to X on a long-term basis subject to the
entire control of X, that is likely to result in X alone being liable.[82]
Another situation is illustrated by *Mersey Docks and Harbour
Board v Coggins and Griffith (Liverpool) Ltd.*[83] D, the harbour
authority, employed A as the driver of a mobile crane, and let the

---

[76] The Police Act 1997 provides for vicarious liability of the Directors-General of the
National Criminal Intelligence Service and the National Crime Squad in respect of officers
under their control.

[77] A company will be vicariously liable for acts of its directors within the scope of their
authority (*NZ Guardian Trust Co Ltd v Brooks* [1995] 1 W.L.R. 96), but where company
A nominates its employee, B, as a director of company X it is not vicariously liable for B's
acts as director even if it allows B to carry out his duties in its time and, as a shareholder
in X, has an interest in B's proper performance of those duties: *Kuwait Asia Bank E.C. v
National Mutual Life Nominees Ltd* [1991] 1 A.C. 187.

[78] It is assumed that there is no dispute that a contract of service exists between A and D.

[79] *Esso Petroleum Co Ltd v Hall Russell & Co Ltd* [1989] A.C. 643 at 686.

[80] Denning L.J. in *Denham v Midland Employers Mutual Assurance Ltd* [1955] 2 Q.B. 437
at 443. In any event, where there is vicarious liability for an agent that may arise without
any contract of employment (see para.20–19, below) and if A is employed by D but X puts
forward A as speaking on his (X's) behalf, there is no reason why X should not be
vicariously liable even though for other purposes only D would be: *MAN Nutzfahrzeuge
AG v Freightliner Ltd* [2005] EWHC 2347 (Comm) at [107].

[81] [2005] EWCA Civ 1151; [2005] 4 All E.R. 1181.

[82] See e.g. *Hawley v Luminar Leisure Ltd* [2006] EWCA Civ 18.

[83] [1947] A.C. 1.

crane together with A as driver to X. The contract between D and X provided that A should be the servant of X but A was paid by D, and D alone had power to dismiss him. In the course of loading a ship C was injured by the negligent way in which A worked the crane. At the time of the accident X had the immediate direction and control of the operations to be executed by A and his crane, for example to pick up and move a piece of cargo, but he had no power to direct how A should work the crane and manipulate its controls. The House of Lords held that D as the general or permanent employer of A was liable to C.[84] At that time it was assumed that it was not possible for both D and X to be liable and this was not therefore argued. However, it is suggested in the *Viasystems* case that the result might still be the same and the sole liability would be in D[85]: A was on D's premises, operating D's crane and exercising his own skill and discretion in that task, even if he was subject to the direction of X as to what loads he should lift and where he should take them.[86] Even in such a case, of course, if X, though he has no authority to do so, expressly directs A to do the act which is negligently done and causes damage, X is generally liable with A as a joint tortfeasor; whether D is vicariously liable will depend on whether A's departure from instructions given by D takes him outside the course of his employment. Although more than one person may now be vicariously liable it seems that it is still true to say that as a starting point there is a presumption that D, the general employer, is liable and X is not.

As the *Mersey Docks* case shows, the fact that the contract between D and X provides that X is to be treated as the sole employer is not determinative of the question whether that is in fact so. However, a term in the contract may entitle D to an indemnity from X in respect of any damages D has to pay to C.[87]

By statute, owners of hackney carriages (including taxi cabs) are made responsible for the torts of the driver while he is plying for hire as if the relationship of master and servant existed between

[84] Both D and X being solvent, it was a matter of indifference to C which one was liable to him and he took no part in the appeal.
[85] [2005] EWCA Civ 1151; [2005] 4 All E.R. 1181 at [80] per Rix L.J. It is also suggested by May L.J. at [32] that *Bhoomidas v Port of Singapore* [1978] 1 All E.R. 956 would also go the same way and the stevedoring company alone would be liable.
[86] See also *Biffa Waste Services Ltd v Maschinenfabrik Ernst Hese GMBH* [2008] EWCA Civ 1257; [2009] Q.B. 725. Contrast *Airwork (NZ) Ltd v Vertical Flight Management Ltd* [1999] 1 N.Z.L.R. 641, NZCA, where the borrower had control over a highly skilled employee.
[87] *Herdman v Walker (Tooting) Ltd* [1956] 1 W.L.R. 209; *Spalding v Tarmac Civil Engineering Ltd* [1966] 1 W.L.R. 156. Because such a contract is not determinative of the question as against C it is not within the Unfair Contract Terms Act 1977 s.2—the allocation of indemnity rights between D and X is not an exclusion of liability: *Thompson v T. Lohan* [1987] 1 W.L.R. 649.

them even though it does not in fact exist,[88] but the tort must be committed in the course of the driver's employment (using the word "employment" in this fictitious sense).[89]

3. Scope of Employment

20–9 Unless the wrong done falls within the scope of the servant's employment the employer is not liable at common law. It may be asked: "How can any wrong be in the scope of a servant's employment? No sane or law-abiding employer ever hires someone to tell lies, give blows or act carelessly"; but that is not what scope of employment means. The focus is not so much on the wrong committed by the servant as upon the act he is doing when he commits the wrong. Traditionally it has been said that the act will be within the scope of the employment if it has been expressly or impliedly authorised by the employer[90] or is sufficiently connected with the employment that it can be regarded as an unauthorised manner of doing something which is authorised,[91] or is necessarily incidental to something which the servant is employed to do. The underlying idea is that the injury done by the servant must involve a risk sufficiently inherent in[92] or characteristic of[93] the employer's business that it is just to make him bear the loss. For example, no one would think of arguing that an employer of a lorry driver should be liable for an accident caused by the driver in his own car when on holiday. "Scope of employment" and "course of employment" tend to be used interchangeably, though the latter expression is often found in legislation dealing with other matters and it is dangerous to assume that authorities from such contexts can be automatically transferred to that of vicarious liability.[94] It may also be the case that statute imposes a liability for the acts of others in a particular context. Whatever form of words is used, the question under the statute is one of construction and it may lay down some wider (or narrower) principle than the common law.[95] It is often an extremely

[88] *Keen v Henry* [1894] 1 Q.B. 292; *Bygraves v Dicker* [1923] 2 K.B. 585; London Hackney Carriages Act 1843 and (outside London) Town Police Clauses Act 1847.
[89] *Venables v Smith* (1877) 2 Q.B.D. 279.
[90] If the act authorised is inherently wrongful (e.g. trespassing on another's land) the employer is liable because he has procured a wrong and there is no need to rely on vicarious liability.
[91] *Kirby v NCB* 1958 S.C. 514 at 533.
[92] *Lister v Hesley Hall Ltd* [2001] UKHL 22; [2002] 1 A.C. 215 at [65] per Lord Millett.
[93] *Ira S. Bushy & Sons Inc v USA* 398 F. 2d 167 (1968) per Judge Friendly.
[94] *Lister v Hesley Hall Ltd*, fn.92, at [40] per Lord Clyde.
[95] *Jones v Tower Boot Co Ltd* [1997] 2 All E.R. 406 (Race Relations Act 1976 but from another point of view the liability is narrower, for there is a "reasonable steps" defence). See also in another context *MacMillan v Wimpey Offshore Engineers & Constructors Ltd* 1991 S.L.T. 515.

difficult question to decide whether conduct is or is not within the scope of employment as thus defined, and, while it would not be correct to say that the question is one of fact (for it involves the application of legal principle to facts[96]) it is not one that lends itself to the imposition of mechanical or precise formulae.[97]

It is necessary that the acts done by the servant within the scope of his employment constitute an actionable wrong in themselves: it is not enough that the wrong is constituted by some acts done by him within and some outside that relationship or that the wrong partly consists of acts done within the scope of employment by the servant and other acts committed by a third party.[98]

The decided cases are not very amenable to any scientific classification and the issue tends to be "fact-sensitive"; the best that can be done is to select and illustrate a few of the more common factual situations to see if one can discern broad trends. A word of warning is also in order. In *Lister v Hesley Hall Ltd*[99] the House of Lords to some extent[100] restated the "test" for scope of employment in terms of whether the act was so closely connected with the employment that it would be just to hold the employer liable. The case concerned wilful wrongdoing of an extreme kind and was intended to extend the scope of liability but it cannot necessarily be confined to that situation[101] and, despite the fact that very soon afterwards in the same court the traditional formula was used and it was said that in this area previous authorities were particularly valuable,[102] some cases cited below which have gone against the claimant are at least open to argument, even if at the end of the day most of them would probably be decided in the same way.

A. Carelessness of Servant

By far the commonest kind of wrong which the servant commits **20–10** is one due to unlawful carelessness, whether it be negligence of the kind which is in itself a tort, or negligence which is a possible

---

[96] *Dubai Aluminium Co Ltd v Salaam* [2002] UKHL 48; [2003] 2 A.C. 366 at [24].

[97] See *Lister v Hesley Hall Ltd*, above, fn.92.

[98] *Credit Lyonnais Bank Nederland N.V. v E.C.G.D.* [2000] 1 A.C. 486.

[99] Above, fn.92.

[100] However, apart from Lord Steyn and Lord Hutton it is not easy to be sure of the view of the court as a whole on the traditional test. In fact Lord Clyde seems to regard it as a correct statement of the law, but cf. *Mattis v Pollock* [2003] EWCA Civ 787; [2003] 1 W.L.R. 2158 at [19] .

[101] The change of approach owes something to the Canadian case of *Bazley v Curry* [1999] 2 S.C.R. 534. However, it is said in *Sickel v Gordy* [2008] SKCA 100; 298 D.L.R. (4th) 151 that the court in that case had no intention to say anything about the straightforward case where the servant is carrying out instructions. For criticism of *Lister* see Hardiman J. in *O'Keefe v Hickey* [2008] IESC 72.

[102] *Dubai Aluminium Co Ltd v Salaam*, fn.96, at [26] at [30]. See also *HSBC Bank Plc v So* [2009] EWCA Civ 296.

ingredient in some other tort. It should be noted also that in some torts intention or negligence is immaterial: the doer is liable either way. In cases of this sort the employer may well be responsible for conduct of the servant to which no moral blame attaches[103]; but, assuming that the tort is negligence or that it is one in which inadvertence is a possible element in its commission, it may still be in the course of employment even if the servant is not acting strictly in the performance of his duty, provided he is not "on a frolic of his own".[104] Thus a first-aid attendant at a colliery was still within the course of his employment while cycling across his employer's premises to go to an office to collect his wages,[105] and so was a person sent to work at a place away from his employer's premises who drove some distance from his place of work to get a midday meal.[106] A number of cases are concerned with deviations by drivers from routes authorised by their employers. We have probably not advanced much beyond the test stated in the old case of *Storey v Ashton*,[107] that it is, "a question of degree how far the deviation could be considered a separate journey" divesting the employer of responsibility.[108] It is unlikely that all the cases are reconcilable but in modern conditions one has to take account not merely of the geographical or temporal divergence from instructions, but how far the servant can still be said to be carrying out the task he was set.[109] A servant travelling between home and work will not generally be in the course of employment[110] unless he is contractually required to use a particular mode of transport[111] or comes out "on call" in his employer's time to deal with emergencies.[112]

> "One must not confuse the duty to turn up for one's work with the concept of already being 'on duty' while travelling to work."[113]

---

[103] *Gregory v Piper* (1829) 9 B. & C. 591.

[104] This famous phrase was coined by Parke B. in *Joel v Morison* (1834) 6 C. & P. 501 at 503.

[105] *Staton v National Coal Board* [1957] 1 W.L.R. 893.

[106] *Harvey v R.G. O'Dell Ltd* [1958] 2 Q.B. 78; *Whatman v Pearson* (1868) L.R. 3 C.P. 422; cf. *Higbid v Hammett* (1932) 49 T.L.R. 104; *Crook v Derbyshire Stone Ltd* [1956] 1 W.L.R. 432; *Nottingham v Aldridge* [1971] 3 W.L.R. 1.

[107] (1869) L.R. 4 Q.B. 476. Contrast *Whatman v Pearson* (1868) L.R. 3 C.P. 422.

[108] *Hilton v Thomas Burton (Rhodes) Ltd* [1961] 1 W.L.R. 705.

[109] Thus in *A.&W. Hemphill Ltd v Williams* 1966 S.C. (H.L.) 31, the deviation was proportionately extensive but the servant was carrying passengers, some of whom had incited it. In *Angus v Glasgow Corp* 1977 S.L.T. 206 it is suggested that the real test is, "has the servant departed altogether from his master's business".

[110] *Smith v Stages* [1989] A.C. 928; but employment may commence as soon as the factory gates are passed: *Compton v McClure* [1975] I.C.R. 378.

[111] See *Nottingham v Aldridge* [1971] 2 Q.B. 739 at 747.

[112] *Blee v LNER Co* [1938] A.C. 126; *Paterson v Costain and Press (Overseas) Ltd* [1979] 2 Lloyd's Rep. 204; but as Lord Lowry admits in *Smith v Stages*, above, fn.110, at 956, the concept of the "employer's time" cannot be applied to salaried workers.

[113] *Smith v Stages*, above, fn.110, at 955 per Lord Lowry.

Where the employment is essentially peripatetic (for example, a travelling salesman or appliance repairer), travel from one location to another during the day will be within the course of employment[114] and the same will be true of the journey between home and the first location if the servant goes directly there rather than to his "base".[115] In these cases driving from place to place is an ordinary and necessary incident of performing the duties of the employment. This was not so in *Smith v Stages*[116] where the servants were normally employed at site A but were sent to perform an urgent job at site B over 200 miles away. Nevertheless they were held to be in the course of their employment in driving home from site B because they were paid wages (and not merely a travelling allowance) for doing so even though they were using a private vehicle[117] and had a discretion as to how and when they would travel.

In *Century Insurance Co Ltd v Northern Ireland Road Transport Board*,[118] the driver of a petrol lorry, employed by the defendants, while transferring petrol from the lorry to an underground tank in the claimant's garage, struck a match to light a cigarette and threw it on the floor and thereby caused a conflagration and an explosion which damaged the claimant's property. The defendants were held liable, for the careless act of their driver was done in the course of his employment. Lord Wright pointed out that the act of the driver in lighting his cigarette was done for his own comfort and convenience; it was in itself both innocent and harmless, but the act could not be treated in abstraction from the circumstances as a separate act; the negligence was to be found by considering the time when and the circumstances in which the match was struck and thrown down, and this made it a negligent method of conducting his work.

B. Mistake of Servant

So far we have been dealing with the incompetent dilettante and we now pass to the misguided enthusiast. *Bayley v Manchester, Sheffield and Lincolnshire Ry*[119] is an illustration. The defendant's **20–11**

---

[114] Yet the salesman is not in the course of his employment when he books into a hotel for the night.

[115] *Nancollas v Insurance Officer* [1985] 1 All E.R. 833 at 838 ("in driving to Aldershot [from home] Mr Nancollas was not going to work. That was part of his work").

[116] Above, fn.110.

[117] The case arose because the driver was uninsured and the time limits in the MIB Agreement had not been complied with.

[118] [1942] A.C. 509, approving *Jefferson v Derbyshire Farmers Ltd* [1921] 2 K.B. 281, where the facts were very similar, and for all practical purposes overruling *Williams v Jones* (1865) 3 H. & C. 602; cf. *Kirby v NCB* 1958 S.L.T. 47.

[119] (1873) L.R. 8 C.P. 148. See also Willes J. in (1873) L.R. 7 C.P. at 420.

porter violently pulled out of a train the claimant who said his destination was Macclesfield and who was in a train that was going there. The porter mistakenly thought it was going elsewhere. The defendants were held liable. The porter was doing in a blundering way something which he was authorised to do—to see that passengers were in the right trains and to do all in his power to promote their comfort. Another application of the same principle is an act done in protection of the employer's property. The servant has an implied authority to make reasonable efforts to protect and preserve it in an emergency which endangers it. For wrongful, because mistaken, acts done within the scope of that authority the employer is liable, and it is a question of degree whether there has been an excess of the authority so great as to put the act outside the scope of authority. A carter, who suspected on mistaken but reasonable grounds that a boy was pilfering sugar from the wagon of the carter's employer, struck the boy on the back of the neck with his hand. The boy fell and a wheel of the wagon went over his foot. The employer was held liable because the blow given by the carter, although somewhat excessive, was not sufficiently so to make it outside the scope of employment.[120] However, while a servant's authority to protect his employer's goods against armed robbery extends to acts done in self-defence against the robber it does not extend to using a customer as a human shield.[121] A servant has no implied authority to arrest a person whom he suspects of attempting to steal after the attempt has ceased, for the arrest is then made not for the protection of the employer's property but for the vindication of justice.[122]

The existence of an emergency gives no implied authority to a servant to delegate his duty to a stranger, so as to make his employer liable for the defaults of the stranger,[123] but it may be that the servant himself was negligent in the course of his employment in allowing the stranger to do his job. In *Ilkiw v Samuels*,[124] a lorry driver in the employment of the defendants permitted a stranger to drive his lorry, and an accident resulted from the stranger's negligent driving. The defendants were held liable, not for the stranger's

---

[120] *Polland v Parr & Sons* [1927] 1 K.B. 236; but it may be that after *Lister v Hesley Hall Ltd* [2001] UKHL 22; [2002] 1 A.C. 215 (para.20–14, below) even a grossly excessive reaction would not take the servant outside the course of his employment.

[121] *Reilly v Ryan* [1991] 2 I.R. 247.

[122] e.g. *Abrahams v Deakin* [1891] 1 Q.B. 516; *Hanson v Waller* [1901] 1 Q.B. 390; *Radley v LCC* (1913) 109 L.T. 162.

[123] *Houghton v Pilkington* [1912] 3 K.B. 308; *Gwilliam v Twist* [1895] 2 Q.B. 84. On the basis of the reasoning of Diplock L.J. in *Ilkiw v Samuels* [1963] 1 W.L.R. 991 at 1003–1006 it may be that these cases would be differently decided today.

[124] [1963] 1 W.L.R. 991; *Ricketts v Thomas Tilling Ltd* [1915] 1 K.B. 644.

negligence, for he was not their servant,[125] but on the ground that the driver himself had been guilty of negligence in the course of his employment in permitting the stranger to drive without even having inquired whether he was competent to do so.[126] Equally, the employer may sometimes be liable even though the servant has usurped the job of another, provided that what he does is sufficiently closely connected with his employer's business and is not too gross a departure from the kind of thing he is employed to do. In *Kay v I.T.W. Ltd,*[127] a storekeeper employed by the defendants needed to return a forklift truck to a warehouse but found his way blocked by a large lorry belonging to a third party. Although there was no urgency and without first inquiring of the driver of the lorry, he attempted to move the lorry himself, and by his negligence in doing so caused an injury to the claimant. The Court of Appeal considered that the case fell near the borderline, for it cannot be for every act, however excessive, that the servant may do in an attempt to serve his employer's interests that the employer is liable.[128] Nevertheless, taking into account the fact that it was clearly within the terms of the storekeeper's employment to move certain obstacles out of the way if they blocked the entrance to the warehouse, and since it was part of his normal employment to drive trucks and small vans, the court held that his act of trying to move the lorry was not so gross and extreme as to take it outside the course of his employment.

C. Wilful Wrong of Servant

Next, as to the servant's wilful wrongdoing.[129] Here two rules are settled.   **20–12**

In the first place the act done may still be in the course of employment even if it was expressly forbidden by the employer.[130]

---

[125] [1963] 1 W.L.R. 991 at 996 per Willmer L.J.

[126] See, however, the different and more complex reasoning of Diplock L.J. [1963] 1 W.L.R. 991 at 1003–1006, referred to by Lord Hobhouse in *Lister v Hesley Hall Ltd* [2001] UKHL 22; [2002] 1 A.C. 215 at [58].

[127] [1968] 1 Q.B. 140; *East v Beavis Transport Ltd* [1969] 1 Lloyd's Rep. 302. Cf. *Beard v London General Omnibus Co* [1900] 2 Q.B. 530 and see the explanation of that case by Sellers L.J.: [1968] 1 Q.B. 140 at 152.

[128] [1968] 1 Q.B. 140 at 151–152 per Sellers L.J. It is, however, odd that the employer may be vicariously liable for a fraud by the servant against the employer's interests, but not liable in some cases when he is seeking to forward those interests: *Iqbal v London Transport Executive* (1973) 16 K.I.R. 329 at 336 per Megaw L.J.

[129] Wilful horseplay may be outside the course of employment: *Duffy v Thanet DC* (1984) 134 N.L.J. 680; *Aldred v Nacano* [1987] I.R.L.R. 292; cf. *Harrison v Michelin Tyre Co* [1985] 1 All E.R. 918, doubted in *Aldred v Nacano*. As to the employer's personal duty in such cases, see para.8–11, above.

[130] *C.P.R. v Lockhart* [1942] A.C. 591 at 600 per Lord Thankerton; *Ilkiw v Samuels* [1963] 1 W.L.R. 991 at 998 per Willmer L.J.; *Stone v Taffe* [1974] 1 W.L.R. 1575.

The prohibition by the employer of an act or class of acts will only protect him from liability which he would otherwise incur if it actually restricts what it is the servant is employed to do[131]: the mere prohibition of a mode of performing the employment is of no avail.[132] It is a question of fact in each case whether the prohibition relates to the sphere of the employment or to the mode of performance, and:

> "[T]he matter must be looked at broadly, not dissecting the servant's task into its component activities . . . by asking: what was the job on which he was engaged for his employer?"[133]

In *Limpus v London General Omnibus Co*,[134] a driver of the defendants' omnibus had printed instructions not to race with, or obstruct, other omnibuses. In disobedience to this order he obstructed the claimant's omnibus and caused a collision which damaged it. The defendants were held liable because what he did was merely a wrongful, improper and unauthorised mode of doing an act which he was authorised to do, namely, to promote the defendants' passenger-carrying business in competition with their rivals.[135] Again, in *LCC v Cattermoles (Garages) Ltd*[136] a garage-hand was not allowed to drive vehicles, but it was part of his duty to move them by hand. His employers were held liable for his negligence while driving a vehicle. However, a fire engine crew engaging in a "go-slow" in support of a pay claim were held not to be acting in the course of their employment when they failed to arrive in time to put out a fire.[137] The question of prohibitions by the employer has given rise to particular difficulty where the servant has

---

[131] The servant is outside the course of employment while performing acts of precisely the character for which he is employed by the employer, if he is in fact working for someone else at the time: *Kooragang Investments Pty Ltd v Richardson & Wrench Ltd* [1982] A.C. 462.

[132] *Plumb v Cobden Flour Mills Ltd* [1914] A.C. 62 at 67 per Lord Dunedin; *C.P.R. v Lockhart*, above, fn.130, at 599 per Lord Thankerton; *LCC v Cattermoles (Garages) Ltd* [1953] 1 W.L.R. 997 at 1002 per Evershed M.R.; *Ilkiw v Samuels*, above, fn.130 per Diplock L.J. at 1004; *Kay v I.T.W. Ltd* [1968] 1 Q.B. 140 at 158 per Sellers L.J.

[133] *Ilkiw v Samuels*, above, fn.130, at 1004 per Diplock L.J.

[134] (1862) 1 H. & C. 526.

[135] "The law casts upon the master a liability for the act of his servant in the course of his employment and the law is not so futile as to allow a master, by giving secret instructions to his servant, to discharge himself from liability": (1862) 1 H. & C. 526 at 539 per Willes J.

[136] [1953] 1 W.L.R. 997. *Ilkiw v Samuels,* above, fn.130; cf. *Iqbal v London Transport Executive* (1973) 16 K.I.R. 329.

[137] *General Engineering Services Ltd v Kingston and St Andrew Corp* [1988] 3 All E.R. 867; but perhaps there is no duty to get there promptly at all: *Capital & Counties Plc v Hampshire CC* [1997] Q.B. 1004.

given a lift in the employer's vehicle to an unauthorised passenger.[138] As Lord Greene M.R. put it in *Twine v Bean's Express Ltd*,[139] giving a lift to an unauthorised passenger:

"[W]as not merely a wrongful mode of performing the act of the class this driver was employed to perform but was the performance of an act of a class which he was not employed to perform at all."

As always, however, this test is capable of producing divergent answers on the simplest facts and did so in *Rose v Plenty*.[140] A milkman had been warned by his employer not to allow children to assist him, nor to allow passengers on his float. In breach of these instructions he engaged the claimant, aged 13, to help him, and the claimant was injured, while a passenger on the float, by the milkman's negligent driving. To Lawton L.J. the situation was indistinguishable from that in *Twine v Bean's Express Ltd*, but the majority of the Court of Appeal, while accepting the correctness of the decision in *Twine*'s case, held that the milkman was acting in the course of his employment because the engagement of the claimant was made to further the employer's business[141]: the milkman was employed to deliver milk, which was precisely what he was doing when he caused the accident. This decision is certainly in accord with the long-standing tendency to apply a very broad description to "course of employment"[142] and it was approved by three judges in *Lister v Hesley Hall Ltd*,[143] but it is questionable whether it is so easily reconcilable with the earlier passenger cases as the majority of the court asserts.[144] It may also be asked in this context whether,

---

[138] One view is that this problem is now of little significance because of the compulsory insurance provisions of the Road Traffic Act 1988 regarding passengers (para.25–10, below): *Rose v Plenty* [1976] 1 W.L.R. 141 at 145 per Lord Denning M.R. However, with respect, it is far from clear that this is the case. In the cases where the employer has been held not liable the reason has not been any antecedent agreement or assumption of risk within s.149 of the Act but the fact that the servant was outside the course of his employment. In any case, similar problems could arise in situations where the Act of 1988 is inapplicable such as use of a vehicle off the road or other forms of transport.

[139] (1946) 62 T.L.R. 458; *Conway v George Wimpey & Co Ltd* [1951] 2 K.B. 266; cf. *Young v Edward Box & Co Ltd* [1951] 1 T.L.R. 789 (driver within scope of employment because foreman gave consent; foreman's consent unauthorised but within ostensible authority).

[140] [1976] 1 W.L.R. 141.

[141] A supposed "benefit" which he has made it very clear he does not want, presumably because his insurers have insisted upon the prohibition.

[142] See particularly *Ilkiw v Samuels* [1963] 1 W.L.R. 991 at 1004. *Stone v Taffe* [1974] 1 W.L.R. 1575 perhaps points the same way, though in that case the employer's prohibition related not to the original entry on to their property but to the duration of the stay.

[143] [2001] UKHL 22; [2002] 1 A.C. 215 (Lords Steyn, Clyde and Millett).

[144] Surely in *Twine* and *Conway* the servants were employed to drive the vehicles, in the course of which activity they injured the claimants?

assuming a prohibition to limit the scope of the servant's employment, the claimant's knowledge of the prohibition is of any significance. In principle, it is submitted that knowledge is not
necessary[145] but that in cases where the servant has ostensible
authority to invite persons into his employer's vehicle a passenger
should not be affected by any prohibition of which he is
unaware.[146]

Whatever the present status of the earlier decisions on unauthorised passengers, it remains clear that even if the servant is acting
outside the scope of his employment with regard to the passenger[147]
he may still be within it with regard to other road users.[148]

20–13 In the second place, it does not necessarily follow that the servant
is acting outside the scope of his employment because he intended
to benefit himself and not his employer. At one time it was generally
thought that this was so[149] but this view was displaced by *Lloyd v
Grace, Smith & Co.*[150] The defendants, a firm of solicitors,
employed a managing clerk who conducted their conveyancing
business without supervision. The claimant, a widow, owned some
cottages. She was dissatisfied with the money which they produced
and went to the defendants' office where she saw the clerk, who
induced her to give him instructions to sell the cottages and to
execute two documents which he falsely told her were necessary for
the sale but which in fact were a conveyance of the cottages to
himself. He then dishonestly disposed of the property for his own
benefit. The House of Lords unanimously held that they were

---

[145] See Asquith L.J. in *Conway v Wimpey*, above, fn.139, but this point in his judgment is
related to the issue of whether the claimant was a trespasser. Strictly, the issue of
knowledge was irrelevant in *Rose v Plenty* because of the majority decision that the
prohibition did not limit the scope of the employment but in view of the differences of
opinion one may assume that it would have been mentioned if it had been regarded as
possessing any significance.

[146] Cf. *Ferguson v Welsh* [1987] 1 W.L.R. 1553. Perhaps this is the reason for the decision in
Stone v Taffe, above, fn.142, that the claimant could succeed in the absence of evidence of
his knowledge of the prohibition. The Court of Appeal regarded the questions whether the
claimant was a visitor and the servant was acting within the scope of his employment as
one and the same thing.

[147] The servant, of course, remains personally liable to the passenger, but his liability is not
one which is required to be covered by insurance: *Lees v Motor Insurers' Bureau* [1952]
2 All E.R. 511.

[148] "In driving his van along a proper route he was acting within the scope of his employment
when he ran into the omnibus. The other thing he was doing simultaneously was something totally outside the scope of his employment, namely, giving a lift to a person who had
no right whatsoever to be there": *Twine v Bean's Express Ltd* [1946] 62 T.L.R. 458 at 459
per Lord Greene M.R. See also para.20–16, below.

[149] Based on *Barwick v English Joint Stock Bank* (1867) L.R. 2 Ex. 259.

[150] [1912] A.C. 716. See, too, *Uxbridge Permanent, etc. Society v Pickard* [1939] 2 K.B. 248;
British Ry, etc. Co Ltd v Roper (1940)) 162 L.T. 217; *United Africa Co v Saka Owoade*
[1955] A.C. 130; *Morris v C.W. Martin & Sons Ltd* [1966] 1 Q.B. 716. Cases such as
Century Insurance Co Ltd v Northern Ireland Road Transport Board [1942] A.C. 509,
para.20–10 above can also be regarded as involving acts done by the servant for his own
benefit.

liable[151]: the clerk was acting as the representative of the firm and they had invited the claimant to deal with him over her property. It cannot be said, however, that as a result of *Lloyd*'s case the question of benefit is invariably irrelevant, for it will still be found in some cases that it is the fact that the servant intended to benefit himself alone that prevents his tort from being in the course of his employment. This will be so, for example, in the case of a driver who takes his employer's vehicle "on a frolic of his own". It is because the journey was made solely for the driver's benefit that the employer is not liable to a person injured by the negligence of the driver.

It has been in the context of wilful wrongdoing that the approach **20–14** of asking whether the servant's acts were an improper mode of doing what he was employed to do has been perceived as giving rise to most difficulty. Many claims have been lodged against local authorities and other bodies in respect of abuse suffered by the claimants while they were children in care.[152] In *Lister v Hesley Hall Ltd*[153] the House of Lords held that the defendant children's home was vicariously liable for the acts of the warden in abusing the claimants: the home had undertaken the care of the children and entrusted the performance of that duty to the warden and there was therefore a sufficiently close connexion between his employment and the acts committed by him. There is a good deal of criticism of the "improper mode" approach and it is even described as "simplistic".[154] With respect this is harsh, for there seems no difficulty in accommodating the facts within the traditional test as it has been applied to matters like fraud or theft: just as the clerk's making off with Mrs Lloyd's money was an outrageous way of performing his duty to attend to her affairs, so also the conduct of the warden in indecently assaulting the children was an outrageous way of carrying out his duty to care for them. What is in fact surprising is the Court of Appeal's decision to the contrary in *Lister*.[155] Whatever view one takes on this issue, the fact remains that it may still be very difficult to determine the range of persons for whom the employer is

---

[151] Equally, the servant is personally liable for fraud even if his object is solely to benefit his employer: *Thomas Saunders Partnership v Harvey* (1990) 7 Tr.L.R. 78.

[152] This litigation phenomenon is not confined to England. See, e.g. *Bazley v Curry* [1999] 2 S.C.R. 534; *NSW v Lepore* [2003] HCA 4; 212 C.L.R. 511; Cane, "Vicarious Liability for Sexual Abuse" (2000) 116 L.Q.R. 21; Feldthusen, "Vicarious Liability for Sexual Torts" in *Torts Tomorrow: A Tribute to John Fleming* (1998).

[153] [2001] UKHL 22; [2002] 1 A.C. 215.

[154] By Lord Steyn at [20].

[155] Of course these cases present serious forensic problems: there seem to be thousands of them (170 in respect of one school in *Re St William's Group Litigation*, QBD, November 3, 2009), involving very large bills for local authorities and insurers; such claims tend to be presented many years after the events, e.g. 15 years in *Lister*; and the substance of the claims is for psychiatric trauma, which presents formidable problems of determining the truth. The distinction between the vicarious liability claim and that for breach of a direct personal duty in choosing and supervising staff had significance for limitation purposes but that problem has been solved: see para.26–18, below.

responsible in these cases. *Lister*, "provides no clear assistance on when . . . an incident is to be regarded as sufficiently work-related" to attract vicarious liability.[156] *Lister* is a comparatively easy case because the warden of the home was entrusted with the care of the children and an ability to influence them and take advantage was inherent in this. At the opposite extreme, if the servant had been, say, a handyman employed by a local authority who had been sent to do repairs at a home run by the authority and had taken the opportunity to commit indecent assaults, the result should be different: he is not employed to deal with children.[157] Nonetheless, there will be intermediate cases, for example, what are we to say if on facts like *Lister* the servant is the resident caretaker at the home; or where a person has the care of one inmate but uses the opportunity created by his position to abuse another?[158] Outside the context of residential homes, the Supreme Court of Canada has held that a Roman Catholic diocese was vicariously liable for abuse by a priest on the basis of the degree of power and influence it conferred on him in relation to children in his parish.[159] These questions are fact-sensitive. In *Maga v Birmingham Archdiocese* the trial judge dismissed a claim in respect of sexual abuse by a priest because the priest, although he had engaged the young claimant for small jobs like cleaning, had made no attempt to involve him in religious activities and his position as a priest merely gave him the opportunity to commit the abuse; but the Court of Appeal was of a different view. Among the factors which pointed the other way were that a priest's role was to "bring the Gospel" to all people, though not necessarily by seeking converts, that the priest in question had a special responsibility for youth work, that he had engaged the claimant in helping with social events at the church, that some of the abuse had taken place at the presbytery and that his priestly status and authority meant that no one would question his being alone with the claimant.[160]

There were a number of cases before *Lister* outside the context of childcare but involving assaults by servants and which seemed to proceed broadly on the basis that the servant's act might be in the course of his employment if his intention was, however wrongly, to

[156] *Dubai Aluminium Co Ltd v Salaam* [2002] UKHL 48; [2003] 2 A.C. 366 at [25].

[157] *Maga v Birmingham Archdiocese* [2010] EWCA Civ 256 at [74]; *B(E) v Order of Oblates of Mary Immaculate* (2003) 227 D.L.R. (4th) 298.

[158] No, according to *B v Jacob* (1998) 166 D.L.R. (4th) 125, decided just before *Bazley v Curry* [1999] 2 S.C.R. 534. In *Jacobi v Griffiths* [1999] 2 S.C.R. 570 the Supreme Court was divided on the application of *Bazley v Curry* to abuse by a youth club leader, most of which took place at his home. However, the majority view that there was no vicarious liability is influenced by the view that to impose liability upon a non-profit institution might call for a more rigorous insistence on a strong connexion between the tort and the employment.

[159] *Doe v Bennett* [2004] SCC 17; [2004] 1 S.C.R. 436.

[160] [2010] EWCA Civ 256.

further his employer's business or assert his employer's authority,[161] but if the assault was a mere act of personal vengeance and not in pursuit of those aims, it would not.[162] After *Lister* the issue arose in *Mattis v Pollock*,[163] where a nightclub bouncer, having been assaulted by disgruntled customers in an incident at the club, went home, got a knife and, about 20 minutes after the incident, stabbed the claimant outside the club. The Court of Appeal held that the stabbing was sufficiently closely connected with the incident under *Lister* to make it within the course of his employment by the defendant. However, it was regarded as important that the defendant had encouraged the bouncer to take an aggressive attitude towards customers[164]; indeed, the court was of the opinion that the defendant was in breach of his personal duty in this respect.[165] So also in *Gravil v Carroll*[166] a rugby club was held liable for a punch by a part-time professional player in a melee which persisted after a scrum but the Court of Appeal was influenced by the fact that such attacks, though unlawful and in breach of the rules, were an "ordinary incident of a rugby match", leading to the conclusion that the assault was "very closely" connected with the employment.[167]

Actions are frequently brought against chief constables in respect of acts of police officers amounting to intentional torts such as assault, false imprisonment and malicious prosecution. The statutory formula[168] is that the chief constable is liable for acts done in the performance or purported performance of the officer's functions. The powers of a police officer are conferred on him by law, by virtue of his office and do not originate in any authorisation by his superiors; it would therefore be artificial and misleading to attribute to the chief constable a "business" in the course of which he gives the officer authority to act.[169] In practice the liability of a Chief Constable for wilful acts by police officers is more extensive than the

---

[161] *Dyer v Munday* [1895] 1 Q.B. 742; *Vasey v Surrey Free Inns* [1995] C.L.Y. 3735; *Fennelly v Connex South Eastern* [2001] I.R.L.R. 390.

[162] *Warren v Henlys Ltd* [1948] 2 All E.R. 935; *Petterson v Royal Oak Hotel Ltd* [1948] N.Z.L.R. 136; *Daniels v Whetstone Entertainments Ltd* [1962] 2 Lloyd's Rep. 1; *Keppel Bus Co Ltd v Sa'ad bin Ahmad* [1974] 1 W.L.R. 1082. See Rose "Liability for an Employee's Assaults" (1977) 40 M.L.R. 420. The victim may of course have a claim under the Criminal Injuries Compensation scheme.

[163] [2003] EWCA Civ 787; [2003] 1 W.L.R. 2158.

[164] Cf. *Brown v Robinson* [2004] UKPC 56 (security officer; pursued unruly fan offsite to teach him a lesson and shot him; no apparent evidence of encouragement of aggression by employers; liable; however, the court clearly contemplated that there could still be "private revenge" cases outside the scope of the rule—at [12]).

[165] It was left open whether the decision the other way in *Daniels v Whetstone Entertainments Ltd*, above, fn.162, where the employer had ordered the bouncer to desist, was correct.

[166] [2008] EWCA Civ 689; [2008] I.C.R. 1222.

[167] The court declined to speculate how facts such as those in *Deatons Pty Ltd v Flew* (1949) 79 C.L.R. 370 would now be decided (barmaid throwing glass at customer).

[168] See para.20–7, above

[169] *Makanjuola v MPC*, *The Times*, August 8, 1989.

vicarious liability of an employer but it is not without limit. For example, it does not extend to blackmail by an officer using information he has acquired in his work.[170] However, an officer "carries his authority about with him", so to speak, so if he purports to assert it in the course of a private quarrel when he is off duty the Chief Constable may be liable.[171] It would be a different matter if he altogether put aside his role as constable and merely used equipment provided for his police duties in order to commit a tort.[172]

D. Theft by Servant

20–15   It was at one time the view that if a servant stole goods his employer could not be vicariously liable to their owner on the ground that the act of stealing necessarily took the servant outside the course of his employment.[173] This view was, however, really inconsistent with *Lloyd v Grace, Smith & Co.* In *Morris v C.W. Martin & Sons Ltd*,[174] where some of the older cases were overruled, the claimant had sent her fur coat to X to be cleaned, and X, with her permission, sent it on to the defendants, who were specialist cleaners.[175] The defendants handed the coat to their servant, M, for him to clean it, and M stole the coat. It was held by the Court of Appeal that on these facts the defendants were liable. Although reliance was placed on the duty owed to the claimant by the defendants themselves as bailees of the coat, so that, in effect, the theft of the coat by the servant, to whom they had delegated their own duty of reasonable care in respect of it, constituted a breach of that duty, yet the case has been regarded as illustrative of the general

---

[170] *Makanjuola*, above, fn.169. Note (1) Henry J. regretted the result, (2) he thought that the initial trespass by unauthorised use of the warrant card prior to the blackmail might have been in purported performance of the officer's functions. See also *N v CC Merseyside* [2006] EWHC 3041 (QB) (off-duty officer raping intoxicated claimant after volunteering to take her to police station).

[171] *Weir v CC Merseyside* [2003] EWCA Civ 111; [2003] I.C.R. 708; *Bernard v Att Gen* [2004] UKPC 47; [2005] I.R.L.R. 398.

[172] *Att Gen v Hartwell* [2004] UKPC 12; [2004] 1 W.L.R. 1273 (but in view of their knowledge of the officer's previous behaviour the defendants were held in breach of their personal duty). When the "employer" provides a police officer with a gun that creates a risk of its misuse, but while the risk created by the employer is a relevant consideration in determining the scope of vicarious liability, it is not a sufficient test of it: *Brown v Robinson* [2004] UKPC 56 at [11].

[173] See, e.g. *Cheshire v Bailey* [1905] 1 K.B. 237; but even the earlier cases recognised that the employer may be primarily liable as, e.g. where the theft can be attributed to his own negligence in employing a dishonest servant or if his own negligence led to the theft: *Williams v The Curzon Syndicate Ltd* (1919) 35 T.L.R. 475; *De Parell v Walker* (1932) 49 T.L.R. 37; *Adams (Durham) Ltd v Trust Houses Ltd* [1960] 1 Lloyd's Rep. 380.

[174] [1966] 1 Q.B. 716. *Mendelssohn v Normand Ltd* [1970] 1 Q.B. 177; *Port Swettenham Authority v T.W. Wu & Co* [1979] A.C. 580.

[175] On the sub-bailment and exemption clause aspects of this case, see *The Pioneer Container* [1994] 2 A.C. 324.

approach of the law to wilful wrongdoing by a servant.[176] That is not to say that in the particular context of theft the bailment was irrelevant: an essential element of the defendants' liability on any ground was that they had been entrusted with the coat and had in turn entrusted it to their servant. Had this not been the case it could not have been said that they had delegated to him their own duty as bailees, nor would the theft have been committed by him in the course of his employment. On the other hand, the principle is not confined to situations where there is a bailment to the defendant and the servant is given physical custody of the goods. There may be liability, for example, where the employer's duty is to take steps to keep property secure and this task is entrusted to the servant. Thus landlords of a block of flats were held liable when a dishonest porter employed by them used his keys to enter the claimant's flat and steal[177]; but the result would have been different if, say, the boiler-man had stolen the keys and used them for the same purpose: it is not enough that the employment gives the opportunity to steal, for there is then insufficient connexion between the employment and the theft.[178]

E. Damage to Goods Bailed

The same approach serves to solve the problem of damage caused by a servant to goods which are the subject of a bailment to his employer. If the goods have been entrusted by the employer to the care of his servant and the servant negligently damages them, his employer will be vicariously liable to their owner, for there is close connexion between the employment and the damage or, to put it another way, the servant has done carelessly what he was employed to do carefully, namely, to look after the goods. For this purpose it makes no difference that the servant at the time of his negligence was using the goods improperly for purposes entirely of his own, as, for example, if he uses a car, bailed to his employer and entrusted to his care, for taking his friends for a ride, and then negligently damages the car in an accident.[179] He is as much guilty of failure to look after the car as he would have been if the accident had occurred

20–16

---

[176] See *Lister v Hesley Hall Ltd*, above, fn.126, at [19] and [76] and *Photo Productions Ltd v Securicor Transport Ltd* [1980] A.C. 827 at 846.

[177] *Nahhas v Pier House Management (Cheyne Walk) Ltd* (1984) 270 E.G. 328; *Fawcett Security Operations (Pvt) Ltd v Omar Enterprises (Pvt) Ltd* [1991] 2 S.A.L.R. (Zimbabwe) (theft by security guard at client's premises).

[178] See *Heasman v Clarity Cleaning Co* [1987] I.C.R. 949 and *Lister v Hesley Hall Ltd*, above, fn.126 at [45]; cf. *Brink's Global Services Inc v Igrox Ltd* [2009] EWHC 1817 (Comm).

[179] *Coupe Co v Maddick* [1891] 2 Q.B. 413; *Aitchison v Page Motors Ltd* (1935) 154 L.T. 128; *Central Motors (Glasgow) Ltd v Cessnock Garage and Motor Co* 1925 S.C. 796. Cf. *Sanderson v Collins* [1904] 1 K.B. 628.

while he was using the car for an authorised purpose. Nevertheless some difficulty has been felt to exist in such a case because the servant would, in relation to a third party injured in the same accident, be held to have been "on a frolic of his own". "How can this be?" Lord Denning M.R. asked.[180] "How can the servant, on one and the same journey, be acting both within and without the course of his employment?" The answer, it is respectfully suggested, is not, as Lord Denning proposed, to abandon the notion of vicarious liability in favour of that of the primary liability of the bailee, but to recognise that the facts relevant to the two claims —that brought by the car owner and that brought by the third party—are different. The car owner's claim is based on the fact that the servant was at fault in looking after the car, which he was employed to do.[181] The third party's claim is based upon the fact that the servant was guilty of negligent driving at the time and place in question, and if the servant was using the car for a joyride then he was not, with regard to the third party, at that place at that time in the course of his employment.

F. Fraud of Servant

20–17   Cases of fraud raise special problems because of the special character of fraud itself. Of its very nature, fraud involves the persuasion of the victim, by deception, to part with his property or in some other way to act to his own detriment and to the profit of the person practising the fraud. Thus in *Lloyd v Grace, Smith & Co*,[182] as we have seen, the defendants' clerk fraudulently persuaded the claimant to transfer her property to him, and what is significant for the purposes of vicarious liability is that it was the position in which he had been placed by the defendants that enabled him to do this. His acts were within the scope of the apparent or ostensible authority with which he had been clothed by the defendants and it is for this reason that they were liable.[183] In *Uxbridge Permanent Benefit Building Society v Pickard*,[184] as in *Lloyd*'s case, the clerk had full authority to conduct the business of a solicitor's office in the name and on behalf of his principal. It was not within his actual authority to commit a fraud, but it was within his ostensible authority to

---

[180] *Morris v C.W. Martin & Sons Ltd* [1966] 1 Q.B. 716 at 724–725.

[181] See also *Photo Productions Ltd v Securicor Transport Ltd* [1980] A.C. 827 (security guard setting fire to premises).

[182] [1912] A.C. 716, para.20–13, above.

[183] "If the agent commits the fraud purporting to act in the course of business such as he was authorised, *or held out as authorised*, to transact on account of his principal, then the latter may be held liable for it": [1912] A.C. 716 at 725 per Earl Loreburn (emphasis added). See also at 738–739 per Lord Macnaghten, at 740 per Lord Shaw, but this does not mean that "scope of authority" is a universal substitute for "scope of employment" in statement cases: *HSBC Bank Plc v So* [2009] EWCA Civ 296.

[184] [1939] 2 K.B. 238.

perform acts of the kind that come within the business conducted by a solicitor.

"So long as he is acting within the scope of that class of act, his employer is bound whether or not the clerk is acting for his own purposes or for his employer's purposes."[185]

However, there must be some statement or conduct by the employer which leads to the claimant's belief that the servant was acting in the authorised course of business. It is not enough that the belief has been brought about solely by reliance on the servant's misrepresentation of the scope of his authority, however reasonable, from the claimant's point of view, it may have been to have acted upon it. In *Armagas Ltd v Mundogas SA*[186] M had authority to sell a vessel belonging to the defendants on terms that it was to be chartered back to them for 12 months. As part of a fraudulent scheme he induced the claimants, the purchasers, to believe that the contract involved a 36-month charter back. Such a transaction was not within the usual class of acts which an employee in his position was entitled to do and, the claimants' belief resting solely on M's statement that he had the defendants' consent for what was being done,[187] it was held that M's employers were not liable for his fraud. M's employment by the defendants to deal with the vessel gave him the opportunity to commit the fraud but, as in the case of theft by a servant of goods bailed to his employer that is not enough.

4. EMPLOYERS' INDEMNITY

Vicarious liability being a form of joint liability, the provisions of the Civil Liability (Contribution) Act 1978[188] may enable the   **20–18**

---

[185] [1939] 2 K.B. 238 at 254 per Sir Wilfrid Greene M.R. "In the case of a servant who goes off on a frolic of his own, no question arises of any actual or ostensible authority upon the faith of which some third person is going to change his position. The very essence of the present case is that the actual authority and the ostensible authority to [the clerk] were of a kind which in the ordinary course of an everyday transaction were going to lead third persons, on the faith of them, to change their position": at 254–255.

[186] [1986] A.C. 717. See also the discussion of ostensible authority in *Freeman and Lockyer (A Firm) v Buckhurst Park Properties (Mangal) Ltd* [1964] 2 Q.B. 480 at 502–505 and in *First Energy (UK) Ltd v Hungarian International Bank Ltd* [1993] 2 Lloyd's Rep. 194 (a case of contract). Ostensible authority in the case of acts by officers of a company has been affected by the fact that the company's memorandum is a public document, but the Companies Act 2006 s.40 provides that, "in favour of a person dealing with a company in good faith, the power of the board of directors to bind the company, or authorise others to do so, is deemed to be free of any limitation under the company's constitution."

[187] Authority was also in issue in *Kooragang Investments Pty Ltd v Richardson & Wrench Ltd* [1982] A.C. 462 (a case of negligence) where the servant was "moonlighting" for X. There was no actual authority to do the acts in question, the employer in no way held out the servant as having authority and, indeed, the claimant was unaware that the servant was in the employ of the defendants. Not liable.

[188] See Ch.21, below.

employer to recover from his servant some or all of the damages he has had to pay on account of the servant's tort.[189] Additionally, however, the employer can in some cases recover damages from his servant at common law, and so, in effect, recoup himself for the damages he has had to pay. In *Lister v Romford Ice and Cold Storage Co*,[190] L was a lorry driver employed by R. Co who by his negligent driving in the course of his employment, had caused an injury to his father, another servant of R. Co. R. Co paid the father's damages and then sued L. It was held that L's negligent driving was not only a tort against his father but also a breach of an implied undertaking in his contract of service that he would exercise reasonable care, for which R. Co were entitled to damages equivalent to the amount which they had had to pay to the father.

> "That an employee who is negligent and causes grave damage to his employers should be heard successfully to say that he should not make any contribution to the resulting damage, is a proposition which does not in the least commend itself to me and I do not see why it should be so. I find that justice, as we conceive justice in these courts, says that the person who caused the damage is the person who must in law be called upon to pay damages arising therefrom."[191]

However, the justice of this decision did not commend itself so strongly to others and the matter was considered by an inter-departmental committee[192] with the result that employers' liability insurers entered into a "gentleman's agreement" not to take advantage of the principle unless there was evidence of collusion or wilful misconduct. Indeed, there are strong grounds for arguing that the *Lister* principle is unjustifiable in modern conditions[193]: the employer would probably rarely wish to take advantage of it because of the disastrous effect on labour relations and the real claimant is likely to be an insurer acting under the doctrine of

---

[189] For cases in which a full indemnity was awarded to the employer under the previous legislation, the Law Reform (Married Women and Tortfeasors) Act 1935, see *Ryan v Fildes* [1938] 3 All E.R. 517; *Semtex v Gladstone* [1954] 1 W.L.R. 945; *Harvey v O'Dell Ltd* [1958] 2 Q.B. 78.

[190] [1957] A.C. 555. See also the judgment of the CA: [1956] 2 Q.B. 180.

[191] *Semtex v Gladstone* [1954] 1 W.L.R. 945 at 953 per Finnemore J., cited with approval in the *Lister* case in the CA [1956] 2 Q.B. at 213 per Romer L.J. In *Harvey v O'Dell Ltd* [1958] 2 Q.B. 78, McNair J. held that a servant's implied undertaking to exercise reasonable care extended only to those acts which he was specifically employed to do and that therefore the negligent driving of the servant, who was employed as a storekeeper, did not constitute a breach of his contract of service.

[192] Report published in 1959. See Gardiner (1959) 22 M.L.R. 652.

[193] It has been abrogated by statute in Australia.

subrogation.[194] If it be objected that to deny the right of indemnity against the servant is to put him above the law, it may be replied that it is sufficient that he is liable to the victim of the tort, though admittedly judgment will rarely be enforced against him.[195]

There is, however, one important limit to the principle of *Lister*'s case. The decision in that case constitutes, in effect, an exception to the common law rule of *Merryweather v Nixan*[196] that there can be no contribution between joint tortfeasors, for that rule was held not to apply in the case of claimants whose liability, "arose solely from the fact that they were answerable for the negligence of the defendant himself".[197] If, therefore, the employer has himself, or through some other servant, been guilty of culpable fault, the principle of *Lister's* case does not apply and the employer can only recover, if at all, under the Act of 1978.[198]

5. LIABILITY FOR AGENTS: VEHICLE DRIVERS

Thus far we have spoken of the relationship under a contract of service. However, many cases on vicarious liability speak in the language of agency and numerous dicta can be found equating agency with a contract of service for this purpose.[199] It has been said on high authority that in principle the law governing vicarious liability for servants and agents is the same and depends upon the question, "was the servant or agent acting on behalf of, and within the scope of the authority conferred by the master or principal?" The answer will often differ simply because the authority of a servant is usually more general.[200] Whatever the validity of this for such matters as fraud,[201] it can hardly be true for liability for accidents,

20-19

---

[194] Despite the "gentlemen's agreement" referred to above, *Lister*'s case is not dead: see *Morris v Ford Motor Co Ltd* [1973] Q.B. 792, where the right was sought to be exercised by a third party who was bound to indemnify the employer. Weir, "Subrogation and Indemnity" (privately published case note, 1973).

[195] Some systems go further and insulate the servant from liability to the claimant: para.20–1, above.

[196] (1799) 8 T.R. 186.

[197] [1956] 2 Q.B. 180 at 210 per Romer L.J. This aspect of the problem was not considered by the House of Lords.

[198] *Jones v Manchester Corp* [1952] 2 Q.B. 852. "A chauffeur who, through negligence, causes damage for which his employer is held responsible, may well be liable to his master. On the other hand, if the chauffeur is young and inexperienced, and is suddenly told to drive another and bigger car or lorry, which he does not understand, and an accident follows, it is by no means certain that the employer will be entitled to an indemnity": at 865 per Singleton L.J.

[199] See Atiyah, *Vicarious Liability in the Law of Tort*, Ch.9. Cf. *Holderness v Goslin* [1975] 2 N.Z.L.R. 46 at 50–51.

[200] *Heatons Transports (St Helens) Ltd v TGWU* [1973] A.C. 15 at 99. The case was not an action in tort, but for an "unfair industrial practice" under the Industrial Relations Act 1971. Lord Wilberforce disclaimed any intention to deal with tort liability: see at 100.

[201] See para.20–17, above.

since it is clearly established that the principal is not liable (except in certain isolated instances) for accidents caused by the negligence of his independent contractors performing the tasks entrusted to them. In fact, agency in its most precise legal sense is a predominantly contractual concept and involves the idea of A, the agent, acting so as to bring his principal, D, into a legal relationship with another, C. It is not, therefore, surprising that D should bear responsibility for A's fraud in purporting to carry out a transaction between D and C. There are undoubtedly other instances in the law of tort of vicarious liability for persons who are not servants[202] and who are sometimes described as agents, but these seem to rest less on any general principle of agency than upon an ad hoc judgment that for one reason or another the principal ought to pay.[203] This perhaps is the basis of the decision that a master of a hunt is liable for trespasses by hunt members.[204]

Whatever may be the correct principle as to liability for agents, it is convenient to treat here a doctrine which fits easily into no existing legal category[205] but which developed because of the insurance position in relation to road traffic liability. The doctrine may be stated as follows. Where D, the owner[206] of a vehicle, expressly or impliedly requests or instructs A to drive the vehicle in performance of some task or duty carried out for D, D will be vicariously liable for A's negligence in the operation of the vehicle.[207] Thus in *Ormrod v Crosville Motor Services Ltd*[208] D, the owner of a car, asked A to drive the car from Birkenhead to Monte Carlo, where they were to start a holiday together. It was held that D was liable for A's negligent driving even though A might be said to be partly

---

202 See para.20–21, below.

203 See *Morgans v Launchbury* [1973] A.C. 127 at 135 per Lord Wilberforce. In *Moores v Bude-Stratton Town Council* [2001] I.C.R. 271, the lay majority of the EAT held a local authority vicariously liable for the conduct of a councillor which led to the constructive dismissal of the applicant.

204 *League Against Cruel Sports v Scott* [1986] Q.B. 240 where control is emphasised. The Supreme Court of Canada held a childcare authority not vicariously liable for abuse of its ward by a foster parent since although the foster parents acted in pursuance of a public goal they could not be regarded as acting on behalf of the authority: *K.L.B. v British Columbia* [2003] SCC 51; [2003] 2 S.C.R. 403.

205 Winfield sought to explain the doctrine in terms of "casual delegation" of the use of a chattel, but the leading case now talks in terms of agency: *Morgans v Launchbury* [1973] A.C. 127.

206 Ownership as such is probably not necessary: *Nottingham v Aldridge* [1971] 2 Q.B. 739. In *Morgans v Launchbury* the husband was held liable for the negligence of the driver and there was no appeal against that decision. If an owner bails his vehicle to A and A gets B to drive it, the owner is not liable for B's negligence: *Chowdhary v Gillot* [1947] 2 All E.R. 541.

207 *Morgans v Launchbury* [1973] A.C. 127.

208 [1953] 1 W.L.R. 1120. See also *Samson v Aitchison* [1912] A.C. 844; *Pratt v Patrick* [1924] 1 K.B. 488; *Parker v Miller* (1926) 42 T.L.R. 408; *The Trust Co Ltd v De Silva* [1956] 1 W.L.R. 376, PC; *Vandyke v Fender* [1970] 2 Q.B. 292; *Candler v Thomas* [1998] R.T.R. 214.

pursuing his own interest in driving A's car. On the other hand, liability was not imposed in *Morgans v Launchbury*[209] where the husband, who normally used his wife's car to go to work, got a third person to drive him home after visits to several public houses. In no sense was the husband acting as his wife's agent in using the car for his work and still less was the third person her agent.[210] It is now clear that mere permission to drive without any interest or concern of the owner in the driving does not make the owner vicariously liable[211] nor is there any doctrine of the "family car".[212] Where, however, the facts of the relationship between owner and driver are not fully known, proof of ownership may give rise to a presumption that the driver was acting as the owner's agent.[213]

The development of a separate head of vicarious liability for **20–20** vehicle drivers was clearly been prompted by a desire to ensure a claim-worthy defendant, but the House of Lords denied that the courts may go on a voyage of discovery into the insurance position in these cases and said that any alteration of the law must be left to the legislature with its superior capacity for making decisions of policy. However, to confine our attention in this context to instances of vicarious liability risks giving a false impression. If there is in force a policy of insurance covering the liability of the driver[214] there will generally be no point in suing the owner. In fact, as far as the claimant is concerned, even if the driver is not covered by the policy, in most cases the owner's insurer must satisfy the judgment against the uninsured driver[215] and if there is no insurance at all the claimant may proceed under the MIB Agreement.[216] The owner may be liable to indemnify his insurer or the MIB (and that will be out of his own pocket) but that is no concern of the claimant.

The question remains of the reach of this principle. While it has certainly been most prominent in the context of motor accidents, it

---

[209] [1973] A.C. 127.
[210] Cf. the valiant attempt of Lord Denning M.R. and Edmund Davies L.J. in the CA to fit the facts into a traditional agency framework: [1971] 2 Q.B. 245.
[211] *Morgans v Launchbury*, above, fn.207; *Hewitt v Bonvin* [1940] 1 K.B. 188 (father permitting son to take girlfriends home in car); cf. *Carberry v Davies* [1968] 1 W.L.R. 1103 (owner suggesting to driver that he take owner's son out in car). A person who has "borrowed" a car, with or without the owner's permission is not acting as his agent when driving it back to him: *Klein v Caluori* [1971] 1 W.L.R. 619.
[212] Cf. the view of Lord Denning M.R. in *Launchbury v Morgans* [1971] 2 Q.B. 245. A wife is not her husband's agent because she is on a family shopping expedition: *Norwood v Navan* [1981] R.T.R. 457.
[213] *Barnard v Sully* (1931) 47 T.L.R. 557; *Rambarran v Gurrucharan* [1970] 1 W.L.R. 556; *Morgans v Launchbury*, above, fn.207, at 139 per Viscount Dilhorne.
[214] e.g. under a "named driver" clause in the policy.
[215] Road Traffic Act 1988 s.151(2)(b).
[216] It should be noted that at the time of the accident in *Morgans v Launchbury* insurance for passengers was not compulsory and therefore fell outside the scope of the MIB Agreement.

has been applied to a boat[217] but even a special rule about "transport" seems out of tune with the style of the common law and the judgments in *Morgans v Launchbury* are couched in quite general terms of agency. On the other hand, a general principle that the owner of a chattel was liable for the negligence of anyone using it at his request would have surprising consequences.[218] The High Court of Australia declined to apply it in a case where the owner of a light aircraft requested a pilot who was not his servant to take a son's friend for a flight,[219] though even its application to the motor car situation in Australia is subject to some uncertainty (at least where the owner is not in the vehicle).[220]

6. EMPLOYER AND INDEPENDENT CONTRACTOR

20–21 In principle an employer is not responsible for the torts of his independent contractor. It is no exception to say that he is liable: (1) for torts authorised or ratified by him or where the contractor is employed to do an illegal act, for here they are both liable as joint tortfeasors[221]; or (2) for his own negligence, for example in failing to take care to select a competent contractor[222] or procure adequate resources; (3) cases of strict liability are sometimes treated as exceptions, but it is doubtful if they are so in theory; (4) nor is it an exception that he is liable if he personally interferes with the contractor or his servants and in fact directs the manner in which the work is to be done, for he is then again liable as a joint tortfeasor.[223]

However, there are certainly cases in which the employer is responsible for damage caused by his contractor's fault even though there is no authorisation or misconduct on the employer's part. The

---

[217] *The Thelma (Owners) v The Endymion (Owners)* [1953] 2 Lloyd's Rep. 613.

[218] See the examples of the cricket bat and the barbecue given by Callinan J. in *Scott v Davis* [2000] HCA 52; 204 C.L.R. 333 at [347]–[348] and *Moynihan v Moynihan* [1975] I.R. 192.

[219] *Scott v Davis*, above, fn.218, with a powerful dissent from McHugh J. The development of the law may have been based on a misunderstanding of the early cases which were said to found it: see the judgment of Gummow J.

[220] See the way *Soblusky v Egan* (1960) 103 C.L.R. 215 is treated by the majority in *Scott v Davis*.

[221] *Ellis v Sheffield Gas Consumers Co* (1853) 2 El. & Bl. 767. The defendants, without authority, employed contractor to dig a trench in the street for gas pipes. Contractor's servants carelessly left heap of stones on the footpath and the claimant fell over them and was injured. The contract was to do an illegal act, a public nuisance, and defendants were liable.

[222] For the scope of this in the context of occupiers' liability see para.9–15, above.

[223] *M'Laughlin v Pryor* (1842) 4 Man. & G. 48; *Hardaker v Idle DC* [1896] 1 Q.B. 335. In *Brooke v Bool* [1928] 2 K.B. 578 the defendant was held liable on the basis of participation in a joint enterprise. It is respectfully submitted that *Scarbrook v Mason* [1961] 3 All E.R. 767 takes this much too far: and it was doubted in *S. v Walsall MBC* [1985] 1 W.L.R. 1150.

conventional analysis, and though it is open to criticism[224] it is best to adhere to it here, is that in these cases the employer is liable not vicariously but because he was in breach of some duty which he himself owed to the claimant.[225] In such cases the employer is said to be under a "non-delegable" duty. Strictly speaking no duty is delegable,[226] but if my duty is merely to take reasonable care, then, if I have taken care to select a competent contractor to do the work, I have done all that is required of me.[227] If, on the other hand, my duty is, for example "to provide that care is taken"[228] or is to achieve some actual result such as the secure fencing of dangerous parts of machinery, then my duty is not performed unless care is taken or the machinery is fenced. It is no defence that I delegated the task to an independent contractor if he failed to fulfil his duties. This is put with clarity by Lord Blackburn in *Hughes v Percival*[229]:

"The law cast upon the defendant, when exercising this right, a duty towards the plaintiff. I do not think that duty went so far as to require him absolutely to provide that no damage should come to the plaintiff's wall from the use he thus made of it, but I think that the duty went as far as to require him to see that reasonable skill and care were exercised in those operations which involved a use of the party-wall, exposing it to this risk. If such a duty was cast upon the defendant he could not get rid of responsibility by delegating the performance of it to a third person. He was at liberty to employ such a third person to fulfil the duty which the law cast on himself, and, if they so agreed together, to take an indemnity to himself in case mischief came from that person not fulfilling the duty which the law cast upon the defendant; but the defendant still remained subject to that duty, and liable for the consequences if it was not fulfilled."

For this purpose, care must be taken to avoid the conclusion that because a duty owed by A to B is non-delegable, so also is a duty owed by A to C. A building contractor may well, as a matter of contract, be responsible to the building owner for deficiencies in the completed building, but it does not follow that he is responsible to

[224] See para.20–1, above.
[225] *D.&F. Estates Ltd v Church Commissioners* [1989] A.C. 177 per Lord Bridge.
[226] *Cassidy v Ministry of Health* [1951] 2 K.B. 343 at 363 per Denning L.J.
[227] See *Phillips v Britannia Hygienic Laundry Co* [1923] 1 K.B. 539; *Stennett v Hancock* [1939] 2 All E.R. 578; *Salsbury v Woodland* [1970] 1 Q.B. 324.
[228] *The Pass of Ballater* [1942] P. 112 at 117 per Langton J. See also *The Lady Gwendolen* [1965] P. 294, where Winn L.J. (at 350) described the duty owed by a shipowner to other ships and to persons who might be affected by the navigation of his own ships as a duty, "that all concerned in any capacity with the navigation of those ships should exercise such care as a reasonable person would exercise in that capacity."
[229] (1883) 8 App. Cas. 443 at 446.

third parties for damage for which they sue in tort[230]: as far as the
first is concerned his duty may be to provide a building according to
specifications, but to the second he owes only a duty of care.

20–22   It is a question of law whether the duty in a given case is "non-
delegable". The categories of instances do not appear to be closed,
but not a great deal by way of principle appears from the cases.
Indeed, it has been said that, "the doctrinal roots of non-delegable
duties are anything but deep or well established".[231] Where there is
a contract then of course all depends upon the proper interpretation
of the contract and there would be nothing unusual in the conclusion
that the defendant had undertaken to produce a result (in which case
negligence on anyone's part is irrelevant) or to secure that care was
taken by all concerned with the matter. The same is true where the
case depends upon implication by law, as in the case of a bailment,[232] but some cases are more difficult to explain. In *Rogers v
Night Riders*[233] the defendants held themselves out as a minicab firm
and undertook to provide a car to take the claimant to Euston. The
defendants in fact relied on independent contractor drivers and were
not much more than a booking agency. The decision that the defendants were liable to the claimant for an accident caused by the bad
condition of the car seems correct on the basis of what they had led
the claimant to believe about the nature of their business, in other
words, although they were not a minicab company they contracted
to provide the services of one.[234] More difficult is the Court of
Appeal's statement that it did not matter whether the case was
framed in contract or in tort. We are, of course, now familiar with
tort liability arising from an undertaking or assumption of responsibility,[235] but there does not seem to be any general rule that such
liability necessarily carries with it responsibility for the defaults of
an independent contractor. In *Aiken v Stewart Wrightson Members
Agency Ltd*,[236] it was held that Lloyd's members agents did not owe
a non-delegable duty in tort in respect of the carrying on of underwriting business by managing agents even though they were contractually liable for the conduct of the managing agents.[237] The tort
duty which they did owe (to exercise reasonable care in selecting
and liaising with the managing agents) therefore fell short of their

---

[230] *D.&F. Estates Ltd v Church Commissioners* [1989] A.C. 177.
[231] *Leichhardt Municipal Council v Montgomery* [2007] HCA 6, 233 A.L.R. 200 at [155] per
Hayne J.
[232] The duty of a mortgagee or receiver to obtain the best price for property sold to meet a debt
is also non-delegable so it is no answer for him to say he instructed a competent valuer:
Raja v Austin Gray [2002] EWCA Civ 1965; 13 E.G. 117.
[233] [1983] R.T.R. 324.
[234] See the judgment of Dunn L.J. The case is referred to without disapproval in *Wong v Kwan
Kin Travel Services Ltd* [1996] 1 W.L.R. 138.
[235] See para.5–34, above.
[236] [1995] 1 W.L.R. 1281.
[237] The point was significant because of limitation.

contractual duty. We now turn to those cases where a non-delegable duty is fairly well established.

A. Withdrawal of Support from Neighbouring Land

This furnished the earliest example of a "non-delegable" duty at **20–23** common law. If A, in the course of work done on his land causes subsidence on B's adjoining land and B's land is entitled to the support of A, A is liable to B, and it is no defence that the work had been entrusted to an independent contractor.[238]

B. Operations Affecting the Highway other than Normal User for the Purpose of Passage

In *Tarry v Ashton*[239] the defendant employed an independent **20–24** contractor to repair a lamp attached to his house and overhanging the footway. As it was not securely fastened the lamp fell on the claimant, a passer-by, and the defendant was held liable, because:

"[I]t was the defendant's duty to make the lamp reasonably safe . . . the contractor has failed to do that . . . therefore the defendant has not done his duty and is liable to the plaintiff for the consequences".[240]

In *Gray v Pullen*[241] the defendant owned a house adjoining a highway and had statutory authority to cut a trench across the road to make a drain from his premises to a sewer. For this purpose he employed a contractor who negligently filled in the trench improperly and the claimant, a passenger on the highway, was injured. The defendant was held liable although he was not negligent. On the other hand, in *Salsbury v Woodland*[242] the defendant had employed an apparently competent contractor to fell a tree in the front garden of his house near the highway. Done competently this would have involved no risk to anyone, but owing to the negligence of the contractor, the tree fouled some telephone wires, causing them to

---

[238] *Bower v Peate* (1876) 1 Q.B.D. 321; *Dalton v Angus* (1881) 6 App. Cas. 740; *Hughes v Percival* (1883) 8 App. Cas. 443; cf. *Stoneman v Lyons* (1975) 133 C.L.R. 550.
[239] (1876) 1 Q.B.D. 314.
[240] (1876) 1 Q.B.D. 314 at 319 per Blackburn J.
[241] (1864) 5 B. & S. 970. *Hole v Sittingbourne Ry* (1861) 6 H. & N. 488 (bridge obstructing navigation); *Hardaker v Idle DC* [1896] 1 Q.B. 335 (gas main broken by failure to pack soil round it while constructing a sewer); *Penny v Wimbledon UDC* [1899] 2 Q.B. 72 (heap of soil left unlighted in road); *Pickard v Smith* (1861) 10 C.B.(N.S.) 314 (cellar flap on railway platform left open); *Daniel v Rickett, etc.* [1938] 2 K.B. 322 (cellar flap left open on pavement); *Holliday v National Telephone Co* [1899] 2 Q.B. 392 (explosion in highway caused by dipping benzoline lamp in molten solder); *Walsh v Holst Co Ltd* [1958] 1 W.L.R. 800 (building operations adjoining highway).
[242] [1970] 1 Q.B. 324.

fall into the highway, and an accident resulted in which the claimant was injured. The Court of Appeal held that these facts did not bring the case within the special category comprising cases of work done on the highway[243] and that there was no equivalent category comprising cases in which work is done near the highway. Accordingly the general principle applied and the defendant was not liable for the negligence of the independent contractor. Cases like *Gray v Pullen* rest on the fact that they involve an obstruction of the highway which is inherent in the very nature of the act the contractor is employed to do.[244]

C. Other Cases of Strict Liability

20–25   The rule of *Rylands v Fletcher*,[245] damage by fire,[246] and, in some cases, nuisance,[247] impose a liability for the default of an independent contractor. The Court of Appeal in *Honeywill and Stein Ltd v Larkin Bros Ltd*[248] stated a further principle whereby there is a class of, "extra hazardous acts, that is, acts which in their very nature, involve in the eyes of the law special danger to others" such as acts causing fire and explosion, where an employer cannot escape liability by delegating their performance to an independent contractor.[249] The claimants, who procured the defendants as independent contractors to take photographs of X's cinema by flashlight, were liable for the defendants' negligence in setting fire to X's cinema. However, while some activities plainly present more hazard than others, it is extremely difficult, if not impossible, to attempt a classification based on inherent risk without at the same time taking account of the necessary precautions, which will minimise that risk. The principle stated in *Honeywill and Stein* has therefore been described by the

---

[243] Widgery L.J. observed that the cases within this category would be found on analysis to be cases where the work done was of a character which would have been a nuisance unless authorised by statute: [1970] 1 Q.B. 324 at 338. Cf. at 348 per Sachs L.J. By statute a highway authority is liable for the negligence of contractors to which it delegates highway maintenance functions, see para.14–42, above. Cf. the position in Australia, where there is no such statutory provision: *Leichhardt Municipal Council v Montgomery* [2007] HCA 6; 233 A.L.R. 200.

[244] *Rowe v Herman* [1997] 1 W.L.R. 1390.

[245] See Ch.15.

[246] *Black v Christchurch Finance Co* [1894] A.C. 48; *Spicer v Smee* [1946] 1 All E.R. 489; *Balfour v Barty-King* [1957] 1 Q.B. 496; *H.N. Emanuel Ltd v GLC, The Times*, March 10, 1971; *Iverson v Purser* (1991) 73 D.L.R. (4th) 33. Cf. *Eriksen v Clifton* [1963] N.Z.L.R. 705.

[247] *Matania v National Provincial Bank* (1936) 155 L.T. 74 (nuisance by dust and noise the inevitable consequence of extensive building operations); *Att Gen v Geothermal Produce NZ Ltd* [1987] 2 N.Z.L.R. 348.

[248] [1934] 1 K.B. 191.

[249] At 197.

Court of Appeal as anomalous and unsatisfactory and its application should be kept as narrow was possible.[250]

D. Employer's Common Law Duties

The employer's common law duties in respect of his servant's **20–26**
safety as laid down in *Wilsons and Clyde Coal Co v English* are
"non-delegable".[251] This matter has already been dealt with.[252]

E. Cases of Statutory Duty

"Where a special duty is laid by statute on an individual or class **20–27**
of individuals either to take care or even to ensure safety (an
absolute duty in the true sense) . . . they cannot in any way escape
from or evade the full implication of and responsibility for that
duty."[253]

Whether the duty is absolute in this sense depends upon the true
construction of the statute. Some of the duties imposed by industrial
safety legislation are absolute.[254] Where a statute authorises something to be done which would otherwise be illegal, the duty is
generally such that there is liability if the work is done by an
independent contractor.[255] However, everything turns on the particular statute,[256] so that, for example, a local authority's duty under

---

[250] *Biffa Waste Services Ltd v Maschinenfabrik Ernst Hese GMBH* [2008] EWCA Civ 1238;
[2009] Q.B. 725. *Honeywill*'s case was said not to be part of Australian law in *Stevens v
Brodribb Sawmilling Co Pty Ltd* (1986) 160 C.L.R. 16. In *Burnie Port Authority v General
Jones* (1994) 179 C.L.R. 520 the High Court declared that the rule in *Rylands v Fletcher*
no longer formed part of the law of Australia, but the defendants were held liable for the
activities of their contractors. However, the duty imposed seems more an enhanced duty
of care than a true non-delegable duty. It has been said that, "outside its proper sphere of
operation, broadly coextensive with that occupied by the former law concerning spread of
fire and *Rylands v Fletcher*, *Burnie* has not detracted from the principle decided in *Stevens
v Brodribb*, that there is no general doctrine in Australian law that a person has a non-
delegable duty to ensure that reasonable care is taken by an independent contractor who
is employed to engage in an extra-hazardous activity": *Transfield Services (Australia) v
Hall* [2008] NSWCA 294 at [90]. See also *Northern Sandblasting v Harris* (1997) 188
C.L.R. 313 (landlord's repairing duties not non-delegable).
[251] [1938] A.C. 57.
[252] See para.8–17, above.
[253] *The Pass of Ballater* [1942] P. 112 at 117, referring to *Smith v Cammell Laird & Co Ltd*
[1940] A.C. 242; *Donaghey v Boulton and Paul Ltd* [1968] A.C.1.
[254] See Ch.8.
[255] *Hardaker v Idle DC* [1896] 1 Q.B. 335 at 351; *Darling v Att Gen* [1950] 2 All E.R. 793
(Minister of Works having statutory power to do work on land liable for negligence of
independent contractor in leaving heap of timber on field which injured claimant's
horse).
[256] In *Rivers v Cutting* [1982] 1 W.L.R. 1146 the police were held not liable for the negligence
of a garage which they had procured to tow away an abandoned vehicle. The statutory
power was to "remove" or "arrange for the removal" of the vehicle and since the
policeman was exercising the latter no question of delegation arose.

childcare legislation was discharged by boarding a child out with foster parents and the authority was not liable for negligence by the foster parents in looking after the child.[257]

F. Collateral or Casual Negligence of Independent Contractor

20-28   There is a recognised exception that an employer is not liable for the collateral or casual negligence of an independent contractor, that is, negligence in some collateral respect, as distinct from negligence with regard to the very matter delegated to be done.[258] The distinction between the two kinds of negligence is sometimes difficult to draw[259] but is established by the cases. To take a simple case, if D employs a contractor on a construction project D would not be liable for the negligent driving of the contractor while going to get supplies. However, in *Padbury v Holliday and Greenwood Ltd*[260] the defendants employed a sub-contractor to put metallic casements into the windows of a house which the defendants were building. While one of these casements was being put in, an iron tool was placed by a servant of the sub-contractor on the window sill, and the casement having been blown in by the wind, the tool fell and injured the claimant in the street below. It was held that the claimant's injuries were caused by an act of collateral negligence and the defendants were not liable. In *Holliday v National Telephone Co*[261] the defendants were laying telephone wires under a street and employed an

---

[257] *S. v Walsall MBC* [1985] 1 W.L.R. 1150; cf. *H v Surrey CC, The Times*, January 27, 1994 (primary liability for statement).

[258] *Pickard v Smith* (1861) 10 C.B.(N.S.) 470 at 480 per Williams J.: "If an independent contractor is employed to do a lawful act, and in the course of the work he or his servants commit some casual act of wrong or negligence, the employer is not answerable . . . The rule, however, is inapplicable to cases in which the act which occasions the injury is the one with the contractor was employed to do." "It is settled law that one employing another is not liable for his collateral negligence unless the relation of master and servant exists between them": per Lord Blackburn, *Dalton v Angus* (1881) 6 App.Cas. 740 at 829; *Cassidy v Ministry of Health* [1951] 2 K.B. 343 at 363–364 per Denning L.J.

[259] See the criticism of Sachs L.J. in *Salsbury v Woodland* [1970] 1 Q.B. 324 at 348. Prosser, *Torts*, 5th edn, p.516, suggests that the test of collateral negligence is not its character as a minor incident or operative detail of the work to be done, but rather its dissociation from any inherent risk created by the work itself. See also Jolowicz (1957) 9 Stanford L. Rev. 690 at pp.707–708.

[260] (1912) 28 T.L.R. 494.

[261] [1899] 2 Q.B. 392. Cf. *Reedie v L & NW Ry* (1849) 4 Ex. 244 (railway company employed contractor to build a bridge; contractor's workman negligently caused the death of a person, passing beneath along the highway, by allowing a stone to drop on him; Ry company held not liable). "I am not liable if my contractor in making a bridge happens to drop a brick . . . but I am liable if he makes a bridge which will not open . . . The liability of the employer depends on the existence of a duty . . . it only extends to the limit of that duty. I owe a duty with regard to the structure of the bridge; I owe a duty to see that my bridge will open; but I owe no duty with regard to the disposition of bricks and hammers in the course of construction": Chapman, "Liability for the Negligence of Independent Contractors" (1934) 50 L.Q.R. 71 at 80–81. That accords with the result of *Padbury* but not of *Holliday*.

independent contractor to make certain connections. A plumber employed by the contractor dipped a blowlamp into molten solder causing an explosion which injured the claimant. In the court below Willes J., in no uncertain terms, treated this as an act of collateral negligence, but the Court of Appeal reversed his decision and held the defendants were liable. The cases are difficult to distinguish save for the delphic statement in the brief report of *Padbury* that:

> "[T]he tool was not placed on the window sill in the ordinary course of doing the work which the sub-contractor was employed to do".

Otherwise, they both involve dangers to users of the highway and incidents in the performance of work rather than any deficiency in the finished work.

CHAPTER 21

JOINT AND SEVERAL TORTFEASORS

1. MULTIPLE TORTFEASORS, CAUSATION AND PROOF

WHERE two or more people by their independent breaches of duty to **21–1**
the claimant cause him to suffer distinct injuries, no special rules are
required, for each tortfeasor is liable for the damage which he
caused and only for that damage.[1] Where, however, two or more
breaches of duty by different persons cause the claimant to suffer a
single, indivisible injury the position is more complicated. The law
in such a case is that the claimant is entitled to sue all or any of them
for the full amount of his loss,[2] and each is said to be jointly and
severally liable for it.[3] If the claimant sues defendant A but not B
and C, it is open to A to seek "contribution" from B and C in respect
of their relative responsibility but this is a matter among A, B and
C and does not affect the claimant. This means that special rules are
necessary to deal with the possibilities of successive actions in

---

[1] See *Performance Cars Ltd v Abraham* [1962] 1 Q.B. 33; *Baker v Willoughby* [1970] A.C.
467, para.6–7, above.
[2] Though he cannot execute judgment so as to recover more than his loss: see below.
[3] This is the general position in common law and European legal systems. See Rogers (ed.),
Unification of Tort Law: Multiple Tortfeasors (2004). The major exception is the United
States, where the position has been radically altered by statute in many states. See Green
in Rogers (ed.), *Unification of Tort Law: Multiple Tortfeasors* (2004) p.261. However,
most Australian states have now gone down a similar road of apportioning liability among
wrongdoers, though not in relation to personal injuries. See, e.g. Civil Liability Act 2002
(NSW) Pt 4. For a broader comparative overview of divisibility issues see Oliphant (ed.)
Aggregation and Divisibility of Damage (2009).

respect of that loss and of claims for contribution or indemnity by one tortfeasor against the others. It may be greatly to the claimant's advantage to show that he has suffered the same, indivisible harm at the hands of a number of defendants for he thereby avoids the risk, inherent in cases where there are different injuries, of finding that one defendant is insolvent (or uninsured) and being unable to execute judgment against him. Even where all participants are solvent, a system which enabled the claimant to sue each one only for a proportionate part of the damage would require him to launch multiple proceedings, some of which might involve complex issues of liability, causation and proof. As the law now stands, the claimant may simply launch proceedings against the "easiest target".[4] The same picture is not, of course, so attractive from the point of view of the solvent defendant, who may end up carrying full responsibility for a loss in the causing of which he played only a partial, even secondary role. Thus a solicitor may be liable in full for failing to point out to his client that there is reason to believe that a valuation on which the client proposes to lend is suspect, the valuer being insolvent[5]; and an auditor will be likely to carry sole responsibility for negligent failure to discover fraud during a company audit. A sustained campaign against the rule of joint and several liability has been mounted in this country by certain professional bodies, who have argued instead for a regime of "proportionate liability" whereby, as against the claimant, and not merely among defendants as a group, each defendant would bear only his share of the liability.[6] While it has not been suggested here that such a change should be extended to personal injury claims, this has occurred in some American jurisdictions, whether by statute or by judicial decision.[7] However, an investigation of the issue by the Law Commission on behalf of the Dept of Trade and Industry in 1996[8] led to the

---

[4] Consider for example the outcome of the Selby rail accident. A driver fell asleep on the M62, veered off the road and caused a rail crash. The driver brought (unsuccessful) contribution proceedings alleging defective design of the motorway bridge. Under the present system the victims' claim was for a simple case of driving negligence. If they had been required to sue the designers of the bridge their case would have been much more complicated: *GNER v Hart* [2003] EWHC 2450 (QB). See also *Roe v Sheffield CC* [2004] EWCA Civ 329 at [34].

[5] See *Mortgage Express Ltd v Bowerman* [1996] 2 All E.R. 836.

[6] Which is in effect the position at sea where cargo on ship A is damaged by the concurrent fault of ship A and ship B (but not where cargo on innocent ship A is damaged by the concurrent fault of ships B and C) under the Merchant Shipping Act 1995 s.187 (replacing the Maritime Conventions Act 1911 s.1).

[7] See DTI Feasibility Investigation (1996) s.6.3 and Green, fn.3, above.

[8] See previous note. There was said to be a case in logic for proportionate liability in the case where C is at fault as well as D1 and D2 (see e.g. *Fitzgerald v Lane* [1989] A.C. 328) though in practice a change would tend to favour defendants: see the Feasibility Study at s.4.14.

conclusion that the present law was preferable to the various forms of proportionate liability.[9]

The question of the scope of joint and several liability is a difficult **21–2** one and there appears to have been some narrowing of the approach in the recent case law, so that although from a medical point of view there is only one injury, there may be a greater willingness to hold that the causative contribution of each defendant can be identified and his liability confined to that. The simplest case of joint and several liability is that of two virtually simultaneous acts of negligence, as where two drivers behave negligently and collide, injuring a passenger in one of the cars or a pedestrian,[10] but there is no requirement that the acts be simultaneous. Thus if D1 driving too fast in icy conditions causes his lorry to "jack-knife" across the motorway and D2, also driving too fast, later comes along and, trying to avoid the obstruction, runs down C, assisting at the scene, both D1 and D2 may be liable for C's injuries.[11] Of course it may be on the facts the act of D1 is held to have lost its causative effect.[12] The acts of the two defendants may be separated by a substantial period of time and yet contribute to one, indivisible injury for this purpose, as where D1 manufactures a dangerous product and D2 uses it without due care years later. In all these case there is no logical or sensible basis for dividing up the causative origin of the claimant's injury between the defendants. If, for example, he is killed in the accident one cannot say that he was half killed by D1 and half killed by D2—he was killed by the effect of the conduct of both of them. However, where an injury is a progressive one it seems a different attitude may be taken. Some of these cases are concerned with the different factual situation where there is only one tortfeasor and the other contributory cause is a natural event or something for which the defendant is not responsible, but the issue is fundamentally the same as that where there are two tortfeasors. In *Holtby v Brigham & Cowan (Hull) Ltd*[13] the claimant had been exposed to asbestos during employment with several employers and

---

[9] For another approach, see the Professional Standards Act 1994 (NSW) allowing professions to draw up schemes of limited liability for professional activities. The Limited Liability Partnership Act 2000 (para.24–24, below) reduces the risk of personal ruin to those practising in partnerships.

[10] "Commonplace": *Ellis v Environment Agency* [2008] EWCA Civ 1117; [2009] P.I.Q.R. P5 at [1].

[11] Based on *Rouse v Squires* [1973] Q.B. 889. See also *Lloyds Bank v Budd* [1982] R.T.R. 80. If, however, C's car had been damaged by a collision with D1's lorry before the arrival of D2 on the scene then D1 alone would be responsible for that loss.

[12] This was the issue in *Rouse v Squires*, above, fn.11.

[13] [2000] 3 All E.R. 421. *Thompson v Smiths Shiprepairers (North Shields) Ltd* [1984] Q.B. 405; *Allen v B.R.E.L. Ltd* [2001] EWCA Civ 242; [2001] I.C.R. 942; *Horsley v Cascade Insulation Services Ltd* [2009] EWHC 2945 (QB). In *Brookes v South Yorkshire Passenger Executive* [2005] EWCA Civ 452 the claimant was exposed by the defendant to conditions causative of vibration white finger from 1982 but the defendant was only at fault in relation to this risk from 1987. The CA declined to reduce the damages because although all

each of these exposures probably made some contribution to the asbestosis which he developed, but only one employer was sued. The Court of Appeal rejected the argument that once the claimant had shown that the defendant had made a material contribution to the disease (which was a virtually inevitable inference) the defendant was liable for the whole of the loss and held that the defendant was liable only to the extent that he had contributed to the disability and that on such facts the correct approach was to attribute responsibility on the basis of the proportionate time the claimant had been exposed while in the defendant's employment. Such cases are distinguishable from the motor collision injuring the passenger (at least pragmatically) on three bases: first, the time exposure approach provides a more or less rational (though often probably unscientific) basis for allocating responsibility; secondly, it seems counterintuitive to hold second or subsequent employers liable in respect of the consequences of what happened before they took the claimant on or to hold any of them liable in respect of what happened after he left them[14]; and thirdly, conditions like asbestosis or deafness are likely to get worse with continued exposure. However, the court does not appear to have regarded the principle it was enunciating as confined to "sequence" cases like this. In the leading case of *Bonnington Castings Ltd v Wardlaw*[15] the claimant suffered injury from exposure to silica dust in the defendants' works. One source of dust was swing grinders and the defendants were in breach of duty with regard to those (the "guilty dust") but the other source was the pneumatic hammers and there was no possible method of eliminating dust from those (the "innocent dust"). The defendants were held liable in full for the damage he suffered even though they were only to blame for part of the dust and probably substantially the lesser part of it.[16] In *Holtby* Stuart-Smith L.J. said that:

> "[W]hat the House of Lords did not consider in [*Bonnington*] was the extent of the defendants' liability, because it was never argued that the defendants were only liable to the extent of the material contribution."

---

exposure made some contribution to the final result, the claimant had a low susceptibility and would probably never have developed symptoms had the defendant taken proper steps in 1987. The objective of an award of damages is not to compensate the claimant for the amount of the damage suffered but for the effects of the damage on him: at [26].

[14] Cf. *Luke v Kingsley Smith & Co* [2003] EWHC 1559; [2004] P.N.L.R. 12 (lawyer D1 by dilatoriness makes C's claim vulnerable to striking out; lawyer D2 then negotiates a settlement for a fraction of C's loss; one single, indivisible loss in respect of which there can be contribution between D1 and D2).

[15] [1956] A.C. 613.

[16] [1956] A.C. 613 at 622.

As we have seen, the court in *Fairchild v Glenhaven Funeral Services Ltd*[17] was faced with a situation where the disease might have been caused by the ingestion of a single asbestos fibre emitted by any one of a number of employers and held that each was liable on the basis that he had materially increased the risk; but it was not disputed for the purposes of the claim that if there was liability each was liable in full. It was later held that even though such injury was indivisible, justice required that each defendant be liable only for the extent to which he had increased the risk and that approach in turn was reversed and joint and several liability reimposed by statute.[18] However, that particular, narrow context tells us nothing about the general rule and *Holtby* has not led to the wholesale abandonment of the proposition that each defendant is liable in full for an indivisible injury. It has been said in the Court of Appeal[19] that the *Holtby* principle is:

"[A]n exception to the general rule intended to do justice in a particular class of case. Although at the fringes the delineation of the class of case may be debateable, in the main it has been applied and in this court at least should be limited to, industrial disease or injury cases where there has been successive exposure to harm by a number of agencies, where the effect of the harm is divisible, and where it would be unjust for an individual defendant to bear the whole of a loss when in commonsense he was not responsible for all of it."[20]

Since the question of whether something made a causative contribution to an injury and to what extent is a question of fact and since it is not necessary that there should be precise mathematical evidence before a result may be apportioned between two causes, the courts may go quite a long way in reducing the claimant's recovery by being more willing to find that an injury is divisible.[21]

---

[17] [2002] UKHL 22; [2003] 1 A.C. 32, para.6–9, above.

[18] See para.6–10, above (mesothelioma cases only).

[19] See also *Wright v Stoddard International Plc* [2007] CSOH 138.

[20] *Ellis v Environment Agency* [2008] EWCA Civ 1117; [2009] P.I.Q.R. P5 at [39]. This is not a multiple tortfeasor case but the point of principle is the same. C's injury was the product of the combined effect of a fall for which D was responsible and another fall for which he was not. There was no "discount" for the contribution of the second fall. However, matters which are not causative may be relevant to damages. In the case C had a pre-existing spinal condition which would have at a later stage have caused disability without the falls and the damages were discounted for this.

[21] See the rather remarkable way in which the expert evidence in *Rahman v Arearose Ltd* [2001] Q.B. 351 attributed different aspects of the claimant's psychiatric trauma to different events. Criticised by Weir [2001] C.L.J. 237. See also *Hatton v Sutherland* [2002] EWCA Civ 76; [2002] I.C.R. 613 at [41] and *O'Neil v van Horne* (2002) 212 D.L.R. (4th) 458. Cf. *Rees v Dewhirst Plc* [2002] EWCA Civ 871.

The burden of proof rests on the claimant to show that the defendant was responsible for the whole or a quantifiable part of his injury, but in practice once it has been shown that what the defendant did make a material contribution he is at risk of being held liable for the whole unless he produces evidence of the contribution of other factors.[22]

2. DISTINCTION BETWEEN JOINT AND SEVERAL TORTFEASORS

21-3 At common law tortfeasors liable in respect of the same damage were divided into "joint" tortfeasors and "several" tortfeasors.[23] This distinction, formerly of importance, has been largely eroded by statute, as we shall see in a moment, but it remains of significance for one purpose and some account of it is necessary.

> "Persons are said to be joint tortfeasors when their separate shares in the commission of the tort are done in furtherance of a common design."[24]

So, in *Brook v Bool*,[25] where two men searching for a gas leak each applied a naked light to a gas pipe in turn and one of them caused an explosion, they were held to be joint tortfeasors[26]; but where two ships collided because of the independent acts of negligence of each of them, and one of them, without further negligence, collided with a third, it was held that they were several tortfeasors, whose acts combined to produce a single harm, because there was no community of design.[27] A seemingly anomalous exception to the requirement of community of design is that where an employer is liable vicariously for his servant's tort, employer and servant are joint

---

[22] *Holtby*'s case, above, fn.13.

[23] "Several or concurrent tortfeasors" is the terminology used by Auld L.J. in *Jameson v C.E.G.B.* [1997] 3 W.L.R. 151 at 156. However, "concurrent tortfeasors" is a convenient phrase to describe both.

[24] *The Koursk* [1924] P. 140, at 151 per Bankes L.J., at 159–160 per Sargant L.J. For the liability of company directors, see para.24–23, below.

[25] [1928] 2 K.B. 578. See too *Arneil v Patterson* [1931] A.C. 560; cf. *Cook v Lewis* [1952] 1 D.L.R. 1.

[26] Hence liable in respect of the damage. Note that the act of only one defendant was the physical cause of the damage. See also *Monsanto Plc v Tilly* [2000] Env L.R. 313 (reconnoitring site and being present at scene explaining matters to press sufficient to make D joint tortfeasor in relation to damage to crops); *Shah v Gale* [2005] EWHC 1087 (QB).

[27] *The Koursk*, above, fn.24. See also *Sadler v GW Ry* [1896] A.C. 450; *Thompson v LCC* [1899] 1 Q.B. 840. For the position where a number of persons are responsible for publication of a libel and only some of them are malicious, see para.12–65, above.

tortfeasors.[28] On the other hand, the parent or custodian of a child whose personal negligence enables the child to commit a tort, though he may be liable for the resulting damage, is not a joint tortfeasor with the child. He is personally negligent and his liability is for his own independent tort.[29] Mere facilitation of the commission of a tort by another does not make the defendant a joint tortfeasor and there is no tort of "knowing assistance" nor any direct counterpart of the criminal law concept of aiding and abetting: the defendant must either procure the wrongful act or act in furtherance of a common design or be party to a conspiracy.[30]

The two principal consequences at common law of the defendants' being joint tortfeasors were, (1) judgment against one of them, even if it remained unsatisfied, barred any subsequent action, or even the continuance of the same action, against the others, and (2) the release of one operated as the release of all, even if the claimant had not recovered his full loss. In each case the reason given was that the cause of action was single and indivisible.[31] Neither rule ever applied to several tortfeasors liable for the same damage. Now, however, the first rule has been abolished by statute.[32] The second rule still exists, though the fact that even joint tortfeasors may be sued in successive actions has "heavily compromised"[33] the logic of unity of liability upon which it rests. However, if the agreement with the first joint tortfeasor can be interpreted as a covenant not to sue or (which for practical purposes amounts to the same thing) contains a reservation of the claimant's rights against the other, then the other is not discharged.[34] Where the defendants were not true joint tortfeasors it has always been clear that if the claimant received from one damages representing his whole loss he could not proceed against the others[35] but it is now the case that the

[28] However, on the basis that joint tortfeasors are liable for the same *tort*, whereas several concurrent tortfeasors are liable for the same *damage* (Gleeson C.J. and Callinan J. in *Baxter v Obacelo Pty Ltd* [2001] HCA 66; 205 C.L.R. 635) perhaps it is not anomalous.
[29] See *Bebee v Sales* (1916) 32 T.L.R. 413; *Newton v Edgerley* [1959] 1 W.L.R. 1031.
[30] *Credit Lyonnais Bank Nederland N.V. v E.C.G.D.* [2001] 1 A.C. 486. See also *C.B.S. Songs Ltd v Amstrad Consumer Electronics Plc* [1988] A.C. 1018 at 1058. D1 is attacking C. D2, a malicious bystander, throws a knife to D1, with which D1 stabs C. It seems extraordinary to suggest that D2 is not civilly liable for C's injury. Yet it is difficult to say that there is any procurement, common design or conspiracy.
[31] *Brinsmead v Harrison* (1872) L.R. 7 C.P. 547; *Duck v Mayeu* [1892] 2 Q.B. 511; *Cutler v McPhail* [1962] 2 Q.B. 292. Cf. *X.L. Petroleum v Caltex Oil* (1985) 155 C.L.R. 448.
[32] Civil Liability (Contribution) Act 1978 s.3, replacing the Law Reform (Married Women and Tortfeasors) Act 1935 s.6(1)(a).
[33] Steyn L.J. in *Watts v Aldington, The Times*, December 16, 1993. Or even destroyed it: *Robinson v Tait* [2002] 2 N.Z.L.R. 30 at [9].
[34] See *Watts v Aldington*, above, fn.33; *Gardiner v Moore* [1969] 1 Q.B. 55; *Apley Estates Ltd v De Bernales* [1947] Ch. 217.
[35] *Clark v Urquhart* [1930] A.C. 28 at 66; *Tang Man Sit v Capacious Investments Ltd* [1996] A.C. 514 at 522; *Mason v Grogan* [2009] EWCA Civ 283.

same is true wherever the settlement with the first defendant is made in full satisfaction of the claim even if the sum is less than the claimant would have received if the case had been pursued to judgment.[36] The settlement with one tortfeasor, even though other tortfeasors are not party to it, is to be taken as conclusively establishing that the sum which has been agreed represents full value for the claim,[37] despite the fact that the settlement makes no mention of the position of other tortfeasors and the sum recovered from the settlor will in practice be discounted to reflect any weaknesses in the claim. Of course the terms of the settlement may show, expressly or by implication, that it is not in full satisfaction and that the claimant is reserving his rights against other defendants.[38] So, where C dismissed D1, its managing director, for gross misconduct amounting to fraud and he compromised their action by surrendering his shareholding, it was held in proceedings by C against D2, their auditors, for failing to detect D1's wrongdoing,[39] that it was quite unrealistic to say that C was giving up its right to bring further proceedings.[40] Even where the claimant may bring successive proceedings, it is obviously desirable that a claimant should, if he reasonably can, sue in the same proceedings all the tortfeasors who are liable to him for the same damage. It is therefore provided that the claimant may not recover costs in any but the first action in respect of the damage unless the court is of the opinion that there was reasonable ground for bringing the further proceedings.[41]

---

[36] *Jameson v C.E.G.B.* [2000] 1 A.C. 455. This difficult case was a rather unsuitable vehicle on which to restate the law in this type of case, because the general rule that sums actually received would reduce the liability of other tortfeasors *pro tanto* did not apply. J recovered £80,000 in settlement from his employer, Babcock, shortly before his death from mesothelioma. After his death his widow commenced proceedings under the Fatal Accidents Act 1976 against C.E.G.B. Although the settlement sum from Babcock passed to the widow, it is provided in s.4 of the 1976 Act that benefits accruing to the claimant (the widow) from the estate of the deceased are not to be brought into account in assessing the damages: para.23–16, below.

[37] [2000] 1 A.C. 455 at 474.

[38] Where C settles with D1 in circumstances where it remains open to him to go against D2 and he does so, D1 is exposed to contribution proceedings by D2 (below). D1 can protect himself by obtaining from C an undertaking not to go against D1 or to indemnify him.

[39] In which D2 sought contribution or indemnity from D1: one defendant cannot resist contribution proceedings by the other by saying that he has settled with C: Civil Liability (Contribution) Act 1978 s.1(3).

[40] *Cape & Dalgleish v Fitzgerald* [2002] UKHL 16, applying *Heaton v Axa Equity & Law* [2002] UKHL 15; [2002] 2 A.C. 329.

[41] Civil Liability (Contribution) Act 1978 s.4. A similar provision appeared in the Law Reform (Married Women and Tortfeasors) Act 1935 s.6(1)(b), but that act went further in providing that the sums recoverable in later actions should not in the aggregate exceed the amount awarded by the judgment first given. The Law Commission (Report on Contribution, Law Com. No.79 (1977)) thought the "damages sanction" an unnecessary complication and potentially unjust, e.g. if P suffered loss at the hands of D1 and D2 he might have a good practical reason for suing D1 first but might be bound by a valid contractual provision for limitation of damages against D1.

3. CONTRIBUTION BETWEEN TORTFEASORS

At common law the general rule was that one concurrent tortfeasor,   **21–4**
even if he had satisfied the claimant's judgment in full, could not
recover indemnity nor contribution towards his liability from any
other tortfeasor liable. The rule was laid down with regard to joint
tortfeasors in *Merryweather v Nixan*[42] and was later extended to
several concurrent tortfeasors.[43] The harshness of this rule was
modified to a limited extent and it does not apply where the tort was
not clearly illegal in itself, and the person claiming contribution or
indemnity acted in the belief that his conduct was lawful[44]; nor does
it apply where even though the tort was clearly illegal in itself, one
of the parties has been vicariously liable for another's wrong to
which he gave neither his authority nor assent and of which he had
no knowledge.[45]

A. Civil Liability (Contribution) Act 1978

The rule in *Merryweather v Nixan* was for most practical pur-   **21–5**
poses reversed by s.6(1)(c) of the Law Reform (Married Women and
Tortfeasors) Act 1935.[46] The operation of the 1935 Act was examined by the Law Commission in the wider context of contribution
generally (including contribution between contractors) and the product of its deliberations is the Act of 1978.[47] As far as contribution
between tortfeasors is concerned the Act continues the same basic
structure as its predecessor but there are some significant changes of
detail.

By s.1(1) of the Act, any person liable in respect of any damage
suffered by another may recover contribution from any other person
liable in respect of the same damage (whether jointly or otherwise)

---

[42] (1799) 8 T.R. 186. The rule was regarded as resting on the maxim *ex turpi causa non oritur actio*: see para.25–18, below.
[43] *Horwell v L.G.O. Co* (1877) 2 Ex.D. 365 at 379 per Kelly C.B.; *The Koursk* [1924] P. 140 at 158 per Scrutton L.J.
[44] See *Adamson v Jarvis* (1827) 4 Bing. 66 (auctioneer innocently selling X's goods at the behest of the defendant, who represented himself as owner). This exception may hold good even where the joint enterprise proves to be criminal: *Burrows v Rhodes* [1899] 1 Q.B. 816.
[45] *Romford Ice and Cold Storage Co v Lister* [1956] 2 Q.B. 180, affirmed [1957] A.C. 555, para.20–18, above.
[46] See Cmd. 4637 (1934). Two statutory exceptions to the rule antedated the 1935 Act: Maritime Conventions Act 1911 s.3, and Companies Act 1908 s.84. Contribution in personal injury cases at sea is now governed by the Merchant Shipping Act 1995 s.189, to the same effect as the 1911 Act.
[47] *Report on Contribution*, Law Com. No.79 (1977). The Act came into force on January 1, 1979.

and for this purpose a person is "liable" whatever the legal basis of his liability, "whether tort, breach of contract, breach of trust or otherwise".[48] So if D1 advises C on the purchase of a computer system and as a result C buys a system from D2 which does not perform the required task satisfactorily and D1 settles C's claim, D1 may be able to seek contribution from D2, even though D2's only liability is in contract, whereas D1's sounds in contract and in tort.[49] However, in order that D1 and D2 are liable in respect of the "same damage" one must generally[50] be able to say that if either of them makes a payment to C on account of his liability that will go to reduce the liability of the other to C.[51] Hence where D1 overvalued a property on the security of which C lent money to D2 and, D2 having defaulted on the loan, D1 settled C's claim for negligence for £400,000, D1 was unable to claim contribution from D2.[52] In such a case D1's liability to C is reduced by the value of D2's covenant to repay[53] but D2's liability (which is not a liability *for damage* or *in damages* at all) is not reduced by the value of the claim against the valuer. If C did recover in full from D2, no doubt it would hold £400,000 on trust for D1. Further, D1 would be subrogated to the extent of £400,000 to C's claim against D2.[54] Considerable uncertainty has developed over the question whether, and if so how far, the Act applies where one party is liable in tort and the other liable

---

[48] Civil Liability (Contribution) Act 1978 s.6(1). "Liability" means a liability which has been or could be established in a court in England and Wales: s.1(6). It includes a judgment, even though given on a false assumption: *BRB (Residuary) Ltd v Connex South Eastern Ltd* [2008] EWHC 1172 (QB); [2008] 1 W.L.R. 2867.

[49] Based on *Brownton Ltd v Edward Moore Inbucon Ltd* [1985] 3 All E.R. 499, a pre-1978 Act case. So also where an architect fails to supervise a builder both he and the builder are liable for the same damage, that is to say the owner being left with a defective building. But an architect whose negligent certification hampers the building owner in a claim against the builder for late completion is not liable for the same damage as the builder (*Royal Brompton Hospital NHS Trust v Watkins Gray International (UK)* [2002] UKHL 14; [2002] 1 W.L.R. 1397); nor is a builder who is exempt from liability under his contract for fire damage but required to restore the works under an insurance policy liable for the same damage as persons who also caused the fire but have no such exemption (*C.R.S. Retail Services Ltd v Taylor Young Partnership* [2002] UKHL 17; [2002] 1 W.L.R. 1419); nor is a solicitor who allows a limitation period to expire liable for the same damage as the tortfeasor: *Wallace v Litwiniuk* (2001) 92 Alta. L.R. (3d) 249. See also *Bovis Construction Ltd v Commercial Union Assurance Co Plc* [2001] 1 Lloyd's Rep. 416 but cf. *Greene Wood & McClean LLP v Templeton Insurance Ltd* [2009] EWCA Civ 65; [2009] 1 W.L.R. 2013.

[50] In the *Royal Brompton* case, above, fn.49, at [28] Lord Steyn pointed out that in the last resort it is the statutory wording which governs and that this "test" might lead to undue complexity in some cases.

[51] *Howkins & Harrison v Tyler* [2001] Lloyd's Rep. P.N. 1, CA.

[52] [2001] Lloyd's Rep. P.N. 1, CA: doubting *Friends' Provident Life Office v Hillier Parker & Rowden* [1997] Q.B. 85.

[53] *Eagle Star Insurance Co v Gale & Power* (1955) 166 E.G. 37.

[54] That had not been pleaded in *Howkins*. A claim by one co-surety against another does not fall within the 1978 Act: *Hampton v Minns* [2001] 1 W.L.R. 1.

in restitution, for example where D1 defrauds C of money and D2 knowingly receives it and/or disposes of it. Doubt has been expressed whether an obligation of D2 to pay C on a restitutionary basis can be described as an obligation to pay "compensation" within the meaning of the Act[55]; but at the moment there are Court of Appeal decisions accepting the applicability of the Act.[56] Further, the defendant and the potential contributor must be liable to the same person, otherwise they are not liable for the same damage. So if D1 is liable to C, he cannot obtain contribution from D2 who is liable to some other party altogether, even if C could himself have claimed contribution from D2.[57] On the other hand "the same damage" must not be confused with "the same damages". Where the vendor of a business is in breach of warranty the measure of damages against him may be different from that against a valuer engaged by the buyer, but that does not preclude the application of the 1978 Act.[58]

The amount of contribution ordered[59] is to be: **21–6**

"[S]uch as may be found by the court to be just and equitable having regard to the extent of that person's responsibility for the damage in question".[60]

The principles are similar to those governing the apportionment of damages between claimant and defendant in the other legislation dealing with concurrent fault, the Law Reform (Contributory Negligence) Act 1945,[61] so that the court must look at both causation[62]

---

[55] Lord Steyn in *Royal Brompton Hospital NHS Trust v Watkins Gray International (UK)* [2002] UKHL 14; [2002] 1 W.L.R. 1397 at [33].

[56] See *Charter Plc v City Index Ltd* [2007] EWCA Civ 1382; [2009] Ch. 313.

[57] *Birse Construction v Haiste Ltd* [1996] 1 W.L.R. 675.

[58] *Eastgate Group Ltd v Lindsey Morden Group Inc* [2001] EWCA Civ 1446. That does not, of course, necessarily mean that it is just and equitable that the vendor should recover contribution from the valuer.

[59] Claims for contribution are brought under Pt 20 of the Civil Procedure Rules. The parties are known as Pt 20 claimants and defendants.

[60] Section 2(1). The statutory right to contribution is not in the nature of a claim in tort. It has been said to resemble a quasi-contractual claim by a person who has been constrained to discharge another's liability: *Ronex Properties Ltd v John Laing Construction Ltd* [1983] Q.B. 398, but in another context the right was said to be "founded on tort": *FFSB Ltd v Seward & Kissel LLP* [2007] UKPC 16.

[61] See para.6–53, above. Where C, D1 and D2 are all to blame both the 1945 and 1978 Acts are applicable. The correct approach is to consider the claimant's fault against the totality of the defendants' conduct. That will give a figure for which the claimant recovers judgment against all defendants and in respect of which they may seek contribution inter se: *Fitzgerald v Lane* [1989] A.C. 328.

[62] Causation of the damage is what is in issue. Hence where a collision is the fault of D1 and D2 but D1 carried C in dangerous conditions which led to the injury, D1 may carry a greater share of the responsibility than D2: *Madden v Quirke* [1989] 1 W.L.R. 702.

and culpability.[63] However, it has been held, somewhat surprisingly, that culpability includes fault which is non-causative, for example attempts to cover up responsibility for the damage.[64] Where one defendant is vicariously liable to the claimant for the fault of his employee that is also the relevant fault for the purposes of a contribution claim against another defendant: the first defendant cannot say his claim should be assessed on the basis that he was free from personal blame.[65] As we have seen, in a road accident case a passenger's failure to wear a seat belt generally leads to a 25 per cent reduction in damages for contributory negligence where the injury would have been prevented by taking that precaution[66] and in *Jones v Wilkins*[67] the Court of Appeal upheld an apportionment of 25 per cent responsibility to a passenger who failed to take adequate steps to restrain her infant child, the claimant,[68] and 75 per cent to the driver of the other car, who was responsible for the collision. The question is one of proportion, involving an individual exercise of discretion by the trial judge and for that reason appellate courts will be reluctant to interfere with an apportionment as determined by the judge[69] unless there has been some error in his approach.[70] If it considers it appropriate, the court may exempt the defendant from any liability to make contribution[71] or direct that the contribution

---

[63] *Jones v Wilkins* [2001] P.I.Q.R. Q12.

[64] *Re-source America International Ltd v Platt Site Services Ltd* [2005] EWCA Civ 665; *Brian Warwicker Partnership v HOK International Ltd* [2005] EWCA Civ 962. However, in the latter case, Arden L.J., who seems to have been unhappy about this conclusion, thought that the result in the *Re-source* case would have been the same even without the non-causative conduct and that that was really relevant as showing the seriousness of the defendants' causative fault.

[65] *Dubai Aluminium Co Ltd v Salaam* [2002] UKHL 48; [2003] 2 A.C. 366.

[66] See para.6–53, above.

[67] Above, fn.63. However, in *Pride Valley Foods Ltd v Hall & Partners* [2001] EWCA Civ 1001 at [69] Sedley L.J., while regarding the result in *Jones* as "inescapable", observed that while the principles for gauging contributory negligence can furnish a template for the apportionment of liability between joint tortfeasors, it does not follow that the converse will be the case because in a case of contributory negligence the claimant's fault may be linked to some unfulfilled duty of the defendant to guard against that.

[68] In practice, the effect (though not the theory) may be the same as identifying the child with the parent for the purposes of contributory negligence, since unless the parent is insured she may not be in a position to pay the contribution and would risk bankruptcy if the judgment were enforced in full against the driver.

[69] *Kerry v Carter* [1969] 1 W.L.R. 1372 at 1376. In determining the apportionment the court must have regard only to the parties before it and cannot take into account the possibility that some other person may also have been to blame: *Maxfield v Llewellyn* [1961] 1 W.L.R. 1119. D1 and D2 may be liable to C in respect of the same damage, but D1 may also sue D2 in respect of his own damage (and vice versa). If this happens after the conclusion of C's suit are the parties to the second action bound by the apportionment in C's suit? "Yes", said Popplewell J. in *Wall v Radford* [1991] 2 All E.R. 741, reviewing conflicting lines of authority. However, a subsequent suit between D1 and D2 might not now be possible: see para.22–3, below.

[70] As in *Andrews v Initial Cleaning Services Ltd* [2000] I.C.R. 166.

[71] Contrast the Law Reform (Contributory Negligence) Act 1945, where, once a finding has been made that the claimant is guilty of contributory negligence, the court is obliged to reduce the damages. The power to exempt a defendant from contribution is plainly directed

recoverable shall amount to a complete indemnity.[72] The Act does
not cease to be applicable because the act of the defendant seeking
contribution amounts to a crime[73] but where a defendant guilty of
wilful wrongdoing seeks a contribution from one who has merely
been negligent the latter may in some cases have a powerful and
perhaps overwhelming case why it would not be just and equitable
to order him to make contribution: it is unlikely that a court would
accede to the request of a burglar for contribution from the security
guard who fell asleep.[74] Nevertheless, there is no rule that a fraudulent defendant is required to bear the whole loss as against a
negligent one.[75] The court's powers in any case are subject to the
overriding principle that one defendant cannot, by way of contribution proceedings, be liable for a greater sum than could be recovered
from him by the claimant. Since the two defendants have caused
indivisible damage they will often be liable for the same amount but
this is not necessarily the case. Thus if C's property worth £1,000 is
destroyed as a result of the combined (and equal) negligence of D1
and D2, there being a binding contract between C and D1 whereby
the latter's liability is limited to £300, the principle just mentioned
means that D2 in contribution proceedings can recover no more than
this amount from D1.[76] A negligent D1 may be able to rely on the
claimant's contributory negligence and/or on a contractual limitation of liability; a fraudulent D2 may do neither. Let us assume that,
(1) the combined conduct of D1 and D2 has produced an indivisible
loss of £15 million, (2) the claimant is guilty of one-third contributory negligence, (3) D1 has validly limited his liability to £5 million
and has paid that to the claimant, and (4) D2's responsibility is
assessed under the Act at 75 per cent. In such a case it has been held

---

at the case where he is nevertheless under a liability to the claimant. Cf. the curious result
in *Hawley v Luminar Leisure Ltd* [2006] EWCA Civ 18. D1 had suffered a default
judgment. D2 was held liable after a trial. D2's contribution claim was dismissed because
D1's minor negligence was insufficiently causally connected with C's loss. In other words,
D1 was not in law liable to C but the court declined to set aside the default judgment
because timely application had not been made.

[72] As in *Semtex Ltd v Gladstone* [1954] 1 W.L.R. 945, and *K.D. v CC Hampshire* [2005]
EWHC 2550 (QB), where the first defendant's liability was only vicarious and in *Wong v
Kwan Kin Travel Services* [1996] 1 W.L.R. 39 under the HK Ordinance. Cf. *Jones v
Manchester Corp* [1952] 2 Q.B. 852.

[73] *K v P* [1993] Ch. 141.

[74] Counsel's example in *K v P*, fn.73.

[75] See *Downs v Chappell* [1997] 1 W.L.R. 426, where, however, some weight is placed upon
the fact that it was D1's negligence rather than D2's fraud which was the direct inducement to buy and where D1's conduct was "reckless". Note, however, that the fraudulent
defendant cannot raise contributory negligence against the claimant.

[76] See Civil Liability (Contribution) Act 1978 s.2(3). Where an offer of amends under the
Defamation Act 1996 has been made and accepted and the person who has made the offer
is sued for contribution by another defendant, he cannot be required to pay by way of
contribution a greater amount than the amount payable in pursuance of the offer:
s.3(9)(b).

that the correct approach is that the starting point is the total loss less the reduction for contributory negligence, i.e. £10 million, even though D2's liability to the claimant is for the full £15 million. As between D1 and D2 the £10 million would be shared in the respective sums of £2.5 million and £7.5 million. Hence since D1 has paid £5 million he is entitled to £2.5 million from D2.[77]

21–7   It often happens that one tortfeasor may be able to recover an indemnity, or damages amounting to an indemnity or contribution, from another person by virtue of a contract between them. Nothing in the 1978 Act affects the enforceability of such an indemnity[78] and it is irrelevant to this contractual claim that the extent of a tortfeasor's liability has been determined as between himself and another tortfeasor in proceedings for contribution. In *Sims v Foster Wheeler Ltd*[79] the claimant's husband was killed when defective staging collapsed, and both his employers and the constructors of the staging were liable in tort. As between these two tortfeasors it was held that the employers were 25 per cent to blame and should bear that proportion of the damages. They were, however, entitled to recover this amount from their sub-contractors by way of damages for breach of an implied warranty that the staging should be properly constructed for safe use as scaffolding. On the other hand, the Act does not render enforceable any agreement for indemnity which would not have been enforceable had it not been passed.[80] This appears to refer to cases where the party seeking indemnity knew or may be presumed to have known that he was committing an unlawful act. In *W.H. Smith & Son v Clinton*[81] the defendants had contracted to indemnify the claimants, a printing and publishing firm, against any claims made against them for libels appearing in the defendants' paper *Vanity Fair*. This indemnity was held to be irrecoverable because the claimants well knew that the matter published was libellous. If the claimants had been innocent they could have recovered under the indemnity clause.[82] Although they could still

---

[77] *Nationwide Building Society v Dunlop Haywards (DHL) Ltd* [2009] EWHC 254 (Comm); [2010] 1 W.L.R. 258. Of course it may be that the fraudulent D2 is not claim-worthy, as was probably so in the case.

[78] Section 7(3) saves, (1) an express contractual right to contribution, (2) an express or implied contractual right to indemnity, (3) an express contractual provision "regulating or excluding contribution". The Act does not affect any right to recover an indemnity otherwise than by contract. This is an obscure area: see *Lambert v Lewis* [1982] A.C. 225; *The Kapetan Georgis* [1988] 1 Lloyd's Rep. 352; *Fletcher v National Mutual Life Nominee Ltd* [1990] 1 N.Z.L.R. 97.

[79] [1966] 1 W.L.R. 156; *Wright v Tyne Improvement Commissioners* [1968] 1 W.L.R. 336. Cf. *Lambert v Lewis* [1982] A.C. 225, where the person seeking indemnity was held to be the sole cause of his own loss.

[80] Section 7(3).

[81] (1908) 99 L.T. 841.

[82] *Daily Mirror Newspapers Ltd v Exclusive News Agency* (1937) 81 S.J. 924.

not recover under the express contract of indemnity,[83] it may be that the court would award contribution under the Act to the printer[84] or publisher of a libel against its more culpable author.[85]

B. Limitation and Contribution

21–8

Under the Civil Liability (Contribution) Act 1978 a defendant may seek contribution notwithstanding that he has ceased to be liable to the claimant since the damage occurred,[86] provided he was so liable immediately before the judgment or compromise in the claimant's favour,[87] but his right to seek contribution is subject to a limitation period of two years from the time when it arises.[88] The other party likewise is liable to make contribution notwithstanding that he has ceased to be liable in respect of the damage in question,[89] unless he ceased to be liable by virtue of the expiry of a period of limitation or prescription which extinguished the right on which the claim against him in respect of the damage was based.[90] This proviso will not apply to most periods of limitation in tort since they merely bar the remedy, not the right.[91] Accordingly, suppose C is injured by the combined negligence of D1 and D2 on December 31, 2006. On December 1, 2009, C recovers judgment against D1. C's cause of action against D2 becomes statute-barred on the last day of 2009,[92] but D1 has two years from the judgment against him to seek contribution from D2. However, conversion is an exception to the principle that the expiry of a limitation period only bars the remedy, for by s.3(2) of the Limitation Act 1980, the owner's title to his chattel is extinguished six years after the conversion.[93] Thus if C's goods are wrongfully converted by D1 and D2 on December 31, 2004, and C recovers judgment against D1 on December 1, 2010,

---

[83] Section 11 of the Defamation Act 1952 provides that agreements for indemnity against civil liability shall not be unlawful unless at the time of the publication the person claiming to be indemnified knows the matter is defamatory and does not reasonably believe there to be a good defence to any action brought upon it.

[84] The printer who is unaware he is publishing a libel and takes reasonable care now escapes liability altogether: para.12–23, above.

[85] Williams, *Joint Torts and Contributory Negligence*, pp.139–145. Cf. Gatley, *Libel and Slander*, 11th edn, para.29–32.

[86] The judgment against the defendant will, of course, extinguish the claimant's right of action against him by merger.

[87] Section 1(2).

[88] Limitation Act 1980 s.10.

[89] e.g. by a settlement with the claimant: *Logan v Uttlesford DC* (1986) 136 N.L.J. 541; *Jameson v C.E.G.B.* [1998] Q.B. 323 (this point not on appeal [2000] 1 A.C. 455).

[90] Section 1(3).

[91] See para.26–16, below.

[92] It is assumed that there is no question of the period being extended under the Limitation Act 1980: para.26–20, below.

[93] There is an exception where the conversion amounts to theft: para.26–16, below.

D1 will be unable to claim contribution from D2 unless he brings proceedings before the end of 2010.

C. Settlements

21–9   The vast majority of tort actions are settled (or withdrawn) before the court pronounces judgment and the machinery of civil justice could not operate if this were not so. As we have seen, in some cases a settlement with one defendant may preclude the claimant from taking further proceedings against others because he will be deemed to have received full satisfaction.[94] However, a defendant who has settled must have the opportunity of seeking contribution against any other person he considers liable. Under the law before the 1978 Act a defendant who settled, with or without admission of liability, could seek contribution[95] but this involved a curious reversal of the normal roles of litigation, for in the contribution proceedings he was required to show that he was liable to the claimant.[96] What was more, if he failed to do this he could recover no contribution even though the evidence showed beyond any doubt that the person from whom he sought it was liable to the claimant. Section 1(4) of the 1978 Act meets this point by providing that a person who has bona fide settled a claim:

> "[S]hall be entitled to recover contribution . . . without regard to whether or not he himself is or ever was liable in respect of the damage, provided, however, that he would have been liable assuming that the factual basis of the claim[97] against him could be established."

One objection to this is that it produces the possibility of a collusive settlement but this is probably not very great in tort actions where the real defendants will usually be insurers.[98]

What is the position if the claimant sues one defendant (D2), fails and then successfully sues the other (D1)? Can D1 claim contribution from D2 notwithstanding the determination of C's claim in D2's favour? This would not create any issue estoppel at common law, but by s.1(5) of the 1978 Act a judgment in C's action against D2:

---

[94] See para.21–3, above.

[95] *Stott v West Yorkshire Road Car Co Ltd* [1971] 2 Q.B. 651.

[96] Section 6(1)(c) of the 1935 Act provided that, "any tortfeasor liable in respect of [the damage] may recover contribution from any other tortfeasor who is, or would if sued have been, liable in respect of the same damage."

[97] Which is to be defined by reference to any pleadings: *BRB (Residuary) Ltd v Connex South Eastern Ltd* [2008] EWHC 1172 (QB); [2008] 1 W.L.R. 2867.

[98] The risk of collusion is probably considerably greater in contract actions, which are brought under the statutory contribution scheme by s.1(1) of the Act.

"[S]hall be conclusive in the proceedings for contribution as to any issue determined by that judgment in favour of the person from whom the contribution is sought".

The effect of this is that if the action against D2 was dismissed on the merits (because C failed to make out the legal basis of his claim) D1 cannot proceed against D2 for contribution, but the position is otherwise if the dismissal was on procedural grounds (for example, for want of prosecution by C[99]) or because of the expiry of the limitation period.[100] In practice there will generally not be successive proceedings, and the issue of contribution will be disposed of in the main action. Either C will sue D1 and D2 or, if he does not and chooses to sue D1 alone, D1 may bring Pt 20 proceedings against D2.[101]

---

[99] *R.A. Lister & Co Ltd v E.G. Thompson (Shipping) Ltd (No.2)* [1987] 3 All E.R. 1032 at 1039.

[100] *Nottingham Health Authority v Nottingham CC* [1988] 1 W.L.R. 903 at 911–912. This is the only way to avoid a conflict between s.1(3) and s.1(5). The wording proposed by the Law Commission was clearer.

[101] CPR Pt 20. If the court finds that one defendant is wholly to blame and exonerates the other, that does not preclude an appeal by the first directed to placing all or part of the blame on the second: *Moy v Pettmann Smith* [2005] UKHL 7; [2005] 1 W.L.R. 581.

CHAPTER 22

REMEDIES

IN this chapter we shall consider the remedies which may be availa- **22–1**
ble to the victim of a tort. Of these the most important is an award
of damages, and the first part of this chapter is devoted to the rules
governing the action for damages and their assessment.[1] In the
second part the other remedies, namely, self-help, injunction and an
order for the specific restitution of property, will be discussed.

---

[1] Damages for fatal accidents are considered in the next chapter.

Part I. Damages[2]

1. DAMAGES RECOVERABLE ONCE ONLY

22–2   The general rule is that the damages to which a claimant is entitled from the defendant in respect of a wrongful act must be recovered once and for all.[3] He cannot bring a second action upon the same facts simply because his injury proves to be more serious than was thought when judgment was given.[4] The principal difficulties arise in actions for personal injuries, because there the judge has so often to base his award of damages upon an estimate of many future uncertainties. Accordingly, the "once for all rule" has already been modified in that context.[5]

A. Qualifications of the Rule

22–3   **i. Where two distinct rights are violated.** It was held in *Brunsden v Humphrey*[6] that where one act of the defendant violated two distinct rights of the claimant (personal injury and property damage) he could bring successive actions in respect of those rights. That remains the law but it must now be qualified by the procedural rule that it may be an abuse of process to return to court to raise issues which could have been raised against the same party in earlier proceedings[7] and if so the second claim will be struck out.[8] Lack of funds to pursue both claims is unlikely in itself to mean there is no abuse, though it is not irrelevant.[9] Failure to raise both issues in the initial proceedings may result in the claimant having an action

---

[2] McGregor, *Damages*, 18th edn; Tettenborn, Wilby and Bennett, *Law of Damages*; Burrows, *Remedies for Torts and Breach of Contract*, 3rd edn; Street, *Principles of the Law of Damages*; Ogus, *The Law of Damages*; and, for personal injuries, Kemp and Kemp, *The Quantum of Damages*. The Law Commission was very active in the field of damages in the late 1990s. The Reports and Consultation Papers are referred to at appropriate points.

[3] Laid down in *Fetter v Beale* (1701) 1 Ld.Raym. 339 at 692; *Fitter v Veal* (1701) 12 Mod. 542. For Winfield's views on the merits of the rule, see the 7th edn of this work, pp.97–98. Nor can the court make a complex conditional order tailored to do justice between the parties: *Patel v Hooper & Jackson* [1999] 1 W.L.R. 1792.

[4] A foreign judgment may preclude further action in England. See, e.g. *Black v Yates* [1992] Q.B. 526.

[5] See para.22–23, below.

[6] (1884) 14 Q.B.D. 141.

[7] *Henderson v Henderson* (1843) 3 Hare 100; *Talbot v Berkshire CC* [1994] Q.B. 290; *Bradford and Bingley Building Society v Seddon* [1999] 1 WLR 1482. The court in *Talbot* (where the claimant had been sued by X, a passenger in his car, and had issued a third-party notice claiming contribution against the highway authority but had not lodged a claim against the authority in respect of his own injuries) thought that *Brunsden v Humphrey* might have been wrongly decided on the facts. Cf. *Sweetman v Shepherd*, *The Times*, March 29, 2000 (not abuse to bring separate claim for contribution).

[8] See *Johnson v Gore Wood & Co* [2001] 2 A.C. 1.

[9] [2001] 2 A.C. 1.

against his legal advisers, but the fact that he has none will again not itself mean that raising the issue in fresh proceedings against the defendant is not an abuse.[10]

ii. Continuing injury. If I wrongfully place something on your land and leave it there, that is not simply a single act of trespass, but is a continuing trespass giving rise to a fresh cause of action from day to day, *de die in diem*.[11] Similarly, a continuing nuisance gives rise to a fresh cause of action each time damage occurs as a result of it, and accordingly successive actions can be brought.[12] In fact in a case of continuing nuisance prospective damages cannot be claimed, however probable the occurrence of future damage may be: the claimant must await the event and then bring fresh proceedings.[13] It follows, somewhat unfortunately, that if the defendant has caused a subsidence of part of the claimant's land, damages can be awarded only for what has already occurred, and the claimant cannot recover damages for the depreciation in the value of his property attributable to the risk of further subsidence.[14] However, he may recover as damages the cost of remedial work to prevent further injury.[15]

22–4

2. KINDS OF DAMAGES

Ordinarily an award of damages is made in order to compensate the claimant for his injury, and the assessment of compensatory damages is considered in detail below.[16] An award of damages may,

22–5

---

[10] *Wain v Sherwood & Sons Transport Ltd* [1999] P.I.Q.R. P159.
[11] *Hudson v Nicholson* (1839) 5 M. & W. 437; *Konskier v B. Goodman Ltd* [1928] 1 K.B. 421. Distinguish the case of a single act of trespass, such as the digging of a hole on the claimant's land, where it is only the consequence of the trespass, not the trespass itself, which continues.
[12] *Darley Main Colliery Co v Mitchell* (1886) 11 App. Cas. 127; *Phonographic Performance Ltd v DTI* [2004] EWHC 1795 (Ch); [2004] 1 W.L.R. 2893 (claim for failure to give effect to Directive subject to this principle).
[13] Cf. *Toronto General Trusts Corp v Roman* (1962) 37 D.L.R. (2d) 16 (Ontario CA) where, notwithstanding a judgment against him in an action of detinue for the return of shares, the defendant nevertheless failed to return them for a substantial period of time. A second action claiming damages for that detention was allowed but damages were not awarded in the second action for a period of detention prior to judgment in the first. Under certain conditions damages in respect of probable future harm may be awarded in lieu of an injunction under Lord Cairns' Act, para.22–53, below. See, however, *Redland Bricks Ltd v Morris* [1970] A.C. 652.
[14] *West Leigh Colliery Co Ltd v Tunnicliffe and Hampson Ltd* [1908] A.C. 27.
[15] *Delaware Mansions Ltd v Westminster CC* [2001] UKHL 55; [2002] 1 A.C. 321.
[16] As will be seen at various points below the courts often award "conventional" or "tariff" sums for things which may not be capable of being valued by reference to a market (e.g. pain and suffering and loss of amenity or loss of liberty). Generally speaking these standard figures are kept in line with inflation. A £1,000 award in January 1990 would be the equivalent of £1,825 at the end of 2009, a £1,000 award in January 2000 the equivalent of £1,308.

however, be avowedly non-compensatory in intention. If not compensatory, damages may be: (1) contemptuous; (2) nominal; (3) exemplary or punitive (this category may be difficult to distinguish in practice from "aggravated" compensatory damages); or (4) restitutionary. However, even this classification probably does not in fact complete the tally of strands in the law of tort damages. A substantial award for libel may be spoken of as necessary to "vindicate" the claimant's right to his good reputation; a substantial award for false imprisonment may be said to "vindicate" his right to liberty. This rather imprecise word has various shades of meaning[17]: in the libel example it means to "clear" the claimant, in the false imprisonment example the sense is decisively to uphold or defend his rights. Common law jurisdictions with written constitutions sometimes award additional, vindicatory damages for violation of constitutional rights, even though there may be parallel liability for torts like battery or false imprisonment (which may include aggravated or exemplary damages) because the violation may add an extra dimension to the claim.[18] Although not the exact equivalent of exemplary damages, such "constitutional" damages share the common element of deterrence and it is therefore not appropriate to combine them with an exemplary award.[19] The closest analogy here is the jurisdiction to award damages against a public authority under the Human Rights Act 1998. However, the guiding principles here are those of the European Court of Human Rights, the awards of which are generally modest by English tort standards and that court quite often regards the vindication as being sufficiently provided by the declaration of violation.[20] A bad instance of oppressive behaviour by the police might quite easily produce a tort award of £50,000 or more but would not, it seems, produce a further award under the Act.[21]

A. Contemptuous

22–6   The amount awarded here is merely derisory—formerly 1 farthing, then 1 halfpenny and now, presumably, 1 new penny—and

---

[17] Its original, technical, legal sense (in Roman Law) was the regaining of property by the *rei vindicatio.*
[18] See *Att Gen of Trinidad and Tobago v Ramanoop* [2005] UKPC 15; [2006] 1 A.C. 628; *Merson v Cartwright* [2005] UKPC 38; *Inniss v Attorney General of Saint Christopher and Nevis* [2008] UKPC 42; *Subiah v Att Gen of Trinidad and Tobago* [2008] UKPC 47; *Taunoa v Att Gen* [2007] NZSC 70; [2008] N.Z.L.R. 429.
[19] *Takitoka v Att Gen of the Bahamas* [2009] UKPC 12.
[20] *R. (Greenfield) v Secretary of State for the Home Dept* [2005] UKHL 14; [2005] 1 W.L.R. 673.
[21] Compare *Merson v Cartwright* above, fn.18, where the JCPC upheld awards of general damages of US$180,000 for assault, battery and false imprisonment and US$100,000 for violation of constitutional rights.

indicates that while a right has technically been infringed,[22] the court has formed a very low opinion of the claimant's bare legal claim, or that his conduct was such that he deserved, at any rate morally, what the defendant did to him. Damages of this kind may imperil the claimant's chances of getting his costs, for although costs now usually follow the event of the action, yet their award is in the discretion of the judge, and although the insignificance of damages is not by itself necessarily enough to justify him in depriving the claimant of his costs, yet it is a material factor in the exercise of his discretion. Where there is a jury it is impermissible for it to be influenced on the quantum of damages by the likely outcome as to costs and the judge should decline to answer questions on the subject.[23] Contemptuous damages are sometimes found in libel actions.[24]

B. Nominal

Nominal damages are awarded when the claimant's legal right **22–7** has been infringed, his conduct is not open to criticism in the above sense, he has suffered no actual damage, but he still has a complete cause of action because the tort is actionable per se, for example, trespass to land, or because his cause of action is breach of contract. In *Constantine v Imperial Hotels Ltd*,[25] the defendants were guilty of a breach of their duty as common innkeepers when they unjustifiably refused accommodation in one of their hotels to the claimant, the well-known West Indian cricketer. Although he was given accommodation elsewhere, he was awarded nominal damages of 5 guineas.[26] An award of nominal damages does not, therefore, connote any moral obliquity on the claimant's part, but even so the judge may in his discretion deprive the claimant of his costs or even make him pay the costs of both sides.[27]

---

[22] It seems that where D libels C it is not possible so to find and to award *no* damages. In *Reynolds v Times Newspapers Ltd* [1998] 3 W.L.R. 862 the trial judge, after the jury's verdict, awarded 1p and the CA said this was correct (on appeal on other points [2001] 2 A.C. 127).

[23] *Pamplin v Express Newspapers Ltd* [1988] 1 W.L.R. 116.

[24] For an example, where the claimant got no costs, see *Dering v Uris* [1964] 2 Q.B. 669, upon which the defendant based a successful book, *Q.B. VII.*

[25] [1944] K.B. 693. See now the Race Relations Act 1976, which expressly allows damages for injury to feelings and might therefore produce a larger award on such facts.

[26] In fact, since this sum would now be at least £100, the case is perhaps better regarded as an example of "small" or "conventional" damages. The standard sum for nominal damages now seems to be £5 or £10.

[27] *Anglo-Cyprian Trade Agencies Ltd v Paphos Wine Industries Ltd* [1951] 1 All E.R. 873 (a case of contract). The real test is probably whether the claimant had a legitimate reason to establish his right and that right has been vindicated by the judgment, for example where an action of trespass is brought with the object of determining a dispute over a right of way.

C. Aggravated and Exemplary (or Punitive)[28]

22–8   In torts like libel or assault damages are often said to be "at large". What is meant by this is that damages cannot be precisely quantified in money terms[29] but the claimant is entitled to a substantial award for the wrong against him[30] and an appellate court will not interfere merely because the award is larger than it would have made (though there is now, as a result of immoderate awards in libel cases, a markedly greater readiness to overturn awards on the ground that they are unreasonable and excessive than was once the case).[31] The issue is, even if the trial is by judge alone, a "jury question". Part of the award in these cases will reflect the injury to the claimant's feelings and the mental distress he has suffered as well as the need to vindicate his rights. The injury to feelings and distress may, however, be increased by the bad motive or wilful behaviour of the defendant and it is then possible to make a corresponding increase in the award as, in traditional terminology, an "aggravation" of damages.[32] Such aggravated damages, unlike exemplary damages, are compensatory in nature.[33] Thus there might be a substantial award of damages for a serious libel published innocently with belief in its truth,[34] a larger award where the defendant published out of malice or persisted at the trial with an insupportable plea of justification[35] and a larger one still where the defendant was out to make a profit from the publication and so

[28] "Exemplary" is now more popular than "punitive": see Lord Devlin in *Rookes v Barnard* [1964] A.C. 1129 and Lord Hailsham L.C., Viscount Dilhorne and Lords Morris and Diplock in *Cassell & Co Ltd v Broome* [1972] A.C. 1027; but the Law Commission has stated a preference for "punitive": Law Com. No.247, s.5.39.

[29] In the individual case there may of course be precisely quantifiable items: the victim of an assault may be off work and lose wages.

[30] As Gaudron and McHugh J.J. said in *Plenty v Dillon* (1990) 98 A.L.R. 353, a case of trespass by public officers, "If the courts of common law do not uphold the rights of individuals by granting effective remedies, they invite anarchy, for nothing breeds social disorder as quickly as the sense of injustice which is apt to be generated by the unlawful invasion of a person's right, particularly when the invader is a government official."

[31] See further, para.12–71, above.

[32] See *Rookes v Barnard* [1964] A.C. 1129 at 1221; *Cassell & Co Ltd v Broome* [1972] A.C. 1027 at 1073.

[33] *Khodaparast v Shad* [2000] 1 W.L.R. 618 at 632; *Rookes v Barnard* [1964] A.C. 1129 at 1221 per Lord Devlin; *Cassell & Co Ltd v Broome* [1972] A.C. 1027 at 1124 per Lord Diplock. The present law of basic compensatory, aggravated and exemplary damages was described in *Gerald v MPC, The Times*, June 26, 1998, as a "muddled jurisprudential amalgam of categories". However, the "muddle" arises from the fact that aggravated damages (or even basic compensatory ones) may be regarded as having the *effect* of punishing the defendant; as far as their purpose is concerned there would seem to be no muddle.

[34] Similarly, damages for false imprisonment may be large even though there is no high-handed behaviour and little pecuniary loss.

[35] The relevance of the defendant's conduct of the trial in defamation is well established. While it has been said not to be a true exception (Sir Thomas Bingham M.R. in *A.B. v South West Water Services Ltd* [1993] Q.B. 507) as a general rule the claimant cannot recover damages for the indignation which he feels at the defendant's behaviour committed after the tort.

brought himself within the net of exemplary damages.[36] The Court of Appeal in 1998 in *Thompson v Metropolitan Police Commissioner*[37] comprehensively restated the law on damages in actions against the police for torts like false imprisonment and malicious prosecution and indicated the guidance that should be given to juries. In a case of false imprisonment the starting point[38] for what the court called "basic damages" should be (in the money of 1998) about £500 for the first hour of detention, £3,000 for the first day and at a declining rate thereafter.[39] Where there are aggravating factors such as humiliation or insult the starting point for aggravated damages would be about £1,000. There can be no mathematical relationship between aggravated and basic damages, but in the ordinary way[40] the former should not be as much as twice the latter. Awards of aggravated damages have also been made in cases of battery,[41] of trespass to land,[42] of deceit,[43] of misuse of private information,[44] and of the statutory torts of discrimination.[45] Aggravated damages are probably not, however, available for negligence[46] even where the conduct of the defendant is "crass"[47] and it is thought that they

[36] At least this is the theory of the matter. The element of vindication in cases of libel is in fact so strong that it is questionable whether even the first category can really be called compensation. See Windeyer J. in *Uren v John Fairfax & Sons Pty Ltd* (1967) 117 C.L.R. 118 at 150: "It seems to me that, properly speaking, a man defamed does not get compensation for his damaged reputation. He gets damages because he was injured in his reputation, that is simply because he was publicly defamed. For this reason, compensation by damages operates in two ways—as a vindication of the plaintiff to the public, and as consolation to him for a wrong done. Compensation is here a solatium rather than a monetary recompense for harm measurable in money."

[37] [1998] Q.B. 498; *Manley v MPC* [2006] EWCA Civ 879.

[38] These are not rules to be applied in a mechanistic fashion and although the threshold for interference has been lowered the jury (or judge) still retains some margin of discretion: *Clark v CC Cleveland, The Times*, May 13, 1999.

[39] The starting point for malicious prosecution is about £2,000. While these figures are only a starting point they have to be increased by about 40 per cent to get end-2009 values.

[40] Cf. *Shah v Gale* [2005] EWHC 1087 (QB).

[41] *W. v Meah* [1986] 1 All E.R. 935 (rape); *Appleton v Grant* [1996] P.I.Q.R. P1 (non-consensual dental treatment). In *Shah v Gale*, above, fn.40, the defendant was a joint tortfeasor in respect of an assault which led to the murder of the deceased. The claim of his estate was presented on the basis of asking for damages for the assault alone, without the concomitant injury. £2,750 general and aggravated damages were awarded.

[42] *Jolliffe v Willmett & Co* [1971] 1 All E.R. 478. See also *Columbia Picture Industries Inc v Robinson* [1987] Ch. 38 (aggravated damages available where defendant executed an Anton Piller order in an excessive and oppressive manner).

[43] *Archer v Brown* [1985] Q.B. 401.

[44] *Campbell v MGN Ltd* [2004] UKHL 22; [2004] 2 A.C. 457 (the damages were not really in issue on the appeal).

[45] *Prison Service v Johnson* [1997] I.C.R. 275.

[46] In *Ashley v CC Sussex* [2008] UKHL 25; [2008] 1 A.C. 962 (para.1–2, above) the defendant conceded the availability of aggravated damages in the negligence claim against him because he was seeking to avoid trial of the battery claim: at [23]. Lord Neuberger at [101] was troubled by the idea that the parties could by agreement confer on the court power to award damages not available at law but thought it was arguable that aggravated damages might be available in some cases of negligence.

[47] *Kralj v McGrath* [1986] 1 All E.R. 54.

should not be available to a corporation, which has no feelings to be hurt.[48]

Some confusion is injected into the terminology of this area by *Richardson v Howie*[49] where the court said that in cases of assault and similar torts it should no longer be the practice to make an award of aggravated damages but to subsume the compensation for the claimant's injured feelings into the award of general damages, save in a "wholly exceptional case". In one sense this is an advance in that it recognises that "aggravated damages" *are* "injury to feelings damages": the defendant's conduct aggravates the (at large) damages beyond what they might otherwise be, rather than leads to a separate head of aggravated damages. However, it is contemplated that there may still be exceptional cases where there could be a separate award but there is no indication of what those might be. At any rate, the courts still go on making separate awards under this head in the sense of identifying a separate sum.[50]

22–9   "Exemplary damages are a controversial topic and have been so for many years."[51] They are not compensatory but are awarded to punish the defendant and to deter him and others from similar behaviour in the future. This distinction, though clear in theory, is obviously difficult to apply in practice[52]; it was also, in the past, relatively insignificant, for it was thought that exemplary damages, like aggravated damages, could be awarded in any case of a deliberate tort.[53] However, in *Rookes v Barnard*,[54] the House of Lords, through Lord Devlin, restated the law regarding exemplary damages and severely limited their scope, and this restriction was affirmed by the House in *Cassell & Co Ltd v Broome*.[55] It is true that Lord Devlin thought that this would not make a great difference to the substance of the law, for aggravated damages can do most of the work of exemplary damages,[56] but, subject to what is said below, it

---

[48] So held in *Collins Stewart Ltd v Financial Times Ltd* [2005] EWHC 262 (QB); [2006] E.M.L.R. 5, suggesting that the apparently contrary decision in *Messenger Newspapers Group Ltd v NGA* [1984] I.R.L.R. 397 was in fact a case of exemplary damages. Indeed, it has been held that even in the case of an individual damages for injured feelings (including aggravated damages) can only be awarded where a purpose of the liability is to protect the claimant's self-esteem or enjoyment: *R. v Secretary of State for Transport, Ex p. Factortame Ltd (No.7)* [2001] 1 W.L.R. 942.

[49] [2004] EWCA Civ 1127; [2005] P.I.Q.R. Q3.

[50] See e.g. *Rowlands v CC Merseyside* [2006] EWCA Civ 1773; [2007] 1 W.L.R. 1065. On the relationship between damages for injury to feelings and damages for psychiatric harm see this case and *Choudhary v Martins* [2007] EWCA Civ 1379; [2008] 1 W.L.R. 617.

[51] *Kuddus v CC Leicestershire* [2001] UKHL 29; [2002] 2 A.C. 122 at [50] per Lord Nicholls. For comparative law see Koziol and Wilcox (eds), *Punitive Damages: Common Law and Civil Law Perspectives* (2009).

[52] It is especially difficult where there is a jury: see *Sutcliffe v Pressdram* [1991] 1 Q.B. 153 per Nourse L.J.; *Gerald v MPC, The Times*, June 26, 1998.

[53] See, e.g. *Loudon v Ryder* [1953] 2 Q.B. 202.

[54] *Rookes v Barnard* [1964] A.C. 1129.

[55] [1972] A.C. 1027.

[56] [1964] A.C. at 1230.

is now clear that, except in the comparatively rare cases where exemplary damages are still allowed, any award must be strictly justifiable as compensation for the injury sustained.

In Lord Devlin's view exemplary damages are in principle objectionable because they confuse the civil and the criminal functions of the law[57] and, apart from cases where they are allowed by statute,[58] exemplary damages can now be awarded in only two classes of case.[59]

The first category is where there is oppressive, arbitrary or unconstitutional action by servants of the Government.[60] A well-known example of this, approved by Lord Devlin, is *Huckle v Money*,[61] one of the cases deciding against the legality of the search warrants which were issued against John Wilkes and others during the latter part of the 18th century. The claimant was detained under one of these warrants for no more than six hours and the defendant, "used him very civilly by treating him with beef-steaks and beer". Yet the court refused to interfere with a verdict for £300 damages, for:

22–10

"[T]o enter a man's house by virtue of a nameless warrant, in order to procure evidence, is worse than the Spanish Inquisition . . . it is a more daring public attack made upon the liberty of the subject".[62]

This class of case covers abuse of executive power. It does not therefore extend to oppressive action by individuals or corporations, no matter how powerful (though it has been suggested that it might extend to oppressive use of the law by private persons[63]), nor does it cover acts by public bodies which are not exercising executive functions, for example a public body supplying water or a local

---

[57] [1964] A.C. at 1221.

[58] Lord Devlin cites the Reserve and Auxiliary Forces (Protection of Civil Interests) Act 1951 s.13(2): [1964] A.C. at 1225. Lord Kilbrandon in *Cassell v Broome*, above, fn.55, at 1133, doubted whether any existing statute contemplated the award of exemplary damages in the proper sense. The Copyright, Designs and Patents Act 1988 s.97, allows the award of "additional" damages. The Inner House in *Redrow Homes v Betts* [1997] F.S.R. 828 held that this did not allow exemplary damages. In the House of Lords the only issue was whether such additional damages could be awarded on a claim only for an account of profits (no). The nature of the additional damages was left open, but in Lord Clyde's view they were probably not exemplary: [1999] A.C. 197 at 209.

[59] A claim for exemplary damages must be pleaded: CPR 16.4(1)(c).

[60] [1964] A.C. at 1226; *Att Gen of St Christopher etc. v Reynolds* [1980] A.C. 637.

[61] (1763) 2 Wils. 205.

[62] (1763) 2 Wils. 205 at 207 per Pratt C.J. Comparison is virtually impossible but on a price inflation basis it might be £40,000 today. See also *Wilkes v Wood* (1763) Lofft. 1. In *Wilkes v Lord Halifax* the jury awarded John Wilkes the then phenomenal sum of £4,000 for false imprisonment: 19 State Trials 1466.

[63] See *Columbia Picture Industries Inc v Robinson* [1987] Ch. 38. See also *Moore v Lambeth County Court Registrar (No.2)* [1970] 1 Q.B. 56); cf. *Al-Rawas v Pegasus Energy Ltd* [2008] EWHC 617; [2009] 1 All E.R. 346.

authority acting in its capacity of employer of staff.[64] On the other hand it does cover the actions of the police[65] even though police officers are not, in strict constitutional law, the "servants of the government".[66] There has perhaps been a tendency to treat the three adjectives used by Lord Devlin as synonymous, all carrying the idea of "high-handedness", but the Court of Appeal has pointed out that grammatically this is incorrect and there may be unconstitutional action which is neither "oppressive" nor "arbitrary".[67] On the other hand, the court was clearly unhappy with the proposition that any false arrest or other unauthorised conduct by a police officer should attract an exemplary award, but rather than attempt to define "unconstitutional" as a matter of law it preferred the approach of relying on the trial judge to indicate to the jury[68] that in the absence of aggravating factors they might consider the case unsuitable for exemplary damages.[69]

Lord Devlin's second category covers cases where the defendant's conduct has been calculated by him to make a profit for himself which may well exceed the compensation payable to the claimant.[70] The purpose of awards in this category is to teach the defendant (and others who might be tempted to behave in the same way) that "tort does not pay". From another point of view the purpose of this category may be regarded as to confiscate the fruits of wrongdoing.[71] The conduct of the defendant may be a crime and since *Rookes v Barnard* there have come into existence extensive mechanisms for enabling the criminal court to make compensation orders and to confiscate the proceeds of crime[72] but these do not preclude the making of an award of exemplary damages against the

---

[64] *A.B. v South West Water Services Ltd* [1993] 507. This case is overruled on the "cause of action" test by *Kuddus v CC Leicestershire* [2001] UKHL 29; [2002] 2 A.C. 122 (see below) but this element of the decision would still seem to stand. Nor does the action of a councillor in a local authority committee necessarily fall within this category: *Shendish Manor Ltd v Coleman* [2001] EWCA Civ 913 at [62].

[65] An award may be made against an officer who acts under colour of authority even though in the circumstances he is pursuing his own ends to such an extent that the chief constable is not vicariously liable for him: *Makanjuola v MPC, The Times*, August 8, 1989.

[66] *Cassell & Co Ltd v Broome*, above, fn.55, at 1077–1078, 1130, 1134 per Lord Hailsham L.C. and Lords Diplock and Kilbrandon.

[67] *Holden v CC Lancashire* [1987] Q.B. 380.

[68] Actions for trespass and false imprisonment against the police will commonly be tried by jury.

[69] The judgment in *Thompson v MPC* [1998] Q.B. at 516 (which does not mention *Holden*) is rather equivocal on this issue.

[70] [1964] A.C. at 1226–1227.

[71] It is, "merely preventing the defendant from obtaining a reward for his wrongdoing . . . the plaintiff is the accidental beneficiary of a rule of law based on public policy rather than on the reparation of private wrongs": *McCarey v Associated Newspapers Ltd (No.2)* [1965] 2 Q.B. 86 at 107 per Diplock L.J.

[72] Now consolidated in the Powers of Criminal Courts (Sentencing) Act 2000. See also the Proceeds of Crime Act 2002.

wrongdoer in a proper case,[73] nor does the gradual development of "restitutionary" damages.[74] In so far as such damages deprive the defendant of his profits they may only do so only in a rough and ready way. The paradigm case in this category is a libel in a newspaper, but in practice it would be a rare case in which the profit attributable to the libel could be shown with anything approaching precision.[75] Furthermore, while the profit made by the defendant is a relevant consideration in arriving at the award,[76] it is not determinative and an award of exemplary damages may be made even if no profit accrues: what counts is the defendant's purpose.[77]

It is not, however, sufficient to bring a case within this category that the defendant was engaged in an activity aimed at profit. There must be something more calculated and deliberate, though it is unnecessary that the defendant should have indulged in any precise balancing of the chances of profit and loss. There must be something in the nature of what is described in one libel direction approved by the Court of Appeal:

"Well, it will help the circulation of our newspaper. He may sue, he may not.[78] If he does not so much the better. If he does we will try to settle and get out as quickly as we can. If we cannot do that and it goes to court we still think that the total cost to us, adding everything, damages . . . and the legal costs, all the lot, will make it worth the gain for us to publish it. So we will go ahead."[79]

However, if this profit motive is absent, exemplary damages may not be awarded (unless the case falls within the other category) no matter how malicious the defendant's conduct.[80] Where the tort is one that may be committed without intention or malice exemplary damages should not be awarded unless the defendant is intentional

---

[73] *Borders (UK) Ltd v MPC* [2005] EWCA Civ 197; *AT v Dulghieru* [2009] EWHC 225 (QB). The method of calculating the exemplary damages in *Borders* showed that it could in fact have been dealt with on a compensatory basis but that was not the way the claim had proceeded.

[74] See para.22–13, below.

[75] Cf. *Att Gen v Guardian Newspapers Ltd (No.2)* [1990] 1 A.C. 109.

[76] *John v MGN Ltd* [1997] Q.B. 586 at 619.

[77] They can be awarded even though the defendant fails in his scheme to profit: *Design Progression Ltd v Thurloe Properties Ltd* [2004] EWHC 324 (Ch); [2004] 2 P. & C.R. 594.

[78] In *Cassell & Co Ltd v Broome* [1972] A.C. 1027 at 1079, Lord Hailsham L.C. said: "It is not necessary that the defendant calculates that the plaintiff's damages if he sues to judgment will be smaller than the defendant's profit . . . The defendant may calculate that the plaintiff will not sue at all because he has not the money . . . or because he may be physically or otherwise intimidated."

[79] The direction in *John v MGN Ltd*, above, fn.76.

[80] Thus it would seem that exemplary damages could not be awarded on such facts as those of *Hill v Church of Scientology* (1995) 126 D.L.R. (4th) 129, where the SCC upheld an exemplary award of CAN$800,000 (in addition to the same amount in general and aggravated damages).

or reckless as to the consequences of his actions. Thus in a case of libel, the defendant must be aware that what he is publishing is untrue or he:

> "[M]ust have suspected that the words were untrue and have deliberately refrained from taking obvious steps which, if taken, would have turned suspicion into certainty".[81]

22–11   For a time there was a further restriction on the award of exemplary damages. In *A.B. v South West Water Services Ltd*[82] the Court of Appeal interpreted the modern authorities in such a way that, even if the case fell within one of Lord Devlin's categories, such damages could only be awarded if they had been awarded for the tort in question before *Rookes v Barnard*—the "cause of action" test. This meant that such awards were not based on principle but on the accidents of past litigation[83] but the restriction was rejected by the House of Lords in *Kuddus v CC Leicestershire*.[84] Exemplary damages may therefore be awarded for misfeasance in a public office,[85] the paradigm example of a tort within the first category above, but which had been almost forgotten in 1964.

The sum awarded by way of exemplary damages should be the minimum necessary to punish the defendant, to show that tort does not pay and to deter others.[86] In the case of actions against the police for trespass to the person and malicious prosecution the Court of Appeal has said that where:

> "[E]xemplary damages are appropriate they are unlikely to be less than £5,000. Otherwise the case is probably not one which justifies an award of exemplary damages at all. In this class of action the conduct must be particularly deserving of condemnation for an award of as much as £25,000 to be justified and the figure of £50,000[87] should be regarded as an absolute maximum, involving   directly   officers   of   at   least   the   rank   of superintendent."[88]

---

[81] *John v MGN Ltd*, above [1997] Q.B. at 618.
[82] [1993] Q.B. 507.
[83] *Kuddus v CC Leicestershire* [2001] UKHL 29; [2002] 2 A.C. 122 at [22].
[84] Above, fn.83. *Design Progression Ltd v Thurloe Properties Ltd* [2004] EWHC 324 (Ch); [2004] 2 P. & C.R. 594.
[85] *Muuse v Secretary of State for the Home Dept* [2009] EWHC 1886 (QB) (£25,000 for basic loss of liberty, £7,500 aggravated damages, £27,500 exemplary damages); but not if there is no actual damage on which to found the claim: *Watkins v Home Office* [2006] UKHL 17. For the CA in *Muuse*, see Preface.
[86] *Rookes v Barnard* [1964] A.C. at 1228.
[87] Money has of course declined in value. £50,000 in 1998 would be approaching £70,000 in 2010.
[88] *Thompson v MPC* [1998] Q.B. at 517.

The court in *John v MGN Ltd* was less prescriptive with regard to libel, and it is clear from the substituted award of £50,000 exemplary damages in that case that libel awards may justifiably be higher,[89] since the conduct of the defendants in that case was not the worst imaginable,[90] but here, too, the tribunal must not cross the threshold of the "necessary minimum". Exemplary damages may, however, exceed any compensatory damages awarded by a large margin.[91] Before making an award the tribunal should ask itself whether the sum which has been set for compensatory (including aggravated) damages is sufficient to punish the defendant.[92]

The fact that the damages will be paid not by the actual wrong-doer but by someone vicariously liable for his actions does not, as the law now stands,[93] prevent an exemplary award being made[94] and while the means of the defendant are in general relevant to the quantum of exemplary damages an award against a newspaper or a chief officer of police is not limited by the means of the journalist or constable directly responsible.[95] Where a policy of liability insurance, on its proper construction, covers an award of exemplary damages, there is no rule of public policy which prevents the insured enforcing the indemnity.[96] Where the claimant sues more than one joint defendant in the same action, the sum which may be awarded by way of exemplary damages is the lowest which the conduct of

---

[89] No doubt because of the profit-making element.

[90] Not as bad as that in *Cassell & Co Ltd v Broome* [1972] A.C. 1027.

[91] A ratio of 2:1 in *John*. However, the ratios in *Thompson* were 0.75:1 and 1.25:1.

[92] *Cassell & Co Ltd v Broome* [1972] A.C. at 1089; *John v MGN Ltd* [1997] Q.B. at 619; *Thompson v MPC* [1998] Q.B. at 517. See *Muir v Alberta* (1996) 132 D.L.R. (4th) 695.

[93] In *Kuddus v CC Leicestershire*, above, fn.83, the majority of the HL declined to deal with the question of vicarious liability for exemplary damages, the matter not having been argued; but see Lord Scott at [123]. The HCA decisively upheld the availability of exemplary damages against those responsible for police officers in *NSW v Ibbett* [2006] HCA 57; 231 A.L.R. 485 (though note that in NSW statute now provides that a police officer is not personally liable for his torts).

[94] It has been argued that large deterrent awards are likely to produce a greater managerial response. "It is desirable as a matter of policy that the courts should be able to make punitive awards against those who are vicariously liable for the conduct of their sub-ordinates without being constrained by the financial means of those who committed the wrongful acts in question. Only by this means can awards of an adequate amount be made against those who bear public responsibility for the conduct of the officers concerned": *Rowlands v CC Merseyside* [2006] EWCA Civ 1773; [2007] 1 W.L.R. 1065 at [47]; but cf. Ipp J. dissenting in *NSW v Ibbett* [2005] NSWCA 445; 65 N.S.W.L.R. 68 at [162]: "it is difficult to comprehend how an award against the State of New South Wales could be said merely to irritate because it is $10,000 but would sting if it were $25,000, particularly if regard is had to the State's annual budget." For HCA, see above, fn.93.

[95] *Thompson v MPC* at [1998] Q.B. 517.

[96] *Lancashire CC v Municipal Mutual Insurance Co* [1997] Q.B. 897. Note that in this case the insurers had agreed by indorsement that injury caused by assaults by constables should qualify as "accidental harm" within the meaning of the force's policy and that it by no means follows that a claim under a policy by the actual wrongdoer would succeed where his conduct constituted a crime. On liability insurance and wilful wrongdoing see also *Hawley v Luminar Leisure Ltd* [2006] EWCA Civ 18 and *KR v Royal & Sun Alliance Plc* [2006] EWHC 48 (QB).

any of the defendants deserves.[97] In the reverse case of multiple claimants the tribunal should arrive at a global sum by way of punishment and that should then be divided among the claimants. While a defendant may deserve more punishment, for example, for libelling 10 than for libelling one, to fix a figure for the individual and multiply it by the number of claimants is likely to lead to an excessive award.[98] It has been held that where the defendant has already been prosecuted and convicted in a criminal court for precisely[99] the conduct which forms the basis of the suit the punitive function is spent and no exemplary award should be made.[100] However, the Court of Appeal has upheld an exemplary award where the defendant had been sentenced to imprisonment for acts which were conversion in the civil law, where very substantial loss had clearly been inflicted on the claimant and where there was no possibility of duplication between the award and sums in respect of which the defendant might be subjected to confiscation procedures in criminal proceedings.[101] Where the defendant has been fined that is a "powerful factor" against the award of exemplary damages, though it may not be conclusive.[102]

D. The Future of Exemplary Damages

22–12   An examination of the speeches in the House of Lords in *Cassell v Broome*[103] will reveal considerable differences of opinion about the desirability in principle of exemplary damages and had it not been for the force of history they might have disappeared in that case or in *Rookes v Barnard*. These differences still exist, as witness *Kuddus v CC Leicestershire*,[104] where Lord Nicholls and Lord Hutton expressed the view that such damages might have a valuable role to play in dealing with outrageous behaviour and the defence of

---

[97] *Cassell & Co Ltd v Broome*, above, fn.92. This result flows from the rule that only a single award of damages may be made against joint tortfeasors, though it is difficult to justify in this context. The rule has been rejected in Australia: *X.L. Petroleum v Caltex Oil* (1985) 57 A.L.R. 639. It does not apply if employer and servant are jointly sued.

[98] *Riches v News Group Newspapers Ltd* [1986] Q.B. 256, where at the trial each of the claimants had been awarded £250 compensatory damages and £25,000 exemplary damages.

[99] Cf. *Ashgar v Ahmed* (1984) 17 H.L.R. 25.

[100] *Archer v Brown* [1985] Q.B. 401. However, legislation in New Zealand now provides that a criminal conviction or acquittal is no bar to a claim for exemplary damages, though the court is to have regard to any criminal penalty imposed: Injury Prevention, Rehabilitation and Compensation Act 2001 s.319. A criminal acquittal followed by a finding of civil liability may occur because the standard of proof is different.

[101] *Borders (UK) Ltd v MPC* [2005] EWCA Civ 197.

[102] *Devenish Nutrition Ltd v Sanofi-Aventis SA* [2007] EWHC 2394 (Ch); [2009] Ch. 390 (on appeal but not on the issue of exemplary damages [2008] EWCA Civ 1086; [2009] Ch. 390). In any event the Community law principles of (i) *non bis in idem* and (ii) the primacy of Commission rulings precluded an exemplary award.

[103] [1972] A.C. 1027.

[104] [2001] UKHL 29; [2001] 2 W.L.R. 1789.

civil liberties,[105] whereas Lord Scott regarded them as an anomaly.[106] The main arguments against them are that they confuse the purposes of the civil and criminal law, import the possibility of punishment into civil litigation without the safeguards of the criminal process and provide an unmerited windfall for the claimant. On the other hand, one should not too readily assume that the boundaries between the civil and the criminal law are either rigid or immutable or that the criminal law alone is an adequate mechanism to deter wilful wrongdoing, particularly where the criminal law is rarely enforced or where the wrongdoing is by the state or its agents. As Lord Wilberforce said in *Cassell v Broome*:

> "[O]ver the range of torts for which punitive damages may be given . . . there is much to be said before one can safely assert that the true or basic principle of the law of damages in tort is compensation, or, if it is, what that compensation is for, . . . or, if there is compensation, whether there is not in all cases, or at least in some, of which defamation may be an example, also a delictual element which contemplates some penalty for the defendant."[107]

The acceptability of "compromising the purity of the distinction" between compensation and punishment in this way has since been confirmed in the Privy Council: "Oil and vinegar may not mix in solution but they combine to make an acceptable salad dressing."[108] Exemplary damages certainly enjoy a continuing vitality in other common law jurisdictions, which, by and large, have rejected the various shackles imposed on them in England and extended them to situations to which they never applied here[109]: in New Zealand, for example, they are available for cases of outrageously bad negligence,[110] though an Australian court has declined to extend them to equitable wrongs like breach of fiduciary duty.[111]

---

[105] At [63] and [75] respectively.

[106] At [95].

[107] [1972] A.C. at 1114.

[108] *The Gleaner Co Ltd v Abrahams* [2003] UKPC 55, [2004] 1 A.C. 628 at [54]. There was no exemplary award in that libel case but in that context the theoretically clear line between (compensatory) vindication and punishment/deterrence tends to break down in practice.

[109] For Canada see *Vorvis v Insurance Corp of BC* (1989) 58 D.L.R. (4th) 193 and *Hill v Church of Scientology* (1995) 126 D.L.R. (4th) 129. For Australia see *Uren v John Fairfax* (1966) 117 C.L.R. 118 and *Gray v Motor Accidents Commission* (1998) 196 C.L.R. 1. They are, of course, firmly and widely established in the United States. Their formal absence from civil law systems may conceal a more complex reality: L.C.C.P. 132, ss.4.19–20 and Rogers (ed), *Damages for Non-Pecuniary Loss in a Comparative Perspective* (2001) at pp.290–291.

[110] *A v Bottrill* [2002] UKPC 44; [2003] 1 A.C. 449.

[111] *Harris v Digital Pulse Pty Ltd* [2003] NSWCA 10; 44 A.C.S.R. 390.

The Law Commission concluded,[112] after a fairly evenly balanced consultation, that exemplary damages should be retained but the law should be restated and rationalised so that they were available for any tort or equitable wrong (but not for breach of contract) where the defendant had, "deliberately and outrageously disregarded the plaintiff's rights".[113] However, the Government has indicated that it is not at present minded to legislate.[114]

E. Unjust Enrichment and Damages

22–13 As we have seen "restitution" is the name now commonly given to that branch of the law dealing with unjust enrichment[115] and part of that is concerned with restitution of benefits obtained through wrongs. A brief historical background is necessary here, though details must be sought in works on restitution.[116] When the forms of action governed procedure, the claimant against whom a tort had been committed was in some cases allowed to "waive the tort" and sue in *indebitatus assumpsit* instead. This remedy was of much more general application than waiver of tort (for example, it governed recovery of money paid under ineffective or unperformed contracts or under a mistake of fact) and involved a wholly fictitious allegation that the defendant was indebted to the claimant and had promised to pay him. Hence the expression "quasi-contract". Like other (to us) barely comprehensible fictions it owed its origin to a combination of competition for business between different courts and a need to develop the law within the constraints of a formalistic system. Waiver of tort did not relieve the claimant of the burden of showing that a tort had been committed but it gave him various procedural advantages—thus he might avoid the effect of a statute of limitations,[117] or of the rules that a tort action died with the defendant or that a claim for unliquidated damages in tort could not be proved in bankruptcy. Virtually all these procedural consequences have disappeared, but another consequence of waiver remains, namely that the sum recovered by the claimant is based not on the loss to the claimant, as in conventional damages, but upon the gain to the defendant. So if D converted C's jewellery and managed

---

[112] *Aggravated, Exemplary and Restitutionary Damages*, Law Com. No.247 (1997).
[113] Note that this would mean that punitive damages would be available even though the cause of action was negligence, provided this element in the defendant's behaviour could be found. See *A v Bottrill*, above, fn.110.
[114] Hansard, HC, November 9, 1999, Col.502. *Kuddus*, above, fn.104, shows that the question of vicarious liability for exemplary damages needs judicial re-examination.
[115] See para.1–10, above.
[116] See for the modern law and its background, Goff and Jones, *Restitution*, 7th edn; Burrows, *Restitution*, 2nd edn; Edelman, *Gain-Based Damages*; Rotherham, "The Conceptual Structure of Restitution for Wrongs" (2007) 66 C.L.J. 172. For history see Jackson, *History of Quasi-Contract in English Law*; Winfield, *Province of the Law of Tort*.
[117] *Chesworth v Farrar* [1967] 1 Q.B. 407 is a modern example.

to sell it above market value C could recover that and even if there was no great difference between these figures, the claimant was saved the trouble of showing what the property was worth.[118] Not all torts could be waived, for the essence of *indebitatus assumpsit* was that the claimant claimed that the defendant "had and received" money which belonged to the claimant[119]—hence the modern terminology that the defendant was unjustly enriched at the claimant's expense. Obviously, therefore, there are some torts in respect of which the defendant receives no "enrichment", even by the most generous interpretation—assault and battery or negligence for example. Conversion or trespass to goods by taking, on the other hand, are obvious candidates for inclusion.

Under modern procedure, the court is less likely to be concerned with the precise labelling of the claimant's claim or remedy and the terminology of waiver of tort seems largely to have disappeared: a court is now likely to say that it is awarding damages assessed on a restitutionary basis rather than awarding a restitutionary remedy for a tort. However, the question arises whether the modern form of restitution for tort is still tied to the old waiver or whether there is now a more general principle, applicable to all torts where a benefit has been gained and perhaps applicable to contract as well, under which the function of the law is to reverse the defendant's gain rather than compensate the claimant's loss.[120] It is well established that where the defendant makes wrongful use of the claimant's property (for example by trespassing and dumping material on it[121] or by taking or detaining it[122]) the court will assess the damages by reference to a fair rental or access payment for the use,[123] even though the claimant has not in any real sense suffered a loss.[124] However, the line between these cases and those where damages are truly compensatory but assessed in a "conventional" form is not

[118] See, e.g. *Hospital Products Ltd v US Surgical Corp* (1984) 55 A.L.R. 417 (not a tort case).
[119] It can be argued that the historical nature of conversion straddled tort and unjust enrichment: see Douglas, "The Nature of Conversion" (2009) 68 C.L.J. 198
[120] One of the two categories of exemplary damages may fulfil this function. Thus exemplary damages may be awarded in some cases of libel (para.22–10, above) but no case suggests that the tort of libel could be waived.
[121] *Whitwham v Westminster Brymbo Coal and Coke Co* [1896] 2 Ch. 538; *Martin v Porter* (1839) 5 M & W 351; *Jegon v Vivian* (1871) LR 6 ChApp 742; *Penarth Dock Engineering Co Ltd v Pounds* [1963] 1 Lloyd's Rep. 359.
[122] *Watson, Laidlaw & Co Ltd v Pott, Cassels and Williamson* (1914) 31 R.P.C. 104 at 119; *Strand Electric and Engineering Co Ltd v Brisford Entertainments Ltd* [1952] 2 Q.B. 246. See also *MoD v Ashman* (1993) 66 P.& C.R. 193 (relationship between restitution and *mesne* profits).
[123] Hence the expression "user" damages. Such damages are "readily awarded": *Pell Frischmann Engineering Ltd v Bow Valley Iran Ltd* [2009] UKPC 45 at [48].
[124] *Att Gen v Blake* [2001] 1 A.C. 268 at 279 per Lord Nicholls.

easy to draw.[125] At present the Court of Appeal is bound by authority[126] that damages cannot be awarded on a restitutionary basis[127]
except in torts where the defendant has misappropriated[128] the
claimant's property rights, so that a claim on this basis failed in
Devenish Nutrition Ltd v Sanofi-Aventis SA,[129] decided as a preliminary issue on the basis that the defendants had operated a cartel in
breach of art.81 of the EC Treaty, a breach of statutory duty in
English law. In fact the case was, in any event, a rather unsuitable
vehicle for a restitutionary claim. Longmore L.J. dissented on the
basic issue of law but was of the view that a restitutionary claim
could be made outside the "proprietary" torts only in "exceptional
cases", as had been held by the House of Lords in the context of a
claim for an account of profits arising from a breach of contract[130]
and there was nothing exceptional about cartels. In so far as the
claimants had paid too much for the goods as a result of the cartel
that would fall within damages based on loss; if they had passed on
the higher price to their customers they had suffered no obvious
loss.[131]

"If . . . the claimant has in fact passed the excessive price on to
its purchasers and not absorbed the excess price itself, there is no
very obvious reason why the profit made by the defendants (albeit
undeserved and wrongful) should be transferred to the claimant
without the claimant being obliged to transfer it down the line to

---

[125] Compare in *Blake* the view of Lord Nicholls at 279 and Lord Hobhouse, dissenting, at 299
on the example put by Lord Halsbury L.C. in *The Mediana* [1900] A.C. 113 of wrongful
detention of a chair when the claimant still has enough chairs for all his needs. For Lord
Nicholls the award of damages based on interest on the capital value is depriving the
defendant of his gain; for Lord Hobhouse it is simply a conventional mode of assessment
of truly compensatory damages. In the "fair rental" case, although the defendant's profits
are relevant to the quantification of this, the claim is not one for a share in the profits:
Severn Trent Water Ltd v Barnes [2004] EWCA Civ 570; [2004] E.G.L.R. 95 at [41];
Forsyth-Grant v Allen [2008] EWCA Civ 505 at [25]. In *Experience Hendrix LLC v PPX
Enterprises Inc* [2003] EWCA Civ 323; [2003] All ER Comm 83 Mance L.J. remarked at
[26]: "Whether the adoption of a standard measure of damages represents a departure from
a compensatory approach depends upon what one understands by compensation and
whether the term is only apt in circumstances where an injured party's financial position,
viewed subjectively, is being precisely restored."

[126] *Stoke on Trent CC v W. & J. Wass Ltd* [1988] 1 W.L.R. 1406.

[127] Lord Nicholls in *Att Gen v Blake* at [2001] 1 A.C. 284 deprecates "restitutionary damages"
as an "unhappy expression". Possibly this was because, as Longmore L.J. says in the
Devenish case, below, fn.129, at [144] to the uninitiated "restitution" may imply restoration to the claimant of what he once had, whereas the true sense is surrender of unjust
enrichment.

[128] Not merely interfered with them: *Forsyth-Grant v Allen*, above, fn.125 (nuisance).

[129] [2008] EWCA Civ 1086; [2009] Ch. 390.

[130] *Att Gen v Blake*, above, fn.127. Longmore L.J. indeed adopts the terminology of account
of profits even for tort cases (though see fn.127, above). We certainly allow an account of
profits for breach of copyright or breach of confidence. The first at any rate involves
interference with intangible property

[131] They might have lost sales but that would be difficult to prove.

those who have actually suffered the loss. Neither the law of restitution nor the law of damages is in the business of transferring monetary gains from one undeserving recipient to another undeserving recipient even if the former has acted illegally while the latter has not."[132]

Again there have been proposals by the Law Commission.[133] Since the law on the recovery of damages on an unjust enrichment basis is undergoing gradual clarification and development by the courts it would not, in the Commission's view, be appropriate to attempt to codify this matter. It has, however, proposed that legislation should specifically state that the court may award "restitutionary damages" for a tort or civil wrong where the defendant's conduct shows a deliberate and outrageous disregard for the claimant's rights.

3. MEASURE OF DAMAGES

A. Scope of Subject

In theory, even if not always in practice, this subject is distinct **22–14** from that of the chapter on remoteness of damage,[134] though, obviously, both topics have a direct bearing upon the amount of money the claimant will ultimately recover. Remoteness of damage concerns the question: "in respect of what consequences of an established breach of duty can the injured party recover?"[135] Now we must see how the law attempts to answer the different question: "how much compensation can the injured party recover for consequences of the breach of legal duty which have already been held to be not too remote?"

In the case of some torts such as conversion and deceit specific rules for the assessment of damages exist, and these have been noticed in their appropriate chapters.[136] For the rest, and most notably so far as damages for personal injury are concerned, the courts were once content to leave the assessment of damages to the jury with only general guidance from the judges, and many statements can be found to the effect that the quantum of damages in each case is a question of fact. It is no doubt still true that ultimately the exact sum which the claimant is awarded in any case is dependent upon all the detailed circumstances of the case, but this does not

---

[132] At [146].
[133] Law Com. No.247, above, fn.112.
[134] See Ch.6, above. See Wilson and see fn.134, "A Re-examination of Remoteness" (1952) 15 M.L.R. 458.
[135] Wilson and Slade, see fn.134.
[136] For the measure of damages in defamation, see para.12–71, above.

mean that the topic is devoid of principle.[137] On the contrary, at least where so-called pecuniary damage is concerned, some quite firm rules have developed, and even in the case of non-pecuniary damage, such as pain and suffering and what is called "loss of amenity", where precise valuation in money terms is obviously impossible, the courts now to some extent elucidate the bases of their awards.[138] In this chapter, therefore, we shall consider some of the rules governing the assessment of damages in cases of personal injury and of loss or damage to property, acting always on the assumptions that a tort has been committed and that the damage in question is not too remote.

B. General and Special Damages[139]

22–15   We have already come across "special damage" as signifying the element of particular harm which the claimant has to prove to sue for slander[140] or public nuisance.[141] However, in the context of pleading special damage is used, in contradistinction to "general damage", to signify:

> "[T]he particular damage (beyond the general damage[142]) which results from the particular circumstances of the case, and of the plaintiff's claim to be compensated, for which he ought to give warning in his pleadings in order that there may be no surprise at the trial."[143]

This is a sensible distinction resulting in a rule proper to the law of pleading but unfortunately it spawned another sub-rule which distinguished between damages which are capable of substantially exact pecuniary assessment and those which are not,[144] which had

---

[137] See the caustic observations of Lord Sumner in *Admiralty Commissioners v SS Chekiang* [1926] A.C. 637 at 643.

[138] Indeed, in comparison with some European systems English law has rather precise rules on these matters.

[139] Jolowicz, "The Changing Use of 'Special Damage' and its Effect on the Law" [1960] C.L.J. 214.

[140] See para.12–4, above.

[141] See para.14–3, above.

[142] Which is what the law will presume. "Every libel is of itself a wrong in regard of which the law . . . implies general damage. By the very fact that he has committed such a wrong, the defendant is prepared for the proof that some general damage may have been done": *Ratcliffe v Evans* [1892] 2 Q.B. 524 at 529 per Bowen L.J.

[143] [1892] 2 Q.B. 524 at 528 per Bowen L.J. A person who claims some specific item of loss as special damages but fails to prove it may nevertheless recover general damages: *The Hebridean Coast* [1961] A.C. 545 (damage to ship; cost of chartering a substitute claimed as special damages but this loss not proved; claimant nevertheless allowed general damages for loss of use).

[144] See *British Transport Commission v Gourley* [1956] A.C. 185 at 206 per Lord Goddard. For yet another variation see *R. (Greenfield) v Secretary of State for the Home Dept* [2005] UKHL 14; [2005] 1 W.L.R. 673 at [11].

the result that, for example, loss of earnings which had accrued by the date of the trial was regarded as special damage (and therefore had to be strictly pleaded) while future loss of earnings fell under the head of general damages. However, under the current Civil Procedure Rules the claimant has to attach to his particulars of claim a schedule of details of all past and future losses which he claims, so the distinction would seem to have disappeared for this purpose.

C. Restitutio in Integrum

The basic principle for the measure of damages in tort as well as in contract is that there should be restitutio in integrum.[145] Apart from the special cases we have considered[146]:　　　　　　　　　　　　**22–16**

> "[W]here any injury is to be compensated by damages, in settling the sum of money to be given for reparation of damages you should as nearly as possible get at that sum of money which will put the party who has been injured, or who has suffered, in the same position as he would have been in if he had not sustained the wrong for which he is now getting his compensation or reparation."[147]

So, in an action for deceit, the proper starting point for the assessment of damages is to compare the position of the claimant as it was before the fraudulent statement was made to him, with his position as it became as a result of his reliance upon the statement.[148] The difference between the two situations is the measure of the damages.[149] In a case of personal injury, too, this criterion can and should be applied to the pecuniary elements of the claimant's loss such as his loss of earnings,[150] but it is difficult to see that it can be applied to the non-pecuniary elements such as pain and suffering.

---

[145] This expression has nothing to do with "restitution" in the sense used in para.1–10 and para.22–13. Here the idea is "making whole".

[146] See paras 22–5 to 22–13, above.

[147] *Livingstone v Rawyards Coal Co* (1880) 5 App.Cas. 25 at 39 per Lord Blackburn; *Monarch Steamship Co Ltd v Karlshamns Oljefabriker (A/B)* [1949] A.C. 196 at 221 per Lord Wright. In *The Albazero* [1977] A.C. 774 at 841 per Lord Diplock. Lord Wright described the principle of restitutio in integrum as "the dominant rule of law". "Subsidiary rules can only be justified if they give effect to that rule." Cf. *Admiralty Commissioners v SS Valeria* [1922] 2 A.C. 242 at 248 per Lord Dunedin.

[148] *Doyle v Olby (Ironmongers) Ltd* [1969] 2 Q.B. 158. See para.11–14, above.

[149] What German law calls the *Differenzhypothese*. Of course one must take care that one brings into the calculation what the claimant saves from the tort. If D destroys C's goods which are in the hands of X for refurbishment C can recover the cost of substitute goods less what he would have had to pay X for the refurbishment: *Re-Source America International Ltd v Platt Site Services Ltd* [2005] EWCA Civ 97; [2005] 2 Lloyd's Rep. 50.

[150] *British Transport Commission v Gourley* [1956] A.C. 185; *Parry v Cleaver* [1970] A.C. 1 at 22 per Lord Morris; *Thompstone v Tameside and Glossop etc NHS Trust* [2008] EWCA Civ 5; [2008] 1 W.L.R. 2207 at [47].

Full restitutio in integrum is not possible there[151] and it may be that even compensation is not a wholly apt expression. What is given has been described as, "notional theoretical compensation to take the place of that which is not possible, namely, actual compensation".[152] There is, "no medium of exchange for happiness"[153] and the exercise of converting pain and loss of function and amenity into money must be an artificial one.[154]

D. Mitigation of Damage

22–17   In determining the loss suffered by the claimant there may have to be brought into the account money or other benefits received by the claimant as a result of the tort. This raises difficult questions of law and policy, particularly in relation to personal injuries and is considered later.[155] Even where no countervailing advantage is in fact received the claimant may not claim damages in respect of any part of his loss that would have been avoidable by reasonable steps on his part. Most of the authorities on the "duty" to mitigate relate to breach of contract, but the broad principles are equally applicable to tort. What is reasonable is a question of fact in each case: while the claimant must not be allowed to indulge his own whims or fancies at the expense of the defendant, it must also be remembered that the defendant is a wrongdoer who has caused the claimant's difficulty.[156] Accordingly, the standard of reasonableness is not a high one.[157]

4. ACTIONS FOR PERSONAL INJURY

A. Heads of Damage

22–18   It was for long customary, even after the decline of the civil jury, to make a global award which did not distinguish between the different aspects of damages. This practice was supported partly on the ground that separate assessment and addition of individual items might lead to "overlapping" and a consequently excessive award. However, the introduction by the Administration of Justice Act 1969

---

[151] *British Transport Commission v Gourley*, above, fn.150, at 208 per Lord Goddard.
[152] *Rushton v National Coal Board* [1953] 1 Q.B. 495 at 502 per Romer L.J.; *H. West & Son Ltd v Shephard* [1964] A.C. 326 at 346 per Lord Morris.
[153] *Andrews v Grand & Toy Alberta Ltd* (1978) 83 DLR (3d) 452 at 475 per Dickson J.
[154] *Heil v Rankin* [2001] Q.B. 272 at 293; an "essentially judgemental question": *Thompstone*, above, fn.150, at [47].
[155] See para.22–31, below.
[156] *Banco de Portugal v Waterlow* [1932] A.C. 452 at 506. For cases on refusal of medical treatment, see Hudson in (1983) 3 L.S. 50.
[157] *Morris v Richards* [2003] EWCA Civ 232; [2004] P.I.Q.R. Q30. For mitigation and remoteness, see para.6–33, above.

of a new basis for the award of interest on personal injury damages[158] and subsequent decisions that different heads of damage should be treated in different ways for this purpose have meant that a judge is compelled to itemise his award at least into pre-trial pecuniary loss, future loss of earnings[159] and non-pecuniary loss. The idea that there can be an overlap between the pecuniary and non-pecuniary elements of an award should probably now be discarded.[160]

Even before the provisions on interest, however, it was the case that a variety of situations, each presenting some unusual feature, had compelled the courts to work out outlines of particular "heads of damage" within the broad categories of non-pecuniary and pecuniary loss and it is to these that we must now turn.

i. Non-pecuniary loss.

(a) *Pain, suffering and loss of amenity*. This category of damage **22–19** consists of the two elements of (a) pain and suffering and (b) loss of amenity (i.e. the damaging effect upon the claimant's ability to enjoy life[161]). In practice in nearly all cases the two elements are lumped together in a global sum (known by the inelegant acronym of "PSLA") and it is not usual to distinguish between them in the award.[162] If, for example, the claimant suffers more pain than would be usual for an injury of the type in question, the court would simply make an increase in the usual overall "tariff" figure rather than award a separate sum for the extra pain. Contrariwise, damages under this head may be lower if the claimant suffered no pain because he remained unconscious.[163] It is theoretically possible that there could be pain and suffering without any loss of amenity and if so the claimant is no doubt entitled to damages; but in practice even temporary pain with no permanent physical effect[164] is likely to lead to continuing mental suffering as the injury is recalled.[165] Pain and suffering includes the suffering attributable to any consequential

---

[158] See para.22–39, below.

[159] Expenses are treated in broadly the same way as loss of earnings.

[160] See *Lim v Camden Area Health Authority* [1980] A.C. 174 at 192.

[161] Or "loss of faculty". *Andrews v Freeborough* [1967] 1 Q.B. 1 at 18 per Davies L.J. This head may include social handicap: *A v National Blood Authority* [2001] 3 All E.R. 289 at 383.

[162] *Heil v Rankin* [2001] Q.B. 272 at 298. In American terminology "pain and suffering" tends to be used to describe PSLA as a whole.

[163] *Wise v Kaye* [1962] 1 Q.B. 638; *West & Son Ltd v Shephard* [1964] A.C. 326. See below.

[164] Even injuries like a broken limb will have a temporary disabling effect.

[165] See, e.g. *Phelan v E Cumbria HA* [1991] 2 Med.L.R. 419 (£15,000 for being awake during surgery and subsequently reliving the experience).

medical treatment, and worry about the effects of the injury upon the claimant's way of life and prospects, including worry attributable to "compensation neurosis" which will cease on the determination of his claim for damages.[166] A person is entitled to damages under this head for the mental suffering caused by his awareness that his life expectation has been shortened by the injuries,[167] but fear and anxiety is not in itself damage which can be the basis of the claim. So where the claimant developed symptomless pleural plaques which indicated penetration of the body by asbestos fibres and a small (but greater than normal) chance of developing disease, the physical condition was too insignificant in its effect to constitute damage and there was no claim[168]; nor is there any cause of action for awareness of impending death in an accident.[169] The separate head of "loss of expectation of life" was abolished by the Administration of Justice Act 1982.[170] Before that Act a claim lay for the shortening of life expectancy even though the claimant was unaware of the loss and, indeed, even in cases of instantaneous death,[171] but the difficulties of valuation of such an item soon persuaded the courts to adopt a modest conventional sum[172] which would rarely be departed from. In fact, the principal function of this head of damage was to provide in an indirect way for damages for bereavement in certain cases. This is now done directly by statute.[173] At one time it was thought that the fact that the claimant is wealthy may be a reason for awarding a smaller sum by way of damages for personal injuries,[174] but this view is now untenable.[175]

It is sometimes said that the claimant is entitled to damages not only for pain and suffering and loss of amenity but for "the injury" itself, but it is very doubtful if this is so, it being unlikely that there could ever be a case in practice of bodily injury unaccompanied by

---

[166] *James v Woodall Duckham Construction Co Ltd* [1969] 1 W.L.R. 903, where it was also held that the claimant could not recover in respect of a period of delay in determining his claim which was due to his own dilatoriness in proceeding with it.

[167] Administration of Justice Act 1982 s.1(1)(b). Such damages were recoverable under this head at common law: *Davies and Davies v Smith and Smith* (1958) CA No.34a; *Forest v Sharp* (1963) 107 S.J. 536.

[168] *Rothwell v Chemical & Insulating Co Ltd* [2007] UKHL 39; [2008] A.C. 281. See further para.5–64, above. Cf. *Fletcher v Comrs of Public Works* [2003] 1 I.R. 465.

[169] *Hicks v CC South Yorkshire* [1992] 2 All E.R. 65.

[170] Section 1(1)(a).

[171] *Rose v Ford* [1937] A.C. 826. Causes of action in tort generally survive for the benefit of the estates of deceased persons under the Law Reform (Miscellaneous Provisions) Act 1934 (para.23–3, below) and the victim was regarded as having acquired a cause of action for the shortening of his life.

[172] £200 in *Benham v Gambling* [1941] A.C. 157.

[173] See para.23–12, below.

[174] *Phillips v LSW Ry* (1879) 5 C.P.D. 280 at 294 per Cotton L.J.

[175] *Fletcher v Autocar and Transporters Ltd* [1968] 2 Q.B. 322 at 340, 361; *West v Shephard*, above, fn.163, at 350 per Lord Morris.

any suffering or loss of amenity.[176] A quite different and valid point is that where the injury is a very specific one, like the loss of an eye or a leg, there is in effect a judicial "tariff", a bracket containing the standard award for non-pecuniary loss (see below). The judge will award as damages for loss of amenities a sum comparable to that awarded in other cases unless the effect on the claimant is markedly different from the norm.

Turning to loss of amenity, it has for long been recognised that if **22–20** the claimant's injuries deprive him of some enjoyment, for example, if an amateur footballer loses a leg, then he is entitled to damages on this account.[177] It has become clear, however, that loss of amenity is to a large extent an objective element of the claimant's loss and distinguishable from pain and suffering, so that even though the claimant never appreciates the condition to which he has been reduced, he may nevertheless recover substantial damages under this head.

In *Wise v Kaye*[178] the claimant remained unconscious from the moment of the accident and was deprived of all the attributes of life but life itself. A majority of the Court of Appeal upheld an award of £15,000 for loss of amenity. In *H. West & Son Ltd v Shephard*[179] the claimant was a married woman aged 41 at the time of her accident and sustained severe head injuries resulting in cerebral atrophy and paralysis of all four limbs. There was no prospect of improvement in her condition and her expectation of life was reduced to about five years. There was evidence that she might appreciate to some extent the condition in which she was, but she was unable to speak. A majority of the House of Lords upheld an award of £17,500 for loss of amenities.[180] As Lord Morris said:

> "The fact of unconsciousness does not . . . eliminate the actuality of the deprivations of the ordinary experiences and amenities of life which may be the inevitable result of some physical injury."[181]

---

[176] See Law Com. CP. No.140 (1995) §2.20. Cf. *Rothwell v Chemical & Insulating Co Ltd*, above, fn.168.

[177] *Heaps v Perrite Ltd* [1937] 2 All E.R. 60; *Manley v Rugby Portland Cement Co Ltd* (1951) C.A. No.286.

[178] [1962] 1 Q.B. 638. Notwithstanding medical advances, such cases may be less frequent after *Airedale HA v Bland* [1993] A.C. 789.

[179] [1964] A.C. 326.

[180] An increase of £2,500 over the award in *Wise v Kaye*, where the claimant had no appreciation of her condition. The trial judge in *Shephard* said that if there had been a normal life expectation the damages would have "come up well into the twenties of thousands" (perhaps £120,000 more than today's maximum, even for a fully conscious claimant).

[181] [1964] A.C. at 349.

Powerful objections have been voiced against *West v Shephard*.[182] The principal objection is that one can no more compensate an unconscious person than a dead one and since there can be no award of damages for non-pecuniary loss in respect of the period after death, there may be a very great difference between the total sum awarded to the estate of a deceased person and that awarded to an unconscious, living one, even though the latter will be unable to use the money for his benefit and the whole sum will probably at some future date pass to his relatives.[183] On the other hand, there is a natural reluctance to treat a living claimant as if he were already dead and there are great difficulties in full and accurate diagnosis in these cases.[184] A more general argument which is not aimed at the present treatment of the unconscious claimant but which supports the "conceptual" or "objective" approach upon which that treatment rests is the undesirability of making compensation depend upon the individual unhappiness caused by loss of amenities. It has been argued that unhappiness is in fact the only logical basis for assessment,[185] but Lord Pearce replied:

"It would be lamentable if the trial of a personal injury claim put a premium on protestations of misery and if a long face was the only safe passport to a large award. Under the present practice there is no call for a parade of personal unhappiness. A claimant who cheerfully admits that he is as happy as he ever was, may yet receive a large award as reasonable compensation for the grave injury and loss of amenity over which he has managed to triumph."[186]

22–21   The arguments are fairly evenly balanced. The Law Commission in 1973 recommended no change in the law,[187] but the Pearson

---

[182] See the dissenting speeches of Lords Devlin and Reid in that case, the dissent of Diplock L.J. in *Wise v Kaye*, above, fn.178, and the decision of the High Court of Australia in *Skelton v Collins* (1966) 115 C.L.R. 94.

[183] The difference became even greater when the Administration of Justice Act 1982 abolished claims for loss of expectation of life; but against the argument based upon the ultimate destination of the damages it must be pointed out: (1) the court has never exercised any general power to control the damages awarded to the victim of an accident; (2) some victims who are conscious but unable to "use" their damages might feel compensated by being able to benefit their relatives.

[184] See Law Com. No.257, *Damages for Personal Injury: Non-Pecuniary Loss* (1999), para. 2.14. Furthermore, the possibility of advances in medical science bringing about some amelioration of the condition may contribute to the current judicial attitude (*Croke v Wiseman* [1982] 1 W.L.R. 71 at 84) and diagnoses of permanent vegetative state may be wrong.

[185] See Diplock L.J. in *Wise v Kaye*, above, fn.178.

[186] *West v Shephard*, above, fn.178, at 368–369.

[187] Law Com. No.56, para.31.

Commission went the other way.[188] In a further review in 1999 the Law Commission recommended no change, a view backed by over two-thirds of the consultees.[189] It is also noteworthy that the majority of European systems allow substantial damages for the comatose victim.[190] The House of Lords had looked at the matter again in *Lim v Camden Area Health Authority*[191] and refused to overrule *West v Shephard*, commenting that this, "should not be done judicially but legislatively within the context of a comprehensive enactment"[192] on damages, but no such enactment now seems imminent. However, it would be wrong to think that *West v Shephard* itself is a case of "all or nothing". The minority in that case would have awarded something for the objective loss of amenity even in a case of unconsciousness, though much less than was in fact awarded[193]; equally, the majority would accept that an award under this head would be increased if the claimant were conscious of his loss.[194] In other words, the disagreement was not so much about the factors making up the award as about the relative weight to be given to these factors. On this basis the result in *Lim* might have been regarded as a modest move in the direction of the minority in *West v Shephard* because, making all due allowance for the greater severity of the injuries in *Shephard*, the award of £20,000 in *Lim*[195] was not much more than a third in real terms. Lord Scarman said:

"An award for pain, suffering and loss of amenities is conventional in the sense that there is no pecuniary guideline which can point the way to a correct assessment. It is, therefore, dependent only in the most general way upon the movement in money values . . . As long, therefore, as the sum awarded is a substantial sum in the context of current money values, the requirement of the law is met."[196]

---

[188] Cmnd. 7054, Vol.1, para.398, recommending that damages for loss of amenities should no longer be recoverable in cases of permanent unconsciousness. However, it is not clear whether this would have extended to the case of the claimant who is, literally, conscious but has suffered such severe brain damage that he is unable to appreciate his loss, or the full extent of that loss. Since the Pearson Commission's proposal was based on the premise that, "when we compensate someone for non-economic loss we are essentially seeking to relieve his suffering, and suffering is by its nature an experience subjective to the victim", logic would dictate similar treatment in such cases. However, while medical science will find it fairly easy to distinguish between consciousness and unconsciousness, "consciousness of loss" will often be a much more speculative matter.

[189] Law Com. No.257, paras 2.19 and 2.24.

[190] Rogers (ed), *Damages for Non-Pecuniary Loss in a Comparative Perspective* (2001), p.257.

[191] [1980] A.C. 174.

[192] [1980] A.C. 174 at 189.

[193] See [1964] A.C. at 341, 363.

[194] Hence the larger award in *West v Shephard*, compared with *Wise v Kaye*.

[195] The trial was in 1977.

[196] [1980] A.C. at 189.

However, the case seems to have had little impact in this respect, for the current "bracket" for very severe brain damage is £180,000–£260,000,[197] depending on the degree of insight, which is comparable for the range for quadriplegia and is at least twice as much as the updated figure from *Lim's* case.

A more fundamental question is whether damages for non-pecuniary loss can be justified in *any* case. It has been argued that they are necessarily arbitrary in amount since there is no market by which to value a limb or brain function; that they are secondary in importance to income losses and they divert limited funds from the replacement of those losses; and that they represent interests which are not so highly valued by the public since the interests are not commonly insured. However, such damages are found almost without exception in developed legal systems and, judging by the responses of accident victims to a Law Commission survey,[198] they provide some sort of solace, however, inadequate, for the real hurt suffered by victims of injury. Few could be found to agree with the view of an Italian court at one time that in the eye of the law, "people without any value can exist, as in the case of those who, because of old age, have no earning capacity".[199]

22–22   (b) *Basis of assessment.* It is in the nature of non-pecuniary loss that it cannot be translated directly into money,[200] but nevertheless the only form of compensation available is an award of monetary damages, and an assessment of damages has to be made.[201] In the past their quantification was a jury question for which, "no rigid rules, or rules that apply to all cases can be laid down".[202] However, in the middle 1960s the courts practically abolished the jury in personal injury actions,[203] principally because juries were considered to be incapable of achieving a measure of uniformity in essentially similar cases.[204] Since then it has become normal for judges to have cited to them previous awards and there is a pattern for various

---

[197] Judicial Studies Board, *Guidelines for the Assessment of General Damages in Personal Injury Cases*, 9th edn.

[198] Law Com. No.225, *How Much is Enough?* (1994).

[199] Trib. Firenze, January 6, 1967, [1969] *Archivio della resposabilità civile* 130.

[200] Unfortunately, the economists' tests of value ("What would you want in return for suffering this?" or "What would you pay to avoid this?") are not of much use to a practical tribunal.

[201] *The Mediana* [1900] A.C. 113 at 116 per Lord Halsbury L.C.

[202] *Admiralty Commissioners v SS Susquehanna* [1926] A.C. 655 at 662 per Viscount Dunedin, but he added that: "in each set of circumstances certain relevant considerations will arise which . . . it would be the duty of the judge in the case to bring before the jury."

[203] *Ward v James* [1966] 1 Q.B. 273. After *H. v Ministry of Defence* [1991] 2 Q.B. 103 it seems unlikely that the discretion to order jury trial in these cases will ever be exercised again.

[204] Though one feels some sympathy for the jury, since counsel could not put awards before it, nor suggest a maximum or minimum figure, nor even any specific figure at all. Cf. the position in libel, para.12–71, above.

common kinds of injury, a tariff,[205] though one with some flexibility, since no two cases are identical.[206] There is no "medical schedule" of disability, though medical evidence is of course admissible as to the extent of the claimant's disability.[207] As a technique the comparison of awards no doubt has drawbacks. How can a realistic comparison be made between cases involving different kinds of injury? If, for example, £87,000 is an appropriate figure for total loss by a right-handed claimant of his right arm, what guidance does that give to the damages appropriate for the loss of the sight of an eye,[208] or for the inability to bear a child,[209] or for loss of the sense of smell?[210] Indeed, one might go further and ask, even assuming a suitable standard for comparison can be found, how we justify a particular datum figure for the injury with which the comparisons are made. Why is our figure £87,000 not £870 or £870,000? As far as this latter question is concerned, one can say little more than that the choice of the right order of figure is empirical and in practice results from a general consensus of opinion of damage-awarding tribunals, though one might add that that consensus has become stronger since the ousting of the jury. As for comparisons, Diplock L.J. said that the standard of comparison which the law applies:

"[I]f it is not wholly instinctive and incommunicable, is based, apart from pain and suffering, upon the degree of deprivation —that is, the extent to which the victim is unable to do those things which, but for the injury, he would have been able to do."[211]

The main concern in recent years has not been over the comparison of one injury with another but with whether the overall scale of awards accords with what public opinion regards as just and whether

[205] For a statement of the function of the Court of Appeal in setting levels of awards for non-pecuniary losses, see *Heil v Rankin* [2001] Q.B. 272. A useful publication is the Judicial Studies Board's *Guidelines for the Assessment of General Damages in Personal Injury Cases*, 9th edn. Awards are summarised in *Current Law* and set out more fully in Kemp and Kemp. For example, the appropriate award for loss of sight of one eye without any complications and assuming perfect sight in the other, is now around £32,000. Obviously the appropriate figure for total blindness is a good deal more than twice this (£172,000). The standard tariff figures assume a claimant in the prime of life. See *Nutbrown v Sheffield HA* [1993] 4 Med.L.R. 188 (claimant aged 76, half standard award).

[206] This is particularly obvious in the case of scarring, where the "range" is about £1,500 (minor scarring male, limbs) to about £62,000 (disfiguring facial scarring of female).

[207] However, insurers use two software systems (COA and COLOSSUS) for the purpose of making initial offers so there is some resemblance in practice with the "medical points" system used in some European countries.

[208] See fn.205.

[209] £11,500 to £23,500 where claimant already has children, otherwise much higher, up to £108,000.

[210] £16,000 to £21,000 (but often higher because of impairment of sense of taste).

[211] *Bastow v Bagley & Co Ltd* [1961] 1 W.L.R. 1494 at 1498.

it has kept up with inflation. As to the latter, there is no doubt that the awards for the worst cases fell in real terms in the 1970s and 1980s,[212] though there was a significant "catching up" in the ensuing 10 years.[213] As to the former, the results of a survey led the Law Commission in 1999 to propose an increase by a factor of 1.5 or 2 in cases where the then award would be above £3,000 and by a smaller tapered factor for awards between £2,000 and £3,000. In *Heil v Rankin*[214] the Court of Appeal accepted that there was a need for some increase but disagreed with some aspects of the Law Commission's reasoning[215] and instead held that there should be a tapered increase (to a maximum of 33 per cent) in awards above £10,000. As a result, the top of the range for the most catastrophic injuries, such as quadriplegia, is now about £260,000, putting England towards the upper end of European awards. Since a disproportionate number of claims are for lesser injuries the overall effect was far less than a 33 per cent rise in the total bill[216] but it should be noted that the decision immediately followed another one in the House of Lords which led to substantial increase in damages for pecuniary loss.[217]

Since the assessment of damages for non-pecuniary loss is not an exact mathematical process the Court of Appeal should not interfere with an award unless the judge has acted on a wrong principle of law, or misapprehended the facts or has for other reasons made a wholly erroneous estimate of the damage suffered.[218]

ii. Pecuniary loss.

22–23   (a) *Introduction: lump sums, structured settlements and periodical payments.* In the case of a serious accident, the greater part of the claimant's loss will be pecuniary, usually loss of earnings and expenses. In so far as these losses have been incurred before the trial or settlement[219] there is unlikely to be much difficulty about their

---

[212] On the level of personal injury damages in general, Mr Prevett, an actuary, calculated that the 1982 value of the £16,000 awarded by the jury in *Phillips v LSW Ry* (1879) 5 C.P.D. 280 (under all heads) would have been £500,000 (probably £1,500,000 now). There are now regularly awards of several millions (without interest) under all heads, pecuniary and non-pecuniary. Medical techniques which enable seriously injured claimants to be kept alive for years have inevitably increased the expenses elements in damages claims.

[213] See *Heil v Rankin* [2001] Q.B. 272 at 308.

[214] Above, fn.213.

[215] See [2001] Q.B. at 302.

[216] The Law Commission thought that an overall rise of 50 per cent in non-pecuniary loss damages would put about 2 per cent on motor premiums and between 7 and 9 per cent on employers' liability premiums.

[217] *Wells v Wells* [1999] 1 A.C. 345, para.22–28, below. For Australian developments see para.1–44, above.

[218] *Pickett v British Rail Engineering Ltd* [1980] A.C. 136; *Heil v Rankin*, above, fn.213.

[219] The larger the claim, the longer the likely delay before settlement.

assessment other than, perhaps, with regard to offsetting other benefits received.[220] However, it is an inveterate principle of the common law that damages may only be awarded on a lump sum, "once and for all" basis[221] which means that the court must therefore also attempt to convert future pecuniary losses into a present capital sum, a process which is inevitably inexact because it involves a host of assumptions, including the claimant's future rate of earning had he not been injured, the period and extent of his disability, and the chance that his earning capacity might have been affected by some other vicissitude even if the accident had not happened. In modern times the difficulty of this task has been exacerbated by unpredictable factors like unemployment and inflation. So the lump sum system was under pressure. The first, limited, exception[222] was the introduction of "provisional awards". Section 32A of the Senior Courts Act 1981[223] applies to an action for personal injuries in which there is proved or admitted to be a chance that at some time in the future the injured person will, as a result of the defendant's tort,[224] develop some serious disease or suffer some serious deterioration in his physical or mental condition. In such a case[225] the court has power to make a provisional award, that is to say, award damages on the basis that the claimant will not suffer the disease or deterioration but with power to award further damages if and when he does. Obviously, this procedure is only of use in those cases where the risk of deterioration in the claimant's condition is known before judgment.[226] The provisions have been interpreted to require a "clear and severable event" (such as, perhaps, the development of epilepsy following a head injury[227]) rather than a gradual deterioration (such as joint degeneration or arthritis, which are common sequelae of orthopaedic injury).[228] This restriction was regarded as justifiable because an extension to gradual deterioration would

---

[220] See para.22–31, below.

[221] See generally, para.22–2, above. In *Watkins v Olafsen* (1989) 61 D.L.R. (4th) 577, the Supreme Court of Canada declined to introduce periodical payments by judicial decision. Specific performance may be ordered of an obligation to make periodic payments of money (*Beswick v Beswick* [1968] A.C. 58) but that can have no application to a case of tort.

[222] The power to make an interim award where the court is satisfied that there would be a substantial award at trial (CPR 25, in particular 25(7)) is only a quasi-exception: the sum is simply an advance on the final award.

[223] Formerly the Supreme Court Act 1981. Introduced by the Administration of Justice Act 1982 s.6.

[224] The court is only relieved of the necessity of assessing a chance in this type of case. If, e.g. the defendant contends that damages should be low because a pre-existing disease may cause the claimant to die prematurely the court must assess the chance and discount accordingly.

[225] See CPR 41 and PD 41.

[226] However, an appellate court has power to receive new evidence, including evidence of events occurring after trial.

[227] Or, presumably, the development of full-blown AIDS following HIV infection.

[228] *Willson v Ministry of Defence* [1991] 1 All E.R. 838.

vastly increase the number of cases in which provisional awards could be made and introduce a serious measure of uncertainty into the system.

Lump sum awards are alleged to have advantages from the point of view of both the claimant and the defendant (or, more usually, his insurer). The claimant, it is said, can concentrate his efforts on recovery from his disability without fear that in doing so he will be reducing his compensation and he is given a degree of choice as to his future financial resources (for example, he may buy a small business). The defendant's insurers, on the other hand, can close their books on a claim and incur no further administrative costs. There is no doubt that there is force in these arguments, but there are also powerful objections to the lump sum system. There is generally no way in which the claimant's use of his damages can be controlled and if he uses his capital improvidently or engages in an unsuccessful business venture the end result may be that he is supported through social security by the community at large.[229] Even where the claimant uses his capital wisely the lump sum system cannot protect him against unforeseen deterioration in his medical condition or in the economic situation after the trial and it becomes difficult to adopt anything but the most arbitrary rule as to offset of social security payments (which are periodic) against tort damages.[230] There may also be a downside in the lump sum system for "self-funding" defendants (like the NHS) who, rightly or wrongly, might see budgetary attractions in paying, say £50,000 a year rather than a lump sum of seven figures. The first major change in the lump sum system came in the form of "structured settlements".[231]

If a claimant with a large award of, say, £500,000 used it to buy an annuity to replace his pre-accident income he would be relieved of the burden of managing a fund and the terms might give him protection against inflation but the annual income received would be subject to income tax in the normal way. If, instead, the defendants were to pay the damages in annual instalments over 25 years that would be the repayment of a capital debt and would not attract income tax. Generally of course such an arrangement was impracticable because a general insurer would not be willing to enter into such a transaction. However, in 1987 the Inland Revenue approved arrangements whereby annuity-based settlements would attract the same tax advantage. Very broadly, the original arrangements were as follows: once a settlement had been agreed the defendant's liability insurer would enter into two contracts: (1) with the claimant, for a lump sum in the normal way, but on the basis that in lieu of the

---

[229] Of course, exactly the same may happen in the case of an uninjured person who wastes his capital and periodical income.
[230] See para.22–34, below.
[231] Lewis, *Structured Settlements* (1993); Law Com. No.224.

greater part of this[232] payments would be made of instalments tied to the Retail Price Index; (2) with a life office for an annuity on the claimant's life. The annuity was payable to the liability insurer, which would use it to make the agreed periodical payments to the claimant, these being free of tax in the claimant's hands. Since the claimant would make a tax saving of up to 40 per cent the liability insurer would be able to negotiate a discount on the sum that would be required for a conventional lump sum settlement. At the same time, in case of long-term disability the structure would yield payments much in excess of an invested lump sum, especially where predictions of the claimant's life expectancy turned out to be pessimistic. It was likely, particularly where the claimant had dependants, that the structure would provide a guaranteed number of payments even if the claimant died early and it was also usual to retain a capital sum to cover contingencies, since the structure could not be altered once it was in place. This system was refined by various legislative developments which allowed the claimant to receive payments directly from the life office and brought them within the scope of the Policyholders Protection Act 1975, giving protection against the failure of the life office,[233] but the court was still unable to *make an award* under which the damages were paid wholly or partly on a periodical basis except with the consent of both parties. However, the system was radically transformed by the amendments to the Damages Act 1996 by the Courts Act 2003,[234] the relevant provisions of which came into force in 2005.

(b) *Periodical payments under the Damages Act 1996 as* **22–24** *amended.* The basic provision is disarmingly simple, though it is supplemented by a mass of statutory instruments, rules and guidance documents—to be followed no doubt by a stream of case law:

"2. (1) A court awarding damages for future pecuniary loss in respect of personal injury[235]—

    (a) may order that damages are wholly or partly to take the form of periodical payments, and

    (b) shall consider whether to make that order.

---

[232] Some actual lump sum transfer will be necessary to cover pre-settlement losses and capital expenditure.

[233] Damages Act 1996 s.4. The Secretary of State was empowered to guarantee "directly funded" settlements such as those by NHS Trusts.

[234] Sections 100 and 101.

[235] The provisions apply equally to fatal accident cases. Non-pecuniary loss damages may be included in an order for periodical payments only with the consent of the parties: s.2(2). It seems that any *damages* for personal injuries paid on a periodic basis are free of tax in the hands of the recipient: Income Tax (Trading and Other Income) Act 2005 s.731.

> (2) A court awarding other damages in respect of personal injury[236] may, if the parties consent, order that damages are wholly or partly to take the form of periodical payments.
>
> (3) A court may not make an order for periodical payments unless satisfied that the continuity of payment under the order is reasonably secure."

Provision for periodical payments has been established in many European legal systems for a long time but the general picture is that the claimant has a choice whether to accept such an award (and the majority apparently go for a lump sum, though the differences in social security and fiscal provisions and security may make it impossible to generalise to any "natural" preference[237]); under English law the decision is that of the court, whatever either (or even both[238]) of the parties may want. No doubt the wishes of a properly advised claimant are entitled to considerable weight. Although periodical payments are concerned with needs, they are not like social security payments: an award of damages is also about indemnifying him for his loss, and his own perceptions of his prospects and that of his family may have a role to play in that. However, at the end of the day the question for the judge is what form of order best meets the claimant's needs and there may be cases in which he is satisfied that, "he knows what is best for the claimant better than the claimant himself knows".[239] In practice, of course, it is very unlikely that any personal injuries judgment will be entirely in the form of a periodical payments order even in respect of future losses, for a very seriously injured claimant is likely to need capital to obtain equipment and accommodation. However, this power to compel only arises if the matter comes before the court for judgment on damages or if a settlement is made on behalf of a minor or person lacking mental capacity, which requires to be approved by the court.[240] The basic position is that it remains open for persons of full age and understanding to make what settlement they wish, whether it is for a lump sum or periodical payments on some other basis than that prescribed by the Act. It is true that where proceedings have been commenced many settlements will be implemented in a consent order so that they are enforceable as a judgment rather than a contract, but this will not attract the court's powers of compulsion

---

[236] i.e. for non-pecuniary loss.

[237] Langstaff, "Structured Settlements, Past, Present and Future" [2003] J.P.I.L. 236.

[238] If only for evidential reasons a court is unlikely to go against the wishes of both parties: *Thompstone v Tameside and Glossop etc NHS Trust* [2008] EWCA Civ 5; [2008] 1 W.L.R. 2207 at [102].

[239] *Thompstone*, above, fn.238, at [103].

[240] All the appeals in *Thompstone* involved claimants subject to legal disability. In subsequent proceedings there was approved a model schedule for periodical payments: [2008] EWHC 2948 (QB).

for generally speaking the court has no role in determining the terms of such a "judgment".[241] That is not to say that in today's climate the impact of the court's powers will not be felt at an early stage even if the matter never proceeds to judgment. If the claimant's lawyers do not consider the possible advantages of periodical payments they are at risk of a suit for negligence; in the case management context, r.41.6 requires the court to indicate as soon as practicable whether it considers periodical payments to be the most appropriate route and claimants may address this issue in the Statement of Case and may be required to do so. Under Pt 36 either party may make an offer to settle, refusal of which may have significant consequences for the costs of further proceedings: for example if a claimant makes an offer at £X, this is refused by the defendant and the claimant "beats" £X at trial the court may award interest at 10 per cent above base rate on the damages and indemnity costs with enhanced interest on those.[242] If the claimant refuses the defendant's offer and fails to beat it at trial the defendant will generally get his costs from 21 days after the offer. Offers by either side may be expressed in alternative terms of lump sum or periodical payments (or a mixture of the two)[243] and it may prove difficult in practice to determine whether, say, a judgment for periodical payments at the rate of £X is "more advantageous" (the term in the Rules) for the claimant than a rejected offer by the defendant of a lump sum of £Y. Nor is it simply a matter of comparing amounts: for example, an offer of £X made early in the proceedings may be regarded as more advantageous to the claimant than a judgment for, say £X+10 per cent recovered later after substantial expenditure.[244]

In deciding whether to give judgment for periodical payments the court must, "have regard to all the circumstances of the case and in particular the form of award which best meets the claimant's needs",[245] and by Practice Direction 41B the relevant factors include:

"(1) [T]he scale of the annual payments taking into account any deduction for contributory negligence;

---

[241] The CA in *Thompstone* at [103] said that it was no longer the right of a claimant of full age and capacity to receive his damages as a lump sum and spend (or squander) them as he wishes, but this statement is presumably contemplating a judgment. However, if the settlement embodied in the consent order involves periodical payments, it seems that the court must be satisfied that continuity is secure: Dept of Constitutional Affairs, *Guidance on Periodical Payments* (2005), para.44.

[242] Rule 36.21.

[243] Rule 36.2A.

[244] *Carver v BAA Plc* [2008] EWCA Civ 412; [2009] 1 WLR 113. This "open-textured" approach has led to considerable uncertainty and the *Review of Costs in Civil Litigation* (2010) has recommended that it should be purely an arithmetical comparison of the offer and judgment: Ch.41, 2.9.

[245] Rule 41.7.

(2) the form of award preferred by the claimant[246] including—

(a) the reasons for the claimant's preference; and
(b) the nature of any financial advice received by the claimant when considering the form of award; and

(3) the form of award preferred by the defendant including the reasons for the defendant's preference."

Periodical payments may be "stepped", i.e. made at such and such a rate for one period and at a different rate for another, to reflect anticipated changes in the claimant's circumstances.[247] The secure continuity of the payments is obviously the matter of most critical importance and the court can only make an order if it is satisfied that this continuity is "reasonably secure".[248] This condition is taken to be satisfied where the payments are underwritten by the compensation scheme in s.213 of the Financial Services and Markets Act 2000 (which will apply to most insurers), or, in the case of public sector settlements, by a Ministerial guarantee or the source of payment is a designated government or health service body.[249] Otherwise the court must be satisfied on this issue by evidence.[250]

We became familiar under the structured settlements regime with indexation of payments. Under the Damages Act payments are linked to the Retail Prices Index unless the court orders otherwise[251] but in *Thompstone v Tameside and Glossop etc NHS Trust,*[252] a long-term care case, the Court of Appeal approved indexation by reference to an index based on care costs[253] and this will be the norm in the absence of good reason to the contrary.[254] The matter is obviously of great significance if a major element of the damages represents something likely to exceed the general rate of inflation. At least a claimant with a lump sum fund can attempt to gear his

---

[246] In *Freeman v Lockett* [2006] EWHC 102 (QB) a lump sum award of £5.5 million (mostly in respect of future care) was made where the claimant had received expert advice and wished to avoid dependence on public funds.
[247] CPR r.41.8; PD41.
[248] Damages Act 1996 s.2(3) as substituted.
[249] The only body named in the third category for England is the NHS Litigation Authority: Damages (Government and Health Service Bodies) Order, SI 2005/474. If an NHS Trust becomes insolvent the National Health Service Residual Liabilities Act 2003 requires the Minister to secure that its residual liabilities are dealt with, but the same is not true of a *Foundation* Trust, which may leave the Clinical Negligence Scheme for Trusts: *Kanu v King's College NHS Trust* [2005] EWHC 2759 (QB).
[250] The court approved the MIB in *Thacker v Steeples*, June 22, 2005 (LTLPI) on the basis that in view of the Second European Motor Insurance Directive it was unlikely that the Government would allow it to be wound up with its liabilities undischarged.
[251] Section 2(8).
[252] [2008] EWCA Civ 5; [2008] 1 W.L.R. 2207.
[253] Known as ASHE 6115.
[254] At [100].

investment policy so as to meet higher costs but the periodical payments claimant cannot do this: "the transfer of [investment] risk away from him results also in a loss of opportunity for gain".[255]

An important feature of the periodical payments regime is the power to vary payments because of changed circumstances,[256] which may be built into a periodical payments order or an agreement for such payments when they are made. As far as deterioration is concerned the law is modelled on the provisional damages regime, that is to say, there is proved or admitted or agreed to be a chance that at some time in the future the injured person will develop some serious disease or suffer some serious deterioration. However, the variation provisions apply equally to the case where there may be some "significant improvement" in his condition,[257] a factor which would obviously influence a claimant in his attitude to the choice between a lump sum and periodical payments. Whether it is deterioration or improvement, the power to vary is confined to changes in the claimant's condition, so it will not cover, for example, changes in the availability or cost of care where these cannot be absorbed by the relevant indexation.[258]

Structured settlements were comparatively rare and confined to "big" cases. It should not be assumed that the new regime will replace lump sum damages in every case involving large long-term losses[259]: for example, a claimant with a large earnings loss but substantial other income or assets[260] or one with a heavy reduction for contributory negligence (which would reduce the income produced by the award) could probably make out a pretty convincing case for a lump sum award. The most obvious area where the periodical payments system has attractions for claimants is in respect of the costs of care: in one case there was a "split" award, earnings as a lump sum, care on a periodical basis.[261] The general assumption seems to be that periodical payments offer less attractions for defendants (apart perhaps from the NHS, which may see a "cash flow" benefit); but it is certainly true that we will no longer have a "clean break" approach. Under the classical lump sum model the defendant's insurers paid the claimant £2 million (or whatever) and that was the end of it, whether he died unexpectedly the

22–25

---

[255] Swift J. at first instance in *Thompstone*. The extended quotation from this judgment in the CA at [18] is a clear explanation of the background to the periodical payments system.

[256] Distinguish the making of an order which initially specifies different rates of payment for different periods.

[257] Damages (Variation of Periodical Payments) Order, SI 2005/841, arts 2 and 9.

[258] It is true that under r.41.8 the payments can be "stepped" to take account of predictable changes but that is unlikely to cover this situation.

[259] The Government's hope that, "the use of periodical payments in appropriate personal injury cases would become the norm" (*Guidance on Periodical Payments*, above, para.8) of course begs the question of what are "appropriate" cases.

[260] Even more so one with a comparatively short period of loss.

[261] *Godbold v Mahmood* [2005] EWHC 1002 (QB).

following year and left his children a fortune, made a miraculous recovery or lived for decades and became a charge on public funds. Now the "relationship" continues (although it may be with some third party providing an annuity to fund the judgment). It is hardly surprising that the claimant will be required to provide evidence that he is still alive before receiving an instalment but in view of the variation provisions there may be cases in which the defendant feels it in his interest to engage in rather more surveillance of the claimant.

Structured settlements existed against the background of a basic lump sum payment system in the sense that the parties' estimate of what the court would award at a trial formed the datum on which the structure was based. The Government's Guidance on the new system says that:

> "[I]t is intended that where a periodical payments order is made or agreed, a 'bottom-up' approach will be adopted, which focuses instead on calculating the annual future needs of the claimant . . . Moving from a 'top-down' to a 'bottom-up' approach means that the claimant should no longer need financial advice on how to 'structure' the payments or on the best priced annuity available to meet his or her needs. The 'bottom-up' approach places the onus on the defendant to decide how to meet the terms of the court order or settlement."[262]

This is most clearly illustrated by the power to make an order under which the payments will change according to anticipated changes in the deceased's circumstances. However, there is some danger of oversimplification here. Defendants will always have to value the claimant's future losses and prospects against a lump sum because they will, directly or indirectly, have to fund the periodical payments, but so may claimants. In reality most big cases either settle or go to judgment after a long period of negotiation and in either event the claimant is likely to be faced with offers (whether or not under Pt 36) which will need to be assessed against the possible alternative, which will certainly involve financial advice.

Lump sum damages for pecuniary loss will be with us for a good while yet, even in some big cases, so we must now turn to see how the courts attempt to assess them.

22–26   (c) *Lump sum awards.* Where the court has to make a final lump sum award for future pecuniary loss it has to capitalise a future stream of income. The normal approach is that of the so-called "multiplier". One first determines the multiplicand in the form of

---

[262] *Guidance on Periodical Payments*, above, para.8.

the claimant's net annual loss. If we assume a case in which the claimant is totally disabled, this is arrived at by deducting from the gross income the claimant was receiving before the accident the amount of income tax,[263] social security contributions[264] and other expenditure the claimant would have had to incur to gain the income (for example, his contribution to a company pension scheme[265]). Logically, a case could be made out for deducting under the last head the claimant's travelling expenses to and from work which he will no longer incur after the accident but, except perhaps in very exceptional circumstances,[266] this is not done.[267]

The annual sum thus arrived at[268] is then multiplied by a number of years' purchase calculated upon the likely duration of the loss.[269] In determining the multiplier, however, the court will not simply adopt the number of years from trial[270] to retirement age or death[271] for that would be to overcompensate the claimant. First, some allowance must be made for the "general vicissitudes of life", that is to say, damaging events like early death or unemployment which might have affected the claimant[272] even if the defendant had not injured him.[273] Secondly, account must be taken of the fact that the lump sum of damages will itself produce an investment income.[274] A reduction of the multiplier will therefore be made to effect a

---

[263] *British Transport Commission v Gourley* [1956] A.C. 185. (1) The damages themselves are not taxable in the claimant's hands. (2) Interest on the damages awarded by the court would be taxable were it not specifically exempted by statute. (3) The income produced by the investment of the award is taxable in the normal way and since this has to go to cover part of the claimant's loss he in effect suffers tax twice over; but this illogicality is tolerated: see Lord Oliver in *Hodgson v Trapp* [1989] A.C. 807.

[264] *Cooper v Firth Brown Ltd* [1963] 2 W.L.R. 418. As to deduction of social security *receipts* by the claimant, see para.22–34, below.

[265] *Dews v NCB* [1988] A.C. 1; but if as a result of the accident the claimant's employment is terminated and he suffers a reduction in pension, this is itself a compensable head of damage: *Parry v Cleaver* [1970] A.C. 1.

[266] Lord Griffiths in *Dews v NCB* suggests as a possible example the case of a wealthy man who commuted daily by helicopter from the Channel Islands to London, but cf. *Eagle v Chambers* [2004] EWCA Civ 1033; [2004] 1 W.L.R. 3081 at [68].

[267] It can be argued that it is no concern of the defendant where the claimant chooses to live but a further practical reason is that such deductions would complicate the settlement and disposal of claims.

[268] Increases in the claimant's earnings which will be produced by inflation are ignored (see below) but likely increases due to promotion, etc. are brought into the calculation. For a complicated example see *Robertson v Lestrange* [1985] 1 All E.R. 950 (a fatal accident case).

[269] There may be differing periods for different heads of claim. Loss of earnings may cease at retirement age but expenses of care may be life-long.

[270] See *Pritchard v J.H. Cobden Ltd* [1988] Fam. 22.

[271] It is assumed here that the disability is permanent.

[272] It must be emphasised that although it is justifiable to make a larger reduction for, say, a person in a hazardous occupation, the general range of reductions under this head is modest unless there is evidence to show some special risk affecting the claimant as an individual: *Herring v MoD* [2003] EWCA Civ 528; [2004] 1 All E.R. 44.

[273] For the position where such a vicissitude occurs before trial, see para.6–7, above.

[274] While alternative contingencies may be relevant to the assessment of past loss this element is not: *Takitoka v Att Gen of the Bahamas* [2009] UKPC 12 at [9].

discount in respect of those factors. Of course, the claimant's circumstances (for example promotion prospects) may call for an increase rather than a reduction in the multiplier. The theoretical aim of the process is to provide a lump sum sufficient, when invested, to produce an income equal to the lost income when the interest is supplemented by withdrawals of capital. Naturally, it is unlikely that this result is actually reached in more than a handful of cases since it involves a double exercise in the art of prophesying—not only what the future holds for the injured claimant, but also what the future would have held for him if he had not been injured.[275]

> "The calculations which [the court] makes will involve the use of arithmetic as the multiplier is applied to the multiplicand. To that extent the exercise will give the impression of accuracy. But the accuracy of the result achieved by arithmetic will depend on the assumptions on which it has been based."[276]

It will be observed that whatever virtues periodical payments have in avoiding the need to make guesses about what *will* happen to the claimant they contribute nothing at all on the question which underlies the determination of his loss—what *would have* happened to him.[277]

22–27 The current practice is to make use of the "Ogden Tables",[278] a set of actuarial tables tailored to assessing a lump sum of damages for continuing loss. Actuarial tables were created by life assurance companies for the purpose of determining what capital sum should be charged for an annuity, since the insurer is obviously vitally concerned to make an estimate of the annuitants' life expectancies. Since the tables are concerned with assessing the capital "price" of a future stream of income, the information on which they are based can easily be used to determine the present capital "value" of a future stream of loss. The use of such evidence has sometimes been criticised because, grounded as it is in the needs of insurers, it is concerned with groups, whereas the court is concerned with an individual. This is of course true in the sense that the insurer providing annuities is concerned to cover his costs and make a profit from the group of annuitants as a whole. He will "lose" some by

---

[275] *Paul v Rendell* (1981) 34 A.L.R. 569 at 571, PC, per Lord Diplock; *Wells v Wells* [1999] 1 A.C. 345 at 363 per Lord Lloyd.

[276] *Wells v Wells* [1999] 1 A.C. at 389 per Lord Hope.

[277] For an extreme example of difficulty in assessing what future earnings would have been, see *Norris v Blake* (1997) 41 N.S.W.L.R. 49 (Australian film actor, possible peak earnings anywhere between AU$300,000 and $40 million pa). See also *Collett v Smith* [2008] EWHC 1962 (QB) and [2009] EWCA Civ 583 (young professional footballer); *van Wees v Karkour* [2007] EWHC 165 (QB); *Leesmith v Evans* [2008] EWHC 134 (QB).

[278] 6th edn, 2007.

granting annuities to people who live to be very old; he will "win" others where the annuitant dies early and he will not be concerned whether any single case is "right" in the sense that the annuitant dies at the moment predicted by the tables. However, the criticism is misplaced for two reasons. First, it is at least as unlikely that the "right" answer is produced for an individual case by an uninformed guess and it may well be that the use of actuarial evidence would lead to a more accurate global answer for tort claimants as a whole. Secondly, while the Ogden Tables themselves are based on general mortality and therefore do not allow for contingencies like unemployment or ill-health, they do contain suggestions as to how they may be adapted to allow in a general way for such risks[279] and in a particular case more detailed actuarial evidence may be available. Although in the past there has been some resistance to using actuarial evidence as the basis for calculating the multiplier, in *Wells v Wells* Lord Lloyd said that while the judge should not be:

"[A] slave to the tables . . . [they] should now be regarded as the starting-point, rather than a check. A judge should be slow to depart from the relevant actuarial multiplier on impressionistic grounds, or by reference to 'a spread of multipliers in comparable cases' especially when the multipliers were fixed before actuarial tables were widely used."[280]

Of course, no matter how sophisticated the tables, there is no guarantee that the answer will be correct for any individual claimant, but assuming that there is no evidence that the claimant, before the accident, was atypical, there seems no reason not to apply to him data based on the general population.

Assessing the duration of the claimant's loss is only half the story; there is also the question of what rate of return he will obtain on his capital sum, for that will go to make up part of his post-judgment income. To take a rather unrealistic example, if C suffers a loss of £100 for one year and receives compensation for it at the beginning of the year, then the higher the rate of interest during the year, the less he will need as a lump sum at the beginning to cover his loss. The multipliers habitually used by the courts in personal injury cases corresponded approximately to an assumed rate of return of 4.5 per cent net (or 6 per cent gross). Much of the period in which the modern law of damages has developed has been

22–28

---

[279] See Section B, "Contingencies other than Mortality" and *Herring v MoD* [2003] EWCA Civ 528; [2004] 1 All E.R. 44.
[280] [1999] 1 A.C. at 379.

characterised by periods of high inflation[281] and it is clear that during at least part of this period a claimant achieving a 4.5 per cent net return could not keep pace with the progressive fall in the value of his fund. However, the law has always been clear, that is to say, money is treated as retaining its value at the date of the judgment. Though surprising at first sight, this approach was defended on the ground that protection against inflation is built into the system, because there is a tendency for high inflation to be accompanied by high rates of interest,[282] so that the claimant whose damages have been calculated on the basis of a 4.5 per cent return will in fact receive a higher rate in times of high inflation and the decline in the capital value of the fund will be offset by an increase in income. While there is undoubtedly some truth in this, there is reason to believe that the machine does not work in quite so efficient a way. First, it does not take account of the "ratchet" effect: high inflation raises prices but when it is brought under control prices do not generally fall (except the price of credit) but the claimant's income does. Secondly, the assumption of a claimant expertly managing a large fund over a long period for maximum advantage may not be a very accurate one.[283] Thirdly, in any event the model only worked if the figure of 4.5 per cent roughly equalled the "real" rate of interest, that is to say, what is left after the rate from time to time has the inflation element stripped out, a proposition which was pretty clearly incorrect.[284]

For a number of years there had been in existence index-linked Government securities (ILGS), which are bonds under which the capital sum is linked to the inflation index so that, in the event of a fall in the value of money, a larger sum is repaid than was lent. Naturally, interest on these investments was lower than the general commercial rate, generally at 2.5 per cent of the nominal value adjusted for inflation. The Law Commission in 1994 recommended that the courts, when determining the return to be expected from investment of damages should take account of the ILGS rate and that this should be adopted unless there were special reasons affecting the individual case.[285] This was taken up by the House of Lords in *Wells v Wells*,[286] where it was held that it should be assumed that

---

[281] When the Retail Price Index began in 1948 money had about 27 times its present value. The peak period was the 1970s.

[282] Due to interest representing not only the sum a lender charges for the use of his money but also his estimate of how much the value of the sum lent will have declined on repayment.

[283] The Law Commission found that 84 per cent of claimants with damages of more than £100,000 had taken some investment advice: Law Com. No.224, s.2.30.

[284] See, in a different context, *Wright v B.R.B.* [1983] 2 A.C. 773.

[285] Law Com. No.224, §2.31.

[286] [1999] 1 A.C. 345.

the claimant would invest his fund in ILGS stocks[287] and that the assumed rate of return should be 3 per cent. While in a sense this gave the claimant a degree of protection[288] denied to the "ordinary, prudent investor" his position was not exactly the same, since he would be likely to depend on the damages fund for the necessities of life. Section 1 of the Damages Act 1996 provides that the court is to take account of, "such rate of return . . . as may from time to time be prescribed by the Lord Chancellor". This was not in force at the time of *Wells* but the Lord Chancellor exercised the power and prescribed a rate of 2.5 per cent from June 28, 2001.[289] The financial impact of this may be judged from a simple example. In the case of a permanently disabled male aged 30 at the time of the trial, with a loss of earnings to an assumed pension age of 65, the Ogden Tables at 4.5 per cent give a multiplier of 17.5; at 2.5 per cent the multiplier is 22.8, an increase of 30 per cent.[290]

(d) *Loss of earning capacity or "handicap in the labour market"*. **22–29** In cases of continuing disability the claimant may be able to remain in his employment but with the risk that, if he loses that employment at some time in the future, he may then, as a result of his injury, be at a disadvantage in getting another job or an equally well-paid job.[291] This "loss of earning capacity"[292] has always been a compensable head of damage but has come into more prominence in recent years, probably as a result of the growth of the practice of "itemising" awards.[293] Assessment of damages under this head may be highly speculative and clearly no mathematical approach is

---

[287] Provided he is of full age and capacity, what he *actually* does with the fund is entirely his own business. In fact many damages funds in very serious cases are managed by the Court of Protection, which invests broadly on the advice of brokers.

[288] In fact they are only risk free if held to maturity and the pattern of their issue makes them a rather inflexible investment.

[289] Damages (Personal Injury) Order SI 2001/2301.

[290] Although s.1(2) of the Damages Act 1996 enables the court to use a different rate where "appropriate" and in reality the claimant will invest in a mixed portfolio, he cannot recover the costs of investment advice, nor can he base his claim on a lower rate because he can show that an element of his loss (e.g. the cost of care) is likely to increase faster than general inflation: *Cooke v United Bristol Healthcare* [2003] EWCA Civ 1370; [2004] 1 W.L.R. 251; *Page v Plymouth Hospitals NHS Trust* [2004] EWHC 11154 (QB); *Eagle v Chambers* [2004] EWCA Civ 1033; [2004] 1 W.L.R. 3081.

[291] This principle is directed at the situation where the claimant remains in employment with no present effect on earnings. To extend it more broadly risks double counting: *Morgan v UPS Ltd* [2008] EWCA Civ 375.

[292] The terminology in this area is not uniform and all loss of future earnings is sometimes included within this expression. On this view, all loss of earnings represents a capital loss, a point which influenced the High Court of Australia in *Atlas Tiles v Briers* (1978) 21 A.L.R. 129 to refuse to follow *Gourley's* case on income tax and damages (para.22–26, above). However, a full court assembled in *Cullen v Trappell* (1980) 29 A.L.R. 1 overruled *Atlas Tiles*. The truth appears to be that earning capacity in the broad sense is a "capital" asset but can only be valued by the income it produces and that *Gourley's* case proceeded pragmatically rather than conceptually.

[293] *Moeliker v A. Reyrolle & Co Ltd* [1976] I.C.R. 253 at 261 per Brown L.J.

possible[294] but the court should be satisfied that there is a "substantial" or "real" risk that the claimant will be subject to the disadvantage before the end of his working life. If so satisfied, the judge must then do his best to value the "chance", taking into account all the facts of the case.[295]

22–30   (e) *The "lost years"*. In some cases the injury suffered by the claimant will reduce his expectation of life. For many years the rule was that while a claimant was entitled to damages for "loss of expectation of life" (a conventional sum)[296] he could not recover any further damages for loss of earnings during the period when, but for the accident, he would probably have remained alive and working. For an adult claimant with dependants the consequences of this might be catastrophic, for his dependants might be left without compensation for a very large part of the loss they have suffered.[297] In the face of prolonged legislative inaction, the House of Lords in *Pickett v British Rail Engineering Ltd*[298] held that damages for loss of earnings were to be assessed on the claimant's expectation of life before the accident, making a deduction in respect of money which the claimant would have spent on his own support during the lost years. Nearly all the cases arose from claims by estates of deceased persons, a context in which *Pickett* has been reversed by statute,[299] but the general approach, although by no means identical to those applicable to the assessment of damages under the Fatal Accidents Act 1976,[300] was at least similar: as one might say, the lost years claim, though generally smaller, would be at least in the same "ball park" as the claim by his dependants for loss of support had he been killed instantly. The courts should not enter the realms of speculation or guesswork: where the claimant is middle-aged with established commitments the task may present no particular novelty or

---

[294] The same applies to a claimant who is injured before his working life has begun: it may be more appropriate to select a global figure which seems fair compensation than to seek a multiplier and multiplicand: *Joyce v Yeomans* [1981] 1 W.L.R. 550.
[295] See *Ashcroft v Curtin* [1971] 1 W.L.R. 1731; *Smith v Manchester Corp* (1974) 17 K.I.R. 1 (this item is commonly known as "*Smith v Manchester* damages"); *Clarke v Rotax Aircraft Equipment Ltd* [1975] I.C.R. 440; *Moeliker v A. Reyrolle & Co Ltd* [1976] I.C.R. 253; *Nicholls v NCB* [1976] I.C.R. 266; *Robson v Liverpool CC* [1993] P.I.Q.R. Q78 ; *Goldborough v Thompson* [1996] P.I.Q.R. Q67. Damages may be awarded under this head even though the claimant is unemployed at the date of the trial: *Cook v Consolidated Fisheries Ltd* [1977] I.C.R. 635.
[296] See para.22–19.
[297] See *Gammell v Wilson* [1982] A.C. 27 at 64–65 per Lord Diplock. Where death is attributable to the defendant's tort the deceased's dependants have a cause of action under the Fatal Accidents Act (para.23–9, below), but this cannot be brought where the victim has already recovered judgment before death.
[298] [1980] A.C. 126.
[299] See para.23–5, below.
[300] *Harris v Empress Motors Ltd* [1983] 3 All E.R. 561, overruling a number of first instance decisions.

difficulty; where the claimant is a teenager about to embark on a career there may be enough material to justify a moderate award but in the case of a very young child the right figure will often[301] be nil.[302] Cases of this type may be particularly suitable for being handled under the periodical payments regime[303] because the court is specifically enabled to order that part of the payments may continue to be made after the claimant's eventual death,[304] thereby avoiding speculation (which may be distressing to him) as to when, exactly he will die.

(f) *Deductions: benefits received.*[305] The principle of mitigation **22–31** requires that the claimant must take reasonable steps to avoid or reduce the loss and if he does not do so he cannot charge to the defendant that part of it which is attributable to failure to do so.[306] It is a necessary corollary of this that the claimant cannot claim from the defendant loss which has in fact been avoided because he has received a countervailing benefit. The problem lies in distinguishing between those receipts[307] which go to reduce the loss and those which are "indirect" or "collateral" and do not do so. The issue is of general application in contract as well as in tort[308] and in non-personal injury cases the modern approach seems to be to ask whether the benefit received is sufficiently causally connected with the defendant's wrongdoing[309] to require it to be brought into

---

[301] In *Gammell v Wilson*, above, fn.297, at 78, Lord Scarman put forward the case of a five-year-old child television star "cut short in her prime" as a possible exception. However, in *Connolly v Camden Area Health Authority* [1981] 3 All E.R. 250, Comyn J. suggested the addition of cases where the child might, but for the shortening of life, have inherited a capital sum.

[302] *Croke v Wiseman* [1982] 1 W.L.R. 71. This decision is inconsistent with *Pickett* and *Gammell* but as a matter of precedent the CA is bound by it: *Iqbal v Whipps Cross University NHS Trust* [2007] EWCA Civ 1170; [2008] P.I.Q.R. P9. Note, however, that the claimant received £25,000 in respect of loss of earnings during the considerable life expectancy that remained to him, during which he would be insensible of his plight. Lord Denning M.R. thought this assessment just as speculative as that for the lost years.

[303] See para.22–24, above.

[304] CPR r.41.8(2). In fact it may not even be necessary to regard the post-death element as resting on the lost years theory. PD41B, para.2–1 provides that an order, "may be made under rule 41.8(2) where a dependant would have had a claim under section 1 of the Fatal Accidents Act 1976 if the claimant had died at the time of the accident".

[305] Lewis, *Deducting Benefits from Damages for Personal Injury* (2000).

[306] See para.22–17, above.

[307] The principle is this area extends to savings made as well as receipts: *Salih v Enfield AHA* [1991] 3 All E.R. 400 is a macabre example.

[308] Well known contract cases are *Erie County Natural Gas Co v Carroll* [1911] A.C. 105 and *British Westinghouse v Underground Electric Railways* [1912] A.C. 673.

[309] In something more than the simple "but–for" sense. Thus in *Hussey v Eels* [1990] 2 Q.B. 227, a negligent survey case, the profit from the disposal of the property for development was not brought into account because it was not part of the original transaction. How fine the line can be is illustrated by *Monroe Schneider Associates v No.1 Raberem Pty* (1991) 104 A.L.R. 397.

account. Causation is certainly a necessary element if a benefit is to be so deducted from damages in a personal injury case, too—no one would suggest that a person who received a legacy from the estate of a relative a week after being injured in an accident should have to bring that into account in a claim against the tortfeasor.[310] However, the deduction issue in personal injury cases has generated a good deal of case law and many receipts are governed by statute so we must examine this area more closely. A distinction has to be drawn between receipts from private sources (governed by the common law) and social security benefits (governed by statute).

22–32   (I) RECEIPTS FROM PRIVATE SOURCES. It has been said to be difficult to, "articulate a single precise jurisprudential principle by which to distinguish the deductible from the non-deductible receipt"[311] but the basic rule is that receipts which have come to the claimant as a result of the injury are prima facie to be set against his loss of earnings and consequential expenses unless they fall within established exceptions.[312] The first of these is that voluntary payments prompted by the benevolence of third parties,[313] whether into a "disaster fund" or directly to the claimant, are not to be brought into account to reduce the damages for the simple reason that otherwise there would be a risk that the springs of charity would dry up.[314] Ex gratia payments by the tortfeasor do not fall into this category.[315] The second exception is that the court will not bring into account monies accruing to the claimant under policies of insurance.[316] These must, however, be paid for by the claimant: receipts will be brought into account if the premiums were paid for by the tortfeasor and if the claimant is, for example, an employee of the tortfeasor he cannot say that he has paid indirectly because the

---

[310] However, it would be brought into account for the purpose of determining entitlement to a number of social security benefits—need is not the same as loss.

[311] *Hodgson v Trapp* [1989] A.C. 807 at 820 per Lord Bridge. The views expressed to the Law Commission were so diverse that it did not feel able to propose any general reform of this area: *Damages for Personal Injury: Medical, Nursing and other Expenses; Collateral Benefits* (1999) Law Com. No.262.

[312] *Hodgson*, above: "It is the rule which is fundamental and axiomatic and the exceptions to it which are only to be admitted on grounds which clearly justify their treatment as such": Buxton L.J. in *Ballantine v Newalls Insulation Co Ltd* [2000] P.I.Q.R. Q327 at Q332.

[313] The donor of the benevolence has no claim: *Esso Petroleum Co Ltd v Hall Russell & Co Ltd* [1989] A.C. 643.

[314] *Redpath v Belfast County Down Ry* [1947] N.I. 167; *Parry v Cleaver* [1970] A.C. 1; *Naahas v Pier House Management (Cheyne Walk) Ltd* (1984) 270 E.G. 328 (property loss).

[315] *Gaca v Pirelli General Plc* [2004] EWCA Civ 373; [2004] 1 W.L.R. 2683. In theory of course the tortfeasor might make the payment on the terms, "This is a gift which is not to diminish any eventual award of damages against me."

[316] *Bradburn v GW Ry* (1874) L.R. Ex. 1.

fruits of the workers' labour enabled the premiums to be paid.[317] By contrast, sick pay received is outside these exceptions and is deductible from damages for loss of earnings, whether or not it is paid by the defendant,[318] even if it takes the form of a very long-term payment which the employer has based on an arrangement with an insurance company[319]: in such a case the claimant has not insured himself against loss of wages, the employer has taken out insurance to cover his liability to pay wages. No deduction is, of course, made if the payment to the claimant is made on condition of repayment in the event of recovery of damages.[320] However, it is necessary to consider the nature of the payment made to the claimant. If, as a result of the injury, the claimant retires from his job and receives a pension, that is not deductible from the claim for lost earnings, for the pension is not of the same nature as the lost wages.[321] This is so even if the defendant provides or contributes to the pension,[322] though it is open to the defendant employer to draft the pension scheme in such a way as to negate this result. It may happen that the claim of a claimant who has to retire early includes not only loss of earnings but also loss of pension rights which he would have accumulated had he worked until the normal retirement age. In that case the pension received is brought into account in so far as it is received in the period after the normal date of retirement.[323]

A reason commonly given for the insurance exception[324] is that **22–33** the claimant is not to be disadvantaged by his own thrift and foresight. However, there is no question of depriving the claimant of his insurance monies, the question is of his right of recovery against the defendant, and in so far as the claimant is allowed to recover damages and to keep the insurance payments it may be argued that he is overcompensated for his loss. There is no such "double recovery" where the policy is one of indemnity, for then if he sues he has to reimburse the insurer out of the damages (though it is more likely that the insurer would sue the tortfeasor by virtue of his subrogation to the insured's rights). It is of course another question whether the insurer's right of subrogation is justifiable, but that issue

---

[317] *Gaca v Pirelli General Plc,* above, fn.315, but it would be surprising if insurance payments were brought into account where the premiums were paid by someone not responsible for the tort: it is hard to believe that the damages of an injured holidaymaker are to be reduced because another member of the party paid (otherwise than as agent) the travel insurance premiums.
[318] *Parry v Cleaver* [1970] A.C. 1.
[319] *Hussain v New Taplow Paper Mills Ltd* [1988] A.C. 514.
[320] *Berriello v Felixstowe Dock & Ry Co* [1984] 1 W.L.R. 695.
[321] *Parry v Cleaver,* above, fn.318.
[322] *Smoker v London Fire Authority* [1991] 2 A.C. 502.
[323] *Longden v British Coal Corp* [1998] A.C. 653; *Parry v Cleaver,* above, fn.318; *Cantwell v Criminal Injuries Compensation Board* [2001] UKHL 36; 2001 S.L.T. 966 (HL (Sc.).
[324] See *Parry v Cleaver,* above, fn.318.

cannot be addressed solely in the context of personal injuries, where many policies (for example for personal accident[325]) are not based on the indemnity principle. Where the policy is not one of indemnity the net result is that there is undoubtedly, in mathematical terms, a double recovery. Whether that is so in substance is debatable. Arguments in favour of the present position are as follows. First, that while there is no question of depriving the claimant of the benefit of his insurance, to deduct it from the damages would at least give the appearance of putting him at a disadvantage in comparison with another claimant who had chosen not to insure. No doubt there is a logical answer to this, namely that the claimant has not "wasted" the premiums for he has had the benefit of the cover, which is likely to have extended much more widely than the risk of injury in circumstances which amount to a tort.[326] If it is thought that the defendant should not escape scot-free it would in theory be possible to require him to reimburse the claimant for all or part of the premiums paid.[327] Nevertheless, the intuitive conclusion that it is unfair to make any deduction probably has widespread appeal. Secondly, it may be thought that the traditional statement that the insurance is *res inter alios acta* does more than express a conclusion in Latin. The point about the scope of the insurance cover which is made above can be turned in support of the present regime: the claimant has taken out cover which may extend more widely than injury by tort and in non-indemnity cases the amount of that cover will be determined by the terms of the policy and need bear no necessary relationship with any objectively determined value of the interest protected. In effecting the policy the claimant may therefore fairly say that he has bought a form of security additional to and wholly different from that which the law of tort provides to him and there is no reason why the defendant should be able to take advantage of this to reduce his liability.[328]

22–34   (II) Social Security Benefits. At the inception of the modern welfare state the relationship between tort damages and social security benefits was dealt with by the compromise embodied in the Law Reform (Personal Injuries) Act 1948 whereby there was a deduction from damages for loss of earnings of one-half of the value of social

---

[325] As in *Bradburn v GW Ry*, above, fn.316.
[326] Note, however, one form of "add-on" cover sometimes found in liability policies, which only covers the insured against the risk of a tort—where the policy promises to pay in the event of the insured having an uncollectable award against an uninsured defendant.
[327] See American Law Institute, Enterprise Responsibility for Personal Injury, Vol.II (1991); *Bristol and West BS v May, May & Merrimans (No.2)* [1997] 3 All E.R. 206 at 226.
[328] See Lord Morris in *Parry v Cleaver* [1970] A.C. 1 at 31.

security benefits receivable by the claimant in the five years following the accident. The Act did not cover all benefits but the courts
gradually moved towards deducting other benefits in full throughout
the period of the disability.[329] This approach prevented double
compensation of the victim, gave a windfall to the defendant but left
the provider of the benefit, the State, the loser. In the late 1980s the
Government came to the conclusion that the State should not sub-
sidise the tortfeasor in this way and the system was radically altered
by the Social Security Act 1989.[330] The current legislation is the
Social Security (Recovery of Benefits) Act 1997. Under this regime
benefits are deducted in full (for a period) from the claimant's
damages but the deduction is used to reimburse the Secretary of
State.

A person ("the compensator"[331]) is not to make any compensation payment in consequence of an accident, injury or disease[332]
until he has applied to the Secretary of State (via the Compensation
Recovery Unit) for a "certificate of recoverable benefits" for the
purposes of the Act. A compensation payment for this purpose is not
confined to damages payable under a judgment but extends to an out
of court settlement, whether or not proceedings have been commenced.[333] However, the Act does not extend to charitable payments made by third parties[334] for the payment must be made, "by
or on behalf of a person who is, or who is alleged to be, liable to any
extent in respect of the accident".[335] The recoverable benefits for the
purposes of the certificate are the specified social security benefits
payable to the victim during the five years immediately following
the accident or until the making of the compensation payment,
whichever is earlier. This sum is to be deducted from the payment
and paid to the Secretary of State.[336] If there is a judgment the court

---

[329] Culminating in *Hodgson v Trapp* [1989] A.C. 807.
[330] See Report of the National Audit Office (Session 1985/86, HC 553) and Public Accounts
Committee (Session 1987/88, HC 120).
[331] In practice in most cases the defendant's insurer.
[332] The Act was held inapplicable to a case where the defendants failed to inform the
claimants of the risk of Down's Syndrome in their unborn child and they incurred expense
(and received benefits) in looking after the child: *Rand v E Dorset HA* [2001] P.I.Q.R.
Q1.
[333] Section 1(2).
[334] Payments made from a disaster fund are treated as exempt payments provided no more
than 50 per cent of the capital sum was contributed by the alleged wrongdoer. Schedule 1,
Pt I.
[335] These words are not very apt to cover the MIB, since the scheme depends on an agreement
between the Motor Insurers' Association and the State which is technically unenforceable
by the victim. However, the statutory definition of compensation payment in s.1(2)(b)
extends to a payment made, "in pursuance of a compensation scheme for motor
accident".
[336] The CRU recovered over £138 million in 2008/2009 from 812,000 cases but this figure
appears to include recovered NHS charges (see below).

is not concerned with the benefits, which it is to disregard—the deduction and accounting to the Secretary of State is a matter for the defendant.[337] As between the claimant and the defendant, the latter is to be treated as having fully discharged his liability to the former by paying him the difference (if any[338]) between the amount of the damages and the recoverable benefits.[339] However, for this purpose like is only to be deducted from like. Under Sch.2 of the Act compensation payments are treated as containing up to three elements—loss of earnings, cost of care and loss of mobility—and the deduction of a particular benefit is only to be made against the equivalent element of the compensation payment. Thus if the compensation payment contains elements of £10,000 for loss of earnings and £5,000 for cost of nursing and the claimant has received £13,000 in income support and statutory sick pay and £2,000 in attendance allowance, the loss of earnings element is extinguished but he still gets £3,000 for cost of nursing.[340] There is no deduction against damages for pain and suffering and loss of amenity,[341] there being no "equivalent" benefits.[342] However, none of this affects the defendant's liability to reimburse the Secretary of State for all specified benefits received by the claimant. Nor is there any offset for contributory negligence, so if the defendant is only 10 per cent liable for the claimant's injuries he still has to reimburse the State for all the benefits.[343] Indeed, there is no requirement that the defendant should actually be liable to the claimant at all and it is certainly now dangerous to make a small settlement offer to buy off a weak, "nuisance" claim.

---

[337] Section 17. The effect of this is that the claimant is entitled to interest on damages which he will not receive and which, in view of the benefits he has received, he has not (under the philosophy of the Act) been "kept out of": *Wisely v John Fulton (Plumbers) Ltd* [2000] 1 W.L.R. 820, but where the benefits exceed the damages payable a deduction may be made against any interest, too: *Griffiths v British Coal Corp* [2001] 1 W.L.R. 1493.

[338] i.e. the benefits may reduce the defendant's liability to the claimant to nil.

[339] See s.8.

[340] Under the regime applying between 1990 and 1997 the claimant would have got nothing for pecuniary loss in such a case, since the deduction was of all specified benefits against all heads of damages.

[341] Thus damages for "loss of mobility" under Sch.2 must be confined to financial costs such as having to take taxis, and does not extend to matters like sadness and frustration at being unable to get around: *Mitchell v Laing, The Times*, January 28, 1998, IH.

[342] Again contrast the pre-1997 position, under which it was not uncommon for claimants to lose their damages altogether.

[343] Though by protecting his damages for non-pecuniary loss the 1997 Act improved the position of the claimant, it worsens the position of the defendant. Under the previous regime the claimant might be advised that his damages would be eliminated altogether by the deduction process and he would then have no incentive to sue, in which case the recoupment procedure would not be triggered, there being no free-standing right in the Secretary of State to seek recoupment. The justice of requiring the defendant to carry the whole burden of the claimant's support by the State when the injury is largely the claimant's fault is not apparent.

Under the regime in force between 1990 and 1997 small pay-   **22–35**
ments (not exceeding £2,500) were outside the scope of the recoupment regime. They remained a matter purely between the parties and
were subject to a modified version of the 1948 Act. Although the
1997 Act contains power[344] to make regulations disregarding small
payments there is at present apparently no intention to implement
this. However, fatal accident cases are entirely outside the scope of
the Act, which reflects the generally more favourable treatment
(from the claimant's point of view) given to such cases in respect of
collateral benefits.[345]

Although the 1997 Act made important changes to the law, it is
essentially a modification of an existing regime, so it is with the
position before the 1989 Act that a comparison should probably be
made. Since there was then no right of recovery the State is never
the loser and sometimes makes substantial gains. Claimants sometimes win and sometimes lose. In smaller cases they generally lose
because the deduction is at the rate of 100 per cent of benefits
received rather than 50 per cent as under the 1948 Act, and there is
no "allowance" for contributory negligence, though their position is
somewhat ameliorated by the protection of damages for non-pecuniary loss by the 1997 Act. On the other hand, in a case of serious
long-term disability the claimant's position is improved, because
certain benefits were deductible in full and in perpetuity at common
law, whereas under the Act they are deductible only for the first five
years or until settlement or payment of compensation, whichever
occurs earlier.[346] It follows, of course, that in these big cases defendants will be losers but they will also be losers in the general run of
cases because the "credit" they get from the claimant carries with it
the duty to reimburse the Secretary of State, perhaps for considerably more than their liability to the claimant. Defendants (or
rather their insurers) will also carry the burden of the "paperwork"
associated with the system.

Some State benefits are not covered by the 1997 Act. If there is
no indication as to their deductibility in the relevant legislation the
issue must be determined under the common law.[347]

---

[344] Schedule 1, Pt II.
[345] See para.23–16, below.
[346] In *Hodgson v Trapp* [1989] A.C. 807 the damages would have been at least £32,000 higher
under the present regime. In *Eagle v Chambers* [2004] EWCA Civ 1033; [2004] 1 W.L.R.
3081 the claimant would receive ongoing mobility allowance. Using that to participate in
the Motability Scheme (which could only be done by payments from the allowance) would
have been cheaper than private vehicle arrangements but the court rejected the argument
that the claimant's failure to take that route would have been a failure to mitigate: the court
was to "disregard" the allowance in the "assessment of damages" and a rule as to
mitigation is just that.
[347] *Ballantine v Newalls Insulation Co Ltd* [2000] P.I.Q.R. Q327.

22–36　　(g) *Expenses.* The claimant is entitled to the cost of medical and similar services which he reasonably incurs as a result of his injuries, and it is enacted that in determining the reasonableness of any expenses the possibility of avoiding them by making use of the National Health Service is to be disregarded.[348] However, if the claimant in fact receives treatment under the NHS he cannot recover the notional cost of private treatment[349] nor can he recover the cost of future private treatment if the evidence shows that he will not take that course, perhaps because it is unlikely to be available.[350] If the NHS is utilised the Health and Social Care (Community Health and Standards) Act 2003 provides for the NHS to recover the cost of treatment from the tortfeasor's insurer up to a current maximum of £41,545.[351]

Damages for expenses may be awarded in respect of both past and prospective expenses and may include not only the cost of medical treatment and attendance but all such matters as increased living expenses: if, for example the claimant has to live in a special institution because of his injuries[352] or to be supplied with special equipment.[353] The fact the claimant may have a statutory right to call upon the local authority for free institutional care does not prevent him electing to pay for such services in the market and recovering the cost from the defendant: such a situation has nothing to do with mitigation.[354] In serious cases it is now the practice to present very detailed schedules of future expenses and awards under this head can be very large indeed, often much larger than those for

---

[348] Law Reform (Personal Injuries) Act 1948 s.2(4).

[349] *Harris v Brights Asphalt Contractors Ltd* [1963] 1 Q.B. 617 at 635 per Slade J.

[350] *Eagle v Chambers* [2004] EWCA Civ 1033; [2004] 1 W.L.R. 3081 (same applies to social services).

[351] The regime does not apply to a disease which is not the result of an injury: s.150(5), (6) of the Act. The system is, like that for recovery of social security payments, operated by the Compensation Recovery Unit. Contributory negligence is taken into account: Personal Injuries (NHS Charges) (General) Regulations and Road Traffic (NHS Charges) (Amendment) Regulations SI 2006/3388. For the background to the 2003 Act see Law Com. No.262 (1999).

[352] *Shearman v Folland* [1950] 2 K.B. 43; *Oliver v Ashman* [1962] 2 Q.B. 210; *Cutts v Chumley* [1967] 1 W.L.R. 742. For the position where the claimant purchases more suitable accommodation, see *George v Pinnock* [1973] 1 W.L.R. 118; *Roberts v Johnstone* [1989] Q.B. 878.

[353] *S. v Distillers (Biochemicals) Ltd* [1970] 1 W.L.R. 114; *Povey v Governors of Royal School* [1970] 1 All E.R. 841, but the claimant cannot recover the cost of an increase in cigarette consumption unless perhaps there is a brain injury which deprives him of all real choice: *Eagle v Chambers* [2004] EWCA Civ 1033; [2004] 1 W.L.R. 3081.

[354] *Peters v E. Midlands Strategic HA* [2009] EWCA Civ 145; [2010] Q.B. 48, distinguishing *Sowden v Lodge* [2004] EWCA Civ 1370; [2005] 1 W.L.R. 2129 and *Crofton v NHSLA* [2007] EWCA Civ 71; [2007] 1 W.L.R. 923. At present the local authority cannot make a charge to a personal injury claimant because his damages are disregarded in the assessment of his resources. If the claimant suffers from lack of capacity (as in *Peters*) it is possible to guard against a change of mind by those responsible for him by ordering that no application for public care be made without the consent of the court.

loss of earnings.[355] However, the financial detriment of a divorce resulting from the injury is, on policy grounds, too remote.[356]

Care must be taken to avoid duplication of damages where a claim for the cost of future medical care is combined with a claim for loss of earnings.[357] The proper course is to make a full award in respect of loss of earnings but deduct from the cost of care award that element of care which may be described as "domestic"[358]: food, laundry and so on. The balance is the expense which is properly attributable to the tort.

It may happen that caring[359] services for which the claimant **22–37** would otherwise have to pay are rendered without payment. As we have seen above, the National Health Service has a statutory right to claim the cost but otherwise the provider of the services has no claim in his own right. So in *Islington London Borough Council v University College London Hospital NHS Trust*[360] the local authority was under a statutory duty to provide care for the claimant, who had suffered a stroke as a result of the defendants' negligence and although she had recovered damages, these were not available for payment of the local authority's charges.[361] A claim for recoupment against the defendants based on negligence failed. A decision in favour of the local authority would have implications which could not be fully explored for all sorts of other bodies and persons, public and private, providing services in aid of misfortune and the specific legislation in relation to NHS charges pointed towards the conclusion that the matter was for Parliament.

Where the services are provided voluntarily by a relative or friend, the practical position is somewhat different. The provider has no claim but the claimant may be able to recover damages in respect of the services even though he has not undertaken a legal obligation to pay for them. In *Donnelly v Joyce*[362] it was held that the requirement for the services was the claimant's own loss and hence could

---

[355] e.g. *Housecroft v Burnett* [1986] 1 All E.R. 332; *Cassell v Riverside HA* [1992] P.I.Q.R. Q168.

[356] *Pritchard v J.H. Cobden Ltd* [1988] Fam. 22.

[357] Where the claimant is maintained in a hospital at public expense the saving to him is offset against his damages for loss of earnings: Administration of Justice Act 1982 s.5. For recoupment of treatment costs by the NHS see above. The assessment of compensation for a victim of miscarriage of justice (para.19–1, above) involves substantial analogy with tort damages and a deduction will be made in respect of saved living expenses attributable to imprisonment: *O'Brien v Independent Assessor* [2007] UKHL 10; [2007] 2 A.C. 313.

[358] *Lim v Camden AHA* [1980] A.C. 174.

[359] The same considerations do not necessarily apply to business services: *Hardwick v Hudson* [1999] 1 W.L.R. 1770.

[360] [2005] EWCA Civ 596; [2006] P.I.Q.R. P3.

[361] On the facts the damages were by way of a structured settlement, but a lump sum of damages for personal injury is to be wholly disregarded under the regulations governing a local authority's power to charge for residential care: *Peters v E Midlands Strategic HA* [2009] EWCA Civ 145; [2010] Q.B. 48.

[362] [1974] Q.B. 454.

Remedies

be recovered by him but the reasoning in that case was substantially modified by the decision in *Hunt v Severs*[363] that the claimant, having recovered the damages, held them on trust for the carer. The theory now seems to be that the loss is the carer's loss, but only recoverable in the action of the victim. The facts of *Hunt v Severs* were rather unusual in that the defendant (who was married to the claimant) was himself providing the care in respect of which the damages were being sought and the trust approach seems to have been seized on as a way of avoiding the apparent absurdity of holding that the defendant could be liable for the cost of what he was already providing gratuitously, for he could not be liable for what he would then receive back. However, this causes potential difficulties where, for example, the care arrangements are altered (and the claimant must surely be able to do this) or dies or becomes insolvent. Perhaps it goes too far to say that the trust is theoretical rather than real[364] but if it is thought that the carer should have a legal claim to the money in the claimant's hands a personal duty in the claimant to account for it would seem better.[365] In any event, the absurdity of the result that on facts like *Hunt v Severs* the defendant should be liable may be more apparent than real. Where, as will usually be the case, the defendant is insured, the reality is that the damages will not come from him and the decision can easily be evaded by the claimant's entering into contractual arrangements with outsiders, though that may be less suitable to meet his needs.[366] Indeed, there seems nothing in the decision to prevent the claimant making a contract for care with the defendant, though the bona fides of that may well be challenged. The Law Commission has concluded that there should be a legislative provision reversing *Hunt v Severs*.[367]

There is no hard-and-fast rule for the sum recoverable under this head. Where the relative has given up paid employment the lost wages should certainly be recoverable, provided they do not exceed the commercial rate for the services. In other cases the sum may be less than the commercial rate (if only because of the absence of tax and national insurance payments) but should be enough to ensure that the relative gets a reasonable recompense and the court should bear in mind the possibility that the relative may not be able to

---

[363] [1994] 2 A.C. 350.

[364] *H v S* [2002] EWCA Civ 792; [2003] Q.B. 965 at [30] criticising *Bordin v St Mary's NHS Trust* [2000] Lloyd's Rep. Med. 287.

[365] This is the law in Scotland: Administration of Justice Act 1982 s.8(2). This would be the effect of a draft Civil Law Reform Bill published at the end of 2009.

[366] As the CA contemplated when coming to the opposite conclusion: [1993] 3 W.L.R. 558.

[367] Law Com. No.262, para.3.76. See also the draft Civil Law Reform Bill referred to above. The High Court of Australia, which has consistently adopted the reasoning in *Donnelly v Joyce*, rejected *Hunt v Severs* in *Kars v Kars* (1996) 141 A.L.R. 37.

provide care indefinitely.[368] There is no doubt that recovery extends to expenses reasonably incurred for the claimant's benefit, such as visits which may assist in the claimant's recovery.[369]

Where a person rendered unpaid household services before the accident but is disabled from doing so, there can be no recovery for loss of earnings. However, it is now the law, by a principle analogous to the above, that he or she may recover as damages the value of substitute services.[370] The action for loss of services formerly allowed a husband to claim for loss of his wife's domestic services but the action was anachronistic in form and was abolished by the Administration of Justice Act 1982; the emergence of the principle that the victim may claim in her own right rendered any statutory substitute unnecessary.

(h) *Other pecuniary loss.* The heads of damage so far mentioned **22–38** are not exhaustive, nor can an exhaustive list be given, for the claimant is entitled to damages for any item of loss he may have suffered provided only that it is not too remote. The following examples provide some indication, however, of the kinds of loss that may have to be considered in any given case. If his employer provided board and lodging[371] or a car available for private use[372] and he has to give up his employment, the claimant may recover the value of those items as well as his actual loss of earnings, and if he has to give up a pensionable employment he can recover for any consequent loss of pension rights.[373] The injury inflicted by the defendant may have made it more difficult for the claimant to obtain life or health insurance.[374] In professions where reputation is significant, damages may be awarded for loss of opportunity of enhancing that reputation.[375] On a less material level, a woman may recover damages for the reduction of her prospects of marriage, which is an item of pecuniary as well as non-pecuniary loss, but it must be borne in mind that if she had married that might have reduced her earning capacity for a time. Rather than make an addition to one side of the equation and a balancing deduction on the

---

[368] *Housecroft v Burnett* [1986] 1 All E.R. 332 (£3,000 pa, against commercial rate of £3,640 pa). 25 per cent below the commercial rate seems common: *A v National Blood Authority* [2001] 3 All E.R. 289 at 390.

[369] *Hunt v Severs* [1994] 2 A.C. at 357. Cf. *Richardson v Schultz* (1980) 25 S.A.S.R. 1 (no recovery where victim unconscious).

[370] *Daly v General Steam Navigation Ltd* [1981] 1 W.L.R. 120. There are, however, certain difficulties with the practical application of this: Law Com. No.262, para.87.

[371] *Lifften v Watson* [1940] 1 K.B. 556. It is immaterial that a relative provides the claimant with free accommodation and food.

[372] *Clay v Pooler* [1982] 3 All E.R. 570 (a fatal accident case).

[373] *Judd v Hammersmith etc. Hospital Board* [1960] 1 W.L.R. 328; *Parry v Cleaver* [1970] A.C. 1.

[374] *A v National Blood Authority* [2001] 3 All E.R. 289.

[375] Cf. *Clayton v Oliver* [1930] A.C. 209 (contract).

other[376] it may be better simply to ignore marriage altogether.[377] Even a person's hobbies have to be considered.[378] If the claimant had a profitable hobby which he can no longer pursue, or if, for example, he formerly tended his own garden and now has to employ another to do it for him, he has suffered a loss for which he is entitled to compensation.[379]

22–39   **iii. Interest on damages for personal injury.** Although there is now power in certain circumstances to order an interim payment on account of damages, it is obvious that there will always be a lapse of time between the injury and the payment of damages, and that frequently the claimant will have to wait a considerable time until his claim has been determined and the damages found due to him are paid. For many years the court had a discretionary power to award interest but this is now mandatory in an action for personal injuries in which the claimant recovers more than £200, unless the court is satisfied that there are special reasons why interest should not be given.[380] In fatal accident claims the pecuniary loss up to the date of the trial should carry interest at half the short-term interest rates current during that period, but no interest should be awarded upon future pecuniary loss because that loss has not yet been sustained.[381] In personal injury cases pecuniary loss should be treated in the same way as in fatal accident cases.[382] As to non-pecuniary loss interest is to be awarded,[383] but only at the moderate rate of 2 per cent.[384] The reason for this low rate is that damages for non-pecuniary loss will be awarded at the rates prevailing at the time of the trial, thus covering any intervening fall in the value of money. What the claimant has therefore lost by late receipt of his damages under this

---

[376] As was done in *Moriarty v McCarthy* [1978] 1 W.L.R. 155.

[377] *Hughes v McKeown* [1985] 1 W.L.R. 963, approved in *Housecroft v Burnett* [1986] 1 All E.R. 332 in so far as the loss of earnings multiplicand is reasonably equivalent to the economic support of the never-to-be spouse. In *Lampert v Eastern National Omnibus Co* [1954] 1 W.L.R. 1047 it was accepted in principle that if a woman's husband leaves her because of disfigurement suffered in an accident this is a compensable head of damage, but it is hard to see how this can survive *Pritchard v J.H. Cobden*, above, fn.356, even though that case concerned a male claimant and was concerned only with the financial consequences of divorce.

[378] i.e. apart from their relevance to the claim for loss of amenities, para.22–20, above.

[379] See also *Morris v Johnson Mathey* (1967) 112 S.J. 32.

[380] Senior Courts Act (formerly known as the Supreme Court Act) 1981 s.35A (added by Administration of Justice Act 1982) replacing the Administration of Justice Act 1969 s.22; County Courts Act 1984 s.69.

[381] *Cookson v Knowles* [1979] A.C. 556. There is also interest on the judgment debt under the Judgments Act 1838.

[382] *Jefford v Gee* [1970] 2 Q.B. 130; *Cookson v Knowles* [1977] Q.B. 913 (on appeal, [1979] A.C. 556). There may be cases in which the award should be at the full, not the half rate: *Ichard v Frangoulis* [1977] 1 W.L.R. 556.

[383] *Pickett v British Rail Engineering Ltd* [1980] A.C. 136.

[384] *Wright v B.R.B.* [1983] 2 A.C. 773.

head is only that element of modern interest rates which truly represent the "use value" of money.[385]

5. DESTRUCTION OF OR DAMAGE TO PROPERTY[386]

As we have seen, the basic principle for the assessment of damages **22–40** is that there should be restitutio in integrum,[387] and in cases of loss of or damage to property this principle can be more fully applied than in cases of personal injury. It is, in fact, the dominant rule to which the subsidiary rules which follow must conform.[388] In working out these subsidiary rules the courts have been mainly concerned with cases involving ships, but the rules are the same in Admiralty and under the common law.[389]

A. Destruction

Where property is totally destroyed as a result of the defendant's **22–41** tort the normal measure of damage is its value at the time and place of the destruction, and at common law this was so even if the claimant had only a limited interest in the property destroyed.[390] In principle the claimant is generally entitled to such a sum of money as would enable him to purchase a replacement in the market at the prices prevailing at the date of destruction[391] or as soon thereafter as is reasonable.[392] Where no precise equivalent is available the claimant may be allowed a recovery which exceeds the amount he could have obtained by selling the property,[393] but the cost of producing an exact replacement will be refused where it is well in excess of the

---

[385] Arguably this should be the figure (2.5 per cent) used as the assumed rate of return on damages for future pecuniary loss, but it is not: *Laurence v CC Staffordshire* [2000] P.I.Q.R. Q349. The court may abridge the period during which interest is payable if the claimant unjustifiably delays bringing the case to trial.

[386] For the measure of damages in conversion, see para.17–27, above.

[387] See para.22–16, above.

[388] *Liesbosch Dredger v SS Edison* [1933] A.C. 449 at 463 per Lord Wright.

[389] *Admiralty Commissioners v SS Susquehanna* [1926] A.C. 655 at 661 per Viscount Dunedin. An English court in an action of tort may give judgment in the currency in which the loss was sustained: *The Despina R.* [1979] A.C. 685; *Hoffman v Sofaer* [1982] 1 W.L.R. 1350 (personal injuries).

[390] *The Winkfield* [1902] P. 42. For the effect of the Torts (Interference with Goods) Act 1977, see para.17–18, above.

[391] *Liesbosch Dredger v SS Edison* [1933] A.C. 449. In *Smith Kline & French Laboratories Ltd v Long* [1989] 1 W.L.R. 1 (a case of deprivation by deceit) the claimants could themselves produce a replacement at less than market cost, because with drugs most of the cost is attributable to research and development but were nevertheless entitled to recover the market value. This seems to be a case of a restitutionary award: para.22–13, above. Cf. para.17–27, above.

[392] The price the claimant paid for the article is not decisive for he may have got a bargain: *Dominion Mosaic and Tile Co Ltd v Trafalgar Trucking Co* [1990] 2 All E.R. 246.

[393] *Clyde Navigation Trustees v Bowring* (1929) 34 Ll.L.R. 319.

value of what was destroyed and a reasonable substitute is available.[394] Merely to enable the claimant to acquire a replacement, however, will often be insufficient to effect a full restitutio in integrum, and he may recover consequential damages which are not too remote, such as the reasonable cost of hire of a substitute until a replacement can be bought.[395] When the property destroyed is used by the claimant in the course of his business then loss of business profits may come into the account. Speaking of destruction of a ship, Lord Wright said that the:

> "[T]rue rule seems to be that the measure of damages in such cases is the value of the ship to her owner as a going concern at the time and place of the loss. In assessing that value regard must naturally be had to her pending engagements, either profitable or the reverse."[396]

In *Liesbosch Dredger v SS Edison*[397] the claimant's dredger, which they were using in the course of contract work at Patras Harbour, was sunk by the negligence of the defendants. It was held that they were entitled to recover the market price of a comparable dredger, the cost of adapting the new dredger and transporting it to Patras, and compensation for disturbance in the carrying out of their contract from the date of the loss until the new dredger could reasonably have been available in Patras.

As Lord Wright pointed out in *Liesbosch Dredger v SS Edison*, in assessing the value of a ship as going concern, care must be taken to avoid awarding damages twice over. The market value of a profit-earning chattel such as a ship will normally recognise that the chattel will be used in a profit-earning capacity and the actual loss of prospective freights or other profits cannot, therefore, simply be added to that market value.[398] What is needed, it may be suggested, is a recognition in the assessment of the damages of the difference between the profit-earning potential of a ship without any engagement but with the chance or probability of making a profit, which will be reflected in the market value, and the actual profits which would have been made by the claimant's ship had it not been

---

[394] *Ucktos v Mazetta* [1956] 1 Lloyd's Rep. 209.
[395] *Moore v D.E.R. Ltd* [1971] 1 W.L.R. 1476; cf. *Watson Norrie v Shaw* (1967) 111 S.J. In a road accident case the claimant may recover the unused portion of his premium which he forfeits on making a claim: *Patel v London Transport Executive* [1981] R.T.R. 29. See also *Ironfield v Eastern Gas Board* [1964] 1 W.L.R. 1125 ("no-claim" bonus).
[396] *Liesbosch Dredger v SS Edison* [1933] A.C. 449 at 463–464; *Jones v Port of London Authority* [1954] 1 Lloyd's Rep. 489 (lorry).
[397] [1933] A.C. 449. See para.6-33, above, where the case is considered from the point of view of remoteness of damage. The claimants' claim for the cost of hire of a substitute dredger failed because this damage flowed from their own impecuniosity but that aspect of the case is now overruled.
[398] *The Llanover* [1947] P. 80.

destroyed.[399] Nevertheless, if a ship is actually under charter at the time of her loss or has charters which would have commenced shortly thereafter, the loss of those charters may be allowed in some cases[400] as damages for loss of use of the ship from the time of its destruction until the time when it could reasonably be replaced.[401] It is submitted that in deciding whether or not these damages may be added to the market value, the manner in which the market value itself has been determined is of critical importance. If it is determined on the basis that the ship was in any case virtually certain of profitable employment, then nothing may be added for the loss of actual charters,[402] but if the market value does not assume the full employment of the ship then the loss of actual charters must be taken into account.

It has been said above that the claimant will generally be entitled to the cost of a substitute even though in practice he will have to pay somewhat more than he would have obtained by selling the now destroyed article. However, that is because by replacing he acts reasonably to mitigate his loss and it would be unfair to impose on him the additional cost of the replacement transaction; but where a ship destroyed the claimants' crane (worth about £665,000), a second hand substitute crane of that type would have had to be obtained from the United States at a cost of nearly £2.4 million and the claimants at no stage intended to effect the replacement because they had bought other, newer cranes before the accident, they were confined to recovering £665,000 plus some consequential expenses.[403]

B. Damage

Where property is damaged the normal measure of damages is the **22–42** amount by which its value has been diminished, and in the case of ships and other chattels this will usually be ascertained by reference to the cost of repair,[404] simply because that is usually the only

---

[399] For this distinction see *The Philadelphia* [1917] P. 101 at 108 per Swinfen Eady L.J.
[400] *The Kate* [1899] P. 165; *The Racine* [1906] P. 273; *The Philadelphia* [1917] P. 101.
[401] See the explanation of Greer L.J. in *The Arpad* [1934] P. 189 at 217; *The Fortunity* [1961] 1 W.L.R. 351.
[402] *The Llanover* [1947] P. 80.
[403] *Southampton Container Terminals Ltd v Schiffahrtsgesellschaft "Hansa Australia" M.B.H. & Co (The Maersk Colombo)* [2001] EWCA Civ 717; [2001] 2 Lloyd's Rep. 275; *Ali Reza-Delta Transport Co Ltd v United Arab Shipping Co S.A.G.* [2003] EWCA Civ 684; [2003] 2 Lloyd's Rep. 450.
[404] *The London Corp* [1935] P. 70 at 77 per Greer L.J. This is of course the reasonable cost of repair. Where the claimant does repairs "in house" he may be entitled to a sum for overheads as well as direct labour costs but what is relevant in causation terms may be a difficult question: *Ulsterbus Ltd v Donnelly* [1982] 13 N.I.J.B.; *British Telecommunications Plc v Geraghty & Miller International Inc*, July 29, 2004, Leeds Mercantile Court.

practical way to do it: there is a market in two-year-old cars of a certain type and mileage, there are no markets in such cars with dented wings or broken mirrors, we just assume that a buyer will reduce his price by the cost of repair. The estimated cost of the repairs can be recovered as indicating the amount by which the chattel's value is reduced. It does not matter that the repairs have not been carried out at the date of the trial,[405] or even that they are never carried out at all, as where a ship is lost from other causes before the repairs are done.[406] On the other hand, if a ship is damaged while on its way to the breaker's yard it is submitted that the cost of repairing the ship could not be recovered, for that cost would not necessarily represent the true reduction in the value of the ship. All that could be recovered would be the diminution, if any, in the value of the ship as scrap.[407] Similarly, if the cost of repairing the chattel exceeds its total value, then, unless the chattel is in some way unique or irreplaceable, no more than its value can be recovered.[408]

Whether it is a case of damage or destruction the defendant cannot rely on the fact that the claimant is entitled to claim on an insurance policy,[409] indeed many marine property damage claims will be brought by subrogated loss insurers and that can only happen if the claimant retains his right of action after claiming on his policy. That accords with the law on personal injuries.[410] That analogy also points to recovery where funds to replace or repair the goods are provided as, say, an act of kindness by a relative. It is also consistent with the proposition that the cost of replacement or repair is generally used as a practical measure of the value lost by the claimant because of the defendant's tort.[411]

22–43 In the majority of cases the claimant will not only have incurred the cost of repairing his chattel, he will also have been deprived of its use for a period of time and for this loss he is entitled to damages. In the case of a profit-earning chattel (such as a commercial ship) the normal measure of damages will be the loss of profits calculated at the freight rates prevailing during the period of detention of the ship or, where the hire of a substitute is a reasonable way of avoiding

---

[405] *The Kingsway* [1918] P. 344.

[406] *The York* [1929] P. 178 at 184–185 per Scrutton L.J.; *The London Corp*, above, fn.404; *Dimond v Lovell* [2000] 2 W.L.R. 1121 at 1140.

[407] See *The London Corp* [1935] P. 70 at 77–78, where Greer L.J. seems to have been in two minds on this point. See also *C.R. Taylor (Wholesale) Ltd v Hepworths Ltd* [1977] 1 W.L.R. 659 (land). In any event it will be for the defendant to prove that the damage he has caused to the claimant's ship has not reduced its value to the claimant.

[408] *Darbishire v Warran* [1963] 1 W.L.R. 1067, distinguishing *O'Grady v Westminster Scaffolding Ltd* [1962] 2 Lloyd's Rep. 238.

[409] *Dominion Mosaics and Tile Co Ltd v Trafalgar Trucking Co Ltd* [1990] 2 All E.R. 246.

[410] See para.22–32, above.

[411] *Burdis v Livesey* [2002] EWCA Civ 510; [2003] Q.B. 36 (on appeal, but not on this point, sub nom. *Lagden v O'Connor* [2003] UKHL 64; [2004] 1 A.C. 1067).

such losses, the cost of that hire.[412] However, the measure based upon prevailing freight rates may in the actual case be too high or too low. It will be too high if the ship was operating at a loss at the time of the damage[413] and too low if the damage prevented the ship from fulfilling an actual charter already entered into at favourable rates.[414]

It was held in *Giles v Thompson*[415] that where a substitute is hired it is no answer that the claimant's obligation to pay for the hire is contingent upon recovery from the defendant[416] but it was also said that the fact of hire (and not merely its quantum or level) must be reasonably undertaken, so that damages could not be recovered where, for example, the claimant spent the period abroad or in hospital,[417] which may mean that if I have two cars for my sole use, I cannot recover the cost of hiring a replacement when one is damaged. In other words, whereas the cost of repair, even if not incurred, is a more or less automatic measure of diminution in value, the cost of hire is not in any sense an automatic measure of loss of use: the first is an immediate, direct loss, the second is consequential.[418] Nevertheless, there is still a real loss. In *The Mediana*[419] Lord Halsbury L.C. was clearly of the opinion that the fact that the claimant would not have used the chattel was no bar to a claim for loss of use.

"Suppose a person took a chair out of my room and kept it for 12 months, could anybody say that you had a right to diminish the damages by showing that I did not usually sit in the chair, or that there were plenty of other chairs in the room. The proposition so nakedly stated appears to me to be absurd."[420]

---

[412] If a substitute is hired and the claimant is thereby enabled to make a greater profit than he would have done if his own chattel had never been damaged, credit for this must be given: *The World Beauty* [1969] P. 12, reversed without affecting this point: [1970] P. 144.

[413] *The Bodlewell* [1907] P. 286. See also *SS Strathfillan v SS Ikala* [1929] A.C. 196.

[414] *The Argentino* (1889) 14 App. Cas. 519. However, it is not yet finally settled whether this rule is independent of the test of remoteness of damage, viz. foreseeability.

[415] [1994] 1 A.C. 142. The case concerned a practice which has given rise to much litigation. A person whose car has been damaged by someone else's fault puts his case in the hands of a car hire company (which is likely to be able to process large numbers of claims comparatively efficiently) on terms that it will handle his claim and he will not have to pay for the hire if it fails. The claimant is relieved of trouble and expense and the risk of non-recovery, which are often a deterrent to hiring a substitute. Hence the opposition of liability insurers.

[416] Contrast *Dimond v Lovell* [2002] 1 A.C. 384, where the arrangement between the claimant and the car hire company fell foul of the Consumer Credit Act 1974. That meant that the claimant could not recover the cost of hire because he would then hold it on trust for the company and that would contravene the policy of the Act.

[417] [1994] 1 A.C. at 167.

[418] See *Burdis v Livesey*, above, fn.411, at [84], referring to *Jones v Stroud DC* [1986] 1 W.L.R. 1141, CA.

[419] [1900] A.C. 113; *Bee v Jenson* [2007] EWCA Civ 923; [2007] 4 All E.R. 791.

[420] [1900] A.C. at 117; *Att Gen v Blake* [2001] 1 A.C. 268 at 278; *Dimond v Lovell* [2000] 2 W.L.R. 1121 at 1139.

This may be reconcilable with the line taken in *Giles v Thompson* on the basis that damages for loss of use need not necessarily be based on the cost of hiring a substitute. As has been said in a different context, it is a fallacy to proceed from:

"[T]he premise that a loss has been suffered which is incapable of economic measurement to the conclusion that it must be compensated by reference to a measure of economic loss . . . which has not been and will not be incurred."[421]

In *The Mediana* a lightship belonging to the claimants was damaged and replaced by a standby vessel kept by them for such an emergency. In such a case it seems entirely reasonable that the defendant should have to pay damages for loss of use, though the suitable measure may vary from case to case,[422] but a calculation based on the daily cost of running the substitute plus depreciation may be suitable.[423] In the last resort the claimant is entitled to interest on the capital value of the chattel for the period during which it is out of use.[424]

Damages for loss of use cannot, of course, be claimed if the loss is not due to the defendant's tort but to some other extraneous cause.[425]

C. Land and Buildings

22–44 The principles considered thus far have been worked out in the context of injuries to chattels; those governing injuries to land and buildings are not fundamentally different though their application must take account of the different character of land. Thus, for example, a claimant is more likely to recover the cost of reinstatement where this exceeds the diminution in value of the property than he is in the case of chattel: where a factory is burned down it may well be the commercially sensible course to rebuild immediately on

---

[421] *Ruxley Electronics and Construction Ltd v Forsyth* [1996] A.C. 344 at 354 (breach of contract; sum for "loss of amenity value" recoverable rather than disproportionate cost of remedial work).

[422] In *Admiralty Commissioners v SS Susquehanna* [1926] A.C. 655 at 661 Viscount Dunedin said that these are jury-type questions on which no rigid rules are possible.

[423] *The Marpessa* [1907] A.C. 242; *Admiralty Commissioners v SS Susquehanna*, above, fn.422; *The Hebridean Coast* [1961] A.C. 545; *Birmingham Corp v Sowsbery* (1969) 113 S.J. 577 (bus); cf. *Alexander v Rolls Royce* [1996] R.T.R. 95 (car).

[424] *Admiralty Commissioners v SS Chekiang* [1926] A.C. 637, but where this applies it is the end of the matter. The damages for loss of use of the chair in Lord Halsbury's example above do not vary according to how often he sits in it: *Voaden v Champion (The Baltic Surveyor)* [2002] EWCA Civ 89; [2002] 1 Lloyd's Rep. 623.

[425] *Carslogie SS Co Ltd v Royal Norwegian Government* [1952] A.C. 292. Cf. *Admiralty Commissioners v SS Chekiang* [1926] A.C. 637.

the same site rather than remove the business to a different location.[426] Ultimately, however, the reasonableness of the proposed expenditure is the issue so that where the cost of reinstatement is out of all proportion to the diminution in value the latter will be taken as the measure.[427] Again, the court may allow a degree of reinstatement but refuse the claimant the extra cost of precise and meticulous restoration which will not increase the utility of the property.[428] The claimant may not claim the cost of repairs which exceed diminution in value where he has no intention of having them carried out.[429]

What has been said above represents a broad principle which may be departed from in particular contexts. For example, the usual measure of damages for negligent survey (where the action will commonly lie concurrently in contract and tort) is the difference between the price paid by the claimant and the actual market value of the property, not the cost of putting the property in the condition described in the report[430] and, as we have seen, in some cases of wrongful interference with property the courts have shown signs of a restitutionary approach by assessing damages so as to deprive the defendant of the fruits of his wrong.[431]

The rapid inflation of the 1970s brought into prominence, particularly on the context of damage to buildings, the question of the date as at which damages were to be assessed, for a judgment representing the cost of repair at the time of the wrong, even with interest, would be unlikely to be sufficient to cover the work when the action came on for trial.[432] While there may still be a general rule that

---

[426] See *Harbutt's "Plasticine" Ltd v Wayne Tank and Pump Co Ltd* [1907] 1 Q.B. 447 at 467, 472, pointing out that the market in land and buildings is more limited and inflexible than in, e.g. secondhand cars. *Ward v Cannock Chase DC* [1986] Ch. 546; *Aerospace Publishing Ltd v Thames Water Utilities Ltd* [2007] EWCA Civ 3 (a goods case—high cost of restoration, low consequential loss; lower diminution in value, higher consequential loss). Contrast *Dominion Mosaics & Tile Co Ltd v Trafalgar Trucking Co Ltd* [1990] 2 All E.R. 246 (rebuilding impracticable; value of destroyed building £60,000; £390,000 cost of lease of new premises recoverable since this was a reasonable way of mitigating loss of profits).

[427] *Jones v Gooday* (1841) 8 M. & W. 146; *Lodge Holes Colliery Co Ltd v Wednesbury Corp* [1908] A.C. 323; *Taylor v Auto Trade Supply Ltd* [1972] N.Z.L.R. 102; *Munnelly v Calcon Ltd* [1978] I.R. 387.

[428] *Dodd Properties Ltd v Canterbury CC* [1980] 1 W.L.R. 433 at 441 (on appeal, without affecting this point, at 447); *Ward v Cannock Chase DC* [1986] Ch. 546. Cf. *Farmer Giles v Wessex Water* [1990] 18 E.G. 102 (loss of development opportunity).

[429] *Perry v Sidney Phillips & Son* [1982] 1 W.L.R. 1297 (though it is not certain that the Court of Appeal would have upheld an award based on cost of repairs even if the claimant had intended to carry them out); *Hole & Son (Sayers Common) v Harrisons* [1973] 1 W.L.R. 345.

[430] *Perry v Sidney Phillips & Son* [1982] 1 W.L.R. 1297; *Patel v Hooper & Jackson* [1999] 1 W.L.R. 1792; but the claimant may recover damages for the inconvenience of living elsewhere while repair work is done.

[431] See para.22–13, above.

[432] In *Dodd Properties Ltd v Canterbury CC* [1980] 1 W.L.R. 433 the cost of repair when the damage was done in 1968 was £10,817. At judgment, 10 years later, it was £30,327. Interest on a judgment at the 1968 cost would have amounted to about £5,500.

damages for tort are to be assessed as at the time when the tort is committed,[433] that rule is subject to exceptions and in a repair case the applicable principle is that the date for assessment of damages is the time when, having regard to all relevant circumstances, repairs can first reasonably be undertaken,[434] and in determining this question it is proper to pay regard to the claimant's financial position.[435]

Consequential losses such as loss of rental or profits, may also be recovered.[436]

D. "Betterment"

22–45   While the broad approach to damages for injury to goods or buildings is clear enough, no mechanical rules can be laid down: given the fundamental principle that the claimant is entitled to, and only entitled to, fair compensation for his loss the application of the broad principles must be "fact sensitive". This is well illustrated by the problem of "betterment". A claimant whose two-year-old car is destroyed is entitled to its value, or in practical terms, the cost of a similar two-year-old car; but if his two-year-old car suffers damage this may have to be repaired with new parts which may make it more valuable than it was before.[437] The real question here is whether the claimant gets any real advantage from the betterment produced by the repairs.[438] Where new parts are fitted in repairs to ships or vehicles[439] or machinery[440] any benefit to the owner is likely to be trivial or speculative. Although such an issue is more likely to arise in a case of repair rather than replacement, because in the latter case the market will commonly provide access to a substitute of comparable age and condition, it may also have to be considered where an equivalent is not available. If a building is destroyed by the defendant the claimant may, as a practical matter, have to rebuild on the same site but the fact that he has a new building which may have a higher market value than the old may not be much of an advantage to him if the business carried on there is to continue.[441] However, if

---

[433] *Miliangos v George Frank (Textiles) Ltd* [1976] A.C. 443 at 468; *Johnson v Perez* (1988) 82 A.L.R. 587.

[434] *Dodd Properties Ltd v Canterbury CC*, above, fn.432.

[435] *Dodd Properties Ltd*, fn.432; *Alcoa Minerals v Broderick* [2002] 1 A.C. 371.

[436] *Rust v Victoria Graving Dock Co* (1887) 36 Ch.D. 113; *Dodd Properties Ltd v Canterbury CC*, above, fn.432. For *mesne* profits, see para.13–18, above.

[437] Of course in many cases the effect of the new parts may be more than offset by the suspicion among buyers of an "accident car" but in principle the point must be true.

[438] *Voaden v Champion (The Baltic Surveyor)* [2002] EWCA Civ 89; [2002] 1 Lloyd's Rep. 623.

[439] *The Gazelle* (1844) 2 W.Rob.(Adm.) 279; *The Munster* (1896) 12 T.L.R. 264.

[440] *Bacon v Cooper (Metals) Ltd* [1982] 1 All E.R. 397.

[441] *Harbutt's "Plasticine" Ltd v Wayne Tank and Pump Co Ltd* [1970] 1 Q.B. 447; *Dominion Mosaics and Tile Co Ltd v Trafalgar Trucking Co Ltd* [1990] 2 All E.R. 246.

there is a substantial and realisable advantage this should be brought into account, for that is the basic principle.[442]

Part II. Other Remedies

6. SELF-HELP

Self-help is apt to be a perilous remedy, for the person exercising it is probably the worst judge of exactly how much he is entitled to do without exceeding his rights.[443] Still, it is well recognised as a remedy for certain torts. A person wrongfully imprisoned may escape. A trespasser,[444] or a trespassing animal, may be expelled with no more force than is reasonable. No doubt there are circumstances in which a structure erected by a trespasser may be demolished, but this is unlikely to be so in cases of minor encroachments by neighbours where the demolition would be out of all proportion to the harm suffered. In any event, the refusal of a mandatory injunction would terminate any right of self-help.[445] By the right of distress damage feasant, chattels wrongfully on the land may be detained as a means of compelling the owner to pay damages, but the right is confined to cases where actual damage has been caused.[446]

22–46

Goods wrongfully taken may be peacefully retaken. This form of self-help has already been considered.[447]

A. Abatement of Nuisance

A nuisance may be abated, i.e. removed, but this is a remedy which the law does not favour, because, as Sir Matthew Hale said—"this many times occasions tumults and disorders".[448] In the first place, before abatement is attempted, notice should be given to

22–47

---

[442] *British Westinghouse Electric and Manufacturing Co Ltd v Underground Electric Railways Co of London Ltd* [1912] A.C. 673. So in the *Dominion Mosaics* case, above, fn.441, where there was 20 per cent more space in the leased substitute the result might have been different if there had been evidence of a realistic prospect of sub-letting this: *The Baltic Surveyor*, above, fn.438, at [85].

[443] *R. v CC Devon and Cornwall, Ex p. C.E.G.B.* [1982] Q.B. 458 at 473. This case contains a review of the powers and duties of the police where a landowner or person with rights over land exercises the right of self-help.

[444] If the trespasser is in a building or land ancillary to a building and the occupier uses or threatens violence to secure entry, the occupier may be guilty of an offence under the Criminal Law Act 1977 s.6: see further, para.13–14, above.

[445] *Burton v Winters* [1993] 1 W.L.R. 1077 (where the claimant received a two-year sentence for contempt because of her efforts to remove an encroachment).

[446] See para.17–10, above. The right of distress over trespassing animals was abolished and replaced with a statutory remedy: para.16–11, above.

[447] See para.17–25, above.

[448] *De Portubus Maris*, Pt 2, Ch.VII.

the offending party to remedy the nuisance, unless it be one of omission and the security of lives and property does not allow time for notice,[449] or unless the nuisance can be removed by the abator without entry on the wrongdoer's land: I may lop the branches of my neighbour's tree which project over or into my land without notice to him,[450] although I must not appropriate what I sever.[451] Secondly, unnecessary damage must not be done: for example tearing up a picture which is publicly exhibited and which is a libel on oneself is too drastic.[452] Thirdly, where there are two ways of abatement, the less mischievous should be followed, unless it would inflict some wrong on an innocent third party or on the public.[453] Fourthly, except in trivial cases which would not justify legal proceedings, the right is confined to urgent cases requiring an immediate remedy.[454] Where abatement is justified, one may recover the costs reasonably incurred in carrying it out.[455]

7. INJUNCTION

22–48 An injunction is a judgment or order of the court restraining the commission or continuance of some wrongful act, or the continuance of some wrongful omission. Originally only the Court of Chancery could issue an injunction, but now any Division of the High Court may do so in any case in which it appears to the court to be "just and convenient".[456] This does not mean that the court has a free hand to restrain conduct of which it disapproves, for the claimant must have some cause of action (whether for a tort or in protection of some legal or equitable right[457]) against the defendant, for if the law were otherwise, "every judge would need to be issued

[449] *Lagan Navigation Co v Lambeg Bleaching Co Ltd* [1927] A.C. 226.
[450] *Lemmon v Webb* [1895] A.C. 1. Roots of a tree projecting into one's soil from neighbouring land may be sawn off, but it is not clear whether notice to the neighbouring land occupier must first be given: *Butler v Standard Telephones, etc. Ltd* [1940] 1 K.B. 399.
[451] *Mills v Brooker* [1919] 1 K.B. 555.
[452] *Du Bost v Beresford* (1801) 2 Camp. 511, where the point was left open, but it may probably be regarded as settled now.
[453] Blackburn J. in *Roberts v Rose* (1865) L.R. 1 Ex. 82 at 89 adopted by Lord Atkinson in *Lagan Navigation Co v Lambeg, etc. Bleaching Co Ltd* [1927] A.C. 226 at 244–246, where the abators satisfied none of these three conditions.
[454] *Burton v Winters* [1993] 1 W.L.R. 1077; cf. *Chamberlain v Lindon* [1998] 1 W.L.R. 1252. For the financial consequences of minor "boundary wars" see *Macnab v Richardson* [2008] EWCA Civ 1631.
[455] *Abbahall Ltd v Smee* [2002] EWCA Civ 1831; [2003] 1 W.L.R. 1472.
[456] Senior Courts Act (formerly known as the Supreme Court Act) 1981 s.37. As to county courts, see the County Courts Act 1984 s.38, as substituted by the Courts and Legal Services Act 1990 s.3.
[457] e.g. an injunction may be granted to restrain a breach of contract or a breach of confidence. For the possibility that there remains a wider jurisdiction to restrain any "unlawful injury to property", see para.7–10, above.

with a portable palm tree".[458] However, the Attorney-General has a "legal right" to bring proceedings in support of the criminal law.[459]

Injunctions are generally sought against such torts as nuisance, continuing or repeated trespass, passing off or interference with contract[460] but there is no theoretical reason why an injunction should not be issued to restrain the repetition or continuation of a tort of any kind.[461] Like other equitable remedies, the issue of an injunction is in the discretion of the court and the remedy cannot be demanded as of right. However, in the context of prohibitory injunctions (i.e. those ordering the defendant to desist from wrongful conduct[462]) it would be wrong to think that a claimant who makes out interference with his rights will face any particular difficulty in getting one. For example, a landowner is prima facie entitled to an injunction to restrain trespass by the defendant in parking his vehicle on the land[463] or running hounds across it[464] or swinging a crane jib through the air above it[465] even though he cannot produce evidence of any particular harm. It is true that an injunction will not be granted where damages are an adequate remedy[466] but this does not mean that the defendant who is willing to pay can demand to buy out the claimant's rights. In *Shelfer v City of London Electric Lighting Co* the operation of the defendant's engines seriously interfered with the enjoyment of the premises of which the claimant was occupier. Granting an injunction, Lindley L.J. commented that the Court of Chancery had repudiated the notion that the legislature, in allowing the award of damages in lieu of an injunction:

> "[I]ntended to turn that Court into a tribunal for legalising wrongful acts or in other words, the Court has always protested against the notion that it ought to allow a wrong to continue simply because the wrongdoer is able and willing to pay for the injury he may inflict."[467]

---

[458] *CC Kent v V* [1983] Q.B. 34 at 45 per Donaldson L.J.

[459] See Feldman (1979) 42 M.L.R. 369. See also s. 222 of the Local Government Act 1972 (local authorities). See also anti-social behaviour orders under the Crime and Disorder Act 1998, proceedings for which are classified as civil: *R. (McCann) v Crown Court at Manchester* [2002] UKHL 39; [2003] 1 A.C. 787.

[460] For injunctions in the context of trade disputes, see para.18–43, above.

[461] See, e.g. *Egan v Egan* [1975] Ch. 218 (injunction to restrain assaults).

[462] For mandatory injunctions, see para.22–51, below.

[463] *Patel v W.H. Smith (Eziot)* [1987] 1 W.L.R. 853 and see *John Trenberth Ltd v National Westminster Bank Ltd* (1979) 39 P. & C.R. 104.

[464] *League against Cruel Sports v Scott* [1986] Q.B. 240.

[465] *Anchor Brewhouse Developments v Berkley House (Docklands Developments)* (1987) 284 E.G. 625, para.13–7, above.

[466] *London and Blackwall Ry v Cross* (1886) 31 Ch.D. 354 at 369 per Lindley L.J. For the statutory power to award damages in lieu of an injunction, see para.22–53, below.

[467] [1895] 1 Ch. 287 at 315–316.

Where the injury to the claimant is trivial[468] or of a very temporary character the court may content itself with awarding nominal damages. It is not, however, enough that the grant of the injunction will inflict more harm on the defendant than the continuance of the activity will upon the claimant.[469]

22–49 An injunction will also be refused if the claimant has acquiesced in the defendant's infringement of his legal rights[470]; but mere delay is not acquiescence: the claimant must have induced the defendant to believe he does not object.[471] A controversial matter has been the significance of the interest which the public at large may have in the continuance of the defendant's activity. While this is relevant[472] there has been strong reluctance to refuse an injunction on this basis. In *Shelfer's* case it was said that:

> "[T]he circumstance that the wrongdoer is in some sense a public benefactor . . . [has never] been considered a sufficient reason for refusing to protect by injunction an individual whose rights are being persistently infringed. Expropriation, even for a money consideration, is only justifiable when Parliament has sanctioned it."

In *Miller v Jackson*,[473] the celebrated case of the village cricket club, two members of the Court of Appeal[474] concluded that the interests of the inhabitants in recreation should prevail over those of the claimants in the enjoyment of their property. Subsequently, however, the Court of Appeal in *Kennaway v Thompson*[475] reaffirmed and applied the principles of *Shelfer's* case and *Miller v Jackson* should probably be regarded as wrongly decided; and it has subsequently been said that it is not appropriate to deny specific

---

[468] Best illustrated by attempts to restrain use of the beach or access thereto: *Llandudno UDC v Woods* [1899] 2 Ch. 705; *Behrens v Richards* [1905] 2 Ch. 614. See *Armstrong v Sheppard and Short Ltd* [1959] 2 Q.B. 384.

[469] Cf. the strange case of *Bank of NZ v Greenwood* [1984] 1 N.Z.L.R. 525 where glare from the defendant's building amounted to a nuisance which could be abated, (1) by major work on the building, or (2) by the claimants installing blinds. Disclaiming any power to award damages in lieu of an injunction, Hardie Boys J. intimated that the installation of blinds at the defendant's expense would satisfy the claimant's rights and adjourned the action sine die.

[470] *Armstrong v Sheppard and Short*, above, fn.468.

[471] *Jones v Stones* [1999] 1 W.L.R. 1739.

[472] *Wood v Sutcliffe* (1851) 2 Sim.(N.S.).

[473] [1977] Q.B. 966.

[474] Lord Denning M.R. and Cumming-Bruce L.J. The former in fact held the defendants' conduct not actionable at all.

[475] [1981] Q.B. 88. However, the injunction was formulated so as to allow the defendants some scope for the continuation of their noisy activities and in *Miller v Jackson*, Geoffrey Lane L.J., dissenting, would have suspended an injunction for 12 months to allow the defendants to find an alternative pitch.

private rights in order to confer indefinite advantages on the public.[476] Of course there are limits to any broad principle: a court is not likely to order the closure of a military airbase because the flying amounts to a noise nuisance.[477]

A. Interim Injunction[478]

An injunction which is issued at the conclusion of a trial upon the merits is known as a perpetual injunction, but an injunction may be issued provisionally until the hearing of the case on the merits, when it is known as an interim injunction.[479] The court on an application for an interim injunction does not profess to anticipate the final outcome of the action and since it is always possible that when the case actually comes to trial the defendant may be found to have been in the right after all, the claimant may be required, as a condition of the grant of an interim injunction, to give an undertaking in damages, i.e. to undertake to pay damages to the defendant for any loss suffered by him while the injunction was in force, should it prove to have been wrongly issued.[480] The principles on which the court acts on an application for an interim injunction are to be found in *American Cyanamid Co v Ethicon Ltd*.[481] A claimant need not establish a prima facie case but merely that there is a "serious question" to be tried.[482] If so, the court must then decide whether the balance of convenience lies in favour of granting or refusing interim relief. The court should consider all the circumstances of the case, particularly whether damages are likely to be an adequate remedy for the claimant, whether the claimant's undertaking in damages gives the defendant adequate protection if the claimant fails at the

22–50

---

[476] *Elliott v Islington LBC* [1991] 10 E.G. 145 (encroachment by ancient tree). See further as to damages and injunctions, Tromans, "Nuisance—Prevention or Payment?" [1982] C.L.J. 87.

[477] *Dennis v MoD* [2003] EWHC 793 (QB); [2003] Env L.R. 34 (though what was in fact sought was a declaration).

[478] For specialised forms of interim injunctions, the search (formerly *Anton Piller*) order (allowing entry to search for property and documents) and the freezing (formerly *Mareva*) injunction (restraining removal of assets beyond the jurisdiction) see Clerk and Lindsell, *Torts*, 19th edn, Ch.30.

[479] Before the CPR 1999 an "interlocutory injunction".

[480] An undertaking in damages will not normally be required where the Crown or a local authority seeks an injunction in aid of the criminal law: *Kirklees MBC v Wickes Building Supplies Ltd* [1993] A.C. 227. In practice the parties often treat the application for an interim injunction as the trial of the action. In cases of great urgency the claimant can obtain an interim injunction in the absence of the defendant which will remain in force for a few days, until there can be a hearing.

[481] [1975] A.C. 396. The case concerned an application for a prohibitory injunction against patent infringement. An interim injunction may be in mandatory (see below) form, but a stronger case is probably required than for a prohibitory injunction.

[482] Cf. *J.T. Stratford & Son Ltd v Lindley* [1965] A.C. 269 at 325, 331, 388, 339, 342–343 and the remarks of Lord Denning M.R. in *Fellowes v Fisher* [1976] Q.B. 122. For trade disputes cases, see para.18–43, above.

trial and whether the preservation of the status quo is important enough to demand an injunction. Curiously, perhaps, the relative strength of each party's case on the affidavits is only to be considered when the other considerations leave the balance of convenience "even".[483]

The practice in libel cases was not affected by the *American Cyanamid* case.[484] Interim injunctions in such cases have always been exceedingly rare because of the public interest in freedom of expression and the fact that the question of libel or no libel is peculiarly one for the jury.[485] It seems that the court will never in practice grant one if the defendant intends to plead justification, or fair comment, or qualified privilege, unless it is crystal clear that the defence will fail.[486] If the defendant contends only that the words do not have a defamatory meaning the court should grant an injunction only if it is clear that any jury verdict for the defendant would be perverse.[487] There is no ground for confining the special treatment of defamation to threatened publication in the media[488] and the demands of free speech go wider than claims for libel properly so-called. It is possible to sue for conspiracy in respect of a defamatory publication[489] but an interlocutory injunction will still only be granted "in the very clearest cases".[490] A similar approach is taken in cases of malicious falsehood, so that if the defendant intends to justify the alleged falsehood no injunction should be granted unless the contention will obviously fail.[491] Under s.12 of the Human Rights Act 1998 no interim injunction is to be granted which might affect freedom of expression unless the court is satisfied that the applicant is likely to establish that publication should not be allowed; and the court is to have particular regard to the importance

---

[483] "I confess that I cannot see how the 'balance of convenience' can be fairly or reasonably considered without taking some account as a factor of the relative strength of the parties' cases, but the House of Lords seems to have held that this is only the last resort": *Fellowes v Fisher* [1976] Q.B. 122 at 138 per Browne L.J.; but cf. *Series 5 Software v Clarke* [1996] 1 All E.R. 853.

[484] *Herbage v Pressdram Ltd* [1984] 1 W.L.R. 1160.

[485] *Coulson v Coulson* (1887) 3 T.L.R. 846; *Bonnard v Perryman* [1891] 2 Ch. 269.

[486] There must be some apparent basis for the defence, it is not something that can be put forward on the insistence of an obsessive client: *Howlett v Holding* [2006] EWHC 41 (QB). The claimant might be a little more likely to succeed in showing this where the defence was comment or privilege because, e.g. it might be clear that the words were not comment or there was no privileged occasion. However, an injunction would still be wholly exceptional.

[487] *Herbage v Times Newspapers Ltd, The Times*, May 1, 1981; *Kaye v Robertson* [1991] F.S.R. 62.

[488] *Holley v Smyth* [1998] Q.B. 726 (threat to expose alleged wrongdoing unless claimants made restitution).

[489] *Gulf Oil (GB) Ltd v Page* [1987] Ch. 327.

[490] *Femis-Bank (Anguilla) Ltd v Lazar* [1991] Ch. 391, explaining *Gulf Oil*, above, fn.489.

[491] *Bestobell Paints Ltd v Bigg* [1975] F.S.R. 421. Cf. *Kaye v Robertson* [1991] F.S.R. 62 and *Compaq Computer Corp v Dell Computer Corp Ltd* [1992] F.S.R. 93 where the claimants established sufficiently strong cases.

of the Convention right to freedom of expression and, where the proceedings relate to material which appears to be journalistic, literary or artistic material, to the extent to which it is in the public domain, to the public interest in its publication and to any relevant privacy code.[492] This does not lower the threshold for defamation cases. The provision is directed at the protection of freedom of expression, not its restriction.[493] Breach of confidence and misuse of private information cases are another matter because it is often the case that once the information is made public the damage is irretrievably done. In that context, s.12 creates no single, rigid standard and there may be occasional cases in which a claimant may succeed even if his case does not pass the "more likely than not" threshold.[494]

B. Mandatory Injunction

Normally injunctions are prohibitory, they forbid the defendant **22–51** from persisting in his wrongful conduct, but the court has power also to grant a mandatory injunction by virtue of which the defendant is actually ordered to take positive action to rectify the consequences of what he has already done. In *Redland Bricks Ltd v Morris*[495] the defendants' excavations on their own land had caused part of the claimant's land to subside and had endangered part of the remainder. In the county court the claimants recovered damages in respect of the subsidence which had already occurred, and the judge also granted them a mandatory injunction requiring the defendants to restore support to their land, the estimated cost of doing which was very great, and, indeed, actually exceeded the value of the whole of the claimant's land. In the House of Lords the defendants' appeal against this injunction was allowed and, while emphasising that the issue of a mandatory injunction is entirely discretionary and that each case depends upon its own circumstances, Lord Upjohn laid down certain general principles.[496] These may be summarised as follows:

1. Damages will not be an adequate remedy for the harm to the claimant.[497]

---

[492] e.g. the code of the Press Complaints Commission.
[493] *Greene v Associated Newspapers Ltd* [2004] EWCA Civ 1462; [2005] Q.B. 972.
[494] *Cream Holdings Ltd v Bannerjee* [2004] UKHL 44; [2005] 1 A.C. 253. See para.12–86, above.
[495] [1970] A.C. 652.
[496] [1970] A.C. 652 at 665–667. The other members of the House of Lords agreed with Lord Upjohn's speech.
[497] *Taylor v Auto Trade Supply Ltd* [1972] N.Z.L.R. 102; *Daniells v Mendonca* (1999) 78 P. & C. R. 401. This is a general principle applicable to all injunctions: [1970] A.C. 652 at 655.

2. If the defendant has acted wantonly or has tried to steal a march on the claimant or on the court,[498] then the expense which the issue of a mandatory injunction would cause the defendant to incur is immaterial, but where the defendant has acted reasonably though, in the event, wrongly, the cost of remedying his earlier activities is a most important consideration.[499]

3. If a mandatory injunction is issued, the court must be careful to see that the defendant knows as a matter of fact exactly what he has to do so that he can give proper instructions to contractors for the carrying out of the work.

C. Quia Timet Injunction

22–52   Normally injunctions are issued only when a tort has already been committed, and, in the case of torts actionable only on proof of damage, it is premature for the claimant to seek an injunction before any damage has actually occurred. Where, however, the conduct of the defendant is such that, if it is allowed to continue, substantial damage to the claimant is almost bound to occur, the claimant may bring a quia timet action, that is, an action for an injunction to prevent an apprehended legal wrong.[500] The existence of the court's power to grant a *quia timet* injunction is undoubted,[501] but it is not often exercised, for the claimant must show both a near certainty that damage will occur[502] and that it is imminent[503]; and even then an injunction will not be issued to compel the defendant to do something which he is willing to do without the intervention of the court.[504]

D. Damages in Lieu of Injunction

22–53   The Court of Chancery had no power to award damages for torts which brought no profit to the wrongdoer, but by Lord Cairns's Act

---

[498] See, e.g. *Daniel v Ferguson* [1891] 2 Ch. 27; *London & Manchester Assurance v O.&H. Construction* [1989] 29 E.G. 65.

[499] *Tollemache & Cobbold Breweries Ltd v Reynolds* (1983) 268 E.G. 52 (claimants displaying extreme pettiness).

[500] *Redland Bricks Ltd v Morris* [1970] A.C. 652 at 664 per Lord Upjohn. In his Lordship's opinion an action is still *quia timet* even though damage has already occurred, if that damage has been redressed by an award of damages: at 665.

[501] For an example, see *Torquay Hotel Co Ltd v Cousins* [1969] 2 Ch. 106 at 120 per Stamp J.

[502] *Att Gen v Nottingham Corp* [1904] 1 Ch. 673; *Redland Bricks Ltd v Morris,* above, fn.500; but something rather less than this appears to be necessary in passing off cases: see, e.g. *Associated Newspapers Plc v Insert Media Ltd* [1991] 1 W.L.R. 571.

[503] *Lemos v Kennedy Leigh Developments* (1961) 105 S.J. 178. Cf. *Hooper v Rogers* [1975] Ch. 43 where the view is expressed that there is no fixed standard of certainty or imminence.

[504] *Bridlington Relay Ltd v Yorkshire Electricity Board* [1965] Ch. 436.

1858[505] the court was enabled to award damages either in addition to, or in substitution for, an injunction, and this jurisdiction now applies to the High Court, the power being contained in s.50 of the Senior Courts Act 1981.[506] Such damages are given in full satisfaction not only for all damage already done in the past, but also for all future damages which may occur if the injunction is not granted.[507] To say that damages may be awarded "in substitution for" an injunction is apt to be misleading for it is fairly clear that the power is not confined to cases in which the Court of Chancery before the Act would have granted the equitable relief.[508] It may be that the power arises whenever the facts of the cases are such as to call into play the exercise of the court's general equitable discretion whether or not to grant an injunction.[509] Damages may be awarded in substitution for an injunction even in a *quia timet* action.[510] This is, in effect, to allow the defendant to purchase the right to commit a tort in the future but, illogical though this may be, it is really no more illogical than the idea, inherent in Lord Cairns' Act itself, that damages can be "adequate" compensation for damage which has not yet occurred, which can be avoided, and to which the claimant does not consent.[511] Practical considerations must, however, be taken into account and on practical grounds there may be considerable advantage in awarding a claimant damages only, where his probable future damage is likely to be much less than the cost to the defendant of preventing it, provided, of course, that the defendant has acted honestly and without the deliberate intention of hurrying on the work so as to present the court with a *fait accompli*. Otherwise there is a danger that proceedings for injunctions will be used by unscrupulous claimants, not to protect their rights, but to extort from defendants sums of money greater in value than any damage that is likely to occur.[512]

---

[505] Section 2. Jolowicz, "Damages in Equity—A Study of Lord Cairns's Act" [1975] C.L.J. 224.

[506] Formerly known as the Supreme Court Act 1981. The legislative history of the original provision was tortuous: see Jolowicz, above, fn.505, pp.228–230.

[507] *Jaggard v Sawyer* [1995] 1 W.L.R. 269, disapproving dicta in *Anchor Brewhouse Developments v Berkeley House Docklands Developments* (1987) 284 E.G. 625.

[508] *Isenberg v East India House Estate Co* (1863) 3 D. & G.J. & S. 263; *City of London Brewery Co v Tennant* (1873) L.R.Ch.App.212; *Wroth v Tyler* [1974] Ch. 30 (substitution for specific performance). The contrary is perhaps implied by Lord Upjohn in *Redland Bricks Ltd v Morris* [1970] A.C. 652 but see Jolowicz, above, fn.505, pp.242–245.

[509] Jolowicz, above, fn.505, pp.241–242. *Hooper v Rogers* [1975] Ch. 43 at 48; *Jaggard v Sawyer*, above, fn.507, at 285; *Marcic v Thames Water Utilities Ltd (No.2)* [2001] 4 All E.R. 326 at [11].

[510] *Leeds Industrial Co-operative Society v Slack* [1924] A.C. 851 (the decision was by a bare majority); *Hooper v Rogers* [1975] Ch. 43. There would, of course, be no cause of action at common law.

[511] *Leeds Industrial Co-operative Society Ltd v Slack*, above, fn.510, at 867–868 per Lord Sumner, dissenting.

[512] *Colls v Home and Colonial Stores Ltd* [1904] A.C. 179 at 193 per Lord Macnaughten; *Jaggard v Sawyer* [1995] 1 W.L.R. 269.

Generally, it has been stated to be a "good working rule" that the jurisdiction under the Act should be exercised if it would be oppressive to the defendant to issue an injunction and if the injury to the claimant's rights is small, is capable of being estimated in money, and is one which can be adequately compensated by a money payment.[513]

"Laid down [over] 100 years ago [this] checklist has stood the test of time,[514] but it needs to be remembered that it is only a working rule and does not purport to be an exhaustive statement of the circumstances in which damages may be awarded instead of an injunction."[515]

There is little authority on the measure of damages in lieu of an injunction, but the Act also allows the grant of damages in lieu of a decree of specific performance of a contract, and in that context it has been held that the principles of assessment are those which apply generally at common law.[516] The same would seem to be true of damages in lieu of an injunction, with the qualification that in awarding damages for future wrongs it is granting a remedy which could not exist at common law.[517]

8. SPECIFIC RESTITUTION OF PROPERTY

22–54 Orders for the specific restitution of property may be for the recovery of land or for the recovery of chattels, but whether it is restitution of land or of goods that is sought, the remedies are confined to cases where one person is in possession of another's property and this limits them to torts infringing such possession. They have, therefore, been considered at appropriate points.[518]

---

[513] *Shelfer v City of London Electric Lighting Co* [1895] 1 Ch. 287 at 322 per Smith L.J. Cf. *Fishenden v Higgs and Hill Ltd* (1935) 152 L.T. 128 at 141.

[514] See *Regan v Paul Properties Ltd* [2006] EWCA Civ 1391; [2007] Ch. 135, where it is said that it is wrong to put the onus on the applicant to show why he should not be confined to damages. In this case the injunction involved demolition of part of a building. Although the courts are reluctant to order demolition it cannot be said that there is any universal rule preventing it: *Site Developments (Ferndown) Ltd v Barratt Homes Ltd* [2007] EWHC 415 (Ch).

[515] *Jaggard v Sawyer*, above, fn.512, Millett L.J.; *Watson v Croft Promo Sport Ltd* [2009] EWCA Civ 15; [2009] 3 All E.R. 249. The checklist is structured around the assumption that the claimant wants an injunction and the defendant resists that. It may not be suitable in a case where the claimant "only wants money" (Lindley L.J. in *Shelfer* at 317): *Marcic v Thames Water Utilities Ltd (No.2)* [2001] 4 All E.R. 326 at [10].

[516] *Johnson v Agnew* [1980] A.C. 367.

[517] *Jaggard v Sawyer*, above, fn.512.

[518] See paras 13–15, 17–29, above.

CHAPTER 23

DEATH IN RELATION TO TORT

CONSIDERED merely as a final catastrophe, death does not require a **23–1** separate chapter in the law of tort, but it does have an important bearing on liability in tort and its legal effects are most conveniently considered in a separate chapter. The death of a person may affect tortious liability in two ways:

1. It may possibly extinguish liability for a tort. Here the question for discussion is: "If I have committed a tort against you (not involving your death), and either of us dies, does your right of action survive?"
2. It may possibly create liability in tort. Here the question is: "If I cause your death, is that a tort either (a) against you, so that your personal representatives can sue me for it or (b) against persons who have an interest in the continuance of your life, e.g. your spouse or children?"

1. Death as Extinguishing Liability

At common law the general rule was that death of either party **23–2** extinguished any existing cause of action in tort by one against the other—*actio personalis moritur cum persona.*[1] Actions in contract

---

[1] For the historical background see Winfield (1929) 29 Col. L.R. 239.

generally escaped the rule, and so too did those in which property had been appropriated by a deceased person and added to his own estate, but it was not until 1934 that the defects of the law were forced on the attention of the legislature by the growth of motor traffic and its accompanying toll of accidents. If a negligent driver was killed in the accident which he himself had caused, nothing was recoverable from his estate or his insurer[2] by those whom he had injured. Accordingly, the Law Reform (Miscellaneous Provisions) Act 1934 was passed to provide generally for the survival of causes of action in tort.[3] Its main provisions may be summarised as follows.

A. Survival of Causes of Action

23–3   By s.1(1) of the Act, all causes of action subsisting against or vested in[4] any person on his death, except causes of action for defamation,[5] now survive against, or, as the case may be, for the benefit of, his estate.[6] The Act does not create a cause of action for death itself and has no bearing on the common law rule that no such cause of action exists. What it does is to provide for the survival of causes of action subsisting when the tortfeasor or the injured person dies.

The exclusion of actions for defamation from the 1934 Act was not so much the result of a conscious decision of policy that such actions should not survive death as of a desire to avoid potentially controversial areas and deal with the urgent issue of deaths in road accidents.[7] A committee which reviewed the whole law of defamation under the chairmanship of Faulks J.[8] considered the issue in some detail and made proposals for survival of claims against the estate of a deceased defamer and for the personal representatives of a deceased person who was defamed in his lifetime to be able to commence an action[9] limited to an injunction and damages for

---

[2] Insurance against third-party risks was first made compulsory in 1930 (now Road Traffic Act 1988 s.143).

[3] The generality of the main provisions of the Act renders superfluous earlier statutory provisions concerning torts against property.

[4] For a curious twist on this see *Daniels v Thompson* [2004] EWCA Civ 307; [2004] P.N.L.R. 638.

[5] Other causes of action were also excluded from the operation of the Act, but these were abolished by the Law Reform (Miscellaneous Provisions) Act 1970 ss.4 and 5.

[6] The fact that the outcome of the claim will not be compensatory (e.g. because the defendant has conceded liability on some other cause of action) does not prevent the claim being for the benefit of the estate: *Ashley v CC Sussex* [2008] UKHL 25; [2008] 1 A.C. 962.

[7] See the Faulks Committee Report, Cmnd. 5909 (1975), Ch.15.

[8] Above.

[9] Where the deceased has commenced an action but dies before judgment the action abates, but a judgment obtained before death may be enforced thereafter: *Rysak v Rysak and Bugasjaski* [1967] P. 179.

pecuniary loss. The Committee also proposed a right of action for certain relatives within five years of the death where an already deceased person was defamed. This would have been limited to a claim for a declaration, injunction against repetition and costs. However, the Supreme Court Procedure Committee re-examined these matters, found serious practical difficulties and concluded that no change in the law was called for.[10]

B. "Subsisting" Action

It may happen that a cause of action is not complete against a **23–4** wrongdoer until after he has in fact died, as, for example, where damage is the gist of the action and no damage is suffered until after the death of the wrongdoer. In such a case no cause of action subsists against the wrongdoer at the date of his death and there is nothing to survive against his estate, so that, were there no provision in the Act to deal with the point, the person suffering the damage would be deprived of his remedy. Section 1(4) provides, however, that where damage has been suffered as a result of a wrongful act in respect of which a cause of action would have subsisted had the wrongdoer not died before or at the same time as the damage was suffered, there shall be deemed to have subsisted against him before his death such cause of action as would have subsisted if he had died after the damage had been suffered. Thus, if on facts similar to those of *Donoghue v Stevenson*,[11] D, the negligent manufacturer of noxious ginger beer, dies before the ultimate consumer, C, suffers damage from drinking it, C's cause of action against D's estate is preserved as it is regarded as arising before D's death.[12]

C. Damages Recoverable

1. Where the injured party dies, the damages recoverable for the **23–5** benefit of the estate may not include any exemplary damages,[13] nor any damages for loss of income in respect of any

---

[10] The Neill Report (see para.12–68, above) Ch.VI. Compare s.39 of the Irish Defamation Act 2009.

[11] [1932] A.C. 562, para.5–5, above.

[12] A right to claim contribution from another tortfeasor is not a claim in tort and survives death without reference to the 1934 Act: *Ronex Properties Ltd v John Laing Construction Ltd* [1983] Q.B. 398.

[13] It is hard to see why the death of the victim should bar punishment of the surviving wrongdoer, while at the same time the death of the wrongdoer does not (apparently) bar civil punishment of his estate. The Law Commission has recommended the correction of this: Law Com. No.247, ss.5.275, 5.278. A similar provision in Victoria produced a historical tour de force on the practice of giving judgment *nunc pro tunc* in *Hartley Poynton Ltd v Ali* [2005] VSCA 53.

period after the victim's death.[14] The explanation of the latter
provision lies in the problem of the "lost years".[15] Once it was
held that the victim of a tort whose life had been shortened
might recover damages for lost earnings during the years of
life of which he had been deprived and that this principle
applied equally to a person who was already dead when the
action was commenced, there arose problems of the relationship between the 1934 Act claim and that of the dependants
under the Fatal Accidents Act. In particular, there was a possibility that the defendant could be liable twice over. The above
provision removes this risk.[16]

It is further provided that where death has been caused by
the act or omission which gives rise to the cause of action,
damages are to be calculated without reference to any loss[17] or
gain[18] to the deceased's estate consequent on his death, except
that funeral expenses may be included.[19] Where, however, the
death is unconnected with the act or omission which gives rise
to the cause of action, it appears that substantial damages can
be recovered even though the deceased himself, had he been
alive when the action was brought, would only have recovered
nominal damages.[20]

The damages which the estate may recover include those for
non-pecuniary items (such as pain and suffering and loss of
amenity) during any significant[21] interval between injury and

---

[14] Law Reform (Miscellaneous Provisions) Act 1934 s.1(2)(a), as amended by the Administration of Justice Act 1982 s.4.

[15] See para.22–30, above.

[16] However, it may be unsafe to assume that this provision removes all possibility of a "lost
years" claim by the estate. It refers only to loss of income and the common law may extend
to loss of the opportunity to inherit capital: see *Adset v West* [1983] Q.B. 826. Further, the
court in *Ward v Foss, The Times*, November 29, 1993, allowed a lost years claim by the
estate to proceed by disapplying the Limitation Act (para.26–19, below): the fact that the
law had subsequently been changed did not make it inequitable to allow old claims to
proceed. It is important to note that the 1982 Act has no application to a claim by a living
claimant, who may still sue for loss of earnings during the "lost years": *Gregg v Scott*
[2005] UKHL 2; [2005] 2 A.C. 176 at [181]. This is essential to allow full compensation
for claimants with dependants who face premature death: para.22–30, above.

[17] e.g. cessation of an annuity or life interest.

[18] e.g. insurance money.

[19] Section 12(2)(c). A living claimant whose life expectancy has been shortened cannot claim
"anticipatory" funeral expenses: *Watson v Cakebread Robey Ltd* [2009] EWHC 1695
(QB).

[20] *Otter v Church, Adams, Tatham & Co* [1953] Ch. 280. This was an action in contract for
professional negligence, which survived at common law. It is submitted, however, that the
result would have been the same even if the plaintiff had had to rely upon the Act of
1934.

[21] Not momentary pain which is effectively part of the process of death itself: *Hicks v CC
South Yorkshire* [1992] 1 All E.R. 65. Cf. *Beesley v New Century Group Ltd* [2008] EWHC
3033 (QB) (£72,000 for 17 months of suffering).

death, but death now terminates these losses for legal purposes.[22]

Damages recovered form part of the estate of the deceased, are available for payment of his debts and pass under his will or upon his intestacy. The Law Reform (Contributory Negligence) Act 1945 applies to claims by estates.

2. When the tortfeasor dies, the ordinary measure of damage applies in an action brought against his estate.

D. Time Limitation

Until 1970 special rules governed the time within which proceed-   23–6
ings in tort had to be started against a deceased person's estate. However, those rules were abolished by the Proceedings Against Estates Act of that year and generally the ordinary law for the limitation of actions applies, whether the action is brought against or for the benefit of the estate.[23]

E. Right of Action is Cumulative

The rights conferred by the 1934 Act are in addition to, and not   23–7
in derogation of, any rights conferred on the dependants of deceased persons by the Fatal Accidents Act 1976.[24]

2. DEATH AS CREATING LIABILITY

We have seen how the Act of 1934 abolished the common law rule   23–8
of *actio personalis moritur cum persona* and allowed the survival of the cause of action of a deceased person, though it did not as such create any cause of action. A quite separate rule of the common law providing that the death could not give rise to a cause of action in other persons, although they were dependent on the deceased, was derived from the ruling of Lord Ellenborough in *Baker v Bolton*[25] that, "in a civil court the death of a human being could not be complained of as an injury".[26] *Baker v Bolton* was only a ruling at

---

[22] Until the Administration of Justice Act 1982 the conventional award for "loss of expectation of life" (para.22–18, above) could be regarded as representing *post mortem* loss of amenity.

[23] See para.26–19, below, but under the Limitation Act 1980 s.11(5), a new, fixed period of limitation arises where the victim dies during the period which commenced with his injury. Provision is made, by rules of court, to enable proceedings to be started against an estate where no grant or probate or administration has been made: CPR 19.8.

[24] Section 1(5), as amended by the Fatal Accidents Act 1976 s.6 Sch.1 para.2(2).

[25] (1808) 1 Camp. 493 (the claimant's wife had been killed in a stagecoach accident).

[26] The rule in *Baker v Bolton* does not apply where the claimant's cause of action is founded upon contract: *Jackson v Watson* [1909] 2 K.B. 193.

Nisi Prius, not a single authority was cited and the report is extremely brief, but it was nevertheless upheld in later cases and the seal of approval placed upon it by the House of Lords in *Admiralty Commissioners v SS Amerika.*[27] Long before that case, however, the legislature had intervened.

A. Fatal Accidents Act 1976[28]

23–9   The development of railways in England led to a great upsurge in the number of accidents, fatal and non-fatal, and this made a change in the law imperative for, while those who survived an accident could recover substantial damages, the dependants of those who were killed could recover nothing. Accordingly, in 1846, the Fatal Accidents Act, otherwise known as Lord Campbell's Act, was passed and virtually overturned the common law so far as those dependants who were specified in the Act and in later legislation were concerned. The present statute is the Fatal Accidents Act 1976, which consolidates the earlier legislation.[29] The Act provides that whenever the death of a person is caused by the wrongful act, neglect or default[30] of another, such as would (if death had not ensued) have entitled the injured person to sue and recover damages in respect thereof, then the person who would have been liable if death had not ensued shall be liable to an action for damages on behalf of the dependants, notwithstanding the death of the person injured.[31]

23–10   **i. Dependants.** As far as concerns financial loss caused by the death the action lies for the benefit of the deceased's dependants, a class of persons which has been considerably enlarged since it was first defined in 1846, most particularly by the Administration of Justice Act 1982.[32] The class now comprehends: (1) the spouse or former spouse[33] of the deceased; (2) the civil partner or former civil partner of the deceased[34]; (3) a person who was living as the spouse or civil partner of the deceased, in the same household, immediately

---

[27] [1917] A.C. 38.

[28] Law Com. No.263, *Claims for Wrongful Death* (1999).

[29] The 1976 Act was amended in important respects by the Administration of Justice Act 1982.

[30] It is now common form in statutes imposing strict liability to provide that a situation giving rise to such liability is "fault" within the meaning of the Fatal Accidents Act: see, e.g. the Animals Act 1971 s.10. A breach of contract causing death is within the statute: *Grein v Imperial Airways Ltd* [1937] 1 K.B. 50.

[31] Section 1.

[32] Substituting a new s.1 in the Fatal Accidents Act 1976.

[33] Including a person whose marriage has been annulled or declared void; the same applies where a civil partnership is annulled or dissolved.

[34] i.e. a person party to a registered same-sex civil partnership under the Civil Partnership Act 2004: s.83 of the Act.

before the date of the death and had been so living for at least two years[35]; (4) any parent or other ascendant of the deceased or person treated by the deceased as his parent; (5) any child[36] or other descendant of the deceased or any person who has been treated by the deceased as a child of the family in relation to any marriage or civil partnership of the deceased; and (6) any person who is, or is the issue of, a brother, sister, uncle or aunt of the deceased.[37] Moreover, in deducing any relationship an adopted person is to be treated as the child of the persons by whom he was adopted,[38] a relationship by marriage or civil partnership as one of consanguinity and a relationship of the half-blood as a relationship of the whole blood. The stepchild[39] of any person is to be treated as his child and an illegitimate person as the legitimate child of his mother and reputed father.[40] The major change introduced by the 1982 Act was the admission of the "common law spouse" to the list of dependants[41] and various amendments were made in 2005 consequent on the general assimilation of the legal status of registered same-sex partnerships with that of marriage by the Civil Partnership Act 2004. The Fatal Accidents Act also gives rise to a claim for damages for "bereavement", but in favour of a much narrower range of persons. This is dealt with below.

An action under the Fatal Accidents Act must normally be brought on behalf of the dependants by the executor or administrator of the deceased[42] but where there is no personal representative, or no action is brought by him within six months, any dependant who is entitled to benefit under the Act may sue in his own name on behalf of himself and the others.[43] Subject to the court's powers under the Limitation Act 1980, the action must in any case be brought within three years of the death.[44]

---

[35] Compare the very much wider residual category under the Inheritance (Provision for Family and Dependants) Act 1975, and see Law Com. No.263, above, §3.18 and *Shepherd v Post Office, The Times*, June 15, 1995. A draft Civil Law Reform Bill published at the end of 2009 would extend eligibility to a person not falling within the other categories who was being maintained by the deceased immediately before the death.

[36] Including a posthumous child: *The George and Richard* (1871) L.R. Ad. & E. 466.

[37] Fatal Accidents Act 1976 s.1(3), as substituted by Administration of Justice Act 1982.

[38] Where a cause of action in respect of the death of the natural parent has accrued, a subsequent adoption does not extinguish the child's claim: *Watson v Willmott* [1991] 1 Q.B. 140.

[39] Including the child of the deceased's civil partner: Civil Partnership Act 2004 Sch.21.

[40] Fatal Accidents Act 1976 s.1(5).

[41] Before the 1982 Act a reduction in the resources of an unmarried mother as a result of the death of the father might constitute a loss to the children: *K. v J.M.P. Co Ltd* [1975] Q.B. 85. This might still be relevant where the conditions of the 1982 Act are not fulfilled.

[42] Section 2. An executor's title to sue dates from the death, but an administrator must first obtain a grant of letters of administration.

[43] Section 2(2). If there is no executor or administrator, the dependants need not wait six months before suing: *Holleran v Bagnell* (1879) 4 L.R.Ir. 740.

[44] See para.26–19, below.

23–11 **ii. Nature of the action.** In comparison with the common law, the right of action created by the Fatal Accidents Act is, "new in its species, new in its quality, new in its principles, in every way new"[45]; it is not the deceased's own cause of action which is caused to survive, it is a new action for the benefit of his dependants. For this new cause of action to exist, however, it is necessary that the circumstances of his death should have been such that the deceased himself, had he been injured and not killed, could have sued for his injury.[46] One must consider the hypothetical ability of the deceased to sue as at the moment of his death, with the idea fictionally that death has not taken place.[47] If, therefore, the deceased had been run over in the street through nobody's fault but his own, there will be no claim on behalf of his dependants nor will there be such a claim if by contract with the defendant the deceased had excluded any possibility of liability to himself,[48] but if the contract merely limited the amount of the defendant's liability, then the deceased could have sued for some damages, the way is open for the dependant's claim, and that claim, being independent of the deceased's, will not be affected by the limitation of liability.[49] Similarly the dependants have no claim if the deceased, before his death,[50] had accepted compensation from the defendant[51] in satisfaction of his claim,[52] or had actually obtained judgment against the defendant,[53] or if by the date of his death his claim had become statute-barred.[54] Nonetheless, so long as the deceased's claim has not become statute-barred when he dies, then the dependants have the full three years from the

---

[45] *Seward v Vera Cruz* (1884) 10 App.Cas. 59 at 70–71 per Lord Blackburn.

[46] For a curious qualification to this, caused by the wording of the MIB agreement, see *Phillips v Rafiq* [2007] EWCA Civ 74; [2007] 1 W.L.R. 1351.

[47] *British Columbia Electric Ry v Gentile* [1914] A.C. 1034 at 1041 per Lord Dunedin; *Pym v GN Ry* (1862) 2 B. & S. 759, 4 B. & S. 396.

[48] *Haigh v Royal Mail Steam Packet Co Ltd* (1883) 52 L.J.Q.B. 640; *The Stella* [1900] P. 161; but since the passing of the Unfair Contract Terms Act 1977 s.2 (para.25–6, below), it is a good deal less likely that such a term will be binding.

[49] *Nunan v Southern Ry* [1924] 1 K.B. 223; *Grein v Imperial Airways* [1937] 1 K.B. 50.

[50] If there is a discontinuance of the deceased's claim after death that does not bar the Fatal Accidents Act claim unless as a matter of construction of the agreement it is intended to do so: *Reader v Molesworths Bright Clegg* [2007] EWCA Civ 169; [2007] 1 W.L.R. 1082.

[51] Not if he has accepted a payment from another tortfeasor unless this in fact fully satisfies his claim: *Jameson v C.E.G.B.* [2000] 1 A.C. 455.

[52] *Read v GE Ry* (1868) L.R. 3 Q.B. 555. This does not contravene arts 6 or 8 of the European Convention on Human Rights: *Thompson v Arnold* [2007] EWHC 1875 (QB); [2008] P.I.Q.R. P1. The view that the dependants are barred was assumed to be correct for the purposes of the appeal in *Pickett v British Rail Engineering Ltd* [1980] A.C. 136. Whether the liability in tort is destroyed from the moment that the agreement to accept compensation is made, even before the money is actually paid is a question of construction: *British Russian Gazette v Associated Newspapers Ltd* [1933] 2 K.B. 616.

[53] The award of provisional damages to the deceased does not bar the dependants' claim: Damages Act 1996 s.3.

[54] *Williams v Mersey Docks and Harbour Board* [1905] 1 K.B. 804; but the court may be able to override the limitation period: Limitation Act 1980 s.33.

death (or, in certain cases, the time when they know they have a cause of action) in which to sue,[55] for their claim, which arises on the death, has no connection with the deceased's. It is thus somewhat illogical, though doubtless good practical sense, that, since the Law Reform (Contributory Negligence) Act 1945, if the deceased was himself partly to blame for the accident which caused his death, the damages recoverable by his dependants are reduced in proportion to his share of responsibility for the accident.[56] Before the Act of 1945, of course, the dependants could have recovered nothing for the deceased could not himself have sued. At the present time, were it not for express statutory provision to the contrary, they would be able to recover the full amount of their loss without reduction.

iii. What is recoverable.[57] The Act provides for recovery in respect of two types of loss. First, since 1982, the spouse or civil partner of the deceased or the parents[58] of a minor[59] who was never married or a civil partner may claim damages for "bereavement", a fixed sum,[60] now £11,800.[61] English law thus now has direct,[62] though conventional, provision for the solatium which was long

23–12

---

[55] Limitation Act 1980 s.12(2).

[56] Fatal Accidents Act 1976 s.5.

[57] The standard works mentioned in para.22–1, above, also deal with damages under the Fatal Accidents.

[58] In the case of an illegitimate child, only the mother.

[59] There is no claim for bereavement if the victim is injured before majority but dies after majority: *Doleman v Deakin, The Times*, January 30, 1990. The Act does not apply to a stillborn child, though since the tort causing the stillbirth will be a tort against the mother she may recover substantial damages (not necessarily limited to the statutory sum) for the effect of the loss of the child on her: *Bagley v North Herts Health Authority* (1986) 136 N.L.J. 1014. Cf. *Kralj v McGrath* [1986] 1 All E.R. 54, where the emphasis seems to be on the mother's grief hindering her physical recovery, and *Kirby v Redbridge HA* [1993] 4 Med. L.R. 178.

[60] Like other damages under the Act, this sum would seem to be subject to reduction on account of the deceased's contributory negligence.

[61] Fatal Accidents Act 1976 s.1A (inserted by Administration of Justice Act 1982 s.3) as amended by SI 2007/3489. These damages are additional to any recoverable by the claimant for psychiatric trauma because there has been a tort to him: *Jones v Royal Devon etc NHS Foundation Trust* [2008] EWHC 558 (QB); 110 B.M.L.R. 154. Where the claim is made by both parents the sum is to be divided equally between them (s.1A(4)), the form of which might suggest that if one parent is the tortfeasor, the other receives the full sum but contra, *Navei v Navei* [1995] C.L.Y., Cty Ct). The statutory damages for bereavement are even more arbitrary than those for pain and suffering and loss of amenity in an injury case. For a dramatically different perspective from the point of view of the economics of happiness see Oswald and Powdthavee, "Death, Happiness and the Calculation of Compensatory Damages" (2008) 37 Jo. of Legal Studies S217 (suggesting figure of the order of £312,000 for first year from loss of spouse).

[62] In effect, though not in theory, the previous law allowed a solatium where the deceased was a young child. The child's action for loss of expectation of life (a conventional sum not exceeding £1,750) survived for the benefit of the estate and passed to the parents, who would, since there was no dependency, generally have no Fatal Accidents Act claim from which it could be deducted.

recognised by Scots common law.[63] It has been recommended that the range of eligible persons be extended and the statutory sum increased (with a global limit of £30,000).[64]

More important in financial terms is the claim for loss of support provided by the deceased which is given by the Act to the much wider class of "dependants". The Act simply says that the court may give damages proportioned to the injury resulting from the death to the dependants[65] it does not say on what principle they are to be assessed, but Pollock C.B., in 1858, adopted the test which has been used ever since, that damages must be calculated: "in reference to a reasonable expectation of pecuniary benefit as of right, or otherwise, from the continuance of the life".[66] If, therefore, the dependants have suffered only nominal damages, or none at all, they can recover nothing,[67] nor can they recover if the deceased had earned his living by crime, for then their claim arises *ex turpi causa.*[68] However, the courts have stretched the concept of pecuniary benefit in holding that a child may claim damages for loss of its mother's care and that in assessing this loss the court is not confined to evaluating her services as housekeeper but may take into account instruction on essential matters to do with his upbringing.[69] Where a son, who worked for his father at full wages under a contract, was killed, his father was held to have no claim for though

---

[63] However, by the Damages (Scotland) Act 1976 s.1(4), the common law claim for solatium was replaced by a claim for, "such non-patrimonial benefit as the relative might have been expected to derive from the deceased's society and guidance if he had not died".

[64] Law Com. No.263, Pt VI. A draft (i.e. for pre-legislative consultation rather than immediate enactment) Civil Law Reform Bill published in December 2009 contains provisions to extend such damages to cohabitants and (at half the standard rate) to minor children of a deceased person. Some European systems award damages to relatives of a living victim for the distress to them: see Rogers (ed.) *Damages for Non-Pecuniary Loss in a Comparative Perspective* (2001) p.262. See also para.2–14, above, in relation to the Human Rights Act 1998.

[65] Section 3(1). A literal interpretation of the Act might mean that it did not apply to a case where the deceased was seriously injured but did not die for some time, for his earning capacity would be destroyed before the death. Naturally, this has been rejected: *Jameson v C.E.G.B.* [1997] 3 W.L.R. 151 (on appeal [2000] 1 A.C. 455).

[66] *Franklin v SE Ry* (1858) 3 H. & N. 211 at 213–214. Hence the dependants are entitled to recover where the deceased has been prevented from accumulating savings which they would have received from him: *Singapore Bus Co v Lim* [1985] 1 W.L.R. 1075. It has been held that where the deceased's estate is substantial and pays estate duty (now inheritance tax) which would otherwise have been avoided, that duty is recoverable by the dependants/beneficiaries from the tortfeasor: *Davies v Whiteways Cyder Co Ltd* [1975] Q.B. 262.

[67] *Duckworth v Johnson* (1859) 29 L.J. Ex. 257.

[68] *Burns v Edman* [1970] 2 Q.B. 541. This decision has come in for a good deal of criticism but, while the claim of the dependants is certainly separate from that of the deceased, it is hard to see how the court can countenance an award of damages in respect of loss of the benefits of criminal activity. See also *Hunter v Butler, The Times,* December 28, 1995 (fraudulent concealment of savings, claimant aware) and para.25–18, below.

[69] *Hay v Hughes* [1975] Q.B. 790 at 802; *Regan v Williamson* [1976] 1 W.L.R. 305; *Mehmet v Perry* [1977] 2 All E.R. 529; *Beesley v New Century Group Ltd* [2008] EWHC 3033 (QB) (principle of recovery for "intangible" benefits also applicable to spouses). See also para.23–15, below.

he had lost the son's services, he could not prove that he had lost any pecuniary benefit since he had paid full wages for them.[70] An additional reason for rejecting the father's claim in that case was that the father could not show any benefit accruing to him from his relationship with his son, but only that he had lost an advantage derived from a contract with him, and this was insufficient.[71] "The benefit, to qualify under the Act, must be a benefit which arises from the relationship between the parties."[72] In *Malyon v Plummer*[73] the claimant widow had been in receipt of a salary of about £600 per annum for somewhat nominal services to her husband's "one-man" company. The Court of Appeal estimated the value of her services to the company at £200 per annum and held that the balance, but only the balance, was attributable to her relationship as wife to the deceased. The £200 represented payment for services rendered under her contract of employment and could not therefore be recovered. Nor is a mere speculative possibility of pecuniary benefit sufficient, as where the person killed was aged four years and his father proved nothing except that he had intended to give the child a good education.[74]

On the other hand, there may be a reasonable expectation of **23–13** pecuniary benefit although the relatives had no legal claim to support by the deceased, as where a son who was killed had voluntarily assisted his father in the father's work,[75] or where he once gave him money during a period of unemployment,[76] or where a wife who was killed had gratuitously performed the ordinary household duties.[77] Indeed, it is not necessary that the deceased should have been actually earning anything or giving any help, provided there was a reasonable probability, as distinct from a bare possibility, that he would do so, as there was where the deceased was a girl of 16 who lived with her parents, was on the eve of completing her apprenticeship as a dressmaker, and was likely in the near future to earn a wage which might quickly have become substantial.[78]

---

[70] *Sykes v NE Ry* (1875) 44 L.J.C.P. 191.
[71] *Burgess v Florence Nightingale Hospital for Gentlewomen* [1955] 1 Q.B. 349.
[72] [1955] 1 Q.B. 349 at 360 per Devlin J.
[73] [1964] 1 Q.B. 330; *Williams v Welsh Ambulance Service NHS Trust* [2008] EWC Civ 81; *Cox v Hockenhull* [2000] 1 W.L.R. 750 (loss of invalid care allowance not recoverable; claimant in effect employed by State to care for deceased).
[74] *Barnett v Cohen* [1921] 2 K.B. 461. Funeral expenses (not including the cost of a wake: *Jones v Royal Devon etc NHS Foundation Trust* [2008] EWHC 558, QB) are recoverable under s.3(5).
[75] *Franklin v SE Ry* (1858) 3 H. & N. 211.
[76] *Hetherington v NE Ry* (1882) 9 Q.B.D. 160.
[77] *Berry v Humm* [1915] 1 K.B. 627. See also *Burgess v Florence Nightingale Hospital for Gentlewomen* [1955] 1 Q.B. 349 at 361–362.
[78] *Taff Vale Ry v Jenkins* [1913] A.C. 1; *Wathen v Vernon* [1970] R.T.R. 471; *Kandella v B.E.A.* [1981] Q.B. 158.

In assessing whether there was a reasonable expectation of benefit in the above sense, the court is not concerned with a balance of probabilities in the same way as when it is adjudicating upon facts. Thus if a wife is separated from her husband at the time of his death, it is unnecessary for her to show that on a balance of probabilities she would have returned to live with her husband. The correct approach is for the court to determine whether there was a reasonable chance, rather than a mere speculative possibility, of reconciliation. If there was such a chance, the award should be scaled down to take account of the probability of the reconciliation taking place.[79] Where the dependant was not married to the deceased but was living with him as his wife the court is directed by statute to take into account the fact that the claimant had no enforceable right to financial support from the deceased.[80]

In a case under the Fatal Accidents Act the court is concerned with assessing what would have happened if the deceased had lived, but since the loss for which damages are awarded is pecuniary loss which will be suffered by dependants in the future, it is also inevitably concerned with the prospects of the dependants: for example, if the dependant himself has a short expectation of life the damages will be small.[81] The most controversial aspect of this matter related to the dependent widow's prospects of remarriage, but there the law has undergone a fundamental alteration by statute. The common law rule was that the court had to estimate the widow's chances of remarriage and reduce the damages accordingly, but some judges tended to revolt against this "guessing game" and a campaign against the rule led to its reversal by the Law Reform (Miscellaneous Provisions) Act 1971. Now, in assessing the damages payable to a widow in respect of the death of her husband in any action under the Fatal Accidents Act there shall not be taken into account the remarriage of the widow nor her prospects of remarriage.[82] As a result of judicial interpretation of s.4 of the Act (dealing with the offsetting of benefits received) it now seems that the provision dealing with the widow's remarriage is in effect redundant and that the same result will be reached where, for

---

[79] *Davies v Taylor* [1974] A.C. 207. See also *Wathen v Vernon* [1970] R.T.R. 471; *Gray v Barr* [1971] 2 Q.B. 554.

[80] Fatal Accidents Act 1976 s.3(4), as substituted by the Administration of Justice Act 1982. The position is the same where there is same-sex cohabitation but no registered civil partnership.

[81] Thus where the deceased's widow actually died before the trial damages were awarded to her estate in respect only of the period during which she actually survived him: *Williams v John I. Thornycroft Ltd* [1940] 2 K.B. 658; *Voller v Dairy Produce Packers Ltd* [1962] 1 W.L.R. 960.

[82] Fatal Accidents Act 1976 s.3(3). A draft Civil Law Reform Bill published at the end of 2009 would take into account actual remarriage.

example, a widower remarries or a widow cohabits without marriage.[83] To ignore remarriage is obviously correct with regard to bereavement damages but with regard to loss of support the situation created by the present law is artificial and strays a long way from the principle of compensation.[84]

iv. Assessment of damages. Damages for bereavement are a fixed sum. What follows concerns pecuniary loss. Although the action is normally brought by the executor or administrator of the deceased, and not by the dependants themselves, the remedy given by the statute is to individuals, not to a class.[85] In calculating the damages, therefore, the pecuniary loss suffered by each dependant should be separately assessed. In practice, however, it will frequently be necessary first of all to determine a figure for the total liability of the defendant and then to apportion the damages between the various dependants[86] and this has been said to be the more usual method.[87]

23–14

The regime for payment of damages by way of periodical payments which has been outlined in relation to personal injury cases also applies to claims under the Fatal Accidents Act[88] where, typically, a higher proportion of the damages will be for pecuniary loss. Where a lump sum award is made, the process of assessment is very similar to that used in assessing future loss in a personal injury action, that is to say the court determines a multiplicand representing the net annual loss and applies to that a multiplier representing the duration of the loss scaled down for contingencies and the value of accelerated receipt in the form of a lump sum. It is, however, more complicated because the court is concerned with the prospects of the dependants as well as of the deceased (for example, whether they would have survived to enjoy the benefit of the deceased's provision)[89] and the period of dependency of individual dependants will vary (for example, that of the spouse will generally be longer

23–15

---

[83] See para.23–16, below. Perhaps for this reason there is no provision dealing with the contingency of a civil partner dependant entering into a new civil partnership, but there are other contexts in which a court may still have to assess a person's prospects of marriage: para.22–38, above.

[84] The High Court of Australia by a majority departed from the common law rule in *De Sales v Ingrilli* [2002] HCA 52; 212 C.L.R. 338.

[85] *Pym v Great Northern Ry* (1863) 4 B. & S. 396; *Avery v London & NE Ry* [1938] A.C. 613; *Jeffrey v Kent CC* [1958] 1 W.L.R. 926; *Dietz v Lennig Chemicals Ltd* [1969] 1 A.C. 170 at 183 per Lord Morris.

[86] *Bishop v Cunard White Star Co Ltd* [1950] P. 240 at 248 per Hodson J. Once the total liability of the defendant has been determined, the apportionment of that sum is no concern of the defendant: *Eifert v Holt's Transport Co Ltd* [1951] 2 All E.R. 655n.

[87] *Kassam v Kampala Aerated Water Co Ltd* [1965] 1 W.L.R. 688 at 672 per Lord Guest.

[88] Damages Act 1996 s.7. See para.22–24, above.

[89] For a full analysis see the judgment of Purchas L.J. in *Corbett v Barking HA* [1991] 2 Q.B. 408.

than that of a child[90]), whereas in a personal injury case, as far as earnings are concerned it is generally only the claimant's working life expectancy that is in issue. As a matter of precedent the multiplier is to be set at the date of the death, not the trial,[91] but the effect is generally to undercompensate and, since both the Law Commission[92] and those responsible for the Ogden Tables[93] take a contrary view, the courts may be persuaded to change their line.[94] Most cases fall into one of two broad categories. The first is where the deceased is the family breadwinner. Traditionally, the approach was to build up the multiplicand item by item by a schedule of expenditure which could be regarded as for the family benefit (mortgage payments, heating, insurance, and so on) and this may still be a valid approach in some cases but it is now more common simply to take the deceased's income, net of tax and other deductions and base the multiplicand on a standard fraction of that—66.6 per cent where the only dependant is a widow, 75 per cent if there are also children.[95] These figures are intended to allow for the expenditure which the deceased incurred solely for his own benefit and recognise the fact that expenditure for joint benefit (for example heating) is not necessarily reduced by the absence of the deceased.[96] It must, however, be stressed that the standard fractions can be varied up or down if there is evidence to justify that. The other type of case is that where the deceased provided valuable but gratuitous service in looking after the home and children. Here there may be[97] no earnings to serve as the baseline for the multiplicand and the proper approach will often be to use as a measure the cost of employing substitute domestic help, if necessary on a "live-in" basis,[98] though it may in some

---

[90] In *Dolbey v Goodwin* [1955] 1 W.L.R. 553 it was held that the damages awarded to the widowed mother of the deceased could not be assessed on the same basis as if she had been his widow, as it was likely that the deceased would have married and that his contributions to his mother's upkeep would then have been reduced.

[91] *Graham v Dodds* [1983] 1 W.L.R. 808; *Cookson v Knowles* [1979] A.C. 556 at 576 per Lord Fraser; *H v S* [2002] EWCA Civ 792; [2003] Q.B. 965; *Fletcher v A. Train & Sons Ltd* [2008] EWCA Civ 413; [2008] 4 All E.R. 699.

[92] Law Com. No.263.

[93] See para.22–27, above.

[94] The alternative approach would be to set the multiplier discounted for early receipt from trial and apply to pre-trial losses the actual period between death and trial, discounted only for the risk (typically very small in the absence of specific evidence) that the deceased might anyway have died from other causes before trial.

[95] *Harris v Empress Motors* [1984] 1 W.L.R. 212. Where both spouses earned and pooled their resources, the fraction is applied to the joint income and the survivor's continuing income deducted: *H v S*, above, fn.91, at [31].

[96] Cf. the assessment in "lost years" cases, which was in issue in *Harris's* case, para.22–30, above.

[97] Of course, as many wives work there may also be a substantial claim for loss of earnings which went to the support of the family.

[98] *Jeffrey v Smith* [1970] R.T.R. 279; *Hay v Hughes* [1975] Q.B. 790. Though in principle a deduction should be made in respect of the living expenses of the deceased, this maybe offset because the courts recognise that a commercial provider may not be "as good as" the deceased: *Reagan v Williamson* [1976] 1 W.L.R. 305.

cases be more apt to take the earnings loss of the other parent who stays at home to look after the children.[99] The fact that commercial help is not engaged (as where the children are looked after by a relative) does not prevent the cost of such help being used as a measure but in this event it should be the net wage without tax and insurance contributions for those are items of expenditure which will never be incurred.[100] In any event the loss by children of the services of their mother is one which is likely to be a declining one so it cannot be valued at a constant figure for the whole of the child's dependency.[101]

v. Deductions. The original position was that benefits accruing to   **23–16**
a dependant as a result of the death were regarded as reducing the loss. A series of legislative amendments reduced the range of such deductions and now s.4 of the Fatal Accidents Act[102] provides that in:

> "[A]ssessing damages in respect of a person's death . . . benefits which have accrued or will accrue to any person from his death or otherwise as a result of his death shall be disregarded".

The law is now therefore very simple: once one has assessed the dependency there is simply no deduction to be made. If the benefit does not arise as a consequence of the death it is irrelevant; and if it does so arise it is excluded from consideration by the statute. This goes even to the extent of refusing any deduction for ex gratia payments made by the defendant, though he can of course express such a payment to be on account of potential liability.[103] We are therefore much more generous to the dependants of the deceased than to claimants in personal injury cases: where the breadwinner is killed the dependants are entitled to a full award based on loss of support from the deceased's earnings, even though as a result of an occupational pension, widow's benefit, insurance money and the devolution of the deceased's estate they may be better off in financial terms than they were before the death. The effect of s.4 has also been in issue where voluntary care is provided by a relative after the death of a parent. In *Stanley v Saddique*[104] the Court of Appeal held that "benefit" was to be given a wide meaning and was not confined

---

[99] *Mehmet v Perry* [1977] 2 All E.R. 529; *Cresswell v Eaton* [1991] 1 W.L.R. 1113.
[100] *Spittle v Bunney* [1988] 1 W.L.R. 847; *Corbett v Barking HA* [1991] 2 Q.B. 408 ("acceptable only on the basis that there is no better means of approaching this difficult and almost unquantifiable aspect of dependency"). It seems that these damages are held on trust for the carer: para.22–37, above.
[101] *Spittle v Bunney*, above, fn.100 (£47,500 reduced on this basis to £25,000).
[102] As substituted by the Administration of Justice Act 1982.
[103] *Arnup v M.W. White Ltd* [2008] EWCA Civ 447; [2008] I.C.R. 1064.
[104] [1992] Q.B. 1; *R. v Criminal Injuries Compensation Board, Ex p. K* [1999] Q.B. 1131.

to direct payments in money or money's worth. Hence when a child lost its mother in an accident but was then looked after by a stepmother, that was a "benefit" under s.4 and was to be ignored[105] even if the stepmother provided better care[106] than the natural mother.[107] It follows that the child has a claim for substitute services to replace those lost and that, in line with the cases on personal injuries,[108] the damages awarded in that respect are held on trust for the carer, provided he is not the tortfeasor.[109]

The existence of a loss of dependency has of course always been anterior to any issue of deduction. If, for example, the deceased maintained himself and his spouse solely from the income of investments and those investments pass to the spouse then the latter will have suffered no pecuniary loss except insofar as the deceased provided skill, which now needs to be replaced, in managing them.[110] However, it is important to remember that loss of dependency is not the same as need. If the claimant was a successful actor who retired upon marriage to the wealthy deceased but resumed her career on his death and made even more money than she had received in support from the deceased, her claim is still based on that loss of support.

> "The dependency is fixed at the moment of death; it is what the dependants would probably have received as benefit from the deceased, had the deceased not died. What decisions people make afterwards is irrelevant."[111]

[105] The decision also seems to take a broader approach to the causative link between the benefit and the death than the decision of the same court in *Hay v Hughes* [1975] Q.B. 790.

[106] However, if the natural mother's care was unreliable that may render the multiplier/multiplicand approach inoperable.

[107] It seems, therefore, that although s.3(3) of the Act (para.23–13, above) directs the court to disregard only the remarriage or remarriage prospects of a widow in assessing damages the same result is reached via s.4 in the case of a widower. For the legislative history see Purchas L.J. in *Stanley v Saddique.* Parliament may have left s.3(3) in the Act notwithstanding the 1982 amendment of s.4 because it had represented a particularly significant policy step. Indeed, it might be said in general, "that the two sections combined are to some degree otiose. It might have been better if there had simply been a statement that the damages in a fatal accident case were to be the loss of dependency. But, historically, the legislation has always provided for assessment in two stages and Parliament has seen fit to retain that format, even though the second stage, section 4, requires the disregard of all benefits which would otherwise have to be brought into account under section 3": *Arnup v M.W. White Ltd,* above at [27].

[108] See para.22–37, above.

[109] *H v S* [2002] EWCA Civ 792; [2003] Q.B. 965. In this case the marriage had broken down and the children went to the father after the mother's death. Quaere as to the position where, e.g. marriage was stable, the mother is killed and father simply provides further services. See *Hayden v Hayden* [1992] 1 W.L.R. 986.

[110] See *Wood v Bentall Simplex* [1992] P.I.Q.R. P332 and *Cape Distribution Ltd v O'Loughlin* [2001] P.I.Q.R. Q73. Pensions can cause difficulties: see *Auty v NCB* [1985] 1 W.L.R. 784 (under previous legislation) and *Pidduck v Eastern Scottish Omnibuses Ltd* [1990] 1 W.L.R. 993.

[111] *Williams v Welsh Ambulance Service NHS Trust* [2008] EWC Civ 81 at [50].

A basic question is whether the present distinctions between fatal and injury cases (which appear to have arisen by historical accident rather than by design) can be defended. There seems no very obvious way of doing so, though as a matter of politics a reform which takes money off widows and orphans in pursuit of principle may not prove popular. The Law Commission has, however, proposed that the law should be brought into line with that governing personal injuries.[112]

vi. Contributory negligence. As we have seen,[113] the contributory negligence of the deceased is taken into account and the damages awarded to the dependants are reduced in proportion. Though the Act is silent on the point, it is fairly clear that the contributory negligence of the dependants is also relevant. The point is not at all far-fetched: suppose Mrs A is being driven in a car by her husband A and is killed in an accident caused by the combined negligence of A and B. It is submitted that in principle the damages awarded to the negligent dependant should be reduced under s.1(1) of the Law Reform (Contributory Negligence) Act 1945, in proportion to his share of responsibility,[114] but that the other dependants should receive their damages in full,[115] since the remedy under the Fatal Accidents Act is given to individuals, not to the dependants as a group. In one case it was held that the damages of a non-negligent dependant were not affected by the fault of another dependant, but there the accident was held to be entirely the fault of the latter and it was conceded by counsel that she had no claim.[116]

23–17

3. RELATIONSHIP OF THE FATAL ACCIDENTS ACT AND LAW REFORM ACT

The rights of action under these Acts are cumulative, with damages under the Law Reform (Miscellaneous Provisions) Act 1934 going to the estate and those under the Fatal Accidents Act going to dependants. In most cases, one or more of the dependants will also be entitled to the deceased's estate. There is no longer any provision for deduction of Law Reform Act claims from those under the Fatal

23–18

---

[112] See Law Com. No.263, Pt V.

[113] See para.23–11, above.

[114] See para.6–53, above.

[115] *Mulholland v McRae* [1961] N.I. 135.

[116] *Dodds v Dodds* [1978] Q.B. 543. There seems no reason why the defendant should not claim contribution from a negligent dependant under the Civil Liability (Contribution) Act 1978, and this would be the better course where the negligent dependant is not the only dependant. It would also be the appropriate course where the executor or administrator of the deceased, i.e. the nominal claimant, has contributed to the death but is not himself the principal dependant.

Accidents Act but since the Administration of Justice Act 1982 damages under the Law Reform Act will, in the case of instantaneous death, be confined to funeral expenses, and since these are anyway recoverable under the Fatal Accidents Act there is no point in bringing a Law Reform Act claim. Where there is an interval between injury and death and hence loss of amenity and earnings and so on, then no doubt a Law Reform Act claim will continue to be presented concurrently with one under the Fatal Accidents Act.

4. MISCELLANEOUS STATUTES

23–19 The development of organised international transport has led to the conclusion of a number of international conventions governing the carrier's liability. The principal English statutes implementing such conventions are the Carriage by Air Act 1961, the Carriage of Passengers by Road Act 1974, the Merchant Shipping Act 1995 and the International Transport Conventions Act 1983. Accounts of these Acts must be sought elsewhere, but some of them set a limit on the damages which may be awarded for death or personal injury.[117]

---

[117] See Clerk & Lindsell, *Torts*, 19th edn, Ch.29.5.g. Note that the liability of EC air carriers is no longer subject to limitation: Council Regulation (EC) 2027/97 and SI 1998/1751. In another context see the Coal Mining (Subsidence) Act 1991 s.32.

CHAPTER 24

CAPACITY

THE title of this chapter is a compendious abbreviation of "Variation   **24–1**
in capacity to sue, or liability to be sued, in tort".

Every system of law and every branch of each system must
recognise variations in favour of, or against, abnormal members of
the community. Who are to be reckoned as abnormal is a question
of policy. In the law of tort the chief variations in capacity are to be
found with the State and its officials, minors, persons of unsound
mind, corporations and trade unions.[1] Married women were abnormal for this purpose until well into the 20th century. That condition
has now disappeared, but there are still some restrictions on actions
between spouses.

1. THE STATE AND ITS SUBORDINATES

A. The Crown and State Officials

At common law no action in tort lay against the Crown[2] for   **24–2**
wrongs expressly authorised by the Crown or for wrongs committed

---

[1] It is convenient to treat trade unions in the chapter on economic torts: para.18–35,
above.
[2] Or against Government departments, for these enjoyed the immunity of the Crown unless
a statute expressly provided otherwise. See *Minister of Supply v British Thomson-Houston
Co* [1943] K.B. 478

by its servants in the course of their employment.[3] Moreover, the head of the department or other superior official was not, and is not, personally liable for wrongs committed by his subordinates, unless he has expressly authorised them, for all the servants of the Crown are fellow servants of the Crown and not of one another.[4] On the other hand, the actual wrongdoer could, and still can, be sued in his personal capacity.[5] In practice the Treasury Solicitor usually defended an action against the individual Crown servant and the Treasury, as a matter of grace, undertook to satisfy any judgment awarded against him for a tort committed in the course of his employment. If the actual wrongdoer could not be identified the Treasury Solicitor would supply the name of a merely nominal defendant for the purpose of the action, i.e. a person who, though a Government servant, had nothing to do with the alleged wrong. However, in *Royster v Cavey*[6] it was held that the court had no jurisdiction to try the case unless the subordinate named by the Treasury Solicitor was the person who apparently had committed the tort. As the Crown had become one of the largest employers of labour and occupiers of property in the country, this system of providing compensation for the victims of torts committed by Crown servants in the course of their employment was plainly inadequate and, finally, some 20 years after it was mooted, the Crown Proceedings Act 1947 put an end to Crown immunity in tort.

B. Crown Proceedings Act 1947

24–3   Under the Act the old maxim that "the King can do no wrong" is retained to the extent that no proceedings can be instituted against the Sovereign in person,[7] and there are savings in respect of the Crown's prerogative and statutory powers,[8] but otherwise the Act went a long way towards equating the Crown with a private person

---

[3] *Canterbury (Viscount) v Att Gen* (1842) 1 Ph. 306. The remedy by way of petition of right was available for breach of contract, and to recover property which had been wrongfully taken and withheld. *France, Fenwick & Co Ltd v R.* [1927] 1 K.B. 52. Proceedings by way of petition of right were abolished by the Crown Proceedings Act 1947 Sch.1 para.2, but only with regard to liability in respect of Her Majesty's Government in the UK. A petition of right may, therefore, still lie in certain cases, but in the common law form used prior to the Petition of Right Act 1860: *Franklin v Att Gen* [1974] Q.B. 185.

[4] *Raleigh v Goschen* [1898] 1 Ch.73 at 83; *Bainbridge v Postmaster-General* [1906] 1 K.B. 178.

[5] He could not, and cannot now, plead the orders of the Crown or State necessity as a defence. *Entick v Carrington* (1765) 19 St. Tr. 1030; *Wilkes v Wood* (1763) 19 St. Tr. at 1153; *M. v Home Office* [1994] 1 A.C. 337.

[6] [1947] K.B. 204, the Court of Appeal acting upon emphatic obiter dicta of the House of Lords in *Adams v Naylor* [1946] A.C. 543.

[7] Section 40(1).

[8] Section 11(1).

of full age and capacity for the purposes of tortious liability.[9] The Crown cannot, however, be liable in tort except as provided by the Act and this cannot be evaded by dressing up the claim as one for a declaration that the Crown is behaving wrongfully.[10] Section 2(1) provides that the Crown shall be liable[11] as if it were a private person: (1) in respect of torts committed by its servants or agents[12]; (2) in respect of any breach of those duties which a person owes to his servants or agents at common law by reason of being their employer; and (3) in respect of any breach of the duties attaching at common law to the ownership, occupation, possession or control of property.[13] Section 2(2) makes the Crown liable for breach of statutory duty, provided that the statute in question is one which binds other persons besides the Crown and its officers. The starting point is still, apart from the Human Rights Act 1998, that the Crown can do no wrong in private law. In the second and third cases enumerated in s.2(1) and that in s.2(2) the Crown can be "institutionally" or "personally" liable[14]; but otherwise the Act makes the Crown liable for the acts of human agents who commit torts. Hence the Crown can only be liable for misfeasance in a public office if the mental element of that tort can be brought home to some individual for whose actions the Crown is answerable.[15] The apportionment provisions of the Civil Liability (Contribution) Act 1978 and the Law Reform (Contributory Negligence) Act 1945, as well as the analogous provisions of the Merchant Shipping Act 1995, apply to proceedings in which the Crown is a party.[16] There is a little doubt whether an action lies against the Crown on behalf of a deceased person's estate under the Law Reform (Miscellaneous Provisions) Act 1934 or on behalf of his dependants under the Fatal Accidents

---

[9] The Civil Procedure (Modification of Crown Proceedings Act 1947) Order SI 2005/2712 removed certain procedural advantages of the Crown, but the 1947 Act does not mean that duties owed by the Crown can in all respects be equated with those owed by private persons: para.5–4, above.

[10] *Trawnik v Lennox* [1985] 1 W.L.R. 532 (where the court had no jurisdiction to hear a claim for a nuisance in Berlin because it did not arise in respect of the Crown's activities in the UK: s.40(2)(b)).

[11] The action is brought against the appropriate government department in accordance with a list published by the Treasury, otherwise the Attorney-General may be made defendant (s.17).

[12] "Agent" includes an independent contractor (s.38(2)) but the Crown is not on this account subject to any greater liability for the tort of an independent contractor employed by it than it would be if it were a private person: s.40(2)(d).

[13] The duties owed by an occupier of premises to his invitees and licensees are now contained in the Occupiers' Liability Act 1957, which binds the Crown. The liability of the Crown under the Act thus falls under s.2(2), but s.2(1)(c) continues to apply to the other duties which attach to the ownership, occupation, possession or control of property such as those in the tort of nuisance.

[14] The statement in *Chagos Islanders v Att Gen* [2004] EWCA Civ 997 at [20] seems to go too far in that it ignores these categories.

[15] [2004] EWCA Civ 997.

[16] Section 4.

Act 1976, but it is submitted that on principle the Crown should be liable.[17]

There are, however, certain limitations on the Crown's general liability in tort. Until 1987 it was not possible for a member of the armed forces to sue the Crown for injuries inflicted by a fellow member in the execution of his duty or arising from the condition of premises or equipment. There was a similar immunity for the actual wrongdoer.[18] These restrictions were removed by the Crown Proceedings (Armed Forces) Act 1987.[19] However, pre-1987 cases may still arise (for example from diseases contracted from exposure to asbestos) and the original restriction has been declared substantive rather than procedural in nature and compatible with art.6 of the European Convention on Human Rights.[20] The remaining limitations are:

1. Officers, that is, servants or Ministers of the Crown,[21] who may render the Crown liable are only those appointed directly or indirectly by the Crown and paid wholly out of moneys provided by Parliament or a fund certified by the Treasury as equivalent. This excludes liability for police officers, who are not paid out of such funds, even in the case of the Metropolitan Police,[22] and also for public corporations which are, normally, liable themselves like any other corporation.[23]

2. The Crown cannot be made liable for an act or omission of its servant unless that act or omission would, apart from the Act, have given rise to a cause of action against the servant himself.[24] This preserves such defences as act of State but does not, it is submitted, extend so far as to exempt the Crown from liability in those exceptional cases where the employer is

---

[17] Clerk and Lindsell, *Torts*, 19th edn, s.5–19; Glanville Williams, op. cit., pp.55–58; Treitel, "Crown Proceedings: Some Recent Developments" [1957] Pub. L. 321, 322–326.

[18] Section 10 of the 1947 Act, which applied only to death or personal injury. On its scope see *Post Traumatic Stress Disorder Litigation, Multiple Claimants v MoD, Re* [2003] EWHC 1134 (QB).

[19] While the law of negligence may be applicable to routine military activities (*Groves v Commonwealth* (1982) 41 A.L.R. 193) it was held in *Mulcahy v MoD* [1996] Q.B. 732 that there was no duty of care in active operations during the Gulf War, even though s.10 had not been revived, as provided for by s.2: para.5–15, above. There is a compensation scheme for service injuries, which does not preclude civil claims where applicable, under the Armed Forces and Reserve Forces (Compensation Scheme) Order SI 2005/439 as amended.

[20] *Matthews v MoD* [2003] UKHL 4, [2003] 1 A.C. 1163.

[21] Section 38(2). The Crown is not expressly defined, but it appears to include all government departments, officers, servants and agents of the Crown.

[22] See now the Police Act 1996 s.88, para.20–7, above.

[23] *Tamlin v Hannaford* [1950] 1 K.B. 18. Cf. *Glasgow Corp v Central Land Board* 1956 S.L.T. 41, HL. See also *Bank Voor Handel en Scheepvaart v Administrator of Hungarian Property* [1954] A.C. 584.

[24] Section 2, proviso. The Crown has the benefit of any statute regulating or limiting the liability of a government department or officer of the Crown: s.2(4).

vicariously liable even though his servant is immune from liability himself.[25]

3. The Crown is not liable for anything done by any person in discharging responsibilities of a judicial nature vested in him or any responsibilities he has in connection with execution of the judicial process.[26]

C. Act of State

It is proposed to deal with this matter briefly since it belongs **24–4** much more to the realm of constitutional and international law than to the law of tort. There is no doubt that no action may be brought either against the Crown or anyone else in respect of an act of State, but there is less agreement on the meaning of this phrase. Certainly an injury inflicted upon a foreigner abroad which is done pursuant to a policy which is not justiciable by the courts[27] and which is either authorised or ratified by the Crown is for this purpose an "act of State" and cannot be made the subject of an action in the English courts,[28] but it is doubtful whether, as an answer to a claim for tort, act of State goes any further than that. It will probably not avail a defendant to plead act of State in respect of an act done within British territory,[29] whatever the nationality of the claimant.[30] There has been some dispute as to whether it may be available against a British citizen abroad, though the only case in which the point appears to have arisen decided that it may be.[31] An act of the Crown may, of course, be lawful as an act of prerogative, and s.11 of the Crown Proceedings Act preserves the Crown's rights to exercise its statutory and prerogative powers, but there is no prerogative power

---

[25] Clerk and Lindsell, *Torts*, 19th edn, s.5–05. Contra, Glanville Williams, *Crown Proceedings*, pp. 44–45.

[26] Section 2(5). In *Quinland v Governor of Swaleside Prison* [2002] EWCA Civ 174; [2003] Q.B. 306, the failure of the Criminal Appeal office to expedite the correction of the judge's error was held to fall within s.2(5) and the suggestion that the subsection does not cover "administrative" responsibilities in *Welsh v CC Merseyside* [1993] 1 All E.R. 692 was disapproved. However, failure to deal with money paid into court is not a judicial act and outside the subsection: *Kirvek Management etc. v Att Gen of Trinidad and Tobago* [2002] UKPC 43; [2002] 1 W.L.R. 2792 (similar legislation). An award of damages may be made against the Crown in limited circumstances under the Human Rights Act 1998: see para.24–9, below.

[27] Not merely "administrative" acts like providing accommodation for troops as in *Att Gen v Nissan* [1970] A.C. 179. There was no reliance on act of state in *Bici v MoD* [2004] EWHC 786 (QB).

[28] *Buron v Denman* (1848) 2 Ex. 167. Cf. *Carr v Francis, Times & Co* [1902] A.C. 176.

[29] *Johnstone v Pedlar* [1921] A.C. 262.

[30] With the rather obvious exception of enemy aliens present in British territory without licence.

[31] *Hilal v Secretary of State for Defence* [2009] EWHC 397 (QB). This at least avoids problems arising from the fact that the old cases spoke in terms of "British subjects", a concept far wider than modern British citizenship.

to seize or destroy the property of a subject without paying compensation.[32] It must be emphasised that all this concerns common
law liability in tort and the Human Rights Act 1998 may have extra-
territorial application to locations abroad where UK authorities are
exercising effective control, thus creating an obligation not to act
inconsistently with the Convention with regard to aliens as well as
British subjects.[33]

D. Post Office

24-5   The Post Office was until 1969 a department of Government, but,
despite the general provisions of the Crown Proceedings Act 1947,
no proceedings in tort lay against the Crown for any act or omission
of a servant of the Crown in relation to a postal packet or telephonic
communication.[34] Nor was there any contract between the Post
Office and the sender of mail. In 1969 the Post Office became a
statutory corporation but the immunity from suit was preserved and,
indeed, somewhat extended.[35] Now the law is contained in the
Postal Services Act 2000. The Post Office became a company, albeit
wholly owned by the Crown and its monopoly on delivery of certain
mail may be broken up by the issue of licences to others. Both these
others and the Post Office company are "universal service providers"[36] and s.90 provides that no proceedings in tort lie against a
universal service provider in respect of loss or damage suffered by
any person in connection with the provision of a universal postal
service because of (a) anything done, or omitted to be done, in
relation to any postal packet in the course of transmission by post,
or (b) any omission to carry out arrangements for the collection of
anything to be conveyed by post. Furthermore, no officer, servant,
employee, agent or sub-contractor of a universal service provider
nor any person engaged in or about the conveyance of postal packets
is subject, except at the suit or instance of the provider, to any civil
liability for (a) any loss or damage in the case of which liability of
the provider is excluded or (b) any loss of, or damage to, an inland
packet to which s.91 applies. Under s.91 the service provider is
liable for loss of or damage to registered inland postal packets where
he has accepted liability under a "scheme" made by it[37] and the loss
or damage is due to the wrongful act, neglect or default of servants,

---

[32] *Att Gen v De Keyser's Royal Hotel* [1920] A.C. 508; *Burmah Oil Co Ltd v Lord Advocate* [1965] A.C. 75; *Att Gen v Nissan*, (above, fn.27) at 227 per Lord Pearce. The common law right to compensation was considerably restricted by the War Damage Act 1965, para.25–36, below.

[33] *R (Al-Skeini) v Secretary of State for Defence* [2007] UKHL 26; [2008] 1 AC 153.

[34] Crown Proceedings Act 1947 s.9(1).

[35] Post Office Act 1969 s.29.

[36] See s.4.

[37] Under s.89.

agents or sub-contractors of the service provider, but such wrongful act, etc. is presumed unless the contrary is shown.[38]

E. Foreign Sovereigns

English law was for long committed to the proposition (which **24-6** derives from general public international law[39]) that a foreign sovereign State enjoyed absolute immunity from liability before an English court unless the immunity had been waived by submission to the jurisdiction.[40] The doctrine was not confined to "acts of State" and had become a serious problem in modern times because of the practice by many countries of carrying on ordinary trading activities through organs of State. Accordingly, attempts were made to restrict the immunity, culminating in the decision of the House of Lords in *The Congreso del Partido*[41] whereby a court was required to analyse the nature of the obligation and breach in question to determine whether it was of a private law or a "governmental" character. However, the law is now contained in the State Immunity Act 1978. The fundamental provision is that a State is immune from the jurisdiction of the English courts except as provided by the Act.[42] Much of the Act concerns matters of contract, but for our purposes the principal exceptions from sovereign immunity[43] are: (1) an act or omission in this country causing death or personal injury; (2) obligations arising out of the ownership, possession or use of property in this country[44]; and (3) Admiralty proceedings (whether in rem or in personam) in respect of ships used for commercial purposes.[45] The residual immunity contained in the Act does not protect an entity distinct from the executive organs of the State[46] unless the proceedings arise out of the exercise of sovereign authority and the State would have been immune.[47] However, the Act does not apply

---

[38] Section 92(7). This section also contains provisions governing who may sue and the amount recoverable.

[39] It, "pursues the legitimate aim of complying with international law to promote comity and good relations between states through the respect of another state's sovereignty" and its recognition does not infringe art.6 of the European Convention on Human Rights: *Al-Adsani v UK* (2002) 34 E.H.R.R. 273 at [54].

[40] *The Cristina* [1938] A.C. 485. As to the immunity of diplomatic officials, see the Diplomatic Privileges Act 1964.

[41] [1983] A.C. 244.

[42] Section 1(1).

[43] The State may still submit to the jurisdiction: s.2.

[44] Sections 5 and 6 respectively.

[45] Section 10. For States parties to the Brussels Convention of 1926, see s.10(6).

[46] Cf. *C. Czarnikow Ltd v Centrala Handler Zagranicznego "Rolimpex"* [1979] A.C. 351.

[47] Section 14(2); but a central bank is equated with a State: s.14(4). The provisions of s.14(2) are fully examined in *Kuwait Airways v Iraqi Airways* [1995] 1 W.L.R. 1147 (a $630 million claim for conversion). The effect of s.14(2) seems to be that the issue is essentially the same as it would have been at common law under *The Congreso del Partido*.

to cases involving visiting forces of a foreign power,[48] which are still governed by the common law.[49]

The law of sovereign immunity rests on the proposition that it would be an affront to the dignity and sovereignty of a State to allow it to be impleaded in a foreign court. It applies even though the acts alleged against the foreign State involve violation of a *jus cogens* or peremptory rule of international law such as the prohibition of torture.[50] That dignity may also be affronted if those who are or were its officials are impleaded in relation to the conduct of its affairs before the courts of another State and therefore the State can "extend the cloak of its own immunity over those officials".[51] Thus in *Grovit v de Nederlandsche Bank*[52] libel proceedings against the central bank's officers alleging malice and arising out of the refusal to register the claimant's company were struck out

Independently of sovereign immunity, there is a principle of English law that the courts may refuse to adjudicate on acts done abroad by virtue of the sovereign authority of foreign States. In *Buttes Gas and Oil Co v Hammer*[53] the House of Lords therefore stayed litigation between private parties when it involved an examination of allegations of conspiracy between one party and a sovereign ruler and acts of assertion of territorial sovereignty by other States in the area.[54] However, this is not an absolute rule which precludes an English court from determining whether there has been a breach of international law where there are recognised standards by which the issue is justiciable.[55]

F. European Community

24–7   Article 288 (formerly 215) of the EEC Treaty renders the Community liable for damage caused by its institutions or servants: "in

---

[48] Section 16(2).

[49] See *Littrell v USA (No.2)* [1995] 1 W.L.R. 92 (treatment not actionable in US law and not justiciable here as interference with sovereign rights of USA over its military personnel) and *Holland v Lampen-Wolfe* [2000] 1 W.L.R. 1573 (provision for education of military personnel a matter within the sovereign immunity of the USA so as to bar a claim for libel).

[50] *Jones v Saudi Arabia* [2006] UKHL 26; [2007] 1 A.C. 270.

[51] *Jones* in the CA at [2004] EWCA Civ [105].

[52] [2005] EWHC 2944 (QB); [2006] 1 W.L.R. 3323.

[53] [1982] A.C. 888. Similar considerations played some part in English law's long adherence to the rule that an English court had no jurisdiction over actions involving trespass to foreign land. See the discussion in *Pearce v Ove Arup Partnership Ltd* [2000] Ch. 403. That rule was abolished by the Civil Jurisdiction and Judgments Act 1982 s.30—there is still no jurisdiction if the action is principally concerned with title to, or the right to possession of such property.

[54] Nor will the English court entertain a claim *by* a foreign State which in substance amounts to an exercise of its sovereign authority: *Mbasogo v Logo Ltd* [2006] EWCA Civ 1370; [2007] Q.B. 846.

[55] *Kuwait Airways Corp v Iraqi Airways Co (Nos 4 and 5)* [2002] UKHL 19; [2002] 2 A.C. 883.

accordance with the general principles common to the laws of the Member States". Jurisdiction over such claims is vested in the European Court of Justice and the topic is a branch of law in its own right.[56] We have already noted that a Member State may incur liability to a citizen damaged by its failure to implement EC measures.[57]

2. JUDICIAL ACTS[58]

The law casts a wide immunity around acts done in the administration of justice. This has been rather infelicitously styled a "privilege", but that might imply that the judge has a private right to be malicious, whereas its real meaning is that in the public interest it is not desirable to inquire whether acts of this kind are malicious or not. It is rather a right of the public to have the independence of the judges preserved rather than a privilege of the judges themselves.[59] It is better to take the chance of judicial incompetence, irritability, or irrelevance, than to run the risk of getting a bench warped by apprehension of the consequences of judgments which ought to be given without fear or favour.[60]

24–8

Despite a valiant attempt by Lord Denning M.R. to rationalise the law into one, unified principle[61] and despite recent legislation, the law is still hard to state concisely or with precision. First, as to judges of the High Court, they are immune from liability for any act of a judicial character even though the act is in excess of or outside their jurisdiction and whether this is a result of mistake of fact or of law. If, however, an act is in excess of jurisdiction and is done in bad faith, then the judge would be liable in damages for what follows from the order made, for example, imprisonment or seizure of property.

> "If the Lord Chief Justice himself, on the acquittal of a defendant charged before him with a criminal offence, were to say, 'That is a perverse verdict', and thereupon proceed to pass a sentence of imprisonment, he could be sued for trespass."[62]

---

[56] See Antoniolli, "Community Liability" in Koziol and Schulze (eds) *Tort Law of the European Community* (2008).

[57] See para.7–12, above.

[58] The topic is dealt with at length in Winfield, *Present Law of Abuse of Legal Procedure*, Ch.7.

[59] *Bottomley v Brougham* [1908] 1 K.B. 584 at 586–587 per Channell J.; *Nakhla v McCarthy* [1978] 1 N.Z.L.R. 291.

[60] For a more sceptical view, see Olowofoyeku (1990) 10 L.S. 271 and *Suing Judges* (1993).

[61] In *Sirros v Moore* [1975] Q.B. 118.

[62] *Re McC* [1985] A.C. 528 at 540 per Lord Bridge.

At the other extreme the liability of justices (including district judges of magistrates' courts[63]) is now governed by the Courts Act 2003, re-enacting provisions first introduced in 1990. It is provided that no action lies for any act in the execution of the justice's duty and "with respect to any matter within his jurisdiction"[64] and that an action lies for an act:

"[I]n the purported execution of his duty . . . but with respect to a matter which is not within his jurisdiction, if, but only if, it is proved that he acted in bad faith".[65]

Putting aside the point that proceedings in magistrates' courts are amenable to review and control by the High Court, whereas a High Court judge is the sole arbiter of his jurisdiction (subject to appeal) it is difficult to see how this differs from the position of a judge of the High Court if the above dictum represents the modern law.

24–9 Unfortunately, there is no legislation governing the position of the majority of professional judges (county court judges, recorders, district judges[66]) and their position has to be discovered from the older cases and by inference from what the House of Lords decided in the context of justices in *Re McC*.[67] A further complication arises from the fact that another distinction cuts across that based upon the status of the judge, namely that between courts which are and are not "courts of record". Thus all trials on indictment are before a court of record, even though very few of them are presided over by High Court judges.[68] For acts within their jurisdiction "inferior" judges have full protection, even if they are actuated by malice.[69] What is less clear is their position with regard to acts outside their jurisdiction. The concept of jurisdiction is a difficult one and its meaning may vary from one context to another. Here what is involved is the power to decide an issue, not the method by which the decision is reached, so that procedural irregularity in reaching a result which the court has power to achieve does not take the case

---

[63] By s.10C of the Justices of the Peace Act 1997, inserted by the Access to Justice Act 1999 a district judge, magistrates' courts (formerly a stipendiary magistrate) is a justice for every commission area.
[64] Courts Act 2003 s.31.
[65] Section 32. There are provisions for indemnity of justices in s.35, which dates from the Justices of the Peace Act 1979.
[66] Other than those of magistrates' courts.
[67] [1985] A.C. 541.
[68] In fact the majority of High Court *civil* actions are now heard by deputy judges, i.e. circuit judges and QCs, but there does not seem any doubt that they enjoy the same immunity as a full High Court judge.
[69] See *Hinds v Liverpool County Court* [2008] EWHC 665 (QB).

outside the jurisdiction.[70] According to *Re McC* this is the true explanation of *Sirros v Moore*.[71] The claimant had been convicted of an offence and recommended for deportation by a stipendiary magistrate, but without an order for his detention. The judge in the Crown Court,[72] wrongly thinking that he had no jurisdiction to hear an appeal against deportation, dismissed it but ordered the claimant to be detained. This did not amount to trespass because he did have power to overrule the initial decision against detention and intended to do so, but implemented that decision by a "hopelessly irregular procedure". On the other hand, by analogy with *Re McC*, if a judge of an inferior court were, in good faith, to pass a sentence which he had no power to pass he would be liable. In modern conditions it is entirely unconvincing to argue as a justification for a professional judge being liable for acts done in good faith outside his jurisdiction, that he is always supposed to know the law (the state of which is in any event often a matter of opinion): if the argument has any validity at all it should surely apply, a fortiori, to judges of the High Court. What is needed, it is suggested, is a bold decision declaring the common law for inferior judges to be the same as that stated for justices in the Act.[73] Enough has been said to show that it will be a rare case in which a person may recover substantial damages in respect of a judicial act. An action in tort is not, however, the only route to compensation. Where a criminal conviction is reversed on the basis of a newly-discovered fact there may be a statutory right to compensation under s.133 of the Criminal Justice Act 1988. Furthermore, an award of damages[74] under the Human Rights Act 2000 may be possible in respect of a judicial act done in good faith in order to compensate a person to the extent required by art.5(5) of the European Convention on Human Rights (which provides for compensation for arrest or detention).[75] However, the damages are awardable against the Crown and the immunity of the judge is in effect preserved.[76]

---

[70] Nor does error as to a collateral matter on which the jurisdiction depends: *McC, Re*, above, fn.67, at 544; *Johnson v Meldon* (1890) 30 L.R.Ir. 15.

[71] [1975] Q.B. 118.

[72] Not being a trial on indictment, the court was not a court of record.

[73] The distinction between judges of the High Court and others seems to have been abandoned in the rarified context of a judge's compellability as a witness: *Warren v Warren* [1997] Q.B. 488.

[74] The award is made against the Crown: Human Rights Act 2000 s.9(4).

[75] Section 9. Proceedings may only be brought by exercising a right of appeal, by judicial review or in such other forum as may be prescribed by rules. However, the decision of an inferior court may be subject to judicial review and a claim for damages may be presented in an application for judicial review. It is not necessarily the case that an erroneous decision gives rise to a claim under art.5: *Benham v UK* (1996) 22 E.H.R.R. 293.

[76] *Hinds v Liverpool County Court* [2008] EWHC 665 (QB).

A. Other Exemptions Connected with the Administration of Justice

24–10   No action for negligence will lie in respect of the evidence of a witness or investigations carried out by a potential witness before any proceedings have been commenced, provided they are made or carried out for the purpose of possible proceedings[77] and there is not even a right of action for one who claims that he has suffered as a result of perjury by a witness.[78] Though the functions involved are not judicial and the decisions have no direct connection with the immunities considered here, it has also been held that a social security adjudicating officer[79] and an investigating officer under the police complaints procedure[80] owe no duty of care to the subjects of their adjudication or investigation. The principal reason is that there are statutory routes of appeal backed up by judicial review but in the case of the investigating officer there is the further reason, comparable to that for judicial immunity, namely the public interest in the "free and fearless" investigation of complaints. One of the torts most likely to be committed in the course of judicial proceedings is defamation and as we have seen,[81] the law casts the protection of absolute privilege over judges, advocates and witnesses.

B. Officers of the Law

24–11   An officer of the law who executes process apparently regular, without knowing in fact the person who authorised him to do so has exceeded his powers, is protected in spite of the proceedings being ill-founded.[82] Again by the Constables Protection Act 1750,[83] no action can be brought against a constable for anything done in obedience to any warrant[84] issued by a justice of the peace until the would-be claimant has made a written demand for a copy of the warrant and the demand has not been complied with for six days. If it is complied with, then the constable, if he produces the warrant at

---

[77] See para.5–60, above. A person who sets the law in motion may be liable for malicious prosecution: Ch.19, above. As to the former immunity of advocates, see para.5–60, above.

[78] *Hargreaves v Bretherton* [1959] 1 Q.B. 45; *Marrinan v Vibart* [1963] 1 Q.B. 234; cf. *Roy v Prior* [1971] A.C. 470.

[79] *Jones v Dept of Employment* [1989] Q.B. 1.

[80] *Calveley v CC Merseyside* [1989] A.C. 1228.

[81] See para.12–41, above. Proceedings of tribunals having essential characteristics similar to those of courts are treated in the same way and they should share the same immunity in respect of other torts. The Parole Board is treated as a judicial body for the purposes of the Human Rights Act 1998 in *R (Giles) v Parole Board* [2003] UKHL 42; [2004] 1 A.C. 1; but cf. *X v South Australia* [2007] SASC 125 (a tort case).

[82] *Sirros v Moore* [1975] Q.B. 118; *London (Mayor of) v Cox* (1867) L.R. 2 H.L. 239 at 269 per Willes J. For detention under a court order based on a mistaken view of the law, see para.4–19, above.

[83] Section 6.

[84] For arrest without warrant see para.4–24, above.

the trial of the action against him, is not liable in spite of any defect of jurisdiction in the justice. However, if he arrests a person not named in the warrant or seizes goods of one who is not mentioned in it, he does so at his peril. His mistake, however honest, will not excuse him. In *Hoye v Bush*[85] Richard Hoye was suspected of stealing a mare. A warrant was issued for his arrest, but it described him as "John Hoye", which in fact was his father's name. Richard was arrested under this warrant and subsequently sued Bush, the constable, for false imprisonment. Bush was held liable, for although Richard was the man who actually was wanted, still the warrant described somebody else and it did not help Bush that John Hoye was not really wanted.[86]

3. MINORS

After an early period of uncertainty, the common law adopted 21 years as the age of majority for most purposes,[87] and it remained at this until 1970, when it was reduced by statute to 18.[88] So far as the law of tort is concerned, only two questions arise concerning minors, namely their capacity to sue and to be sued for tort. **24–12**

A. Capacity to Sue: Unborn Children

In general no distinction falls to be taken between a minor and an adult so far as their respective capacities to sue for tort are concerned, save that a minor must sue by his "litigation friend".[89] **24–13**

That a child born with a disability as a result of injuries suffered while *en ventre sa mere* could sue,[90] even though before birth it was

---

[85] (1840) 1 M. & G. 775.
[86] Contrast *McGrath v CC, RUC* [2001] UKHL 39; [2001] 2 A.C. 731 (under s.38 of the Criminal Law Act 1977 arrest of C, who was named in the warrant, was lawful, even though the person wanted was X, who had given C's name). Both cases are consistent with a policy of requiring the constable to exercise the warrant at its face value. Contrast the matter of the *timing* of the execution of the warrant, where the constable may have a discretion: *Henderson v CC Cleveland* [2001] EWCA Civ 335; [2001] 1 W.L.R. 1103.
[87] Holdsworth, HEL iii, pp.510–511.
[88] Family Law Reform Act 1969 s.1.
[89] There is no bar to a child suing a parent: see below, and para.5–29, above. A number of claims have been brought against parents (as opposed to those having institutional care) for sexual abuse (see, e.g. *Stubbings v Webb* [1993] A.C. 498; *Pereira v Keleman* [1995] 1 F.L.R. 428) though for obvious reasons most of them have gone to the Criminal Injuries Compensation Board. On claims by parents wrongly suspected of abuse see para.5–53, above.
[90] It was held at an early date that a posthumous child of a deceased father could maintain an action under the Fatal Accidents Act: *The George and Richard* (1871) L.R. 3 Ad. & E. 466. Winfield thought that if a tort were committed before a child's birth to property to which he became entitled on birth, he could sue, but cf. para.5–40, above.

not a legal person, was put beyond doubt by the Congenital Disabilities (Civil Liability) Act 1976, which applies to all births on or after July 22 in that year. However, the Limitation Act allows claims by children to be brought many years after injury is suffered and the common law position was not finally determined in England[91] until 1992 when the Court of Appeal in *Burton v Islington Health Authority* held that an action lay.[92] It seems unlikely that an English court will have to grapple with questions such as how far an action lies against the mother,[93] or whether a claim might lie on behalf of a stillborn child since these issues are specifically dealt with by the Act and the common law is now a virtually obsolete category.[94] The principal provisions of the Act may be summarised as follows. In the first place, an action only lies if the child, the claimant, is born alive and disabled.[95] Secondly, the liability to the child is "derivative", in other words it only arises if the defendant was under an actual or potential tort liability[96] to either parent of the child for the act or omission which led to the disability, but for this purpose:

"[I]t is no answer [to a claim by the child] that there could not have been such liability because the parent suffered no actionable injury, if there was a breach of legal duty which, if accompanied by injury, would have given rise to the liability".[97]

In other words, if a pregnant woman takes a drug which has been manufactured or developed negligently or in circumstances which contravene the Consumer Protection Act 1987 and this causes her child to be born disabled, the child may recover damages from the manufacturer even though the mother suffers no injury herself from

---

[91] There were favourable decisions in the Commonwealth.
[92] [1993] Q.B. 204.
[93] See e.g. *Dobson v Dobson* [1999] 2 S.C.R 753. In *Preston v Chow* (2002) 211 D.L.R. (4th) 756, Man. CA, the defendants were sued for failing to prevent the claimant child becoming infected with genital herpes via the mother. The defendants' claim for contribution or indemnity against the mother because of her fault in engaging in unprotected sex failed because the mother could not have been liable to the child.
[94] No common law liability can arise in respect of births after the commencement of the Act: s.4(5).
[95] The mother may have an action in respect of a stillbirth: *Bagley v N Herts HA* (1986) 136 N.L.J. 1014. For definition of "disabled" see s.4(1). The damages referred to in s.4(4) for "loss of expectation of life" were abolished by the Administration of Justice Act 1982: para.22–19, above.
[96] This liability will commonly be for negligence, but there is nothing in the Act to confine it to this. Section 3 extends the provisions of the Nuclear Installations Act 1965 (para.15–24, above) to prenatal injury. The running of time against the parent is irrelevant: s.1(3) ("or would, if sued in time, have been so"). While the child's cause of action accrues upon birth (s.4(3)) the Limitation Act would prevent time running against him until he reached majority: para.26–17, below.
[97] Section 1(3).

the drug.[98] In practice the commonest situation giving rise to liability[99] is likely to be that where the child is injured during its mother's pregnancy but the Act extends more widely than this to cover an occurrence which affects either parent in his or her ability to bear a normal, healthy child,[100] so that, for example, a negligent injury to the mother's reproductive system before conception could found an action by a child conceived thereafter and born disabled as a result.[101] The mother herself is not generally liable under the Act so that there is no possibility of, say, an action being brought in respect of disabilities said to have caused by the mother smoking during pregnancy.[102] The good sense of this immunity is clear: not only is the possibility of liability revolting to normal feelings but there is a risk of the liability being used as a potent weapon in husband-wife disputes. The Law Commission thought that on balance the immunity should not be extended to the father, and the Act so provides, but the Pearson Commission disagreed and proposed an amendment on this point.[103] The policy arguments in favour of immunity are nothing like so strong when the potential parental liability would be covered by insurance[104] and s.2 of the Act accordingly provides that a woman driving a motor vehicle when she knows or ought to know herself to be pregnant is to be regarded as under a duty of care towards her unborn child.[105]

The derivative nature of the child's action in cases other than **24-14** those involving negligent driving by the mother is emphasised by the supplementary provisions of s.1, which "identify" the child with the parents for the purposes of defences. Thus, in the case of an occurrence preceding the time of conception, knowledge by either

---

[98] In many cases it would be impossible for the mother to suffer any physical injury from the drug and it then perhaps looks odd to say that there has been any breach of legal duty, but it is inconceivable that such a case falls outside the Act. Perhaps the possibility of psychiatric trauma to the mother may allay doubts on this point.

[99] This is not to suggest that it will be very common for the Act to be invoked at all. The Pearson Commission estimated that no more than 0.5 per cent of all severely disabled children would have grounds for claiming tort compensation. The British Medical Association said that: "the vast majority of congenital defects and diseases are of unknown causation and the number of instances which can be unequivocally ascribed to any particular act of omission or commission are few". See Cmnd. 7054, Vol.1, Ch.26 and Annexes 12 and 13.

[100] Section 1(2)(a).

[101] In this situation there is a high likelihood that the action could be met by the defence of knowledge of the risk by the mother: s.1(4).

[102] Proving cause and effect in an individual case might be impossible, anyway.

[103] Cmnd. 7034, Vol.1, para.1471.

[104] In form the claim is one against the parent, but most people would regard the "real" defendant as the insurer (cf. *Hunt v Severs*, para.22–37, above). Now in motor cases there is a direct right of action against the insurer: para.1–30, above. Under the present law, claims by children injured as passengers in cars negligently driven by parents are not uncommon.

[105] Should knowledge be required? Other drivers will have no means of knowing the mother is pregnant and it seems far-fetched to assume that the mother would desist from driving if she knew she was pregnant.

parent of the risk of disablement will bar the child's action[106]; where the parent affected shared responsibility for the child being born disabled, the child's damages are to be reduced according to the extent of the parent's responsibility[107]; and any contract term having the effect of excluding or restricting liability to the parent is equally effective in respect of liability to the child.[108]

Since the Act was passed there have been major developments in the treatment of infertility and the possibility arises of a disability being caused by some act or omission in the course of such treatment but which would not fall within s.1, for example during the keeping of the gametes or the embryo outside the body. Section 1A of the Act, inserted by s.44 of the Human Fertilisation and Embryology Act 1990, covers these cases and provides a virtual mirror image of s.1. So far we have been dealing with cases where, but for the defendant's wrongful act or omission, the claimant would have been born without the disability or with a lesser degree of it; but another situation presents much more acute legal problems, that is to say, where the claimant contends that he should never have been born at all, the so-called "wrongful life" case. Such a case could conceivably be advanced against a person responsible for the child's conception[109] but is more likely to arise from failure during the early stages of pregnancy to detect some deformity or disability which, if it had been detected, would have led to an abortion.[110] Such was one of the claims in *McKay v Essex Area Health Authority*,[111] decided at common law since the birth was before the 1976 Act. In striking out this claim, the court referred to various objections of a public policy nature (for example, the dangers of a legal assessment of the life of a handicapped child as less valuable than that of a "normal" child

---

[106] Section 1(4); but not where the father is responsible for the injury to the mother and she does not know of the risk. If a woman is the child's other parent, under the Human Fertilisation and Embryology Act 2008 she is treated in the same way as the father: s.1(4A).

[107] Section 1(7). Cf. a case under s.2, which would follow the normal rule of non-identification (para.6–51, above), allowing the child to recover in full against either defendant and consigning the final allocation of loss to contribution proceedings between the defendants. The effect of s.1(7) might be to raise by a side-wind the very issue of maternal responsibility which had prompted the grant of immunity to the mother. Accordingly, the Pearson Commission recommended its repeal: Cmnd. 7054, Vol.1, para.1477, but it would still be open to that defendant to allege that the injury was solely the mother's fault.

[108] Section 1(6). This provision is likely to be of very limited effect in view of the Unfair Contract Terms Act 1977 s.2(1) (para.25–6, below), and is anyway inapplicable to cases under the Consumer Protection Act 1987: see s.6(3)(c) of that Act.

[109] See, e.g. *Zepeda v Zepeda* 190 N.E. 2d 849 (1963).

[110] The risk of serious handicap is a ground for lawful abortion. Since the amendment of the Abortion Act 1967 by the Human Fertilisation and Embryology Act 1990 s.37, there is no specific time limit for these cases, nor is the Infant Life Preservation Act 1929 applicable (cf. *Rance v Mid-Downs HA* [1991] 1 Q.B. 587) but there might still be practical or medical grounds ruling out a late abortion.

[111] [1982] Q.B. 1166. An alternative basis of the case was unproblematical: that if the mother had received treatment the disability would have been less.

and the prospect of a claim against the mother where, informed of the danger, she declined to have an abortion) but that which most strongly influenced all the members of the court was the impossibility of assessing damages on any sensible basis, for the court would have to, "compare the state of the plaintiff with non-existence, of which the court can know nothing".[112] In so far as this might be taken to imply that such a comparison is impossible in all legal contexts[113] it may have been overtaken by *Re J*,[114] in which the Court of Appeal held that in extreme circumstances it could be lawful to withhold life-sustaining treatment because of the poor quality of the life the patient would have to endure. In other words, the law accepts that there are circumstances in which it is in a person's best interests to die. However, no doubt was cast on the correctness of *McKay*'s case: the fact that the court might be compelled to engage in a comparative balancing exercise on the treatment issue did not alter the fact that the problem of assessment of damages remained insuperable.[115]

The 1976 Act replaces:

> "[A]ny law in force before its passing, whereby a person could be liable to a child in respect of disabilities with which it might be born",

words which, it is thought, are wide enough to prevent any future cases at common law even in the unlikely event that the House of Lords were to overrule *McKay's* case and the limitation problems could be overcome. In *McKay* the Court of Appeal said, obiter, that no such claim could be made under the Act because it imports the assumption that but for the occurrence giving rise to the disabled birth, the child would have been born normal and healthy, not that it would not have been born at all. This is certainly true of

---

[112] [1982] Q.B. 1166 at 1193 per Griffiths L.J. Cf. *Cherry v Borsman* (1992) 94 D.L.R. (4th) 487 (attempted but unsuccessful abortion caused claimant's injuries).

[113] At the time of the case damages were recoverable in a fatal accident case by the estate of the victim for "loss of expectation of life", i.e. for the fact of death itself (these damages have now been abolished, see para.22–19, above). The court was in essence comparing life with death by setting a value on the former but the assumption was that the former was preferable to the latter in all cases and the claimant was hardly likely to challenge this. The problem of valuation was sidestepped by awarding a more or less fixed, conventional sum.

[114] [1991] Fam. 33; but cf. Ward L.J.'s view of this case in *A, Re* [2001] Fam. 147.

[115] That was also the view of the majority of the High Court of Australia in *Harriton v Stephens* [2006] HCA 15; 226 C.L.R. 52, which contains an exhaustive discussion. French law granted a claim to the child (the *Perruche* case, Cass., Ass. Plén., November 17, 2000, Bull. Ass. Plén., No.9). Legislative action to reverse this fell foul of art.1 of the First Protocol to the European Convention on Human Rights in *Draon v France* [2005] 3 F.C.R. 409.

s.1(2)(b),[116] which deals with the most obvious case, that where there is negligence towards the mother during pregnancy. However, no such assumption is expressly built into s.1(2)(a) dealing with pre-conception events, nor into the new s.1A. Indeed, one of the specified matters dealt with by the latter ("the selection . . . of the embryo . . . or of the gametes used to bring about the creation of the embryo") seems to point to a situation where the defect is already inherent in the "material" used. Nearly all the discussion in the English and American cases has been in terms of general damages. In some American cases damages have been allowed in respect of medical expenses caused by the disability[117] but in practice such claims are likely to be presented by parents, whose claims are clearly not affected by the 1976 Act. It is to claims of parents that we now turn.

24–15   From the mid-1980s the courts faced claims by parents (usually arising out of unsuccessful sterilisation operations) for the cost of upbringing of children. These were allowed, damages being based upon the parents' station in life and therefore sometimes amounting to very substantial sums. This line of cases was overturned by the House of Lords in *McFarlane v Tayside Health Board*.[118] The reasons were various: to award damages representing the cost of upbringing was disproportionate to the wrong committed (negligent advice to the father that his vasectomy had been successful); it would fail to take account of the real (though incalculable) counter-vailing benefits brought to the family by the birth of a healthy child, benefits which were still present even if the parents' intention had been to have no more children[119]; and it would offend against the

---

[116] "An occurrence . . . which . . . affected the mother . . . or the child . . . so that the child is born with disabilities which would not otherwise have been present."

[117] In *Turpin v Sortini* 182 Cal. Rptr. 337 (1981), the claimant's parents alleged that they would not have conceived her but for the negligence of the defendants in respect of the risk of the disability. The Supreme Court of California held that a claim by the claimant for medical expenses in treating her condition stated a cause of action but one for general damages did not. Suppose a doctor, dealing with a patient who may become pregnant, fails to advise her properly of the risk of medication to a foetus if she does become pregnant. The mother would otherwise have taken effective steps not to become pregnant or would have discontinued the treatment. Now the doctor has caused (at least in a factual sense) both the disability and the birth. The fact that recognising a duty to the child risks a conflict with the mother's health has been used to deny liability: *Lacroix v Dominique* [2001] MBCA 211; 202 D.L.R. (4th) 121; *Paxton v Ramji* [2008] ONCA 697; 299 D.L.R. (4th) 614. Again the argument can hardly be applied to the claim of a parent denied the freedom to make a decision.

[118] [2000] 2 A.C. 59. The majority of the High Court of Australia took a contrary view: *Cattanach v Melchior* [2003] HCA 38; 215 C.L.R. 1. The court was divided 4:3 and the differences between the members were profound. However, the effect of the decision has been reversed by statute in most states: see, e.g. Civil Liability Act 2002 (NSW) s.71.

[119] Hale L.J. in *Parkinson v St James Hospital Trust* [2001] EWCA Civ 530; [2002] Q.B. 266 at [87] said, referring to *Mcfarlane*, that, "at the heart of it all is the feeling that to compensate for the financial costs of bringing up a healthy child is a step too far."

idea of distributive justice, which in suitable cases had a role to play in the mosaic of tort law alongside the more usual corrective justice.[120] However, the mother was allowed to recover damages for the pain, suffering and inconvenience of pregnancy and birth and for the loss of earnings and expenses immediately attendant on those processes.[121] A little later in *Rees v Darlington Memorial Hospital NHS Trust*[122] the majority of a divided House of Lords modified the position somewhat by holding that it was necessary to do more to recognise that the mother in such a situation had suffered a legal wrong and an interference with her autonomy in being deprived of the freedom to limit her family as she wished and that this should take the form of an award of a conventional sum of damages[123]: £15,000 was awarded. This is a curious decision, which verges on judicial legislation. There have been other common law examples of such conventional awards, most notably the damages for loss of expectation of life which were formerly awarded in fatal accident cases[124] but the sum in *McFarlane* was substantially greater in real terms. Perhaps the closest analogy is the statutory sum (now £11,800) for bereavement.[125]

Where, in such cases the child is born with a serious disability, whether mental or physical, a parent may recover as damages the extra expenses of upbringing associated with that disability, over and above the costs attached to bringing up any child.[126] It may also happen that the child is normal but the mother's disability makes it more difficult and expensive for her to look after the child but in that case no damages are recoverable beyond those immediately associated with the birth and the conventional sum referred to above. Such a situation was what was in issue in *Rees v Darlington*, where the mother was blind and had sought sterilisation because of the burden motherhood would impose on her; but this did not justify a different result, for a balance sheet of benefit and detriment still could not be drawn up—just as the law could not distinguish between the impact of an "unwanted" child on wealthy parents and poor parents, so it could not distinguish between parents who were fit and well and those whose disability might cause them to incur

[120] See also *Frost v CC South Yorks* [1999] 2 A.C. 455, para.5–69, above.
[121] The mother's loss of earnings during the upbringing of the child is not recoverable: there is no material distinction between such loss and the expenses of upbringing: *Greenfield v Flather* [2001] EWCA Civ 113, [2001] 1 W.L.R. 179 (where an attempt to rely on art.8 of the European Convention on Human Rights was also rejected).
[122] [2003] UKHL 52; [2004] 1 A.C. 309.
[123] In *Rees* the mother was disabled (see below) but the proposition is plainly not confined to such cases.
[124] See para.22–19, above.
[125] See para.23–12, above.
[126] *Parkinson v St James Hospital Trust* [2001] EWCA Civ 530; [2002] Q.B. 266.

further expense.[127] Indeed, the correctness of the proposition that the "extra" cost of bringing up a disabled *child* is recoverable is a matter of controversy. In *Rees* Lord Scott said:

> "The possibility that a child may be born with a congenital abnormality is plainly present to some degree in the case of every pregnancy. But is that a sufficient reason for holding the negligent doctor liable for the extra costs, attributable to the abnormality, of rearing the child? In my opinion it is not. Foreseeability of a one in 200 to 400 chance does not seem to me, by itself, enough to make it reasonable to impose on the negligent doctor liability for these costs. It might be otherwise in a case where there had been particular reason to fear that if a child were conceived and born it might suffer from some inherited disability. And, particularly, it might be otherwise in a case where the very purpose of the sterilisation operation had been to protect against that fear. But on the facts of *Parkinson* I do not think the Court of Appeal's conclusion was consistent with *McFarlane*."[128]

B. Liability to be Sued

24–16   In the law of tort there is no defence of infancy as such and a minor is as much liable to be sued for his torts as is an adult. In *Gorely v Codd*,[129] Nield J. had no hesitation in holding that a boy of 16 had been negligent when he accidentally shot the claimant with an air rifle in the course of "larking about", and it is obvious that a motorist of $17\frac{1}{2}$ is as responsible for negligent driving as one six months older. However, where a minor is sued for negligence, his age is relevant in determining what he ought reasonably to have foreseen. In an action for negligence against a young child, therefore, it is insufficient to show that he behaved in a way which would amount to negligence on the part of an adult. It must be shown that his behaviour fell below the standard of an ordinarily reasonable and prudent child of his age[130] and even though one cannot fix the age precisely, it is obvious that a tiny infant cannot be liable in tort at all.

[127] In the earlier case of *A.D. v East Kent Community NHS Trust* [2002] EWCA Civ 1872; [2003] 3 All E.R. 1167 the court had dismissed a claim where the child was cared for by a relative of the disabled mother.
[128] At [147]; and Lord Bingham at [9] said that, "it is arguably anomalous that the defendant's liability should be related to a disability which the doctor's negligence did not cause and not to the birth which it did". Contra Lord Nicholls at [35] ("The legal policy on which *McFarlane* was based is critically dependent on the birth of a healthy and normal child."), Lord Hope at [57] and Lord Hutton at [91] (both dissenting on the main issue). Lord Millet at [112] left the point open.
[129] [1967] 1 W.L.R. 19; *Buckpitt v Oates* [1968] 1 All E.R. 1145 at 1149 per John Stephenson J.
[130] *Mullin v Richards* [1998] 1 W.L.R. 1304, adopting *McHale v Watson* (1966) 115 C.L.R. 199.

C. Tort and Contract

In general contracts entered into by minors are void and unen- **24–17**
forceable, and the question arises, therefore, whether if the facts
show both a breach of a (void) contract and a tort, the contract rule
can be evaded by framing the claim against the minor in tort. The
answer seems to be that a minor cannot be sued if the cause of action
against him arises substantially *ex contractu* or if to allow the action
would be to enforce the contract indirectly, but if the wrong is
independent of the contract, then the minor may be sued even
though but for the contract he would have had no opportunity of
committing the tort.[131] In *R. Leslie Ltd v Shiell*[132] a minor had
fraudulently represented to the claimants that he was of full age and
had thereby persuaded them to lend him money. He was held not
liable for deceit or on any other ground, for a judgment against him
would have amounted to the enforcement of the contract of loan in
a roundabout way. On the other hand, in *Burnard v Haggis*,[133] the
defendant, an undergraduate of Trinity College, Cambridge, and a
minor, was held liable in the following circumstances. He hired
from the claimant a mare for riding on the express stipulation that
she was not to be used for "jumping or larking". He nevertheless
lent the mare to a friend who, while they were galloping about fields
in the neighbourhood of Cambridge, tried to jump her over a fence,
on which she was staked and she died from the wound. The defendant's conduct was, as Willes J. said[134]:

> "[A]s much a trespass, notwithstanding the hiring for another
> purpose, as if, without any hiring at all, the defendant had gone
> into a field and taken the mare out and hunted her and killed her.
> It was a bare trespass, not within the object and purpose of the
> hiring. It was not even an excess. It was doing an act towards the
> mare which was altogether forbidden by the owner".[135]

If in *R. Leslie Ltd v Shiell* the minor had still been in possession of
the money lent equity would have ordered its restoration on the
ground of fraud. Now, under s.3(1) of the Minors' Contracts Act
1987 the court has a discretion to order the transfer back of any
property acquired under the contract (or its proceeds) even without
fraud, but if the money has been spent and there is nothing to show
for it, nothing can be done.

---

[131] Pollock, *Contract*, 13th edn, pp.62–63, approved by Kennedy L.J. in *R. Leslie Ltd v Shiell*
    [1914] 3 K.B. 607 at 620.
[132] Above, fn.131.
[133] (1863) 14 C.B.(N.S.) 45. Cf. *Jennings v Rundall* (1799) 8 T.R. 335; *Fawcett v Smethurst*
    (1915) 84 L.J.K.B. 473.
[134] (1863) 14 C.B. (N.S.) 45 at 53.
[135] See too *Ballett v Mingay* [1943] K.B. 281.

D. Liability of Parent

24–18   A parent or guardian[136] is not in general liable for the torts of a child[137] but to this there are two exceptions. First, where the child is employed by his parent and commits a tort in the course of his employment, the parent is vicariously responsible just as he would be for the tort of any other servant of his. Secondly, the parent will be liable if the child's tort is due to the parent's negligent control of the child in respect of the act that caused the injury,[138] or if the parent expressly authorised the commission of the tort, or possibly if he ratified the child's act. Thus, where a father gave his boy, about 15 years old, an airgun and allowed him to retain it after he had smashed a neighbour's window with it, he was held liable for the boy's tort in injuring the eye of another boy with the gun.[139] Where, however, a boy aged 13 had promised his father never to use his air rifle outside the house (where there was a cellar in which the rifle could be fired) and subsequently broke that promise, the Court of Appeal refused to disturb the trial judge's findings that the father had not been negligent.[140] Nor will he be liable to one who is bitten by a dog which belongs to his daughter who is old enough to be able to exercise control over it, and this is so even if the father knows of the dog's ferocious temper.[141] Where, however, the child is under the age of 16 a different rule prevails by statute.[142]

4. SPOUSES

24–19   It is now over 70 years since the abolition of the special rules governing a married woman's liability in tort and making her husband liable for her torts during marriage.[143] Suffice now to say that as far as third parties are concerned there are no special rules governing husband and wife and neither is liable for the other's

---

[136] Note in this connection that it has been said that school authorities are under no greater duty than that of a reasonably careful parent: *Ricketts v Erith BC* [1943] 2 All E.R. 629; *Rich v London CC* [1953] 1 W.L.R 895. However, while this may be true for ordinary supervision in the classroom, it seems unrealistic in modern conditions to apply it to, say, the organisation of a school trip.

[137] Such liability is common in Europe, e.g. in France and the Netherlands. Nor is it simply "vicarious". Thus under para.6–169 of the Dutch Civil Code a parent of a child under 14 is liable for an act of the child where, "but for the child's age, [it] could be imputed to him as an unlawful act". See Martin-Casals, *Children in Tort Law Part I: Children as Tortfeasors* (2006).

[138] If a juvenile court imposes a compensation order it is to be paid by the parent or guardian unless the court considers this unreasonable: see *T.A. v DPP* [1997] 2 F.L.R. 887.

[139] *Bebee v Sales* (1916) 32 T.L.R. 413; *Newton v Edgerley* [1959] 1 W.L.R. 1031.

[140] *Donaldson v McNiven* (1952) 96 S.J. 747.

[141] *North v Wood* [1914] 1 K.B. 629.

[142] See para.16–4, above.

[143] Law Reform (Married Women and Tortfeasors) Act 1935. For a summary of the common law see the 11th edn of this work.

torts, though he or she may of course be liable as a joint tortfeasor if this is in fact the case. As between themselves, the common law rule was that no action in tort was possible, but in modern times this was productive of serious anomalies and injustices[144] and it was abolished by the Law Reform (Husband and Wife) Act 1962.[145] Each of the parties to a marriage now has the same right of action in tort against the other as if they were not married,[146] but, in order to prevent them from using the court as a forum for trivial domestic disputes, the proceedings may be stayed if it appears that no substantial benefit will accrue to either party from their continuation.[147] The proceedings may also be stayed if it appears that the case can be more conveniently disposed of under s.17 of the Married Women's Property Act 1882, which provides a summary procedure for determining questions of title or possession of property between husband and wife.

5. CORPORATIONS

A corporation is an artificial person created by the law. It may come **24–20** into existence either by the common law, by royal charter, by Parliamentary authority, or by prescription or custom. Whatever their origin may be, the characteristics common to most corporations are a distinctive name, a common seal and perpetuity of existence. This existence is quite independent of the human beings who are members of the corporation. Fellows of a college and shareholders of a brewery company may perish, but the college and brewery company still continue.

A. Capacity to Sue in Tort

A corporation can sue for torts committed against it,[148] but there **24–21** are certain torts which, by their very nature, it is impossible to commit against a corporation, such as assault or false imprisonment. A corporation can sue for the malicious presentation of a winding-

---

[144] See Law Reform Committee, 9th Report, Cmnd. 1268 (1961).

[145] Section 1(1). In *Church v Church* (1983) 133 N.L.J. 317, £9,605 damages were awarded in an action for battery between spouses

[146] This means, of course, that even if proceedings are not brought against the spouse, a co-tortfeasor with him may have a right of contribution.

[147] Section 1(2)(a) (there are equivalent provisions for same-sex formalised relationships in s.69 of the Civil Partnership Act 2004). See *McLeod v McLeod* (1963) 113 L.J. 420. The Civil Procedure (Modification of Enactments) Order SI 1998/2940, para.4 repealed s.1(3), requiring the court to consider a stay at an early stage of the proceedings. However, s.1(2) remained untouched, so the power to order a stay still exists.

[148] *Semble*, even if engaged in an ultra vires undertaking at the material time: *National Telephone Co v Constable of St Peter Port* [1900] A.C. 317 at 321 per Lord Davey, obiter, a decision of the Privy Council on appeal from the Royal Court of Guernsey.

up petition[149] or for defamation, though the precise limits of the latter are unclear. It is certain that a trading corporation may sue in respect of defamation affecting its business or property,[150] and perhaps in respect of anything affecting its conduct of its affairs[151] but a governmental authority cannot sue for defamation.[152]

A rather different point is that the corporation (and not its members) is the only proper claimant in respect of a tort against the corporation. To some extent this is simply a reflection of the elementary principle that C cannot bring an action against D to recover damages for an injury done by D to A, C (the member) and A (the corporation) being different persons. A shareholder is not an owner of the company's assets but merely has a right to participate in them on winding up. So if the defendant infringes patents belonging to a company the company can sue but a shareholder cannot. The shareholder and the company may, of course, have separate and distinct claims arising out of the same conduct of the defendant. If D carelessly burns down the company premises and C, a shareholder who happens to be present at the time, is injured, the fact that the company has a claim for the cost of rebuilding does not affect C's claim for personal injuries. However, even though a tort has been committed against the shareholder, the loss suffered by him may be a diminution in the value of his shareholding and this is only a reflection of the loss to the company caused by the diminution of its assets. To allow both the company and the shareholder to sue would be to allow double recovery; to allow the shareholder to sue and then bar the company from further action would be to harm the company's creditors, for they are entitled to the company's assets in dissolution in priority to the shareholders and by allowing the shareholder to sue the company's assets would in effect be diminished. Hence English law does not allow such a "reflexive" claim. If the sole asset of a company is a box containing £100,000 and the claimant owns 99 of the 100 shares in the company he cannot sue the thief who appropriates the contexts of the box.[153] However, the same would be true in that example even if the contents were misappropriated by the thief fraudulently obtaining the key from C

[149] *Quartz Hill Consolidated Gold Mining v Eyre* (1883) 11 Q.B.D. 674.
[150] *Metropolitan Saloon Omnibus Co v Hawkins* (1859) 4 H. & N. 87; *Jameel v Wall Street Journal Europe Sprl* [2006] UKHL 44; [2007] 1 A.C. 359.
[151] *D.& L. Caterers Ltd v D'Ajou* [1945] K.B. 364; *National Union of General and Municipal Workers v Gillan* [1946] K.B. 81; *Willis v Brooks* [1947] 1 All E.R. 191; *South Hetton Coal Co Ltd v NE News Association Ltd* [1894] 1 Q.B. 133, though inconclusive on the point, seems to support this view. Dicta in *Manchester Corp v Williams* (1891) 63 L.T. 805 at 806 (the fuller report) and *Lewis v Daily Telegraph Ltd* [1964] A.C. 234 at 262, seems to support the narrower view.
[152] See para.12–18, above.
[153] This is so even if the company chooses not to sue. However, where a wrongdoer is in control of the company a shareholder may be able to bring a "derivative" action on behalf of the company, but this is not a personal claim.

and thereby committing an actionable wrong against him. C has still suffered no loss other than the diminution of the value of his shareholding in the company which will arise as a result of the loss of the company's assets.[154] If, on the other hand, the value of the shareholder's holding is diminished by a tort against him which is not actionable by the company there is nothing to prevent him suing for that loss.[155]

B. Liability to be Sued

It has always been generally accepted that a chartered corpora-   **24–22** tion[156] has all the powers of a natural person[157] but most companies were incorporated under statute and were expressly limited by the terms of their incorporation as to what they might lawfully do. While this is still true as far as the internal affairs of the company are concerned, s.39 of the Companies Act 2006 provides that:

> "[T]he validity of an act done by a company shall not be called into question on the ground of lack of capacity by reason of anything in the company's constitution".

This would seem to render otiose any distinction for the purposes of the law of torts between intra vires and ultra vires acts, though the distinction had in fact been largely effaced under the old law.[158] A company will be liable for the acts of its servant committed within the course of employment[159] (and where relevant in tort, for the acts of its agent within the scope of his authority[160]) and no doubt the objects for which the company was incorporated may be very relevant in determining the limits of the employment or authority of the servant or agent.[161] However, there are acts or omissions which, for the purposes of the law, are to be regarded as those of the company itself.

---

[154] *Johnson v Gore Wood & Co* [2001] 2 A.C. 1 (though there were some differences of opinion in the HL on what the law ought to be and Lord Cooke thought the rule was of narrower scope); *Prudential Assurance Co Ltd v Newman Industries Ltd (No.2)* [1982] Ch. 204. Cf. *Christensen v Scott* [1996] N.Z.L.R. 273). Where the claimant is sole owner of the company matters like loss of salary and pension or liability on guarantees may be affected by this principle: *Humberclyde Finance Group Ltd v Hicks*, November 14, 2001; *Rushmer v Smith* [2009] EWHC 94 (QB).

[155] *Lee v Sheard* [1956 1 Q.B. 192; *Fischer (George) GB Ltd v Multi-Construction Ltd* [1995] 1 B.C.L.C. 260; *Gerber Garment Technology Inc v Lectra Systems Ltd* [1997] R.P.C. 443.

[156] e.g. the older universities.

[157] *Case of Sutton's Hospital* (1613) 10 Co Rep. 23a.

[158] See the 13th edn of this work, p.675.

[159] See Ch.20, above.

[160] *New Zealand Guardian Trust Co Ltd v Brooks* [1995] 1 W.L.R. 96 (directors).

[161] Under the Companies Act 2006 s.40 (originating in 1989), "in favour of a person dealing with a company in good faith, the power of the board of directors to bind the company, or authorise others to do so, is deemed to be free of any limitation under the company's constitution".

Thus it may incur a personal liability when it fails to take reasonable care for the safety of persons even if no allegation of negligence is made against any individual servant of the company[162] and it has been held, where a liability depended upon the "actual fault or privity" of the company, that this condition was satisfied if the persons who constituted the "directing mind" of the company were at fault, for the act or omission was then that of the company itself.[163] The metaphor of the "directing mind" does not, however, mean that there is a particular person or group of persons whose acts are to be regarded as those "of the company" for all purposes[164] for this question depends on the purpose for which it is sought to attribute the acts of a human being to the company, which will generally be a matter of statutory construction.[165] Thus in *The Lady Gwendolen*[166] the question was whether a collision at sea was with the "actual fault or privity" of brewers (a minor part of whose business was owning ships to carry their product to England), so that the claimants might escape the limitation of liability generally granted by statute to shipowners.[167] For this purpose the inaction of the director who had supervision of the transport department was attributed to the brewers, but his acts and omissions would not have had this effect if the matter had been one outside his supervision under the company's organisation.[168] Contrariwise, the purpose of the statutory rule might lead to the conclusion that the act of someone well below board level should be attributed to the company.

Under this principle of "attribution" there is no legal difficulty in finding company liable for deceit, even though it obviously has no natural capacity to be dishonest.[169] So in *Stone & Rolls Ltd v Moore Stephens*[170] it was uncontroversial that the company was liable to a bank where its sole executive director and presumed sole beneficial owner used it as a vehicle of fraud to extract money from the bank. What provoked disagreement in the House of Lords was the question whether the director's act was also to be regarded as the company's act so as to prevent it, on the basis of ex turpi causa non

---

[162] See para.8–9, above.

[163] *Lennard's Carrying Co Ltd v Asiatic Petroleum Co Ltd* [1915] A.C. 705; *The Lady Gwendolen* [1965] P294 (limitation provisions in merchant shipping legislation).

[164] Though for practical purposes this may be true of a resolution of the board or of a meeting of the company.

[165] See *Meridian Global Funds Management Asia Ltd v Securities Commission* [1995] 2 A.C. 500.

[166] [1965] p.294.

[167] The current legislation, the Merchant Shipping Act 1995, adopts a different test for breaking limitation.

[168] These questions are less important in the context of tort than they are in crime, because vicarious liability is more extensive in the former.

[169] Or for battery: *KR v Royal & Sun Alliance Plc* [2006] EWCA Civ 1454; [2007] P.I.Q.R. P14 (where the question arose from an exclusion in a liability insurance policy in respect of the assured's deliberate acts).

[170] [2009] UKHL 39; [2009] 3 W.L.R. 455.

oritur actio,[171] suing its auditors for failure to discover the fraud, to which the majority answered that it did.[172]

In modern conditions a business may be carried on by a group of companies, perhaps in the form of a holding company with subsidiaries in many different jurisdictions. In principle these are as much separate entities as the companies and their shareholders and directors[173] and one is not liable for the acts of another. However, where one company in the group is involved in the management of another it may owe a duty of care to persons (for example workers or consumers) affected by the activities of the other.[174]

C. Liability of Directors[175]

As a company is a separate legal person its directors are not, apart from statute, personally liable on contracts made by the company, nor for torts of company servants for which the company is vicariously liable. To identify the director with the company would be too great a brake on commercial enterprise and adventure, however small the company and however powerful the control of the director. Nevertheless, where directors order an act by the company which amounts to a tort they may be liable as joint tortfeasors on the ground that they have procured the wrong to be done.[176] Where the tort in question requires a particular state of mind the director must have that, but there is no general principle that a director must know that the act is tortious or be reckless as to that.[177] If a company servant were to trespass on the claimant's land believing it to belong to the company that would be trespass and there is no reason why a director who, with the same state of mind, instructed him to do the act should escape liability. The director is also, of course liable if he

24–23

---

[171] See para.25–18, below.

[172] Cf. *Safeway Stores Ltd v Twigger* [2010] EWHC 11 (Comm) (not directing mind).

[173] See below.

[174] See *C.S.R. Ltd v Wren* (1997) 44 N.S.W.L.R. 463; *James Hardie & Co v Hall* (1998) 43 N.S.W.L.R. 554. Such an issue underlay *Lubbe v Cape Plc* [2000] 1 W.L.R. 1545 but the only point before the HL was whether England was a proper forum.

[175] For a very full examination of the authorities see *Johnson Mathey (Aust) Ltd v Dacorp Pty Ltd* [2003] VSC 291; 9 V.R. 171.

[176] See, e.g. *Mancetter Developments Ltd v Germanson Ltd* [1986] Q.B. 1212 (waste); *Global Crossing Ltd v Global Crossing Ltd* [2006] EWHC 2043 (Ch) (incorporation of company, trade mark infringement). A company and its directors may be conspirators: para.18–25, above; but if C makes a contract with the D Co and the directors resolve not to perform it, C cannot sue them for inducing breach of contract: para.18–6, above. It has been said that there is a general principle that a director will not be liable in tort if he does no more than carry out his constitutional function in governing the company by voting at board meetings: *MCA Records v Charly Records* [2001] EWCA Civ 1441; [2002] F.S.R. 26 at [49]; applied, *Società Esplosivi Industriali v Ordnance Technologies (UK)* [2007] EWHC 2875; [2008] R.P.C. 12.

[177] *C. Evans & Sons Ltd v Spriteband Ltd* [1985] 1 W.L.R. 317. *Johnson Mathey (Aust) Ltd v Dacorp Pty Ltd*, above, fn.175 (conversion). *Joiner v George* [2002] EWHC 90 (Ch) turns on the way the case was pleaded and perhaps on the erroneous view of the CA in *Standard Chartered Bank*, below, fn.178.

commits the tort himself. In some cases company law will regard an act of the directors as an act of the company itself. If the director of a company were to assault the director of a rival business in the course of a dispute about sales that could hardly be regarded as an assault by the company and any liability of the company would have to be truly vicarious, that is to say for the director qua employee. On the other hand, if the board of a company were to induce someone to make a contract by fraudulent misrepresentation that would be a fraud by the company. However, that fact does not mean that the individual directors are not also liable.

"No one can escape liability for his fraud by saying: 'I wish to make it clear that I am committing this fraud on behalf of someone else and I am not to be personally liable.'"[178]

In such a case the director would not be liable for the company's fraud but for his own fraud, as indeed would a non-director employee who participated.[179]

As far as negligence is concerned, it has been held that a director may be liable as a joint tortfeasor with the company when he sends a vessel to sea in an unseaworthy condition causing personal injury[180] but a liberal approach to director's liability will have the effect that the limited liability which is the main object of incorporation for a small, "one man" company will be set at naught. In *Williams v Natural Life Health Foods Ltd*[181] the House of Lords held that to justify liability of a director for advice there must be some special facts showing a personal assumption of responsibility,[182] which the court declined to find in the combination of the active part which the director played in preparing the financial projection in question and the representation in the company's brochure that the company's expertise in the trade was based upon the director's experience gained in a personal capacity independent of the company. There were no exchanges between the director and

[178] *Standard Chartered Bank v Pakistan National Shipping (Nos 2 and 4)* [2002] UKHL 43; [2003] 1 A.C. 959 at [22].
[179] "The maxim *culpa tenet suos auctores* may not be the end, but it is the beginning of wisdom in these matters": [2002] UKHL 43; [2003] 1 A.C. 959 at [40] per Lord Rodger. "Attribution provides a basis for imposing liability on a company, not conferring an immunity on an individual": *Body Corporate 202254 v Taylor* [2008] NZCA 317; [2009] 2 N.Z.L.R. 17 at [30]
[180] *Yuille v B.&B. Fisheries (Leigh) Ltd* [1958] 2 Lloyd's Rep. 596. It is usually regarded as self-evident that a servant whose negligence in the course of employment causes personal injury is personally liable even though the employer is vicariously liable.
[181] [1998] 1 W.L.R. 830.
[182] Cf. *Standard Chartered Bank*, above, fn.178, a case of deceit, which is not based on a duty of care.

the claimants which could have led them reasonably to believe that he was assuming a personal responsibility to them.[183]

6. PARTNERS

In English law a partnership is not a legal person distinct from its members and consequently has no capacity to sue or be sued,[184] but each partner is liable jointly and severally with his co-partners for any wrongful act or omission committed by any of them against an outsider while acting in the ordinary course of business of the firm.[185] If a partner in a firm of solicitors were to commit fraudulent misrepresentations in the course of persuading someone to buy double glazing the other partners would not be liable for that because selling double glazing is not within the description of activities which a solicitors' firm ordinarily carries out.[186] Even where the transaction is one within that general description it may be that its details are so unusual that it is not within the ordinary course of business[187] but the mere fact that the partner intends to behave dishonestly does not take it outside the scope of vicarious liability.[188] The Limited Liability Partnerships Act 2000 introduced a new form of legal entity known as a limited liability partnership, which is a body corporate (with legal personality separate from that of its members and with unlimited capacity) and which is formed by being incorporated under the Act.

24–24

7. CLUBS[189]

In the case of proprietary and incorporated clubs, it would seem that the ordinary rules as to the liability of employer or principal for the

24–25

---

[183] Cf. *Merrett v Babb* [2001] EWCA Civ 214; [2001] 3 W.L.R. 1, para.11–22, above (employee). The root of the problem is of course our readiness to accept concurrent liability in contract and tort. Cf. *Trevor Ivory Ltd v Anderson* [1992] 2 N.Z.L.R. 517, where the director of a small company was held not liable for advice. *Fairline Shipping Corp v Adamson* [1975] Q.B. 180 is perhaps a rather clearer case for liability.

[184] The partners may sue or be sued in the name of the firm: CPR r.5A.3.

[185] Partnership Act 1890 ss.10 and 12. See *Dubai Aluminium Co Ltd v Salaam* [2002] UKHL 48; [2003] 2 A.C. 366. The partners may, of course, also be liable for the torts of their servants or agents under ordinary principles: see, e.g. *Lloyd v Grace, Smith & Co* [1912] A.C. 716.

[186] *J.J. Coughlan Ltd v Ruparelia* [2003] EWCA Civ 1057; [2004] P.N.L.R. 4 at [25].

[187] *J.J. Coughlan Ltd*, above, fn.186.

[188] See *Dubai Aluminium Co Ltd v Salaam*, above, fn.185, especially at [120].

[189] Lloyd (1953) 16 M.L.R. 359. For the position of trade unions, see para.18–35, above.

torts of his servants or agents apply.[190] In the case of an unin-corporated club, which is not an entity known to the law and which cannot be sued in its own name, liability involves a question of substantive law and one of procedure. The first question is, who is liable for the wrongful act or breach of duty?[191] This depends on the circumstances of the particular case, and it may be the members of the committee, or someone such as a steward who is in control of the club or possibly the whole body of members. Membership of the club and even membership of the committee does not involve any special duty of care towards other members of the club nor, it seems, towards a stranger but neither is it a ground of immunity for one who has assumed a responsibility.[192] So, members of the committee (at the time when the cause of action arose) will be liable personally to the exclusion of other members, if they act personally, as by employing an incompetent person to erect a stand as the result of which a stranger is injured.[193] In the case of torts involving vicarious liability, apart from the actual wrongdoer's liability, the question depends upon whose servant or agent the wrongdoer was at the material time.[194] Where liability arises out of the ownership or occupation of property, as in nuisance or under the Occupiers' Liability Act 1957, the occupiers of the premises in question will normally be the proper persons to sue. If the property is vested in trustees they may be the proper persons to sue, but in the absence of trustees it is a question of fact as to who are the occupiers of the premises.[195] As to the procedural point, the need for a representative action only arises where it is desired to sue the whole body of members, and a representation order may be made, provided that the members whose names appear on the writ are persons who may fairly be taken to represent the body of club members and that they

---

[190] Halsbury, *Laws of England*, 5th edn (2009), Vol.136; for different kinds of clubs, see para.204. In a proprietary club the property and funds of the club belong to a proprie-tor, who may sue or be sued in his own name or in the name of the club. The members are in contractual relation with the proprietor, and have a right to use the club premises in accordance with the rules, but they are not his servants or agents. An incorporated club may sue or be sued in its corporate name. An unincorporated members' club has no legal existence apart from its members, who are jointly entitled to the property and funds, though usually the property is vested in trustees. It cannot sue or be sued in the club name, nor can the secretary or any other officer sue or be sued on behalf of the club.

[191] For an extensive review (in the context of the Roman Catholic Church in Australia) see *Trustees of the Roman Catholic Church v Ellis* [2007] NSWCA 117.

[192] *Prole v Allen* [1950] 1 All E.R. 476; *Shore v Ministry of Works* [1950] 2 All E.R. 228 ; *Jones v Northampton BC, The Independent*, May 25, 1990; *Grice v Stourport Tennis etc. Club*, February 28, 1997, CA cf. *Robertson v Ridley* [1989] 2 All E.R. 474.

[193] Halsbury, *Laws of England*, above, para.231; *Brown v Lewis* (1896) 12 T.L.R. 445; *Bradley Egg Farm Ltd v Clifford* [1943] 2 All E.R. 378.

[194] Lloyd, above, fn.189, p.359.

[195] Lloyd, above, fn.189, p.360.

and all the other club members have the same interest in the action.[196]

8. PERSONS OF UNSOUND MIND

There is singularly little English authority as to the liability[197] of **24–26** persons of unsound mind for torts committed by them.[198] Sir Matthew Hale thought that dementia was one of several other forms of incapacity which might exempt a person from criminal liability, but which ordinarily do not excuse him from civil liability, for that, "is not by way of penalty, but a satisfaction of damage done to the party"[199] and there are dicta in the older cases which regard lunacy as no defence.[200] More to the purpose is a dictum of Lord Esher M.R., in 1892,[201] that a mentally disordered person is liable unless the disease of his mind is so great that he cannot understand the nature and consequences of his act. In *Morriss v Marsden*[202] the defendant, who attacked and seriously injured the claimant, had been found unfit to plead in earlier criminal proceedings. He was then sued by the claimant for damages for assault and battery. Stable J. found that the defendant's mind was so disturbed by his disease that he did not know that what he was doing was wrong, but that the assault was a voluntary act on his part and that the defendant was therefore liable.

Unsoundness of mind is thus certainly not in itself a ground of immunity from liability in tort, and it is submitted that the true question in each case is whether the defendant was possessed of the requisite state of mind for liability in the particular tort with which he is charged. In trespass to the person it is enough that the defendant intended to strike the claimant and the defendant in *Morriss v Marsden* was therefore rightly held liable but had his disease been so severe that his act was not a voluntary one at all he would not

---

[196] *Campbell v Thompson* [1953] 1 Q.B. 445. See Lloyd, above, fn.189, pp.360–363 and CPR r.19.6. A representation order may also be made in favour of persons as claimants.

[197] A person suffering from mental disorder has the capacity to sue in respect of a tort against him, proceedings being conducted by his litigation friend. However, a claim in respect of action taken under the Mental Health Act 1983 will only lie if the act was done, "in bad faith or without reasonable care" and leave of the High Court is required. See *Winch v Jones* [1986] Q.B. 296; *Johnston v CC Merseyside* [2009] EWHC 2969 (QB). See also para.4–9, above.

[198] See Fridman, "Mental Incompetency" (1963) 79 L.Q.R. 502 (1964) 80 L.Q.R. 84.

[199] 1 *History of Pleas of Crown* (ed. 1778), pp.15–16. So too, in effect Bacon (Spedding's edition of his works, vii, 348).

[200] e.g. *Weaver v Ward* (1616) Hob. 134.

[201] *Hanbury v Hanbury* (1892) 8 T.L.R. 559 at 569. Cf. *Mordaunt v Mordaunt* (1870) L.R. 2 P. & D. 103 at 142 per Kelly C.B.

[202] [1952] 1 All E.R. 925. *Morriss v Marsden* was followed in *Phillips v Soloway* (1957) 6 D.L.R. (2d) 570 and in *Beals v Hayward* [1960] N.Z.L.R. 131. See also *Squittieri v De Sautis* (1976) 75 D.L.R. (3d) 629; *Att Gen v Connolly* (1993) 64 D.L.R. (4th) 84.

have been liable.[203] In defamation it is enough that the defendant published matter defamatory of the claimant and it would certainly be no defence that in his disturbed mental state he believed it to be true. Again, as Stable J. said:

> "I cannot think that, if a person of unsound mind converts my property under a delusion that he is entitled to do it or that it was not property at all, that affords a defence."[204]

The tort of negligence probably creates the greatest difficulty. The standard of negligence is said to eliminate the individual character-istics of the defendant,[205] but this does not mean, for example, that a driver who suffers a sudden, unexpected[206] and disabling illness is liable for the damage he does: even the reasonable man can have a heart attack.[207] No English court appears to have been required to deal in this context with what might be called "unsoundness of mind" in the generally accepted sense but there have been cases of inability to drive caused by a hypoglycaemic episode. In *Mansfield v Weetabix Ltd*[208] the Court of Appeal held that the defendants were not liable when their driver had a crash caused by such an episode, of the onset of which he was unaware. There was no requirement of a "sudden, disabling event" and it was wrong to bring in the criminal law test of automatism.[209] The position is still unclear where the defendant is fully conscious and has the physical capacity to control his vehicle but is suffering from an insane delusion, for example that the vehicle is subject to external control.[210] Where there is likely to be liability insurance it is perhaps tempting to judge the defendant's behaviour purely objectively, but to do that would invite the application of the same standard to a driver who was stung by a bee or who suffered a heart attack, and that would sever all

---

[203] [1952] 1 All E.R. at 927 per Stable J. See also *Carrier v Bonham* [2000] Q.D.C. 226 (District Court).

[204] [1952] 1 All E.R. 927.

[205] See para.5–75, above.

[206] This is important, because if he has reason to believe that he will have an attack he may be negligent in setting out: *Jones v Dennison* [1971] R.T.R. 174.

[207] See *Waugh v James K. Allan Ltd* [1964] 2 Lloyd's Rep. 1. In *Morriss v Marsden*, above, fn.202, at 927, Stable J. said, "If a sleepwalker, without intention or without carelessness, broke a valuable vase, that would not be actionable." His Lordship thus evidently contemplated negligent and non-negligent sleepwalkers as legal possibilities.

[208] [1998] 1 W.L.R. 1263.

[209] *Roberts v Ramsbottom* [1980] 1 W.L.R. 823 was said to be wrong in this respect, though the decision is correct on the basis that the defendant should have been aware of his unfitness to drive before he lost control of the vehicle.

[210] In *Fiala v Cechmanek* (2001) 201 D.L.R. (4th) 680 the Alberta CA declined to impose negligence liability where the defendant could show that he did not understand what he was doing or lacked the capacity to control his actions. See also *Buckley v Smith Transport Ltd* (1946) 3 D.L.R. 721 and *Adamson v Motor Vehicle Insurance Trust* (1957) 58 W.A.L.R. 56. In *Att Gen v Connolly*, fn.202, above, the somewhat curious conclusion was that the defendant was liable for battery but not for negligence.

connection between negligence in name and negligence in reality.[211]

9. Persons having Parental or Quasi-Parental Authority

Parents and other persons in similar positions are necessarily **24–27** immune against liability for many acts which in other people would be assault, battery or false imprisonment. They have control, usually but not necessarily, of a disciplinary character, over those committed to their charge. The nature of the control varies according to the relationship and, provided that it is exercised reasonably and moderately,[212] acts done in pursuance of it are not tortious. By s.58(3) of the Children Act 2004 it is specifically provided that an act causing actual bodily harm (i.e. something which is more than temporary and trifling) cannot be justified.

Parental authority[213] certainly ceases when the child attains 18 years, but is a dwindling right as the child approaches adulthood and for this purpose may well cease at an earlier age.[214] Quasi-parental authority is exemplified by the control of schoolteachers over pupils.

At common law a schoolteacher had power to discipline pupils **24–28** and this probably rested upon the need to maintain order and discipline at the school,[215] so that a parental veto upon corporal punishment would not render its use unlawful.[216] However, by statute corporal punishment is no longer a defence to a civil action against a school, whether state or independent, even where the parent authorises the school to administer it.[217] It remains the law, however, that reasonable force may be used to avert personal injury or damage to property: that is not "punishment".

---

[211] The *Restatement of Torts* 3d in §11 makes an allowance for physical disability but not for mental or emotional disability because it would be "one-sided" to do so. Unlike the physically disabled person, one subject to mental disability cannot take extra precautions to counter the disability. See also *Carrier v Bonham*, fn.203, above.

[212] *R. v H* [2001] EWCA Crim 1024; [2002] 1 Cr.App.R. 7.

[213] The rights, duties and authority of father and mother of a legitimate child are equal: Children Act 1989 s.2.

[214] *Gillick v West Norfolk AHA* [1986] A.C. 112. See *R. v Rahman* (1985) 81 Cr.App.R. 349 (false imprisonment).

[215] Disciplinary powers are not necessarily confined to conduct on school premises: *Cleery v Booth* [1893] 1 Q.B. 465; *R. v Newport (Salop) JJ.* [1929] 2 K.B. 416.

[216] Cf. the decision of the European Court of Human Rights (*Campbell and Cosans v UK* (1982) 4 E.H.R.R.) that the European Convention on Human Rights is violated where a school administers corporal punishment against the wishes of parents.

[217] Education Act 1996 s.548, as amended. This does not conflict with the European Convention on Human Rights, one cannot apply *Campbell and Cosans* (above, fn.216) in reverse: *R. (Williamson) v Secretary of State for Education etc.* [2005] UKHL 15; [2005] 2 A.C. 246. It was once the law that a husband might beat his wife moderately as a mode of correction or confine her. Those rights are wholly obsolete. It was once said: "For that is a poynt of an honest man, For to bete his wife well nowe and than." *Johan Johan* (one of Heywood's Comedies, circa 1533). For ships' masters see the 15th edn of this book, p.842.

CHAPTER 25

DEFENCES

A CLAIMANT who fails to prove the necessary ingredients of the **25–1** particular tort or torts on which he relies will, of course, fail in his action. Even if he does prove these ingredients, however, he may still fail if the defendant shows that he is entitled to rely upon some specific defence. Some of these defences are peculiar to particular torts, as is justification to the tort of defamation, and these have been noted in their appropriate chapters. We must now consider those defences which apply more generally throughout the law of tort.[1]

1. CONSENT. VOLENTI NON FIT INJURIA

There are many occasions on which harm—sometimes grievous **25–2** harm—may be inflicted on a person for which he has no remedy in tort, because he consented, or at least assented, to the doing of the

---

[1] Winfield described these as "conditions which in general negative liability".

act which caused his harm.[2] Simple examples are the injuries received in the course of a lawful game or sport, or in a lawful surgical operation. The effect of such consent or assent is commonly expressed in the maxim volenti non fit injuria, which is certainly of respectable antiquity. The idea underlying it has been traced as far back as Aristotle,[3] and it was also recognised in the works of the classical Roman jurists,[4] and in the canon law. In English law, Bracton in his *De Legibus Angliae* (c. AD 1250–1258) uses the maxim, though not with the technicality that attached to it later,[5] and in a Year Book case of 1305 it appears worded exactly as it is now.[6] So far as actual citation of the maxim goes, most of the modern cases use it in connection with harm to the person rather than to property. The explanation seems to be that if the assent is to the infliction of harm on, or at any rate to, the use of the claimant's property, such assent is more usually styled leave and licence of the claimant, but this phrase expresses much the same idea.[7]

Though the terminology in the case law is by no means consistent, "consent" is normally the expression used in relation to intentional torts and volenti non fit injuria in relation to negligence, though the modern "voluntary assumption of risk" is now perhaps more popular.[8]

A. Consent and Intentional Torts

25–3   A fair blow in a boxing match, an inoculation, a welcome embrace are not torts, because the claimant consents to them. Consent is commonly spoken of as a defence but in the case of trespass to the person this may not be quite accurate because a defence is something which it is incumbent on the defendant to plead and prove and it has been held in England[9] (though not in Canada[10]) that

---

[2] "One who has invited or assented to an act being done towards him cannot, when he suffers from it, complaint of it as a wrong": *Smith v Baker* [1891] A.C. 325 at 360 per Lord Herschell.

[3] T Beven in *Journal of Comparative Legislation* (1907), p.185 Ingman [1981] J.R. 1.

[4] Dig. 47, 10.1.5: "*nulla injuria est quae in volentem fiat*". See, too Dig. 9.2.7.4: 50.17.203.

[5] Ed. Woodbine (1942) Vol.4, p.286: "*cum volenti et scienti non fiat injuria*".

[6] 33–5 Edw. 1 (Rolls Series), 9 Hunt *arguendo*, "*volenti non fit injuria*".

[7] e.g. *Park v Jobson & Son* [1945] 1 All E.R. 222. Cf. *Armstrong v Sheppard and Short Ltd* [1959] 2 Q.B. 384.

[8] Nothing turns on the terminology. Thus where an intentional act is not imminent but there is only a risk of it, it is natural to speak of voluntary assumption (or acceptance) of risk: *Arthur v Anker* [1997] Q.B. 564; *Vine v Waltham Forest LBC* [2000] 1 W.L.R. 2383 (notices warning of wheel-clamping). Or one may say "consent to the risk": *Blake v Galloway* [2004] EWCA Civ 814; [2004] 1 W.L.R. 2844 at [24].

[9] *Christopherson v Bare* (1848) 11 Q.B. 473 at 477; *Freeman v Home Office (No.2)* [1984] Q.B. 524 at 539. So also in New Zealand: *H. v R.* [1996] 1 N.Z.L.R. 299.

[10] *Non-Marine Underwriters, Lloyd's of London v Scalera* [2000] SCC 24; [2000] 1 S.C.R. 551. This is probably also the law in Australia: *Secretary, Dept of Health etc. v J.W.B.* (1992) 106 A.L.R. 385 at 453.

it is for the claimant to prove absence of consent: because an assault must be something against the will of the person assaulted, it cannot be said that a person can be assaulted by his permission.[11] As a practical matter, however, the defendant may need to lead evidence to lay a foundation from which the court will infer consent and in modern pleading he would have to raise consent as a specific issue in his defence to the particulars of claim.[12] In this sense, therefore, it may be proper to refer to it as a "defence".

It is clear that consent may be implied from conduct as well as expressed in words so that the defendant escapes liability if he was justified in inferring that the claimant consented even though, secretly, he did not.[13] The very acts of taking part in a boxing match or presenting one's arm for injection,[14] for example, clearly convey consent.[15] The consent, however, must be freely given so that one obtained by wrongful threats sufficient to overbear the claimant's will would not be effective.[16] We have already seen that an adult of full understanding may choose whether or not to receive medical treatment even if the treatment is necessary to save his life and we have considered the capacity of minors and mentally disordered persons to give consent.[17]

B. "Informed" Consent

Consent to one medical procedure does not justify another, as **25–4** where a condition is discovered and treated for mere convenience during the authorised treatment of another condition[18] or where an operation authorised by patient A is performed on patient B by

---

[11] In old pleading terminology, consent could be raised by a plea of "not guilty" to the general issue.

[12] As was, indeed, done in *Freeman v Home Office*, above, fn.9. See [1984] Q.B. 524, 548. Under CPR r.16.5(2) a defendant who denies an allegation must state his reasons for doing so and if he intends to put forward a different version of events from that given by the claimant, he must state his own version.

[13] In the criminal law the issue of the defendant's belief in the victim's consent on a charge of rape was subjective. Now, however, under s.1 of the Sexual Offences Act 2003, a defendant is guilty even if he believes there is consent where his belief is unreasonable.

[14] However, where non-trivial medical procedures are involved it is customary to require the patient to sign a consent form.

[15] Cf. *Freeman v Home Office (No.2)* above, fn.9, at 557, where Sir John Donaldson M.R. suggests that "consent" applies if the claimant does consent, but volenti non fit injuria applies if he does not consent but so conducts himself as to lead the defendant to believe that he does.

[16] Obviously, a threat might vitiate the will of a child but not of an adult. *Latter v Braddell* (1881) 50 L.J.Q.B. 448 seems unduly narrow in insisting on threats of violence.

[17] See para.4–9, above.

[18] The terms of the consent may authorise such further treatment as the doctor considers necessary or desirable. For consideration of this, see *Brushett v Cowan* (1990) 69 D.L.R. (4th) 743.

mistake.[19] However, so long as the patient understands the broad
nature of what is to be done, his consent is not vitiated by failure to
explain the risks inherent in the procedure,[20] for it would be deplor-
able to deal with such cases under the rubric of trespass to the
person.[21] In this sense English law does not require "informed
consent". However, going beyond the basic duty to give sufficient
information to enable understanding of the nature of the treatment,
there is a further duty, sounding in negligence, to explain the
procedure and its implications in the way a careful and responsible
doctor would do. It is important to note that, in common with other
issues of professional negligence,[22] the test is not what risks would
appear material to a prudent patient but what is the normal practice
of the medical profession or, where opinion is divided, the practice
of a respectable section of the profession—the so-called *Bolam*
test.[23] Since the consequence of a failure to perform the duty to warn
of risks is that the claimant may succeed, even though the operation
has been carried out with all due care and skill, if he can show that
he would not[24] have consented[25] had a proper explanation been
given, the House of Lords in *Sidaway's* case clearly feared the
growth of a new category of medical litigation and of yet more
defensive medicine by way of detailed explanations which would
probably be beyond the comprehension of most patients. However,
though the court will pay great deference to medical practice, the
medical profession is not the final arbiter of what patients should be
told: it seems that if a patient asks a specific question he is entitled

---

[19] *Chatterton v Gerson* [1981] Q.B. 432.

[20] Cf. *Canterbury v Spence* (1972) 464 F.2d 772.

[21] *Chatterton v Gerson* [1981] Q.B. 432; *Hills v Potter* [1984] 1 W.L.R. 641; *Sidaway v
Bethlehem Royal Hospital* [1985] A.C. 871; *Reibl v Hughes* (1981) 114 D.L.R. (3d) 1
(Sup. Ct. of Canada). Cf. Tan, "Failure of Medical Advice: Trespass or Negligence?"
(1987) 7 L.S. 149. If there is no consent, the defendant's act is actionable even if the
claimant would have consented if he had been aware of the truth.

[22] See para.5–81, above.

[23] *Sidaway v Bethlehem Royal Hospital* [1985] A.C. 871. Named after *Bolam v Friern
Hospital Management Committee* [1957] 1 W.L.R. 582, para.5–81, above. Teff, "Consent
to Medical Procedures" (1985) 101 L.Q.R. 432; Brazier, "Patient Autonomy and Consent
to Treatment" (1987) 7 L.S. 169. There is no distinction for this purpose between
therapeutic and non-therapeutic contexts: *Gold v Haringey HA* [1987] 32 W.L.R. 649.

[24] For the position where the patient would or might have undergone the procedure on
another occasion see para.6–12, above.

[25] However, the court must be alive to the risk of self-serving (albeit honest) testimony from
the patient. Also in favour of the "subjective" test of causation, *Rosenberg v Percival*
[2001] HCA 18; (2001) 178 A.L.R. 577. In *Reibl v Hughes* (1981) 114 D.L.R. (3d) 1 the
Supreme Court of Canada adopted the test of what a reasonable person would have done,
but on any view a pure "but-for" causation would be unsuitable. If the defendant fails to
inform the patient of highly significant risk A and what occurs is injury from risk B which
the defendant could legitimately omit to mention, he should not be liable. Cf. *Banque
Bruxelles Lambert SA v Eagle Star Insurance Co Ltd* [1997] A.C. 191, para.6–27,
above.

to an adequate answer[26] and in the last resort it is the court, not the profession, that sets the standards. As Lord Bridge said:

"[E]ven in a case where . . . no expert witness . . . condemns the non-disclosure as being in conflict with accepted and responsible medical practice . . . the judge might in certain circumstances come to the conclusion that disclosure of a particular risk was so obviously necessary to an informed choice on the part of the patient that no reasonably prudent medical man would fail to make it."[27]

The High Court of Australia declined to follow *Sidaway* in *Rogers v Whittaker*[28] and rejected the *Bolam* approach as being relevant to treatment but not to information or advice. In the High Court's view the correct principle is that a doctor has a duty to warn a patient of a material risk inherent in treatment and a risk is material if, in the circumstances of the case, a reasonable person in the patient's position, if warned of the risk, would be likely to attach significance to it, or if the doctor should be aware that the particular patient would attach significance to it. At the end of the day the choice of the correct approach is a matter of degree rather than a choice between absolutes: no one suggests that a patient should be told nothing even if he asks, nor that a patient should be given a course of medical lectures on his condition, but the Australian view leans more heavily towards patient autonomy than the practice of the profession.

C. Vitiating Factors

What if consent to what would otherwise be a trespass is obtained **25-5** by fraud? Or if the actor fails to disclose some fact (for example that he has a contagious disease) which would have led to the other party to withhold consent? The view long prevailed that the consent was valid so long as the claimant was aware of the essential nature of the act done (which includes the identity of the actor, where that is relevant). Thus if, as happened in one criminal case, the defendant

---

[26] [1985] A.C. 871 at 898, 895, 901; *Pearce v United Bristol Healthcare NHS Trust* (1998) 48 B.M.L.R. 118; the patient cannot expect all the information at the doctor's disposal and therapeutic discretion must have a part to play even in responding to a direct question: see *Blyth v Bloomsbury AHA, The Times*, February 11, 1987.
[27] At 900; *Pearce v United Bristol Healthcare NHS Trust*, above, fn.26. See also *Bolitho v City and Hackney HA* [1998] A.C. 232, dealing with treatment, para.5–81, above. In *Chester v Afshar* [2004] UKHL 41; [2005] 1 A.C. 345 a duty to warn of a 1 or 2 per cent risk in spinal surgery was not contested. On comparative risks of different procedures see *Birch v University College etc NHS Foundation Trust* [2008] EWHC 2237 (QB).
[28] (1992) 175 C.L.R. 479. This has survived recent statutory restrictions on tort liability (para.1–44, above). See, e.g. Civil Liability Act 2002 s.5P (NSW); Wrongs Act 1958 s.60 (Vic).

took liberties with the naive claimant, falsely representing that he was performing a procedure to improve her voice,[29] that would be battery on this approach, but not if the defendant persuaded the claimant to have intercourse with him by falsely representing that he was free from disease.[30] However, in *R. v Dica*[31] it was held that if a person had sexual intercourse knowing he was HIV positive and concealed that fact and the partner contracted the condition, the former would be guilty of inflicting grievous bodily harm under s.20 of the Offences against the Person Act 1861. It would be surprising if the same conduct were not now civilly actionable (though not necessarily as battery[32]). On the other hand, if D induces C to have intercourse with him by falsely[33] promising money or by falsely promising to marry her, or by representing that he is married to her, it is thought that this should be no more battery than it is rape.[34] In such cases there might of course be liability for deceit.[35] In *R. v Richardson*[36] a criminal conviction for assault was quashed when the defendant continued to treat patients after her suspension from dental practice and it is thought that the result should have been the same in a civil action for battery.[37] On the other hand, it was held in *Appleton v Garrett* at first instance that a dentist was liable for trespass to the person when he undertook extravagant and wholly unjustified work on patients' teeth,[38] which might possibly be supported by saying that on the facts what the claimants consented to was treatment that was reasonably necessary.

The criminal law places limits on the effectiveness of consent when the public interest so requires. Thus fighting (otherwise than in

---

[29] *R v Williams* [1923] 1 K.B. 340.

[30] In *Hegarty v Shine* (1878) 14 Cox CC 145 the defendant concealed his disease when he had intercourse with the claimant but the case was partly decided on the basis that the claim was barred by ex turpi causa non oritur actio, which can hardly be the law today: para.25–18, below.

[31] [2004] EWCA Crim 1103; [2004] Q.B. 1257.

[32] The difficulty is that complainants' consent was valid for the purposes of a charge of rape and, it seems, of other charges requiring an assault (s.20 does not so require). The conclusive presumptions relating to consent in s.76 of the Sexual Offences Act 2003 (rape and kindred offences) speak of the nature and *purpose* of the act.

[33] i.e. having no intention of fulfilling the promise at the time it is made.

[34] *R. v Linekar* [1995] Q.B. 250, where the court applied the "nature of the act/identity of the actor" test; and see *R. v Harvinder Singh Jheeta* [2007] EWCA Crim 1609; [2008] 1 W.L.R. 2582 under the 2003 Act. "The most heartless bigamist has not been considered guilty of rape": *Papadimitropoulos v R.* (1957) 98 C.L.R. 249 at 260.

[35] As in *Graham v Saville* [1945] 2 D.L.R. 489 (bigamy); and see *P v B (paternity: damages for deceit)* [2001] 1 F.L.R. 1041.

[36] [1999] Q.B. 444. Cf. *R. v Tabassum* [2002] 2 Cr. App. R. 328, where D had no medical qualifications at all.

[37] Though the judgment seems to suggest otherwise. No doubt it is correct to say that the failure to disclose the suspension might found a civil claim (at 450) but that would most obviously be under *Sidaway* and if there were no ill effects from the treatment it is not obvious what the damage would be.

[38] (1995) 34 B.M.L.R. 32. The issue arose because the claimants sought aggravated damages.

the course of properly conducted sport) is unlawful if bodily harm is intended or caused, notwithstanding the consent of the participants,[39] as are activities likely to cause harm in the course of sado-masochistic sexual encounters.[40] However, it seems that in such a case the consent may still be effective to bar a civil claim.[41] So, for example, it is a criminal offence to have intercourse with a girl aged 15 even if she has the practical capacity to consent and does so, but it is hard to believe that where this is the case her partner commits battery. One case took a different line where the claim arose out of sexual abuse by a foster parent[42] but that could be justified on the basis that public policy requires the consent to be ignored, even in a civil action, where one person is in a position of dominance and influence over another. In any event there may be other circumstances where an unlawful fight can give rise to a civil action. In *Lane v Holloway*,[43] after a verbal altercation, the elderly claimant struck the young defendant on the shoulder and the defendant replied with an extremely severe blow to the claimant's eye. The claimant recovered damages,[44] for although each party to a fight takes the risk of incidental injuries the claimant had not consented to the risk of a savage blow out of all proportion to the occasion.

D. Negligence: Exclusion of Liability and Volenti Non Fit Injuria

i. **Express exclusion of liability.** Since, on one view at least, **25–6** volenti is based upon an agreement between the claimant and the defendant that the former shall run the risk of the latter's negligence, it seems sensible to start with those cases where there is an express provision to that effect, even though most of them are probably correctly regarded as examples of a separate defence of exclusion of liability or disclaimer.[45]

---

[39] *Att Gen's Reference (No.6 of 1980)* [1981] Q.B. 715.
[40] *R. v Brown* [1994] 1 A.C. 212; *Laskey, Jaggard and Brown v UK* (1997) 24 E.H.R.R. 39, ECHR; but consent to run the risk of infection with HIV from sexual intercourse is valid: *R v Dica* [2004] EWCA Crim 1103; [2004] Q.B. 1257.
[41] *Murphy v Culhane* [1977] Q.B. 94.
[42] *M (M) v K (K)* (1989) 61 D.L.R. (4th) 392.
[43] [1968] 1 Q.B. 379.
[44] Although the Law Reform (Contributory Negligence) Act 1945 probably applies to intentional trespass to the person the disproportion between the conduct of the two parties in *Lane v Holloway* prevented any reduction of the damages: see *Murphy v Culhane*, above, fn.41. See, too, *Barnes v Nayer, The Times*, December 19, 1986 (insufficient provocation for murderous attack with machete).
[45] Such cases are distinguished from volenti proper by Lord Denning M.R. in *Barnett v British Waterways Board* [1973] 1 W.L.R. 700. It is also implicit in the Unfair Contract Terms Act 1977 s.2(3), that the defences are separate.

At common law, in the absence of duress or some other vitiating factor, entry into a contract which exempted the defendant from liability for negligence was a complete defence and the same attitude was adopted where the claimant entered another's land by licence subject to a condition exempting the occupier from liability.[46] For this purpose the question was not whether the claimant did in fact agree to run the risk of negligence, but whether the defendant had given sufficient notice to make the excluding term part of the contract or licence: if he had done so, the claimant was bound even though he might not have troubled to read the terms and hence was unaware of the excluding one. This remains the basic rule, but in most cases it is now heavily qualified by the Unfair Contract Terms Act 1977. Where the defendant acts in the course of a business[47] or occupies premises for business purposes[48] he cannot, by reference to any contract term or notice,[49] exclude or restrict his liability for death or personal injury resulting from negligence,[50] and in the case of other loss or damage caused by negligence can only exclude or restrict his liability in so far as the term in the contract or notice is reasonable.[51] It is also provided that:

> "[W]here a contract term or a notice purports to exclude or restrict liability for negligence a person's agreement to or awareness of it is not of itself to be taken as indicating his voluntary acceptance of any risk."[52]

The implication of this is that the defence of volenti non fit injuria is still available, but it remains to be seen what evidence of voluntary acceptance of the risk beyond the making of the agreement (which is not enough)[53] will be required. In 1993 the Council of the EC issued a Directive on Unfair Terms in Consumer Contracts,[54] which is now in England given effect by the Unfair Terms in

---

[46] Similarly, where a person accepted a lift in a car which carried a prominent notice that passengers travelled at their own risk, he could not sue the driver for negligence: *Buckpitt v Oates* [1968] 1 All E.R. 1145. Such notices became ineffective as a result of the Road Traffic Act 1972 s.148(3) (now the Road Traffic Act 1988 s.149(3)). Disclaimers in relation to the giving of advice are discussed, para.11–30, above.

[47] Which, "includes a profession and the activities of any government department or local or public authority": s.14.

[48] Section 1(3). For a modification of this restriction in relation to premises, see para.9–19, above.

[49] Which, "includes an announcement, whether or not in writing, and any other communication or pretended communication".

[50] Section 2(1).

[51] Section 2(2).

[52] Section 2(3).

[53] In *Johnstone v Bloomsbury HA* [1992] Q.B. 333 the CA held that an agreement to work excessive hours might be construed as an "express assumption of risk" and might arguably be subject to s.2(1) of the 1977 Act.

[54] Directive 93/13 [1993] O.J. L95/29.

Consumer Contracts Regulations 1999.[55] These are mainly concerned with matters of pure contract, but they cover terms excluding
or limiting the legal liability of a seller of goods or supplier of
services in the event of the death of a consumer or personal injury
resulting from an act or omission of the seller or supplier. Though
other parts of the Directive go considerably further than the Unfair
Contract Terms Act, this particular provision adds nothing to what
is already contained in s.2 of the Act. In fact, it does not go so far,
since such a term is prima facie unfair but not automatically void.

The defendant sometimes seeks to shelter behind an excluding **25–7**
term which is not in a contract between him and the claimant but
between the claimant and a third party (as where a stevedore claims
the protection of a provision limiting liability in a contract of
carriage by sea made between the carrier and the consignor or
consignee of the cargo). Details of this must be sought in works on
the law of contract but the courts have generally insisted that the
defendant be able to show contractual privity between himself and
the claimant if he is to succeed in relying on the term.[56] However,
in *Norwich CC v Harvey*[57] a building was damaged by fire as the
result of the negligence of a sub-contractor. The main contract
between the building owner and the head contractor provided that
the former should bear the risk of loss by fire and the Court of
Appeal concluded that this was a reason for denying any duty of
care in respect of the fire between the sub-contractor and the building owner. Unfortunately, the contract cases are not referred to in
Harvey, so it is difficult to say how far it extends beyond the context
of building contracts. However, in many cases a person will now be
able to shelter under an exclusion clause in someone else's contract
by virtue of the Contracts (Rights of Third Parties) Act 1999. The
conditions are (a) that the contract expressly provides that he may
rely upon the term in question *or* that it purports to confer a benefit
on him[58] and (b) that he is expressly identified in the contract by
name or by reference to a class or by description.[59]

---

[55] SI 1999/2083.

[56] Though in *New Zealand Shipping Co Ltd v A.M. Satterthwaite & Co Ltd* [1975] A.C. 154
the Privy Council made it fairly easy to establish such privity in the stevedore situation.
The court declined to express an opinion on the, "argument that, quite apart from contract,
exemptions from, or limitations of, liability in tort may be conferred by mere consent on
the part of the party who may be injured". See also *The Mahkutai* [1996] A.C. 650.

[57] [1989] 1 All E.R. 1180, distinguished in *British Telecommunications v James Thomson &
Sons (Engineers)* [1999] 1 W.L.R. 9.

[58] However, in the latter case it is open to the contracting parties to provide that the third
party may not enforce the term. This is not subject to the Unfair Contract Terms Act
1977.

[59] See s.1. The Act is of course primarily concerned with the enforcement of "positive"
benefits by the third party, e.g. a promise between A and B to pay money to C. The
provisions on the "negative" benefit of an exclusion clause are in fact rather wider than
in the other case: s.6(5).

25–8 **ii. Implied assumption of risk.** If the circumstances warrant the inference that the claimant has voluntarily assumed the risk of the defendant's negligence he cannot sue—volenti non fit injuria. That, at least, is a commonly accepted view, but we should note at the outset that there is some disagreement about the nature and scope of this defence in the context of negligence. It is clear that there are cases in which, in a sense, the claimant has assumed a risk but in which it is unnecessary (indeed improper) to call in aid the defence to explain why the defendant is not liable. If, for example, I undertake to repair the roof of your house and while doing so I fall off and injure myself, the reason I cannot sue you is not that I have consented to the risk of injury but that you did not in the first place owe me any duty to instruct me on how to go safely about my task.[60] To take this further, suppose that a spectator at a cricket match is struck and injured by a ball which the batsman, having little control of precisely where it will land, has hit as hard as he can. Most lawyers would agree that the claimant has no claim against the batsman and some might say that this was because the spectator had agreed to assume the risks of cricket. However, Diplock L.J. in *Wooldridge v Sumner*[61] was of the view that in such a case the claim would fail not because of volenti but because the conduct was not, in the circumstances of the case, negligent.

> "The matter has to be looked at from the point of view of the reasonable spectator as well as the reasonable participant not because of the maxim volenti non fit injuria, but because what a reasonable spectator would expect a participant to do without regarding it as blameworthy is as relevant to what is reasonable care as what a reasonable participant would think was blameworthy conduct in himself . . . A reasonable spectator attending voluntarily to witness any game or competition knows, and presumably desires, that a reasonable participant will concentrate his attention on winning, and if the game or competition is a fast-moving one will have to exercise his judgment and attempt to exert his skill in what, in the analogous context of contributory negligence, is sometimes called 'the agony of the moment'. If the participant does so [act] . . . in circumstances of this kind which are inherent in the game or competition in which he is taking part, the question whether any mistake he makes amounts to a failure to take reasonable care must take account of those circumstances."[62]

---

[60] See the Occupiers' Liability Act 1957 s.2(3)(b), para.9–12, above.
[61] [1963] 2 Q.B. 43.
[62] [1963] 2 Q.B. 43 at 66.

Of course, it might be said that it is still the spectator's voluntary decision to attend which lies at the root of the failure of his claim (after all, the batsman would plainly be liable if he took his bat and ball into the High Street and performed the same feat[63]) but even this does not seem to be correct, at least in a case of this type: the answer would plainly be the same if the person struck were a reluctant child dragged along to the game by a parent or even one who was too young to understand the risk.[64] Diplock L.J. went so far as to say that:

"[T]he maxim in the absence of expressed contract has no application to negligence simpliciter where the duty of care is based solely upon proximity or 'neighbourship' in the Atkinian sense."[65]

There are even some cases in which the claimant voluntarily encounters a hazard which the defendant has already created which could be handled without reference to a separate concept of volenti. For example, suppose the operator of a roller coaster is in breach of his duty to his customers to maintain the safety bars on the cars in proper condition but the claimant, instead of falling from the car, takes advantage of the defective bar to leap out and commit suicide. In order to hold the defendant not liable[66] one might simply say that the claimant's own conduct was the sole effective cause of his death—a novus actus interveniens. Neither approach leads to this result, of course, if one has decided in the circumstances that the defendant owes the claimant a duty to protect him against the risk of self-harm. In *Reeves v Metropolitan Police Commissioner*[67] the deceased committed suicide while in police custody, the subsequent litigation by his dependant being fought on the basis of two assumptions or concessions: first, that he was not suffering from any mental disorder such as to render him irresponsible[68] and secondly, that the police owed him a duty of care to protect him against the suicide risk. Given the second point a majority of the Court of Appeal held

---

[63] Cf. *Bolton v Stone*, para.5–84, above, where P was injured outside the ground by activity inside the ground.

[64] As appears to have been the case in *Murray v Harringay Arena Ltd* [1951] 2 K.B. 529.

[65] [1963] 2 Q.B. at 69. As between the claimant and the organisers of the game or as between one participant and another, his Lordship regarded the matter as resting on an implied term in the relationship between them, e.g. that, "the occupier need take no precautions to protect the invitee from all or from particular kinds of risks incidental to the game or competition which the spectator has come on the premises to watch." In *Murray v Harringay Arena*, above, fn.64, the action was against the occupier and the court seems to have regarded the six-year-old claimant as a party to a contract. Sed quaere.

[66] It is assumed that, unlike in the case of *Reeves v MPC*, below, the operator's duty does not extend to guarding against suicide.

[67] [2000] 1 A.C. 360.

[68] Cf. *Kirkham v CC Greater Manchester* [1990] 2 Q.B. 283.

that it was impossible to apply volenti because that would "empty the duty of meaningful content"[69] and the same went for the causation argument.[70] Volenti was not pursued as an independent issue by the defence in the House of Lords, it being accepted that if they failed on causation (which they did) they failed on the other defence, too—a concession which the majority of the court clearly thought correct.[71] However, there are other cases where, if the desired end is to reach a conclusion adverse to the claimant, it would be difficult to do so on the basis of causation, as where the claimant embarks in a light aircraft with a pilot whom he knows to be incompetent through drink.[72] In such a situation it seems natural to say that the claimant fails simply because he consents to run the risk of injury[73] and thereby waives any right to sue the defendant.[74]

E. Is an "Agreement" Necessary?

25–9 In *Nettleship v Weston*, Lord Denning M.R. speaking of a case where an amateur instructor embarked on a lesson with a learner driver, said that:

> "[N]othing will suffice short of an agreement to waive any claim for negligence. The plaintiff must agree, expressly or impliedly, to waive any claim for any injury that may befall him due to the lack of reasonable care by the defendant: or more accurately, due to the failure of the defendant to measure up to the standard of care that the law requires of him."[75]

However, on the assumption, which is implicit in the context, that what is meant is a bilateral agreement between claimant and defendant, it is very difficult to reconcile with the case law without resort

---

[69] [1999] Q.B. 169 at 197 per Lord Bingham C.J.

[70] On causation see further, para.6–41, above.

[71] Or there might be a case in which volenti would be inapplicable but the claim would fail on causation grounds. In *Calvert v William Hill Credit Ltd* [2008] EWCA Civ 1427; [2009] Ch. 330 D had undertaken to prevent C making telephone bets with them, but the evidence showed that even if they had performed this he would have ruined himself by betting with others.

[72] *Morris v Murray* [1991] 2 Q.B. 6. In the more obvious example of taking a lift with a drunken driver the defence is now precluded by statute: para.25–10, below.

[73] Suppose the claimant is suicidal and hopes there will be a crash. The terminology of "assumption of risk" is then artificial, but, "a person who is *volens* as to the actual harm he intentionally does to himself is manifestly an *a fortiori case*, indeed the paradigm case, of this defence, though for obvious reasons it rarely comes to court": Weir, [1998] C.L.J. 241, commenting on *Reeves v MPC* in the CA.

[74] Compare the judgment of Salmon L.J. in *Nettleship v Weston* [1971] 2 Q.B. 691 at 704, dealing with the incompetent driver, where he took the view that the passenger's knowledge could prevent him asserting that the driver owed him any duty to drive carefully. In *Morris v Murray*, above, fn.72, at 15 Fox L.J. thought there was not much difference between this and the "waiver" approach.

[75] [1971] 2 Q.B. 691 at 701.

to fiction, because the parties typically give no thought to the matter. The requirement of agreement meant that on the facts volenti could not be found in getting into a vehicle as instructor of a driver known to be completely inexperienced, though since a contract is not necessary it is not clear why such a situation should not give rise to an implied agreement.[76] Certainly volenti has been found on the basis of no more promising material. In *Imperial Chemical Industries Ltd v Shatwell*[77] the claimant and his brother, James, decided to disregard the employers' clear safety instructions and also certain statutory duties imposed directly on them. In the result an explosion occurred which injured the claimant and he sought to hold the employers vicariously liable for James' negligence and breach of statutory duty. Had the claimant been working alone, the accident would have been entirely his own fault[78] and he would have failed on that ground, but there was no doubt on the facts that it was at least partly James' fault. The House of Lords held that the defence of volenti would have been available to James if he had been sued, and therefore that the defendants were not vicariously liable. The claimant had consented to the very conduct which had caused his injury and, moreover, had fully appreciated the risk of injury to himself by explosion which it entailed. Furthermore, there are certainly cases in which volenti has been regarded as applicable even though there has been no communication or even opportunity of communication between the parties and which therefore support the view that it is the claimant's consent to run a risk rather than agreement, that is at the basis of the defence. So in *Titchener v British Railways Board*[79] the House of Lords assumed that volenti could be applicable to a case where the claimant is injured while crossing the defendant's property by an activity carried out thereon.[80]

Nettleship v Weston was a case of a passenger in a vehicle, a situation which was also involved in the controversial case of *Dann v Hamilton*,[81] where Asquith J. rejected the defence against a claimant who had taken a lift with a driver who was, to her knowledge, the worse for drink, though he left open the possibility that volenti might operate where the drunkenness was so extreme that to accept

25–10

---

[76] Putting aside the fact that now statute covers the field: see below. For Salmon L.J. the critical factor was the parties' prior conversation about insurance cover, which rebutted the inference of volenti. While Lord Denning M.R. refers to this, he implies that volenti should be inapplicable to the non-professional instructor in the absence of an express agreement.

[77] [1965] A.C. 656.

[78] See para.7–16, above.

[79] [1983] 1 W.L.R. 1427.

[80] See also *Ratcliffe v McConnell* [1999] 1 W.L.R. 670.

[81] [1939] 1 K.B. 509. Cf. *Insurance Comr v Joyce* (1948) 77 C.L.R. 39.

a lift was like "meddling with a bomb".[82] Now, however, s.149 of the Road Traffic Act 1988 provides that where a person uses a motor vehicle in circumstances in which liability insurance is required (and this includes liability to passengers) then:

"[A]ny antecedent agreement or understanding between them (whether intended to be legally binding or not) shall be of no effect in so far as it purports or might be held—

(a) to negative or restrict any such liability of the user in respect of persons carried in or upon the vehicle as is required . . . to be covered by a policy of insurance, or

(b) to impose any such conditions with respect to the enforcement of any such liability of the user."

It is further provided that:

"[T]he fact that a person so carried has willingly accepted as his the risk of negligence on the part of the user shall not be treated as negativing any such liability of the user."

It is now plain that this section is not confined to an express agreement or notice, but extends to the case where volenti arises from an inference of consent drawn from the circumstances rather than any agreement or notice. In *Pitts v Hunt*[83] Beldam L.J. put it:

"[I]t is no longer open to the driver of a motor vehicle to say that the fact of his passenger travelling in a vehicle in circumstances in which for one reason or another it could be said that he had willingly accepted a risk of negligence on the driver's part, relieves him of liability for such negligence."

The Act, however, has no effect on illegality,[84] nor on the contributory negligence which would almost inevitably arise from travelling with a drunken driver.[85]

The 1988 Act is inapplicable to aircraft, boats and other means of transport. In *Morris v Murray*[86] the claimant accompanied the

---

[82] Asquith J. made it plain, extra-judicially, that there was no plea of contributory negligence (at that time a complete defence): (1953) 69 L.Q.R. 317.

[83] [1991] 1 Q.B. 24.

[84] See para.25–18, below.

[85] See, e.g. *Owens v Brimmell* [1977] Q.B. 859, but it would be difficult to describe the conduct of a professional driving instructor in embarking on a course of lessons with a new driver (as opposed to mishandling them) as "contributory negligence".

[86] [1991] 2 Q.B. 6.

defendant on a flight in the defendant's light aircraft after an after-noon's drinking in which the defendant had consumed the equiva-lent of more than half a bottle of whisky. Piloting an aircraft is a far more complex and demanding task than driving a car and the risks of misjudgment are correspondingly greater. The Court of Appeal held that the defence of volenti was made out, distinguishing *Dann v Hamilton* on the basis that the activity was so inherently dangerous that it was like Asquith J.'s example of tampering with a bomb.

F. Knowledge does not Necessarily Imply Assent

The claimant must have information that indicates, at least in a **25–11** general way, the risk of injury from the defendant's negligence. The mere fact that he is aware that the activity in which he participates carries risks does not mean that he has licensed the defendant to be negligent[87]: the knowledge that aircraft sometimes crash does not make out a case of volenti non fit injuria where the claimant has no reason to know of any defect in the plane or the pilot. So, for example, in *Slater v Clay Cross Co Ltd*, where the claimant was lawfully walking along a narrow tunnel on a railway track owned and occupied by the defendants where she was struck and injured by a passing train owing to the negligence of the driver, Denning L.J. said:

"It seems to me that when this lady walked in the tunnel, though it may be said that she voluntarily took the risk of danger from the running of the railway in the ordinary and accustomed way, nevertheless she did not take the risk of negligence by the driver."[88]

The requirement of knowledge may mean that, paradoxically, the claimant who is completely drunk is in a better position than one who is sober.[89] However, provided he has the capacity to understand the risk it does not matter that the alcohol he has taken makes him more willing to take risks than he would normally be, nor even, perhaps, that he gives no thought to the risk.[90] However, the maxim

---

[87] Legislation in all Australian states now provides that a person cannot sue in respect of the materialisation of an obvious risk of a dangerous recreational activity whether or not he was aware of the risk (see, e.g. ss.5K and 5L of the Civil Liability Act 2002 (NSW). This is not easy to interpret: *Fallas v Mourlas* [2006] NSWCA 32; 65 N.S.W.L.R. 418.

[88] [1956] 2 Q.B. 264 at 271.

[89] The account of the facts of *Pitts v Hunt* [1991] 1 Q.B. 302 in the judgment of Beldam L.J. can be taken as indicating that the claimant was too drunk to realise that the defendant was unfit to drive, but the facts relevant to volenti are not fully examined in view of the court's conclusion that the defence was excluded by the Road Traffic Act.

[90] The last point is not entirely clear, given the limited extent to which the issue was covered in argument in *Morris v Murray*, above, fn.72. See also *Bennett v Tugwell* [1971] 2 Q.B. 267 at 273.

is volenti non fit injuria, not scienti non fit injuria, and it does not follow that a person assents to a risk merely because he knows of it. The most conspicuous illustrations of this have occurred in cases of harm sustained by workers in the course of their employment. Until the latter half of the 19th century, very little attention was paid by the law to the safety of manual labourers, and several of the decisions on volenti non fit injuria went near to holding that knowledge of risk in the employment invariably implied assent to it. Protective legislation began to make notable headway from about 1860 onwards, and, quite apart from legislation, the courts, beginning with the judgment of Bowen L.J. in *Thomas v Quartermaine*,[91] declined to identify, as a matter of course, knowledge of a risk with acceptance of it.

This doctrine was driven home by the House of Lords in *Smith v Baker*,[92] where it was held that volenti non fit injuria had no application to harm sustained by a workman from the negligence of his employers in not warning him of the moment of a recurring danger, although the man knew and understood that he personally ran risk of injury if and when the danger did recur. He worked in a cutting on the top of which a crane often jibbed (i.e. swung) heavy stones over his head while he was drilling the rock face in the cutting. Both he and his employers knew that there was a risk of the stones falling, but no warning was given to him of the moment at which any particular jibbing commenced. A stone from the crane fell upon and injured him. The House of Lords held that the defendants were liable. Lord Herschell admitted that:

"Where a person undertakes to do work which is intrinsically dangerous, notwithstanding that reasonable care has been taken to render it as little dangerous as possible, he no doubt voluntarily subjects himself to the risks inevitably accompanying it, and cannot, if he suffers, be permitted to complain that a wrong has been done to him, even though the cause from which he suffers might give to others a right of action";

but he added:

"[W]here . . . a risk to the employed, which may or may not result in injury, has been created or enhanced by the negligence of the employer, does the mere continuance in service, with knowledge of the risk, preclude the employed, if he suffers from such negligence, from recovering in respect of his employer's breach of duty? I cannot assent to the proposition that the maxim, 'Volenti

[91] (1887) 18 Q.B.D. 683.
[92] [1891] A.C. 325.

non fit injuria', applies to such a case, and that the employer can invoke its aid to protect him from liability for his wrong."[93]

G. Consent Must be Freely Given

The main point to notice here is that: **25–12**

"[A] man cannot be said to be truly 'willing' unless he is in a position to choose freely, and freedom of choice predicates, not only full knowledge of the circumstances on which the exercise of choice is conditional, so that he may be able to choose wisely, but the absence of any feeling of constraint so that nothing shall interfere with the freedom of his will."[94]

The claimant in *Imperial Chemical Industries Ltd v Shatwell*[95] was obviously under no pressure from the defendants to adopt the dangerous method of work which caused his injury, for they had, to his knowledge, specifically forbidden it; but usually there will be economic or other pressures upon a worker which will make it unjust for an employer to say that he ran the risk with his eyes open, being fully aware of the danger he incurred.[96] Indeed, some modern statements of the employer's duty of care to his workers go even further and seem inconsistent with the very existence of the defence in the employment context, even where the worker is willing to continue to encounter an inevitable risk rather than leave the employment.[97] In the absence of some such relationship as employer and worker between the parties it will, no doubt, be easier to establish the necessary freedom of consent, but if such consent is absent the defence of volenti non fit injuria cannot prevail.[98]

H. Consent and the Standard of Care

Whether or not we regard them as properly falling under volenti **25–13** non fit injuria, there are clearly cases in which the claimant may have consented to a certain degree of disregard for his safety by the

---

[93] [1891] A.C. 325 at 360, 362. Cf. *Johnstone v Bloomsbury HA*, para.25–6, above.

[94] *Bowater v Rowley Regis Corp* [1944] K.B. 476 at 479 per Scott L.J., cited with approval by Lord Hodson in *Imperial Chemical Industries Ltd v Shatwell* [1965] A.C. 656 at 681–682; *Merrington v Ironbridge Metal Works Ltd* [1952] 2 All E.R. 1101. For a case where constraint was put upon an employee by someone other than his employer, see *Burnett v British Waterways Board* [1973] 1 W.L.R. 700.

[95] [1965] A.C. 656, above.

[96] [1965] A.C. 656 at 681 per Lord Hodson at 686 per Lord Pearce. Stuart-Smith L.J. in *Johnstone v Bloomsbury HA* [1992] Q.B. 333 at 344 (para.25–6, above) adverts to the pressure which the NHS can bring on trainee doctors because it is, as far as training is concerned, a monopoly employer.

[97] See para.8–16, above.

[98] *Hambley v Shepley* (1967) 63 D.L.R. (2d) 94 (Ont. CA) is an interesting example.

defendant but has not given him complete carte blanche. This point is obvious with regard to participants in sports. As Barwick C.J. said in *Rootes v Shelton*[99]:

> "By engaging in a sport . . . the participants may be held to have accepted risks which are inherent in that sport . . . : but this does not eliminate all duty of care of the one participant to the other."

The same may apply to a spectator who is injured in the course of some game or sport which he is watching. A spectator does not consent to negligence on the part of the participants,[100] but:

> "[P]rovided the competition or game is being performed within the rules and requirements of the sport and by a person of adequate skill or competence the spectator does not expect his safety to be regarded by the participant."[101]

In *Wooldridge v Sumner*[102] the claimant, a photographer at a horse show, was struck by a galloping horse whose rider had allegedly taken the corner too fast. It was held that there was no negligence. Had the defendant acted in disregard of all safety of others so as to have departed from the standards which might reasonably be expected in anyone pursuing the competition, he might well have been liable[103] but all he had done was to commit an error of judgment in the course of doing his best to win. The result is summarised by Diplock L.J. in these words:

> "A person attending a game or competition takes the risk of any damage caused to him by any act of a participant done in the course of and for the purposes of the game or competition not-withstanding that such an act may involve an error of judgment or

---

[99] [1968] A.L.R. 33 at 34.
[100] See *Cleghorn v Oldham* (1927) 43 T.L.R. 465 and the unreported cases referred to by Sellers L.J. in *Wooldridge v Sumner* [1963] 2 Q.B. 43 at 55–56. For the position of the occupier of the premises where the game or sport is taking place, see *Murray v Harringay Arena Ltd* [1951] 2 K.B. 529; *Wilks v Cheltenham Home Guard Motor Cycle and Light Car Club* [1971] 1 W.L.R. 668.
[101] *Wooldridge v Sumner*, above, fn.100, at 56 per Sellers L.J., at 67 per Diplock L.J.
[102] Above, fn.100.
[103] [1963] 2 Q.B. 43 at 57 per Sellers L.J.: "There would, I think, be a difference, for instance, in assessing blame which is actionable between an injury caused by a tennis ball hit or a racket accidentally thrown in the course of play into the spectators at Wimbledon and a ball hit or a racket thrown into the stands in temper or annoyance when play was not in progress."

a lapse of skill, unless the participant's conduct is such as to evince a reckless disregard for the spectator's safety."[104]

The same approach will be taken where injury is inflicted by one participant upon another. In *Condon v Basi*[105] the issue arose between participants in an amateur league football match and substantial damages were awarded for injuries arising from a tackle which was described by the trial judge as:

"[M]ade in a reckless and dangerous manner not with malicious intent towards the claimant but in an excitable manner without thought of the consequences".[106]

The rules of the sport are of course very relevant in determining what is a proper standard of care[107] but they should not in all cases be decisive: contravention of a rule designed only to produce fair play should not automatically amount to negligence[108]; equally, conduct may be dangerous even though it does not infringe any particular rule.[109] This approach is not confined to organised sports with clear rules: it may apply where the parties engage in horseplay with tacit understandings or conventions.[110] Whether one regards such cases as involving a departure from the normal duty of care on the basis of the implied consent of the participants, or as illustrating the proposition that in determining what amounts to reasonable care all the circumstances of the case must be taken into account, has been said not to make the slightest difference.[111] English courts have, however, declined to adopt a variable standard of care as between drivers of vehicles and their passengers where the latter have reason to doubt the competence of the former, probably because of the universality of insurance.[112]

---

[104] [1963] Q.B. 43 at 68. Cf. *Harrison v Vincent* [1982] R.T.R. 8, where the negligence lay in preparation of equipment.

[105] [1985] 1 W.L.R. 866; *Caldwell v Maguire* [2001] EWCA Civ 1054; [2002] P.I.Q.R. P6.

[106] By implication, therefore "reckless" does not have the sense of conscious advertence to the risk. See also *McCord v Swansea City AFC, The Times*, February 11, 1997; *Watson v Gray, The Times*, November 26, 1998.

[107] See e.g. *McCracken v Melbourne Storm Rugby League Football Club* [2005] NSWSC 107.

[108] In *McCord*, above, fn.106, Ian Kennedy J. said that, "those who play football . . . consent to the risk of injury from the great majority of errors of judgment, mistakes and even intentional fouls." Note, however, that the referee owes a duty of care to players (*Smoldon v Whitworth* [1997] P.I.Q.R. P133) and the organising body may also do so in relation to the rules and requirements for safety (*Watson v British Boxing Board of Control Ltd* [2001] Q.B. 1134, para.5–36, above).

[109] *Affutu-Nartey v Clarke, The Times*, February 9, 1984.

[110] *Blake v Galloway* [2004] EWCA Civ 814; [2004] 1 W.L.R. 2844. The position would have been different if the defendant had, say, substituted a stone for the piece of bark.

[111] *Condon v Basi* [1985] 1 W.L.R. 866 per Sir John Donaldson M.R., though he stated a preference for the latter.

[112] See para.5–76, above.

I. Rescue Cases

25–14   Rescuers are not a specially privileged category of persons in tort law.[113] Nevertheless, their presence may be foreseeable when that of others would not be and they deserve some further treatment here, too, for the "rescue cases" straddle three branches of the law —volenti non fit injuria, causation and contributory negligence—and the two latter may, for the sake of convenience, be considered here as well as the first. Rescue cases are typified by C's death or injury in rescuing or endeavouring to rescue X from an emergency of danger to X's life or limb created by the negligence of D. Is D liable to C? Or can D successfully plead: (1) volenti non fit injuria; or (2) that C's conduct is a novus actus interveniens which makes his injury too remote a consequence of D's initial negligence; or (3) that C's injury was due to contributory negligence on his own part?

Until 1924, our law was almost destitute of any decision on these questions.[114] The American law reports, on the other hand, from 1871 onwards had contained numerous cases which, subject to the limitations stated below, conferred a right of action upon the rescuer or his representatives. In 1935, in *Haynes v Harwood*[115] the Court of Appeal adopted a similar principle.

We can best consider the three arguable defences of D to such an action separately.

25–15   **i. Volenti non fit injuria.** Dr Goodhart, in summarising the American cases, said:

> "The American rule is that the doctrine of assumption of risk does not apply where the plaintiff has, under an exigency caused by the defendant's wrongful misconduct, consciously and deliberately faced a risk, even of death, to rescue another from imminent danger of personal injury or death,[116] whether the person endangered is one to whom he owes a duty of protection or is a mere stranger to whom he owes no such special duty."[117]

This was accepted as an accurate representation of English law by Greer L.J. in *Haynes v Harwood*,[118] where the Court of Appeal

---

[113] *Frost v CC South Yorkshire* [1999] 2 A.C. 455 at 508. Thus they have no special status in relation to psychiatric injury: para.5–69, above.

[114] *Roebuck v Norwegian Titanic Co* (1884) 1 T.L.R. 117 seems to have been forgotten soon after it was reported.

[115] [1935] 1 K.B. 146.

[116] This phrase should not be taken as implying that the claimant must literally be doing something like pulling the victim from danger. A person who is engaged in dangerous conditions in a search for the victim is within the rescue principle.

[117] Goodhart, "Rescue and Voluntary Assumption of Risk" (1934) 5 C.L.J. 192 at 196.

[118] [1935] 1 K.B. at 156–157.

affirmed a judgment in favour of a policeman who had been injured in stopping some runaway horses with a van in a crowded street. The defendant had left the horses and van unattended on the highway and they had bolted. The policeman, who was on duty, not in the street, but in a police station, darted out and was crushed by one of the horses which fell upon him while he was stopping it. It was also held that the rescuer's act need not be instinctive in order to be reasonable, for one who deliberately encounters peril after reflection may often be acting more reasonably than one who acts upon impulse.[119]

There are several reasons why volenti non fit injuria is no answer to the rescuer's claim. In the first place, it is now clear that he founds upon a duty owed directly to himself by the defendant, and not upon one derived from that owed to the person imperilled, so that, for example, the claimant has recovered damages for injury suffered in going to the rescue of a trespasser who, as the law then stood, had no claim.[120] If the defendant ought to have foreseen an emergency and that someone would expose himself to danger in order to effect a rescue, then he owes a duty directly to the rescuer. To go on to hold that the rescuer was volens would be flatly self-contradictory.[121] In the second place, a rescuer acts under the impulse of duty legal, moral or social, and does not therefore exercise that freedom of choice which is essential to the success of the defence.[122] Thirdly, it is in the nature of a rescue case that the defendant's negligence precedes the claimant's act of running the risk. The claimant does not assent to the defendant's negligence at all, and, indeed, may be wholly ignorant of it at the time. All he knows is that someone is in a position of peril which calls for his intervention as a rescuer.[123]

ii. Novus actus interveniens. The policeman's act was that of a normally courageous man in the like circumstances, and therefore was both the direct and foreseeable consequence of the defendant's unlawful act; hence the injury which he suffered was not too remote.

25–16

"The reasonable man here must be endowed with qualities of energy and courage, and he is not to be deprived of a remedy because he has in a marked degree a desire to save human life when in peril."[124]

[119] [1935] 1 K.B. 146 at 158–159 per Greer L.J., at 164 per Maugham L.J.
[120] *Videan v British Transport Commission* [1963] 2 Q.B. 650.
[121] Cf. *Reeves v MPC*, para.6–41, above.
[122] *Frost v CC South Yorkshire* [1999] 2 A.C. 455 at 509.
[123] *Baker v T.E. Hopkins & Son Ltd* [1959] 1 W.L.R. 966 at 976 per Morris L.J.
[124] [1935] 1 K.B. at 162 per Maugham L.J.

Even if his duty to intervene were merely a moral one, still:

"[T]he law does not think so meanly of mankind as to hold it otherwise than a natural and probable consequence of a helpless person being put in danger that some able-bodied person should expose himself to the same danger to effect a rescue."[125]

This covers the case, not only of a policeman or a fireman, who may be expected to be involved in a rescue, but also that of any other person who makes such an attempt with any reasonable prospect of success.[126] So, in *Chadwick v British Railways Board*[127] the defendant railway authority was held liable where the claimant's husband, who lived near a railway line, had gone from his home to the scene of a major railway disaster and, having played a major part in rescue operations there, subsequently became psychoneurotic as a result of his experiences.[128] On the other hand, the principle does not sanction any foolhardy or unnecessary risks, such as an attempt to stop a runaway horse on a desolate country road.[129] Here, as elsewhere in innumerable legal relations, the test is: "What is reasonable?" and it is unreasonable to go to the assistance of a driver of a horse and cart merely because he shouts for help to pacify a restive horse which has bolted into a field but which is endangering nobody.[130] Furthermore the injury suffered by the rescuer must be a reasonably foreseeable consequence of his attempt to assist.[131]

The fact that members of the emergency services are in a sense employed to take risks has led some American courts to deny liability to them on the part of the person whose negligence creates the danger. This, the so-called "fireman's rule", was decisively rejected by the House of Lords in *Ogwo v Taylor.*[132] Of course, some

---

[125] Pollock, *Torts*, 15th edn, p.370, adopted by Maugham L.J. in *Haynes v Harwood* [1935] 1 K.B. 146 at 163.

[126] It is no defence that hindsight shows the attempt to have been futile so long as it appears reasonable at the time: *Wagner v International R.R.* (1921) 133 N.E. 437.

[127] [1967] 1 W.L.R. 912. In *Urbanski v Patel* (1978) 84 D.L.R. (3d) 650 the first claimant lost her only kidney as a result of the defendant's negligence. The second claimant recovered damages in respect of an unsuccessful kidney donation by him.

[128] The case is now explained on the basis that although the psychiatric injury was suffered as a result of what he saw (no longer enough) he was nevertheless in the zone of physical danger: para.5–63, above.

[129] [1935] 1 K.B. 146 at 163 per Maugham L.J.

[130] *Cutler v United Dairies (London) Ltd* [1933] 2 K.B. 297. That seems to be the interpretation of this case by the Court of Appeal in *Haynes v Harwood*.

[131] *Crossley v Rawlinson* [1982] 1 W.L.R. 369. Cf. *Chapman v Hearse* (1961) 106 C.L.R. 112.

[132] [1988] A.C. 431.

fires may present no foreseeable hazard to a trained fireman acting with skill and care but if the risk is unavoidable (as it was on the facts) he is not to be disadvantaged because of his calling.

iii. Contributory negligence. In *Haynes v Harwood* this was set up but was not much pressed. Indeed, the earlier case of *Brandon v Osborne, Garrett & Co Ltd*[133] had made it improbable that it would have met with any success. There, X and his wife were in a shop as customers. Owing to the negligence of the defendants who were repairing the shop roof, some glass fell from a skylight and struck X. His wife, who was unharmed herself, but who reasonably believed X to be in danger, instinctively clutched his arm and tried to pull him from the spot, and thus injured her leg. Swift J. held that there was no contributory negligence on her part, provided, as was the fact, she had done no more than any reasonable person would have done.

> "Bearing in mind that danger invites rescue, the court should not be astute to accept criticism of the rescuer's conduct from the wrongdoer who created the danger."[134]

Do the rules just stated apply where the person who is rescued is the person who was negligent, instead of being some third party endangered by the negligent person's conduct? So far we have been considering a case in which C is injured in trying to rescue X from the effects of D's negligence, but is the position the same if C is injured in trying to rescue D himself from peril caused by D's own negligence? Would it have made any difference in *Haynes v Harwood* if the person by whose negligence the horses had bolted had been imperilled and had been saved by the policeman? On principle, it seems that there ought to be no difference, bearing in mind that the rescuer's right in the more usual three-party situation is an independent one and is not derived from that of the person imperilled, and that D ought to be just as much liable in the one case as in the other. It was so held at first instance in *Harrison v British Railways Board*.[135]

Another question is whether someone would be justified in running risks to life or limb in order to save his own or other people's

25–17

---

[133] [1924] 1 K.B. 548.
[134] *Baker v T.E. Hopkins Ltd*, above, fn.123, at 984 per Wilmer L.J.
[135] [1981] 3 All E.R. 679; *Canadian National Ry v Bakty* (1978) 82 D.L.R. (3d) 731. Barry J. had expressed the same view obiter in *Baker v T.E. Hopkins Ltd* [1958] 1 W.L.R. 993 at 1004. The Court of Appeal did not consider the point.

property from evil consequences threatened by the wrongful conduct of another person. In *Hyett v GW Ry*,[136] the claimant was injured in attempting such a rescue and the Court of Appeal held that, on the facts, his conduct was reasonable and that the defendants were liable; the court held that the doctrine of *Haynes v Harwood* applies to rescue of property as well as to rescue of the person and pointed out that in either case it is necessary for the court to consider the relationship of the rescuer to the property in peril, or to the person in peril, and also to consider the degree of danger.[137] Goodhart suggested that the only difference between the life and the property cases is that a rescuer would not be justified in exposing himself to as great danger in saving property as he would in saving human life.[138] In general, this seems sound in principle, though particular cases are imaginable in which the rescuer might reasonably encounter just as much danger in trying to preserve property as to preserve life, for example where documents of great national importance, and of which no copies exist, are in peril of being destroyed by a fire caused by the tortious conduct of some person other than the rescuer.[139]

2. PUBLIC POLICY. ILLEGALITY

25–18   It is a well known principle of the law of contract that if the claimant has to found his claim on an illegal act or agreement he will fail: ex turpi causa non oritur actio. Though that maxim may be properly confined to cases involving contracts[140] there are also certainly cases of tort in which to allow recovery to a claimant implicated in illegality is against public policy.[141] The difficulty arises in determining when a claim (or part of it, for illegality may affect only one element of the damages claimed) will be rejected for this reason. As

---

[136] [1948] 1 K.B. 345. See *Hutterly v Imperial Oil and Calder* (1956) 3 D.L.R. (2d) 719; *Russell v McCabe* [1962] N.Z.L.R. 392. In the Scottish decision *Steel v Glasgow Iron and Steel Co* 1944 S.C. 237, such an action was held to be maintainable subject to the conditions that (1) the rescuer's act ought reasonably to have been contemplated by the defendant, and (2) the risk undertaken must be reasonable in relation to the interests protected

[137] [1948] 1 K.B. 345 at 348 per Tucker L.J. Note that the industrial injuries scheme includes in the "course of employment" steps taken by the insured person to rescue persons or property on his employer's premises.

[138] 5 C.L.J. at 198.

[139] See *Russell v McCabe* [1962] N.Z.L.R. 392 at 404 per North J.

[140] *Smith v Jenkins* (1970) 119 C.L.R. 397 at 410 per Windeyer J.

[141] The same idea may surface in "no-fault" or social security compensation. The Criminal Injuries Compensation Scheme (para.4–2, above) allows payments to be reduced or withheld on account of the applicant's character or conduct and under the New Zealand Accident Compensation Scheme (para.1–40, above) the compensation authority may decline to give compensation where, "it would be repugnant to justice for... such compensation to be paid". Compensation can never be entirely about need.

is so often the case, it may make no difference whether one rests the decision on lack of a duty of care or upon a separate ground of illegality, since the nature of the claimant's behaviour is a matter which is relevant to the question of whether it is fair, just and reasonable to impose a duty.[142]

One statutory provision which takes into account the claimant's **25–19** criminal behaviour may be noted at the outset. Under s.329 of the Criminal Justice Act 2003 a person has a defence to a claim in respect of a trespass to the person brought by a claimant who he believed was committing an imprisonable offence if there was a conviction and his act was not grossly disproportionate.[143] This provision is of comparatively narrow scope and it is now necessary to examine the common law.

There are two principles in play here: first that tort law must not **25–20** contradict the criminal law by giving the claimant an indemnity or compensation for a penalty imposed on him by the latter, secondly (a broader principle) that a claimant may not recover damages for a loss which is regarded by the law as the consequence of his own illegal act.

The first principle may be illustrated by *Gray v Thames Trains Ltd.*[144] The claimant was involved in a rail crash caused by the negligence of the defendants, suffered psychiatric trauma and, nearly two years later and under the influence of this, killed a person in a "road rage" incident, which led to his conviction for man-slaughter on the ground of diminished responsibility for which he was sentenced to be detained indefinitely in hospital. He was sane in the legal sense and responsible for his actions, the diminished responsibility merely preventing the offence being murder. There was no doubt that the defendants' negligence was a cause in fact of his detention but the House of Lords held that he was not entitled to recover his lost earnings from the time of the detention. In such a situation:

"If the [claimant] has been convicted and sentenced for a crime, it means that the criminal law has taken him to be responsible for his actions and has imposed an appropriate penalty. He or she should therefore bear the consequences of the punishment,[145]

---

[142] *Vellino v CC Greater Manchester* [2001] EWCA Civ 1249; [2002] 1 W.L.R. 218 at [62].

[143] See para.4–27, above.

[144] [2009] UKHL 33; [2009] A.C. 1339. See also *Clunis v Camden and Islington Health Authority* [1998] QB 978; *British Columbia v Zastowny* [2008] SCC 4; [2008] 1 S.C.R. 27.

[145] There may be losses arising from conviction rather than penalty which do not fall within this principle: *Griffin v Uhy Hacker Young & Partners* [2010] EWHC 146 (Ch). Nor does it apply to a fine imposed even though the claimant was in no way at fault: *Osman v J. Ralph Moss Ltd* [1970] 1 Lloyds Rep 313; *Safeway Stores Ltd v Twigger* [2010] EWHC 11 (Comm).

both direct and indirect. If the law of negligence were to say, in
effect, that the offender was not responsible for his actions and
should be compensated by the tortfeasor, it would set the determination of the criminal court at nought. It would generate the sort
of clash between civil and criminal law that is apt to bring the law
into disrepute."[146]

An award of damages would amount to the law, "giving with one
hand what it takes away with the other".[147] It was not necessary to
decide what the position would have been if the claimant had been
legally irresponsible by reason of insanity but had still been indefinitely detained.[148]

This, however, is not quite the end of the story for in *Gray* the
claimant's alternative argument was that even if his claim for lost
earnings as such during his detention was barred, yet his earning
capacity had already been diminished by his injury and there was
therefore a "partial" or "continuing loss" for which he was entitled
to be compensated notwithstanding his detention. However, this
counter-factual assumption was regarded as unrealistic, for the situation was regarded as comparable to that in *Jobling v Associated
Dairies*[149] where the claimant was denied damages for the effects of
an injury in the period after the onset of a disease occurring before
trial and which had a greater disabling effect. However, the two
cases are not identical, for in *Gray* there was no doubt that the injury
was a cause of the detention in the factual sense, whereas in *Jobling*
the disease was unconnected with the tort. Nevertheless, as Lord
Browne said:

"In the last analysis there is no logical basis on which . . . . [C]
could be regarded as responsible and [D] in no way legally liable
for the full consequences of his detention ([C's] inability to earn
the full [sum] he would have earned but for his accident) and yet
be entitled in respect of the continuing loss claim to disregard his
responsibility for his supervening detention and thus ignore it as
a vicissitude terminating his claim."[150]

---

[146] *State Rail Authority of New South Wales v Wiegold* (1991) 25 NSWLR 500 at 514, cited
by Lord Hoffmann at [40] and Lord Rodger at [67] in *Gray*.
[147] *Hall v Hebert* [1993] 2 SCR 159 at 178.
[148] See *Clunis* above, fn.144 at 989 and *Hunter Area Health Service v Presland* [2005]
NSWCA 33; 63 NSWLR 22, where the majority of the court denied liability in such a
case.
[149] [1982] AC 794, para.6–8, above.
[150] [2009] UKHL 33; [2009] A.C. 1339 at [101]. "If one cannot get 'direct' compensation for
the non-economic or economic loss resulting from imprisonment, one should not be able
to receive 'indirect' compensation for lost earning capacity after imprisonment by treating
the fact of imprisonment as irrelevant to the assessment of economic loss" : *State Rail
Authority of New South Wales v Wiegold* (1991) 25 NSWLR 500 at 515.

In many cases the first principle does not come into play, either **25–21** because the criminal law has not been invoked at all or because the loss suffered by the claimant is plainly not the product of any sentence—as where the claimant suffers injury during the commission of an offence.[151] Probably few people would disagree with the remark of Lord Asquith in *National Coal Board v England*[152] that:

"If two burglars, A and B, agree to open a safe by means of explosives, and A so negligently handles the explosive charge as to injure B, B might find some difficulty in maintaining an action for negligence against A."

There are, however, a number of problems here which make it difficult to state the law in a simple fashion likely to produce predictable results.

In the first place it is not very clear what is the theoretical basis of the defence. In some of the cases involving negligence by the defendant in the course of a joint illegal activity with the claimant the law has been said to rest on it not being feasible for the court to determine an appropriate standard of care.[153] However, what this means is not that the court *cannot* determine a standard of care, merely that it *will not* do so. Thus a car might be driven at very high speed to get someone to hospital and in that situation there can be no doubt that the court would examine the circumstances to determine what was a proper standard of care in the emergency, perhaps modifying the normal standard of careful driving so as to allow the taking of certain risks. If, therefore, it refuses to examine the incidents of the activity of driving at precisely the same speed in order to escape from a robbery it must be because, as between the robbers, it is inappropriate for it to do so.[154] Furthermore, a principle based on refusing to examine the required standard of care would seem to be inapplicable to cases where some other tort is complained of.

In Canada the Supreme Court rested the effect of illegality upon the need for consistency between different parts of the law. This has obvious affinities to the approach taken to claims for compensation

[151] See those parts of the claim in *Gray v Thames Trains*, above, fn.144, relating to the claimant's feelings of remorse and an indemnity against a claim by relatives of the victim (though since no claim had been made by them, the basis of the latter is not entirely clear).

[152] [1954] A.C. 403 at 429.

[153] *Jackson v Harrison* (1978) 138 C.L.R. 438; *Gala v Preston* (1999) 172 C.L.R. 243; Balcombe L.J. in *Pitts v Hunt* [1991] 1 Q.B. 24 at 50.

[154] The point is obvious if one bears in mind that the court might have to consider a case in which the escaping robbers collided with an innocent motorist.

for the consequences of criminal punishment but in the case in question the claim was for the injuries suffered in an accident.

" . . . [T]o allow recovery [where the claim arises from the claimant's illegal conduct] . . . would be to allow recovery for what is illegal. It would put the courts in the position of saying that the same conduct is both legal, in the sense of being capable of rectification by the court, and illegal. It would, in short, introduce an inconsistency in the law. It is particularly important in this context that we bear in mind that the law must aspire to be a unified institution, the parts of which—contract, tort, the criminal law—must be in essential harmony. For the courts to punish conduct with the one hand while rewarding it with the other, would be to 'create an intolerable fissure in the law's conceptually seamless web' . . . We thus see that the concern, put at its most fundamental, is with the integrity of the legal system."[155]

The point may be illustrated by *Stone & Rolls Ltd v Moore Stephens*,[156] where the C Company defrauded X in a scheme set up by its sole controller Y and then sued its auditors, D, for negligence in failing to spot what Y was doing, the damages claimed being the sum for which it was liable to X.[157] The claim failed because to allow it would have been to say that what was recoverable from C in the action against it for fraud was damage to it for the purposes of its claim against D.[158]

25–22 Some of the cases have spoken in terms which figure large in the contract cases, of asking whether the claimant needs to rely on his illegality in order to make out his cause of action. That will fit the case where the claimant's loss arises directly from the consequences to him of his criminal act[159] or where he is complaining of being deprived of income from a criminal source[160] (though most such cases are covered at least in part by the "inconsistency" principle discussed above). However, this approach is not merely a matter of

---

[155] *Hall v Hebert* (1993) 101 DLR (4th) 129 at 165 per McLachlin J.
[156] [2009] UKHL 39; [2009] A.C. 1391.
[157] Assuming this to amount to damage at all: see Lord Phillips at [5].
[158] No one contested that this was the result had Y acted as a natural person, but the fact that the vehicle of fraud was the company produced profound disagreement on the result. The majority took the view that (a) Y's acts were to be attributed to the company, so that it was directly and not merely vicariously liable for the fraud on X and (b) that a decision the other way would outflank the principle that auditors do not owe a duty of care to the company's creditors (see para.11–25, above), the company being insolvent and X being the likely beneficiary of any judgment.
[159] *Clunis v Camden and Islington Health Authority* [1998] Q.B. 978.
[160] Neither a burglar nor his dependants if he is killed can claim as damages the loss of income from his trade: *Burns v Edman* [1970] 2 Q.B. 541. As Clarke L.J. put it *Hewison v Meridian Shipping Services Pte Ltd* [2002] EWCA Civ 1821; [2003] I.C.R. 766 at [28] it is not so much ex turpi causa non oritur actio as ex turpi causa non oritur damnum.

what the claimant needs to prove to make out a prima facie cause of action. While it is true that if the complaint is of interference with property rights the defendant cannot defeat the claim by contending that the claimant acquired his title to the property by an illegal transaction,[161] a person who has obtained employment by fraudulent misrepresentation about his health cannot, when injured during the course of that employment, recover damages for future lost earnings therein, even though his pleadings would not need to say anything about the circumstances in which he obtained the employment and the matter will have been raised by the defendant.[162] In *Cross v Kirby*[163] Beldam L.J. said:

"I do not believe that there is any general principle that the claimant must either plead, give evidence of or rely on his own illegality for the principle to apply. Such a technical approach is entirely absent from Lord Mansfield's exposition of the principle [of ex turpi causa in *Holman v Johnson* (1775) 1 Cowp. 341]".

More frequently the matter has been determined by asking whether the loss suffered by the claimant is "inextricably linked" with the illegality in which he was engaged, though it has been said that the matter is probably best expressed as an issue of causation.[164] The claimant would not be barred from recovering damages for loss of earnings because he would have failed to pay tax on them[165] nor would the owner of a damaged car be precluded from recovering damages because it was illegally parked[166]; and in *NCB v England* Lord Asquith, having given the example of one safe-cracker blowing the other up immediately gave an example on the other side of the line:

---

[161] *Bowmakers Ltd v Barnet Instruments Ltd* [1945] K.B. 65; *Singh v Ali* [1960] A.C. 167; *Tinsley v Milligan* [1994] 1 A.C. 340; *Webb v CC Merseyside* [2000] Q.B. 427.

[162] *Hewison v Meridian Shipping Services Pte Ltd* [2002] EWCA Civ 1821; [2003] I.C.R. 766: *Romantiek BVBA v Simms* [2008] EWHC 3099 (QB). Cf. *Major v MoD* [2003] EWCA Civ 1433. (Claimant suffered injury from the defendants which produced a pathological mental condition. She concealed this in order to join the RAF and was discharged when this was discovered. *Hewison* was distinguished on the ground that she could frame her claim for the injury prior to entry to the RAF on the basis of "loss of value in the labour market" and her earnings in the service were merely evidence of that so that the deception to gain entry was causally irrelevant to the loss.)

[163] *The Times*, April 5, 2000; *Stone & Rolls Ltd v Moore Stephens* [2009] UKHL 39; [2009] A.C. 1391 at [23].

[164] *Gray v Thames Trains Ltd* [2009] UKHL 33; [2009] A.C. 1339 at [54] per Lord Hoffmann.

[165] *Hall v Woolston Hall Leisure Ltd* [2001] 1 W.L.R. 225; *Finnis v Caulfield* [2002] EWHC 3223 (QB). The damages recoverable would be net of tax, so there is no question of the claimant benefiting from his wrongdoing.

[166] Lord Hoffmann's example in *Gray* at [53]. See *Kelly v Churchill Car Insurance* [2006] EWHC 18 (QB); [2007] R.T.R. 26.

"But if A and B are proceeding to the premises which they intend burglariously to enter, and before they enter them, B picks A's pocket and steals A's watch, I cannot prevail upon myself to believe that A could not sue in tort."[167]

In these cases the illegality is simply part of the background, but in other cases it is not obvious what the criterion is to be applied to this causal issue. For example, suppose that the claimant is injured in a car accident caused by the fault of the defendant but the claimant was driving under the influence of alcohol and well above the speed limit, this factor also contributing to the accident. It does not seem to have occurred to anyone to contend that the claim is barred by illegality, as opposed to the damages being reduced for contributory negligence. On the other hand, in *Pitts v Hunt*[168] after an evening's drinking, C and D set off home on a motorcycle which D was, to C's knowledge, neither licensed nor insured to ride. D's alcohol level was twice that permitted. D, encouraged by C, drove in a reckless and hazardous manner in order to frighten members of the public. Their conduct, as well as infringing the road traffic law, would have amounted to manslaughter if some third party had been killed. An accident occurred in which C was seriously injured. The Court of Appeal held that C's action failed on the ground of public policy.[169] It is hard to see any differences between our hypothetical case and *Pitts v Hunt* beyond the facts that the claimant and the defendant were engaged on a joint venture and they were out to scare other road users. In other words, their conduct was worse than that in our hypothetical example.

25–23   In some cases the statutory context in which the illegality arises may point towards it not barring a tort claim. Thus sometimes a worker commits an offence by disobeying safety regulations. *NCB v England* put paid to the idea that illegality could be invoked in such a case and the Law Reform (Contributory Negligence) Act 1945 includes breach of statutory duty in the definition of "fault". In *Revill v Newberry*[170] the Court of Appeal declined to apply the illegality defence where a burglar was shot negligently by the occupier, though the damages were reduced by two-thirds on account of contributory negligence.[171] A very respectable argument

---

[167] [1954] A.C. 403 at 429.

[168] [1991] 1 Q.B. 24.

[169] *Volenti* was inapplicable because of what is now the Road Traffic Act 1988 s.149 (para.25–10, above), contributory negligence would have led, at the most, to a 50 per cent reduction in C's damages.

[170] [1996] Q.B. 567. See para.9–27, above.

[171] See also *Marshall v Osmond* [1983] Q.B. 1034. The suggestion by Lord Denning M.R. in *Murphy v Culhane* [1977] Q.B. 94 that even if a burglar is deliberately shot by a householder acting beyond the bounds of self-defence he has no claim clearly goes too far.

can be made from the point of view of policy that given the provisions of the Occupiers' Liability Act 1984 governing liability to trespassers the claimant should not be made an outlaw for participation in such an offence.[172] It is true that people generally would probably be startled to be told that a householder could be liable to a burglar who injured himself on the householder's rotten ladder while gaining entry but the flexibility of the formula in the 1984 Act probably means that this result could generally be avoided without recourse to illegality. Sometimes it has been suggested that one should look at the question of proportionality between the illegal conduct and the harm suffered by the claimant[173] but in other cases the issue has been put in terms of disproportion between the fault of the claimant and the defendant,[174] though this, too, has been denied.[175]

At one time there was a tendency to deal with the matter by asking whether recovery by the claimant would "shock the conscience of the court". This was disapproved by the House of Lords in the context of contract and title to property in *Tinsley v Milligan*.[176] It is not wholly clear how far it survives in the context of tort. It was subsequently referred to in a tort context by the Court of Appeal in *Reeves v Metropolitan Police Commissioner*[177] where it was held that the deceased's suicide in custody did not bar a claim in respect of his death; a decision in favour of the claimant would neither encourage others down the same road nor shock the conscience. However, later cases indicate that it has gone for all purposes.[178] Nevertheless, while it may be the case that there is no true "discretion" about illegality, which is a matter of law with an all or nothing effect upon the claim, it is hard to escape the feeling that the imprecise nature of the present law might very well be described as a principle of "public conscience".

Common sense would seem to indicate that the degree of gravity **25–24** of the misconduct must be an important factor but it is very difficult

---

[172] In NSW damages cannot be awarded to a person who suffers injury while committing an offence punishable by six months' imprisonment if his conduct "contributed materially" to his injury: Civil Liability Act 2002 (NSW) s.54. Presumably the conduct of the claimant in *Revill* satisfied this?

[173] *Saunders v Edwards* [1987] 1 W.L.R. 1116 at 1134; *Hewison v Meridian Shipping Services Pte Ltd* [2002] EWCA Civ 1821; [2003] I.C.R. 766 at [86]

[174] *Revill v Newbery* [1996] Q.B. 567 and see *Lane v Holloway* [1996] 1 Q.B. 379.

[175] *Vellino v CC Greater Manchester* [2001] EWCA Civ 1249; [2002] 1 W.L.R. 218 at [70]: "there is no question of proportionality between the conduct of the claimant and defendant" (injury during escape attempt from police custody).

[176] [1994] 1 A.C. 340.

[177] [1999] Q.B. 169. The point was not pursued in the HL: [2000] 1 A.C. 360. For facts see para.6–41, above.

[178] *Hewison v Meridian Shipping Pte Ltd* [2002] EWCA Civ 1821; [2003] I.C.R. 766; *Stone & Rolls Ltd v Moore Stephens* [2008] EWCA Civ 644; [2008] 3 W.L.R. 1146. In the latter case in the HL it is impliedly rejected at [2009] UKHL 39; [2009] A.C. 1391 [97] and [129]. No mention of it has been traced in *Gray v Thames Trains Ltd*.

to state any principle upon which the line is to be drawn.[179] It is suggested in one case[180] that a crime punishable by imprisonment would normally attract the public policy principle but it is difficult to understand the further remark that if the crime is relatively trivial it would be unlikely to be sufficiently closely connected with the claim: in the example above the speeding by the claimant is just as much part of the essential story as the fault of the defendant. In any event, it seems that the illegality defence may sometimes arise from conduct which is not criminal.[181]

25–25   Enough has been said to show that the limits of the illegality defence are very difficult to state, probably because the underlying policy issues are equally difficult. The matter was examined by the Law Commission, which made provisional proposals[182] for the court to have a "structured" discretion to reject a tort claim when it arises from or is connected to an illegal act on the part of the claimant, based upon matters like the seriousness of the illegality, the knowledge of the claimant, the deterrent effect of rejection, whether rejection would further the purpose of the law making the conduct illegal and whether denying relief would be proportionate to the wrongdoing. However, in a further consultative report[183] it concluded that legislation was not necessary and that the law should continue to be developed by the courts, suggesting that they should consider in each case whether the application of the illegality defence can be justified on the basis of the policies that underlie that defence, these including (a) furthering the purpose of the rule which the illegal conduct has infringed; (b) consistency; (c) that the claimant should not profit from his own wrong; (d) deterrence; and (e) maintaining the integrity of the legal system.

3. Mistake[184]

25–26   Mistake, whether of law or of fact, cannot be said to be a general ground of exemption from liability in tort. There is no need to discuss the rule that ignorance of the law does not excuse, for that is not peculiar to the law of tort. As to mistake of fact one must

---

[179] The cases are reviewed in *Griffin v Uhy Hacker Young & Partners* [2010] EWHC 146 (Ch).

[180] *Vellino v CC Greater Manchester* above, fn.175, at [70].

[181] *Standard Chartered Bank v Pakistan National Shipping Corporation* [2000] 1 Lloyd's Rep 218 (non-criminal fraud); on appeal on other issues [2002] UKHL 43; [2003] 1 A.C. 959; *Safeway Stores Ltd v Twigger* [2010] EWHC 11 (Comm). In *Stone & Rolls Ltd v Moore Stephens*, above, fn.178, the criminal liability of the claimant company (as opposed to Y) must have been purely theoretical.

[182] L.C.C.P. No.160 (2001).

[183] L.C.C.P. No. 189 (2009).

[184] Trindade (1982) 2 O.J.L.S. 211.

examine the elements of whatever tort happens to be in question. There are several torts in which liability hangs upon whether a reasonable person would have done what the defendant did, and mistake becomes relevant here, because a person may quite well make one and yet be behaving reasonably. Thus the claimant in malicious prosecution must prove lack of reasonable and probable cause for the prosecution, and in false imprisonment the defendant may in certain circumstances be able to escape liability if he can show that he had reasonable cause to believe that the claimant was guilty of an offence. In defamation, mistake is relevant in some instances of publication and privilege. A mistaken belief may remove the requisite mental element for the tort of deceit, and a judicial officer may be immune from liability for his judicial acts even though he acts under a mistaken belief as to his jurisdiction. Yet there are torts which go the other way, and matters have gone too far to make mistake a general defence in the law of tort, for a good deal of the law relating to trespass, conversion and wrongs of strict liability would need recasting. Thus an auctioneer who inno-cently sells A's goods in the honest and reasonable belief that they belong to B on whose instructions he sells them, has been held liable to A[185]; and a surgeon who, as a result of an administrative mix-up, carries out the wrong operation is liable in trespass to the patient,[186] though in both cases the innocent wrongdoer would be entitled to be indemnified by the person responsible for the mistake. In fact, it is wrong even to think in terms of the desirability of a general rule about mistake. Each area of liability depends upon a proper assess-ment of the balance between the interests of potential claimants and defendants and it is not surprising that "mistake" will vary in significance from one tort to another.[187]

4. INEVITABLE ACCIDENT

Inevitable accident was defined by Sir Frederick Pollock as an accident, "not avoidable by any such precautions as a reasonable man, doing such an act then and there, could be expected to take".[188] It does not mean a catastrophe which could not have been avoided by any precaution whatever, but such as could not have been avoided by a reasonable man at the moment at which it occurred, and it is common knowledge that a reasonable man is not credited by the law with perfection of judgment. "People must

25–27

---

[185] *Consolidated Co v Curtis* [1892] 1 Q.B. 495, see para.17–22, above.
[186] *Chatterton v Gerson* [1981] Q.B. 432 at 443.
[187] See also para.25–30, below.
[188] Pollock, *Torts*, 15th edn, p.97.

guard against reasonable probabilities, but they are not bound to guard against fantastic possibilities."[189]

To speak of inevitable accident as a defence, therefore, is to say that there are cases in which the defendant will escape liability if he succeeds in proving that the accident occurred despite the exercise of reasonable care on his part, but it is also to say that there are cases in which the burden of proving this is placed upon him. In an ordinary action for negligence, for example, it is for the claimant to prove the defendant's lack of care, not for the defendant to disprove it, and the defence of inevitable accident is accordingly irrelevant[190] and it is equally irrelevant in any other class of case in which the burden of proving the defendant's negligence is imposed upon the claimant. Nor is the position different in a case of res ipsa loquitur, for that merely raises a prima facie case.[191] It was for long thought that the burden of proof in trespass to the person rested with the defendant and that trespass, therefore, offered scope to the defence of inevitable accident, but it has now been held that here too the burden is with the claimant.[192] In trespass as well as in negligence, therefore, inevitable accident has no place. In these cases inevitable accident is irrelevant because the burden is on the claimant to establish the defendant's negligence, but it does not follow that it is any more relevant if the claimant has no such burden. If, as in *Rylands v Fletcher*,[193] the defendant is liable notwithstanding that he has taken reasonable care, it can avail him nothing to prove inevitable accident and the same is true in those cases where liability for nuisance is strict, and, subject to ss.1 and 4 of the Defamation Act 1996 in cases of defamation. It therefore seems that the conception of inevitable accident has no longer any useful function and it is doubtful whether much advantage is gained by the continued use of the phrase (which anyway seems to have dropped out of use[194]).

---

[189] *Fardon v Harcourt-Rivington* (1932) 146 L.T. 391 per Lord Dunedin.

[190] "I do not find myself assisted by considering the meaning of the phrase 'inevitable accident'. I prefer to put the problem in a more simple way, namely has it been established that the driver of the car was guilty of negligence?": *Browne v De Luxe Car Services* [1941] 1 K.B. 549 at 552 per Greene M.R. This should not be understood to mean that the defendant in an action for negligence need never bring any evidence to exculpate himself. The claimant's evidence may raise a presumption or prima facie case which, if nothing more appears, will entitle the court to infer that the defendant was negligent, but the legal burden of proof remains with the claimant and when all the evidence has been heard the court must decide, whether it has been discharged: *Brown v Rolls-Royce Ltd* [1960] 1 W.L.R. 210 at 215–216 per Lord Denning.

[191] See para.5–89, above and the previous note.

[192] See para.4–33, above.

[193] (1868) L.R. 3 H.L. 330, Ch.15, above.

[194] It is still occasionally used as a description of an accident which could not have been prevented by the exercise of care (e.g. *Arnott v Sprake* [2001] EWCA Civ 341 at [50]) but nothing seems to turn on the point.

5. ACT OF GOD

This defence is limited to negation of liability under the rule in **25–28**
Rylands v Fletcher and has already been dealt with.[195]

6. PRIVATE DEFENCE

Reasonable defence of oneself,[196] of one's property, and of those **25–29**
whom one is bound or entitled to protect negatives any liability in
tort. Sometimes this is regarded as a species of self-help, i.e. as one
of the remedies for tort. Certainly what begins as self-defence often
ends as self-help, but the better view is that private defence is
allowed, "not for the redress of injuries, but for their prevention",[197]
and much more injury may in certain circumstances be incidental to
the expulsion of a trespasser than would ever be permissible in
merely keeping him out.

A. Defence of the Person

There is no doubt that the right extends to the protection of one's **25–30**
spouse and family, and, whatever the limits of this defence, almost
certainly anyone can be protected against unlawful force for the
independent reason that there is a general liberty, even as between
strangers, for the use of such force as is reasonable in the circumstances in the prevention of crime.[198]

It must always be a question of fact, rather than of law, whether
violence done by way of self-protection is proportionate to warding
off the harm which is threatened. On the one hand, I am certainly not
bound to wait until a threatened blow falls before I hit in self-
defence; thus my blow may be justified when my assailant does no
more than shake his stick at me, uttering taunts at the same time[199];
much less do I commit any assault by merely putting myself in a
fighting attitude in order to defend myself.[200] On the other hand, not
every threat will justify a blow in self-defence; still less can D be
excused, "if upon a little blow given by [C] to [D], [D] gives him a

---

[195] See Ch.15, above.
[196] Including defence against an unlawful arrest: "If a person is purporting to arrest another
without lawful warrant the person arrested may use force to avoid being arrested, but he
must not use more force than necessary": *R. v Wilson* [1955] 1 W.L.R. 493 at 494 per Lord
Goddard C.J.; *Kenlin v Gardiner* [1967] 2 Q.B. 510.
[197] Pollock, *Torts*, 15th edn, pp.135–136.
[198] Criminal Law Act 1967 s.3; *R. v Duffy* [1967] 1 Q.B. 63.
[199] *Dale v Wood* (1822) 7 Moore C.P. 33.
[200] Lord Lyndhurst C.B. in *Moriarty v Brooks* (1834) 6 C. & P. 684.

blow that maims him".[201] What if D uses force on C because of a mistake (for example he believes C is attacking him when in fact he is not)? The criminal law provides that D is not guilty of a crime if his action would have been justified if the facts had been as he believed them to be[202] but in the case of a civil action by C then D's belief must be a reasonable one because the civil law is concerned not with the punishment of D but with the protection of C's rights.[203] Indeed, it is arguable that the civil law is even more restrictive and that D only escapes liability if he is actually in danger of attack, whatever his belief may be.[204]

B. Defence of Property

25–31   Actual possession (whether with a good title or not), or the right to possession of property is necessary to justify force in keeping out (or, for that matter, expelling) a trespasser. Thus, in *Holmes v Bagge*,[205] the claimant and defendant were both members of the committee of a cricket club. During a match in which the defendant was captain and the claimant was a spectator, the defendant asked the claimant to act as substitute for one of the eleven. He did so, but being annoyed at the tone of the defendant in commanding him to take off his coat, he refused either to remove the garment or to leave the playing part of the field. He was then forcibly removed by the defendant's direction. The defendant, when sued for assault, pleaded possession of the ground, but the plea was held bad because possession was in the committee of the club. Note, however, that a person who does not have possession of the land may use reasonable force against persons thereon who obstruct him in carrying out statutory powers,[206] and it may be that if the defendant in *Holmes v Bagge* had pleaded that he removed the claimant for disturbing persons lawfully playing a lawful game he would have been justified.[207]

---

[201] *Cockroft v Smith* (1705) 2 Salk. 642; *Lane v Holloway* [1968] 1 Q.B. 379; but the law should not grade the levels of permissible response to an assault with too much nicety: *Cross v Kirkby, The Times*, April 5, 2000. In NSW damages are not to be awarded in respect of a disproportionate response unless the case is exceptional and refusal of damages would be "harsh and unjust"; and even then there can be no damages for non-pecuniary loss: Civil Liability Act 2002 (NSW) s.53.

[202] The Criminal Justice and Immigration Act 2008 s.76 restates the law on this basis but it was the common law.

[203] *Ashley v CC Sussex* [2008] UKHL 975; [2008] 1 A.C. 962.

[204] See at [20], [55] and [90]. See also *Hepburn v CC Thames Valley* [2002] EWCA Civ 1841. The claimants in *Ashley* did not advance this view of the law. Compare the law of arrest where, subject to the rule in *Walters v W.H.Smith*, a reasonable mistake of fact is clearly a defence to an action for false imprisonment and, presumably, for any associated and necessary assault or battery: para.4–24, above.

[205] (1853) 1 E. & B. 782; see also *Dean v Hogg* (1834) 10 Bing. 345 and *Roberts v Taylor* (1845) 1 C.B. 117.

[206] *R. v CC Devon and Cornwall, Ex p. C.E.G.B.* [1982] Q.B. 458.

[207] [1982] Q.B. 458 per Lord Denning M.R.

The idea that a burglar may be shot at sight[208] or that a trespasser must always take premises as he finds them goes beyond what the law allows. The broad test here, as elsewhere in private defence, is reasonableness. One is not necessarily bound to make one's premises safe for trespassers at least to the level necessary for lawful visitors[209] but there is a difference between harm suffered from what may be called the ordinary condition of the premises and harm suffered from means of defence deliberately adopted. These means must be reasonable, i.e. proportionate to the injuries which they are likely to inflict. Such would be broken glass or spikes on a wall, or a fierce dog,[210] but not deadly implements like spring guns.[211] The infliction of grave bodily harm is too high a price to demand for keeping one's property intact. Even at common law a trespasser wounded in this way could recover damages[212] unless he knew that the guns were somewhere on the land and it is an offence against the Offences Against the Person Act 1861[213] to set a spring gun or similar device. Consistently with the principle of proportion in the means of defence, more latitude is permissible in protecting premises by night than in the daytime, or when the occupier is not in the presence of the trespasser than when he is. Thus an intruder who tears himself on a spiked wall has no ground of complaint, but he certainly would have one if he, being peaceable and unarmed, had a spike thrust into him by the occupier.[214]

> "Presence [of the occupier] in its very nature is more or less protection . . . presence may supply means [of defence] and limit what it supplies."[215]

C. Injury to Innocent Third Person

Suppose that in protecting myself from an unlawful attack by A, I injure you, an innocent passer-by. On what principles ought my liability to you to be discussed? Certainly not on those of private   **25–32**

---

[208] As to illegality, see para.25–18, above.

[209] For the liability of occupiers to trespassers generally, see para.9–25, above.

[210] *Sarch v Blackburn* (1830) 4 C. & P. 297. The position is now governed by the Animals Act 1971 s.5(3)(b), which is to the like effect, though the position may have indirectly affected by the Guard Dogs Act 1975: para.16–8, above.

[211] A, "possessor of land cannot do indirectly and by a mechanical device that which, were he present, he could not do immediately and in person": *Katko v Briney* 183 N.W. 2d 657 (1971), but that could hardly apply to the spikes.

[212] *Bird v Holbrook* (1828) 4 Bing. 628.

[213] Section 31, re-enacting Spring Gun Act 1827.

[214] In *Pickwick Papers*, Captain Boldwig's mode of ejecting Mr Pickwick, whom he found asleep in a wheelbarrow in his grounds, was excessive. He directed his gardener first to wheel Mr Pickwick to the devil and then, on second thoughts, to wheel him to the village pond.

[215] *Deane v Clayton* (1817) 7 Taunt. 489 at 521 per Dallas J. For the defences available to the occupier of land who kills or injures a dog, see Animals Act 1971 s.9.

defence, for I cannot "defend" myself against one who has done me no unlawful harm. It would seem that the true principles applicable are that I committed no tort if I did not intend to harm and was not negligent, and that I may rely on the defence of necessity[216] if I did, but this does not mean that whatever I may do is justifiable under the one head or the other. Provided I acted reasonably I am excused, and not otherwise.

In *Scott v Shepherd*,[217] D threw a lighted squib into a crowded market house. It fell upon the gingerbread stall of Yates. A bystander, Willis, to prevent injury to himself and the wares of Yates, instantly picked up the squib and threw it away. It fell upon the gingerbread stall of Ryal, who, to save his own goods from injury threw the squib farther. It struck C in the face, exploded and blinded him in one eye. Now it was held without any difficulty, except as to the exact form of action, that D was liable to C for trespass and assault. No proceedings were taken against Willis or Ryal, but supposing that they had been sued by C, would they have been liable? Two of the judges thought not, because they acted, "under a compulsive necessity for their own safety and self-preservation". No exact technicality was attached by the judges to "necessity" or "self-preservation",[218] but one difficulty is the question whether Willis and Ryal really did behave as reasonable men would have done. Willis, it will be noted, acted to prevent injury to himself as well as the wares of Yates, and it must be recollected that a person may well act reasonably even if he shows no great presence of mind. A cooler person would have stopped the danger by putting his foot on the squib, but perhaps Willis did all that the lawyer, if not the moralist, could expect of him; Ryal, on the other hand, appears to have acted merely to preserve his goods, and we may doubt whether a man of ordinary presence of mind would throw a squib into a crowd to save his gingerbread from ruin.

7. NECESSITY

25–33 This negatives liability in tort, provided, of course, that the occasion of necessity does not arise from the defendant's own negligence,[219] though the authority on it is fairly scanty. It differs from private defence in that in necessity the harm inflicted on the claimant was

---

[216] See below.
[217] (1773) 2 W.Bl. 892.
[218] (1773) 2 W.Bl. 892 at 900 per De Grey C.J., at 898 per Gould J.
[219] *Southport Corp v Esso Petroleum Ltd* [1954] 2 Q.B. 182 at 194 per Singleton L.J., at 198 per Denning L.J.; *Esso Petroleum Ltd v Southport Corp* [1956] A.C. 218 at 242 per Lord Radcliffe. For a case where there was no negligence in creating the occasion so that necessity applied but the defendants' conduct in responding to the necessity was negligent, see *Rigby v CC Northamptonshire* [1985] 1 W.L.R. 1242.

not provoked by any actual or threatened illegal wrong on the claimant's part and that what the defendant did may be entirely for the good of other people and not necessarily for the protection of himself or his property. Its basis is a mixture of charity, the maintenance of the public good and self-protection, and it is probably limited to cases involving an urgent situation of imminent peril.[220] It does not, for example, furnish a defence to an action for trespass brought against homeless persons who enter and "squat" in unoccupied premises[221]; still less does it justify "direct action" by self-appointed guardians of what they perceive to be the public interest, like persons destroying genetically modified crops.[222]

Familiar examples from the cases are pulling down a house on fire to prevent its spread to other property,[223] destroying a building made ruinous by fire to prevent its collapse into the highway,[224] throwing goods overboard to lighten a boat in a storm[225] or the removal of the claimant's barge because it is frozen hard to the defendant's barge which he is lawfully moving.[226] However, what may be justified in one age is not necessarily justified in another: nowadays, for example, there is an efficient public fire service so it would require the most exceptional circumstances for a private person to destroy another's property to prevent the spread of fire.[227]

The measures which are taken must be reasonable, and this will depend, amongst other things, upon whether there is human life or merely property in danger.[228] In *Kirk v Gregory*,[229] X died in a state

---

[220] For a useful summary of common law rights of entry to land in case of necessity, see *Dehn v Att Gen* [1988] 2 N.Z.L.R. 564 at 580 (on appeal on damages only, [1989] 1 N.Z.L.R. 320).

[221] *Southwark LBC v Williams*, above, where the Court of Appeal was concerned that the defence of necessity should not become a "mask for anarchy". In *John Trenberth Ltd v National Westminster Bank* (1979) 39 P. & C.R. 104, the defendants were liable in trespass although entry to the neighbouring land was the only way of repairing their ruinous building, but see now the Access to Neighbouring Land Act 1992, para.13–11, above.

[222] *Monsanto Plc v Tilly* [2000] Env L.R. 313.

[223] Shelley *arguendo* in Y.B. Trin. 13 Hen. 8, f.15, pl. 1, at f.16a; Kingsmill J. in Y.B. Trin. 21 Hen. 7, f.27b, pl. 5; *Saltpetre Case* (1606) 12 Rep. 12 at 13; *Sirocco v Geary* (1853) 3 Cal. 69.

[224] *Dewey v White* (1827) M. & M. 56 (A, whose adjoining house was inevitably damaged had no remedy).

[225] *Mouse's case* (1609) 12 Rep. 63. It should be noted that this case took place on an inland waterway. The position as to jettison at sea may be affected by the principle of general average.

[226] *Milman v Dolwell* (1810) 2 Camp. 378. Defendant lost his case because he did not plead necessity. Cf. *Romney Marsh v Trinity House* (1870) L.R. 5 Ex. 204.

[227] See *Burmah Oil Co (Burmah Trading) Ltd v Lord Advocate* [1965] A.C. 75 at 164–165.

[228] "The safety of human lives belongs to a different scale of values from the safety of property. The two are beyond comparison and the necessity for saving life has at all times been considered a proper ground for inflicting such damages as may be necessary upon another's property": *Esso Petroleum Ltd v Southport Corp* [1956] A.C. 218 at 228 per Devlin J.

[229] (1876) 1 Ex.D. 55.

of *delirium tremens*. His servants were feasting and drinking in the house. X's sister-in-law removed X's jewellery from the room where he lay dead to another room for safety's sake. Some unknown person stole it. The sister-in-law was held liable to X's executor for trespass to the jewellery because there was no proof that her interference was reasonably necessary. On the other hand, the justification for interference depends upon the state of things at the moment at which interference takes place. Subsequent events may show that interference was not needed at all, but that will not deprive the doer of his defence. In *Cope v Sharpe*,[230] a fire broke out on C's land. While C's servants were trying to beat it out, D, the gamekeeper of X (who had shooting rights over C's land) set fire to some strips of heather between the fire and some nesting pheasants of X. Shortly afterwards, C's servants succeeded in extinguishing the fire. C sued the gamekeeper for trespass. He was held not liable, for there was real and imminent danger to the game at the moment at which he acted, and what he did was reasonably necessary.

25–34   A landowner may defend himself against an incursion of water by erecting barricades or heightening banks on his own land even if the foreseeable result is the flooding of his neighbour's land by the diverted water.[231] The law allows a kind of reasonable selfishness in such matters.[232] Altruism is not demanded; ordinary skill and care are.[233] This applies not only to private landowners but also to any authority charged with protecting landowners from the incursion of water.[234] Nor is it material that the barriers were erected at some distance within the boundaries of the land instead of on the edge of it for it would be illogical to allow a landowner to protect the whole of his land against floods and yet to hold him liable because he had set his embankment farther back and so had left part of his land undefended.[235]

However, this repulsion of a temporary incursion must be distinguished from accumulating water on one's land and then getting rid of it by artificial means in such a way as to flood a neighbour's land. That is not lawful[236] and this is so even if the accumulation of the water is due, not to the act of the landowner, but to an extraordinary rainfall. Thus, in *Whalley v Lancashire and Yorkshire Ry*,[237] an unprecedented storm and rainfall flooded the drains bordering on the

---

[230] [1912] 1 K.B. 496.
[231] *Home Brewery Plc v William Davis & Co (Leicester) Ltd* [1987] Q.B. 339; cf. *Green v Somerleyton* [2003] EWCA Civ 198; [2004] 1 P & C.R. 520.
[232] *Nield v L & NW Ry* (1874) L.R. 10 Ex. 4 at 7 per Bramwell B.
[233] *Maxey Drainage Board v GN Ry* (1912) 106 L.T. 429.
[234] *R. v Pagham* (1828) 8 B. & C. 356
[235] *Gerrard v Crowe* [1921] 1 A.C. 395 at 400 per Viscount Cave.
[236] *Hurdman v NE Ry* (1878) 3 C.P.D. 168; *Maxey Drainage Board v GN Ry*, above, fn.233; *Gerrard v Crowe*, above, fn.235.
[237] (1884) 13 Q.B.D. 131.

railway embankment of the defendants so that a large quantity of water was dammed up against the embankment. The water afterwards rose so as to endanger the embankment. The defendants then pierced it with gullies and the water flowed away and flooded the claimant's land. The defendants were held liable, although the jury found that if they had had only the preservation of their own land to consider their act would have been reasonable. They could lawfully have turned away the flood if they had seen it coming, but:

"[T]here is a difference between protecting yourself from an injury which is not yet suffered by you, and getting rid of the consequences of an injury which has occurred to you".[238]

Greyvensteyn v Hattingh,[239] an appeal case from South Africa, related to a plague of locusts. They entered the claimant's land, and the defendants, in the reasonable belief that they were trekking towards their land, entered a strip of land belonging to third parties and turned away the locusts so that they re-entered the claimant's land and devoured his crops. The defendants were held not liable because they were repelling an extraordinary misfortune or because, if locusts were to be regarded in South Africa as a normal incident of agriculture, the defendants were entitled to get rid of them just as they would be allowed to scare away crows regardless of the direction they took in leaving.[240]

So far we have been dealing with harm inflicted on property. **25–35** Necessity as a justification for interference with the person is much more likely to arise in a criminal law context and the law is discussed at length in *A (Children) (Conjoined Twins: Surgical Separation), Re*[241] where necessity was held to be justification for an operation to separate Siamese twins, where otherwise they would both have died, even though the inevitable consequence of the operation was the death of the weaker one, who was inevitably "designated for death". This would equally have been a defence to a civil action by the parents.[242] Though the matter is now largely governed by statute, necessity was used at common law as the basis for justifying medical treatment of an incapable person[243] and in *R. v Bournewood etc. NHS Trust*[244] the House of Lords accepted that

[238] (1884) 13 Q.B.D. 131 at 140 per Lindley L.J.
[239] [1911] A.C. 355.
[240] Scaring crows is a normal incident in the occupation of land; piercing a railway embankment is not an ordinary use of the embankment: *Whalley v Lancs & Yorks Ry* (1884) 13 Q.B.D. 13 at 138.
[241] [2001] Fam.147. See also the well-known criminal cases of *R. v Dudley* (1884) 15 Cox C.C. 624 and *US v Holmes* (1842) 1 Wall Jr. 1.
[242] For the statutory sum for bereavement under the Fatal Accidents Act 1976.
[243] See para.4–9, above.
[244] [1999] 1 A.C. 458. But as to the European Convention on Human Rights see *HL v UK* [2004] E.H.R.R. 32.

common law necessity could justify the detention of a mentally disordered person who is a danger to himself or others, notwithstanding the existence of a statutory regime for detention. However, this situation is now governed by the Mental Capacity Act 2005.[245]

25–36 Where property is destroyed it is clear that no damages can be claimed in tort where the defendant's act is justified by necessity; but that does not necessarily settle the question whether the defendant is liable to make some form of compensation. Perhaps a distinction exists between (1) an act done for the common weal, and (2) an act done simply in protection of one's person or property. As to (1), in the *Saltpetre Case*,[246] it was said that every man, as well as the King and his officials, may, for the defence of the realm, enter upon another man's land and make trenches or bulwarks there:

"[B]ut after the danger is over, the trenches and bulwarks ought to be removed, so that the owner shall not have prejudice in his inheritance";

and in *Burmah Oil Co (Burmah Trading) Ltd v Lord Advocate*[247] it was held by a majority of the House of Lords that the Crown must pay compensation for property destroyed, by an exercise of the Royal prerogative during the War, in order to prevent it from falling into enemy hands. The effect of this decision was, however, removed by the War Damage Act 1965, which provides that:

"No person shall be entitled at common law to receive from the Crown compensation in respect of damage to, or destruction of, property caused . . . by acts lawfully done by, or on the authority of, the Crown during, or in contemplation of the outbreak of, a war in which the Sovereign was, or is engaged."

Notwithstanding the dictum in the *Saltpetre Case* it may be doubted whether a private person, who, of course, does not act under the prerogative and is unaffected by the Act of 1965, need ever have made any compensation for acts justifiably done in defence of the realm.[248] It is, in any case, exceedingly difficult to conceive that today a private citizen could justify an otherwise tortious action on

---

[245] Under s.4B (inserted by the Mental Health Act 2007) deprivation of liberty is only justified under a court order or while a court order is being obtained if necessary to give life-sustaining treatment or to prevent serious deterioration in the person's condition.

[246] (1606) 12 Rep. 12 at 13 per the justices consulting in Serjeants Inn.

[247] [1965] A.C. 75.

[248] The whole passage in 12 Rep. 12–13 is rather confused and the earlier authorities do not support Coke, who reported the case. See, e.g. *Maleverer v Spinke* (1538) Dyer 35b at 36b, para.40.

the ground that it was done in defence of the realm.[249] Where a claim is made for a taking or destruction in emergency against a public authority it is nowadays much more likely to involve the guarantee of protection of property under the First Protocol to the European Convention on Human Rights[250] (to the effect of which even statutory authority is not immune) than the common law. As to (2), in *Southport Corp v Esso Petroleum Co Ltd*[251] Devlin J. was not prepared to hold without further consideration that a person is entitled to damage the property of another without compensating him merely because the infliction of such damage is necessary to save his own property. Possibly bare restitution or compensation for the use or consumption of property might be claimed on unjust enrichment grounds: for example using a neighbour's fire extinguisher to put out a fire on one's own house.[252] Alternatively, one might say that necessity gives an "incomplete privilege" against tort liability. On this basis, on either view:

> "[T]he skier who is lost in a snow storm may enter your cabin for shelter without liability. But if he burns the furniture to stay warm he must pay for its destruction".[253]

8. DURESS

Duress, or threatened injury to a person unless he commits a tort, **25–37** was held many years ago to be no defence if he does commit it. In *Gilbert v Stone*,[254] 12 unknown armed men threatened to kill the defendant unless he entered the claimant's house with them, which he did. To an action for trespass he was held to have no defence:

> "[F]or one cannot justify a trespass upon another for fear, and the defendant hath remedy against those that compelled him."

---

[249] See *Burmah Oil* (above, fn.247), at 164–165 per Lord Upjohn. Lord Reid at 99 conceded that there might be occasions when a subject is entitled to act on his own initiative in defence of the realm, particularly if there is no one in authority there to direct him, but he thought it impossible that any subject could have been entitled to carry out the major demolitions with which the case was concerned.

[250] Deprivation of property is justified, "in the public interest and subject to the conditions provided for by law" but it seems that a lawful taking without any compensation would be exceptional: *Holy Monasteries v Greece* (1994) 20 E.H.R.R. 1.

[251] [1965] A.C. 218 at 227.

[252] An example put by Lord Mansfield in *Hambly v Trott* (1776) 1 Cowp. 371 at 375 is consistent with the suggestion. The *American Restatement of Restitution*, s.122, is to the like effect and applies the rule also where A harms B's property in order to preserve C or C's property, for, "a person is not entitled to be a good samaritan at the expense of another". Section 122, however, exempts A from any obligation to make restitution to B if A's act appeared reasonably necessary to avert a *public* catastrophe.

[253] Dobbs, *Torts* (2000) §107.

[254] (1647) Aleyn 35.

Actual physical compulsion as distinct from mere threat of it, was a defence.[255] It is difficult to believe that there is now any such absolute rule where the threat is out of all proportion to the damage the claimant is required to do. Duress, after all, has been said to be only a species of the genus of "necessity".[256]

9. STATUTORY AUTHORITY

25–38 When a statute authorises the commission of what would otherwise be a tort, then the party injured has no remedy apart from the compensation (if any) which the statute allows him. Statutory powers are not, however, charters of immunity for any injurious act done in the exercise of them. In the first place, courts will not impute to the legislature any intention to take away the private rights of individuals without compensation, unless it be proved that there was such an intention and the burden of proving it is said to rest with those who exercise the statutory powers.[257] On the other hand, the court must beware lest it interfere with the administrative discretion which may have been granted by the statute.[258] Most of the cases have concerned liability for nuisance and the matter has been considered under that head.[259]

---

[255] *Smith v Stone* (1647) Style 65; dictum in *Weaver v Ward* (1616) Hob. 134.
[256] *R. v Howe* [1987] A.C. 417 at 429. In the criminal law context necessity is sometimes labelled "duress of circumstances" (as opposed to duress by threats).
[257] *Farnworth v Manchester Corp* [1929] 1 K.B. 533 at 556 per Lawrence L.J. For proceedings in the House of Lords, see [1930] A.C. 171, but the question would seem to be one purely of statutory construction and as such not to involve questions of the burden of proof at all. The point is that unless the clearest language is used it is to be assumed that Parliament did not intend an encroachment upon the liberties of the subject: *Att Gen v Nissan* [1970] A.C. 179 at 229 per Lord Pearce.
[258] See *Marriage v E Norfolk Catchment Board* [1950] 1 K.B. 284 and para.14–34, above.
[259] See para.14–34, above. One must bear in mind that the European Convention on Human Rights now figures in the picture.

CHAPTER 26

EXTINCTION OF LIABILITY IN TORT

EXTINCTION of liability in tort may take place in several ways, some of them by act of the parties, others by operation of law.[1] **26–1**

1. WAIVER

"Waiver" is a term used in a number of different senses in the law. **26–2** It may mean conduct by the claimant which signifies an intention to give up a right of action for a legal wrong. Subject to the doctrine of promissory estoppel (which cannot be pursued here and the applicability of which to money claims is a matter of some doubt[2]) a right of action for tort can only be "waived" in this sense by an

---

[1] For extinction of liability by death, now more the exception than the rule, see para.23–2, above.
[2] See the standard works on contract.

agreement for valuable consideration or a release by deed.[3] Mere demand for payment of what is due is not a waiver of the right of action for the wrong[4] nor is receipt of part payment of what is due, unless it is accepted as full discharge.[5] Waiver is also used to mean an election between inconsistent rights, as when the claimant, having ratified the unauthorised act of his agent and sued a third party to judgment (which went unsatisfied) was barred from suing his agent for going beyond his authority.[6] There will be an election between inconsistent rights whenever the claimant has done an unequivocal act showing that he has chosen to assert one right rather than the other.[7] Another sense is of choosing between inconsistent or non-cumulative remedies. A claimant in a claim for passing off, for example, may claim damages based upon the loss he has suffered or an account of the profits made by the defendant from the tort, but he cannot have both. However, the claims may be pursued in parallel until the time when liability is established and an election between the two remedies is not generally required until judgment,[8] though it should not be unreasonably delayed to the prejudice of the defendant.[9] It is in this last sense that waiver is used in the special sense of "waiver of tort". As we have seen,[10] the claimant is sometimes allowed to base a claim on the principles of unjust enrichment (or quasi-contract as it was previously called) in order, inter alia, to claim the gains made by the defendant from his wrongdoing. While this may be historically different from an account of profits the two remedies have essentially the same purpose.[11] The claimant is certainly not waiving the tort in the sense of forgiving it, for showing that a tort was committed is a necessary basis of his restitutionary claim,[12] nor is there any binding election in pursuing the claim on one basis rather than the other. Indeed, even a judgment, unless satisfied, may not be a bar. In *United Australia Ltd v Barclays Bank Ltd* C's secretary endorsed a cheque payable to C in favour of D1 and D2 paid the cheque. C, claiming that the secretary had no authority, brought a claim against D1 for money had and received but discontinued it before judgment. The House of Lords held that

---

[3] See para.26–3, below.
[4] *Valpy v Sanders* (1848) 5 C.B. 886; *Morris v Robinson* (1824) 3 B. & C. 196.
[5] *Burns v Morris* (1834) 4 Tyrw. 485; *Lythgoe v Vernon* (1860) 5 H. & N. 180.
[6] *Verschures Creameries Ltd v Hall and Netherlands SS Co* [1921] 2 K.B. 608.
[7] See *United Australia Ltd v Barclays Bank Ltd* [1941] A.C. 1 at 29–30.
[8] *United Australia*, above, fn.7; *Tang v Capacious Investments Ltd* [1996] A.C. 514 (not a tort case).
[9] *Island Records Ltd v Tring International Plc* [1996] 1 W.L.R. 1256.
[10] See para.22–13, above.
[11] "The purpose of ordering an account of profits . . . is to prevent an unjust enrichment": *My Kinda Town Ltd v Soll* [1982] F.S.R. 147 at 156.
[12] See Lord Atkin in *United Australia* [1941] A.C. at 28.

C was not barred from bringing an action for conversion of the cheque against D2 and Lord Simon said that he did not:

"[T]hink that [D2] would escape liability, even if judgment had been entered in [C's] earlier action against [D1]. What would be necessary to constitute a bar . . . would be that, as the result of such judgment or otherwise, the appellant should have received satisfaction".[13]

2. ACCORD AND SATISFACTION

Tortious liability can be extinguished by agreement for valuable **26–3** consideration between the injured party and the tortfeasor.[14] This is styled accord and satisfaction but is really little more than a specialised form of contract and so, to be effective, it must comply with the rules for the formation of contract.[15] "Accord" signifies the agreement, "satisfaction" the consideration which makes it operative. The satisfaction may be either executed, for example "I release you from your obligation in consideration of £100 now paid by you to me" or it may be executory, for example "I release you from your obligation in consideration of your promise to pay me £100 in six months."[16]

Accord and satisfaction may be conditional. A person injured in an accident brought about by the negligence of the defendant may accept an offer of compensation, reserving to himself the right to renew his claim if his injuries turn out to be worse than they were at the time of the accord.[17]

---

[13] [1941] A.C. at 21.

[14] *Peytoe's Case* (1611) 9 Rep. 77b. It is most important to note that since the claim will be for unliquidated damages an accord and satisfaction will be effective even though a court might have awarded more or less in the way of damages. "The agreed sum is a liquidated amount which replaces the claim for an illiquid sum. The effect of the compromise is to fix the amount of his claim in just the same way as if the case had gone to trial and he had obtained judgment.": *Jameson v C.E.G.B.* [2000] 1 A.C. 455 at 474 per Lord Hope. It is also possible for the parties, by an agreement falling short of full accord and satisfaction, to limit the issues between them, as in *Tomlin v Standard Telephones and Cables Ltd* [1969] 1 W.L.R. 1378, an action for damages for personal injuries, where it was agreed that the defendants would pay 50 per cent of the claimant's damages, leaving only the amount of those damages to be determined.

[15] See *D&C Builders Ltd v Rees* [1966] 2 Q.B. 617.

[16] *British Russian Gazette, etc. Ltd v Associated Newspapers Ltd* [1933] 2 K.B. 616 per Scrutton L.J.; at 650 per Greer L.J.

[17] *Lee v L&Y Ry* (1871) L.R. 6 Ch. 527; *Ellen v GN Ry* (1901) 17 T.L.R. 453; *North British Ry v Wood* (1891) 18 R. 27, HL. On the effect of an agreement with D1 where C also has a claim against D2 see *Jameson v C.E.G.B.* [2000] 1 A.C. 455, para.21–3, above.

A. Non-performance of Accord and Satisfaction

26–4   What is the position of the parties if the accord and satisfaction are not carried out? Are they in the same situation as if it had never been made or must the party aggrieved sue upon the broken accord and satisfaction and upon that only? The answer is that it depends upon the construction of the agreement which embodies the accord and satisfaction.[18] If the satisfaction consists of a promise on the part of the tortfeasor, the interpretation of the agreement may be, "I accept this promise as an absolute discharge of your tortious liability"; if so, all that the injured party can sue upon in the event of the tortfeasor not carrying out his promise, is the contract which has been substituted for the tortious liability.[19] Alternatively, the interpretation of the agreement may be, "I accept this promise as a discharge of your liability provided you carry it out" in that case, if the promise is not fulfilled, the injured party has two alternative remedies: he can either fall back upon his original claim in tort, or he can sue upon the contract which was intended to take its place. Somewhat different considerations apply to an accord and satisfaction which is expressed to be conditional in the first instance, as in the example given above of provisional acceptance of compensation in an accident. Here the injured party cannot have recourse to his action in tort unless the condition is not fulfilled. If it is fulfilled within the time specified by the agreement or, if no time is specified, within a reasonable time, then the tortious liability is extinguished. If it is not thus fulfilled, then the injured party can either rely upon his claim in tort or sue upon the conditional agreement which was substituted for it and which has been broken.

B. Release

26–5   Closely akin to accord and satisfaction is release of tortious liability given by the injured party. In fact, there seems to be little difference between the two except that a release is usually, but not necessarily, embodied in a deed and the necessity for consideration is thus avoided.[20] Release is apparently effective whether it is given before or after an action against the tortfeasor is commenced.

---

[18] Although the agreement will usually be contained in "without prejudice" correspondence, which means that the correspondence cannot be used in evidence, this correspondence can be produced to the court if the question is whether a binding agreement has actually been reached between the parties (*Tomlin v Standard Telephones and Cables Ltd* [1969] 1 W.L.R. 1378) and, presumably, also when a question of the interpretation of the agreement has to be decided.

[19] On the position in such a case regarding a claim against another tortfeasor see *Jameson v C.E.G.B.* at [2000] 1 A.C. 481 per Lord Clyde.

[20] *Phillips v Clagett* (1843) 11 M. & W. 84.

3. JUDGMENT

Final judgment by a court of competent jurisdiction extinguishes a **26–6** right of action. It has a twofold effect. First, it estops any party to the litigation from disputing afterwards the correctness of the decision either in law or in fact.[21] Secondly, it operates as a merger of the original cause of action in the rights created by the judgment and these are either to levy execution against the defendant or to bring a new action upon the judgment (not upon the original claim, for that has perished).

The reason why judgment wipes out the claimant's original cause of action is put on either of two grounds. One is public policy: *interest reipublicae ut sit finis litium*; the other is private justice: *nemo debet bis vexari pro uno et eodem delicto.*[22]

4. LIMITATION

Whether a person's claim is based upon tort or upon any other form **26–7** of injury, he will lose his remedy if he falls asleep on it. The reasons for this are twofold. In the first place, no one ought to be exposed to the risk of stale demands of which he may be quite ignorant and which, owing to changed circumstances, he may be unable to satisfy. Secondly, it may have become impossible or difficult, owing to the loss of documents or the death of witnesses, to establish a defence which would have negatived the claim if it had been presented more promptly. These considerations point to a short, definite time limit for the presentation of claims, but they have always been counterbalanced by other considerations of justice to the victim of the tort—suppose, for example, he is suffering from a disability which renders him unable to pursue his claim, or he is unaware of the damage he has suffered (which may or may not be because the wrongdoer has concealed it)? Further, considerations of justice to defendants may be less compelling now than in former times since in the great majority of cases the "real" defendant will be a liability insurance company with large resources and the ability to keep extensive records. In fact, the recent trend of law has been towards the softening of rigid time limits and the use of greater discretion in allowing the presentation of old, but meritorious

---

[21] Provisional damages (para.22–23, above) are a practical, if not theoretical, qualification of this.

[22] It is in the interest of society that there should be an end to litigation and no one should face the risk of being sued more than once for the same wrong. Bower, *Res Judicata* (1924), pp.1–2. Even a technically separate cause of action may now be barred by judgment if it could, with reasonable diligence, have been asserted in the original proceedings: para.22–3, above.

claims. However, these conflicting demands have produced a system of great complexity and the Law Commission has produced proposals for a radical revision of limitation law.[23]

The principal Act today is the Limitation Act 1980,[24] with substantial amendments brought in by the Latent Damage Act 1986. Broadly speaking, actions founded on tort[25] must be brought within six years from the date when the cause of action accrued. In the case of personal injuries claims, however, the period is three years. Defamation has gone from the original period of six years, first to three years and now to one year.[26] The strictness of these rules is ameliorated in various ways, for example by postponing the running of time where the claimant was ignorant that he had a claim and, in personal injury cases, by giving the court a discretionary power to override the time limits altogether. Personal injury limitation will be dealt with separately.

The defendant must plead the Limitation Act if he wishes to rely on it,[27] for the court will not of its own motion take notice that the action is out of time,[28] but if it is pleaded, the claimant has the burden of showing that his claim accrued within the period.[29] A claimant who begins an action within the time allowed may still find that the proceedings are dismissed if conducted in a dilatory manner, for under the Civil Procedure Rules the courts are less tolerant of delay than was formerly the case, whether or not there has been significant prejudice to the defendant. Furthermore, there may be rare cases in which, even though the limitation period still has some time to run, the court will entertain an application by the defendant for a negative declaration that he is *not* liable to the claimant.[30]

---

[23] Law Com. No.270 (2001). See para.26–26, below.

[24] The earliest comprehensive legislation was the Statute of Limitations 1623, discussed at length in the first edition of this book. The 1980 Act consolidated the Limitation Act 1939 with subsequent amending Acts, most notably the Limitation Act 1975 and the Limitation Amendment Act 1980. For the 1980 reforms, see the Law Reform Committee's 21st Report, Cmnd. 6923 (1977). For the 1986 reforms, see the Law Reform Committee's 24th Report, Cmnd. 9390 (1984).

[25] An action for damages for an infringement, contrary to s.2 of the European Communities Act 1972, of rights conferred by Community law is in the nature of a breach of statutory duty and is therefore be considered "an action founded on tort" for this purpose: *R. v Secretary of State for Transport, Ex p. Factortame Ltd (No.7)* [2001] 1 W.L.R. 942.

[26] The first reduction was introduced with effect from December 30, 1985 by the Administration of Justice Act 1985 s.57(2). See now the Limitation Act 1980 s.4A, as substituted by the Defamation Act 1996 s.5. This also applies to malicious falsehood.

[27] CPR, PD 16, para.14–1.

[28] *Dunsmore v Milton* [1938] 3 All E.R. 762. If the defendant decides to contest the case on its merits, it is not open to him to amend to plead limitation at a later stage when it becomes apparent that he is likely to lose on the merits: *Ketterman v Hansel Properties Ltd* [1987] A.C. 189.

[29] *London Congregational Union v Harriss and Harriss* [1988] 1 All E.R. 15; *Crocker v British Coal* (1996) 29 B.M.L.R. 159. However, the burden of proof where the issue of actual or constructive knowledge is raised under s.14 of the Limitation Act 1980 (see para.26–18, below) is not entirely clear: *AB v MoD* [2009] EWHC 1225 (QB) at [482].

[30] *Toropdar v D* [2009] EWHC 567 (QB).

A. Commencement of the Period

According to the Act of 1980 the period of limitation runs, "from **26–8** the date on which the cause of action accrued". No further explanation of "accrued" is given, but authorities from earlier legislation show that the period begins to run, "from the earliest time at which an action could be brought".[31] " 'Cause of action' means that which makes action possible".[32] A cause of action arises, therefore, at the moment when a state of facts occurs which gives a potential claimant a right to succeed against a potential defendant.[33] There must be a claimant who can succeed, and a defendant against whom he can succeed,[34] subject to the qualification that a merely procedural bar to bringing a suit will not prevent time running.[35] Thus, for example, when goods belonging to a person who has died intestate have been converted after his death, the proper party to sue is the administrator and time does not begin to run until he has taken out letters of administration.[36] So, too, where the tortfeasor is entitled to diplomatic immunity, time does not run in his favour until the termination of his period of office, for until then no action will lie against him.[37] If, however, time has once begun to run, it will continue to do so even over a period during which there is no one capable of suing or of being sued.[38] The fact that the potential claimant is unable to

---

[31] *Reeves v Butcher* [1891] 2 Q.B. 509 at 511 per Lindley L.J. The day on which the cause of action arose is excluded: *Marren v Dawson, Bentley & Co Ltd* [1961] 2 Q.B. 135. If the last day of the period is one when court offices are closed the claimant has until the first following day when they are open (*Kaur v S. Russell & Sons* [1973] 1 Q.B. 336) and proceedings are started when the claim form is received in court even if there is delay in its issue: *Barnes v St Helens MBC* [2006] EWCA Civ 1372; [2007] 1 W.L.R. 879.

[32] Preston and Newsom, *Limitation of Actions*, 3rd edn, p.4, citing Lord Dunedin in *Board of Trade v Cayzer, Irvine & Co Ltd* [1927] A.C. 610 at 617. Or in terms of pleading, "Every fact which it would be necessary for the plaintiff to prove, if traversed, in order to support his right to the judgment of the court": *Read v Brown* (1888) 22 Q.B.D. 128 at 131 per Lord Esher M.R.

[33] Our theory of judicial decisions may have a curious impact here. Suppose D is negligent in advising C in 1995, at a time when the settled view of the law is that D is immune from suit in such a case. In July 2000 the HL departs from this view. C issues proceedings in May 2006, just within the six-year period from July 2000, and argues that the immunity was removed from July 2000 and that was the first point at which C could sue D. C's claim is dismissed on the basis that the limitation period expired in 2001: the basic rule is that when the court "changes" the law it declares that the "new" law it states has always been the law: *Awoyomi v Radford* [2007] EWHC 1671; [2008] Q.B. 793. A claim under the *Francovich* principle for failure by the UK to implement a EU Directive arises at the time of the relevant injury to the claimant, even though the failure may not be apparent until his rights against the wrongdoer prove illusory: *Spencer v Secretary of State for Work and Pensions* [2008] EWCA Civ 750; [2009] Q.B. 358.

[34] Preston and Newsom, *Limitation of Actions*, 3rd edn, p.4, referring to dicta of Vaughan Williams L.J. in *Thomson v Clanmorris* [1900] 1 Ch. 718 at 728–729.

[35] *Sevcon Ltd v Lucas CAV Ltd* [1986] 1 W.L.R. 462 (sealing of patent necessary before action could be brought).

[36] *Pratt v Swaine* (1828) B. & C. 285. The principle was laid down in *Murray v East India Co* (1821) 5 B. & Ald. 204, which, however, was not an action in tort.

[37] *Musurus Bey v Gadban* [1894] 2 Q.B. 352.

[38] *Rhodes v Smethurst* (1838) 4 M. & W. 42; (1840) 6 M. & W. 351.

identify the defendant does not, in principle, prevent a cause of action accruing,[39] though this is now qualified in many cases.[40]

Typically,[41] the tortious conduct of the defendant will be a single act or omission but the damage suffered by the claimant will continue unless and until it is remedied by damages. Once some damage has been suffered from the tort time begins to run and the claimant cannot evade the limitation period by confining his claim to losses which have occurred within the prescribed period before he commences proceedings.[42]

B. Latent Damage

26–9   When the tort is actionable per se, as in trespass and libel, time begins to run, in general, at the moment the wrongful act was committed, whether the injured party knows of it or not, provided there is no fraudulent concealment.[43] This applies though the resulting damage does not occur or is not discovered until a later date, for such damage is not a new cause of action, but is merely an incident of the other.[44] On the other hand, where the tort is actionable only upon proof of actual damage, as in nuisance, deceit and negligence, time runs from the damage.[45] If, therefore, you were injured by drinking my negligently manufactured ginger beer more than three years after it was made you could bring an action against me without asking the court to exercise its special dispensing powers for personal injury cases, because no cause of action would have accrued to you until you drank. This rule of negligence contrasts with that applicable to actions for breach of contract, where time runs from the date of the breach, so that a claimant whose contractual claim is time-barred may yet save himself by asserting a concurrent right of action for tortious negligence. So, if a defective part is supplied for a chemical plant time starts to run for the purpose of the Sale of Goods Act as soon as the part is delivered even though its defective condition is then unknown. However, for the purposes of a claim in negligence it does not run until the part fails and causes damage to the plant.[46] Damage may, however, be suffered, even for the purposes of tort, before it is apparent to the claimant. In *Bell v Peter*

---

[39] *R.B. Policies at Lloyd's v Butler* [1950] 1 K.B. 76.
[40] See para.26–18, below.
[41] Leaving aside those cases, like continuing trespass, where there is a continuing wrong and a fresh cause of action arises each day. For an example from another context see *Phonographic Performance Ltd v DTI* [2004] EWHC 1795; [2004] 1 W.L.R. 2893.
[42] *Khan v R.M. Falvey & Co* [2002] EWCA Civ 400; [2002] P.N.L.R. 28. On this basis, in a case of negligence in not proceeding with a claim time may begin to run before the claim is struck out for delay once it becomes at risk of suffering that fate.
[43] *Granger v George* (1826) 5 B. & C. 149.
[44] *Howell v Young* (1826) 5 B. & C. 259.
[45] *Backhouse v Bonomi* (1861) 9 H.L.C. 503.
[46] See *Nitrigin Eireann Teoranta v Inco Alloys Ltd* [1992] 1 W.L.R. 498.

Browne & Co[47] a husband and wife upon the breakdown of their marriage in 1978 agreed that the matrimonial home should be transferred into the wife's name but that the husband's interest in the proceeds of sale should be protected by some legal mechanism. No steps were in fact taken by the husband's solicitors to effect this protection and eight years later the wife sold the house and spent all the proceeds. Even on the basis that the husband had concurrent claims in contract and tort against his solicitors, time began to run for the tort claim at the latest when, after the completion of the transfer, a competent solicitor would have taken steps to protect the husband's interest, as by lodging a Land Registry caution against the property. It was true that the situation was remediable until sale of the property, but the ability to remedy it depended upon knowledge of the problem on the part of the husband and this was more theoretical than real.

However, there must be a present loss, not merely the contingency of one at some time in the future. In *Bell v Peter Browne* the claimant failed to get what he bargained for when the defendants failed to put the protective mechanism in place, even though the loss of his money when his wife spent the proceeds was a contingency which had not then occurred. In *Law Society v Sephton & Co*,[48] on the other hand, the defendant between 1988 and 1995 wrongly certified to the claimants compliance by a solicitor with the accounts rules, which led to the claimants paying compensation to clients.[49] The first claim on the compensation fund was made in July 1996 but proceedings were issued in in May 2002, within six years of the first claim but more than seven years after the last certification. The House of Lords held that time did not begin to run until the first claim on the compensation fund was made. Even though it was true that had the claimants known the truth they would have exercised their statutory powers of intervention in the practice and prevented misappropriation of funds, there had been no transaction changing the claimants' legal position or diminishing their assets. Similarly, time would not begin to run in respect of advice given on a personal guarantee (as opposed to one secured on the guarantor's property[50]) until the lender made a call on the guarantee,[51] though it is hard to see why the guarantor who gives no security should be in a better

26–10

---

[47] [1990] 2 Q.B. 495.

[48] [2006] UKHL 22; [2006] 2 A.C. 543 at [45]. See also *Wardley Australia Ltd v Western Australia* (1992) 175 C.L.R. 514.

[49] For the cause of action see *Law Society v KPMG Peat Marwick* [2000] 1 W.L.R. 1921, para.11–25, above. Strictly, the payment of compensation in *Sephton* was a public law matter but nothing turns on this.

[50] *Forster v Outred & Co* [1982] 1 W.L.R. 86.

[51] *Axa Insurance Ltd v Akther & Darby* [2009] EWCA Civ 1166 at [17]; *Wardley Australia Ltd v Western Australia*, above, fn.48.

position against his adviser than one who does not.[52] The line is of course hard to draw. In *Knapp v Ecclesiastical Insurance Group Plc* it was held that where a policy of insurance was voidable for non-disclosure because of the broker's negligence the cause of action arose when the policy was effected, not at the later stage when it was repudiated[53] and this was approved in *Sephton*; but in *Nykredit Mortgage Bank Plc v Edward Erdman Group Ltd*[54] a valuer was responsible for the claimant having made a loan on the basis of an inadequate security. The issue was not limitation but when the cause of action accrued for the purposes of interest on damages and on the facts the borrower defaulted immediately and the cause of action in respect of the inaccurate valuation was held to arise from the time of the transaction or very soon thereafter. However, the House of Lords was of the view that in general the question whether the lender had suffered a loss could not be determined without taking account of the value of the borrower's covenant to repay. That might be worthless (as on the facts); it might be of some, though uncertain, value; or it might be perfectly adequate to protect the lender's interests. It seems that at least in the last case there would be no loss at the time of the transaction even though the lender did not "get what he paid for" from the valuer. Indeed if the borrower continued to pay until the loan was discharged there never would be a loss. Tempting though it is to equate these cases with that where a buyer has received sub-standard goods for his money, this result shows that the analogy cannot be pressed too far.[55] The difficulty of untangling the current concepts is demonstrated by *Axa Insurance Ltd v Akther & Darby*.[56] The assumed facts for the purposes of the preliminary issue were that the defendants were in breach of duty to NI (which had assigned its claims to Axa) in assessing the prospects of success of legal claims for the support of which NI issued ATE policies.[57] Seven thousand-odd of these policies leading to £19 million of loss[58] were issued more than six years before proceedings were started. The majority of the Court of Appeal held that the cause of action accrued when the policies were issued and that this was not a case of a contingent liability.

[52] "Within the bounds of sense and reasonableness the policy of the law should be to advance, rather than retard, the accrual of a cause of action. This is especially so if the law provides parallel causes of action in contract and in tort in respect of the same conduct. The disparity between the time when these parallel causes of action arise should be smaller, rather than greater": *Nykredit Mortgage Bank Plc v Edward Erdman Group Ltd* [1997] 1 W.L.R. 1627 at 1633..
[53] [1998] P.N.L.R. 172.
[54] [1997] 1 W.L.R. 1627.
[55] *Law Society v Sephton*, above, fn.48, at [45].
[56] [2009] EWCA Civ 1166.
[57] See para.1–27, above.
[58] The total size of the claim was £65 million: [2009] EWHC 635 (Comm); [2009] P.N.L.R. 25 at [3].

"If as a result of the vetting breaches the policy results in a loss
to the insurer, it carried that risk from inception and thus (using
hindsight as a valuer is entitled and bound to do) a valuation of
the policy on inception would always have reflected that inherent
risk."[59]

Unlike *Sephton*, this was a case where the claimants had entered into
a transaction as a result of information provided by the
defendants.

"The most that can be said . . . is that the loss suffered by the
claimant insurers is contingent upon the claim, which is (ex
hypothesi) likely to fail, actually failing. But that does not make
the case a case of a 'mere contingent liability' because the
claimants have entered into a flawed transaction which they ought
not to have entered into. To my mind that is the damage which the
claimants have suffered and that occurred at the time of the
inception of the policies."[60]

For Lloyd L.J. dissenting, on the other hand, the insurers:

"[S]ustained no loss, of any kind, on entry into the policy other
than that resulting from incurring the contingent liability to pay
sums of money under the policy. It seems to me that *Sephton* . . .
binds this court to hold that incurring such a liability does not
constitute actual damage."[61]

Those cases exemplify latent economic damage. For personal   **26–11**
injuries there was legislative intervention, first in 1963 and then in
1975 and the law is examined below. The recurrence of the problem
in the 1970s in the context of defective premises led to further
legislative action in the Latent Damage Act 1986, amending the
Limitation Act 1980 by the insertion of ss.14A and 14B. Ironically,
it now seems that most of the cases upon which the 1986 Act was
intended to operate do not raise any cause of action at all since the
decision of the House of Lords in *Murphy v Brentwood DC*[62] that
claims for structural defects in buildings do not generally sound in

---

[59] At [61] per Arden L.J.
[60] At [82] per Longmore L.J. See also *Shore v Sedgwick Financial Services Ltd* [2008]
EWCA Civ 863; [2008] P.N.L.R. 37; *Pegasus Management Holdings v Ernst & Young*
[2010] EWCA Civ 181.
[61] At [160]. It may be observed that if the Law Commission's proposals (para.26–26, below)
were implemented these problems would disappear because the *base* period of limitation
would run from the discoverability of the claim. Now there is an alternative, secondary
period on that basis which may or may not be available depending on the facts: see
below.
[62] [1991] 1 A.C. 398, para.9–33, above.

tort. However, the added sections are generally applicable to actions for damages for negligence (other than one which includes a claim for damages for personal injuries) where latent damage is involved, though not to actions for breach of contract, even though the claim is based on breach of an express or implied term to take reasonable care.[63]

To the basic period of six years from the accrual of the cause of action, s.14A(4)(b) adds[64] an alternative period of three years from the earliest date (the "starting date") on which the claimant had not only the right to sue but also knew or reasonably could have known about the damage and its attributability to the act or omission alleged to constitute negligence.[65] This is only relevant if the alternative period expires later than the basic period of six years from the accrual of the cause of action.[66] Hence, if the facts of *Bell v Peter Browne & Co* were to recur, the six-year period would commence and finish at the same times as it did in that case but the claimant would then have three years from the point, after the sale of the house by the wife, when the problem came to light. The alternative, three-year period may commence while the initial six-year period is still running or may start time running afresh after the initial period has expired, but superimposed upon both periods is the so-called "long-stop" provision of s.14B, which bars any claim for negligence (other than in respect of personal injuries) 15 years from the date of the last act of negligence to which the damage is attributable. The operation of the two sections may be illustrated in the context of a *"White v Jones"* claim[67] by a disappointed beneficiary against

[63] *Iron Trade Mutual Insurance Co Ltd v J.K. Buckenham Ltd* [1990] 1 All E.R. 808; *Société Commerciale de Reassurance v ERAS (International) Ltd* [1992] 2 All E.R. 82n. It is not obvious why contract claims are excluded, given that the claimant may have concurrent claims in contract and tort. Furthermore, the greater laxity shown to the tort claim is also liable to elevate its importance in comparison with the contract claim, even though that should be the primary matter governing a relationship which is, ex hypothesi, consensual. It is even harder to defend the exclusion of other torts such as nuisance and breach of statutory duty. The answer seems to be that the legislative exercise was dominated by the problems of negligently constructed buildings. However, this makes it doubly hard to justify the exclusion of liability under the Defective Premises Act 1972 from the scheme of s.14A.
[64] Technically, s.14A removes all latent damage cases from the basic provision of s.2 and then re-enacts a six-year basic period for these cases (s.14A(4)(b)). This appears to be solely for drafting convenience and there appears to be no difference of substance between s.2 and s.14A(4)(b).
[65] This is a considerable oversimplification of the complex provisions of s.14A(5)–(10). These are modelled closely on s.14, dealing with personal injury: para.26–18, below and *Haward v Fawcetts* [2006] UKHL 9; [2006] 1 W.L.R. 682. Knowledge includes knowledge the claimant might reasonably have been expected to acquire. It is *not* necessary that the claimant should have known that the acts or omissions constituted negligence in law, it is enough if he knew of the facts which are now the basis of his claim for negligence.
[66] For this reason s.14A was no use to the claimants in *Law Society v Sephton & Co* [2006] UKHL 22; [2006] 2 A.C. 543, above.
[67] See para.5–37, above.

a solicitor who fails in 2000 to carry out his client's instructions to confer a benefit upon the beneficiary by will, the testator dying in 2007. It is unclear whether time starts running against the beneficiary when the will is executed or when the testator dies[68] but even if it is the former, a new, three-year period will begin when the problem comes to light on the testator's death in 2007. If, however, the testator dies in 2016 the beneficiary's claim would be extinguished in any event.[69]

We have already noted that the change in the law in 1986 was largely prompted by cases about defective buildings but that the premise of that change seems to have been falsified by *Murphy v Brentwood*. However, there may still be "building" cases for which s.14A has some significance. The most obvious—though probably rare in practice—are those in which operations by the defendant cause latent damage to an existing building owned by the claimant.[70] In addition, there may be cases in which the claimant can found a claim on *Hedley Byrne v Heller* against someone involved in the design or building of premises which are defective from the start. Lord Keith in *Murphy v Brentwood*[71] thought that the decision of the House in *Pirelli General Cable Works Ltd v Oscar Faber & Partners*[72] (where the defendants were consulting engineers for a factory chimney built by a third party) might be explained in this way.[73] In *Pirelli* it was held that the cause of action arose, not when the chimney was designed or built but when damage in the form of cracks appeared, even though at that stage they were neither discovered nor discoverable by any reasonable means.[74] Where all this stands today is not easy to state.[75] The view that there was physical damage for tort purposes when cracks occurred is irreconcilable with the view of the nature of such damage in *Murphy v Brentwood*; if, however, *Pirelli* is to be explained as based on *Hedley Byrne* then the liability can embrace economic loss. Unfortunately, that does not take us very much further. In some cases of economic loss time has

26–12

---

[68] See *White v Jones* [1993] 3 W.L.R. 730 per Nicholls V.C.

[69] There may be circumstances in which a professional person owes a continuing duty to a client, but it is not thought that this could be called in aid for the beneficiary's claim in tort.

[70] It is assumed that if the claimant can show negligence in fact, he is entitled to take advantage of s.14A even though the situation might fall under the rubric of nuisance, to which the Act has no application.

[71] [1991] 1 A.C. 398 at 466.

[72] [1983] 2 A.C. 1.

[73] A similar argument was rejected on the facts in *Nitrigin Eireann Teoranta v Inco Alloys Ltd* [1992] 1 W.L.R. 498.

[74] A further complication in this area is the suggestion in *Pirelli* that time might begin to run even before damage occurred if the building was "doomed from the start" but this was strictly interpreted and it is not clear that it was actually applied in any case.

[75] For a full discussion see McKendrick, "Pirelli Re-Examined" (1991) 11 L.S. 326. On facts indistinguishable from *Pirelli* the CA in *Abbott v Will Gannon & Smith Ltd* [2005] EWCA Civ 198; [2005] P.N.L.R. 30 considered itself bound by the case.

been held to run before the loss was discoverable and it is arguable that taking over a building at the end of construction is analogous to entering into the transaction in cases like *Bell v Peter Browne*. On the other hand, the Privy Council on an appeal from New Zealand (where common law liability for defective buildings is more extensive than it is here) accepted that classification of the loss as economic pointed towards time running from the point where the defect became apparent to an ordinarily observant owner,[76] for it is not until then that the value of the property is depreciated. However, the decision is expressly made only in the context of the New Zealand law governing defective buildings.[77]

26–13   Another provision of the Latent Damage Act 1986 may be yet more flotsam left behind by the wreck of the earlier building cases in *Murphy*. Property may be disposed of during the limitation period and before the defect is discovered. In *Pirelli* the House of Lords introduced the novel concept of "class limitation" whereby if time began to run against an owner it also continued to run against his successors in title. The House of Lords was not, however, directly concerned with the question of whether such successors had claims at all. If, after *Murphy*, the original owner's claim has to be based upon *Hedley Byrne v Heller* one would have thought that would be a serious obstacle to a claim by a successor in title.[78] However, s.3(1) of the Latent Damage Act provides that:

"[W]here—

   (a) a cause of action ("the original cause of action") has accrued to any person in respect of any negligence to which damage to any property in which he has an interest is attributable (in whole or in part) and

   (b) another person acquires an interest in that property after the date on which the original cause of action accrued but before the material facts about the damage have become known to any person who, at the time when he first has knowledge of those facts, has any interest in the property;

a fresh cause of action in respect of that negligence *shall accrue*[79] to that other person on the date on which he acquires his interest in the property."

---

[76] *Invercargill CC v Hamlin* [1996] A.C. 624.

[77] Note, however, that Lord Nicholls, sitting as a judge of the Hong Kong Court of Final Appeal (albeit dissenting) in *Bank of East Asia Ltd v Tsien Wui Marble Factory Ltd* 2000–1 H.K.C. 1 regarded *Pirelli* as outdated.

[78] See para.11–25, above; but cf. *Bryan v Maloney* (1995) 128 A.L.R. 163.

[79] Emphasis added. By s.3(2)(a) such a fresh cause of action, "shall be treated as if based on breach of a duty of care at common law to the person to whom it accrues".

In effect, therefore, provided the first owner had no knowledge of the defect but had a cause of action, his transferee has a new, statutory claim. Although the second owner only acquires his cause of action when he acquires the property, there is no risk of extension of the limitation period because for the purpose of s.14A of the 1980 Act it is deemed to accrue at the same time as that of the first owner.[80]

C. Fraud and Concealment

Related to the problem of latent damage are special provisions in the Limitation Act 1980[81] dealing with fraud and concealment. First, where the claimant's action is based on the fraud of the defendant or his agent[82] or of any person through whom he (or his agent) claims, time does not run until the claimant has discovered the fraud or could with reasonable diligence have discovered it.[83] This part of the section is limited to cases where the action is actually founded on fraud (for example, where it is a claim for damages for deceit or to rescind a contract) and does not extend to causes of action in which "dishonest" or "fraudulent" conduct may figure (for example conversion),[84] but by s.32(1)(b) the same postponement of the running of time applies[85] where, "any fact relevant to the claimant's right of action[86] has been deliberately concealed from him by the defendant" and this includes a case of, "deliberate commission of a

26–14

---

[80] That is to say, both the primary, six-year period and the 15-year long-stop period will run from the time when the damage occurred when the property was in the first owner's hands. There can be no question of the running of part of the alternative three-year period while the property is in the first owner's hands since it is a pre-condition of the application of s.3 that he should not have had actual or constructive knowledge of the damage. On its face, s.3 is not confined to buildings. Indeed, it has been suggested that it applies so as to create a cause of action where D damages goods belonging to X which are at the risk of C (see para.5–42, above).

[81] Section 32, replacing Limitations Act 1939 s.26. Section 32 was intended by the Law Reform Committee to restate the 1939 Act provision as it had been interpreted in the courts: Cmnd. 6923, para.2–22. However, the section differs somewhat from the Committee's original draft and see *Sheldon v R.H.M. Outhwaite (Underwriting Agencies) Ltd* [1996] A.C. 102 at 145.

[82] Which includes an independent contractor: *Applegate v Moss* [1971] 1 Q.B. 406.

[83] Section 32(1)(a). On reasonable diligence, see *Peco Arts Inc v Hazlitt Gallery Ltd* [1983] 1 W.L.R. 1315 (a s.32(1)(c) case) and *Barnstaple Boat Co Ltd v Jones* [2007] EWCA Civ 727.

[84] *Beaman v A.R.T.S. Ltd* [1949] 1 K.B. 550 at 558 per Lord Greene M.R., at 567 per Somervell L.J. Cf. *Grahame Allen & Sons Pty Ltd v Water Resources Commission* [2000] 1 Qd. R. 523 (misfeasance in a public office).

[85] See also s.32(1)(c) which applies to actions "for relief from the consequences of a mistake".

[86] This has been interpreted to mean a fact which it is necessary to allege and prove to establish a cause of action. It is not enough that the defendant has concealed facts going to the strength of the claimant's case or the availability of a defence: *Johnson v CC Surrey, The Times*, November 23, 1992; *C v MGN* [1997] 1 W.L.R. 131 (same words in former s.32A); *AIC Ltd v ITS Testing Services (UK) Ltd* [2006] EWCA Civ 1601; [2007] 1 Lloyd's Rep 555.

breach of duty in circumstances in which it is unlikely to be discovered for some time".[87] In other words, there must either be a deliberate breach of duty (the second limb) or there must be a deliberate concealment[88] of a prior breach of duty which may only have been negligent (the first limb).[89] It is not enough to satisfy the first limb that what the defendant did was deliberate if he did not realise it was a breach of duty.

Section 32(1)(b) applies where the defendant commits a tort which is not at the time known to the claimant and then, at a later date, conceals that. The ideal answer in such a case would be to "stop the clock" at the time of the concealment and to restart it when the wrong is discovered (or becomes discoverable) by the claimant. However, the words of the Act will not bear this interpretation, so the result is that a new limitation period starts from the date of discovery.[90]

The principle of s.32 will prevent the running of time in many cases where there is a wrongful dealing[91] with goods by a person who has custody of, or a limited interest in, them and hence the opportunity to conceal that dealing. However, it would be hard if the running of time were also suspended against innocent purchasers. Therefore, notwithstanding that fraud or concealment will generally affect persons who claim through the actual wrongdoer, s.32(3)(b) provides that nothing in the section shall enable an action to be brought to recover property or its value[92] against the purchaser of the property or any person claiming through him, in any case where the property has been purchased for valuable consideration by an innocent third party since the fraud or concealment.[93]

D. Fiduciary Obligations

26–15   We have seen that the law of limitation has been a fertile source for the presentation of concurrent claims in contract and tort.[94]

---

[87] Section 32(2). See Preface for complex case of two losses, one concealed, the other not.

[88] Clearly a defendant can only conceal something he knows. As to whether there may be concealment by failure to disclose see *Williams v Fanshaw Porter and Hazelhurst* [2004] EWCA Civ 157; [2004] 1 W.L.R. 3185 at [29] and *AIC Ltd v ITS Testing Services (UK) Ltd* [2006] EWCA Civ 1601; [2007] 1 Lloyd's Rep 555 at [319].

[89] *Cave v Robinson Jarvis & Rolfe* [2002] UKHL 18; [2003] 1 A.C. 184.

[90] *Sheldon v R.H.M. Outhwaite (Underwriting Agencies) Ltd* [1996] A.C. 102. Logically this applies even if the claim was statute-barred before the concealment took place.

[91] It is assumed in this discussion that the wrongful dealing does not amount to theft. If it does, time does not run because of the provisions of s.4: see below. Section 32 is not applicable in the normal case of theft where the thief is unknown or untraceable: *R.B. Policies at Lloyd's v Butler* [1950] 1 K.B. 76.

[92] This is an extension of the previous proviso: see the remarks of Lord Denning M.R. in *Eddis v Chichester Constable* [1969] 2 Ch. 345 at 358.

[93] It seems, therefore, that where a custodian knowingly commits conversion by sale to innocent C and conceals this from the owner, C does not get the benefit of the proviso since his purchase is contemporaneous with the fraud or concealment.

[94] See para.1–8, above.

Nowadays it is not uncommon for claims based on professional liability to be run on the basis of breach of fiduciary duty as well as in contract and tort.[95] Historically, such claims are equitable and the Limitation Act 1980 does not provide any fixed periods in respect of equitable relief. Section 36(1) states that the periods applicable to contract and tort do not apply to any such claim:

"[E]xcept in so far as any such time limit may be applied by the court by analogy in like manner as the corresponding time limit under any enactment repealed by the Limitation Act 1939 was applied before 1 July 1940".

In *Cia de Seguros Imperio v Heath (REBX) Ltd*[96] the claim was brought in respect of alleged breaches of duty by the defendants in the operation of a "pooling" arrangement among insurers and was based on alleged dishonest breaches of fiduciary duty as well as on breach of contract and negligence. The Court of Appeal held that, the contract and tort claims being time-barred,[97] the claim for "equitable compensation" was also time-barred by analogy since they corresponded to the common law damages claims.[98]

E. Extinction of Title: Theft[99]

Before 1939 it was only in cases concerning title to land that **26–16** expiry of the limitation period affected title. In all other cases it merely barred the claimant from pursuing his remedy before the courts, so that a person wrongfully deprived of his goods whose action was time-barred might recover them by extra-judicial means and have a right of action in respect of subsequent wrongful dealings with them. The Act of 1939 changed this with regard to conversion and there are further modifications in the 1980 Act.

First, it is enacted by s.3(1) that once a cause of action for conversion has accrued in respect of a chattel, no action may be brought for any subsequent conversion after the expiry of six years from the accrual of the original cause of action unless, of course, the owner has recovered possession of it in the meanwhile. Secondly, s.3(2) provides that once the period of limitation in respect of the original cause of action has expired, then the owner's title is extinguished. So, if you convert my goods wrongfully and later sell them

---

[95] See para.1–11, above.
[96] [2001] 1 W.L.R. 112.
[97] The judge below held that the facts allegedly concealed by the defendants could have been discovered by the claimants for the purposes of s.32 of the 1980 Act.
[98] See also *Coulthard v Disco Mix Club Ltd* [2000] 1 W.L.R. 707.
[99] There is a major international dimension to this in terms of art: see Law Commission Consultation Paper No.151 (1998) §13.47.

to someone else, once six years have elapsed from the taking, not only have I lost the right to sue either you or the person who bought the goods from you, but he is in a position to deal with them as absolute owner notwithstanding that at the time of the sale to him you had no title which you could pass on to him. However, the Law Reform Committee was troubled at the prospect of time running in favour of a thief or receiver and we now have the further and rather complicated provisions of s.4 of the 1980 Act. The effect of the section is that time does not run against the owner in respect of the theft[100] of his chattel or any conversion "related to the theft", which latter phrase means any subsequent conversion other than a purchase in good faith.[101] Thus if property is stolen and then sold by the thief to X (who is aware of its origin) and then given by X to Y, the owner's rights of action against the thief and X and Y continue indefinitely and his title will never be extinguished. However, the occurrence of a good faith purchase starts time running against the owner in favour of the good faith purchaser (and any converter from him). After six years the owner will no longer be able to sue the good faith purchaser or anyone who subsequently dealt with the goods[102] and his title to the goods will be extinguished. However, he retains his right to sue the original thief and other converters who preceded the good faith purchaser.[103]

F. Disabilities

26–17   One of the longest standing derogations from standard limitation periods occurs where the claimant is under disability. If, on the date when the right of action accrued, the person to whom it accrued was under a disability, time does not begin to run until he ceases to be under a disability or dies (whichever first occurs).[104] For these purposes, the law now recognises only two forms of disability, infancy and lack of mental capacity (formerly unsoundness of mind).[105] Infancy presents no difficulty, for it means simply a person under the age of 18.[106] The question whether a person has the mental

---

[100] Which includes fraud and blackmail: s.4(5)(b).

[101] Any conversion following the theft is presumed to be related to the theft unless the contrary is shown: s.4(4). A purchase in good faith may itself give the purchaser a good title, but will by no means necessarily do so: para.17–22, above.

[102] If this person is a thief, all the provisions of the section will apply over again vis-a-vis the good faith purchaser, who is now the owner.

[103] Section 4(1): " . . . but if his title . . . is extinguished under section 3(2) . . . he may not bring an action in respect of a theft preceding the loss of his title, unless the theft in question preceded the conversion from which time began to run for the purposes of section 3(2)."

[104] Section 28(1).

[105] Section 38(2).

[106] In *O'Driscoll v Dudley HA* [1998] Lloyd's Rep. Med. 210 the problems arose because of the family's mistaken belief that the age of majority was 21.

capacity to conduct legal proceedings is to be determined by reference to the Mental Capacity Act 2005.[107]

What is the position of a claimant who had mental capacity when time began to run but later loses it; or of a claimant who was an infant when his cause of action accrued and suffered loss of mental capacity before he reached the age of 18; or of a claimant who is under a disability at the moment when he succeeds to the title of a predecessor who was under no disability? The Act provides that unless the right of action first accrues to a person who is then disabled the disability has no effect.[108] Where, however, there are successive disabilities in the same person (lack of mental capacity supervening on infancy) time does not run until the latter of the disabilities has ended, provided that there is no interval of ability between the disabilities.[109]

G. Special Periods of Limitation

i. Personal injuries and death.[110] The law is now to be found in   **26–18**
ss.11 to 14 and 33 of the Limitation Act 1980, re-enacting the Limitation Act 1975.[111] The provisions apply (s.11(1)) to:

"[A]ny action for damages for negligence, nuisance[112] or breach of duty (whether the duty exists by virtue of a contract or of

---

[107] See para.4–9, above.

[108] Section 28(1), (2). If the claimant is immediately mentally incapable by the tort itself he is disabled when the cause of action accrues, for the law takes no account of parts of a day: *Kirby v Leather* [1965] 2 Q.B. 367. Aliter if the incapacity, though caused by the tort, comes on some days later. However, that might be a pointer towards the court's exercising its discretion under s.33 of the Act, para.26–20, below. Nor, if the right of action accrues to disabled C1 who then dies and it passes to disabled C2 is any further extension of time allowed in respect of C2's disability: s.28(3).

[109] This is the effect of s.28(1), which refers to the claimant's ceasing to be under a disability. See also *Borrows v Ellison* (1871) L.R. 6 Ex. 128.

[110] Even where a claim is not time barred because of one of the qualifications discussed below to the basic rule that it must be brought within three years of the accrual of the cause of action, there may be an issue of which, if any, liability insurer is on risk. A common form of cover applies to injury "occurring during the currency of the policy". In *Bolton MBC v Municipal Mutual Insurance Ltd* [2006] EWCA Civ 50; [2006] 1 W.L.R. 1492 G was exposed to asbestos during the 1960s, when Bolton was insured by CU. G became fatally ill around 1981, though malignancy was not apparent until 1990, at both of which times Bolton was insured by MMI. MMI was liable to indemnify Bolton but CU was not—the cause of the injury occurred during its cover but not the injury itself.

[111] The 1975 Act was based upon the 20th Report of the Law Reform Committee, Cmnd. 5630 (1974). There is a review of the history of this matter in *AB v MoD* [2009] EWHC 1225 (QB).

[112] It seems that this can now only refer to public nuisance: para.14–3, above. There may be special periods for particular contexts. Thus claims by air accident passengers are subject to a fixed two-year period under the Carriage by Air Act 1961 and associated legislation: see *Laroche v Spirit of Adventure (UK) Ltd* [2009] EWCA Civ 12; [2009] 3 W.L.R. 351.

provision made by or under a statute or independently of any contract or any such provision) where the damages claimed by the claimant[113] for the negligence, nuisance or breach of duty consist of or include[114] damages in respect of personal injuries to the claimant or any other person."

For a long while it was held that these words did not include actions for intentional trespass to the person,[115] and in this case the basic six-year period of s.2 applied. As we shall shortly see, although the basic period under the personal injury provisions is shorter, the fact that the claim fell under s.2 was by no means necessarily to the claimant's advantage, because there could be no extension of the period.[116] However, in *A v Hoare*[117] the House of Lords reversed this view of the law so that the provisions of ss.11 to 14 and 33 now apply to trespass.[118] The personal injury provisions also include a case where the owner of a car is sued for allowing an uninsured person to drive, even though he has not caused the accident.[119] The expression "personal injuries" includes any disease and any impairment of a person's physical or mental condition.[120] This covers a claim based on failure to diagnose and treat learning difficulties such as dyslexia[121] and an unwanted pregnancy and

---

[113] Consider the following Machiavellian plan. C, a litigant in person, sues for property loss (extending over more than three years) and for personal injury on the basis of a tort for which personal injury damages are not in fact recoverable. D submits to judgment for damages to be assessed and then contends that his liability for the property loss is limited to a three-year period: *Vukelic v Hammersmith & Fulham LBC* [2003] EWHC 188 (TCC).

[114] If, therefore, the claimant claims damages for personal injuries and damage to property in the same action both claims are governed by s.11.

[115] *Stubbings v Webb* [1993] A.C. 498..

[116] See s.33 (below).

[117] [2008] UKHL 6; [2008] 1 A.C. 844. To similar effect (though divided): *Stingel v Clark* [2006] HCA 37; 228 A.L.R. 229.

[118] Presumably not to cases of purely technical battery where there is no harm at all beyond the invasion of rights. The decision does not fit the words of the statute very well but the law had got itself into a mess in the context of child abuse. If D was the employer of X, who abused C, then under the previous regime D's liability would be governed by the fixed six-year period; hence C often sought to establish defects in D's system of supervision to turn the claim into one for negligence. In *A v Hoare* itself, however, the claim was a direct one against a rapist, who had won a fortune on the National Lottery shortly before the end of his sentence. The claimant's case was allowed to proceed under s.33: [2008] EWHC 1573 (QB).

[119] *Norman v Ali* [2000] R.T.R 107. For this liability see para.7–9, above; but it seems that a claim against a solicitor for failure to pursue his client's personal injury action is not generally within the three-year period (though see *Bennett v Greenland Houchen & Co* [1998] P.N.L.R. 458—solicitors' negligence alleged to have caused depression).

[120] Section 38(1). Where the injured person dies without commencing an action before the expiry of the three-year period, then the period applicable to a claim by his estate under the Law Reform (Miscellaneous Provisions) Act 1934 is three years from (1) the date of death or (2) the date of the personal representative's knowledge (see below) whichever is the later.

[121] *Adams v Bracknell Forest BC* [2004] UKHL 29; [2005] 1 A.C. 76.

confinement is also a "personal injury" for this purpose[122]; but a claim in respect solely of loss of stored substances obtained from a person's body is not one for personal injury,[123] though a claim for psychiatric injury arising from such loss is.[124]

Where s.11 applies the limitation period is three years from the date on which the cause of action accrued, or the date (if later) of the claimant's "knowledge".[125] By virtue of s.14, a person has knowledge under s.11 when he knows all the following facts (though as is explained below, knowledge may be constructive):

(a) that the injury in question was significant;
(b) that the injury was attributable in whole or in part to the act or omission which is alleged to constitute negligence, nuisance or breach of duty;
(c) the identity of the defendant[126] and
(d) if it is alleged that the act or omission was that of a person other than the defendant,[127] the identity of that person and the additional facts supporting the bringing of an action against the defendant.[128]

However, the claimant's knowledge that any acts or omissions did or did not, as a matter of law, involve negligence, nuisance or breach of duty is irrelevant.[129] An injury is "significant"[130] under paragraph (a) if the claimant would reasonably have considered it sufficiently

---

[122] *Walkin v South Manchester HA* [1995] 1 W.L.R. 1543. Where damages for the cost of upbringing of the child are still available that claim, too, falls within this provision though whether that is consistent with the reasoning in *McFarlane v Tayside Health Board* (see para.24–15, above) is debatable: see *Godfrey v Gloucestershire Royal Infirmary NHS Trust* [2003] EWHC 549 (QB).

[123] *Yearworth v North Bristol NHS Trust* [2009] EWCA Civ 37; [2010] Q.B. 1.

[124] *Yearworth* (where the issue was not one of limitation) at [18].

[125] Section 11(4). On the burden of proof see *AB v MoD* [2009] EWHC 1225 (QB) at [482].

[126] Complications can arise where there is a group of companies under common control: *Simpson v Norwest Holst Southern Ltd* [1980] 1 W.L.R. 968; *Cressey v E Timm & Son Ltd* [2005] EWCA Civ 763; [2005] 1 W.L.R. 3926.

[127] e.g. where the defendant is an employer who is vicariously liable.

[128] Section 14(1).

[129] Section 14(1). Thus the advice of the claimant's solicitors that the defendant's conduct does not amount to a tort does not prevent time running, though the claimant might have an action for professional negligence against them. Similarly, time runs even if the advice is correct at the time but a subsequent appellate decision makes the conduct actionable: *Robinson v St Helens MBC* [2002] EWCA Civ 1099; [2003] P.I.Q.R. P128. "To interpret section 14(1) ... so that the three-year period runs from the date when the law first recognised such a claim by means of a judicial decision, would bring into existence a host of stale claims, some of which could be 20, 30 or more years old, and so give rise to great unfairness to defendants": *Rowe v Kingston-upon-Hull CC* [2003] EWCA Civ 1281; [2003] E.L.R. 771 at [24]; and see *Awoyomi v Radford* [2007] EWHC 1671; [2008] Q.B. 793.

[130] It has been held that if the claimant knows that one injury is significant, time runs even in respect of another, of the significance of which he is unaware: *Bristow v Grout, The Times*, November 3, 1986.

serious to justify his instituting proceedings for damages against a defendant who did not dispute liability and was able to satisfy a judgment.[131]

This has not proved easy to interpret[132] but in *Spargo v North Essex District Health Authority*[133] the Court of Appeal distilled the earlier case law into what have been described as not merely guidelines but a binding set of rules[134]:

> "(1) The knowledge required to satisfy section 14(1)(b) is a broad knowledge of the essence of the causally relevant act or omission to which the injury is attributable;
>
> (2) 'Attributable' in this context means 'capable of being attributed to', in the sense of being a real possibility;
>
> (3) A plaintiff has the requisite knowledge when she knows enough to make it reasonable for her to begin to investigate whether or not she has a case against the defendant. Another way of putting this is to say that she will have such knowledge if she so firmly believes that her condition is capable of being attributed to an act or omission which she can identify (in broad terms) that she goes to a solicitor to seek advice about making a claim for compensation;
>
> (4) On the other hand she will not have the requisite knowledge if she thinks she knows the acts or omissions she should investigate but in fact is barking up the wrong tree: or if her knowledge of what the defendant did or did not do is so vague or general that she cannot fairly be expected to know what she should investigate; or if her state of mind is such that she thinks her condition is capable of being attributed to the act or omission alleged to constitute negligence, but she is not sure about this, and would need to check with an expert before she could be properly said to know that it was."

26–19 A firm belief may amount to knowledge even if the claimant receives medical advice adverse to a claim.[135] However, the reference to, "negligence, nuisance or breach of duty" in paragraph (b)

---

[131] Section 14(2). It follows that even a quite minor injury with no long-term effects of which the claimant is then aware may justify the institution of proceedings: *Albonetti v Wirral MBC* [2008] EWCA Civ 783.

[132] Similarly with the closely comparable Irish legislation: *Gough v Neary* [2003] 3 I.R. 92.

[133] [1997] P.I.Q.R. P235. See also *Haward v Fawcetts* [2006] UKHL 9; [2006] 1 W.L.R. 682 on the similar s.14A. *Spargo* has been said to be consistent with *Haward*: *AB v MoD* [2009] EWHC 1225 (QB).

[134] *Griffin v Clwyd HA* [2001] EWCA Civ 818; [2001] P.I.Q.R. P31; *Corbin v Penfold Metallising* [2000] P.I.Q.R. P247.

[135] *Sniezek v Bundy (Letchworth) Ltd* [2000] P.I.Q.R. P213.

merely identifies the acts of which the claimant now complains: it does not impart a requirement that time does not run until the claimant knows the acts are actionable, for that would stultify the general proviso to s.14(1).[136]

"Knowledge" includes knowledge which the claimant might reasonably have been expected to acquire from facts observable or ascertainable by him or from facts ascertainable by him with the help of medical or other appropriate expert advice which it is reasonable for him to seek. However, he is not fixed with knowledge of a fact ascertainable only with the help of expert advice so long as he has taken all reasonable steps to obtain (and, where appropriate, to act on) this advice.[137] Thus, where the claimant suffered injury by a piece of metal flying off a hammer in 1957, the failure of the expert who later conducted a hardness test to notice the defect which was in fact the cause of the accident prevented time running against the claimant with the result that the claimant's personal representative was able to bring a successful action in 1975.[138] At one time the view was taken that the issue of knowledge under s.14 should be considered on a basis that was "partly subjective and partly objective"[139] taking account of matters like the claimant's intelligence and the effect on him of his injury. However, the current view is expressed by Lord Hoffmann in *A v Hoare*[140] in the following terms:

"I respectfully think that the notion of the test being partly objective and partly subjective is somewhat confusing. Section 14(2) is a test for what counts as a significant injury. The material to which that test applies is generally 'subjective' in the sense that it is applied to what the claimant knows of his injury rather than the injury as it actually was. Even then, his knowledge may have to be supplemented with imputed 'objective' knowledge under section 14(3). But the test itself is an entirely impersonal standard: not whether the claimant himself would have considered the injury sufficiently serious to justify proceedings but whether he would 'reasonably' have done so. You ask what the claimant knew about the injury he had suffered, you add any knowledge

---

[136] *Broadley v Guy Clapham & Co* [1994] 2 All E.R. 439; *Dobbie v Medway HA* [1994] 1 W.L.R. 1234, but if the defendant is charged with negligence by omission, the claimant cannot have knowledge until he knows something could have been done: *Forbes v Wandsworth HA* [1997] Q.B. 402.

[137] Section 14(3).

[138] *Marston v BRB* [1979] I.C.R. 124.

[139] See *McCafferty v Metropolitan Police Receiver* [1977] 1 W.L.R. 1073.

[140] [2008] UKHL 6; [2008] 1 A.C. 844 at [34]–[35]. The shift had in fact occurred earlier as a result of *Adams v Bracknell Forest BC* [2004] UKHL 29; [2005] 1 A.C. 76: see e.g. *McCoubrey v MoD* [2007] EWCA Civ 17; [2007] 1 W.L.R. 1544.

about the injury which may be imputed to him under section
14(3) and you then ask whether a reasonable person with that
knowledge would have considered the injury sufficiently serious
to justify his instituting proceedings for damages against a defendant who did not dispute liability and was able to satisfy a
judgment.

It follows that I cannot accept that one must consider whether
someone 'with [the] plaintiff's intelligence' would have been
reasonable if he did not regard the injury as sufficiently serious.
That seems to me to destroy the effect of the word 'reasonably'.[141] Judges should not have to grapple with the notion of the
reasonable unintelligent person. Once you have ascertained what
the claimant knew and what he should be treated as having
known, the actual claimant drops out of the picture. Section 14(2)
is, after all, simply a standard of the seriousness of the injury and
nothing more. Standards are in their nature impersonal and do not
vary with the person to whom they are applied."[142]

A reason for this shift is that even if the claimant fails on the date
of knowledge issue it has since 1975 been open to the court to
override the limitation period under s.33 and that is the right place
to deal with, for example, the question of the impact of the injury on
what the claimant could reasonably be expected to have done,[143]
though it should not, "be supposed that the exercise of the court's
section 33 discretion will invariably replicate" the position that
prevailed under the former interpretation of s.14.[144]

If the claim is under the Fatal Accidents Act 1976 in respect of a
death caused by the defendant's tort the time limit is found in s.12
of the 1980 Act. First, no action can be brought under the Fatal
Accidents Act unless the deceased himself could have maintained an
action at the date of his death.[145] Subject, therefore, to the court's
power to override the time limit,[146] any potential right of action
under the Fatal Accidents Act will disappear three years after the

---

[141] Cf. Baroness Hale, who had doubts on this issue, at [58]: "This does not deprive the word 'reasonably' of all meaning, because the test is still what the reasonable outsider would expect of the claimant rather than what the claimant would expect of himself."

[142] Section 14(3) dealing with the knowledge which the claimant might reasonably be expected to acquire is, however, to some extent different: "You do not assume that a person who has been blinded could reasonably have acquired knowledge by seeing things" (at [39]).

[143] See at [45].

[144] At [87] per Lord Brown.

[145] Section 12(1).

[146] See below. The court can override the time limit if the deceased's own claim is barred by s.11 but not if it was barred by any other statute, e.g. Carriage by Air Act 1961 Sch.1, art.29 (two years from intended date of arrival at destination).

accident or the date of the deceased's knowledge if later.[147] If the deceased has a cause of action at the date of his death, then the dependant may bring an action, again subject to the court's power to override the time limit,[148] within three years of the date of the death or the date of the dependant's knowledge, whichever is the later.[149] In most cases of course, there is more than one dependant and in that event the provision regarding the date of knowledge is to be applied to each of them separately and anyone debarred by this is to be excluded from the action.[150]

A much more fundamental development in the law of limitation is the court's power, conferred by s.33, to override the statutory time limits if it appears to the court to be equitable to do so having regard to the degree to which the primary limitation rules prejudice the claimant and any exercise of the power would prejudice the defendant.[151] This discretion applies only to cases where the limitation period is prescribed by s.11 or s.12, though as we have seen s.11 is now regarded as embracing claims for intentional trespass to the person.[152] Where the discretion applies, the court is directed to have regard to all the circumstances of the case and in particular to: **26–20**

1. the length of, and reasons[153] for, the delay[154] on the part of the claimant;
2. the effect of the delay upon the evidence in the case;
3. the conduct of the defendant after the cause of action arose, including his response to the claimant's reasonable request for information;
4. the duration of any disability of the claimant arising after the accrual of the cause of action[155];

---

[147] Section 11. By s.12(1): "where any such action by the injured person would have been barred by the time limit in section 11 ... no account shall be taken of the possibility of that time limit being overridden under section 33." Claimants under the Fatal Accidents Act must therefore ask the court to override the time limit under s.33 if three years have elapsed since the injury or the deceased's knowledge.

[148] Section 33(1).

[149] Section 12(2). The question whether the injury was "significant" naturally has no application for the purposes of the dependant's knowledge.

[150] Section 13. This is less significant than it might seem, because the dependants will normally include children, against whom time would not run until majority.

[151] Section 33(1). The actual term used in the Act is "disapply". "Parliament has now decided that uncertain justice is preferable to certain injustice": *Firman v Ellis* [1978] Q.B. 886 at 911 per Ormrod L.J.

[152] See para.26–18, above.

[153] Which may include not only the express reasons given by the claimant, but also the subconscious factors which may have prevented him from litigating: *McCafferty v Metropolitan Police Receiver* [1977] 1 W.L.R. 1073.

[154] Which means the delay after the primary limitation period has expired: *Thompson v Brown* [1981] 1 W.L.R. 744 at 751; *Donovan v Gwentoys Ltd* [1990] 1 W.L.R. 472; *McDonnell v Walker* [2009] EWCA Civ 1257; but prior delay is part of the "circumstances of the case".

[155] Cf. *Kirby v Leather*, para.26–17, above.

5. the extent to which the claimant acted promptly and reasonably once he knew[156] he might have an action for damages;
6. the steps, if any, taken by the claimant to obtain medical, legal or other expert advice and the nature of any such advice as he may have received.[157]

There is evidence that the Law Reform Committee intended s.33 to apply only to "residual" or "difficult" cases[158] but the Court of Appeal in *Firman v Ellis*[159] soon held that the words were too plain to admit of any such restrictive interpretation even if it were possible to categorise such cases, and this broader approach has been upheld by the House of Lords.[160] Accordingly it has been frequently relied on and not infrequently applied.[161]

26–21   Subject to the duty to act judicially, the judge's discretion is unfettered[162] and the matters set out in s.33(3) are by way of example and not definitive.[163] Although it has been said that the greater emphasis on sticking to time limits under the Civil Procedure Rules does not fetter the court's discretion under the Act,[164] yet the question of proportionality is now important in the exercise of any discretion and courts:

"[S]hould be slow to exercise their discretion in favour of a claimant in the absence of cogent medical evidence showing a serious effect on the claimant's health or enjoyment of life and employability."[165]

Furthermore:

---

[156] Which means actual knowledge, not the deemed knowledge which may arise under s.14, above: *Eastman v London Country Bus Services, The Times*, November 23, 1985.

[157] Section 33(3). Legal advice is privileged, but the claimant may be interrogated as to whether the advice was favourable or unfavourable: *Jones v G.D. Searle & Co* [1979] 1 W.L.R. 101.

[158] Cmnd. 5630, paras 38, 56 and 57. What Griffiths J. (a member of the Committee) described in *Finch v Francis* (Unreported, July 2, 1977) as "the occasional hard case".

[159] [1978] Q.B. 886.

[160] *Thompson v Brown* [1981] 1 W.L.R. 744; *Horton v Sadler* [2006] UKHL 27; [2007] 1 A.C. 307.

[161] *Walkley v Precision Forgings Ltd* [1979] 1 W.L.R. 606 held that if the claimant issues proceedings in time but fails to serve them or the claim is dismissed for want of prosecution there is no discretion under s.33 because he is not then prejudiced at all by the primary limitation provisions of the Act but by his dilatoriness or that of his advisers. But *Walkley* was departed from in *Horton v Sadler*, above, fn.160. The primary limitation periods do prejudice him in respect of his second action, which is what counts.

[162] *Donovan v Gwentoys Ltd* [1990] 1 W.L.R. 472; *Horton v Sadler*, above, fn.160.

[163] *Nash v Eli Lilly & Co* [1993] 1 W.L.R. 782.

[164] *Steeds v Peverel Management Services Ltd* [2001] EWCA Civ 419 at [9].

[165] *Robinson v St Helens MBC* [2002] EWCA Civ 1099; [2003] P.I.Q.R. P128 at [33]; *Adams v Bracknell Forest BC* [2004] UKHL 29; [2005] 1 A.C. 76.

"[T]he court should never lose sight of the public policy considerations underlying the legislative regime governing limitation periods. Public authorities, as well as commercial entities and individuals, should not remain exposed indefinitely to the threat of litigation based upon historic allegations. Fairness requires a balancing of all relevant factors and their interests have to be taken into account. There is a public interest in certainty and finality and such considerations must not be lightly discounted, especially not on the basis of sympathy for an individual litigant—even where there is, or might be, a strong case on liability and causation."[166]

The exercise is essentially a balancing one and the balance will come down heavily in favour of the defendant where, for example, he is required to meet a claim which is first presented years after the wrong[167] and the longer the delay after the occurrence of the matters giving rise to the cause of action the more likely it is that the balance of prejudice would swing against the exercise of the discretion in the claimant's favour. Thus in *Adams v Bracknell Forest BC*[168] the House of Lords declined to exercise the discretion in respect of a claim alleging that the defendants were at fault in failing to diagnose and treat the claimant's dyslexia: the claim was brought 14 years after his last contact with the defendants and 12 years after he had reached majority, there were no records to enable the defendants to rebut the allegations and in view of the uncertainties of proof of causation of the claimant's current condition and its effect on his life and employment the damages would be likely to be modest. The mere fact that the exercise of the discretion will deprive the defendant of a limitation defence is not of itself "prejudice" to him: if, for example, he has had early notice of the possibility of a claim he will have had opportunity to investigate it and some delay in issuing

---

[166] *TCD v Harrow Council* [2008] EWHC 3048 (QB) at [35], where the proceedings were commenced in 2006 and the last act complained of occurred in 1981; *Kamar v Nightingale* [2007] EWHC 2982 (QB). The CA gave guidance on the exercise of the s.33 discretion in child abuse cases in *AB v Nugent Care Society* [2009] EWCA Civ 827; [2010] P.I.Q.R. P3.

[167] Even though the "delay" referred to on s.33(3) is that occurring after the expiry of the limitation period (fn.154, above) delay before then is relevant in determining the prejudice to the defendant. "A defendant is always likely to be prejudiced by the dilatoriness of the plaintiff in pursuing his claim . . . The fact that the law permits a plaintiff within prescribed limits to disadvantage a defendant in this way does not mean that the defendant is not prejudiced. It merely means that he is not in a position to complain of the prejudice he suffers. Once a plaintiff allows a prescribed time limit to elapse, a defendant is no longer subject to that disability": *Donovan v Gwentoys Ltd*, above, fn.162, at 479 per Lord Oliver. Compare *Thompson v Brown*, above, fn.160, where, although the writ was issued outside the limitation period, the claim had been notified at an early stage and negotiations pursued.

[168] Above, fn.165.

proceedings after the expiry of the limitation period will have had no effect on his ability to defend.[169] Although the fact that the defendant is insured is a relevant consideration, it is wrong to take the line that an insured defendant cannot establish prejudice, because only his insurers will suffer and they are not parties to the action. The correct approach is to treat the defendant and his insurers as a composite unit: insurers should not be penalised by being made to fight claims that an uninsured defendant would not be held bound to fight.[170] The fact that the claimant has a claim[171] for professional negligence against his solicitors in failing to issue proceedings[172] is a highly relevant circumstance,[173] and prima facie it is the claimant, and not the defendant, who should bear the consequences of their default,[174] though the court must bear in mind the difficulty, delay and expense which may be caused to the claimant by having to change horses in midstream[175] and the fact that the solicitor will have a greater knowledge of the weaknesses of the case than will the defendant.[176]

26–22   **ii. Maritime cases.** The Merchant Shipping Act 1995[177] fixes two years as the period of limitation for damage to a vessel, her cargo, freight or any property on board her, or for damages for loss of life or personal injuries suffered by any person on board caused by the fault of another vessel. The court may, however, extend this period to such extent and upon such conditions as it thinks fit,[178] but the Act only applies to actions brought against ships other than that on which the damage actually occurred, and, accordingly, where an

---

[169] *Cain v Francis* [2008] EWCA Civ 1451; [2009] Q.B. 754. In such a case the limitation defence is sometimes referred to as a "windfall". *Cain* is an extreme case: liability was quickly admitted, interim payments were made and proceedings were issued only one day late.

[170] *Kelly v Bastible* (1996) 36 B.M.L.R. 51.

[171] Cf. *Das v Ganju* [1999] P.I.Q.R. P260.

[172] *Donovan v Gwentoys Ltd*, above, fn.162. Not every error is negligence, but the inference arising from allowing a limitation period to expire is difficult to rebut. A solicitor must be taken to know the simpler limitation provisions "off the cuff".

[173] *Thompson v Brown*, above, fn.160, at 752; *McDonnell v Walker* [2009] EWCA Civ 1257.

[174] *Horton v Sadler* [2006] UKHL 27; [2007] 1 A.C. 307 at [53] doubting *Das v Ganju*, above on this point.

[175] *Thompson v Brown*, above, fn.160, at 750; *Firman v Ellis*, above, fn.159. As has often been pointed out, the real issue in such a case is not whether the claimant will recover damages, but which liability insurer will pay them.

[176] *Hartley v Birmingham City DC* [1992] 1 W.L.R. 968.

[177] See s.190, re-enacting the Maritime Conventions Act 1911 s.8. A number of other statutes provide their own periods of limitation, e.g. Carriage by Air Act 1961, Nuclear Installations Act 1965, Carriage by Railway Act 1972, Carriage by Road Act 1974.

[178] Section 190. For a case on the exercise of the discretion, see *The Alnwick* [1965] P. 357.

action was brought against shipowners in respect of the death of a seaman on their ship, it was held that the general law of limitation (the three-year period) applies.[179]

iii. Liability under the Consumer Protection Act 1987. We   **26–23**
have seen that this Act imposes strict liability for defective products.[180] Though applying to some private property damage it is
likely in practice to be overwhelmingly concerned with personal
injury.[181] It adds a new s.11A to the Act of 1980 and the main rules
are identical to those generally applying in personal injury cases,
that is to say, a primary three-year period from the damage, an
alternative period running from the claimant's knowledge and a
power to override the limitation period. However, there is one major
difference: no action can be brought in any case more than 10 years
from the date when the product was put into circulation.[182] This bar
is absolute, that is to say, it cannot be overridden by the court under
s.33 of the 1980 Act and it applies even if the claimant was under
a disability or there was fraud, concealment or mistake—or even if
no cause of action could have arisen within the 10-year period
because there was no damage.[183] None of these provisions, however,
affects an action for common law negligence.

iv. Defamation and malicious falsehood. By s.4A of the Limita-   **26–24**
tion Act 1980, as substituted by s.5 of the Defamation Act 1996,
there is a limitation period of one year from the accrual of the cause
of action in cases of libel, slander and malicious falsehood. Under
s.32A of the 1980 Act (also substituted by s.5 of the 1996 Act) the
court may in its discretion allow a case to proceed outside this time
if it would be equitable to do so having regard to the relative
prejudice to the claimant and the defendant.[184]

---

[179] *The Niceto de Larrinaga* [1966] P. 80.

[180] See Ch.10, above.

[181] Where property damage alone is sued for the limitation period is three years, not the usual six: Limitation Act 1980 s.11A(4), inserted by the Consumer Protection Act 1987 Sch.1 Pt I para.1. The Latent Damage Act 1986 does not apply because this is not an action for negligence, but by s.5(5) of the 1987 Act time runs from the date when the damage occurred or the earliest time at which a person with an interest in the property had knowledge of the material facts (as to which see subss.(6) and (7)).

[182] This means the moment when it leaves the production process and entered a marketing process in which it was offered to the public for use or consumption: *O'Byrne v Sanofi Pasteur MSD Ltd* [2006] 1 W.L.R. 1606 (ECJ).

[183] See Limitation Act 1980 ss.11A(3), 28(7) and 32(4A), all inserted by the Consumer Protection Act 1987 Sch.1 Pt I.

[184] This is modelled on s.33 and s.32A(2) directs the court to have regard to certain factors comparable to those listed in s.33(3). See *Steedman v BBC* [2001] EWCA Civ 1534; [2002] E.M.L.R. 17.

26–25   **v. Cases of contribution.** Section 10 of the Limitation Act 1980 provides that a claim to recover statutory contribution[185] must be brought within two years of the date when the right to contribution first accrued.[186] If the tortfeasor claiming contribution has himself been sued by the victim of the tort, then the right to contribution accrues when judgment is given against him which quantifies his liability[187]; if he compromises the action the right accrues when the amount of the payment to be made by him to the victim is agreed.[188] In the case of claims for contribution between shipowners in respect of their liabilities for loss of life or personal injuries aboard ship, which are governed by the Merchant Shipping Act 1995, however, the period of limitation for contribution is one year from payment only.[189]

H. The Law Commission's Exercise on Limitation

26–26   The Law Commission in 2001 concluded[190] that the law of limitation should be overhauled and rationalised on the basis of a general "core regime" applicable to most causes of action (tort, contract and others) of a three-year period of limitation to run from the date when the existence of a claim was discoverable by the claimant. This would be balanced by an absolute long-stop of ten years from the accrual of the cause of action or from the time of the act or omission giving rise to the claim. The long-stop would not apply where the defendant has dishonestly concealed relevant facts. However, in the case of personal injury (whether arising from negligence or intentional wrongdoing) the court would have a discretion to disapply the primary limitation period and there would be no long-stop. As now, there would be provision for postponement in cases of disability, though modified in a number of respects.[191]

5. ASSIGNMENT OF RIGHT OF ACTION IN TORT[192]

26–27   This topic may conveniently be treated here, although it relates not

---

[185] The legislation thus gives added importance to the possibility of a common law claim between tortfeasors, e.g. by virtue of an express contract between them (para.21–7, above) or under *Lister v Romford Ice & Cold Storage Co Ltd* [1957] A.C. 555 (para.20–18, above) since the limitation period for such claims remains at six years.

[186] Section 10(1). The provisions of the Act on disability and on fraud, concealment and mistake apply to contribution claims: s.10(5).

[187] Section 10(3), as interpreted in *Aer Lingus v Gildacroft Ltd* [2006] EWCA Civ 4; [2006] 1 W.L.R. 1173.

[188] Section 10(4). "Payment" includes a payment in kind (e.g. remedial work) provided a value can be placed on it: *Baker & Davies Plc v Leslie Wilks Associates* [2005] EWHC 1179 (TCC); [2005] 3 All E.R. 603.

[189] Merchant Shipping Act 1995 s.190(4).

[190] See Law Com. No.270.

[191] Inclusion of these measures in a draft Civil Law Reform Bill was promised in 2008. However, the draft Bill produced at the end of 2009 does not contain them.

[192] Winfield, *Present Law of Abuse of Procedure*, pp.67–69.

so much to extinction of liability in tort, but to transfer of a right of action in tort.

It is a long-standing rule in the law of assignment of choses in action that, while property can lawfully be assigned, a "bare right to litigate" cannot,[193] because to allow such an assignment would be to encourage undesirable speculation in law suits.[194] Indeed, the agreement would savour of maintenance and champerty, which, formerly, were themselves torts and are still grounds for striking down a contract[195] and providing a defence to the assignee's action.[196] This is not to say, however, that there can never be a valid assignment of a right of action in tort and the basic rule must be read in the light of the following qualifications and exceptions.[197]

A. "Proper Interest of Assignee"

It has been held that if A transfers property to B he may also **26–28** assign a right of action for breach of contract[198] (for example breach of covenant to repair in a lease) in relation to that property, for then, it has been said, the assignee buys not in order to obtain a cause of action but in order to protect the property he has bought.[199] Notwithstanding certain statements denying the assignability of any tort claim, it is submitted that at the present day such a case should be treated in the same way if the cause of action is in tort.[200] It is more difficult to know how far there may be applied to a case of tort the doctrine stated in the House of Lords in *Trendtex Trading Corp v Credit Suisse*,[201] a case of assignment of a claim for breach of contract. It was said that an assignee who has a "genuine commercial interest" in the enforcement of a claim may take a valid assignment of it so long as the transaction is not champertous and it seems that a genuine commercial interest may be present simply

---

[193] Reaffirmed in *Trendtex Trading Corp v Credit Suisse* [1982] A.C. 679.
[194] Some reasons formerly given for the rule are either unconvincing or obsolete. Thus it was said in argument in *Anon.* (1600) Godbolt 81 that damages in the assigned action are too uncertain at the date of assignment, or that the assignee, "may be a man of great power, who might procure a jury to give him greater damages".
[195] See para.19–15, above.
[196] *Laurent v Sale & Co* [1963] 1 W.L.R. 829.
[197] For statutory transmission on death, see Ch.23, above. A liability to pay damages for personal injuries passes under the Transfer of Undertakings legislation: para.8–9, above.
[198] *Ellis v Torrington* [1920] 1 K.B. 399.
[199] [1920] 1 K.B. 399 at 412–413 per Scrutton L.J.
[200] See the comments of Lord Denning M.R. in the Court of Appeal in *Trendtex Trading Corp v Credit Suisse* [1980] Q.B. 657.
[201] [1982] A.C. 679; *Brownton Ltd v Edward Moore Inbucon Ltd* [1985] 3 All E.R. 499, another contract case; but see Lloyd L.J. at 509, whose statement of the principle of the *Trendtex* case applies to contract and tort alike. In *24 Seven Utility Services Ltd v Rosekey Ltd*, February 18, 2004 (QB) an assignment of a property damage claim by the owner to its maintenance contractor was upheld; and see *Khan v R.M. Falvey & Co* [2002] EWCA Civ 400; [2002] P.N.L.R. 28 at [28].

because the assignee is a creditor of the assignor.[202] On this basis, unless an arbitrary line is to be drawn between contract and tort, it may be that, for example, an assignment to a bank of the assignor's claim for damages for negligent misstatement inducing a contract which the bank has financed, and on which it stands to lose, would be valid.[203] In any event a trustee in bankruptcy and a liquidator have statutory power to sell a cause of action on terms that the assignees will pay a share of the proceeds (this statutory power necessarily precluding any challenge on the grounds of maintenance or champerty)[204] and this can extend, for example, to a tort claim for negligent advice.[205] By contrast, it is thought that the law should still refuse to give effect to the assignment of, say, a claim for libel or for personal injuries even though the assignor was indebted to the assignee.[206]

B. Judgment

26–29 No such problems arise with regard to the assignment of a judgment in an action for tort. If the judgment has already been given, the rights of the creditor are assignable like any other debt.[207] Similarly, a person may assign the fruits of an action yet to be commenced for this is no more than the assignment of property to be

---

[202] The action was an attempt by the assignor to set aside the assignment, when a settlement of the assigned claim produced some 10 times what the assignor had sold it for. The agreement was in fact champertous because its purpose was not merely to enable the assignees to recoup their losses in financing the abortive deal made by the assignors with the contract breaker, but to allow them to sell the claim to a third party and divide the spoils. On the facts, however, the proper law of the agreement was Swiss.

[203] There are essentially the facts of the *Trendtex* case with a change in the cause of action and the removal of the champertous element; but suppose the claim is for fraudulent misrepresentation? Cf. Turner L.J. in *De Hoghton v Money* (1866) L.R. 2 Ch.App. 164 at 166. No objection seems to have been made to the assignment of the tort claim in *Axa Insurance Ltd v Akther & Darby* [2009] EWCA Civ 1166, though it seems that the assignor insurer had been owned by Winthertur, which was acquired by Axa. See also *Auckland City Council as Assignee of Body Corporate 16113 v Auckland City Council* [2008] 1 N.Z.L.R. 838.

[204] *Grovewood Holdings Plc v James Cappel & Co Ltd* [1995] Ch. 80 at 86; *Norglen Ltd v Reeds Rains Prudential Ltd* [1999] 2 A.C. 1.

[205] *Ramsey v Hartley* [1977] 1 WLR 686. There is a full review of the law in *Empire Resolution Ltd v MPW Insurance Brokers Ltd*, February 23, 1999 (TCC).

[206] Lord Roskill in the *Trendtex* case at 702 refers to the principle that, "causes of action which were essentially personal in their character, such as claims for defamation and personal injury, were incapable of assignment" but he is speaking in terms of the law 80 years ago and his general point is that the law of maintenance was then more severe. In the Court of Appeal in the *Trendtex* case ([1980] Q.B. 629) Lord Denning M.R. and Oliver J., who would have abandoned the "bare right of action" approach altogether, would have maintained a rule against the assignability of "personal tort" claims. It seems that if A makes a voluntary payment to B to compensate B for loss caused by C, A may take a valid assignment of B's claim in tort against C: *Esso Petroleum Co Ltd v Hall Russell & Co Ltd* [1988] 3 W.L.R. 730 at 738.

[207] *Carrington v Harway* (1662) 1 Keb. 803; *Goodman v Robinson* (1886) 18 Q.B.D. 332.

acquired. Thus, in *Glegg v Bromley*[208] an assignment *pendente lite* of the fruits of an action for slander was upheld.[209]

C. Subrogation[210]

The commonest example of subrogation in this connection is in   **26–30** the law of insurance. An insurance company which has compensated a policyholder under an indemnity insurance policy stands in his shoes with regard to his claims against the person who caused the injury. Hence if A by negligent driving of his car damages B's car, and the X company, with whom B is insured, compensates him, the X company can exploit B's action for negligence against A.[211] The payment by the insurer under the policy does not provide the tortfeasor with a defence to a claim by the insured,[212] but if the latter recovers damages they are subject to a proprietary lien or charge in favour of the insurer.[213]

6. INSOLVENCY

A. Insolvency of Defendant

The original rule was that a claim for unliquidated damages in tort   **26–31** was not provable as a bankruptcy debt so that the claim remained alive against the bankrupt (who might acquire assets after his discharge) and liability did not pass to his trustee.[214] A similar principle applied to the winding-up of an insolvent company, though since the company would generally then cease to exist there was no equivalent to the personal liability of the individual bankrupt. Now, by the

---

[208] [1912] 3 K.B. 474.
[209] *Cohen v Mitchell* (1890) 25 Q.B.D. 262 can also be supported on this ground, although other reasons were given for the decision.
[210] For a statement of the principle, see *Castellain v Preston* (1883) 11 Q.B.D. 380 at 387 per Brett L.J.; *Burnand v Rodocanachi* (1882) 7 App. Cas. 333 at 339 per Lord Blackburn; *Morris v Ford Motor Co* [1973] Q.B. 792.
[211] See para.1–20, above, for the former "knock for knock" agreement. In *Lister v Romford Ice and Cold Storage Co Ltd* [1957] A.C. 555 the action was in fact brought by the employer's insurers, and the employers themselves were not consulted about the action: [1956] 2 Q.B. 180 at 185 per Denning L.J. Normally the action is brought in the name of the insured, but if there has been an assignment which complies with the requirements of the Law of Property Act 1925 s.136, the insurer can bring the action in his own name: *Compania Colombiana de Seguros v Pacific Steam Navigation Co* [1965] 1 Q.B. 101 at 121–122 per Roskill J. *Esso Petroleum Co Ltd v Hall Russell & Co Ltd* [1988] 3 W.L.R. 730 at 738 per Lord Goff.
[212] See para.1–19, above.
[213] *Lord Napier and Ettrick v Hunter* [1993] A.C. 713.
[214] Tort claims became provable against the insolvent estate of a deceased person by the Law Reform (Miscellaneous Provisions) Act 1934 s.1(1)(b).

Insolvency Act 1986,[215] a liability in tort is a "bankruptcy debt"[216] so that the claimant may seek to share in the assets along with the other creditors and discharge from the bankruptcy[217] extinguishes the personal liability of the bankrupt. The Third Parties (Rights Against Insurers) Act 1930 (an exception to privity of contract) transfers to the claimant the rights of the bankrupt against his insurers and it has been held that for this purpose the liability, though not enforceable against the bankrupt, is not totally extinguished by the discharge and, if not already established, may be established in the bankruptcy even after discharge so as to allow the claimant to proceed against the insurers.[218] In any event, discharge does not, unless the court otherwise directs, release the bankrupt from his liability for damages for personal injuries arising from, "negligence, nuisance or breach of a statutory, contractual or other duty".[219]

By the Insolvency Rules[220] made under the authority of the Companies Act 1985 tort claims which have accrued[221] are likewise provable in the winding-up of an insolvent company but after winding-up the company ceases to exist[222] and the Third Parties (Rights Against Insurers) Act 1930 is of no assistance to a claimant who has not sued before the dissolution.[223] That Act transfers to the claimant the rights of the insured against the insurer, it does not make the insurer liable for the torts of the insured[224]: hence if there is no one who can be sued for the tort the Act has no application. However, there is power to restore the defunct company to the register.[225]

---

[215] Replacing equivalent provisions of the Insolvency Act 1985.

[216] See s.382. By subs.(2): "in determining ... whether any liability in tort is a bankruptcy debt, the bankrupt is deemed to become subject to that liability by reason of an obligation incurred at the time when the cause of action accrued."

[217] Which may be on order of the court or by mere passage of time (now generally one year).

[218] *Law Society v Shah* [2007] EWHC 2841 (Ch); [2009] Ch. 223. The Third Parties (Rights Against Insurers) Act 2010 will replace the 1930 Act and among other things will enable the claimant to bring proceedings directly against the insurer in which he may establish the insured's liability.

[219] Section 281(5). See also Road Traffic Act 1988 s.153.

[220] To a very large extent the Rules correspond closely with the provisions for individual insolvency in the Insolvency Act.

[221] Potential future claims are not provable: *Re T & N Ltd* [2005] EWHC 2870 (Ch); [2006] 1 W.L.R. 1728 (potential asbestos claims).

[222] Subject to a power in the court to restore the company to the register within six years: Companies Act 2006 s.1030.

[223] This will change under the 2010 Act, since liability can be established directly against the insurer. Cf. *Law Society v Shah*, above, fn.218.

[224] Neatly illustrated by *Firma C-Trade SA v Newcastle Protection and Indemnity Association* [1991] 2 A.C. 1 ("pay to be paid" clause in rules of Marine P. & I. Club).

[225] Generally within six years but no time limit where a claim for personal injuries is brought: Companies Act 2006 s.1030.

B. Insolvency of Claimant

Under the Insolvency Act the bankrupt's property[226] forms, with **26–32**
certain exceptions, his estate, available for distribution among creditors. If the injury is a purely personal one, like general damages for
libel, the right of action for it remains exercisable by the injured
party himself and does not pass to his trustee in bankruptcy but
when the tort is to property, for example conversion of goods, then
the right to sue for it passes to the trustee, who can sell or assign it
to anyone as he, in his discretion thinks fit. In some cases the claim
is a "hybrid" one, for example a case of personal injury may involve
damages for loss of amenity and for loss of earnings. Since there is
only one cause of action and it includes a claim for "property", the
whole claim passes to the trustee[227] but if the latter brings proceedings he holds any damages representing the purely personal loss on
trust for the bankrupt.[228]

---

[226] Defined in s.436 to include "things in action".
[227] In the case of statutory discrimination claims the claimant may pursue the personal
element of the claim in his own right: *Khan v Trident Safeguards Ltd* [2004] EWCA Civ
624; [2004] I.R.L.R. 961.
[228] *Ord v Upton* [2000] Ch. 352. For an example of the practical difficulties facing the
bankrupt in these circumstances see *Kaberry v Freethcartwright* [2003] EWCA Civ 1077;
[2003] B.P.I.R. 1144. It should not be assumed that in all circumstances a claim for
financial loss is non-personal: *Mulkerrins v Price Waterhouse Coopers* [2003] UKHL 41;
[2003] 1 W.L.R. 1937.

INDEX

[all references are to paragraph number]

1211

Occupiers
see also **Occupiers' Liability Act 1957; Occupiers' Liability Act 1984anan**
nuisance, 14–15, 14–18
Occupiers' Liability Act 1957
"common duty of care"
children, 9–10—9–11
generally, 9–8—9–12
independent contractors, 9–15, 9–16
persons exercising calling, 9–10, 9–12
warning, 9–14
common law, 9–2
contracts
third parties, and, 9–22, 9–23
contributory negligence, 9–18
current relationship with common law, 9–3
damage
property, to, 9–24
exclusion of liability, 9–19—9–21
generally, 9–1—9–24
occupier, 9–4
Tomlinson's case, 9–17
visitors
generally, 9–5—9–7
implied permission, 9–6, 9–7
Occupiers' Liability Act 1984
current relationship of 1984 Act with common law, 9–27
generally, 9–25—9–29
persons exercising "right to roam", 9–29
persons who are neither trespassers nor visitors, 9–25
trespassers
common law, 9–25
duty of care, 9–26
generally, 9–25—9–29
Oil pollution
strict liability, 15–25
Omissions
see **Duty of care**

Parental authority
generally, 24–27
Particulars of claim
generally, 2–5
Partners
generally, 24–24
Passing off
generally, 18–44—18–52
goodwill, 18–50
limits, 18–51
remedies, 18–52
representation likely to confuse, 18–45
variants, 18–46—18–48
Pecuniary loss
see also **Damages**
damages, 22–23—22–38
Periodical payments
generally, 22–24—22–25

Personal injury
cost of system, 1–27
criticism of system
delay, 1–35
deterrence, 1–29—1–31
expense, 1–34—1–36
fault liability, 1–36
"fault principle", 1–28
generally, 1–28—1–36
inefficiency, 1–34—1–36
Pearson Commission, 1–41
responsibility, 1–32—1–33
damages
see **Damages**
defective products, 10–1
generally, 1–21—1–42
limitation, 26–17, 26–18
Picketing
generally, 18–42
Police
arrest powers of, 4–24
duty of care
omissions, 5–19
vicarious liability, 20–7
Pollution
waste
liability, 15–26
Possession
interference with goods, 17–4, 17–16
negligence and property damage, 5–40
trespass to land, and, 13–2—13–3
Possession claims (land)
generally, 13–15—13–16
Post office
generally, 24–5
Privacy
see also **Misuse of private information**
confidence, 12–82
data protection, 12–81
defamation and , 12–87
generally, 12–78—12–87
Human Rights Act 1998, 2–12, 12–80
indirect impact of other torts, 12–79
misuse of private information, 12–82
no specific tort of invasion of privacy, 12–78
Private nuisance
generally, 14–4
Protection from Harassment Act 1997
generally, 4–38
Proximity
duty of care and, 5–11
Psychiatric harm
duty of care
claimant physically threatened, 5–63—5–65
claimant shocked by defendant's exposure of himself to danger, 5–70
claimant witness of danger to others, 5–66—5–68

Trade disputes—*cont.*
    unprotected acts, 18–41
Trade unions
    trade disputes, 18–35
Trespass
    see also Trespass to goods; Trespass to
        land; Trespass to the person
    action on the case and, 2–2
    directness, 2–2
Trespass *ab initio*
    generally, 13–12
Trespass on the case
    see Trespass
Trespass to goods
    damage, 17–3
    generally, 17–3—17–5
    possession,
        essential, 17–4—17–5
        exceptions, 17–5
Trespass to land
    defences
        generally, 13–9—13–12
        justification by law, 13–11
        licence, 13–9
        revocation of licence, 13–10
    interference
        airspace, with, 13–7
        continuing trespass, 13–8
        generally, 13–4—13–8
        trespass on highway, 13–5
        trespass to subsoil, 13–6
    meaning, 13–1
    possession
        generally, 13–2—13–3
        immediate right to possess, 13–3
        trespass by relation, 13–3
    remedies
        action for recovery of land,
            13–15—13–16
        ejectment, 13–15—13–16
        generally, 13–13—13–18
        jus tertii, 13–17
        mesne profits, 13–18
        re-entry, 13–14
    trespass ab initio, 13–12
Trespass to the person
    criminal injuries compensation,
        4–2—4–4
    intention, 4–1, 4–33
    forms of
        see Assault; Battery; False
            imprisonment
    generally, 4–1—4–37
    meaning, 4–1
    negligence and
        burden of proof, 4–33—4–34
        fault, 4–33
        generally, 4–1, 4–33—4–35
        highways, 4–34
    other acts intended to cause physical
        harm, 4–36—4–37

Trespassers
    Occupiers' Liability Act 1984,
        9–25—9–29
Trustees
    generally, 1–11

Unjust enrichment
    damages, and, 22–13
    tort and, 1–10

Vendors (of land and buildings)
    common law
        "complex structure", 9–35
        economic loss and, 9–33—9–3
        generally, 9–32—9–36
    Defective Premises Act 1972,
        9–37—9–38
    generally, 9–31—9–38
    limitation, 9–38
    NHBC Scheme, 9–38
Vicarious liability
    agents, 20–19—20–20
    contract of service
        control test, 20–4
        generally, 20–3—20–8
        indicia, 20–5
        lending a servant, 20–8
    employer's indemnity, 20–18
    generally, 20–1—20–28
    hospitals, 20–6
    independent contractors
        casual negligence, 20–28
        collateral negligence, 20–28
        employer's common law duties, 20–26
        generally, 20–21—20–28
        non-delegable duty, concept of, 20–1,
            20–21
        operations affecting highway other
            than normal use for purpose of
            passage, 20–24
        statutory duty, 20–27
        strict liability, 20–25
        withdrawal of support from
            neighbouring land, 20–23
    meaning, 20–1, 20–2
    police, 20–7
    scope of employment
        carelessness of servant, 20–10
        damage to goods bailed, 20–16
        fraud by servant, 20–17
        generally, 20–9—20–17
        mistake of servant, 20–11
        theft by servant, 20–15
        wilful wrong of servant,
            20–12—20–14
Volenti non fit injuria
    agreement,
        necessary, whether, 25–9—25–10
    breach of statutory duty, 7–17
    exclusion of liability
        generally, 25–6—25–7